The People's
Medical
Manual

THE PEOPLE'S MEDICAL MANUAL

Everything You Need to Know About Health and Safety

HOWARD R.
and MARTHA E. LEWIS

Fast-Action Illustrations by _Neil O. Hardy_

Additional illustrations by _Ralph Moseley_

A Clinical Communications Book

DOUBLEDAY & COMPANY, INC., GARDEN CITY, NEW YORK   1986

Library of Congress Cataloging in Publication Data

Lewis, Howard R.
  The people's medical manual.

  (A Clinical Communications Book)
  1. Medicine, Popular—Handbooks, manuals, etc.
I. Lewis, Martha E.   II. Title.
RC82.L48   1986   610   83–24003
ISBN 0-385-27649-4

Published by
Doubleday & Company, Inc.
Garden City, New York

FOR DAVID AND EMILY
Who've Lived with This Book
All Their Lives

HOW TO GET THE MOST OUT OF THIS BOOK

A Note from the Authors

This is intended to be the most useful, comprehensive health book ever published for laymen, a single source that you can consult for practical, consumer-oriented advice about virtually any health-related problem you may face. It is a book that not only tells you how your heart or liver works, but it also details the symptoms of the most common diseases that can affect those organs and all the other parts of your body. It tells you how your doctor may diagnose your condition and what treatment he may prescribe.

This book may forestall unnecessary visits, but no book can replace your doctor. Indeed, we often alert you to conditions calling for a physician's prompt care and call your attention to self-medication that can be dangerous. At the same time we do give you simple, practical advice about what to do before you reach the doctor in case of illness or accident—with specific details and brand names.

In addition, this book can usefully supplement the information your doctor gives you. Sometimes it can tell you virtually all you need to know about your condition after the doctor has diagnosed it and prescribed treatment. At the very least the information in this book will provide you with a basis of discussion so you'll have a better idea of what questions to ask on your next visit.

Money-saving advice: The cost of health care is rising faster than the rate of inflation and is taking an ever larger slice of your income. Yet much of what you are offered in health products and services is worthless if not actually hazardous. Wherever possible we report the least expensive way of accomplishing an end. We sound frequent warnings against quackery, a little-recognized national disgrace. About $1 of every $9 spent on health care goes for frauds, which are not only wasteful but potentially dangerous (see the entry QUACKERY).

Misleading advertising is the norm for health products. The field is meagerly regulated, and otherwise respectable publishers and broadcasters do scant screening of the health-related ads they carry. Yet 3 Americans in 8 believe that the ads must be correct or the advertisers "wouldn't be allowed to say them," reported the Food and Drug Administration in "A Study of Health Practices and Opinions." We name hundreds of widely advertised products in this book, telling you which ones work, which are good values, which are worthless or wasteful, which may be dangerous.

In addition we include many pointers about the economics and practice of medicine. How do you select a doctor and then deal with him on tricky questions like services and fees? See PHYSICIAN for specific advice. Is hospitalization necessary, and if so what precautions should you take? Read HOSPITAL and HOSPITALIZING CHILDREN to find out. Learn about HEALTH INSURANCE and MEDICAL DEDUCTIONS.

New health discoveries: You'll find subjects not ordinarily covered in health books. The treatment of sex-related disorders has undergone a revolution with the pioneering work of Masters and Johnson and the sex therapists who have followed them. This book can help you apply to your own life the practical results of their research (see SEX DISORDER; IMPOTENCE; FRIGIDITY; PREMATURE EJACULATION; MASTURBATION). We also deal with the sexual aspects of many illnesses, as for example how soon after a heart attack you can have sexual relations.

Emotional stress is a factor in many physiological conditions. Yet medical guides have not generally caught up with the findings of investigators in psychosomatic medicine. We attempt to correct this. See STRESS for how your emotions can damage your bodily health—and how you can ward off such problems.

Safety and accident-prevention are similarly ignored in most health books. This flies in the face of a compelling fact: accidents are the fourth largest cause of death of all Americans and are the leading killer of children. Therefore, see ACCIDENTS and related entries. We have detailed the hazards of scores of activities common in home and recreation. We provide sensible, practical advice on how to avoid many of these dangers. And we supply vital information about what to do when accidents do occur.

Care of the skin and hair is something of a stepchild in medicine, having rarely been taken seriously as a health subject. Because of its importance to many consumers, we bring you practical tips on dermatology and cosmetics. SKIN DISORDER can start you off on this subject.

Nutrition is likewise widely ignored as a major health topic. As a result it has fallen prey to widespread quackery. We include a number of entries aimed at giving you a thorough, scientifically based understanding of food and diet. Begin by reading NUTRITION.

As you read this book, expect surprises. To write an accurate health book is to explode many popular beliefs. As medical writers, even we were amazed at how many things that we had always "known" to be true were in fact myths or are no longer true because of modern medical science. This book brings you up to date on many new developments. Some are as simple as they are effective. For example, PLAQUE control (not only TOOTHBRUSHING) is now the key to dental health, and many dentists are just beginning to tell their patients about it. Plain soap and water, not ANTISEPTICS, is the best means of CLEANSING MINOR WOUNDS. Ice water can prevent scars and pain of BURNS. Hot water relieves ITCHING. A teaspoon of sugar can cure HICCUPS.

And then there are handy bits of information that you need when you need them. Ever wonder what to do if you're in a plane crash? See AIR TRAVEL. Or how to act when you meet wild animals in a national park? See BEARS (and WOLVES for a real surprise). TRAVEL HEALTH is an important consideration for anyone planning a trip. A number of entries deal with INSECTS and other pests.

How to use this book: The book is organized to lead you to information in a hurry. For easy access, the 532 entries are in alphabetical order. In addition, they're listed with page numbers up front in "Entries at a Glance."

Where appropriate, entries lead off with what you need to know right away for emergencies. This is true not only for entries obviously pertaining to first aid (ARTIFICIAL RESPIRATION; HEART STOPPAGE; SHOCK; etc.). FIRE begins by telling you what to do if your clothes catch fire; HEART ATTACK, what to do if you have a coronary; CHILDBIRTH, what to do if a woman starts giving birth before you can get her to a hospital; DRUGS, how to handle a bad drug reaction.

First aid: When you need help in a hurry, the entries are accompanied by illustrations that show at a glance how to handle many emergencies and other home medical problems. They are like miniposters, combining brief instructions with clear pictures. Merely by looking at a fast-action illustration you often know what to do.

Furthermore illustrations and text are aimed at the reader who has no previous knowledge of first aid—and no special first aid equipment. To be as practical as possible we show how you can use in emergencies materials that are likely to be immediately available: rolled-up newspapers to splint FRACTURES; ties and belts when no BANDAGE may be handy; bare hands when you have nothing else to stop BLEEDING.

In general we title entries with the terms most likely to be used by a layman: WHOOPING COUGH rather than pertussis; HIVES, not urticaria. For further convenience we title related entries so that they fall close together, whenever possible. This device creates groupings for such subjects as CANCER; EAR; EYE; HAIR; HEART; TOOTH.

Within and at the end of entries we use cross-references extensively, marked by SMALL CAPITALS. Thus you are reminded you can go from CANCER to SMOKING to HEART DISEASE to OVERWEIGHT to NUTRITION ad infinitum. Like human health itself, the book is an integrated whole.

The entries are written to invite skimming and are in language that you, the patient and consumer, can understand. As patients and consumers ourselves we have learned that the most useful information is worthless unless it is clear to the reader. We know that jargon can be avoided.

For the sake of readability we use he-him-his in referring to a physician at large. Let it be clear that our use of these pronouns refers not necessarily to a man but to (as Webster's says) "that one whose sex is unknown or immaterial." More than 30 percent of all medical students are women, a wave of future practitioners (now about 15 percent female), and the pronouns could well be she-her-hers.

We wish to thank the many physicians, dentists and other specialists, and the many medical journalists, whose work we have drawn on. The citations in our entries hardly do them justice. Special thanks go to the consultants who reviewed the material for accuracy. Reflecting the nature of this book—scientific plus practical—our consultants include both researchers in medical centers and clinicians in office practice. In seeking insights gained in the day-to-day realities of patient care, we've drawn heavily on practitioners in our own representative corner of the United States as well as consulting many other clinicians across the country. Every one of our consultants is in the first rank of his field, and they have our gratitude for joining into the spirit of a consumer-oriented book.

Howard R. and Martha E. Lewis
Shady, New York

CONSULTANTS

The following individuals and organizations have reviewed material in this book for accuracy. We thank them for their generosity in sharing their expertise in a manner of benefit to consumers. Their enthusiasm, comments, and suggestions have been invaluable. All statements of judgment and fact, of course, rest with us.—H.R.L. and M.E.L.

Chief Medical Consultant
James M. Sullivan, M.D.
Albany Medical College

American Academy of Facial Plastic and Reconstructive Surgery: Ferdinand F. Becker, M.D.
American Academy of Orthopaedic Surgeons
American Academy of Pediatrics
American Cancer Society: Irving Rimer
American College of Radiology: Raymond L. Del Fava, M.D.
American Dental Association
American Heart Association
American Lung Association
American Medical Association
American Podiatric Medical Association: Norman Klombers, D.P.M.; Richard B. Patterson, D.P.M.
American Thyroid Association: William M. McConahey, M.D., Mayo Clinic, Rochester, Minnesota
American Tinnitus Association
Arthritis Foundation: Frederic C. McDuffie, M.D.
Association for Children With Retarded Mental Development
Paul L. Cerrato, B.S., M.A., Director of Clinical Nutrition, *RN* Magazine
Dominick D. Davalos, M.D., cardiologist, Memorial Hospital and St. Peter's Hospital, Albany, New York
Deafness Research Foundation: Walter A. Petryshyn, M.D.
Armando DeMoya, M.D., obstetrician, gynecologist, and sex therapist, Georgetown University School of Medicine and George Washington University School of Medicine and Health Sciences, Washington, D.C.

Dorothy DeMoya, M.S.N., obstetric-gynecologic nurse and sex therapist, Georgetown University School of Medicine and Catholic University School of Nursing, Washington, D.C.
Electric Energy Association
Epilepsy Foundation of America
Mark R. Feldman, M.D., gastroenterologist, Kingston, New York; New York Medical College
Joseph J. Forno, pharmacist, Woodstock, New York
Paul Heller, M.D., hematologist, University of Illinois College of Medicine and V.A. West Side Medical Center, Chicago, Illinois
Leon A. Krakower, M.D., psychiatrist and family physician, Poughkeepsie, New York
Sanford Krotenberg, D.D.S., Woodstock, New York
Leukemia Society of America: Kenneth B. McCredie, M.D.
March of Dimes Birth Defects Foundation
Norman B. Medow, M.D., ophthalmologist, Manhattan Eye, Ear and Throat Hospital, New York, New York
Robert F. Moseley, M.D., orthopedist, Salt Lake City; University of Utah School of Medicine
Arnold Erik Nathanson, O.D., Hudson, New York
National Center for the Prevention of SIDS
National Council on Alcoholism: Sheila B. Blume, M.D.
National Cystic Fibrosis Foundation: Robert J. Beall, Ph.D.
National Hemophilia Foundation: Jeanne M. Lusher, M.D.
National Kidney Foundation
National Migraine Foundation: Seymour Diamond, M.D.
National Multiple Sclerosis Society: Robert Slater, M.D.
National Society to Prevent Blindness
New York League for the Hard of Hearing: Jane R. Madell, Ph.D.
Parkinson's Disease Foundation

Jamshid Payman, M.D., pediatrician and allergist, Kingston, New York

Randall Rissman, M.D., family physician, Woodstock, New York

Leon E. Schwartz, M.D., dermatologist, San Bernardino, California

Robert L. Schwartz, C.P.A., Kingston, New York

Spina Bifida Association of America

Samuel J. Stein, M.D., allergist and dermatologist, Kingston, New York

United Cerebral Palsy Associations: Leon Sternfeld, M.D.

ENTRIES AT A GLANCE

A

abdominal injuries   1
abortion   1
accidents   3
acne   4
acoustic neuroma   6
AIDS   6
air pollution   9
air travel   9
alcohol   11
allergy   17
amblyopia   22
amebiasis   22
amphetamines   23
analgesics   23
anemia   24
animal bites   25
animal disease   26
ankylosing spondylitis   27
antacids   27
antibiotics   28
anticoagulants   30
antihistamines   31
antiseptics   31
ants   32
appendicitis   32
arm fractures   33
arteriosclerosis   33
arthritis   35
artificial respiration   38
arts and crafts   59
asbestos   59
aspirin   59
asthma   62
astigmatism   65
athlete's foot   65
axes   66

B

baby-sitters   67
backache   67
back fractures   71
bags under the eyes   71
bandages   71

barbiturates   71
bathing   72
bats   73
bears   74
bedbugs   74
bed rest   74
bedsores   79
bedwetting   80
bicycles   82
birth control   83
birth defects   90
birthmarks   92
black eyes   93
bleeding   93
blisters   94
blood clot   94
blood pressure   94
blood transfusion   98
boating   99
boils   100
botulism   101
breastfeeding   101
breast sagging   103
breast smallness   103
breath-holding   104
bronchiectasis   104
bronchitis   105
brucellosis   105
bruises   106
bunions   106
burns   106
bursitis   108

C

calluses   109
camping   109
camps   110
cancer   111
cancer in children   118
cancer of the bladder   119
cancer of the bone   120
cancer of the brain   120
cancer of the breast   121

cancer of the colon and
   rectum   124
cancer of the larynx   126
cancer of the lung   126
cancer of the mouth   127
cancer of the prostate   128
cancer of the skin   129
cancer of the stomach   130
cancer of the testicles   131
cancer of the uterus   132
canker sores   133
canned food   133
carbohydrates   134
cars   135
cataract   140
caterpillars   141
cat scratch disease   141
centipedes   142
cerebral palsy   142
charley horse   142
chest injuries   142
chest pain   142
chickenpox   144
chiggers   144
childbirth   145
chiropractors   148
choking   150
cholera   153
Christmas trees   154
circles under the eyes   154
circumcision   154
cleansing minor
   wounds   155
cleft lip   156
cleft palate   156
coccidioidomycosis   156
cockroaches   157
colds   158
cold sores   161
cold weather   161
colitis   162
collarbone fracture   163
color blindness   163
compresses   164

congenital heart
    defects   165
constipation   167
contact dermatitis   168
contact lenses   170
convulsions   173
corns   175
coronary artery
    disease   175
coughing   175
crib death   177
cribs   178
crossed eyes   178
croup   178
cuts   179
cystic fibrosis   180
cysts   181

D

dandruff   183
death   183
dehydration   187
dentures   187
dermographism   189
diabetes   189
diaper rash   196
diarrhea   196
diathermy   197
diphtheria   197
dislocations   198
diverticulitis   198
dizziness   199
Down's syndrome   199
drowning   200
drug allergy   202
drugs   203
dust disease   208

E

earache   210
ear deformities   210
ear infections   210
ear piercing   211
earwax   211
eclipses   212
eczema   212
edema   213
electric shock   213
emergency medical
    identification   215
emphysema   216

encephalitis   217
epilepsy   218
erosion of the cervix   219
erysipelas   220
erythema multiforme   220
exercise   220
eye disorder   226
eye donation   228
eye exercises   228
eyeglasses   228
eye injuries   230
eye makeup   231
eyestrain   232
eyewashes   232

F

fainting   233
fallen arches   234
falls   234
falls through ice   235
farsightedness   236
fatigue   236
fats   237
fever   238
fiber   241
finger fractures   241
fingernail brittleness   242
fire   242
fireworks   246
first aid supplies   246
fishing   248
fleas   248
flies   249
floods   249
fluoridation   249
food additives   251
food allergy   252
food poisoning   254
football   256
foot problems   257
fractures   259
freckles   260
frigidity   261
frostbite   262

G

gagging   266
gallbladder disease   266
gas   266
gas poisoning   267
giardiasis   268

gingivitis   268
glass   269
glaucoma   269
glue sniffing   271
golf   271
gonorrhea   271
gouges   273
gout   273
growing pains   274
gunshot wounds   274

H

hair bleaching   276
hair brushing   276
hair curling   276
hair dryness   277
hair dyeing   277
hairiness   278
hair loss   280
hair oiliness   283
hair straightening   283
hair washing   283
hairy tongue   284
Halloween   284
hand, foot, and mouth
    disease   284
hangover   284
hay fever   285
headache   287
head injuries   288
health clubs   288
health food   289
health insurance   291
hearing aids   295
hearing loss   297
heart attack   300
heart block   303
heart disease   304
heart failure   306
heart murmurs   307
heart palpitation   307
heart stoppage   308
heat cramps   308
heat exhaustion   308
heat stroke   309
hemophilia   310
hemorrhoids   310
hepatitis   311
hernia   313
herpes   313

hiccups   314
hiking   315
histoplasmosis   316
hives   317
hoarseness   318
Hodgkin's disease   318
hookworms   319
hospital   320
hospitalizing children   322
hot weather   323
humidity   325
hydrocephalus   326
hyperventilation   326
hypoglycemia   326
hysterectomy   327

I

ice skating   329
ichthyosis   329
immunization   329
impetigo   332
impotence   332
indigestion   334
infectious disease   334
infertility   337
influenza   338
ingrown hairs   340
ingrown toenails   340
insects   340
insect stings   343
iron   345
itching   345

J

jellyfish   347
jet lag   347
jock itch   348

K

keloids   349
kidney disease   349
kidney stones   350
kites   351
knives   351

L

lead poisoning   352
leeches   352
leg fractures   353
leg pain   354
leprosy   354
leptospirosis   355
leukemia   356

lice   357
lighting   358
lightning   359

M

machines   360
malabsorption   360
malaria   360
malocclusion   361
masturbation   363
measles   363
medical deductions   364
medical supplies   365
Ménière's disease   366
meningitis   366
menopause   367
menstruation   368
mental retardation   370
microwave ovens   371
migraine   371
minerals   372
minibikes   373
mold allergy   373
moles   375
mononucleosis   375
mosquitoes   376
motion sickness   377
motorcycles   377
mouth cleft   378
mouth odor   378
mouth sores   379
mouthwashes   379
moving the injured   379
mowers   381
multiple sclerosis   381
mumps   382
muscular dystrophy   383
myasthenia gravis   384

N

nail-biting   385
nausea   385
nearsightedness   385
neck fractures   386
neuritis   386
noise   386
nosebleed   387
nose deformities   388
nose drops   388
nose fractures   389
nose obstructions   390
nutrition   390

O

osteoarthritis   404
osteoporosis   404
overweight   405

P

paint removers   415
paralysis   415
Parkinson's disease   415
pelvic fractures   416
pemphigus   417
peptic ulcer   418
periodontal disease   419
perspiration odor   419
physical examination   420
physician   422
pink eye   427
pinworms   428
PKU   429
plague   429
plaque   430
plaster casts   432
pleurisy   432
pneumonia   433
poisoning   434
poison ivy   437
poisonous plants   439
polio   440
postnasal drip   441
pregnancy   441
premature birth   446
premature ejaculation   447
presbyopia   447
prickly heat   448
prostate trouble   448
protein   449
psoriasis   450
pulse   451
punctures   452

Q

quackery   454

R

rabies   458
radiation   459
rats   459
refrigerators   460
respiratory disease   460
Rh disease   462
rheumatic fever   463
rheumatism   463

rheumatoid arthritis   464
rib fractures   465
ringworm   466
Rocky Mountain spotted
   fever   467
roundworms   467
rubella   467

S

salmonellosis   469
scabies   469
scarlet fever   470
scars   470
scarves   470
schistosomiasis   470
sciatica   471
scissors   471
scorpions   471
scrapes   472
scuba diving   472
seborrheic dermatitis   473
severed parts   473
sex disorder   474
shaving   478
shigellosis   478
shingles   479
shock   479
shortness   480
shortness of breath   481
sickle cell anemia   482
sinusitis   483
skiing   484
skin disorders   485
skin dryness   488
skin oiliness   489
skull fractures   489
skunks   489
sleeplessness   490
sleepwalking   491
slipped disc   492
smallpox   492
smoking   492
snakebite   498
snoring   502
snowmobiles   503
sodium   503
solar plexus blows   505
sore throat   505
spider bites   506
spider veins   507
spina bifida   507

splinters   508
sports   508
sprains   509
spray cans   510
steroids   510
stiff neck   511
stingrays   512
strains   512
stress   513
stroke   516
styes   518
sunburn   518
sunglasses   521
surgery   522
sweaty palms   525
swimming pools   525
syphilis   525
systemic lupus
   erythematosus   527

T

tapeworms   528
tattoos   528
teeth and mouth
   disorders   528
television   531
tennis elbow   531
testicle blows   531
tetanus   532
thrombophlebitis   532
thyroid disease   533
tic douloureux   534
ticklishness   534
ticks   534
tinnitus   535
tonsillitis   535
tools   537
toothache   537
toothbrushing   537
tooth decay   539
tooth extraction   540
toothpaste   540
tooth salvaging   541
tornadoes   542
tourniquet   542
toxoplasmosis   543
toys   543
trachoma   545
trains   545
tranquilizers   546

travel health   547
trench foot   550
trench mouth   551
trichinosis   551
trichomoniasis   552
trick knee   553
tuberculosis   553
tuberculous arthritis   554
tularemia   554
typhoid   554
typhus   555

U

unconsciousness   556
underweight   556
undescended testicles   557
urinary tract infection   557

V

vaginal douching   559
vaginal infection   559
vaginal odor   560
varicose veins   561
vasectomy   562
vegetarianism   563
venereal disease   563
vitamins   564
vitiligo   568

W

warts   569
water contamination   569
water on the knee   570
webbed fingers   570
webbed toes   570
whiplash   570
whooping cough   571
wolves   571
wrinkles   571

X

xanthoma   574
X rays   574

Y

yeast infection   576
yellow fever   576

Z

zippers   578

A

ABDOMINAL INJURIES are often accompanied by shock and internal bleeding. A blow—from a car crash, from a thump in a schoolyard scuffle—may rupture or damage internal organs such as the liver, spleen, kidneys or intestines. Symptoms usually appear within six hours, but may not show up for several days.

Deep cuts (lacerations) of the abdomen may cause organs, particularly intestines, to spill out. Gently cover protruding organs with a damp cloth, and keep the cloth moist and warm. Alternatively, cover the wound with aluminum foil or another nonsticking material (see illustration).

Don't touch the organs with your fingers or try to put them back; by doing so you're likely to cause further injury. Control bleeding with a pressure bandage.

See also ACCIDENTS; BANDAGES; BLEEDING; CUTS; SHOCK.

IF THE ABDOMEN IS OPENED

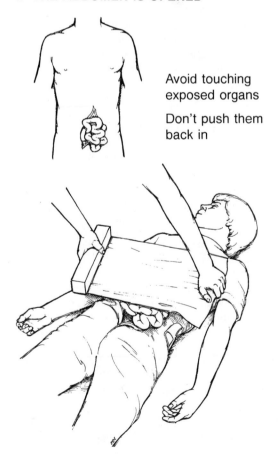

Avoid touching exposed organs

Don't push them back in

Cover with nonsticking material
(Aluminum foil, damp cloth, plastic wrap)

ABORTION is the termination of a pregnancy.

A spontaneous abortion, or miscarriage, occurs without outside interference in about 25 percent of all pregnancies, usually during the first three months. The most common reasons for miscarriages are a medical condition in the pregnant woman or an abnormality of the pregnancy. Call a doctor if you are pregnant and develop vaginal bleeding or abdominal cramps.

Induced abortion is the deliberate removal of the fetus to end the pregnancy. In the controversy surrounding legal abortion those who oppose abortion for any reason contend that the interruption of pregnancy constitutes murder. On the other side are those who believe that a woman has a right to choose whether or not she wants to bear a child.

While the moral debate still rages, some of the legal problems are being resolved. Until the 1973 Supreme Court decision legalizing abortion most states would permit legal abortions only to save the life of the mother. Thus women wishing to terminate a pregnancy had the choice of either bearing an unwanted child or obtaining an illegal abortion with considerable risk to health and life. An estimated 1.2 million illegal abortions were performed in the United States annually, with many women dying as a result.

Liberalized abortion laws have brought about a sharp decline in maternal death and injury rates. When abortion became available on demand in New York City, the maternal death rate there dropped 68.6 percent in one year. There was also a decline in illegitimate births and in injuries from incomplete abortions. Overall, legal abortion in the United States is safer than childbirth. The vast majority of women having legal abortions develop no complications of any kind.

The Supreme Court decision legalized abortion during the first three months of pregnancy. Abortions after three months also became legal, but subject to individual state regulations.

Don't confuse abortion with birth control—it's not a safe substitute.

Abortion may in some cases have an adverse effect on future childbearing. Although not conclusive there is evidence that repeated or improperly performed abortion increases the chances of premature delivery in subsequent pregnancies. But studies of uncomplicated abortions done with current medical techniques find no connection between abortion and any later pregnancy problems.

Consider abortion only when contraception fails.

Never try to abort yourself. Abortion is safe only in competent medical hands. Attempting to dislodge a fetus with knitting needles or coat hangers can be fatal. Nor should you attempt do-it-yourself suction with a vacuum cleaner. This could perforate your uterus and suck out part of your intestine.

If you suspect that you're pregnant, get medical confirmation before arranging for an abortion. A menstrual period may be skipped for many reasons other than pregnancy.

Early abortions. Up to 12 weeks the most commonly used abortion procedure is suction, or vacuum aspiration. The procedure is usually done under local anesthesia. The cervix (the opening of the uterus) is usually anesthetized, then dilated (enlarged). A vacuum pump attached to a thin tube is then inserted into the uterus. Gentle suction dislodges the fetus. The woman may feel some cramps during the dilating, but the suction is usually quick (five or ten minutes) and painless.

The procedure might involve an overnight stay in a hospital. More commonly it takes a half day at an abortion clinic. Prices vary depending on the type of facility used.

Dilation and curettage (usually referred to as D & C) was formerly the most common abortion procedure in the United States but is now used in only a small percentage of cases. For D & C the cervix is dilated more than for suction and the uterus is scraped with a curette.

Late abortions. Beyond the twelfth week a woman's risks increase. Saline is used for most abortions after 16 weeks. In this procedure the physician applies a local anesthetic and inserts a long, hollow needle through the abdominal wall into the amniotic sac surrounding the fetus. He draws out some amniotic fluid and replaces it with a concentrated saltwater solution. The salt injection induces an abbreviated form of labor within three days.

Hormonelike chemicals called prostaglandins have been approved by the Food and Drug Administration (FDA) for use in inducing labor between the twelfth and twenty-fourth weeks. Like saline the prostaglandin technique involves an injection into the amniotic sac, but of a much smaller amount of fluid. Most women experience some degree of nausea and vomiting.

Major complications of the saline and prostaglandin methods include infection and retained placental tissue, often with bleeding and

fever. Infection can usually be treated with antibiotics; retained placenta usually requires a D & C.

Dilation and evacuation (D & E) is another method of late abortion. Similar to D & C, it involves dilating the cervix with graduated metal dilators. Then suction curettage is used, frequently in conjunction with crushing forceps or sharp curettage. The relative safety of saline, prostaglandin, and D & E is still being debated.

Hysterotomy, a miniature cesarean section, is an abortion technique usually performed only in conjunction with sterilization by tying the fallopian tubes. The surgeon makes an incision through the abdomen and uterus and removes the fetus and placenta. The operation, four times as risky as a saline abortion, usually requires general anesthesia and several days of hospitalization.

A small number of abortions are performed by hysterectomy, surgical removal of the uterus. This is major surgery and is usually done only when the uterus is diseased.

Aftercare. A menstruallike flow of blood is normal after abortion. It may stop completely for a few days, then resume. A woman should wear sanitary pads, not tampons. She needs to report to her doctor any bleeding heavier than the heaviest menstrual flow she's experienced, and any passage of large clots.

She should also report severe cramps that begin later than a day after the abortion. Other danger signs: fever; a greenish, foul-smelling vaginal discharge; and burning or frequent urination. She should have a follow-up examination about two weeks after the abortion.

A woman can safely resume intercourse about 48 hours after the cessation of all bleeding. This usually occurs a week to ten days after the abortion.

Abortion help. Several agencies can help a woman obtain a safe, low-cost abortion. Planned Parenthood and the National Clergy Consultation Service on Abortion have affiliates in most states. Both are nonprofit agencies and charge no fee for referrals. If there is no local listing for these organizations, call their national offices in New York City to get the location of the nearest facility.

Stay away from private abortion referral services. Such commercial enterprises charge women up to $150 for abortion referral—the same information the nonprofit organizations offer free of charge.

Abortion can be an upsetting experience for any woman, and particularly for teen-agers. Talking about one's feelings of fear and guilt can help to alleviate them, and many abortion clinics include some kind of counseling as part of the procedure.

In general, though, studies show that most women who undergo abortions do not have any lingering emotional problems, even though they may experience mild feelings of depression. One British study of several hundred women found that women who really wanted the abortions "had remarkably little psychiatric disturbance." Conversely, many women who experience the stress of bearing an unwanted child often had to be hospitalized for severe psychiatric problems.

See also CHILDBIRTH; HYSTERECTOMY; MENSTRUATION; PREGNANCY.

ACCIDENTS injure more than 10 million Americans a year. Accidents are the leading cause of death in children under 15, each year killing about 15,000. In the total population accidents take more than 100,000 lives a year, making them the fourth leading killer (after heart disease, cancer, and stroke).

In helping an accident victim, no matter what the cause, these are your first aid priorities:

1. Clear air passages. Remove debris, mucus, blood from the mouth and throat.
2. Try to restore breathing and heartbeat with ARTIFICIAL RESPIRATION (which see), preferably using mouth-to-mouth resuscitation.
3. If there is still no heartbeat, use closed-chest massage (see HEART STOPPAGE).
4. Stop BLEEDING (which see) with direct pressure. Use a tourniquet only when an emergency justifies sacrificing a limb (see TOURNIQUET).
5. Treat for SHOCK (which see). For more detailed first aid instructions, see the end of this entry.

Causes of accidents. Cars and other motor vehicles account for nearly half of all accidental deaths. Motorcycles are statistically the most hazardous vehicle, causing the greatest number of deaths per number of machines, and minibikes pose dangers that make them unsafe for the youngsters for whom they are supposedly designed.

Falls are the second greatest cause of accidental deaths, particularly hazardous to the elderly.

Drowning follows in frequency. Watch yourself and children around water. People drown not only while swimming in pools, lakes, or oceans, but also while fishing, boating, and scuba diving.

Burns and other deaths from fire are next in prevalence. Using fireworks, often illegally, adds to the toll.

Choking, the next largest category, among adults usually involves bits of food stuck in the airway. For children suffocation is the leading cause of death in home accidents. Infants may strangle in their cribs, and too many children die when they are accidentally locked in abandoned or empty refrigerators.

Poisons take the next greatest toll. A multitude of household products can cause death, and attractive poisonous plants that bloom in nearly every garden are often sampled by children.

Gunshot wounds, which follow poisoning as a cause of death, kill many hunters but many more people at home.

There are many mechanical causes of accidents. Power lawn mowers are particularly dangerous. Spray cans and glass bottles often explode. Be cautious while using tools and arts-and-crafts materials. Check the end of this entry for specific kinds of accidents, hazards, and first aid measures.

When will accidents occur? Be extra careful on Saturdays and between 3:00 and 6:00 P.M. That's when accidents most often happen, according to the Boston Children's Hospital Medical Center. The hospital's study dealt with accidents to children, but most of the findings apply equally well to adults.

Accidents are most likely to occur when the family has departed in some degree from its usual routine, or under any of the following circumstances:

The family members are hungry or tired.
The mother is ill, about to menstruate, or pregnant.
The mother must take care of an ill family member.
The mother is rushed.
The child is in the care of another person.
The family is moving or taking a trip.
The parents are under emotional stress.
The parents overestimate or underestimate what a child is capable of. A mother may not realize that with a bit of ingenuity her two-year-old can reach a high shelf containing poisons. Or she may not understand that a simple warning, such as "Don't play with matches," is unlikely to deter a child under five.

To avoid accidents accommodate to these situations. For instance, if family members are hungry because dinner is delayed, fix a quick, cold snack. During periods of stress simplify your schedule.

See also ABDOMINAL INJURIES; ANIMAL BITES; ARTIFICIAL RESPIRATION; ARTS AND

CRAFTS; AXES; BABY-SITTERS; BICYCLES; BLACK EYES; BLEEDING; BLISTERS; BOATING; BRUISES; BURNS; CAMPING; CAMPS; CARS; CHOKING; CHRISTMAS TREES; COLD WEATHER; COMPRESSES; CRIBS; CUTS.

DROWNING; ELECTRIC SHOCK; FAINTING; FALLS; FALLS THROUGH ICE; FIRE; FIREWORKS; FIRST AID SUPPLIES; FISHING; FLOODS; FOOTBALL; FRACTURES; FROSTBITE; GAS POISONING; GLASS; GOLF; GOUGES; GUNSHOT WOUNDS; HALLOWEEN; HEAD INJURIES; HEART STOPPAGE; HEAT CRAMPS; HEAT EXHAUSTION; HEAT STROKE; HIKING; HOT WEATHER.

ICE SKATING; INSECT STINGS; KITES; KNIVES; LEAD POISONING; LIGHTNING; MACHINES; MEDICAL SUPPLIES; MINIBIKES; MOTORCYCLES; MOVING THE INJURED; MOWERS; NOSEBLEED; NOSE OBSTRUCTIONS; PAINT REMOVERS; POISONING; POISONOUS PLANTS; PUNCTURES; REFRIGERATORS.

SCARS; SCISSORS; SCORPIONS; SCRAPES; SCUBA DIVING; SHOCK; SKIING; SNAKEBITE; SNOWMOBILES; SOLAR PLEXUS BLOWS; SPIDER BITES; SPLINTERS; SPORTS; SPRAY CANS; SUNBURN; SWIMMING POOLS; TESTICLE BLOWS; TOOLS; TOYS; TOURNIQUET; TRAINS; TRENCH FOOT; UNCONSCIOUSNESS; WATER CONTAMINATION; ZIPPERS.

ACETAMINOPHEN See ASPIRIN.

ACETYLSALICYLIC ACID See ASPIRIN.

ACID INDIGESTION See INDIGESTION.

ACNE (acne vulgaris) Few adolescents entirely escape this skin problem, and even a moderate case can last for five to ten years or more. It usually begins at just the time of life when youngsters are most self-conscious about their appearance, and can cause untold agony. Adolescents with acne may feel stigmatized and socially outcast. They often become withdrawn and depressed. Consider counseling if your youngster is unusually troubled by having acne.

For a small number of acne sufferers the disorder begins after adolescence. If it begins abruptly in middle age, a hormone disorder may be the cause, and a physician should be consulted. Adults are more prone than adolescents to a severe form of acne called cystic acne, characterized by purple cysts the size of quarters.

Cause of acne. Acne is usually triggered by hormonal changes of puberty. Despite folklore, it has nothing to do with masturbation, "bad" thoughts, sexual problems, constipation, or indigestion.

Acne is a disorder of the sebaceous glands. These glands, which nestle around hair follicles, secrete a waxy lubricant called sebum. The glands are most numerous on the face, chest, and back.

Sex hormones produced in increasing amounts in adolescence stimulate the glands to enlarge and secrete excess sebum. This plugs the follicle. Result: one whitehead or blackhead.

Blackheads have nothing to do with dirt. The color comes from dark melanin pigment at the pore opening. In a whitehead, the top is closed, with no melanin visible.

A whitehead develops into a pimple when the excess secretion breaks down the wall of the follicle, and oils and fatty acids inflame the surrounding tissue. If pus gathers in pimples, you may get boils.

Acne flare-ups often accompany menstruation, emotional upsets, or too little rest. If teenagers become overconcerned about their acne, help them understand that the worrying itself may aggravate the condition.

Treating acne. There is no quick cure for acne, but you can help control it by doing the following.

See a physician if you have more than a few blackheads or pimples. A physician can evaluate the degree of acne and determine whether you need to be referred to a dermatologist. Most doctors who treat acne advise a regimen that includes many of these following measures.

Wash your face two or three times a day. While oil and dirt do not cause acne, they may contribute to it. To remove grease and plugs use hot water and rub gently with a washcloth.

Ordinary soap will usually suffice. If not try an abrasive soap (Brasivol, Pernox). The irritating granules of these products may promote peeling—but may be too harsh if your skin is sensitive. Soaps that contain sulfur and salicylic acid promote peeling and dry the skin and may have some value in controlling acne.

On the other hand, excessive drying may delay clearing of acne lesions. Indeed, many dermatologists advise you to avoid excess moisturizers and to use water-based makeups. Some dermatologists recommend against using water at all. Instead they advise their patients to use an emollient cream (such as Eucerin), rubbing it into the skin and then wiping it off.

Be gentle—irritating the skin may cause inflammation. The AMA warns that mechanical face cleansers won't cleanse the skin any better than a washcloth and soap and water. Automatic or manual complexion brushes can irritate, causing redness and scaling. No device can clean beneath the surface of the skin, so be skeptical of claims for "super deep-pore" cleansing.

Similarly, warns the AMA, there's no evidence that "facial saunas" (which are actually facial steam baths) will relieve acne or remove skin blemishes. Steam won't take the place of soap and water. Nor will sweating flush out pores. Indeed the steam and excess sweating may worsen the condition and produce a severe form called tropical acne.

Use drying creams or lotions. They create a continuous mild peeling of the skin that helps keep pores open. Products that contain benzoyl peroxide are considered most effective. Over-the-counter preparations with various strengths of benzoyl peroxide include Benoxyl, Clearasil Antibacterial, Oxy, and Persadox. Different formulations of benzoyl peroxide (Benzagel, Persa-Gel) are available with a doctor's prescription.

Products that contain salicylic acid, sulfur, resorcinol, or combinations of these drugs are also considered effective, although less so than benzoyl peroxide. Such over-the-counter products include Fostex, Fostril, Listerex, Acnaveen, and many others. Follow package directions carefully.

Drying preparations are usually applied every night, then washed off in the morning. Girls can use them during the day as well, in place of makeup.

It's best not to use cosmetics. If you do, use a water-based product and apply as little of it as possible.

Soak up sunshine. Sunbathing may cause too much skin dryness for some people, but it is a boon to acne sufferers.

In northern winter climates take ultraviolet treatments twice a week with an ordinary 275-watt RS sunlight bulb. To avoid sunburn keep the bulb at least 2 feet from your skin, cover your eyes, and limit exposure to five minutes. You seek a reddening and slight scaling of the skin. If none results, increase the exposure to six or seven minutes. Don't confuse ultraviolet rays with infrared heat, which is of no value in acne.

Before you sunbathe, ask your doctor if any medication you are taking—for acne or another condition—can increase your susceptibility to sunburn.

Don't squeeze blackheads or pimples. You can spread infection and cause deep-pitted scars.

If you want to remove blackheads, ask your physician if he recommends home use of an extractor, which can be bought at pharmacies. Before you use the extractor, soften the plugs with hot wet compresses for about ten minutes.

Watch your diet. Some foods—particularly sweets, starchy and fatty foods, shellfish, and pork—may possibly aggravate acne for some people.

Some dermatologists advise acne sufferers to omit all of the following: pastries, pies, cakes, ice cream, soda-fountain drinks, cream in any form, jams, jellies, fried foods, gravies, alcoholic drinks, peanut butter, nuts, chocolate, cocoa, mayonnaise, corned beef, pork, ham, bacon, and all shellfish. In addition they advise limiting sugar, butter or other shortening, beef, macaroni, noodles, spaghetti, potatoes, bread, rice, and cheeses.

However most dermatologists believe that the role of diet in acne has been overemphasized. A University of Pennsylvania study demonstrated that even chocolate, a traditional villain, may actually have little or no effect. The researchers could find no difference in acne between people who ate a daily candy bar containing ten times the amount of chocolate in a typical bar, and those who ate an identical-appearing bar containing no chocolate at all.

The effect of diet seems to vary with each individual, so experiment by following a safe and healthy diet—cereals, eggs, fish, chicken, vegetables, fruits. Introduce one omitted item at a time to see if it causes a flare-up. Do so in small portions, since excessive amounts may cause a reaction while moderate amounts will be well tolerated.

Ask your doctor about drugs. Small doses of some antibiotics have been helpful in controlling moderate to severe acne. Tetracyclines have been particularly effective but may cause sensitivity to the sun. In such small doses antibiotics have been used for many months or even years with minimal side effects. To absorb the tetracycline properly take it one hour before or two hours after a meal and never with milk. The drug should not be used by pregnant women.

For mild to moderate acne topical antibiotic lotion may be prescribed. Among the topical antibiotics commonly used are clindamycin phosphate (Cleocin T), erythromycin (Staticin), tetracycline (Topicycline), and meclocycline sulfosalicylate (Meclan). Some consultants for *The Medical Letter* believe that topical clindamycin may be more effective than other topical antibiotics.

The use of topical antibiotics sometimes results in burning and irritation. Topical tetracycline causes a faint yellowing of the skin and skin fluorescence that can be seen under the "black light" of discotheques.

X-ray therapy should be avoided. Topical corticosteroids may worsen acne. When a woman's acne seems related to her menstrual cycle, and other measures have failed, birth control pills that contain estrogen may bring relief. But because estrogen may stunt growth, it should not be given to girls under 16.

Vitamin A acid applied to the skin has relieved some severe cases of acne, especially when used in tandem with benzoyl peroxide. Initially vitamin A acid worsens acne; improvement may not be seen for two months or more. Since vitamin A acid makes your skin more sensitive to sunlight, stay out of the sun as much as possible.

Vitamin A tablets are of questionable value in acne. Consult a physician before attempting treatment with vitamin A, which in large doses can be toxic. Taking vitamin E or rubbing it into the skin has no scientific basis whatever.

For very severe acne the dermatologist may use surgery to drain large pimples or abscesses. Liquid nitrogen or solid carbon dioxide may be applied to the skin. Corticosteroids may be injected into acne cysts. Also available is a synthetic vitamin A known as 13-*cis*-retinoic acid (Accutane), which holds promise in cases of severe, resistant acne.

Iodides and bromides may make acne worse, so avoid cough medicine containing iodides, and remedies for insomnia that contain bromides. Prescription drugs containing some hormones, such as ACTH and steroids, may cause acne flare-ups.

Keep your hair off your face. Bangs and long hair make it hard to keep the skin clean and to apply medications. Hair also shields the face from the sun's rays. Whether it is long or short, wash your hair often to get rid of excess oil. Avoid hair dressings with greasy or lanolin bases that can cause "pomade acne" on the forehead and temples.

Also keep your hands off your face. Acne can flare up on your chin if you frequently rest your chin on your hand.

Whiskers, too, can be a problem. Follow these suggestions for shaving: Shave with the grain and as seldom as possible (maybe once or twice a week). Some acne sufferers are helped by changing from a blade razor to an electric shaver, but in general a wet shave seems best. Use a new blade each time, and shave as lightly as possible to avoid nicking pimples. Soften the beard by washing carefully first with plenty of soap and hot water. After shaving rinse with hot, then cold, water. Apply witch hazel or after-shave lotion.

Don't pluck ingrown hairs. Gently loosen the free ends so they do not grow back into the skin.

Removing acne scars. Mild or moderate acne often disappears without a trace. More severe cases may leave behind pits and scars. These can often be reduced. In skin planing (dermabra-

sion), the top cell layers of the skin are scraped down by a sanding or planing device or by a rapidly rotating wire brush. After swelling and crusting disappear, usually within two weeks, the smoother, softer underlying skin is revealed. The technique is rarely successful for leathery, pitted, wide-pored skin. Occasionally dermabrasion leaves a person with darkened areas of skin.

To reduce the danger of scarring, skin planing should be done only by a physician, generally a dermatologist or plastic surgeon.

Avoid "chemical face peels" and never go to a layman such as a beautician or health spa operator for any kind of chemosurgery. Peels—which involve applying a burning agent such as carbolic acid to the skin—are occasionally recommended for removing minor wrinkles and freckles, but must be done only by a physician.

See also BOILS; HAIR OILINESS; SKIN DISORDER; SKIN OILINESS.

ACOUSTIC NEUROMA is a benign ear tumor that grows around the acoustic nerve. The acoustic nerve affects balance as well as hearing, and symptoms of the neuroma include dizziness, tinnitus (noise in the ear), loss of hearing, headache, and trouble with eyesight. Since the acoustic nerve is close to the facial nerve, there may be some loss of skin sensation or movement of the facial muscles.

Acoustic neuroma is not a cancer and will not spread to other parts of the body. But it can be fatal. If untreated the acoustic neuroma may continue to grow, pressing on the brain until it destroys some function necessary to life.

The tumor may be removed by surgery. If the neuroma is small (perhaps the size of a pea), removal may improve hearing and cure dizziness. If the tumor is large, however, a section of the nerve may have to be removed, which could cause permanent hearing loss in the affected ear.

Acoustic neuroma is believed to affect some 2 percent of the population. But in most cases the growth is so small that it never causes any symptoms and is not life-threatening.

See also HEARING LOSS; TINNITUS.

ADAMS-STOKES SYNDROME See HEART BLOCK.

ADENOIDS See TONSILLITIS.

AEROBICS See EXERCISE.

AEROSOLS See ARTS AND CRAFTS; SPRAY CANS.

AIDS (acquired immune deficiency syndrome) is a disruption of the immune system, which defends the body against infection. When AIDS was first diagnosed in the summer of 1981 it seemed confined to certain groups.

The people at highest risk included homosexual men with many sex partners, users of intravenous drugs, and hemophiliacs who require frequent blood transfusions. Those groups remain most susceptible to AIDS.

Now, however, the virus is spreading rapidly into the general population, mainly through these pathways:

Contaminated blood. In Pennsylvania, a hemophiliac received a blood product donated by someone carrying the AIDS virus. He transmitted the virus to his wife. She passed it on to their son in the womb or through her milk. The husband and son showed signs of succumbing rapidly to AIDS, while the wife had early symptoms.

Bisexual contact. In Washington, D.C., a man contracted the AIDS virus from a gay partner. He entered into a relationship with a woman. During their year-long affair, she contracted the virus from him. Now she's dying of AIDS. She's selected the urn to hold her ashes after her cremation.

Heterosexual carriers. In Belle Glade, Florida, prostitutes harbor the AIDS virus. They are presumed to spread it to farm workers, who carry it in their migrations up the eastern seaboard. Also among the prostitutes' customers are long-distance truckers, who are thought to convey the virus all over the country.

By such routes has AIDS infected the drug-free heterosexual majority. Authorities already warn that no one is entirely safe from the syndrome. Each year the number of heterosexual patients increases. Dr. William A. Blattner of the National Cancer Institute forecasts a day when more heterosexuals than homosexuals will have AIDS.

What causes AIDS? In AIDS, a virus attacks white blood cells called T lymphocyte "helper" cells. These cells normally activate the defense system. In addition, the AIDS virus decreases the effectiveness of antibodies, which are important in the body's defenses.

Another destructive effect: The body normally has "suppressor" lymphocytes that chemically turn *off* the immune system. The AIDS virus does not attack this type of lymphocyte, so relatively more and more suppressor cells are involved in weakening the immune system. A person with AIDS is thus more vulnerable to many diseases.

Signs and complications. A person with AIDS generally feels run-down, with unexplained tiredness and weight loss. He may have persistent fever, night sweats, and diarrhea. He's likely to have a dry, hacking cough and be short of breath. Mild infections such as a cold or cold sores are more severe and last much longer than normal.

Because the immune system is weakened, AIDS patients are open to attack by bacteria, viruses, and other organisms in the environment. Normally, people can resist such germs. But in AIDS the germs seize the opportunity offered by the person's weakened defenses. They can cause "opportunistic infections" that can be extremely difficult to cure.

The most common opportunistic infection results from an invasion of the lungs by a parasite called *Pneumocystis carinii.* Pneumonia caused by the organism is marked by fever, breathing difficulties, weight loss, and a dry cough. Treatment is difficult because the drugs used against the parasite often cause AIDS patients to suffer many side effects.

AIDS patients also may suffer pneumonia, colitis, and other infections from an agent called cytomegalovirus, for which there is no effective treatment. Herpes viruses also commonly strike AIDS patients, causing severe infections. AIDS patients may further have candidiasis, a fungus infection of the mouth, throat, esophagus, and rectum. Bacteria may cause meningitis and widespread, often fatal, infections. The AIDS virus may also damage the brain, causing a dementia resembling Alzheimer's disease.

Cancer also may result. The AIDS patient may develop painless red to purple bruises or sores. These may occur on his body or inside his mouth, nose or anus. Such lesions are signs of a type of cancer called Kaposi's sarcoma. Ordinarily Kaposi's sarcoma is a rare and relatively benign skin cancer. It chiefly affects elderly men of Mediterranean ancestry, in whom it grows slowly.

In AIDS patients, however, Kaposi's sarcoma spreads rapidly and may be widely disseminated. It can involve the skin, lymph nodes, and abdominal organs. AIDS patients are also more vulnerable to cancers of the lymph nodes, lip, tongue, and anus.

Treatment for AIDS-related cancers and infections is only partly effective. Thus the prognosis for AIDS patients is grave. Death within two years is virtually certain with some opportunistic infections, especially if combined with Kaposi's sarcoma.

Protecting yourself. Preventive measures may especially benefit people who are in high-risk populations. The following are particularly important for gays in areas where AIDS is most prevalent:

The safest forms of sexual activity include

massage, snuggling, and mutual masturbation. In general, homosexual men should avoid anonymous partners, diminish the total number of partners, and—most important—avoid the exchange of bodily secretions. IV drug users should refrain from sharing needles.

Avoid the exchange of semen via oral or anal intercourse. Oral sex presents minimal risk as long as the skin of the mouth and penis are unbroken. However, partners should ejaculate outside the mouth, or at least not swallow the semen. Anal intercourse is a high-risk activity for the spread of AIDS, especially for the receiving partner. It is best avoided for the time being, or at the minimum a condom should be used.

There is debate about the role of saliva in the transmission of the AIDS virus. Some authorities advise avoiding intimate kissing until more is known. Other authorities argue that kissing is not linked to the spread of AIDS because, if kissing were a common route, the AIDS epidemic wouild be much more widespread.

In addition, keep your general health in top condition. Get plenty of rest. Eat a well-balanced diet. Exercise regularly. Make sure your hepatitis-B, influenza, and other immunizations are up-to-date. Avoid crowds where you might pick up a viral infection. Keep clean. Avoid recreational drugs such as alcohol, poppers, and marijuana.

Condoms may not offer protection against AIDS. Recommendations from the Centers for Disease Control state that the "efficacy of condoms in preventing infection with HTLV-III is unproven, but the consistent use of them may reduce transmission." The virus is so small that it could theoretically pass through the pores in a condom.

Dealing with AIDS patients. Pregnant women should avoid close contact with AIDS patients. This is important not because they can contract AIDS but because AIDS is often associated with cytomegalovirus, which can harm the fetus. Otherwise, AIDS patients require the continued support and comfort of family and friends. It is safe to provide such assistance to these gravely ill people.

Beware of panic. AIDS has been found to be spread only through the direct exchange of body fluids: blood, semen, breast milk, and the like. It cannot be spread through the air or by objects. Even prolonged close contact with AIDS patients has not transmitted the infection to family members. Thus there is little reason to exclude AIDS patients from home, job, school, and similar settings.

Nonetheless, people with AIDS have been the subject of much hysteria and anxiety—shunned by relatives, schools, employers, landlords, even hospital personnel. Comments Dr. Constance B. Wofsy of the AIDS Clinic at the University of California, San Francisco: "This ostracism and sense of alarm are unfortunate, and distract from the necessary and rational infection control measures that can be implemented safely."

Carriers of AIDS. Many people carry the AIDS virus without showing symptoms. Or their immune system may be only slightly weakened. They may suffer relatively minor problems, from which they may recover. Indeed, one cause for concern with AIDS is its long incubation period.

A person can harbor the virus for years before showing any symptoms. Meanwhile, he might infect others.

A blood test can detect the presence of antibodies to the AIDS virus—which is variously termed HTLV-III (for human T-cell lymphadenopathy virus-3); LAV (lymphadenopathy-associated virus); and ARV (AIDS-related virus). If antibodies are present, it suggests that the person has been exposed to the AIDS virus and can possibly be carrying the virus. The test is mainly used for screening blood donors.

This test, however, has a high number of false positives, results that wrongly show the person has antibodies. The test may thus be repeated several times to verify a positive result. Moreover, the test doesn't tell for certain if the person is actually carrying the virus. Nor can it predict if the person will develop AIDS symptoms.

In a report on the screening tests for AIDS, *The Medical Letter* sums up the findings: "The availability of screening for antibodies to the AIDS virus may increase the safety of blood transfusions, but will also cause a great deal of fear and anxiety when tests are positive. Asymptomatic . . . patients can be told that they might remain well for years and perhaps indefinitely. Until more data become available, however, they must be considered potentially capable of infecting others."

If your test is positive. Obviously, if an AIDS test shows the presence of HTLV-III antibody, you should not donate blood. Also, be on the alert for any symptoms suggestive of AIDS. Since many of the complications of AIDS are treatable, and early diagnosis may decrease the severity of the illness, put yourself under a physician's care.

Since many people with positive test results have the HTLV-III virus in their blood, semen, or saliva, they may be able to transmit the infection to others, even though they may have no symptoms themselves. *The Medical Letter* believes that such patients "must be considered potentially infective for an indefinite period."

If your test results are positive, you should not share razors, toothbrushes, needles, or other utensils that could be contaminated with blood or saliva. Clean with household bleach any surface contaminated with your blood or semen. Inform any sex partners you've had for at least the last 6 months, and encourage them to go for health evaluation. Alert your dentist, physician, and other medical personnel, so that measures can be taken to protect them.

See also VENEREAL DISEASE.

AIR POLLUTION One clear day at noon a New York City Department of Sanitation tugboat chugged through the narrows separating Staten Island from New Jersey. Most of the tug's five-man crew were on deck eating lunch, oblivious of what appeared to be a patch of fog billowing ahead. The pilot merely checked his navigational equipment and headed into it.

Suddenly panic exploded among the crew. The fog burned their eyes, skin, noses, and throats. Some of the men choked, writhed on deck, and vomited. As investigators determined later, the "fog" was a classic example of air pollution, caused by sulfuric acid mist emitted by a New Jersey chemical plant.

The waste products of man's activities often contaminate the air we breathe. A community's air is considered polluted when the contamination is strong enough to interfere with health, comfort, or safety.

Air pollution can cause mass death. In one instance 4,000 residents of London died as a result of a five-day temperature inversion, when pollutants were trapped under a lid of warm, still air. A similar three-day inversion was blamed for more than 400 deaths in New York City.

Even small cities are subject to buildups of pollution. One of the first recognized air pollution disasters occurred in Donora, Pennsylvania, where almost 6,000 people fell ill out of a total population of 14,000. The death rate was ten times normal during a ten-day period when polluted air hung over the community.

Invisible pollutants. Not long ago, people thought of air pollution only in terms of smoke and soot. We now believe that invisible pollutants may be even more damaging to health. These unseen chemicals, which result from the burning of coal, fuel oil, and gasoline, include sulfur dioxide, hydrocarbons, nitrogen oxides, and carbon monoxide.

The exhaust from automobiles also contains lead and other additives. When the sun acts on that exhaust, a photochemical smog containing irritating ozone may be formed. Dust and other fine particles come from many industrial processes, as do a wide range of harmful chemicals.

These pollutants can slow down, even stop, the action of the cilia, hairlike cells that sweep germs and dirt out of the respiratory tract. Irritants in the air increase the production of mucus; they can constrict the airways into the lungs and can cause a loss of several layers of cells.

Pollution and disease. Air pollution plays a role in a number of diseases. It can precipitate asthma attacks and can make you more susceptible to infectious respiratory diseases such as colds, influenza, and pneumonia.

Air pollution also aggravates many chronic diseases that cannot be attributed to a single cause. Emphysema, chronic bronchitis, and cancer of the lung are all worsened by air pollution. The American Lung Association cites studies concluding that illness and death from respiratory diseases would be reduced by 25 percent if air pollution in big cities were cut in half.

Heart disease, too, is linked to air pollution. When your lungs can't do the job of getting enough oxygen into your bloodstream, your heart has to make up for it by pumping harder. For people with a heart condition the strain can be too great. Most of the people who have died in air pollution disasters were elderly or had heart and lung ailments. Air pollution multiplies the already great hazards of cigarette smoking. Toxic chemicals in the air cause an estimated 2,000 cancer deaths a year.

Fight for clean air. The U.S. Environmental Protection Agency has set limits on emissions from cars and industrial plants, and has set air-quality standards for specific pollutants. These measures have considerably reduced air pollution in recent years.

Nonetheless, ozone and nitrogen oxides are still major problems. Worse yet, there has been increasing pressure from industry to lower air-purity standards. To protect yourself and your family from the hazardous effects of air pollution, join citizens groups that are fighting to maintain these strong air-quality regulations.

See also ALLERGY; ASTHMA; CANCER; HEART DISEASE; RESPIRATORY DISEASE.

AIRSICKNESS See MOTION SICKNESS.

AIR TRAVEL, even in pressurized airplanes, subjects you to reduced air pressure, roughly that of an altitude of 8,000 feet. If a plane cabin maintained ground-level air pressure in the thin air of high altitudes, it might explode like an overinflated balloon.

Most people adjust to this change in pressure without even noticing it, but there are times when it is wise to discuss your travel plans with your doctor.

You may do well to avoid flying when you have hay fever, a cold, or other upper respiratory disease. Sudden changes in pressure may spread an infection into your ears and sinuses. Congestion may prevent equalizing of pressure in your ears or sinuses, causing considerable discomfort. If you already have sinusitis, pressure changes can cause pain. The doctor may advise using decongestant nose drops or inhalers before or during a flight.

Gas in the body will expand as air pressure is reduced. Sufferers from emphysema should discuss with their physicians the possibility that distended air sacs in their lungs might burst under reduced pressure.

As bubbles of trapped gas expand, they may cause pressure on surrounding tissues, with pain and possible interference in circulation. An unreduced hernia may enclose gas. So might a perforating wound of the eye or skull. So, too, might recent abdominal or lung surgery. If you have any of these conditions, check with your doctor when planning your trip.

You breathe less oxygen with the lowering of cabin pressure. This can present a hazard to people with breathing difficulties or with tissues already short of oxygen—as from emphysema, chronic bronchitis, heart disease, anemia, or gas poisoning. A sudden deficiency in oxygen may precipitate an epilepsy seizure. If your doctor thinks it advisable, arrange with the airline for an oxygen tank and mask to be available for you in flight.

People whose tissues are starved for oxygen need to rest during a flight. On the other hand prolonged sitting is hazardous for people with thrombophlebitis and some other types of circulatory disorders. Such passengers need to move about frequently during long flights. Exercising is also helpful if you suffer from "traveler's ankle," a swelling resulting from unrelieved bending of the knee for long periods.

A fractured jaw should be kept immobile only with a device capable of quick release. Otherwise, if the jaw can't be opened in case of severe motion sickness, the victim may inhale his vomit.

Be aware of the emotional tension related to air travel. A calming drug may be in order for sufferers from some psychiatric disorders and from conditions often worsened by stress, such as high blood pressure and asthma.

Keep jet lag in mind when making your plans.

Aside from the foregoing precautions, air travel presents no special problems for pregnant women. Normal infants tolerate air travel well.

In a plane crash. If you are a survivor in a crash, stay with the plane when you are sure there will be no fuel explosion or fire. The plane is large, and may be spotted by air searchers. Leave it, even for a short trip, and you may not find your way back.

For survival in a frigid climate avoid the common error of bundling up with everything you can put on. Perspiring will bring on frostbite faster; you're best off slightly chilly, with your head covered.

If you come down in a burning desert, conserve all your body moisture possible. Sit in the shade of the plane and remain motionless to keep from sweating. Keep your clothes on to retard evaporation. Do no unnecessary talking, since breath from the mouth wastes moisture. Urine is sterile, so you may safely drink it to reclaim water.

On a lifeboat at sea your greatest threat is dehydration. If your water runs out, drink the blood of seabirds. They'll come down and peck at a fishline in water with almost anything shiny on its hook. Or squeeze fluid from raw fish. Don't drink seawater, which can damage your kidneys and will make you thirstier.

In a wilderness follow the survival tips as if you were lost while hiking.

Handicapped travelers. If you are physically handicapped, ask the airline in advance what services they provide. Some airlines try to place handicapped persons on lightly booked flights so cabin attendants will have more time to devote to them. Seating may be arranged to provide you with more space, closeness to the washroom, an empty seat adjoining yours.

Passenger service staffs en route can be notified to give you special assistance when you deplane. At stopovers where passengers ordinarily leave the aircraft, ask to remain aboard if it's more convenient.

Airlines recommend that a passenger unable to move about freely or attend to personal needs travel with a friend or attendant. Wheelchair users should not travel alone until they develop know-how and at least have someone help them board and deplane.

Advise the airline that you are a wheelchair user when you book your flight. Try to get a nonstop flight or at least a straight-through one; this eliminates extra loading and unloading. Check for a jetway that connects the terminal with the plane door without steps.

To avoid trips to the toilet don't drink anything after bedtime for a morning flight and take little or no fluid during flight. Use the toilet at the terminal before getting aboard. When you land, drink extra fluids to compensate for the dehydration.

Arrive at the terminal early. This allows you to double-check on seating, arrange to board in advance of other passengers, and make sure that the agent wires ahead regarding your needs at your destination point. If you have a transfer point, check your wheelchair only to that point and insist on using it between flights to ensure it will not be lost. Better yet, carry aboard a fold-up chair.

Access Travel: Airports—A Guide to Accessibility of Terminals lists for 220 airport terminals in 27 countries the design features, facilities, and services of importance to the handicapped. For copies write to the Architectural and Transportation Barriers Compliance Board, U.S. Department of Health and Human Services, Washington, D.C. 20201.

See also JET LAG; MOTION SICKNESS; TRAVEL HEALTH.

ALCOHOL is a drug that acts on the central nervous system and affects mood, judgment, behavior, and motor coordination. In high doses alcohol is a general anesthetic. Before the discovery of ether it was virtually the only drug available to dull the pain of surgery. Very rapid intake of a large quantity of alcohol (more than a pint) can be fatal.

Symptoms of intoxication. Most people think of alcohol as a stimulant because it initially produces a feeling of well-being and light-headedness. But it is actually a depressant. The euphoric feeling results because alcohol depresses inhibitions.

As intoxication increases, alcohol impairs coordination. Typically it causes an unsteady gait, speech disturbance, and reduced manual skill. This comes about because alcohol tends to slow down the area of the brain that controls muscular coordination.

The drinker's memory, learning ability, concentration, and perception become dulled. At the same time, his confidence in his mental and physical abilities may increase, leading him to become reckless.

As the concentration of alcohol builds up, the depressant action increases, and the feeling of well-being may give way to an overall depression.

Alcohol both irritates the stomach directly and stimulates gastric juices. Therefore it can inflame the stomach lining and cause nausea and vomiting. Continued overindulgence may cause

the drinker to pass out (become unconscious). The morning after a drinking spree he may find himself with the combination of headache and abdominal symptoms known as a hangover.

Even small amounts of alcohol can have a powerful, dangerous, and sometimes fatal effect when taken in combination with other drugs: sedatives, tranquilizers, antidepressants, narcotics, and stimulants. Barbiturates in particular have frequently been associated with alcohol deaths, especially when taken at bedtime.

Other drugs may have unpleasant effects when taken with alcohol—such as nausea, vomiting, abdominal pain. The effectiveness of some drugs is reduced by alcohol. If your doctor prescribes medication of any kind, always ask if it is safe to drink while you are taking the drug.

Reactions to alcohol. Alcohol acts quickly. It is absorbed into the bloodstream directly through the stomach and intestinal walls, and then the blood rapidly carries it to the brain.

It generally takes about one hour for the body to burn up about half an ounce of alcohol, the amount contained in an average highball, glass of wine, or can of beer. Any alcohol in excess of half an ounce an hour will remain in the bloodstream and continue to affect the brain.

Different people react differently to the same amount of alcohol. Even the same person may react differently to the same amount of alcohol under different circumstances. A person may be influenced by how fast he or she drinks, whether drinking is done before or after eating, the type of beverage, body weight, body chemistry. Other influences may be the situation a person is in, mood, attitude toward drinking, drinking experience.

If you drink with or after a large meal, for example, the presence of solid food in your stomach will delay the rate at which the alcohol is absorbed into your bloodstream. With an empty stomach the alcohol can pass through the stomach walls much more quickly.

How much you weigh makes a difference. Since alcohol moves quickly from the digestive tract into the entire circulatory system, someone who weighs 180 pounds will have smaller concentrations throughout his bloodstream and body than someone who drinks the same amount, but weighs only 120 pounds.

What you use as a mixer also matters. The carbonation in soda water or ginger ale will speed the passage of alcohol through the stomach. The alcohol in a drink diluted with plain water is absorbed somewhat slower.

Switching or mixing drinks won't make you drunker because the degree of drunkenness is determined by the total amount of alcohol your blood absorbs, not by the type of beverage. However for some people switching drinks will increase the possibility of nausea and vomiting, perhaps because of the different flavorings and mixers used.

Alcohol and driving. Figures from the National Safety Council point to alcohol as a cause in about half of the car accidents fatal to drivers and one third of those fatal to adult pedestrians. Studies have shown a definite correlation between traffic accidents and the amount of alcohol in the blood. The combination of poor coordination, impaired judgment, and overconfidence, all symptoms of alcohol consumption, make it dangerous for anyone who has been drinking to drive a car.

All 50 states have laws against driving under the influence of alcohol, with various penalties. Most states base evidence of intoxication on a person's blood alcohol concentration, and usually a blood alcohol concentration of .10 percent is considered evidence of being intoxicated. For a 120-pound person this represents about three bottles of beer, or three and a half 1-ounce shots of whiskey, or one and a half martinis in less than an hour. However it may be dangerous to drive even after drinking smaller quantities.

Studies at Indiana University have shown that an increase in traffic accidents is discernible with a blood alcohol level of .04 percent. Accidents are twice as likely at .06 percent and at least 6 times as likely at .10 percent. At .15 percent the chances of having an accident are 25 times greater.

The best way to avoid being intoxicated at the wheel is to avoid drinking when you expect to drive. General tips for the social drinker:

Eat while you drink. This slows down the rate at which the alcohol is absorbed into your bloodstream.

Drink slowly. Sip, don't gulp, your drinks. Drink no more than what your body can handle at one time: about one drink an hour.

Decide how much to drink. Plan beforehand to stop after a certain number of drinks. Make this a firm resolution, for once you've begun drinking, your judgment becomes impaired.

Don't drive if you feel the alcohol. If you know or suspect that you are under the influence of alcohol, arrange for a sober person to drive you. Notes Dr. Sheila B. Blume of the National Council on Alcoholism: "People *never* think they're 'drunk' but *can* feel the influence of alcohol."

What's in a drink. In all the major alcoholic beverages—beers, table wines, cocktail or dessert wines, liqueurs, cordials, and distilled spirits —the chief ingredient is identical: ethyl alcohol, known also as ethanol, or simply as alcohol.

However the beverages are made from two different processes—fermentation and distillation. The fermented beverages, wines and beers, contain lower concentrations of alcohol. Most beer made in the United States contains about 4 percent pure alcohol. Ordinary table wines, such as Burgundies or sauternes, contain up to 14 percent. Dessert or cocktail wines (ports and sherries, for instance) are fortified with extra alcohol, increasing the alcohol content to 18 or 21 percent.

The distilled liquors—rum, gin, vodka, brandy, and whiskey (rye, bourbon, Scotch)— usually contain between 40 and 50 percent pure alcohol. In this country a liquor is labeled by its "proof," which is double its alcoholic strength; "100 proof" means 50 percent alcohol.

The distinctive flavor of each liquor is due to the ingredient from which it is made. Whiskey is made from grain such as corn, barley, and rye; vodka from corn, other cereals, and potatoes; rum from molasses; and gin from alcohol flavored with juniper berries. But all liquors have roughly the same alcohol content: one-half ounce of pure alcohol in each ounce. The other half-ounce includes a variety of chemical substances. Some come from the original grains, grapes, or other fruits; others are produced during fermentation, distillation, or storage. Flavoring or coloring agents may also be added.

Alcohol is highly caloric. Each ounce of absolute alcohol contains about 280 calories. A 12-ounce can of beer (much diluted with water) contains about 150 calories.

But the calories add very little nutritionally. Thus a person who habitually overindulges is likely to be either overweight or undernourished. If he eats a well-balanced diet and drinks as well, he will be taking in an excessive number of calories. On the other hand if he substitutes the calories in alcohol for nutritionally balanced foods, he may suffer from malnutrition.

Except for the danger of causing an automobile accident, most people can drink on occasion and in moderation without any permanent ill effects. There is no difference in life expectancy between moderate drinkers and abstainers.

But some drinkers cannot control their intake, and develop the chronic and progressive disease called alcoholism.

How to recognize alcoholism. The National Council on Alcoholism defines an alcoholic as a "person who is powerless to stop drinking and whose drinking seriously alters his normal living pattern."

In recent years the concept of alcoholism as a disease has been gaining ground. It is now regarded more as a health problem than a moral problem, and the alcoholic is increasingly treated as a person in need of medical and psychological help rather than someone who just needs a little willpower.

The essential element of alcoholism is compulsive, uncontrollable drinking. Others can decide whether to drink or not, whether to keep on drinking after the second or third drink. The alcoholic cannot.

Out of 96 million people who drink in the United States, there are an estimated 10 million alcoholics. The great majority are average middle-class Americans. They reside in respectable neighborhoods, belong to the country club, attend church, pay taxes. They continue to perform more or less effectively as bank presidents, housewives, farmers, salesmen, machinists, stenographers, teachers, clergymen, physicians. Only about 5 percent of all alcoholics are the stereotyped skid row down-and-outers.

The rate of alcoholism seems to be rising steadily. A recent study by the National Institute of Mental Health shows an increase in the rate of admissions of alcoholics to state mental hospitals. At least one in seven newly admitted patients suffers from alcoholism, an increase of 18 percent in ten years. In some states alcoholism is the leading diagnosis in mental hospitals.

Women alcoholics. Alcoholism was long thought to be much more prevalent among men than women. Now authorities estimate that it is almost as serious a problem among women as men.

Women alcoholics frequently drink alone, keeping their addiction secret even from their families. In some cases the family of a woman alcoholic may, from shame, shield her instead of urging her to get help.

Mrs. Marty Mann, a recovered alcoholic and the founder of the National Council on Alcoholism, feels that women alcoholics go underground because society "will tolerate the male who can't handle his liquor, often until he reaches the last stages of alcoholism, but any woman who drinks too much in public is automatically disgraced." In recent years, however, more female alcoholics have become willing to seek treatment.

Miscarriage rates are greater among pregnant alcoholic women. Children of alcoholic mothers who drink heavily during pregnancy are more prone to growth abnormalities, learning disabilities, hyperactivity, physical deformity, and brain damage—the fetal alcohol syndrome.

Warnings of alcoholism. The disease takes an average of ten years to become firmly established. Most alcoholics go through several stages, summarized by the Japanese proverb: "First the man takes a drink. Then the drink takes a drink. Then the drink takes the man." Often drinkers ignore or rationalize the warning signals that their drinking is on the verge of getting out of hand.

Here—in the rough order of their occurrence—are some of the danger signs:

Drinking more than the other members of your group.

Drinking to feel better or solve problems.

Beginning to experience blackouts or temporary amnesia during and following drinking episodes.

Drinking more rapidly than others. Gulping drinks.

Drinking surreptitiously and sneaking drinks.

Beginning to lose control as to time, place, and amount of drinking. Drinking—and often getting drunk—at inappropriate times and places when you did not intend to.

Hiding and protecting your liquor supply so you will never be caught short.

Drinking to overcome the hangover effects of prior drinking.

Drinking alone.

Developing an elaborate system of lies, alibis, excuses, and rationalizations to cover up or to explain drinking.

Promising yourself you'll stop drinking, but being unable to keep your promise.

Personality and behavioral changes—even when not drinking—which adversely affect your family situation, friendships, or on-the-job relationships. Accidents, job losses, family quarrels, broken friendships, and trouble with the law may take place.

Finally, extended binges, physical tremors, hallucinations and deliria, complete rejection of social reality, and malnutrition with accompanying illnesses and diseases.

The alcoholic becomes both psychologically and physiologically addicted. He (or she) often develops a tolerance to the drug so that the same amount produces progressively less effect, and he craves larger and larger quantities. Eventually he must keep on drinking in order to avoid the severe and painful symptoms that result from abrupt withdrawal. These symptoms include weakness, severe tremors, fever, hallucinations, convulsions, and, in some cases, delirium tremens.

Causes of alcoholism. Most authorities agree that the illness results from a complicated combination of physiological, psychological, and sociological factors.

Alcohol alone is not the cause of alcoholism. It is true that some of alcohol's effects can contribute to the development of psychological or physical dependence on the drug. But it is an indisputable fact that the vast majority of people who drink alcohol never become alcoholics.

Alcoholism is not caused by drinking a particular beverage. Preference for a specific type or brand of liquor is most frequently a matter of taste, availability, or price. As time goes on, it is common for an alcoholic to resort to cheaper and more available forms of liquor. A person can become an alcoholic on any beverage or solution containing any amount of alcohol.

Alcoholism is not an allergy, but you can become allergic to the constituents of any form of liquor, such as the basic ingredients from which it is made, the aromatics that help provide flavors, or the materials that are used in processing. Some people may become allergic to alcohol itself, but these allergic reactions do not seem to be a basic cause of the inability to control intake.

Some researchers have been pursuing the possibility that there might be a specific biological reason for alcoholism. They are looking for a defect in the body chemistry, a nutritional deficiency, or perhaps a metabolic disturbance that would cause an unmanageable craving.

One reason for their suspicions is that certain families seem prone to alcoholism; more than half of all alcoholics have an alcoholic parent. Recent evidence suggests that this susceptibility might be inherited.

But the reasons for a family tendency might also be environmental; conditions in the home of an alcoholic could pave the way for the children to become addicted. Of course just the opposite happens frequently: children of alcoholics often become determined never to drink at all.

Psychological factors of many kinds seem to play a major role in the development of the disease. One theory holds that alcoholism is the result of early emotional disturbances and deprivation, with consequent emotional immaturity. Frequently an alcoholic relies on drinking to relieve feelings—anxiety, hostility, inferiority, and depression—that may reflect much deeper and usually unrecognized patterns of marked insecurity, rage, and guilt.

The pressures and tensions of everyday life also contribute to alcoholism, as do the pressures of some social groups that encourage heavy drinking.

Some studies have tried to identify characteristics common to all alcoholics so that future alcoholism might be predicted—and prevented.

However no description of an "alcoholic personality" has emerged that would set alcoholics apart from the rest of the population. Alcoholics who have been studied share certain traits: emotional immaturity, preoccupation with self, insecurity, guilt, low tolerance of frustration, low self-esteem. On the other hand no one knows whether these traits existed before they became alcoholics, and many people who have some or all of these traits never become addicted.

Effects of alcoholism. The disease severely damages the health of its victims. However it is often not diagnosed. The average alcoholic visits the family doctor three times a year, complaining of gastrointestinal upsets, aches, and pains—but not alcoholism. Doctor and patient frequently fail to recognize that alcohol is the underlying cause. Medical schools have often failed to prepare physicians to recognize alcoholism in its early stages.

High concentrations of alcohol in the blood exert a strong depressive effect on the brain, producing incoordination, confusion, disorientation leading to stupor, anesthesia, coma, or death. Chronic alcoholics often suffer from disturbances of the nervous system, such as alcoholic polyneuropathy, characterized by weakness, numbness, pain, and wasting away of the leg muscles. Recovery is a slow process and permanent damage is common.

One set of symptoms is called Wernicke's disease: The alcoholic suffers from muscular incoordination, eye abnormalities, and mental confusion. This is generally followed by Korsakoff's psychosis, in which the alcoholic suffers from severely impaired memory and learning. He is generally inert and apathetic. Typically, islands of past memory remain, but out of sequence. The majority of those with Korsakoff's psychosis can expect only limited improvement, taking a long period of time.

Chronic users of alcohol frequently suffer from gastrointestinal disorders, such as gastric or duodenal ulcers. Inflammation of the pancreas is also common.

They often have nutritional deficiencies, leading to diseases like pellagra. The calories in alcohol provide a certain amount of energy, but little else that is nutritionally valuable.

As the alcoholism progresses, the small intestine's ability to absorb nutrients decreases to a serious extent. Thus fats, fat-soluble vitamins, B vitamins, and proteins may not be effectively

15

used. Also alcohol increases the urinary loss of some minerals and amino acids.

Prolonged drinking is particularly damaging to the liver, even if the diet is otherwise adequate. Alcoholics develop cirrhosis of the liver—a potentially fatal inflammation—about eight times as frequently as nonalcoholics. Those who have only a mild liver impairment may recover completely after a few weeks if they stop drinking and eat nourishing food. With more severe damage there is less chance of full recovery.

Chronic heavy drinking causes a decrease in levels of the male hormone testosterone. This may explain sex problems widely observed in men who are heavy drinkers. Among the damage resulting from prolonged alcohol intake: impotence, withering of the testicles, and enlargement of the breasts.

Alcoholics become more susceptible to pneumonia and other infectious diseases, most likely because of their malnutrition. However researchers at Cornell University have found that even well-nourished heavy drinkers have lowered resistance; they speculate that alcohol may directly interfere with immunity mechanisms.

Suicide is common among alcoholics. Their suicide rate is many times that of nonalcoholics. Fully a third of all who take their own lives are alcoholics.

Treating alcoholism. Successful treatment programs usually involve a combination of medication, psychotherapy, community aid programs, and the support of family and friends. Recovery rates vary from 20 to 80 percent. The earlier help is sought, the greater the chance of recovery.

Most alcoholics should be hospitalized in the early phases of treatment, especially when there are physical complications or when active intervention is needed to interrupt drinking patterns.

Be wary of drugs or other products that claim to cure alcoholism. There are no easy or secret treatments, no drugs conclusively demonstrated to remove or overcome addiction to alcohol permanently and safely, or to make it possible for the alcoholic to drink normally.

A drug called Antabuse (disulfiram) has been used with some degree of success. It does not "cure" alcoholism, but creates a sensitivity, so that anyone who drinks while taking it will experience disagreeable and sometimes violent reactions, such as a rapid rise in blood pressure, headache, chest pain, nausea, and vomiting. Antabuse should be taken only after an examination by a doctor and according to directions. And it must be taken regularly to be effective. Doctors have found that some alcoholics merely

stop taking the drug in order to be able to drink again.

Recovery requires total abstention. Those who have recovered say that it's the first drink that gets you drunk. Most specialists hold that no alcoholic can ever learn to drink moderately. For almost all alcoholics a return to any drinking, even after many years of complete sobriety, will often trigger all of the old symptoms. Recovered alcoholics should also avoid cough medicines and other over-the-counter drugs that contain alcohol.

Withdrawal from alcohol usually requires medical assistance. An alcoholic who abruptly cuts out alcohol after a prolonged period of heavy drinking will enter an acute withdrawal state. Within hours or days he will experience some combination of the following symptoms: lack of appetite, nausea, vomiting, sweating, flushing, insomnia, tremulousness, irregular heartbeat, agitation, irritability, apprehension, weakness, fever, and confusion.

If untreated the alcoholic is likely to proceed to a more dangerous stage of withdrawal. He may experience convulsions like those in epilepsy, and may suffer from delirium tremens, characterized by delusions, hallucinations, profuse sweating, and high fever. These conditions can be fatal.

Under medical supervision some drugs, including tranquilizers, are used to help the alcoholic through this critical period. However, they are used in outpatients only with careful supervision and observation. Vitamins may also be prescribed to replace possible vitamin deficiencies.

Psychotherapy can be very helpful. It is almost impossible for a person who has become dependent on alcohol to break away from it completely without emotional support and guidance. Group psychotherapy has proved very effective for some alcoholics, but others respond better to individual therapy.

Whatever method is employed, psychiatric treatment will give the patient very practical support, especially early in the treatment program, when help is needed with immediate problems. Ultimately treatment should equip the alcoholic to deal with, and adjust to, the everyday pressures of living without the need to drink.

Organizations and programs. Local community programs, particularly Alcoholics Anonymous, can be invaluable. AA's program, offering mutual help and understanding by fellow alcoholics, has probably produced more recoveries than all other methods combined. There are no dues or fees for joining. The only requirement is a desire to stop drinking. AA has more than 1,000,000 members in 114 countries, with local groups in practically every city, town, and community in the United States. Larger communities have many such groups. They may be located by consulting the telephone book, under "AA" or "Alcoholics Anonymous." If AA is not available locally, information can be obtained from:

Alcoholics Anonymous General Service
  Headquarters
P.O. Box 459, Grand Central Station
New York, New York 10017

The National Council on Alcoholism, a voluntary organization, brings together physicians, scientists, and laymen to work for the prevention and control of alcoholism through education, community services, and research. Throughout the country local chapters may be listed in telephone directories under "Council on Alcoholism" or "Alcoholism Information Center." If there is no local council or center, write to:

National Council on Alcoholism
12 West 21st Street
New York, New York 10010

In many states, commissions or agencies on alcoholism operate clinics, hospitals, or units in state hospitals specifically for alcoholics. These are usually found in more heavily populated areas. A number of cities also now have their own programs.

Other organizations that often can help the alcoholic include mental health clinics, mental health centers, state hospitals, and the Salvation Army. Many churches and religious organizations sponsor active education programs, and several give direct services to the alcoholic and his or her family. Information about such services available in any community usually can be obtained through direct contact with the churches and local church federations.

Resources for families of alcoholics include Al-Anon Family Groups, which usually work with Alcoholics Anonymous, though they are not formally affiliated. Relatives or friends of persons with alcoholism are eligible for membership in Al-Anon. Problems associated with the alcoholic family member are discussed in a group situation.

The Alateen movement tries to help children understand their parents' drinking problems and find mutual support in a group situation.

A wide variety of other agencies and organizations not specifically concerned with the problems of alcoholism may be available to assist family members. These include state and county medical societies, mental health centers and clinics, health departments, family service agencies, welfare departments, and churches.

An increasing number of industrial concerns have developed assistance programs for their alcoholic employees. These programs help to catch the disease in its early stages and later contribute to the rehabilitation of employees. Even when a formal program does not exist, employers frequently can help their employees to recognize their alcohol problem, to seek treatment, and to recover sufficiently to return to productive work.

Helping an alcoholic recover. The support of family and friends can spell the difference between success and failure in the treatment of alcoholism.

The National Council on Alcoholism offers these tips on what the family of an alcoholic can do to help the alcoholic recover:

Learn the facts about alcoholism.

Accept the alcoholic as a sick person in need of help.

Talk to someone who understands alcoholism.

Go to a treatment center for alcoholics or AA.

Maintain a healthy atmosphere in your home.

Encourage the alcoholic's new interests. A person who gives up drinking has a lot of time on his hands.

Take a relapse lightly if there is one.

Pass your knowledge of alcoholism on to others.

At least as important as what to do is what *not* to do:

Don't preach and lecture. The alcoholic is probably already guilt-ridden about his or her family. The motivation for treatment should come from the alcoholic, not from a nagging spouse.

Don't have a holier-than-thou attitude. Any feelings you have of scorn or suspicion are easily picked up by the alcoholic, and are likely to make him or her sullen and resentful and resistant to treatment.

Don't use the "if you loved me" appeal. After all, you wouldn't say to a diabetic, "If you loved me, you'd get well." Remember that an alcoholic's drinking is compulsive and can't be controlled merely through willpower.

Don't hide liquor or pour it out. This is likely to lead the alcoholic to rage and desperation, and a determination to find more alcohol.

Don't make threats you won't carry out, such

as threatening divorce if the alcoholic doesn't stop drinking.

Don't allow the alcoholic to persuade you to drink with him (or her) on the grounds that he will drink less. He rarely does, and your drinking with him condones his drinking and allows him to avoid seeking treatment.

Don't argue with him when he is drunk.

Don't make an issue over his treatment. Let him take the initiative and the responsibility for seeking help. The alcoholic needs to make his own decisions and to feel he has as much freedom of choice as any adult. At the same time, let him understand that you believe he is going to do something.

Don't expect an immediate, 100 percent recovery. Relapses are common and the recovery period is a difficult time.

Don't try to protect him against alcohol, such as warning other people not to serve him drinks. This may push the recovering alcoholic into a relapse by stirring up old feelings of resentment and inadequacy. The alcoholic must take responsibility for himself, making his own adjustment to being in situations where alcohol is served.

See also DRUGS; HANGOVER; PREGNANCY; UNCONSCIOUSNESS.

ALLERGIC DERMATITIS   See ECZEMA.

ALLERGIC RHINITIS   See HAY FEVER.

ALLERGY is a condition of unusual sensitivity which anyone may develop to substances that are ordinarily harmless.

About one person in seven is allergic to something encountered routinely in everyday life. Foods, pollens, molds, and house dust are among the most common offenders, but there are hundreds of possible sensitizing substances—called allergens—including animal dander (bits of skin and fur), house dust mites, feathers, cosmetics, household chemicals, medicines, plant oils, and even heat, cold, and sunlight.

Allergens can gain access to the body by being swallowed or inhaled. They may also enter via the skin, or by injection (as with drugs and serums).

When an allergic person is exposed to an allergen, his tissues produce antibodies. Some antibodies are beneficial—they are defenses produced by the body to fight invading germs or viruses that cause disease. But in addition to attacking such invaders antibodies may injure your tissues. In an allergic person antibodies react to the allergen as if it were a threatening microbe or foreign body, often causing inflammation and cellular damage.

Allergic symptoms usually appear only after the person has been exposed to the allergen repeatedly. Once these antibodies have been developed, further contact with the allergen produces irritation in such particularly sensitive tissues as the nose, eyes, skin, bronchial tubes, or digestive tract. An initial contact may also cause symptoms, typically of a lesser magnitude.

People vary in their reactions to allergens. Someone allergic to eggs might become violently ill from the amount of egg he would get in a trace of mayonnaise dressing. Another might be able to eat as much as one egg a day with only a slight upset. You do an allergy victim a disservice if you try to persuade him to try the food or other allergen "just this once." An allergy is hardly imaginary.

If you have an allergy, carry emergency medical identification for protection. If you are unconscious or unable to communicate, the information will be valuable to the first-aider and may even be a lifesaver, especially if you are allergic to drugs or insect stings.

Allergic reactions may involve any part of the body, but occur most frequently in the respiratory system and skin. Asthma, hay fever, and allergic rhinitis (year-round perennial hay fever) are all respiratory diseases triggered by an allergic reaction. Eczema, contact dermatitis, poison ivy, and hives are allergic conditions that affect the skin. Itching of any sort is commonly an allergic symptom.

Allergic factors may also be present in diseases of the gastrointestinal tract, of the eye and ear, of the heart and blood vessels and the blood, of the urinary tract, and of the nervous system (including epilepsy and migraine).

In rare instances allergic reactions can be life-threatening. Some people experience anaphylactic shock when exposed to an allergen, most often a medication or an insect sting. Its onset is usually sudden, with swelling and redness of the skin. Hives may develop. The victim may experience abdominal cramps, vomiting, diarrhea, and feelings of anxiety. The larynx may swell, causing breathing difficulties. A swift drop in blood pressure may lead to fatal shock.

Anaphylactic shock is a medical emergency. Get help as soon as possible. Treatment is an injection of epinephrine and antihistamines and the administration of oxygen and of intravenous fluids.

Heredity in allergies. Many people with allergies come from families where the parents or other close relatives have had some form of allergic manifestation. Although people do not inherit a specific disease such as hay fever, they can inherit the tendency to become sensitive to certain things. Members of the same family who have inherited such a tendency may develop altogether different allergic diseases.

Some specialists in this field believe that an individual who suffers from an allergy can expect half his children to have a major allergy in childhood. If you know and accept this hereditary factor, you have taken the first step toward prevention. There are numerous effective means of treatment and prevention. However refusal to face the diagnosis often makes proper care very difficult.

If asthma in childhood is not treated, it may lead to disabling lung disease in adult life. The popular belief that the allergic child will outgrow this condition is dangerous. Without early diagnosis and correct treatment he may become physically retarded and—as an indirect result—may develop emotional disorders.

Do not discount an allergy that appears in adult years. While the symptoms are most apt to show up in childhood, the first attack may erupt at any age. On record is one man who developed his first allergic symptoms at the age of 80.

The emotional factor. Another common fallacy is that allergy is "only emotional." It is true that intense emotions—anxiety, fear, anger, strong excitement—may precipitate allergic attacks. Many patients improve when they receive psychotherapy. However most authorities believe that the physical basis of the allergy must be present first.

Clear-cut differentiations between physical and emotional factors are not always possible. Consider the allergic child with eczema. His skin itches and he scratches, aggravating the lesions and making him scratch more. The buildup of nervousness and tension cause more sweating and other bodily reactions, which increase the itchiness and the scratching. If his condition is unsightly, his anxiety about his appearance then becomes a major factor in the persistence of the illness.

Making the diagnosis. To identify the allergen the most important clue is the medical history taken by the doctor. Often a physician can recognize that certain allergic symptoms appear in conjunction with exposure to a suspected allergen.

A variety of detailed studies may be required to establish an exact diagnosis. These may include blood and skin tests and a thorough investigation of the potential allergens you might encounter in your daily life.

Skin tests are made by making light scratches on the arm or the back and dropping on the scratch a powdered or liquid extract of a common allergen. Another method involves injecting a small amount of liquid allergen between the layers of the skin. These tests give little pain, do not scar, and all traces disappear in a few days. If you are sensitive to the allergen, a small hive resembling a mosquito bite will develop.

Skin tests are general guides which may help the doctor narrow down the field of the suspected causes. To pinpoint the exact cause, the doctor will follow up the skin tests by actual trial—exposing you to the allergen. Most likely he will try to single out the most suspected ones and cautiously add them one by one, watching carefully for any reaction.

Studies such as these have identified sensitivity to the most unlikely substances, such as a toothpaste that had never been used before. In one recorded case the patient discovered that he had become allergic to quinine when he began drinking gin and tonic—the tonic is made with quinine water.

Treatment for allergic diseases. First the allergen must be removed as completely as possible, even if it means giving away an offending pet dog or cat. Use nonallergenic bedding and keep house dust at a minimum. If a child is allergic to a favorite stuffed toy, you can make the toy reasonably nonallergenic by removing the stuffing, cleaning the covering, and then restuffing with discarded nylons.

Special treatment such as removal of nasal polyps is sometimes called for. Certain drugs may be prescribed to relieve symptoms temporarily: antihistamines, inhalers, and hormones—notably steroids. But they do not get at the underlying condition, and all produce side effects that may become bothersome. These drugs should be used only as directed by your physician, even if they can be bought without prescription.

Hyposensitization—i.e., reduction of sensitivity—provides longer-lasting relief. It is particularly valuable when the allergen can't be avoided because of its wide distribution or your habits or occupation.

Your doctor may try hyposensitization (also called desensitization or immunotherapy) by giving you injections of the offending allergen in small but gradually increasing amounts. Biweekly or monthly injections may be continued for several years or more. With proper care hyposensitization is safe and successful for large numbers of patients as long as there is only normal exposure to the allergen.

Moving: not a sure cure. Should you move to a different section of the country? Running away from an allergy is not the proper first step. A change of climate, although sometimes beneficial, is not advisable unless you have first had a thorough investigation of your condition and a reasonable period of hyposensitizing treatment. If you respond well, you may not need to move at all.

Often it is not the change in climate itself that brings about an improvement. If you seem to find relief when away from home, try to spend time in another house in the same community. Your symptoms may disappear, and you will know that climate alone is not the culprit. For example, insulation, wood shavings, and plaster dust can be a problem in recently built homes. If you are sensitive to house dust and other aller-

14 WAYS TO FIGHT BEDROOM DUST

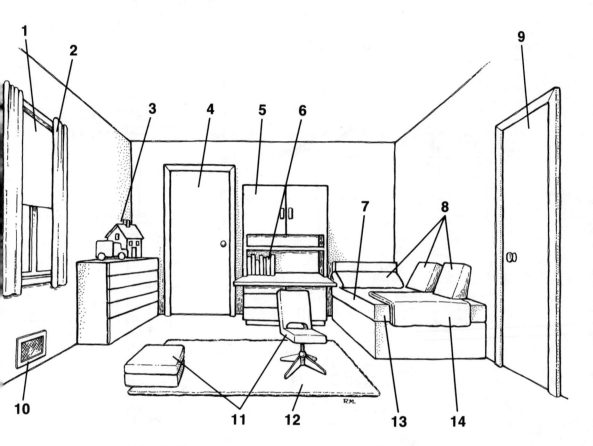

1. Use washable window shades instead of venetian blinds
2. Hang easily washed curtains rather than thick drapes
3. Toys should be plastic, wood, or metal, not fabric
4. Weatherstrip room door, and keep it closed
5. Keep furniture simple
6. Dust books frequently
7. Use zippered plastic cover over mattress
8. Pillows should be foam rubber or synthetic—avoid feather or kapok
9. Keep all clothes in closet and keep closet door closed
10. Put filter over air inlet if you have forced-air heat
11. Use plastic instead of upholstery on chair and hassock
12. Avoid wall-to-wall carpeting. Scatter rugs should be cotton and washable
13. For bedspread, use washable cotton instead of chenille
14. Use washable cotton or synthetic blankets—avoid fuzzy blankets

gens that may be present wherever you go, a change of climate is useless.

Tree and grass pollens are so prevalent everywhere that it is difficult to escape them except by an ocean voyage. Although people sensitive to eastern ragweed move to California, they often soon develop sensitivity to new pollen. Moving to a region free of a particular pollen may possibly be of value only if you are sensitive chiefly to regional pollens.

The dry, warm climate of southern California, Arizona, or New Mexico and parts of Florida may prove beneficial to those people with recurrent asthma who also suffer from sinusitis or other respiratory problems, and who have frequent attacks in damp, cold weather.

No one can predict if you will find relief in a new area. So even if advised by a doctor to seek a change of climate, give yourself a trial period of six months or more. Choose an area not only as free as possible of allergens known to affect you, but also as free as possible of air pollution. Look for a spot where the climate is dry and there are no factories, fields, or woods nearby.

8 ALLERGY HINTS FOR THE KITCHEN

1. If you're allergic to one spice, you're probably allergic to others
2. Allergic to wheat flour? Substitute oat or barley
3. While preparing food, allergic people should wear rubber gloves with white cotton gloves underneath
4. Fish is a common food allergen
5. Use exhaust fan to get rid of cooking odors
6. Use an air conditioner to reduce heat, which can cause or intensify skin sensitivity
7. An electric range is preferable: you may be sensitive to unburned gas
8. Young children may be sensitive to dust, mold, and insect debris which accumulate under and behind the refrigerator—clean area often

Housekeeping for allergic patients. You can reduce daily exposure to many contaminants (see illustrations). To reduce dust, give your living quarters a thorough cleaning at least once a week. If you are the sufferer, remain away from the home until the cleaning has been completed.

Bedrooms require special attention since you spend eight or more hours a day in them. They should contain a minimum of furnishings. Remove upholstered chairs or recover with nonallergenic material. Remove all pictures and other dust-catchers, such as knickknacks and venetian blinds. Use only washable rugs and the simplest curtains, preferably plastic, and launder these once a month. Avoid dust-catching fabrics like velvet or corduroy. Bid farewell to plants that are fragrant or give off pollen. Remove artificial plants, which collect dust.

Mattresses and pillows, even if nonallergenic, should have dust-proof covers. Don't risk sleep-ing on feather pillows or even having them in the house. The pillows of choice are Dacron or Acrilan. Foam rubber may harbor molds.

Eliminate waffle pads under rugs. They are often made out of animal hair and collect a great deal of dust. Rugless rooms are desirable. If carpeting is a must, make sure it can be lifted and the floor beneath it vacuumed every three months.

To prepare a dust-free room wipe down the ceiling and walls. Wax the floors with caution— some people are sensitive to floor wax and polish. Wash furniture or clean with a damp or oiled cloth. Pay special attention to bedsprings and slats and to the backs of dressers and other furniture. To maintain a dust-free room after a major cleaning job, clean it lightly every day, using a damp cloth or an oiled mop.

Conventional window air conditioners will screen out some pollens from a room. But they

9 TIPS TO DESENSITIZE DRIVING

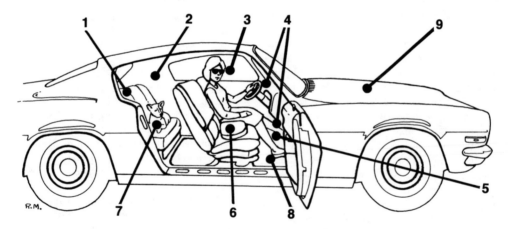

1. Cover seats with vinyl or tightly woven cloth, nylon, or rayon
2. No smoking in car
3. Dark glasses can relieve eyes, especially for hay fever sufferers
4. Use air conditioning
   If outside air is polluted, recirculate interior air
   Keep drafts off allergic passengers
5. Vacuum heater outlets before winter
   Keep car interior clean
   Check frequently for exhaust fume leaks
6. For pillows, use dacron or other synthetic
   Avoid kapok, feathers, foam rubber
7. Leave animals at home

8. Clean floor mats often
   Seal car leaks to prevent water on floor
   Air out mats in sun
   Spray mats with mold inhibitor
9. While driving, try to avoid:
   · Farm areas recently sprayed with insecticides
   · Rural areas during pollen season
   · Freshly tarred roads
   · Gasoline fumes (stay in car with windows up when refueling)
   · Following diesel trucks, buses, or cars emitting blue smoke or visible exhaust
   · Tunnels, busy intersections, heavy traffic
   · Areas with industrial smoke and fumes

are ineffective in removing microscopic dust molds, bacteria, animal hairs, and insect particles. These can be effectively removed only by special electronic filters. In homes heated by a forced-air system you may want to insert within the ducts a two-stage electronic air cleaner that will filter out most household air contaminants, particularly dust and molds.

But beware of so-called air purifiers that claim to prevent or aid in the treatment of allergies. These small units do not have sufficient capacity to remove dust and pollen.

See also AIR POLLUTION; ANTIHISTAMINES; ASTHMA; CONTACT DERMATITIS; DRUG ALLERGY; ECZEMA; EMERGENCY MEDICAL IDENTIFICATION; FOOD ALLERGY; HAY FEVER; HIVES; INSECT STINGS; ITCHING; MIGRAINE; MOLD ALLERGY; POISON IVY; QUACKERY; RESPIRATORY DISEASE; SINUSITIS; STEROIDS.

ALLERGY, DRUG   See DRUG ALLERGY.

ALLERGY, FOOD   See FOOD ALLERGY.

AMBLYOPIA (lazy eye, amblyopia ex anopsia) is a decrease of vision caused by not using one eye. It is one of the leading causes of sight loss in children.

The child's eyes may look straight, bright, and clear and appear normal in regular medical examinations. The child will play, look at TV, and even begin to read without obvious difficulty. But if his eyes aren't examined in early childhood, by the time he gets his first eye examination, the damage may be irreparable.

Amblyopia is caused by an abnormality that interferes with normal use of both eyes and with visual development. This abnormality—such as nearsightedness, farsightedness, astigmatism, eye disease, crossed eyes, or a congenital defect —may cause the child to see a double image, or images of different shape, size, or clarity. To be freed of these two confusing pictures the youngster may unconsciously suppress the weaker eye and use only the stronger one. If the suppression becomes deep-seated, the vision in the weaker eye fails to develop properly and may be permanently diminished.

Affected is the central vision—the type of vision needed for reading, doing work that requires fine discrimination, and seeing straight ahead and for distances. Ordinarily this acute vision develops between the ages of one and seven, or not at all.

There are degrees of amblyopia, and most cases are mild. Typically an amblyopic child sees blurrily with his weak eye. He has poorer depth perception than he would have with two good eyes.

A child should be examined at 6 months and again at age 3, at age 5, and periodically through the school years. In some communities preschool children are screened free in a volunteer program. Because other eye defects may develop as a child grows, his eyes need to be reexamined at least once a year by an eye specialist.

An aid to screening the vision of preschool youngsters is offered by the National Society to Prevent Blindness, 79 Madison Avenue, New York, New York 10016. The organization will send an eye-test kit free of charge to any parent or physician who requests it. The kit includes a scale version of the standard Snellen E chart, along with instructions for its use.

If amblyopia is detected early enough, it is possible to correct it by forcing the lazy eye to see. Sometimes, the strong eye is covered with a patch or blurred with eyedrops. To force the weaker eye to get to work and learn to see again, some children may need to wear special glasses or do prescribed exercises.

See also EYE DISORDER; EYE EXERCISES; EYEGLASSES.

AMEBIASIS (amebic dysentery) is an infectious disease that results from swallowing cysts of *Entamoeba histolytica,* microscopic one-celled animals, in contaminated food or water. The amebas may burrow into the wall of the large intestine, causing small ulcers. Unlike shigellosis (bacillary dysentery), the symptoms of the disease develop slowly, not being evident for three or four weeks after exposure.

Amebas can become widespread and infect large numbers of people. In South Bend, Indiana, a contaminated water system infected more than half the population of the city.

Diarrhea is the most common symptom, but it does not have to be dramatic. Other symptoms may be transitory or misleading.

A person with amebiasis may suffer from tiredness, and constipation alternating with diarrhea. He often has cramps, backache, indigestion, nausea, low fever, and gas, and may lose weight. There may be a general feeling of being unwell.

In severe cases there may be an explosion of dysentery—an inflammation of the large intestine marked by abdominal pain and watery diarrhea with discharges of blood and mucus. Amebic abscess of the liver may result if the bloodstream carries the parasite from the intestine.

About 1 person in 20 in the United States is thought to carry the parasite, though without having signs of illness. The disease is especially prevalent in the Southwest and can be a threat to travelers in tropical areas with poor sanitation.

Infected food handlers may spread the disease by not adequately washing their hands. Food can be contaminated by flies, cockroaches, and other insects carrying the parasite. Leafy vegetables may be contaminated if fertilized with human excrement or washed in polluted water.

There is also a considerable amount of sexual transmission resulting from oral-anal contact. Statistically, sexual transmission of amebiasis occurs most frequently in male homosexual communities.

Drugs can usually bring about the disappearance of symptoms and get rid of the amebas.

To help prevent amebiasis follow safeguards against water contamination and food poisoning. Use proper screening to protect against insects.

See also ANIMAL DISEASE; DIARRHEA; FOOD POISONING; INFECTIOUS DISEASE; INSECTS; TRAVEL HEALTH; VENEREAL DISEASE; WATER CONTAMINATION.

AMNIOCENTESIS See BIRTH DEFECTS.

AMPHETAMINES (bennies, dexies, speed, pep pills, ups) are drugs that stimulate the central nervous system. An overdose or prolonged use can cause excitation and irritability, increased blood pressure, frequent urination, sleeplessness, diarrhea, tremors, headache, and other effects.

An acute psychosis—almost indistinguishable from paranoid schizophrenia—is another mark of amphetamine overuse. The victim may experience auditory and visual hallucinations and periods of semiconsciousness. He may be aggressive and violent. His behavior may be bizarre. Take a person in this state to the emergency room of a hospital as soon as possible.

Don't drive while on amphetamines. If you have taken the drug, tremors and excitation can affect your reflexes and impair your judgment—an invitation to an accident. As the drug wears off, you're likely to feel drowsy.

What amphetamines do. In ordinary amounts amphetamines give a temporary sense of alertness and well-being. A very tired person may experience mental clarity and be able to perform tasks well for a brief period.

But at the same time, his judgment may be impaired. His heart rate, pulse, and breathing may be speeded up. His pupils may dilate. His mouth may be dry. He may sweat and have a headache. He's unlikely to feel like eating. When the drug wears off, he may "crash"—suffer a letdown that can lead him to take the drug again.

Amphetamines are legally available only through a physician's prescription. They are used mainly to treat narcolepsy, a disease characterized by the overwhelming need to sleep.

They are sometimes prescribed for mild depression, and for some hyperactive children with behavior disorders.

While some doctors prescribe amphetamines for treatment of overweight, this use is widely disputed in the medical community and illegal in many states. These drugs rarely control appetite for more than a few weeks. Nor do they help an obese person acquire lifelong eating habits that will maintain proper weight. Amphetamines should never be the foundation of a weight-reducing program.

Amphetamine reactions. Amphetamines can create a psychological dependence. Though the drugs are not considered physically addictive, some people develop an intense need to repeat the "up" experience. They may develop a tolerance requiring escalating doses to produce the same effect.

Amphetamines usually come in tablets or capsules. But they can also be injected in large doses into veins for a more rapid and intense experience. Those who practice this form of drug abuse—"speed freaks" or "meth heads"—may become physically debilitated and suffer from malnutrition. They may also become more susceptible to infections, particularly viral hepatitis from contaminated needles.

Death from the drug alone is rare. But speed freaks are likely to become progressively incapacitated, unable to work or take proper care of themselves. Some die from accidents during paranoid delusions or from contaminated substances mixed with the amphetamines.

Withdrawal can be unpleasant. Heavy users may need to be hospitalized. Withdrawal symptoms may include extreme restlessness, severe depression (sometimes suicidal), and psychosis. Some of these can be alleviated by the drug Thorazine.

Speed freaks, like other drug abusers, often relapse. Medical and psychiatric help may be required. Group-therapy sessions run by ex-users are beneficial for some people.

Pseudo amphetamines, marketed by mail order, usually contain phenylpropanolamine and caffeine. In high doses, they can cause dangerous increases in blood pressure.

See also DRUGS; OVERWEIGHT.

AMPICILLIN See ANTIBIOTICS.

AMPUTATIONS See SEVERED PARTS.

ANALGESICS are drugs that relieve pain. Many are available without prescription and consumers spend more on them than on any other medication.

No known drug or combination of drugs will

relieve all pain. Moreover, effectiveness varies greatly with patient and conditions. A healthy adult with occasional headache, an arthritis sufferer with congestive heart failure, an infant with high fever—each may do best with a different preparation.

Be skeptical when you read analgesic labels and ads. Manufacturers often exaggerate circumstances under which their product may help. Very likely you'll be best off with plain aspirin, acetaminophen (e.g., Tylenol) or ibuprofen (Advil, Nuprin). Ibuprofen, now sold over the counter after a favorable history as a prescription drug (Motrin, Rufen), seems effective for menstrual cramps and inflammatory disorders as well as headache.

Watch out for products that claim to cure or bring long-lasting relief for symptoms of arthritis, bursitis, fibrositis, lumbago, neuralgia, neuritis, or sciatica. Nonprescription analgesics will provide only temporary relief for these conditions. And nonprescription analgesics are relatively ineffective for pains of cuts and other wounds, for muscle spasms and cramps, or for very severe pain.

In general, limit your use of over-the-counter analgesics to the treatment of simple headache; the temporary relief of minor aches and pains associated with rheumatism, arthritis, bursitis, sprains, and neuralgia; the temporary relief of minor aches and pains due to overexertion, fatigue, sinusitis, or common colds; and the temporary relief of toothache and of minor cramps from menstruation.

Use of analgesics may mask a condition requiring medical attention. Pain, no matter how mild, may be a symptom of a serious disease. If pain persists, suspend self-medication and consult a physician.

See also ASPIRIN; DRUGS.

ANAPHYLACTIC SHOCK See DRUG ALLERGY.

ANEMIA is a condition in which the blood has too few red cells or too little hemoglobin, the iron-containing red substance that carries oxygen to the tissues.

Typical symptoms are rather vague. They include fatigue, lack of pep, a washed-out feeling, shortness of breath. The skin may appear sallow. The palms of the hands, the fingernails, the inner parts of the eyelids, may be unusually pale. Some anemia victims develop a craving for ice, eating a tray or more a day; cravings for cornstarch, dirt, and clay may also appear.

If you believe you may be anemic, consult your doctor. Anemia can be a symptom of other conditions that require treatment such as cancer, hemorrhage, or tuberculosis. Some infectious diseases, such as malaria, and some bacterial infections may affect the blood and cause anemia. A person whose intestines are infected with hookworm or tapeworm generally is anemic.

Only a competent physician can prescribe proper treatment for specific types of anemia. Blood tests are invariably needed to pinpoint the diagnosis.

Beware of patent medicines for "tired blood." So-called iron remedies may do harm by masking the anemia while the disease of which anemia is only a symptom goes unchecked.

No one should take iron except on doctor's orders. But if prescribed, iron tablets should be in child-proof containers. In massive doses iron can destroy stomach and intestinal tissue. Jaundice, bloody diarrhea, a severe drop in blood pressure, and convulsions may occur within hours. The dangerous dose is much smaller for a child, and unless treated quickly the child may die.

It is a myth that iron taken for anemia will lead to arteriosclerosis.

Bleeding and anemia. Bleeding accounts for about three out of four cases of anemia, and for nearly all cases where anemia is marked by a deficiency of iron for the manufacture of hemoglobin. The typical patient with iron deficiency anemia is a woman in her childbearing years, and the most common cause is excessive menstrual bleeding.

The second most common source of blood loss—and the most important in adult males and postmenopausal females—is gastrointestinal bleeding. Just the loss of a little blood daily can easily result in iron deficiency.

Hemorrhoids account for about 10 percent of such bleeding. Irritation from taking aspirin, a peptic ulcer, hiatus hernia, and diverticulosis are also frequent causes. An anemic patient may have to go through a complete gastrointestinal checkup to find a possible bleeding site.

Donating blood for blood transfusions at medically approved intervals will not lead to anemia. However excessive donation may dangerously remove iron from the body. Anyone with anemia ought not give blood.

Diet and anemia. Improper diet may contribute to anemia, especially in some children who drink great quantities of milk and skimp on other foods. While milk contains many nutrients essential for growth, it is lacking in sufficient iron. An iron preparation prescribed by a physician usually corrects the anemia, and the child's diet may be rounded out with iron-enriched cereals and iron-rich foods.

Pregnant women may similarly become anemic through diet deficiency. An expectant mother needs additional iron to build extra blood cells for herself and the baby. A diet deficiency can tip the balance and cause anemia in a person who has a minor hemorrhoid or ulcer that causes a small amount of bleeding. To prevent iron deficiency anemia during pregnancy, many physicians prescribe supplemental iron tablets.

Foods rich in iron include meat (especially liver), eggs, dried peas and beans, nuts, fruits, green leafy vegetables, and whole grain or enriched cereals and cereal products.

Anemia may also result from injury to the bone marrow, which manufactures red cells. X rays used without proper safeguards may damage bone marrow; so may some chemicals, especially benzene, which is present in most gasolines and is a common ingredient of paint and varnish removers. If these products are accidentally drunk, or inhaled over a long period or in a single high concentration, bone marrow may be injured. Use benzene products cautiously, with plenty of ventilation.

The blood-building marrow can also be injured by the antibiotic chloramphenicol (see ANTIBIOTICS).

Other anemias. Pernicious anemia is a specific disease that results from poor absorption of vitamin B_{12} because of the absence from the gastric juice of a substance termed "intrinsic factor." In addition to the symptoms of ordinary anemia someone with pernicious anemia may also have special warning signs: slightly yellowish skin, sore and smooth tongue, stomach distress, diarrhea. He may have numbness and tingling in his fingers and toes, walk with an unsteady gait, and show other evidence of the injury that pernicious anemia sometimes does to the spinal cord. Pernicious anemia can also mimic almost any psychosis or neurosis.

The illness used to be fatal. Now, however, the patient gets injections of vitamin B_{12} at regular intervals and can lead an otherwise normal life.

A similar anemia, actually more frequent than pernicious anemia, is due to a deficiency of folic acid, a B vitamin. It generally occurs with a diet devoid of fresh vegetables and fruits and is especially common in alcoholics.

Cooley's anemia. Also known as Mediterranean anemia or thalassemia major, Cooley's anemia is a hereditary blood disorder. It is characterized by the body's inability to produce red blood cells with a sufficient amount of hemoglobin. Normal red blood cells have a life span of 120 days, and as they die, they are continuously replaced by new cells. In Cooley's anemia the red blood cells cannot survive for more than a few weeks, resulting in anemia that appears shortly after birth and becomes progressively worse as time passes.

Both parents must carry and transmit the trait for Cooley's anemia to their child if the child is going to develop the disease. People whose ancestors were natives of the countries surrounding the Mediterranean Sea, particularly Italy and Greece, are most likely to inherit Cooley's anemia. The American "melting pot" has distributed the gene defect through intermarriage to about 200,000 Americans of varied backgrounds. In the past, 1 in 1,000 American children of Mediterranean descent inherited Cooley's anemia. But the frequency of the disease has been reduced by genetic counseling and a simple test that can detect a carrier.

People who inherit the hereditary defect from only one parent are considered to be carriers. Their condition (thalassemia minor) can manifest itself as a mild form of anemia or may present no symptoms at all. The condition never worsens or converts to thalassemia major, and is not a threat to a normal life span or to normal health.

The earliest signs of Cooley's anemia are similar to those of any anemia. Children with the disease are usually small for their age because their bone growth is poor. Their bones are sometimes so fragile that fractures occur almost spontaneously.

The only way to maintain a blood count sufficient for survival is to administer periodic blood transfusions, for some patients every two to four weeks, for others at longer intervals. This lifesaving treatment may create a buildup of an excessive amount of iron, which becomes deposited in the patient's body and vital organs, including the heart. The resulting iron overload can cause the development of such conditions as cardiac and liver failure, kidney failure, diabetes, and hepatitis.

See SICKLE CELL ANEMIA, another hereditary blood disorder; See also BLEEDING; IRON.

ANGINA PECTORIS See CHEST PAIN.

ANIMAL BITES should always be reported to a doctor. Anyone bitten by a warm-blooded animal—especially a dog, cat, bat, skunk, or fox— should follow precautions for rabies. Bites also can cause tetanus and cat scratch disease.

You can reduce the chances of infection if you

wash the wound with soap under warm running water for at least ten minutes (see illustration). Thereafter treat as a cut. Treat human bites the same way.

Of all animal bites, human bites are the most dangerous. Bacteria in the mouth can cause rapid infection. Some people suffer a bite-like injury when they punch someone in the mouth. See a doctor if you're bitten by another person.

Also see a doctor if you're bitten by a cat. Cat bites are extremely infectious, second only to human bites.

By far, dogs account for most animal bites. To prevent such accidents:

Avoid strange dogs. An animal may misinterpret your innocent movement as a threat. A cat or dog may close its mouth on your hand or arm as an expression of affection—and hang on, thereby "biting" when you pull away.

Never run away from a dog. Dogs are predatory meat eaters and may regard your running as typical prey behavior that rouses them further. If threatened walk away. If you're riding a bike and a dog pursues you, stop. If the dog continues to behave aggressively, get off the bike and walk slowly away.

Speak to an aggressive dog in a friendly tone. Don't scream, yell, or scold. Don't try to wave off an aggressive dog with a stick. Doing so is more likely to provoke an attack than frighten it.

Never romp with more than two large dogs at once. When several dogs get together, pack behavior may take over. Humans have been killed by packs of normally docile, well-behaved neighborhood dogs.

If attacked strike at the dog's head, especially the sensitive nose. Yell wildly—the noise may help scare it off. If it knocks you down, roll onto your stomach. Protect your face, head, and neck with your arms.

Wild animals. Discourage children from trying to make pets of wild animals. Chipmunks, woodchucks, squirrels, and the like are excitable in captivity and prone to bite. Raccoons captured when young generally become vicious around the age of two.

Teach children not to bother a pet that's eating and to be careful of their fingers when feeding an animal by hand. Even rabbits can inflict a mean injury. Hamsters are often vicious when pregnant, and all animal mothers may snap at a hand reaching for their young.

Warn children not to push fingers through the bars or wire mesh of a cage. Most animals will nibble any object pushed into a cage if only out of curiosity.

See also ANIMAL DISEASE; CAT SCRATCH DISEASE; CUTS; RABIES; TETANUS.

ANIMAL DISEASE (zoonosis) With an estimated 75 million house pets, 195 million farm animals, and many millions of wild animals, the potential for zoonoses (pronounced zo-ON-o-sees)—diseases harbored by animals which may be transmitted to people—in the United States is enormous.

Epidemics among animals, called epizootics, break out frequently and are often contagious to humans. Anthrax has spread to farmers from diseased cattle. Plague, mankind's most feared disease for centuries, is carried by animals, and the occasional rare case in the United States is usually traceable to an outbreak among wild rodents. Rabies is also generally spread by wild animals. Tularemia (rabbit fever) principally afflicts outdoorsmen.

Diseases transmitted by pets. Pets are often a source of human illness. They spread parasite infections that include tapeworms, pinworms, hookworms, toxoplasmosis, and amebiasis. Cats can transmit ringworm. Biting, scratching, or licking by infected cats can lead to cat scratch disease.

One woman underwent psychiatric treatment for 18 months because her itchy, pimply rash was thought to be of emotional origin. During treatment the rash became worse, and the woman finally decided to have her dog examined. Both the dog and its mistress were found to be infested with a scabies mite that usually lives in the hair coat of dogs, cats, and rabbits. Three weeks of washing with a medicated lotion and thorough cleaning of possibly contaminated house furnishings rid both the woman and her pet of their common affliction.

Allergies to animals are common, and continued exposure to skin, fur, and feathers may worsen the sensitivity. Children have been known to develop allergies to gerbils. Monkeys and apes can be carriers of tuberculosis, encephalitis, infectious hepatitis, measles, yellow fever, and salmonellosis.

Birds are the principal reservoir of encephalitis. Diseased parrots, parakeets, and farm fowl can be sources of psittacosis (parrot fever), producing symptoms like those of pneumonia, with headache and high fever. People who handle birds are also prone to an allergic respiratory problem called bird fancier's lung.

Domestic animals spread leptospirosis and brucellosis. Pet turtles are a major source of salmonellosis. Trichinosis is caused by a parasite consumed in some undercooked meats.

With the tremendous increase in the dog population there has also been an increase in the incidence of toxocariasis—human infestation traced to the roundworm in dogs.

The roundworm is a parasite that exists throughout the country, but with higher concentrations in the Southeast. The most common victims are young children, who typically get the infection by playing with dirt containing dog feces with roundworm eggs.

Symptoms are recurrent fever, cough, mild loss of appetite, and asthma symptoms. Treatment is rarely necessary. In some instances, however, the infection is more severe, with encephalitis, inflammation of the muscular tissue around the heart, and eye inflammation. Cats may sometimes pass this parasite as well.

Heartworm infestation from dogs is also increasingly recognized as a danger to dog owners. The person with this parasite has no symptoms, but routine lung X rays show a lesion. Since the lesion resembles that of early cancer, surgical exploration is necessary to make proper diagnosis.

Pet health. Since owners tend to live intimately with their pets, pet health is more important than generally realized. With good veterinary care the risk of contracting an animal disease is minimal. Follow your vet's advice about checkups, immunization, and deworming.

Isolate sick animals and birds from your family. If the illness is more than minor or persists beyond three days, have the pet examined by a vet. If the disease is transmissible to humans, check with your physician about safeguards for your family.

Pets can acquire and transmit several common childhood diseases, including measles, mumps, and possibly streptococcal infections (see SORE THROAT). Keep animals away from children who have these illnesses. Diseases are transmitted most frequently when pets are young.

Clean dogs and cats regularly to free them of ticks, fleas, and lice. Guard against contact with feces, through which an infected animal can transmit eggs of intestinal parasites. Keep dogs from excreting where food is grown or where children play. Many children contract parasites by putting soil in their mouth or going barefoot in places contaminated by pets' excreta. Raw animal excrement is unsafe to use as fertilizer.

In general, it is best not to get too intimate with pets. Kissing them, or holding food for them between your lips, is unwise.

Importing pets. To prevent infectious animals from coming into the United States, there are restrictions on importing animals, even for returning with a pet you've taken abroad. Most questions are answered in a pamphlet you can order from the Government Printing Office, Washington, D.C. 20401. Ask for Public Health Service Publication 1766, *How to Import Pets But Not Disease.*

For pet entry requirements of foreign countries get in touch with the nation's embassy in Washington or its consulate nearest you. Most airlines and ship companies can provide information on international shipment of animals.

See also ALLERGY; AMEBIASIS; ANIMAL BITES; BRUCELLOSIS; CAT SCRATCH DISEASE; ENCEPHALITIS; FLEAS; HEPATITIS; HOOKWORMS; INFECTIOUS DISEASE; LICE.

MEASLES; MUMPS; PINWORMS; PLAGUE; RABIES; RINGWORM; SALMONELLOSIS; SCABIES; TAPEWORMS; TICKS; TOXOPLASMOSIS; TRICHINOSIS; TUBERCULOSIS; TULAREMIA; YELLOW FEVER.

ANKLE FRACTURES See LEG FRACTURES.

ANKYLOSING SPONDYLITIS (also called Marie-Strümpell disease) is a form of arthritis that affects primarily the spine, causing pain and progressive stiffening of the back. The name means an immobilizing inflammation of the vertebrae. Low-back and leg pain is the earliest symptom in most cases. Stiffness may increase until there is complete rigidity of the spine. Other joints of the extremities, particularly the hips and the shoulders, sometimes become involved. Inflammation of the eyes and damage to the heart valves can be complications.

The cause is not known. It affects men more severely and about ten times as often as women and almost always begins in young adults. The disease attacks the small joints connecting the vertebrae and also the sacroiliac joints.

There is no specific cure but treatment will relieve the symptoms. Drugs used to control discomfort include aspirin, phenylbutazone, and indomethacin. Patients must follow a daily program of exercise to prevent deformities. Heat applications also may be helpful.

The disease usually becomes arrested after several years, when the pain subsides, although stiffness persists. Most patients are able to carry on and lead productive lives.

See also ARTHRITIS.

ANOREXIA NERVOSA See UNDERWEIGHT.

ANTACIDS neutralize stomach acids and are used mainly to relieve discomfort associated with heartburn, sour stomach, and/or acid indigestion. They may also be recommended for hiatal hernia and peptic ulcer.

Don't routinely use antacids except on your doctor's recommendation. While all antacids are safe and effective for occasional use, long-term use of many antacids can have side effects.

Read the label before you buy an antacid. Some antacids contain analgesics and are necessary only if you have a headache as well as an upset stomach. Take recommended dosages seriously.

See a physician if you experience repeated episodes of indigestion, even if they are as infrequent as a few times a month for several months. Also get medical help if you experience a single episode of severe or persistent discomfort, especially if it is accompanied by sweating, weakness, or breathlessness—signs of a possible heart attack. If indigestion is ever accompanied by vomiting of blood, see your doctor.

For prolonged use. The safest antacids for long-term use contain aluminum hydroxide combined with magnesium compounds. These include Maalox, Mylanta, Gelusil, and Di-Gel. The liquid form is more effective, but the tablets are more convenient to carry with you.

Magnesium hydroxide alone (as in Phillip's Milk of Magnesia) is safe for long-term use but may cause diarrhea. If you have a kidney disease, ask your doctor if you should take any product that contains magnesium. Also check with your physician if you are taking the anticoagulant dicumarol—antacids containing magnesium may interact with the drug to cause bleeding. Avoid magnesium hydroxide if you are being treated with the drug Kayexalate.

Use only occasionally. Sodium bicarbonate (baking soda), the main ingredient of Alka-Seltzer, Bromo-Seltzer, and Brioschi, can create changes in body chemistry if used frequently or over a long period of time. It may contribute to stone formation in the urinary tract and is potentially dangerous for people with kidney problems.

Rolaids contain an ingredient similar to sodium bicarbonate. They are all right for occasional use, but don't munch on them constantly. Rolaids are high in sodium and unsafe for anyone on a salt-restricted diet.

Calcium carbonate is an ingredient of Tums, Titralac, and Pepto-Bismol tablets. These are fine for occasional use. But prolonged use can cause constipation, excessive calcium in the blood, and impaired kidney function. And through a rebound effect, calcium carbonate may even cause an *increase* in stomach acid secretion after the antacid action has taken place.

When to be wary. If you're on a sodium-restricted diet, be extremely cautious in your use of antacids. Sodium content is high in many antacids and is a particular consideration for pa-

tients with cardiovascular and kidney problems. The liquid antacids with by far the lowest sodium content are Gelusil and Riopan Plus. Tablets containing relatively little sodium are Riopan Plus and Titralac.

Use antacids with caution if you are taking digitalis for heart disease, since antacids seem to reduce the effects of digitalis. If you must take an antacid, take it several hours before or after your dose of medication.

Antacids can render the antibiotic tetracycline ineffective. Take an antacid two hours before or after the tetracycline.

Some antacids contain aspirin and should be avoided by anyone with an active peptic ulcer, or with an allergy to aspirin.

When diabetic patients take antacids, they may unwittingly consume sugar that could interfere with their control; sugar is considered an "inactive" ingredient that needn't be listed on the label. For sugar-free antacid tablets diabetics can use Camalox, Maalox No. 1, Riopan swallow tablets, and Trisogel. Liquid antacids that contain no sugar include Basaljel, Camalox, Gelusil, Maalox, Phillips Milk of Magnesia, Phosphaljel, Riopan, and Silain-Gel.

Several kinds of antacids can interfere with tranquilizers such as Thorazine and other phenothiazines. Take the antacid one hour before or two hours after the tranquilizer.

If you are taking high dosages of aspirin, as for rheumatoid arthritis, antacids may interfere with their effect. You may have to increase your aspirin dosage to keep pain and inflammation under control.

See also DRUGS; HERNIA; INDIGESTION; PEPTIC ULCER; SODIUM.

ANTHRACOSILICOSIS See DUST DISEASE.

ANTHRAX See ANIMAL DISEASE.

ANTIBIOTICS are the main weapons for combating infection and infectious disease. "Antibiotic" means "against life," and one or more of these drugs kill or stop the growth of most disease-causing bacteria, fungi, and rickettsias. The drugs are so generally effective that it is tempting to overlook their limitations and hazards.

Many people experience allergic reactions to antibiotics. Before taking an antibiotic inform your physician about any adverse reactions you have had to any antibiotic in the past. (Also inform your physician about any other medications you are taking.)

Most of these reactions are relatively minor—generally rashes, nausea, and vomiting. But about one in seven reactions cause anaphylactic shock—an explosive and potentially fatal drug allergy. Penicillin and cephalosporin are the antibiotics most likely to cause a fatal allergic reaction.

Sometimes adverse reactions develop only after repeated administrations of a drug. Sensitivity to penicillin often worsens with each exposure until a full-blown allergy appears, making it unsafe for you to ever use the drug again.

Side effects of antibiotics can last for weeks after you discontinue the drug. Problems include a sore mouth, "furry" tongue, cramps, diarrhea, anal and vaginal itch, nausea, and vomiting. Wear a sun-blocking lotion if you're exposed to the sun while taking sulfa or tetracyclines, which can produce severe sunburn reactions. Tetracycline can stain the teeth of young children and retard their bone growth. It should be avoided by women in the last half of pregnancy.

More serious—and more rare—side effects of antibiotics include blood disorders, kidney failure, deafness, and liver damage.

Moreover, both in an individual and in a hospital or community, overprescribing of an antibiotic can speed up the development of resistant strains of bacteria. The strains that succumb to the drug die off and the ones that survive may possibly be even more injurious. Penicillin G used to be able to wipe out *Staphylococcus aureus* in hospitals. Now hospital staph infections are so resistant that they are said to eat the drug like candy.

Reducing risks from antibiotics. Urge your doctor not to prescribe antibiotics unless necessary. Testifying at a Senate hearing, Dr. James Visconti of Ohio State University Hospital's drug information center cited several studies indicating that more than 60 percent of patients given antibiotics in several hospitals "showed no evidence of infection." One of the studies found more than 65 percent of the antibiotic administrations "irrational"—wrong drug, wrong dose, wrong route of administration, or no sign of infection.

Why do physicians overprescribe? Because they want to do something positive—and because some patients demand a "miracle drug" to cure their complaints.

You can help by waiting for a lab report. A culture in which a specimen is grown and tested can pin down which type of bacteria is responsible for an infection, usually in two to five days. Then the doctor can prescribe the best antibiotic for eliminating it.

It's rarer than most laymen realize for an infection to be identified merely from its outer signs. For example, at least seven organisms can invade the kidneys and cause the damage, pain, and fever of pyelonephritis. A drug that works against one of the seven may be ineffective against another. To find out whether he should ideally prescribe kanamycin, ampicillin, or a cephalosporin, the doctor must first learn if the infective organism is an enterobacteriaceae, or *Proteus mirabilis,* or klebsiella—each as different from the other as an elephant is from a giraffe.

When no bacteriological studies can be conveniently made or the patient demands immediate treatment, the doctor may prescribe a so-called broad-spectrum antibiotic, which is effective against several types of bacteria. But this shotgun approach may be completely off target, and raises the risk of developing bacteria resistant to the drug.

The patient may then develop a hard-to-cure superinfection—a worse infection caused by a microorganism resistant to the drug.

Women on broad-spectrum antibiotics often suffer minor yeast infection, with distressing vaginal itching—caused by antibiotic-resistant fungi that thrive after the destruction of the "good" bacteria that normally keep them in check.

Waiting for a lab report of a culture also may save you money. Pneumonia caused by pneumococci bacteria can normally be treated with penicillin for less than $1 a day. Some broad-spectrum antibiotics may cost over $20 a day, but are no more effective than penicillin against pneumococci.

Don't insist on "preventive medicine." Antibiotics are not like immunization—they can treat an infection but don't generally protect you from getting one.

Don't expect a shot of penicillin to cure a cold or any other virus-caused diseases. Antibiotics don't work against viruses. Hard evidence shows that treating viral infections with antibiotics does *not* ward off such bacterial complications as ear infections or sinusitis.

Antibiotics *are* useful to prevent complications following a streptococcal sore throat. Penicillin is normally taken for ten days to reduce the chance of kidney involvement leading to glomerulonephritis, or the development of rheumatic fever and subsequent rheumatic heart disease. In some cases of heart disease or congenital heart defects antibiotics are administered judiciously before surgery, dental work, and childbirth.

One preventive step you can always take with antibiotics is to complete a full course of medication, even though symptoms seem to disappear before all the pills are gone. The best way to prevent a relapse or the development of resistance is to wipe out the infection rapidly and thoroughly. Too little antibiotic can help breed a strain of resistant bacteria. A low dosage also can provoke bacteria to produce more toxins injurious to cells.

Challenge any prescription for Chloromycetin. This is the major brand of chloramphenicol, an extremely potent but also potentially dangerous drug. Other brand names to beware are Amphicol and Mychel.

If one of these is prescribed for you, ask your doctor, "Is this drug necessary? Can a less hazardous one be used?"

Chloramphenicol can cause several blood disorders—including aplastic anemia, a usually fatal blood disease in which the bone marrow no longer makes white cells, red cells, and platelets (necessary for proper clotting). Ordinarily the chances of dying of aplastic anemia are less than 1 in 500,000; with chloramphenicol the risk increases by 12 to 20 times.

Newborn and premature infants given chloramphenicol can develop "gray baby syndrome," which results from failure of blood to circulate properly. It is often fatal.

At Senate hearings medical authorities testified that chloramphenicol was uncalled for in 90 percent of the cases in which it had been prescribed. One doctor reportedly told a woman to take chloramphenicol whenever she had a cold. She died of aplastic anemia.

It is therefore recommended that chloramphenicol be the drug of choice only for severe typhoid fever. Otherwise it should be used only for certain life-threatening conditions—such as meningitis in a patient allergic to penicillin, or severe Rocky Mountain spotted fever—or where less dangerous drugs have failed.

If you need to take chloramphenicol, inform your doctor of any unusual bleeding or bruising, weakness or fatigue, fever, pale skin, or sore throat. If a baby taking the drug develops gray skin color, low body temperature, bloated stomach, uneven breathing or drowsiness, stop the medicine and contact your doctor immediately.

See also DRUG ALLERGY; DRUGS; INFECTIOUS DISEASE.

ANTIBIOTICS—GENERIC AND BRAND NAMES

Your doctor diagnoses infection and scribbles a prescription he says is for penicillin. You pick up the medicine from the drugstore and note that the label says Compocillin-V. Drugs go by two names—a generic (chemical) one, and the brand name given to the drug by the manufacturer. Below is a sampling of antibiotics by generic name, and a partial listing of brand names for the same drugs.

Generic Name	Brand Name
Amoxicillin	Trimox; Amoxil
Amphotericin B	Fungizone
Ampicillin	Amcill; Penbritin; Polycillin; Principen; Omnipen
Cephaloglycin	Kafocin
Cephalothin	Keflin
Chloramphenicol	Chloromycetin; Amphicol; Mychel
Chlortetracycline	Aureomycin
Cloxacillin	Tegopen
Demeclocycline (demethylchlortetracycline)	Declomycin
Dicloxacillin	Veracillin; Dynapen; Pathocil
Doxycycline	Vibramycin
Erythromycin	Erythrocin; Ilosone; Ilotycin; Pediamycin; Erythromycin; E-mycin
Gentamicin	Garamycin
Griseofulvin	Grisactin; Grifulvin V; Fulvicin
Kanamycin	Kantrex
Lincomycin	Lincocin
Methicillin	Staphcillin; Dimocillin
Nafcillin	Unipen
Nystatin	Mycostatin
Oxacillin	Prostaphlin; Resistopen
Oxytetracycline	Terramycin
Penicillin G	Pentids
Penicillin G (benzathine)	Bicillin
Penicillin V	Compocillin-V; V-Cillin; Veetids; Pen-Vee
Phenethicillin	Syncillin
Polymyxin B	Aerosporin; Polymyxin B
Sulfamethoxazole and trimethoprim	Bactrim; Septra
Sulfonamide	Gantanol; Gantrisin; Sulla
Tetracycline hydrochloride	Achromycin; Sumycin

ANTICOAGULANTS prolong the time needed for blood to coagulate, or clot. These drugs can reduce the possibility of thrombosis: a blood clot forming in an artery, a vein, or in the heart itself, blocking the flow of blood. Anticoagulants also help prevent embolism, or blockage resulting from a clot breaking loose from the inner wall of the artery or heart and traveling downstream to become wedged in smaller blood vessels.

Anticoagulants are often prescribed to prevent conditions caused or complicated by clots: heart attack, stroke, thrombophlebitis, leg pain. After surgery anticoagulants are often administered to prevent pulmonary embolism, caused by a clot entering a blood vessel in the lung.

Precautions. If you're taking an anticoagulant, list the drug's name and dosage on any emergency medical identification you carry with you. This is essential information in case of an accident, since physicians treating you need to take special precautions if your blood won't clot normally.

Your doctor may prescribe an antidote, such as Vitamin K_1, should bleeding occur. Always carry it and take it only as instructed.

Ask your physician before taking any drugs whatever. Some increase, some lessen, the action of the anticoagulant. This includes aspirin; remedies for colds and coughing; vitamins in any form; and antibiotics. Also ask your doctor about smoking or alcohol.

Mention to your dentist and any physician who treats you that you're on anticoagulants.

Be prepared to have periodic blood tests. The effectiveness of anticoagulants varies from individual to individual, even from time to time in the same person. You need to have your prescription regulated so the drug will be effective without causing bleeding.

Watch for complications. Tell your doctor at once if you have any of these signs of possible internal bleeding:

Red or dark brown urine.

Red or black bowel movements.

Unusually large amounts of bleeding during menstruation.

Unusually severe or prolonged headache or abdominal pain.

Bleeding of any kind (such as from gums).

Illnesses, notably diarrhea, can reduce your tolerance for anticoagulants. Get in touch with your doctor if you feel sick, unusually tired, faint, or dizzy. He also needs to know if you think you might be pregnant.

Notify him if you discover spontaneous bruises or "blood blisters," or if you've received any blows or other injuries, even if there are no visible signs of bleeding.

See also DRUGS; EMERGENCY MEDICAL IDENTIFICATION; HEART DISEASE.

ANTIHISTAMINES are chemical compounds—there are about 50 types—that counteract symptoms caused by a destructive substance called histamine.

In the course of allergic reactions and in a number of diseases histamine results from the breaking down of histidine, a compound produced in the intestines and normally found in most body tissues. Histamine acts to cause such symptoms as itching, headache, falling blood pressure, constriction of the bronchial tubes, and reddening and heating of the skin.

Antihistamines block these effects and are widely used to bring relief in allergy attacks. The drugs help dry mucous membranes and ease the symptoms of hives and hay fever as well as reactions to poison ivy and related plants. They may be useful in a purely local reaction to an insect sting, but when the victim is in real danger because of such an allergy, the drug of choice is Adrenalin.

When antihistamines first came out, the press publicized them as cold cures: if taken at the first sign of a cold, it was said, they would ward off the attack. This was false. The drugs can ease discomfort but can't influence the course of the infection or appreciably reduce coughing.

Antihistamines cause drowsiness. Most antihistamines can make you sleepy or reduce your mental responses and nerve reactions. While this side effect may disappear with continued use, it is sometimes so troublesome that the drug must be withdrawn. If taking an antihistamine, you may be unable to properly drive a car, operate machines, or perform other duties requiring keen reactions.

Other major side effects of antihistamines include impairment to the nervous system: dizziness, ear noises, fatigue, nervousness, blurred vision. In very rare instances these drugs have serious adverse effects on the blood and blood-forming organs.

While ordinarily a sedative, in some people the drug can bring on sleeplessness. Similarly, despite wide use in allergies, antihistamines themselves can cause reactions, especially if applied to the skin.

Among over-the-counter antihistamines you may get best results with Benadryl and other products containing diphenhydramine, formerly available only by prescription.

See also ALLERGY; DRUG ALLERGY; DRUGS.

ANTISEPTICS, long believed essential to any stock of family medical supplies, are usually unnecessary and sometimes dangerous. They may irritate the wound, retard healing, and trigger a drug allergy or skin irritation.

You can usually treat scratches, cuts, and other small injuries by cleansing with soap and water and covering with a small bandage for protection against bumps and additional contamination. In most instances the normal skin is capable of preventing invasion by any disease-causing bacteria that are not removed by the painless cleansing action of soap and water.

If you feel that treatment won't be complete unless you use an antiseptic, choose rubbing alcohol or iodine. Both are among the most potent antiseptics available and are inexpensive in their generic forms.

Alcohol evaporates quickly, so rub it on the skin for about two minutes for maximum effectiveness. Drying or skin irritation may occur with repeated use. Allergies to alcohol are rare.

Iodine solution USP has very little sting when applied to breaks in the skin. Iodine tincture USP (iodine in alcohol) is even more effective, but causes stinging and irritates the skin with repeated use.

Mercurial compounds (such as Mercurochrome and Merthiolate) are less effective antiseptics and may irritate the skin. Allergic skin reactions are fairly common.

Hydrogen peroxide solution is a poor antiseptic. But if you have a particularly dirty wound, its frothing action may help cleanse it.

Avoid phenols (carbolic acid, cresol). They must be used in such high concentrations to be effective that they irritate the skin.

Quaternary ammonium compounds work against some organisms, but do little to prevent the growth of many other bacteria that can also cause infection. Proprietary products containing this class of antiseptic include Bactine and Zephiran Chloride.

Be cautious in your use of antibiotic preparations intended for use on the skin without a doctor's prescription. Neomycin is the most commonly used such antibiotic, and though it is quite effective against some bacteria, it is less effective against others. Further, there may be little wisdom in using antibiotics without medical supervision. When used repeatedly antibiotics may encourage the development of resistant strains of bacteria and would then be useless if these strains later caused a serious infection.

See also DRUGS; MEDICAL SUPPLIES.

ANTS become a nuisance primarily when they proliferate. However the bite of the red ant, which is prevalent in southern states, can cause a severe reaction in people who are allergic to insect stings.

The key to ant extermination is finding the nest. Many species of ants establish regular lines of march, so you can often track down the approximate location of their community. If they are headquartered outdoors, prevent them from gaining entrance to your house by sealing off the cracks they travel through. If the ants start coming again, they may have changed routes, and you will have to block another section.

Indoors, pinpointing a nest may be difficult. Ants nest within walls and partitions, behind baseboards, and under flooring. Using a brush apply a 2 percent chlordane liquid to the cracks

from which the ants emerge and to their surface runways.

Allow a few days for the treatment to take effect, especially if you have not been able to get directly at the nest. If the ants still show up, they may be traveling by another route, which you will have to locate and brush insecticide onto.

If the ants return again, you may have to pry loose a baseboard or doorframe to treat the nest directly. If the nest is outside the kitchen, spray it with a 2 percent chlordane liquid brand. In the kitchen—where chlordane is likely to contaminate food or food preparation equipment—spray and dust with pyrethrin-based products, which are harmless to man.

You may need a professional exterminator for out-of-reach nests—those between partitions or under floors—or for a row house or apartment building.

Do not use ant traps, baits, or syrups. They are not as effective as surface treatment with chlordane, and they often contain extremely dangerous poisons such as thallium sulfate.

See also INSECTS, INSECT STINGS.

ANT STINGS See INSECT STINGS.

ANXIETY See STRESS; TRANQUILIZERS.

AORTA, COARCTATION OF THE See CONGENITAL HEART DEFECTS.

APOPLEXY See STROKE.

APPENDICITIS is inflammation of the appendix, a functionless worm-shaped organ that is attached to the large intestine. Appendicitis can occur at any age, but is most common in young people.

Untreated, the inflamed appendix may rupture, causing severe illness or death. Most deaths from appendicitis occur because of delay in seeking treatment, largely because the early symptoms are dismissed as indigestion or constipation.

An appendicitis attack often begins with pain around the navel. There often is nausea and vomiting.

Frequently the pain shifts to the lower right-hand side of the abdomen after several hours, generally to a spot about 2 inches from the hipbone. The tenderness is not necessarily severe at first, but in most cases it gradually becomes more so. There is typically "rebound tenderness"—the victim feels more pain when the hand is quickly removed than when pressure is applied. The victim generally likes to remain still because the pain is worse when he walks or otherwise moves.

Most people experience only slight fever (99° F–101° F) or none at all. Constipation is common and is often considered the cause of the pain.

Call a doctor. Get medical attention if abdominal pain is severe or lasts more than a day. Don't take laxatives or enemas: they increase the chance of rupture. Nor should you eat or drink.

For temporary pain relief until you can see a doctor, put ice compresses on the abdomen. Don't apply heat.

Appendicitis is usually treated by prompt surgery to remove the inflamed appendix. Don't be surprised if after an appendectomy you are told that the appendix was normal. It can be virtually impossible to distinguish acute appendicitis from other conditions that cause pain in the lower right abdomen—a ruptured ovary, an inflammation of lymph nodes, an intestinal infection. A prudent surgeon who can't rule out appendicitis may be afraid to take the chance of leaving the appendix in.

Except in rare instances, such as an expedition into the wilds, don't have a normal appendix removed merely as a "preventive measure." A healthy appendix is likely to be less of a threat than the surgery for taking it out.

Peer review has reduced the number of unnecessary appendectomies. Even so, if a surgeon tells you, "You'd better have it out now before it gets infected," ask for another opinion. An official of the American College of Surgeons used the term "chronic remunerative appendicitis" to describe an operation in which a normal appendix is removed merely to enrich the surgeon.

See also GALLBLADDER DISEASE; SURGERY.

ARCHES, FALLEN See FALLEN ARCHES.

ARM FRACTURES can often be identified by the strange angle at which the arm is hanging. This is particularly true of a fracture of the elbow.

Do not attempt to straighten or bend the arm in any direction. To give first aid handle the arm very gently.

Splint it with a board, magazine, or pillow. Then support it against the body with a sling tied around the neck (see illustration). A simple sling can be made from a large scarf or a torn sheet folded into a triangle.

See also FRACTURES; PLASTER CASTS.

ARRHYTHMIA, CARDIAC See HEART PALPITATION.

ARTERIOSCLEROSIS refers to changes in arteries resulting in thickening and hardening of their walls and loss of their elasticity.

In atherosclerosis, the most common form of arteriosclerosis, the inner walls of the arteries are gradually thickened and roughened by deposits of fats, particularly cholesterol and triglycerides. As more layers build up, they narrow the channel through the artery. This may block the flow of blood. A blood clot may form on the rough areas and block circulation at that point.

Most heart attacks can be traced to atherosclerosis of the special heart arteries, the coronaries, which carry blood to nourish the heart muscle with oxygen. The most frequent cause of stroke (arterial thrombosis) is atherosclerosis in the arteries that deliver blood to the brain.

Atherosclerosis develops over a long time. It may be present in a young person but not become apparent until middle age or later, when a

IF AN ARM MAY BE BROKEN

1. Splint the break

2. Immobilize with sling

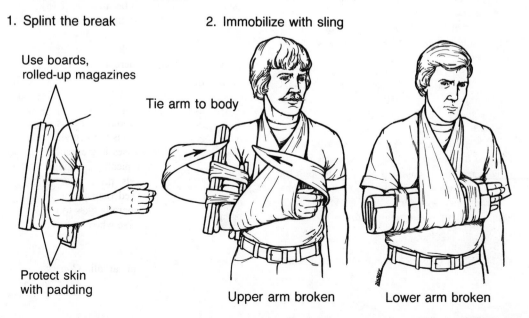

Use boards, rolled-up magazines

Tie arm to body

Protect skin with padding

Upper arm broken

Lower arm broken

symptom such as chest pain (angina pectoris) occurs.

Often when the coronary arteries become narrowed, nearby arteries may get wider and even open up tiny new branches to deliver blood to the area of heart muscle that needs it. This collateral or substitute circulation helps to prevent some people from developing chest pains or heart attacks even though they have atherosclerosis.

No drug can reverse arteriosclerosis, though a low-cholesterol diet may offer some protection against further fat buildup. Medical treatment after a heart attack often consists of anticoagulants to prevent blood from clotting within the narrowed arteries.

There is a strong hereditary factor. A family history of heart disease should serve as a warning to take precautions, such as following a low-cholesterol diet.

The "clay pipe stem" type of arteriosclerosis, in which calcium deposits build up in the blood vessels, seems limited largely to very old people.

Coronary bypass surgery. This is a common surgical procedure for improving the blood supply to the heart muscle. Coronary bypass surgery is often done to relieve the pain of severe angina pectoris. About 60 to 70 percent of people with severe angina who have bypass surgery are completely free of pain after the surgery; another 15 percent have much less pain. For a small minority surgery does not relieve angina pain.

Coronary bypass surgery may also be done for a blockage that could cause a heart attack, even if the person does not have angina pain or has it only occasionally.

In effect bypass surgery is similar to building a detour around a blocked section of a tunnel. The surgeon takes a piece of a blood vessel from another part of the body—usually a vein from the leg—and uses it to "bypass" the blocked part of the artery.

Before surgery the obstructed areas of coronary arteries can be identified through coronary arteriography. In this diagnostic procedure the doctor guides a catheter—a thin, flexible plastic tube—through an artery of the arm or leg into the coronary arteries. An X-ray opaque dye is injected through the catheter. High-speed X-ray movies record the course of the dye through the arteries and point up any obstructions. The procedure is done with the patient awake and takes about an hour. Fatal complications are rare—about 1 in 1,000.

Bypass surgery usually takes about three to six hours. An incision is made along the midline

of the chest through the breastbone. Most patients stay in the hospital about two weeks, then convalesce at home for two to four weeks, gradually resuming normal activities.

Nationwide the mortality rate for coronary bypass surgery is about 1 to 3 percent. A small number of bypass patients suffer heart attacks in the period surrounding the surgery; such attacks, however, seem to be less severe than those that would occur naturally from obstructed heart arteries. There may also be a number of less serious complications.

Once you are discharged from the hospital, call your physician if you experience any signs of infection around your incision, fever, chills, increased fatigue, shortness of breath, swelling, excessive weight gain, or changes in heart rate or rhythm. Most people can return to work in four to six weeks.

For most people who undergo bypass surgery, the quality of their lives is substantially improved: They have little or no chest pain, and more energy for daily activities and exercise. It is not yet clear, however, whether the surgery also averts heart attacks and thus prolongs life. In any case it makes sense to reduce risk factors of heart attack after you've had bypass surgery: Don't smoke. Control high blood pressure. Reduce stress. Eat less salt, cholesterol, and saturated fats. Exercise (under your doctor's guidance). Keep your weight down. Even with such precautions, however, blockage may recur.

In a new technique that might spare many patients painful and costly surgery, doctors are opening blocked arteries with balloons. The balloon is inserted into the damaged area of a blood vessel, then inflated and deflated several times, each time with increasing pressure. When the balloon is removed, obstructions caused by fatty deposits have been compressed, and more oxygen-rich blood can flow through the blood vessel.

The technique—called angioplasty—has been in use for relieving cramps and saving legs by opening obstructions in leg arteries. It can also treat, and sometimes cure, a type of high blood pressure resulting from blockage of an artery to the kidneys.

Now angioplasty is becoming more commonly used to compress obstructions in coronary arteries—although this use is still considered experimental and requires a backup team ready to do open-heart surgery in case of complications. For most patients who have undergone angioplasty, the technique removes the obstruction and relieves symptoms. But in about 16 percent of patients the blockage recurs, usually within the first six months after the procedure.

See also ANTICOAGULANTS; BLOOD CLOT; CHEST PAIN; CORONARY ARTERY DISEASE; FATS; HEART ATTACK; HEART DISEASE; STRESS.

ARTERIOSCLEROSIS OBLITERANS See LEG PAIN.

ARTHRITIS means inflammation or damage of a joint. It has become the popular name for a number of conditions involving pain and inflammation of joints.

More than 38 million Americans have some form of arthritis. About 3.5 million of them are limited in their activities, and close to a million of these are unable to work, keep house, or carry on a major activity.

Types of arthritis. The most painful and crippling form is rheumatoid arthritis. Another type, osteoarthritis, is believed to result from aging and normal stresses on joints; in some degree it attacks the joints of nearly everyone over 50.

Gout most often affects the joint of the big toe and develops from excessive uric acid in the tissues. In ankylosing spondylitis the chief symptoms are pain and stiffening of the spine. Systemic lupus erythematosus is an inflammatory disorder of the body's connective tissues; arthritis is frequently associated with it.

Arthritis sometimes accompanies other diseases, as in gonococcal arthritis (associated with gonorrhea), tuberculous arthritis, and psoriatic arthritis. The term *rheumatism* is used widely by laymen for any condition producing pain in joints, nerves, and muscles. Bursitis is often associated with a sore shoulder.

Controlling symptoms. While most forms of arthritis cannot be cured, they can be relieved with painkilling and anti-inflammatory drugs. Aspirin is used most widely. It often must be taken in large doses (usually 10 to 16 tablets a day) and only under a doctor's supervision. Nonaspirin salicylate tablets may be used as alternatives to aspirin for people who are unable to tolerate large doses of aspirin. They include magnesium salicylate, choline magnesium trisalicylate, and salsalate. These drugs cost considerably more than plain aspirin.

Other drugs commonly used in arthritis treatment include indomethacin, ibuprofen, naproxen, fenoprofen, tolmetin and sulindac. If arthritis symptoms fail to respond, physicians may prescribe still other drugs: Phenylbutazone, antimalarial compounds, gold salts, or corticosteroids, are used in some forms of arthritis. All can have serious side effects. Phenylbutazone, for example, may give rise to kidney disease and

severe blood disorders. Corticosteroids may produce a wide range of side effects—including mental disturbances, high blood pressure, lowered resistance to infection—and are generally reserved for short periods during acute flare-ups.

Proper exercise is extremely important in helping the arthritic retain maximum motion in a joint.

For instance, if one hip joint is allowed to become overly stiff and painful, you are likely to favor that hip and the muscles will weaken. Then more powerful muscles on the other side of the body tend to take over.

What may have begun as a slight favoring of one side can become a twisting of the body that may later result in a permanent defect in posture. Abnormal stresses are set up, and joints that were not originally affected may become troublesome. To help avoid this, your doctor may prescribe a series of exercises to make sure the affected joints are moved through their full range of motion several times a day.

Casts, splints, and metal braces are sometimes used to give joints added rest and to help prevent contractions, shortening of muscles and ligaments resulting in an inability to straighten the joint. Removable devices are often used at night and for periods during the day. Light splints can support afflicted joints. For example, a splint on the wrist permits active use of fingers and hands while giving the wrist protection.

Some joints, like those of the feet, take a good deal of the body weight when you stand or walk. A doctor may recommend special shoes or distributing weight with the use of canes or crutches. Don't use these aids without first getting instruction. If maneuvered improperly they can create stresses that may injure the joints.

Hydrotherapy can reduce inflammation and soreness. In many hospitals arthritis patients find relief and are exercised gently in tanks of warm, bubbly water. Smaller whirlpool tanks are available for treatment of arms, hands, feet, and legs. Warm swimming pools can also be therapeutic. Equipment of this type is available for home use, but don't buy any without first consulting a physician.

Heat is an old and effective means of relaxing muscles and relieving pain in arthritic joints. Doctors often prescribe a 20-minute hot bath early in the morning, when joints are likely to be particularly stiff and painful. Half-hour submersions in paraffin melted at low heat can bring relief to hands, wrists, and feet. To prevent burns be sure the paraffin is cool enough to keep a half-dollar-sized fragment of wax unmelted at all times.

Hot compresses, electric mitts, heat lamps, electric pads, and blown hot air are among other useful methods. For an acutely inflamed joint ice packs may bring relief.

There is no evidence that a warm, dry climate will improve arthritis. Thus physicians generally advise patients against changing climate in an effort to find relief.

Surgery to repair damaged joints can be effective in relieving pain and correcting deformities. In some cases joints can be replaced by artificial devices of metal or plastic.

Rest is an important part of arthritis therapy. Several times a day arthritis sufferers should lie down for short periods. It's also important to minimize the strain on joints by simplifying your daily routine. Stop doing chores that don't really need to be done; find easier ways to perform essential tasks.

Arthritis sufferers can make or purchase a wide variety of special tools to make daily life easier—long-handled combs or toothbrushes, for example.

If arthritis affects the fingers, clothing with front openings will be easier to put on. Fastenings should be easy to handle—large buttons or Velcro tape.

Quack remedies. Arthritics are particularly vulnerable to quack claims. It has been estimated that they spend an average of $1 billion a year on worthless medications and treatment.

The arthritic is often frustrated by the long-term and uneventful treatment offered by legitimate practitioners. No matter how valueless a

IF ARTHRITIS HAMPERS YOUR HOUSEWORK

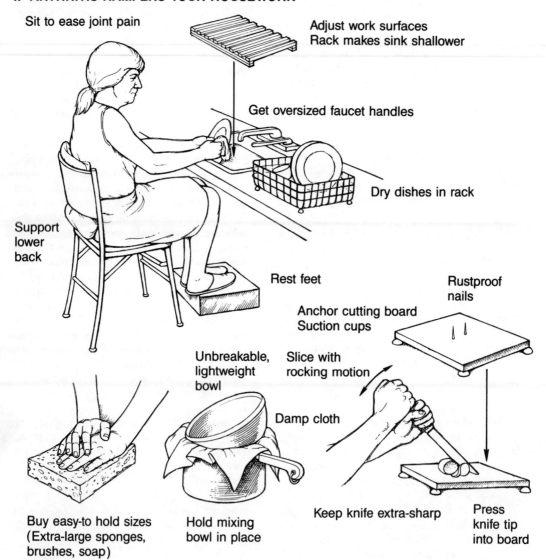

Sit to ease joint pain

Adjust work surfaces
Rack makes sink shallower

Get oversized faucet handles

Dry dishes in rack

Support lower back

Rest feet

Rustproof nails

Anchor cutting board
Suction cups

Unbreakable, lightweight bowl

Slice with rocking motion

Damp cloth

Buy easy-to hold sizes
(Extra-large sponges, brushes, soap)

Hold mixing bowl in place

Keep knife extra-sharp

Press knife tip into board

quack preparation may be, it can gain his confidence if taking it happens to coincide with one of the spontaneous remissions common in the disease.

Arthritis sufferers are often in such pain that they are tempted to try anything that holds out the promise of relief. Besides the economic waste, the menace to health is enormous, for arthritics are encouraged by misleading claims to attempt dangerous self-medication. Some products are actually harmful.

Dangerous drugs have been manufactured outside the country, then imported by arthritis sufferers. One such drug was dispensed by a Mexican physician in unlabeled ampules, and thousands of patients in five southern states were taking it. Analysis showed it was the drug dipyrone, which often causes agranulocytosis, a blood disease in which the white blood cell count drops rapidly and infection follows. At least four people with arthritis taking the imported drug died of this disorder.

Misleading claims sometimes suggest that a product has general medical approval: "an amazing new discovery," "used by doctors," or "now available without prescription." Any such claim should be checked with your doctor.

False claims extend to the names companies give themselves. The words *research* or *medical* or *clinic* may be included in the name of the concern marketing the phony product.

Some drugs claiming to relieve arthritis pain are nothing more than ordinary aspirin. But they usually cost far more—in one case, $5.95 for 25¢ worth of aspirin.

Lotions and ointments can often provide temporary relief, but that's all. Many such products, however, falsely claim to give "deep, long-lasting" relief and other therapeutic benefits—and are priced accordingly.

Bee venom, once widely used in Europe, has been discredited for relief of arthritis pain. First used in this country in the 1930s, it has been found ineffective in studies.

Liefcort occupies a special chapter in the annals of quackery. It is among the most dangerous yet widely used of fraudulent drugs available to arthritis patients.

The drug—a combination of prednisone (a corticosteroid) and sex hormones testosterone and estradiol—was developed by Robert E. Liefmann, who was then an unlicensed Canadian doctor. In a magazine article, which gave the drug favorable publicity, Liefmann describes how he created this remedy for an arthritic friend: "I just went downstairs and mixed it up. By God, I hit it right on the head."

When the friend's arthritis symptoms subsided, Liefmann mixed up additional supplies of his secret formula in his home "laboratory" and prescribed it for any arthritis victims who happened to show up.

Liefmann's practice flourished, and he was estimated to gross as much as $250,000 annually. American arthritis patients streamed across the border to buy Liefcort for as much as $180 for 6 ounces.

Serious adverse reactions and a number of deaths among patients were reported. In 1969 Dr. Liefmann was convicted of violating Canada's Food and Drug Act, and ordered to pay a fine. He died in 1972. But clinics in the United States, Canada, Mexico, and the Dominican Republic continue to use his therapy.

These and other clinics lure large numbers of victims. Many clinics subject the patient to a series of worthless treatments—kerosene and iodine baths, alfalfa-seed diets, and so on—and charge exorbitant prices.

Quack food remedies. No special diet or food supplement can cure the disease. The claims for juice and herbal concoctions and an endless variety of food-faddist offerings are not based on any evidence.

One widely advertised, and useless, "treatment" consisted of three separately packaged items: a laxative, a vitamin formula, and a concoction of acids. The cost was $12.50 for a two-month supply.

"Immune" milk is another misrepresented product. According to its promoters the milk gets its immunity from antibodies produced in the udders of cows injected with streptococcus and staphylococcus vaccines. Scientifically controlled studies show this milk has absolutely no effect on the disease.

Other miracles that don't work. Over the years a wide variety of useless mechanical devices have attracted arthritis sufferers in search of a cure. One contraption was supposed to expand all the atoms of the body with its "Z-Ray" and so produce perfect health, all for $50. Another consisted of a plastic lampshade and bulb. The blue plastic, when placed over the lampshade, was supposed to produce a glow that would cure arthritis and rheumatism.

Metallic and electromagnetic bracelets also lure arthritis patients. Copper bracelets in particular have enjoyed a long vogue.

Other false devices include metal plates fitted into shoes and supposedly setting up electronic waves that dissolve calcium deposits in diseased joints, stainless steel wristwatch bands with their own "miniature thermopiles," and dangerous spine stretchers.

Vibrating machines can no longer advertise that they relieve or prevent arthritis, as they have proved to be ineffective and often dangerous. Vibrator machines range in price from perhaps $15 for a pillow, to $600 and more for a chair.

A recent development in potential arthritis quackery is the acupuncture clinic. Acupuncture has been shown to produce only temporary relief of arthritis in particularly suggestible people. But many people are lured by false claims into expensive and possibly hazardous treatment.

Another treatment that may or may not prove beneficial for arthritis patients is the use of dimethyl sulfoxide, or DMSO. Proclaimed as a wonder drug for a wide range of ailments, the claims have yet to be scientifically substantiated. What's more, self-treatment with DMSO may be risky. Many arthritis sufferers are treating themselves with strong solutions intended for veterinary or industrial use. For human use the drug is currently approved only for the treatment of chronic bladder disease.

Books about arthritis. Erroneous and misleading books are the source of many quack arthritis diets as well as other false information about the disease.

Some books *not* recommended by the Arthritis Foundation include *The Arthritic's Cookbook* by Colin M. Dong, M.D., and Jane Banks; *Arthritis Can Be Cured* by Bernard Aschner, M.D.; *Arthritis, Nutrition and Natural Therapy* by Carlson Wade; and *Bees Don't Get Arthritis* by Fred Malone.

By contrast, the following books *are* among those recommended by the foundation and other reliable sources in medicine as being among the most informative and accurate on arthritis: *Understanding Arthritis* by The Arthritis Foundation (Scribner's); *Arthritis: A Comprehensive Guide* by James F. Fries, M.D. (Addison-Wesley Publishing Company); *Beyond the Copper Bracelet: What You Should Know About Arthritis* by Louis A. Healey, M.D., Kenneth R. Wilske, M.D., and Bob Hansen (Charles Press); *Living With Your Arthritis* edited by Alan M. Rosenberg, M.D. (Arco Publishing); *The Arthritis Handbook—A Patient's Manual on Arthritis, Rheumatism and Gout* by Darrell C. Crain, M.D. (Exposition Press); and *Understanding Arthritis and Rheumatism: A Complete Guide to the Problems and Treatment* by Malcolm I.V. Jayson, M.D. and Allan St. J. Dixon, M.D. (Pantheon Books).

See also ANKYLOSING SPONDYLITIS; ASPIRIN; BURSITIS; CHIROPRACTORS; COMPRESSES; DRUGS; EXERCISE; FRACTURES; GOUT; OSTEOARTHRITIS; PSORIATIC ARTHRITIS; QUACKERY; RHEUMATISM; RHEUMATOID ARTHRITIS; SYSTEMIC LUPUS ERYTHEMATOSUS; TUBERCULOUS ARTHRITIS.

ARTIFICIAL RESPIRATION (rescue breathing) has the highest priority in first aid. It's the first step of CPR (cardiopulmonary resuscitation), preceding closed-chest heart massage. After 4 to 6 minutes without breathing, a victim is likely to suffer irreversible brain damage or death.

For someone age 8 or older who may need rescue breathing, do the following (see illustrations—"CPR Review: To Restore Breathing and Heartbeat for Victims Age 8 and Older"—starting on page 39):

1. Determine that he's unconscious. Shake his shoulder and shout, "Are you all right?" If he doesn't respond, shout for help. Have someone phone 911 or your local emergency number.

2. Turn him onto his back, face up. Roll him as a unit so that his head, shoulders and torso move simultaneously, positioning his arms and legs as shown in the illustration.

3. To open his airway, tilt his head. This maneuver prevents obstruction by his tongue: With one hand, gently lift his neck or chin. With your other hand, push down on his forehead.

4. Kneel at his side, and place your ear close to his mouth. Look at his chest or stomach for movement. Listen for sounds of breathing. Feel for breath on your cheek. If you don't detect any of these signs, assume he's not breathing.

5. Using your hand that's on his forehead, pinch his nostrils shut. Keep his head tilted with the heel of that hand plus the neck or chin lift.

   Place your mouth on his. If you wish, you can place a handkerchief between your lips and his.

6. Give 4 full, rapid breaths. As you do so, check if his chest rises and falls.

   If the chest doesn't rise, again open the airway (as in Step #3) and again give 4 full, rapid breaths.

   Emergency: If the chest still fails to rise and fall, follow instructions in "When the Airway Is Blocked" (page 44).

7. Check the pulse in his neck to see if his heart is beating. Locate his larynx by finding the bony point (Adam's apple) in the front of his neck. In the side of the neck, feel for

CPR REVIEW: TO RESTORE BREATHING AND HEARTBEAT FOR VICTIMS AGE 8 AND OLDER

Caution: Never practice CPR without proper instruction!

1. Determine if victim is unconscious
If so, yell for help—and proceed with CPR

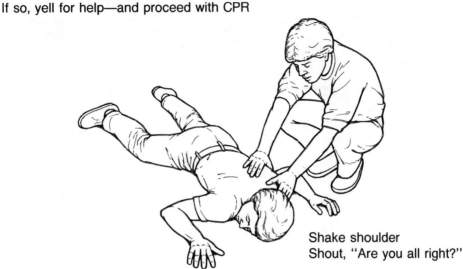

Shake shoulder
Shout, "Are you all right?"

---

2. Turn him on his back, face up
Roll head, shoulders, and torso all at once

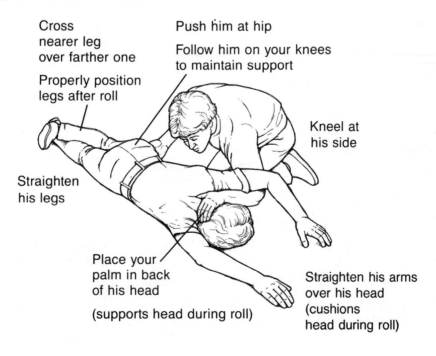

Cross
nearer leg
over farther one

Push him at hip

Follow him on your knees
to maintain support

Properly position
legs after roll

Kneel at
his side

Straighten
his legs

Place your
palm in back
of his head

(supports head during roll)

Straighten his arms
over his head
(cushions
head during roll)

3. Open airway
Tilt his head far back

4. Check if he's breathing

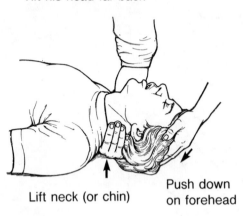
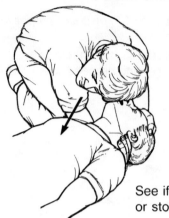

Place your ear close to his mouth

Listen for sounds of breathing

Feel for breath on cheek

Lift neck (or chin)   Push down on forehead

See if chest or stomach moves

5. Start rescue breathing

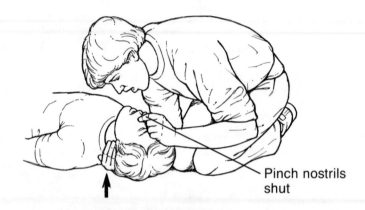

Pinch nostrils shut

Keep head tilted, airway open

6. Give 4 full, rapid breaths

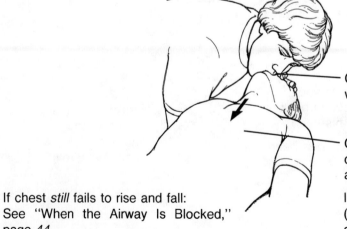

Cover victim's mouth with your lips

Check whether chest rises and falls

If chest *still* fails to rise and fall:
See "When the Airway Is Blocked,"
page *44*

If not, again open airway
(Step 3) and
again give 4 breaths

7. Check pulse in side of neck

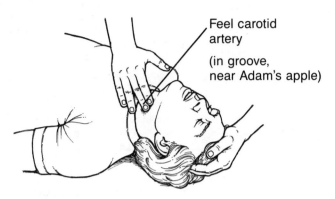

Feel carotid artery

(in groove, near Adam's apple)

If you *can* find pulse
Perform rescue breathing (as in Step 5)
Give 1 full mouth-to-mouth breath every
5 seconds

If you *can't* find pulse
Begin heart massage (Steps 8 to 11)

---

8. To begin heart massage
Find notch below sternum (breastbone)

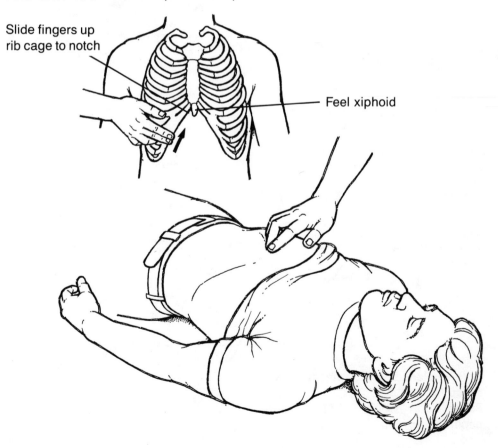

Slide fingers up
rib cage to notch

Feel xiphoid

9. Place hands on breastbone
Don't press fragile xiphoid

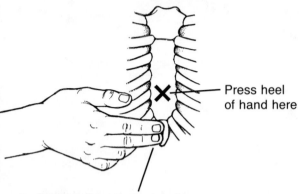

Press heel
of hand here

Place 2 fingers on xiphoid
Your other hand goes alongside those fingers

the groove where the carotid artery is usually evident.

If you *can* find the pulse, give 1 full mouth-to-mouth breath every 5 seconds.

If you *can't* find the carotid pulse, begin closed-chest heart massage in addition to rescue breathing:

8. With your hand that's closest to his waist (say it's your left hand), locate the notch at the lowest portion of the sternum (breastbone). You can do this by sliding the fingers of your left hand up his rib cage. Feel the arrow-shaped xiphoid process.

9. Place 2 fingers on the xiphoid. Alongside those fingers, on the midline of the sternum, place the heel of your right hand. This gives you the correct spot to apply pressure. If you pressed farther down, you could break the xiphoid and pierce internal organs.

10. Put your left hand on top of your right. Keep the tips of your fingers off the chest—they could damage the chest wall. Keeping your arms straight, bring your shoulders directly over the sternum.

Compress the chest with the weight of your upper body, rocking back and forth. Without removing your hands from the sternum, allow the chest to return to its normal position between compressions. Relaxation and compression should be of equal duration.

10. Compress chest with weight of your upper body
Rock back and forth from your hips

Depress chest 1½ to 2 inches,
60 times per minute

Compress and relax for
equal periods

Keep arms
straight

(Keep tips
of fingers
off chest

Don't remove
hands from chest

They may
damage
chest wall)

Stack one hand
on top of other

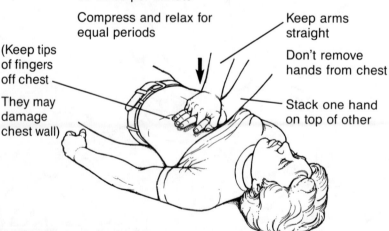

11. Give cycles of heart massage and rescue breathing
Follow "Your Quick Guide to CPR,"
page 58

11. For depth and frequency of compressions and other details, follow "Your Quick Guide to CPR" (page 58). In general, for an adult, depress the sternum about 1½ to 2 inches.

If you're the only rescuer, you must provide both rescue breathing and chest compression. Give 15 chest compressions, then 2 quick breaths. Compress at the rate of 80 times per minute (because you must stop compressing when you give breaths).

If you have another rescuer helping you, position yourselves on opposite sides of the victim. One of you compresses the chest, at the rate of 60 compressions a minute. The other rescuer interposes a breath after every 5 compressions, while the chest relaxes.

For infants and small children, see "CPR Review: For Youngsters to Age 8," page 49.

To determine that the youngster is unconscious, gently tap or shake him.

In performing *rescue breathing,* when opening the airway be careful not to tilt the head too far back. A very young child's neck is so pliable that you might pinch off the breathing passages. You can prevent this by keeping the child's head on the same level as his back, as if he were sleeping on his back.

To avoid overinflating the lungs give small breaths.

For an infant (birth to one year) cover the mouth and nose with your lips making an airtight seal. Give one small breath every 3 seconds.

For a child age 1 to 8 cover the mouth and breathe every 4 seconds.

Check an infant's pulse by feeling the brachial artery on the inside of the upper arm midway between the elbow and underarm. Check an older child's pulse in the same way as an adult's.

In giving *closed-chest heart massage,* use only one hand for compression. Apply pressure midway between the nipples, in the center of the sternum. You may use your other hand to provide a firm support for the back. Administer breaths after every 5 compressions, while the chest relaxes.

For an infant (birth to one year) use only the tips of your index and middle fingers to compress the chest. Depress the sternum between ½ and 1 inch, at a rate of 100 times per minute.

For children age 1 to 8, use only the heel of one hand to compress the chest. Depress the sternum between 1 and 1½ inches, depending on the size of the child. Do this at a rate of 80 times per minute.

If the stomach inflates, breathing may be more difficult because of the internal pressure against the lungs. For a person age 8 or older turn the victim on his side and press his upper abdomen briefly but firmly.

For a child to age 8 turn him face down on your arm (or on his side if he's too large to carry). Press his abdomen between his ribs and navel.

In either case, be prepared to clear the mouth of vomit.

If the victim's mouth is injured, you may have to breathe into his nose, holding his mouth closed to make a leakproof seal.

Use the manual method of artificial respiration only if severe face injuries make mouth-to-mouth or mouth-to-nose breathing impossible. See illustration for the least tiring manual method, which employs arm lifts and chest pressure.

In all other cases, mouth-to-mouth is the method of choice. You can give it to a drowning victim while still in the water. You can usually keep it up for hours without fatigue. You can better control the amount of air given. A small person can readily administer it to a large one.

To be sure that you can do CPR properly, you need to take a short course in proper techniques for airway clearing, rescue breathing and heart compression. To meet performance standards, you need to practice on a training mannequin.

Under no circumstances should you attempt to practice CPR on a friend or relative. Severe injuries can occur if rescue breathing or chest massage is applied to someone who doesn't need it.

See also CHOKING; HEART ATTACK; HEART STOPPAGE.

FAST-ACTION
ILLUSTRATIONS
CONTINUE
ON
NEXT PAGE

WHEN THE AIRWAY IS BLOCKED (AND VICTIM IS UNCONSCIOUS)
If victim is conscious, see "If Someone Is Choking," page 151

1. Give 4 hard back blows

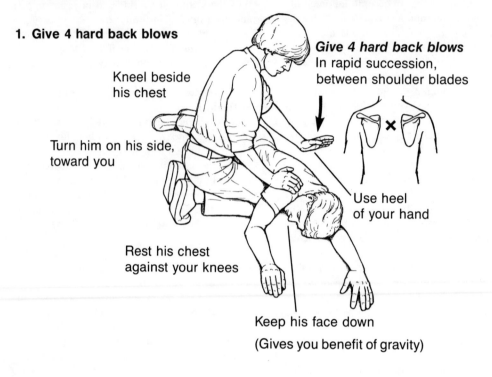

Kneel beside
his chest

Give 4 hard back blows
In rapid succession,
between shoulder blades

Turn him on his side,
toward you

Use heel
of your hand

Rest his chest
against your knees

Keep his face down

(Gives you benefit of gravity)

---

2. Give 4 rapid thrusts against abdomen or chest
Against abdomen

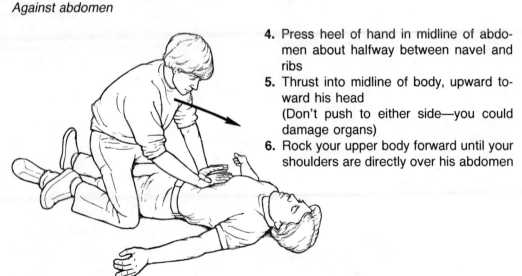

4. Press heel of hand in midline of abdomen about halfway between navel and ribs
5. Thrust into midline of body, upward toward his head
   (Don't push to either side—you could damage organs)
6. Rock your upper body forward until your shoulders are directly over his abdomen

1. Place him on his back
2. Straddle his thighs
   (Or kneel beside his hips)
3. Stack one of your hands on top of the other

Against chest

Slide fingers up
rib cage to notch

Feel xiphoid

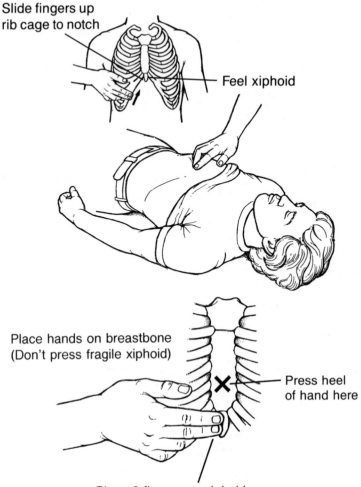

Place hands on breastbone
(Don't press fragile xiphoid)

Press heel
of hand here

Place 2 fingers on xiphoid
Your other hand goes alongside those fingers

Compress chest with
weight of your upper
body
Rock back and
forth from your hips

Depress chest 1½ to 2 inches,
60 times per minute

Compress and relax for
equal periods

Keep arms
straight

Don't remove
hands from chest

(Keep tips
of fingers
off chest

They may
damage
chest wall)

Stack one hand
on top of other

3. Clear out mouth and throat

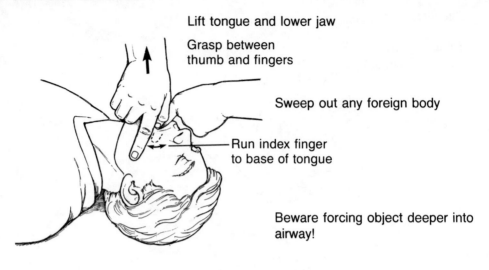

Lift tongue and lower jaw

Grasp between
thumb and fingers

Sweep out any foreign body

Run index finger
to base of tongue

Beware forcing object deeper into
airway!

4. Check if airway is unblocked

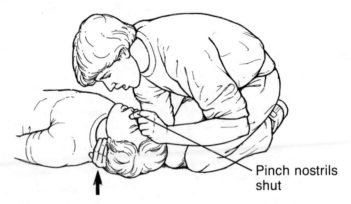

Pinch nostrils
shut

Keep head tilted, airway open

5. Give 4 full, rapid breaths

**If airway is *un*blocked, perform
rescue breathing**
Give 1 full mouth-to-mouth breath
every 5 seconds

**If airway is still blocked,
repeat Steps 1 to 5**

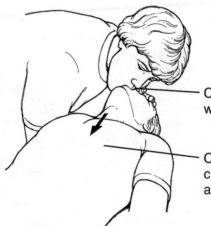

Cover victim's mouth
with your lips

Check whether
chest rises
and falls

LAST RESORT: CUT INTO THE WINDPIPE
Caution: For your legal protection, attempt this only if the patient would otherwise die

1. Expose membrane in windpipe
Tilt head
all the way back

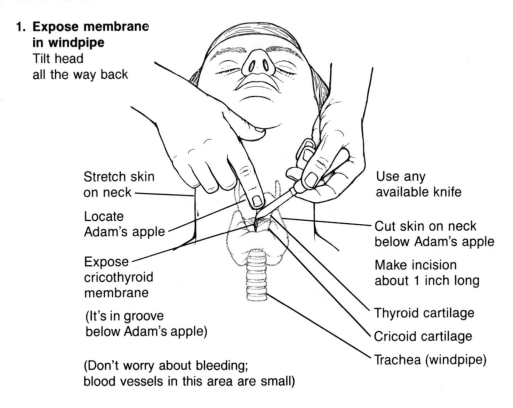

Stretch skin
on neck

Locate
Adam's apple

Expose
cricothyroid
membrane

(It's in groove
below Adam's apple)

(Don't worry about bleeding;
blood vessels in this area are small)

Use any
available knife

Cut skin on neck
below Adam's apple

Make incision
about 1 inch long

Thyroid cartilage

Cricoid cartilage

Trachea (windpipe)

---

2. Cut into membrane
Hold incision
apart

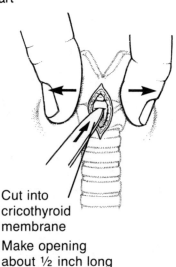

Cut into
cricothyroid
membrane

Make opening
about ½ inch long

3. Keep cut open
Insert any
available object
(Key, knife handle, pen, stick, etc.)

MANUAL METHOD: WHEN RESCUE BREATHING IS IMPOSSIBLE
Use for severe face injuries
(Avoid in chest injuries and arm fractures)

1. Lay victim on back
   Clear out mouth
   and throat

Keep his head to side
(to expel vomitus,
fluids, etc.)

Grasp his arms
above wrists

Tilt head far back

Raise shoulders

---

2. Force air out
   Keep your arms vertical

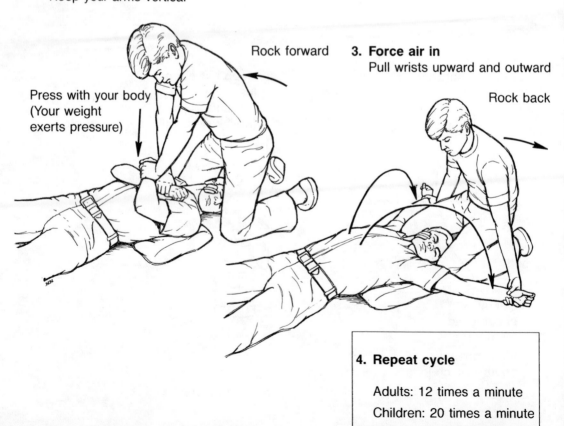

Rock forward

3. Force air in
Pull wrists upward and outward

Press with your body
(Your weight
exerts pressure)

Rock back

4. Repeat cycle

Adults: 12 times a minute

Children: 20 times a minute

CPR REVIEW: FOR YOUNGSTERS TO AGE 8

Caution: Never practice CPR without proper instruction!

NOTE: CPR care varies with age. As used here, an "infant" is from birth to 1 year of age. A "child" is from 1 to 8. Above 8, a youngster gets the same CPR care as an adult (see page 39).

1. Determine if child is conscious

Gently tap or shake him

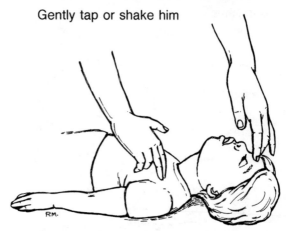

If he's unconscious, yell for help—and proceed to Step 2

---

2. Open his airway

INFANT

Support neck and back with your hand

Tilt his head back *slightly* (Too much tilt may pinch off airway)

CHILD

Place child face up on table or floor (You can place a smaller child across your thighs)

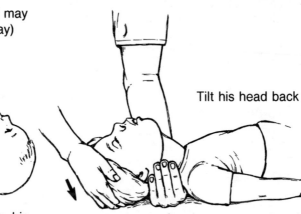

Tilt his head back

Have his head on same level as his back (As if he's sleeping on his back)

Push down on forehead   Lift his neck (or chin)

3. Check his breathing

Place your ear close to his mouth
Listen for sounds of breathing

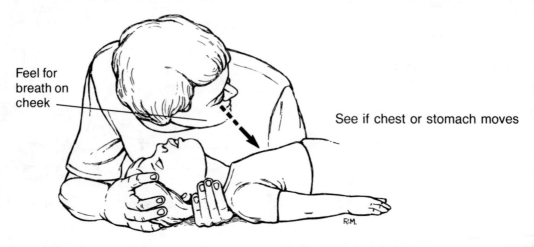

Feel for breath on cheek

See if chest or stomach moves

If breathing is obstructed or absent, proceed to Step 4

4. Give 4 breaths

Be sure airway is open (Step 2)

For CHILD: Cover mouth with your lips
Pinch nostrils with thumb and forefinger

For SMALL CHILD or LARGE INFANT:
Cover mouth with your lips
Seal nostrils by pressing against your cheek

For SMALL INFANT: Cover both mouth and nostrils with your lips

For CHILD: Give shallow breaths
Enough to make chest rise

For INFANT: Give gentle puffs from your cheeks
Avoid overinflating small lungs!

Check whether air goes into lungs

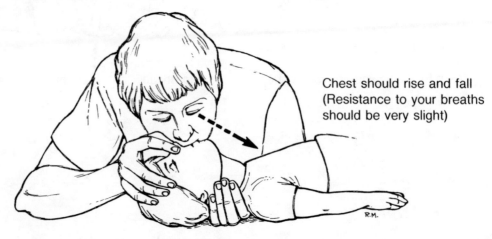

Chest should rise and fall
(Resistance to your breaths should be very slight)

5. Does air go into lungs?

YES—but he's not breathing: Go to Step 12 (page 55)

NO: · Again open airway (repeat Step 2, page 49)

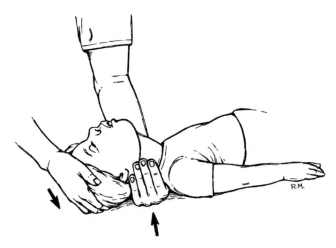

· Again check his breathing (repeat Step 3)

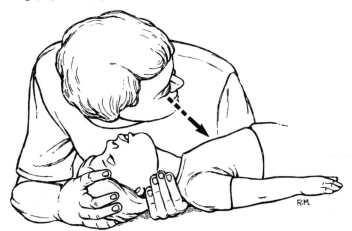

· Again give 4 breaths (repeat Step 4)

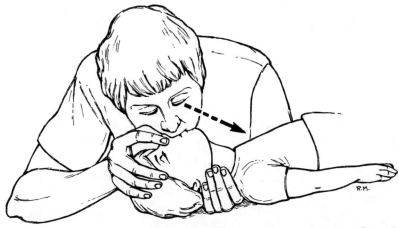

If airway remains blocked, proceed to Step 6

IF THE AIRWAY IS BLOCKED

6. **Give 4 hard back blows**

In rapid succession, between shoulder blades

INFANT

Turn him head down over one of your forearms

Pound with heel of your hand

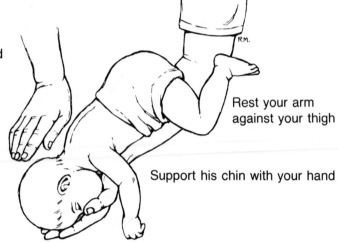

Rest your arm against your thigh

Support his chin with your hand

CHILD

Place him on floor

Kneel beside him

Pound with heel of your hand

Turn him on his side, toward you

Keep his face down

Extend his arm
(Gets it out of the way, cushions his head)

Rest his chest against your knees

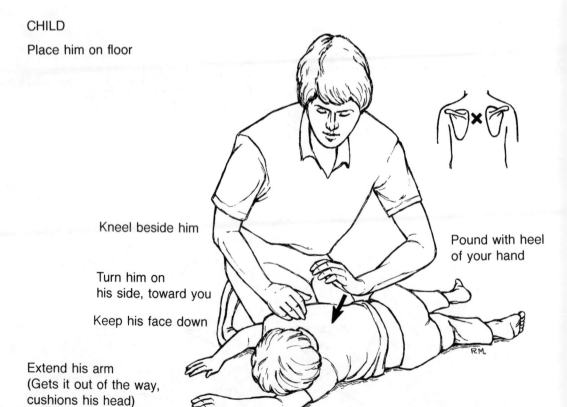

7. Check his breathing (as in Step 3)

If breathing is obstructed or absent, proceed to Step 8

---

8. Give 4 rapid thrusts against chest
INFANT
Place him face up on your forearm

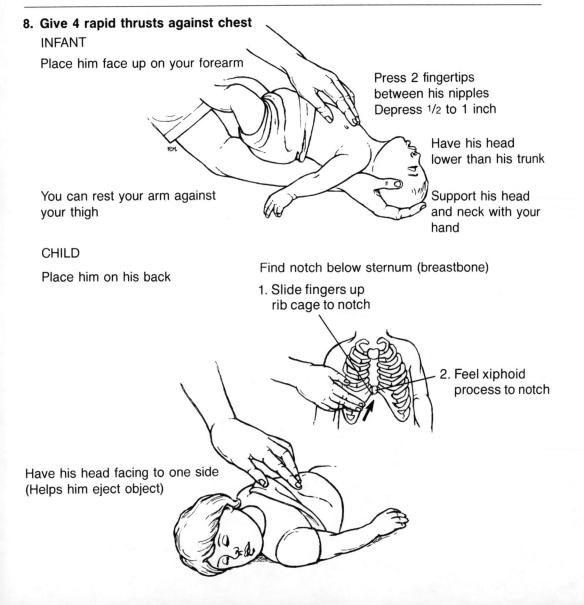

Press 2 fingertips between his nipples
Depress 1/2 to 1 inch

Have his head lower than his trunk

You can rest your arm against your thigh

Support his head and neck with your hand

CHILD
Place him on his back

Find notch below sternum (breastbone)

1. Slide fingers up rib cage to notch

2. Feel xiphoid process to notch

Have his head facing to one side (Helps him eject object)

8. Give 4 rapid thrusts against chest (continued)

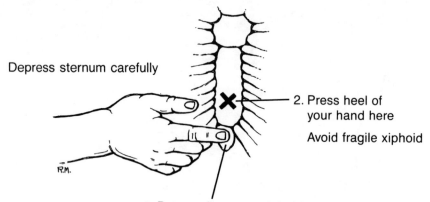

Depress sternum carefully

2. Press heel of
   your hand here

Avoid fragile xiphoid

1. Put one finger on xiphoid

(Your other hand goes
alongside that finger)

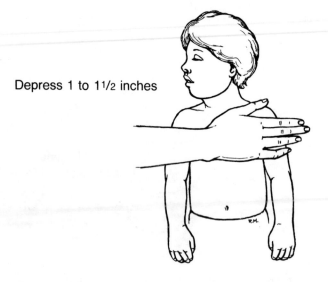

Depress 1 to 1½ inches

9. Check his breathing (as in Step 3)

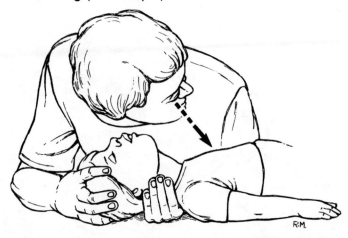

If breathing is obstructed or absent, proceed to Step 10

10. Open his mouth
Can you SEE object that's causing choking?

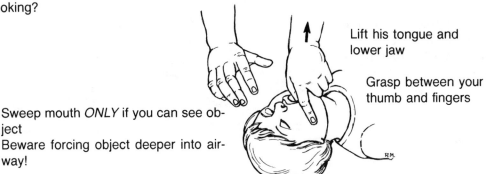

Lift his tongue and lower jaw

Grasp between your thumb and fingers

Sweep mouth *ONLY* if you can see object
Beware forcing object deeper into airway!

---

11. Check his breathing (as in Step 3)

If breathing is obstructed or absent, repeat Steps 3 through 10

IF THE AIRWAY IS OPEN—BUT THERE'S NO BREATH

12. Check whether there's a pulse

INFANT

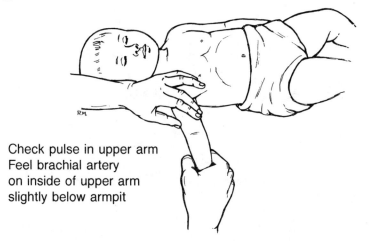

Check pulse in upper arm
Feel brachial artery
on inside of upper arm
slightly below armpit

12. Check whether there's a pulse (continued)

CHILD

Check pulse in side of neck
Feel carotid artery
in groove near Adam's apple

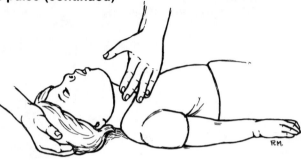

If There Is a Pulse
Perform rescue breathing (as in Step 4)
For INFANT: Give 1 puff every 3 seconds
For CHILD: Give 1 shallow breath every 4
seconds

If There's No Pulse
Give closed-chest heart massage *and*
rescue breathing
Give 5 heart compressions, then 1 breath
Repeat this cycle until professional rescu-
ers take over

INFANT

Place him face up on table

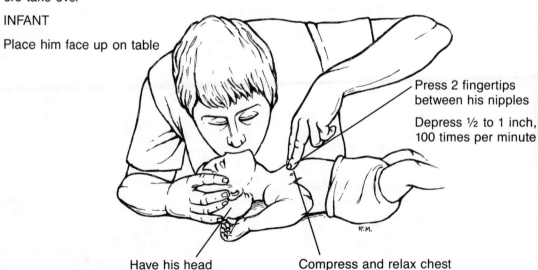

Press 2 fingertips
between his nipples

Depress ½ to 1 inch,
100 times per minute

Have his head
level with his back

(Helps keep airway open)

Compress and relax chest
for equal periods

Don't remove fingers from chest

If There's No Pulse (continued)

CHILD

Place him on back (as in Step 2)

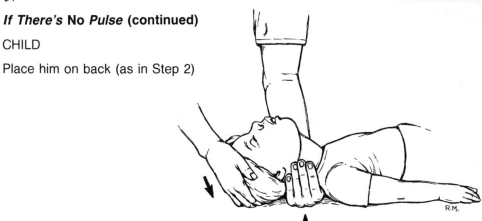

Have his head tilted back
(Helps keep airway open)

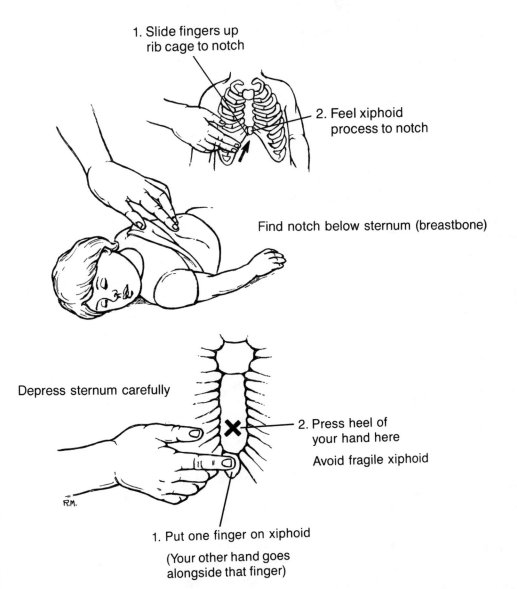

1. Slide fingers up
   rib cage to notch

2. Feel xiphoid
   process to notch

Find notch below sternum (breastbone)

Depress sternum carefully

2. Press heel of
   your hand here

   Avoid fragile xiphoid

1. Put one finger on xiphoid

   (Your other hand goes
   alongside that finger)

If There's **No** *Pulse* **(continued)**

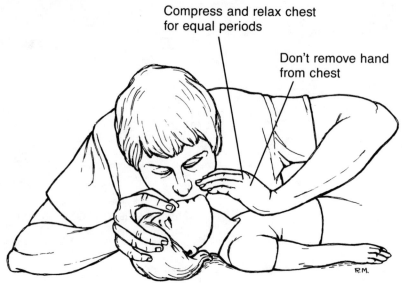

Compress and relax chest
for equal periods

Don't remove hand
from chest

Depress 1 to 1½ inches, 80 times per
minute

Your Quick Guide to CPR

	Adults	**Children** (Age 1 to 8)	**Infants** (Birth to 1 year)
RESCUE BREATHING (victim has pulse): Give 1 breath every	5 seconds	4 seconds	3 seconds
HEART MASSAGE (no pulse): Locate this spot for compressing	Above notch at bottom of sternum	Mid-sternum	Mid-sternum
APPLY PRESSURE WITH	Heel of one hand, other hand on top	Heel of one hand	Tips of index and middle fingers
NUMBER OF COMPRESSIONS PER MINUTE	60	80	100
COMPRESSION DEPTH	1½ to 2 inches	1 to 1½ inches	½ to 1 inch
COMPRESSIONS : BREATHS 1 rescuer 2 rescuers	15 : 2 5 : 1	5 : 1 5 : 1	5 : 1 5 : 1

ARTS AND CRAFTS materials and equipment often require special care for safety.

You can avoid most accidents by working in a room that is well ventilated with an exhaust fan, or by using masks or other respiratory protective equipment. Clean your hands and fingernails after working with dangerous materials and keep contaminated hands away from your face. Don't lick or shape the ends of brushes with your lips to obtain a fine point.

Solvents represent the greatest threat to painters, mainly through inhalation of toxic vapors or the danger of fire. The vapors of carbon tetrachloride and benzene are especially harmful. Don't use them. Acetone is much less toxic, but is highly flammable.

Pigments may contain such toxic compounds as lead, mercury, and arsenic. Painters who prefer to grind their own pigments might easily inhale toxic dust and possibly develop poisoning from the metals.

Synthetic media such as resins, glass fibers, and curing agents can cause skin irritations.

Aerosols—spray coatings, fixatives, and adhesives—may be irritating to eyes or skin, are toxic in varying degrees, and are fire hazards. Spray cans may explode.

Stone dust from prolonged chipping and grinding in sculpturing can produce dust disease, especially silicosis. A sculptor's repeated use of pneumatic tools may affect hearing and may call for noise-control devices.

Wood used for carving may cause contact dermatitis.

Clay may contain silica, leading to silicosis. Grinding or sanding dry clays creates a potential hazard from inhalation of poisonous materials. Binders in some clays used for modeling may trigger an allergy.

Metal casting requires you to guard against toxic fumes. Wear clothing that protects you against burns from hot metal.

Welding calls for precautions against burns, eye injuries, and gas poisoning. Wear safety glasses or goggles and protective clothing when welding.

Soldering and brazing fumes may be poisonous, particularly from solders containing cadmium. Some fluxes may irritate the upper respiratory system. Acid fluxes can burn the skin on contact.

See also ACCIDENTS; ALLERGY; BURNS; CONTACT DERMATITIS; DUST DISEASE; EYE INJURIES; GAS POISONING; LEAD POISONING; NOISE.

ASBESTOS is extremely dangerous to inhale. The mineral fibers can become lodged in your air passages, where they set up chronic, enlarging areas of irritation. This can lead to asbestosis, characterized by shortness of breath, coughing, and strain on the heart.

Worse yet, even relatively brief exposures to asbestos dust can lead to several types of cancer. Mesothelioma, an incurable cancer of the chest or abdominal lining, occurs almost exclusively among people who have been exposed to asbestos dust. Studies at the Mount Sinai School of Medicine found that asbestos workers suffer nearly seven times the rate of lung cancer and three times the rate of stomach cancer and cancer of the colon and rectum as the general population.

Once asbestos gets in the lungs, it stays there forever, and the cancer may take 20 or more years to develop. Some people who worked with asbestos in World War II shipyards are only now beginning to develop mesothelioma.

Asbestos is a special hazard to workers who process the fibers into thousands of industrial products, such as fireproof insulation, floor tiles, wallboard, filters, linings, and paddings. But the material threatens the general public as well.

Asbestos insulation sprayed on high-rise buildings under construction is particularly menacing. Elementary schools have been closed because asbestos on the ceiling came loose and mixed with the air.

To protect yourself, avoid all asbestos dust. Steer clear of areas where asbestos insulation is being sprayed and insist that contractors control asbestos dust by wetting it down, using blankets, and so on.

Don't drill or cut asbestos building material yourself. Have it done at a lumberyard—and, since the danger is not widely known, warn the yard to take precautions.

Read labels of fireproof products to see if they contain asbestos. If an asbestos product starts to disintegrate with age, get rid of it. Hire an experienced contractor for removal of asbestos insulation from buildings.

See also AIR POLLUTION; CANCER; RESPIRATORY DISEASE.

ASCARIASIS   See ROUNDWORMS.

ASCORBIC ACID   See VITAMINS.

ASPIRIN (acetylsalicylic acid), the most widely used of all drugs, relieves pain and headache and reduces fever and inflammation. But like all drugs it should not be used indiscriminately.

Don't take too much aspirin. The recommended dosage for adults is one to two tablets every three to four hours. Except on a physician's advice don't take more than 12 tablets in

24 hours; don't take aspirin for more than ten days without consulting a physician. Overdoses in adults often cause ringing in the ears, hearing loss, and dizziness. These symptoms lessen when the dosage is reduced.

Some people experience nausea or indigestion after taking aspirin. To reduce the possibility of stomach irritation you can dissolve aspirin in milk or water and swallow the fluid. This is more effective (but worse tasting) than the more familiar method of taking tablets immediately after meals or with a full glass of milk or water (carbonated if possible).

Frequent use of aspirin may result in minor gastrointestinal bleeding, iron deficiency anemia, liver damage, and the aggravation of stomach ulcers. Chronic aspirin use occasionally provokes severe hemorrhage.

Special dangers. Don't give aspirin to children with chickenpox or flulike symptoms, the surgeon general advises. Studies have linked aspirin used to treat these diseases to Reye's syndrome, a rare but often fatal children's disease. Reye's syndrome generally strikes children between 5 and 16. There are an estimated 600 to 1,200 cases a year. The disease is characterized by the sudden onset of fever, severe headache, vomiting, and lethargy. It may rapidly progress to delirium and coma. Death occurs in 20 to 30 percent of reported cases. In four studies sponsored by the Centers for Disease Control, a total of 137 of 144 children with Reye's syndrome had recently been treated with aspirin.

To be on the safe side avoid giving your children aspirin during the flu season, or when there is a chickenpox outbreak in your area. Also make sure that throat lozenges, cold remedies, and cough medicines you give your children contain no aspirin. To be even safer avoid giving your children aspirin at any time; use acetaminophen for headache, fever, or pain. Aspirin may be required, however, for children with juvenile rheumatoid arthritis.

Avoid aspirin during pregnancy, especially during the third trimester. Aspirin late in pregnancy has been associated with prolonged pregnancy and labor, increased blood loss at delivery, and increased infant mortality.

Since aspirin retards blood clotting, avoid taking it for one to two weeks before elective surgery.

Check with your doctor if you suffer from gout, stomach ulcers, liver or kidney disease, or bleeding problems. He may recommend a smaller dose of aspirin or an aspirin substitute such as acetaminophen.

If you are taking any medication, ask your physician if aspirin might interact with the drug. Be especially wary if you are taking anticoagulants, oral antidiabetics, or the drugs methotrexate, probenecid, or sulfinpyrazone.

Don't take aspirin and alcohol at the same time. Both can irritate the stomach lining. Combining the two may increase the risk of gastrointestinal bleeding. Aspirin taken with large doses of vitamin C may also be more damaging to the stomach than aspirin alone.

Aspirin allergy. If you are allergic to aspirin, avoid it in any form. See the accompanying partial list of products containing aspirin. Allergic symptoms may include hives, asthma, swelling of the tissues of the throat, and occasionally bleeding into the skin or gums. In the most severe cases there is falling blood pressure, shock, and death. Emergency injection of Adrenalin may be required. Note your aspirin allergy on your emergency medical identification.

There is a higher incidence of aspirin allergy among people with chronic asthma, nasal polyps, allergic rhinitis, and hives. Anyone allergic to aspirin may also have a reaction to indomethacin (Indocin), ibuprofen (Advil, Motrin, Nuprin, Rufen), and other nonsteroidal anti-inflammatory drugs frequently used for arthritis. Any food, beverage, or medication that is colored yellow, orange, or green may contain tartrazine, to which about one in seven aspirin-sensitive people react. Sodium benzoate, a common food preservative, may cause reactions in some people sensitive to aspirin.

When aspirin helps. Aspirin is the most widely used nonprescription analgesic. Americans take more than 20 billion aspirin a year. It can relieve tension headache, muscle ache, and rheumatic pain. It reduces fever and discomfort of colds and influenza, and is often effective for toothache, sore throat, and menstrual discomfort.

It sometimes works as a mild sedative, if only because of the strength of suggestion. It may give temporary relief of minor aches and pains associated with arthritis, bursitis, fatigue, sinusitis, and sprains. Besides relieving pain, aspirin can reduce inflammation in rheumatoid arthritis and osteoarthritis, and in acute rheumatic fever. Researchers are investigating the possibility that aspirin may protect against heart attack and stroke.

Buying aspirin. Buy the least expensive *fresh* USP aspirin you can find. All aspirin prepared to the USP (United States Pharmacopeia) formula is the same, brand names notwithstanding.

In fact there are only a handful of chemical companies that actually make aspirin. The lowest-priced aspirin and the most expensive may come from the same vat. The chief difference in most of the final products is the gimmickry with which the advertiser packages and promotes the drug before selling it, often at a greatly inflated price. Bayer aspirin, for example, costs two to five times as much as some unadvertised brands, yet—like other heavily promoted brands—it is not more effective.

Since aspirin decomposes, buy no more than you're likely to use over the next several months. Buy an even smaller quantity if the drug is to be stored in high temperature or humidity, which makes it decompose faster. Decomposing aspirin smells vinegary and is less effective and more irritating than fresh aspirin. Avoid high-priced "extra strength" or "maximum strength" products. If you need more relief, take three plain aspirin instead of two.

Some people prefer aspirin capsules to tablets —they may be easier to swallow, and you may avoid aspirin aftertaste. Effectiveness of capsules and tablets is the same, but capsules are 20 to 30 percent more expensive.

Alka-Seltzer, an effervescent aspirin, contains sodium and should not be used by anyone on a sodium-free diet. Further, Alka-Seltzer contains antacids and should not be taken for prolonged periods. It is no better than plain aspirin taken with food or drink, and much more expensive.

There is no reliable evidence that buffered aspirins (such as Bufferin) combat stomach irritation and speed passage through the stomach. Buffered aspirin products may possibly ease stomach upset for arthritic patients who must take heavy aspirin doses daily. Buy a generic version.

Aspirin compounds. Combining other drugs with aspirin is expensive—and has not been shown to be more effective. Anacin, for example, combines aspirin with caffeine—which has no analgesic effect, has not been shown to add to aspirin's effectiveness, and thus is not worth paying extra for.

Excedrin contains aspirin, caffeine—and acetaminophen, another analgesic most useful to people allergic to aspirin. Combining it with aspirin destroys its use as a nonallergenic. Acetaminophen, moreover, costs much more than aspirin, and combining it with aspirin has not been shown to be more effective than either ingredient alone.

Enteric-coated aspirin products (for example, Ecotrin) wear a chemical armor intended to pass the tablet intact through the stomach for disintegration in the small intestine, thereby avoiding heartburn and stomach bleeding. But you can't always count on it. Investigators have found that the coating sometimes dissolves prematurely or fails to dissolve at all. Pain relief is delayed with enteric-coated aspirin. But these products may be beneficial for arthritics and others who need to take aspirin in large amounts.

Timed-release aspirin—at about $2\frac{1}{2}$ times the price of regular aspirin—do not offer any reliable benefit. These products (such as Measurin and Bayer Time-Release) contain twice as much of the drug in each tablet as in an ordinary aspirin tablet. They are supposedly useful as a substitute for having to take a dose of aspirin during the night. But release and absorption depend on many factors, and you cannot depend on getting the dosage you need when you need it. Toward the end of the recommended six- or eight-hour interval between doses the analgesic effects may be less than you'd get with more frequent smaller doses of regular aspirin.

Furthermore the double dose of aspirin is excessive for some conditions, such as headaches and minor pains that often require no more than a single small dose of plain aspirin. The timed-release aspirin may prolong any toxic effects or allergic reaction. On the other hand timed-released aspirin may be convenient as nighttime doses for arthritics, who must maintain a steady aspirin level in the blood.

The dangers of children's aspirin. Candy-flavored aspirin sold for children is a poison hazard. Symptoms of overdosage in children include deep breathing, vomiting, lethargy, and confusion. Call a doctor if your child shows any of these symptoms after taking aspirin.

Small children who swallow candied aspirin account for the nation's largest category of accidental poisoning; 80 percent of the aspirin deaths occur among preschoolers. In more than half of the children treated for aspirin poisoning, children's flavored aspirin was the culprit.

Always keep all aspirin out of the reach of children, preferably in a locked cabinet. Don't give small children any aspirin except with the approval of your physician. Not every fever calls for it, and many parents inadvertently overdose their children.

When a child is receiving aspirin, check other medications to avoid overdosing. In one recorded case a child received only a small amount of an aspirin tablet. But he died of an aspirin overdose after his mother gave him cough medicine. She didn't realize it contained additional salicylate.

To get youngsters to take unflavored aspirin, crush the drug into a spoonful of jelly or honey. Wash it down with half a glass of water, milk, or orange juice. This amount of fluid gets rid of any medicinal aftertaste, and also avoids possible stomach irritation.

Administer aspirin to children no more than four times in any 24-hour period, in doses spaced three to four hours apart. The weight of a child is your best guide to size of dose: generally, children weighing under 30 pounds should get less than half a regular (5-grain) tablet—and only under a doctor's prescription. Between 30 and 60 pounds—½ regular (5-grain) tablet. More than 60 pounds—1 tablet.

Flavored liquid analgesics are even more dangerous than candy aspirin, since the chance of taking dangerous overdoses is greater. The flavored liquid form of acetaminophen products such as Tylenol and Tempra don't belong in homes with small children. When acetaminophen is prescribed, unflavored tablets are safer.

"Safety" packaging only slightly diminishes the hazards of having candy aspirin in the home. Manufacturers have agreed to sell candy aspirin in bottles of no more than 36 tablets, with each tablet no more than one quarter regular size. But the contents of such a bottle could still be lethal to some children. Moreover, supposedly tamperproof caps are often no real barrier. Many small children have little difficulty with such a "safety" cap.

Acetaminophen (sold as Tylenol, Datril, and others) is the best nonprescription alternative to aspirin. Clinical tests show acetaminophen comparable to aspirin in reducing fever and relieving pain. However acetaminophen is not as effective in suppressing inflammation in arthritis—although it may reduce some other types of inflammation and swelling.

Acetaminophen is particularly useful for people who are allergic to aspirin, and for those who cannot take aspirin because of ulcer or other medical conditions. Allergy to acetaminophen is rare.

In general, acetaminophen is a somewhat safer drug than aspirin. It is less irritating to the stomach and has fewer potentially serious side effects.

Take acetaminophen in the dosage and at the intervals indicated. Overdose can cause liver damage. A single large overdose (as in a suicide attempt) can cause permanent, and sometimes fatal, liver injury. If you suffer from liver disease or alcoholism, ask your physician about taking acetaminophen.

Keep acetaminophen out of the reach of children, especially in its syrup form. In general, poisoning from acetaminophen is much less serious in children than in adults.

Acetaminophen is considerably more expensive than plain aspirin. If you prefer to take acetaminophen, it's least expensive in its generic form.

See also ANALGESICS; DRUGS.

THESE DRUGS CAN CAUSE ASPIRIN REACTIONS

If you're sensitive to aspirin, avoid any product on this partial list of aspirin-containing products, prepared by rheumatologist L. Maxwell Lockie of Buffalo, New York, and internist Stephen C. Weisberg of Minneapolis. Virtually all remedies for headache, common colds, menstrual pain, and hangover contain aspirin—so before you take any such preparation, check the ingredients for aspirin or its chemical name (acetylsalicylic acid).

Acetidine	Darvon Compound
Acetylsalicylic Acid	Darvon Compound 65
Alka-Seltzer	Darvo-Tran Pulvules
Anacin	Doan's Pills
Anahist	Ecotrin
A.S.A. Enseals	Empiral Tablets
A.S.A. Pulvules	Empirin Compound w/
A.S.A. Suppositories	Codeine, # 1, 2, 3, 4
A.S.A. Compound w/	Empirin Tablets
Codeine	Equagesic Tablets
Ascriptin	Excedrin Tablets
Aspergum	Fiorinal Capsules
Aspirin Aluminum	Fiorinal Capsules w/
(children's chewable)	Codeine, # 1, 2, 3
Aspirin Compound	Fiorinal Tablets
Capsules	4-way Cold Tablets
Aspirin Compound	Inhiston
Tablets	Measurin
Aspirin Tablets	Midol Tablets
B-C Headache Powder	Momentum
Bromo-Quinine	Mobigesic
Bromo-Seltzer	Pabalate
Bufferin	Pepto-Bismol
Cope	Percodan Tablets
Coricidin D Tablets	Percodan-Demi Capsules
Coricidin Pediatric	Persistin
Medilets	Robaxisal Tablets
Coricidin Tablets	Sine-Off
Coricidin Tablets w/	Super Anahist
Codeine	Vanquish
Darvon w/A.S.A.	Zactirin Tablets

ASTHMA is a lung disease in which "twitchy," overreactive bronchial tubes narrow, swell, and become clogged with mucus. During an attack the asthmatic has difficulty inhaling fresh air and exhaling spent air, often creating a wheezing or whistling sound. He (or she) is also likely to cough uncontrollably, have a tight chest, and be short of breath. Oxygen deprivation can make him anxious and fatigued.

First aid. If you're with someone having an asthma attack, speak calmly and softly to help him relax. Encourage him to sit up or stand up straight, and to breathe from his abdomen and lower chest. Loosen his clothes and take him to a well-ventilated space. Assist him in taking his antiasthma drugs, but be alert to a tendency of some asthmatics to overdose themselves during an attack. Have him drink a lot of fluids, especially water.

If the attack is severe or if it fails to respond to drugs, take him to an emergency room. Extreme, resistant respiratory distress, called status asthmaticus, can lead to death.

Hospitalization is generally necessary when severe symptoms cannot be controlled by usual methods. The patient is usually given oxygen, and injections of Adrenalin and steroids. Other antiasthma drugs may be administered intravenously.

During attacks. Throughout a period of impaired breathing, it's important to drink plenty of fluids, perhaps as much as two quarts a day. The labored breathing and heavy perspiring that are part of asthma attacks can make the body lose considerable amounts of water, depleting blood plasma and congealing mucus. The easiest way to drink a large amount of liquid is to have small sips of favorite beverages throughout the day. Warm and room-temperature drinks are preferable; iced drinks may send the bronchial tubes into spasm.

Asthma attacks may last for a few hours, or for days or even weeks. They may occur in frequent spells, or a single one may become continuous.

Although the attack itself is rarely fatal, asthmatics are less resistant to other diseases of the respiratory system, and they face extra risks in surgical procedures. Their average life span is less than that of nonasthmatics.

To get the best care, consult a board-certified allergist, pediatrician, or pulmonologist (specialist in lung diseases). Physicians in these specialties are usually experts in controlling asthma with drugs while keeping side effects to a minimum. The specialist also may be able to recognize factors that are precipitating attacks.

Don't be surprised if you develop asthma as an adult. Contrary to popular belief it need not begin in childhood. Adult-onset asthma is common after 35 and should be suspected in any man or woman who suffers episodes of shortness of breath.

If you're the patient, you're likely to undergo pulmonary-function tests to evaluate your degree of obstruction or exhaling. You may be given skin tests to determine if you're sensitive to substances that can cause a reaction in your respiratory system. During the visit tell your physician if there is a history of asthma in your family; a predisposition to the disease may be hereditary.

It's sometimes difficult to distinguish asthma from other diseases that have similar symptoms. Heart disease, emphysema, and chronic bronchitis may also cause wheezy, difficult breathing.

To prevent or relieve symptoms your physician may urge you to reduce emotional stress. Indeed he may recommend psychological counseling. Emotional upset can precipitate attacks, although it's unlikely that psychological problems alone can produce the disease.

Further, for asthma of allergic origin, your doctor may advise you on the value of immunotherapy. This mode of therapy seeks to build tolerance to asthma-provoking substances by injecting them in larger and larger amounts.

Drug therapy may prevent or control most of your attacks. Be careful to take only the recommended dose of antiasthmatic drugs. Using too much can rebound, producing shorter periods of relief and longer attacks. You then may be tempted to take ever larger amounts, building up to a toxic level that's potentially fatal. The problem is particularly severe with inhalers, which can make it easy for you to overdose yourself without realizing it. If an inhaler is prescribed for a child, it should be used only under the supervision of a parent or, at school, a teacher or nurse.

Aminophylline agents are often the first drugs prescribed for asthmatics with mild to moderate attacks. You might get theophylline (Accurbron, Bronkodyl, Slo-Phyllin, Theo-Dur among many others), oxtriphylline (Brondecon, Choledyl), or dyphylline (Airet, Lufyllin, Neothylline). All are potent bronchodilators, drugs that relax the bronchial muscles and keep the airways open.

Report any stomach upset, vomiting, diarrhea, rapid heartbeat, or irritability. These side effects can usually be diminished by lowering the dosage. Beware of concurrently taking the antibiotics erythromycin (E.E.S., Erythrocin, Pediamycin) and troleandomycin (Tao), which can intensify the aminophylline effect; conversely, barbiturates and the cardiac drug propranolol (Inderal) can weaken the antiasthmatic action.

Adrenergic drugs, another class of bronchodilators, may help you if your attacks remain uncontrolled or if you can't tolerate aminophylline. The most frequently prescribed oral medications include albuterol (Proventil, Ventolin), terbutaline (Brethine, Bricanyl), metaproterenol (Alupent, Metaprel), and ephedrine (Bronkotabs, Marax). You could be given an inhaler of albuterol or metaproterenol or of isoetharine (Bronkosol), isoproterenol (Isuprel, Medihaler-Iso, Norisodrine), epinephrine (AsthmaHaler, Bronkaid, Primatene), or bitolterol (Tornalate).

Tell your physician of any increase in your heartbeat, flushing of your skin, or feelings of nervousness, the most common side effects. Avoid taking these drugs with propranolol (Inderal). Antidepressants can interact with some of these drugs to raise blood pressure to emergency levels.

Corticosteroids seem to enhance bronchodilator effects and may be prescribed if you suffer from severe asthma. You may get tablets of prednisone (Deltasone, Meticorten) or methylprednisolone (Medrol), or an inhaler of beclomethasone (Beclovent, Vanceril). Short-term use is usually free from side effects (see STEROIDS).

Cromolyn sodium (Aarane, Intal) is useful for preventing attacks, especially in children. This inhaled drug can inhibit allergic reactions and ward off asthma induced by exercise. It should never be used *during* an attack. The first toxic signs are usually dizziness, headache, nausea, rashes and hives. Steroids make side effects more likely to occur.

Avoid allergens. If you suffer from asthma, the chances are about three to one that you're allergic to one or more substances. By avoiding these most common allergens, you may protect yourself against attacks:

Dust and mold. Make your home, especially your bedroom, as free from dust and mold as possible. Remove upholstered furniture, draperies, carpets, stuffed toys, and any unnecessary objects.

Use smooth washable fabrics, such as cotton and synthetics, for blankets, bedspreads, and curtains. Enclose dust-retaining mattresses, box springs, and pillows in dustproof covers. Install a central air filter on your furnace, and clean or replace it frequently.

Animals and birds. Fur, feathers, and dander can be highly sensitizing. It's often necessary to get rid of a pet.

Foods. Be watchful of what you eat, and forgo any foods that seem to be followed by breathing distress. Especially be wary of eggs and milk—and the vast number of foods that contain them, often in disguise: all dairy dishes, most baked goods, many cold cuts and other meat products,

innumerable desserts. Wheat and corn products also frequently provoke asthma.

Drugs. Take drugs only under your physician's supervision. Among the drugs most likely to cause severe attacks are penicillin and related antibiotics (e.g., ampicillin, cloxacillin, methicillin). Avoid aspirin and all aspirin-containing compounds; the odds are at least one in five that you're sensitive to the pain reliever.

Pollen. An allergy to pollen can cause you to suffer both hay fever and asthma at the same time. If you're sensitive to pollen, stay indoors as much as possible during pollen season, and keep doors and windows closed. Since most air-conditioner filters are not fine enough to eliminate all pollen, set your air conditioner to recirculate household air rather than to take in fresh air from outside.

Breathe clean air. Virtually any insult to the respiratory tract can spur an asthma attack. Steer clear of such irritants as paint fumes, pine oil, insect spray, household cleaners, strong cooking odors. Don't smoke, and avoid the smoke of others. Reduce your exposure to air contaminated by industrial pollutants and car exhaust.

Protect yourself from respiratory infections. Asthma attacks can be set off by a bacteria or virus invasion, especially of the nose, throat, or sinuses. Stay out of drafts. Avoid overexertion. Be extra cautious during a change of weather.

Do breathing exercises at the first sign of an impending attack. You may be able to ward off the attack entirely. Also do the following exercises regularly to strengthen your diaphragm and increase your lung capacity. Perform them in the morning before breakfast and at night before going to bed.

Before beginning these exercises clear your nasal passages. Start each exercise with a short, gentle inhaling through your nose, then a prolonged exhaling through your mouth. When you inhale, keep your upper chest immobilized. When you exhale, pull in your abdominal muscles. During the exercises do *not* inhale deeply—but see how long you can prolong the exhalation. Repeat each exercise 8 to 16 times. Rest one minute. Then do the exercise again.

Abdominal breathing. (1) Lie on your back with your knees drawn up, your hands on your upper abdomen. (2) Exhale slowly through your mouth, gently sinking your chest and then your upper abdomen. (3) Relax your upper abdomen, letting it bulge. Meanwhile inhale briefly through your nose. Your chest should not rise.

Side expansion breathing. (1) Sit relaxed in a chair with your palms on each side of your lower ribs. (2) Exhale slowly through your mouth. This should contract the upper part of your chest and lower your ribs. (3) Press your palms against your ribs. (4) Inhale, expanding your lower ribs against slight pressure from your hands.

Forward bending. (1) Sit with your feet apart, arms relaxed at your sides. (2) Exhale slowly. Let your head drop forward to your knees. Meanwhile retract your abdominal muscles. (3) Inhale, and raise your head slowly. Meanwhile expand your upper abdomen. (4) Exhale quickly, sinking your chest and abdomen. Remain erect. (5) Inhale, expanding your upper abdomen.

Asthmatic children should be encouraged to take part in virtually all childhood activities. The American Academy of Pediatrics urges parents to resist the natural impulse to overprotect asthmatic youngsters. If you're a parent of an asthmatic child, treat him as a normal youngster who occasionally needs special care. Teach him to manage for himself as much as possible rather than be dependent on you.

Most asthmatic children can take part in at least one sport. Swimming is especially beneficial. The fatigue and emotional upheaval caused by competition can precipitate attacks. But these can usually be avoided or treated with medication—and needless restricting of activities may do far more harm.

Secure treatment for an asthmatic child immediately. Some parents put off seeking medical help because they've heard that children "outgrow" asthma. In fact it's much more likely that untreated childhood asthma will worsen. The younger the patient, the better his prospects. When asthma does seem to go away spontaneously, it's likely that what triggered the condition has been removed from the environment.

Beware of quackery. Charlatanism abounds in connection with asthma. Avoid over-the-counter medications that claim to prevent or relieve asthma symptoms. They're ineffective, and some may cause allergic reactions. No drug can cure the disease.

The Food and Drug Administration (FDA) has questioned the reliability and effectiveness of the drug stramonium, better known as jimsonweed, for use as an inhalant. Some stramonium products are manufactured in the form of cigarettes, pipe mixture, and a powder with instructions to burn and inhale. The drug can be hallucinogenic, with such toxic effects as delirium, visual disturbances, and coma.

Also steer clear of psychoquacks who exploit the association sometimes existing between emotional stress and asthmatic attacks. Attempts at hypnosis are rarely successful in relieving asthmatic suffering.

Beware, too, of the fanciful claims made by so-called air cleaners and "ionic devices." There is no proven value to asthmatics in adding or removing ions (electrically charged particles) in the air.

Nor is there any truth in the folk belief that having a short-haired dog (such as a chihuahua) in the home will cure asthma.

See also ALLERGY; RESPIRATORY DISEASE.

ASTIGMATISM results from distortion of light-transmitting surfaces of the eye. The lens and the cornea (the transparent front of the eye) ideally focus light rays on the retina to make a sharp image. In astigmatism the curvature of the lens or cornea is irregular. Some light rays are thus diffused, producing a blurred, distorted image. An attempt to see clearly may result in headaches.

Astigmatism may accompany farsightedness or nearsightedness. By itself this condition can produce eyestrain, blurred vision, and abnormal sensitivity to light. Eyeglasses or contact lenses for correcting astigmatism have a cylinder incorporated in them to focus some light rays more sharply. Since the cylinder must always be at a definite axis (position), these glasses must fit properly and be kept in good alignment.

When astigmatism is first corrected, the glasses often make things look funny. The room seems crooked, the curb jumps up, and the wearer is disoriented. This disappears after a short period of adjustment.

Astigmatism tends to appear in members of the same family. Sometimes it results from an injury or inflammation that changes eye curvature. See also EYE DISORDER; EYEGLASSES; EYESTRAIN.

ATHEROSCLEROSIS See ARTERIOSCLEROSIS.

ATHLETE'S FOOT is a term devised by an advertising man in the early 1930s to promote a patent remedy for fungus infections of the feet. The name usually refers to a type of ringworm technically called dermatophytosis or tinea of the feet.

In the most common form the areas between the toes become red and crack, with itching and burning. The ringworm fungus may also cause a blistering eruption of the sole of the foot.

Almost everyone harbors this fungus on the skin, and it is usually kept in check by bacteria. The warm, dark, humid environment of the sock and shoe promotes the growth of the fungus.

Athlete's foot is not necessarily picked up at

public showers and pools. Such places are merely among many that provide the moisture on which the organisms thrive.

Treatment of athlete's foot. Try Tinactin or Aftate, nonprescription antifungal preparations that are preferred by consultants to *The Medical Letter.* Apply an antifungal cream or ointment overnight and a powder during the day.

Avoid antihistamines, antiseptics, or cortisone creams, which may intensify and prolong the infection. Organic mercurial antiseptics are among the common offenders. Other strong chemicals or salicylic acid ointments can lead to severe inflammation.

Moreover, your condition may not even be athlete's foot. Cracked, peeling, or blistered skin can develop with other skin conditions such as contact dermatitis, psoriasis, or eczema. The wrong remedy can lead to serious secondary infections.

Preventing athlete's foot. The best preventive is to keep your feet dry. Dry your feet thoroughly after bathing, especially between toes and around nails. Let children run barefoot around the house after bathing before they put on socks and shoes. Dust your feet regularly with foot powder and sprinkle it in your shoes. As a preventive, nonprescription powders for athlete's foot can help retard the growth of fungus.

Alternate shoes daily and allow them to air out in a well-ventilated place. Avoid tight, ill-fitting shoes and nonporous socks and stockings that keep air from circulating around your toes.

Cotton or wool socks or cotton Peds help absorb moisture. When you wear nylon or other synthetic stockings, insert small pieces of absorbent cotton or lamb's wool between your toes.

Sneakers and other rubber-soled shoes impede ventilation and evaporation, promoting the moist environment fungi thrive in. If you're prone to athlete's foot, wear cotton or acrylic socks with your sneakers and change once or twice during the day. Take sneakers off when you can, or alternate them with open sandals. Stay with leather soles if you can't change your footwear often.

Wear clogs when using public showers or pools. Avoid footbaths or other efforts to "sterilize" your feet, shoes, or socks. They are useless and may irritate the skin. This is also true of strong chemicals that are supposed to disinfect floors in and around showers or swimming pools. Washing with plenty of soap and water at frequent intervals will clean the floors more effectively and safely.

See also RINGWORM.

AXES rank high among causes of accidents while camping and hiking. When chopping with a short-handled ax, you're close to the action. If the ax is dull, it can glance off the wood and inflict ragged, hard-to-heal cuts.

So sharpen your ax before using. Test its sharpness by running your fingers across the blade, not along it. If you're cutting wood in wet weather, oil the blade to prevent rust. Keep the handle tight with wedges (soaking will help temporarily).

When using a hand ax, kneel on one or both knees, with a block under the wood you are cutting to protect the blade. When you are finished, store the ax and sheathe the blade. Never leave it stuck in a log for an unwary camper to trip over.

The National Safety Council suggests that you use a bow saw or a folding saw instead of an ax. For cutting wood a saw is not only simpler and safer, but also less wasteful of firewood. Cover the saw teeth when not in use; a simple scabbard can be made from a split length of rubber or plastic hose.

See also ACCIDENTS; CAMPING; CUTS; HIKING; KNIVES.

BABY-SITTERS have a big responsibility. So do you when you entrust your children to a sitter who may be a youngster not much older than your own.

To make sure your children will be fine when you return, here are pointers for parents:

Know your sitter. If she or he is new, ask for references and check them out.

Brief her thoroughly. Take a few minutes to tell her what she needs to know. Give her time to get acquainted with your children. Let her know if the child is active, shy, fretful—or requires any special help or preventives. Also be sure your kids know the baby-sitter's in charge when you leave.

Tour the house with her. Point out phones, first aid supplies, escape routes in case of fire, and any hazards that attract your child. Give her a flashlight.

Don't expect her to do extra chores. Her primary concern should be your children's safety.

Prohibit sleeping. Ask her to tour the house and the children's rooms every half hour or so.

Leave her a memo. Write down where you're going and a telephone number where you can be reached. If you can't be reached, leave the name and number of a friend or neighbor. Also write down phone numbers of your doctor, police, and fire department.

No guests unless you give permission. Caution her in particular not to admit strangers. Lock doors and be sure she locks the door you leave by.

Phone while you're out. Check at least once to see how things are going. If you're going to return later than you expected, call again and let the sitter know.

See also ACCIDENTS.

BACILLARY DYSENTERY   See SHIGELLOSIS.

BACKACHE most commonly results from placing too much stress on the back—as in lifting a heavy object, bending and digging for many hours, or sitting, standing, or sleeping in incorrect positions.

The spinal column is made up of 23 or 24 bones called vertebrae. Each has a number of bony projections to which are attached ligaments and muscles. Between the vertebrae are discs of a firm but cushiony substance that serve as shock absorbers.

Excessive pressure or strain on the back may result in strains or sprains. A ligament stretched beyond its limit will flash pain signals. A muscle given too difficult or unnatural a job will respond with a severe tearing pain. It and nearby muscles may go into a temporary contraction— or "spasm"—to discourage continued use. The pain may make you tense, which can tighten your muscles and cause more pain, and so on to cause a chronic problem. On the other hand if treatment doesn't work, it may indicate the muscle's need to stay in spasm so that motion will continue to be restricted.

Discs also may be damaged—they can degenerate and collapse, become ruptured or "slipped," and often press into a nerve.

Back pain and other illness. Backache can be a symptom of a serious illness such as cancer or arthritis. Back pain is often one of the earliest signs of osteoporosis. Pain may come from an infection or congenital defect in the bones of the back.

Sometimes back pain signals that something is wrong in another part of the body. Kidney disease, heart disease, prostate trouble, problems in the uterus, ovaries, pancreas, stomach, or liver— all may have backache as a symptom.

During the last months of pregnancy women often suffer from low-back pain. The weight of the child may cause a "swayback" that cannot be compensated for by a change in posture.

Tell your doctor about any backache that limits your activity and lasts more than two or three days.

Emotional causes. Emotional problems often contribute to the development of backache. This seems particularly true of a type of low-back pain that is accompanied by stiffness, difficulty in bending and moving, and shooting pains in the buttocks and legs.

Backache is widely considered a symptom of overburdened people. A muscle spasm may be the result of depression or anxiety. Suspect depression as an underlying cause if your backache is accompanied by constipation, sleeping difficulties, loss of appetite or weight, and impotence or loss of interest in sex. Other clues to depression include sadness, feelings of guilt, and thoughts of suicide or death. A stressful life-style is often marked by problems with memory, concentration, and decision-making. Look for an emotional cause if around the time your backache begins, you crave being alone, you neglect your appearance, you fall down on your job, or you lose interest in favorite activities.

When emotional problems contribute to backache, psychotherapy and medication are often beneficial.

Much psychogenic backache is due to the failure of the back muscles to balance correctly because of abnormal tension. With the pain further muscular contraction occurs, intensifying the symptoms. A study of workers in heavy industry found that four out of five of the backaches were caused wholly or largely by emotional factors.

Treating back pain. To relieve low-back pain rest your back on the floor with your head on a pillow. Lie between the legs of a straight-back chair, propping your legs on a pillow over the rungs (see illustration). This is also a good position for a half-hour daily rest break. If you're more comfortable with your legs higher up, set the chair upright and rest them on the seat.

HOW TO REALLY REST YOUR BACK

Sleep on your back
Thick pillow raises knees

No pillow under head
(Use thin pillow if necessary)

If you can't sleep on back
Sleep on side

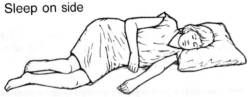

Knees bent   Pillow shoulder height

Take ½-hour rest break daily

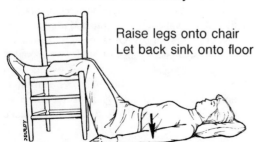

Raise legs onto chair
Let back sink onto floor

Look for a trigger point, a spot where tenderness is most extreme. Have someone press hard on the trigger point with a bare knuckle or a cylindrical hard object like a cigar casing. Maintain the pressure for a minute or two until the point is numb. At first this pressure can be excruciatingly painful and cause pins and needles in your arms and legs. Physicians often treat trigger points with ultrasound or injections of local anesthetics and steroids.

If your backache is diffuse, have someone rub the painful area and surrounding skin with ice four times a day. Without drying the skin rub until the area is numb, for 20 to 30 minutes. Use crushed ice in a pillowcase or other cloth bag. Or, for easy handling, make an ice pop by freezing a Popsicle stick or knife blade in a paper cup of water, then tearing away the paper. For cold therapy doctors often use ethyl chloride spray.

Heat may work if cold fails. Take a 30-minute soak in a hot bath four times a day—not more because excessive heat can make your pain worse. If you can't get in and out of the bathtub easily, have someone apply a hot pack: Over the painful area place a moist towel. Cover it with a sheet of plastic, then a heating pad set to medium or low—all topped by a lightweight blanket.

To avoid burns and electric shock use only a pad that carries an Underwriters Laboratory seal. Never set the pad at high or put it under your body. Apply the heat for at least 20 minutes but never more than 30. Physicians sometimes prescribe heat in the form of whirlpool baths, diathermy, and infrared radiation.

Ask your doctor to demonstrate a simple range-of-motion maneuver that can bring you quick relief at home with the help of a family member or friend. Sit on a stool. If your pain's toward your left side, bring your left hand across your chest and grasp your right shoulder (vice versa if your pain's to your right). Find a comfortable position, preferably leaning into the pain. Your helper faces your painful side—one of his hands on your tender area, his other hand supporting your opposite shoulder. Very gently, he bends, straightens, and rotates your trunk. Then he holds you in a comfortable position for two or three minutes. Repeat several times to relax a spasm.

Two or three days' complete bed rest may be helpful. You may be more comfortable in bed lying flat on your back with a pillow placed under your knees. Or you may find relief lying on your side with your knees bent. A bed board may also help—you can put a sheet of plywood under your mattress, or put the mattress on the

69

floor. Complete bed rest means getting up only to go to the bathroom. If you have no one to bring you meals, you may need to go to a hospital.

A corset is often useful to relieve a mild back problem. Wear one for a long drive or airplane flight. Braces, which are heavier and more rigid than corsets, may ease severe back problems, especially if you need to do heavy labor. The elderly and the obese can often bear up under a corset but not a brace.

Physicians often recommend massage and mild analgesics like aspirin. A drink or two of alcohol may be an effective muscle relaxant. Tranquilizers may be prescribed to combat anxiety and depression. In unusual cases, when back pain is due to a skeletal disorder, surgery may be needed.

Preventing backache. Here are some suggestions that may help you avoid an aching back.

When picking up a heavy object, let your legs do the lifting, not your back (see illustration). The strong muscles and bones of your legs can withstand strain far better than your back.

If you are subject to back pain, as a reminder to squat rather than bend from the waist, keep a small smooth object—such as a short comb or a half-dollar—in your shirt pocket. If you bend over, the object will fall out; if you bend your knees to do the task, the object remains in place.

Carry matched loads, equal weights in both hands. Students do well to carry books in a backpack, rather than under one arm. If you're having back problems, avoid carrying heavy packages or bulky packages even if they're light. A large package that needs to be supported far from your body can cause more strain than a smaller, heavier one.

Exercise to build up your abdominal muscles. When stomach muscles are flabby, the weight of the abdominal contents is thrown forward, tending to pull the spine with it. Do situps, with your knees bent, not straight. A straight-leg situp can put a tremendous strain on your lower back.

If you tend to get backaches, ask your physician to recommend a back-exercise program geared to your needs. Also follow a general exercise program to maintain strength and flexibility. Swimming is an ideal exercise, but brisk walking or running may be more practical.

It's a strain to keep both feet on the floor when sitting or standing. Sit with your legs crossed, or with a telephone book under one foot.

Make countertops at home or work high enough so you needn't bend. If you must bend for a long time, a low stool under one foot may relieve the strain on your back. Try never to stay in one position for a long time.

See that your mattress is flat and free of hollows and lumps.

Be comfortable when you drive. Place a small cushion in the hollow of your back, and pull the seat farther forward. Or support your lower back with a smooth square of ¼-inch plywood

LIFT WITH YOUR LEGS!

3. Raise body slowly

1. Take this position   **2. Bring body close to object**

Tuck chin in

Keep back straight

Hold arms and elbows close to ribs

Grasp with palms

Start push with rear foot

Keep spine straight

One foot alongside object

Center body weight between feet

Put load on leg muscles

STRAIGHTEN YOUR SPINE TO PREVENT BACKACHE
Do this posture exercise 6 times daily

1. Brace against wall

Touch wall with . . .

Back of head

Shoulder blades

Buttocks
(tighten muscles)

Heels a few
inches from wall

Feet comfortably
apart

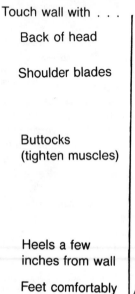

2. Slide down—flatten lower back

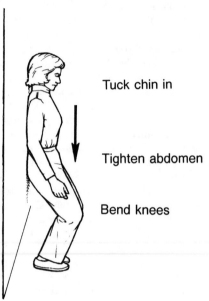

Tuck chin in

Touch wall
with small
of back

Tighten abdomen

Bend knees

3. Stand erect for 5 seconds

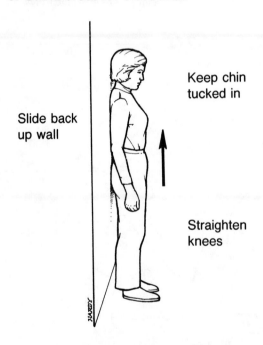

Slide back
up wall

Keep chin
tucked in

Straighten
knees

Practice walking with straight spine

12 inches on a side. Seat belts set firmly across the lap will often improve car seat comfort, as well as helping to prevent injury in an accident. A plastic car seat sold by medical supply houses is a boon to many back sufferers.

Better posture may take the stress off your back. Standing or walking, put most of your weight on your heels. Practice tightening your buttocks. Stand tall, tucking in your pelvis.

Avoid low, soft chairs, which are difficult to get out of without putting pressure on your back.

Avoid very high-heeled shoes, which put a strain on the back.

Do warming-up exercises before giving your back a workout. Follow the practice of wise athletes, who always warm up before strenuous exercise.

If you plan to plant shrubs, for example, first accustom your back to some of the bending and shoveling it's going to be taxed with. Bend forward at the waist and rotate your arms to help loosen up tight muscles and relax tension. Then take the tool you plan to work with and swing it easily back and forth around your head and shoulders. Start with small motions, gradually increasing the range of motion. Swing it in all the positions you expect to use for the job.

Physicians are seeing more low-back pain after strenuous nights on the disco-dance floor—especially among generally inactive people over 30 who dance only on weekends. Weekend skiers are also vulnerable to backache. Don't forget to do warmup exercises before these activities.

See also ANALGESICS; ARTHRITIS; BED REST; DIATHERMY; DRUGS; EXERCISE; RADIATION; SPRAINS; STRAINS; STRESS; TRANQUILIZERS.

BACK FRACTURES call for precision handling, since a wrong move can injure the spinal cord and cause serious and permanent disability.

The victim of a fracture of the spine is likely to be in pain, with swelling and tenderness over the injury. Legs or arms may be paralyzed when the spinal cord is injured.

If at all possible, refrain from moving the injured person. Keep him lying flat until medical help arrives. Never twist his body, head or neck. If you must move him, as in a diving accident, use a stretcher, plank, or door to carry him. Four to eight people should lift him to or from the stretcher, taking care to keep his body in a straight line.

See also FRACTURES; MOVING THE INJURED.

BACTERIA See INFECTIOUS DISEASE.

BAD BREATH See MOUTH ODOR.

BAGS UNDER THE EYES usually develop with advancing age. Muscles and tissues of the eyelids degenerate, and the lower lid tends to fall in folds. Underlying fat pushes through the weakened muscles, causing the baggy tissue to balloon out.

Cosmetics offer little or no help. The only method to improve this condition is plastic surgery of the eyelids called blepharoplasty. Swelling and discoloration generally subside within ten days, and scars are usually well camouflaged.

The operation is often performed along with face-lifting for wrinkles, and the effects last longer than those of face-lifting because the skin on the upper part of the face stretches less with age than the skin on the lower part of the face.

Don't confuse bags under the eyes with the puffy eyelids that may signal a severe kidney disease. Puffiness may also occur if fluid accumulates in the eyelids during sleep on the side of the face that is down.

An allergy or chronic skin condition may also cause puffiness, since the loosely attached skin under the eyes is apt to accumulate fluid.

See also SKIN DISORDER; WRINKLES.

BALDNESS See HAIR LOSS.

BANDAGES protect wounds during healing. Keep them clean and dry. For most purposes all you need is a simple covering of sterile gauze and adhesive tape.

Use plastic-coated gauze, which won't stick to the wound. Avoid medicated gauze, which may trigger a drug allergy. Don't use plastic adhesive tape or let a bandage be airtight. Moisture given off by the skin, or water trapped under the bandage, may damage the skin and encourage the growth of bacteria.

Change the bandage as often as it gets dirty or wet. If a bandage is complicated, ask your doctor to show you how to change it.

Your goal is to aid the formation of a scab, which helps protect new cells during healing. Pulling a scab loose to change a bandage can retard healing and increase the danger of infection. If the wound bleeds under the bandage and becomes stuck, leave the bandage on as long as possible. If a stuck bandage must be changed, soften the scab with hydrogen peroxide.

You can remove sticky tape from a hairy area painlessly, without shaving or uprooting the hair. Before applying the tape, smooth the hair in the direction of its natural angle with the skin. Then peel off the tape by pulling slowly and steadily in the direction the hair lies, from root to tip.

See also ACCIDENTS; CLEANSING MINOR WOUNDS; CUTS; SCRAPES.

BARBITURATES and other hypnotics (drugs that are used to induce sleep) are a leading cause of suicide, accidental as well as intentional.

In case of an overdose see POISONING, with nonpetroleum products, or see DRUGS. Treat for an overdose if you don't know how much was swallowed.

Don't administer coffee—it may be harmful in barbiturate poisoning. Don't try to walk the person around to keep him awake. After a siege of vomiting he's better off resting.

Never drink alcohol before or along with barbiturates. Both are depressants—they slow down the activity of the central nervous system, the respiratory system, and the nerves and muscles, including the heart muscle. The actions of barbiturates and alcohol enhance one another, and barbiturates interfere with the body's normal disposing of alcohol. Together they can cause death from respiratory and cardiovascular failure much faster than barbiturates might alone.

An estimated half the cases of barbiturate poisoning are suicide attempts. The rest are thought to be accidents. Typically a person who fails to fall asleep after one or two pills becomes confused and takes additional doses.

Since the lethal dose of barbiturates is about

ten times the normal dose, physicians are advised to prescribe only six doses at a time. This precaution reduces the possibility of accidental overdosage and protects people who attempt suicide on impulse.

Addiction. Barbiturates can be addictive. A chronic user of barbiturates needs increasingly larger amounts to obtain the same effects. After a while he is likely to develop both psychological and physical dependence on the drug, as in alcoholism.

Large doses produce the same neurological signs as alcohol intoxication, and the same sluggishness and poor judgment and impaired coordination. As with alcohol, if you've taken barbiturates, don't drive or operate dangerous machinery.

Withdrawal from barbiturates needs to be supervised by a physician. Abrupt withdrawal can cause fatal convulsions. Other effects may include delirium tremens (as in alcoholism), nausea, confusion, muscle twitching, and sudden drop in blood pressure.

Many adults are caught in a cycle of barbiturates to get them to sleep and amphetamines to wake them up. The habit often needs a physician's intervention to break safely.

Encourage a friend or family member to see a physician if he's addicted to barbiturates. Since the drugs are cheaper and often more available to children than liquor, a sizable subculture has grown up around barbiturate use.

On the street the drugs are called "goofballs," "sleepers," or "downers." They appear in a variety of colored capsules or tablets. Seconals are dubbed "red devils"; Nembutals, "yellow jackets"; Tuinals, "rainbows"; Amytals, "blue angels." The dangers of these drugs are much greater when bought on the street—they are often badly synthesized, even cut with poisons like arsenic and strychnine.

Even for their legal purpose use barbiturates with caution. In small doses barbiturates usually induce sleep within half an hour. In somewhat smaller doses they (especially phenobarbital) can be effective tranquilizers for the relief of anxiety. Phenobarbital taken for seizure disorders is generally safer and less addicting than the "short-acting" barbiturates taken as sleeping pills.

For insomnia use barbiturates only occasionally and as a last resort. The sleep produced by barbiturates usually lasts four to eight hours, varying with the individual and with the drug and dosage. You may awaken refreshed with proper use—but often there is nausea, lassitude, dizziness, headache, and diarrhea the following day, even after a moderate dose. Skin eruptions and lesions of the mouth sometimes occur.

Even when there is no obvious hangover, some degree of mental impairment may persist for a few hours after awakening. Another objection to barbiturates is that they reduce the amount of dream-stage (rapid eye movement, or REM) sleep. Sleepers deprived of dreaming sleep for several nights tend to become hostile, irritable, and anxious, even though they sleep the requisite number of hours.

Barbiturates are effective for insomnia for only about two weeks. After that a tolerance develops, and the drug becomes ineffective.

An irony of barbiturate use is that when the drug is discontinued, or when the patient develops a tolerance to it, the "dreaming debt" is made up—often with intense, disturbing nightmares that awaken the dreamer.

Another irony is insomnia rebound. Withdrawing barbiturates usually results in very poor sleep for a few weeks. Other remedies for sleeplessness can help the insomniac get through this crucial period without pills.

To use barbiturates more safely, take the following precautions:

- Do not increase the dosage or take the drug more frequently than directed.
- Inform your physician if you may be pregnant, or if you are breastfeeding.
- Keep no more than one night's supply of the medication on your bedside table.
- Consult your physician before you take any other medication, since barbiturates may interact with other drugs, including over-the-counter medications. Be particularly cautious if you are taking steroids, tetracyclines, heart drugs derived from digitalis, or anticoagulants.
- Contact your physician if you develop a skin rash, mood changes, frequent nightmares, or depression.
- Don't smoke after you've taken a barbiturate.

See also ALCOHOL; DRUGS; POISONING; SLEEPLESSNESS.

BATHING daily is necessary only for special purposes, not for ordinary cleanliness. Too frequent bathing is one of the common causes of skin dryness, especially in cold weather and for the elderly, and may aggravate some skin disorders.

Unless perspiration odor is likely to be a problem—as in hot weather or after sweaty activities—a bath or shower once or twice a week, can usually keep your skin clean and odor-free. Or take a quick daily shower or sponge bath, limiting the use of soap (which is drying to skin) to your underarms, genitals, and feet.

Soap. You're best off with the simplest, cheapest soap. Brands differ principally in color and odor. Soaps that float have air bubbles in the cake, which have nothing to do with purity.

All soaps are "deodorant" in that they remove perspiration and bacteria. Some soaps claiming special deodorant properties contain perfumes that may cause photosensitivity reactions akin to sunburn. Avoid medicated soaps unless they're prescribed by a doctor—they may trigger a drug allergy.

"Castile" is now a meaningless term; it once meant that the soap was made according to an ancient Spanish formula using olive oil. Manufacturers now use the term because it suggests quality, though the soap does not contain olive oil and is not necessarily purer or milder than other soap.

To get rid of soap rings around your bathtub, add a softener to your water system. Unlike soaps, detergents do not combine with the minerals in hard water and thus deposit no hard-water scum. Some detergents can contribute to housewives' eczema, an allergy that is a form of contact dermatitis.

Bubble-bath preparations in high concentrations can inflame the penis and vagina, especially in children. Use the least amount that will make water foam, and be sure the bath is well mixed before sitting in it.

Benefits of bathing. Warm baths can help you sleep. For an effective home remedy for insomnia and nervous tension bathe for a half hour in water kept as close as possible to normal body temperature, or slightly over 98° F. This probably will feel hot since the skin temperature of a healthy person is only 93° F.

If the bath is too hot, it can cause sleepless nights instead of curing them. A very hot bath can be as stimulating as an icy plunge.

A hot bath relaxes your muscles. If you gently massage a sore muscle during a hot bath (98° F to 104° F), you may get relief.

Hot baths can be used for the treatment of arthritis, backache, neuritis, gout, and bronchitis. They can relieve pains of hemorrhoids and vaginal problems. Check with your doctor before trying this kind of treatment, and see if hot compresses are preferable.

Don't stay in a hot bath longer than 20 to 30 minutes. After you get out, wrap up warm and lie down for a while. If the bath is as hot as 104° F and if it is prolonged, your body temperature begins to rise. Body temperature over 102° F can be dangerous, especially for sufferers of heart disease. Also you can lose quarts of perspiration in a long hot bath. The loss of fluid and salt is apt to shock an elderly or debilitated person.

Follow a hot bath with a rinse in cool (65° F to 80° F) water, especially if you are going out into a cold temperature. If you prefer, you can get the same results by an alcohol, witch hazel, or cologne rubdown.

Alternating warm and cool showers can improve circulation and reduce fatigue. While following a hot shower with a cold one can be refreshing, contrary to myth it does not "close the pores." Pores are the openings onto the skin's surface of the sweat and oil glands and hair follicles. They can't be opened and closed, nor can their size be altered.

Cold baths. Cold baths (below 65° F) can be dangerous. Underweight, run-down, or elderly people, as well as those with high blood pressure, need to abstain from any kind of cold bath. Even if you're young and healthy, consult your doctor before embarking on a regimen that calls for cold plunges.

If you insist on the invigorating shock of a cold bath or shower, don't let it last more than four minutes. Warm up afterward with a few minutes' vigorous exercise, even if it consists only of knee bends and some energetic drying with a coarse towel.

To help reduce fever from disease or heat stroke, use a cool—not cold—sponge bath. It is dangerous to let the body temperature drop too quickly. Washing with cool water is preferable to alcohol or ice water sponge baths. Don't submerge a feverish person in cold water, although wrapping him in a cold wet sheet or large towel may help.

See also PERSPIRATION ODOR; SKIN DISORDER; SLEEPLESSNESS.

BATS native to the U.S. are normally shy creatures that fly only at night and never attack man unless they have rabies. The sole exception is the vampire (bloodsucking) bat, which is extremely rare in the United States and in this country is found only in Texas.

If a bat bites you, scrub the wound with soap and water as you would other animal bites—and see a doctor. If possible, bring the bat with you for a rabies check. Capture it with gloves to avoid more bites. Even if the bat is dead, handle it only with gloves.

Rabid bats may sometimes be found lying on the ground, apparently sick or dead. Never pick one up without heavy gloves or other protection. It still might be able to bite.

Wear a mask in bat caves. The rabies virus may be airborne and cause infection even without bites. Bat droppings also may harbor fungi that cause histoplasmosis, ringworm, or athlete's foot.

To bat-proof a house: Close all openings in walls, roofs, and floors larger than three eighths inch in diameter. Moth flakes, crushed mothballs, and bird and rodent repellents help discourage bats. Blow glass fiber insulation into wall spaces occupied by bats to drive them out.

When a building is infested, shut all but a few entrances. After four days the bats will become accustomed to leaving by these openings. After they fly out one evening, close these holes.

Bat-proof only in the early spring or fall. During other times of the year young bats may be trapped inside a building and die.

Don't kill bats, advises the Public Health Service. "Because they eat insects and therefore help in pest control, bats are useful. But they should be kept away from houses, barns, and other buildings."

See also ANIMAL BITES; ANIMAL DISEASE; RABIES.

BEARS—all bears—are unpredictable and dangerous. If you meet one while hiking or camping, fall down and play dead. The bear may come up and smell you, but that's likely to be all.

If you run, the bear may chase you. If you climb a tree, it may come after you. Throwing rocks at a bear or yelling at it in an attempt to scare it away will only incite the animal to bite or maul you.

Discourage bear cubs from playing around your camp, lest their mother nearby become aroused. Don't get between a cub and its mother.

Bears in parks can be especially dangerous, since they've often lost their fear of humans. Don't feed bears or leave food out where they can get it.

Cook bear meat well; it can harbor trichinosis.

See also ANIMAL BITES; ANIMAL DISEASE; CAMPING; HIKING; TRICHINOSIS.

BEDBUGS are roundish, red-brown, and wingless. Although they are not known to spread any disease, they nonetheless have a disagreeable odor and their bites ordinarily produce itching red blisters. Some people are allergic to them, breaking out in hives.

The bugs live in beds, bedding, upholstered furniture, walls, and draperies. They are drawn to victims by the odor of the body. Since they feed along their way, their bites may appear in a line on the skin, generally in spots not covered by nightclothes.

Bedbugs are vulnerable to relatively safe insecticides like those containing pyrethrins. You may need several cans for a full treatment. Remove the mattress and lightly spray all of its surface, penetrating folds, tufts, and seams. Spray all of the bedstead, including frames, springs, and slots, and every crevice. Allow at least two hours before making up the bed or occupying it.

Also spray any upholstered furniture in the room. Spray walls up to several feet from the floor. Search for specific signs of hiding places, revealed by telltale brown or black spots on surfaces near a crevice. Spray liberally here, until there is a wet runoff of the liquid.

Repeat this entire procedure weekly for several weeks. A month after apparent disappearance of the problem, you may need to repeat the spraying treatment to wipe out newly hatched bugs.

See also INSECTS.

BEDBUG

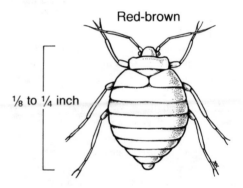

Red-brown

⅛ to ¼ inch

BED REST, though sometimes essential, should not be overdone. Don't stay in bed, completely inactive, for more than three days unless you have specific orders from your physician. Dr. Richard Asher, an English clinician, wrote in rhyme when urging his colleagues to limit time in bed for ill patients:

> Teach us to live
> That we may dread
> Unnecessary time in bed.
> Get people up and we may save
> Our patients from
> An early grave.

Complications of bed rest. A number of conditions may develop, or worsen, during prolonged stays in bed. Bedsores can be a nightmare. Maintaining one position in bed encourages the development of pneumonia and impairs reexpansion of a lung damaged by a respiratory disease. Lack of exercise can lead to thrombophlebitis and blood clot in the lung.

The contraction of some muscles and stretching of others can cause crippling knee stiffness and also a type of paralysis called foot drop. These can take weeks to correct. There is a general weakening of the muscles and joints. When bones are not used, the calcium drains from them, inviting osteoporosis and fractures.

The drain of calcium can lead to kidney and bladder stones. A horizontal position can make it difficult for men particularly to urinate. Such urinary retention can then cause bedwetting.

After a few days in bed indigestion often develops, along with loss of appetite. Constipation is almost inevitable with the absence of muscular movement and the difficulties in using a bedpan. The retained mass of feces may then overflow as diarrhea.

Sleeplessness at night results from too much inactivity and napping during the day. Staying in bed can cause emotional stress marked by irritability and hypochondria, often leading to lethargy and depression.

Resist unnecessary confinement to bed in a hospital. "Too often," notes Dr. Asher, "a nurse puts all her patients back to bed as a housewife puts all her plates back in the plate rack—to make a generally tidy appearance." After surgery ask your surgeon not "How long should I stay in bed?" but "How soon can I get up?"

Care for the bedridden patient. Here are tips on easing home care: See the accompanying illustrations for aids you can improvise. Basic techniques for caring for the bedridden:

Using a bedpan. The patient lifts himself slightly. You slide under him a bed protector—a plastic shower curtain or tablecloth works fine.

Then help him raise his hips. Slip in the bedpan, open end toward the foot of the bed. Adjust for comfort, and leave the room so he'll have privacy.

Ask your doctor about encouraging a patient who can walk to use a bathroom or portable commode. Arrange heavy chairs, tables, and other furniture to give him a handhold on his route from bed to toilet.

14 AIDS FOR THE SICKROOM

Raised bed

It is easier to take care of the patient if he is in a single bed raised on blocks to bring the mattress up to the level of your elbows.

1. Use blocks of wood with portion in the center hollowed out to fit each bed leg (remove casters). Or use tall fruit juice cans filled with sand

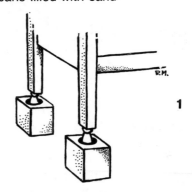

2. Or use two mattresses

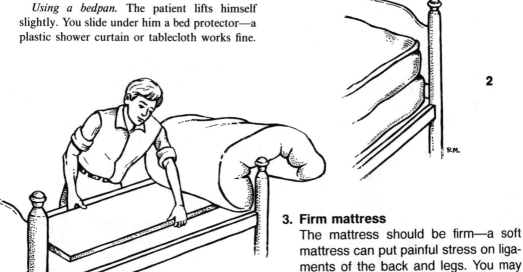

3. **Firm mattress**
   The mattress should be firm—a soft mattress can put painful stress on ligaments of the back and legs. You may need to put a bed board between springs and mattress. Buy a standard bed board or make one from several table leaves or a piece of plywood.

4. Backrest

Improvise a backrest by covering a board or folded card table with canvas and tying it in place against the head of the bed. Satisfactory backrests are available from mail order houses or hospital supply stores. Some department stores sell folding backrests for use on beaches. For good support, the backrest should be higher than the patient's head. To keep the backrest from slipping, it is helpful if the canvas comes down under the buttocks.

4

5. Footrest

To prevent foot drop, which can begin after a few days in bed, improvise a footboard, or padded board that will provide firm support for the patient's feet. A pillow does *not* give enough support. His feet need to be kept at right angles to the mattress with his toes straight up. The footboard extends several inches above the toes to prevent the bedclothes from pressing down upon the toes or upon a painful ankle. Fasten ropes to the footboard. Tie them to the head of the bed so that the board can be moved toward the head of the bed when the patient sits up.

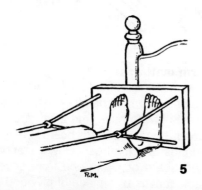

5

6. Bed cradle

When the footrest is higher than the toes, it may also serve the purpose of a bed cradle by keeping the weight of the covers from the feet and ankles. If protection is needed for painful joints, use a cardboard box.

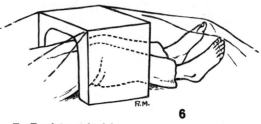

6

7. Bed tray/table

Improvise. Some suggestions: A table leaf resting on two chairs. A board resting on blocks or books. A heavy carton. An orange crate.

7

8. Commode

Make a hole in an old straight chair and place it over a pail. Pad the seat and cover it with oilcloth.

8

9. Storage bag

Possessions can be kept in order, easily available, and out of the way when not in use. Commercially available shoe bags may suit your purpose. Or cut a piece of canvas, duck, or heavy denim to the width of the head of the bed. Fit it with pockets of various sizes and with some means of attaching it to the top of the bedstead.

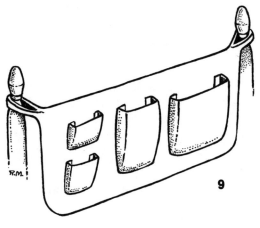

11. Heel rest

To prevent heels from becoming chafed, place a folded soft towel beneath the ankles just above the heels. This will raise the heels just enough to relieve the pressure of the mattress.

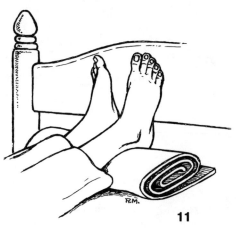

Pillows

12. Small pillows can be made and stuffed, or cut from foam rubber. Place a small pillow behind the patient's neck when he leans against the backrest.

10. Wheelchair

When your patient can sit up but is not allowed to walk, put a chair on casters or roller skates to wheel him to the bathroom, the family table, or onto the porch. Add a footrest for comfort.

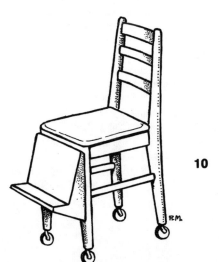

13. An ordinary pillow wedged between his back and the mattress will support him when he lies on his side.

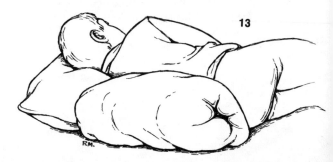

14. A small pillow between the knees will add comfort. When he sits up or bends his knees he may want a soft rolled pillow under them.

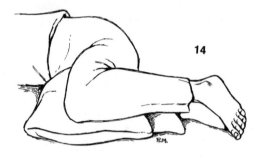

14

Getting out of bed. Lowered blood pressure and muscular weakness may make the patient fall if he tries to sit up and jump out of bed. Instead have him slowly push himself up on one arm, then slide his legs over the side of the bed and gently lower his feet to the floor.

Bathing in bed. Alcohol-impregnated towelettes such as Wash 'n Dri can give a good, neat wash. For a more thorough scrubbing, use soap and keep the water warm. Wring out a washcloth and wash, then dry, only one part of the patient's body at a time. Protect the bed with towels.

Sharing the patient's care. Divide up a bedridden person's care. The whole burden shouldn't rest on one person. Others in the family are less likely to resent the time given to the patient if they have some share in caring for him too.

Even children can pitch in. Perhaps one can serve meals to him, another can fill his water pitcher, an older child can read to him. Set up a schedule in which family members visit with the patient, a time he can count on.

Ask your doctor or local health department about visiting nurse services. If a housewife is sick, some communities have agencies that provide Meals-on-Wheels, homemakers, and household helpers.

Relocate a patient to a room of his own near family activities. In a two-story house having him on the first floor will save you a lot of running up and down and keep him in the swim of things. Ideally, have him close to a bathroom.

Help the patient keep in touch with friends. Arrange for visits, however brief, and letters or postcards. Having a phone beside the bed is a great relief for isolation. Ask associates to record tape cassettes over lunch, in class, at work—to let him listen in on familiar voices.

If he's feeling up to it, take him for a drive with you when you go shopping. Move a television and radio into the sickroom. Borrow books, magazines, phonograph records from the library. For a child lay in a stock of inexpensive model kits, arts and crafts supplies, puzzles— and dispense them one at a time so they don't get used up too quickly. A booklet called *Have Fun . . . Get Well,* available from the local heart association, contains suggestions for many hobbies and activities, including household tasks a child can do in bed. Or write to:

American Heart Association
7320 Greenville Avenue
Dallas, Texas 75231

You need to be an amateur psychologist. "When you are taking care of an ill person at home, you must cope with both the physical and psychological problems of being sick," said M. Lucille Kinlein, R.N., of the Georgetown University School of Nursing. "You must . . . build his self-esteem, keep him occupied, listen to his complaints and troubles, and encourage a positive attitude among the other members of the family."

Expect childish behavior. Most people regress when sick. Let a patient cry. It's an indication of fear and of frustration. Sick people often fail to realize their limitations and become disappointed in themselves when they're unable to do something well.

If you're exposed to chronic complaints, advises Nurse Kinlein, pull up a chair, sit down, and just listen and agree. Don't take the complaints personally. The patient is doing a natural thing in feeling sorry for himself.

For a sick child. To keep a sick child quiet it is effective to say: "If you run around now, your temperature will go up again and you'll stop feeling good. Then it will take you a lot longer to get well enough to go outdoors and play."

Promise a child a special treat if he stays in bed until the next meal. Then if he merits the reward, give him a favorite dessert or a new toy.

If a child must do something he doesn't like to do, the American Heart Association advises letting him choose between two ways of doing it. Don't ask him, "Do you want to take your medicine?" Instead say: "It's time to take your medicine. What would you rather have after it, orange juice or chocolate milk?"

If you warn a child that certain behavior will be punished, stick to your word. Possible punishments for a bedridden child are no television, no dessert, time alone in his room with the door closed, or brief deprivation of a favorite toy.

"Above all," cautions the Heart Association, "don't tell him he will have heart trouble [or any other long-lasting condition] if he does not behave."

See also BEDSORES.

BEDSORES are most likely to afflict people who are underweight and in bed for long periods. The skin and underlying tissues are pressed between the bed and prominent bones, such as those in the buttocks, heels, elbows. This decreases circulation, and the tissue deteriorates.

Tell your physician immediately if you notice any redness or tenderness, first signs of a bedsore. Once it develops, a bedsore is extremely slow to heal.

Preventing bedsores. Make a "poor man's water bed." A commercial water bed costs about $1,000, but for $20 to $30 you can buy an ordinary camper's air mattress and partially fill it

MAKING THE BED TO AVOID SORES
How to make the bed with the patient in it

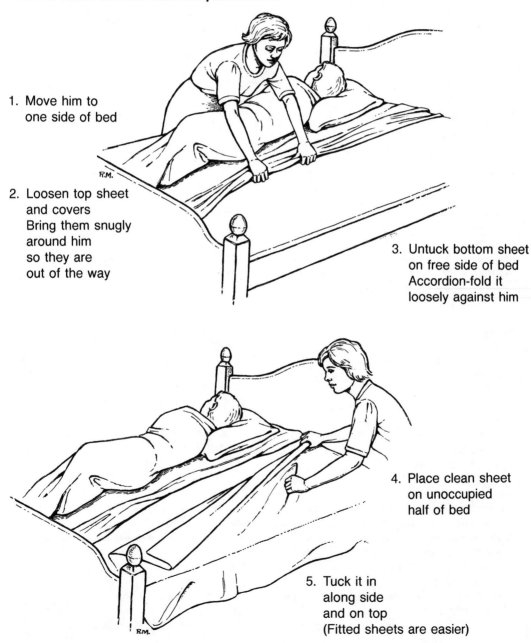

1. Move him to one side of bed

2. Loosen top sheet and covers Bring them snugly around him so they are out of the way

3. Untuck bottom sheet on free side of bed Accordion-fold it loosely against him

4. Place clean sheet on unoccupied half of bed

5. Tuck it in along side and on top (Fitted sheets are easier)

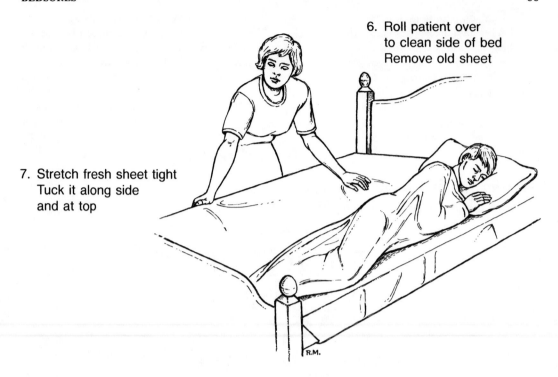

6. Roll patient over
   to clean side of bed
   Remove old sheet

7. Stretch fresh sheet tight
   Tuck it along side
   and at top

with water, which "floats" the patient, easing pressure on the skin.

Fill the mattress on the bed where it's to be used (the water will weigh about 250 pounds), using a garden hose. Add enough water—about 3 inches in depth—so the mattress is loose and, with weight on it, the top and bottom surfaces don't meet. Keep a stick of chewing gum handy to make a temporary plug if there's a leak. A swimming-pool repair kit can fix leaks permanently.

To maintain the proper temperature fill the mattress with water that's 94° F to 98° F. Keep a thermometer under the mattress. When a patient stays in bed, his body heat will hold the water at the right temperature. When he gets off the mattress, a heating pad or electric blanket can maintain the warmth. If the mattress cools, bleed off about a fourth of the water and restore it with hotter water.

Other ways to avoid bedsores. Move a bedridden person from side to side at least every two hours (three hours on a water bed), so he is not left on his back too long. Keep the sheet beneath him smooth and free of crumbs and other irritants. (See the accompanying illustration on how to make a bed with a patient in it.)

Dampness promotes bedsores. Every time you move the patient, and after bathing him, rub the danger areas lightly with baby oil or alcohol (alcohol may be too drying for the elderly). If bedwetting is a problem, give him a bedpan frequently and change the sheets as soon as they become moist.

Prop pillows to help him stay on his side. A pillow between his knees can keep the sides of the knees from rubbing. A pillow or rolled-up towel under his heels and knees reduces their chafing on the mattress.

From a surgical supply store buy "flotation pads," miniature water beds, for use as pillows. Steer clear of the "doughnut," an air-inflated rubber ring, which cuts off skin circulation from all directions. Use a cloth covering to avoid skin contact with nylon, plastic, or rubber surfaces, which promote sweating and dampness.

Teach a person on a wheelchair to do "push-ups" every 15 minutes or so. By pressing down on the chair arms and lifting himself off the seat cushion for a few seconds, he'll relieve the constant pressure on his buttocks.

See also BED REST.

BEDWETTING (enuresis, incontinence) is far more the norm among children than worried parents realize.

Often parents become concerned when the child is only two or three. By the time he is four or five, their concern is intensified by the specter of accidents at school, camp, or on overnight visits with friends. If he's still wetting the bed at six or older, getting him to stop may become a family problem of gigantic proportions. Many parents feel guilty if their child wets the bed, afraid that it is a symptom of emotional disturbance.

Actually most bedwetting generally indicates only physical immaturity. Delayed maturation of the bladder is often hereditary. It may be indicated by frequent urination during infancy.

Two studies in hospital clinics revealed that fully 25 percent of all patients over five years old wet the bed. Any child of any age may wet the bed occasionally. Some children wet the bed only during stressful times—after a move, for example, or during the first few weeks of a new school year.

The condition usually abates by itself as the child matures, both physically and mentally, or is relieved of a disturbing emotional problem.

Organic causes of bedwetting. Organic problems, such as disease or physical defects, are the cause of bedwetting in a small percentage of cases. These require a physician's attention, and enuresis will usually disappear after the physical disorder is treated.

Diabetes is one such cause, since the diabetic's great thirst leads to great consumption of water. Convulsions may also be a cause; bladder control is frequently lost during seizures. Other physical problems may prompt the child to retain urine—in boys, an undersized opening in the penis; in girls, irritating adhesions in the vaginal lips.

Fever is one clue to an infection that may be causing enuresis. Another clue is wetting or spotting in the daytime.

In cases of physical defect a slow, intermittent voiding may signal an obstruction. A girl is likely to have dribbling at the end of urination, whereas normally a girl voids in a steady stream with a noticeable concluding squirt. A boy with a urinary tract defect may stop and start—ordinarily a boy urinates in a steady stream, diminishing toward the conclusion.

Curing bedwetting. Aim for a partnership with the child. Adopt an easy, unconcerned attitude. Don't punish, show anger, or belittle. Avoid commenting on a wet bed. A relaxed approach will encourage the child to regard controlled urination as a natural process about which there is no need to be apprehensive.

Give the child a private pep talk to instill self-confidence. A child will often respond to exercises in muscle control. Get him to flex an arm muscle, then relate the action to his buttocks, knees, and bladder. Thereafter have him work on tightening his buttocks and pressing his knees together until he can reach the bathroom.

Children who continue to wet the bed often have small bladder capacities—they cannot hold more than 5 or 6 ounces of urine before they get the urge to void. To go through the night a child must be able to hold 12 to 14 ounces of urine.

Suspect a small bladder if, on an automobile trip, you have to stop often for the child. You can test his bladder capacity simply by measuring the amount of urine he can hold in the bladder up to the point of marked discomfort. All you need is an inexpensive pint measuring cup marked in ounces. If your child can't hold 12 to 14 ounces during the day, begin a regimen to increase his bladder capacity.

Urge him to drink lots of fluids. A good program includes an 8-ounce glass of liquid with each meal, two full glasses of water between breakfast and lunch, a full glass of water within an hour after lunch, a large soda or diluted fruit juice in midafternoon, and a glass of water an hour before dinner.

With this intake of fluid your youngster will have to urinate frequently. Tell him not to urinate when the first urge comes, but to hold off as long as he can—preferably 20 to 30 minutes. Check his improvement by measuring his bladder capacity once or twice a week. Make it a game. Give him a calendar and stars to paste on the dates of his dry nights. At the end of each month, if he has shown progress, reward him.

Following the hour hand on a large clock may help your child achieve longer intervals between voiding, and thus increased amounts for each urination. Set an initial goal of two hours between voidings. Once he has achieved this, lengthen the interval by half an hour each week until he reaches his maximum capacity. The total regimen ordinarily lasts about six months.

Let him drink all he wants in the evening. After all, you want to stretch his bladder at night as well as during the day. The treatment costs practically nothing and has been successful in a large number of cases. The rare child who fails to respond needs to be seen by a pediatrician.

If your child's enuresis appears to be due to profound sleep, wake him to go to the bathroom an hour and a half after bedtime. He must be fully awakened so that he feels his full bladder and recalls emptying it in the bathroom, thus increasing his confidence. A good test of his awakeness is to give him a "magic number" when he's up and ask him to repeat it in the morning. A child who never wakes, although he may use the toilet, is not being trained for dryness—he is only saving laundry.

Some doctors recommend battery-operated signaling devices to wake the child. These are activated by the salt in the urine and sound an alarm at the first drop. The alarm bell is so placed that the child has to get out of bed to turn it off.

Drug control. Drugs may aid in treating bedwetters. Antidepressant drugs sometimes help the overly relaxed sleeper. They need to be given just at bedtime; if given an hour or so earlier they may keep him from going to sleep. The hyperactive, tense child who urinates as a nervous outlet may benefit from tranquilizers. Anticholinergic drugs block the passage of impulses through the parasympathetic nervous system and thus keep certain muscles from contracting. Their muscle-relaxant action can help develop increased bladder capacity.

If there is no improvement after a month or six weeks of treatment with drugs, buzzers, or interruption of sleep, abandon the attempt for six months to a year. For some children psychotherapy and/or hypnosis have been effective.

Be wary of commercial claims for enuresis control. Dealers who sell and lease devices, and publishers of "techniques," often prey on parents of bedwetters. The FTC has cracked down on fraudulent advertising in this field.

Ads often make bald claims like "Bedwetting stopped"—with no indication that all such devices are useless for organic disorder.

Manufacturers of buzzer devices often boast of a "new" technique. Actually virtually all electrical enuresis-control systems work on the same principle: the completion of an alarm circuit by the sleeper's discharge of urine. The manufacturers are likely to charge as much as the traffic will bear. Not uncommon are leasing charges of more than $75 a month, even more if there are additional bedwetters in the family.

A company may seek to link itself with science by including an unfounded "Research" in its name. One distributor of a device admitted it deceptively threw around titles like "Research Department," "Analytical Department," and "analysts" to suggest activity by academic, medical, or psychological personnel.

In a pseudomedical ploy the representative would claim there were up to 300 bedwetting and sleep patterns into which an enuretic could be classified. Supposedly as a continued service, users of this device were offered the opportunity to send periodic reports to the distributing company covering such information as when the enuretic retires, when he awakens on the sounding of the alarm, and the size of the spot caused by urine discharge. In response they would get written counsel on the future use of the device.

None of this had a shred of medical validity, and served solely to lure customers.

Adult bedwetting. In adults bedwetting may result from disease or genitourinary tract abnormality. The use of some drugs may cause incontinence.

Some older women, particularly women who have borne children, may wet their beds occasionally, or lose urine when bending or lifting, coughing or sneezing. This is usually the result of stretching and relaxation of the muscles of the floor of the pelvis. The condition responds well to exercise and surgery. Some women may require a pessary, a soft rubber internal support. In men incontinence—usually temporary—may follow surgery for prostate trouble.

Various surgical procedures, mechanical devices, prostheses, and exercise regimens are available to aid adults with incontinence problems.

BEE STINGS See INSECT STINGS.

BELCHING See GAS.

BENDS See SCUBA DIVING.

BENNIES See AMPHETAMINES.

BERIBERI See VITAMINS.

BERYLLIOSIS See DUST DISEASE.

BICYCLES are the most hazardous product listed by the Consumer Product Safety Commission. The commission estimates that bikes are responsible for 460,000 accidents a year requiring emergency hospital treatment. The National Safety Council counts some 850 bike deaths a year.

Dangerous and safe bikes. Many deaths and injuries are caused by dangerous design. Bikes are not toys but potentially lethal vehicles.

Avoid the high-rise "banana" seat, which makes it harder to balance the bike. It also encourages riding double, which hampers both balancing and turning. The so-called sissy bar, a long vertical backrest behind the seat, makes it almost impossible to get off by throwing one foot over the rear of the seat. Gearshift levers that stick out from the crossbar can injure the genitals. And the little front wheel of high-rise bikes can make the bike hard to steer.

Buy a closed-frame bike—a "boy's" bike with a bar between the seat post and steering post. It's the best bike for girls as well as boys because the bar contributes substantially to the bike's strength and rigidity.

Be sure the bike is the right size: Divide your height in inches by three to get the correct frame size. When seated, you should be able to place both sets of toes on the ground simultaneously.

If you can't, the seat's too high; if you can sit flat-footed, the seat's too low. The handlebars should be far enough away so your elbows don't rub against your ribs, and close enough so you won't have to stretch forward uncomfortably.

Look for good safety features like handle grips that won't come off, reflectors on all sides of the bike and on its wheel, a front light, and nonskid pedals. Buy only a bike whose front and rear wheels have the same diameter, and whose gearshift is located either on the handlebar or way up front on the horizontal bar. Insist on coaster brakes or hand brakes small enough for a child to grasp, and a seat that cannot be raised or lowered enough to make the bike unstable.

Riding in traffic. When you venture into traffic, be extremely alert. Dr. Reynald Chase, a Manhattan GP usually makes house calls on a three-speed bike. He notes that in disagreements with cars, bikers always lose.

"You're utterly exposed," says Dr. Chase, "with cabbies shaving you, little cars in particular bearing down on you unwittingly, and motorcyclists crowding you off and buffeting you in their way. Then suddenly the door of a parked car opens, or a parked car suddenly pulls out, or you're up against a red light. You're often bounced off course by potholes, and you can't stop on a dime like a motorized vehicle can."

Dr. Chase is concerned about the safety of pedestrians too. "A bike can be a lethal weapon attacking a walker. Kids especially don't realize that when their ten-speeders zoom along at 20 or 25 miles an hour, they develop the weight and momentum of a lethal force. And when cyclists also jump lights or cut in and out of traffic, you can see the potential for serious accidents."

Think of yourself as a bicycle driver, not a rider. The National Safety Council believes this sense of responsibility would correct many causes of accidents.

Eighty percent of the bicycle "riders" now killed or hurt in traffic accidents are breaking traffic laws at the time, says the council. Some 20 percent of the bicycles involved in accidents have a mechanical defect.

Resist stunting. Some TV commercials encourage accidents by showing youngsters performing dangerous acts like "popping a wheelie" —in which the rider places himself near the rear wheel, shifts his weight back, and lifts the front wheel off the ground. Another common stunt is curb jumping, which often leads to loss of control.

On a slippery or wet surface, avoid braking or turning. Instead, with a firm hold on the handlebars, coast through the bad spot in as straight a line as possible. Hand brakes become almost useless when wheel rims are wet. You can stop better by dragging your feet than by applying the brakes. A fine mist can make brakes as ineffective as riding through a puddle. If you ride a bike with hand brakes in wet weather, go extra slowly and walk the bike down hills.

Other rules for safe bicycling:

Observe all traffic regulations. Be ready to yield the right of way. Use motorists' hand signals when turning, stopping, or slowing. Be aware of traffic behind as well as in front of you.

Keep to the right and close to the curb. Ride in a straight line, single file.

If you must drive at night, have a white headlight in good working order, and a red rear reflector. Wear white or light-colored clothing.

Give pedestrians the right of way. Have and use a horn or bell for signaling. If you must use a sidewalk, walk your bike through congested areas.

Never hitch onto other vehicles. Never stunt or race in traffic.

Don't carry riders. Carry packages in a basket or rack. Except when signaling, keep hands on handlebars at all times.

Slow down at all intersections. Look both ways: left, then right, then left again before crossing.

See also ACCIDENTS.

BIRTH CONTROL (contraception) For fertile people, abstaining from sexual intercourse is the only foolproof method of preventing pregnancy.

Aside from this extreme there are many safe, convenient, and generally effective means of birth control. Each method has its advantages and disadvantages, and not all contraceptive techniques are psychologically or physically suited to everyone. Discuss with your doctor your own problems and preferences before selecting a contraceptive method.

The two most effective contraceptive measures are surgical sterilization and oral contraceptives.

Sterilization is meant only for people who will never want any more children. At least one American couple in six in the main childbearing years (ages 20 to 39) has had a surgical sterilization. The most common form of female sterilization is tubal ligation, or tube-tying. It is performed in a hospital, usually under general anesthesia. With only isolated failures, it is considered 100 percent effective.

Tubal ligation involves tying off or cauterizing (burning) the fallopian tubes between the ovaries and the uterus. This prevents the egg from reaching the uterus and the sperm from traveling up the tubes.

The most generally recommended method is laparoscopy. A long, tubelike instrument called a laparoscope is inserted through a small abdominal incision. With the mirrors and lights on the laparoscope the surgeon locates the tubes and cauterizes, clamps, or cuts them.

Laparoscopy is sometimes called a "Band-Aid operation" because the incision is so small. It requires at most an overnight stay in the hospital —many women go home the same day. Cauterizing presents a slight risk of burning the large intestine. If a clamp is used, there's a better chance of reopening the tubes if you wish to have more children.

In the traditional method of tubal ligation, called laparotomy, a larger incision is made in the abdominal wall. The surgeon cuts each fallopian tube and ties each separated end. While the operation can be performed at any time, it is often done just after delivery, when the uterus is enlarged and the tubes are easily reached.

Laparotomy entails two to four days in the hospital. It is the procedure of choice for women who are 50 pounds or more overweight and for women who suffer marked heart or lung disease.

A newer technique is called minilaparotomy, or "mini-lap." A small incision (1 to 2 inches) is made in the lower abdomen.

Using an instrument inserted into the uterus by way of the vagina, the surgeon rotates and lifts the tip of the uterus, bringing the fallopian tubes to the incision site. Various techniques are suitable to close off the tubes. In the most frequently used technique each tube is grasped and lifted out of the abdomen. A loop of the tube is tied off and a small segment of the loop is removed. Each tube is then returned to the abdomen and the small incision is closed.

After a mini-lap operation you can expect to feel pain and soreness in your abdomen for a few days. Medication can help to relieve the discomfort.

The mini-lap is often done on an outpatient basis in a clinic or hospital.

Complications of tubal ligation are rare. Consult your physician at once if you develop fever or severe abdominal pain.

Sexual response is not affected by tubal ligation. Menstruation continues; hormones are secreted normally; ovaries, uterus, and vagina are not affected. An egg is produced and released every month, but when it reaches the cut portion of the fallopian tube, it can go no farther; it disintegrates and is harmlessly absorbed by the body.

Although it is possible to reverse the tubal ligation, only one in four reversal operations is successful. Don't have a tubal ligation unless you are absolutely sure you don't want any more children.

A woman also becomes sterile after the removal of her reproductive organs: both fallopian tubes, both ovaries, or the uterus (see HYSTERECTOMY). These operations are usually performed to remove damaged or diseased tissue. Rarely are they done specifically as a birth control measure.

The sterilization procedure for males is VASECTOMY (which see).

For more information, contact the Association for Voluntary Sterilization, Inc., 122 East 42nd Street, New York, New York 10168.

The Pill. Oral contraceptives, or birth control pills, are nearly 100 percent effective. Commonly known as "the Pill," the oral contraceptive is a combination of hormones that prevent conception mainly by suppressing ovulation, the production of the woman's egg cell.

Oral contraceptives are available only by prescription and need to be taken under a doctor's direction.

The Pill's major advantage is its high degree of effectiveness. It is more effective than the IUD, although it presents more potential problems. The Pill is a method appropriate for mature women with established sex lives and regular daily habits.

A woman is a candidate for the Pill only if her menstrual cycle is established and reasonably regular. Most oral contraceptives combine the two kinds of female sex hormones: estrogens and progestogens. They prevent ovulation; they also thicken the mucus in the neck of the uterus, obstructing sperm. Further, they change the lining of the uterus so that it cannot receive a fertilized egg. The combined pill is effective because, if one of the reactions fails to occur, another will do the trick. Combination brands include Brevicon, Demulen, Enovid, Loestrin, Lo/Ovral, Modicon, Norinyl, Norlestrin, Ortho-Novum, Ovral, Ovulen, Zorane. A "mini-pill" contains progestogen only. It does not stop ovulation, but works by thickening the liquid in the cervical canal so that sperm have more difficulty in reaching the egg. Major mini-pill brands: Micronor, Nor-Q-D, Ovrette.

Before getting a prescription for the Pill you need a gynecological examination. Your doctor needs to take a careful medical history to find out whether you have a tendency toward any condition that would make it best for you not to take the Pill. He should also take blood pressure, examine your breasts for lumps, and take a Pap smear to check for cervical cancer.

You start your first course of pills on the fifth day after your period begins. You should use another method of contraception as well for the first two weeks. Until then you are not fully protected by the Pill alone.

If she misses even one pill, a woman risks becoming pregnant until her next period. After such a lapse she should take the pill or pills missed, then continue taking pills daily for the rest of the month—but also use another contraceptive method, such as condoms, spermicidal preparations, or a diaphragm. Contrary to popular belief there is no medical reason to give her body a "rest" by periodically stopping for a month or two. A woman should never use someone else's prescription.

A physician can prescribe an oral contraceptive tailored to a woman's individual needs. Thus, if a woman tends to be hairy, he is likely to prescribe a pill with a low progestogen content. If she develops complications such as vaginal bleeding, he may switch her to a pill with a higher estrogen content.

Many brands of the Pill are available in 21- or 28-day packets. It is a good idea for the doctor to prescribe the 28-day packet, the last 7 pills of which are inactive. That way a woman gets used to taking a pill every day. If she goes off the Pill, she needs to start another method of contraception right away. Even if she wants to conceive, a miscarriage is more frequent in the first two or three months following stoppage of the Pill. She should use another method of contraception for at least three months.

Common side effects. About one in five users experiences reactions to the Pill. Many of these side effects are similar to the symptoms of early pregnancy and may disappear after a few months. They may include nausea and vomiting, a bloated feeling, and tender breasts. Many users complain of being perpetually damp from excessive vaginal secretions. This vaginal dampness is related to estrogen and may be relieved by switching to a pill higher in progestogen.

The skin may darken irreversibly, especially on exposure to sunlight. This reaction is especially common among brunettes. Headache, dizziness, acne, and emotional depression are less common complaints associated with the Pill. Loss of scalp hair is an uncommon side effect.

At unexpected times of the month a woman may experience some breakthrough vaginal bleeding, marked by staining of her underpants. There is often a tendency to gain weight, probably caused by an increase in appetite and water retention. A change of hormone combination may eliminate or reduce specific side effects. So may a change in the dosage or the taking of concurrent drugs, like diuretics to reduce the bloating. The Pill may interfere with the absorption of vitamins and minerals. Supplements may be required.

On the plus side, women usually report an absence of premenstrual tension and menstrual cramps. There is likely to be a lesser amount of menstrual bleeding and a more regular menstrual cycle. Some Pill users, however, stop menstruating entirely—a side effect that can make them fear they're pregnant.

When not to take the Pill. If you have a chronic health problem, it may be made worse by an oral contraceptive. Migraine, depression, and asthma are often aggravated by the Pill. Among other contraindications: High blood pressure; fibroid tumors in the uterus; and heart, liver, or kidney disease.

Nor should you take birth control pills if you have any tendencies toward blood-clotting disorders, cancer of the breast or uterus, a serious liver condition like hepatitis, or undiagnosed vaginal bleeding.

Don't take oral contraceptives if you are nursing a baby. When you are breastfeeding the baby, hormones from the Pill pass in your milk to your baby, and the long-range effects on infants is not known. Furthermore the Pill may decrease your milk supply.

Serious side effects. These are relatively rare, but can be life-threatening. Women on the Pill face an increased risk of developing thrombophlebitis—blood clots in the veins possibly leading to loss of limb, paralysis, or death. Contact your doctor immediately if you ever experience severe headaches, shortness of breath, blurred vision, or pain in the legs or chest. Also, while you are taking the Pill, report any unusual swelling, and any color changes, such as brownish spotting or yellowish discoloration of the skin or eyes.

About 450 women die each year in this country from the effects of the Pill on the heart and blood vessels. The overwhelming percentage of those complications occur among women who smoke. Studies suggest that at least half of these deaths could be avoided if women who used the Pill did not smoke.

A Pill user is three times more likely than a nonuser to have a fatal heart attack. Among 100,000 women age 20 to 29 years old who use the Pill, 3 would be expected to have a heart attack each year; 2 of the 3 attacks would be attributable to the Pill. Among 100,000 women aged 40 to 44 who take the Pill, 75 will have a fatal heart attack, with 50 of the deaths attributable to the Pill.

The use of the Pill by women over 40 is generally not recommended. Nor is it advisable for a woman who is already at risk of heart attack—one, for example, who smokes, has high cholesterol, and a family history of coronary artery disease.

Pregnancy after the Pill. Most women have no trouble becoming pregnant after they stop taking the Pill. A small percentage of women have delayed menstruation and ovulation for a few months. A number of studies have shown no increase in the occurrence of birth defects in offspring born to women after they stopped oral contraceptive use.

Benefits of the Pill. Before thinking about taking the Pill, you need to face whether its benefits offset its risks. Certainly you should not consider the Pill if you have intercourse only at great intervals. Its risks are too great to take it "just in case." *The Medical Letter* recommends that "the risks in the use of oral contraceptives should be weighed against the psychological effects of fear of pregnancy and the possible physical consequences of pregnancy or abortion."

Numerous studies have shown that for healthy women under 30 the benefits of oral contraceptives outweigh the risks. Risks can be sharply reduced if patients are screened for conditions that can compound any health risks from the Pill (obesity, high blood pressure, diabetes), if they are given the lowest effective dosage, and if they do not smoke.

There is no evidence supporting earlier fears that Pill use might increase the risk of breast or any other cancer. The overwhelming majority of studies that have examined the issue find no evidence that the Pill use causes cancer of the ovaries, uterus, or breast.

On the contrary, the evidence suggests that the Pill may protect against ovarian and endometrial (uterine lining) cancer. According to several recent studies users of oral contraceptives appear to have only half the risk of contracting both endometrial and ovarian cancer. For both the protective effect may persist for ten years after discontinuation of Pill use.

Studies suggest that Pill use may also help protect women against benign breast disease; ovarian cysts; iron deficiency anemia (partly because of the fact that Pill users usually have reduced menstrual flow); pelvic inflammatory disease; rheumatoid arthritis; and ectopic pregnancy (since Pill use usually prevents ovulation).

Other birth control methods. Consider these other highly effective methods of birth control:

Diaphragm. This saucer-shaped device is made of soft thin rubber with a flexible metal rim. It is placed in the vagina before intercourse and covers the entrance to the uterus.

Always use the diaphragm with spermicidal cream or jelly. Properly used, the diaphragm-spermicide combination is about 97 percent effective. However diaphragm users are nearly 20 times as likely as Pill takers to become pregnant because so many women neglect to insert their diaphragms, or use them improperly.

The diaphragm must be fitted by a physician, who will also instruct you in how to use it. You can insert the diaphragm several hours before intercourse, and need to leave it in place for at least six hours afterward.

Spermicide is effective for about one to two hours. If you have intercourse more than an hour or so after insertion, you'll be safest if you leave the diaphragm in place but introduce more spermicide into your vagina. Each application protects against the sperm in one ejaculation. Before each additional intercourse another application of spermicide is needed.

Correctly placed, the diaphragm will not be felt by either the woman or the man. Remove it within 24 hours after intercourse.

Properly cared for, diaphragms last for several years. After removing your diaphragm, wash it with mild soap and water, pat it dry with a towel, and lightly powder it with cornstarch before you put it back in its container. Check it for holes every month by holding it up to the light or filling it with water.

The diaphragm can fail to protect a woman from conceiving if it is improperly inserted or if it is too small. It is also possible for the diaphragm to be displaced during intercourse.

Have your doctor check your diaphragm size 12 to 16 weeks after each childbirth, when the vaginal canal often stretches. Also have your diaphragm checked if you lose more than 15 to 20 pounds. Have your insertion technique checked annually.

IUD (intrauterine contraceptive device). This is a small, flexible plastic device that is inserted into the uterus. IUDs are about 98 percent effective, though it is not known exactly how they prevent pregnancy. One theory is that the IUD causes changes in the endometrium (the lining of the uterus), possibly altering the time of month when it is ready to accept implantation. Or the

IUD may increase the movement of the fallopian tubes so as to prevent fertilization of the egg.

Several different kinds are in use, differing in size, shape, and type of material. The most commonly used are the Lippes Loop and the Saf-T-Coil.

They are 98 to 99 percent effective in preventing pregnancy. IUDs containing copper may also help prevent gonorrhea.

Insertion of IUDs is quick and usually painless, though it can be somewhat uncomfortable. A complete gynecological examination makes sure there is no reason why you should not use an IUD. The doctor opens the vagina with a speculum and inserts the device with a special introducer. Most doctors prefer to insert the IUD during menstruation when there is no chance of pregnancy, and when insertion will be less uncomfortable.

Once it is in place, you should not feel the IUD, nor should either partner be aware of it during intercourse.

The IUD can remain in the uterus for many years. It should be checked twice a year to make sure it is properly placed. IUDs containing copper should be replaced every two to three years.

Between 2 and 20 out of every 100 women—depending on the device used—spontaneously expel IUDs, usually within the first three months. Women who have never been pregnant are more likely to expel the device, but as long as they retain it, it is effective.

An expulsion generally occurs during menstruation. Check your sanitary napkins or tampons to make sure the IUD has not been passed out. If your IUD has a stringlike appendage that can be felt in the vagina, try to check it after every menstrual period. See your doctor if you believe that the device has been expelled or changed position. Roughly half the women who expel IUDs can retain a different type.

Most women experience some spotting of blood for a week or two after the IUD is inserted. Menstrual-type cramps and backache are also common. The first few menstrual periods after insertion are likely to be earlier, heavier, and longer. There may be spotting between periods. These discomforts tend to disappear after a few months.

A small percentage of women experience severe cramps and heavy bleeding from the IUD and must have it removed.

Pelvic inflammatory disease (PID) occurs more often among women who use IUDs. The incidence of such infections becomes lower with increasing age and duration of IUD use. PID appears to be highest in women with multiple sex partners. Most cases of PID can be successfully treated with antibiotics. The device may have to be removed for the duration of the infection. PID sometimes causes sterility. For this reason many doctors recommend against the use of the IUD in young women who have not had children, particularly if they have many sex partners.

An extremely rare complication of IUD, occurring about once in every 2,500 insertions, is perforation of the uterus: the device penetrates the uterine wall, often as a result of faulty insertion. In most instances there is no pain or any other symptom. An IUD that has entered the abdominal cavity should be removed.

There are no known cases of uterine or cervical cancer resulting from IUDs, and available information indicates that they do not cause any other abnormalities.

If you wish to become pregnant, have the IUD removed by a doctor. The IUD has no effect on your fertility after it is removed.

A small number of women become pregnant with the device still in place. Consult your doctor as soon as you suspect you're pregnant. There is a higher risk of ectopic (outside the uterus) pregnancy in IUD users. This requires surgery. In many normal pregnancies the IUD presents no danger to the baby and is delivered along with the baby. But it's safest to have the IUD removed. Women who continue pregnancy with the IUD in place are 50 times more likely to die of a spontaneous abortion than are women whose IUDs were removed.

IUDs are generally not recommended for women who have had recent pelvic inflammatory disease or other gynecological infections such as venereal disease. The IUD is also ruled out for women who have heavy menstrual bleeding or abnormal uterine bleeding, cancer of the uterus, or fibroid tumors in the uterus. A woman with an abnormally small or irregularly shaped uterus may not be able to wear an IUD.

To increase the effectiveness of IUDs, some doctors recommend using a spermicidal preparation for seven to ten days around the high-fertility midpoint between periods.

Condom. Probably the most widely used contraceptive product in the United States—it can be bought without prescription—the condom is one of the safest and least expensive. Also commonly called a rubber or prophylactic, the condom is a thin latex rubber sheath that is worn over the erect penis during intercourse.

Regular use of the condom is about 96 percent effective as a contraceptive technique. The condom also provides some protection against venereal disease.

The original condoms were made in England in the eighteenth century from sheep intestines. In recent years such "skin" condoms have been largely replaced by latex, but they are still available at about three times the cost of latex ones. Their advantage is that they conduct heat better than latex condoms and are thought less likely to dull the man's sensitivity.

Condoms are about 7 or 8 inches long and generally come rolled and powdered. Some come with a small reservoir at the tip for collecting ejaculated semen. If yours doesn't have a reservoir, leave 1/2 inch loose at the end when putting it on. Lubricated condoms are widely available.

Condoms should last up to a year in an unopened box. But they deteriorate with exposure to light and heat, so don't store them in a pocket or a wallet. Buy condoms from a drugstore—not a machine, which may have old or inferior condoms.

Condoms are under the jurisdiction of the Food and Drug Administration and have to meet strict standards. There is no need to test a condom before using it. You are likely to damage it by needless stretching or inflating.

On the negative side, the condom must be fitted over the penis while it is erect, interrupting sexual foreplay. A way around this is to have the woman put the condom on the man as part of foreplay. Some men claim that the condom dulls sensation. It may feel confining and get tangled in the man's pubic hair.

There is a small chance that the condom will break during use, usually from dryness—an argument for using lubricated condoms. It may slip off inside the vagina as the penis shrinks after ejaculation; thus it is a good idea for a condom wearer to withdraw within a few minutes. To keep the condom from slipping off during withdrawal, hold the edge of the condom.

If you think any semen leaked into the vagina, the woman needs to immediately insert an application of a spermicidal jelly, cream, or foam. Vaginal douching is unlikely to help.

When a man is using a condom, the woman may wish to use a contraceptive jelly, cream, or foam for added protection. This will also help to lubricate the condom if it is dry. Don't use petroleum jelly or oils, since they can cause the condom to deteriorate, and have no spermicidal properties.

Natural family planning (rhythm method). This is the only contraceptive method sanctioned by the Roman Catholic Church. It is an effective means of contraception (possibly as high as 95 percent) only when used correctly and diligently.

All four methods of natural family planning involve calculating the fertile days within the menstrual cycle and abstaining from sexual intercourse for a certain number of days.

Determining the time of ovulation (when the woman is most fertile) is difficult and time-consuming. Attempt natural family-planning methods only under the guidance of a physician experienced in their use.

Calendar rhythm method. This method is based on three assumptions: (1) that ovulation (release of the egg from the ovary) occurs some 12 to 16 days before the beginning of menstruation; (2) that the egg survives for 24 hours; and (3) that sperm are capable of fertilizing an egg for a period of 48 to 72 hours.

The calendar method is based not on signs and symptoms of ovulation, but rather on mathematical calculations involving the length of at least 6 to 12 previous menstrual cycles.

Once a woman observes the longest and shortest cycles, she then calculates that her fertile period begins on the eighteenth day before the end of the shortest likely cycle. The last day of the fertile period is calculated by figuring the longest cycle minus 11 days.

Thus a woman whose menstruation begins every 28 to 32 days must abstain from intercourse on the tenth through the twenty-first day after her period starts. (She subtracts 18 from 28 to get 10; then subtracts 11 from 32 to get 21.) The method is unsuitable for a woman with irregular menstrual periods.

The disadvantage of this method is that there is always the possibility that there will be a change in the length of the menstrual cycle, thus resulting in miscalculation of the fertile time. The calendar method, although practiced by many couples for many years as the only form of natural family planning, is now considered obsolete—the failure rate is very high.

Basal body temperature method. This method involves charting on a temperature graph the changes in body temperature, which may indicate fertile and infertile days.

While this method cannot identify exactly when ovulation occurs, a slight rise in temperature usually means that a woman has started to ovulate. Before ovulation her temperature is likely to range from 96.6° F to 98.2° F. During and after ovulation, the range is 97.6° F to 99.2° F. A woman should not engage in intercourse until three consecutive days after this temperature rise begins.

The temperature is best taken by a basal body temperature thermometer, which is calibrated in tenths of a degree and measures temperatures between 96° F and 100° F. Temperature can be taken either orally, rectally, vaginally, or under the arm—but it should be taken at the same site and at the same time daily, preferably in the morning on awakening.

Fluctuations in temperature may be influenced by illness, stress, drugs, alcohol, and sleeplessness. These factors should also be noted on the temperature chart.

Ovulation method. This method is based on the changes that occur in the mucus of the cervix in the course of a woman's menstrual cycle.

Also called the vaginal mucus method, it requires a woman to examine her cervical mucus for changes. Following her menstrual period, the mucus will be scant. After that she will have a sticky discharge. As she draws closer to ovulation, her mucus increases in amount. A clear, slippery mucus that looks like egg white and can be stretched between the fingers indicates the peak period in which she can conceive. About the fourth day after ovulation the mucus becomes cloudy and sticky and reduces in volume or dries up entirely. This shows her safe period for intercourse, which lasts until her next menstrual period.

When a woman first begins the method, she must abstain from sexual intercourse for one month. This allows her to become aware of how her cervical mucus changes in the course of her menstrual cycle. During her menstrual flow and the first phase of her cycle she should abstain every other day, so that she can accurately identify the fertile mucus when it occurs. After she identifies the fertile mucus, she should wait four days before engaging in intercourse.

Sympto-thermal method. This is a combination of methods to help a woman identify her time of ovulation. She can observe changes in her cervix and cervical mucus; basal body temperature changes; and secondary signs of ovulation, which may include increased sexual desire, breast tenderness, abdominal bloating, vulvar swelling, slight pain in the ovary, and some vaginal spotting.

At the time of ovulation the cervix thickens and increases its slippery mucus discharge. It also elevates and dilates slightly. A couple can observe and record these and other signs of ovulation and should abstain from intercourse until a few days after these changes occur.

Further information, counseling, and instruction may be obtained by consulting the following:

Human Life and Natural Family Planning Foundation
1511 K Street, NW
Washington, D.C. 20005

National Family Planning Federation of America, Inc.
1221 Massachusetts Avenue, NW
Washington, D.C. 20005

Less effective methods. Contraceptive methods with only medium to fair effectiveness include:

Withdrawal (coitus interruptus). This is the oldest method of birth control. In theory it costs nothing and is always available. Withdrawal involves withdrawing the penis from the vagina just before ejaculation, so that the semen is deposited away from the woman's vagina.

But this method can easily fail if the male is slow in withdrawing and deposits even a drop of semen in the vagina. Sperm may also escape before ejaculation.

Withdrawal makes great demands on the man's self-control. The split-second timing required can seriously interfere with a couple's enjoyment of sex. Some doctors observe that the stress connected with the frequent use of withdrawal may lead to sexual and psychological problems.

Vaginal spermicide. A preparation that contains sperm-killing chemicals is inserted into the vagina before intercourse. Spermicides come as foams, creams, jellies, foaming tablets, and suppositories. A small number of men and women are allergic to spermicides. Some women are bothered by the messiness of these products, especially when the creams and jellies leak during or after intercourse.

Spermicides are available without prescription from drugstores. Most come with applicators to ease insertion.

Insert a vaginal spermicide about ten minutes before intercourse. If you get off the bed before intercourse, apply additional spermicide, since a large quantity may leak out. If you don't have intercourse within an hour after inserting the spermicide, give yourself another application, for by then most spermicides lose their effectiveness. Don't douche for at least six hours after intercourse.

Vaginal foams are more effective in preventing pregnancy than creams or jellies. Vaginal foaming tablets and suppositories are least effective, and should be used only when other spermicides are not available. All spermicides are more effective when used in conjunction with other birth control methods such as diaphragm, condoms, or rhythm.

Contraceptive sponge. About as effective as foam (the failure rate is 15–18 percent), the sponge is made of polyurethane and shaped like a doughnut. It can be bought without a prescription and comes in one size for all women. The sponge is inserted deep into the vagina so that it covers the cervix. It releases a spermicide that may also provide some protection against venereal disease.

An advantage of the sponge over spermicides is that it provides protection for 24 hours. Each sponge can be used only once. It should be left in the vagina for at least six hours after the last act of intercourse.

Some women experience allergic reactions or irritations. In a few cases, sponges have broken apart and had to be removed by physicians. A few cases of toxic shock syndrome have been associated with sponge use (see MENSTRUATION).

Methods that don't work. Among the least effective methods of contraception are:

Douching. Flushing out the vagina with a large amount of water after intercourse is virtually useless for preventing pregnancy.

For douching to be effective at all, it must be done immediately after intercourse, since sperm can reach the cervix in less than 90 seconds after ejaculation. Use douching only as an emergency measure. It is a shade better than using no birth control method at all.

Breastfeeding. Some women are under the mistaken impression that breastfeeding will prevent conception indefinitely. It is true that if you nurse your baby, menstruation and ovulation are not likely to return for several months. Without contraception women who breastfeed their babies are less likely to conceive in the year after delivery than women who don't. But don't rely on this as a method of birth control. You can ovulate and become pregnant even before your first postpartum menstrual period.

The morning-after pill. A controversial "morning-after" contraceptive has been approved by the Food and Drug Administration (FDA) for use in emergency situations such as rape and incest. The pill, a large dose of a synthetic estrogen compound called diethylstilbestrol or DES, is about 90 percent effective in preventing pregnancy. It should be administered within 72 hours after intercourse.

DES should not be considered as a routine means of contraception because of possibly severe side effects. It generally causes violent nausea and vomiting. If you take the DES treatment once, don't ever take it a second time: the con-traceptive dose is equivalent to about ten months of birth control pills.

The major hazard of DES is its cancer-causing potential. It was banned as a growth hormone for cattle and other food animals after it was found capable of causing cancer in some animals. At one time DES was used to prevent miscarriages. Daughters of women who received DES during pregnancy suffer an unusually high incidence of a rare type of vaginal cancer.

There are no data to show that DES causes cancer in the woman who takes it. The FDA believes that DES, used as a contraceptive, does not pose a "significant threat to the patient."

On the other hand the cancer-causing potential of DES has not been fully explored. Drs. Roy Hertz and Mort Lipsett, experts in hormonal cancer at the National Institutes of Health, have stated that "DES is such a powerful carcinogen that it is used as a model for producing artificial cancers in animals."

Avoid DES if you or any member of your family have ever had cancer of the breast or of the genitals. You are also at added risk from DES if you have taken other estrogens, such as birth control pills.

Before taking DES have your doctor check to see if you are already pregnant. If DES is ineffective and you do become pregnant, the FDA advises that you consider abortion. If you consider the risks of DES too great, you may prefer to wait and see if you become pregnant, bearing in mind the possibility of abortion.

See also ABORTION; HYSTERECTOMY; PREGNANCY; THROMBOPHLEBITIS; VASECTOMY; VENEREAL DISEASE.

BIRTH DEFECTS afflict about 250,000 American babies each year, or about 1 in 15. They account for half the deaths of preschool children.

There are at least 2,000 different birth defects, ranging from very mild to life-threatening. Among the most common are mental retardation, congenital blindness, deafness, genitourinary anomalies, congenital heart defects, cleft palate, and cleft lip. Some children are born with limb deformities—especially club foot—missing limbs, disfiguring birthmarks, cystic fibrosis, or sickle cell anemia.

Others have bone, muscle, or joint diseases, or metabolic disorders like PKU. Some conditions, like diabetes, may not show up for many years. Many children have more than one type of birth defect.

Genetic counseling. If you have a family history of serious birth defects, seek genetic counseling before becoming pregnant. Many medical centers, universities, hospitals, and clinics provide such services. To find a genetic counselor near you, contact your local chapter of The March of Dimes Birth Defects Foundation or its headquarters at 1275 Mamaroneck Avenue, White Plains, New York 10605.

The genetic counselor, working with a physician, can assess the risk of your having a child with a particular birth defect if it runs in your family, or if you've already had one child with the defect, or experienced unexplained miscarriages, stillbirth, or infant death. This can be done through a family and personal medical history and various medical tests. Chromosome analysis, for example, can determine whether you or your mate is carrying a chromosome abnormality that does not affect you but may seriously affect your offspring.

Women in their mid-thirties and older are at increased risk of having babies with certain chromosome abnormalities, and should consider genetic counseling.

After evaluating family and personal medical histories and the results of any medical tests, the counselor may be able to reassure you that the abnormality is unlikely to be repeated. If he finds that you run a considerable risk of having a child with the defect, the counselor will discuss your range of options for avoiding or dealing with such an outcome.

Genetic counseling ethics strongly discourage advising you to do (or not do) anything. Counselors should provide you with explanations, estimates of risks if possible, and discussion of whatever options apply in hard situations: childlessness, artificial insemination, prenatal testing, abortion, giving the offspring up for adoption, expectations of treatability, and so on. When clients ask, "What would you do in my position?" a counselor is likely to reply in effect, "I'm not you. My job is to inform, not advise."

When a child is born with a birth defect, immediate diagnosis and treatment can be very important. Many abnormalities can be surgically improved or corrected. With others early training can help prevent future disabilities. Special schools and vocational training centers are widely available. Ask your pediatrician or health department.

A severely handicapped child can put severe emotional stress on a family. For information, counseling, and the support of other families with similar problems seek out a local organization of parents with handicapped children. The local March of Dimes chapter may be able to refer you to such a group.

Causes of defects. Some birth defects are connected with poor prenatal care and malnutrition in the mother. Spina bifida, for example, is sometimes associated with the mother's poor diet and poor health.

Women with chronic medical conditions such as diabetes, alcoholism, or hypertension are more prone to have babies with birth anomalies. A woman who contracts rubella during early pregnancy runs a high risk of having a child with defects such as cataracts and hearing loss. Birth defects are also linked to other infectious diseases during pregnancy, including toxoplasmosis, genital herpes, and cytomegalovirus.

Untreated venereal disease in the mother may result in defects in the child. Rh disease can cause fetal abnormalities. Alcoholism in the mother is associated with a greater chance of birth anomalies.

Multiple, excessive X rays during pregnancy, or prolonged X-ray therapy before pregnancy, may cause chromosomal changes that result in birth defects. Some drugs taken during the first three months of pregnancy may be implicated in fetal abnormalities.

Premature babies or those with low birth weight are more prone to suffer from abnormalities. Teen-aged mothers and women over 40 have more babies with birth defects than women of intermediate ages. Environmental pollutants—chemical wastes, pesticides, air pollution, water contamination—are suspected of playing some part in causing birth defects.

The causes of most birth defects are unknown. Often it is impossible to pinpoint one specific cause, since it may be due to a combination of factors.

Minimize the risk. You can substantially reduce your chances of giving birth to a baby with anomalies. Here are some precautions you can take:

Seek good prenatal care as soon as you suspect you are pregnant. Follow your doctor's prescribed diet. Take only the drugs that he prescribes for you. Avoid X rays if possible.

Get diagnosis and treatment immediately if you suspect you have venereal disease.

Avoid smoking and alcohol during pregnancy.

Before pregnancy be vaccinated against rubella if you have never had the disease.

Before pregnancy be tested for rubella antibodies, and be vaccinated against rubella if necessary.

If you have a cat or if you like rare meat, be tested before pregnancy or in the early weeks for antibodies against toxoplasmosis. Unless you're proved immune, avoid rare meat and contact with cat litter, which can transmit this infection.

If you have Rh-negative blood, and have had an induced or spontaneous abortion or an Rh-positive baby, get the vaccine that can prevent resulting birth defects in future pregnancies.

A diagnostic procedure called amniocentesis, which involves drawing amniotic fluid through the abdominal wall with a needle, can detect or rule out various birth defects in the fourth month of pregnancy. The fluid—which contains cells shed by the fetus—is cultured and then analyzed for genetic abnormalities.

See also ABORTION; BIRTHMARKS; CEREBRAL PALSY; CLEFT LIP; CLEFT PALATE; CONGENITAL HEART DEFECTS; CYSTIC FIBROSIS; DIABETES; MENTAL RETARDATION; PKU; PREGNANCY; Rh DISEASE; RUBELLA; SICKLE CELL ANEMIA; SPINA BIFIDA; TOXOPLASMOSIS.

BIRTHMARKS (vascular nevi, hemangiomas) rarely call for medical treatment. The great majority disappear spontaneously or can be camouflaged with masking cosmetics.

Vascular birthmarks result from improper development of small blood vessels of the outer skin surface, and may be visible at birth or soon after.

The exact cause of birthmarks remains unknown. But one thing is sure: They are not caused by a pregnant woman's having a nightmare, or being frightened by an animal, or taking medication, or being injured in the process of childbirth. These old wives' tales have long been disproved.

The major types of vascular birthmarks are:

Port-wine stain, the most common, usually appears at birth. It is usually lifelong, seldom fading or disappearing with age. Perhaps one out of three newborns may have a pale form of such a birthmark on the back of the scalp or neck; this form usually disappears.

The stains are flat and usually some shade of the red that gives them their name. They can be as small as quarter of an inch, or large enough to cover a whole arm or half of the face. If the mark covers a large area, a physician may try to determine whether there is abnormal development of underlying large blood vessels.

The argon laser is being used successfully to treat some port-wine stains. It is most effective after adolescence. By contrast, scarring may result from other methods such as freezing the skin with dry ice or scraping the mark off. Tattooing with skin-colored pigments may some-times prove helpful, but should be done only by a physician.

The AMA recommends teaching a child to accept a birthmark and to understand that a cosmetic preparation may successfully disguise it.

Strawberry hemangioma has a distinct border around a reddish, soft, compressible swelling that looks like a strawberry. These hemangiomas can occur anyplace on the body. They are usually 1 or 2 inches in diameter but have been known to cover an entire arm or leg.

They may appear at birth or during the first months of life, and may grow rapidly to several times their original size. For a short while they remain stable, without either increasing or decreasing in size. Then they spontaneously disappear over a period of from two to six years, leaving little if any mark to show where they had been.

Treatments to try to hasten the spontaneous regression of strawberry hemangiomas are uncomfortable and not always satisfactory. Sometimes, if one is very small, treating it with dry ice may result in an improved appearance that warrants the discomfort.

Cavernous hemangioma has an elevated surface and bluish color. It feels like a mass of dough beneath the skin, only partly compressible and without sharply defined borders. It is usually from 1 to 3 inches in diameter.

It follows much the same pattern of growth and disappearance as the strawberry hemangioma, except that cosmetic results are often not as pleasing. After the birthmark regresses, a soft hanging pouch of skin may remain. This may improve over the years, though a person who doesn't want to wait may undergo plastic surgery.

A baby with a hemangioma should have a thorough physical examination, since he may have internal lesions. See a doctor if you note any sudden enlargement, bleeding, infection, or spreading of the stain to nearby vital structures such as the eye, nose, or mouth. Bleeding following an injury to the birthmark is common and rarely requires special treatment. In an emergency apply a gauze bandage firmly but not tightly in place until you can get your baby to a doctor.

Parents often find it difficult to watch a birthmark enlarge without demanding that a doctor do something about it. See a dermatologist, even a plastic surgeon, if you'll be helped by a specialist's reassurance that you're best off letting nature take its course.

Most authorities recommend waiting at least four years before treating the ordinary straw-

berry or cavernous hemangioma. By that time
you may be able to see spontaneous improvement. Since birthmarks have no relation to cancer, there is no urgency for treatment.

See also SKIN DISORDERS.

BITE, FAULTY See MALOCCLUSION.

BITES, ANIMAL See ANIMAL BITES.

BITES, HUMAN See ANIMAL BITES.

BLACK-AND-BLUE MARKS See BRUISES.

BLACK DEATH See PLAGUE.

BLACK EYES should be treated as bruises. Applying raw beefsteak or liver to a black eye only
benefits the butcher. It is no more useful than
other types of cold compresses for limiting the
discoloration. See a doctor if vision is fuzzy, or
the eye is painful or cut.

See BRUISES; EYE INJURIES.

BLACK LUNG See DUST DISEASE.

BLADDER CANCER See CANCER OF THE
BLADDER.

BLEEDERS' DISEASE See HEMOPHILIA.

BLEEDING (hemorrhage), when heavy, must be
stopped as quickly as possible. An accident victim can die in less than five minutes if large
blood vessels are cut. In giving first aid, control
of heavy bleeding has priority right after restoration of breathing and heartbeat (see ARTIFICIAL
RESPIRATION; HEART STOPPAGE).

Immediately close the bleeding vessel by applying pressure directly on the wound (see illustration). If necessary, use your bare hands and
press directly into the wound to compress the
artery. Press with the palm of your hand, keeping your fingers flat. Danger of infection can be
dealt with later. Raise the bleeding area higher
than the rest of the body unless there may be
fractures.

If possible make a pad with a clean bandage—
or cloth, tissue, paper towel, or sanitary napkin
—and hold it in place firmly with one or both
hands. If the bleeding persists, add additional
layers of padding to soak up the blood and help
the wound clot. Don't remove old layers of padding. Nor should you disturb any clots that
form.

If the bleeding slows or stops, tie the pad
firmly in place with a bandage, necktie, or anything similar. Also tie the pad in place if you
must keep your hands free to give artificial respiration or treat for heart stoppage.

Be prepared to treat for SHOCK (which see).
Provide fluids and warmth as precautions.

When the injury is to a leg or an arm, apply
enough pressure to control the bleeding, but not
so much as to obstruct the flow of blood to the

STOP BLEEDING WITH DIRECT PRESSURE

Press with cloth as soon as possible
Add layers to soak up blood
Don't disturb clots
Keep pressure on wound

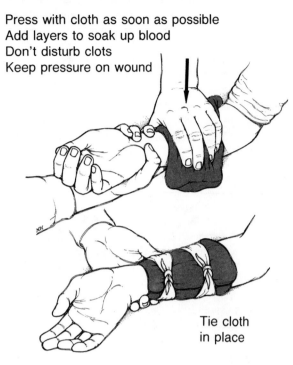

Tie cloth
in place

Don't waste time!
If necessary:
· Use your bare hand
· Compress artery with fingers

rest of the limb. Make sure you can feel a pulse
below the point where the dressing was applied.
If not, loosen the dressing until a pulse can be
felt.

If direct pressure on the wound does not stem
the flow sufficiently, supplement it with pressure
on the artery supplying the wounded area. These
"pressure points" are most likely to be effective
for controlling bleeding in arms and legs.

Because a tourniquet can result in loss of a
limb, don't use one unless the bleeding cannot be
controlled in any other way and the victim
seems likely to bleed to death. Nosebleed is
rarely serious and usually can be quickly remedied with simple measures.

Internal bleeding is extremely serious and requires immediate medical attention. If it is severe, internal bleeding can be controlled only by
emergency surgery. A person may bleed to death
internally—bleed into the chest or into the abdominal or pelvic cavities or into any of the organs—without a drop of blood ever leaving the
body.

Internal bleeding may be caused by a bruising force that tears one of the internal organs. It may result from a hole cut in a blood vessel, as when a bullet or knife passes through the abdominal wall. Fractures may cut into surrounding tissues. Heavy internal bleeding may also accompany such conditions as peptic ulcer, tuberculosis, cancer, and anemia.

Suspect internal bleeding if a person has cold, clammy skin, is restless and thirsty, suffers from faintness and dizziness. Other signs are dilated pupils; shallow or irregular breathing; thin, rapid, weak, and irregular pulse; and feelings of anxiety. You can be fairly certain of internal hemorrhage if the person coughs up or vomits blood, has bloody urine and stools, or if the stools are black and tarry.

Call for medical help immediately. In the meantime treat the victim for SHOCK (which see). Do not give anything to eat or drink. Be prepared to give ARTIFICIAL RESPIRATION (which see).

See also ACCIDENTS; ANEMIA; ARTIFICIAL RESPIRATION; BANDAGES; CANCER; CUTS; NOSEBLEED; PEPTIC ULCER; PULSE; SHOCK; TOURNIQUET; TUBERCULOSIS.

BLISTERS caused by burns should be treated as open wounds. After immersing the area in ice water to relieve pain and avoid scars, apply a bandage with several thicknesses of sterile gauze to keep out air and prevent infection. Avoid opening a blister caused by a burn.

Don't tamper with blisters caused by mouth sores or frostbite. See a doctor if any blister shows signs of infection.

Blisters caused by friction (generally on the hands and feet) are usually best left alone unless located where the surface is apt to be rubbed off, or where continued abrasion might irritate them. In less vulnerable spots all that's required is a light covering while the blister heals and the fluid in it dries up.

If you need to open a friction blister, pierce the edge with a needle that's been sterilized in an open flame. Press the fluid out. Wash the deflated blister and the area around it with soap and water. Keep it covered with a plastic-coated gauze pad or bandage strip until healed.

Prevent friction blisters by wearing work gloves when handling tools like wrenches or rakes. If a shoe chafes your foot, wear a protective pad until you have the fit adjusted—two pairs of socks may give adequate protection. When hiking or taking part in an active sport, wear a lightweight pair of socks under your sweat socks.

See also ACCIDENTS; BURNS; FROSTBITE; MOUTH SORES; SPORTS.

BLISTERS, FEVER See COLD SORES.

BLOOD CANCER See LEUKEMIA.

BLOOD CLOT—a thickened wad of blood—that blocks circulation to the heart is a major cause of heart attack. When a clot obstructs the blood supply to the brain, it commonly causes a stroke.

Clots may also block circulation to the lungs. Such a pulmonary embolism may develop when a patient is allowed to remain virtually inactive after surgery, especially after abdominal or pelvic operations. It also may occur when immobilization is needed—after a leg fracture, for example.

A clot, or portion of a clot, may break loose, then be carried in the bloodstream to the pulmonary artery. This vessel divides within the lung, and its branches subdivide, each division progressively smaller. The clot will finally reach a blood vessel through which it cannot pass, and cut off the blood supply to the part of the lung. If the clot cuts off a large part of the pulmonary artery, the victim could die almost immediately. Even a small clot can cause severe respiratory distress.

Women in childbearing years—especially if taking birth control pills—and men over 60 are most susceptible to pulmonary embolism.

Any condition that involves long periods of bed rest may lead to a clot on the lung.

To prevent embolism anticoagulants are often prescribed. Getting out of bed as soon as possible—or at least exercising the legs while in bed—is invaluable following surgery or childbirth. Wearing elastic stockings after surgery for support of the veins can help prevent postoperative emboli.

Smoking adds to your risk of blood clots. Constricting clothing such as tight garters and boots can interfere with circulation in the legs and lead to blood clots in the veins. As a general rule, avoid such risk factors.

See also ANTICOAGULANTS; BED REST; BIRTH CONTROL; HEART ATTACK; HEART DISEASE; STROKE; THROMBOPHLEBITIS.

BLOOD PRESSURE that's high (hypertension) is a grave—but widely neglected—health hazard. Your blood pressure is the force your blood exerts against your artery walls. If abnormally great, this pressure may scar your arteries, and can force your heart to pump harder and so become inefficiently enlarged.

To detect hypertension get a blood pressure check at least once a year for every member of your family—including children. In addition ask to have your blood pressure read every time you see any physician, whatever the reason for your visit. If you have hypertension, scrupulously stay on medication to control it. This requires self-discipline, since hypertension has no outward signs to motivate you.

According to some studies, if you have high blood pressure, your risk of a stroke is four times higher than normal; of heart attack or heart failure, five times higher. Hypertension is also a major contributor to eye conditions that lead to blindness, and to fatal kidney disease.

Some authorities consider hypertension the nation's leading cause of death. Untreated, it can cut 17 years off a 35-year-old man's life expectancy. For blacks it *is* the leading cause of death.

The silent disease. Hypertension is called the "silent" disease because it can do its damage for years without symptoms. Contrary to popular belief, hypertension does *not* produce such warning signals as dizziness, heart palpitation, headache, shortness of breath, or insomnia. When such a symptom does accompany hypertension, it is from the heart or kidney complications of an advanced hypertensive condition, not from the high pressure itself.

It has been estimated that perhaps seven out of eight people who suffer from hypertension are not being properly treated. The American Heart Association says apathy over hypertension "probably represents the major health care challenge in the country today."

Myths about high blood pressure. Contributing to the neglect are some common misapprehensions:

It's not true that mild high blood pressure is nothing to worry about. This was so widely believed until recently that physicians called the condition "benign hypertension" to indicate that it was harmless. Now physicians recognize—and are trying to convince patients—that even a slight continued elevation of blood pressure is a risk factor that needs lifelong care. Laymen, alas, persist in poohpoohing the disease—or in believing that they are "cured" after brief medication.

It's not only a disease of the elderly. Indeed, the younger you are when hypertension develops, the more years by which it reduces your life expectancy. Large numbers of children have elevated pressures. Without treatment they can suffer strokes or develop hypertensive heart disease or other symptoms before they're out of their twenties.

It's not true that women don't get it. While women are substantially less likely than men to get it in early life, after age 45 the incidence is virtually the same for both sexes.

It's not caused by an ailing heart. Quite the reverse: Heart damage often results from hypertension.

It doesn't necessarily involve anxiety. While emotional stress is often a factor, hypertension can afflict even the tranquil and secure.

What causes it? The cause of most hypertension is unknown, but it is thought that the kidneys or adrenal glands send into the bloodstream substances that cause a contracting of the arterioles. These microscopic arteries regulate blood pressure with the stretching and contracting of muscles in their walls. When they clamp down, more pressure is needed to force blood through them.

In perhaps 15 percent of cases hypertension can be traced to a specific disease: toxemia of pregnancy, coarctation of the aorta (see CONGENITAL HEART DEFECTS), lead poisoning, an adrenal-gland tumor called pheochromocytoma, obstructions of blood flow to the kidneys. Such "secondary" hypertension disappears when the condition is cleared up. The 85 percent of hypertension not related to any other disease is called "primary" or "essential."

Secondary hypertension may result from drugs. Any woman taking birth control pills should get pressure checks at least twice a year.

If you're taking antidepressants that inhibit monoamine oxidase (MAO), ask your doctor about the need to steer clear of certain foods and drugs (see TRANQUILIZERS). These contain compounds that, in combination with the drug, can cause a hypertensive crisis—a sharp, life-threatening rise in blood pressure. Such a crisis is marked by convulsions, stupor, coma, head pains, and vision problems—and needs immediate care in a hospital emergency room.

Have you a close relative with hypertension? If so, you may be at greater than average risk, since hypertension tends to run in families. It's twice as common among brothers, sisters, and children of hypertensives as among relatives of people with normal pressure.

Overweight greatly increases your susceptibility to hypertension. So may chronic emotional stress.

A *brief* rise in blood pressure because of short-term stress is often normal. Be sure you get readings over several weeks before you're diagnosed as hypertensive—your blood pressure may rise merely from tension you feel over having it checked. Also tell your physician if you've recently experienced anger or frustration, or problems related to your work or family.

HOW TO TAKE YOUR BLOOD PRESSURE AT HOME

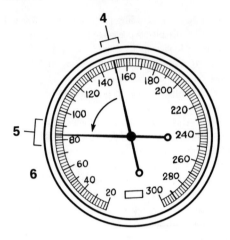

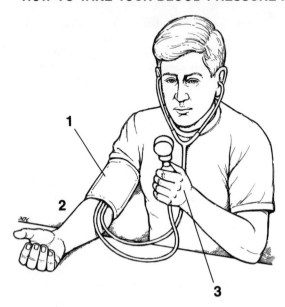

1. **Wrap cuff.** Wear a short-sleeve shirt. Apply the blood pressure cuff directly to the skin around your upper arm. The bottom edge of the cuff should be above your elbow.
2. **Apply stethoscope.** Feel for the arterial pulsation at the bend of your arm. Place the stethoscope (or microphone) gently but firmly over it.
3. **Inflate cuff.** Pump air into the blood pressure cuff with the squeeze bulb until you can no longer feel the arterial pulse.

4. **Release air.** Allow air to escape slowly from the cuff. Watch the numbers on the pressure gauge and listen for the blood pressure "tapping" sounds.
5. **Tapping starts.** When the first tapping sound is heard, note the number on the pressure gauge. This is your systolic (pumping) pressure—or the top number of the blood pressure. It represents the pressure that is generated by the heartbeat that pumps blood to the rest of the body.
6. **Tapping stops.** Note the number on the gauge when you stop hearing the tapping sounds. This is your diastolic (relaxing) pressure, the bottom number of your blood pressure. It represents the pressure in the artery when the heart is filling with blood for the next beat.

Your blood pressure is likely to be lowest when you're lying down. It rises somewhat when you sit up, still more when you stand. It is apt to rise a bit after unusual exercise, though normally it quickly subsides.

Blood pressure range. The magic number is 140/90. That's the high end of the normal blood pressure range for most adults, measured by millimeters of mercury rising in a glass tube. The first and higher number in a reading is always the systolic pressure, resulting from the heart's contraction (systole). The second number is the diastolic pressure, from the between-beat relaxation phase (diastole). The diastolic reading is generally the more critical since it can disclose pressure that's high even when the heart's at rest.

A borderline hypertensive consistently has a diastolic pressure in the 90 to 95 range. Readings chronically above that are considered moderate to severe hypertension.

If you have borderline hypertension, your doctor may initiate therapy, or may ask only to see you at least once a year to check if drug therapy is required. He's more likely to be aggressive in your treatment if your borderline readings persist, or if you are under 45, male, black, have a family history of hypertension, have high blood levels of cholesterol, have diabetes, or show any heart, kidney, or eye damage. All these are risk factors foretelling complications.

If you're hypertensive, you're almost certain to need to stay at normal weight. Merely taking off excess pounds may restore your blood pressure to normal. In addition you may need to modify your diet to keep it low in sodium and saturated fats. Merely cutting down your intake of salt may lower your blood pressure and make medication more effective (see SODIUM).

In a widely used stepped-care approach the first drug you may be prescribed is a thiazide-type diuretic (Esidrix, HydroDIURIL, Hygroton, among many others). These drugs reduce sodium levels and stimulate frequent urination (see EDEMA). Because essential potassium is also excreted, you may need to take a potassium supplement—or eat each day a banana or other foods rich in potassium. A potassium-sparing diuretic (e.g., Aldactone, Dyazide, Midamor) may be used with a thiazide.

If diuretics alone don't work, you may also be prescribed antihypertensive drugs (e.g., Inderal, Lopressor, Tenormin) in increasing dosage and potency. These drugs affect the autonomic nervous system, causing the arteriole walls to relax and thereby lower blood pressure. For many patients these may be the first drugs used.

Tranquilizers may be prescribed to reduce psychological stress, though they are not a substitute for antihypertensive therapy. A drink or two of alcohol before dinner can be relaxing and is sometimes recommended by physicians. Meditation and biofeedback are increasingly being used as methods for lowering your own pressure.

Tell your doctor about any side effects you experience. About half the hypertensives who begin therapy drop out of treatment because the drugs can bring on diarrhea, impotence, dizziness, nausea, fatigue, hives, headache, heart palpitation, cramps, and mental depression.

But the side effects can often be relieved. Your medication can be individualized from the battery of drugs available. Where you may be lethargic and depressed under drug A, you may do beautifully with drug B or with a combination of C plus D. Ask your doctor to seek the combination that gives the most benefits with the fewest possible side effects.

Some doctors find that patients do better on a simple regimen. The fewer pills a day, the better. Conversely, the more frequently you have to take medication, the more likely you are to forget doses. If one drug isn't enough to control your blood pressure, ask your doctor if he might give you a combination tablet rather than two separate pills.

You may be asked to measure your own blood pressure (see the illustration for instructions).

Taking your own pressure is a way to get your true readings over a long period. Readings taken when you're relaxed at home are likely to be more accurate than those taken under stress in a doctor's office. Taking your own readings may encourage you to stay on medication. You see for yourself that your pressure goes down when you take your pills and goes up when you don't.

You may be asked to take six readings a day—while standing and while lying down at each of three times: in the morning upon arising; during the afternoon (if you can't do this on your job, take it upon arriving home); and at bedtime. Bring the record each time you see your doctor.

Also bring your blood pressure monitoring device, termed a sphygmomanometer, for checking and possible resetting. A mercury column is generally more accurate than an aneroid (nonliquid) gauge. Most devices for home use are aneroid, which are less expensive. The greater accuracy, however, can make mercury models worth the extra money. Near-automatic models, using a flashing light or beeper to signal readings, are also available, at higher cost.

If you take your own pressure, expect fluctuations and isolated high readings. Never change the dosage of your medication without checking with your doctor.

Sometimes it's helpful to teach a relative or friend to take your blood pressure. It may not only be easier, but will also involve another person who'll encourage you to adhere to a lifetime of blood pressure control.

Low blood pressure. In contrast to hypertension, low blood pressure is usually an asset. It places less strain on your heart and arteries. In most people lucky enough to have low blood pressure, possibly the only drawback is mild, brief dizziness if you abruptly stand straight after lying down or kneeling. This light-headedness, called orthostatic hypotension, results from a momentary deficiency of blood to the brain. It ordinarily needs treatment only if it causes fainting.

Disabling low blood pressure, accompanied by blackouts and coldness of skin, may be a side effect of treatment for hypertension. It indicates that the dosage needs correcting.

Blood pressure may be lowered dangerously in shock associated with injury, heavy bleeding, poisoning, anemia, thyroid disease, and other glandular defects. Here the pressure may be too low to circulate the blood properly. The pressure is likely to be raised to normal levels with treatment of the underlying condition.

See also DRUGS; HEART ATTACK; HEART DISEASE; HEART FAILURE; KIDNEY DISEASE; PHYSICAL EXAMINATION; STROKE.

BLOOD SUGAR, LOW   See HYPOGLYCEMIA.

BLOOD TRANSFUSION is one of medicine's miracles and can be lifesaving. On occasion it can be dangerous and expensive.

Everyone about to get a transfusion gets his blood typed for its ABO group. This is determined by the presence or absence on red cells of two substances labeled A and B. The cells may contain both substances, in which case your type would be AB. Or they may have only A or only B, making you type A or type B. Or they may be lacking in both substances, and then your blood would be type O. In addition blood is routinely typed for another substance, termed the *Rh factor*. A test determines if the most important Rh factor, $Rh_0(D)$, is present (Rh positive) or absent (Rh negative).

See the table for a guide to safe transfusions. The donor's blood type must be compatible with yours—either the same type or type O, popularly called the "universal donor." Furthermore you and your donor must match as to Rh factor. Note your blood type on your Emergency Medical Identification to save time in case of an accident where you may be unconscious and need transfusions.

There is a slight risk of getting blood of the wrong type. Transfusion practices have improved to such a degree that reactions because of giving the wrong type of blood are infrequent. The patients most likely to have reactions are those who receive multiple transfusions.

In the most common transfusion reaction the patient develops chills and fever. There may also be anxiety, difficulty in breathing, a bursting sensation in the head, and severe pain in the neck, chest, or lower back. Some patients show signs of shock, with cold clammy skin, rapid feeble pulse, a drop in blood pressure, nausea, and vomiting. Reactions to wrong blood type occur during or immediately after the transfusion. While rarely fatal, the reactions are distressing to the patient, who faces repeated transfusions and requires immediate treatment.

One of the risks of blood transfusions is hepatitis. Tens of thousands of Americans who have a transfusion this year will develop this illness from contaminated blood. Many recipients of transfusions will have none of the symptoms, but will unknowingly become carriers of the hepatitis virus, capable of infecting others.

Other dangers arise from drugs a donor has been taking, which may adversely affect the recipient. If you are in shock, with abnormally low blood pressure, blood from a donor who has been taking drugs to relieve high blood pressure might be harmful. Drug-allergy reactions are also possible. When a donor has taken a normal dose of aspirin during the week before donating, it can prolong the recipient's bleeding time for five days or more.

FOR A TRANSFUSION TO BE SAFE

Consider *both* of these	If your blood is	You can get blood from	You can donate blood to
ABO Type	A	A, O	A, AB
	B	B, O	B, AB
	AB ("Universal Recipient")	A, B, AB, O	AB
	O ("Universal Donor")	O	A, B, AB, O
Rh Factor	+ (Positive)	+, −	+
	− (Negative)	−	−, +

Commercial blood. Blood from commercial suppliers is more likely to be contaminated than blood from volunteer donors. Merchants who buy and sell human blood as a commodity supply some 10 percent of the 6.5 million pints transfused each year. In some large cities they provide more than half of all the blood used in hospital transfusions.

By offering a fast $15 or so for a pint of blood, such firms frequently attract donors with a high probability of hepatitis: alcoholics and derelicts living in unsanitary surroundings, narcotic addicts whose contaminated needles spread disease with epidemic velocity. Because of their urgent need for cash, such donors may conceal their past health history.

Blood from commercial sources is 10 to 20 times more likely to cause hepatitis than blood from voluntary donors.

There is no reliable way to detect unsafe blood. The FDA requires blood banks and commercial blood suppliers to test blood for a factor associated with hepatitis, but the test leaves about three out of four cases undetected.

Shortages and expense compound transfusion problems. Hospitals continue to use high-risk blood chiefly because there isn't enough donated voluntarily. Shortages are particularly critical during year-end holidays and summer vacation months, when the most blood is needed and the least is given.

Shortages may worsen as more blood is required each year to meet the needs of a larger population and to keep pace with advances in medical know-how. Open-heart surgery, for example, can require 20 pints of blood.

The cost of blood continues to rise. In addition to the charge for the blood hospitals often add administration costs. The total can run to about $100 per unit.

Transfusion of whole blood is generally needed only for a newborn infant's exchange transfusion, or for a hemorrhage severe enough to cause shock and lack of sufficient oxygen in the blood. More often the patient needs certain specific blood components that have been separated out, such as concentrated red blood cells, platelets (which aid in clotting), Factor VIII concentrate or cryoprecipitate (also called antihemophilic factor or AHF), and plasma (the liquid portion of blood). Plasma can be further broken down to yield other components. Through transfusion of blood components a patient with severe anemia because of hemorrhage can be given red cells alone; one with a low platelet count, platelets; one with classical hemophilia, AHF. This is safer and more economical than administering whole blood to everyone.

Preventing blood hazards. Your safest tactic is to store your own blood. If you are scheduled for elective surgery, give blood weeks in advance. If you are going to have cardiac surgery, for instance, give a unit, wait a month, then give another unit. Because blood ordinarily has a shelf life of three to four weeks, this method can be used only when a freezing process is available.

Another way to reduce the possibility of getting a harmful agent or allergy is to use blood drawn from reliable voluntary donors. Recruit donors from your family and friends, from co-workers, from members of organizations you belong to.

Don't ask anyone to give blood who has frequent and severe allergic reactions. Substances in his blood that are responsible for the reactions can initiate a similar sensitivity in you. Anyone suffering from malaria, anemia, or a fever should not give blood. Chronic disorders such as heart disease or kidney disease make blood donation inadvisable.

You'd do well to join a local blood bank. Under most Red Cross and blood bank plans, donation of a single pint assures you and the members of your family all the blood any of you need during the next year.

If you have other than O-positive or A-positive blood—which account for 75 percent of the population—join the National Rare Blood Club, 164 Fifth Avenue, New York, New York 10010. This is a nationwide blood bank for people with

AB negative (1 person in 200), B negative (1 in 70), AB positive (1 in 25), A negative (1 in 17), O negative (1 in 16), and B positive (1 in 11). Club members appear on short notice to provide fresh blood for other "raries."

See also BLEEDING; EMERGENCY MEDICAL IDENTIFICATION; HEMOPHILIA; HEPATITIS; RH DISEASE.

BLUE BABY See CONGENITAL HEART DEFECTS.

BOATING   If you are thrown from a boat, don't swim for a faraway shore. The odds are heavily against your making it.

Stick with the boat even if it is capsized. Nearly all overturned boats—motorboats, canoes, metal or wood rowboats—will float and are your best life preservers. They also attract rescuers.

If another person was thrown from a capsized boat, lock hands with him over the boat's bottom. This gives you a surer grip and helps prevent exhaustion.

If the boat is still upright but you can't climb aboard, grasp the edges of the boat with your fingers. Submerge to your nose and paddle toward shore. Even a swamped boat will support about as many people as it was designed to normally carry. Hold the boat lightly and let the water support most of your weight.

Cold water survival. To survive in cold water, your best bet is a thermal flotation jacket, insulated with a foamed plastic waterproof lining. These not only keep you warm—they help keep you afloat.

Avoid unnecessary movement in cold water. Thrashing won't warm you. On the contrary, it drains your reserves more quickly, making you more vulnerable to the cold. If help is expected, remain as still as possible in the water. This doubles your chances of survival.

If several people are in the water with life jackets, huddle together to help preserve body heat. If you are alone, bring your knees to your chest.

Your clothing traps a substantial amount of air which provides temporary insulation and flotation. Discard clothes only when they begin to drag you down.

Consider swimming to shore only as a last resort. In 50° F water a person in a standard life jacket and light clothing can swim less than a mile before succumbing to the effects of the cold.

A person who is rescued from cold water should be quickly dried and wrapped in warm clothing and blankets. He should be given hot drinks and a warm bath. An electric blanket will also help warm him. If the person shows signs of hypothermia (see COLD WEATHER), get immediate medical attention.

To avoid accidents. Take a course in safe boat handling. Know and obey Rules of the Road, the standard traffic laws for boats.

Never overload a boat. Place passengers toward the centerline and distribute them evenly so the boat will be slightly down by the stern.

Don't stand in a boat. Kneel while fishing. The higher your center of gravity in a boat, the likelier you are to topple overboard.

Only an experienced person should be in a boat alone. Children need to be accompanied by an adult. Provide a flotation cushion for each person, and see that a Coast Guard–approved life preserver is worn by children and nonswimmers. Of some 1,200 drownings resulting from boating accidents in one year, more than 300 victims did not have a lifesaving device available —and more than 500 others had one but failed to use it.

Before venturing forth, leave a "float plan" with friends or family ashore. Tell when and where you will depart, where you will be cruising, and when and where you will return. If you fail to return in a reasonable time, the person holding your plan can notify the Coast Guard or other authorities.

Include in the float plan a full description of your boat, the name and address of everyone on board, and frequencies or channels you have available on marine radio.

Remember that an offshore wind may make the center of a lake dangerously rough even though the water is smooth near shore. River current or tide is equally dangerous. If you are just going for a ride, go upwind or upstream first, then return with the wind or current.

Keep away from larger, less maneuverable craft, especially at night. Before large swells reach your boat, head into them and slow down so that they will slide under you from end to end. Stay away from steep or rocky shorelines against which you might be thrown.

Have your motor checked before the first trip of the season. Carry an emergency supply of fuel in a National Fire Protection Association (NFPA)–approved can that has a safety spout. To prevent fire, never refuel with the motor running or while smoking. Dry any spilled fuel before starting the motor. A spark may make the boat an inferno.

Reduce the speed of power-driven boats when passing bathing beaches, canoes, or other small boats. Stay as far as possible from other boats, docks, and beaches. Allow a minimum of 100 feet from the red scuba-diving flag bearing a white diagonal stripe running from upper left corner to lower right.

See also DROWNING; FIRE; FISHING; FROSTBITE; SCUBA DIVING.

BOILS were one of Job's afflictions and a curse of God upon the Egyptians. A boil is an enclosed infection of the skin caused by pus-forming bacteria, and generally forms in an infected hair follicle.

The lesion is a tender, hot, red mass with a cone of pus. There may be a small central white area, or a draining area. Unlike CYSTS (which see), the material that drains from a boil is a mixture of germs, cells, and tissues that have been destroyed in the inflammatory reaction.

The staphylococci bacteria that cause the infection usually find entry through the skin via tiny cuts or a constant irritation at the base of hair follicles. Any site of friction, such as the back of the neck or the buttocks, is particularly susceptible. An acne pimple, if squeezed or further infected, may develop into a boil.

An *abscess* is a boil that involves deep tissues under the surface of the skin, whereas a simple boil is on the surface. A *furuncle* is a small boil. A *carbuncle* is a cluster of boils. A *felon* is a painful type of boil near a fingernail. Because the pus cannot discharge through the thick skin, it can damage bone if not cared for.

In most cases a wall around the boil prevents its spreading into surrounding tissue. You should not squeeze a boil because you might break down that wall. The veins of the face connect with the veins of the brain, and fatal brain abscesses have been known to develop from the squeezing of a simple face boil.

Treatment. Don't try to lance or cut open a boil yourself. This is a surgical procedure and requires a physician to remove the core and effect complete drainage of the infection. He may prescribe penicillin or any other suitable antibiotic. In rare cases the doctor may have a vaccine made from some of the pus and then give you injections to build up your body's immunity.

If you have diabetes or heart disease and develop a boil, it is imperative to see a doctor at once.

If the boil is not complicated by other diseases and is not too painful, there are safe home treatments you may try: Use a medicated salve that softens the skin and encourages the infection to drain earlier than it otherwise might. Apply hot compresses to the affected area. This increases circulation, encourages the building of the protective wall, and hastens drainage.

Keep the skin areas around boils clean. Wash your hands each time you touch the affected area. Avoid contact with people with chronic infections like sinusitis—you may reinfect each other.

As a preventive avoid constant friction that may cause irritation in vulnerable areas like the back of the neck. Wash such areas especially often. Never squeeze pimples.

If boils recur or if your whole family comes down with the condition, use an antiseptic soap and wash all underclothing, sheets, and pillowcases in boiling water. Dry-clean blankets and outer clothing.

Frequent bathing by every member of the boil-plagued family is important. Don't let anyone do any cooking who has a boil on the hands or fingers, for the bacteria in the infection may cause food poisoning.

See also SKIN DISORDER.

BONE CANCER   See CANCER OF THE BONE.

BOTULISM is the deadliest form of food poisoning. It almost always results from eating improperly canned food.

The villain is a type of bacteria, *Clostridium botulinum,* which can survive heat that kills most other bacteria, and thrives in an airfree environment such as exists in cans. Waste products released by the bacteria attack nerve centers controlling the muscles of the eyes, throat, and lungs.

A victim generally has drooping eyelids and blurred vision. His muscles are weak. He has a stiff, tight throat, with difficulty speaking, swallowing, breathing. Death usually results from respiratory failure.

A tracheostomy may be lifesaving first aid (see CHOKING). But for survival the victim needs antitoxin and often a mechanical respirator to help him breathe.

Be wary in home canning. Boiling at 212° F destroys the bacteria but not their seedlike spores, which will hatch in the preserved food. To destroy the spores you need to use a pressure cooker to reach a temperature of at least 249° F for 15 minutes.

This is essential for preserving all low-acid foods—meats, most vegetables, mildly acid fruits. The bacteria will not grow in an acid medium, so highly acid foods—some fruits, some foods made with vinegar or lemon juice—can be processed in water-bath canners, in which food is merely boiled.

Freezing is also safe, since the botulism bacteria won't grow at low temperatures. Foods most frequently found to harbor the botulism bacteria are string beans, spinach, corn, peas, asparagus, beets, and some meats—especially home-canned sausage.

Boil home-canned food for a few minutes before serving. That will get rid of any bacteria and toxin. Don't taste the food until it's been boiled. One woman sampled beans she'd put up in a jar before cooking them for her family. She died, whereas none of her family experienced difficulty.

Even a small amount of tainted food can cause poisoning. A woman in San Jose, California, became ill after a mere teaspoonful of infected chili sauce. A man at the same Thanksgiving dinner consumed a few tablespoonsful of the sauce and died.

Stay on guard even if other canned jars in the same batch prove safe. It's not unusual for toxin to be present in only a single jar of several prepared at the same time. In Louisville, Kentucky, an amateur gardener prepared 28 cans of tomato juice. He drank 27 without ill effect. With the last he developed botulism from a single swallow.

Throw out any food that has a suspicious odor or appearance. Be especially wary of spicy food whose strong taste may mask spoilage. Smoked fish causes many outbreaks of botulism.

Although botulism is rare from commercial canning, don't be lulled by commercially canned foods of even a high-priced brand. A Westchester County, New York, couple had vichyssoise soup of the Bon Vivant gourmet line. The husband died of botulism. His wife, who ate only a small amount because she thought it tasted spoiled, became critically ill. The company went out of business.

See also CANNED FOOD; FOOD POISONING.

BRAIN CANCER   See CANCER OF THE BRAIN.

BRAIN FEVER   See ENCEPHALITIS.

BRAIN TUMOR   See CANCER OF THE BRAIN.

BRANCHIAL CYSTS   See CYSTS.

BREAST CANCER See CANCER OF THE BREAST.

BREASTFEEDING (nursing) is generally better for your baby than bottle feeding. The American Academy of Pediatrics has recommended that all physicians encourage all mothers to breast-feed their infants, declaring that breast milk is "the best food for every newborn infant."

Breast milk is a natural vaccine. It temporarily transmits to the infant the mother's defenses against harmful bacteria and viruses. It also appears to trigger the infant's own defense system.

A nursed baby is less likely to suffer from diarrhea and other intestinal upsets; is less prone to allergy; and is less likely to suffer from infections such as severe colds, bronchitis, and croup. Breast milk is a more complete food for babies than formula from cow's milk. A breast-fed baby is less likely to be an obese child or develop weight problems as an adult.

Breastfeeding is also more convenient than bottle feeding. All the mother need do is accompany the baby—and the source of supply is available, clean, and free. Breastfeeding is a valuable hygienic measure where sanitary conditions are inadequate.

Many women report that the nursing experience is intensely pleasurable. Nursing mothers are more likely than bottle feeders to touch their babies, rock them, cuddle them, rest with them. This enhances mother-infant relations, and provides the baby with the maximum opportunity for beneficial sensory stimulation.

Breastfeeding also causes the uterus to return faster to its prepregnancy size. Nursing mothers don't face the slightly increased risk of blood clots associated with the use of estrogens to suppress milk flow.

If you plan to breast-feed your baby, discuss it with your doctor or your pediatrician during your pregnancy. Contact your local LaLeche League, an organization that provides information and support to nursing mothers. Go to meetings before your baby is born and ask for some good books about breastfeeding.

Milk supply has nothing to do with breast size. You can have extremely small breasts and still breast-feed your baby. Nor does a nursing infant cause your breasts to sag. A good nursing bra provides comfort and easy access to the breast for nursing.

You may not begin to menstruate for many months while breastfeeding, but don't consider it a method of birth control. You may begin to ovulate even before your periods resume. But don't use birth control pills while you're nursing.

Avoid all drugs as much as possible while you're nursing. Almost every drug you take passes to your baby through your breast milk, with possibly harmful effects. Consult your pediatrician if it becomes necessary for you to take drugs.

If you must take an aspirin or over-the-counter cold remedy, do so just after nursing. Don't nurse your baby if you are taking anti-cancer drugs, steroids, or therapeutic doses of radioactive iodine. (Also avoid breastfeeding if you suffer from tuberculosis, severe malnutrition, or a chronic debilitating disease.)

Ordinarily you can have a drink or two of alcohol without its adversely affecting your child.

Nursing hints. Don't wash your nipples with soap or alcohol. Use a breast cream such as Masse Cream or lanolin after each feeding. This will help prevent cracking and soreness. You needn't wipe it off before nursing your baby. If your nipples do become red and irritated—a common complaint of nursing mothers—it helps to expose them to the air as much as possible between feedings. Nipples heal very rapidly and the baby can probably continue nursing as usual while the nipples heal. Shorter, more frequent feedings will be more comfortable if your nipple is sore.

Get into a comfortable, relaxed position to nurse your baby. This will prevent neck and back strain. For each feeding alternate the breast you start the baby on: if you offer the left breast, then the right, for one feeding, start with the right breast for the next. Drink about 1½ quarts of milk or its equivalent in cheese or yogurt daily. Get as much rest as possible.

To begin nursing support your breast with one hand, grasping the nipple between your thumb and forefinger. Draw your baby close until his cheek is touching your breast, with the nipple next to his mouth. He will turn his head toward it and open his mouth. Then pull him closer until he can get the nipple and some of the areola into his mouth. Make sure his nose is not covered by your breast; if it is, use a finger of your free hand to push your breast away from the baby's nose so he can breathe easily.

Sometimes your breast may be so full of milk that your nipple and areola are hard (engorged), making it difficult for the baby to grasp the nipple. Express some of the milk by hand before nursing the baby. Shorter, more frequent feedings will help relieve engorgement.

Don't worry that your baby is not getting enough milk. Some women are concerned— since they can't tell how much milk the baby is getting—that their milk supply is inadequate. Let your baby tell you how much he needs. Generally breast-fed babies need to nurse every three hours for the first few weeks. A baby is generally getting enough to drink if he's not crying a lot between meals and is urinating normally.

Breast milk operates on the principle of supply and demand. The more a child nurses, the more the supply increases. As your baby grows and his need for nourishment increases, he'll nurse more frequently to increase the supply. Once the increased supply is established, the baby will want to nurse less often.

If you'll be away during your baby's usual nursing time, your baby can be given a bottle of premixed formula—or, for babies over five or six months, regular cow's milk. (Do not give skimmed or low-fat milk to a child under two.) Alternatively, your baby can be fed milk that you've previously expressed and frozen. You can safely freeze your milk for up to a month, or store it in the refrigerator for up to 48 hours.

Bottle feeding. If you bottle-feed your baby, hold him nestled partially sitting up against one arm while you hold the bottle with the other hand. Your baby needs the closeness of being held during feeding.

Don't prop the bottle for the baby to drink and leave him unattended. He might swallow a lot of air, have difficulty swallowing, or even choke. A propped bottle can also lead to tooth decay—milk or formula may remain in the mouth all night.

Don't let your baby drink while he's lying down. In this position liquid can flow from the mouth into the middle ear, possibly causing ear infection.

See also BIRTH CONTROL; CHILDBIRTH; PREGNANCY.

BREAST SAGGING may develop following pregnancy, most likely because their elastic tissues are repeatedly stretched by increases in size during pregnancies. A great weight loss can also cause breasts to sag and flatten.

Surgery can temporarily relieve severely sagging breasts. The first stage raises the breasts by cutting out excess skin and tissue and ordinarily takes two to three hours and requires several days in the hospital. After two or three months' healing time implants are inserted to augment the size of the breasts if needed. Within three to five years, however, the sag usually returns.

To avoid breast sag wear a bra. Some degree of flattening is part of the normal aging process, and currently, physicians disagree as to whether the problem may be accelerated in women who habitually go braless.

Bralessness is particularly hazardous for large-breasted women, and those who have had several pregnancies or large weight losses. Without the added support of a bra, the fragile breast ligaments may gradually weaken, giving the breasts a flat, pendulous appearance.

Enlarged breasts. In rare cases a woman of normal weight develops extremely enlarged breasts. There is no known cause, nor is there any drug, hormone, or other medical treatment for reducing the size of the breasts.

Special brassieres, available through a surgical supply company, will help most women with over-large breasts to be comfortable.

For women who suffer physical and/or psychological discomfort from huge breasts, surgery is available. Excess skin and breast tissue is removed, and the nipple is often transplanted. Breast reduction is a lengthy surgical procedure —about four or five hours—and usually requires about ten days of hospitalization.

See also PREGNANCY.

BREAST SMALLNESS (flat-chestedness) is a social rather than biological problem. Many women feel inadequate and self-conscious about what they consider undersized breasts. Yet the size of a woman's breasts is no indication of her femininity, her sexual capacity, or her ability to bear children or to nurse them. It is not true that breastfeeding causes breasts to decrease in size with each child nursed.

A thin woman with small breasts may increase her breast size merely by gaining some weight. Otherwise there is no known preparation, exercise plan, or mechanical device that can affect breast size.

If you want your breasts enlarged, see a plastic surgeon. An operation called breast augmentation is the only way to increase breast size to any significant degree. It takes about two hours and usually requires about a week in the hospital. Some doctors do it as an office procedure.

The surgeon cuts an incision at the underfold of the breast and inserts a silicone-rubber bag filled with silicone gel. The bag, which closely duplicates the shape and consistency of breast tissue, is harmless.

There will be fairly small and inconspicuous permanent scars beneath the breasts. You'll have some degree of discomfort and pain during the two- to four-week healing process.

Some women experience discomfort and drainage from the surgical incision that may persist for many months. In such cases the implants may have to be removed.

Implanted breasts feel firmer than normal breasts, especially if you have little breast tissue of your own. The more tissue over the implant, the more natural it feels. The same procedure is used in part of the relief for breast sagging.

Purely for psychological reasons, many women who have had their breasts surgically enlarged report strong feelings of increased adequacy and a greater interest in sex.

Liquid silicone prohibited. The injection of liquid silicone for increasing breast size is prohibited by the Food and Drug Administration (FDA). Don't believe any doctor who tells you it's safe, nor confuse liquid silicone with the silicone gel implants used in augmentation surgery.

The results of injectable silicone are unpredictable. Deaths have occurred. Some women have had to have both breasts removed to save their lives.

Injected silicone may mask malignancy. Globules of the plastic form pseudocysts, which may be hard to differentiate from cancerous tumors.

By contrast, in accepted plastic surgery procedure the material is inserted under the woman's own breast tissue, and thus does not interfere with the detection of malignancy.

Some physicians illegally offer liquid silicone injections to uninformed women. The liquid silicone used by these nonauthorized physicians is not the pure medical-grade product available only to the registered investigators. Injection with a substitute liquid exposes the women to further unnecessary hazards.

For women who have had silicone injections, it is often possible to remove the injected silicone and replace it with a silicone-gel implant.

Exercise plans don't work. Be wary of products that purport to increase breast size. Some mail-order operations advertise exercise plans for breast development—they are almost entirely worthless.

Since the breast has no muscles, exercises can merely tone up the chest-wall muscles beneath them. This may contribute to the overall prominence of the breasts, but it may also give a woman a barrel-chested appearance. It cannot improve her breast contour.

Often these come-ons are accompanied by impressive before-and-after photographs: on the left a small-breasted woman; on the right the same woman presumably after the exercise plan, with huge breasts. The difference may be merely a change in posture. Or it may be a matter of trick photography. Sometimes women who resemble each other are used in the before-and-after pictures.

Other mail frauds for breast enlargements may pose an actual threat to your health. One gadget was a suction device that forced temporary swelling of the breast tissue. Users were encouraged to believe that if they persevered, some of the temporary swelling would become permanent.

At Post Office hearings the government's medical witness testified that the device was not only worthless, but possibly dangerous. It might cause unknown cancer to spread more rapidly.

Other dangerous breast-enlargement products may contain female hormones like estrogen. These products can upset the body's own hormone balance, possibly disrupting menstruation and accelerating unsuspected breast cancer.

See also BREAST SAGGING; CANCER OF THE BREAST.

BREATH, BAD See MOUTH ODOR.

BREATH-HOLDING rarely causes children any harm even if they faint, turn blue, or go into convulsions.

It's a tactic frequently used by a child trying to get his own way. Your best course is to display an attitude of purposeful neglect to prevent the child from using the spells as a means of dominating the family.

The habit generally begins before age 18 months, frequently during the early weeks of life. It may happen anywhere from several times a day to only once a month. Attacks usually are brought on by anger, frustration, pain, or fear.

In an episode the child cries violently. Then the crying halts abruptly and he stops breathing. He turns blue and may become unconscious and twitch convulsively from too little oxygen.

Breath-holders usually are active, energetic children who react vigorously to many situations. The placid child usually is immune. In most cases breath-holding spells taper off gradually and stop before age six, with the child's cessation of violent crying.

During a spell place the child in a safe position. As he recovers, leave him to himself. Display an attitude of unconcern to prevent him from gaining satisfaction from his performance.

Convulsions last only a few seconds and require no treatment. If the child has serious behavior problems, call them to the attention of your doctor. He may recommend a consultation with a neurologist or psychiatrist.

See also CONVULSIONS; RESPIRATORY DISEASE.

BREATHLESSNESS See SHORTNESS OF BREATH.

BRIGHT'S DISEASE See KIDNEY DISEASE.

BROKEN BONES See FRACTURES.

BRONCHIECTASIS is a respiratory disease in which the air passages (bronchi) balloon out into little pockets that collect mucus. This sets the stage for infection, which aggravates the condition and produces still more mucus.

The main symptom is coughing that sends the victim into a sudden, violent spasm. It usually comes every morning, with any change in the body's position, especially following a laugh. While the bronchiectasis patients feel well despite their "graveyard cough," they occasionally are unable to hold jobs in which they meet the public.

The coughs usually bring up a great amount of thick mucus, frequently foul-smelling. Spitting up of blood may occur. Colds develop easily into pneumonia.

Many cases begin with such respiratory diseases as influenza or tuberculosis. A severe attack of whooping cough or measles can weaken the walls of the bronchial tubes and cause the pockets of infection to form.

An obstruction that presses on the bronchial tubes from the outside or blocks them from the inside may cause bronchiectasis. Sometimes a child swallows a peanut "the wrong way." It is trapped in the bronchial tubes, cuts off air, and injures the walls of the tubes.

Treatment generally includes inhaling substances to make the mucus more liquid, thus easier to cough up. Postural drainage is a simple way of getting relief: Lie down several times a day, with your head hanging far over the side of a bed or table. The bronchial tubes drain more easily in this upside-down position.

Surgery is effective if the disease is confined to one portion of the lung. Then the damaged part can be removed. Since bronchiectasis victims are susceptible to acute bronchitis and pneumonia, the doctor may prescribe antibiotics.

See also CHOKING; COUGHING; RESPIRATORY DISEASE.

BRONCHITIS isn't usually considered a killer. Thus many people neglect chronic bronchitis until it is in an advanced stage. Often by the time a victim goes to his doctor, his lungs have been severely injured. Then he may be susceptible to other types of respiratory disease and resulting heart disease.

Bronchitis is an inflammation of the lining of the bronchial tubes, which connect the windpipe with the lungs. When the bronchi are inflamed and infected, the airflow to and from the lungs becomes labored and you cough up a heavy mucus (phlegm).

Acute bronchitis is not ordinarily cause for concern. Marked by fever, coughing, and spitting, it is often a complication of colds. These infections make you more susceptible to bacteria in your throat, permitting them to invade your bronchial tubes. Sinusitis and hoarseness frequently accompany the bronchial inflammation.

Acute bronchitis may occur with influenza, whooping cough, measles, and chickenpox. It also can result from inhaling smoke, chemical fumes, or irritating gases.

Acute bronchitis can threaten the life of a child in poor health or an adult with emphysema or heart disease. Otherwise severe complications are rare. As the original condition clears up, acute bronchitis generally becomes less severe. It seldom lasts more than a few weeks.

Chronic bronchitis is another story. The term *chronic* is applied when the coughing and spitting continue for several months and return each year, lasting slightly longer after each winter cold. The cough is usually loose and rattling, worse in the morning and evening than middle of the day, and worse in damp or cold weather than in warm, dry periods. It may be wrongly dismissed as a "smoker's cough." Chronic bronchitis is almost always associated with heavy use of cigarettes. The other common source of irritation is air pollution. Most victims live in cities where polluted air is a problem.

The condition creeps up on you. Often without your noticing it, the amount of phlegm and the duration of coughing increase from year to year until there is never a complete remission. If there is no change in environmental conditions, the disease tends to lead to emphysema.

Bronchial pneumonia may occur as a complication. Abdominal hernia may be produced or made worse by the chronic cough.

The disease is likely to begin in middle age and to get worse as the years go on unless you seek help from a doctor early. Almost four times as many men get chronic bronchitis as women.

To clear up and prevent chronic bronchitis you need to give up smoking. If you are exposed to dust and fumes at work, your doctor may urge you to move to another job and perhaps to a warm, dust-free climate. Before making a permanent move visit a new area for a month to see if the changed climate really helps.

Avoid fatigue. Sleep in a warm bedroom free of drafts. Maintain adequate humidity in your home. A general upbuilding of health, including a high-vitamin diet and mild daily exercise, help increase resistance to infections. Ask your doctor about being vaccinated against influenza and pneumonia. Avoid exposure to colds and flu.

During attacks bronchodilators prescribed by a physician can make breathing easier by shrinking the swollen linings of the airways. Antibiotics are effective against bacterial infections.

See also AIR POLLUTION; EMPHYSEMA; RESPIRATORY DISEASE; SMOKING.

BRUCELLOSIS (undulant fever, Malta fever, Mediterranean fever) came to light in the last century, when British soldiers and sailors on the Mediterranean island of Malta were falling ill with what seemed to be a type of madness.

Victims were extremely irritable and depressed. They suffered from fatigue and sleeplessness, and literally shook from nervousness. Their problem proved to be a bacterial animal disease caught from drinking raw milk.

Labeled *brucellosis* after Sir David Bruce, an early investigator, this infectious disease remains fairly common in agricultural areas, especially as an occupational disease among farm workers. It is widespread among cattle, hogs, goats, and sheep. Many farmers know brucellosis as "contagious abortion" because it causes cows to lose their unborn calves.

Symptoms of brucellosis. In humans it was formerly called *undulant fever* because the fever that accompanies it undulates, or comes and goes in waves, between 98° F and 104° F in a day. Symptoms may begin after a 5- to 21-day incubation period with a general feeling of tiredness and possibly a slight fever. Other victims may have a sudden onset of chills, night sweats, pain in the joints, nervousness.

Extreme weakness is the most common symptom. The sufferer may feel comfortable while resting. But the slightest exertion induces overpowering exhaustion.

Often the victim becomes distraught in the belief that brucellosis is a chronic, debilitating disease for which there is no satisfactory treatment. It is important to reassure him he is almost certain to recover, although it may take time.

The disease may last from a few days to many years, depending on the severity of the case. With antibiotics about 85 percent of victims recover within three months. In some cases there are flare-ups of earlier symptoms, an allergic response to contact with the brucella organism. Deaths from brucellosis are extremely rare.

See a doctor. Call a physician immediately if symptoms occur. The earlier treatment begins, the shorter the course is likely to be.

A doctor can distinguish brucellosis from mononucleosis, influenza, and a host of other diseases (including tuberculosis, typhoid fever, and Hodgkin's disease) having similar symptoms.

Your physician can help locate the sources of infection and prevent the spread of the disease to other members of your family or to the community. He can report the case to local public-health authorities as required by most states, so these officials can disinfect contaminated areas and search for infection among livestock and packinghouses.

Protection and prevention. To protect yourself against brucellosis, drink only milk that is pasteurized. When only raw milk is obtainable, boil it before drinking.

Eat only cooked meat and meat products. The bacteria that cause the disease are readily killed by normal cooking temperatures. Smoked ham, processed at high temperatures, is generally safe. Insist that any meat you buy be U.S. Government–inspected.

Brucellosis in cattle is now rare, thanks to a program of eradicating diseased herds. But among swine the disease is on the rise, and infected hogs cause most of the brucellosis in the United States. Sheep and goats spread the disease more in other parts of the world.

Most U.S. cases occur among people who are exposed to diseased animals through work on hog farms and in meat-packing or processing plants. The brucella bacteria may enter the body through the mouth, eyes, or air passages, even through unbroken skin. In some areas the infection rate is estimated as high as 20 percent of hog producers.

See also ANIMAL DISEASE; INFECTIOUS DISEASE.

BRUISES (black-and-blue marks, contusions) commonly occur after accidents in which a blow breaks tiny blood vessels beneath the skin. The escaped blood often appears blue-black.

To limit the discoloration apply cold wet compresses. Some authorities recommend hot compresses. Applying a towel with ice packs may help. If the skin is broken, treat for cuts as well. See a physician for bruises behind the ear or on the abdomen, which might indicate a serious injury.

See also ACCIDENTS; COMPRESSES; CUTS.

BUBONIC PLAGUE See PLAGUE.

BUCK TEETH See MALOCCLUSION.

BUERGER'S DISEASE See SMOKING.

BUNIONS are deformities at the big toe joint, causing the toe to slant outward. The bony structure of the foot is inherited, and if the bulge is there, it may be aggravated by wearing shoes that are too tight or too short. This causes pressure on the bones, causing an inflammation of the bursa, the fluid-filled sac at the joint. Bunions can become swollen and painful, and the bulging bone can make wearing normal shoes impossible.

Corrective shoes and padding may relieve the discomfort of a bunion. In more severe cases surgery is often required to remove a spur or wedge of bone. No corn-remover can cure a bunion, nor can any known product dissolve or reduce it.

See also FOOT PROBLEMS.

BURIAL See DEATH.

BURNS should be immediately treated with cold water. This reduces pain, prevents blisters and scars, and aids in healing.

For mild and moderate burns run cold water over the burn for 30 minutes. Or immerse a burned hand or foot in a tub of water. For other parts of the body remove clothing and apply cold compresses. Don't bathe in cold water—

RX FOR BURNS: COLD WATER—IMMEDIATELY!

Soak at least 30 minutes
Remove rings

For large burns

Apply cold wet towels

prolonged bathing in cold water can be injurious. Don't apply ice to the burn or you may cause frostbite.

You can safely treat at home only first-degree burns and second-degree burns covering a small area.

First-degree burns are the most mild. They are characterized by redness, mild swelling, and pain. The skin is unbroken and there are no blisters.

After treating with cold water cover the first-degree burn with a clean bandage. Do not apply grease or oil to any burn. For all burns remove any jewelry, such as rings or watchbands, since there is likely to be swelling.

Second-degree burns are characterized by a red, blotchy or streaking appearance. The area swells and blisters. The surface of the skin is moist and oozy, and the burned area is painful.

After treating with cold water cover the burned area with a dry, sterile bandage. Elevate burned arms or legs. Do not break blisters.

Larger second-degree burns call for a doctor's immediate attention. An adult who has suffered burns over 15 percent of his body surface requires hospitalization. So does a child with 10 percent of his body burned.

Cover large second-degree burns with a clean dressing—towels, sheets, pillowcase, etc. If the burn is on the face, check the victim's breathing frequently. Swelling of the respiratory tract may obstruct breathing. Give artificial respiration if necessary.

Burns accompanying electric shock may cook the tissues and also are medical emergencies. Deep sunburn, too, may require prompt physician's care.

Third-degree burns, the most serious, destroy all layers of the skin. There is little pain, since nerve endings are destroyed. The burned area appears white or charred.

Seek medical help immediately. See a doctor for even a very small third-degree burn.

Cover the burned area with thick, sterile dressings—such as clean towels, sheets, disposable diapers. Do not remove clothes that are stuck to the burn.

Place a cold cloth or cool water on burns of the face, hands, or feet. Elevate burned hands and feet. Do not allow the victim to walk on burned feet.

SHOCK (which see) is a major threat in burn cases. Keep a victim lying down, with his feet up. If he is conscious and medical help is more than one hour away, give a solution of 1 teaspoon salt and ½ teaspoon baking soda mixed into 1 quart water: 4 ounces every 15 minutes for an adult, 2 ounces for a child. Clear juices may also be given.

Give artificial respiration if the burn victim has stopped breathing. Avoid breaking burn blisters.

Never put ice or ice water on third-degree burns. If a victim has burns on his neck or face, have him sit or prop his head up with pillows. Check his breathing frequently.

For chemical burns, wash off the chemical with plenty of water. Flush the eyes first. Continue to flush with water while removing clothing from burned area. If container of chemical causing burn is available, follow instructions on label. Seek medical help.

Besides shock and respiratory distress, dehydration and infection are major problems in severe burns. Of the 130,000 people who are hospitalized with burns each year, 12,000 of them die.

To treat burns in hospitals or in specialized burn centers, antibiotics are given to guard against infection. Temporary skin grafts—from skin taken from pigs or the victim's close relatives—offer lifesaving protection against fluid

FLOOD CHEMICAL BURNS WITH WATER

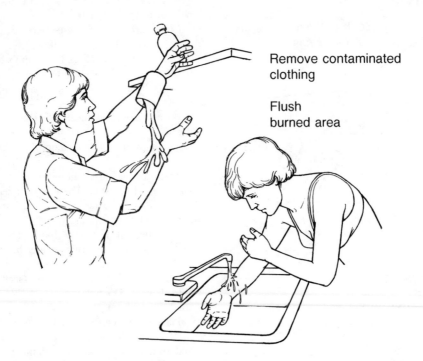

Remove contaminated clothing

Flush burned area

loss or infection. Later the patient's own skin from unburned areas is permanently grafted.

Artificial skin is a promising new development. Made of two layers—of silicone and proteins taken from shark cartilage—it is eventually replaced by the patient's body, just as natural skin is continually renewed.

To prevent burns, the National Safety Council recommends that parents teach toddlers the meaning of *hot.* "Say 'Hot!' if you see a youngster about to touch a hot pan or a lighted cigarette—or something else that'll hurt a little, but not give a bad burn," advises the council. "If he touches it, he'll feel what 'hot' is—and he'll learn to respect your warnings."

To avoid many accidents causing burns follow precautions against FIRE (which see). Also keep your water heater below 120° F. Hot tap water is often kept at scalding temperatures, and has caused many burns and deaths in the bath or shower.

See also ACCIDENTS; ARTIFICIAL RESPIRA-TION; BLISTERS; COMPRESSES; ELECTRIC SHOCK; FIRE; SHOCK; SUNBURN.

BURPING See GAS.

BURSITIS is a common and sometimes very painful condition in which injury or inflammation of a bursa (a small sac between tendon and joint), tendons, and tendon sheaths may cause a pain in the shoulder or other area. Even a mild injury or strain can bring on pain. Bursitis may occur in other joints of the body, such as the hips or elbows. Depending on the nature of the problem, pain-relieving drugs, injections of cortisone, physical therapy, and perhaps surgery are used for relief.

See also ARTHRITIS.

CAISSON DISEASE See SCUBA DIVING.

CALCIUM See MINERALS.

CALLUSES are most common on the soles of the feet. They usually come from pressure produced by poorly fitted shoes or structural problems of the foot.

A callus is a hard mass of skin surrounded by an inflamed rim. The area of callus does not stretch when you flex your feet, and the result may be a burning sensation.

To speed the disappearance of calluses you can file them down with an emery board two or three nights a week after a bath. Don't use a knife, razor blade, or liquid chemical.

Unmedicated callus pads, available at drugstores and shoe stores, may bring relief by adjusting the weight distribution to different parts of the foot. A large, persistent callus may require the help of a family physician or a podiatrist.

See also FOOT PROBLEMS.

CAMPING outdoors is a safe and healthy pastime as long as you follow some simple guidelines.

Choosing a site. Ideally, locate your camp area on high ground where there is natural drainage and more chance of a breeze to keep insects away. Don't dig a ditch around your tent for drainage—it causes soil erosion, damages trees, and makes a mudhole for future campers.

Avoid swampy, low sites in which mosquitoes breed. Canyons and dry streambeds can become death traps in flash floods. Don't get too close to any stream that may overflow and get chilly at night. Cliffs, including overhanging ones, are an obvious danger.

To avoid accidents scout the area for hazards. Ask questions of custodians, other campers, or nearby residents. When you get the lay of the land, instruct your children about what they may do and where they may go. Have your family wear footwear, since campgrounds are often covered with glass, cans, and sharp rocks.

Fire and gas. Before you build a fire, be sure it is not prohibited because of dry conditions. Select a spot where it can be built on sand, clay, loam, or rocks and there is no danger of it spreading through underground humus. Clear away leaves, pine needles, or any combustible material for several feet around the site. Locate it downwind from your campsite, and avoid building it next to a log, stump, or low branches.

A small fire is safer and best for cooking and comfort. Building it on a slight mound provides drainage and helps keep it going in a shower or if a pot is spilled. Dig a trench if it is windy or if you have no stones for a windbreak.

To avoid burns don't wear loose, floppy clothing while tending the fire, or let children play near it. And watch those marshmallows—they carry flame and can be exceedingly hot (the pointed sticks are dangerous, too).

When extinguishing a fire, let it die down. Break up the coals. Soak them several times with water. Cover them with dirt or sand.

Keep fuel for a camp stove in an approved metal container outdoors out of the sun. Refill the stove only outdoors and when it is cool.

When using a fuel-burning stove, heater, or lantern in a closed tent or trailer, have plenty of ventilation to avoid carbon monoxide poisoning (see GAS POISONING). Tent or camper stoves require a flue to carry smoke and fumes outside. Keep a stove or lantern away from tent walls.

Flora and fauna. Take along a snakebite kit, and don't play with animals. Unusually docile, friendly wild animals may be carrying a form of rabies.

Discourage animals from coming into your camp by storing food in your car with the windows closed. Deeper in the woods, store your food in a sturdy box and hang it from a stout tree limb. Wash your dishes as soon as you've finished eating. If animals come into camp, scare them with a flashlight, beating on a pan, or yelling.

Be prepared to cope with insect bites. Divert flies, hornets, and bees by placing bits of food away from the campsite.

Watch out for poison ivy. Before foraging from nature, be certain you know poisonous plants from safe ones.

First aid supplies. Assemble a kit of medical items for emergencies. Keep medical supplies in a separate box or suitcase with strong catches to discourage children from opening it. A fishing-tackle box will easily accommodate all the following except the splints:

Adhesive bandages such as Band-Aids—the nonmedicated type.

Roll bandages, in 1-inch and 2-inch sizes.

Sterile gauze pads, 3 by 3 inches, wrapped separately. Take about a dozen.

Sterile gauze pads impregnated with petroleum

jelly, wrapped separately, for covering minor burns.

Adhesive tape, in 1-inch or 2-inch size.

Elastic bandage, about 3 inches wide, for splinting sprained joints.

Splints, including a board at least 4 feet long, 6 inches wide, and ½-inch thick, for splinting a leg or spine, and several thin basswood splints for arm fractures.

Large triangular bandage. A piece of sheet about 4 feet square will serve. The Red Cross first aid book shows many uses for this bandage, but it is most commonly used as a sling.

Large safety pins for fastening the triangular bandage when used as a sling.

Tongue depressors. These serve also as finger splints.

Scissors, large and sharp enough to cut gauze or cloth.

Tweezers for removing splinters. A large needle (and matches to sterilize it) may also be useful for dealing with small embedded splinters or thorns.

Clinical thermometer, in a case to keep it from being broken.

Aspirin or acetaminophen.

Phenolated calamine lotion USP, to soothe insect bites and skin eruptions.

Rubbing alcohol, the only antiseptic needed for ordinary first aid measures—to be used around, not in, wounds. It also has a number of other first aid applications.

Cascara sagrada extract tablets NF. This laxative will take up less room than milk of magnesia, which is usually recommended. Many people find a trip constipating and a mild laxative can help them through the transition period. Use sparingly.

Tincture of opium USP (a prescription drug), for treatment of acute diarrhea.

See also ACCIDENTS; ANIMAL BITES; AXES; CHIGGERS; COLD WEATHER; FLIES; FOOD POISONING; GUNSHOT WOUNDS; HIKING; HOT WEATHER; INSECTS; INSECT STINGS; MOSQUITOES; POISON IVY; POISONOUS PLANTS; SCORPIONS; SNAKEBITE; SUNBURN; TICKS; WATER CONTAMINATION.

CAMPS "David is missing," the camp director telephoned the parents of 15-year-old David Kurman.

The boy had been canoeing on the Penobscot River in Maine when his canoe overturned. He drowned in the accident. Mitch Kurman, David's father, investigated.

He found the Penobscot was a torrent of white water and jagged rocks. The counselor leading the boys had been warned by a forest ranger not to attempt the Penobscot. He was unfamiliar with its waters. His own canoe smashed into rocks at the start of the outing. Yet he persisted in leading his charges on the trip.

Could such an accident happen at the camp where you plan to send your youngster? Mitch Kurman believes so. As a result of David's death, he has become an authority on camp safety—and a crusader for eliminating the many hazards he's uncovered.

There are at least 250,000 accidents reported each year at the 12,000 summer camps attended by some 8 million boys and girls. Many more accidents are not reported.

Laws regulating camp safety are inadequate. Nor do camp owners regulate themselves. Some of the most conscientious belong to the American Camping Association. But association inspectors have found that one in eight member camps fail to live up to the association's minimal, voluntary safety standards.

Don't believe the words *certified* or *approved* stamped on camp brochures. Most likely the camps do their own "approving." Nor does a high price guarantee adequate safety standards or personnel. Expensive camps are no more or less likely to be safe than nonprofit ones like those run by the YMCA or Boy Scouts.

Checking on a camp. Before sending your child off to camp, find out all you can about it. Question the parents of children who have vacationed there before. The director of a well-run camp will not hesitate to supply you with names in your area to call.

Visit the camp before you entrust your child's life to it. You can have little idea of how a camp functions unless you see it in operation. Following are minimum precautions to insist on:

Adequate medical precautions. A doctor or registered nurse should be on call at all times. Someone should always be available who has a Red Cross certificate in advanced first aid.

Physical examinations should be required of campers and counselors. Records should be kept of first aid and other medical treatment.

Adequate fire prevention. There should be frequent fire drills, fire patrols at night, and at least two emergency exits for each ground-level bunkhouse.

Buildings more than one floor high should have readily accessible fire escapes. All inflammables like gasoline and pool chemicals should be stored far from activity centers, and kept under lock.

Adequate water safety. Every camp with a swimming program needs a waterfront director over 21 years old with a current Red Cross water safety instructor's certificate. There should be at least 1 senior lifeguard on duty for every 25 swimmers. Bathing areas should be marked off according to the swimming ability of various groups, and located at a distance far enough away from rocks or tricky currents to avoid accidents.

All boats should be locked when not in use. All campers should be required to take an advanced swimming test before being allowed to participate in water sports, and also required to wear life preservers when boating or water-skiing.

Sufficient competent camp personnel. The director should be at least 25 years old, with training in administration and a minimum of 16 weeks experience in supervising an organized children's camp.

Counselors at day camps should be at least 18, at overnight camps 19, and at travel camps 21. At overnight camps there should be 1 counselor for every 6 campers.

Safe motorized transportation. All camp vehicles should be kept in good condition and state-inspected. No open trucks should be used to carry children.

Carefully supervised games and activities. Archery and rifle ranges should be a safe distance from other activities. Craft shops should be supervised by a counselor when campers are using dangerous tools such as power saws and lathes. Baseball players should be required to wear protective equipment, and spectators protected at the field. Foot trails should be laid out far from heavily traveled roads, with barriers placed so as to protect hikers from cliffs and swamps.

See also ACCIDENTS.

CANCER, perhaps more than any major disease, requires prompt treatment for the patient's survival. While a malignant cancerous growth still is limited to one area, it often can be destroyed or removed. If undetected or ignored because it is small, it will often spread and cause death. Many thousands of lives are being lost to cancer that could be saved with medical knowledge and techniques that are available right now.

More than 2 million Americans alive today have been cured of cancer. By "cured" it is meant they are without evidence of the disease at least five years after diagnosis and treatment. The cure rate may now be as high as 49 percent (up from 25 percent in 1950), making cancer one of the most curable of chronic diseases. Moreover, many patients whose cancers persist can lead relatively normal lives, receiving treatment that allows them to survive with minimal complications of the disease.

Yet patients'—and doctors'—fatalistic attitudes hold down treatment successes in cancer.

Some people are so terrified by the thought of having cancer that they simply cannot accept the doctor's diagnosis, and therefore disregard his instructions. Others shut their eyes and pretend the problem will vanish if they ignore it. In a California survey four patients in ten waited more than three months to seek medical help after noticing the symptoms of cancer. One in every five waited longer than a year—during which time the cancer spread. In such cases fear itself may be the biggest obstacle to recovery.

Cancer prevention. A periodic physical examination can save many lives from cancer. At prescribed intervals have your doctor examine you thoroughly, even if you feel well (see PHYSICAL EXAMINATION).

Quitting smoking is another smart move. Cigarette smoking is thought to be a major contributing cause of lung cancer and an important factor in several other diseases.

The American Cancer Society emphasizes the Seven Warning Signals. These signals don't mean that cancer is necessarily present, but they do indicate a need for medical attention. Consult a doctor if you have any of the following:

*C*hange in bowel or bladder habits.
A sore that does not heal.
*U*nusual bleeding or discharge. Blood in the urine should be investigated immediately.
*T*hickening or lump in breast or elsewhere.
*I*ndigestion or difficulty in swallowing.
*O*bvious change in wart or mole.
*N*agging cough or hoarseness.

Pain is seldom an early cancer signal. Don't wait for pain if the warning signals persist.

The disease called cancer. Cancer is not a single disease. Rather it is a group of more than one hundred different diseases that have in common an abnormal, unrestricted growth of body cells. Each of the billions of cells that make up your body has a special job: skin cells give protection, red blood cells carry oxygen, bone cells build the skeleton.

These cells multiply rapidly during the growth spurts of childhood. But after you reach maturity they divide and reproduce themselves only to replace worn-out tissues or to repair wounds.

Cancer cells seem to be runaway cells that multiply rapidly and without purpose. The cancer growth takes nourishment needed by normal cells. It compresses and invades healthy tissues.

Cancer cells may break off from the original cancerous mass. They move, via the bloodstream or lymphatic system, to other parts of the body.

There they form secondary sites (metastases). If important organs such as the liver or kidneys are affected by the metastases, life expectancy will be shortened drastically. Because the ancient Greeks thought that spreading cancerous growths resembled the claws of a crab, they called it the crablike disease, *karkinos*. The Latin translation of the word was *cancer*.

Different kinds of cancer have different characteristics. Cancer of the lip, of the stomach, of the rectum—each is as different as, say, a cold sore is from a peptic ulcer is from a hemorrhoid.

Some cancers are slow to grow and spread to neighboring tissues. Others grow rapidly and spread swiftly to distant sites. What cures one type of tumor (growth) may be ineffective for another. Moreover, one part of the body may give rise to several different types of cancer, each following its own course and requiring different treatment.

Not all tumors are malignant (cancerous). Benign tumors are clumps of cells that grow in a limited area and do not spread. They are harmful only when they press against other organs and disturb their normal functions. Ordinarily benign tumors can be removed without complications.

Who gets cancer? Cancer is the second most frequent cause of death in the United States. Only heart disease surpasses it. In a typical year about 910,000 people develop cancer and some 462,000 die of it. At the present rate, about one in four persons will eventually have cancer and about one out of every six deaths in the United States will be caused by cancer.

The effect of age is important. The number of cancer deaths in the United States has increased steadily during the past 50 years. In large part this is due to deaths in aged persons, who in previous generations would die earlier from diseases that have since been conquered. The actual rate of cancer in terms of deaths per 1,000 persons has changed but little.

Since 1936 the cancer death rate has been declining slowly but steadily among American women. During the same period, however, the male rate has increased, and is especially higher among blacks.

The decline among women is traceable to a sharp reduction in mortality from cancer of the uterine cervix and a drop in cancers of the stomach and rectum. The rise among men is due mainly to a large increase in lung cancer. The higher male incidence is also attributed to a marked increase in cancer of the prostate and of the colon.

The cancer rate in blacks is markedly higher than in whites, particularly among men. Black men show considerably higher rates for cancers of the prostate and esophagus. Black women have a higher rate of uterine cervix cancer but lower rates of breast and uterine cancers. During the past two decades the cancer death rate for blacks has jumped alarmingly: over 50 percent for black men, and 20 percent for blacks of both sexes. Howard University researchers suggest that black Americans' recent mass migration to cities may be at least partly responsible. In addition everything works against an inner-city black's detecting a cancer early: He tends to think of cancer as a "white disease." He's unfamiliar with early warning signs. He's likely to use public-health facilities, which are geared to treating symptomatic conditions, not detecting asymptomatic cancer.

Nearly all forms of cancer are more common in urban areas. There is an unusually high rate of cancer of the respiratory system and esophagus among urban men. Death rates from cancer are generally above average in the Northeast and below average in the South and Southwest. On the other hand the South has an above-average death rate from skin cancer, probably because of greater exposure to sunlight.

Low socioeconomic groups are generally likeliest to develop cancer and die from it. Low-income groups seem particularly prone to cancers of the uterine cervix, esophagus, and stomach. The poor's greater vulnerability may be due to higher exposure to cancer-causing agents, lower-quality medical care, and poorer personal hygiene.

Causes of cancer. The causes of cancer include many chemical compounds. In 1775 a prominent English surgeon, Percivall Pott, broke a leg and spent his time of recovery writing a book on his observations. He devoted a few pages to the subject of cancer of the scrotum in chimney sweeps, which he attributed to long exposure and intimate contact with soot.

This was the first clear description of an occupational cancer. It has since been observed that bladder cancer occurs frequently in aniline-dye workers who handle certain compounds. Cancer of the bone was much more frequent among workers who painted luminous dials of watches with radium. Lung cancer may be caused by inhalation of chromium compounds, radioactive ores, asbestos, arsenic, and iron. Cancer of the nasal sinuses and the lung is common in nickel-mine workers. Skin cancer may result from handling some products of coal, oil shale, lignite, and petroleum.

Hazards to which industrial groups are exposed have implications for the general population. For example, air pollution from industrial wastes represents a potentially important source of carcinogens (cancer-producing agents). When the air contains impurities, your lungs ordinarily get rid of them by coughing, or by cleansing processes within the lining of the bronchial tubes or lung tissue. But excessive or continuous exposure to inhaled impurities brings about changes in the bronchial linings and the lungs that may eventually result in disability and illness. If the impurities contain cancer-producing substances, prolonged exposure may lead to cancer.

The higher cancer death rates in urban areas are believed to be at least partly due to the polluted air, which often contains chemicals known to cause cancer in laboratory animals.

Excessive radiation is a major cause of cancer. The commonest source of radiation is the sun, specifically the ultraviolet wavelengths. People with light skins or who spend a great deal of time in the sun have a higher incidence of skin cancer than dark-skinned people or those whose occupations keep them indoors.

With increasing use of radioactive materials in industry and medicine, and fallout from nuclear-weapons testing, man-made radiation hazards have become a major environmental problem. Large doses of radiation can cause many types of cancer. It is now generally assumed that even very small amounts of radiation may produce some injury in a few individuals.

Viruses may be cancer-causing. These minute parasites (see INFECTIOUS DISEASE) can induce a wide range of experimental cancers in animals. Evidence suggests that they can produce cancer in humans.

Does cancer run in families? Cancer is a common disease, and some "clustering" of cases in families will occur by chance alone.

Scientists have not been able to show any significant family clustering for most kinds of cancer. One exception is retinoblastoma, a rare cancer of the eye. The chances that a patient cured of retinoblastoma will have a child with this tumor are very high.

If one identical twin develops leukemia, it is a one in six chance that the other twin will also develop leukemia, usually within a year. An abnormal sensitivity of the skin to ultraviolet radiation, called xeroderma pigmentosum, almost inevitably develops into cancer, and is a hereditary disease. So is multiple polyposis of the colon, which develops into cancer during the second and third decade of life.

Among the more common types scientists believe that relatives of patients with cancers of the stomach, ovary, female breast, or colon and rectum run an increased risk of developing these cancers. But they do not know whether such family clustering is due to inherited characteristics or to environmental factors, such as diet or occupation, which may continue unchanged from one generation to the next.

Misconceptions about cancer. A single injury, no matter how severe, will not cause cancer or stimulate its growth. The belief that injury is likely to bring on cancer seems especially strong in respect to cancer of the breast. Most women can recall one or more instances when a breast sustained an injury through a bump, a blow, a fall. If cancer of the breast appears, it is natural —but not correct—to associate it with that injury.

Cancer is not contagious. Now and then a husband and wife, or two otherwise closely associated persons, both have cancer. But such coincidences are bound to occur in a disease as prevalent as cancer.

There is no such thing as a "cancer house," supposedly a building where occupants get struck by cancer. Nor are there "cancer districts," usually mythologized as low, marshy areas where the night air is laden with a harmful "miasma."

Cancer is not a "wage of sin." The belief that cancer is a consequence of wrongdoing stems from the notion that cancer is a shameful social disease.

Tomatoes, canned goods, preserves, spices, refined sugar, white flour, cooked food, and numerous other staples of the table—all have opponents who hold them responsible for cancer, in spite of the utter lack of serious evidence. Similarly, fertilizer used in agriculture has no credible link with cancer.

Aluminum pots and dishes have no connection with cancer. Nor has the use of steel wool.

Fluoridation, vaccinations, or other immunization procedures are not related to cancer.

Cancer diagnosis is a difficult problem because symptoms usually do not manifest themselves until the disease has progressed for some time.

Every diagnosis of cancer is subject to confirmation by a biopsy. In this surgical procedure a small piece of suspect tissue is removed, cut in very thin slices, stained with special dyes, and examined under the microscope. The biopsy may be performed while the patient is still in the operating room so that the operation can be continued for removal of the tumor if the presence of cancer is established.

For specific kinds of cancer, laboratory procedures are useful as clues to diagnosis. Best known is the Pap smear (after its originator, Dr. George N. Papanicolaou) for cancer of the uterine cervix. This technique involves the microscopic examination of cells scraped from the cervix or collected in fluid from the vagina. This procedure has been extended to other sites by examining body fluids, such as the urine and the sputum, smears from the nose and mouth, and washings of the stomach.

Treating cancer. A person with cancer has the best chance of a favorable outcome if his care is directed by an oncologist, a specialist in cancer therapy who usually is connected with a cancer treatment center or medical center. Team therapy is the norm in cancer treatment. Cancer patients are treated by surgeons, radiotherapists, a host of other specialists.

Rarely, then, does the patient have greater need for a personal physician who can serve as his medical manager. Ideally the family doctor makes the initial referral to the oncologist, and keeps in close touch throughout the course of treatment. He may administer anticancer drugs, especially if the oncologist is too far for convenient travel. He commonly acts as the patient's advocate, because oncologists often remain strangers to their patients and treatment centers tend to be impersonal.

The following major forms of therapy may be used alone or in a variety of combinations:

Surgery is the most frequent treatment for cancer (see SURGERY). Contrary to widespread belief, cancer is not spread or stimulated by being cut with the surgeon's scalpel. A metastasis appearing after surgery did not get there because the surgeon's knife put cancer into the bloodstream; the cancer already had access to the circulatory system and almost certainly would have metastasized anyway.

When surgery is undertaken in hopes of removing all the cancerous tissues, it is called "specific" surgical treatment. It is performed to treat patients with most of the major forms of cancer, especially if the disease has been diagnosed in an early stage. The surgeon needs to remove a margin of healthy tissue while preserving the organ's ability to function.

"Supportive" surgery is performed mainly to sustain the cancer patient or alleviate his discomfort. Surgery is sometimes necessary to remove glands that, although healthy, secrete hormones that contribute to the tumor's growth.

Surgery also can treat complications incidental to cancer, such as abscesses, intestinal perforation and bleeding, and tumor-related bone fractures. It is often done to "debulk" the tumor, reduce its mass to keep it from impinging on vital organs, and to aid in chemotherapy.

In advanced cancer the surgeon may perform an operation to relieve pain. He may sever nerves at the area where the cancer started, at the area of spread, or centrally to make the cancer-bearing area insensitive.

Radiotherapy destroys the reproductive mechanism of cancer cells, so that once they die, no new tumors develop (see RADIATION). In external radiation a source of energy such as X rays is located outside the body and directs a radioactive beam toward the tumor. In internal radiation a radioactive substance such as radium is inserted into a body cavity or implanted in tissues with needles, capsules, wires.

Radiotherapy is extremely delicate—too much destroys healthy tissue; too little permits tumor growth. Temporary nausea, blood disorders, and internal tissue changes are frequent side effects. Pelvic irradiation may cause diarrhea; skin irradiation may cause itching; mouth irradiation may cause soreness and swallowing problems.

Before undergoing radiotherapy, ask your family physician to check the radiotherapist's qualifications. There are many more machines

---

CANCER AND CIGARETTES

Some highlights of the surgeon general's *Report on Smoking:*
- Smoking causes about 130,000 cancer deaths a year.
- It is the major cause of cancer of the lung, larynx, mouth, and esophagus.
- It is a contributory factor to cancer of the bladder, kidneys, and pancreas.
- Overall cancer death rates are directly related to the number of cigarettes smoked. Those smoking more than one pack a day are three times as likely to die of cancer as nonsmokers.
- Quitting smoking reduces the risk of cancer.

suited to radiotherapy than there are well-trained radiotherapists. Diagnostic radiologists are *not* experts at therapeutic radiology; their training is quite different even if they have access to radiotherapy machines.

Chemotherapy, the use of drugs, chiefly attacks cancers that have spread beyond the reach of surgery or radiation. The major classes of drugs mainly seek to slow down or stop the formation of cancer cells, so the cell doesn't replace itself as it dies off. The drugs are often used in combination.

For a cell to reproduce there must be a division in its genetic material, DNA. The creation of DNA is obstructed by *antimetabolites* (e.g., fluorouracil [5-FU, Efudex, Fluoroplex], methotrexate [Mexate], thioguanine [Lanvis]) and *antibiotics* (bleomycin [Blenoxane], doxorubicin [Adriamycin], dactinomycin [Cosmegen]). Further, to keep DNA from dividing, its twin spiral strands may be bound together by *alkylating agents* (busulfan [Myleran], cyclophosphamide [Cytoxan], melphalan [Alkeran]).

After DNA divides, there's a division of the cell nucleus, which can be inhibited by *alkaloids* (vincristine [Oncovin], vinblastine [Velban]). Other anticancer drugs have similar actions at various points in the cell cycle. Steroids and hormones can create an unfavorable environment for some types of tumors.

Most anticancer drugs act on the body at large and can be extremely toxic to healthy tissues. Before beginning chemotherapy you need baseline blood counts to signal dangerous reductions in red and white blood cells and blood platelets. While undergoing chemotherapy you need frequent physical exams. Tell your doctor immediately of any sores in your mouth, or diarrhea—some drugs can cause sloughing of the intestinal tract and require that you drink at least two quarts of fluid a day.

Almost all the drugs cause nausea and vomiting. You stand the best chance of reducing this if you start an antiemetic and perhaps some codeine a day or two before beginning chemotherapy.

Chemotherapy may cause your hair to fall out. Before treatment you can prepare for such hair loss by buying a wig of your normal hair color and having it shaped to your usual style. A wig bought for this purpose is tax-deductible as a medical expense.

Insist that any nurse who gives you injections be specially trained in administering chemotherapy. Some drugs can destroy muscle and other tissue if they are infused outside the bloodstream. Repeated injections can be painful and can damage veins. One alternative to repeated sticking with a needle is a tube (a shunt or catheter) that provides access to a blood vessel throughout chemotherapy.

Cancer quacks. Noted an editorial in the *Journal* of the AMA: "Of all the ghouls who feed on the bodies of the dying, the cancer quacks are the most vicious and the most heartless."

The huge sum squandered on worthless products isn't the worst aspect of cancer quackery. More important, a patient who relies on false cures usually leaves the care of a competent doctor to do so, thus depriving himself of the sound medical treatment that could ease his pain or lengthen his life.

In cancer loss of time can mean loss of life. Therefore the cancer patient who wastes time being treated with a worthless remedy may be risking his life, which could be saved by early diagnosis and prompt treatment with well-proven methods.

Fear, more than any other reason, is why people go to proponents of unproven remedies, concludes the American Cancer Society. Fear of expense—many think it is less expensive to procure and use unproven remedies than to place themselves under the care of a reputable physician. Fear of the knife or radiation—many prefer the illusion of painless, prompt medical "miracles." Fear of social stigma—many still feel it is a disgrace to have cancer. Fear that their own doctor has given up hope—they are ready to clutch at any straw.

Testimonials are often used as lures. An unproven remedy is likely to be attested to by congressmen, actors, or other prominent people. While generally well intentioned, these proponents are not experienced in the care of patients with cancer or with scientific methodology.

Books and articles often promote the use of unproven cancer remedies. Some are printed by organizations, such as the International Association of Cancer Victims and Friends, the Cancer Control Society, the National Health Federation, and the Committee for Freedom of Choice in Cancer Therapy. Moreover, cancer is a sensational subject, and less-than-conscientious publishers find it profitable to attract readers with cancer "cures."

Some of these books are artfully written. Facts are set forth against as well as in favor of the method. The reader gets the impression that the author is impartial despite the fact that the argument is heavily weighted in favor of the method. The American Cancer Society blames such seemingly factual books for giving big boosts to the unproven remedies Krebiozen, Laetrile, and the Gerson method.

Don't take the word of a patient about the value of unproven treatment—he might not have had cancer at all. The nonexistent cancer could have been misdiagnosed by an unqualified person or by the use of a discredited test. Two such tests with typically fanciful names are the Gruner Blood Smear Test and the Zuccala Lytic Test. Both are worthless.

The patient who really had cancer is another source of misleading testimonials. One woman was undergoing X-ray therapy for cancer of the uterine cervix. She thought her condition was worsening, largely because she felt ill from the X-ray treatment. She lost confidence in her physicians and went to a quack. He gave her a tonic.

Shortly her weakness and nausea stopped, and her cancer disappeared. The woman credits the tonic. Actually she had received enough X-ray therapy to destroy the cancer. Her strength and appetite returned as soon as the side effects of the X rays wore off.

Cancer is a capricious disease. Its growth may be halted temporarily because of the nature of the cancer itself. Mere cessation of symptoms is not necessarily a proof of improvement or cure.

Investigations were made several years after the publishing of some testimonials of cures by a quack product or method. A number of these testimonial-givers had died of cancer, some only months after publication of the testimonial, and a few before the testimonial even had appeared in print.

Cancer quacks tend to run to type. Be skeptical of anyone treating cancer if:

He claims to have an exclusive method. There is no such thing. Reputable doctors share their knowledge and experience and make approved treatment widely available. The charlatan often refuses consultation with local physicians. He frequently proclaims that he is battling the "medical trust"—that his "discovery" is being kept from the public.

His "cured" patients have only his word that they had cancer. An honest medical man is prepared to provide proof if he says he has found cancer. He welcomes checking and always verifies suspected cancer with a biopsy.

His scientific standing seems questionable. Some proponents of unproven methods hold Ph.D. or M.D. degrees. But they tend to be isolated from established scientific facilities or associates, and are more likely to work behind the name of a high-sounding foundation or other "scientific" organization.

They do not use regular channels of communication between cancer specialists, such as reputable scientific journals or reports to medical meetings. Often they have questionable degrees —N.D. (doctor of naturopathy); Ph.N. (philosopher of naturopathy); M.T. (medical technologist); DABB-A (diplomate of American Board of Bio-Analysts); Ms.D. (doctor of metaphysics) —which may have been received from correspondence schools.

Dangerous, worthless cures. Beware of corrosives, one type of unproven cancer remedy. These corrosive or caustic agents are usually salves, poultices, or plasters. Some charlatans claim their burning chemicals will "draw out" cancers, "roots and all." The usual result of caustic agents in the hands of a quack is incomplete removal and recurrence of an external cancer, plus needless scarring and disfigurement.

The Hoxsey method cures no one. Using burning agents, plus other medications, Harry M. Hoxsey, a coal miner who left school after the eighth grade, promoted his cancer treatment for more than 30 years. It consists primarily of arsenic trisulfide for external cancers, and an assemblage of herbs and flavorings (licorice, red clover, buckthorn, bark, etc.) in pills.

All scientific testing discredits the method completely. The federal government secured a court ban on its sale, but it and related methods still hang on.

Worthless diets. Many special diets of an unproven nature have been advocated for the treatment or cure of cancer. None of them work.

The Gerson method requires hourly drinks of freshly prepared vegetable juice and calves' liver juice, combined with frequent coffee enemas. It was proposed by Max B. Gerson, M.D., and used at his sanatorium near New York City. Variations are still offered by fringe practitioners around the country and in Mexico.

The so-called grape cure limits a patient to a diet of grapes or grape juice for one to two weeks.

The method is not new. A grape diet was advanced as a cancer treatment in England more than 100 years ago. In more recent years one of its strongest proponents was a naturopath, Johanna Brandt, whose book *The Grape Cure* has undergone over 20 editions. Drugless practitioners and health spas use the method, sometimes adding other fruit and throwing in fraudulent claims for cures of such conditions as high blood pressure, faulty eyesight, and gray hair. It cures nothing.

Some quacks claim that cancer is caused by an imbalance of acids and alkalis in the body. Often they advocate a "natural food" diet to correct such an imbalance. Others claim to correct it by administering medicines that have an opposite chemical reaction.

There is no scientific evidence that such an imbalance is a cause of cancer, or that correcting an acid-alkaline imbalance improves or cures it.

Fasting for periods varying from one to two days to several weeks is another ineffective method of cancer treatment. Indeed the fasting weakens the patient, and may spur the growth of the tumor.

Worthless drugs. A number of supposed drugs have received wide notice in the public press as cancer cures. But their effectiveness has not been proven by scientific tests.

Laetrile has had wide publicity. It is principally amygdalin, a compound obtained from peach and apricot kernels. In theory when amygdalin comes in contact with an enzyme occurring in malignant tissues, hydrogen cyanide is formed that kills the cancer. Thorough scientific testing has pronounced Laetrile worthless for the treatment of cancer. Worse yet, it has caused deaths from cyanide poisoning.

Government court actions have banned Laetrile in Canada and in interstate commerce in the United States. But individual states permit the drug, and cancer sufferers cross the border into Mexico to be treated with Laetrile at supposed clinics in Tijuana and other border cities.

Krebiozen, promoted as a miraculous cure, has been found to have no anticancer activity in man. Moreover, scientists identified what the promoters claimed was Krebiozen powder as creatine, an amino acid derivative that is plentifully available from meat in an ordinary diet.

Still another investigator checked sample vials. He could not find even creatine in them. What was being sold was plain mineral oil.

Worthless devices. Unscientific devices are widely promoted for the diagnosis, treatment, or cure of cancer.

The Vrilium Tube, or "magic spike," contains a penny's worth of barium chloride, whose sole medical use in proper dosages is as a heart stimulant. Nonetheless the tube is sold for both cancer and arthritis. Gullible patients have paid $300 for it.

The impressive-appearing Detoxacolon machine has been sold to hundreds of chiropractors and naturopaths for $2,500. It is nothing but a device for irrigating the colon under pressure. But it is purported to treat cancer and 38 other

---

CAN DIET HELP YOU PREVENT CANCER?

An expert panel of the National Academy of Sciences concludes that these changes in eating habits can improve your chances of avoiding cancer:

EAT MORE:

Foods rich in vitamin C (citrus fruits, tomatoes, peppers), which seem to lower the risk of cancer of the stomach and esophagus.

Foods rich in beta-carotene (dark-green leafy vegetables such as broccoli and spinach, and deep-yellow fruits and vegetables such as peaches and carrots), which are associated with a reduced risk of cancer of the lung, breast, bladder, and skin.

Vegetables in the cabbage family (including broccoli, cauliflower, kale, brussels sprouts), which contain cancer-inhibiting substances.

EAT LESS:

Smoked food (sausages, including frankfurters, bologna, and other cold cuts; bacon; smoked ham and fish), which increase exposure to such cancer-causing substances as nitrosamines and polycyclic hydrocarbons, and are associated with cancer of the digestive tract.

Fat (both saturated and unsaturated, as in dairy products, beef and pork, cooking oils), which is linked to cancer of the colon, breast, and prostate.

diseases, although it has no value for any medical purpose.

The Film-O-Sonic machine, another worthless device, has been sold to the patient for as much as $500. The machine plays a tape with the song "Smoke Gets in Your Eyes."

The patient applies two pads wired to the device over the region of his body presumably affected by cancer. The Lord's Prayer can be a second selection used for certain types of cancer. Before the fraud was exposed, the promoters netted over $200,000.

Ozone machines, promoted as "God's Gift to Humanity," have been sold for $150 each. Not only are they worthless as therapeutic instruments, but ozone is a poisonous gas that can be dangerous.

Uranium treatments in nonmedical clinics are attempts to cash in on legitimate radiotherapy. Uranium treatment centers consist of cubicles lined with low-grade uranium ore, or beds with trays of uranium ore under them. The uranium ore generally has a radiation emission less than that of a common luminous dial watch—it will cure nothing.

Some such devices are hazardous in themselves. A device called a radon generator consists of a rod whose top was attached to the lid of an ordinary picnic jug. The jug is filled with ordinary tap water and the rod immersed in it for 12 hours, resulting in a "radium-impregnated" liquid. When taken internally, it has been guaranteed to cure almost any ailment, including cancer, restore hair to bald heads, and revive virility. The manufacturer has bragged that some 9,000 generators had been sold in the United States.

Analysis of the rod reveals it to contain a minute amount of radium mixed with iron oxide, but of sufficient strength to cause the water in which it is suspended to pose 305 times the maximum permissible safe concentration of radioactivity.

For reliable information about cancer, write the American Cancer Society, 90 Park Avenue, New York, New York 10016, and the Office of Cancer Communications, National Cancer Institute, Bethesda, Maryland 20014.

See also AIR POLLUTION; CANCER IN CHILDREN; CANCER OF THE BONE; CANCER OF THE BRAIN; CANCER OF THE BREAST; CANCER OF THE BLADDER; CANCER OF THE COLON AND RECTUM; CANCER OF THE LARYNX; CANCER OF THE LUNG; CANCER OF THE MOUTH; CANCER OF THE PROSTATE.

CANCER OF THE SKIN; CANCER OF THE STOMACH; CANCER OF THE UTERUS; DRUGS; HODGKIN'S DISEASE; LEUKEMIA; PHYSICAL EXAMINATION; QUACKERY; RADIATION; SMOKING; SURGERY; X RAYS.

CANCER IN CHILDREN kills more youngsters between ages 3 and 14 than any disease. However with dramatic improvement in survival rates about 50 percent of childhood cancer patients grow into healthy adults.

Cancer in a child is often hard to recognize, since it may masquerade as a trivial disorder of the sort children are prone to. Further, since children's tumors are comparatively rare, they are less understood and less readily suspected than those that appear in older people.

Between regular examinations report to your doctor any out-of-the-ordinary symptoms that do not subside in two weeks. The following conditions warrant investigation:

Swellings, lumps, or masses in any part of the body.

Pains, or the persistent crying of a baby or child, for which no reason can be found.

Any change in the size or appearance of outward growths, such as moles or birthmarks.

Nausea and vomiting for which there is no apparent cause.

A marked change in bowel or bladder habits.

Bloody discharge of any sort; blood in the urine; heavy spontaneous nosebleeds or other type of hemorrhage; failure of bleeding to stop in the usual time after a cut or injury.

Unexplained stumbling in a child who has been walking well.

A general "run-down" condition.

The most common children's cancer is LEUKEMIA (which see).

Neuroblastoma is the most common form of cancer in children after leukemia. It arises in nerve fibers and may occur anywhere, usually in the abdomen. Among the warning signs may be swelling of the abdomen. Many young patients, especially infants, treated with a combination of surgery and drugs, have an excellent chance of recovery.

Retinoblastoma, an eye tumor, usually occurs under the age of four. The first symptom may be the widening of the pupil of the child's eye, resembling a squint. Later a pearly glint may be noted within the eye. If detected early, cure is possible. Treatment may consist of surgery or X-ray therapy, sometimes in combination with drugs.

Wilms's tumor, a cancer of the kidney, is usually detected by a swelling or lump in the child's abdomen. With the use of surgery, radiotherapy, and sometimes chemotherapy, success in the treatment of this tumor has greatly improved.

Emotional problems. In general, a child with cancer should be told the diagnosis. At Children's Hospital Medical Center, Boston, 70 percent of childhood cancer patients and 90 percent of their parents favored informing the youngster of his condition.

Young cancer patients may find that their best friends refuse (or are forbidden) to play with them. They also may be ridiculed by classmates for wearing wigs, scarves, baseball caps covering hair loss. Pediatricians at Memorial Sloan-Kettering Cancer Center, New York, find that peer acceptance of the condition is aided if patients take off the coverings and show their bald heads —and if the teacher gives a little explanation in class.

Often parents wrongly blame themselves for the disease, on the grounds that they lived in a polluted area, or let the child have X rays, or fed him the wrong foods. Siblings commonly resent the displacement caused by illness. Marriages are sometimes threatened. And even if the youngster's treatment is successful, he and his family may suffer a lifelong "Damocles syndrome," marked by uncertainty over whether the sword of cancer will fall.

To counter such stress, families do well to seek professional counseling, especially at these eight crisis points: (1) at the time of diagnosis; (2) at the onset of treatment; (3) during negative physical reaction to treatment; (4) when treatment is ended; (5) when the child reenters school; (6) during recurrence of the disease; (7) at the time research treatments are given; and (8) when the decision is made to end treatment. Social workers at cancer-treatment centers are often skilled in providing help during such situations.

For other common tumors in children and young adults, see CANCER OF THE BONE, HODGKIN'S DISEASE, and CANCER OF THE BRAIN. See also CANCER.

CANCER OF THE BLADDER's most common first symptom is bloody urine. It usually appears suddenly and without pain. Depending on the amount of blood present, the color of the urine can vary from a smoky or rusty hue to deep red. The amount of blood does not seem to depend on the stage of the cancer. In one individual a highly advanced cancer might cause only a little bleeding, while in another an early tumor could result in profuse bleeding.

The blood may be present one day and absent the next. Although weeks or months may go by during which the urine is clear, sooner or later blood reappears. The recurrence of blood in the urine is the single most characteristic symptom of bladder cancer.

Usually the bleeding is painless, but it may be accompanied by some discomfort and increased frequency of urination. Sometimes blood clots form, causing painful muscle spasms in the bladder.

Infection of the urinary tract is a common complication of bladder cancer. This causes fever, weight loss, and tenderness in the bladder area.

Bloody urine does not always mean cancer. Other conditions, such as infection, benign tumors, or bladder stones, may be responsible. To examine the inside of the bladder, doctors use a cystoscope, a slender tube fitted with a lens and a light that can be introduced into the bladder through the passage, the urethra. If any suspicious-looking areas are seen, a bit of tissue is removed for a biopsy. If a bladder tumor is large, it can sometimes be felt during a rectal or vaginal examination.

There are two types of cancerous bladder tumors. The papillary type is the most common and also the most easily cured. It does not grow right on the bladder wall but is attached to it by a mushroomlike stem. Benign bladder tumors often have the same appearance and may later become cancerous.

The other type of tumor arises directly on the bladder wall and quickly invades underlying muscles. This type of tumor also tends to become ulcerated and infected. Even though metastasis is rapid, most patients die not because of widespread cancer but because of accompanying infection.

Bladder cancer is most frequent in persons between 50 and 70 years old. Some 70 percent of the patients are men. Cancer of the bladder and kidney strike some 55,000 people a year, of whom about 17,000 die of the disease.

An association between smoking and cancer of the bladder in men has been reported in several studies. Researchers have found a marked increase in the amount of cancer-causing agents in the urine of cigarette smokers. Another study found that cigarette smokers are about five times more apt to get kidney cancer than those who don't use tobacco. The risk for pipe and cigar smokers, who don't usually inhale, is half that run by cigarette smokers.

Bladder cancer seems directly related to schistosomiasis. In Egypt, where the bladder cancer rate is one of the highest in the world, it is estimated that from 70 to 90 percent of the population is infected with the schistosoma fluke, a parasite worm that infests the Nile waters, covering fields where farmers must wade to sow their crops. The parasite enters the body through the skin and finds its way to the bladder, where it buries itself in the wall. There it produces irritation and chronic changes that may finally terminate in cancer (see SCHISTOSOMIASIS).

Another suspected cause of bladder cancer is the compound betanaphthylamine, used in aniline-dye manufacturing. Betanaphthylamine and similar chemicals are absorbed into the bloodstream, then converted into a more dangerous form that is excreted in the urine. The bladder, as the storage organ for urine, is directly exposed to the cancer-causing substance for long periods of time.

Curing bladder cancer. There is a good possibility of cure if bladder cancer is detected in an early stage. Of men whose tumors did not spread at the time of treatment, 70 percent are alive and well five years later.

A single, superficial papillary tumor may be successfully treated by electrically destroying the tissue. Multiple tumors, even at an early stage, are best treated by surgical removal of the surrounding tissue as well as the tumor itself. When the tumor is large or has already invaded much normal tissue, a cystectomy—total removal of the bladder—is performed. The ureters are then diverted so that the output from the kidneys can drain into the large intestine instead of the bladder, or into a plastic pouch through an opening in the abdominal wall.

The development of supervoltage radiation in the past two decades has made easier the radiotherapy of deep-seated tumors such as bladder cancer. Radiation can now be delivered to the bladder without excessive damage to overlying tissues, permitting the cure not only of many early cancers but also of some advanced tumors not suited for surgical removal.

See also CANCER; SCHISTOSOMIASIS.

CANCER OF THE BONE develops most frequently in young people 10 to 20 years old. Unlike nearly all other types of cancer, which are painless, a common early symptom of bone cancer is pain.

Sometimes the pain seems to be relieved by exercise, but at other times it is aggravated by motion. The pain may come and go. Although pain may develop in any area of the skeleton, the predominant sites are the knee, thigh, arm (especially the upper part), ribs, and pelvis.

Other symptoms include swelling from the expanding tumor, and fever. Depending on the type of bone tumor, swelling may precede or follow pain. Fever is not usually present when the tumors are small.

Primary bone cancers, called sarcomas, originate in the skeletal tissues. Osteogenic sarcoma, the most common, most often arises in the bone in the lower end of the femur (thighbone) or upper end of the tibia (shinbone). Chondrosarcoma affects the cartilage, most commonly in the pelvis or femur. Ewing's sarcoma occurs in the pelvis or one of the long bones of the body.

Secondary bone cancers are those that arise from primary tumors elsewhere in the body and reach the skeleton through metastasis. These are much more common than primary bone tumors. The most common sources of the metastases are cancers of the breasts, kidneys, lung, thyroid, and prostate gland, cancers that ordinarily occur in middle-aged and older persons.

The symptoms of bone cancer and many benign conditions are similar. A few benign bone tumors may develop into cancer. Chondromas (cartilage tissue tumors) and giant cell tumors of bone have the greatest tendency to change from benign to malignant. A physician usually treats these with surgery or radiation as a preventive measure. Paget's disease of the bone is an inflammatory condition that sometimes precedes the development of bone cancer.

Bone cancers used to always require amputation of the affected body part. Increasingly limbs are being saved—only bone sections are removed, often in combination with chemotherapy and radiation.

However most bone cancers have a high fatality rate. The tumor metastasizes soon after its onset and is usually at an advanced stage when first discovered.

It is natural for parents to take the vaguely painful early symptoms lightly, especially when the complaints are made by a healthy-looking child. Parents often ascribe the pain to a bruise or a sprain—certainly common enough in active children—or to the mythical old standbys rheumatism and growing pains.

Take a child to the doctor when such complaints persist beyond a week. Even if the cause seems clear, an injury severe enough to be followed by pain for a week means that the child should be taken to the doctor anyway. Also be suspicious of swelling over the knee, thigh, or other bone, which may be caused by an expanding tumor. Similarly, see a doctor if the skin over a bone feels considerably warmer than other body skin, or if veins become prominent.

See also CANCER.

CANCER OF THE BRAIN and central nervous

system may have headache and seizures as early symptoms. Other frequent signs include double or blurred vision, difficulty in walking, and unexplained nausea.

The brain is the center of consciousness, sensation, and emotion. It directs all voluntary acts and controls all thought processes. The brain and spinal cord make up the central nervous system. All their functions—thinking, acting, feeling—may be impaired by a tumor.

Many victims are children or young adults. While some tumors are curable if caught early, many are fast-growing and lead to death within just six months or a year from the time symptoms begin. Of all deaths attributed to diseases of the central nervous system, those due to brain tumor rank second only to stroke. Each year about 12,500 Americans develop brain tumors and about 10,500 die.

The brain's unique anatomy, which normally protects it, presents special problems in brain-tumor treatment. The cerebrospinal fluid cushions and lubricates the brain, but may carry away cancer drugs before they have become concentrated or had time enough to destroy malignant cells. The skull rigidly confines the brain so that slight swelling or small amounts of abnormal growth may cause irreversible damage to nerve tissue.

Tumors that originate elsewhere and metastasize to the brain make up more than 20 percent of the brain tumors. They usually arise from breast or lung cancer. Even though the primary tumors may be life-threatening in themselves, critically located brain metastases may be the ultimate cause of death.

Surgery currently offers the best chance for cure of brain tumors following early diagnosis. However, surgical damage to the nervous system may be as great as that caused by the tumor, including severe disabilities such as paralysis or blindness.

To avoid the damage that may result from surgery, neurosurgeons often attempt to remove surgically only as much of the tumor as is possible without damaging normal nerve tissue. The remaining tumor cells are often treated with varying degrees of success by radiation therapy. See also CANCER.

CANCER OF THE BREAST, if treated early enough, offers excellent prospects for survival—indeed for possibly saving the breast. The disease strikes about 1 out of 11 women and occurs more often (some 119,000 cases a year) than any other form of cancer. If localized to the breast, its five-year survival rate is nearly 96 percent.

But few women examine their breasts every month or make any other systematic effort at detection. The disease causes more deaths (38,400 a year) than any other form of cancer and is the leading cause of death of women between ages 40 and 44.

Daughters and sisters of breast cancer patients run a somewhat greater risk of developing the disease than do other women—and therefore need to be especially watchful. In addition, the risk is highest for women over age 50. A somewhat lower risk faces women who've never had children or who had their first child after age 30. There also seems to be an increased risk for women who've undergone menopause with their ovaries intact and are taking high doses of estrogens.

Breast cancer is the subject of many myths. Contrary to widespread belief, it cannot be caused by a blow or injury to the breasts. It is never caused by caressing or fondling. It is not contagious. It is unrelated to breastfeeding or the use of oral contraceptives. It is extremely uncommon in children and occurs only rarely in men.

There is no known preventive against developing breast cancer. Brassieres that make cancer-prevention claims are outright frauds.

Surviving breast cancer. If the cancer is detected early, while still localized, nearly nine out of ten women will survive five years or more. However by the time most breast cancers are discovered, they've already spread to the armpit lymph nodes. When this happens, the survival rate is less than 50 percent.

Metastasis is twice as likely to be present when the tumor is the average size at which tumors are discovered—about the size of a pea—than when it is only a third the diameter. Thus it is vital to discover the tumor at the earliest possible stage.

Immediate medical attention is needed by anyone who notices a breast lump or any thickening, swelling, irritation, or dimpling of the skin. Another worrisome sign is enlargement of the pores so that the surface of the breast resembles an orange skin. It's also important to report any changes in the shape or size of the breast, or any pain or tenderness. Similarly, watch the nipple for flattening, scaliness, discharge.

Self-examination. Many women have discovered breast cancer at a curable stage by giving themselves a monthly breast examination (see illustration). The best time for this examination is at the end of each menstrual period.

Most breast lumps are not cancerous but symptoms of cystic mastitis, or fibrocystic breast disease. This is a minor inflammation involving the milk ducts, which become obstructed and produce fluid-filled cysts of various sizes. Fibrocystic breast disease is not associated with cancer. Women who have this condition, however, should be meticulous about examining their breasts. Should cancer develop, a Harvard School of Public Health study suggests, such women run a two and a half times greater chance of dying from breast cancer than other women in the population.

One in 20 women have cystic disease of the breast during the years in which they menstruate. When these cysts are removed surgically, they do not return. There is no reason to believe that these lumps themselves will become cancerous or that a breast will have to be removed.

Women aged 20 to 40 do well to have their breasts examined by a physician or nurse at least once every three years. Women over 40 need a professional exam every year.

Between 35 and 40 every woman should have a baseline mammography, an X ray showing the normal condition of the breast for future comparisons. From 40 to 50 the American Cancer Society recommends mammograms every 1 to 2 years. After 50 an annual mammogram is widely recommended.

Immediate mammography is required for any woman showing a symptom that could suggest breast cancer.

Treatment. Surgery and radiation are both used for the treatment of breast cancer. Chemotherapy also is often helpful, especially if the cancer has metastasized.

Radical (Halsted) mastectomy removes the breast, the underlying layer of pectoral muscles, all of the underarm lymph nodes, and some additional fat and skin. The procedure leaves sunken areas in the chest. Often patients experience significant arm swelling and reduced overall strength. Long the standard surgery for breast cancer, it is being resorted to less and less

HOW TO DO BREAST SELF-EXAMINATION

Examine your breasts every month

If you menstruate, check your breasts 2 or 3 days after the *end* of your period. If you no longer menstruate, pick a certain day each month: the first of each month is an easy day to remember.

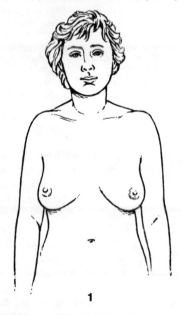

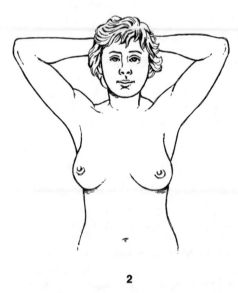

1   2

1. **Study breasts.** Stand before a mirror. Observe both breasts for anything unusual, such as any discharge from the nipples, puckering, dimpling, or scaling of the skin.

2. **Raise hands.** Watching closely in the mirror, clasp hands behind your head and press hands forward. Study both breasts again.

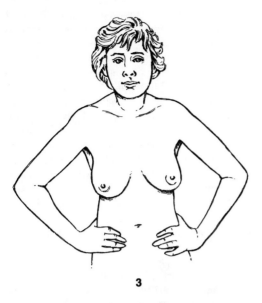

3

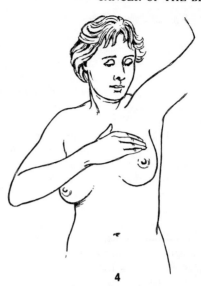

4

3. Lean forward. Next, firmly press hands on hips and bow slightly toward your mirror as you pull your shoulders and elbows forward. Again look for unusual signs.

4. Feel for masses. Raise your left arm. Use three or four fingers of your right hand to explore your left breast firmly, carefully, and thoroughly. Beginning at the outer edge, press the flat part of your fingers in small circles, moving the circles slowly around the breast. Gradually work toward the nipple. Be sure to cover the entire breast. Pay special attention to the area between the breast and the armpit, including the armpit itself. Feel for any unusual lump or mass under the skin. Some women find it easier to do this step in the shower.

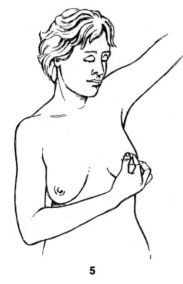

5

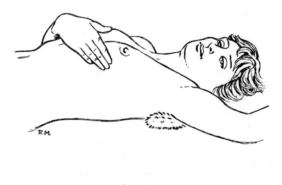

6

5. Squeeze nipple. Gently squeeze the nipple and look for a discharge. Then repeat the examination on your right breast.

6. Option: Lie flat. You may also do Steps 4 and 5 lying down. To do so, lie flat on your back, left arm over your head and a pillow or folded towel under your left shoulder. This position flattens the breast and may make it easier to examine. Use the same circular motion described in Step 4 to examine your left breast. Repeat on your right breast.

often, especially for cancers diagnosed in early stages.

Modified radical mastectomy involves removing the breast, some or most of the underarm nodes, and merely the lining over the pectoral muscles. Sometimes the smaller of the two pectoral muscles is also removed to permit access to underarm nodes. The modified mastectomy is largely replacing the Halsted procedure for cancers localized to the breast and underarm nodes. It leads to less disfigurement and weakness.

Total (simple) mastectomy removes the breast only. Underarm nodes closest to the chest may also be removed to see if chemotherapy or other treatment may be advisable.

Minimal tumors, usually diagnosed through mammograms, may be treated by extremely limited surgery combined with precise, high-energy doses of radiation. In a *segmental (partial) mastectomy* only the tumor plus a wedge of normal surrounding tissue may be removed. The *wide excision* is more limited yet, sparing overlying skin and the lining of the adjacent muscle. *Tumor excision (tumorectomy)* removes only the tumor. After such conservative surgery it often is difficult to tell which breast was operated on.

As part of therapy, the patient's ovaries may be removed. These organs are the principal source of female sex hormones affecting the growth of breast tissue. Synthetic hormones developed in the laboratory are often beneficial in treating breast cancer.

After surgery. A mastectomy patient who has undergone removal of lymph nodes in the armpit often needs to protect her hand and arm, since the arm may become more susceptible to infection and swelling. She should pamper her arm, carrying her purse and heavy articles with the unaffected arm.

Some more advice: Get someone else to do heavy work like digging or moving furniture. Wear a loose-fitting rubber glove when washing dishes. To avoid burns use your unaffected arm when reaching into hot ovens or smoking cigarettes.

Sew using a thimble to avoid pinpricks. Apply insect repellent when you may be exposed to insect bites. Don't permit injections, vaccinations, or blood samples to be done on your affected arm, unless specifically recommended by a doctor who knows you have had breast surgery.

Every mastectomy patient will have some fear, anxiety, and depression following her operation. Adjustment to family, marriage, and the community poses great emotional problems for a woman who has had a breast removed. She will be helped by a warm doctor-patient relationship and a loving and understanding husband and family. Some women need psychological consultation.

Many benefit from seeing and talking with another woman who has had the operation and has fully recovered physically and psychologically.

Use the Reach to Recovery program of the American Cancer Society. Volunteers—mastectomy patients themselves—visit the patient shortly after surgery. During two visits the volunteer discusses exercises, cosmetic devices, clothing adjustment, and listens to the patient ventilate her concerns. For information about this program contact your local division of the American Cancer Society.

Breast reconstruction, preferably performed by a board-certified plastic surgeon, is also an option to explore. Many women can attain a breast through the placement of a silicone gel mound into existing tissue. If the cancer was small enough to need only modified mastectomy, the breast may be reconstructed within a week after removal. In the meantime the healthy nipple and surrounding areola may be preserved through a graft in the groin or elsewhere on the body. An extensive mastectomy usually requires the transfer of new skin and muscle into the area to allow for the creation of an adequate breast mound.

See also CANCER.

CANCER OF THE COLON AND RECTUM is often called "the cancer nobody talks about."

Bowel movements and toilet hygiene are among the most private activities of the day. Thus many people, when they find blood on the toilet paper, or signs of blood in their stools, fail to report this to members of their family or even to their doctor. Further, bleeding from the rectum is most often associated in people's minds with hemorrhoids. Therefore many victims of colon-rectum (or colorectal) cancer seek to treat themselves in privacy with ineffective "pile cures."

Such excessive modesty costs lives. Colorectal cancer strikes some 138,000 Americans each year, almost the same number as lung cancer, and more than any type of cancer except skin cancer. Each year there are about 60,000 deaths.

The tumor tends to grow slowly and remain localized for a long time. Thus more than three out of four patients with colorectal cancer can be saved when the disease is found early and treated promptly. Yet the actual five-year survival rate is under 50 percent. The principal reason is that patients fail to act on their symptoms —or if they go to a doctor, they are not checked for colorectal cancer.

The symptoms often result from a cancer's obstructing the feces. Bleeding appears as clots of blood in the stool. The stool is often reddish. There may be changes in bowel habits—either constipation or diarrhea or both alternately. Intestinal gas may cause varying degrees of abdominal discomfort.

Any symptoms that persist more than two weeks need to be brought to the attention of a physician. Digested matter in the lower colon and rectum becomes increasingly solid. Therefore the closer the cancer is to the rectum, the more pronounced will be the symptoms.

The gas pains associated with bowel cancer are usually not steady in early cases, but become more frequent and crampy as the cancer enlarges. If bleeding continues over a long period, the patient may become weak and short of breath, due to anemia from blood loss.

Detecting colorectal cancer. If you're age 40 or over, every year have a physician perform a digital rectal examination. The doctor inserts a lubricated gloved finger into your rectum to feel for abnormal tissue that may be malignant. Digital exams find 12 to 15 percent of colorectal tumors.

Starting at least at 50, preferably at 40, an annual at-home test (e.g., Hemoccult II) is recommended for detecting hidden blood in your bowel movements. In a folder-type kit, using wooden applicators, you smear samples from three consecutive stools, which you then have analyzed by a doctor or lab. These are sometimes called "guaiac" tests, after one chemical that discloses the presence of blood. For four days, starting at least 24 hours before the first sample, it's advisable to follow a meat-free diet that's high in fiber and to avoid products (iron, vitamin C, aspirin-containing drugs) that can interfere with test results.

A flexible sigmoidoscopy is the most definitive direct exam for detecting colorectal cancer. Through a slim, lighted tube, the doctor explores your rectum and a large portion of your lower left colon, the site of two out of three tumors. It is more comfortable as well as more complete than a "procto" (short for proctosigmoidoscopy), which employs a rigid tube. Drawbacks: It's more expensive than a procto, and is more likely to be performed by a gastroenterologist than a family physician.

Starting at age 50, the American Cancer Society recommends you undergo a procto each year for 2 years, followed by one every 3 to 5 years. For even greater safety, starting at 50, have a flexible sigmoidoscopy every 3 years.

You require the most frequent scheduling of such exams if you have a tendency to grow polyps in your colon or rectum. These tiny pendulums of tissue may become malignant, and can be removed through the instrument. You also need frequent direct exams if you have ulcerative colitis, familial polyposis, Gardner's syndrome, or a close blood relative who's had colorectal cancer.

If the physician suspects a tumor of the colon or rectum, he may recommend an X-ray examination. The bowel is filled with a liquid barium compound, which shows up the colon and rectum on X-ray film. Any tumor that may be present would appear as an irregularity or obstruction. He also may advise a fiberoptic colonoscopy, employing a flexible tube that can examine the entire length of the large intestine.

The treatment is surgery. The operation consists of removing the part of the bowel containing the tumor and rejoining the healthy segments. Surgery may also take place through a proctoscope.

When the operation involves extensive surgery of the rectum, an opening called a colostomy can be made in the abdominal wall to permit elimination of body wastes. After adjusting to inconvenience the patient with a colostomy can lead an otherwise normal, active life. Considerable help can be had from a local Ostomy Club, which offers members social activities as well as medical services and advice.

Changing your diet. Preliminary studies suggest that you may reduce your risk of getting colorectal cancer if you eat bran-containing cereals and breads, and lots of fruits and vegetables. These foods are rich in dietary fiber, an indigestible, water-absorbing material that helps speed waste through the large intestine (see FIBER). Without enough fiber in the diet, warns English researcher Denis Burkitt, waste accumulates in the colon, encouraging the growth of abnormal bacteria—which produce chemicals that can lead to the development of cancer.

The refining of grains removes fiber (bran is the fibrous coat of the seed, normally removed in processing). Dr. Burkitt links increasing consumption of refined grains to the rise in colorectal cancer. By contrast, he's found that people who consume large amounts of fiber have an extremely low rate of the disease.

In addition there is a suspicion that cholesterol, widely implicated in heart disease, also may promote colorectal cancer. Some researchers believe that the end products of the digestion of cholesterol are carcinogenic. Thus by avoiding cholesterol (see FATS), you may be fending off not only a heart attack but also cancer.

See also CANCER; FATS; FIBER; PHYSICAL EXAMINATION.

CANCER OF THE ENDOMETRIUM See CANCER OF THE UTERUS.

CANCER OF THE ESOPHAGUS See CANCER OF THE STOMACH.

CANCER OF THE LARYNX, or voice box, can generally be cured if diagnosed early, when it is limited to one vocal cord.

Symptoms usually develop when the tumor is still small and localized. However it is tempting —and dangerous—to ignore the early signs because they are frequently mild.

Prolonged hoarseness may be noted first—a direct result of a tumor growing on the vocal cords, the most common early site of the disease. Any hoarseness that lasts more than three weeks should be investigated by a physician.

Growths often occur elsewhere on the larynx, causing symptoms such as a change in voice pitch, lump in the throat, or coughing. There may be difficulty and pain in breathing or swallowing. Sometimes there will be an earache. In these instances hoarseness may not develop until much later, if at all.

There are about 11,000 new cases a year, and some 4,000 deaths. Nine out of ten patients are men, chiefly in their fifties and sixties. Habitual smoking, and heavy drinking combined with smoking, are among the most important factors linked with laryngeal cancer.

Other factors are exposure to wood and metal dusts, and repeated inhalation of some chemical substances. The disease keratosis, which produces wartlike growths on the larynx, is believed to be a precancerous condition. Those with the disease need to be examined regularly.

A preliminary examination for laryngeal cancer can be made by the physician in his office using the laryngeal mirror. This device resembles a dentist's mirror with a long handle, and enables the doctor to see into the larynx.

When the cancer is diagnosed early, the treatment is generally radiation, and the patient's voice returns to normal in 90 percent of all cases. For more advanced cases surgery may remove only one vocal cord, altering the voice but preserving the ability to speak.

If the cancer has spread to other areas of the larynx or throat, treatment often involves laryngectomy. Because this surgical removal of the larynx closes off the windpipe, the surgeon creates an opening, called a stoma, in the lower part of the neck. The patient can eat and drink normally but must breathe, cough, and sneeze through the neck opening. Air inhaled through the stoma goes directly to the lungs, so the laryngectomee should avoid extreme heat or cold, gases, fumes, or dusts. He can't swim, since there is nothing to stop the water from flowing through the stoma into his lungs. The laryngectomee is unable to speak or sing or laugh out loud, and—because there is no way to temporarily lock in breath—may find it hard to lift heavy loads.

After this operation most patients can learn to speak through a technique known as esophageal speech, produced by expelling swallowed air from the esophagus. A well-trained and practiced esophageal voice produces intelligible speech of good quality. The method is best learned from a qualified speech therapist.

Across the country those who have undergone a laryngectomy have formed Lost Chord Clubs, Anamilo, and New Voice Clubs, many of which are affiliated with the International Association of Laryngectomees (IAL), an autonomous agency supported by the American Cancer Society. The IAL has been especially helpful in seeking out laryngectomees who have secluded themselves from society.

Mechanical devices are available for those patients who are unable to learn esophageal speech. Artificial larynxes, both mechanical and electric, and a device that attaches to the upper dental plate are among aids that may produce an intelligible voice.

So generally successful are the means of rehabilitation that the great majority of patients who have undergone laryngectomy are able to return to full employment activity and lead relatively normal lives.

See also CANCER; SMOKING.

CANCER OF THE LUNG was a rare disease only 50 years ago. Today, among American men, it is the most common cause of death from cancer. About 144,000 people develop lung cancer each year; 126,000 die of it. Lung cancer deaths have increased more than 20 times in less than half a century, and account for more than 25 percent of all cancer deaths.

The symptoms of lung cancer vary depending on where the cancer occurs. If it starts in the air passages, the bronchi, it will cause partial obstruction and irritation and the symptom probably will be a cough. The sputum may contain blood. But lung cancer can also start in any other part of the lung, and may not be detected until it shows up on X rays.

Sometimes coughing may occur, sometimes not. There may be vague chest pain, shortness of breath, and loss of weight and strength.

Because most of these symptoms are so commonplace, early diagnosis of the disease is difficult. Moreover, in its earliest stages lung cancer is a silent disease. It gives no warning of its presence and may not be found even by examination.

A biopsy for lung cancer may be performed with the aid of a bronchoscope, a tube through which the examining physician can see a limited portion of the bronchial tubes. If an area looks suspicious, a bit of tissue can be removed by means of another instrument inserted through the bronchoscope. On the basis of X-ray or bronchoscopic examination, the physician may decide that an exploratory chest operation is necessary.

The treatment of choice for lung cancer is surgical removal of the tumor. The disease is often so far advanced that chances for recovery are not good—less than 13 percent survive more than five years after treatment.

Smoking and lung cancer. The most widespread cause of lung cancer is cigarette smoking. At least 85 percent of all primary lung cancer cases occur in people who smoke cigarettes.

The cigarette smoker's risk of getting lung cancer is in proportion to the number of cigarettes smoked, the amount of time he has smoked, his age when he started, and how deeply he inhales. The death rate from lung cancer for men who are heavy smokers—more than two packs a day—15 to 20 times greater than that for men who do not smoke.

Occupational hazards, air pollution, and other environmental factors have also been implicated as causes of lung cancer.

A greater chance of developing lung cancer exists for persons exposed frequently and over a long period of time to asbestos, chromium compounds, radioactive ores, nickel, and arsenic. The chances of developing lung cancer increase when such exposure is accompanied by cigarette smoking.

Proportionately more cases of lung cancer are found in urban than in rural areas, most likely due to air pollution.

The best way to prevent lung cancer is to give up smoking. Even people who have been heavy smokers over long periods of time benefit by quitting, eventually reaching almost the same level of safety as those who have never smoked at all.

Any cough that lasts for more than two weeks should be actively investigated, including "cigarette coughs" and coughs resulting from colds, pneumonia, or any other respiratory illness.

Lingering so-called "virus pneumonia" and any unexplained persistent respiratory symptoms in adults, especially cigarette smokers, need to be checked by a doctor as soon as possible.

See also ASBESTOS; CANCER; COUGHING; RESPIRATORY DISEASE; SMOKING.

CANCER OF THE MOUTH (oral cancer) most commonly signals its presence by a sore on the mouth, lips, or tongue that fails to heal and bleeds easily. It may or may not be painful.

Other signs may be a lump or thickening, whitish patch, or sore throat. There may be bleeding, difficulty or pain in chewing or swallowing food, or the sensation of something in the throat. Movement of the tongue or jaw may be restricted, and there may be discomfort in wearing dentures.

Symptoms that may appear outside the mouth are a lump or swelling around the ear or in the upper neck, a sore, or facial paralysis. Report any such symptoms to a physician.

Oral cancer can occur in men and women of any age, but most frequently strikes men over 40. There are about twenty-seven thousand new cases a year, and nine thousand deaths.

Cancer of the pharynx (throat), which affects the part of the digestive tract between the mouth and the esophagus, accounts for about 25 percent of all oral cancer. About 20 percent is cancer of the tongue; 15 percent, the lip; 10 percent, the salivary glands. Other sites include the floor of the mouth, gums, palate, tonsils, lower jaw, and cheeks.

The survival rate averages about 40 percent but depends on the site. About 84 percent of men treated for lip cancer are alive five years later, but only 22 percent of those treated for cancer of the pharynx.

Many victims delay getting medical attention for mouth lesions because these conditions are so common. But most mouth cancers grow and spread quickly. For the most effective treatment early diagnosis is essential.

Surgery and radiation are the principal methods of treatment, the choice depending on the site and stage of the disease. Sometimes either form of treatment may be used effectively, and often one is used to supplement the other. For example, radiation is sometimes used to shrink tumors of the cheek or floor of the mouth before surgery.

When surgery is the method of treatment, the lymph nodes in the neck are often removed with the primary cancer. These nodes, into which the lymph system of the mouth drains, often trap spreading cancer cells. Their removal may help prevent further spread.

To help ensure removal of all malignant tissue, extensive surgery may be necessary. Although such procedures are sometimes disfiguring, highly developed techniques of reconstructive surgery can be used to rebuild or repair facial features or other affected areas. If a complete reconstructive procedure is not advisable at the time of cancer surgery, temporary artificial devices of a cosmetic nature can often be employed.

Preventing mouth cancer. Mouth cancer may be largely preventable. Safeguards include the following:

Every few months, check your mouth and lips for sores, scales, thickenings, or changes in color. Tilt your head back to inspect the hard and soft palate. Grasp your tongue with a gauze or tissue and examine all surfaces. Look for white, red, or dark patches on the inside of your cheeks and lips. Check for tenderness or small lumps by applying light pressure to your cheeks, the small rise just below each ear, and the lymphatic glands on your neck.

Give up tobacco. There is a significant link between mouth cancer and smoking. The death rate from mouth cancer is about four times higher for cigarette smokers than for nonsmokers. Mouth cancer is also strongly linked with pipes and cigars—the heat from burning tobacco may be a factor.

Chewing tobacco or snuff is also hazardous. It brings tar residue into direct contact with mouth tissues.

See a dentist regularly. He may spot a developing cancer. Chronic irritation, such as that caused by sharp, jagged teeth, a projecting filling, or badly fitting dentures, should be promptly corrected. It is possible that such irritation could lead to cancer.

Protect yourself against the elements. Among farmers, sailors, and other outdoor workers, exposure to sunlight over many years sometimes results in lip cancer as well as skin cancer. Excessive exposure to wind and frost may also be a contributing factor.

Cut down on alcohol. Excessive drinking, with or without tobacco use, is a definite factor in the development of mouth cancer.

Practice good oral hygiene. Noncancerous mouth conditions that tend to become malignant include leukoplakia of the mouth, which may result from improper care of the teeth. Leukoplakia is a disorder in which a painless white patch of cells (resembling a bit of wet tissue paper) forms on the lip, tongue, or mouth lining. If leukoplakia does appear, it should be biopsied and checked regularly. Some physicians believe that the white patches should be removed.

Follow a good diet. Plummer-Vinson syndrome, a wasting away of mucous membranes of the mouth, pharynx, and esophagus caused by diet deficiencies, frequently precedes mouth cancer.

See also ALCOHOL; CANCER; SMOKING.

CANCER OF THE PROSTATE occurs in a gland about the size of a chestnut that is part of the male genital system.

The prostate lies just below the urinary bladder and surrounds the first inch or so of the urethra, the canal that carries urine from the bladder. The secretion of the prostate provides most of the semen ejaculated during male sexual activity.

After age 55 prostate cancer becomes the third highest cause of cancer deaths among men, and after age 75 the second highest. The disease is responsible for some 25,500 deaths annually in the United States. An estimated 86,000 new cases are discovered each year.

A great number of prostate cancers are not diagnosed. Particularly in elderly men, they progress so slowly that they present no symptoms. They are discovered at autopsy in 15 to 20 percent of all men over 50.

Prostatic cancer may produce urinary symptoms, including a weak or interrupted flow of urine and the need to urinate frequently, especially at night. There may be inability to urinate or difficulty in starting urination. Blood may appear in the urine. The flow may not be easily stopped. Urinating may be painful or burning.

Though these symptoms may occur with cancer, more often they result from a noncancerous enlargement called benign prostatic hypertrophy. More than half the men in the United States over 50 suffer from such benign enlargement, which often requires surgical removal of part or all of the gland. Only a physician can tell if the symptoms are due to a benign or malignant enlargement or other illnesses.

Pain in the pelvis, lower back, or upper thighs may also be a sign of prostate cancer. Sometimes such pain is the first or major symptom.

A rectal examination is the first step in diagnosis. During an internal examination of the rectum the physician can feel irregular or unusually firm areas that may indicate a tumor. Increasingly physicians are routinely using a relatively new test called CIEP (counterimmunoelectrophoresis) for detecting elevated levels of acid phosphatase, a prostatic enzyme that increases with tumors. Further tests may include a biopsy extracting prostate cells through a needle, and also X rays checking if the cancer has invaded bone. The patient needs to consult a urologist, who may carry out additional tests and who will probably be responsible for providing necessary treatment.

If a cancer is confined to the prostate gland, the patient can usually be treated successfully by radiotherapy or by surgical removal of the gland. Surgery especially interferes with the nerve supply to the penis. The resulting impotence may be relieved with a penile prosthesis producing an erection.

Controlling prostate cancer. If the cancer has spread, it can very often be checked for long periods of time, or until death from other causes, by controlling the body's supply of male hormones, which stimulate the growth of prostate cancer.

Female hormones suppress the manufacture of these male hormones and counteract their effects. In some cases the testicles, which are the main source of male hormones, will be removed. Sometimes steroids will be used to suppress the action of the adrenal glands, which also contribute to the body's supply of male hormones.

These methods usually cause dramatic improvement—shrinking the tumor, relieving symptoms, and greatly improving the feeling of well-being. However some treatment seems to increase the risk of heart disease and stroke, so the physician must decide whether the potential benefits outweigh the hazards.

Every man over 40 should have a rectal examination as part of his annual physical examination. If prostate cancers can be discovered while still confined to the prostate gland, before they display symptoms, the great majority can be treated successfully.

If benign prostatic hypertrophy is diagnosed, it does not rule out the possibility of prostate cancer, since they often occur simultaneously. When a benign tumor is removed surgically, the urologist probably will do a biopsy to find out if cancer is present.

Most operations for benign tumors do not remove the whole prostate. Unless a man has undergone a total prostatectomy, it is still possible for him to develop prostate cancer.

Wives of men with prostate cancer may face a higher than usual risk of developing cancers of the breast and genital organs. Therefore such women should have frequent checkups for these diseases.

See also CANCER; STEROIDS.

CANCER OF THE SKIN is the most common form of cancer, striking some 400,000 Americans a year. It also has the highest cure rate of any type of cancer. Nonetheless about 7,500 die of skin cancer each year.

The skin's main surface layer is the epidermis. The underlying layer of connective tissue is the dermis. Most of the epidermis is composed of squamous cells, which are flat. Basal cells, which are spherical, are found in smaller numbers in the lowest epidermal layer. The two main kinds of skin cancer correspond to these cell types: squamous cell cancer and basal cell cancer.

Basal cell cancer occurs more frequently and grows more slowly. It rarely metastasizes, but if left untreated it can extend to the underlying bone. Squamous cell cancer occurs much less frequently, but is a greater hazard, because it often metastasizes.

Either type can appear in almost any area of the skin, but the exposed parts of the body—face, neck, forearms, and backs of the hand—are the most common sites.

The two types are similar in outward appearance. In general, a skin cancer is characterized by a dry, scaly patch or by a shallow ulcer that persists. It may appear as an inflamed area with a crusting center. Or it may look like a pale, waxy, pearly nodule that may eventually ulcerate.

Two main forms of therapy are radiation and surgery. Other methods of treatment include tumor destruction by heat, freezing, and ointments or lotions containing drugs.

Other skin cancers. Some skin conditions tend to become malignant. The most common of these is senile or actinic (sun-ray) keratosis, a scaly thickening that develops in a small area, usually on the face, neck, and hands, invariably among older people. Comparatively few keratoses degenerate into skin cancer, but when they do, they can be safely removed.

If you see any changes in the appearance of a keratosis, or any inflammation, go to your doctor immediately.

Two other malignant conditions appear in the skin: malignant melanoma and mycosis fungoides.

Malignant melanoma can arise anywhere on the body, including the soles of the feet. It is usually dark brown or black, although some lesions may lack pigment. It commonly occurs as a small, molelike growth that increases in size. It may become ulcerated and may bleed easily upon slight injury (see MOLES).

Malignant melanoma metastasizes quickly and can involve many organs. Early diagnosis and surgical removal are essential, so bring any change in size or color of any skin patch promptly to the attention of a physician.

Mycosis fungoides is marked by the development of reddish tumors on the skin which have a tendency to spread and ulcerate. Although the disease usually remains confined to the skin for years, it eventually spreads to involve internal organs.

Sun and skin cancer. The sun is the leading cause of skin cancer. Other less common causes are coal tar, pitch, arsenic compounds, paraffin oil, radium, and X rays—all products with important industrial, commercial, and medical value. As with sunlight their cancer-producing effects are proportional to the degree of exposure.

Skin cancer occurs most often in people who have fair, ruddy, or sandy complexions and are exposed to a great amount of sun.

People with fair complexions are more susceptible because their skin lacks sufficient quantities of the pigment substance melanin, which filters out the harmful rays of the sun. The darker brown the skin, the greater the amount of melanin. Blacks, in whom skin cancer is rare, have sufficient melanin to protect them from ultraviolet rays.

Precautions against skin cancer are much the same as those against sunburn. If you have fair skin, take your sun in small doses.

If long exposure is necessary, make it less harmful by wearing protective clothing such as sun hats and long sleeves. Use a beach umbrella. Apply lotions or ointments that aid the body's natural sun-shielding mechanisms. Deliberate tanning increases the chances of skin cancer.

Outdoor workers—farmers, construction workers, policemen, mailmen, seamen—should use screening ointments and protective clothing.

See a doctor for any sore that does not heal, or for a change in the size or color of a wart or mole.

If you're exposed to tarry and greasy materials, cleanse the skin afterward with plenty of soap and water. Avoid wearing clothing soaked with tars or greases. Skin cancer often strikes people exposed to tars—roofers and other workers who handle materials impregnated with tars, such as tarred ropes.

See also CANCER; MOLES; SKIN DISORDERS; SUNBURN.

CANCER OF THE STOMACH (and esophagus) has been occurring less frequently in the United States. Today only about 5 percent of all cancer deaths can be attributed to stomach cancer, compared to 20 percent 20 years ago. Nonetheless it is one of the most lethal cancers. Some 24,000 Americans develop the disease each year, and about 14,000 die of it.

To protect yourself ask your doctor about frequent medical checkups if you're in a high-risk ethnic group. Countries reporting the highest rates of stomach cancer are Japan, Chile, Portugal, Austria, Italy, Germany, and Finland. Persons from these nations who immigrate to the United States run a higher risk of stomach cancer than do native-born Americans or immigrants from other countries. You also need close watching if you have pernicious anemia or achlorhydria (the absence of hydrochloric acid from stomach secretions) because these conditions often predispose people to stomach cancer. In the United States the risk of developing stomach cancer seems to be greater for nonwhites than for whites, and to occur more often among low-income persons than among those higher up on the economic scale.

Diet may be protective. Improved diet is believed to be at least partly responsible for the downward trend in stomach cancer in this country. In the past 50 years there has been a greatly increased use of citrus fruits and lettuce and a decreased consumption of potatoes, wheat flour, and cabbage. Upper- and middle-income people tend to have well-balanced diets. Poorer people, by contrast, continue to have starchy diets—and higher rates of stomach cancer.

The variation in incidence found geographically and ethnically may be largely explained on the basis of differences in food habits. Methods of preparing or preserving food may be as important as the foods themselves. Studies in Japan and Iceland show a relationship between the high rate of stomach cancer and consumption of smoked and singed foods.

It has long been suggested that cancer of the stomach runs in families. Studies show that close relatives of stomach cancer patients are two or three times as likely to develop the disease as are persons in the general population. But this increased risk may be due more to a shared environment, including diet, than to any inherited susceptibility.

Similarly, popular belief holds that excessive consumption of alcoholic beverages, habitual drinking of very hot or very cold liquids, and use of chewing tobacco might cause stomach cancer. There is no scientific proof that any of these factors is involved.

Symptoms and diagnosis. First symptoms of stomach cancer are much like those of less serious digestive illnesses: vague digestive discomfort aggravated by eating, mild nausea, bloating, heartburn, a distaste for food ordinarily liked. If stomach pain or digestive discomfort continue more than two weeks, always consult a doctor. This especially applies to someone over age 50 who suddenly develops stomach trouble.

Other symptoms of stomach cancer—blood in the stools or vomiting, rapid weight loss, and pain—are of such a dramatic nature that they are not likely to be ignored. By this time a malignant tumor may have been present for many months, and may have started to spread to the adjacent lymph glands and to other organs such as the liver or lungs.

A thorough physical examination for stomach cancer includes laboratory tests such as a comlete blood count and chemistry profile. The doctor also checks for blood in the bowel movement.

The most important of all diagnostic methods is gastroscopy, which permits direct visualization of the stomach lining. A flexible instrument, the gastroscope, is passed down the throat and into the stomach where all areas can be viewed by the examining physician. Tissue may be gathered for microscopic examination (biopsy).

Ulcers and stomach cancer. Most authorities believe that stomach cancers start as cancers, and doubt that a peptic ulcer is precancerous except perhaps under unusual circumstances. But they warn that the ulcer symptoms may mask stomach cancer and thus delay proper treatment.

A duodenal ulcer, the most common type of peptic ulcer, can be treated conservatively for a long time without fear of cancer. A stomach ulcer should not be. Even if ulcer pain is relieved by medication, repeated direct visualizations with possible biopsies are important in order to be sure a malignant tumor is not present and growing.

The only successful treatment is prompt surgical removal of the malignant tumor. This operation involves the removal of a part or all of the stomach, depending on the location of the malignancy. Sometimes parts of other abdominal organs, such as the spleen and pancreas, are removed if they are believed to be affected.

Survival from stomach cancer is closely related to the stage of the disease at the time treatment is begun. Of patients whose tumors are localized at the time of surgery, 40 percent are alive and well five years following treatment. When adjacent tissues or lymph nodes are involved, the survival rate falls to 13 percent. Unfortunately, most cases are advanced when treatment starts.

Cancer of the esophagus, the tube that leads from the throat to the stomach, occurs most frequently in persons over the age of 55. Especially affected are men, blacks, and city dwellers. Most people who develop it are heavy smokers or drinkers.

The earliest symptom is typically difficulty in swallowing. Weight loss is a common sign. To catch the cancer early, the slightest difficulty in swallowing should be investigated promptly and thoroughly. Largely because of delays in reporting that symptom, the five-year survival rate for esophageal cancer is only about 4 percent.

For cancer of the lower portion of the esophagus surgery usually offers the best chance for complete removal of the growth. The esophagus can be replaced by constructing a new tube from a section removed from the colon. Radiation therapy is generally used when the tumor is in the upper part of the esophagus.

See also CANCER; PEPTIC ULCER.

CANCER OF THE TESTICLES is the most common malignancy in men between 25 and 44. Only a short time ago this form of cancer was often fatal because of its rapid spread to vital organs, usually the lungs. But largely because of recent advances in chemotherapy, testicular cancer has become one of the most curable of cancers, particularly if found at an early stage.

To catch the disease early, starting by age 15 men should take about one minute every month to examine their testicles, much as women check their breasts for tumors. Best time is after a hot bath or shower, when the scrotal skin is relaxed and a pea-sized nodule may be felt anywhere in the testicle. The procedure:

1. Stand in front of a mirror. Look for obvious lumps or swelling of the scrotal sac, or growth of the breasts (a danger sign).
2. Examine each testicle gently with the fingers of both hands by rolling the testicle between the thumb and the fingers. Feel for any lumps or swelling. A normal testicle is oval and firm but not hard and has a regular surface.
3. Identify the epididymis (the ropelike structure which collects the sperm) on the top and back of each testicle. Don't confuse this structure with an abnormal lump.

Repeat the exam on the other testicle. The testicles should feel the same and be approximately the same size. It is normal for one testicle to hang lower.

Abnormal lumps are often painless, as small as the size of a pea, usually located in the front part of the testicle.

If you find a lump or note enlarged breasts, contact your doctor or clinic right away. Other danger signals to report immediately are a heavy feeling in the testicles, a dragging sensation in the groin, or a sudden accumulation of fluid or blood in the scrotal sac. Sharp pain in the scrotum, while requiring medical attention, is almost never a symptom of cancer.

Increased risk. An undescended testicle increases the risk of testicular cancer. The malignancy occurs in as many as 5 percent of men with one testicle that has remained in the abdominal cavity instead of descending into the scrotal sac.

In addition researchers at Massachusetts General Hospital estimate that mumps could increase the risk of developing testicular cancer by nearly six times; an undescended testicle by almost five times; tight, heat-trapping jockey shorts by more than three times; and prenatal radiation to the mother's abdomen and pelvis by nearly two times. Testicular cancer may also be more likely to develop in men who were exposed in the uterus to hormones such as DES and progesterone.

Treatment of testicular cancer usually includes surgical removal of the affected testicle only—it's extremely rare for both testes to be affected. Depending on the type of tumor, some patients may also need to have the testicular lymph nodes removed. Following surgery, chemotherapy and radiation are commonly used to prevent a possible spread of the tumor to other parts of the body.

It is important to remember that removal of a testicle need not diminish sexual activity. An artificial testicle made of medical plastic may be placed in the scrotum during surgery or at a later time. This helps the patient look and feel normal. In addition his ability to have children is not affected since one testicle is adequate for reproductive functions.

See also CANCER.

CANCER OF THE UTERUS (cervix, endometrium) is potentially one of the most curable forms of cancer, yet is commonly fatal. It usually begins in the cervix, or neck—the narrow part where the pear-shaped uterus (or womb) opens into the vagina. The cancer proceeds slowly. For years before it includes surrounding tissues—indeed, while cells are still merely abnormal—the condition can easily be detected by a simple, painless Pap test.

Named for developer Dr. George N. Papanicolaou, the test requires only the microscopic examination of uterine secretions. Sloughed-off cancer cells may be present even though the woman has no symptoms. If their presence is detected before the cancer invades healthy tissue, the disease can be cured in almost every case. Cancer of the endometrium (the lining of the uterus) may sometimes be detected by the same test.

Yet among the women in this country some 55,000 cases of uterine cancer occur each year, with about 9,700 deaths—6,800 from cancer of the cervix, 2,900 from cancer of the endometrium. Dr. Hugh J. Davis of the Johns Hopkins School of Medicine observes: "Practitioners are 'too busy' to make routine smears; women are 'too busy' to seek prophylactic examinations; hospital laboratories are 'too busy' to organize screening services. Only the invasive cancers seem to have enough time to make themselves monotonously manifest."

Cervical cancer most often strikes women ages 40 to 49. At higher risk are women who have unusual bleeding or vaginal discharge between periods. Victims particularly include more who had frequent sex before age 20, or have had sex with many partners, or have had more than one child. Vaginal infections (notably herpes) may contribute to the condition by injuring normal cells and bringing about the first changes leading to cancer.

Endometrial cancer usually affects women between 50 and 64. At higher risk are women who have a history of infertility or failure of ovulation. Extra risks also face a woman who has a late menopause (after 55), or who has unusual bleeding or discharge during or after menopause, or who has estrogen therapy during or after menopause. Special hazards are posed for women who have a combination of diabetes, high blood pressure, and overweight.

For maximum protection, the American College of Obstetricians and Gynecologists recommends that every woman age 20 or over have a Pap test and pelvic exam every year.

Because of the cancer's slow development, some authorities feel that less-frequent testing would be adequate at lower cost. The American Cancer Society advises two Pap smears a year apart for women between 20 and 40, plus those under 20 who are engaging in sexual intercourse. If both these tests are negative, women thereafter should have a Pap smear at least every three years until age 65. Pelvic exams are recommended every three years from 20 to 40, and anually thereafter. Women may need more frequent testing if they had their first intercourse before age 17 or have such other risk factors as infertility, overweight, failure of ovulation, abnormal bleeding, or estrogen therapy.

At menopause a woman at a high risk of developing endometrial cancer should have a Pap test, pelvic exam, and endometrial tissue sample.

Symptoms. The first visible signs of the disease are irregular bleeding or unusual vaginal discharge. There may be spotting of blood after intercourse or douching. These warning signals are the same as those of other, less urgent conditions such as the common erosion of the cervix. But report such symptoms promptly to a physician, since the possibility of cancer is too great a risk to ignore.

Because the cancer usually develops slowly, patients may live for years in good general condition. Irregularities in menstrual cycles, profuse periods, and the recurrence of a period after several months without periods are symptoms that call for checking with a physician.

Diagnosis is often aided by colposcopy, the visual examination of the vagina and cervix with a magnifying instrument called a colposcope. Endometrial cancer may be diagnosed with a tissue sample obtained by scraping (dilation and curettage) or suctioning (aspiration curettage).

Treatment. If the uterine cancer has not spread, the best treatment is hysterectomy, surgical removal of the uterus.

Radiation can be used alone or in combination with surgery to help cure uterine cancer; to control tumor growth; or to alleviate pain. Drugs are used in treating some cases of advanced uterine cancer.

See also CANCER; CIRCUMCISION; EROSION OF THE CERVIX; VAGINAL INFECTION.

CANKER SORES are blisterlike sores inside the mouth and on the lips, accompanied by intense pain and burning sensation. The medical name —aphthous stomatitis or aphthous ulcers—is derived from the Greek word *aphthae,* which comes from words meaning "to set on fire." It is estimated that at least one person in five suffers from them.

Sores appear on the lining of the cheeks, edge of the tongue, floor of the mouth, and palate. Syphilis has no relation to canker sores, though the sores may remotely resemble the mucous patches found in the mouth in secondary syphilis.

In the early stages a small blister forms, but it often goes unnoticed. After the blister breaks, the typical sore (or canker) develops. It is a small oval, light yellow or yellow in color, surrounded by a red margin. Some people may have only an occasional single canker. At the other extreme are those who have a mouthful of painful sores and blisters that rarely have time to heal before the next crop appears. The victim can be debilitated by the disease, for eating and drinking become difficult with repeated outbreaks.

Causes of canker sores. It was once thought erroneously that eating chocolate or some varieties of fruit caused canker sores to erupt. A more promising theory is that the sores are related to physical or emotional stress. Another theory is that canker sores result from an autoimmune reaction.

The sores tend to heal spontaneously in about 10 to 14 days. In the meantime a protective dental paste can prevent irritation of the sores by teeth or dentures. If eating is difficult, a topical anesthetic in a mouthwash taken before meals will provide relief.

If you get recurrent canker sores, your dentist or physician may prescribe triamcinolone acetonide in an emollient paste (Kenalog in Orabase). Applied at the first sign of a lesion, this medication can abort its formation and reduce discomfort. Tetracycline oral suspension may also help avert an acute canker sore.

Various other agents—such as vitamin C in high dosages, antimicrobial drugs, gamma globulin, iodides, and gentian violet—have been used with only limited success. Patent ointments and mouthwashes may do more harm than good by increasing pain and injuring tissues.

See also MOUTH SORES; TEETH AND MOUTH DISORDERS.

CANNED FOOD may not be safe to eat if the can is dented or swollen. The swelling may result from gas produced by bacteria that can spoil food or cause food poisoning.

Cans also may bulge from hydrogen gas released when defective tinning on the can interior allows the steel of the can to react with food. This may produce metallic salts in the food, which can spoil the taste.

Return any bulging can to the retailer or manufacturer for a refund. Also return any can that is contaminated by foreign material like wood or stones. If you have trouble getting a refund, complain to your local health department.

Improper canning at home is a major cause of botulism, a possibly fatal type of food poisoning.

Open cans. Contrary to myth, it is safe to leave foods in an open can. In fact if the can was properly sterilized, it is probably cleaner than a jar or dish. Put it in the refrigerator or freezer right away as you would any other cooked food. Cover it with a plastic bag to reduce drying.

If you don't plan to use up an acidic food like grapefruit slices or orange juice in a short time, empty the contents of the can into a glass jar or other nonmetal container. When left in the refrigerator for more than a day or two, acidic foods may dissolve a little iron from the can. It's probably not harmful, but will cause a metallic taste.

Outside rust or dents don't affect the contents of a can as long as the can is not leaking or bulging. Sometimes the inside of a can shows blue, black, or brown stains, caused by the release of sulfur during food processing. This discoloration is not harmful. Also harmless is an etched pattern on the inside of fruit juice cans.

Store cans in a dry, moderately cool place. When food is stored at relatively high temperatures, slow deterioration of some vitamins will occur.

Freezing and thawing of cans may impair the texture of food, but not its overall safety—unless the freezing causes the can to bulge and leak. After thawing, check that a can has returned to its normal shape.

How long will canned foods keep? According to the FDA: "Generally speaking, if the can itself is normal in appearance, the food inside should still be wholesome. However, a regular turnover about once a year is suggested."

See also BOTULISM; FOOD POISONING; VITAMINS.

CARBOHYDRATES—starches and sugars—are necessary for proper nutrition. They contribute the major source of energy in the diet.

Many people mistakenly consider all carbohydrates "fattening." Carbohydrates, they reason, merely provide the body with calories. Hence overweight people frequently begin diets by cutting out all bread, potato, pasta, as well as desserts.

But if you eliminate virtually all carbohydrates, your body starts drawing on its own fat and protein reserves, which may cause fatigue and irritability.

Good carbohydrate foods. Many high-carbohydrate foods are nourishing and low in calories. A medium-sized potato, for example, provides you with some vitamins and some protein for only 90 calories. A banana—at 100 calories—gives you several vitamins and minerals, including important potassium.

Whole grain or enriched bread gives you B vitamins, protein, and iron. It's a nutritional bargain at 10 to 75 calories for a slice. So, too, is enriched cereal: Roughly 100 calories for an average portion (3/4 cup).

Sugar: empty calories. If you're like most Americans, you eat too much sugar. Americans consume an average of 128 pounds per person annually (over 600 calories a day)—in soda, ice cream, cakes, candy, cookies, cereals, syrups, jams, crackers, juices, coffee, tea, and countless other foods.

Unlike the many high-carbohydrate foods that contain valuable nutrients, sugar is simply "empty calories" (16 a teaspoon, 48 a tablespoon, 768 a cup). It has no nourishment.

Honey and brown sugar—substituted for white sugar by many people, including some health food enthusiasts—are scarcely better nutritionally and are less sweet. Blackstrap molasses is the sweetening product that retains the most nutrients—some calcium, iron, and B vitamins.

Excess sugar you eat is likely to be taking the place of essential nutrients and may cause nutritional deficiencies. You may be courting trouble if, say, you habitually skimp on dinner to save the calories for rich dessert. Besides contributing to overweight and poor nutrition, sugar promotes tooth decay and can precipitate diabetes in susceptible people.

To cut down on sugar: For dessert it's best to eat fresh fruits or fruits canned in their own juices (not syrup). Soft cheese with fruit makes a nutritious dessert. Have heavily sugared desserts sparingly. If you can't do without sweet desserts, select such relatively nutritious ones as cheesecake, peanut butter cookies, ice cream, custard.

If you are cooking a dessert, reduce the amount of sugar called for in any recipe. You probably won't be able to tell the difference.

Check labels carefully. Sugar is an ingredient in canned and frozen food, catsup and relishes, salad dressings, cured meats, and many other foods. Several different sugars may be among the ingredients in a product; listing them individually is a device used by some manufacturers to avoid having to list "sugar" as the first ingredient. Any word ending in "ose" is likely to be a sugar—as in dextrose or maltose. Corn syrup is also a sugar.

Beware heavily sugared cereals hawked to children on TV. Some are little better than candy—as much as 50 percent sugar. Nutritionist Jean Mayer of Harvard called such cereals "sugar-coated nothings." Television commercials, he said, equate "goodness with sweetness." Children become conditioned to require a great deal of sugar in cereals and other foods, a bad eating habit that may persist into adulthood.

It's best to buy an unsugared brand of ready-to-eat cereal. If you require sweetening, add a small amount of sugar at home. Better still, add a natural sweetener—raisins, bananas, berries, cantaloupe, pineapple, etc.

See also DIABETES; NUTRITION; OVERWEIGHT; TOOTH DECAY.

CARBON MONOXIDE See AIR POLLUTION; GAS POISONING; SMOKING.

CARDIAC ARREST See HEART STOPPAGE.

CARDIAC ARRHYTHMIA See HEART PALPITATION.

CARDIAC INSUFFICIENCY See HEART FAILURE.

CARDIOPULMONARY RESUSCITATION See ARTIFICIAL RESPIRATION; HEART STOPPAGE.

CARIES, DENTAL See TOOTH DECAY.

CARS are the fourth largest U.S. cause of death after heart disease, cancer, and stroke. Each year automobile crashes take the lives of some 50,000 Americans and injure about 2 million. They account for about half of all deaths from accidents.

If you are first on the scene of a crash: Resist your impulse to drag victims from the wreckage or off the road—moving an injured person can cause severe complications (see MOVING THE INJURED). Attempt it only if a victim is threatened by fire or if he is bleeding badly and you can't reach the wound (see BLEEDING; FIRE). Otherwise wait for an ambulance or physician.

Turn off the ignitions of the wrecked vehicles to prevent fires. To prevent pileups, station helpers 500 to 1,000 feet on both sides of the wreckage to warn oncoming motorists. Try to make victims comfortable by keeping them warm (a preventive against SHOCK, which see). Loosen their clothing. Talk to them.

Use seat belts. Fasten your safety belt when riding in a car or driving. The lap belt protects you from being thrown against the windshield, other parts of the car interior, or out of the car. Shoulder straps can prevent your head and chest from striking the steering wheel, dashboard, and windshield.

Worn together, lap and shoulder belts more than double your chances of surviving a crash and cut your risk of severe injury by about half.

But to be effective, belts should be replaced every three years. Because of deterioration due to sunlight, moisture, and wear, the odds are one in four that a belt over three years old will fail to protect you adequately.

You need to belt up even if you're driving slowly or going a short distance. More than half of accidents causing injury or death occur at speeds of less than 40 miles per hour. Some three out of four fatal accidents occur within 25 miles of home.

Pregnant women should wear safety belts snugly over the lower abdomen. Belts will not injure the unborn child. Actually a fetus is better protected than its mother—it is well encased by the uterus and a cushion of water that can generally absorb impact against a safety belt. Moreover, the unborn child as well as its mother benefits from the fact that seat belts prevent ejection.

Safety seats for children. Small children require special restraints. Highway accidents are the leading cause of child deaths. In a crash children can become human projectiles, killing themselves and adults they strike.

Some states mandate child safety seats that must meet federal standards. Check *Consumer Reports* for specific recommendations. The April issue of each year concerns cars, and generally carries an article about car restraints for children.

In general, transport an infant who cannot yet sit in a specially constructed infant carrier secured by safety belts. Those that face the child toward the rear are best. Ordinary infant seats should not be used. Children up to about four should ride in a safety-tested child car seat. The child is safest riding in the rear.

An adult lap belt may be used for a child more than 50 pounds (on a smaller child, a belt might cause abdominal injury). Use a shoulder strap only for a child more than 55 inches. A strap could cause a shorter child neck or face injuries.

Throw away a car seat that merely hooks over the back of the passenger seat, or a harness that is secured only by looping a strap around the back of a seat. Never hold a child on your lap in a moving car—a sudden stop can result in his being crushed by your body. Parents who let children play or sleep in the back of a station wagon or truck are inviting tragedy.

Don't speed. Keep your speed down. Driving too fast for road conditions is a factor in about three in ten fatal accidents. Speed can kill because it increases the force of impact. What would be a mere bump on the forehead at 20 mph can be a crushed skull at 60. Above 50 mph your chances of dying in a highway crash double with each 10-mph increase in speed. So if you drive at 70 (which many people do despite the 55-mile-per-hour speed limit), you have a four times greater chance of getting killed than at 50.

Speed also increases the likelihood of your plowing into a vehicle, pedestrian, or tree (see graph). In an emergency on a dry, level road the average three-fourths-of-a-second reaction time before you hit your brakes will carry you 22 feet at 20 mph, 66 feet at 60 mph. At 20 mph the total distance you travel will be perhaps 44 feet. At 60 it will be as much as 268 feet.

Excessive speeds generally save less time than most drivers expect. Averaging 60 rather than 50 on a 25-mile trip will save at most five minutes. Even that minimal gain in time is hard to realize. The speeding motorist is constantly forced to brake for signals and traffic conditions,

Slow Down for Safety

At this
speed   You take this long to stop

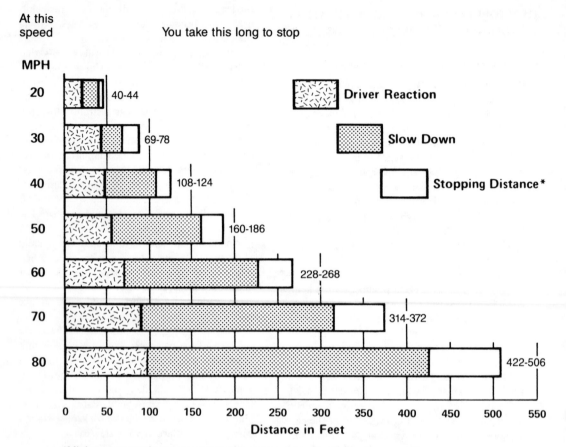

*Minimum to maximum stopping distances on dry, clean, level pavement.
Source: Illinois Rules of the Road

thus ends up at just about the average speed for the road.

Regard the legal speed limit as the maximum in ideal conditions. Though 40 or 50 may be allowable normally, on an icy, foggy night even 20 may constitute reckless driving.

Leave three car lengths (about 60 feet) between you and the car in front of you for every 10 mph of speed. The old guideline of one or two car lengths has proved inadequate to guard against "blindgating" accidents: If the car in front of you, without braking, switches to a neighboring lane to expose a stalled car or other obstruction dead ahead, you'd probably hit it if you're too close behind.

Keep awake. At the first sign of fatigue stop and stretch your legs. Run in place for two or three minutes to refresh yourself. Droopy eyelids, stiff neck muscles, decreased awareness—even in broad daylight the symptoms of "high-

way hypnosis" may creep up on you during a long trip, especially if you're alone. Falling asleep behind the wheel is blamed for about 10 percent of single-car accidents.

Take deep breaths. Get a cup of coffee. If you're still drowsy, nap for an hour or so. If this isn't possible, open the windows to drive with a blast of fresh air in your face. Turn your radio on loud. Sing to yourself.

If driving fatigue tightens your neck muscles, pull off the road and do six-second isometric exercises, repeating each three times. First press your forehead against your hands. Do this with your head straight, then tilted up, down, and toward each side.

Next push-pull with your hands clasped behind your head. Finally rotate and stretch your neck in every direction as far as you can without pain.

If your shoulders or shoulder blades are tired,

grasp the front edge of your seat. Shrug your shoulders and try to pull up the seat. Then, keeping your arms and back straight, try to lift the steering wheel to the ceiling.

Don't take stay-awake pills. The lift they give eventually wears off, leaving you more dangerously fatigued than before. With amphetamines you can literally fall asleep with your eyes open.

Other drugs—antihistamines, tranquilizers, medications for colds and coughs—may dull reflexes, make you nervous, or cloud your judgment. Don't drive without knowing the side effects of drugs you're taking.

You'll reduce chances of fatigue if you switch off with another driver every two hours. Wear sunglasses during the day to lessen glare. A relaxed, steady pace is less exhausting than speeding and frequent braking. Have light, easily digested meals while driving. Never start a journey on an empty stomach. Low blood sugar is a common source of fatigue and drowsiness, seldom suspected. Munch fruits to help keep alert.

Driving at night. Take special precautions in night driving. Deaths per mile more than double after dark. Fatal accidents increase sharply between 4:00 and 8:00 P.M., when darkness often coincides with rush-hour traffic. Twilight is a special trap—daylight has faded and headlights don't do much good. Drive at least 10 mph slower at night than you normally do in daylight, slower still on wet roads or in bad weather. Gauge your speed so you can comfortably stop within the distance illuminated by your headlights: 55 mph is about tops for average high beams on an open road.

Always use headlamps, never parking lights, when in motion, even in twilight or on rainy days. For maximum vision keep your windshield and headlamps clean—merely a day's buildup of dust and bugs can cut visibility in half.

Avoid glare blindness by keeping your eyes on the shoulder or lane marking. Never wear sunglasses at night. Lower your beams when an oncoming car is 500 feet away, or when you come within 300 feet behind a car. Keep the instrument panel dimly lit and dome light off.

If your headlights fail, slow down and stop as soon as possible. Pull well off the road, and set out warning flares. Check battery terminals for a loose connection. If this isn't the trouble, get a repairman. Don't drive without lights.

Watch for pedestrians. Pedestrian accidents account for one out of five vehicle deaths. They rise sharply at night. When you're a pedestrian, in the dark wear something white or reflective, or carry a light.

Day or night, walk on roads so you're facing oncoming traffic. Cross only at intersections. Jaywalking is the most common cause of pedestrian deaths. Other practices to avoid are ignoring traffic signals, coming into the street from behind parked cars, waiting in the street for traffic to pass instead of on the curb.

Caution children against playing in the street, and against running suddenly into the street after balls or pets. Don't allow children to play in, around, or under parked cars. It's easy for a child to disengage the parking brake and cause the car to roll down a driveway or hill.

Bad-weather driving. Prepare for winter weather. In some states as many as two out of every three traffic accidents occur when ice or snow is on the ground. On an icy pavement tires can lose all but 5 percent of their grip, making it impossible to brake to a sudden stop.

Use chains when roads are slippery. Reinforced chains on the rear tires can reduce braking distances of regular tires by half (see graph). Studded tires front and rear can cut stopping distances by about a quarter. National Safety Council studies showed that conventional snow tires on rear wheels, while helpful for accelerating, actually had slightly longer stopping distances than regular tires.

To slow down on ice without skidding, pump the brake pedal with fast, hard jabs. If you skid, take your foot off the gas and steer in the direction of the skid—if your rear is headed toward the center of the road, turn your wheels in that direction. Never slam on the brakes in a skid or you may throw the car out of control.

If you're stranded in a blizzard, stay in your car rather than brave the storm on foot. Conserve gas by running the engine enough to warm the car (about ten minutes each hour), then turn it off until the car gets cold. Keep two windows open when the engine's on, for without air circulation you risk gas poisoning by carbon monoxide.

For winter emergencies stock your car with food, blankets, and warm clothes. Pack a shovel in the trunk. If you get stuck in snow, clear under the car so the tires rest on little mounds. Then gas gently (spinning the wheels will only dig you in deeper)—and you'll often have enough momentum to get free. Also keep several small bags of sand distributed throughout the trunk. The extra weight will help traction, and if stuck you can use sand under your tires to help you move.

Driving in the rain increases the accident rate three to five times. Highways that have been dry for extended periods can be especially treacherous. Oil drippings and fine tire dust that accu-

Chains and Studs Brake Best on Ice

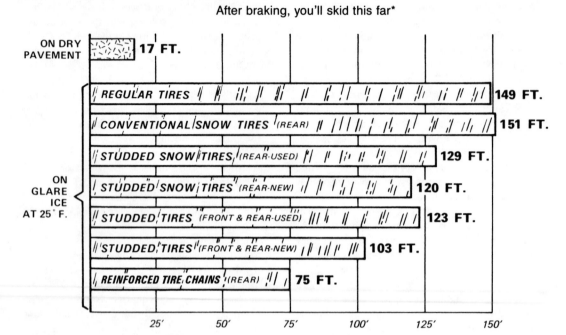

After braking, you'll skid this far*

ON DRY PAVEMENT	17 FT.
REGULAR TIRES	149 FT.
CONVENTIONAL SNOW TIRES (REAR)	151 FT.
STUDDED SNOW TIRES (REAR-USED)	129 FT.
STUDDED SNOW TIRES (REAR-NEW)	120 FT.
STUDDED TIRES (FRONT & REAR-USED)	123 FT.
STUDDED TIRES (FRONT & REAR-NEW)	103 FT.
REINFORCED TIRE CHAINS (REAR)	75 FT.

ON GLARE ICE AT 25° F.

25'   50'   75'   100'   125'   150'

*From 20 mph. Distances don't include normal reaction time (22 additional feet).
Source: National Safety Council Committee on Winter Driving Hazards

mulate during dry periods produce an extremely slick road surface when rain begins.

In heavy rains tires often leave the road at speeds of 50 to 60 miles per hour and skim along the surface of the water, resulting in loss of steering and braking ability. This can occur at speeds as low as 35 miles per hour if the car is overloaded in the rear or if front tires have inadequate tread. If you must drive in a heavy rain, slow down, allow extra space between you and the car ahead, and at the first opportunity increase tire pressure by about one third (don't try this on cheap or badly worn tires).

Wet-weather driving can also result in wet brake linings that lose their braking ability. Check braking ability often, especially after going through deep water. Repeated light applications of the brakes to generate heat will speed up the drying of brake linings.

Mountain driving. Mountain driving robs a car engine of 8 to 10 horsepower with every 1,000-foot increase in altitude. You can lose half your car's horsepower in mountain driving, so allow extra latitude for acceleration and passing.

Higher altitude and extra strain on the engine can cause your car to overheat. Turn off air conditioning, and pull off the road. If the engine is steaming, stop immediately. The cooling system has probably lost coolant, and continued running will ruin the engine.

If no steam is evident, don't turn the engine off. Put the transmission in neutral and run the engine at well above idle speed until temperature returns to normal. Don't stop an overheated engine after a heavy pull except for loss of coolant or an emergency. To do so will stop air and coolant circulation, overheating the engine further, and possibly causing serious damage.

Stay where you are until the engine cools down. Then with the conditioner off proceed to a service station for a checkup. Don't remove the radiator cap—you may be scalded by a geyser—or pour cold water on a hot engine—it may split.

The braking system may fade from overheating because of higher altitudes and heavy usage. As soon as the brake pedal feels mushy, pull off the road and wait for at least half an hour. Always try brakes before long downgrades and apply them intermittently and sparingly to avoid overheating. Downshift the car to a lower gear to let the engine help with braking on long or steep inclines.

Emergency tips. Could you handle these

emergencies? Here's what the National Safety Council recommends:

Your car plunges into water. A car with windows and doors closed will float from three to ten minutes. Escape through a window. Power windows may short out, so try to open them immediately. Tempered glass in the side and rear windows can be broken only with a heavy, hard object.

If the car does sink before you can get out, an air bubble will form in that section of the passenger compartment closest to the surface. You can get a breath of air from this bubble before making your exit. When pressure inside and out is equalized, it is easier to open a door.

Your gas pedal sticks. Turn off the ignition and brake to a stop. If your car is equipped with power brakes and steering, they will go off with the ignition, so be ready to bear down against the stiffness in steering and braking.

If you need the power assist for steering and braking, shift to neutral. But get stopped quickly before the racing engine causes damage.

Your brakes fail. Pump the brake pedal. You may regain some pressure. If this doesn't help, shift to a lower gear—so engine compression can help slow the car—and apply the parking brake.

If that doesn't work, throw the car into reverse. This will bring most cars to a stop. It may damage the transmission, so do it only in an emergency.

If you are traveling down a hill and can't reduce speed, drive into heavy brush or snow, or sideswipe a guardrail, sandbank, or even parked cars. Avoid a head-on collision at all costs.

You have a blowout. Don't slam on the brakes or you may go into a spin. Apply careful pressure on the brake pedal and keep a firm grip on the wheel.

Avoid oversteering to correct a swerve or pull. If it's a front tire, the car may pull to the side of the blowout. A rear tire may cause the car to weave.

Pull onto the road shoulder and limp along until you find a level spot on which to change the tire.

Your car catches fire. Most fires are the result of a short circuit in the car's electrical system. Don't waste time trying to disconnect the battery, which usually requires tools.

If you don't carry a fire extinguisher, rip loose any burning wires with a jack handle and smother with a blanket or coat. Don't grab the wires with your bare hands or you may suffer electrical burns. Flag down a trucker—trucks usually carry efficient extinguishers.

If the fire burns out of control and endangers the gas tank, get away from the car immediately.

Note: You're driving with dynamite if you carry a can of gasoline in the trunk of your car. The cans are easily ruptured in a collision and can drench the car and occupants with highly flammable fluid.

You're on a collision course. Another car is speeding toward you in your lane.

Brake hard—every mile you take off your speed reduces the impact force. Head for the right shoulder and give him the entire road. Lean on the horn and flash your lights.

If he continues toward you, take the ditch or any open ground to the right free of solid obstructions. Even a roll-over gives you a better chance than a head-on collision.

Don't try to outguess him and swerve to the left around him. He may recover at the last instant and instinctively veer back into his own lane—to hit you head-on.

You must stop on a highway. To keep someone from crashing into you, get your car off the road before the car stops rolling. Turn on taillights, four-way flashers, and interior lights at night. To signal for help, raise the hood and tie something white to the antenna or left door handle.

If the car is close to a traffic lane, on a curve, or over a hill, get everyone out and well away from it. Place a flare 10 feet in back of the car and another flare 300 feet to the rear, or still farther back if a hill or curve interferes with normal sight distance.

Driving and drinking. Your worst enemy on the road is the tipsy driver. Alcoholism or problem drinking is implicated in 35 percent of all major crashes. An additional 15 percent are related to social use of alcohol, mainly among teen-agers and young adults.

Alcohol leads to impulsiveness and risk-taking. It reduces coordination, reaction time, tolerance to glare, ability to estimate speed and distance. It tends to exaggerate any emotional instability. It reduces attentiveness and causes drowsiness.

About one in five cardiovascular patients is a high-risk driver. Some 15 percent of fatal single-vehicle crashes are thought to be caused by sudden death from heart disease.

Cardiovascular patients have twice the crash rate of other drivers, some because of heart attack or stroke behind the wheel. Others may lose control because of pain or blackout; or have a tendency to fatigue or inattentiveness; or suffer from reduced reaction time, lower breathing capacity, decreased ability to react to stress.

You do not belong behind a wheel if you suffer from a condition causing blood-vessel constriction or dilatation; if your blood pressure is higher than 180/110; if you've had a stroke (or any other impairment of the circulation of the brain), congestive heart failure, carotid sinus syndrome, or cor pulmonale, as from emphysema.

High-risk drivers. Teen-agers have the worst record on the road. Males under 25 account for 50 percent more than their share of accidents, the highest crash rate of any group by sex or age. A major cause is inexperience in driving plus adolescent irresponsibility expressing a desire to prove oneself, show off, be independent.

If possible insist that your child take driver training at school. These courses teach not only driving skills, but also all-important attitudes, and students completing this training have fewer accidents.

If your child in general respects the rights of others and is trustworthy in following instructions, he's likely to be courteous on the highway. If not you owe it to him and to those he may injure to deny him use of a car until he shows greater maturity.

Other high-risk drivers: Sufferers of epilepsy and diabetes may suddenly lose consciousness behind the wheel. Epileptics need to get off the road immediately and not drive again before seeing a doctor, if they have a grand mal aura or peculiar neuromuscular or digestive sensations. Diabetics also need to avoid driving and see a physician on experiencing these emergency symptoms: dizziness, light-headedness, clammy skin, unusual sweating.

Emotional problems can make you a road hazard because they may distort perceptions and impair judgment and mechanical skills. Don't drive to relieve anger or violent feelings.

Aging may cause driving risks if accompanied by senility, depression, forgetfulness, or by physical impairments such as joint stiffness or reduced breathing capacity. Decreased vision (less than 20/40 or 140-degree peripheral field) should signal an elderly person off the road.

Since the aged rarely notice signs of deterioration in themselves, younger relatives or friends need to watch for signs that an oldster should stop or limit driving. These include a tendency to become easily confused, especially in bad weather or at intersections; an increasing number of near misses in traffic; ever more passing or horn-blowing by other motorists because an aged person's driving is erratic.

What to do in an accident. Here's legal advice if you're in a crash. Get the license-plate number of the cars involved. If there's a pileup, note each car's location.

Get the names and addresses of witnesses, three or four if you can. Don't quiz them or you may scare them off, and say as little as you can yourself. Let your lawyer or insurance company do as much talking as possible for you.

From other drivers and passengers get names and addresses and other drivers' insurance identification (if you can—they're not obliged to give it to you). Carry your own proof of insurance coverage. It may save your car from being impounded.

Note the badge number of the policeman who appears, in case you need him as a witness or he fails to file his report. Make your own notes on accident details: place, time, directions, highway conditions, weather, position of cars. Note the precise seat locations of everyone in the other cars. They may claim serious injury later on, and the information can be meaningful.

Phone the nearest office of your insurance company, or your agent at home. Then write directly to your company's home office, using certified mail, return receipt. Give them simple notice of the accident, and your policy number.

If you're in serious difficulty, phone your lawyer. If you're away from home, let him set up a contact with a local attorney. Let your lawyer file your accident report. Because of the chance of later injury claims, it's wise to fill one out even if no one seems hurt or if property damage is below a statutory minimum. But, in filing, the less said, the better.

See also ACCIDENTS; ALCOHOL; BLEEDING; FIRE; GAS POISONING; MOVING THE INJURED; SHOCK; SUNGLASSES; TRAINS; WHIPLASH.

CARSICKNESS   See MOTION SICKNESS.

CARTILAGE CANCER   See CANCER OF THE BONE.

CASTS, PLASTER   See PLASTER CASTS.

CATARACT is a clouding of the lens of the eye and is a leading cause of blindness in the United States, accounting for about one in four cases.

The opaque areas may increase in number and size until the lens becomes completely clouded. At this point the victim has lost all detailed vision and can usually only distinguish between light, dark, and bright colors.

The most common type of cataract is associated with aging. More and more people are living long enough to have "senile" cataract—an unfortunate term since most cataract sufferers are otherwise healthy and independent.

Children may be born with cataract from hereditary influences or because their mothers had infections such as German measles during the first three months of pregnancy. Among other causes of cataract are eye injuries and radiation. Sometimes glaucoma and diabetes are involved. Those in certain occupations, such as glassblowers and others who work near heat, may be vulnerable because the lens is subjected to intense infrared rays.

Contrary to popular misconceptions, cataract is not caused or worsened by using the eyes for reading, sewing, TV, or movies. It is not a cancer. It is not contagious. It is not a film growing over the lens, but a change in the lens itself.

In advanced cases, an obvious sign may be a whitish spot in the pupil. Usually you won't notice this change yourself unless you gaze in the mirror, since cataract is painless and the affected area at first is usually small. Other symptoms:

Blurred vision. Since less light can now reach the retina, you may have trouble finding a light bright enough to read by. You may need to hold objects closer to your eye to see them.

Double vision or spots. You may not see lights clearly outlined, but as if there were two or more. You may experience loss of detail.

Frequent change of eyeglasses. This may indicate the presence of a cataract near the center of the lens.

Removing cataracts. Surgery is the only treatment. The operation has a success rate well above 90 percent.

Consult with your ophthalmologist to determine the best time for cataract surgery. The decision to operate is usually made when vision is impaired to the point where it interferes with normal activity.

Don't be misled by fraudulent claims that salves, drops, or pills will dissolve a cataract. Advice to use such preparations may delay receiving proper treatment or retard its progress. There are no special eyeglasses that can prevent a cataract from developing.

Sight after surgery. The eye can no longer focus after the lens is removed. To replace the function of the lens there are three possibilities: glasses, implanted lenses, or contact lenses.

Cataract glasses are thick and may feel heavy and uncomfortable. Color and size of familiar objects are noticeably different, and the thick lenses have a tendency to distort straight lines. Peripheral (side) vision is limited. When only one eye is operated on, glasses cannot be used.

If possible most practitioners prefer to provide their cataract patients with either implanted lenses or contact lenses.

Implanted lenses are plastic lenses that are inserted in the eye at the time of surgery in place of the opaque lens that's removed. An implant improves vision, permitting a thinner eyeglass correction, and is more convenient to use than other methods of cataract correction. Implants are generally used in patients above 40 and also in younger patients whose jobs and eye problems preclude glasses or contact lenses. Implants cannot be used with diabetic retinopathy, uncontrolled glaucoma, and other diseases.

Contact lenses provide the same good vision as implanted lenses, with the advantage of easy removal in case of complications. But they may be hard for elderly people to insert and remove daily. A good choice may be contact lenses that can be worn for up to two weeks at a time.

See also CONTACT LENSES; EYE DISORDER.

CATERPILLARS of many moths and butterflies have hollow venom-containing hairs that can poison humans on contact, causing hives and contact dermatitis. Some people who believe they are suffering from poison ivy actually have come in contact with caterpillars, their nests, or windblown hairs. The pain from a poisonous caterpillar falling on the skin can be excruciating, with blisters and reddening. Epidemics of caterpillar dermatitis occasionally occur during caterpillar migration.

For treatment immediately apply cellulose tape over a sting to remove some of the spines. You may be able to reduce swelling and relieve itching with ice compresses. Physicians called in on severe cases often administer Adrenalin and prescribe steroids.

Wash any clothing and bedding that may have been contaminated with caterpillar hair.

See also INSECTS.

CAT SCRATCH DISEASE is generally caused by contact with an infected cat's saliva. This is transmitted to the paws and nails as the cat licks them, and may be deposited in your skin with a bite or scratch. If a cat licks an open wound, it may also lead to infection.

The first symptom is usually a pimple at the site of the wound. Within two weeks there is a swelling of lymph nodes, with fever, headache, loss of appetite, and general malaise. Sometimes blocked nodes need to be removed by surgery. Healing generally occurs spontaneously within a month.

There is evidence that many if not most cats carry the infective organism, thought to be a virus, though not every scratch results in this disease. Your best protection is to avoid being scratched, bitten, or licked. If you are so brought in contact with a cat's saliva, wash the area with soap and water.

See also ANIMAL DISEASE; INFECTIOUS DISEASE.

CAVITIES See TOOTH DECAY.

CELIAC DISEASE See MALABSORPTION.

CENTIPEDES have forelegs bearing fangs through which they can inject venom when they bite. Small species produce only local inflammation, generally with itching. Swelling may be relieved with ice compresses. Bites of the large tropical species can cause painful inflammation of the lymph vessels, vomiting, fever, and headache, and generally require a physician's attention.

Warn children against picking up centipedes —the fact that they are poisonous is not generally known. Centipedes are often confused with millipedes, which are nonpoisonous, nonbiting vegetarians.

To discourage an invasion, remove low vegetation or mulch from the immediate surroundings of your home. Where these pests congregate, use spot applications of insecticides containing 2 percent malathion to control centipedes, 2 percent chlordane to control millipedes.

See also INSECTS.

CEREBRAL PALSY (CP) refers to a number of conditions in which brain damage affects muscular control. Such birth defects affect about 3 of every 1,000 U.S. infants.

The most common forms of CP are *spastic,* in which the muscles are rigid and tense, causing the person to move stiffly and with difficulty; *athetoid,* in which the muscles move involuntarily and continuously; and *ataxic,* in which the person's balance and depth perception are damaged, making him prone to falls. Many people with CP have a combination of several types.

Symptoms can range from a mild, nearly unnoticeable tremor of one muscle to virtually total loss of muscle control. The most common effects of cerebral palsy are an awkward, shambling gait, speech difficulties, grimacing and drooling, tremors and spasms. People with cerebral palsy may also have defects in teeth, vision, and hearing. Learning difficulties and behavioral problems are common. Some people with cerebral palsy suffer from mental retardation.

Rubella in pregnancy can lead to the defect. Other predisposing factors include diabetes in the mother, poor nutrition and poor health during pregnancy, Rh disease, premature birth, and low birth weight.

Another possible cause is oxygen deprivation in the fetus because of complications during childbirth, such as premature separation of the placenta or a long and difficult labor.

Sometimes cerebral palsy develops in a child after meningitis. It may also result from severe head injuries received in an accident, fall, or child abuse.

If your child has cerebral palsy, get help for him as soon as possible. Early treatment and management can help him make better use of his remaining abilities and prevent further disabilities.

There is no cure for CP, but exercises, drugs, braces, and surgery can help. The United Cerebral Palsy Associations, Inc., 66 East 34th Street, New York, New York 10016, can provide you with information, vocational counseling, and psychological help.

See also BIRTH DEFECTS.

CEREBRAL VASCULAR ACCIDENT See STROKE.

CERVICAL CANCER See CANCER OF THE UTERUS.

CHAPPED SKIN See SKIN DRYNESS.

CHARLEY HORSE is a strain that causes a muscle spasm. It frequently develops in the calf and is followed by aching and stiffness. Unaccustomed exercise is the most common cause.

If you suspect you'll suffer a charley horse after unusually strenuous exercise, *before* the activity apply heat to the area or soak in a hot tub. After the activity, apply an ice pack. If you're uncomfortable in the morning, try aspirin.

See also SPORTS; STRAINS.

CHEEK CANCER See CANCER OF THE MOUTH.

CHEST INJURIES are extremely serious if air sucks through the wound into the cavity enclosing the lung. The lung will collapse, causing grave breathing difficulties.

As the first emergency step seal the wound (see illustration). Place a bandage or cloth pad over it. Aluminum foil or a piece of plastic bag or wrap will help make the wound airtight. Draw a belt or cloth strip firmly around the chest to hold the covering in place.

Be ready to administer artificial respiration. Watch for rib fractures that may impede breathing or damage the lungs.

See also ACCIDENTS; ARTIFICIAL RESPIRATION; RIB FRACTURES.

CHEST PAIN most often is *not* a sign of heart disease or impending heart attack. Many cases of heart trouble used to be overlooked or misdiagnosed, but increased awareness of heart disease has led to the opposite tendency of erroneously diagnosing numerous other conditions as heart attack.

See a physician for any persistent chest pain. Among the commonest causes are strains of the muscles of the chest wall or shoulder, and chest injuries including unsuspected rib fractures.

IF A CHEST WOUND IS DEEP

Keep lung from collapsing

1. Pad the wound
Use bandage, clothing, rags

2. Make airtight
Cover with aluminum or plastic wrap
Seal with tape

3. Tie in place

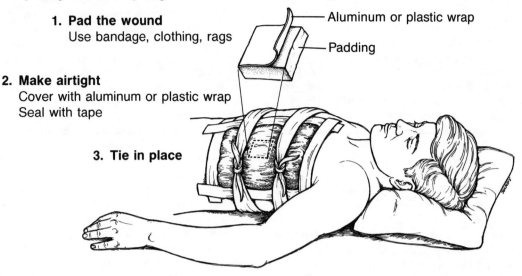

— Aluminum or plastic wrap

— Padding

Emotional stress accounts for much chest pain, especially among people concerned about getting a heart attack.

Many respiratory diseases—asthma, bronchitis, coughing, emphysema, pleurisy—are likely to cause pains in the chest. So may a blood clot in the lung. Chest pain is one late sign of cancer of the lung and cancer of the breast. It can also come from hiatal hernia, indigestion, choking, food poisoning, shingles, or a pinched or inflamed nerve.

It can be a referred pain, the result of the brain's getting mixed up as to the true source of a pain impulse. Gallbladder disease, peptic ulcer, and appendicitis may be felt in the chest.

Angina pectoris. The pain of angina pectoris is a sign that the heart muscle is not getting enough oxygen. *Angina* means "strangling"; *pectoris* refers to the breast or front chest wall. The most frequent underlying cause is coronary artery disease.

Angina sufferers often describe their pain as a sensation of tightness. They say: "I feel a pressure like somebody is sitting on my chest." "Like an elephant's got his foot on my chest." "My heart's in a vise."

An angina attack often starts in the pit of the stomach and may radiate to the neck and lower jaw or shoulders and arms. It generally is accompanied by oppressive feelings of fear and apprehensiveness. The degree of impairment ranges from mild, occasional Class I pain to frequent, debilitating Class IV pain, which can make the least effort an exhausting ordeal.

If you suffer from angina pectoris: Suspect a heart attack if the frequency, duration, or severity of your angina increases; if your angina is accompanied by heavy perspiration; or if you take 3 nitroglycerin tablets within 15 minutes but get little or no relief.

Otherwise pursue your normal work and social life. When angina occurs, rest for 10 to 15 minutes. After 3 minutes the discomfort should subside.

Pace yourself, and avoid unnecessary stress. Running to catch a plane is likely to provoke an angina attack. So is trying to change a tire in a hurry. Beware excessive exercise. Sidestep situations that make you angry, frustrated, or overexcited.

Eat moderately. A heavy meal can place a strain on your heart, especially at night. Take lighter meals, perhaps four instead of three a day, and rest afterward. Many overweight people's angina lessens or disappears with weight reduction.

Steer clear of carbon monoxide—from smoking, air pollution, gas poisoning. The colorless, odorless gas can bring on and aggravate angina. "Secondhand" cigarette smoke makes angina worse.

You may need nitroglycerin, which despite its explosive name is a safe and effective drug (glyceryl trinitrate USP). Placed under the tongue at the first sign of discomfort, it usually brings relief in minutes. Rest for about ten minutes when taking it, since it can cause dizziness. Propanolol (Inderal), generally in combination with other drugs, may be prescribed for someone whose angina is not relieved by nitrates alone. Propanolol, however, can worsen cases of heart failure.

Angina can sometimes be relieved by taking a deep breath and forcing it against your closed throat for about 15 seconds, a motion much like pushing against a hard bowel movement. Don't try the method—called the Valsalva maneuver—without your doctor's permission. In cases of severe angina, coronary bypass surgery may be recommended (see ARTERIOSCLEROSIS).

See also CORONARY ARTERY DISEASE.

CHICKENPOX (varicella) is an extremely common childhood infectious disease. It is caused by a virus that spreads so readily that most people have the disease by the time they are 15 years old. A person almost never has chickenpox twice. The name is thought to come from the Latin word *cicer,* which means chick-pea.

The virus is spread by direct contact with infected persons or articles freshly soiled by the fluid from their blisters, or by airborne droplets expelled from their noses and throats when they cough or sneeze. A person can pass on the disease for about a week or ten days, possibly beginning one day before the rash appears and continuing until no new spots develop. The dry scabs are not infectious.

A susceptible person will break out with chickenpox two or three weeks after he has been exposed. A child may also contract chickenpox from exposure to a person with shingles, which is caused by the same virus.

Symptoms. A rash is usually the first sign that a child is coming down with chickenpox. Occasionally there may be a slight fever (seldom over 101° F), headache, irritability, or loss of appetite for a day or two before the rash appears. The pink spots, which resemble small blisters, usually start on the trunk, then spread to the face and other exposed parts of the body. In severe cases they appear on all the body surfaces, including the scalp and the lining of the mouth, throat, and eyelids.

The blisters do not all come at the same time, but develop in crops. They take from one to four days to form, break, and crust over. Each lesion starts as a spot or blemish. It changes to a pimple at first, next to a blister filled with pus. When it dries, the lesion becomes a crust which will slough off or is brushed away.

Keep the young patient from picking and scratching. It's not easy, since the itching is often intense, but every scratch means a possible scar. Many parents put mitts on the hands of very young children or slip paper tubes (such as mailing tubes or those inside a roll of paper towels) over their elbows to keep them from scratching.

To avoid infection from scratching, keep the child's skin scrupulously clean, fingernails clipped short, and hands scrubbed. Give him a tub bath every day, change his clothing and bedding daily. If the physician prescribes soothing ointments or powders, apply them to all eruptions on the skin, including those on the scalp and sex organs.

Until no new spots appear, keep the patient away from people who have not had the disease. Particularly from adults, since an adult attack can be severe and long-lasting. Members of the family who have had the disease are usually not restricted in any way. Your physician or health department will advise you about local health and school regulations concerning others in the family who have not had the disease.

Protect very young or weak children from exposure to chickenpox, since they may develop chickenpox's rare complications—pneumonia, encephalitis, or eye, ear, and kidney involvement. A person with leukemia or other forms of cancer—or someone taking steroids or antimetabolite drugs—is very susceptible to chickenpox. So is anyone whose normal bodily immunities are not functioning.

Such people may benefit from immunization with zoster immune globulin (ZIG), a blood extract taken from convalescent victims of shingles. ZIG is extremely scarce, and requests are screened by American Red Cross regional blood centers.

See also INFECTIOUS DISEASE; SHINGLES.

CHIGGERS are tiny red larvae of mites. These arachnids—close relatives of spiders—hook onto unprotected skin, injecting a substance that softens the tissue. Red blotches and blisters form, with considerable itching.

TO AVOID BITES OF THE CHIGGER

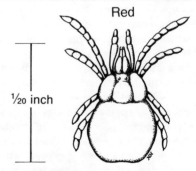

Red

1/20 inch

Use insect repellent
Wear long pants, thick socks
Bathe immediately after exposure

Chiggers infest fields, bushes, swamps in summer, especially in the South. After a walk through such areas bathe with a brush and soapy water as soon as possible. Chiggers usually wait an hour or more before attaching to the body, and prompt cleansing may ward off infestation. Disinfect clothing with a pesticide.

If you are bitten, these measures may help: When bathing leave lather on for ten or more minutes. Dab colorless nail polish over affected areas. Apply an ice cube to each spot.

To avoid an attack use insect repellent on your skin and clothing. When walking in the woods or through undergrowth, wear long pants, thick stockings, and shoes or boots. Avoid sitting or lying on grass that may be infested with chiggers.

See also INSECTS; ITCHING.

CHILDBIRTH   If you ever have to help deliver a baby in an emergency:

1. Let nature take its course. In most normal deliveries the mother can do most of the delivering herself. Don't try either to delay or hasten the birth.

2. Wash your hands thoroughly with soap and water. There's no need for boiling water.

3. Encourage the mother to breathe deeply through her mouth during contractions, and relax between contractions.

   Have her lie on her back with her knees up and legs spread apart. Or, if she's more comfortable, sitting with pillows propped behind her back. Some women prefer a squatting position.

4. As the baby's head emerges, gently support it with your hands. Don't pull on it.

5. Support the emerging baby by the head and shoulders. Make sure your grip is gentle but firm—the baby may pop out, and his natural fluids make him slippery.

6. If you can get medical assistance within a few minutes, wait. Don't wash the baby or cut his umbilical cord.

   Instead cover him with a clean cloth. Place him on his side between his mother's thighs, with his head lower than his trunk. This allows blood and mucus to drain from his nose and mouth.

7. Most babies spontaneously start to breathe and cry as soon as they are born. If the baby needs encouragement, slap the soles of his feet. If he doesn't respond within a minute or two, use artificial respiration, first clearing the airway of mucus, then gently puffing small breaths into his nose and mouth (see ARTIFICIAL RESPIRATION).

8. If you must cut the umbilical cord, wait two or three minutes until it stops pulsating. Then tie a cord (such as a shoelace) about 6 to 8 inches from the baby's navel, tight enough to stop circulation.

   Tie another cord about 2 inches farther from the navel. Cut the umbilical cord between the two ties with a clean scissors or knife. If you can, boil the instrument beforehand.

9. Most women deliver the placenta (afterbirth) a few minutes after the baby is born, but it may not emerge for as long as 15 or 20 minutes. It is usually accompanied by a loss of about half a pint of blood. If you can get the mother to a hospital within a few minutes, don't attempt to deliver the placenta.

   If there's no chance of medical assistance, help deliver the placenta by gently massaging her lower abdomen. You'll feel the uterus as a grapefruit-sized object, which contracts as you massage it. These contractions will help expel the placenta. Do not pull on the cord.

   Wrap the placenta in a towel or plastic bag, and take it to the hospital for examination. A physician must check to see that all of the placenta has been delivered, for any part left in the uterus can cause hemorrhaging and infection.

10. Get the mother and infant to a hospital as soon as possible.

Common complications. You may have to handle one or more of the common complications of childbirth. In case of excessive bleeding treat for SHOCK (which see).

In breech presentation, the most common abnormal delivery, the buttocks emerge first instead of the head. As the baby's buttocks and trunk come out, support the legs and trunk with your palm under the trunk and the legs dangling on either side of your arm. The head will then follow. Pressure on the mother's abdomen, just above the pubic bone, is usually helpful in delivering the head.

In some cases the head will take more than three minutes to deliver. With its head pressing down on the umbilical cord, the baby is getting little or no blood and oxygen. To keep it from suffocating, put your hand into the birth canal and relieve the pressure against the umbilical cord. Maintain this space until the head is born.

If one arm or one leg presents, don't attempt delivery even though the infant is sacrificed. This complex problem requires skilled medical help if only to save the mother. Get her to a hospital as soon as possible.

A baby born prematurely requires special care (see PREMATURE BIRTH).

Onset of labor. Labor usually begins with noticeable contractions of the uterus 10 to 15 minutes apart. Over several hours the contractions gradually become stronger and more frequent. There may be a large discharge of fluid or a slow seepage as the amniotic sac breaks, and a show of blood. This is the time to call your doctor.

At the hospital you'll be examined internally to see how far your labor has advanced, gauged by how much your cervix has dilated. Your blood pressure will be taken, and you'll probably be given an enema to reduce the bowel's bulging into the birth canal.

Your vaginal area may be shaved. (Shaving is not necessary, but many doctors prefer it.) Your baby's heartbeat will be listened to at intervals. If this is your first labor, expect it to last 12 to 16 hours. Subsequent labors are likely to be shorter, but are not always.

During labor you may suffer from backache, leg cramps, and shaking, dizziness, or nausea. As the contractions become more intense, they usually become more uncomfortable. During the most active stage of labor contractions occur at about two- or three-minute intervals and can last a minute or longer.

Generally the doctor performs an episiotomy. Before the baby's head emerges, he cuts the perineum—the skin between the opening of the vagina and the anus—to prevent a jagged tear as the head is delivered. The cut is stitched up while you are still on the delivery table.

A local anesthetic is usually given to dull the pain. The stitches will dissolve by themselves.

Sedation, analgesia, and anesthesia can reduce the discomforts of labor and delivery. All drugs used in childbirth carry a small risk to the mother and the child. Any medication passes through the placenta to the fetus. Among the most commonly used pain-relieving agents are tranquilizers and narcotics like Demerol and several types of spinal anesthetics.

Low spinal (saddle block), caudal, and epidural anesthesia block all sensation of pain—but not pressure—in the pelvis. The woman remains awake through delivery. But these types of anesthesia sometimes obliterate the bearing-down reflex, so that the doctor must use a metal obstetrical tool called a forceps to help pull the baby out. Spinal anesthesia leaves about 5 percent of women with a severe headache for days after delivery.

Not all types of anesthesia are suitable for all women. Discuss with your physician the best method for you. Many doctors use different types of pain-reducers at different stages of labor. The final decision is the anesthesiologist's, not the obstetrician's.

General anesthesia, in which the woman is put to sleep, is now generally used only in special situations.

Cesarean delivery. Some women are unable to deliver through the birth canal. This may be because of a small pelvis, a medical problem such as diabetes, in which babies grow very large, or an obstetrical emergency. In such cases an operation called a cesarean section is performed. The abdominal wall and the wall of the uterus are opened, and the baby and placenta are delivered through the opening. It is possible to have several babies by cesarean delivery. A woman who has a baby by cesarean need not necessarily have subsequent babies by cesarean as well. Cesareans can be done under local anesthesia, and some hospitals now allow fathers to remain with their wives during cesarean delivery.

Natural childbirth. Consider natural childbirth. Courses in childbirth preparation educate the woman about her body in pregnancy and birth. The goal is an emotionally satisfying experience, preferably with little or no painkilling agents. This is generally healthier for mother and baby.

The most popular and successful technique is the Lamaze method, also called psychoprophylaxis. Named after the French obstetrician Fernand Lamaze, this method works on Pavlovian reflex theories.

Women are taught to respond to a contraction by counting, breathing in certain ways, and massaging the abdomen. These reflex reactions occupy the brain to such an extent that its capacity to register the pain of the contraction is lessened. Some women feel no discomfort at all.

The Lamaze course teaches women how to gauge the different stages of labor and breathe appropriately, and how to help push the baby out. Relaxation and massage techniques also help in the birth process. The advantages of childbirth without anesthesia are that the woman can be awake and aware throughout the delivery, and both parents can actively participate in the birth of their baby.

Husbands are encouraged to take the course with their wives and are expected to play a large part in the training and at the delivery. More and more hospitals are allowing fathers into the delivery room. If you are interested in the Lamaze method or other childbirth preparation, ask your local hospital about courses.

Another innovation to consider is a gentle method of introducing newborns into the world, pioneered by French obstetrician Frederick Leboyer. After reading about Leboyer's technique in his book, *Birth Without Violence,* an increasing number of couples are asking that the delivery room be quiet and darkened, and that the infant be massaged and placed in a warm bath right after delivery.

Leboyer's method seeks to remove the fear of childbirth for the infant—a fear Leboyer concludes is real, despite the admitted lack of concrete evidence. He believes that a gentler birth might produce happier children. In a Leboyer-type delivery newborns often smile instead of cry. While skeptical about the scientific basis of Leboyer's techniques, many U.S. obstetricians feel they probably can't hurt and may indeed help—and so will go along with parents who ask for them.

More and more hospitals now provide a "birthing room" for delivery—an attractively furnished room that resembles a bedroom more than a hospital room.

Most obstetricians discourage home delivery. Proponents of home birth argue that in the rare emergency the woman could easily be taken to a hospital. But some studies show that there are dangers to both mother and newborn in transporting a woman to a hospital during a crisis.

The newborn. Don't be alarmed at the appearance of your newborn baby. He won't look anything like the babies in the ads.

When first born he is covered with a cheesy, greenish-gray fluid. He is puffy, with thin, dry, red skin, which mottles when he cries. He may have whiteheads on his nose and chin. Many babies are born with rashes, hives, or welts.

His veins may throb and swell. His lips and nails are bluish. There may be a temporary growth of hair on his face, arms, and shoulders.

His genitals are enlarged. So are his breasts. Small amounts of fluid may come from the baby's breasts during the first few weeks of life. Don't massage the breasts or express the liquid.

After a day or two he'll most likely have a slightly yellow, jaundiced look. This will disappear after a few days.

Your newborn will have a temporarily elongated head from its passage through the narrow birth canal. His arms are longer than his legs. His nose is likely to be broad and flat, and his jaw is undersized. His trunk and neck are stubby; his skull is soft.

A newborn baby's eyes are always blue at first. They may change color within a few months. He'll look as if he has crossed eyes until seven or eight months.

His breathing is rapid and irregular, seeming to stop at intervals. His abdomen bounces when he breathes. His chest seems to cave in when he has hiccups.

The stump of his umbilical cord protrudes from his abdomen. Wash it several times a day. Keep it uncovered—it will fall off by itself. Don't give the baby a tub bath until a week after it has fallen off.

The hair on his head will fall out. The hair that replaces it may be of an entirely different color.

Before he leaves the hospital, he'll lose several ounces of his original birth weight. This is perfectly normal.

After childbirth. After your baby is born, you may feel discomfort in the area around your stitches. Your doctor may prescribe a soothing cream. Hot sitz baths several times a day may help. You're also likely to be more comfortable sitting on a pillow than on a hard chair.

Sweating, especially at night, is common. You may have some loss of appetite.

If you are breastfeeding, your breasts may feel overfull and sore as the milk comes in. Constipation may be a problem—walking soon after the baby is born is helpful. If any of these problems are more than a little troubling, tell your doctor.

You'll bleed from the vagina for several weeks. Wear sanitary napkins, not internal tampons.

In the first weeks after delivery get as much rest as you can. Don't do heavy housework or heavy lifting. Limit stair climbing. Use your common sense. Don't do anything that overtires you.

Most doctors recommend waiting until the six-week postpartum checkup before resuming sexual intercourse. But if your vaginal area feels okay earlier, check with your doctor about resuming sex sooner.

Intercourse may be uncomfortable the first few times you try it. Proceed slowly. If your vagina does not lubricate easily, a common complaint after childbirth, increase foreplay or, if needed, use a water-soluble jelly like K-Y. A side position may be most comfortable at this time. Alternatively, intercourse with the woman on top gives her more control of movement.

You may experience mood swings or mild depression. You may be irritable and hypersensitive, crying for no apparent reason.

Like many other new mothers you are likely to experience the feeling of having lost control of your life. Chances are you'll get little sleep, and all your time may seem taken up with catering to your baby's needs. You may feel exhausted and overwhelmed, and it may seem to you as if life will always be this way.

Postpartum depression (also called after-baby blues) is normal. It usually disappears by itself within a few weeks.

You can help yourself get over it by arranging for time away from your baby at frequent intervals. Just a couple of hours of freedom a day may make you feel refreshed and renewed. Make an effort to maintain outside interests. At the same time, limit your outside responsibilities and simplify household routines as much as possible.

If your depression is severe or prolonged, get professional psychiatric help. For a few women postpartum depression develops into a serious emotional disturbance.

See also PREGNANCY; PREMATURE BIRTH.

CHINESE RESTAURANT SYNDROME See FOOD ADDITIVES.

CHIROPRACTORS are extremely limited in their ability to treat illness.

If you're ill, see a qualified physician. If you need physical therapy, your physician can refer you to a skilled physiotherapist. If you feel a simple massage will help you relax, go to a licensed masseur or masseuse.

It's prudent to avoid chiropractors even though they may be licensed and easily confused with physicians whose training has a scientific basis. The chiropractor calls himself "doctor" and uses the initials *D.C.* (for doctor of chiropractic).

Don't confuse chiropractors with osteopaths, whose tradition includes emphasis on musculoskeletal disorders. Today's D.O. (doctor of osteopathy) gets professional training comparable to that of an M.D. In most states D.O.'s are fully licensed to do anything an M.D. can do, and in some states D.O.'s have merged with the medical profession. Osteopaths are granted medical commissions in the armed forces and are employed as physicians in the Veterans Administration and Public Health Service—none of which is possible for a chiropractor.

While chiropractors are legally barred from doing surgery and prescribing or administering drugs, some state laws are so general as to leave their scope of practice open-ended.

What is chiropractic? B. J. Palmer, son of the founder of chiropractic, summed up its theory: "To the Chiropractor, there is only *one* disease, *one* cause, *one* cure." Not a shred of scientific evidence supports chiropractic's basic premise: that all disease is caused by "subluxation," misalignment of the spine that supposedly interferes with nerve function because of pressure, strain, or tension.

The theory itself is scientifically unsound. The faculty of medicine of McGill University put it this way: "To reduce [the complex science of human biology] to one primary mechanical concept is simple-minded and dangerous."

Indeed the condition as described by chiropractors is unknown to medical science. *(Subluxation* when used as a bona fide medical term means a slight dislocation in a bone or joint.) Despite chiropractors' claims, misalignment of the spine is no cause of heart disease, cancer, infectious disease—indeed, with very few exceptions, of any other medical problem.

The rare exceptions are a handful of conditions that do involve deviation of the spine: kyphosis (humpback), lordosis, excessive front-to-back arching, scoliosis, side-to-side twisting. Chiropractic procedures have shown no success in treating any of these. Concluded the U.S. Department of Health, Education, and Welfare: "There is no valid evidence that subluxation, if it exists, is a significant factor in disease processes."

To cure a presumed subluxation—and thereby a disease—chiropractors perform "adjustments," manual manipulations of the muscles and bones.

But, even under a skilled physiotherapist's hands, permanently relieving a misalignment of the spine is often impossible. Many such conditions result from degeneration of the cartilage discs between vertebrae, the bones of the spinal column. No amount of manipulation can restore a degenerated disc.

Furthermore chiropractic is wrong in its belief that misaligned vertebrae can necessarily press on spinal nerves. Actually many nerves leave the spinal column through openings that are solid rings of bone. These openings cannot constrict a nerve. Nor can they be altered by chiropractic manipulation.

In recent years some chiropractic organizations have modified Palmer's original theory of disease to include, for example, the role of germs in the development of disease. But chiropractic stresses that mechanical disturbances of the nervous system impair the body's defenses and allow the germ entry. While the theory of disease may have been modified, the primary chiropractic treatment for all ailments remains spinal adjustment.

Chiropractors are now divided into "straights," who do only adjustments; and the far more numerous "mixers," who in addition might use colonic irrigation, transcutaneous electric nerve stimulation, diathermy, health food, vitamins, and supposed psychotherapy.

Chiropractic can injure and kill. One of the standard chiropractic manipulations is a sharp twist of the head. This can damage arteries leading to the brain, and patients of chiropractors have died as a result. Others have had brain damage like that from a stroke.

Manipulation of the spine is hazardous to the elderly, whose bones are brittle. A chiropractic adjustment can easily break the bones of someone with osteoporosis.

No substitute for medicine. Some chiropractors presume to treat conditions that need medical attention. When a chiropractor cares for people with potentially fatal diseases such as heart conditions and high blood pressure, leukemia and other forms of cancer, stroke, diabetes, and many infectious diseases, the patients are being kept from treatment that could cure them. In other diseases lack of prompt medical treatment may lead to unnecessary complications.

You run the risk of a chiropractor's not recognizing a disease that calls for prompt medical care. Many people go to chiropractors for backache. But backache is not due only to sprains and strains that can conceivably be relieved by massage. Back pain is commonly a symptom of kidney disease, peptic ulcer—even lung and stomach cancer. All pelvic conditions, especially those of the ovaries and uterus, may be accompanied by low-back pain.

In accumulating data for his book, *At Your Own Risk: The Case Against Chiropractic,* investigative reporter Ralph Lee Smith went to the clinics of two chiropractic schools. At one he presented the symptoms of a damaged vertebral disc. This potentially disabling condition can be aggravated by pushing and jerking of the spine. Nonetheless Smith was subjected to manipulation that left him sore for two weeks.

At the other clinic Smith described the classic symptoms of an impending heart attack, including radiating chest pain and other warning signs. None of the chiropractors who treated him recognized the symptoms. Their diagnosis: The muscles of his left side were overdeveloped, causing subluxations that would take a number of adjustments to fix.

Why some patients are helped. How to account for the fact that many patients claim to have been helped by chiropractors? A wide variety of factors may account for a chiropractor's supposed success. For one thing many patients never had a disease in the first place. About one third to one half of all people who consult a physician have miscellaneous aches and pains

for which no organic cause is found. For another thing most illnesses are self-limiting. It is estimated that about two thirds of all illnesses get better without any intervention. Then, too, a number of serious ailments—such as arthritis or multiple sclerosis—often go into remission. A chiropractor treating the ailment at the time may thus get credit for a cure.

Investigators also believe the placebo effect plays a part in chiropractic success. About a third of patients treated for an ailment with a placebo—usually a sugar pill—will improve. Other patients improve because of the physical attention chiropractors provide. There is often physical and psychological comfort in the laying on of hands.

Others may be helped more by a chiropractor's manner than by his treatment. Most people who consult chiropractors find them amiable, patient, and eager to explain. By contrast they may find physicians abrupt, distant, and condescending.

The one area where chiropractic may have some value is in the treatment of some muscle and joint problems. For example, people with tense and aching back muscles may find that chiropractic manipulation eases the pain.

Chiropractors' "professionalism" is in dispute. Because of their numbers and purported medical training, chiropractic has taken on the trappings of a profession. But what kind of training have most practicing chiropractors received?

Several studies over the last two decades reported inadequate admission requirements, poor teacher-student ratios, many instructors with chiropractic degrees but no college education, lack of research, and lack of student contact with patients with a wide range of ailments. Chiropractic schools offer no in-hospital training, an essential for learning diagnosis and treatment. Nor can chiropractors use many of the sophisticated diagnostic tools available to physicians.

Standards recently set by a government-recognized accrediting agency, the Council on Chiropractic Education, have served to upgrade chiropractic education to some degree. Most chiropractic colleges now require two years of college (although a C average is acceptable); teacher-student ratios are somewhat better; teachers are often better trained. Still chiropractic education does not begin to equal education for physicians, and the typical chiropractor is grossly unqualified to treat serious illness.

A scrupulous chiropractor will refer patients with serious ailments to physicians. But a concern of chiropractic's critics is that even a well-intentioned chiropractor may not be qualified to distinguish a serious ailment from one that may be helped by chiropractic.

Expensive, unnecessary X rays. Some chiropractors take worthless X rays as part of each examination. These "spinographs" are 14-by-36-inch full-spine X rays. Radiologists rarely take such large plates to analyze conditions in a specified area of the spine. A smaller plate focused from a number of angles on the afflicted area not only yields far clearer and more detailed information, but exposes you to much less radiation. Spinographs are of poor definition and generally can reveal little of value, even if the chiropractor were qualified to read them.

Chiropractors often claim spinographs show up pinched nerves. In fact spinographs are taken at the wrong angle and are too undetailed to reveal most such conditions. Moreover, nerves are not visible on X-ray films unless injected with a contrast dye—a complex procedure only radiologists should attempt.

Chiropractors also contend that spinographs aid them in diagnosing subluxations. One test of this was conducted by the National Association of Letter Carriers health insurance program. The union was insuring chiropractic services but found that chiropractors were milking the plan with claims for treating subluxations causing measles, mental retardation, and sundry other ailments.

Representatives of the major chiropractic organizations were shown 20 sets of X rays submitted by chiropractors. Each film was purported to show one to six subluxations. With radiologists looking on, the chiropractors could not identify a single subluxation. The union stopped covering chiropractic services.

Hard sell. Many of the chiropractors in the United States have attended success courses conducted by James W. Parker, millionaire owner of 18 chiropractic clinics in Texas. Parker set down his advice in a textbook on supersalesmanship. Here are tricks chiropractors are taught to use on you:

The free consultation. If you ask what the chiropractor charges, you're told by his assistant that there's no charge for the consultation of the first visit. That gets you into the office, so the chiropractor can make a complete sales pitch in person.

The "yet" disease. This is one of the many ploys intended to scare the daylights out of you. "If the patient has a pain in his left shoulder," Parker says, "ask, 'Has the pain started in your right shoulder yet?'"

The search for chronicity. Parker urges chiropractors to describe symptoms as "an acute flare-up of a chronic condition."

He wants the D.C. to be a Doctor of Chronics rather than a Doctor of Acutes—"You'll make a lot more money." One question the hapless patient may be asked: "How long has it been since you really felt good?"

The spinal connection. If there's pain in your arm, the chiropractor may say, "There doesn't seem to be anything wrong with the arm itself. . . . Let's trace the nerves back to the spine and check there." Inevitably: "I'm glad we found the trouble here, because this is my specialty."

The laying on of hope and fear. After the examination you're told something like, "It's possible this could be the beginning of something serious. It wouldn't make you mad if we stopped this pain for you, would it?"

See also PHYSICAL EXAMINATION; PHYSICIAN; QUACKERY; X RAYS.

CHLORAMPHENICOL See ANTIBIOTICS.

CHOKING A choking victim typically grasps his throat. His breathing may be gasping and noisy. He may cough. If he can't breathe, his skin will become pale, gray, or blue. He's likely to panic. Within a few minutes, he'll become unconscious.

If you are with someone who is choking, at first do nothing. Encourage him to stay calm. Urge him to inhale *slowly,* then exhale hard with a cough. Let him attempt to cough up the obstruction. The reflex muscle spasms of the voice box at the entrance to the windpipe will often be enough to dislodge it.

Attempt the following rescue measures only if an adult victim can't speak (Ask, "Can you speak?"), is coughing ineffectively, or is turning pale, gray, or blue. (On a black person, check the inside of the lip or the fingernail beds.)

To dislodge an object give back blows. Support the victim's chest with one arm. Have him leaning over. (See illustrations.) With the heel of the other hand, give him 4 quick, forceful blows on his back between his shoulder blades. Keep one foot in front of the victim, so that you can help support him if he starts to fall.

After the back blows, again ask the victim, "Can you speak?" If he shakes his head no, or if his breathing is rasping and his skin is bluish, give him 4 rapid thrusts against his abdomen or chest.

For abdominal thrusts (also called the Heimlich maneuver) you suddenly compress the victim's lungs to increase air pressure and thus pop out the object.

Wrap your arms around the victim's waist from behind. If he's sitting, wrap your arms

IF SOMEONE IS CHOKING

1. Find out if he needs rescuing

Proceed only if you see these signs of choking
- He can't cough out object
- He can't speak
- He's turning pale, gray, or blue

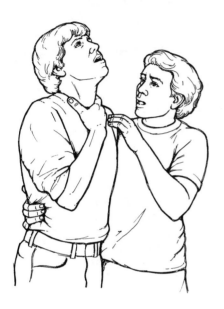

2. Give 4 hard back blows

Give them in rapid succession

Place his head at chest level or lower (Gives you benefit of gravity)

Use heel of your hand

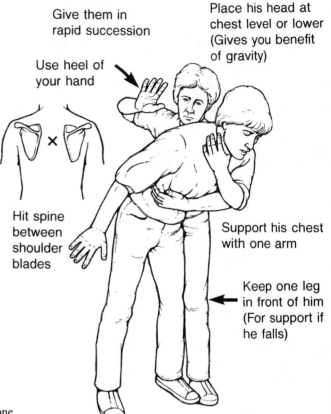

Hit spine between shoulder blades

Support his chest with one arm

Keep one leg in front of him (For support if he falls)

around the chair back. Make a fist with one hand, and grasp it with the other. Place the thumb side of your fist just above his navel, below the rib cage. With a quick, upward thrust, press your fist into his abdomen. Do this 4 times in quick succession. Caution: Don't use abdominal thrusts with pregnant women, infants or children, or obese people. Use chest thrusts instead.

For chest thrusts stand behind the victim and slide your arms under his armpits around his chest. Make a fist with one hand and place it, thumb in, in the middle of the victim's sternum (about halfway between the bottom of the rib cage and the collarbone). Cover your fist with your other hand, and give 4 quick, forceful inward thrusts. (If you're alone and choking try anything that applies force just above your navel. Use your own fist, or press your abdomen sharply into a table or sink.)

If the victim still cannot speak or cough effectively repeat the sequence of back blows followed by either chest thrusts or abdominal thrusts. Continue until the obstruction is dislodged or the victim falls unconscious. Even if

3. Check breathing (as in Step 1)

If choking persists, proceed to Step 4

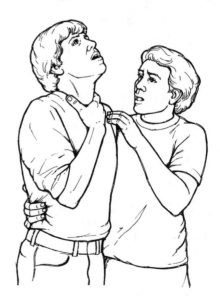

4. Give 4 rapid thrusts against abdomen or chest

Pull sharply with your clenched hands
Grasp your fist with your other hand

Press with
thumb side
of fist

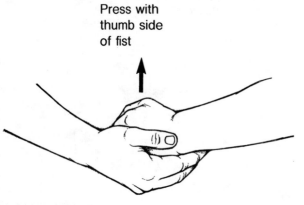

Against abdomen

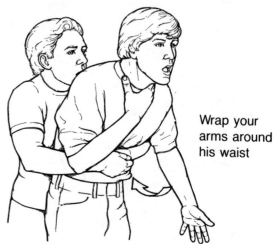

Wrap your
arms around
his waist

Apply thrusts
slightly above
navel
about halfway
below xiphoid
(tip of breastbone)

Against chest
Use if your arms can't encircle the abdomen (e.g., victim is pregnant or obese)

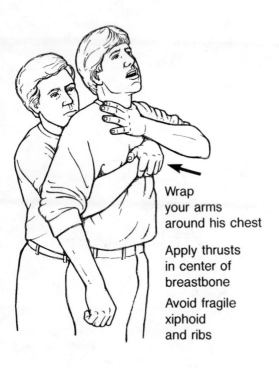

Wrap
your arms
around his chest

Apply thrusts
in center of
breastbone

Avoid fragile
xiphoid
and ribs

5. Check breathing and consciousness

If choking persists, repeat Steps 1 to 4
If victim is unconscious, follow "When the Airway Is Blocked," page *44*

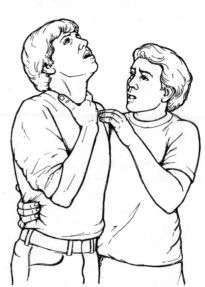

the object is dislodged and breathing restored, the victim should see a physician as soon as possible.

If the victim becomes unconscious. After a few minutes without breathing, the choking victim will lose consciousness. Slide him down on your leg and lay him gently on the floor on his back. For rescue measures see "When the Airway Is Blocked," page 44.

If a child seems to be choking and has a fever and a history of illness, air passages may be swollen. Call an ambulance or take the child to a hospital emergency room.

To dislodge an object and restore breathing and heartbeat see "CPR Review: For Youngsters to Age 8," page 49.

Choking on food. The National Safety Council numbers food inhalation the sixth leading cause of accidental death. Choking is a common cause of "restaurant deaths" in people over 45. In many cases these fatalities have been attributed—wrongly—to heart attacks.

The so-called cafe coronary can come after drinking too much—it makes people careless in their eating habits. Improperly fitting dentures or missing teeth are also major culprits, because they impede chewing.

Gulping large pieces of food, often hunks of steak, is yet another cause. Dr. Roger K. Haugen, medical examiner for Broward County, Florida, found that in deaths from choking, food pieces averaged 3 inches in diameter. In most cases, the food was stuck in such a way that only the tip of it jammed the air passage, while the larger portion was still on the tongue, where it could have been reached by rescuer's fingers.

Elderly people may have frequent episodes of choking because the flap of tissue that prevents food or liquids from going down the windpipe works less efficiently. Sometimes the choking makes old people eat as little as possible, resulting in undernourishment. An aging person should never hurry when eating, and should not be distracted at mealtime. He needs to cut his food into small pieces.

Prevent choking in children. Don't give children under 2 nuts (even candy bars with nuts), popcorn, raw carrots, or crisp bacon. They may inhale these foods instead of swallowing them. Be particularly careful not to serve a child dried beans, since, if taken into the respiratory tract, they can swell and obstruct air passages.

Keep small objects out of the reach of very small children. Don't leave purses, sewing baskets, or other containers of small objects within a baby's reach. Inspect floors for needles, pins, coins, and other objects before you place a baby

there to play. Remove small, detachable parts of toys like the wheels of toy cars and the button eyes of dolls.

Don't use thin plastic film as a waterproof sheet in cribs. Never keep plastic bags—the kind dry cleaners use—around the house. Tie them in knots and throw them away.

Don't use a crib pillow. An infant may bury his nose and mouth in it.

Don't store refrigerators without making it impossible for children to play in them.

See also ACCIDENTS; ARTIFICIAL RESPIRATION; CROUP; REFRIGERATORS; RESPIRATORY DISEASE; SCARVES; TOYS; UNCONSCIOUSNESS.

CHOLERA, after many years, has again become epidemic. Recent outbreaks of this bacteria-caused infectious disease have involved much of Asia, the Middle East, Africa, and parts of Europe (chiefly Italy). Several cases have occurred in the United States for the first time since 1911.

Cholera is acquired mainly from food or water contaminated by cholera-infected human feces. Its most prominent symptom is watery, mucus-laden diarrhea, which dehydrates the victim and causes severe chemical imbalances in tissue fluids.

Travel precautions. If you travel to an infected area, you're unlikely to get cholera if you keep clean and live and move in sanitary surroundings. In epidemic areas consume only cooked food and take precautions against water contamination.

Before going to an infected area get immunization. A few countries affected or threatened by cholera require proof of vaccination upon entry. Some countries bar travelers from infected areas unless they're vaccinated. So even if immunization adds to your protection only slightly, it may ease your coming and going. An International Certificate of Vaccination against cholera must be validated for it to be acceptable to quarantine authorities.

Cholera vaccination consists of two injections spaced a month apart. The vaccine is about 50 percent effective and provides protection for three to six months. There is usually discomfort at the site of the injections and fever and malaise for a day or two.

To determine if a country you are going to has cholera, check your local health department or the Public Health Service. Nations often deny the presence of the disease because they fear it will scare off tourists and businessmen.

Such official refusal to face facts may cost lives. Cholera victims require prompt treatment. Its course is so rapid that a victim may be stricken and killed within four hours, whereas antibiotics and replacement of salt and fluids—if begun quickly—are generally effective therapy.

The literal outpouring of body fluids led people for centuries to view cholera as a divine punishment inflicted on the intemperate and immoral. In six great epidemics of the nineteenth century the disease burst from Asia and caused mass death in Europe and North America. As sanitary conditions improved in Europe and North America, the disease withdrew to around the Ganges delta and remains endemic to Burma, India, Nepal, and Pakistan. Since 1961 a strain called El Tor has attacked more than 20 countries where cholera was previously limited or unknown. A Mideast outbreak killed 14,000 people in a few months.

See also IMMUNIZATION; INFECTIOUS DISEASE; TRAVEL HEALTH; WATER CONTAMINATION.

CHOLESTEROL See FATS.

CHRISTMAS TREES can be as dangerous as a fire bomb. Tests show that a dry tree can blaze to its maximum heat before any effort can be made to combat it.

If you buy an evergreen—fir, spruce, pine—get one that's fresh and therefore less flammable. Look for one that's green, whose needles are hard to pull from branches, whose branches when bent are springy rather than brittle, and whose trunk butt is sticky from resin.

Saw 2 inches off the trunk, cutting diagonally from the butt. Keep the tree standing in water until you throw it out. Check the water level daily—trees absorb large amounts of water indoors. Mount the tree firmly, attaching guy wires to the walls and ceiling if the tree is large. Set it out of the way of traffic and away from a fireplace, stove, or radiator that will dry it out.

Lighted candles have no place on or near a tree. Always use fireproof holders. Keep them where they can't be knocked over, away from other decorations and paper.

Trimming materials. In trimming a tree use only noncombustible or flame-retardant materials. Wear gloves while decorating with spunglass "angel hair." It can irritate your eyes and skin. You're better off with flame-retardant cotton. Artificial snow from spray cans may irritate your lungs. Angel hair plus artificial snow make a combination that's extremely flammable. Avoid spray products that contain asbestos.

When trimming keep in mind what children might swallow or inhale. Keep trimmings with small removable parts out of reach. Avoid those that resemble candy or food. Don't trim with poisonous plants such as mistletoe berries or jequirity or castor beans. Because of the risk of lead poisoning choose tinsel and artificial icicles of plastic or nonleaded metals.

Avoid decorations that are sharp or breakable. Keep bubbling lights away from youngsters. They invite handling and can cause cuts if broken and poisoning if the chemical is drunk.

Use only lights with the UL label from Underwriters Laboratories. Electric shock is a major hazard of the Christmas season. Avoid any strings of lights that appear to be cheaply constructed, badly insulated, or have flammable plastic parts.

Use no more than three sets of lights per single extension cord. Turn off all lights when you go to bed or leave the house. The lights could short out and start a fire.

Use a floodlight rather than electric lights on a metallic tree. If the lights short out, a person touching a branch could be electrocuted. If you buy a plastic or metalized plastic tree, be sure it's marked as made of slow-burning materials. Look for the UL label for those with built-in electrical systems.

See also ACCIDENTS; ELECTRIC SHOCK; FIRE; POISONOUS PLANTS; SPRAY CANS; TOYS.

CIGARETTE COUGH See COUGHING; SMOKING.

CIRCLES UNDER THE EYES are rarely caused by disease. Blood passing through veins close to the surface of the eyelids produces a bluish-black tint.

Circles may be accentuated when you are tired and pale. The condition is often pronounced during menstruation and late pregnancy. With aging the discoloration may become more obvious.

Cosmetics are available to cover dark circles. If you wear eyeglasses, tinted lenses or sunglasses help make circles less noticeable.

See also EYE DISORDER; SKIN DISORDER; SLEEPLESSNESS.

CIRCUMCISION, removing the foreskin of the penis, has been practiced as part of religious ritual among Jews and other groups for thousands of years. With parents' consent U.S. obstetricians circumcise about four out of five newborn boys within a few days after birth. Recently some doctors have begun questioning the wisdom of the operation, and circumcision is now a subject of medical controversy.

Circumcision is clearly needed when there is a decided abnormality of the foreskin, or when the foreskin cannot be pulled back over the head of the penis. Contrariwise, when a child has an infection or is of indeterminate sex, doctors recommend against circumcision, at least until the child's problems are resolved.

When the child's penis and general health are normal, the decision about circumcising rests with the parents. Some arguments on both sides of the question:

There is a firm link between a lowered incidence of cancer of the penis and circumcision at birth. Smegma, an odorous, irritating cheeselike secretion that accumulates under the foreskin, may be implicated.

On the other hand frequent bathing may also prevent penis cancer. Studies do not confirm a widespread belief that circumcision prevents cancer of the cervix in the female sex partner.

Circumcision tends to prevent repeated penis infections. Urologists in military service find that uncircumcised men have substantially more infections, particularly in hot climates. But good personal hygiene also cuts down the incidence of infection.

Circumcision evidently has some protective value against venereal disease.

There is no evidence that the circumcised man is deprived of any sexual pleasure. Nor is it necessarily true that intercourse is more prolonged for him than for the uncircumcised male. It is sometimes argued, without basis in fact, that the tip of a circumcised penis becomes less sensitive because clothing continually rubs against it.

Circumcision is a relatively simple surgical procedure, but it requires skill and careful aftercare. There may be complications such as infection. The most serious complication, death from hemorrhage, is extremely rare.

Upshot: In general doctors feel that babies should be circumcised if the family prefers it for religious or esthetic reasons. The procedure seems especially warranted if busy parents feel circumcision will spare them—and their sons—the effort required to keep the area under the foreskin clean.

When a child is not circumcised, high standards of personal hygiene are needed. About once a week, starting when a child is about three, gently push against the foreskin with a washcloth, pulling the foreskin gradually back over the penis. Don't force or tug since this can cause tearing, with bleeding and possible scarring.

Wash the exposed tip of the penis with soap and water and then rinse. Return the foreskin to normal position. If it does not go back down easily, try squeezing the rounded tip of the penis. If the foreskin still doesn't go down, call a physician immediately, before painful swelling occurs.

Psychiatrists urge fathers to supervise the bathing of a son until he can do it himself. From about age ten the boy needs to retract his foreskin daily and wash with soap and water.

Circumcision is sometimes needed by older boys and adults. Among the reasons for circumcising are repeated infection and difficulty in retracting the foreskin. Psychiatrists recommend against circumcising a child between four and seven years of age, a crucial stage of psychosexual development.

Adults need to abstain from intercourse for ten days after the circumcision. Doctors often provide patients with a drug to avoid erections.

After circumcision. During the first ten days after a child is circumcised, keep the area clean and dry so that it will heal well.

Change diapers often, or leave the child undiapered. Use a dressing or ointment if your doctor prescribes it. Call your doctor if the baby has a fever over 101° F or bright-red bleeding.

See also CANCER OF THE CERVIX; CHILDBIRTH.

CLAP See GONORRHEA.

CLEANSING MINOR WOUNDS calls for washing the area with ordinary soap and water—not alcohol, iodine, or other antiseptics, which can be injurious (see illustration).

See a doctor for wounds with heavy bleeding. Those large enough to leave scars may require

TO CLEANSE A MINOR WOUND

Wash with soap and water
Avoid alcohol, iodine, other antiseptics

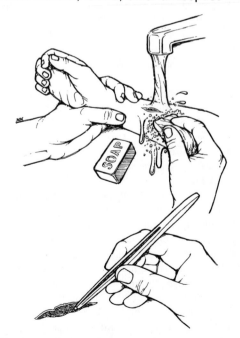

Remove dirt particles
(Sterilize tweezers by boiling)

stitches. Deep punctures also require a doctor's attention because they are difficult to clean through the small break in the skin.

Because of the risk of infection and further damage, don't try to cleanse open ABDOMINAL INJURIES, CHEST INJURIES, or FRACTURES (see these entries for emergency care).

In cleansing minor injuries be gentle—but remove foreign bodies, which generally complicate healing, even though you may cause further injury. Bathing the wound in a tub or under a faucet will usually do a good job of cleaning it out. Lift remaining bits of foreign matter out with clean tweezers. Bleeding helps cleanse the wounds.

Let the wound dry in air. Then apply a bandage.

See also ACCIDENTS; ANTISEPTICS; BANDAGES; PUNCTURES; SCARS.

CLEFT LIP (harelip) is a congenitally divided upper lip, suggestive of a hare. It can generally be corrected by surgery. Sometimes a second operation is needed to improve a child's appearance or to relieve problems of breathing, speaking, or swallowing.

Parents commonly feel guilty and resentful when a child is born with this type of condition, which may harm the child's emotional health. Such feelings are best aired in talks with the family physician.

See also BIRTH DEFECTS; MOUTH CLEFT; TEETH AND MOUTH DISORDERS.

CLEFT PALATE In the normal development of the unborn child, the parts of the head that form the roof of the mouth meet and grow together. When these structures fail to unite, the child is born with an opening: a cleft palate.

Absence of the intact surface between the mouth and nose causes difficulty in chewing and swallowing. Infants may have difficulty sucking. Teeth and mouth problems often develop because the teeth may be in poor position or may be missing entirely. Hearing and speech are often impaired.

Until the cleft is repaired, the tissues of the eustachian tube—the passageway from the nose to the ear—are not fully protected. Food, fluid, and infection can cause damage that may harm hearing. In addition the muscles in the palate cannot work properly to relieve obstructions in the eustachian tube or to even the pressure.

Speech is also impaired. To produce most speech sounds the roof of the mouth and the throat work together to block off the nose and direct air and sound into the mouth. In cases of cleft palate the air leaks into the nose.

The sounds *p, t,* and *k* are difficult to make because they normally are formed by little explosions of pent-up air from the mouth. The sounds *s, sh,* and *f* cause similar problems because they are ordinarily made by a controlled flow of air.

Repair and therapy. A cleft palate may be repaired by a plastic surgeon. Or it may be covered by an orthodontic appliance resembling a denture with an extension added to the back edge. When front teeth are missing, they can be replaced as part of the appliance.

To compensate for the speech impediment caused by a cleft palate, a child learns to use his mouth and throat in an abnormal fashion. These habits continue even after the cleft has been remedied, so his speech may continue to sound strange. The help of a certified speech therapist is often needed; the therapist generally prescribes training that the parents can carry out at home. An orthodontist or pediatrician often can refer you to a speech therapist experienced with children having cleft palates. Other members of cleft palate teams widely include oral surgeons, plastic surgeons, psychologists, and social workers.

A cleft palate need not pose difficulty in feeding a young child. If the mother holds the baby in a sitting position, feeding him a bottle will be fairly easy, and in this upright position milk will rarely run out of the nose. Although a soft nipple with large holes helps the infant suck, its use is discouraged by many speech therapists because it may cause abnormal tongue and swallowing habits.

When a child is born with a defect like a cleft palate, the parents' first reaction is often guilt, compounded by resentment toward the child. Specialists counsel that cleft palates are absolutely unavoidable and unpredictable, and advise parents to talk out their feelings with a family physician.

See also BIRTH DEFECTS; MOUTH CLEFT; TEETH AND MOUTH DISORDERS.

CLIMACTERIC See MENOPAUSE.

CLOT, BLOOD See BLOOD CLOT.

CLUSTER HEADACHE See MIGRAINE.

COARCTATION OF THE AORTA See CONGENITAL HEART DEFECTS.

COCCIDIOIDOMYCOSIS (valley fever, desert fever, San Joaquin Valley fever) In the early days of World War II the Army Air Corps faced a medical problem. The sunny Southwest, because of its many days of good flying weather, had been chosen as the site of several large flying fields. But so many fliers and their crews became ill with symptoms like those of influenza that the good weather was of little value.

The disease that attacked the fliers was coccidioidomycosis (kok-SID-ee-OI-do-my-KO-sis), familiarly called coccy (KOK-see). Today it is believed that two thirds of all adults living in the area from western Texas through New Mexico and Arizona to the San Joaquin Valley in California have been infected with coccy.

This infectious disease is harbored only in this region in the United States. But people who handle articles with infective particles from the area may be exposed to the organism. A freight handler in Georgia developed coccy after unloading raw cotton from west Texas.

A fungus infection. Coccy is a fungus infection. It usually develops as a respiratory disease when tiny seeds, called spores, are inhaled into the lungs. But it can spread to other parts of the body and occasionally begins when fungus-filled dust settles in a skin scratch.

Deep in the lung, the spores begin to grow. They develop into pods that are filled with even tinier seeds. The pods burst open and the seeds pour out and scatter throughout the lung, sometimes to other parts of the body.

Wherever the spores settle down, the body reacts with inflammation. In the lungs patches of pneumonia develop around the spores. Cavities or scars may result, and eventually deposits of calcium.

When the spores stay in the lungs, the disease is said to be in its primary form. When the fungus spreads throughout the body—to the internal organs, bones, brain, and even the skin—coccy is in its disseminated form.

Most people infected with coccy develop no symptoms. Some 30 to 40 percent do get sick, usually within one to three weeks after the spores invade the body. Fever may go as high as 104° F. There are usually aches and pains and coughing.

A week or two after the fever soars, some patients get a rash that resembles the measles. There may also be sores on the shins, called "the bumps," and pains in the joints, called "desert rheumatism." Usually symptoms disappear within a month or so.

The disseminated form of the disease is a great deal more serious, with very high fever and extreme fatigue. It is estimated that less than 1 percent of white patients develop the disseminated form of the disease. But in 2 to 4 percent of dark-skinned patients—Negroes, Mexicans, and Filipinos—coccy progresses to its disseminated form. It can be fatal.

Treatment. If you suffer from coccy in its primary form, you'll probably be sent to bed. Treatment is generally confined to relieving symptoms such as cough and fever.

For the disseminated form of the disease a specific drug—amphotericin B—is available. This drug must be injected slowly into the bloodstream almost daily over a period of from one to six months. It may have disturbing side effects, including kidney damage. For this reason the drug's use is reserved for the more complicated cases, and hospitalization is required.

Occasionally surgery is recommended to remove a diseased portion of the lung.

Anyone living in the Southwest should be aware of coccy and be suspicious of flulike symptoms—fever, aches and pains, and a cough. If the symptoms don't disappear in a day or two, check with a doctor. The disease can be detected with a skin test.

New people coming into the area should be informed about the disease. Those who have lived there since childhood may well have developed a kind of immunity that newcomers do not have. Once you've developed the disease, you can't get reinfected.

See also INFECTIOUS DISEASE; RESPIRATORY DISEASE.

COCKROACHES have traveled with man to most parts of earth.

These insects expel unpleasant-smelling secretions that spoil the flavor of food. They are suspected of transporting disease organisms much as flies do. There is evidence that an allergy to cockroaches can precipitate attacks of asthma.

Don't equate roaches with "dirty" housekeeping. The insect will invade any house or apartment to its liking. They frequently come into homes in delivery cartons or grocery bags, or travel through buildings along water and heat pipes from one apartment to another. The roach hides during the day and feeds at night on practically anything—crumbs, glue, soiled clothing, garbage, grease drippings, litter.

Be especially alert if you live in an apartment house, for your neighbors may give you a roach problem. In many buildings the tenants live in delicate balance with the roach population. A paint job or exterminator's visit in one apartment may displace roaches, causing an explosion elsewhere in the building.

To discourage roaches store food in closed containers. Avoid accumulating even small amounts of grease or garbage. Fill in cracks in walls and block openings around doors, pipes, and wire and cable connections.

For a quick kill of a large population: Use spray cans of pyrethrin, a relatively safe insecticide. Spray pyrethrin in hiding places and crawlways.

To find where these are, scout your rooms at night. Quietly enter a dark room, snap on the light, and watch where the roaches disappear to. Their favorite hideouts include electric clocks, TV and radio cabinets, and appliance motor compartments; areas around stoves, water heaters, and hot-water pipes; behind mirrors, loose baseboards, and moldings; in cupboard cracks and shelves; in the undersides of furniture.

Boric acid for roaches. The insect learns to avoid deposits of conventional pesticides and will go around them. But it will track through boric acid freely while traveling to and from feeding areas. Particles of the powder adhere to the insect's body. When the insect cleans itself, it swallows the powder, which is a stomach poison.

To apply boric acid (readily available from drugstores), use a plastic ketchup or mustard dispenser. Cut off part of the nozzle tip so the opening is large enough for the powder to go through. Fill the dispenser half full and dust the powder lightly in hiding places and crawlways.

As long as the powder remains dry, it will last indefinitely—an advantage over commercial insect sprays, which break down. Boric acid has been used to eliminate colonies of roaches that were overrunning public-housing projects. But it is so slow-acting that wiping out a colony may take weeks.

If you use boric acid, do so with extreme caution because it is poisonous. Ingestion of as little as a teaspoonful has killed adults. In concentrated form, boric acid can also poison by entering the body through cuts.

See also INSECTS.

COITUS INTERRUPTUS See BIRTH CONTROL.

COLDS Despite the isolation of a spacecraft, all three *Apollo 7* astronauts developed bad colds while orbiting above the earth. The common cold is widespread and insidious.

It is man's most prevalent medical complaint. Americans suffer an average of three colds a year, accounting for perhaps a fourth of all acute illnesses. Colds begin—and are catching—one to three days before symptoms appear. One of the astronauts probably brought the cold virus aboard and spread it to the others.

Headache, sneezing, stuffy nose, sore throat, a general feeling of fatigue, coughing, and sniffles—these are the symptoms of the common cold. Temperatures rarely increase more than 1° in adults or go higher than 102° F in children. A cold normally runs its course in 2 to 14 days.

Cold complications. A cold can be a serious threat to infants, older people, heart patients, and the chronically ill—particularly patients with such chronic lung diseases as asthma, chronic bronchitis, and emphysema. Call a doctor if any such patients develop a fever of more than 1°, or if there is chest pain or excessive coughing.

Also call your doctor if you develop any of these symptoms: A fever that lasts more than three days, a severe headache, chest pains, hard coughing spells, earache, or rusty-looking sputum.

If colds occur frequently, or last much longer than a week, they may not be colds at all, but an allergy or sinusitis. A cold and an allergic reaction may occur together, particularly in cold-susceptible children who tend to have asthma.

There is a stage at the onset of some diseases, such as measles, rubella, chickenpox, pneumonia, influenza, and whooping cough, which cannot be distinguished from the common cold. In children consider all upper-respiratory illness to be more than "just a cold" until the diagnosis is reasonably certain.

Vitamin C and colds. Ever since 1970, when Nobel prize winner Linus Pauling advocated large doses of vitamin C to prevent and treat colds, the debate over its merits as a cold fighter has often produced more heat than light. Based on subsequent studies the most authoritative advice about vitamin C and colds is as follows:

Consume an average of 500 mg of vitamin C a week, about double the amount needed by a normal male adult. On the first day of a cold take 1,500 mg (1½ grams). On each of the next four days, take 1,000 mg (1 gram).

University of Toronto investigators found that at those dosages vitamin C makes colds easier to live with, even though it doesn't significantly prevent colds. Volunteers who took vitamin C had only slightly fewer colds than controls, but lost nearly a third fewer working days. They apparently suffered less severe generalized symptoms, such as fever, chills, and muscle aches.

Dr. Terence W. Anderson, who directed the Toronto experiments, theorizes that the body's requirement for vitamin C rises at times of certain illnesses or stress. By saturating your tissues with vitamin C, you have a store to meet such an increased need.

Alternatively you can saturate your tissues with vitamin C by consuming an average of 120 mg a day. You can get all the vitamin C you need from broccoli, Brussels sprouts, orange juice, or other foods (see table under NUTRITION). If you prefer to take supplements, buy the cheapest brand of USP ascorbic acid tablets or powder.

Don't take the massive doses proposed by some of Pauling's followers. At best your body will simply excrete the excess. Worse, however, are possible dangers that accompany large doses of vitamin C. Large amounts could form stones in the urinary passages and cause painful, serious obstructions. (Pauling says any such effect can be avoided by taking an alkalizing agent like bicarbonate of soda.) High doses also may lead to kidney problems, vitamin B_{12} deficiency, and adverse effects on unborn infants when taken by pregnant women.

Cases of stomach upset and diarrhea have occurred among people who take large doses of vitamin C. The vitamin interferes with tests for urine sugar in diabetes. It should be avoided by people with gout.

Care of a cold. The only treatment is to relieve your symptoms. Keep warm and rest for twenty-four hours, partly to avoid spreading the virus around, partly because rest may avert complications.

Take aspirin or acetaminophen to ease your headache and achiness. Blow your nose gently, one nostril at a time, or you risk ear infections.

A vaporizer may relieve congestion. A hot bath can help too. It dilates small arteries in your skin and relaxes your muscles.

Sucking hard candy and gargling with warm salt water can soothe your throat. Cough syrup can ease a troublesome cough. Liquids—fruit juice, soup, or water—may make you feel better generally.

Medicines for colds are no better than home remedies—and may be harmful. Antihistamines can give you relief if allergic reactions such as those of hay fever accompany your cold. But don't use antihistamines merely for colds. Studies show they neither shorten the duration of a cold nor significantly relieve symptoms. While they may help a nose run less in the early stages of a cold, they probably don't reduce nasal congestion in later stages.

Worse, they dry mucous membranes and thicken secretions, causing a bad cough while making expectoration difficult. For people with asthma, chronic bronchitis, and emphysema, this can lead to increased bronchial infection.

Never take cold remedies containing sulfa or antibiotics, *The Medical Letter* warns. There is no proof that either relieves a cold—and you run the risk of developing a drug allergy or having a severe reaction.

Be skeptical of cold-remedy ads. The FTC re-

ported that the "children's aspirin" advertised in Congespirin is just a smaller dose of aspirin.

The summer cold is a "different animal" (as Contac claims) only because most people *think* it is. Colds are colds, summer or winter.

Dristan tablets contain "the decongestant most prescribed by doctors," phenylephrine—according to the ads. This can be misleading, since the drug, when prescribed by doctors, is in the form of nose drops. Moreover, Dristan contains less than a fourth the dosage found effective in oral form.

Caffeine is present in some products, supposedly to help relieve pain. In fact there is no acceptable evidence that caffeine eases pain, improves breathing, or has any value whatsoever in the treatment of any cold symptoms.

Shotgun remedies are even less effective. Some cold preparations contain combinations of numerous ingredients such as decongestants, antihistamines, analgesics, anticholinergics, caffeine, and others.

Not all the individual components of these mixtures have been demonstrated to be effective for colds. Fixed combinations prevent establishing an effective dose of any one constituent without affecting the dose of the other ingredients. Thus if there is severe muscle aching, you cannot double or triple the dose of the aspirin without increasing the levels of the other components. This not only may be unnecessary but may cause toxic effects.

Furthermore, in the interest of safety, the dose of individual drugs is about half the usual therapeutic dose, invariably too low to be adequate for *any* purpose: common cold, allergy, or what have you.

"Continuous action" capsules contain what appear at first to be full therapeutic doses. But the timed-release form retards absorption so that therapeutic blood levels are an impossibility.

In addition timed release of drugs from such formulations is so variable from person to person as to be regarded as highly unreliable by physicians who have studied the matter. Label warnings suggest that the products may be dangerous for children, for elderly people, and for others with high blood pressure, heart disease, diabetes, and thyroid disease.

Aerosol medications are a waste of money. These products release a spray compounded of menthol (a mild anesthetic), glycols (antibacterial agents without therapeutic value when sprayed in the air), and flavoring oils. Even if the ingredients were effective medications, you could hardly get a large enough dose from the room air with these products. No published reports of controlled trials indicate that these preparations can give the relief from congestion that is claimed.

Prevention. To prevent colds avoid people with colds whenever possible. Infants under one year particularly need to be protected, since they are least able to bear up under disease. Women may be more vulnerable just before their menstrual period.

Even though colds are now known to be less contagious than was formerly believed, they are spread by intimate personal contact in which you inhale cold viruses. Virus-laden droplets are expelled when the cold victim sneezes, coughs, even speaks. Droplets may be spread as far as 20 feet by one sneeze, remain in the air for half an hour, be stirred up in dust.

Wash your hands often, especially before eating and after touching a person with a cold. Research has suggested that the main way colds spread from one person to another is via virus-laden objects touched by the hands. The virus is then carried to the eyes or mouth.

Don't use a drinking glass or towel which may have been soiled by a person with a cold. Avoid stress and fatigue—students have an upsurge in colds around examination time. Give your body every possible advantage via adequate diet and rest when there are more than the usual number of colds around you.

Keep indoor humidity at around 45 percent. Autumn's sudden rise in colds is linked to the lowered humidity in heated rooms, which dry out mucous membranes and impair their defenses against infection. Despite popular myth, experiments show that low temperatures, inclement weather, dampness, and chills have little to do with precipitating colds. Sudden changes in temperature may be more significant.

When you have a cold, cover your coughs and sneezes. Use disposable tissues and get rid of them immediately by putting them into a closed paper bag or flushing them down the toilet. Have your own drinking glass, towel, other personal items. Above all stay away from other people.

Take time-honored rituals with a grain of salt. "Sure-fire" but ineffective methods for preventing or aborting a cold include regular exercise and drinking lots of water. Some hopeful people swear by cod-liver oil, alcoholic beverages, and citrus fruit juices. But these and other bits of witchcraft have never been verified by scientific research.

Face masks have not proved effective in preventing spread of airborne diseases. The gauze traps few germs. Since a mask is quickly contaminated with germ- or virus-laden saliva, it becomes a source of infection rather than a protection.

Wrapping a piece of flannel around your throat at the first sign of scratchiness will do nothing. Lots of remedies—hot milk is another example—that seem to have a beneficial effect may be psychologically comforting, reinforced by the fact that the cold is self-limiting and may be over in a short time.

Taking a laxative won't budge a cold virus.

If you get under a pile of blankets and sweat, there is no proof that you will flush out the poisons produced by the infection. Drinking liquids would accomplish the same purpose and is pleasanter.

Cold baths and winter sleeping porches don't seem to build you up so that you won't get colds. Cold bath and cold air enthusiasts get as many and as severe colds as comfort lovers.

"Feed a cold and starve a fever" is another popular myth. A light, well-balanced diet will make you feel most comfortable. Diet has no effect on fever or on the course of a cold.

Cold vaccine. Don't pin your hopes on a cold vaccine. Researchers at the National Institutes of Health have for the most part given up trying to find a vaccine for the common cold. Under present technology there is no feasible way of combining a significant number of the 113 cold-causing viruses in a single "cocktail" vaccine. Thus immunization against colds is unlikely in the near future.

Similarly, a penicillin shot is no protection. Antibiotics are effective only against bacteria, which play no significant part in the development of a cold. Doctors may prescribe antibiotics for the complications—the secondary, bacterial infections—but not for the cold itself.

So-called cold vaccines have long been marketed by major drug houses in both oral and injectable form. The vaccines contain a miscellany of killed bacteria and are claimed to be effective not against the cold itself, but for protection against bacteria commonly found in the upper-respiratory tract and assumed to be capable of causing complications or prolonging symptoms. But neither clinical experience nor controlled trials provide evidence that the vaccines are useful.

Don't fall for quack devices that purport to kill the cold virus in the air with special ultraviolet lamps, or with chemical sprays or with germicidal filters. "Air purifiers" that supposedly generate negative ions will merely give the cold viruses a good laugh.

See also ANTIHISTAMINES; ASPIRIN; COUGH-

ING; EAR INFECTIONS; FEVER; HEADACHE; NU-
TRITION; RESPIRATORY DISEASE; SORE THROAT;
VITAMINS.

COLD SORES (fever blisters, herpes simplex) are
a virus disease that is highly contagious but
rarely has lasting effects. Almost half the population suffers from it or has antibodies against it.
Some authorities consider the infection to be second only to colds in prevalence.

The first attack by the virus ordinarily occurs
in very young children, one to three years old.
This initial infection, called primary herpes, may
cause only one or two sores to develop and may
go unnoticed.

In many cases, however, the child has a slight
fever, pain in the mouth, increased salivation, an
odor to the breath, and a general feeling of illness. The inside of the mouth becomes swollen
and the gums inflamed. Many sores appear simultaneously on the lips, inside the cheeks, on
the tongue and gums. The sores are yellow and
irregularly shaped. Later in the course of the disease a red ring of inflammation forms around
them.

The first attack of herpes simplex is the only
time the sores occur over a widespread area
within the mouth. There is no specific treatment
for primary herpes. Healing begins naturally
within 3 days and usually the illness is over in 7
to 14 days. A doctor can advise how to make the
child more comfortable, relieve the pain, and
prevent complications.

Following this initial infection the virus lies
dormant. It reappears later in life as the familiar
cold sore. In this second stage of the disease, the
characteristic sore usually appears on the outside of the lip, at the point where the red part of
the lip meets the adjoining skin.

The sore virtually always develops at the same
place. Blisters rarely occur inside the mouth. A
burning sensation, itching, or feeling of fullness
usually develops about 24 hours before the sore
appears. The lip becomes swollen and red. The
sore is small, covered with a yellow scab.

The blisters erupt when your general resistance is lowered or when you have a cold or
fever. Exposure to sunlight or dry, cracked lips
are also predisposing factors. The sores heal by
themselves in seven to ten days, usually leaving
no scar.

Patent medicines put forth as cold-sore cures
are ineffective and may cause complications. For
relief it may help to place a soaking hot tea bag
on the sore overnight. If the sore is oozing, use a
drying skin lotion or liquid. In cases where the
sore is infected, topical antibiotic ointments may
be applied. While the symptoms are relieved, the

virus is not eliminated, and the condition may
flare up again.

Most cold sores are caused by herpes simplex
virus I. The strain causing most genital HERPES
(which see) is herpes simplex virus II. However,
either strain may attack both the mouth and the
genitals, with identical symptoms. Genital infection may result from oral-genital contact with a
person who harbors the cold sore virus.

See also HERPES; MOUTH SORES; TEETH AND
MOUTH DISORDERS.

COLD WEATHER   Your body is its own heating
plant—merely standing still, you generate about
as much heat as a 100-watt bulb. Clothing furnishes the insulation to keep your heat from escaping. The Army tells soldiers stationed in
frigid areas that the key to staying warm is the
word *C-O-L-D:*

Keep it	*C*lean
Avoid	*O*verheating
Wear it	*L*oose in layers
Keep it	*D*ry

Keep clothes clean because dirt and grease
clog the air spaces in your clothing and reduce
your insulation. Overheating makes your clothes
damp with sweat, and dampness conducts cold.
Loose clothing allows your blood to circulate
freely, warming your limbs.

Layers of clothing trap air warmed by your
body, and also can be removed one at a time to
avoid overheating. Stay dry from the outside by
wearing rain-repellent gear and guarding against
melting snow. Don't let snow collect on your
clothing because the heat from your body will
melt it. Good cold-weather garb consists of an
undershirt topped by one or more shirts and
sweaters, and a light waterproof windbreaker.

Put on a hat or other head covering. Cover
your neck and ears as well, and put on mittens.
Most loss of body heat is from the bare head and
hands.

How warm a garment will keep you is determined by its thickness, not its weight. A
1-pound down-filled ski parka that's almost 2
inches thick will keep you warmer than a
4-pound woolen overcoat that's only ½ inch
thick. The parka traps more air between its fibers. You'll keep your feet warmer by wearing
one pair of fluffy socks than two closely fitted
pairs. Wool and cotton hold more air than
synthetics like nylon.

For other hints on winter dressing and cold
weather emergencies, see FROSTBITE.

Hypothermia. Hypothermia is chilling and
freezing of the entire body. The body's temperature falls to 95° F or below. If not detected and

treated promptly, such a drop in internal body temperature can be fatal.

Signs of hypothermia include shivering and numbness. The victim may be drowsy and weak, uncoordinated and confused. Typically his breathing is slow and shallow; his pulse is weak; his skin is pale and waxy. If the body is severely chilled, the person may be unconscious or semi-conscious.

People suffering from hypothermia do not necessarily feel cold. Indeed they may seem unaware of the cold and insist they are comfortable while others shiver and put on sweaters.

To give emergency treatment to a victim of hypothermia, give ARTIFICIAL RESPIRATION (which see), if necessary. Bring the victim to a warm room as soon as possible. Remove clothes if they are wet. Wrap the victim in warm blankets, towels, or additional clothing. Seek medical attention promptly.

If you are in the wilderness, sandwich the naked hypothermic person between two naked people in a sleeping bag. Get medical help as soon as possible.

If the victim is conscious, give him warm drinks—coffee, tea, soup. Never give alcoholic beverages. Check the person for signs of frostbite and give appropriate first aid care.

Most victims of hypothermia are people who are exposed to severe cold without adequate clothing. But in some people—particularly the elderly and chronically ill—hypothermia may occur in weather as warm as 55° F to 60° F. Chances of hypothermia are greater if the person's clothing becomes wet.

Medical conditions that may predispose a person to hypothermia include illnesses such as severe arthritis and Parkinson's disease, which limit activity; conditions that may reduce awareness, such as stroke or paralysis; hormonal disorders, such as hypothyroidism; any condition that severely impairs normal constriction of blood vessels; alcoholism and drug abuse.

If you are elderly or ill, take extra precautions against hypothermia. Stay indoors on very cold days. Keep your thermostat at 68° F to 70° F. Dress warmly even when indoors. Wear a hat indoors if it's chilly. Stay as active as possible. Eat properly. Wear bedclothes (including a nightcap) and use blankets at night. Ask friends or neighbors to look in on you once or twice a day if you are alone during a cold spell.

If you are taking medication to treat anxiety, depression, nervousness or nausea, ask your doctor if the medication might affect your body's ability to control body temperature. A change in prescription may avert a problem.

See also ACCIDENTS; CHRISTMAS TREES; FALLS; FALLS THROUGH ICE; FIRE; FROSTBITE; ICE SKATING; SKIING; SNOWMOBILES; SUNBURN; SUNGLASSES; TRENCH FOOT.

COLITIS is an inflammation of the large intestine (colon).

Ulcerative colitis is an inflammatory disease. The disorder can appear or worsen during periods of emotional stress. The typical sufferer is a young adult between 18 and 35, but the disease also strikes children and older people.

Symptoms include cramps and intestinal gas, chronic diarrhea, sometimes with as many as 20 bloody bowel movements a day, weight loss, vomiting, weakness, and anemia. With severe loss of body fluids and minerals the disease can be fatal.

Ulcerative colitis can be controlled in four out of five cases. For mild cases bed rest, judicious use of antidiarrheal drugs, and diet may relieve the symptoms. Avoid foods that may cause the patient to suffer flare-ups. Some individuals are sensitive to spicy foods, raw fruits and vegetables, candy, and alcohol.

More severe cases may require other drugs, including sulfasalazine and steroids. Researchers have been experimenting in selected cases with the use of immunosuppressive drugs, which suppress the body's natural tendency to fight off attacks by foreign substances. This research suggests that a cause of ulcerative colitis is an autoimmune process, in which the body's defense mechanisms attack its own tissues.

Report any diarrhea you experience while taking antibiotics. These drugs may cause pseudomembranous colitis, a potentially fatal condition resulting from overgrowth of *Clostridium difficile* bacteria in the intestine. Treatment generally consists of discontinuing the offending antibiotic and using vancomycin against the clostridia.

Ulcerative colitis is characterized by frequent remissions and recurrences, making it hard to evaluate drug therapy.

Only in the most severe cases is surgery necessary. The large intestine is removed and an opening (ileostomy) is cut into the abdominal wall. Feces pass into a bag worn at the opening. The surgery also helps avoid the increased risk of cancer of the colon and rectum, associated with many years of ulcerative colitis. Some surgeons create a reservoir out of a portion of the small intestine, and attach it to the anal sphincter.

If you must have such surgery, join a local Ostomy Club of people who've had similar operations. Their support and experience can help you adjust to the use of the bag. Ask your physician or public-health department about the nearest group.

Mucous colitis. Stress is the probable cause of mucous colitis. This condition is more correctly called spastic colon, irritable colon syndrome, and irritable bowel syndrome.

Mucous colitis is a functional disorder—physicians can find no organic cause for the symptoms. Most believe it is an emotionally triggered condition. Sufferers may experience abdominal pains, belching, and flatulence. Constipation or hard, small stools may alternate with loose stools or diarrhea.

Treatment usually consists of adding fiber to the diet in moderation and psychotherapy for the underlying emotional disorder.

Don't self-treat colitis. No over-the-counter drugs are safe or effective for home treatment.

See also DIARRHEA; FIBER; STRESS.

COLLARBONE FRACTURE is common in children and athletes. There is usually pain, swelling, or a lump and a black-and-blue color in the shoulder area and some disability of the arm on the side of the injury.

Immobilize the fracture by using a sling on the arm on the injured side (see illustration). Take the victim to a doctor or hospital.

See also FRACTURES.

COLON CANCER   See CANCER OF THE COLON AND RECTUM.

COLOR BLINDNESS was first investigated by John Dalton, a Quaker and an eminent scientist, who bought himself some scarlet stockings that he thought were dark brown. Dalton was surprised when a brother Quaker took him to task for wearing such bright colors in public.

The most common type of color blindness involves difficulty in distinguishing red from green. Both green grass and a red rose may be seen as brownish, yellowish, or gray.

A few people have trouble distinguishing between blue and yellow. Rarer still is total color blindness. Such individuals can see only shadings of gray and black.

A special kind of color blindness is blue blindness, in which a person has difficulty seeing blue lines and printing. Most youngsters outgrow it. But in the meantime diagnosis is often missed and many children are mistakenly labeled slow learners because they make errors. The condition may be triggered by diabetes, malnutrition, tranquilizers, and other drugs.

About 1 in every 10 males is color-blind, about 1 in every 100 females. Most red-green color blindness is hereditary and follows sex-linked patterns. A man will be color-blind if his mother merely carries the gene even if she her-

IF A COLLARBONE MAY BE BROKEN

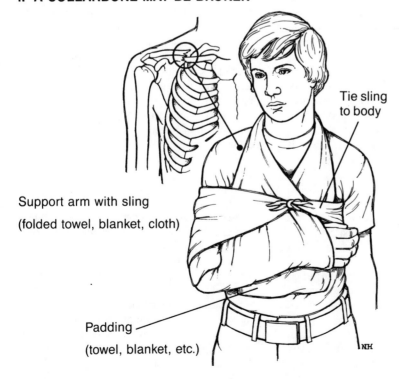

Tie sling
to body

Support arm with sling
(folded towel, blanket, cloth)

Padding
(towel, blanket, etc.)

self isn't color-blind. A woman will be color-blind only if both her parents carry the gene.

Most commonly color blindness skips a generation. It is transmitted from an affected man to his daughters, in whom the condition does not develop. Half of any boys born to the daughters are likely to be color-blind. Color blindness also can be caused by disease or injury of the retina.

You can adapt to color blindness but never cure it. A color-blind person needs to take special care wherever color may be used as a warning. He needs to learn that the red is on top in traffic signals, that yellow lines on roads may not be clear to him.

Eye exercises are of no help. A special contact lens can correct some red-green color blindness. Some promoters offer a "light and filter" treatment, offering as proof people's improved ability to pass the standard color-blindness test. The test consists of sets of tiny colored discs, which to the normal eye form numbers in contrasting colors. Actually the person is trained not to see colors better but to pass the test. Warns the National Society to Prevent Blindness: "This may be dangerous, as in the case of the man who, after 'passing' a test, is unable to distinguish colored safety signals while operating a plane or locomotive."

See also EYE DISORDER.

COMPRESSES can be cold or hot. Use cold immediately after accidents, to prevent bleeding and swelling and to reduce pain. Use heat no sooner than 5 to 7 days later, to absorb bleeding and swelling. Use heat also to localize infection and to reduce the pain of muscle spasm.

Use heat with extreme care on the elderly, and on those with marked disease of the peripheral blood vessels. In such people a heating pad may increase pain in the area with faulty circulation, cause a burn, or spur the development of gangrene.

Don't apply heat to any area in which there is internal or external bleeding. The heat may start the bleeding again.

Cold compresses. Start these immediately following trauma: Fractures, strains, sprains, bruises. Swelling after a blow or twisting injury is most commonly caused by blood and fluid leaking into the tissue. Cold constricts blood vessels and can help reduce this.

Cold applications can relieve pain. After as little as 15 minutes of cold application you're likely to suffer less discomfort moving an injured knee, ankle, or elbow.

But the absence of pain may mask serious injury. If you've applied ice to the apparently twisted ankle of a young athlete, don't let him go back into the game until you're certain that you're not dealing with an injury more serious than a simple strain or sprain.

Most doctors suggest using applications of cold intermittently—10 to 20 minutes, 4 to 5 times daily. Others use cold continuously for 12 hours or longer. Under any circumstances check the skin under the pack often for signs of frostbite.

Don't apply ice directly to the skin. Put it in plastic bags, hot-water bottles, or ice caps, wrapped in a towel, or frozen into paper cups. A can of frozen juice concentrate, wrapped in waxed paper and held in a gloved hand, also serves well for ice massage or a specific point of pain. Even in the emergency treatment of burns cold water is recommended, rather than the application of ice itself.

You can make your own reusable ice packs by breaking or crushing 10 to 12 ice cubes, placing them in a plastic bag, and closing the bag with a rubber band, string, or wire tie. Mold this pack to the part to be treated, and place the pack in the freezer over something that will help it stay molded—a loaf of bread for a leg or arm pack, for example. When it is time to apply the pack, take it from the freezer, wrap it in its cover, and reapply for the prescribed time. Then return it to the freezer for the next application.

Cold sprays are convenient and effective—but hazardous. Ethyl chloride spray is flammable, Freon is nonflammable, but both ethyl chloride and Freon spray have toxic fumes. If not used properly, both can cause skin burns.

Hot compresses. Heat helps localize infection and improves blood circulation. Most doctors suggest local application of heat when the affected area feels hot and is red—for example, inflamed joints due to arthritis, bursitis, or gout. Heat is also considered helpful in achieving the localization of infection in abscesses, boils, and cellulitis.

While relief may not be as marked as that achieved with cold, heat is beneficial for pain and spasm. It is also restful. Heat dilates blood vessels. That brings more blood to the part, improves circulation, carries off waste products, and thereby makes it easier for muscles to relax.

Switch from cold applications to heat no sooner than 5 to 7 days after an injury. If you apply heat earlier, you may prolong swelling. Some physicians hold off using heat until the patient starts rehabilitation, perhaps 3 to 6 weeks after a severe sprain. A physician might, however, advise you to switch to heat earlier if the area becomes red hot and shows signs of a worsening underlying disease.

Don't apply heat if there's a cancer in the area of the injury—the heat may spur cell growth. Switch back from heat to cold if discomfort worsens.

Moist heat is generally better than dry heat. It is less drying to the skin and less likely to cause burns and blisters. It does not result in an excessive loss of fluid and salt through perspiration. It is less apt to raise overall body temperatures above 101° F to 102° F, as dry heat may.

Before applying hot packs, lubricate the skin with baby oil or mineral oil over the area to be treated. The oil will act as an insulator.

Moist heat in the form of hot wet towels and compresses cools rapidly. To hold in heat wrap the affected part in a hot wet towel, cover it with a waterproof material such as wax paper, plastic wrap, plastic bags, or oilcloth, and cover the waterproof wrap with a dry towel.

Another method: Fill a hot-water bottle so it is not too hot to place against your face. Wring out a towel or washcloth in hot water. Wrap that cloth around the affected part, place the hot-water bottle over it, and wrap plastic around the whole pack. A dry towel placed on top of the entire pack will hold the heat in.

Most convenient of all is to cover a hot moist towel with an electric, shockproof, *waterproof* heating pad. But beware the possibility of electric shock from frayed cords and wet outlets.

With most forms of dry heat the disadvantages outweigh the advantages. The hot-water bottle is preferred to the electric heating pad. If a hot-water bottle is hot enough to inflict a burn, you feel that heat as soon as you come in contact with it. From then on the hot-water bottle only gets colder.

A heating pad can feel comfortable at first. You can then become accustomed to a degree of heat that if prolonged can give you a severe burn. Except under specific doctor's orders, a pad is not advised for elderly people, people with poor circulation to the arms or legs, people with diabetes, and people taking steroids. Such people tend to have skin that is especially vulnerable to heat.

Don't use a heating pad with any linament. The combination of the two can produce considerable blistering and skin damage, even disfigurement and disability.

A heating pad may burn you if the heat indicator is set too high or is faulty. You may also be burned if the pad is applied for more than 20 minutes at a time, and especially if you put weight on the pad—even with the thermostat set on LOW. Don't lie on a pad or fall asleep with one.

Don't stick pins into a heating pad. Don't use it without its outer cover. Avoid crushing or bending it.

You may, however, use a heating pad on the abdomen to ease distension and griping pain, as in attacks of irritable colon. Even if such abdominal pain turns out to be acute appendicitis, it is doubtful that a heating pad would have any adverse effect unless it delayed medical diagnosis.

If you have arthritis of the hands and feet, consider paraffin baths, which have the advantage of delivering more heat than other methods. Paraffin also provides its own insulation to keep heat in, keeps the skin well lubricated and supple, and keeps swelling down. Use it only on your physician's instructions.

People whose hands are arthritic, or who are elderly, may have trouble handling the large coffee can or other container of paraffin. If the container tips over on a gas stove, the paraffin could flare up. Also some people develop contact dermatitis from the oils in paraffin sold expressly for paraffin baths.

A novel heat treatment uses a 100-watt bulb in a gooseneck lamp—the area requiring heat is held about 6 inches away from the bulb. Dr. Adam G. N. Moore of Squantum, Massachusetts, finds that his patients prefer this to using a heating pad, or hot-water bottle, or soaking in a hot tub.

See also ACCIDENTS; BATHING; BURNS; DIATHERMY.

CONDOM   See BIRTH CONTROL.

CONGENITAL HEART DEFECTS are malformations in the heart or large blood vessels near the heart. Although present at birth, some give no symptoms until later and may not be discovered until adulthood.

A congenital heart defect is not necessarily fatal or crippling. Some 25,000 U.S. children a year are born with one. Most survive infancy. For some the malformation causes impairment of the circulation, ranging from mild to severe, and the child's growth is slowed and his physical activity limited. But for many others the defect is so slight that it causes no difficulty.

Most often the cause is unknown. Some inborn heart defects may be hereditary, although it is rare for a congenital heart defect to afflict more than one child in a family—a reassurance to parents who might fear "bad heredity." Other inborn defects are caused by virus diseases, such as rubella, occurring in the mother during the first three months of pregnancy.

Surgery can help about three in four. The following are the most common congenital defects that may be remedied by surgery.

Patent ductus arteriosus. Every newborn baby has a passageway—a ductus arteriosus—between the two major blood vessels that leave his heart: the pulmonary artery (which carries blood from the right side of the heart to the lungs) and the aorta, which carries blood from the left side of the heart to the rest of the body. This connection, useful during fetal life, normally closes within a few weeks after birth.

When it remains open ("patent"), some of the blood that should be circulated through the body shuttles uselessly back and forth between the heart and lungs. The heart must work harder to pump sufficient blood through the body to nourish all tissues and organs. Before the child reaches school age, normal circulation can usually be established with an operation to tie shut or cut the passageway that was left open.

Septal defects are openings in the septum, the muscle wall that separates the interior of the heart into a left and right side. The hole may be between the two upper heart chambers (atrial septal defect) or between the lower chambers (ventricular septal defect).

Unless small, such a hole interferes with normal blood circulation and places an increased load on the heart. How much of a load depends on size and location of the hole, but sometimes the heart cannot meet the demand that it work much harder. With the aid of a heart-lung machine, open-heart surgery is successful in sewing shut these septal openings, or in closing them with synthetic patches.

Coarctation of the aorta. The aorta is the largest artery in the body, carrying the full load of blood away from the heart. When the aorta is narrowed (coarcted) at birth, the amount of blood it can transport may be severely reduced.

When symptoms of such a harmful constriction of the vessel show up, surgery can usually remove the narrow segment. If a long section is cut out, the surgeon may replace it with an artificial vessel made from synthetic materials.

Valvular stenosis. Some babies may be born with a narrowing (stenosis) of one of the valves regulating blood flow inside the heart. Narrowing may occur in the valve itself, most commonly in the aortic and pulmonary heart valves, or in an area near a valve. Smooth flow of blood is obstructed by the constriction.

This means an increase in the heart's pumping to push blood through the crippled valve, or possibly inadequate oxygenation of the blood. A stenosed valve can be cut open. An irreparably damaged valve may be replaced with an artificial one.

Transposition of the great vessels. In this defect the two "great vessels"—the pulmonary artery, which carries blood to the lungs to pick up oxygen, and the aorta, which transports blood to the body—originate on sides of the heart opposite their proper source.

The outlook for a newborn infant with this defect used to be extremely grave. Surgery can now help some of them by creating an opening between the upper heart chambers to help balance the circulation. Total correction is sometimes possible after the child has reached a favorable size and state of health.

Tetralogy of Fallot. This name is given to a combination of four defects causing a "blue baby": a ventricular septal opening; an "overriding aorta" that straddles both ventricles, instead of originating solely in the left ventricle; a stenosed pulmonary valve; and an enlarged right ventricle. The main result is a short circuit of the blood flow inside the heart so that not enough blood gets to the lungs to pick up oxygen. Oxygen-poor blood circulating in the body gives the skin a blue color and deprives the body tissues of as much oxygen as they need.

Closed-heart operations often relieve a blue baby's condition but do not correct the heart defects themselves. In these operations the surgeon provides a channel through which more blood can reach the lungs. When the child is of proper age and health, it is increasingly possible to repair tetralogy of Fallot with open-heart operations in which the narrowed pulmonary valve is cut open and the septal defect sealed with a plastic patch.

Special for parents. After heart surgery children usually require a convalescent period ranging from a few weeks to a few months. The youngster generally does not return to school until three to four months after the operation. The need for special medical supervision varies widely after such surgery.

In a few cases of congenital heart defects you may need to arrange adjustments in the school program, at least temporarily. These might include restricted activity during recess and physical education periods, scheduling of special rest periods, and providing of between-meal snacks.

A youngster with a congenital heart defect may be advised to keep out of competitive sports because in the excitement of the game they may not heed warning signals of fatigue. Ordinarily, however, most children with congenital heart malformations limit their own activity when necessary. Physicians find those who tire easily tend to slow down spontaneously. Nagging or imposing restrictions beyond the doctor's recommendations is not only unnecessary but harmful. The child needs to be allowed as normal a school life as possible within his limitations.

Have a cardiac child's condition reevaluated by his physician from time to time. It is likely that his condition will improve and more activity will be allowed.

When children with heart defects undergo tooth extraction, tonsillectomy, or other operations, they generally need penicillin or other antibiotics to guard against a heart infection called bacterial endocarditis. This infection is not common, but it can be life-threatening if it occurs.

A child with a heart defect may have bluish skin. Some of the blood that is meant to go first to the lungs for oxygen is pumped directly from the heart to the body. Since blood low in oxygen is bluish-red, this gives the skin or mucous membranes a blue tinge.

This coloring, termed cyanosis, is not of itself dangerous, though it can be alarming. The youngster with cyanosis may vary in the amount of exercise he can undertake on different days.

Hot and cold weather may affect him. He will have his good days and bad days. These children usually restrict their own activities, and need not have their program limited beyond what the doctor advises.

Children with severe heart problems need early guidance and job counseling. Physical limitations may narrow their choices. Since many unskilled jobs are physically taxing, children who are left with heart difficulties need as much schooling as possible to prepare them for skilled work. Encourage such a child to finish high school and to seek as much additional preparation as is feasible for him.

Vocational counselors take a firm stand against drawing up lists of "jobs for cardiacs." They believe that it is more important to match the individual to specific work than to rule out certain vocational fields. On the other hand vocational plans of these young people are frequently unrealistic in view of their probable physical limitations in the future.

Many families cannot meet the total costs of treatment for children with congenital heart disease. Two major sources of help are the state divisions of vocational rehabilitation and the state crippled children's programs, which parents may contact directly. Family physicians, health departments, and local heart associations can help parents get in touch with the appropriate agency.

See also BIRTH DEFECTS; HEART DISEASE; HOSPITALIZING CHILDREN.

CONGESTIVE HEART FAILURE See HEART FAILURE.

CONJUNCTIVITIS See PINK EYE.

CONSTIPATION is often imaginary. Convinced that a daily bowel movement is essential, many people fear they're constipated if their bowel movement comes every two or three days.

Actually normal bowel movement frequency can range from three times daily to once every four or five days.

Constipation alone is rarely harmful. You may feel some bowel fullness or pass gas, but this is not dangerous. There is no truth in the notion that poisons from the retained bowels get into the bloodstream and damage the brain and other organs.

To relieve constipation eat prunes. Foods high in fiber—such as bran and many raw fruits and vegetables—also stimulate the bowel. Increase your fiber intake gradually to avoid gas and bloatedness. A cup of strong coffee may push along a reluctant bowel movement.

If discomfort makes you urgently need to defecate, take an enema with a pint or so of warm tap water. A bulb-shaped rubber enema syringe can be a good investment, especially when traveling.

Prevention. Help ensure regular bowel movements by eating a wide variety of foods rich in fiber. Getting sufficient rest, exercising daily, drinking plenty of water—these classic measures influence not so much the bowel as the mind. Their psychological effect often aids bowel function.

Heed the urge to defecate. If you disregard it, the impulse grows weaker and the fecal mass becomes hard and dry. Many people become constipated because they're "too busy" to respond to nature's call.

If you tend to have an urge to move your bowels around the same time every day, leave enough time for a leisurely bowel movement. You may find it easiest to have a bowel movement after breakfast. Food on an empty stomach tends to activate the bowels.

Don't spend more than about 10 or 15 minutes on the toilet waiting for a bowel movement. Never strain hard to push it out. This may increase your chances of developing hemorrhoids and hernia. Sit with a footstool under your feet and your knees up—squatting is a more natural way to defecate.

In some people retention of bowel movements is a sign of anger, tension, or other emotional stress. Constipation may also plague the elderly and bedridden, largely because they are deprived of normal physical activity and their eating habits may have altered.

Constipation is common in pregnancy, after childbirth, and after surgery.

People who go on crash diets may also notice that they move their bowels less frequently. If you diet, make sure your diet remains nutritionally balanced and includes raw fruits and vegetables, breads and cereals. Some drugs containing narcotics can cause constipation, which is relieved if the medication is changed.

Don't use laxatives. Laxatives are almost never necessary. Indeed regular use of laxatives can *cause* constipation.

Laxatives evacuate more fecal matter than normal. Thus it may be several days before the colon fills sufficiently for a bowel movement. After a day or two, though, a person may once again be concerned about lack of bowel activity and take another laxative.

The chronic use of laxatives can overstimulate intestinal muscles to the point of exhaustion, making it difficult to have a bowel movement without further use of laxatives. The laxatives become virtually addictive.

Laxatives can mask medical conditions causing constipation. Chronic constipation can be a symptom of diverticulosis, appendicitis, congenital disorders of the intestinal tract, and obstruction caused by cancer. Most constipated people, though, are *not* suffering from any illness.

Laxatives may interfere with proper absorption of foods from the small intestine, causing deficiencies of potassium and other vital nutrients.

Laxatives can cause chronic irritation of the intestines and diarrhea. Hemorrhoids and anal fissure may also result from the habitual use of laxatives. Fluid loss is also a potential problem. Laxatives containing mineral oil may be aspirated (inhaled)—especially by the elderly or ill —and irritate the lungs or cause pneumonia.

A number of over-the-counter laxatives can cause mercury poisoning, according to a team of researchers at Johns Hopkins Hospital. The AMA warns that laxatives containing calomel, a mercury compound, are "unsafe and unreliable."

Since laxatives are almost never necessary, take one only on your doctor's advice. Safest but relatively slow (12 to 36 hours) are bulk laxatives, which work by absorbing water and expanding. Among major brands having virtually no adverse effects are Effersyllium, Hydrocil, Konsyl, and Metamucil.

Milk of magnesia is the mildest of the faster-acting laxatives (two to six hours). Use the smallest dose recommended on the label. If it works, take less next time. Magnesium laxatives can be dangerous for people with chronic kidney disease.

Avoid all other laxatives—especially such strong ones as castor oil, Cas-Evac, Dulcolax, Dorbane, Doxan, Ex-Lax, Feen-A-Mint, Fletcher's Castoria, Gentlax, Nature's Remedy, and Senokot. Also avoid laxatives containing two or more active ingredients, like Haley's M-O, Correctol, and Carter's Little Pills. With a single-ingredient product you run less risk of side effects.

Steer clear of commercial enema preparations with soap, salt water, or other irritants. They can cause severe irritation of the mucous membranes of the anus and rectum. So can glycerine suppositories, if taken more than just occasionally.

If you have a laxative habit, try cutting out laxatives entirely. Most people who do so have a normal bowel movement within a week or so.

Take your child to a doctor if he has frequent problems with bowel movements. Medication to soften the bowels is helpful in many cases. Where the problem is largely a matter of stress, psychotherapy may be necessary. Never give a child laxatives, enemas, or suppositories except on a physician's advice.

Children sometimes develop chronic constipation because of enforced toilet training. A child who is scolded or punished for soiling may withhold his bowel movements until they become hard and painful to eliminate. A sore or crack (fissure) in the rectum or around the anus may also cause a child to retain bowel movements.

Some constipated people develop fecal impaction: the compressed feces become dry, hard, and rubbery. Watery fecal material may be eliminated, but no substantial movement can get through. The sufferer may experience cramps and rectal pain. Under a doctor's supervision treatment is usually a mineral or olive oil enema followed by an irritant enema, such as soapsuds. If enemas don't work, the impacted mass may have to be removed by hand, sometimes under anesthesia.

See also FIBER; HEMORRHOIDS; STRESS.

CONSULTATIONS See PHYSICAL EXAMINATION; PHYSICIAN.

CONTACT DERMATITIS is an allergic skin reaction. After touching such substances as chemicals, metals, or cosmetics, some people erupt with blisters, scaling, and itching.

The most common single cause of contact dermatitis is poison ivy. The nearly universal symptom is itching. With many allergens the eruption may lead you quickly to the source of trouble. If you're sensitive to rubber, for instance, the sites of lesions will be where rubber touches the skin —under a strap or rubber stocking. Also look to your job. An estimated 100,000 workers in hundreds of industries are victims of occupational dermatitis.

The hidden sources of allergens are numerous. A typical housewife lives in a sea of potentially allergenic chemical ingredients. In a single day she may contact at least 800 different substances. Fortunately most of these are weak allergens and affect only the highly susceptible.

Household irritants. Housewives' eczema (or housewives' dermatitis) is a widespread skin irritation of the hands. It is most common in winter among women whose hands are frequently in and out of cleaning solutions.

Repeated exposure to water, with continual wetting and drying, causes the skin to be more susceptible to substances commonly encountered in household work. Detergents, metal polishes, floor waxes, furniture polishes, house dust, vegetable and fruit juices, food and other allergies, mold spores, cold weather and chapping— all have been suggested as potential causes.

The true cause in a particular case often can't be pinpointed. It can occur in men, and sometimes develops on the hands of those who have little contact with water. It may spread to other parts of the body.

The first symptom often is intense, intermittent itching on the back or sides of one or more fingers. The itching site may show slight redness or possibly a patch of tiny, scattered water blisters. If the blisters open, a raw oozing results, which may become inflamed and painful. A crust tends to form.

If the blisters dry up without breaking, the damaged skin becomes dry and scaly. Infections are common, for the damaged skin is no longer able to combat microorganisms. With minimum precautions the skin will eventually heal on its own.

Avoid wet work. Use an unscented white soap, and only when hands definitely need cleansing. Where such chores as dishwashing and hand laundry are unavoidable, wear either cotton-lined rubber gloves or rubber gloves over cotton gloves. Don't wear rubber gloves for more than 15 minutes at a time. They make the hands too moist, and rubber is a common allergen. When possible wear lightweight loose-fitting cotton gloves for dry work. Avoid tightly woven bandages and nonporous adhesive tape, since they tend to make the underlying skin soggy.

It is questionable whether a silicone protective cream would be of use in the ever-changing conditions to which a housewife's hands are subjected. Many silicone creams on the market contain too little of the protective agent to be of any use. Two that have a substantial amount of silicone are Silicote and Silconex. After the affected area becomes rough and scaly, resist the temptation to apply a hand cream or lotion to counteract the dryness, since the itching may return and new water blisters may appear.

After the skin has returned to normal, use a simple emollient cream or lotion before engaging in housecleaning chores, before exposing the hands to soapy water, and before prolonged outdoor activity. Especially in winter an emollient may reduce dryness and chapping.

If you are allergic to synthetic detergent use one of the very few soap products with no synthetic detergents in them. Look for a package that clearly says "soap." Among those manufactured by major producers are Lux Flakes, Ivory Flakes, Ivory Snow, and Duz Soap (as distinguished from Duz Detergent).

Allergy to metals. Metals that may cause allergy include chrome and mercury. A young woman, who knew she was allergic to mercurial antiseptics, broke a thermometer. Unthinkingly she touched a small amount of mercury. A generalized, severe rash followed in a few hours. Mercury in antiseptics, vaccines, preservatives, and ointments may prolong a dermatitis.

Nickel is in such varied use that nickel dermatitis is extremely common. Reactions spring from handling coins as well as from wearing jewelry, buckles, zippers, or garters made with nickel alloys.

Nickel-sensitive women need to use solid gold posts in pierced earrings (see EAR PIERCING). Coating nickel-plated objects with clear fingernail polish may provide protection from the metal. Sprinkle talcum powder under a nickel-plated object to reduce the contact of sweat, which increases sensitivity to nickel.

Nickel is capable of causing a generalized reaction. Itching eruptions may appear anywhere on the body, and the eyes may become irritated. The metal may also bring about an immediate and potentially fatal collapse (an anaphylactic reaction) characterized by hives, vomiting, anxiety, and breathing difficulties.

Plastics and resins frequently produce dermatitis. Some adhesive tapes contain a resin to which many people are allergic.

Several doctors have reported allergic skin reactions from spandex, a synthetic elastic fiber. Spandex is considered to have better washability and wearability than rubber, so is replacing rubber in many stretch fabrics. It is found in swimsuits, foundation garments, stretch pants, and stockings. The material is also being used in men's clothing in such items as elastic tops of socks, and waistbands of pants and underwear. Most of the reported reactions have been caused by garments that come into close contact with the skin.

Allergies to cosmetics. Cosmetics are not as potentially allergenic as they once were, thanks largely to FDA regulation and improved formulas. Nonetheless one or another ingredient of lipstick, especially an indelible brand, may be responsible for lip inflammation.

One corrective is to use specially formulated lipstick minus the offending component. "Nonpermanent" lipsticks are available for women allergic to the ordinary staining dyes. "Unscented" lipstick is sold for women with perfume allergy.

Nail polish, whether tinted or colorless, is a frequent offender, as are nail hardeners. Hair dyes, bleaches, and eye cosmetics may all cause severe reactions on the scalp, ears, and eyelids. Many people experience mild skin reactions from antiperspirants.

"Hypoallergenic" cosmetics are rarely worth the extra cost. They were originally formulated about 35 years ago, after a few manufacturers began to produce cosmetic lines from which known sensitizing agents were omitted. These manufacturers cooperated with dermatologists by publishing the formulations of their products and by providing supplies of individual ingredients for sensitization tests, as well as specially formulated products. The term *hypoallergenic* was coined to indicate that these cosmetics were less likely to produce allergic reactions than others available at that time.

Since then many dermatologists have challenged the term as misleading. Allergic reactions may occur even when so-called hypoallergenic cosmetics are used, since there is no method by which a nonallergenic cosmetic can be produced. Moreover, the ingredients most likely to cause sensitization have been eliminated from the great majority of cosmetic products.

A sensitivity to one brand of cosmetic may be resolved simply by switching to another ordinary brand, which is likely to cost less than a brand advertising itself as hypoallergenic. Different brands, however, may contain the same preservative or fragrance that you've become sensitized to. If reactions persist, an allergist or dermatologist may patch-test for the offending chemical.

The difference between the original hypoallergenic cosmetics and the usual consumer product is now narrowed to the services that the manufacturers of hypoallergenic cosmetics offer physicians. A severely sensitive person may find these services worth the extra cost, although many dermatologists counsel patients to try a less expensive, standard brand first.

Prevention is the most practical cure. Desensitization to prevent contact dermatitis is attempted only in connection with severe poison ivy allergy. No matter what the origin, the first step in treatment is to identify and avoid the allergen.

If a lesion is dry, follow the suggestions given for housewives' dermatitis. If it is oozing, you may get relief from wet dressings of Burow's solution or warm salt water. Use the wet dressings continuously for 2 days, allowing the skin to air-dry for 30 minutes every 12 hours. As the reaction subsides, apply the dressings 4 times a day for periods of 1 hour. For the first 2 days, during waking hours, apply the wet dressings 1 hour on, 1 hour off. Thereafter, until the lesion dries, apply wet dressings 3 or 4 times daily for an hour at a time.

In addition your doctor may prescribe a topical steroid. Patients are ordinarily counseled to use these drugs sparingly. Report any sign of infection immediately.

See also ALLERGY; ITCHING; POISON IVY; SKIN DISORDER.

CONTACT LENSES can do a better job than eyeglasses for many types of eye disorder. But the cost may be more than you care to bear in dollars and discomfort.

About 14 million Americans wear contact lenses. Some people adjust to them successfully; others give up the eye-smarting ordeal and slip the lenses into a drawer.

There are three types of contact lenses. All cover the cornea, the clear part of the eye in front of the pupil and iris. The *hard* lens, in decreasing use, is made of a form of semirigid plastic. The *gas-permeable* lens is like the hard lens but much more comfortable because it allows oxygen to pass through to the cornea. The *soft* lens is of a plastic hydrophilic polymer, which when wet is very pliable.

In addition, lenses may be *daily-wear* (taken out at night) or *extended-wear* (kept in for long periods).

Before investing in contact lenses, you need to consider: (1) Do you really want them? (2) If so, which kind of contact lens would you be better off with?

Contacts versus glasses. The first problem is

price. The initial cost of hard contact lenses will vary between $100 and $400. Soft and gas-permeable lenses run about $200 to $700. Complex, time-consuming examinations and fittings account for the major part of the cost of contacts. Because of possible changes in the fit, contacts require more frequent visits to the doctor than do glasses.

The tiny, transparent lenses are more easily lost or misplaced than eyeglasses. One doctor has reported that nearly half his patients lost at least one lens after several months. For an additional charge you can buy insurance for lenses (but rarely for professional services). The insurance is likely to be practical for costly soft and gas-permeable lenses, less so for hard. An alternative is to find an eye doctor who will replace lost contacts at a reduced cost plus his fee.

All this is in addition to charges for your regular glasses. You need to retain one or more pairs of glasses for when you can't wear contacts, or when you've lost one.

When contacts won't work. Not everyone can wear contacts. You probably won't be a good candidate for contact lenses if you:

Are pregnant or on birth control pills—conditions that cause the cornea to swell.

Are unusually susceptible to infection.

Have hand tremor or severe arthritis, which would interfere with inserting or removing lenses.

Have an eye condition such as chronic dryness, recurrent sties, inflammation, or infection.

Have hay fever, asthma, or another allergy that makes the eyes water excessively.

Have a visual defect so slight that you normally wear glasses only for special tasks.

Are taking diuretics, antihistamines, or decongestants, which may produce eye dryness.

Are psychologically unable to tolerate a foreign body in the eye.

Have a job where accidental dislodgement of a lens could be dangerous.

Are unlikely to endure the adjustment period.

Have only one eye and engage in high-speed activities during which a sudden jolt might dislodge the lens.

Work in an environment with irritating dust, chemicals, or vapors.

Some conditions may bar you from one type of lens. The hard and daily-wear gas-permeable lens can't be worn when the eye is closed for prolonged periods since it may cause corneal abrasion. Thus if you are subject to periods of unconsciousness, you're a poor candidate for such lenses. But even people with diabetes, epilepsy, and severe high blood pressure can consider soft lenses, especially the extended-wear type. Even for daily-wear soft lenses, 24-hour wearing (though not recommended) does not appear to harm the eye.

Soft lenses fit much closer than do hard or gas-permeable lenses and are not susceptible to popping out, as are the hard or gas-permeable lenses. But they too are not suitable for swimmers and scuba divers, since they can absorb contaminants in water.

Even a perfectly fitted contact lens is a foreign body in the eye. During the adjustment period—particularly for hard or gas-permeable lenses—you're likely to experience the discomforts of having something in your eye—tearing, blinking, swollen lids, and bloodshot eyes. Your eyes may become sensitive to light.

You may have to return to the doctor five or six times (or more) during the adaptation period for hard or gas-permeable lenses to get them just right. Even after successful adaptation contacts may be uncomfortable in heavy air pollution, smoke-filled rooms, or when you have a cold or other respiratory infection. Women may experience difficulty wearing them during pregnancy.

Improper insertion or removal might cause corneal scratches. If undetected these can result in permanent damage to the eyes. There is also a risk of infection from contaminated contacts.

Advantages of contacts. The psychological uplift the wearer gets from seeing and being seen without spectacles is probably the greatest advantage of contacts. A survey by Michigan doctors found that 90 of 100 patients bought lenses solely for cosmetic reasons. Feeling less self-conscious, youngsters who get contacts may increase their social activities and improve their grades.

Many people won't wear glasses even when they have severe visual impairment. Their choice is not between glasses and contact lenses, but between contact lenses and not seeing.

Contacts are better than glasses for severe nearsightedness. The spectacle lenses are thick at the edge and thin in the center. They make things look smaller than they are and distort light passing through their edges so that the wearer must constantly turn his head for clear vision. Contact lenses have none of these drawbacks.

Contact lenses often give more satisfactory correction than glasses for the most common form of farsightedness; aniseikonia, a condition in which one eye sees a bigger image than the other; and anisometropia, unequal refractive power of the eyes.

Contact lenses are a good choice for those who have had cataract surgery, where the crystalline lens of the eye has been removed.

Contacts help the athlete, providing better side vision and making sports considerably safer. In cases of blows to the face contact lenses are much less likely to cause eye injuries.

Contacts are often preferred by people whose occupations involve very close work, especially with cameras, microscopes, or telescopes. Contacts don't irritate the ears or the bridge of the nose.

Which type of lens? If you decide to go for contacts, these facts can help you make a choice:

The considerably lower price is one advantage hard lenses have over soft. Hard and gas-permeable lenses give better correction of vision. While clear 20/20 vision is the norm for those lenses, soft lenses are more likely to give you 20/25. Hard and gas-permeable lenses can be polished to remove scratches, while soft lenses cannot.

Hard and gas-permeable lenses can correct high degrees of astigmatism. Some soft lenses can correct only moderate astigmatism, and tend to be harder to fit.

Since the soft lens flexes, you may experience unstable vision each time you blink, a problem nonexistent with hard and gas-permeable lenses.

Soft lenses tend to be more fragile than hard and gas-permeable lenses. If kept wet, they are very flexible and not easily damaged, but when dry, they are as brittle as a cornflake. Women with long fingernails must exercise care in handling the lenses, since their nails can nick the soft surface. Mascara, other eye makeup, or hair spray may soil a hard lens surface, causing blurred vision and irritation, but will ruin a soft lens. Soft lenses must usually be replaced every year or so.

The soft lens is highly absorbent, and medications cannot be placed in the eye while you are wearing it. This rules out soft lenses for people taking eyedrops for such conditions as glaucoma. You can, however, continue to wear hard or gas-permeable lenses during such treatment.

The same absorbency that allows soft lenses to retain medication might prove dangerous in the presence of strong fumes or vapors, such as paint solvents, industrial chemicals, or tear gas. Those who work with such substances should not wear soft lenses. Instead of being washed away quickly by tears, chemicals might be absorbed and held against the eye until the lenses are removed.

Soap and hand cream also might be irritating if they come in contact with the lenses. Serious corneal damage could also result from wearing a soft lens that has been soaked in a conventional hard-lens cleaning solution that contained preservatives.

Hard and gas-permeable lens care is relatively simple. The lenses are simply stored overnight in a specially designed case which the patient fills with soaking solution. Some specialists recommend dry storage to reduce the possibility of contamination by bacteria in the solution.

Soft-lens care is far more complicated, since the danger of infection is great if bacteria get into the absorbent lenses. You need to carefully disinfect soft lenses each day. The lenses must be either boiled or treated with a chemical solution, a particular nuisance for travelers.

The outstanding feature of soft and gas-permeable lenses is the short adjustment period they may require.

It usually takes about two weeks to adjust to hard lenses, adhering to a schedule of wearing the lenses longer and longer each day. Fitting may be complicated. You may not take the lenses home until the third or fourth visit.

By contrast, with soft and gas-permeable lenses very little adjustment may be necessary. You can possibly wear the lenses for several hours the first day and may not have to follow a rigid adjustment schedule. Soft lenses are not custom-ground to prescription, as hard and most gas-permeable lenses are, but are manufactured in varying powers. After a trial-and-error process taking several hours you walk out with the lenses most suited to you.

Hard-lens wearers have to cut their wearing time back if they do not wear the lens for a day or two. Soft and gas-permeable lens wearers can wear the lenses relatively few hours a week if they wish.

If you wish to switch back to glasses intermittently, with hard lenses you'll have blurred vision for minutes to hours. With soft and gas-permeable lenses any blurring is usually minimal.

Special soft lenses are available for extended wear—up to several weeks at a time. Extended-wear gas-permeable lenses are a more recent development. While they are a promising advance, wide experience with soft lenses points up serious disadvantages. They must be taken out every two to four weeks for cleaning. They require careful professional supervision in the first six months to see if they can be worn successfully. They need to be replaced frequently. Some people suffer corneal damage from extended-wear soft lenses. Such lenses may be especially useful for people with handicaps that make daily insertion and removal difficult.

Soft or gas-permeable lenses may be for you if you're a hard-lens dropout. If you still want the benefits of wearing contact lenses and can afford the price, you may not have the same difficulties in adjusting to soft or gas-permeable lenses.

In addition you'll probably do better with soft than hard or gas-permeable lenses if:

You want to wear the lenses solely for cosmetic purposes for limited periods each week.

You're elderly and have just undergone cataract surgery. Soft lenses are larger and easier for the elderly to handle.

You're an athlete and want to reduce the possibility of losing a lens during physical activity. Unlike hard lenses soft lenses are not prone to pop out.

If you opt for contacts, go to a qualified ophthalmologist or optometrist. Avoid bargain contact lenses at clinics. The price advertised may be very low, but hidden costs will raise the price considerably. You're also more likely to get poorly fitted lenses and improper follow-up care at a clinic. Confirm that trying soft lenses doesn't obligate you to buy. Any ethical practitioner should be willing to discuss beforehand what his fee will be if you find the quality of vision with soft lenses unacceptable. Ask specifically if you may sit in his office for a while—a few hours, if necessary—to assess the acuity and comfort of the soft lenses.

Tips for contact lens wearers: In case of an accident you need to carry emergency medical identification signaling you as a contact lens wearer.

Overuse of contacts may impair vision. A contact lens can scratch the cornea of the eye. The cornea becomes easily infected once its thin protective layer is torn, and a corneal infection that goes unnoticed can cause a vision-impairing scar or even the loss of an eye. If you wear contact lenses for more than the prescribed number of hours a day, you may not be aware of a scratch because overuse of contacts deadens the sensitivity of the eye to pain.

Most people should wear daily-wear contacts at most for 10 to 14 hours each day. Even then remove the contacts for a few minutes after 6 or 7 hours to rest your eyes.

Unless you have extended-wear lenses, never wear contacts while sleeping or napping. Don't wear them while sunbathing or using a sunlamp either, because of the possibility of accidentally falling asleep.

Never moisten a lens with saliva. This places bacteria directly on the eye, inviting infection. Use cleansing or wetting agents recommended by your doctor.

Don't wear contact lenses if you have pink eye or other eye infection. If you get a foreign body under the lens, or if your eye becomes irritated, consult your doctor.

If you lose a lens, you may be able to find it easily by following this method: Fashion a filter in a vacuum cleaner hose by inserting the foot and ankle of a nylon stocking. Roll the top of the stocking over the hose nozzle and secure it with rubber bands. Vacuum the floor. Then remove the stocking filter and invert it over a white surface. In most cases the lens will have been picked up.

Avoid deep-tinted hard contacts to change your eye color from, say, brown to green. A slight tinting makes it easier to find lenses when they are accidentally dropped. Deep tinting decreases the amount of light transmitted through them and, as with sunglasses, decreases vision. Moreover, the color additives are irritating to some eyes.

Don't wear contacts in a beauty shop. That way you avoid possible damage and irritation from cosmetics and you won't wear the lenses under a hair dryer, where the intense heat might damage them. Hair sprays and other aerosols can adhere to soft contacts.

Avoid using creams and oils when wearing lenses. Use cosmetics sparingly around the eyelids. Use only waterproof mascara. Don't use "lash extender" mascara—it contains tiny fibers which may become trapped under the lenses and produce discomfort.

When hair spray is used, keep your eyes closed during application and for a few minutes afterward. This will allow the mist to settle out of the air.

See also CATARACT; EYE DISORDER; EYE-GLASSES.

CONTRACEPTION See BIRTH CONTROL.

CONTUSIONS See BRUISES.

CONVALESCENCE See BED REST.

CONVULSIONS (seizures) If you're with someone who's having a convulsion (see illustration):

1. Keep him from falling. Gently lay him down.
2. Protect him from injuring himself by pushing away nearby objects. Put a flat pillow or other padding under his head.
3. Optional: If his mouth is open, you may prevent him from biting his tongue or cheek by gently placing a folded cloth between his teeth on one side. If you do this,

IF SOMEONE HAS A CONVULSION

Keep him from hurting himself

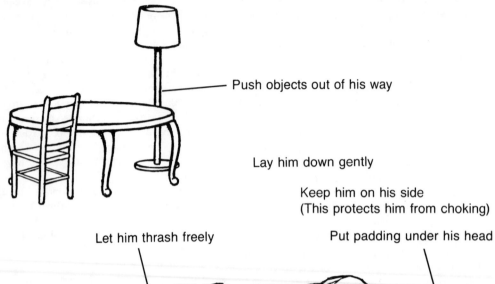

Push objects out of his way

Lay him down gently

Keep him on his side
(This protects him from choking)

Let him thrash freely

Put padding under his head

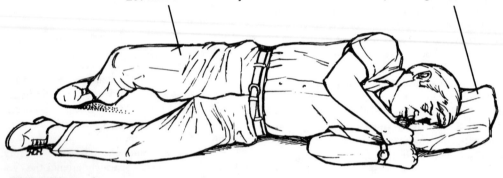

After seizure is over
Loosen his clothing
Let him rest

watch that the cloth does not get inhaled or otherwise obstruct his breathing.

Don't try to force his mouth open. Don't insert a hard object, which could damage his teeth or jaw. (Note: The Epilepsy Foundation of America recommends against putting anything in the mouth.)

4. Turn him on his side. This way his limp tongue won't block his air passages. Nor, if he vomits, will the vomitus be inhaled into his lungs.

5. Don't try to restrain any rigid, spastic movements he may make. Don't slap him or try to wake him. Don't give liquids. When the violent jerking subsides, loosen his clothing about the neck.

6. After the convulsion let him rest.

Convulsions are associated with many conditions, including epilepsy, head injuries, cancer of the brain, heat disorders, and poisoning.

Convulsions in children often result from infection. Frequently the convulsion occurs with high fever (a febrile convulsion). Convulsions may appear at any time during the acute stage or may be the first sign of an infectious disease such as ear infections, colds, tonsillitis, whooping cough, scarlet fever, or pneumonia.

While frightening to parents the convulsion itself is rarely a threat to the child's life. There is no conclusive evidence that a single, brief convulsion causes brain damage.

In a typical febrile convulsion the child lapses into unconsciousness. His limbs stiffen and jerk. His eyes may roll up. His lips and face may turn blue. His breathing may seem slightly labored. The convulsion is usually over in a few minutes, rarely more than 15, leaving the child stuporous. He may fall asleep.

After your child has a convulsion, cover him lightly and call your doctor. He may advise you to give him a fever-reducing medicine and sponge him with tepid water to bring down the fever.

You may be able to reduce the chances of your child's having a febrile convulsion by taking care to reduce high fever (103° F or more) during illness.

Arrange for your child to have a physical examination to determine the cause of the convulsion. Children with one or more convulsions may need an EEG (electroencephalogram or brain-wave test) and follow-up testing.

As a child gets older, he usually gets fewer febrile convulsions. Unless there is an underlying neurological cause, a child over five rarely has them.

Phenobarbital may be prescribed as a preventive for a child who tends to have convulsions with fever and has other neurological problems, or for a child who has had a convulsion of more than 15 or 20 minutes' duration. Such children have a greater chance of developing epilepsy. In any event anticonvulsant medication must be prescribed by a physician.

See also ACCIDENTS; EPILEPSY; FEVER.

COOLEY'S ANEMIA See ANEMIA.

CORNS are thickenings of skin that develop on feet from the pressure and friction of ill-fitting shoes. When your shoe rubs repeatedly against the skin of a toe, the skin thickens and scars, forming a horny growth. The corn may have a central core surrounded by an inflamed ring of thickened skin.

Corns can be extremely painful. Small corns may be treated with the use of corn pads available in drugstores. To keep the corns from recurring, change to a properly fitting shoe.

If the corn does not quickly yield to these self-treatment techniques, consult a family physician or a podiatrist (increasingly known as a podiatric physician). Some cases of recurring corns involve a bone deformity in which a bony growth rubs against the underside of the skin. A surgical procedure may correct this.

A "soft corn" is a corn between the toes that has become infected, often associated with athlete's foot.

Keep the area dry with foot powder. Cotton, lamb's wool, or other soft material between the toes will help reduce pressure. If the soft corn becomes painful, red, and swollen, consult a podiatric or family physician.

See also FOOT PROBLEMS.

CORONARY ARTERY DISEASE is a type of heart disease marked by clogging of the arteries supplying the muscles of the heart. It is almost always a stage of atherosclerosis, a form of arteriosclerosis. It occurs most frequently between ages 40 and 60, about three times as often in men as women.

Pains in the chest (angina pectoris) may signal that the heart is not getting enough oxygen through the clogged arteries. If the narrowed coronary arteries become blocked by a blood clot, a heart attack may occur. Coronary bypass surgery may be recommended as a possible preventive.

Autopsies on young victims of accidents and soldiers killed in battle show that even people in their teens and twenties and in generally good physical condition can have advanced cases of the disease. As the atherosclerosis worsens, the condition is variously termed coronary heart disease, coronary atherosclerotic heart disease, atherosclerotic artery disease, or ischemic heart disease.

See also ARTERIOSCLEROSIS; CHEST PAIN; HEART ATTACK; HEART DISEASE.

CORONARY BYPASS SURGERY See ARTERIOSCLEROSIS.

CORONARY OCCLUSION See HEART ATTACK.

CORONARY THROMBOSIS See HEART ATTACK.

COUGHING is an automatic defense mechanism for expelling excess mucus or irritating debris from the nose, throat, and lungs.

The vast majority of coughs are due to colds or acute bronchitis. They become a nuisance when they hang on for two or three weeks after other symptoms have disappeared.

But many other coughs may be an early indication of serious respiratory disease, such as tuberculosis, lung cancer, emphysema, chronic bronchitis, or pneumonia. Other serious causes of cough are asthma, bronchiectasis, pleurisy, croup, and heart disease.

Even though your cough may not have lasted more than a few days, see a doctor immediately if you are short of breath with the cough, have any pain, or find any blood in the stuff you cough up.

See a doctor if your cough lasts for a month or more. It doesn't matter that you cough only in the morning when you get up, or only at night when you lie down. Such a chronic cough may be a sign of a severe respiratory ailment.

A cigarette cough can mask more serious conditions. It sounds the same as a cough due to tuberculosis, bronchitis, or cancer. The only way to end a cigarette cough—and be sure it has no other cause—is to completely stop smoking for at least four weeks.

Dust and pollen may trigger an allergic cough; air pollution may also start it off.

Hot, dry air indoors or out parches delicate throat and bronchial membranes, leading to a cough. Exposure during the winter may start you coughing if your mucous membranes are sensitive to cold air.

Some coughs originate from emotional stress. Under tension the muscle that closes the larynx before swallowing may not function properly—thus producing a cough.

Most coughs result when an irritation or foreign body triggers a cough center at the base of the brain to seal off the windpipe, contract the chest muscles, and release a blast of air measured as high as 268 miles per hour. The explosion, well above hurricane velocity, has caused rib fracture, hernia, hemorrhage, and fainting.

Treatment for coughs. To relieve a cough home remedies usually suffice. Your goal is a "useful" or "productive" cough that brings up phlegm. This helps vacuum-clean mucus or obstructions from the bronchial passages. A useless or unproductive cough wears you out and itself can be an irritant to your airways.

Other suggestions:

Stay in bed. Not only does this conserve your energy, but the cilia (hairlike projections of the breathing passages that carry mucus to the throat) move much more rapidly when you're horizontal, making each cough more productive.

Increase room humidity. Moist, warm air usually soothes the impulse to cough. It also thins out secretions so they require less coughing to eliminate.

Drink lots of hot sweet fluids and suck hard candy. They relax throat muscles and reduce irritation, help to break up thick mucus.

If a cough is serious enough to require cough medicine, see a doctor. The only remedies likely to be beneficial are those available on prescription.

Bronchial spasm is often the problem. This happens when persistent, jerky contractions replace the regular contractions in the air passages. Adrenaline relaxes spasm and restores normal muscle movement.

When thick, sticky mucus is the cause, a class of drugs known as expectorants loosen a cough by increasing the bronchial solutions so that they thin out the thick material.

If the problem is to stop a nonproductive cough, or if it's necessary to bring under control a useful but exhausting cough, a different approach is used: cough suppressants.

Cough medicines. The chief benefit of patent cough medicines appears to be psychological.

Experiments have shown that patients who thought they were getting a dose of a drug responded as quickly as those who actually received it. In other studies patients got great satisfaction from cough remedies even though the frequency and intensity of their coughing remained unchanged.

Most patent remedies contain too little of effective ingredients. Only two drugs—nocapine and dextromethorphan—are considered both safe and effective as cough suppressants, and only four are safe and effective expectorants: ammonium chloride, ipecac syrup, guaifensen, and terpin hydrate. The most sensible—and least expensive—approach would be to offer a single such suppressant and/or expectorant in full therapeutic doses. Not one patent remedy on the market does this.

When the foregoing ingredients are used at all, they generally are in doses too small to work. Mainly what patent remedies contain—and sell for a premium price—are ineffective compounds. The FTC asked the Bristol-Myers Co. to tell how its Silence Is Golden cough syrup, with "pure honey and natural lemon," works. The concern replied at length on the soothing benefits of honey, but of lemon it only said, "Lemon is added to the honey in Silence Is Golden to make a more palatable mixture"—to make it taste better.

The remedies may mask a severe condition. In lung cancer, tuberculosis, and several other grave disorders cough is the only early symptom. If you take enough of a proprietary suppressant, you may stifle the cough and neglect a condition that requires immediate attention. Further, there is the danger of adverse reactions to the hodgepodge of ingredients in each mixture. Codeine, a cough suppressant, is a narcotic. Long-continued use of even the small amounts available in patent remedies can lead to physical dependence.

A similar problem may arise from the alcohol content of many cough preparations. Cough elixirs are favorite "kick-inducers" among adolescents who can't legally buy liquor. Some contain as much as 50 percent ethyl alcohol, the equivalent of 100-proof whiskey.

Antihistamines are included in many cough mixtures. But antihistamines may actually worsen coughing because of their drying action on mucus, making it harder to bring up. Moreover, since cough mixtures are often used in large amounts, the marked sedative effects of antihistamines may cause you to become drowsy while driving or operating machinery.

See also RESPIRATORY DISEASE; SMOKING.

COXSACKIE VIRUS   See INFLUENZA.

CPR   See ARTIFICIAL RESPIRATION; HEART STOPPAGE.

CRADLE CAP   See SEBORRHEIC DERMATITIS.

CRETINISM   See THYROID DISEASE.

CRIB DEATH (sudden infant death syndrome, SIDS) is one of medicine's most tragic and challenging mysteries. In the typical case an apparently healthy, well-cared-for baby is put to bed. In the morning the baby is found dead in its crib, of no apparent cause. There appears to be no suffering or crying out. Death occurs rapidly, usually during sleep.

Crib death affects about 7,000 U.S. babies each year, or about 1 of every 500 infants born alive. It is the greatest cause of infant death between one week and seven months of age. Most crib-death victims are between two and six months of age, and the syndrome is more common among boys than girls.

Crib death is more likely to occur in the winter than in the summer. Infants born prematurely or with low birth weights are more susceptible than others. So are infants born to teenage mothers and to mothers who received no medical care during pregnancy. In about half the cases the babies had sniffles or other signs of minor colds for a few days before the sudden death.

Crib death cannot be reliably predicted. Because warning signs appear in only a small minority of crib deaths, there is nothing a parent—with present knowledge—can do to prevent a crib death. If you have a "near-miss" baby—one who was saved from an episode in which he stopped breathing—your physician may recommend a home breathing monitor to attach to the baby in his crib. You'll also be taught resuscitation techniques in the event your baby has a subsequent episode.

Babies born into families previously struck by the syndrome have a slightly greater risk than the general population.

The cause of crib death remains unknown. Among the possible causes that have been explored and rejected are allergy to cow's milk or breast milk, bacterial infections, radiation fallout, modern medicines and drugs, smoking, use of bleach in washing diapers, whiplash injury to the spinal cord, air pollution, and fluoridation. Repeat: None of these cause crib death.

In most cases autopsy reveals absolutely no evidence of illness. There may be minor inflammation of the upper respiratory tract, but not sufficiently serious to account for the death.

Crib death is not caused by vomiting and choking. Nor is it caused by suffocation—even when infants are covered by bedding, they can still obtain enough oxygen.

Promising findings. SIDS research suggests that the syndrome may be due to many different causes.

SIDS research suggests that many babies who succumb may have had subtle physiological problems from before birth—such as central nervous system abnormalities, particularly of the brain stem. These may result in irregularities in respiration, feeding, temperature regulation, and other problems.

One hypothesis is that the syndrome may sometimes be related to a low-grade respiratory infection. Studies by several researchers suggest that the syndrome is triggered by a virus. For unknown reasons the virus may cause the baby's larynx to constrict, closing the air passage so that the infant cannot breathe. The vocal cords also are constricted and rendered useless, so the baby cannot cry out.

Another line of research is exploring the sleep patterns of infants. Some studies suggest that breathing patterns may play a part in some cases of SIDS. Babies who had periods of prolonged lulls in breathing (20 seconds or more) seemed more prone to crib death.

Botulism poisoning, some researchers believe, may account for about 5 percent of crib deaths. Adults can safely ingest the botulism spores without harm—sickness or death result only from eating improperly preserved food in which the botulism toxin has been produced (see BOTULISM).

In infants, however, ingested botulism spores can produce toxin in the intestines. Some babies have a greater resistance to the organism. It grows slowly, and the infants become ill. Most recover with hospitalization. In others the course is very rapid, and the infant may die suddenly, presumably of paralysis of the air passages.

It is impossible to try to prevent your baby from swallowing botulism spores—they are all around. But avoid giving your baby honey, known to contain the organism.

Coping with SIDS. Families may face a major crisis following a crib death. Almost inevitably parents feel responsible and guilty. They may blame each other, baby-sitters, or the doctor. Friends or relatives may imply that the parents were negligent. Police may cause needless suffering by questioning the parents with hostility and suspicion, suggesting that they were careless or guilty of child abuse.

Many parents are left with a profound depression after the initial shock and numbness. They may find it difficult to eat, sleep, or concentrate. They may experience physical symptoms, such as fatigue, headaches, stomachaches.

Professional counseling may be necessary to help a family through this period. Often it is helpful for parents to talk to other families who have been struck with crib death.

Organizations that can help families cope with the death of their infant from the syndrome include your state's department of maternal and child health, the Guilds for Infant Survival, P.O. Box 3586, Davenport, Iowa 52808; the National SIDS Foundation, 2 Metro Plaza, Landover, Maryland 20785; and Compassionate Friends, P.O. Box 1347, Oakbrook, Illinois 60521. For reliable, up-to-date information prepared for new and expectant parents, contact the National Center for the Prevention of Sudden Infant Death Syndrome through its national SIDS hotline (800-638-SIDS).

CRIBS, instead of protecting a baby, can cause its death. Infants have strangled when caught in the vertical slats or between the mattress and crib frame. Others have suffered brain damage from head injuries after toppling over the side.

To avoid crib accidents:

Be sure there is no more than 2³/₈ inches between the vertical bars. This is a requirement of the U.S. Consumer Product Safety Commission for cribs manufactured for interstate sale. If you have an older or noncomplying crib, use bumper pads at least 4 inches high all around, secured with at least six ties.

Don't be fooled because the baby's diapered bottom seems too large to fit through the slats. The diaper can generally compress, allowing the baby to slip through feet first until he's caught by his head, which is usually his largest part.

Check that the crib mattress fits snugly. If you can insert two fingers between the edge of the mattress and the sides of the crib, fill the space with rolled towels.

Guard against falls. Don't buy a crib with a horizontal bar—the child can use it as a ladder. Cover the top with netting.

Keep out of the crib large toys or boxes that may give the baby a boost over the side. Keep the mattress well below the top rail—and graduate a child over 35 inches tall to a youth or regular bed.

Check that a drop side has a childproof latching system, which can't be operated by the baby in the crib or by small children outside. A foot latch is especially susceptible to release by children playing on the floor. It not only can open a crib, but can crack the head of the youngster who trips it.

Sand wooden cribs to avoid splinters. Tape or file down sharp metal or plastic edges. Because of the risk of poisoning, especially lead poisoning, from an infant's chewing on a crib, use only leadfree, nontoxic paint.

See also ACCIDENTS; FALLS; LEAD POISONING.

CROOKED TEETH See MALOCCLUSION.

CROSSED EYES (strabismus, squint, wall-eyes) may result from an inborn imbalance of the muscles governing eye motion. A muscle may be too weak, or not attached properly to the eyeball, and thereby causes the eye to turn inward, outward, or upward.

Crossed eyes require prompt treatment by an ophthalmologist, the earlier the better. If left untreated, amblyopia almost always develops, leading to sight loss in the weaker eye. Moreover, cruel fun is often poked at the cross-eyed child, and can lead to emotional problems.

For some children wearing an eye patch may be the treatment. For others the doctor may advise surgery; two or more operations are often necessary. Eyeglasses (even before one year of age) may be prescribed—especially if farsightedness, astigmatism, or nearsightedness is making one eye cross in the struggle to see better. Eye exercises may be an important part of treatment.

Babies sometimes seem cross-eyed because of the broad, flat ridge of their nose. If this is the reason, it usually disappears by the sixth month, and this possibility accounts for the myth that an older child will outgrow his crossed eyes. If the condition persists, the child needs to be seen by an ophthalmologist, especially if others in his family have had it—there's a strong hereditary tendency in crossed eyes.

See also AMBLYOPIA; EYE DISORDER; EYE EXERCISES; EYEGLASSES.

CROUP is a viral respiratory disease that causes swelling of the tissues of the larynx and of air passages above and below. The swelling makes it difficult for the child to breathe, resulting in a barking cough and noisy breathing. It is particularly life-threatening in the very young because the air passage is so small.

A croup attack often comes suddenly, usually in the evening or night and more often in the winter and spring months. Some children—especially those suffering from an allergy—are prone to croup, developing hoarseness and croupy cough whenever they get a cold. The predisposition may run in families. Croup occurs most frequently in children between the ages of two and four. It's rare after six.

Treatment. Never neglect a croupy cough. Keep a croupy child indoors, warm, and resting. Close windows and raise the humidity of the air. Don't give sedatives to a child with croup unless your doctor orders them. A child who has had a case of croup is likely to have it again.

Stay awake with the child as long as there are symptoms of croup. Sleep in the same room with him for three nights. Wake yourself every two hours after the croup attack is over to make sure that he is breathing comfortably.

During an attack, take your child into the bathroom and close the door. Turn on the hot water in the shower or tub. Let the room fill up with steam.

Sit in the steam—not in the hot water—with your child, with the water still running, for ten minutes. If he is still making noise as he breathes, call the doctor.

If the tap water isn't hot enough, make steam with an electric vaporizer (a "croup kettle") or by boiling a pan of water on a hot plate. As a last recourse take him to the kitchen and hold him close while you boil water on the stove. Keep the moist air around him by covering his head and the boiling saucepan with an umbrella.

Be on guard for an emergency. Swelling and mucus may cut off the child's oxygen supply suddenly. Rush him into a steamy room and call the doctor immediately if *any* of the following occurs:

His symptoms get worse fairly fast—more noise, higher fever, difficulty in inhaling.

He becomes very restless—sitting up, lying down, jumping about trying to find a comfortable position.

You notice sharp movement around his collarbones or just below his ribs as he struggles to breathe.

His lips or fingernails become bluish, his color otherwise poor.

He appears to be very sick regardless of the degree of breathing difficulty.

If you can't reach your doctor immediately, call another or call an ambulance with oxygen equipment and take the child to the nearest hospital. If blockage becomes complete, it may be necessary for the doctor (or you, in a crisis) to perform a cricothyrotomy—cutting an opening in the windpipe to prevent the child from strangling to death (see CHOKING).

After breathing has improved, use a cold-air vaporizer. If the child sleeps in a crib, place a sheet or umbrella over the top of the crib and direct the stream of vapor under the sheet. If he sleeps in a bed, place a card table over his head and drape a sheet over the card table. Keep one side of the crib or table open so he won't get too hot.

While he is having the attack, offer liquids that you know he likes every hour he's awake. Drinking plenty of fluids is very important in helping him get over croup.

Let him choose the position in which he's most comfortable. Don't insist that he lie down. An infant seat may be comfortable for a small baby.

If your child has croup due to allergy, keep the house temperature between 65° F and 70° F, particularly in his bedroom at night. Prevent cold drafts in his room. Avoid any marked temperature variation. If possible humidify the air in the house.

See also ALLERGY; CHOKING; HUMIDITY; RESPIRATORY DISEASE.

CRYPTORCHIDISM See UNDESCENDED TESTICLES.

CUTS (lacerations)   Clean with soap and water, not antiseptics, following procedures for cleansing minor wounds. Stop bleeding via direct pressure on the wound with a sterile pad.

Bring the edges of the wound together and bandage them in place. Replace the bandage to keep the wound clean and dry. Butterfly tapes are generally best for holding wound edges together (see illustrations).

Resist the impulse to put a cut in your mouth or blow on it. The mouth harbors germs that could cause infection.

Control heavy bleeding. Get to a doctor immediately if bleeding is heavy. In the meantime control the bleeding as much as possible with direct pressure and guard against shock.

Also see a doctor if foreign matter is lodged under the skin, or if your immunization against tetanus is out of date. Tetanus shots are good for about 10 years. You're protected if you get a shot within 72 hours of the injury.

Call your doctor if the pain becomes throbbing, if the redness and swelling around the cut increase, or if there is a yellowish secretion that indicates an infection. Hot compresses, which increase circulation, may help.

See a doctor if there is any question whether stitches (sutures) are required, as when the cut is long or wide. Stitches may be needed on the forehead, chin, or knee, even though the cut is small. Suturing is often desirable when a cut occurs on the face or other part of the body where scars would be conspicuous. A wound should be stitched within seven hours.

After four or five days it is normal for stitches

WHY BRING WOUND EDGES TOGETHER?

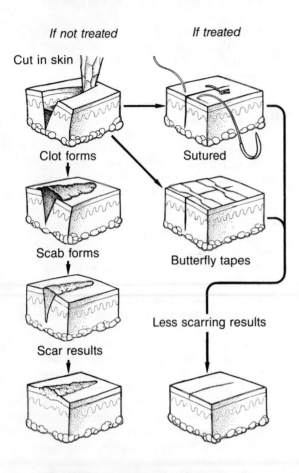

If not treated   If treated

Cut in skin

Clot forms   Sutured

Scab forms

Butterfly tapes

Scar results

Less scarring results

TO MAKE BUTTERFLY TAPES
They're also available commercially

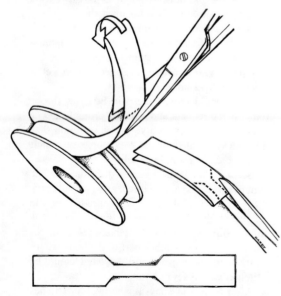

1. Cut length to fit wound
2. Snip thin bridge
3. Large areas anchor tape to skin

HOW TO TAPE WOUND EDGES CLOSED

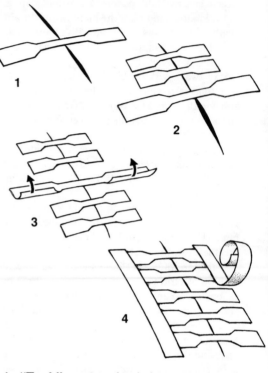

1. **"Tack" center.** Apply large tape to center of wound as temporary holding device.
2. **Anchor edges.** Apply smaller, permanent tapes.
   Wipe away any oozing blood.
3. **Remove "tack."** Gently pull off temporary tape.
   Replace with a permanent tape.
4. **Secure edges.** Use strips of tape.

to "draw," causing an itching or tingling sensation. While less likely than commonly feared, it is possible for stitches to tear out if there is considerable swelling or stretching caused by excessive activity. If this happens, call your doctor.

To avoid cuts be especially cautious when using axes, glass, knives, power lawn mowers, scissors, or any machine or tool.

See also ACCIDENTS; BLEEDING; CLEANSING MINOR WOUNDS.

CYSTIC FIBROSIS (mucoviscidosis, CF) is an inherited disease that primarily affects the lungs and pancreas. They become clogged with abnormal secretions of mucus, which interfere with respiration and digestion.

CF is believed to be the most common lethal inherited disease of white children. In the United States an estimated 5 percent of the population carries the CF gene and 1 of every 1,600 to 2,000 infants is born with the disease. In the past most children with CF died before they reached 15. Now, with early diagnosis and treatment in special care centers, about half can expect to reach adulthood.

Symptoms. The major symptoms are usually evident in the first two years of life, but can vary greatly from child to child. Moreover, CF symptoms resemble those of other diseases. A child exhibiting any symptoms of CF should be referred to a center specializing in diagnosis of the condition. CF's major complications are as follows:

Respiratory. Thick mucus clogs passages in the lungs, interfering with breathing and often causing chronic coughing and wheezing. Bacterial lung infections may result in bronchitis and pneumonia. If not treated properly CF's respiratory complications can lead to progressive deterioration of lung tissue, with such signs of chronic lung disease as bluish lips, clubbed fingers, and a barrel chest.

Digestive. Mucus also plugs the ducts of the pancreas, thus obstructing the passage of enzymes essential to digestion. Some foods cannot be broken down and used by the body, but instead are passed in bulky, foul-smelling bowel movements. Despite a good appetite, the child may have retarded growth and other signs of malnutrition.

Sweat gland involvement. The child's perspiration, saliva, and tears contain excessive amounts of salt. In summer this constant loss of salt by sweating may lead to heat exhaustion. Often parents are the first to give doctors a hint that the child has CF—they report that his skin tastes salty when kissed. CF is diagnosed by measuring the amount of salt in the child's sweat.

The heredity factor. The disease is inherited from parents who carry the trait. A carrier can pass this trait to his children, but does not show symptoms himself.

When only one of the parents is a carrier, their children will not inherit the disease though the odds are that half will be carriers. If both parents are carriers, chances are one in four that each of their children will have CF. In families where one child is affected, the chances are one in four that later offspring will also have the disease.

These statistics make genetic counseling possible, and known carriers can decide whether or not they wish to risk having more children. There is at present no way of definitely determining who is a carrier of the CF gene other than having a child with the disease.

Treatment. While there is no cure for CF, there are effective methods of treatment, especially when the condition is diagnosed early.

Aerosol inhalation therapy, involving the breathing of medicated mist, may be used to help loosen the mucus from the lungs, and to deposit antibiotics, decongestants, and other medications directly into the bronchial tubes.

Physical therapy includes positioning the body to elevate clogged parts of the lungs, allowing gravity to help clear the passages, and clapping and vibrating the chest in each position. This procedure is often carried out two or three times daily. To be effective it must be taught to patient and parents, so it can be practiced at home.

Breathing exercises are often part of the treatment program. Physical activity often is effective in loosening mucus and sputum. Sports and active play should be encouraged.

Commercially available pancreatic extracts from animals can be taken with meals to supply the needed enzymes. Supplementary vitamins and nutrients, plus a well-balanced diet, sometimes with a high calorie intake, is usually prescribed. To offset excessive loss of salt, extra salt is given with foods, particularly in hot weather.

In general, every effort should be made to permit the youngster to live a normal life. He should be encouraged to attend school if his condition permits. His activities should be limited only by his tolerance. He should be given the usual protective immunization.

Further information is available from the Cystic Fibrosis Foundation, 6000 Executive Boulevard, Suite 510, Rockville, Maryland 20852.

See also BIRTH DEFECTS; HOSPITALIZING CHILDREN; RESPIRATORY DISEASE.

CYSTIC MASTITIS See CANCER OF THE BREAST.

CYSTS are noninflamed, saclike structures completely lined with a layer of skinlike material.

Cysts may begin as plugged glands or may result from pieces of skin being buried beneath the surface. There may be a small opening in the cyst through which the contents may drain. In contrast to boils, a cyst is usually neither tender nor hot.

The draining material results not from infection but consists of the products of the cells that form the cyst wall. Sometimes cysts may rupture or become infected and inflamed, and have the same appearance as a boil. They have no relation to cancer.

The most common types:

Sebaceous cysts may be found anywhere on the body, often on the scalp (termed wens) and the face, chest, and back following acne. They develop in sebaceous glands, which normally produce an oily secretion (sebum) that helps prevent skin dryness. When the duct leading from the gland gets stopped up, the sebum collects, forming a protrusion. Sebaceous cysts can become as large as a lemon. If there is pain, temporary relief may be obtained by hot compresses.

The only permanent treatment is surgical removal. If not removed, such cysts tend to become larger, more painful, and possibly infected.

Pilonidal cysts occur at the base of the spine. One of these cysts can be present for some time without causing any trouble. Then repeated jolting or pressure, such as produced by long periods of driving, may activate the cyst, causing itching and an odorous discharge. Pilonidal cysts are common among soldiers who have to take frequent rough trips in jeeps and trucks.

The cause is a congenital folding inward of skin and hair cells beneath the skin surface. Long coils of hair are often found inside pilonidal cysts. Infection may occur, calling for antibiotics. Only surgical removal will effect a permanent cure.

Branchial cysts are on the neck, and get their name from *branchia,* which means "gills." At an early stage in the development of the human fetus there is a row of gills on each side of the embryonic neck, but they are of no use and normally disappear.

In some cases a small piece of them may remain. When this tissue produces a secretion that forms a cyst, it may show up in later life. It can be removed permanently by an operation. There is no connection with the bronchial tubes in the chest, in spite of the similarity of name.

See also SKIN DISORDER.

D

DANDRUFF, according to countless ads, is a social disgrace. Actually almost everyone past puberty who isn't bald has it.

All over the body the skin continuously sheds bits of its dead outer layer. The fragments are generally too small to be seen; they fall or are brushed off immediately. But on the head the flakes are larger and tend to become trapped in the hair, where they also collect oil from the scalp's sebaceous glands as well as dust and soot from the air. The combination forms oily yellow or dry gray-white scales: dandruff.

Some people give off unusually large flakes, perhaps the effect of hormones or microorganisms. The condition can be more pronounced at some periods than others, can affect only part of the scalp, and may be influenced by emotional stress and bodily disease.

The kind of dandruff experienced by most people is an esthetic rather than a medical problem. Contrary to popular belief, dandruff is not a cause or harbinger of hair loss. It is not caused by soap or hair sprays. Often soap residue or dried spray flake off the hair and are confused with dandruff.

Nor is dandruff shed more in winter than in summer. But in winter you generally shower, bathe, and swim less, giving flakes more chance to accumulate. And your clothing tends to be darker, showing up dandruff.

There is no way to stop dandruff from forming, but you can usually keep it under control. Massage your scalp for a few minutes nightly to free flakes. Then brush your hair with 20 or 30 strokes of a fairly stiff brush to remove the accumulation.

Wash your hair with a good shampoo once or twice a week, more often if you have severe dandruff. If you continue to have excessive dandruff with a regular shampoo, try a dandruff shampoo. Make sure you massage the shampoo right into your scalp.

An AMA publication and other medical sources report that zinc pyrithione in shampoos (Head & Shoulders, Zincon, Breck One, and others) is usually effective, as are shampoos that contain selenium sulfide (Selsun, Sul-Blue, and others). But products that contain selenium should be used with caution, since they can cause eye damage. Some studies also report hair loss with frequent use. Prolonged use tends to leave a residual smell and may make hair more oily.

Coal tar shampoos are also effective, but many people find their smell offensive.

Because dandruff shampoos may irritate the scalp with prolonged use, some dermatologists suggest that you try controlling dandruff by washing hair alternately with a dandruff shampoo and a regular shampoo. Discontinue the dandruff shampoo once your dandruff clears up.

Dandruff, however, isn't always simple and can signal an abnormal scalp condition such as seborrheic dermatitis, psoriasis, eczema, and ringworm. These are often accompanied by severe dandrufflike symptoms, as well as by redness, itching, and other skin changes. Such severe dandruff conditions require medical treatment and shouldn't be doctored at home with a shampoo.

See also ECZEMA; HAIR BRUSHING; HAIR WASHING; PSORIASIS; RINGWORM; SEBORRHEIC DERMATITIS; SKIN DISORDERS.

DEAFNESS See HEARING LOSS.

DEATH cannot reliably be determined by a layman. If you suspect someone has died, phone for a physician, ambulance, or policeman. Meanwhile keep up efforts to restore life with artificial respiration and closed-chest heart massage (see ARTIFICIAL RESPIRATION; HEART STOPPAGE).

Don't stop even if the victim has no pulse. Don't stop even if there's no sign of his breathing (ordinarily detectable by movement at the lower sides of the chest). Don't stop even if his pupils fail to constrict under a flashlight.

These commonly used tests are not conclusive —and can lead to abandoning a person who might be saved. Unless halted breathing and heart action are compensated for artificially, the irreversible changes of death generally occur in less than ten minutes.

A sign of death is cooling of the body to the surrounding temperature. Rigor mortis (stiffening of the muscles) sets in sometimes less than an hour after death—but usually between four and ten hours after death—and lasts three or four days.

Extending your life. Within limits you can delay your death. Researchers at the Methodist Hospital of Indiana in Indianapolis have developed a medical actuarial system called the health hazard appraisal. From basic facts about you—such as your blood pressure, smoking habits, cholesterol level (see FATS)—your doctor can determine from a form how much risk you run of succumbing to each of the most common causes of illness and death. From how these risks affect your life expectancy, you find out your "health hazard age" as opposed to your calendar age.

Suppose you are 43, overweight, smoke heavily, and never wear seat belts in cars. You are chopping so many years off your life that in terms of health hazards your age may be the equivalent of 47 or higher.

But you can take defensive measures. Stop smoking, lose weight, and fasten your seat belt. And the years you add to your life expectancy may in effect make you *younger,* dropping your hazard age to 39. (See table for estimating average remaining lifetimes.)

Consider hospice programs. A new approach to meeting the needs of people who are dying and their families is hospice care. The hospice movement has mushroomed in the last few years —from a handful of programs to many hundreds.

Hospice advocates feel that hospice care is the most compassionate way of dealing with death. Its goal is to enhance the quality of life for the terminally ill. The care may be provided in the patient's own home, in a special part of a hospital or nursing home, or in a separate hospice building. Most patients have a prognosis of less than six months to live, after all medical treatment has failed. Many are elderly people, and nine out of ten have cancer.

Hospice programs vary greatly, but in general are characterized by:

· A team approach. A typical hospice program provides or coordinates the services of physicians, nurses, home health aides, social workers, and others. Many hospice programs also provide the services of trained volunteers.
· Home care. Many hospice programs provide home care for patients, and involve family members in helping to provide care. Backup care is arranged if the family needs a respite.
· Support for the family. The hospice team provides emotional support during this difficult time, as well as practical information about caring for the patient.

Bereavement counseling is an important part of the support hospice programs provide. A hospice worker typically stays in contact with a family for up to a year.

Most experts agree that grieving is part of the healing process. It is a normal, necessary, beneficial transition. Generally over a period of about six months to a year, a bereaved person frees himself from being bound to the deceased person, and readjusts to a life in which the person is no longer present. Most people experience a temporary sense of disorganization and despair. They may be frequently tearful and find it hard to sleep.

Some people experience grief that is unusually painful or prolonged; they may be deeply depressed or suicidal. In such instances counseling or psychotherapy should be sought.

Causes of death. The ten leading U.S. causes of death, in order, are:

1. Heart disease
2. Cancer
3. Stroke
4. Accidents
5. Pneumonia and influenza
6. Diseases of early infancy
7. Diabetes
8. Arteriosclerosis
9. Bronchitis, emphysema, and asthma
10. Cirrhosis of the liver

WHAT'S YOUR LIFE EXPECTANCY?

From this sampling of ages you can get an idea of your average remaining lifetime. Your individual estimate varies greatly with your family history, health practices, etc.

| | Average Remaining Lifetime | | | |
| | White | | Nonwhite | |
Age	Male	Female	Male	Female
Birth	68.3	75.7	61.3	69.4
1	68.6	75.8	62.4	70.3
5	64.8	72.0	58.7	66.6
10	60.0	67.1	53.8	61.7
15	55.1	62.2	49.0	56.8
20	50.5	57.4	44.5	52.1
25	46.0	52.6	40.4	47.4
30	41.3	47.7	36.2	42.9
35	36.7	43.0	32.2	38.5
40	32.1	38.3	28.3	34.3
45	27.7	33.7	24.7	30.2
50	23.6	29.2	21.3	26.3
55	19.7	25.0	18.1	22.8
60	16.2	20.9	15.1	19.2
65	13.2	17.0	12.8	16.2
70	10.5	13.4	10.9	13.9
75	8.3	10.2	10.3	12.5
80	6.5	7.5	9.8	10.6
85	4.9	5.3	9.3	8.8

Source: National Center for Health Statistics

Prepare for death. If you prepare now for your death, you can spare your family an ordeal—and save them thousands of dollars.

If you don't have an up-to-date will, draft one with a lawyer. Otherwise your survivors may be shortchanged by outdated provisions of your existing will. If you have no written will, state inheritance laws may distribute your assets in a way that will make you turn over in your grave.

You owe your heirs a letter about your business affairs. Write what your survivors should know about insurance, property, and other legal and financial matters—including any money you owe, or any due them from whatever source (debtors, savings, investments, Social Security). Be specific about what they should do. Give names of people they should get in touch with. Update this letter frequently.

Give one copy to your spouse or other principal survivor. Put another in a safe-deposit box with your important papers (which you'd explain as needed in your letter). Also spell out what you'd like done with your body.

Arrange your own funeral. Macabre? Not when you realize your family will have enough on their minds without worrying about selecting a coffin and cemetery plot. A grieving survivor can be easy prey for an undertaker out to sell a $5,000 funeral ("After all, it's the last thing you'll be able to do for your loved one"). If *you* choose your coffin, chances are you'll resist a sales pitch for one with a posture-pleasing mattress, padded interior, and burnished bronze case.

The least expensive funeral you can arrange is likely to be through a memorial society, a non-profit membership association that contracts with undertakers for services at modest rates. To find the society nearest you consult the phone book or write the Continental Association of Funeral and Memorial Societies (Suite 1100, 1828 L Street, NW, Washington, D.C. 20036). Your local society will refer you to cooperating undertakers and provide a form in which you can specify the type of burial you wish.

Lowest in cost is cremation prior to a memorial service. Cremation following a funeral costs more, since a coffin (and perhaps embalming) is required. Most expensive is burial after a funeral.

You can pay for your funeral in advance by setting up a bank trust account. The interest is likely to compensate for rising prices. Any surplus reverts to your heirs.

In like manner select your cemetery plot. Because you may have moved by the time you die, make sure the cemetery is a member of the Lot Exchange Plan of the National Association of Cemeteries. Through this plan you or your family can trade your old plot for one in your new locale.

Social Security benefits include payment toward burial costs. If you're a veteran, find out from the Veterans Administration if you and your immediate family are eligible for free burial in a national cemetery. For many veterans the VA pays part of the burial expenses and furnishes a grave marker.

Consider signing a "Living Will" (see illustration), an expression of your wish that—when death is imminent—your body not be kept alive by an artificial lung, mechanical heart, or other

TO MAKE A "LIVING GIFT"

If you wish to bequeath your body or organs, photocopy this sample, fill it out, and carry it with you.

UNIFORM DONOR CARD

OF _____
                        Print or Type name of donor
In the hope that I may help others, I hereby make this anatomical gift, if medically acceptable, to take effect upon my death. The words and marks below indicate my desires.
I give: (a)_____any needed organs or parts
           (b)_____only the following organs or parts

_____
                    Specify the organ(s) or part(s)
for the purposes of transplantation, therapy, medical research or education;
           (c)_____my body for anatomical study if needed.
Limitations or
special wishes, if any: _____

Signed by the donor and the following two witnesses in the **presence of** each other:

_____   _____
    Signature of Donor   Date of Birth of Donor

_____   _____
    Date Signed   City & State

_____   _____
    Witness   Witness

This is a legal document under the Uniform Anatomical Gift Act or similar laws.

For further information consult your physician

"heroic" measures. The Euthanasia Educational Council has distributed more than 750,000 such documents, chiefly to people who hope to die in peace and save their families needless guilt and expense.

Since a rush to heroics is routine medical treatment, if you sign a Living Will, give a copy to your doctor as well as to your next of kin.

Although the Living Will isn't legally binding in most states, it's widely respected as a valid assertion of your right to refuse treatment. Have the document witnessed by two adults, to establish if necessary that you signed it voluntarily while of sound mind. Every year or so redate and initial the will to make clear that your wishes are unchanged.

A LIVING WILL

By signing this document, you notify others well in advance that you don't want your dying prolonged by artificial means. Keep copies with your family and physician. Photocopy this sample, or get copies from the Euthanasia Educational Council, 250 West 57th Street, New York, New York 10019.

**TO MY FAMILY, MY PHYSICIAN, MY LAWYER, MY CLERGYMAN
TO ANY MEDICAL FACILITY IN WHOSE CARE I HAPPEN TO BE
TO ANY INDIVIDUAL WHO MAY BECOME RESPONSIBLE FOR MY HEALTH,
WELFARE OR AFFAIRS**

Death is as much a reality as birth, growth, maturity and old age—it is the one certainty of

life. If the time comes when I, _____

_____

can no longer take part in decisions for my own future, let this statement stand as an expression of my wishes, while I am still of sound mind.

If the situation should arise in which there is no reasonable expectation of my recovery from physical or mental disability, I request that I be allowed to die and not be kept alive by artificial means or "heroic measures". I do not fear death itself as much as the indignities of deterioration, dependence and hopeless pain. I, therefore, ask that medication be mercifully administered to me to alleviate suffering even though this may hasten the moment of death.

This request is made after careful consideration. I hope you who care for me will feel morally bound to follow its mandate. I recognize that this appears to place a heavy responsibility upon you, but it is with the intention of relieving you of such responsibility and of placing it upon myself in accordance with my strong convictions, that this statement is made.

Signed _____

Date _____

Witness _____

Witness _____

Copies of this request have been given to _____

_____

_____

_____

Body and organ bequests. Consider bequeathing your body or organs. A humanitarian way of easing the high cost of dying is to donate your body to a medical school for anatomical study. Ultimately the body is cremated at the school's expense. Such a donation does not interfere with your having a memorial service.

Some states permit your next of kin to control your remains, so you must trust that your survivors will carry out your wishes. In any event make an alternate plan with a memorial society in case your body is not suitable for donation—if it is damaged by accident or fire, or if an autopsy has been performed.

A Uniform Donor Card (see illustration) is a means of willing all or part of your body for research, transplantation, or placement in a tissue bank. You can revoke the gift merely by tearing up the card, and you can change its terms at will.

You may also donate organs as needed, such as kidneys, corneas, skin, and bone for transplantation, or hormone extract from the pituitary gland for the treatment of hypopituitary dwarfs. Promising fields of research involve transplantations of the heart, lungs, liver, pancreas, and bone marrow. No disfigurement results from removing any of these parts, so funeral arrangements can proceed in any way you wish.

Keep the donor card with you, attached to your emergency medical identification. Organs must be removed very soon after death to be usable. When being admitted to a hospital, ask that your status as an anatomical donor be included in your chart. Because you might die away from a hospital, alert your physician, relatives, or friends to immediately get your body to a hospital where the organs can be extracted and properly kept.

See also EMERGENCY MEDICAL IDENTIFICATION.

DEGENERATIVE JOINT DISEASE See OSTEOARTHRITIS.

DEHYDRATION—excessive water loss—can cause fatigue, confusion, and impaired coordination. Death usually results after a little more than a week without water.

To make sure you're getting enough water, drink six 8-ounce glasses of water or other liquid every day.

You need at least 2 quarts of fluid every day. You get this not only from tap water, but also from water in other beverages, fruit juices, soups, and from solid foods. Boiled potato, for example, is 78 percent water. Lettuce and tomatoes are more than 90 percent water.

Sufficient water is particularly important during hot weather. Water and salt lost through sweating can lead to heat exhaustion and heat stroke.

You lose roughly a quart of fluid a day through urination, a small amount in bowel movements. About a pint is lost just by breathing. During normal activity you lose about a pint by sweating. But during very hard labor you may lose as much as a gallon a day.

Don't rely on thirst. Thirst is not always a guide to how much water you need. Ordinarily the parched mouth and throat signals the need to replace fluid. When you quench your thirst, your water balance is restored.

But under certain circumstances—for example, when you're sick—your thirst signal may not be working properly. Similarly, after you've done a lot of hard, sweaty work, you may feel satisfied with much less water than your body needs. Steel workers who lose up to 2 quarts of sweat a day will often replace only about half by relying on thirst. If this situation continues, they can become dangerously dehydrated.

To be on the safe side drink past when you've quenched your thirst on days when you do an unusual amount of hard work, particularly when it's hot. If you've sweated a lot and are very thirsty after hard exertion, sip long but slowly to avoid cramps.

Illness can lead to dehydration. Any disease causing fever can result in dehydration, as can chronic vomiting and endocrine disorders. Dehydration is common after prolonged or chronic diarrhea.

For quenching thirst your best bet is water, or beverages containing a high percentage of water: club soda, tea, or coffee. Sweet drinks are generally not as thirst quenching as tart drinks or diet sodas.

Alcoholic beverages are usually not good thirst quenchers, since alcohol itself has a dehydrating effect. Of the alcoholic drinks, your best choice would be beer because it has a much higher water content than whisky or wine.

See also HOT WEATHER; NUTRITION.

DEMECLOCYCLINE See ANTIBIOTICS.

DEMEROL See DRUGS.

DENTAL CARIES See TOOTH DECAY.

DENTURES are artificial substitutes for one or more teeth. The lay term "false teeth" is frowned on by dentists, since it emphasizes merely the cosmetic function of tooth replacement.

YOUR DENTURES NEED CHECKING

See a dentist
- At least once a year
- Immediately if dentures loosen

Proper fit
(Natural expression)

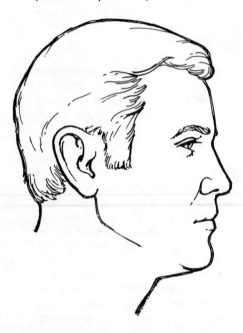

Poor fit
(Aged, wrinkled look)
   Upper-lip depression
   Compressed, protruding lips
   Chin forward and upward

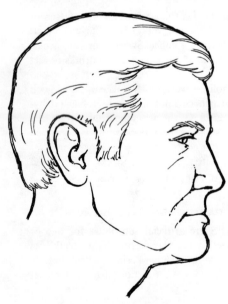

Actually it is important to replace even a missing back tooth although it may not show. If a missing tooth is not replaced with a fixed partial denture (fixed bridge), adjacent teeth tend to drift into the empty space. Once they are out of their proper position, there is likely to be too much stress on teeth when food is chewed. This causes further malocclusion, and eventual injury to the bone and to the tissues that attach the teeth to the jaws.

Also food is more likely to become packed into the spaces between irregular teeth, and this promotes tooth decay and injures the gums and the bone.

Only dentists should make or fix dentures. Quackery especially abounds in relation to removable partial and full dentures, appliances that replace a number of teeth. A layman connected with a dental laboratory may claim there is no need for you to see a "middleman"—the dentist. The promoter promises you rapid service and a perfect fit for less than a dentist would charge.

Responsible dental auxiliary personnel, such as dental technicians working for reliable labs, would never make such claims.

A common result is that you suffer needless pain, often with irreparable damage to your mouth tissues and jawbones. Ill-fitting dentures can impair hearing and speech, even give rise to mouth cancer.

Moreover, the victim rarely saves money. At additional expense he generally needs a dentist to restore his mouth and finally fit him with proper dentures. Indeed restoration may be possible only with implants because of the erosion of the bony ridges of the mouth. The savings offered by quacks are often minimal to begin with. An American Dental Association study showed that complete upper dentures obtained from dentists cost only about 20 percent more than those obtained from quacks.

Such quackery flourishes largely because many laymen fail to recognize the complexity of designing proper dentures. X rays are needed to determine the condition of the soft tissues and of the bone that must support the appliance. The denture and existing teeth must mesh. The jaws must function naturally. The facial appearance must be maintained.

Before fitting a denture, oral surgery may be required. Afterward there may be a need for many adjustments and corrections. In short only a dentist is qualified to design your dentures. Similarly, only a dentist has the training to refit and repair them.

Dangers of home reliners. Because the tissues of the mouth are continually changing, dentures normally become ill fitting and need periodic adjustment by a dentist. Popular misbelief holds that the ill fit results from changes not in the mouth but in the dentures, so to save money many people buy relining kits.

But such do-it-yourself kits for relining and repairing dentures can irreversibly destroy mouth tissues. Jawbones can disintegrate from pressure exerted by home relining pads. Some victims suffer so much bone loss that not enough ridge is left to support new dentures.

Users of home reliners often become trapped in a vicious circle. The reliner may restore comfort temporarily. But the accompanying destruction of bone produces a loose fit again. The sufferer again resorts to a reliner, and again the process repeats.

The ADA has called home reliner kits a "menace to dental public health" and has urged the Food and Drug Administration (FDA) to bar their sale.

Denture adhesives. Use denture adhesives briefly if at all. Dentists sometimes recommend adhesives as a temporary measure. But prolonged use is discouraged. As with all ill-fitting dentures the penalty be irritation, bone loss, and possibly cancer.

Anyone who expects to wear dentures successfully needs to break down mouth and tongue habits that dislodge dentures and also build up habits that support them. The use of adhesives creates a false retention and inhibits development of habits of denture support.

Eating with dentures. For the first few days eat soft foods cut into small pieces. Avoid sticky or very hard foods. Chew food on both sides with the back teeth.

Practice speaking with your new dentures by reading aloud. If your teeth click together when you talk, try speaking more slowly. If the problem persists, your dentures may need adjustment.

Dentures are usually removed at night. But if you leave your dentures out of your mouth for longer periods, irritated places in your mouth may swell, making reinsertion difficult. Ask your dentist for advice.

Care of dentures. Take hygienic care of dentures. Artificial teeth, like natural teeth, need to be kept clean and free from deposits to preserve the health of the mouth and avoid unpleasant "denture breath." Purchase a brush made especially for dentures at any drugstore. Scrub with caution or you may scratch the denture.

Brush and wash in running water with toilet soap or a cleansing agent. Use one agent to clean dirty dentures (Denalan, Kleenite), another to keep them clean (Polident Tablets, Polident Effervescent Powder).

Don't use laundry bleach. Exposed metal may corrode if allowed to remain in a chlorine-containing solution, and the black stain can spread to visible tooth material.

Brush the denture over a washbowl about half full of water. Then, should the denture slip from your hand, the water will act as a cushion and prevent damage.

Don't place dentures in hot water or pour hot water over them to sterilize them. They may soften out of shape. When the dentures are out of your mouth, place them in water or a cleansing solution.

You may save yourself much discomfort and embarrassment while your denture is being repaired if you keep a spare set.

See also MOUTH ODOR; TEETH AND MOUTH DISORDERS.

DEPRESSION   See STRESS; TRANQUILIZERS.

DERMATITIS, ALLERGIC   See ECZEMA.

DERMATITIS, CONTACT   See CONTACT DERMATITIS.

DERMATITIS, SEBORRHEIC   See SEBORRHEIC DERMATITIS.

DERMOGRAPHISM (skin writing) is an exaggerated skin response to trauma. Itching wheals —raised, red skin areas—appear in skin to which normal pressure has been applied. Tight, binding clothes such as bra straps, girdles, belts, or waistbands will induce whealing. Scratching, even the mere applying of pressure on the skin with a fingernail or a blunt object, produces raised, red streaks.

Dermographism is believed to result from an allergy and often occurs following other allergic reactions. But it also occurs in nonallergic people, without apparent cause.

The condition is harmless but annoying. There is no cure, but prescription medications can relieve itching and suppress welts.

See also ITCHING; SKIN DISORDERS.

DESERT FEVER   See COCCIDIOIDOMYCOSIS.

DIABETES (sugar diabetes, diabetes mellitus) is a condition in which the body cannot use carbohydrates (sugars and starches) as well as protein and fat in a normal way because of a deficiency in the quantity or action of the hormone insulin. Normally the body changes food carbohydrates into the form of sugar called glucose. It may burn this right away to supply heat or energy. Or it may store the glucose in a different form, called glycogen, for use later on.

But in uncontrolled diabetes glucose accumulates in the blood, creating a condition called hyperglycemia. The kidneys expel sugar from the body by way of the urine.

Physicians of ancient Greece knew about this disease and named it *diabetes,* which means "siphon" in Greek. This refers to one of the most prominent symptoms of the ailment—frequent urination. In the seventeenth century the adjective *mellitus* was added to the name to distinguish it from other diseases marked by frequent urination. *Mellitus* comes from the Latin word for "honey" and it refers to the fact that diabetics have sugar in their urine. (Early diagnosis involved tasting the urine to see if it was sweet.) For general use today "diabetes mellitus" has been shortened back to the original "diabetes," and even among physicians the terms are virtually interchangeable.

The most common symptoms of diabetes, especially among children, are frequent urination accompanied by unusual thirst and excessive drinking of fluids; weight loss with easy tiring, weakness, irritability or nausea; and uncontrollable craving for food, especially sweet foods and candy. These symptoms appear suddenly—and signal the urgent need for prompt treatment.

Other symptoms of diabetes, common among adults, include frequent infections of the skin, foreskin, gums, or urinary system; unusual changes or blurriness of vision; pain or cramps in the legs, feet, or fingers; slow healing of cuts and bruises; intense vaginal itching; or drowsiness. Any *one* of these signals may mean diabetes and calls for a checkup by a doctor.

Diabetes ranks as among the seven leading causes of death in the United States. It develops most frequently in middle and old age. After the age of 25 women are more likely to have it than men. The prevalence of diabetes is greater in overweight people. For every 20 percent of excess weight the risk of diabetes doubles.

More than 11 million people are estimated to have the disorder, though nearly half these cases are thought to be undiagnosed and getting no care. Yet diabetes can be detected by a glucose tolerance test before symptoms appear, and early detection and treatment may reduce complications. An increasing number of communities and industries are offering diabetes screening programs in which you can be tested, often free.

Cause of diabetes. The cause of most cases of diabetes is unknown. The condition runs in families, but the pattern of heredity is not completely understood. Evidence is mounting that viruses play a role in the development of diabetes in susceptible people.

Other cases of diabetes may be traced to particular circumstances such as pancreatitis, an inflammation of the pancreas. Insulin is produced in the islets of Langerhans in the pancreas, and diabetes can develop when the pancreas is diseased or is surgically removed. In addition, viruses produce antibodies that destroy the islet cells and result in diabetes.

An increase in the rate at which insulin is used up or destroyed in the body may lead to diabetes. There also may be a drop in the efficiency of insulin because of liver disease or the use of drugs—like steroids and pituitary and adrenal hormones—that impede insulin activity. A hormone, glucagon, may in rare cases make the liver—the body's sugar storehouse—release more sugar into the blood than a normal insulin supply can handle.

Types of diabetes. *Type 1* (juvenile-onset, insulin-dependent, ketosis-prone) diabetes occurs when the pancreas produces little or no insulin. It's the most severe and difficult to control type, affecting about 10 percent of people with diabetes. It usually arises between infancy and age 40, although it can appear in older people as well. It generally begins abruptly and progresses rapidly. Type 1 diabetes requires insulin injections at least once a day.

Type 2 (maturity-onset, non–insulin-dependent, ketosis-resistant) diabetes results from a sluggishness or insufficiency of insulin production, and from other impairments in the metabolism of blood glucose. It usually begins later in life, is milder, progresses more slowly. It can often be controlled by diet, weight loss, and exercise. Some people with type 2 diabetes require insulin or oral medication.

(Two other types of diabetes tend to be temporary: *Stress* diabetes follows surgery, trauma, heart attack, burns, or other such episodes. *Gestational* diabetes appears during pregnancy and generally ends with delivery. Because the condition may be asymptomatic yet cause problems to the fetus, it's prudent for a blood-sugar test to be given to every pregnant woman between 24 and 28 weeks of pregnancy—especially if she's overweight, has a family history of diabetes, and in the past has miscarried or delivered a premature or oversized infant.)

For optimum treatment it's advisable to consult a diabetologist (diabetes specialist), even if regular care is managed by a family physician. With proper care people with diabetes can live almost normally, although statistically their life expectancy tends to be less than for the general population.

The disease varies greatly in severity. Many people with insulin deficiencies are barely discomforted by their condition. At the other extreme, as a direct cause of death, diabetes takes the lives of more than 30,000 Americans a year, and its indirect toll is much greater—about 300,000.

Complications of diabetes. People with diabetes are particularly susceptible to diseases involving the heart and small blood vessels. Coronary disease is three times more prevalent than among the general population. A person with diabetes is also much likelier to develop severe arteriosclerosis of the legs, especially in diabetes of over ten years' duration.

Gangrene in the legs can result from damaged blood vessels or infection. The skin does not resist injury well, and small blisters, cuts, or bruises may not heal readily. Infection develops easily and may become extensive. If the blood vessels are not normal, then a deficient blood supply may make matters worse.

Diabetes may lead to failing eyesight. Small, painless hemorrhages can occur from the capillaries of the retina, often blurring vision. A more serious stage, called proliferative retinopathy, begins when new blood vessels grow along the surface of the retina. If they break, blood leaking into the vitreous, the fluid-filled center of the eye, causes "specks" or "cobwebs" in the field of vision. A large hemorrhage may lead to sudden blindness. In addition diabetics are more prone than average to develop glaucoma and cataracts.

If you have diabetes, it's important to see an ophthalmologist at least once a year, even if you perceive no changes in your eyesight. Most specialists advise treating proliferative retinopathy early, before bleeding occurs. Photocoagulation cauterizes the newly formed vessels with a laser. If bleeding has clouded the vitreous, in a surgical procedure called vitrectomy the fluid may be removed with a syringelike instrument and replaced with clear fluid.

People with diabetes are prone to kidney complications, generally resulting from scarring and leakage of the glomeruli, the clusters of kidney capillaries that filter out wastes. Routine urinalyses are essential once diabetes is diagnosed. The persistent presence in urine of protein is usually the first sign of early diabetic nephropathy (kidney disease), which can proceed rapidly to kidney failure if not treated.

A referral to a nephrologist (kidney specialist) is often needed. If kidney function is severely impaired, the patient generally requires dialysis and may be a candidate for a kidney transplant.

If excess glucose enters the nerve cells, one result may be diabetic neuropathy—a nerve disorder marked by numbness, burning, tingling, and decreased reflexes. Any time blood sugar is

poorly controlled, the diabetic may suffer a dull leg pain, numbness, tingling, and other "funny feelings" in the feet.

Advanced neuropathy may not appear for some years after the onset of diabetes. It is often accompanied by excruciating leg pains (sciatic neuropathy), which may sometimes be relieved by phenytoin (Dilantin) or analgesics. There also may be problems with muscles—foot drop, wrist drop, palsies of the face—which may be remedied with physical rehabilitation. Some types of weakness, as of the legs and eyelids, often improve spontaneously after a few months.

Impotence occurs frequently among men with diabetes, because of interference with the nerves or blood supply of the penis. Difficulties with erections may be a man's first sign of diabetes. Because interference may be only partial, and thus may permit a semierection, a diabetic's impotence may be misdiagnosed as emotional in origin.

Pregnancy puts a woman with diabetes at special risk of complications. Her hormonal changes and the demands of the fetus can raise and lower her blood sugar excessively, and can accelerate eye and kidney problems. Compared with nondiabetics she is more likely to retain excessive amounts of water, develop high blood pressure, miscarry, and suffer preeclampsia.

The infants of diabetic mothers are generally larger than normal. Chances for successful delivery are usually improved if the baby is delivered two to three weeks before the due date by induction or cesarean. The infant may be born with birth defects—malformations of the lower limbs, heart and nerve disorders, cleft lip and palate—especially if the mother's diabetes was poorly controlled during the first two months of pregnancy.

The best safeguard against such complications is meticulous control throughout pregnancy. If you have diabetes and become pregnant, select an obstetrician who's experienced in providing the extensive care that diabetes calls for. Expect to see him at least biweekly during your first trimester, and weekly or more often from then on. You need frequent monitoring of blood sugar, constant readjustment of insulin dosage, and careful supervision of diet. In addition the fetal growth must be watched closely, via ultrasonography and lab tests.

Foot care. In diabetes, the feet seem particularly prone to infection. Nerve damage raises the risk of a blister or other injury going unnoticed, and impaired circulation may cause such injuries to heal so slowly as to promote the growth of germs. Simple fungus infections like athlete's foot must be prevented if possible and cared for promptly, because they provide a point of entry for more serious infections.

To help prevent foot infection, if you have diabetes, wash your feet daily with mild soap and lukewarm water. Blot them dry with a clean, soft towel—don't rub. After washing inspect your feet for any redness, sores, or cracks.

Use a small amount of moisturizing lotion to soften dry skin on the soles, heels, and tops of your feet—but not between your toes. You can make an effective, inexpensive foot cream from solid vegetable shortening mixed with a few drops of water. Wear comfortable, well-fitting, low-heeled shoes. Change shoes in the course of the day. Wear socks made of cotton or a cotton blend. Avoid wearing open-toed sandals or going barefoot. Steer clear of rubber soles—they provide insufficient ventilation.

Trim toenails straight across after washing and drying your feet. Do not cut corns or calluses or treat them with over-the-counter medications; instead see a podiatrist.

Any untreated toe infection that does not heal in about ten days may lead to infection of the bone or joint, and then healing without an operation is almost impossible. Serious infections can also develop into gangrene, necessitating amputation. Early treatment with antibiotics may help prevent such complications.

Insulin injections. Injections of insulin provide a person with diabetes with a substance lacking in his own body, and thus enable his system to make use of sugars and starches. Some people with diabetes maintain control over their condition with one insulin injection a day, but most require two or more injections for good control.

The best area for injections is the abdomen, which gives the most reliable absorption of insulin. The thighs also are suitable for self-administration, but should be used cautiously by people who run or jog frequently because the exercise may speed up insulin absorption. Other suitable areas are the upper arms and upper buttocks, but these require the assistance of another person.

Within one area vary the exact spots for injection. Keep the sites 1½ inches apart, and don't use the same spot for at least three weeks. This helps avoid lumps in the skin brought about by too many injections in the same spot.

A money-saving tip: Most U.S. diabetic patients use disposable insulin syringe-needle units, and are taught to discard them after one use. In fact, University of Virginia medical researchers have found, you can safely use a unit at least

three times. Some patients succeed in using units for as long as a week, disposing of them only when the needle is blunted.

Insulin demands a regular eating schedule. A person on insulin must eat at the proper times imposed by the action of the insulin he takes. Meals may not be skipped or delayed. Nor may they be consolidated. Injections need to be made at the same time each day: for example, if an injection of long-acting insulin is delayed several hours one day, the extended action into the following day may cause too rapid a drop in blood sugar if the next injection is taken on time.

In a new development some patients are wearing portable infusion devices that pump insulin under the skin around the clock on a preset schedule. The device—about the size of a pack of cigarettes and weighing a few ounces—attaches to the patient's belt. Able to regulate blood sugar more accurately than insulin injections, the infusion pump is particularly useful for people who are anxious to attain perfect control, such as pregnant women. An insulin pump implanted within the body seems the wave of the future.

Oral substitutes for insulin have been the goal of diabetes researchers for many years. The breakthrough came with the marketing of the drug tolbutamide (sold as Orinase). Like insulin, a drug taken by mouth is no cure for diabetes. It is unlikely to be effective in controlling severe diabetes or diabetes in a person who is suffering from another severe illness or is undergoing surgery. Further, oral antidiabetics can work only when some part of the pancreas is functioning. They seem to ease diabetic symptoms by stimulating the islets of Langerhans to produce more insulin, by making the tissues more sensitive to insulin and by improving the glucose metabolism within body cells.

In addition to Orinase, oral antidiabetic drugs include acetohexamide (Dymelor), tolazamide (Tolinase), chlorpropamide (Diabinese), glyburide (Micronase and Diabeta) and glipizide (Glucatrol).

Such oral drugs are not used in type 1 diabetes. They work best for people whose blood sugar levels are not perfect despite diet and exercise.

Diabetic emergencies. If you or a member of your family has diabetes, you need to be on guard against two opposite and severe reactions (see chart, "Handling Diabetic Emergencies"):

Hypoglycemic reaction (also called hypoglycemia, insulin reaction, and low blood sugar) can affect people with either type 1 or type 2 diabetes. It results from taking too much insulin or oral medication, leading to rapid, extreme drop in blood sugar. It can come about if you miss a meal and thus have too much insulin in your body. Or it can result from more exercise than usual, which decreases the amount of available blood sugar for the insulin to work on. Or it can be a matter of an overdose of insulin or oral medication.

An insulin reaction is usually sudden, although it can appear slowly in type 2 diabetes. The person may feel light-headed and hungry. You're likely to see that his breathing is rapid and shallow, his skin pale and moist, his behavior marked by confusion and mood changes.

A mild reaction can usually be corrected by six or seven Life Savers or other small candies; 2 teaspoons of sugar dissolved in ½ cup of lukewarm water; 1 tablespoon of honey, corn syrup, or maple syrup, alone or in a half cup of orange juice; or any other available candy or sweet such as jam or jelly. People with diabetes should always carry some sweet in case of an insulin reaction: sugar cubes, hard candy, a tube of commercial cake frosting.

A severe insulin reaction—in which the patient may become confused and unconscious—calls for an injection of intravenous glucose or glucagon, which raises the blood-sugar level. A glucagon package, containing the glucose-promoting hormone and injection kit, should always be available.

Ketoacidosis (also called diabetic coma) occurs only in type 1 diabetes. It can result from taking too little insulin—or from stress caused by illness, accident, surgery, emotional upset. To provide the body with extra energy and heat such stress leads to a rise in blood sugar even while reducing insulin supply. Unable to adequately mobilize the sugar, the body then reacts to the stress by metabolizing fat, sending acidic compounds called ketones into the blood.

Ketoacidosis develops slowly over 8 to 24 hours. At first there may be no symptoms. To detect it as early as possible, test your blood sugar as often as your doctor recommends—at least every day without fail. If urine is being tested, the first warning signs are large amounts of sugar—2–5 percent—in your urine, accompanied by a positive test for ketones. At this point call your doctor immediately or get to a hospital.

During the early stages of ketoacidosis there also may be excessive thirst and urination, and often nausea, vomiting, stomach pains, and deep, rapid "air hunger" breathing. Later you may feel drowsy, and your breath will have a sweet, fruity odor. Coma may follow. Hospital care is essential.

People with diabetes should carry emergency medical identification warning of their condition. Too often diabetic emergencies are mistaken for drunkenness. If a hypoglycemic reaction leads to coma, the patient is in danger of being thought to have had a stroke.

Testing blood sugar is essential to let you and your doctor know if your diabetes is under control, and if any changes are necessary for your treatment.

Urine testing (as with Clinitest, Diastix, Tes-Tape) reflects blood-sugar levels via color changes in chemicals or impregnated tape. For some time after diabetes is first diagnosed, urine is usually tested four times a day: Before the morning insulin shot; before lunch; before the afternoon or suppertime insulin shot if you're on two shots a day; and before bed. Later on the doctor may reduce the number of tests required. Ketones should also be tested (as with Acetest or Ketostix) whenever two consecutive urine tests show 2 percent sugar or more, or as your doctor advises.

For a person on only one test a day many doctors recommend rotating the times of testing (one day, before breakfast; the next day, before lunch; and so on), so as to record patterns reflecting a whole day. To get a more accurate measure of the blood sugar at the time of urinating some doctors also recommend "double voiding": emptying the bladder of stored-up urine without testing it, and then urinating again 30 minutes later for the test.

One test result may mean little. The real measure of whether diabetes is under control is the pattern of blood sugar over days or weeks. To show this keep a "diary," a notebook chart recording in parallel columns the results of each day's tests (for sugar and ketones). Also have a column noting "Unusual Occurrences," such as any illness, emotional upset, unaccustomed exercise.

You can reduce the cost of routine urine-glucose testing by cutting each tape into small strips, ¼ or ½ inch long. While testing, you can hold the smaller strips of tape with a pair of tweezers or small plastic clothespin.

Blood-glucose monitoring, which tests the sugar content of a drop of blood, is more accurate than urine testing. High marks for convenience and reliability have been given Visidex and Chemstrip bG, in which a drop of blood is placed on a test strip and wiped off after 60 seconds; the color change is then compared with a reference chart. Also available are machines (e.g., Accuchek, Glucometer, Glucoscan), which can read a test strip and display the glucose level in digits.

Home blood testing is especially recommended for people with type 1 diabetes—who need extremely careful control—and for diabetic women during pregnancy, to reduce hazards to the fetus. It is essential for people who use the insulin pump. People with kidney disease should test their blood because their urine may not reflect blood sugar reliably. Color-blind people, who can't gauge color changes, often find blood-monitoring machines their only way to get essential readings.

Importance of diet. Diet and exercise alone, without insulin, can control some 30 percent to 40 percent of cases, especially overweight people and those with a mild condition that was diagnosed early. Because of the strong association between type 2 diabetes and obesity, much diabetes meal planning is aimed at decreasing caloric intake. A person who takes insulin requires three meals and two to three snacks a day. People who take insulin or oral medication should be consistent day to day in when and how much they eat.

In the ideal diabetic diet, 50 to 55 percent of the calories should come from carbohydrates. Starchy foods such as corn, rice, potatoes, and wheat have been found to cause a slow rise in blood sugar. Fats (30 to 35 percent of calories) and protein (15 to 20 percent) are kept at low levels because of their possible involvement in cardiovascular problems.

You can get a varied, well-balanced diet by referring to a booklet called *Exchange Lists for Meal Planning,* available from the American Diabetes Association and the American Dietetic Association. There are six exchange lists, each for a different food category (milk, vegetables, fruit; bread and cereal; meat and protein; and fat). A measured portion, called an "exchange," is specified for each food listed. Within each list the exchanges have roughly the same food value. So if a prescribed diet calls for 1 bread exchange as a bedtime snack, you could select a slice of bread, 1/2 cup cooked cereal, 1/2 cup macaroni, a small baked potato, etc.

Every issue of *Diabetes Forecast,* a magazine published by the American Diabetes Association, contains suggestions for eating well and still keeping within any limits the doctor sets. Other aids for meal planning are the American Diabetes Association/American Dietetic Association *Family Cookbooks,* Volumes I and II.

There's also evidence that diabetics in poor control should take a B-complex multivitamin with supplements of the growth factor inositol.

These water-soluble nutrients are likely to be lost with excessive urination. If malabsorption is a problem, vitamins D and K may be required as well. Vitamins also may be desirable for people on weight-reducing diets of less than 1,000 calories a day.

What about alcohol? It's important to confer with a physician as to how drinking might affect your condition. Also, when taken with Diabinese, alcohol can cause an "Antabuse reaction," marked by headache, vomiting, and shortness of breath.

Travel tips. Bring along enough insulin or oral drugs for the entire trip. Be sure to take all necessary supplies, including urine- and blood-testing equipment, and keep them readily at hand, not in a luggage compartment. Because your suitcases might go astray, carry supplies on board with you.

Even if you normally use long-acting insulin, carry some regular insulin for emergencies. Also bring sugar snacks in case of a hypoglycemic reaction.

As a precaution get a doctor's prescription, specifying the product's generic name; a particular brand may not be available, especially outside the U.S. For foreign travel also take a note from your doctor to help you clear syringes through customs and obtain additional syringes from pharmacies. If you'll need to buy insulin outside this country, learn in advance which strengths are available and how to switch from one strength to another.

Get all required vaccinations weeks before you leave, so immunization reactions don't disturb diabetic balance during the trip. Jet travel can upset your eating and insulin schedule. Your doctor can help adjust insulin shots to travel time. From the airline you may be able to get a special meal, or at least learn what in-flight meals will be so you can adjust your medication for it.

At home prepare for hurricanes, floods, snowstorms. Stock nonperishable foods that fit into your diet. Also keep carbohydrates in your car, to consume if you're delayed. Be sure you have enough insulin or oral drugs for several months. Store some at your place of work in the event you're stranded there. It's important that you let at least one coworker know you're a diabetic, so you can receive appropriate help if you have an emergency on the job.

Diabetic children. Families with diabetic children face special problems, and typically need help in coping with the ramifications of a child's illness. Children are usually afflicted with the more severe type 1 diabetes and require careful

HANDLING DIABETIC EMERGENCIES

Hypoglycemic reaction (hypoglycemia, insulin reaction, low blood sugar)	Ketoacidosis (diabetic coma)

CAUSES

Too much insulin or oral medication Not enough food	Not enough insulin Severe stress

ONSET

Sudden	Gradual

SIGNS

Pale, moist	*SKIN*	Flushed, dry
Excited, nervous, irritable, confused }	*BEHAVIOR*	Drowsy
Normal	*BREATH*	Sweet, fruity
Normal to rapid, shallow }	*BREATHING*	Deep, labored, fast ("air hunger")
Absent	*VOMITING*	Present
Moist, numb, tingling	*TONGUE*	Dry
Present	*HUNGER*	Absent
Absent	*THIRST*	Present
Headache	*PAIN*	Abdominal
Absent or slight	*SUGAR AND KE-TONES IN URINE*	Large amounts

TREATMENT

Consume sugar. If patient is unable to swallow, give glucagon. If patient is not alert and able to eat within 25 minutes after glucagon injection, take him to a hospital.	Call a doctor. If no doctor is available, take to doctor.

monitoring and daily insulin. But youngsters may fail to follow their daily regimen; teen-agers are especially likely to resist feeling different and may eat junk food at odd hours like their friends. Some parents overprotect their diabetic children and unnecessarily make invalids of them.

It's generally advisable for a diabetic child to manage his own care as early as possible. Some children can keep their own records by five to six years of age, and most can inject their own insulin by the time they're ten.

Diabetes may be extremely disturbing to family life, especially in a child. It's common for parents to feel overwhelmed by the responsibilities for proper testing, diet, and shots. Wrongly, they often feel somehow to blame for the child's having the disease.

Affiliates of the American Diabetes Association have support groups that may prove invaluable to diabetic youngsters and their families. Included are parent-and-youth groups, parents-of-diabetics clubs, young adult discussion groups, and special summer camp programs. The Juvenile Diabetes Foundation also provides programs and educational materials.

Adults with diabetes may similarly benefit from support groups, educational programs, and other special services.

For helpful information write the American Diabetes Association, 18 East 48th Street, New York, New York 10017 and the Juvenile Diabetes Association, 23 East 26th Street, New York, New York 10010.

See also ANTIBIOTICS; ARTERIOSCLEROSIS; ATHLETE'S FOOT; EMERGENCY MEDICAL IDENTIFICATION; FIBER; HEART ATTACK; HYPOGLYCEMIA; QUACKERY; STEROIDS; STROKE.

DIAGNOSIS See PHYSICAL EXAMINATION.

DIAPER RASH occurs when a baby is left in wet diapers for prolonged periods. It is thought that bacteria in the urine and on the skin overgrow, causing redness and irritation in the diaper area. In severe forms there may be deep, oozing ulcerations.

To help prevent diaper rash change the child as soon as possible after each bowel movement or urination, even if it means more than a dozen times a day. Cleanse the baby with plain water—soap or alcohol may damage the skin, increasing the susceptibility to diaper rash. Sprinkle the diaper area with plain talc—medicated talc may trigger a drug allergy. It is unknown whether ointments such as zinc oxide or A & D Ointment reduce irritation from wet diapers.

If your child is subject to frequent diaper rash, use cloth diapers rather than disposable paper diapers. Leave plastic pants off. At night use three cloth diapers—without plastic pants—and put a protective rubber pad under the child.

In washing diapers use a mild laundry soap rather than a strong detergent, which may cause a skin reaction. Then rinse diapers in diluted vinegar. Or impregnate diapers with a chlorine diaper rinse during the final rinse. Then permit them to dry with the chemical remaining on the cloth. The antiseptic won't hurt the child, but may kill bacteria that cause diaper rash. Methylbenzethonium chloride in ointment or powder may also help prevent diaper rash.

Relieving diaper rash. If your child has a mild diaper rash, take all the above measures. In addition set your alarm so that you can change the child's diaper at least once during the night. During the day expose the child's diaper area to the air as much as possible. Avoid the use of cornstarch; it can serve as a medium for the growth of yeast.

Be cautious in your use of over-the-counter .5 percent hydrocortisone cream. Many parents overuse it because they find it so effective in clearing up diaper rash. But topical steroids can be absorbed through the skin and have potentially severe side effects. Absorption is speeded when the area is wet and tightly covered with a diaper. If you use hydrocortisone cream, limit its use to twice daily applications. Leave the child's diaper area exposed as much as possible.

Avoid boric acid and mercury preparations. They have been associated with systemic poisoning.

If the diaper rash is severe or persists for more than a few days after you've taken these measures, take the child to the doctor. Diaper rash may sometimes be complicated by other skin conditions, such as a yeast infection, that require medical treatment.

See also CONTACT DERMATITIS; SKIN DISORDERS.

DIAPHRAGM See BIRTH CONTROL.

DIARRHEA is usually brought on by an irritation of the intestine. This speeds bowel action, so fecal matter is discharged with increased frequency and before fluids have been absorbed.

If you suffer from diarrhea, take a cool or lukewarm drink after each movement to make up for loss of fluids. Drink water, tea, flat cola or ginger ale, soup. Ice-cold beverages may irritate your stomach. Avoid milk and solid foods.

When the diarrhea seems under control, eat low-residue foods that won't irritate your stomach or spur your bowels. These include meat, chicken, and fish (baked or broiled, never fried or highly spiced), poached or boiled eggs, rice, bananas, baked potato. Avoid alcohol until symptoms subside.

In a bout of diarrhea you may make your anal region sore with the frequent wiping. Guard against this by not wiping with toilet paper. Instead rinse the area with soap and water. Then dab it dry with facial tissue. Use petroleum jelly to relieve soreness.

If your diarrhea is mild and unaccompanied by other symptoms, you may get relief with Pepto-Bismol.

Use antidiarrhea drugs with restraint, however. Diarrhea is a mechanism like coughing, in which your body seeks to rid itself of an irritant.

Studies of the disease shigellosis at the University of Texas show that antidiarrheals give microorganisms a chance to dig into the intestinal wall, worsening the infection instead of being excreted.

Don't add to your fluid losses by using a laxative to "clean out the poisons."

Causes. Most cases of ordinary diarrhea stem from overeating, eating unripe or overripe fruit, or consuming large quantities of vegetables. Alcohol, especially wine and beer, can trigger a bout of diarrhea. Viral infection or mild food poisoning are also common causes of diarrhea.

Many people suffer diarrhea as a reaction to emotional stress—in student dorms there are often lines outside the bathrooms at exam times. Diarrhea is a frequent result of antibiotics killing bacteria that are essential to digestion. To repopulate your intestine, eat yogurt. (Make sure it contains live cultures.)

Diarrhea may be a sign you find certain spices irritating. Or you may be experiencing a food allergy or an intolerance to milk sugar (lactose) or other food components (see MALABSORPTION). To uncover the offending food or condiment, keep a food diary. If diarrhea recurs, chances are it's caused by a food you ate within the last 48 hours. Sample any food you suspect and, if diarrhea ensues, eliminate it from your diet.

Diarrhea frequently occurs during travel (see TRAVEL HEALTH). Don't try using so-called intestinal prophylactics. Any drug that suppresses diarrhea may conceal infections, especially amebiasis.

Infant diarrhea. Dehydration from diarrhea and related complications can kill a small child in a few days. So, too, diarrhea can be perilous for an elderly person or one weakened by disease.

Call a physician if you observe any of these signs of dehydration: lethargy, decreased urination, sunken eyeballs, absence of tears, no saliva.

Also call a doctor if your child is under six months and has diarrhea or abdominal pain that continues more than 12 to 24 hours, or if there is blood in the stool.

For simple diarrhea give the child nothing to eat or drink for four to six hours. Then give small amounts of liquid at room temperature, about 1/4 cup of liquid every half hour. The next day, give the child small amounts of easily digested foods. An infant with diarrhea can continue breastfeeding, but formula and cow's milk should not be given for ten days. A soy-based formula can be substituted.

Call the doctor if these measures do not control the diarrhea within 24 hours. Give the child no medications except on your doctor's advice.

For an adult call the doctor if diarrhea lasts for more than two days. Consult one right away if diarrhea is accompanied by fever, nausea and vomiting, headache, severe indigestion or abdominal pain, or extreme fatigue. Also see a doctor immediately if the bowel movements are bloody, tarry, or frothy.

See also ALLERGY; AMEBIASIS; ANEMIA; COLITIS; FOOD ALLERGY; FOOD POISONING; INFECTIOUS DISEASE; MALABSORPTION; POISONING; SALMONELLOSIS; SHIGELLOSIS; TRAVEL HEALTH.

DIATHERMY treatments are a source of great controversy. Diathermy is the therapeutic use of an oscillating electric current of high frequency to produce local heat in the body tissues below the surface.

Proponents point out that deep heat can be achieved anywhere in the body without heating surface tissue, and that chemical changes produced by diathermy can be beneficial in a wide range of disorders. Diathermy can relieve pain and provide greater mobility for patients with slipped disc or arthritis, after trauma from sprains and strains, and in certain abdominal infections, such as pelvic inflammatory disease.

Opponents of diathermy agree, but emphasize that too often you don't receive the close supervision diathermy requires—and so are less likely to suffer accidents if you stick with moist hot compresses. In many doctors' offices the equipment is used by personnel who do not understand it thoroughly and the potential for severe burns is great.

If you are to undergo diathermy, take the following precautions:

Allow it to be administered only where there are trained personnel to watch you and the equipment.

Don't undergo diathermy if you have sensory impairment or are not fully alert. Pain is an indication that there is excessive heating.

Diathermy is not for you if you have metal implants or wire sutures. They may localize heat and cause burning. Don't wear contact lenses, which may localize heat if your eye is exposed to shortwave.

Be undressed, and don't wear any metallic objects such as watches and other jewelry.

Diathermy is ruled out for anyone with cancer or thrombophlebitis or who is pregnant. Applied to a woman's lower back or abdomen, diathermy may cause a marked increase in menstruation.

See also COMPRESSES; RADIATION.

DIPHTHERIA patients complain initially of fever, sore throat, and hoarseness. The doctor may note patches of grayish membrane forming in the throat, giving off a strange, sweet odor. The membrane may interfere with swallowing and threaten to block air passages.

The bacteria causing this infectious disease throw off a powerful toxin that is especially harmful to the heart, blood vessels, nerves, and kidneys. Diphtheria victims may suffer paralysis lasting as long as four months.

Despite antibiotics, adults who have let their immunization lapse may suffer fatal nerve damage from diphtheria. You need a booster shot every ten years.

DTP—for diphtheria, tetanus, and pertussis (whooping cough)—vaccine should be given to a child at two to three months before he loses temporary immunity inherited from his mother. Three doses are required at intervals of four to six weeks, with a fourth a year after the third. Children should get a booster shot when they enter school.

DTP vaccine could wipe out diphtheria in this country. But it hasn't, because about one child in four is never vaccinated and most adults let their immunization lapse.

Symptoms usually begin two to seven days after exposure. The disease spreads in droplets of moisture from the mouth, nose, or throat of someone infected—usually by coughing, sneezing, or kissing. Infection can also be spread by drinking cups, eating utensils, handkerchiefs, towels, pencils, or anything that has touched the mouth of an infected person or been sprayed with discharges from his mouth, nose, or throat.

An infected person can spread the disease after he seems entirely well. Half of the people who recover from diphtheria will continue to have the germ for more than two weeks; one fourth will be able to infect others for more than a month. Members of a patient's family may pass on the germ, whether or not they become ill. The disease can spread by a carrier, an apparently healthy person who harbors the germs in his throat or nose.

The disease is commonest in cold months. But an epidemic, once started, may continue regardless of the season.

See also IMMUNIZATION; INFECTIOUS DISEASE.

DISABILITY INSURANCE See HEALTH INSURANCE.

DISC, SLIPPED See SLIPPED DISC.

DISLOCATIONS result from a twist or blow that forces the bones of the joint to stretch or tear the connective tissue that holds the joint together. First aid advice:

Don't try to push the bones back into place. Neither should you lift or rotate the joint to test for dislocation. This can further damage the connective tissue, perhaps permanently.

For a dislocated shoulder make an arm sling —or tie the arm to the body as it hangs, taking care that it doesn't push the elbow upward.

For a dislocated knee, ankle, or elbow, splint the limb.

Get to the doctor or hospital for X rays and medical attention.

Dislocations most frequently occur in the joints of the shoulder and the jaw. Other common sites are joints of elbows, fingers, hips, knees, ankles, and toes.

In a ball-and-socket joint—like the shoulder —the ball part may push through the connective tissue and slip out of the socket. This type of dislocation often occurs after falling on an outstretched palm, and happens quite frequently during athletic activities.

Dislocation of the jaw may result from a blow to the lower jaw while the mouth is open. It may also occur when the mouth is opened too wide: yawning, opening for the dentist, eating a triple-decker sandwich.

After a fall or blow suspect a dislocation if you have swelling and feel severe pain in the joint. You may find that the limb is either longer or shorter than usual and the joint looks unnatural. The joint may be rigid and its range of motion greatly reduced.

Take care not to dislocate a child's arm— most often the elbow—by lifting him up over a curb, holding him when he stumbles, pulling his arm through a sleeve, pulling a toy away from him, or swinging him around by the hands. When this happens, the child may refuse to use the arm. He'll experience pain at the elbow, possibly also at the wrist and shoulder.

See also ACCIDENTS; SPORTS.

DIVERTICULITIS is an infection involving small pouches that develop in the digestive tract, usually in the lower portion of the large intestine (colon).

The pouches (diverticula) develop as a result of weaknesses in the intestinal walls. The pressure of feces and gas may cause these weak portions to bulge out, forming the pockets. Chronic constipation and powerful laxatives may increase the pressure.

The condition affects some 30 percent of people over 45, about 80 percent of people over 60. Most people with diverticulosis are not troubled by it, indeed even aware of it. But one person in four with the condition has diverticula large enough to trap food and feces.

Infection can develop, causing diverticulitis. Its chief symptoms are abdominal pain, often on the lower left side; fever; nausea and vomiting; and constipation. Since the symptoms are much the same, diverticulitis is sometimes confused with appendicitis. In diverticulitis, however, the pain is more on the left side, and the typical sufferer is an older person.

Diverticulitis can usually be controlled with antibiotics. Your physician may order hospitalization and resting the bowel with a liquid diet.

Drink plenty of water. Eat foods high in fiber, including bran breads and cereals, raw fruits and vegetables. Low-fiber feces tend to be hard, dry, and difficult to move—a strain on the intestinal muscles. Diverticula are thought to occur when the strain increases and the intestinal wall herniates. Diverticulitis is extremely rare where diets are high in fiber. A high-fiber diet often relieves symptoms.

Avoid foods with seeds and hard particles, which can lodge in the pockets. Stay away from figs, nuts, raisins, strawberries, tomatoes, grapes, cracked wheat, and oatmeal. Refrain from using enemas and laxatives, which can perforate the bowel.

Occasionally diverticula burst and the infected contents spill into the abdominal cavity, causing peritonitis and abscesses. This requires immediate surgical attention.

See also APPENDICITIS; CONSTIPATION; FIBER.

DIZZINESS is a feeling of unsteadiness, confusion, fullness in the head, and disorientation in space. The feeling that you are rotating, or that the world is rotating around you, is a more violent form of dizziness called vertigo.

You may experience a few seconds of dizziness when you turn your head suddenly or get out of bed abruptly. Such momentary, infrequent dizziness is no cause for concern. It may result from low blood pressure and can usually be avoided by turning your head or rising from bed more slowly. Exercising your legs for a few moments before rising may also help. See a physician if you're troubled by this condition.

Another common cause of dizziness is overindulgence in alcohol. The dizziness disappears as the alcoholic intoxication wears off.

Dizziness can be a sign of serious illness. See a physician if you experience frequent and severe dizziness, particularly if it is accompanied by nausea.

Dizziness is often caused by disturbances of the inner ear. Delicate mechanisms that are largely responsible for your sense of balance are located in your inner ear. Any infectious disease that involves the ear—including mumps, measles, and whooping cough—can cause dizziness. Accumulations of fluid in the ear may result in dizziness.

Dizziness is one sign of Ménière's disease, a disorder of the inner ear. A tumor that presses on nerves in the ear—such as in acoustic neuroma—can cause dizziness. Diseases such as diabetes or pernicious anemia may account for dizzy spells.

Episodes of dizziness may also result from circulatory disturbances affecting the ear, as in heart disease or poor blood circulation in old age. Emotional stress or nutritional upsets can affect the blood level in the ear. Dizziness may also result from blows to the ear or head or from hyperventilation. Cancer of the brain and other neurological disorders can cause dizziness.

Food allergy may be responsible for dizziness, as may allergy to chemicals and drugs. Fumes from air pollution, paint, etc., can make you dizzy.

Dizziness can generally be relieved by curing the conditions that cause it. Drugs that dilate blood vessels often bring relief. For people with severe vertigo, surgery or treatment with ultrasonic waves often relieves the dizziness.

See also the following conditions and diseases that may cause dizziness: ACOUSTIC NEUROMA; AIR POLLUTION; ALLERGY; ANEMIA; BLOOD PRESSURE; CANCER OF THE BRAIN; DIABETES; FOOD ALLERGY; HEART DISEASE; HYPERVENTILATION; INFECTIOUS DISEASE; MÉNIÈRE'S DISEASE; STRESS.

DOCTOR   See PHYSICIAN.

DONATING ORGANS   See DEATH.

DOSE   See GONORRHEA.

DOWNERS   See BARBITURATES.

DOWN'S SYNDROME (mongolism) is one of several birth defects involving mental retardation. It occurs once in about 700 live births. There is no cure for it.

Down's syndrome is usually diagnosed at birth. A child with this condition has slanting eyes, a flattened face and nose, short and stubby hands and feet. His tongue may be large and his lower lip protruding. Light-colored flecks in the eyes are common. Most children with Down's syndrome have 25 to 50 percent of normal mental capacity.

Other birth defects are common in children with Down's syndrome, particularly cataracts and crossed eyes, congenital heart defects, and hernia. These children have a much greater susceptibility to ordinary colds, and the incidence of leukemia is 20 times greater among them.

Slow development. Expect a child with the syndrome to develop more slowly than other children. At eight months, for example, he may have the skills of a normal two-month-old. He may not speak until the age of four, if at all. He may not be toilet-trained until five. His eventual achievement will also be limited, but with special education some such children reach eighth-grade levels.

The development and general health of a Down's syndrome child is usually better if he is raised at home. Affected children generally have a cheerful, affectionate disposition and are unlikely to be behavior problems.

The cause of Down's syndrome is not completely understood. Most children with this condition have an extra chromosome in each cell. Excessive X rays during early pregnancy or large doses as in X-ray therapy are thought to be responsible for the chromosome change in some cases. Virus diseases such as hepatitis and influenza in a pregnant woman may damage the chromosomes of the fetus, as may some drugs taken during pregnancy. The age of the mother appears to have an effect on the development of the condition: Mothers of Down's syndrome children are typically 35 years or older.

One form of Down's syndrome appears to be hereditary. If you have a child or a brother or sister with the condition, it's wise to get the advice of a genetic counselor before deciding to become pregnant. Chromosomal studies can help determine the risk of your having a child with the syndrome. If you do become pregnant, a technique called amniocentesis (see BIRTH DEFECTS; PREGNANCY) can diagnose Down's syndrome in the fetus, allowing you the opportunity to consider ABORTION (which see). It is also considered advisable to seek amniocentesis if you are 35 or older.

For more information contact the National Clearinghouse for Human Genetic Diseases (805 15th Street, NW, Suite 500, Washington, D.C. 20005); The National Association for Retarded Citizens (2709 Avenue E East, P.O. Box 6109, Arlington, Texas 76011); and March of Dimes Birth Defects Foundation (1275 Mamaroneck Avenue, White Plains, New York 10605).

See also BIRTH DEFECTS; MENTAL RETARDATION.

DROPSY See HEART FAILURE.

DROWNING If the victim has stopped breathing, clear his mouth of sand, muck, and weeds. Begin ARTIFICIAL RESPIRATION (which see) as soon as you can do it effectively—even before removing him from the water. Send someone to call for an ambulance and for blankets to keep the victim warm.

Keep up the rescue breathing until equipment arrives. In case of HEART STOPPAGE (which see) apply external heart massage.

In diving accidents beware neck fractures. Don't drag the diver out of the water. Support the victim in the water until help arrives. If necessary give mouth-to-mouth resuscitation in the water. If he must be removed from the water before an ambulance arrives, use a rigid stretcher (or a surfboard, door, or wooden plank) to keep head and body level.

Don't assume a near-drowning victim is dead. Vigorous and prolonged resuscitation has saved many people who appeared past help. People who have been submerged in cold water (under 70° F) may be particularly slow to respond to resuscitation efforts. In some cases three hours or more of artificial respiration and heart massage have been necessary. But some near-drowning victims have survived without brain damage after being completely submerged in cold water for up to 38 minutes. This is possible because in cold water a reflex most prominent in children slows the heartbeat and reserves oxygen in the blood for the heart and brain. Thus don't stop your rescue efforts until an ambulance arrives, even if the victim seems to be dead.

All drowning victims, even those who seem to recover at the scene, require hospitalization. Inhaling fluid leads to oxygen loss and increased acidity of the blood.

Fresh water absorbed into the body in large quantities tends to dilute blood chemicals and cause the red cells to swell slightly and in some cases to burst. Saltwater is more concentrated than blood and tends to pull fluid out of the blood into the lungs, causing pulmonary edema. Dirty water, chemicals, and salt residue all cause irritative lung problems that must be treated at a hospital.

In many cases only a small amount of water—perhaps as little as a teaspoonful—reaches the lungs. An individual's first reaction when water enters his mouth and nose is to cough and swallow while trying to catch a breath. In doing this some water may enter the trachea (windpipe) and larynx (voice box), causing a spasm of the larynx, which seals the air passageway and thus causes unconsciousness.

To rescue a drowning person. Don't jump in after the victim unless you've had training in lifesaving. He may pull you under.

Instead toss him a life preserver or life jacket if available. Throw him anything that will float

—a beach ball, spare tire, chunk of wood, vacuum jug, picnic chest. The National Safety Council points out that many drownings could be avoided if people were aware of the dozens of such commonplace objects that float well enough to support a drowning person.

Extend a fishing pole, stick, or any other long object that is handy. If necessary wade out as far as possible. Extend a pole, your shirt, and as a last resort your hands.

If you're in a boat or there's one handy, use it for rescue. Turn the boat so he can grab the stern (rear) or a side near the stern. Stay seated and balance the boat as you pull him aboard.

Swimming precautions. To save your own life, practice "drownproofing." This is a new technique for conserving strength in swimming emergencies (see illustrations).

Instead of weighing you down in water, clothes—even heavy clothes—trap air and help you float. Paddle to safety with a breast stroke. Allow most of your body to remain underwater. The more of your body you try to keep above water, the more energy you waste. Overcome the urge to thrash about, which wastes energy and lets air escape.

If you get a cramp while swimming, draw your knees up to your chest while floating, and massage the cramped muscle. Keep away from swift-moving water and watch for an undertow. If caught in a current, swim with it and at the same time angle toward shore.

Determine the depth of water before swimming or diving. Don't dive into unknown waters. Rocks or stumps may be concealed beneath the surface.

Avoid swimming alone—use the buddy system. Don't swim at night except in lighted pools. Don't go swimming when tired. Wait at least an hour after meals. Don't dive into extremely cold

HOW TO FLOAT FOR LONG PERIODS
Drownproofing can save your strength

1   2   3   4   5   6

1. Rest
Take a deep breath and sink vertically beneath the surface. Relax your arms and legs. Keep your chin down and allow fingertips to brush against knees. Keep neck relaxed and back of head above the surface.

2. Get set
Gently raise arms to a crossed position with backs of wrists touching forehead. At the same time step forward with one leg and backward with the other.

3. Rise, exhale
Without moving your arms and legs from the *get set* position, raise your head quickly but smoothly to the vertical and exhale through your nose.

4. Inhale
To support your head above the surface while you inhale through your mouth, gently sweep your arms outward and downward and step downward with both feet.

5. Sink
As you drop beneath the surface, put your head down and press downward with your arms and hands to arrest your fall.

6. Rest
Relax completely as in Step 1 for 6 to 10 seconds.

water. The shock may cause muscle cramps. Prolonged immersion in water below 65° F can cause death from loss of body heat.

If you fall into cold water, avoid unnecessary thrashing. Activity will drain your heat reserves. By floating as still as you can, you'll also retain air in your clothing, which provides some insulation and buoyancy.

Stay with an overturned boat instead of trying to swim a long distance to shore. If you can't right the boat, grasp the edge and kick-paddle toward shore. Don't exhaust yourself to the point of not being able to hang on.

Prevent children from drowning. Teach kids to swim early. Even very young children can learn with good instruction.

Youngsters shouldn't fear water, but it's worse to let them think they're unsinkable, comments the National Safety Council. "A noseful of water while splashing in the tub is a good lesson for a little one. He'll learn that water *can* hurt him if he's not careful."

Never leave a small child alone in the tub. It takes only a few moments for an infant to drown in small amounts of water, so let the doorbell or telephone ring. Hang a sign BATHING BABY— COME BACK LATER on your front door to keep neighbors from dropping in at bath time.

Keep the bathroom door shut to keep out crawling infants and toddlers. Never let them play in the bathroom unattended.

Always supervise swimming and wading. Cover or drain unused pools; earth-fill old cisterns and wells.

See also ACCIDENTS; ARTIFICIAL RESPIRATION; BOATING; CAMPING; FALLS THROUGH ICE; FISHING; HEART STOPPAGE; NECK FRACTURES; SCUBA DIVING; SWIMMING POOLS.

DRUG ALLERGY Ironically nearly every chemical that aids in the fight against disease is also a potential cause of allergic illness. An emergency medical identification can be a lifesaver in known drug allergies. Unless a warning is prominently displayed, an accident victim may be given a drug that can kill him.

Severe allergic responses to drugs include a life-threatening reaction called anaphylaxis, which can occur within seconds. The symptoms may include generalized itching and body flushing, followed by shock and occasionally death.

Serum sickness is a delayed reaction that may appear as long as two weeks after medication was discontinued; it is marked by hives, enlargement of lymph glands, joint pains and swelling, and fever.

Other reactions to drugs include asthma and inflammation of the skin. Some drugs induce excessive, sunburnlike sensitivity to sunlight. Inflammation of the heart muscle (myocarditis) and other heart ailments are occasionally associated with allergic symptoms and may be the result of drug sensitivity. Blood vessels and connective tissues in almost any organ of the body may be affected by drug reactions with resulting disturbance of function.

Allergic drug reactions usually have no direct relationship to dosage, and may often result from very small amounts. Symptoms can be caused by potent new compounds or by ordinary household remedies like aspirin.

Chances of sensitization increase as treatment with a particular drug continues or as courses of treatment are repeated frequently. The fact that you have tolerated a drug on previous occasions is no guarantee that allergic symptoms will not occur after the next dose. Indeed it is rare to have an allergic reaction to a medication you have not encountered in the past. In long-term treatment with a drug reactions are most prone to occur during the first six weeks of therapy.

Penicillin sensitivity. Be especially cautious of penicillin. It is the most effective antibiotic for treatment of many diseases. But the penicillins and the widely used sulfonamides are the drugs most likely to cause allergic reactions.

Doctors are advised not to use penicillin when the patient has had a previous penicillin reaction of any kind.

Active cases of some types of fungus infections, notably ringworm, may flare up with the use of penicillin. Inform your physician when you encounter suspicions of further penicillin allergy. This could come from foods containing penicillin mold, such as beer, bleu and Roquefort cheese, milk, fowl; from viral vaccines that may have sensitizing properties; even from an infection that you may develop.

Neomycin may also be troublesome. Increasing reports of skin allergies from neomycin creams and ointments suggest that sensitivity to this widely used antibiotic is more of a problem than was previously recognized. Neomycin is an ingredient of more than 100 products for skin, ear, and eye infections. A particularly high incidence of sensitization appears to be associated with the long-term use of neomycin in the treatment of leg ulcers.

In addition many people are allergic not to the drug itself but to the fluid containing it—like the horse serum that is the medium for tetanus antitoxin. Sensitivity to medication can sometimes be determined beforehand with a skin test.

Liver damage may occur as the result of sensitivity to certain tranquilizers, sulfonamides, antituberculous agents, some antibiotics, hormones (especially testosterone), gold salts used in the treatment of arthritis, and drugs used to treat overactivity of the thyroid gland. Fever is a common symptom of drug reactions, usually associated with other symptoms of allergy. Among the more common causes of drug fever are quinine, sulfonamides, and certain blood pressure and antithyroid medications.

Handling a drug allergy. Discontinuation of a suspected drug will result in improvement within 48 hours in most instances. If symptoms produced by the drug reaction are extremely severe or unduly prolonged, drugs used to control allergic symptoms are employed, including Adrenalin, antihistamines, and cortisone.

For reasons not entirely understood there is less likelihood of allergic reactions to penicillin and some other drugs when taken by mouth than by injection.

Skin creams, lotions, and ointments are even more prone than injections to cause sensitivity.

If you're sensitive to a drug, be sure your medical records in your family doctor's office note your allergy. Remember that any *new* doctor (in a hospital emergency room, one you consult while on vacation or in the military) will not know about it.

Always remind any physician or nurse—before he or she gives you any injection—that you have had a previous reaction.

If you're allergic to penicillin, you needn't worry about what your doctor will do if you should ever need penicillin to fight an infection. There are many other antibiotics he can choose from.

See also ALLERGY; ANTIBIOTICS; DRUGS; EMERGENCY MEDICAL IDENTIFICATION.

DRUGS are two-edged swords. They may cause problems as well as bring relief.

Every drug poses the threat of a reaction—allergic or otherwise.

Without delay phone your physician or get to a hospital emergency room for any severe change in your condition—including any that may be attributable to a medication.

First aid for overdose. In case of drug poisoning or overdosage: Induce vomiting. (Keep an emetic such as Ipechar—ipecac syrup and activated charcoal—among your medical supplies.) Alternate doses of emetic (vomit inducer) and water until only clear fluid is thrown up. Drinking additional large amounts of water can help speed elimination of the drug.

If the victim is unconscious, don't try to force vomiting or give him fluids. To keep spontaneous vomiting from clogging his breathing passages, lay him facedown with his body inclined so his feet are higher than his head. Summon a doctor or ambulance or get him to an emergency room.

Show the doctor the drug container; the name and dosage of the drug can speed proper treatment.

Have a physician look over anyone who's been drug poisoned or possibly overdosed. Aspirin poisoning in children, and toxic doses of barbiturates and other drugs may not show their effects for several hours. (See box for ways to prevent drug accidents.)

Reactions to illegal drugs. Marijuana in rare cases leads to panic and disorientation. If someone is frightened by his reaction, encourage him to keep his eyes open, since this generally reduces the intensity of the fantasies.

Hold him in your arms. Speak to him softly and reassuringly. You may speed his return to reality by asking simple questions: "What's your name?" "Who am I?" "What color are my eyes?"

Use the same "soft landing" technique with other hallucinogens as well. LSD, psilocybin, and mescaline are more likely than marijuana to produce "bad trips," particularly since these drugs are often badly synthesized.

If the person is extremely agitated and can't be "talked down," seek medical help. (Calling the police may start a legal proceeding.) Hospital emergency rooms are used to handling drug reactions and can provide the proper tranquilizer and keep the person under observation. Also seek medical assistance if there is a severe physical reaction, usually from impurities.

The "flashback" or sudden recurrence of an LSD-like state is "usually transient or harmless," according to *The Medical Letter*. A flashback may be triggered by marijuana and antihistamines. Occasionally, despite supportive psychotherapy and sedation, there's a prolonged state of confusion. Severe depression or a psychosis sometimes follows use of LSD.

Heroin—and other narcotics like Demerol (meperidine), morphine, and methadone—can severely depress breathing and heart action. Be prepared to give artificial respiration and treat for heart stoppage and shock. An emergency room may administer a drug like Nalline or Narcan, which blocks the effects of narcotics.

An addict withdrawing from narcotics is in no special physical danger, though he is likely to suffer from anxiety. Physical discomfort, likened to that of influenza, generally passes in a day or two. Withdrawal may be helped by participation in a methadone-maintenance or other drug program.

For handling reactions to other drugs see AM-PHETAMINES; BARBITURATES; GLUE SNIFFING. See also ARTIFICIAL RESPIRATION; HEART STOP-PAGE; SHOCK.

Cautions about drugs. In addition to allergies there are other problems related to drugs—the information about any specific drug is available in the descriptive literature inserted in the package, and in *Physicians' Desk Reference,* a widely distributed directory of drugs. When your doctor prescribes a drug, discuss any potential problems with him.

In addition to a record of your drug allergies your medical records should carry a running drug history (see sample). Have each doctor you see read it and update it with the drugs he prescribes. Such a chart indicates what drugs you have taken safely—and can protect you from getting drugs that are unsafe for any condition you might have or are incompatible with each other. You ought to know about any of the following:

Contraindications. These are medical indications *against* your taking particular drugs. For example, pregnancy contraindicates most nonessential drugs, since they may injure the unborn infant. Infectious disease, diabetes, and a host of other ailments may contraindicate steroids, which can worsen these conditions.

Side effects. Some drugs have such severe possible reactions that you need frequent monitoring by your doctor—for example, chloramphenicol (Chloromycetin), which can interfere with blood cell production.

Others—like tranquilizers and antihistamines—can cause drowsiness, making it unsafe for you to operate a car or machine. Still others, including amphetamines and steroids, can cause personality changes. Some prescription analgesics can lead to addiction. Often a drug regimen can be adjusted to reduce side effects, as in treatment for high blood pressure.

You'll also want to be reassured about side effects that could cause worry but are harmless—iron for anemia blackens bowel movements; Pyridium for urinary tract infection turns urine orange.

It's helpful to know about self-limiting reactions to many drugs—minor rashes, mouth dryness, headache—that may disappear even before the drug is discontinued.

Drug interactions. Tell your doctor of any drugs you're taking. Ask him about any you should avoid.

One drug may keep another from working. For example, Aureomycin blocks penicillin; barbiturates inhibit anticoagulants. Conversely, drugs may have an additive effect—alcohol enhances antihistamines, barbiturates, and tranquilizers.

Warnings and precautions. Ask your physician or pharmacist about the oddities of any drugs you're to take. Some drugs can interact with foods, and should be taken on an empty stomach. By contrast, some are irritating to the stomach, so should be taken just after meals. Some should be swallowed whole without chewing, because they have special coatings or can stain your teeth or irritate your mouth. Also ask how alcohol may interact with the medication.

Some drugs require unusually large amounts of fluids. But some are inactivated by milk and milk products. Some are destroyed by the acids in fruit juice—whereas with some diuretics and steroids you're advised to drink lots of orange juice to add potassium to your diet.

Dangers of self-medication. Don't doctor yourself with any nonprescription medication for more than ten days. If a problem persists beyond that or is unusually intense, you need a physician.

Self-medication may prevent recognition of a serious disease. A person suffering from gas may dose himself with antacids—until his peptic ulcer perforates. Someone may take cough syrup to ease his chronic coughing and postpone diagnosis of tuberculosis. A headache of unusual severity may be self-treated with aspirin when it's actually a symptom of hypertension, demanding prompt care by a physician.

Without consulting a physician, never take a drug prescribed for another person. When a doctor writes a prescription, he considers not only the illness, but also the body size and drug history of the individual to be taking them.

You may have an idiosyncratic response, an unpredictable bad reaction to a drug that was harmless for the person it was prescribed for. Or someone else's prescription—even an old one of your own—may be for another condition entirely, though to a layman symptoms seem the same.

Beware the temptation to quit taking your medicine prematurely. An infection may be down but not out. Going off antibiotics too soon may open you up to a relapse. Hypertension and diabetes are notoriously free of symptoms that might otherwise spur victims to stay on medication.

Many patients slip into noncompliance because they don't understand the physician's instructions. If your doctor tells you, "Take these pills three times a day with meals," ask if it's more important to take them thrice daily or take them when you eat. Many medical dropouts don't accept the reality of an illness, thus resent the changes it brings to their way of life. It may help you stay on medication if you ask, "What will happen to me if I don't take it?"

If you are tempted to stop taking medication because you choke or gag when swallowing tablets or capsules, try this nonstick trick: Place the pill under the tip of your tongue behind your lower front teeth. As you swallow the water, your tongue normally turns upward and the pill follows the water without adhering to your mouth or throat. You can place several tablets under your tongue together and swallow them all at once.

Don't overdose. People tend to believe that if a small amount is good, more will do better. But if consumed in excessive amounts many otherwise safe medications can be toxic. The margin of safety is often relatively low.

Be especially cautious about playing doctor to your children. Children are not little adults from the standpoint of disease. When sick, children are less able to tolerate many drugs than adults are, and dosage for children is more critical than for adults. If a child balks at taking medicine, as last resort employ an immobilizing "hug" (see illustration).

Nonprescription drugs. Over-the-counter (OTC) drugs rarely do more than relieve symptoms of self-limiting conditions. Unlike prescription drugs these patent medicines can't "cure"— do away with the basic cause of an illness.

But, like prescription drugs, OTCs can cause adverse reactions. If you use an OTC drug, follow directions exactly. A major reason the Food and Drug Administration (FDA) does not require prescriptions for such drugs is that they're safe "for most people if used according to instructions that can be put on a label."

Pay particular heed to contraindications, side effects, drug interactions, and other warnings. Responsible manufacturers emphasize signs that indicate you should stop taking the drug and call a doctor (for example, "Discontinue if rapid pulse, dizziness, or blurring of vision occurs").

If you have a history of drug allergy, examine the label to make sure the product does not contain the agent to which you're sensitive. If you can't positively identify the ingredients of a preparation as being safe for you, don't take it.

Keep within the recommended dosage. Avoid using more than one OTC drug at a time. You may be taking the same ingredients twice and thus go over the limit. For example, two antihis-

WHEN A CHILD WON'T TAKE MEDICINE

How to give drugs gently but firmly
Immobilize youngster, control mouth

tamines in different preparations may combine to produce drowsiness where one alone may not.

If your doctor has prescribed one drug for you, don't self-medicate with an OTC compound at the same time. You may have a reaction to the combined medications.

Save money on drugs. Take the following steps to keep your drug bills down:

Check that a prescription is really needed. Though a medicine is available over the counter, some doctors fear that without prescription (Rx), patients will forget to buy it or neglect instructions for taking it.

However as soon as a drug becomes a prescription item, its cost goes up if only because of the pharmacist's handling. Some cough syrups handled as prescriptions cost 50 percent more than if bought off the shelf.

Ask for samples. Physicians are deluged with free samples from pharmaceutical houses. Often they're put in a cabinet and forgotten until they're thrown away. Most doctors are only too happy to give you drugs they have on hand.

Cautions: Make sure the sample hasn't expired. And ask about side effects, which may not appear on the professional package or be comprehensible to laymen.

Find out if you can use leftover drugs. Whenever a member of your family gets a prescription, ask the doctor to have it labeled with the names of the drug, its concentration, and the expiration date (after which the medication is no longer sure to be effective). Then if it's needed again, the doctor may permit you to use it.

To preserve medicines keep them in your bedroom. The bathroom is generally a poor place for drug storage, because high temperatures and humidity speed up drug deterioration.

For the same reason use only the original container. After more than a day or so, pillboxes and other substitute containers may not preserve drug quality. Don't transfer drugs to containers formerly used for foods or other medicines; a wrong label can lead to confusion, and the new and old contents may interact.

Suggest that your doctor prescribe by chemical name. A brand-name drug almost always costs more than the identical preparation sold by its generic (chemical) name. A Senate subcommittee found that the same antihypertensive cost fully 30 times more if sold as Serpasil rather than as plain reserpine.

When you bring a generic Rx to your pharmacist, look for a further saving by asking him to fill it with the least expensive make of the drug he has on hand from a reliable manufacturer. Some drugstore owners claim that generic drugs are inferior. In general, however, the FDA Bureau of Drugs has been unable to find a significant difference in quality between the generic and brand-name products that have been tested.

Ask for the lowest-priced brand when no generic equivalent is available.

Compare ingredients before buying OTC drugs. Forget brand names and read labels. As with aspirin identical products may have great variations in price.

If honestly labeled all items marked USP are made to the same formula. Additional ingredients—like caffeine added to aspirin—may be junk that will not help you. Your best bargain is likely to be the house brand in a large store.

Seek the most economical sizes. Typically, doctors prescribe a round number of tablets, perhaps 25 or 100. This means that if you need a change of drug, or if you recover before the prescription runs out, you're stuck with the nonreturnable remainder.

The best strategy is to start out with a small quantity—a few days' dosage, with an authorization on the Rx for refills. Thereafter, if you're going to be on the medication for a long time, seek a prescription for a large amount—500 tablets, say. That way you get a lower per-tablet or per-ounce rate and you pay for the pharmacist's services less often.

Larger-dosage tablets are proportionately cheaper. Suppose your doctor instructs you to take two 25-mg tablets so many times a day. The prescription will cost you less if you can take one 50-mg tablet instead.

For continuing treatment request medication you can take yourself. You'll save the cost of the office visit and injection if oral medication will do just as well as regular shots. In some cases tablets are preferable—if vitamins are needed, for example, daily tablets are generally more effective than weekly injections.

Shop around for a drugstore? Ideally, you'd have a family pharmacist much as you'd have a family physician. A strong case can be made for choosing a pharmacist—a specialist in the uses of drugs—according to his service and accessibility rather than his charges. It can be priceless to have a pharmacist whom you can confide in and who gives you adequate instructions and maintains your drug history (your "patient profile") to guard against adverse reactions. If you have a traditional community pharmacy available, consider buying all your drugs, including OTCs, from that one source.

However, for many patients such pharmacies are not readily available or price is a pressing issue. Then it can pay to shop around.

An AMA survey of Chicago pharmacies found that some charged 12 times as much as others to fill identical prescriptions. On the same street in Los Angeles, *Money* magazine discovered one store charging twice as much as the other for the same Rx.

Ask your pharmacist what a prescription will cost before he fills it. If you feel the price is too high—or if he refuses to give you the price in advance—get on the phone and try other stores. For refills, if your state's laws allow it, move your prescription from one store to another if you can get a better price.

You're likely to find the pharmacies that generally charge least in discount department stores or in high-volume stores in business districts and shopping centers. Different branches of a chain may have different prices, so check each store individually.

Also, be mindful that chain discounters often have a "top 100" list: fast-moving drugs that are discounted and give a low-price image. For a less frequently prescribed drug, however, they may charge higher fees than a community pharmacy, making up for lost profit. Further, many chains won't stock or order drugs that community pharmacies routinely keep on hand.

Avoid hospital pharmacies unless you're a patient. They tend to be high-priced because they must stock hundreds of medications that may never be used. When you're discharged as a pa-tient, get your going-home prescriptions filled elsewhere.

Consider mail-order pharmacies. Even cheaper than your least expensive nearby phar-macy may be one hundreds of miles away that can serve you by mail. Mail-order druggists can especially benefit you if you're housebound, lack transportation, or need continuous medication

---

PROTECT YOURSELF FROM DRUG DISASTERS

Make a card on which every doctor you see can review and update the information indicated on this running drug-history form, devised by internist Gerard J. Aitken, Jr., of Hightstown, New Jersey.

Drug Reactions and Allergies:

LIST ALL:

Date	R Medicine and Size	Sig. Dose	For Prescriptions		
			R No.	Disp.	Rfills
	1				
	2				
	3				
	4				
	5				
	6				
	7				
	8				
	9				
	10				
	11				
	12				
	13				
	14				
	15				
	16				

HOW TO AVOID DRUG ACCIDENTS

1. Discard all prescriptions on their expiration date. Dump any drug that has changed color, odor, consistency, or shows signs of mold or other deterioration.
2. Store medicines in a cabinet or drawer, preferably locked, away from the reach of children. Most drug poisoning takes place when children find medicine that is not in its usual safe place. Remind relatives to put drugs and other potential poisons out of reach of visiting children.
3. Replace torn or lost drug labels. Cover labels with transparent tape to keep them legible. Pour liquid label side up to keep the label clean. Put a big red X on medicines that shouldn't be swallowed.
4. Read the label in a good light before opening the bottle or box. Read it again before taking the medicine. Be especially careful at night when you're too sleepy to read and understand labels.
5. Keep just one night's supply of pills on your nightstand. Otherwise, in the confusion of darkness and sleep, you can take a dangerously wrong amount.
6. Don't take or give medicine in front of a child, who may mimic you. Never refer to medicine as candy to get a child to take it, or make the giving of medicine a game. Keep purses out of reach of children—they often contain medicine.

---

for chronic conditions. About the only drugs you'll have difficulty buying by mail are amphetamines, narcotics, and some other controlled substances.

Pharmaceutical Services, Inc. (127 West Markey Road, Belton, Missouri 64012), is a large mail-order pharmacy serving the general public. An organization-sponsored mail-order distributor is the pharmacy service of the National Retired Teachers Association and American Association of Retired Persons (1909 K Street, NW, Washington, D.C. 20006). You may qualify for membership in the AARP—its age-50 requirement is well below normal retirement age. The pharmacy's low prices more than offset the AARP's nominal dues.

Bargain over the price of refills. Seek a quantity discount because of the total amount you'll be buying. You're in the best bargaining position if you need constant refills for a chronic illness.

Take advantage of drug benefits you're entitled to. The Veterans Administration has a free drug service for beneficiaries. Many health-insurance plans have pharmacy services.

If you're a senior citizen, pharmacies may give you discounts.

See also ACCIDENTS; ALCOHOL; AMPHETAMINES; ANALGESICS; ANEMIA; ANTACIDS; ANTIBIOTICS; ANTICOAGULANTS; ANTIHISTAMINES.

ARTIFICIAL RESPIRATION; ASPIRIN; BARBITURATES; BLOOD PRESSURE; DIARRHEA; DRUG ALLERGY; EMERGENCY MEDICAL IDENTIFICATION; GLUE SNIFFING.

HEALTH INSURANCE; HEART STOPPAGE; IRON; MEDICAL DEDUCTIONS; POISONING; PREGNANCY; QUACKERY; SHOCK; STEROIDS; TRANQUILIZERS; VITAMINS.

DUODENAL ULCER See PEPTIC ULCER.

DUST DISEASE (pneumoconiosis) is a category of respiratory disease caused by inhaling the heavy, often harmful dusts produced by various kinds of mining or in certain types of jobs. Unless the worker's nose and mouth and throat are protected, bits of dust can work their way down to the air pockets of the lung.

The dust of asbestos, which can lead to asbestosis and some types of cancer, is most dangerous to the general public.

The most common dust disease is silicosis—the result of inhaling silica, or quartz dust. The disease is also known as miner's phthisis, potter's asthma, grinder's rot, or stonecutter's disease. It is insidious, sometimes not showing symptoms—shortness of breath, coughing—until after 30 years of exposure. It is irreversible.

All types of mining in which the ore is found in quartz rock can produce silicosis. This includes the mining of gold, lead, zinc, iron copper, anthracite coal, and some bituminous coal. Other jobs that have often led to silicosis are sandstone grinding, sandblasting, pottery and china making, granite carving, and various foundry jobs.

Silicosis develops in direct proportion to the amount of silica you breathe in and the length of time you are exposed to it. It is believed that silica slowly dissolves within the lungs and produces a chemical reaction that poisons the cells, causing damage and scarring. Complicating diseases such as tuberculosis and emphysema may develop.

Other major dust diseases are:

Bagassosis. From inhaling bagasse (sugarcane fibers) in insulating and accoustical material, fertilizer, explosives, animal feed. Shows symptoms within a week of exposure. Marked by shortness of breath and wheezing.

Berylliosis. From fumes of beryllium salts, dust from beryllium ore; working on electronic instruments, aircraft engines, rocket and atomic energy materials. Acute form may develop after a few weeks with symptoms of colds and sore throat. Chronic after 6 to 18 months, with shortness of breath, coughing, weight loss.

Byssinosis. From cotton, flax, and hemp fibers. May occur within weeks of initial exposure or almost immediately. Shortness of breath, chest tightness.

Black lung (coal workers' pneumoconiosis, anthracosilicosis). From coal dust. Onset after exposure of as little as two years. Worsening shortness of breath, coughing, chest tightness.

Discontinue exposure. The progress of these diseases cannot be stopped unless exposure to dust is discontinued. Young workers often do best to find another type of work. Older workers may be able to get another job within the company, away from dust exposure.

Anyone with dust disease needs to give up smoking. Weight watching is in order, since excess weight places a burden on already strained lungs. Physical examinations every three months are needed to guard against complications and worsening of the condition.

Nearly all cases of dust disease are preventable through proper controls. Sometimes the dust level can be reduced by such means as face masks; piping of clean air into a closed hood over the worker's head; removing dust by suction as it is produced; wetting down materials before they are worked on; switching from a harmful material to a safe one.

See also ASBESTOS; CANCER OF THE LUNG; COUGHING; EMPHYSEMA; RESPIRATORY DISEASE; SHORTNESS OF BREATH; SMOKING; TUBERCULOSIS.

DYSENTERY, AMEBIC See AMEBIC DYSENTERY.

DYSENTERY, BACILLARY See SHIGELLOSIS.

DYSPNEA See SHORTNESS OF BREATH.

EARACHE is a common symptom of ear infections. Children often suffer from earache with fever as a result of colds and other upper respiratory infections. With prompt medical treatment serious complications can almost always be avoided.

To relieve the pain of earache until you can reach a doctor, try aspirin. Resting the ear on hot compresses—a hot-water bottle or an electric heating pad—may bring some relief. Codeine in cough medicine is an effective painkiller and may relieve the earache. But give the cough medicine only to the person for whom it was prescribed. All these remedies may be used simultaneously if the earache is especially severe.

Sometimes distress is caused by an insect trapped in the ear. First kill the insect with a few drops of rubbing alcohol (vodka would do in a pinch). Then gently flush it out with water at body temperature.

Earache can also be a "referred pain," arising from a problem outside the ear. Persistent earache without ear disease requires a doctor's evaluation.

See also COLDS; EAR INFECTION; HEARING LOSS.

EAR DEFORMITIES such as large, flattened, or protruding ears can often be corrected by plastic surgery (otoplasty).

The operation is most commonly performed on children with protruding ears, improving their appearance and aiding their social adjustment. The physician usually makes the incision behind the ears so that scar tissue is hidden.

The procedure is often done on an outpatient basis, or the patient is usually discharged from the hospital the day after the operation. A bandage is worn over the ears for a few days while the swelling and bruising subside. Feelings of numbness may persist for several weeks.

Look for a surgeon trained to perform otoplasty, either a general plastic surgeon or an otolaryngologist specializing in facial plastic surgery. Most such specialists belong to the American Association of Plastic Surgeons, the American Society of Plastic and Reconstructive Surgeons, or the American Academy of Facial Plastic and Reconstructive Surgery.

See also SURGERY.

EAR INFECTIONS can result in hearing loss, especially in children under ten years old. Children commonly develop infections of the middle ear (otitis media) following an upper respiratory infection. Sometimes allergy is a precipitating factor. Middle-ear infections may also follow childhood diseases such as chickenpox, measles, and scarlet fever.

The first symptoms of an ear infection are earache and a high fever. The pain is usually worse at night. There may be nausea and vomiting. An

HOW TO GIVE EARDROPS

Avoid trapping air in ear canal
(Bubbles keep drops from penetrating)

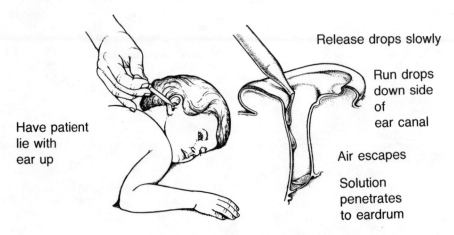

Have patient
lie with
ear up

Release drops slowly

Run drops
down side
of
ear canal

Air escapes

Solution
penetrates
to eardrum

infant with an aching ear may signal by pulling on the ear or turning the head from side to side.

Ear infections can result from improperly blowing the nose. Gently blow one nostril at a time. Holding both nostrils closed and blowing hard can force the infected mucus from the back of the nose into the middle ear.

If untreated, serious infections of the middle ear can spread, possibly rupturing the eardrum and causing mastoiditis, a potentially fatal condition. Eardrops are commonly required (see illustration). Early treatment with antibiotics can prevent these complications. The medication should be taken for the full time prescribed, usually ten days.

Occasionally an infected ear will have to be drained to relieve discomfort and prevent possible hearing loss. This procedure is called a myringotomy.

Infections of the ear canal may be caused by fungi or bacteria that thrive in warm, moist earwax. Any hard, encrusted wax should be removed before going on a vacation that includes swimming—the precaution may prevent a form of ear canal infection called "swimmer's ear."

An ear canal infection may lead to swelling and boils in the membranes that line the canal. Intense itching may be a symptom of ear canal infections. Don't scratch—you may worsen the infection. If itching persists, see a doctor. An untreated outer-ear infection can travel to the eardrum and the middle ear.

Infection can also result from small objects lodged in the ear. Young children sometimes push beads or pencil erasers into the ear canal. Any attempt to dislodge such an object may push it farther into the ear. Have a doctor remove it.

See also HEARING LOSS.

EAR PIERCING should be done by a physician. Although the jeweler, a friend, or Grandma may be good with a needle and ice cube, they are not as equipped as a physician to prevent infections and scars that can be disfiguring. Nor are they likely to spot the person for whom ear piercing could bring trouble.

Self–ear-piercers are similarly unsafe. These devices have sharp points that are supposed to pierce the ears within a few days while they are worn. Although some self-piercers advertise that they won't cause infections because the points are made of 14-karat gold, a number of severe infections have been traced to their use.

If piercing is done outside a physician's office, hygiene needs to be especially strict. The needle —and the trainers for keeping the puncture open —need to be sterilized by being boiled for 20 minutes. Merely washing them off with alcohol or hydrogen peroxide falls far short of required sanitation. The ears need to be scrubbed with an antiseptic, and the hair draped back to avoid contaminating the puncture site.

Special care is needed in marking the puncture spot to make the earrings look even despite differences of shape and size between the earlobes. This is another hazard of self-piercers. Without help it's almost impossible to place them evenly.

Avoid ear piercing if your ears have any type of rash or infection. Also be warned away by a bad case of acne or the presence of small sebaceous cysts in your earlobes. Any of these conditions predispose you to infection, which can result in severe scarring:

Don't have your ears pierced at all if you have a tendency to form keloids, which are excessively thick outgrowths of tissue. This tendency is commonest among girls with dark skin and may be evident in old scar formations.

Another common problem is a skin reaction because of a nickel allergy. Nickel is an ingredient in many alloys, including gold. Even if you've shown no previous metal allergy, it's safest to use pure gold, silver, or stainless steel for ear wires.

Silver wire earrings, sold in many jewelry stores, are the best trainers. If swelling occurs, they cause less pain and pressure than training earrings with posts. However the thin wire earrings need to be worn from three to four weeks, a week or so longer than earrings with posts.

Newly pierced ears have two puncture wounds, opening them to contamination on both sides of the ear lobe. Wear your hair back from your ears, and don't use hair coloring or bleach until the openings are completely healed. Wash your hands before touching the ears. Three times a day, cleanse the lobes with alcohol and rotate the trainers to keep them free. Otherwise keep fingers away from the site. Immediately report to your doctor any tightness, swelling, pain, redness, or loss of part of a trainer. Check with him before removing the trainers.

See also CONTACT DERMATITIS; EAR INFECTIONS; KELOIDS.

EARWAX is a normal secretion that accumulates in the external ear canal. It protects the canal from moisture, insects, and other objects.

If too much wax accumulates, it sometimes fills the ear canal and impairs hearing. When the wax forms a hard plug in the ear, water can get trapped behind it and cause irritation and discomfort. A doctor's help is needed to remove a large accumulation of hardened earwax.

Doctors recommend never putting anything smaller than an elbow in an ear. Cotton tips, hairpins, and toothpicks tend to push the wax farther into the ear canal and can easily damage the eardrum.

For routine removal of normal accumulations of wax doctors recommend softening it with a drop or two of olive oil or mineral oil. Or the doctor may recommend a commercial preparation, such as Debrox or Cerumenex, for loosening wax. Another preparation that works is Milkinol (mineral oil and dioctyl sodium sulfosuccinate), sold as a laxative.

Then the softened wax can be flushed out under the shower or with a gentle stream of body temperature water from a soft rubber syringe.

Some physicians report good results using a dental irrigator—such as Water Pik, which comes with a special attachment for ear cleaning at little additional cost. If the patient's eardrum is intact, the physician may add an ounce of isopropyl alcohol or baking soda to the water in the reservoir of the dental irrigator to aid in cleaning.

See also EAR INFECTIONS; HEARING LOSS.

ECLIPSES During an eclipse of the sun, visible in Australia, no fewer than 170 people suffered eye injuries. Many had used sunglasses and other filters. Some had viewed the eclipse for as little as ten seconds.

The moon's passing in front of the sun blocks out visible rays that might normally deter you from looking into the sun. But the eclipse does not eliminate the sun's infrared rays, which can be just as damaging. The rays can burn blind spots into the retina, the delicate layer of tissue in the back of the eyeball where visual images are focused before transmission to the brain. There is no immediate discomfort to warn you, since the retina lacks nerve endings capable of transmitting pain.

The only safe way to avoid this is to watch an eclipse by means of a simple reflective viewer fashioned from two pieces of white cardboard. Punch a pinhole in one piece and, with the sun over your shoulder, hold it several feet above the other. Manipulate the top cardboard until the sun's image is focused through the pinhole onto the second cardboard.

Avoid colored glasses, smoked glasses, and sheets of exposed photographic film—none of these are sufficiently effective as filters.

See also EYE DISORDER; EYE INJURIES.

ECZEMA (allergic dermatitis) produces red scaling, oozing, and severely itching eruptions that may appear anywhere on the body. Chronic eczema leads to thickening and discoloring of the skin, which becomes progressively more resistant to treatment.

Itchiness comes first. A rash appears and becomes worse when scratched and rubbed. The skin cracks, may "weep" or be constantly moist, then crusty as the moisture dries. There are likely to be repeated flare-ups.

Eczema in children. One of the most common types of allergy, eczema usually begins in infancy as an itching rash on the face, then on the neck, folds of elbows, and knees. Severe cases may spread over the whole body.

Most cases, especially the mild ones, disappear spontaneously or become less severe before the child is two years old. If the first attack occurs well before puberty, the chances are good that the child may outgrow it.

The most stubborn cases may persist through adult life, and the skin will become dry and rough, grayish or sallow in color, with crusting, scaling, or thickened areas.

A large percentage of those who have had eczema in infancy develop other allergies, such as hay fever and asthma. Sufferers usually come from families with an allergic history.

In many cases the cause remains unknown. Food allergy is believed the most common cause in infants. Older patients may be allergic to airborne substances such as dust, pollen, and molds. Wool clothing and blankets produce trouble when against the skin.

Emotional factors may aggravate the condition, but there is no proof that these by themselves actually cause eczema. Marked changes in weather also seem to aggravate it.

Treating eczema. Hot water, wet compresses, and starch baths often relieve the itching. Bland lotions and ointments may also help. Corticosteroid creams are used for limited periods in some cases. Antihistamines may be prescribed to suppress the itch.

It is helpful to prevent the skin from becoming excessively dry, which is a problem during the winter in heated houses. Someone with eczema will do better if the temperature can be kept at a steady, moderate degree and the humidity at 30 to 50 percent. (Use a humidifier if necessary.)

Precautions. It may be possible to prevent or minimize eczema. Breastfeeding decreases the possibility of a food allergy, though the nursing mother may transmit some food traces to the infant. In allergic families give the infant the common allergy-producing foods with caution— egg and fresh cow's milk, for example. Evaporated milk or goat's milk might be better. Some children require substitutes such as protein formula (e.g., Nutramigen) or soy milk (Isomil, Nursoy, ProSobee).

Be especially careful with any new chemical, or any chemical used in a new way that brings it into closer contact with a person's skin. Some of the culprits are new finishes being used in clothing, such as the finishes that produce a permanent press.

See also ALLERGY; FOOD ALLERGY; HUMIDITY; ITCHING.

EDEMA is the abnormal collection of fluid in tissue spaces. Often there is swelling of the legs and ankles. Fluid may collect in the lungs (pulmonary edema) and abdomen. A common form of edema is found in a swollen finger (see illustration).

Unless the blood is kept moving regularly through the arteries, capillaries, and veins, the fluid portion will begin to leak out, chiefly in the capillary beds. A most common reason blood flow becomes sluggish is heart failure. Physicians sometimes prescribe diuretics to help remove through the kidneys some of the accumulated fluid. Sodium, which tends to promote the retention of body fluid, is also eliminated, and its intake restricted.

Another common cause of edema is blockage of a blood vessel, most often a vein, by a clot. Such a block will cause the blood to back up, with leakage of fluid into the tissues.

Edema may also result from inflammation and be a result of infectious disease.

See also BLOOD CLOT; HEART DISEASE; HEART FAILURE; RESPIRATORY DISEASE; SODIUM.

EDEMA, ANGIONEUROTIC See HIVES.

ELBOW FRACTURES See ARM FRACTURES.

ELBOW, TENNIS See TENNIS ELBOW.

ELECTRIC SHOCK can kill. Large currents can cause muscular contractions that keep the victim from letting go of the source of electricity.

Immediately separate a victim from the current. Switch it off or pull out the plug. Never cut a live wire. You may be burned by the flash or whipped by the hot end.

Don't touch the victim when the current is on unless your hand is thickly insulated with rubber, dry cloth, or paper—or you may be endangered too. If no other method is handy, remove him from the contact or pull away the wire with a dry rope or a long dry stick such as the handle of a broom or mop (see illustration).

Make sure your hands are dry and you are standing on a dry board or are protected by a dry, nonconducting material such as rubber—a mat or rubber soles. Beware any moisture—it conducts electricity. Wood that's green or damp is a better conductor than many metals.

Outdoors the danger from high-tension wires is much greater. You can be electrocuted merely by walking near a downed wire. Telephone the power company to turn off the current before you attempt rescue. If you're in a car that has knocked down a utility pole, stay in the car until the power is off. Because of the conductivity of green wood, steer clear of any tree touching a power line.

Electric shock can cause unconsciousness, absence of breathing, a weak pulse or none at all, burns, and violent muscular spasms. The shock can paralyze nerves so that the heart stops beating or pumps ineffectively.

As soon as the victim is free of the current, start artificial respiration. If his heart has

TO UNSCREW A RING FROM A SWOLLEN FINGER

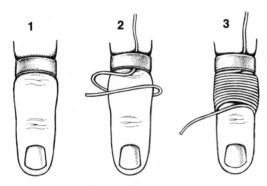

1. Push ring to knuckle
   Lubricate finger with soap, oil, grease
2. Slip string under ring
3. Wrap lower end tightly

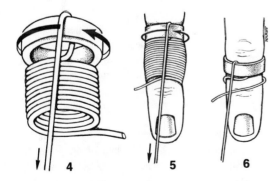

4. Pull down upper end
5. Ring moves down finger
   Follows unwrapping string
6. Ring slides over joint

IN CASE OF ELECTRIC SHOCK

Break contact with current!

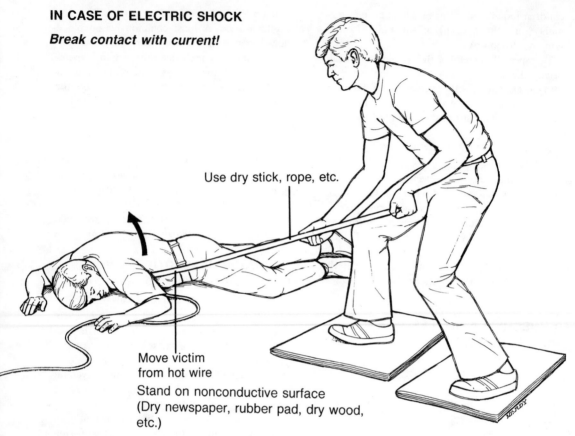

Use dry stick, rope, etc.

Move victim
from hot wire

Stand on nonconductive surface
(Dry newspaper, rubber pad, dry wood,
etc.)

stopped beating, begin heart massage for heart stoppage. Have someone call a physician.

Survivors of electric shock often show symptoms of panic. They may be trembling, pale, and sweating. Paralysis of an arm or leg may last up to four hours. Pain and stiffness may continue for months.

The most obvious injuries that result from electric current passing through the body are heat burns of the skin and superficial tissues. Damage to tissues deep within the body may not be immediately obvious. There should be careful X-ray follow-up because bone damage may appear months or even years later. A pinpoint skin burn may give little warning of extensive damage that may have occurred.

Electrical safety. To avoid electric shock keep wires of household appliances in good repair. When the nonconducting rubber or fabric covering is frayed, you may be exposed to the current. The point of exposure need be only a tiny fraction of an inch to cause shock. Wires fray most when they're under carpets, knotted, or bent around corners.

Protect children from electrical accidents. Many children suffer disfiguring mouth burns

after chewing through plugged-in cords. Others are severely burned when they try to pull plugs from electric cord sockets with their teeth. Still others are badly shocked when they stick pins, paper clips, even fingers into wall outlets.

Avoid using extension cords. If you must use one, buy the kind with self-closing outlets. Cord shorteners are useful in keeping extension cords to the required length, preventing a family pet from pulling the socket from behind a piece of furniture and exposing it to a curious baby.

Insert safety caps into unused outlets or cover them with tape. Don't leave the socket of a lamp exposed—it's safer to fill it with a burned-out bulb than to leave it empty for exploring fingers.

Beware leakage of current. Sometimes the insulation in an appliance is badly made or becomes damaged. A slight tingling or unpleasant shock is a warning that electricity is leaking. Have appliances checked when this happens.

An electric appliance with a short circuit may have an outer metal shell as electrically live as the power line to which it is connected. If you touch this shell, you'll feel a shock if another portion of your body simultaneously touches a ground—any electricity-conducting material that enters the earth or touches a conductor that enters the earth. Electricity takes the shortest and easiest path through good conductors such as metal—or human beings.

Stay dry. Typical grounds are water and gas pipes, storm drains, or any metallic device connected to any of these, such as a faucet, sink, or radiator. Avoid using electrical appliances where it is possible to touch appliance and water faucet simultaneously.

Water and electricity don't mix. A damp concrete basement or patio floor is a potentially dangerous ground. If you are standing on damp earth, you are certainly grounded. Wet or sweaty hands increase the likelihood of shock.

Keep radios and other electrical appliances out of reach of persons in bathtubs.

A flooded basement can electrocute you. When under water, plugged-in appliances, lights and other electrical equipment, plus the wiring system itself, can give off a fatal current. Avoid this danger by learning which electrical circuits should be disconnected at the fuse or circuit-breaker box to shut off power in the basement. Never enter a flooded basement when water is high enough to have reached appliance motors or any electrical circuit.

Avoid using electrical tools or appliances where wet conditions exist. If necessary to do so, be sure equipment is properly grounded or double insulated.

Grounding equipment can often eliminate the possibility of electric shock. Connect a length of wire between a screw on an exposed metal part of the device and a suitable ground. Disconnect the appliance while attaching the grounding wire.

Don't ground an appliance like a toaster or broiler that has an accessible open-coil heating element. In such appliances the open coil is a live wire (in some cases even when the appliance is switched off). If you touched the heating element with a fork and the grounded shell with your hand, your body would complete the circuit.

Ground all electrical devices whose heating elements are *not* exposed. The rule holds for all appliances in the garage or basement, on the patio, or anyplace where you stand on the earth or on concrete in contact with the earth. Ground all portable power tools such as electric drills, which are likely to be held with a sweaty hand.

Use ungrounded electrical devices only where no grounds or grounded appliances are within reach. When you use an ungrounded device, like a vacuum cleaner, near a ground—say a clothes dryer—don't touch the dryer while you are holding the vacuum: electrical leakage in the vacuum would go through you to get to the grounded dryer. Unplug small appliances when not in use—especially in kitchens or bathrooms, where grounds are often abundant.

The best way of avoiding shock is through the use of a three-wire power cord—the usual two-prong plug with a third prong for grounding. A wire attached to the third prong connects the casing of the appliance to a ground for your entire electrical system. Have an electrician convert your outlet boxes so they are properly grounded and will accept three-prong plugs. If a grounded appliance blows a fuse when you plug it in, you have uncovered a potentially lethal shock hazard. Have the appliance repaired.

At Christmas watch out for electric shock from metal trees and from lights and metallic decorations.

See also ACCIDENTS; ARTIFICIAL RESPIRATION; BURNS; HEART STOPPAGE.

ELEMENTS, TRACE   See MINERALS.

EMERGENCY MEDICAL IDENTIFICATION refers to a system for calling attention to crucial medical information that an ill or injured patient may not be able to communicate. A person in coma from diabetes may die if thrown in jail as a drunk. Someone with an allergy to penicillin may get a fatal dose after an injury. A patient with heart disease on anticoagulants may bleed to death in an accident unless given medication to help his blood to clot. Contact lenses may damage the eyes if left on an unconscious person for 24 hours or more.

Two types of emergency identification systems are in wide use—one operated by the Medic Alert Foundation (Turlock, California 95380), the other devised by the AMA for you to set up yourself. Each employs a medallion worn on a chain around the neck, wrist, or ankle. Emblazoned in red is a symbol (see illustration) which

"LOOK FOR EMERGENCY INFORMATION!"

That's the message this AMA-devised emblem seeks to convey to first-aiders. The symbol appears on medallions, bracelets, and other medical ID systems.

the AMA has designed to be a universal sign indicating the presence of information important to the life and health of the wearer. On the reverse side is a medical warning: DIABETIC, ALLERGIC TO PENICILLIN, TAKING ANTICOAGULANTS, WEARING CONTACT LENSES, or whatever condition needs to be known. The wearer carries a wallet-size ID card listing essential medical information.

Medic Alert medallions also contain a serial number assigned you and the instruction "PHONE 209-634-4917," the number of the central file where Medic Alert keeps records on more than 200,000 members. Collect calls from anywhere in the world are accepted at any hour from physicians, hospital employees, police officials. The serial number enables Medic Alert personnel to pull your medical history immediately and relay its contents.

A fee of roughly ten dollars covers the telephone-information service as well as a medical ID card and a stainless steel medallion and chain. For a higher fee you can get a sterling silver or gold-filled medallion. A one-line engraving (EPILEPSY, HEMOPHILIA, etc.) is included; additional lines cost extra.

A do-it-yourself ID system does not provide for central-file service. In addition to your major health problems, the AMA recommends noting on your medallion the phone numbers of your physician and next of kin. Many drugstores and other outlets sell durable metal or plastic medallions, some for around one dollar. Obtain the names of sellers by writing to Emergency Identi-

fication, American Medical Association, 535 North Dearborn Street, Chicago, Illinois 60610.

The AMA medical ID card costs a dime or so. You can make your own by heading a plain card IN CASE OF EMERGENCY and noting your medical problems, medicine you take regularly, any dangerous allergies you have, last immunization dates, and other important information. Display it prominently in your wallet (see sample). In addition, with a red marker, print the most urgent information—"ALLERGIC TO PENICILLIN," for example—on your driver's license and other places where it's likely to be seen.

Medic Alert's 24-hour availability is worth the money if you have any medical problems that may cause trouble in an emergency. Too, Medic Alert's detailed record on you will be useful if you are separated from your ID card—as is likely to be the case in a swimming accident or in a car crash or fire.

In general, even if you have no special medical problem, you're well advised to carry the name and address and phone numbers of your doctor and next of kin.

See also ANTICOAGULANTS; CONTACT LENSES; DIABETES; DRUG ALLERGY; DRUGS; EPILEPSY; HEMOPHILIA; IMMUNIZATION.

EMPHYSEMA (pronounced em-fih-SEE-ma) is rated by the U.S. Public Health Service as "the fastest growing crippler disease in the United States today," constituting a "public health menace" of potentially epidemic proportions. Only heart disease surpasses it as a cause of total disability.

KEEP THIS INFORMATION IN YOUR WALLET

For each member of your family, make a card noting the information indicated on this sample, or photocopy the sample. In filling it out, check doctor for accuracy.

Emergency Medical Identification

My name is _____

Please call _____

My Doctor is _____

Medical Information

Last Immunization Date

diphtheria _____ mumps _____ tetanus toxoid _____

German measles _____ polio Sabin _____

measles _____ small pox _____ typhoid _____

Present Medical Problems _____

Medicine Taken Regularly _____

Dangerous Allergies _____

Other Information _____

It is by far the most common chronic lung condition, more frequent than tuberculosis and lung cancer combined. More than a million Americans lead lives restricted because of emphysema.

In emphysema the walls of tiny air sacs (alveoli) within the lungs are gradually destroyed. The lungs lose elasticity and can no longer expand and contract easily to draw in and force out air. The disease develops so slowly that its victims are generally unaware that anything serious is wrong until much of their lung function is impaired.

An emphysema victim may feel winded in the morning or evening. Exertion as slight as a routine walk may exhaust him. He is likely to feel suddenly tired for no apparent reason. Gradually he becomes sluggish, depressed, irritable.

All these are early signs of oxygen deprivation. As the condition develops, the number of breaths per minute may double to make up for the shortage of oxygen.

The severe emphysema victim's breathing occasionally sounds like a rapid series of gasps—as if he'd just run the four-minute mile. Neck muscles thicken from overworking to help move the enlarged chest through its rapid motions.

Moreover, the heart enlarges because it must work harder to pump blood into the damaged lungs. Meanwhile the tissues of the heart, like all other tissues in the body, are starved for oxygen. A condition called cor pulmonale—pulmonary heart—develops, and ultimately the heart fails.

Since many emphysema sufferers die of heart failure, a heart ailment is often set down as their cause of death. One large medical center found that about 30 percent of the patients who had been listed as dying of congestive heart failure actually had emphysema as their primary disease.

Emphysema and smoking. A frequent cause of emphysema is repeated exposure to lung irritants. Smoking is a major factor. Emphysema is about 13 times more prevalent among cigarette smokers than among nonsmokers.

Most sufferers are men over 40 who are smokers and who have a history of repeated "colds" and bronchial troubles. Many have been heavy smokers disinclined to give up the habit. Those who continue smoking are more likely to die of the disease than those who give up the habit.

Living with emphysema. If you have emphysema, you need to stop smoking entirely. Also steer clear of smoke-filled rooms, which are almost as bad for your irritated bronchial tubes as smoking yourself.

Avoid all other types of irritants to the bronchial tree. These include smog, house dust, street dust, industrial fumes, and air pollution of any type. You may need to change your job if it exposes you to dust or fumes.

Protect yourself against colds. Take shots against influenza. Emphysema worsens whenever you get a respiratory infection. What might be a slight strain on the lungs of a normal person may be a catastrophe for someone with emphysema. Antibiotics are extremely useful in helping an emphysema victim combat infection.

Body chilling causes spasm of the bronchial tubes and should be avoided. But adequate humidity is necessary to help liquefy thick, viscid secretions.

Seek out a pulmonary rehabilitation program. You'll benefit from moderate exercise if it increases your muscle tone without causing excessive fatigue. If you are overweight, reduce to ease the burden on your entire cardiorespiratory system. If you are thin and undernourished, a little gain in weight can help improve your inhaling by raising your diaphragm somewhat.

Adrenalin-type drugs may help control your bronchial spasm and the swelling of the bronchial lining. Expectorants and humidifying agents help in liquefying your thick, sticky secretions.

Drink 10 to 12 glasses of water per day to help loosen secretions. Avoid milk, since it thickens mucus. A cup of hot coffee or tea on arising in the morning helps thin the mucus that has collected during the night.

Breathing retraining can help you master an improved breathing pattern to make your breathing less labored and more efficient. You learn to breathe by moving your abdomen, not your chest; you learn to relax and budget your energy.

Above all, since emphysema can be slowed down if treated early, see a physician if you have colds that hang on, sneezing or coughing spells that turn into spasms, or shortness of breath after mild exercise.

See also RESPIRATORY DISEASE; SMOKING.

ENCEPHALITIS (sleeping sickness, brain fever, encephalomyelitis) comes in several forms.

Eastern equine encephalitis is caused by a virus harbored chiefly in the blood of birds and rodents. An animal disease, it principally afflicts horses (thus the *equine* in its name). It is spread chiefly by mosquitoes (less often by mites and ticks). Other types of encephalitis, similarly caused, include western equine encephalitis, St. Louis encephalitis, California encephalitis, and Venezuelan equine encephalitis. Cases occur most frequently in late summer and fall.

About two in three cases of encephalitis—the general term for inflammation of the brain and spinal cord—are not caused by the viruses carried by mosquitoes and other pests, but develop in the course of an infectious disease in which the brain is affected. Among these diseases are chickenpox, influenza, malaria, measles, mumps, polio, Rocky Mountain spotted fever, and toxoplasmosis.

Treatment depends on the specific organism causing the encephalitis. Rehabilitation is often needed by survivors of severe attacks. Damage to the nervous system can impair walking, talking, and eating. Vision, breathing, and blood pressure may be affected. There may be involuntary movements and rigidity of the body and limbs. Some survivors suffer mental retardation and emotional instability.

See also INFECTIOUS DISEASE.

ENDOMETRIAL CANCER See CANCER OF THE UTERUS.

ENEMAS See CONSTIPATION.

ENTEROBIASIS See PINWORMS.

ENURESIS See BEDWETTING.

EPILEPSY If you are with someone having an epileptic seizure, give first aid for convulsions (which see).

The term epilepsy describes episodic abnormal discharges of the central nervous system. Such discharges can take many forms. But, contrary to popular belief, epilepsy does not necessarily involve convulsions. In some seizures, for example, the person may engage in automatic, sometimes odd-looking, behavior.

Epilepsy comes from the Greek word meaning "to be seized." It affects about 2 million Americans, and many of them are victims of irrational fear and prejudice. The centuries-old myth that the person with epilepsy is possessed by the devil has often made him a social outcast. He may find himself rejected in childhood and unnecessarily kept from employment in adulthood.

Epilepsy alone does not cause mental illness or mental retardation. Most people with epilepsy are of normal intelligence. Some, indeed, have been people of outstanding achievement: Julius Caesar, Alexander the Great, Napoleon, Dostoevski, van Gogh.

Most people on epilepsy medication can attend regular school, work full time, and have normal, active lives. Safety studies show they tend to be more careful than fellow employees. At the same time, people with epilepsy are unsuited to some jobs: airplane pilot, for example. Unless seizures are completely controlled, they should not work near unprotected moving machinery, open flame, or hot metals, or at heights.

Types of epilepsy. In a mild form of epilepsy, called *absence* seizures, the person may experience just momentary loss of consciousness. He may appear disoriented for no more than a few seconds; he may stare fixedly at an object or blink his eyes rapidly. His muscles may twitch briefly. Most sufferers are between 4 and 14 years old. Absence (formerly called petit mal) seizures may be hard to recognize. They may be mistaken for daydreaming or inattentiveness.

In a more common and severe form of epilepsy, *generalized tonic-clonic* seizures, the person becomes unconscious and rigid, followed by massive jerking of the whole body. Breathing through saliva gives the appearance of foam around the mouth. The seizure usually passes in a few minutes, and the person falls asleep.

The tonic-clonic seizure (formerly called grand mal) is often preceded by warning signals called an aura: feelings of doom, odd sounds and smells, tingling skin, spots before the eyes. This warning allows the person to lie down before he falls.

Other types of seizure include *simple partial* seizures, which are confined to only one part of the brain. The person's hands or feet may jerk convulsively. He may feel dizzy, speak nonsense, or experience unusual sounds, smells, or tastes. He usually remains conscious.

In *complex partial* seizures the person experiences mental confusion. He may have hallucinations at the beginning and often engages in automatic, pointless movements, such as pacing or hand-rubbing. He may seem dizzy and irritable and is often mistaken for an alcohol or drug abuser. The seizure usually lasts a minute or two, but the confusion afterward can last longer.

All people subject to seizures should carry an EMERGENCY MEDICAL IDENTIFICATION CARD (which see).

Seizures vary in frequency. Some sufferers have them no more than once or twice a year, while others may have absence seizures more than 100 times a day. Emotional stress may sometimes trigger seizures, but in most cases no precipitating factor can be found.

Some people with epilepsy are subject to more than one type of seizure. And sometimes epilepsy spontaneously disappears completely after a few years.

Epilepsy that has no identifiable cause is called idiopathic epilepsy, and usually develops in childhood. There seems to be a hereditary predisposition toward some types. Relatives of idiopathic epilepsy sufferers have an incidence of seizures six to ten times greater than the general population.

A smaller number of people suffer epilepsy resulting from identifiable causes, such as brain tumors or head injuries. Surgery may control the seizures in such cases. Others may suffer epileptic seizures because of endocrine or metabolic disorders. Birth defects account for epilepsy in some people, as do the complications of infectious disease such as meningitis and measles. Poisons—including lead and alcohol—can cause seizures.

Epilepsy is diagnosed by a complete physical and neurological examination, including an electroencephalogram (EEG)—a record of the brain's electrical activity.

Treating epilepsy. Eighty-five percent of people with epilepsy can be helped. Drugs can eliminate seizures in about 50 percent of epilepsy patients, and significantly reduce them in another 35 percent. The drugs most commonly used are phenobarbital and phenytoin (Dilantin). These, plus several others, may be prescribed singly or in combination.

While you are taking anticonvulsant medication, do not use alcohol. Also be alert for common side effects: drowsiness, vertigo, nausea, vomiting, double vision, irritability. Discuss these and any other problems with your physician. A change in dosage or drug may eliminate unpleasant side effects.

If your child is taking phenobarbital, hyperactivity may be a problem. Bring it to the doctor's attention. If Dilantin is prescribed for your child, take him to the dentist. Teeth and gum problems are common in children taking this drug, and a dentist can suggest a program of good preventive care.

Epilepsy treatment requires careful medical supervision. Steer clear of mail-order treatment. Several promoters have offered phenobarbital, a habit-forming barbiturate, as epilepsy treatment through magazine advertisements. But phenobarbital is not appropriate for all people with epilepsy, and its unsupervised use can be dangerous.

People who still have seizures should not drive because lapses of consciousness may cause them to lose control of cars. But since epileptic seizures can so often be controlled with medication, all states now issue drivers licenses to people with epilepsy on an individual basis. Depending on the state, a person is considered a safe driver if he's been seizure-free for three months to two years.

A person subject to seizures should swim only in the company of someone who is aware of his condition. Young children should be constantly watched while in the bathtub. Water levels should be kept low. An older child can safely take a private bath or shower, but the bathroom door should be unlocked, and an adult should be alert for any problems.

Because of the danger of head injury from falls, people prone to seizures need to avoid climbing and horseback riding. Most sports are safe, but rough contact sports, such as hockey and football, may be unwise.

If your child has epilepsy, raise him in a relaxed atmosphere so he can develop normal emotional traits that will help him cope with an often prejudiced society. Treat him as naturally as possible, without overprotecting him or giving him preferential treatment.

In informing teachers and camp supervisors about his disorder, describe exactly what is likely to occur when he has a seizure. Once a person in charge understands that your youngster is an ordinary person except for occasional, brief attacks, he is likely to be more accepting of the child and his condition.

There is no medical reason for an otherwise normal person with epilepsy not to marry, unless the seizures are so handicapping that the spouse would be unable to cope with them. Nor is epilepsy necessarily a bar to having children. Prior to marriage a couple would do well to meet with a physician and frankly discuss any questions about epilepsy and marriage.

For information about epilepsy clinics and physicians in your vicinity, contact the Epilepsy Foundation of America (4351 Garden City Drive, Suite 406, Landover, Maryland 20785). You can get information about employment services for epileptics from The Foundation or your state's vocational rehabilitation agency.

See also CONVULSIONS; EMERGENCY MEDICAL IDENTIFICATION.

EROSION OF THE CERVIX is a gynecological condition that affects perhaps one out of every four American women.

The cervix is the narrow tip, or neck, of the uterus, at the top of the vagina. An erosion is a sore—a worn-away grainy-looking area of redness—on the cervix.

Erosion of the cervix is almost always present after childbirth. Uterine contractions repeatedly force the baby's head against the cervix, causing it to bear a great deal of abnormal pressure. In some cases the cervix is injured during the delivery. Erosion that develops after childbirth usually heals itself within a few months.

Cervical erosion may also be caused by vaginal infection. Changes in the acid-alkaline ratio of the vagina may destroy cervical tissue, leading to inflammation and subsequently erosion. In intercourse the normal acidity of the cervix is changed toward alkaline by the semen. Bacteria may also be introduced into the vagina and the cervix during intercourse.

The chief symptom is a whitish, odorous discharge. The discharge may be bloody if the erosion is deep. Inflammation around the erosion can cause pelvic pain or backache. Generally the symptoms are so unspecific that women are unaware of the erosion.

You need a semiannual gynecological examination to detect the presence of erosion and other abnormal conditions. An erosion is always benign, but many gynecologists consider neglected erosion a potential forerunner of cancer of the cervix.

Treating erosion. Vaginal douching is often recommended as treatment of mild erosion. Use 1 tablespoon of white vinegar in 1 quart of water to help maintain the normal acid content of the vagina.

Common methods for treating cervical erosion include electric cautery with a fine-tipped needle, the application of silver nitrate to the erosion, the application of creams, and electrocoagulation. These office procedures cause little or no discomfort and require no anesthetic. For a few hours after treatment some women note cramping like that of menstruation, which can be relieved with aspirin.

The newest method of treatment is cryosurgery—freezing of the cervix. It's as painless as other treatments and generally more effective.

See also CHILDBIRTH; VAGINAL INFECTION.

ERYSIPELAS is an infectious disease caused by streptococcal bacteria that are thought to enter minute abrasions in the skin. Most often victims are below age 6 and above age 30.

Usually it begins with abrupt onset of shivering and fever, accompanied by rash and swelling of the skin around the nose or around a wound. The affected area is red and glistening and often forms blisters.

On the face the infection rarely spreads past the eyelids and cheeks, then is likely to subside. On the trunk or extremities the infection spreads rapidly and if untreated may lead to death.

The disease ordinarily can be cured within ten days by antibiotics. Call a physician at first signs.

See also INFECTIOUS DISEASE.

ERYTHEMA MULTIFORME is a severe ulceration of the skin and mucous lining of the mouth, common in children and young adults.

The sores appear most frequently in winter and spring.

The disease may develop suddenly, causing a general sick feeling, sore throat, and arthritic or rheumatic pains. There may be a slight fever, or a temperature as high as 104° F to 105° F.

Sores develop first in the mouth—on the cheek, palate, and tongue—then on the lips. The affected areas show an intense reddening with the appearance of the sores, which are blisters of varying size. Later these blisters break, leaving an ulcerated, irregular surface, coated by a yellowish membrane. Sores on the lips become bloody and encrusted.

Similar blisters can appear on the skin on almost any part of the body, frequently on the genital membranes. These blisters are bright reddish-purple at first, fading to deep purple as the disease progresses. The sufferer may be ill for three or four days. Because his mouth is very painful, he has great difficulty eating and drinking.

Several attacks of blisters may follow one another. In a rare form of the disease the characteristic sores are very large blisters. When they break in the mouth the whole area becomes red, as if the victim had been burned. In very severe cases blisters may form in the eyes, perhaps causing blindness.

In many instances the cause is unknown. Among adults it often results from a drug allergy. In children and young adults viruses are often the cause.

The disease usually runs its course in 10 to 20 days. Anesthetic mouthwashes may make eating less painful. In severe cases a liquid diet or intravenous feeding may be necessary. Penicillin, sulfa drugs, and vitamin B complex have been used to reduce pain and make the sufferer more comfortable. Avoid patent medicines; they may cause further pain and damage.

See also MOUTH SORES; TEETH AND MOUTH DISORDERS.

ESOPHAGEAL CANCER See CANCER OF THE STOMACH.

EXAMINATION, PHYSICAL See PHYSICAL EXAMINATION.

EXERCISE adapted to your age and physical condition can be as important to your health as diet or drugs.

It's not too late to reap the benefits of exercise. Your *current* physical condition is what's pertinent to your health. Get in shape and your body will forgive you past excesses and sloth.

The opposite is also true: You get no credit for having been an athlete once upon a time. Indeed many athletes stop exercising but continue eating at their former level. They often wind up fatter and weaker than people who've never exercised. As a rule the older people get, the more sedentary they become and the more they need exercise.

Exercise for your heart. Exercise is good for your heart. It can help protect you against heart attack. Regular exercise conditions heart muscle so that the body can perform more work while placing less demand on the heart. Exercise permits heavier work at a lower pulse rate.

Exercise improves the efficiency of heart muscle. It's also theorized that, to provide heart muscles with oxygen, the principal arteries to your heart are enlarged with increased activity. Also thought to be enlarged are smaller blood vessels feeding your heart, promoting "collateral circulation." The enlarged arteries presumably are less likely to become obstructed. Even if they do, collateral circulation may keep your heart functioning normally, averting what might have been a heart attack.

When you pump your legs during exercise, the muscles squeeze your leg veins. This helps ward off thrombophlebitis and reduces the chance of a blood clot cutting off circulation through an artery.

Exercise may lower the blood level of fats, including cholesterol, reducing your risk of developing coronary artery disease.

Statistical studies confirm that regular, strenuous exercise lowers the risk of heart attack. For example, farmers have a much lower rate of coronary heart disease than town residents. Farm laborers have a lower coronary heart disease rate than farm owners. Owners who work their farms have a lower rate than owners who hire laborers to work for them.

A long-term Public Health Service study in Framingham, Massachusetts, showed conclusively that the more active you are, the less likely you are to suffer a heart attack and the smaller is your risk that the heart attack will be fatal.

Burning up fat. Exercise burns up flab. As your tissues need energy, they draw on calories you've stored in the form of fat.

If you're overweight, you're likeliest to lose weight via exercise if you take your physical activity in reasonable doses. A program of 15 minutes in the morning and 15 minutes in the evening is much easier to stick to than a 3½-hour marathon once a week. Yet it expends exactly the same number of calories, and poses less of a strain on your heart.

If you walk at a modest pace (2 miles per hour) for an hour, you work off 150 to 240 calories, roughly the equivalent of two glasses of beer, one breast of chicken, or a cup of spaghetti. If you walk at this rate a mere half hour a day—and eat and drink no more than usual—by the end of the month you'll have lost perhaps a pound (1 pound of body fat = 3,500 calories). If you exercise regularly you'll probably lose even more weight than the caloric expenditure indicates. There's evidence that exercise revs up your metabolism—you continue to burn up food at a faster rate for some time after a bout of activity. (See the accompanying table for how many calories different activities consume.)

All this assumes that your caloric intake remains constant. If you drink those two beers after your hour walk, you're pretty much back where you started. However a moderate exercise program (e.g., walking 2 miles a day, 4 days a week, at about 3 miles per hour) seems to put your body at a long-lasting "set point," where it will automatically adjust your metabolism to stay at a lower weight.

People vary greatly in how quickly they burn up calories. In general, a heavier person uses up proportionally more energy to move his greater weight; a lighter person, less. This explains why if you're dieting, as you get closer to your ideal weight, it takes longer and longer to lose the same number of pounds. Having less weight to haul around, you burn up fewer calories.

Conversely, if you cut down on your physical activity, you need to lower your caloric intake or you'll gain weight. Many cases of overweight begin with a decline in exercise. A person begins to commute by car rather than walk to and from buses. He moves to a home or office where he takes elevators instead of climbing stairs. His job changes to one that keeps him sitting more. Inclement weather keeps him indoors. Every calorie that used to be burned as energy now gets stored as fat.

Contrary to myth, moderate exercise does not increase your appetite. Inactive people tend to eat more than those who exercise. Below a certain level of activity your appetite-regulating mechanism fails to reduce your food intake despite your lower energy requirements.

In a study of 300 workers nutritionist Jean Mayer of Harvard found that those engaged in light regular activity eat least and keep their weight normal. Laborers performing heavy work eat most but burn up so much energy that their weight remains low. Sedentary workers—merchants, supervisors, clerks—eat almost as much as laborers and are by far the fattest of the occupational groups.

Psychological benefits. Exercise reduces emotional stress. This relief from tension and anxiety is one reason people who eat out of nervousness tend to eat less after they begin to exercise.

Moreover, an exercise program tends to keep you thinking about weight control. Thus you're likely to eat with less compulsiveness, and more awareness and selectivity. A commitment to an exercise program may make you feel in control of your life, which is helpful to people who eat to relieve feeling defeated or inadequate.

The AMA calls enjoyable exercise a "safe and natural tranquilizer." Moderate exercise helps you sleep better and may help in overcoming impotence.

Muscular benefits. Exercise tones up your muscles. It can protect you from backache resulting from sedentary living.

Increased strength and endurance reduce fatigue, enable you to perform daily tasks with greater ease. Skill and agility gained through exercise provide for more economy of movement. There's less sag to your body.

You can do more, and recover from exertion more rapidly. Your respiratory rate is lower for a given work load. Breathlessness is delayed.

With increasing exercise your liver more rapidly releases glucose, essential for energy. Your kidneys improve their capability to excrete metabolic acids, ridding your body of wastes.

Women and exercise. In contrast with the push boys generally get to be athletes, girls are widely assigned a passive role—with little or no encouragement toward vigorous exercise and competitive sports.

However women need to exercise at least as much as men. It's good for a woman's figure. Fat bulges, but muscles curve—a woman who exercises loses more girth in fat than she gains in muscle.

Women athletes tend to have fewer complications in pregnancy and shorter duration of labor in childbirth. They are less subject to low-back pain after delivery.

It is a myth that exercising makes women more masculine—women athletes tend to get married and bear their first child at ages comparable to average women. Menstruation does not affect sports performance.

There's a strong link between gynecologic complaints and lack of exercise. Studies have shown that women who complain of menstrual discomfort, irregularities, and backache generally had little physical education in school, led inactive lives, and had physically unfit constitutions and poor muscle tone.

Strenuous exercise is beneficial to the health of preadolescent girls and does not ordinarily affect the onset of their menstruation. Extremely lean girls—gymnasts, ballet dancers, track team members—tend to get their periods later than average, with no adverse health affects. There's thus no physiological reason preadolescent girls can't compete in the same sports as boys, be it track, Little League baseball, even football. Indeed before puberty the average girl is stronger, taller, and can run faster than the average boy of the same age.

Strenuous exercise is best. The best exercise is both prolonged and strenuous. To be considered physically fit, you need to be able to maintain a pulse rate of 114 to 164, depending on your age, for at least 1 hour a week (see chart). This 1-hour minimum of strenuous activity may be divided into no fewer than 3 sessions of 20 minutes, or 4 sessions of 15 minutes. If you can meet this level of exertion, chances are your heart and circulation are developed enough to provide substantial protection against heart attack.

An aerobics program is the most realistic exercise plan for people who are busy and not especially athletic. Aerobics exercises are those aimed at building your heart and lung capacity through gradually increasing levels of exertion. Walking, running, swimming, and cycling are typical aerobic exercises.

In *The New Aerobics,* by Kenneth H. Cooper, M.D. (hardcover: M. Evans & Co.; paperback: Bantam Books) you will find a variety of exercise programs geared to your age and physical condition.

For example, in a walking regimen if you're 30 to 39 and out of condition, in the first week you walk 1 mile in 17 minutes 30 seconds on 5 occasions. In the second week you walk the mile in 15 minutes 30 seconds, 5 times. After the sixteenth week you walk 3 miles in 43 minutes 30 seconds or under, 5 times. Or you can do the equivalent activity, measured by "aerobics points." The usual minimum goal is 24 aerobics points a week for women, 30 for men.

A running program. Running may fit most easily into your life. You can run indoors or out, in place or moving. To combat boredom—the bane of exercisers—you can run while watching TV, or to music to make it like dancing.

An all-purpose daily program, recommended by cardiologist Lawrence E. Lamb of Baylor University College of Medicine, calls for you to maintain a pace of 75 to 100 steps a minute, counting 1 step each time your left foot hits the floor. On the first 4 days run 1 minute. Increase the period by 1/2 minute every 4 days until you're at 15 minutes. Comments Dr. Lamb:

WHAT'S THE BEST EXERCISE GOAL FOR YOUR HEART?

If you're this age	Maintain this pulse rate for at least 1 hour per week*			
	120	**130**	**140**	**150**
25-29			135 to 164 →	
30-34			132 to 161 →	
35-39		129 to 157		
40-44		126 to 153		
45-49		124 to 150		
50-54		122 to 148		
55-59	← 119 to 144			
60-64	← 117 to 142			
65-69	← 114 to 138			

* In three 20-minute sessions or four 15-minute sessions for healthy people.

"Almost everyone can afford to use 15 minutes a day to help maintain the function of his heart and circulation." You can get the same training effect by running 10 minutes in the morning and 10 minutes in the evening, 5 days a week.

When you run, lift your feet at least 8 inches. Allow your heel to sink to the floor gently, to reduce the shock to your heel and calf. If you suffer leg soreness, drop back by 1/2 minute until the soreness disappears. "Usually, the exercise will become easier once you have passed the . . . 5-minute level," notes Dr. Lamb.

Another way of beating boredom is recommended by cardiologist Irvine H. Page, who exercises with a stationary bicycle. You don't have to steer, which means you can read while you pedal. "I ride a stationary bicycle 20 minutes a day, and to me that means 20 minutes of unadulterated, uncluttered reading," reports Dr. Page. "I just hold a book and read while I'm pedaling. It's painless; I'm amazed at the number of books I'm reading; and I'm getting quite a bit of exercise."

Aerobics and sports. What about sports? If played for the proper amounts of time, sports that require a lot of running can develop your heart-lung capacity. Dr. Kenneth Cooper has figured out aerobic programs for basketball, handball, and squash—games in which the action is fast and continuous.

But sports as played by most people are of little if any help in providing protection against heart attack. For example, you can play golf all day without having to draw a deep breath. If you use a caddy or golf cart, your heart may never come close to the desired rate of 130. Conversely, an all-out effort—like dashing 100 yards in 10 seconds—gives your heart too little time to exert itself.

The action in bowling, baseball, volleyball, badminton, and most games of tennis is too intermittent to provide the necessary sustained exertion. Because of the many breaks in play in football, for example—not to mention the difficulty in getting a game together—you're likely to find it more convenient and less time-consuming to gain aerobic points by walking or running.

The great value of sports and calisthenics generally lies not in their aerobic value but in other areas: They're fun and provide a release from tension. They burn up calories. They increase muscular strength, agility, coordination.

Isometrics can't do it all. Isometrics can develop your muscles. An isometric exercise aims to increase the size and strength of muscles by tensing one set of muscles against another, or against an immovable object. Though your body is immobile, the intensity of effort can make the affected muscles grow.

Isometrics are well suited to shaping parts of the body, like flabby stomach muscles. Under a physician's direction they have a therapeutic use in keeping immobilized parts of the body from atrophying, such as limbs encased in plaster casts as a result of fractures. And isometrics require very little time—eight seconds is tops for each exercise.

On the other hand, isometrics have been grossly oversold. They are no answer to all your exercise needs. Indeed they not only fail to help develop your cardiovascular system, but can dangerously raise your blood pressure and are often hazardous to victims of heart disease. They develop specific muscle areas, but in no way prepare you for exertion requiring increased heart-lung reserve.

Moreover, they are hardly effortless as claimed. A brief round of isometrics can be as exhausting as a much longer stint of vigorous exercise. Keeping at them is difficult because they're boring and produce results very slowly. Strength built through isometrics is quickly lost unless you maintain an isometrics program or its equivalent.

Thus be skeptical of books with titles like *Five Minutes a Day to Keep Fit* or phonograph records purporting to teach you "How to Exercise Without Moving a Muscle." Isometrics gadgets like exercise bars and stretching devices are unnecessary. All the isometrics equipment you need is your own body or a readily available object like a wall or doorjamb.

Begin with caution. Check with your doctor before beginning an exercise program. A physical examination is especially needed if you're over 40, overweight, or have a history of heart disease. Unaccustomed exercise can put a fatal strain on your heart and circulation.

See a physician right away if while exercising you can't catch your breath, suffer chest pains, can't make your legs or arms do what you want them to, or are white around your mouth while your face is flushed. Also see a doctor if shortness of breath and pounding of the heart are still noticeable ten minutes after you stop.

Other danger signals that require a physician's attention: Marked weakness persisting after two hours; a broken night's sleep attributable to exercise; a definite sense of fatigue the following day.

Chances are you'll stay out of trouble if you follow these precautions:

Wait at least two and a half hours after a meal. You may overtax your circulatory system by demanding blood for your muscles on top of that needed by your digestive system. But physical activity just *before* a meal tends to lower your appetite and is an excellent way to combine diet and exercise.

Proceed slowly. To avoid a shock to your circulatory system, warm up with three to five minutes of light calisthenics. Build up your performance very gradually. Trying to move too quickly in a program is not only hazardous but discouraging. You may quit in frustration if your goals are unrealistic.

Stop well short of exhaustion. If your heart rate approaches 170, slow down. You're probably overdoing it if, 2 minutes after you stop, your pulse still exceeds 110.

Be noncompetitive or compete only with yourself or a closely matched peer. An urge to keep pace with someone in better shape than you can be dangerous. Merely the outpouring of adrenaline in competition can rob your heart muscle of oxygen.

Exercise at least three times a week. Exercise benefits begin to reverse themselves if two or more days go by between sessions. Don't be a weekend athlete.

If you lay off for a week or more, restart at a lower level than you were at when you stopped. If you're going to keep starting and stopping an exercise program, you're safer not starting at all.

Wear supportive clothing. Good jogging or walking shoes can protect you from leg and foot problems. Women should wear a bra to keep breast ligaments from stretching.

Don't exercise in extreme temperatures. Your heart works much harder from activity in very hot or very cold weather. Drink plenty of fluids to avoid dehydration.

Beware seasonal hazards like shoveling snow in winter or doing heavy household chores in summer. On vacation don't overdo swimming or tennis.

Taper off as you finish. Wind down by walking around and breathing deeply. If you stop abruptly, with so much blood in your leg muscles you risk fainting, even heart attack.

Don't use steam baths, saunas, or hot showers

HOW MANY CALORIES DO YOU BURN?

The table at right shows the number of calories expended in various types of activity. See the table of food values under NUTRITION for the number of calories in many kinds of food, and you can figure out how much of what activities will work off last night's dinner.

Adapted from Fox, S. M., Naughton, J. P., and Gorman, P. A., "Physical Activity and Cardiovascular Health" (Table 5), *Modern Concepts of Cardiovascular Disease*, April–June 1972.

Calories per Minute	Exercise	Work	Play
2–2½	Standing, walking at 1 mph, operating a car under ordinary stress	Ordinary desk work, operating an electric office machine, sewing, knitting	Playing cards
2½–4	Level walking (2 mph), level bicycling (5 mph)	Manual typewriting, auto or radio-TV repair, light janitorial work, bartending, riding a lawn mower	Playing billiards, shuffleboard, or piano; bowling; skeet-shooting; light woodworking; powerboat driving; playing golf (with power cart); horseback riding at a walk; canoeing at 2½ mph
4–5	Walking at 3 mph, cycling at 6 mph	Machine assembly-line work, driving a trailer truck in traffic, moderate welding, window cleaning, bricklaying, plastering, pushing a small power mower or light wheelbarrow load	Horseshoe pitching, six-man noncompetitive volleyball, playing golf (pulling a bag cart), archery, sailing a small boat, fly fishing at a stand, noncompetitive badminton (doubles)
5–6	Walking at 3½ mph, cycling at 8 mph	Painting, paperhanging, light carpentry, raking leaves, hoeing	Table tennis, playing golf (carrying clubs), badminton (singles), or tennis (doubles)
6–7	Walking at 4 mph, cycling at 10 mph	Digging a garden, light dirt shoveling	Ice or roller skating at 9 mph, fishing against a light current, canoeing at 4 mph, horseback riding at a trot
7–8	Walking at 5 mph, cycling at 11 mph	Shoveling dirt at the rate of ten 10-lb. loads/min., pushing a hand mower, splitting wood, snow shoveling	Playing competitive badminton or tennis (singles), folk dancing, light downhill skiing, cross-country skiing at 2½ mph in loose snow, water-skiing
8–10	Jogging at 5 mph, cycling at 12 mph	Sawing hardwood, digging ditches, carrying an 80-lb. work load	Horseback riding at a gallop; vigorous downhill skiing; playing basketball, ice hockey, touch football, or paddleball; canoeing at 5 mph; mountain climbing
10–11	Running at 5½ mph, cycling at 13 mph	Shoveling dirt (10 14–16-lb. loads/min.)	Playing noncompetitive squash or handball, vigorous basketball, fencing, cross-country skiing at 4 mph in loose snow
11	Running at 6 mph	Shoveling dirt (10 16-lb. loads/min.)	Competitive handball or squash, cross-country skiing at 5 mph

immediately after exercise. The heat brings blood to your skin, possibly straining your circulation. No squatting or breath-holding, which can adversely affect your blood pressure and heartbeat.

Exercise frauds. Shun exercise gimmicks. There's no shortcut to physical fitness. Avoid fake drugs like "body magic creams," represented as a muscle developer—and declared a fraud by the Post Office Department.

Nor is massage of any value in building muscle or losing weight. For a muscle to be strengthened, it must be actively engaged in movement, not merely acted *upon,* as in massage.

Dream machines that promise exercise without effort are a waste of money. If there is no effort, you are not exercising.

Vibrating belts do nothing to build muscle or take off weight. Nor do other machines in the arsenal of health clubs: barrel rollers, electric exercise bicycles, electric joggers. Passive exercise machines have little or no value. They cannot "break up fat deposits" and "take off inches," as some reducing salons claim.

Some exercise machines are hazardous. One delivered electrical shocks to the body through contact pads. The electricity supposedly contracts your muscles, in theory exercising them without effort. The machine, 400,000 of which were sold, was ordered off the market by the Food and Drug Administration (FDA). It could cause miscarriage and aggravate epilepsy, hernia, peptic ulcers, varicose veins, and a wide variety of other conditions.

See also FATS; HEALTH CLUBS; HEART DISEASE; OVERWEIGHT; SPORTS.

EYE DISORDER of many kinds can be detected with routine eye checkups.

No later than age three a child needs at least one good eye exam. Visual defects such as crossed eyes and amblyopia can lead to permanent loss of vision in the affected eye if not treated, preferably by age six. Eye exercises, eyeglasses, contact lenses, or in some cases surgery may be required before a child enters school.

A child may have normal vision one year and need glasses the next. From age 6 to 20 a once-a-year exam is advisable. Unless corrected promptly, nearsightedness, farsightedness, and astigmatism can impair learning ability and personality development. It is also well to learn of color blindness early so that a child can learn to accommodate to it.

Have a child of any age examined by an eye specialist if he has red-rimmed or watery eyes; squints, scowls, or blinks; often stumbles or falls;

rubs his eyes a lot; or seems sensitive to bright lights. A young child with eye trouble may show little interest in things at a distance or close up, and may continually overreach or underreach for an object. He may have double vision, showing it by shutting or covering one eye. He may try to brush away the blur.

An older child may be tired, dizzy, or have headaches after doing work. Suspect eye trouble if he is falling behind in school or has difficulty doing other work that requires close use of the eyes. Be suspicious if his writing is off line; if he uses unusual colors in artwork; if he complains that printed lines run together or jump around.

Adults may have many of the preceding symptoms. Other signs of trouble are blurred or foggy vision, loss of side vision, or rainbow-colored rings around lights. You may be unable to adjust to darkened rooms such as theaters. You may undergo frequent changes of glasses, none of which is satisfactory.

After age 35 you need a regular eye exam once every one to two years. This is essential to detect presbyopia, glaucoma, and cataract, which most often start developing in the middle and late years.

If you wear glasses or have a vision problem, you need regular eye checkups between 20 and 35, ages when people with normal vision generally needn't bother. But it's a rare soul who lives out his days without needing glasses. A recent survey indicated that 97 percent of Americans over 45 need corrective lenses.

Contrary to popular belief, 20/20 vision does

HOW TO APPLY EYE OINTMENT

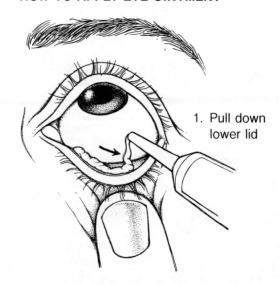

1. Pull down lower lid

2. Apply ointment inside lid (not on eyeball)
3. Close eyes—and roll them

HOW TO GIVE EYE DROPS

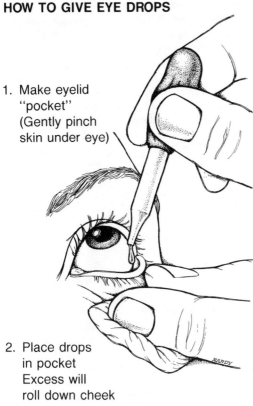

1. Make eyelid "pocket" (Gently pinch skin under eye)

2. Place drops in pocket Excess will roll down cheek

3. Close eyes—and roll them

not mean perfect eyesight. It simply means that when you're sitting 20 feet from an eye chart, you can read the letters you're supposed to read according to a standard. Thus 20/100 vision means that sitting 20 feet from the eye chart you can read only what a person with 20/20 vision could read at 100 feet. It does not indicate the quality of depth perception, color blindness, night vision, and other conditions of the eye.

Eyes and health. General medical as well as eye exams are needed to preserve eyesight. Medical conditions such as diabetes, circulatory ailments, and infections are leading causes of blindness.

Conversely, the eyes are a window into the body. Physicians often peer into your eyes to measure your general state of health. If a doctor finds clear, bright eyes, he will feel less concern than if you have lackluster eyes, heavy eyelids, sluggish eye movement, constantly contracted or dilated pupils, or other symptoms arising from disorders elsewhere in the body. An ophthalmologist is often the first to detect such systemic diseases as diabetes and high blood pressure, especially in people who don't have regular physical checkups.

The eyes are one of the few parts of the body

where the physician can get a good idea about the condition of the blood vessels. As he sees the retina through the ophthalmoscope, he can observe pulsations of the tiny capillaries and see whether they appear soft and supple. If there is notching or indentation of a vein where an artery crosses it, this suggests arteriosclerosis.

If the pulsations are especially strong, or if there are tiny hemorrhages in some areas, then high blood pressure or diabetes is suspected. Such findings lead to a more general examination, including blood pressure readings and perhaps X rays to determine whether the larger blood vessels are affected.

Eyes of the newborn. Most newborn infants have a slight discharge from the eyes the first five days after birth. This often is related to the drops used in the eyes at the time of birth to prevent the development of infection. Occasionally a newborn develops an infection in both eyes, with discharge, redness, and swelling. If this occurs after leaving the hospital, consult your physician at once.

Also watch for a lump under the skin at the inner corner of the baby's eyes. Pressure on the lump discharges mucus into the eye socket—it indicates an infection of the tear sac caused by a blockage.

See a doctor. He can cure the blockage in almost every instance by giving the child a light anesthetic and passing a small silver probe down the tear ducts to the nose to relieve the obstruction.

Which eye doctor? Where should you go for a checkup? An *ophthalmologist* (or *oculist)* is a medical doctor specializing in diagnosing and treating all visual defects or diseases, both medical and surgical. Often he'll use eyedrops or other medications. He also may prescribe glasses.

An *optometrist* (O.D.) examines eyes for visual impairments (particularly focusing defects such as nearsightedness or amblyopia) and prescribes lenses or other optical aids. He also may prescribe (and provide) eye exercises. The optometrist is expected to make a preliminary search for eye diseases and abnormalities. He is not qualified to provide medical or surgical treatment, but is ethically bound to refer you to an ophthalmologist.

An *optician* grinds, fits, and supplies glasses on prescription from an ophthalmologist or optometrist. He is not qualified to give medical or surgical treatment. Nor should he prescribe lenses or other aids except under direct supervision of an ophthalmologist or optometrist.

Examination fees by ophthalmologists range

about twice that of optometrists. The cost of glasses, contact lenses, and exercises is extra.

If you suspect some eye ailment or you're in the vulnerable age for glaucoma and other eye diseases, consult an ophthalmologist recommended by your family doctor. But if you're sure it's a visual problem and that all you need is glasses, pick a reliable optometrist.

See also AMBLYOPIA; ARTERIOSCLEROSIS; ASTIGMATISM; BLOOD PRESSURE; CATARACT; COLOR BLINDNESS; CONTACT LENSES; CROSSED EYES; DIABETES; ECLIPSES; EYE DONATION; EYE EXERCISES; EYEGLASSES; EYE INJURIES; EYE MAKEUP; EYESTRAIN; EYEWASHES; FARSIGHTEDNESS; GLAUCOMA; LIGHTING; NEARSIGHTEDNESS; PINK EYE; PRESBYOPIA; STYES; SUNGLASSES; TRACHOMA.

EYE DONATION   A national organization, the Eye-Bank for Sight Restoration, 210 East 64th Street, New York, New York 10021, coordinates eye donations to obtain the cornea, the clear tissue on the front of the eyeball, as well as other parts of the eye. Kept refrigerated after removal, the tissue can be used to replace parts that have been scarred by disease or injury, and thus restore vision.

A special form is available if you wish to make the donation. Relatives should be informed so they can provide the necessary cooperation, which means calling the Eye-Bank collect (212–TE8–9200) immediately after the donor's death. The eyes should be removed within 24 hours of death. The earlier they are removed, the more suitable the tissues will be for grafting.

Since the eyelids are closed when the body is viewed before burial, no mutilation will be apparent.

See also EYE DISORDER.

EYE EXERCISES (visual training) are the subject of many extravagant and possibly dangerous claims.

On one hand exercises can often help correct such muscle-related defects as crossed eyes and heterophoria, a failure to use both eyes at once. Exercises for these conditions are called orthoptic training, and may be prescribed in conjunction with surgery or eyeglasses.

In addition, visual training can be valuable for children with learning problems and adults with reading difficulties, who often don't use their eyes efficiently. Their eyes may move jerkily and focus sluggishly. They also may have problems coordinating their vision with their hearing or their hand or body movements.

On the other hand there is no basis in fact for claims that exercises can cure nearsightedness (except in extremely rare cases), farsightedness, or astigmatism. Some exercises are advertised as a cure for glaucoma, which leads to blindness if not arrested early. Any delay in treatment because of misplaced hope in exercises or similar efforts usually is disastrous.

Eye exercises are equally valueless for cataracts, color blindness, and eye injuries.

Much "eye training" actually trains your mind rather than your vision. It teaches you to interpret blurred images more accurately. Your vision, however, remains blurred.

This may have serious consequences if, with a false sense of security, you encounter a situation demanding effective sight. Comments the National Society to Prevent Blindness: "The man who didn't see a car coming will find small comfort in the fact that he was taught to read an eye chart in spite of poor vision."

As with many forms of quackery ineffective exercises are surrounded by a lot of mumbo jumbo and get credited for coincidental improvements. Some people's sight improves as they get older. If such improvement follows a course of eye exercises, the person may attribute the improvement to the exercises.

Some people have pseudomyopia. Eye exams erroneously found them nearsighted, and they've developed the habit of straining their eyes to see extra well with eyeglasses. Exercises may help them relax their eyes so that their normal 20/20 vision is restored, and they credit the exercises with a dramatic cure for their supposed nearsightedness.

The Bates method is perhaps the most widespread questionable exercise system. Its most prominent exponent was novelist Aldous Huxley.

Huxley had poor vision because of cloudiness of the cornea, the clear covering of the eyeball, from old inflammation. He consulted many ophthalmologists, with unsatisfactory results. After treatment by one of the followers of Bates, Huxley reported marked improvement.

Judged by the scientific measurement of visual acuity, the Snellen charts, Huxley read very little more than he did before treatment. Judged by his own impressions, he could see better—he could use his eyes with much more comfort and do more work with them.

While this is a worthwhile gain, it is not an improvement in the eyes, the ocular part of vision, but in the cerebral, mental part of vision.

See also EYE DISORDER.

EYE FATIGUE   See EYESTRAIN.

EYEGLASSES   If you have an eye disorder caused by the imperfect shape of your eyeball—

such as astigmatism, farsightedness, nearsightedness, or presbyopia—glasses or contact lenses may help you see clearly. But they must be correctly prescribed and fitted or they will be of little value.

Your first move in replacing broken glasses—or getting new ones after several years of wearing one pair—is an eye exam by your optometrist or ophthalmologist. A checkup is necessary unless you've had one in the last two years. If you haven't saved a copy of the prescription for your old glasses, you will have to call your optometrist or ophthalmologist for a duplicate.

When you travel, take a copy of your eyeglass prescription with you. To avoid eye injuries be sure your glasses and sunglasses are made of plastic or impact-resistant glass.

Adjusting to new glasses. New glasses often require an adjustment period. Especially among children, frames that irritate the nose and ears may result in attempts to avoid wearing the glasses. The world may suddenly look quite different. And some types of corrections may at first produce severe headache.

Let your child know that you realize he has a problem—scolding or punishing may make him resist even more. Make sure that his prescription was ground correctly and that the frames are adjusted properly.

Begin with short wearing periods each day. If the doctor is willing, allow the child to remove the glasses at play. Encourage him by telling him how good he looks with them on.

It is not true that a child will harm his eyes if he puts on another person's glasses. The correction will usually be uncomfortable and he will remove them in a matter of a few moments. If your child wants to wear someone else's glasses all the time, have his eyes examined. It might be he needs a correction and gets some comfort from the glasses of others.

Clean glasses by washing them in warm—not hot—soapy water and drying them on a lint-free cloth. Children's glasses often get filthy and finger-marked, so teach your child to wash his glasses at least once a day, before he leaves for school. A cleaning is often needed again in the evening before he reads, does his homework, or watches television.

Most eyeglass lenses are made of glass, but plastic lenses are becoming more popular. Plastic weighs about half as much as glass, an advantage to people who are bothered by the weight of glasses on the bridge of the nose.

Look for plastic lenses that are scratch-resistant and replaced free for the life of the prescription. Most plastic lenses are easily scratched and

more difficult to clean. Paper lens tissue—such as Sight Savers—should not be used to clean plastic lenses. Cost is roughly the same for both glass and plastic, and both can be tinted.

Choose frames carefully. Cheaply made frames have flimsy plastic pin hinges instead of the more durable, metal barrel hinges. Sturdy frames will generally have five or seven barrels held together by a screw, not a pin. Earpieces should have a metal core.

Be sure the frames center your line of sight and feel comfortable, otherwise your glasses may cause you grief. Odd shapes won't hurt the eyes if the lens correction is good, though the correction may not have the needed result if fitted into very oddly shaped frames.

Rimless glasses are making a comeback. But if they're made of glass, they often chip and break. Try plastic lenses.

Ask the optician for burn-resistant "safety frames." Highly flammable cellulose-nitrate eyeglass and sunglass frames are imported from several foreign countries. There is no way to differentiate them from safer, slow-burning frames. The imported frames carry no identification as to the materials they are made of, nor do they warn of their flammability.

If necessary ask the optician to snip off a fragment of plastic from the earpiece of a sample set of lenses. Try igniting it. If it bursts into flames, it doesn't belong on your face.

Say no to ready-mades. Don't waste your money on ready-made glasses. Warns the National Society to Prevent Blindness: "You might accidentally get a pair which meets the needs of your own two eyes, but a $2 bet on a horse is more likely to pay off."

Ready-made eyeglasses, outlawed in some states, virtually never contain any correction for astigmatism, a condition that needs correction in 65 percent of cases. Further, most eyes are different optically from their mates; in ready-mades, the two lenses are generally of equal power.

Worst of all, by giving some improvement the use of ready-made (so-called Grandma) glasses may mask the underlying causes of changes in vision. Especially in the elderly, vision problems may be symptomatic of eye conditions or bodily diseases that a competent eye examination would uncover and lead to early treatment.

Those who use ready-mades leave themselves open to undetected glaucoma, which may worsen irretrievably; diabetic retinopathy, a potentially blinding complication of diabetes; and other disabling or fatal diseases.

Mail-order eyeglasses are no better. A typical

"self-test optometer" kit purports to allow you to measure your own vision and fit yourself for frames. Instructions in the kit urge you to get orders from others in your neighborhood. But in fact no layman can accurately or safely prescribe his own glasses. People who fall for such schemes play Russian roulette with their vision.

See also EYE DISORDER.

EYE INJURIES cause about 10 percent of all blindness.

An estimated 90 percent of the 500,000 eye injuries occurring each year in the United States could be prevented if people wore glasses with protective lenses. When buying eyeglasses or sunglasses, be sure they meet the required Food and Drug Administration (FDA) standards for impact-resistant lenses. The regulations do not apply to contact lenses or to goggles and face masks such as used in skiing and snorkling. If your glasses were made before January 31, 1972, when the FDA regulation took effect, replace them with safety lenses.

Glass lenses may be made impact-resistant by heat treatment, chemical treatment, or making them thicker. Plastic, especially polycarbonate, lenses are more impact-resistant than glass, on a weight-for-weight basis, but may be scratched more easily if not properly handled.

Eye accidents are a particular threat to youngsters. The junior high school years bring the greatest risk of accidental injuries to youngsters' eyes. Boys are involved in three out of four eye accidents during these years.

Warn your children about the dangers of pointed sticks, pellet guns, bows and arrows, and fireworks. Be sure your children's toys are safe for their ages. Avoid hazardous toys with sharp points and those put together so loosely they might come apart, leaving dangerous edges.

Keep sharp-pointed pencils, scissors, icepicks, and knives out of the reach of small children. A four-year-old hasn't yet learned how to play safely. Scissors in his hands are a dangerous weapon.

Beware of the sun. Sunburn of the eye is a greater danger than generally realized. Although the injury is painless, areas of the retina may be blinded by even brief exposure to the sun's direct rays. When sunning a baby, make certain it is not facing the sun.

Sunglasses will provide relief from the sun's glare, but not from the harmful rays that can damage the delicate retina of the eye. Never look directly at the sun—even while wearing sunglasses.

Here's how to handle the most common eye injuries:

Specks and splinters (the most common causes of permanent eye damage): Don't rub the eye. You may embed the dirt in the eyeball surface or scratch the cornea (the transparent covering over the pupil), causing permanent damage. Lift the upper lid and pull it down over the lower lid, allowing the tears to wash out the speck. If this is unsuccessful, wash the eye with lukewarm water.

Despite irrigation and watering of the eye you may not be able to locate the speck. It may have been carried away in tears, but the irritation continues. Or the trouble may be an eye infection, which in the beginning often feels as if a foreign body were in the eye.

Sometimes a speck adheres under the upper eyelid. If the particle doesn't come away at once, it probably is lodged in the surface.

Bandage the eye and see a physician. A splinter, however tiny, may cause permanent loss of vision—especially if it penetrates the cornea. *Don't* follow the familiar advice of turning back the eyelid against a cotton swab, matchstick, or pencil. Unless you've been specially trained, you may damage the eye.

Blows: If you are hit in the eye by a blunt object such as a fist or ball, apply cold compresses immediately to the area. See a physician at once. Black eyes are often accompanied by unsuspected ruptures, deformities, even fractures of bone around the eye—any of which can result in permanent defects in vision.

IF AN EYE IS BURNED
Immediately after exposure to chemical or flame:

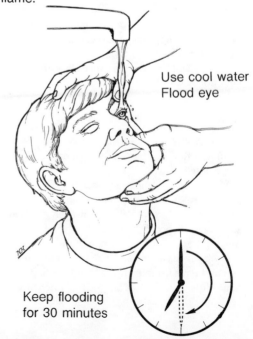

Use cool water
Flood eye

Keep flooding
for 30 minutes

Buying raw beefsteak or liver to put on a black eye benefits only the butcher. It is a waste of time for the eye, and the effort may keep you from consulting a physician.

Cuts, punctures, scrapes: Bandage your eye lightly and immediately call a physician, if possible an ophthalmologist. He may want to meet you in a hospital emergency room.

Don't wash the eye or try to remove any object stuck in it. Treat a torn eyelid the same way, since the wound may extend to the eye.

Skull X rays are often needed before an object impaled in the eye is removed. A pencil or twig may have penetrated the brain.

Don't be surprised if *both* eyes are bandaged following a penetrating wound. This may be done to prevent blinking.

Chemical or flame burns: Keep your eye open, and for at least 30 minutes flood it with cool water by any means whatever—by holding your head under a faucet or shower, by spraying the eye with a sink spray, by holding your face in a basin of water (see illustration).

Don't use an eyecup—it's too small to be effective. Nor try to neutralize an acid by using an alkali, or vice versa. The heat generated by the chemical reaction may lead to further damage.

See a physician, preferably an ophthalmologist, but only after you've finished flooding the eye. Immediate flushing is as important as subsequent medical care.

See also EYE DISORDER.

EYE MAKEUP   Any makeup that contains a dye may be dangerous to your sight. In one case a woman had her hair done before a PTA dinner in her honor. At the beauty shop she was persuaded to have her brows and lashes touched up with a dye.

Two hours after the treatment her eyes were so irritated from the dye that had gotten into them that she could barely see. That night she had to leave the celebration in her honor early because of the pain. The following morning she could not open her eyes. She was never able to see again.

When buying an eyelash preparation avoid any product that is obviously a dye. Even if a product is not called a dye, you can identify it as such. It will claim to produce "permanent" color, meaning that the color will be unaffected by water, tears, or abrasion for several months, as compared with a mascara, which must be reapplied at least daily. There are usually directions for application, and sometimes gadgets are included to protect the eyes during the dyeing.

Precautions for eye makeup. Because eyelids are easily irritated, remove eye makeup with care. Too-frequent or harsh cleansing may irritate the lid surface. Don't remove and reapply eye makeup repeatedly at one session. If you are not satisfied with the initial application, either make do or remove it completely and wait a few hours before reapplying.

The thin skin of the eyelids is particularly susceptible to contact dermatitis. Allergic reactions near the eyes often are caused by cosmetic preparations designed for use on other body areas—especially hair preparations and nail polish. However some people are allergic to eye makeup as well. If the skin becomes red, itchy, or swollen whenever an eye cosmetic is applied, then you may be allergic to one or more of the ingredients in the product and you should stop using it.

Sometimes an allergy may be caused by ingredients used in only one brand of cosmetics, and changing brands will solve the problem. In a few cases use of eye makeup must be stopped altogether.

Some women invite trouble by applying eyeline pencil to the border of the eyelids inside the lashes, rather than to the surface of the eyelid behind the lashes. This may lead to permanent pigmentation of the conjunctiva (membrane lining the lids and covering the eye), redness, itching, tearing, and blurring of vision.

One ophthalmologist says, "I have not seen a patient who used cosmetics inside the lashes who had completely normal conjunctivas." He advises women to confine cosmetics to the lashes themselves, and to the skin outside them.

Infections are another hazard. The preservative in mascara can lose its ability to kill dangerous bacteria. If the eyeball is scratched, as by a mascara brush, an infection may cause serious eye problems.

To reduce the risk of infection the Food and Drug Administration (FDA) advises women to heed the following precautions in the use of eye cosmetics:

Discontinue immediately the use of any eye product that causes irritation. If irritation persists, see a doctor.

Wash your hands before applying cosmetics to your eyes.

Make sure that any instrument you place in the eye area is clean.

Don't allow eye cosmetics to become covered with dust or contaminated with dirt or soil. Wipe off the container with a damp cloth if visible dust or dirt is present.

Don't use old containers of eye cosmetics. If you haven't used the product for several months, it's better to discard it and purchase a new one.

Don't spit into eye cosmetics. Boiled water can be added to products that have thickened.

Don't share your cosmetics. Another person's microorganisms in your cosmetic can be hazardous and spread such diseases as trachoma.

Don't store cosmetics at temperatures above 85° F. Cosmetics held for long periods in hot cars, for example, are more susceptible to deterioration of the preservative.

Avoid using eye cosmetics if you have an eye infection or the skin around the eye is inflamed. Wait until the area is healed.

Take particular care in using eye cosmetics if you have an allergy.

When removing eye cosmetics, be careful not to scratch the eyeball or some other sensitive area.

See also EYE DISORDER.

EYES, CROSSED See CROSSED EYES.

EYE, PINK See PINK EYE.

EYESTRAIN (eye fatigue, tired eyes) can usually be avoided with proper lighting. Don't expect any eyewash to help.

This condition, marked by aching or irritated eyes and accompanied by headache, generally results from excessive demands on eye muscles to accommodate to glare, contrast, or inadequate illumination. Eyestrain may also be caused by wearing sunglasses indoors.

Air pollution, dust, and other irritants can intensify the problem. And often it is a sign that a person needs glasses.

Simple eyestrain generally clears up in a day or so. There are no permanent effects. Contrary to the age-old warning of mothers, you don't "ruin your eyes" by straining them.

Children have especially strong eye muscles and seem resistant to eyestrain. They can read comfortably in poor light, in dark corners, and in all positions.

Watching TV. Television may cause eyestrain but no permanent damage. It is a myth that TV causes eye defects or that you can "wear out" your eyes by watching it. Avoid eyestrain by following these viewing guidelines:

Use some room lighting. The contrast between a totally darkened room and a bright TV screen is too great for comfortable vision. On the other hand very bright lights may wash out the picture.

Sit away from the screen. Experts recommend viewing from a distance of at least five times the width of the screen.

Place the TV at eye level and away from the glare or reflection of lamps and windows.

Keep it in focus. The most common cause of television headache is an improperly adjusted picture. When the picture is blurred, snowy, or vibrating, a heavy burden is placed on the eyes.

Other tips for avoiding eyestrain. Try larger-wattage electric bulbs. Stop an hour earlier on long car trips so that you won't be driving at dusk or night. In low-lighted areas carry a small flashlight.

Give yourself an "eye break" as you would a coffee break. You don't have to cut down on TV viewing, reading, or sewing provided you let your eyes relax from time to time. Shift positions. Look off into the distance. Close your eyes.

Have your eyeglasses checked. You may need to step up to bifocals or trifocals for more comfortable vision. Special hobbies and visual tasks often require extra glasses. Tell an eye doctor about your individual problems and consult him if eyestrain recurs or persists.

See also EYE DISORDER.

EYEWASHES and their advertising claims are often hogwash. While proprietary eyewashes can in fact produce a slight, brief soothing effect, normal eyes do not need cleansing, soothing, or refreshment by solutions of astringent and antiseptic chemicals.

Simple irritation or eyestrain will disappear of its own accord in a day or so. No synthetic solution can match your tears for washing away small bits of dust, dirt, and irritating material. And tears contain an enzyme that kills bacteria at least as well as the antiseptics in proprietary eyewashes.

If you have boric acid in your medicine cabinet, throw it out. It is not effective as an antiseptic or eyewash. Worse yet, it is poisonous and many people have become gravely ill from drinking it by mistake.

Another fault of eyewashes is that their use may lead to the neglect of symptoms that indicate serious types of eye disorder. Glaucoma is often neglected, causing increasing loss of vision while the victim attempts self-treatment with eyewashes.

If you want an eyewash to relieve simple irritation caused by smog, strong light, sea bathing, or bathing in chlorinated water, place one or two drops of cold tap water in the lower lid with a clean eyedropper. The same treatment, or the application of iced wet compresses for 15 minutes or so, will safely relieve "tired" though otherwise healthy eyes. If symptoms persist, consult a physician.

See also EYE DISORDER.

F

FAINTING If you feel faint, lie down with your feet up. If you can't lie down, control the sensation of giddiness, dizziness, or light-headedness by sitting and lowering your head between your knees (see illustration).

Stay in this position until you feel fully recovered. Get up with caution, because fainting can recur. If you faint often, see a doctor. Smelling salts or other ammonia inhalants have little if any real value—and may be harmful in severe heart or respiratory disease.

If a person you're with faints and does not recover at once on lying down with his feet up, or if there is evidence of underlying illness or injury, you may need to treat him for UNCON-SCIOUSNESS (which see).

Be aware of the possibility of heat exhaustion or heat stroke if the temperature and humidity are high.

Simple fainting is a brief loss of consciousness that can occur in a healthy person if the blood supply to the brain is abruptly reduced. When the blood supply replenishes, the person will recover. Fainting often results from rhythm disturbances of the heart and from use of tranquilizers and drugs for reducing blood pressure. Fainting also can be a result of sudden pain or emotional stress.

A few people with low blood pressure feel faint if they arise quickly from a seated or lying-down position. Fatigue, hunger, or inactivity in a stuffy room can also predispose you to faintness. You're likely to feel better if you eat something or get some fresh air.

Hysterical fainting occurs almost entirely in young women. The attack usually occurs in the presence of others, the girl gracefully and dramatically falling to the ground in a swoon. Unlike simple fainting the attack may last an hour or more and there are no abnormalities of pulse,

IF YOU FEEL FAINT—OR SOMEONE ELSE FAINTS
Most effective

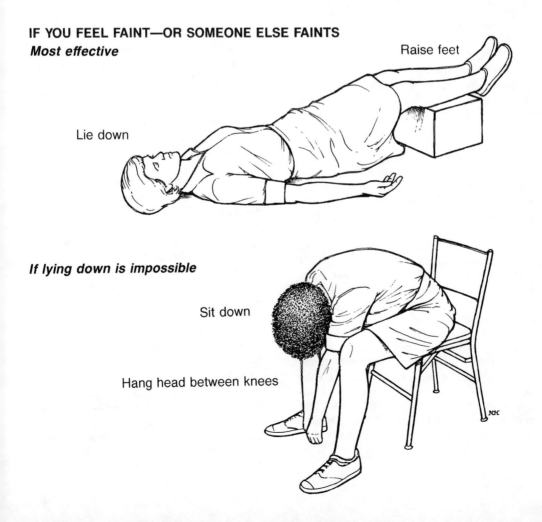

Raise feet

Lie down

If lying down is impossible

Sit down

Hang head between knees

blood pressure, or skin color. Much hysterical fainting occurs in groups of girls during mass excitement, as at a performance of a current teen-age idol. Repeated hysterical fainting can be a symptom of emotional illness and signal a need for counseling.

See also BLOOD PRESSURE; HEART DISEASE; HEAT EXHAUSTION; HEAT STROKE; HOT WEATHER; STRESS; UNCONSCIOUSNESS.

FAITH HEALING   See QUACKERY.

FALLEN ARCHES (flat feet) don't necessarily hurt. Many men have been rejected from military service merely on the basis of their flat feet, so the notion persists that flat feet mean trouble. Actually the foot pain associated with fallen arches can usually be traced to other problems with the foot.

Fallen arches refers to a foot condition in which the muscles and ligaments of the arch of the foot are weakened. Some people are born with weak arches. Many develop the condition. Children usually have no clearly defined arch. The arch develops as they grow older.

An orthopedic shoe may help reduce discomfort from flat feet. A shoe that doesn't give good support under the arch will aggravate the flat-footed condition. Look for sturdy shoes with built-in supports.

If foot pain persists, consult your family doctor or an orthopedist.

See FOOT PROBLEMS.

FALLS can often be sustained without injury if you relax while falling to overcome the natural tendency to stiffen up, practice falling on a mat or rug, loosening your back and shoulders as you fall.

When falling backward, never drop into a sitting position. A sitting jolt is hard on the end of the spine and can cause pain or even back fracture. Try to turn your body to land on a well-padded or large-muscle part—on one side of the buttock, or on the thigh or shoulder. Or stop your fall before you sit down hard—with your arms outstretched, fingers spread wide.

If falling forward, catch your weight on as broad a surface as possible. To take up the shock fall as if you were doing a push-up exercise: Spread your fingers and let your arms give and fold in toward your body. Then let the momentum roll you onto your thigh or shoulder.

In a drop or jump from a height touch ground on the balls of your feet. As your feet touch the ground, bend your knees and ankles and curl your body. Put spring in your body by bending your legs, hips, arms. Roll sideways. Or slow down the momentum by straightening your legs and trotting forward.

Accidental falls kill about 17,500 Americans a year, more than half of them in their own homes, and are the leading cause of accidental deaths for people over 65. Children and people under emotional stress or with physical handicaps are also especially likely to be injured in falls.

Have good lighting throughout the house, with special attention to hallways and heavily trafficked areas. Put night-lights in bathrooms and bedrooms.

Keep floors free of hazards. About two thirds of fatal home falls occur at floor level, usually because the victim slipped on toys or other objects or on spilled liquids, grease, mud, or sand.

Bathroom tile floors are a major threat when wet. Keep them wiped dry and use a nonskid mat on the floor; use nonskid strips and grab bars for the tub or shower.

Polish waxed floors thoroughly according to the manufacturer's instructions. It's the poorly polished floor, coated with slippery wax, that's hazardous. Contrary to popular belief, shiny, highly polished floors are generally safe because they've been rubbed dry, giving them a high-friction surface.

Spray or coat the underside of scatter rugs with antiskid compounds. Keep scatter rugs away from stairways unless they're firmly anchored. If the edges of a rug curl, tack or tape them down before someone inevitably trips.

Stairways are the second leading site of fatal home falls. Poor visibility is frequently at fault. Install light switches at top and bottom.

Painting wood steps is safer than varnishing them or covering them with rubber mats. Watch out for carpeting that's loose or torn. For basement stairs paint the bottom step or a patch of the floor at the bottom of the stairs shiny white. Mix sand or an abrasive with paint to give basement stairs a nonskid surface.

Provide banisters or hand rails 2 to 3 inches from the wall for a solid grip. Don't allow objects to be left on the steps. Be doubly cautious when carrying on stairs an awkward load you can't see around.

When building an addition to a room, try to keep floors level. Abrupt changes in floor level are hazardous, especially the unexpected single step.

Ladder wisdom. Use a ladder to reach high places. You're likely to be headed for a fall if you climb a chair or pile of boxes. Make sure the ladder is on solid footing—a board will help on soft earth. Angle the ladder so the distance from its base to the building is about one fourth of its length (the base of a 16-foot ladder should be 4 feet from the building).

When climbing, hold on with both hands. Hoist tools and materials with a rope. Wear non-slip shoes that are sturdy, since rungs can tire and numb your feet.

Reach no farther than arm's length on either side of the ladder. Move the ladder rather than stretch over. And stay off the top rung. If you need to reach higher, get a taller ladder. Allow a 4-foot overlap for the sections of an extension ladder; if you want to reach 20 feet, get a 24-foot ladder.

Get rid of any ladder that's split or otherwise weakened. When buying a new ladder, look for an American Ladder Institute sticker, which indicates that the ladder meets minimum standards of manufacture. Get one that's at least 15 inches wide, for stability, and has a rung for every foot (a 12-foot ladder should have 12 rungs —fewer rungs may indicate a cheapie).

Aluminum ladders are much lighter than wood, but pose a severe electric shock hazard if used around electricity. Wood ladders too can conduct electricity if wet, and may deteriorate if left outdoors.

Winter falls. "Snow falls gently—people don't!" warns the National Safety Council. Get rid of snow on sidewalks and driveways and sprinkle icy spots with salt or sand.

Clean your shoes on entering a building. Slush on shoes, or tracked on floors, can cause slips.

When walking on ice, keep your body slightly forward. Put your feet down flat, not on the heels. Take short steps. Wear overshoes with heavy-tread soles.

Pedestrian accidents skyrocket in winter. Be careful crossing over streetside snowdrifts or icy curbs. Oncoming traffic may not be able to stop in time if you slip and fall into the street.

Children's falls. Children have a 50–50 chance of falling from a high place before they're a year old. Tumbles from cribs, beds, dressing tables, can cause serious damage. Babies tend to fall headfirst, and their thin skull wall may be easily injured (see HEAD INJURIES).

Don't underestimate an infant's mobility once he's around five months old—and can roll over, sit up, often stand and climb. Hold a baby firmly on a dressing table when you reach to get something from a drawer beneath him.

Never leave a baby unattended unless you are sure that he cannot hurt himself. Take him with you to answer the door. You can't expect a baby to keep still for even a few seconds, and you can't rely on the care of a little brother or sister. A baby lying calmly on the middle of your bed can wriggle to the end and fall off in a much shorter time than it takes you to answer the phone.

See also ACCIDENTS.

FALLS THROUGH ICE can be deadly. The cold water lowers body temperature and may cause a person to go into shock and drown within 15 minutes (see DROWNING).

If you go through the ice, don't attempt to grasp the edge of the ice to pull yourself out, for your weight is likely to break off more of it. Instead spread your weight over as much ice as possible. Stretch your arms forward and kick hard, trying to propel your upper body over the unbroken ice.

If you have a spiked object (screwdriver, pencil, nail file), chip out some ice to get an anchor and pull yourself out. In the absence of any such aids allow your gloves to touch the ice until they stick. Then use the frozen gloves as an anchor.

Once on solid ice don't stand up near the break. Roll or crawl to safety. Quickly get warm and dry to avoid FROSTBITE (which see).

To rescue someone else: resist the impulse to run to him and extend your hand. The edge of the ice is likely to break off beneath you. Phone for help if you can.

Then get a pole, ladder, long board, or similar object, and crawl on the ice until you are close to the victim. Lie prone and inch forward. This distributes your weight over a larger section.

Extend the pole or board so that the victim can grab it. Pull him slowly forward, breaking ice if necessary, until he reaches a firm spot. Help him out when you can do so without breaking through.

Or toss him a rope, preferably with a handhold tied to it. A stick or a spare tire are good handholds. To improvise a rope, tie scarves, belts, ties, coats, or towels together.

If the victim's hands are too numb to grasp a rope, try to loop it over his head and under his arms. If there are several people on the scene, lie down and form a human chain. Each hold the ankles of the person ahead, and inch across the ice to the victim.

Treat all ice as treacherous. A solid-seeming mass may be "candle" ice, made up of long vertical needles that can cave in on touch. Or the ice may be undermined by cracks, or it may be left suspended in thin air by a drop in water level.

Be especially careful around saltwater ice, which is particularly fragile. Also steer clear of sagging ice, new ice, ice formed over swift currents, discolored ice, and ice on inlets and outlets to lakes. The National Safety Council regards 3 inches of hard ice as the minimum for safe foot travel. Other authorities recommend at least a foot of solid ice for rivers and lakes, at least 6 inches for coves and ponds. Before venturing out on ice, test it thoroughly, especially the first ice of winter and ice remaining into warming weather of spring.

See also ACCIDENTS; COLD WEATHER; DROWNING; FROSTBITE.

FARSIGHTEDNESS (hyperopia), difficulty in seeing close objects clearly, is a condition most babies are born with. Thus infants tend to be more attracted to objects at arm's length and fairly blind to those close up, a normal pattern that can needlessly worry parents. As the eye grows and develops, farsightedness lessens until in early school years only a small amount is left.

The farsighted eye is shorter than the normal eye, causing light rays to focus at a distance behind the retina (see illustration). The lens must work hard to refract light rays from near objects so that they produce a clear image on the retina. The stress of constantly accommodating for the farsighted eye may cause headache and eyestrain, especially during close work such as reading.

IF YOU'RE FARSIGHTED
Your eye focuses behind retina

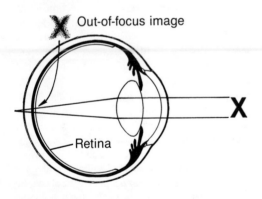

X Out-of-focus image

Retina

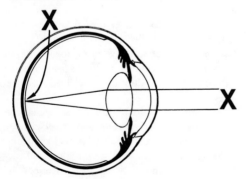

Normal

Farsightedness may be indicated by sleepiness while trying to read and by blurring of the printed page. In children it may be difficult to spot because they can easily read the eye charts. Farsighted children often dislike reading because of the physical strain it entails. Unlike those whose nearsightedness might be a handicap, farsighted children may be skillful in outdoor sports that require sharp distance vision.

Farsightedness is often associated with crossed eyes. A child may need glasses for farsightedness if an eye that is ordinarily straight turns in when he is tired, ill, or has used his eyes a great deal.

Convex lenses in eyeglasses or contact lenses usually can correct farsightedness, bending light rays to focus farther forward. Farsighted people often need glasses only for reading. Eye exercises have not been found to have any effect.

See also EYE DISORDER.

FATIGUE is extreme tiredness. Ordinary fatigue, brought on by hard work or exercise, can be corrected by rest and sleep.

Chronic fatigue, on the other hand, is a persistent and debilitating state that does not respond to ordinary amounts of rest and sleep. It is frequently accompanied by muscle weakness.

See a physician if you are "always tired." Often seeming to have no cause, it can be an early symptom of many types of infectious disease, among them hepatitis and mononucleosis. Chronic fatigue may also be brought on by other conditions, including alcoholism, anemia, diabetes, pregnancy, overweight, rheumatoid arthritis, or heart disease. Hypothyroidism, backache, and a host of other disorders may also account for the fatigue. Malnutrition can result in chronic tiredness, as can the use of some drugs, such as barbiturates.

But more than 90 percent of all fatigue has no organic cause. Boredom and lack of physical exercise can contribute to fatigue. It can also be caused by emotional stress. Living or working in the midst of too much noise, bad lighting, poor ventilation, or oppressive heat or cold may also lead to excessive tiredness.

"Battle fatigue" is an extreme example of living in a stressful situation, applicable to arduous civilian situations as well. The front-line soldier is always threatened with death or mutilation. He must often go hungry, cold, and sleepless. When exposed to these conditions long enough, almost every man will develop anxiety, become tense and easily startled, and his judgment will become poor. He may suffer from headache, diarrhea, lack of appetite. Most victims of battle fatigue recover after a time away from battle.

One clue that fatigue is of psychological origin is that you wake up more tired in the morning than when you went to bed. The overtiredness is often accompanied by a miscellany of other symptoms: headaches, backaches, stomach trouble, sleeplessness, unusual loss or gain of weight, frequent colds.

The "tired housewife syndrome" is a common type of emotionally caused fatigue. The largest group who suffer from this condition are women in their late twenties and early thirties. Typically they have two or more small children and are overwhelmed by both the physical and emotional stress of the responsibility, possibly because of a feeling of inadequacy.

Other tired housewives are in their later thirties and a little more successful financially. Their children are usually adolescents and the gratifications of motherhood have begun to pale.

Yet another group of emotional fatigue sufferers is made up of women in menopause or about to undergo it.

To avoid or relieve emotional fatigue try to spend some time doing things you like. Women who are full-time homemakers and mothers of small children will benefit from having regular baby-sitters. For some women a full- or part-time job may be the answer—or a social group or volunteer work. It may be enough to take a mini-vacation—away from the kids—once a month for a weekend, or even overnight. Also be sure to eat properly, get enough sleep, and follow a regular program of conditioning exercise.

Chronic fatigue may be a symptom of mental illness. Extreme frustration, anxiety, or depression can account for the exhaustion, and it may be accompanied by tics, cramps, tremors, pain. Fatigue of severe psychological origin cannot be eliminated without treating the underlying causes through psychotherapy.

See also STRESS.

FATNESS   See OVERWEIGHT.

FATS (lipids) almost certainly need to be reduced in your diet. For proper nutrition and avoidance of overweight they should supply no more than 35 percent of your total calories. Currently, for most Americans, they supply 40 to 45 percent.

Fats are the most concentrated form of food energy, supplying about 270 calories per ounce, more than twice that of proteins and carbohydrates. You need some fat in your diet—particularly a kind called linoleic acid—for proper growth and well-being.

Fats carry vitamins, specifically A, D, E, and K. They make food taste better, satisfy the appetite, delay the return of hunger pangs. A minimum amount of body fat is needed to insulate you against temperature changes and provide padding around your organs and nerves.

Cholesterol is a fatlike substance that is manufactured by the body and that also enters the bloodstream from foods. Too much of some types of cholesterol can clog the arteries supplying the heart (see ARTERIOSCLEROSIS), possibly leading to a heart attack. Statistical studies confirm that the higher your total blood cholesterol is, the more likely you are to suffer a heart attack.

Cholesterol is also suspected of promoting cancer. Some investigators believe that end products of fat digestion can create carcinogens (cancer-causing substances) when combined with bile acid or acted on by bacteria in the large intestine. Fats are especially implicated in cancer of the colon, breast, and ovary.

Cut down on high-cholesterol foods like egg yolks. Eat no more than three egg yolks a week, including eggs used in cooking, cakes, batters, sauces.

Egg whites contain virtually no cholesterol, and you may find egg-white products (e.g., Egg Beaters) an acceptable substitute for real eggs, bearing in mind that the substitutes are nutritionally inferior and contain additives.

Also avoid or use sparingly shellfish like shrimp, clams, lobster, crab, oysters, scallops. While low in fat, they are high in cholesterol. Organ meats—liver, kidney, heart, sweetbreads—are very high in cholesterol.

When fats are unavoidable, eat polyunsaturated rather than saturated fats. Saturated fats raise your level of blood cholesterol. Polyunsaturated fats lower it. A fat is "saturated" if its chemical bonds are filled with hydrogen; "polyunsaturated," if two or more such bonds are unfilled. Saturated fats are usually solid animal fats—the fat in meat, butter, cheese, cream, whole milk.

Chicken, turkey, and fish are high in polyunsaturates. Veal is low in total fat. Eat any of these instead of food that is high in saturated fats: beef, lamb, duck, goose, pork and pork products such as cold cuts and sausages.

Before you cook meat, trim off fat you can get at, then drain off fat while it's cooking. Skim off the fat in gravies, stews, soup stocks—it will harden and be easier to remove if you cool the food. Baste with wine, tomato juice, or bouillon instead of fatty drippings. Broil rather than fry hamburgers, steak, lamb or pork chops.

Buy dairy products that are low in milk fat: skim milk, nonfat dry milk, buttermilk, yogurt made from skim milk. Eat cottage cheese, farmer's, baker's or hoop cheeses, mozzarella and sapsago cheeses—all made from skim milk.

Ordinary whole milk and whole-milk products—ice cream, cheeses, butter—are high in saturated fats. So too are chocolate, solid fats and shortenings like lard, and coconut oil used in nondairy creamers. So-called 2 percent milk is only slightly better than regular milk, which is 3.25 to 3.8 percent fat.

Polyunsaturated oils. Use polyunsaturated vegetable oils as shortening. Buy safflower oil, corn oil, cottonseed oil, soybean oil. Select a margarine (in preference to butter or lard) that lists one of the foregoing liquid vegetable oils as its first ingredient.

Read labels and be wary of "hydrogenated" fats, as in some peanut butters and margarines. These contain oils that have had their chemical bonds artificially filled to make them harder, improve flavor, retard spoilage. Like saturated fats they raise your cholesterol. "Partially hydrogenated" fats, on the other hand, usually have an acceptable proportion of polyunsaturates.

Peanut oil and olive oil are "unsaturated." They neither raise nor lower cholesterol, although they may benefit blood lipids. They are best used occasionally for flavor.

Look for breads made with a minimum of saturated fats. This describes nearly all white, whole wheat, French, Italian, pumpernickel, oatmeal, and rye breads on the market. Avoid commercially prepared butter rolls, biscuits, muffins, doughnuts, egg or cheese breads.

Pasta—spaghetti, macaroni, noodles (but not egg noodles)—are good low-fat, low-cholesterol choices. So too is cereal.

Physical activity can reduce cholesterol. Swiss studies found that the average city dweller's blood-cholesterol level was more than one and a half times that of mountaineers—on exactly the same diet. Merely losing weight can help many overweight people reduce serum cholesterol.

Reduce emotional stress. Psychological disturbance affects your body's hormone production and interferes with the metabolism of cholesterol, promoting its buildup in arteries.

If you have persistently high blood fats, your doctor may prescribe such lipid-lowering drugs as clofibrate (Atromid-S) or cholestyramine (Questran). With a low-cholesterol diet these drugs help reduce cholesterol levels. Some people, however, go off their diets as soon as drug therapy begins, thereby bringing about a net gain of zero.

Reduce cholesterol now. The sooner you reduce cholesterol the better. In a classic study Norwegian cardiologist Paul Leren reduced saturated fats and cholesterol in the diet of heart-attack victims. In contrast to comparable heart-attack victims who did not change their diet, the dieters suffered a third fewer second heart attacks, half as many heart-attack deaths. But it took two years of such dieting before differences in heart-attack rates became statistically significant.

For your children, start a polyunsaturated fat diet in childhood. Autopsies of American GIs killed in Korea and Vietnam found that 77.3 percent of these lean, seemingly healthy young men had gross coronary disease, largely attributable to their childhood diet.

An example of what you can do with your own youngsters was provided by New England boarding schools that cut their students' rise in cholesterol levels by 50 percent. On most days the schools used egg substitutes instead of eggs, polyunsaturated margarine instead of butter, ice milk (made with skim milk) instead of ice cream, fish and poultry instead of beef and pork. The boys accepted the changes without complaint. When they went home to a "good family diet," their cholesterol levels tended to go back up. Children under two, however, should not be given lowfat milk.

Lumberjacks and farmers in North Karelia, Finland, have one of the world's highest heart-attack rates, despite their healthful outdoor living and physical activity. Investigators from the World Health Organization and Finnish Government blame the heart-attack epidemic on the North Karelians' high-fat diet, which is loaded with butter and cream.

See also CANCER; HEART DISEASE; NUTRITION; OVERWEIGHT.

FEE SPLITTING See SURGERY.

FEET, FLAT See FALLEN ARCHES.

FEVER is a warning sign. Call a doctor when a child or adult develops a high temperature.

Fever most often results when an infectious disease affects the body's thermostat (in the hypothalamus at the base of the brain), causing changes in the oxidation of fuel, and loss of heat through evaporation. The ensuing rise in heat is often one of the earliest indications of illness. Cancer and some drugs may also disturb your thermostat.

There is no relationship between the severity of a disease and the degree of fever. A trivial infection may have a high fever. A low fever, or none, may accompany a severe condition.

Most laymen believe 98.6° F is the normal reading. Actually there is no single "normal," because temperature varies during the day and differs in various parts of the body. It runs highest when taken rectally, about .5° to 2° lower when taken orally, and perhaps .5° lower than that in the armpit or groin.

Your temperature will fluctuate about 1° during every day—lower after midnight, higher in the late afternoon. Vigorous exercise, eating a large meal, and very hot weather can cause elevations in body temperature. If your temperature has subsided after you've remained quiet for an hour or so, you're probably all right.

Physicians tend to consider a range between 97° F and 99° F, taken orally, as a normal zone. There is an increasing effort among doctors to have thermometers redesigned, changing the red line at 98.6° F to a green band covering a range from 96.8° F to 99.5° F. This zone would encompass most normal temperatures while excluding most of the abnormal. Dr. William F. M. Wallace, a British physiologist who originated this proposal, argues that the emphasis on 98.6° F is "arbitrary" and "misleading."

Chills with shivering and goose pimples can be one effect of fever. At high temperatures the blood vessels contract and this in turn keeps warm blood from reaching the skin. The surface temperature will be lower and you may feel cold.

As the fever rises, blood vessels in the skin dilate, causing a hot, flushed face (which is why feeling a forehead may detect a fever). The heart may beat more rapidly, which could be dangerous for someone with heart disease. Increased sweating introduces the threat of dehydration and loss of essential salt. Convulsions may occur with persistent fevers, sometimes even if temperatures are only a little above 100° F.

Above 103° F in adults temporary mental derangement is common, ranging from impaired judgment to delirium. A person with a high fever needs to be watched and not be allowed to administer his own medicines or make important decisions. As temperature rises above 104° F—which is extremely rare except in heat stroke—circulation begins to fail in adults.

Children are subject to much higher temperatures than adults. A mild infection can bring temperatures over 100° F, and bad colds can bring on a fever of 105° F. While such a temperature would indicate a life-threatening condition in adults, a child out of infancy may be in no special danger. Even in children, though, high fever may bring on dehydration and convulsions.

Headache, nausea, and loss of appetite also may result from fever. None by itself is hazardous. Nor, contrary to myth, is there any danger of brain damage from a fever.

ASPIRIN OR ACETAMINOPHEN DOSAGE

Instructions on an aspirin or acetaminophen container base the amount of medication on the child's age. But since children of the same age may have vastly different weights, it's best to calculate the dose on the basis of your child's weight:

Weight of child	Dose of aspirin or acetaminophen
11 to 22 pounds	60 to 120 mg
22 to 44 pounds	120 to 240 mg
44 to 66 pounds	240 to 360 mg
66 to 88 pounds	360 to 480 mg
88 to 110 pounds	480 to 650 mg

The package will tell you how many milligrams (mg) are in each tablet, teaspoonful, or milliliter.

Treating fever. Drink plenty of fluids to ward off dehydration. Give a child soft drinks, juices, ices, or Popsicles (an average Popsicle has about 2 ounces of fluid in it). Gelatin desserts are also a good source of liquids.

For mild fever aspirin or acetaminophen often brings temperature down within an hour. Bed rest will help build up strength, though stay out of bed if you feel like it. That will help the body lose heat by evaporation.

Use light bedcovers and keep the bedroom comfortably cool with adequate humidity. "Sweating out" a fever by bundling up in an overheated room will only increase fluid loss and discomfort, and make it harder for excess body heat to escape. Put on just enough clothing to keep you from getting chilled. In summer that may mean dressing a child in diapers or underpants.

"Starving a fever" is a poor way of handling it. High temperature quickly burns up reserves of protein, fat, and carbohydrates. Rather than cutting down on what you eat, increase your intake of meat, eggs, and other high-protein, high-vitamin foods.

To cool off take a sponge bath or compresses of tepid water. The water should feel just slightly cool to your elbow. Help a child lose body heat by sponging him for three to five minutes at a time, or put him in a tub containing 2 to 3 inches of tepid water and gently slosh water over his body.

An alcohol rub may make you feel better, but will do little to reduce the fever. Don't try to reduce a child's fever by sponging or rubbing with alcohol. Alcohol can be absorbed through skin, causing intoxication, and the fumes may irritate a child's delicate mucous membranes.

To cool a twitching, feverish child, with a physician's permission, put him in a tub of water at 75° F with careful constant attendance. A too-rapid drop in temperature may cause heart stoppage, so keep in touch with the doctor. In 10 to 15 minutes the child's fever should drop by 2° to 3°. Don't use ice packs. Shock from the drastic cold may be harmful.

Fever thermometers. For taking body temperature buy a clinical thermometer with a short, stubby bulb. The stubby bulb can be used either rectally or orally. It is less breakable than a rectal (short, blunt) or oral (long, thin) bulb, and is safest for children and for emotionally disturbed adults.

Check that any thermometer you buy complies with U.S. Department of Commerce Standard CSI-52. A flat stem or a triangular projection at the end of the stem is a useful feature—it keeps the thermometer from rolling off a table. A flat model is easier to read, as is a model with a red-reflecting index that contrasts more vividly with a white background than does a silver index. A good thermometer case does not roll. It permits the thermometer to be slipped in or out with ease, but without rattling.

You can't be sure that the particular thermometer you buy is accurate. Consumer tests have found great variations in quality even among thermometers made by the same manufacturer.

Before using any thermometer, be sure it registers below 96° F. If it reads more than 96° F, hold the end opposite the bulb and give it a few brisk, downward shakes. An oral thermometer should be inserted under the tongue, rotated a few times to assure complete contact, and left there for three minutes, while the patient's lips are closed. Do not take an oral reading immediately after the patient ingests hot or cold foods or liquids. Wait at least 20 minutes.

A rectal thermometer—or a stubby model used rectally—is safer for children or severely ill adults, who may bite or swallow an oral model. Lightly grease the thermometer with petroleum jelly and insert it no more than half its length (less if the patient is a child) while the patient is lying on his side with his knees bent. Keep it in place three minutes, and don't leave a child or seriously ill adult unattended.

Hold a very young child while his temperature is being taken, keeping your palm on his

TAKE A BABY'S TEMPERATURE SAFELY

Hold thermometer in place

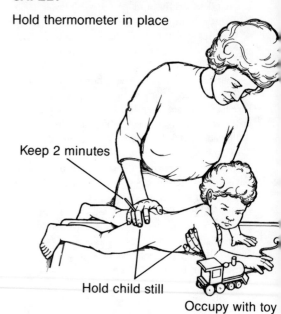

Keep 2 minutes

Hold child still

Occupy with toy

buttocks and the thermometer between two fingers (see illustration).

If your child is younger than three months or protests against rectal temperature taking, use the axillary method—taking the temperature under the child's arm. While axillary readings are somewhat less accurate than rectal or oral readings, the method is preferable when the child's age or behavior increase the risk of the thermometer breaking.

Use an oral thermometer, placing the bulb high up in the armpit, about halfway between the front and back of the arm. Hold the child's arm down gently but firmly at the side of the body. Keep the thermometer in place for five minutes.

Wash any thermometer after each use with soap and cold or lukewarm water (never hot water, which could break it), and rinse.

Steer clear of a new method of temperature taking: plastic fever strips placed on the forehead. They often result in fever readings that are too low.

Centigrade vs. Fahrenheit. If you buy a thermometer overseas, its calibrations may be in degrees Centigrade (also called Celsius) rather than Fahrenheit. On the Centigrade scale the freezing point of water (32° F) is 0° C and the boiling point (212° F) is 100° C.

To convert Centigrade to Fahrenheit: Multiply by 1.8, then add 32. Thus $37°$ C = $37 \times 1.8 + 32 = 66.6 + 32 = 98.6°$ F. If Centigrade reading goes up (or down) $1°$, add (or subtract) $1.8°$ to Fahrenheit: $38°$ C = $98.6 + 1.8 = 100.4°$ F.

To convert Fahrenheit to Centigrade: Subtract 32 and multiply by 0.555. So $98.6°$ F = $(98.6 - 32) \times 0.555 = 66.6 \times 0.555 = 37°$ C. If Fahrenheit reading goes up (or down) $1°$, add (or subtract) $0.56°$ to Centigrade: $99.6°$ F = $37.56°$ C.

See also CONVULSIONS; HEAT STROKE; INFECTIOUS DISEASE; PHYSICIAN.

FEVER BLISTERS See COLD SORES.

FEVER, BRAIN See ENCEPHALITIS.

FEVER, DESERT See COCCIDIOIDOMYCOSIS.

FEVER, GLANDULAR See MONONUCLEOSIS.

FEVER, MALTA OR MEDITERRANEAN See BRUCELLOSIS.

FEVER, RABBIT See TULAREMIA.

FEVER, UNDULANT See BRUCELLOSIS.

FEVER, VALLEY See COCCIDIOIDOMYCOSIS.

FIBER (roughage, vegetable fiber). A diet high in fiber may, according to many researchers, help prevent cancer of the colon, constipation, coronary artery disease, diverticulitis, hemorrhoids, ulcerative colitis, and varicose veins. These conditions occur far more frequently in industrialized nations than in less-developed countries, where the average daily intake of fiber is about seven times as great.

Fiber is the part of grains, vegetables, fruits, and nuts that resist digestion. It consists of cellulose and other components that are low in nutrients but high in bulk.

Fiber holds water. With a high-fiber diet large soft stools pass quickly through the bowel without exerting abnormal pressure or altering normal intestinal bacteria. In contrast, a diet low in fibrous foods results in so hard a stool that your colon has to squeeze to move it along. The slow passage also may give bacteria a chance to convert wastes into injurious substances.

Milling removes most fiber from grains. Little fiber remains in such refined products as white flour, used for white bread and most pastries, cakes, and pies; white rice; cereals such as farina and cream of wheat; and pasta that includes spaghetti, macaroni, and noodles.

Your richest source of fiber is whole grain cereals and bran. Raw bran, the seed coat sifted from refined flour, may be bought in bulk from health food stores. Commercially, the highest percentage of wheat bran is found in Kellogg's All-Bran, Bran Buds, and Nabisco 100% Bran.

Other good sources of fiber are commercial 100 percent whole wheat breads; homemade, whole grain wheat flour breads; whole grain pancakes; and muffins made with whole ground cornmeal or a combination of whole wheat flour and bran cereal. Other sources include oatmeal, brown rice, buckwheat groats, and whole wheat pasta.

Fruits that are high in fiber include apples, apricots, berries, dates, figs, peaches, plums, and prunes. Among high-fiber vegetables are beets, broccoli, brussels sprouts, cabbage, carrots, cauliflower, eggplant, squash, sweet potatoes, and tomatoes.

See also NUTRITION.

FIBROSIS, CYSTIC See CYSTIC FIBROSIS.

FINGER FRACTURES are often mistaken for sprains. The symptoms include acute pain, tenderness, and swelling. The knuckle of the injured bone may be much larger than the other knuckles. The finger may be crooked.

If you suspect a fracture, immobilize the finger with a small splint (an ice cream stick, pencil or spoon will do—see illustration) and have it X-rayed. Treat a mashed fingertip by soaking it in ice water, then wrapping it in a bulky dressing (see illustration).

See also FRACTURES.

IF A FINGER MAY BE BROKEN

Immobilize with small splint
(Ice-cream stick, pencil,
spoon handle, etc.)

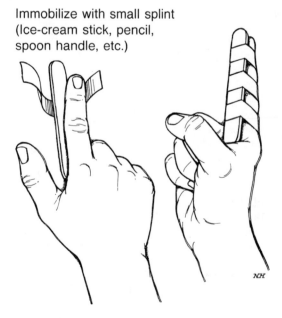

WHEN A FINGERTIP GETS MASHED

Reduce pain, swelling

1. Keep injured part in ice water
   Whole hand: 10 to 15 minutes
   One finger: 20 to 30 minutes

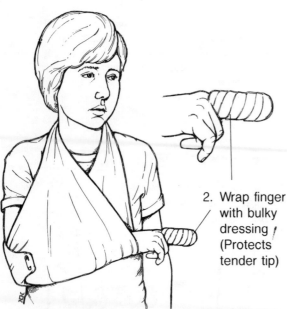

2. Wrap finger
   with bulky
   dressing
   (Protects
   tender tip)

3. Apply sling
   (Raises arm, prevents throbbing)

FINGER INJURIES See FINGER FRACTURES.

FINGERNAIL BRITTLENESS is generally due to chemicals such as detergents, cleansers, and solvents in polish removers. Nail brittleness also increases as a person gets older.

To prevent or reduce nail damage, wear rubber gloves with cotton linings while performing wet household chores. Regularly massage a hand cream into the skin around the nails.

Nail polish or nail-coating products can act as a splint or shield to protect nails. For added insurance against splitting brush polish over and under the nail tip. Soft and weak nails that split easily may be helped by a commercial nail builder made with a protein similar to keratin.

Applying creams and oils for nails every few days will help counteract surface drying, but will not cure brittle nails. No electric manicuring device will promote healthier nails or improve circulation in the fingers.

Avoid fingernail-hardening preparations that contain formaldehyde. Formaldehyde may not actually harm the nail itself, but on live tissue it can cause contact dermatitis and other skin problems, including discoloration, bleeding under the nail, pain, dryness, and loosening and perhaps loss of nails. Even if you use such a preparation with care, you run a risk of getting some on the skin.

If your nail splits or breaks off, you may want to secure it with a strong glue such as epoxy resin. This will hold the nail together until it grows long enough to be trimmed away.

White spots on fingernails have no relation to brittleness. They are believed to be associated with blood circulation and diet. As the nails grow out, the white spots go with them.

See also SKIN DISORDERS.

FINGERS, WEBBED See WEBBED FINGERS.

FIRE If your clothes catch fire, lie down and roll back and forth to smother the flame (see illustration). Or smother the fire with a rug, blanket, or coat. Don't run—you'll only fan the flames.

If you discover a fire, immediately evacuate everyone from the building, even if the fire is small. Gas poisoning from fumes and smoke—a bigger killer than burns in home fires—can cause the death of occupants in minutes. And fire can build up superheated gas and leapfrog explosively, quickly, turning a house into an inferno.

Call the fire department even if you think the fire is minor. Only if you're sure the fire is small and contained should you try to put it out.

Keep in the living room or kitchen (scenes of most home fires) a multipurpose dry chemical extinguisher, in a 1- to 5-pound size for portability. It is useful for all three categories of fires: Class A—involving ordinary combustibles such as paper, wood, fabric, trash; Class B—grease, oil, gasoline, other flammable liquids; and Class C—electrical fires. Buy only an extinguisher with UL (Underwriters Laboratory) approval, and check once a year to see that it's working.

If no dry chemical extinguisher is handy, or if the fire rages on after the extinguisher is spent, use a hose or buckets of water for burning wood,

IF YOUR CLOTHES CATCH FIRE

Don't run
(You'll fan the flames)

Smother flames with wrapping

Cover with rug,
blanket, coat

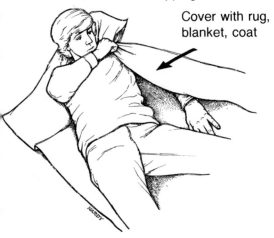

Roll on ground if you have no wrapping

cloth, or paper. For petroleum products smother the fire with a blanket or rug. Don't use water; it can splatter the fire. For electrical fires turn off the current—and only then use water.

For snuffing out grease blazes on your kitchen range keep nearby a pound of baking soda (bicarbonate of soda)—not baking powder, which can explode. A handful of baking soda thrown on an oven and skillet fire will usually release enough carbon dioxide to extinguish it.

If you have an old fire extinguisher either containing carbon tetrachloride or with contents unspecified, take it to your fire department. Carbon tet, now banned by the Food and Drug Administration (FDA), forms fumes that can be fatal or

result in damage to the liver, kidneys, heart, lungs. An Oregon woman died after inhaling fumes from a broken carbon tet extinguisher.

Buy smoke detectors for your home. These devices, no larger than small ceiling-light fixtures, can alert you to a fire by sounding an alarm. Most range from $10 to $50, and are mounted on ceilings or walls.

Photoelectric models are best at detecting slow, smoldering fires. Ionization models respond best to the smoke of fast, flaming fires. For better protection, buy one of each. Place an ionization detector in a hallway outside the bedroom doors. Put the photoelectric model in the general living area, where it can detect smoke from smoldering upholstery or rugs. For maximum protection install both a photoelectric and an ionization detector on each level of your house. If you smoke in bed, put an extra photoelectric in your bedroom.

If your house burns. Sleep with your bedroom doors closed to protect you from a spreading fire. Most fires occur between midnight and 6:00 A.M.

If you awaken and smell smoke, don't fling open the bedroom door. First feel the panels and doorknob. If they are warm, keep the door shut. Heat and smoke could rush in and overcome you in seconds.

Call loudly to warn everyone in the house of the danger. Make your escape through a bedroom window. If this is impossible, stuff blankets and rugs under the door to keep out smoke while awaiting rescue.

If the door is cool, cautiously open it and be ready to slam it shut again should you encounter a blast of heat. If the way is clear, lead the family out of the house. If smoke is heavy, put your handkerchief over your nose and mouth and crawl along the floor where the air is cooler and less smoky.

Don't jump from windows except as a last resort. If possible, throw out a mattress to soften your fall. Slide out backward on your stomach, hang briefly and let go.

Call the fire department from a neighbor's house—many people die of smoke poisoning or are engulfed by flames while phoning firemen from their burning home. Don't reenter a burning building. Many people die attempting to save possessions or rescue persons who are already safe.

If you are caught in a fire in a modern highrise building, use the stairs, not an elevator. If the elevator fails, you're trapped, and the elevator shaft will act like a chimney flue and suck flames into the car. Automatic elevator buttons are often heat-activated and will take you straight to the fire floor. The doors will not close again if smoke renders the electric eye inoperative.

In a theater fire don't scream, talk loudly, or rush madly for an exit. The danger in a crowd is panic—often more deadly than fire itself. Sit or stand still for a moment, letting others bypass you until you decide which way to go. Head for a secondary exit, clearly marked in all public buildings. Don't try to leave the same way you entered.

Nearly everyone in a theater fire dashes for the main exit, often causing a tragic pileup while other exits are ignored. The National Safety Council recommends that whenever you enter a public building such as theater, church, or school auditorium, you should note the exit nearest you and plan to use it in an emergency.

In a hotel locate the exit nearest to your room. Use a portable smoke detector if you do a lot of traveling.

Conduct frequent family fire drills. They're "just as necessary at home as in schools," says the National Safety Council. "A person who knows what to do in case of fire is not so likely to panic and become trapped."

With your family practice at least two escape routes from every room, especially bedrooms. Window ladders are a good investment for upper-floor rooms. Even a heavy rope, knotted for easy climbing, is better than nothing. Don't count on using stairways for escape because they are usually the first to be flooded with smoke and heat.

Teach everyone to do the bedroom-door heat test. Decide on a meeting point outside the house so no one will be tempted to return for someone who is already safe. Assign beforehand who is responsible for taking out young children, who should call the fire department, who should alert the neighbors.

Burn prevention. Fires and burns are the leading cause of death from nontraffic accidents to children 1 to 4 years old and the second leading cause of death to people 5 to 14 and 45 and older. Almost 8,000 fire and explosion deaths occur each year.

Writing in the *Journal of the American Medical Association,* three Texas physicians analyzed the results of a study of 368 burned children. Most of these cases happened under parents' noses, with 90 percent of the children studied having suffered burns in or near their homes. Among the causes they found, space heaters, matches, and outdoor fires were implicated in just more than half the cases. Flammable fabrics and flammable liquids were involved in 70 percent of the cases, with some overlapping of these two factors.

Cotton dresses and nightgowns were the clothing items that most often caught fire and injured children. Gasoline was the most common flammable liquid, with others including paint thinners, lighter fluids, and barbecue fire starters. In some cases gasoline helped ignite clothing.

Be especially cautious if you have an overweight son. A study by Dr. Douglas W. Wilmore and Basil A. Pruitt, Jr., of the Brooke Army Medical Center showed that heavier-than-average boys are far more likely than other children under 13 to suffer severe burns.

"With many of these children, the accident resulted from playing with matches or fire," the investigators noted. "Although this is a common cause of burns in children, the proportionally high number of heavy-for-age boys who sustained accidents in this manner suggests that they are more mischievous, not dexterous enough to prevent an accident, or too slow to avoid serious injury."

Burns are at their most damaging if clothing ignites. Clothing-fire victims suffer burns covering nearly twice as much body surface as fire victims whose clothing does not catch fire, with correspondingly greater scarring and difficulties in recuperation.

Select clothing to guard against ignition. The more tightly woven and heavy a fabric, in general the less likely it is to burn. It is the filmy nets and gauzes, the sheer, lightweight fabrics that burn most readily. Denim is much less flammable than organdy, while a fuzzy or napped fabric ignites much more readily than a smooth surface.

The farther the garment is from your body, the more air surrounds it and the more likely it is likely to ignite. Be cautious with loose-fitting robes, flaring skirts, blousy sleeves, ruffles, and frills. All are not only more flammable but also more likely to brush against a stove burner or lighted cigarette. Little girls' flared and many-petticoated party dresses are especially risky.

Beware cotton. Although the most common fabric for clothing and furnishings, cotton is highly flammable.

Most other fibers will also burn. Rayon, acetate, and triacetate (Chromspun, Celanese, Acele, Arnel) have about the same high flammability as cotton. Rayon-blend blankets are a particular hazard. Linen and paper are almost as flammable. Silk is not very flammable in its natural state, but is made more flammable by material added for color or body.

Nylon polyesters (Dacron, Fortrel, Kodel, Vycron) and acrylics (Acrilan, Creslan, Orlon, Zefran) are moderately flammable. Once ignited, they melt as they burn, forming a sticky, syrupy substance that can produce deep burns. Nomex, a form of nylon, is flame-resistant.

Wool is the least flammable of natural fibers. It resists igniting, burns slowly, and goes out by itself. Glass fibers and saran (Rovana, Velon) won't support combustion. Modacrylics (Verel, Dynel) and olefins (Herculon, Polycrest, Volpex) burn only when in contact with flame, then extinguish themselves. But even such flame-resistant fibers burn if treated with flammable finishes or blended with flammable fiber.

Look for garments that have been treated to retard flame. This is especially important for children and the elderly, who are most vulnerable to clothing fires. Children's sleepwear through size 6X must be made fire-retardant under the law. But you need to search out baby clothes or a blanket for Grandma that has been so treated.

While permanent treatment of fabrics is preferable, you can temporarily make cotton fabrics —especially children's costumes—flame-retardant in a bathtub or washing machine. Saturate the fabric with a solution of 7 ounces of borax, 3 ounces of boric acid, and 2 quarts of water, and allow to drip dry. Repeat the treatment if the garment is washed or dampened by rain.

Smoking and fires. Careless use of cigarettes and matches accounts for one in four fires. Don't smoke in bed or while drowsy in a chair. If flames from a dropped cigarette don't get you, smoke and fumes from smoldering padding can asphyxiate you before heat wakes you up.

Keep handy plenty of large, noncombustible ashtrays. Flush ashtray contents down the toilet. Don't throw them into a wastebasket, since they may be smoldering invisibly. Make a habit of bending or breaking each match before discarding it, so you'll know it's cooled off. Before going to bed, make sure no one has left a cigarette, cigar, or pipe burning anywhere. Check where smokers have sat for embers in the upholstery.

Allow only safety matches in your home. And keep them (and lighters) where children can't reach them. Store several flashlights wherever they may be needed—it's dangerous to use matches for illumination in attics, closets, or other dark spots.

Electrical fires. Investigate fuses that blow, lights that dim, TVs that flicker. They're signs that electrical circuits are dangerously over-loaded, causing wires to heat and possibly ignite inside your walls. Don't overload circuits with an electrical "octopus," a multiple receptacle that allows you to connect more than one plug to an outlet. Make sure air conditioners and other major appliances have adequate wiring.

Use fuses of recommended amperage, using 15 amperes (amp.) for lighting and small appliances. Fuses are like safety valves—they blow to disconnect the circuit before wires get hot enough to burn. If a fuse is oversized, or if a coin is used in place of a fuse, circuits can get hotter and hotter.

Most household extension-cord sets are not adequate for many loads. They have only 18-gauge wires, heavy enough for a total of 7 amperes or less, though the label usually proclaims that the set's receptacle and plug are rated 15 amperes. Use heavy-duty cords—at least 16-gauge—for appliances drawing a total of more than 7 amperes. To determine the amperage of an appliance, consult the nameplate; if only the wattage is given, divide by the voltage in your electrical service (generally 115).

Don't run electrical wires under rugs, over hooks or nails, or in other places where they may be subject to wear or damage. Check frequently and replace damaged cords. For prevention of electric shock as well as fire, buy only electric appliances and cords okayed by Underwriters Laboratories. Leave ventilation space around a TV set, and be sure that your TV antenna is properly grounded against lightning damage.

Have a licensed electrician do all electrical jobs. "Unqualified handymen are indirectly responsible for many electrical fires," warns the National Board of Fire Underwriters.

Heating-equipment fires. Have your furnace checked once a year. About one in five home fires can be traced to improperly functioning heating equipment. Overheating—pushing a furnace beyond its capacity—can cause a breakdown and fire. If flue pipes are less than 18 inches from flammable materials like wood, shield the combustible surface with asbestos, plaster, or metal.

Buy only portable heaters with broad bases that resist being toppled. Place the heaters where they won't be bumped into, and away from furnishings. Because of the risk of suffocation, extinguish an oil or gas heater before going to bed.

Teach children not to play near space heaters or floor furnace grates.

If you smell gas from a stove or furnace, call the gas company—tinkering by nonexperts can cause explosions.

In the kitchen instruct children to play away from the stove. Turn the handles of cooking pots toward the center of the stove so children can't reach them. Keep the stove clear of grease cans, matches, curtains, paper. Don't hang clothes over a stove to dry.

The National Safety Council has found that many children touch the heating units of electric ranges while they are still hot, though not glowing red. The council recommends keeping a teakettle with water on the stove. After turning off the burner, place the kettle on it to cover the unit while it cools.

Treat flammable liquids like dynamite. Gasoline has no place inside your house—not for a fuel, dry cleaner, or any other use. Its invisible vapors can travel near floor level, then explode on contact with a flame, hot surface, or electric spark. To reduce fire risks of power lawn mowers, fill a mower outdoors.

Kerosene can explode if heated above 100° F. The Food and Drug Administration (FDA) tells of one man who used kerosene as a starter for a coal stove. Some hot coals were already in the stove, causing the kerosene to explode and sending the man to the hospital for eight weeks.

Never fill a kerosene lantern or heater while it's burning. Or a fondue pot while it's still hot. Or squirt barbecue fluid once the charcoal is lighted—the flame can travel up the stream and explode the can in your hand.

Other such flammables include alcohol, turpentine and other paint removers, lighter fluid, oil-based paints, naphtha, some antifreeze solutions. Store all the foregoing in their original containers or in airtight metal containers (not glass, which can break and produce a Molotov cocktail), preferably in an outdoor locker well away from a furnace or other source of ignition. Anyone who smokes around volatile fluids is asking to be burned.

Oily rags bunched up in confined spaces can ignite spontaneously, building up heat from slow oxidation and then bursting into flame. Throw them away. Otherwise store them in tight metal containers, or draped so as to get plenty of air. Clean oil drippings promptly or cover them with sand.

Frequently get rid of old newspapers, broken furniture, and other fire-breeding rubbish. Burn trash and leaves in a metal waste burner. Start an open fire only on a clear day, away from buildings and fences. Keep it under close watch, and keep a garden hose connected in case of an emergency.

See also ACCIDENTS; BURNS; CHRISTMAS TREES.

FIREWORKS A 14-year-old boy intended to launch a homemade rocket with fuel made from match heads, cherry bombs, and shotgun powder. His hand was torn apart.

On the Fourth of July an 11-year-old boy who thought of fireworks as toys bought bootlegged firecrackers, which are widely available despite local prohibitions. After lighting them and dropping them into a hose, he put his eyes to the nozzle to see what was wrong. The explosion embedded gunpowder and fragments into the boy's eyes, permanently scarring his cornea.

At a public fireworks display one operator was killed and 57 spectators standing at a "safe" distance were injured by explosions.

A Minneapolis man lost his left foot after he stepped on a lighted firecracker a friend had tossed near him.

A five-year-old in Jacksonville, Florida, suffered burns on his back when his clothing was ignited by a sparkler.

In Vienna, Virginia, five people died in an apartment fire that started when a child tossed a firecracker against the stairway.

Pointing to such accidents, the National Fire Protection Association warns, "There is no such thing as a 'safe' firework!" Despite attempts to make them less dangerous, fireworks still contain the basic elements of gunpowder—sulfur, charcoal, saltpeter, and fulminate of mercury. Sparklers are sulfur-coated wires which burn at 1650° F and have a steel core hot enough to leave permanent burns and disfigurement.

Moral: Stay away from fireworks altogether.

However if you do use fireworks, take the following precautions:

· Store fireworks in a cool dry place, and out of the reach of children.
· Follow directions carefully.
· Light fireworks one at a time.
· Move away quickly once you've lit one.
· Never allow a child to use fireworks without an adult present.
· If fireworks don't function, douse water on them. Don't pick them up or try to relight.
· Never take fireworks apart to see how they work.

See also ACCIDENTS; BURNS; FIRE.

FIRST AID SUPPLIES can be a lifesaver in accidents at home or away. The AMA recommends that you keep these emergency supplies. Wrap the items listed below in a moisture-proof covering. Place them in a child-resistant box such as a fishing-tackle box or toolbox with a strong latch. Store it in the trunk of your car so it will be generally accessible to you at home and on outings. Quantities are for a family of four or fewer:

Item	Quantity	Use
1. Sterile first aid dressing in sealed envelope, 2 in. × 2 in., for small wounds	Box of 12	For open cuts or dry dressings for burns.
2. Sterile first aid dressing in sealed envelope, 4 in. × 4 in., for larger wounds and for compress to stop bleeding	Box of 12	These are packaged sterile. Do not try to make your own.
3. Roller bandage, 1 in. × 5 yds.	2	Finger bandage.
4. Roller bandage, 2 in. × 5 yds.	2	To hold dressings in place.
5. Adhesive tape	1 roll	To hold dressings in place.
6. Large bath towels	2	For bandages or dressings. Old soft towels and sheets are best. Cut in sizes necessary to cover wounds.
7. Small bath towels	2	Towels are burn dressings. Place over burns and fasten with triangular bandage or strips of sheet.
8. Bedsheet	1	Towels and sheet should be laundered, ironed, and packaged in heavy paper. Relaunder every 3 months.
9. Triangular bandage, 37 in. × 37 in. square, cut, or folded diagonally, with 2 safety pins	4	For a sling, as a covering, for a dressing.
10. Mild soap	1 bar	For cleansing of wounds, scratches, cuts. Antiseptics are not necessary.
11. Table salt	Small package	For shock—dissolve 1 tsp. salt, 1/2 tsp. baking soda in 1 qt. water.
12. Baking soda	Small package	
13. Measuring spoon	1 set	
14. Paper drinking cups	25	
15. Flashlight	1	
16. Safety pins, 11/2 in. long	1 dozen	
17. Scissors with blunt tips	1 pair	For cutting bandages or clothing.
18. Tweezers	1	To remove stingers from insect stings.
19. Splints 1/4 in. thick, 31/2 in. wide, 12–15 in. long	12	For splinting broken arms and legs.
20. Tongue blades, wooden	12	For splinting broken fingers and for stirring solutions.
21. Tourniquet: wide strip of cloth, 20 in. long	1	For use in severe injuries when no other method will control bleeding.
22. Short stick	1	To use with tourniquet.
23. Instant cold compresses	Package	For sprains, strains, swelling.
24. Fever thermometer	1	For illness, infection.
25. Antiseptic cream	1	For cuts and scrapes.
26. Ipecac syrup	1	To induce vomiting in case of poisoning.
27. Essential personal prescriptions.		

Also keep a Thermos of water and a stack of clean newspapers in your car. In an emergency clean newspapers are good ground covers. Spread newspaper under and around the victim to prevent contamination.

If you're going on vacation, assemble a kit from the foregoing and from home medical supplies.

See also ACCIDENTS; BANDAGES; BLEEDING; BURNS; CAMPING; FRACTURES; MEDICAL SUPPLIES; SHOCK; TOURNIQUET; TRAVEL HEALTH.

FISHING If a fishhook gets embedded in your flesh, don't try to pull it out. The barb will rip the flesh when pulled back.

Instead have the hook removed by a physician, who will check for protection against tetanus and other infections.

If you can't get to a doctor immediately, remove the hook yourself this way (see illustration): Push the hook through your skin in its natural arc until the point and barb protrude.

HOW TO REMOVE A FISHHOOK

Don't pull!

The barb will rip your flesh
1. Press wood against skin
   (This reduces pain)

2. Let point break through

   Push hook through

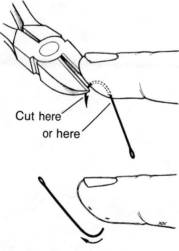

Cut here
   or here

Pull out remainder

Breaking the skin will be easier and less painful if you hold a block of wood against the exit area.

Cut the barbed end off the hook (make wire-cutting pliers part of your fishing equipment for just such emergencies). Remove the hook's shank and curve at the original point of entry. Treat the wounds as for punctures.

Most injuries in fishing accidents are inflicted by hooks. Be especially careful when baiting the hook—slippery worms, minnows, and grasshoppers are particularly hard to handle. Multiple hooks require extra caution.

Other fishing precautions. Handle a fishing rod and reel like a loaded gun: Disassemble the rod to and from the fishing site. When changing locations, carry the rod through underbrush with the reel and handle first. Secure the hooks with a hook keeper or cork cover.

When fishing, point the rod tip toward the water unless you're casting. Overhead casting gives the most effective control, especially when fishing from a boat. Never cast over anyone's head, and be sure there's plenty of room for backcasting.

Drowning, often while boating, is the greatest cause of death in fishing accidents. The National Safety Council advises against wading in a stream when you're alone. Wear cleated or felt-soled waders or boots to get maximum traction on slick surfaces. Don't trust flat underwater rocks—they're usually slippery.

See FALLS THROUGH ICE and FROSTBITE for precautions for winter fishing. Also see ACCIDENTS; BOATING; DROWNING; PUNCTURES.

FISH SCALE DISEASE See ICHTHYOSIS.

FLAT-CHESTEDNESS See BREAST SMALLNESS.

FLAT FEET See FALLEN ARCHES.

FLATULENCE See GAS.

FLEAS in the United States are primarily parasites of animals. They may take to biting you only after your cat or dog has died or run away. The connection may not be obvious, since the flea can go for three months before it gets hungry enough to change its diet from animal to human blood.

These wingless insects often reveal themselves through sores on a pet's skin caused by flea bites and the animal's tormented rubbing. To humans fleas can spread infectious disease, notably bubonic plague, tularemia, and typhus. As their most frequent symptom, fleabites raise blisters that are red and itching.

Many people suffering a flea invasion are needlessly embarrassed, since fleas are erroneously associated with poverty and filth. As a preventive follow insect-control precautions. Fleas can be wiped out with relatively safe insecticides. If the home is infested, first clean affected rooms with a vacuum cleaner, paying special attention to upholstered furniture. Then spray pyrethrins-based bug killers on baseboards and to walls to a height of about 1 foot. This treatment may need to be repeated in about a week.

On dogs, cats, puppies, and kittens use a product, labeled for the type of pet, containing 0.75 percent to 1 percent rotenone; or a product with 0.2 percent pyrethrins fortified with synergists; or 0.75 percent to 1 percent pyrethrins without synergists. It is safe to rub this into the animal's fur for treatment.

Rotenone works slowly. But pyrethrins work so fast that in a few minutes fleas start evacuating, so treat and comb or brush the animal on a sheet of newspaper. Then burn the paper and paralyzed fleas.

You may need to repeat treatments weekly if the animal runs free. Otherwise a single treatment should suffice. Clean and treat animal bedding and doghouses as well.

If you rent a house vacated by a family with a dog or cat, be careful you're not also renting fleas they left behind. Before you move in, consider asking your landlord to hire an exterminator.

See also INSECTS.

FLIES are practically designed to carry infectious disease. Their digestive tracts incubate germs, and flies breed in moist organic material like garbage and excrement, great reservoirs of pathogenic organisms. By providing an air express service between filth and foods, flies transmit cholera, food poisoning, infectious hepatitis, polio, tuberculosis, and typhoid.

Some tropical flies cause maggot infestation (myasis) by laying their eggs on people, especially babies sleeping outdoors. The eggs hatch and the larvae burrow beneath the skin, producing growths that resemble boils. Flies also may deposit eggs on open wounds and on the mouth, nose, ears, and vagina. Surgical removal of the larvae is usually necessary. Infestation can usually be avoided by personal cleanliness, and if a baby is sleeping outdoors, by protecting him with mosquito netting.

As a general preventive keep food covered. Screen all doors and windows. Fill in cracks in walls and floors.

Store garbage in a tightly covered can, and wash the can every few weeks. Enclose the garbage in a plastic bag if collections are less often than twice weekly. Since flies breed in decaying organic matter, bury or otherwise dispose of all stacked lawn clippings, fallen fruit, dog or cat excreta, and other organic refuse. Screen any outdoor privy and cover the contents of the pit with quick lime, crude oil, or an insecticide in oil.

The fly swatter is preferable to towels, rags, and other improvised swatters, which may spread contamination when used for their normal purposes. When more flies invade your rooms than you can control with a swatter, use sprays of pyrethrin, allethrin, or rotenone.

See also INSECTS.

FLOODS are dangerous, not only because of the damage caused by rising waters, but also because flooding frequently leads to disastrous fires. If flood waters are likely to reach your house, turn off all gas stoves and electric appliances. After the flood has receded, don't use matches or open flames until gas mains are checked by authorities for breakage and escaping gas. To avoid electric shock, before connecting appliances be sure they are dry and safe.

Be aware of the possibility that municipal or home water supplies may become contaminated. Flood waters often contain backed-up sewage. Destroy food and medicines that have been under water. Thoroughly wash cans before opening. It is not unusual for typhoid fever to break out in the aftermath of a flood.

At the first flood warning make sure your first aid supplies are at hand. Promptly treat cuts from debris that may be coated with contaminated residue.

If you are trapped in a building, go to the roof or highest floor and wait for help. Because of the risk of drowning the National Safety Council warns: "Don't attempt to swim or use makeshift rafts except as a final extremity."

See also ACCIDENTS; DROWNING; ELECTRIC SHOCK; FOOD POISONING; TYPHOID; WATER CONTAMINATION.

FLUORIDATION should be used in every community water supply. That it is not is a triumph of fear over reason.

Fluoridation is the controlled addition to drinking water of a fluoride, a chemical that is known to increase resistance of tooth surfaces to decay. All drinking water and many foods contain some fluoride—a compound of the element fluorine with another element like sodium or tin. But it generally appears in such small amounts that most people do not get enough to ward off decay.

Scientists now know that tooth decay is noticeably low in communities where the fluoride content of water is naturally high. However only a few areas have enough natural fluoride in their drinking supply to significantly reduce decay. After intensive study, it was decided to add sufficient fluoride to the drinking water of several cities (Grand Rapids, Michigan; Newburgh, New York; and Brantford, Ontario) to bring the level of the chemical up to one part per million gallons.

The plan worked better than investigators had hoped. Follow-up studies found 65 percent less tooth decay in children who drank fluoridated water from birth. In addition there was 45 percent less decay in children who were five or six years old when the programs started, and 20 percent less decay in those who were teen-agers at the start of fluoridation.

This success story has been repeated in virtually every community that has fluoridated its water. The overall conclusion is that people who drink fluoridated water for the first eight years of life average at least 60 percent less decay than those who grow up without benefit of fluorides.

Fluoride improves the structure of bone as well. After a lifetime of fluoridated water aged persons appear to be less susceptible to bone fractures and less likely to develop degenerative bone diseases such as osteoporosis.

Consumer groups call fluoridation a classic example of a good public-health procedure: It serves the whole population. It calls for no conscious effort from the people it benefits. It automatically restricts individual consumption of fluoride to levels proved safe for all ages and for the chronically ill as well as the healthy. The annual cost per capita is only a dime, about one fiftieth of the price of the simplest silver filling.

Fluoridation is safe. Even water containing as much as eight times the amount of fluoride recommended for decay prevention does not injure health. There is no reliable evidence that fluoridation harms people with kidney disorders or allergies, or those already getting occupational exposure to fluorides.

Too much fluoride in water, which occurs in some areas where natural fluoride must be *removed,* can cause teeth to develop harmless though unattractive brownish mottling or opaque white flecks. But concentrations must greatly exceed those used in controlled fluoridation before even that much discoloration will take place. The addition of fluoride in the recommended quantity actually improves the appearance of teeth, making them whiter and shinier.

In sum, concluded Dr. Nicholas C. Leone, chief of medical investigation of the National Institute of Dental Research, "We know without question or doubt that one part per million fluoride in a water supply is absolutely safe, is beneficial, and is not productive of any undesirable systemic effect in man."

Most of the nation's big cities have fluoridated water. Among them are New York, Chicago, Philadelphia, Baltimore, St. Louis, and Washington, D.C. Connecticut, Illinois, and Minnesota have passed laws making mandatory the fluoridation of all public water supplies.

Recent studies show that fluoride—in water supplies, tablets or drops, toothpaste, and special fluoride treatments—is the main reason tooth decay in American children was reduced by a third in the last decade. The National Institute for Dental Research reports that 59 percent of children between the ages of 5 and 11 have never had a cavity.

The American Dental Association, the American Medical Association, the U.S. Public Health Service, the American Academy of Pediatrics, and virtually all other scientific and professional organizations having competence in the field recommend the fluoridation of public water supplies. Former surgeon general Dr. Luther L. Terry has called water fluoridation "one of the four great, mass preventive health measures of all time"—in the same league as the pasteurization of milk, the purification of water, and immunization against disease.

Why not more fluoridation? Despite such endorsement any proposal to introduce community fluoridation arouses bitter opposition, and militant antifluoridationists more often than not raise enough doubts to defeat the measure. Fluoridation is voted down in three out of five communities having referenda on the issue.

Foes of fluoridation often resort to scare tactics. A frequent charge is that fluorides are poisonous substances found in rat poison and insecticides, and their effects may not be noticed for 20 years. The rallying cry "KEEP RAT POISON OUT OF YOUR WATER!" is fallacious, as is "DON'T BE A GUINEA PIG!"—another common (and potent) slogan against fluoridation, which is one of the most painstakingly proved health measures in history.

Only in the most extreme sense is fluoride a poison—in the same sense that table salt, oxygen, even plain water are all poisons. Taken in excessive amounts, any could cause illness or death. Some 7 million Americans drink naturally high concentrations of fluoride in untreated water all their lives, but long-term studies of thousands of them show no adverse effect on general health.

Fluoride treatment. Other ways of getting fluoride can provide some protection. It's wise to seek alternative sources of fluoride if your community water supply is not fluoridated, or if your water comes from a private well.

Families can have teeth painted with fluorides by a dentist or dental hygienist. Even in fluoridated areas children may benefit from fluoride treatments.

Taking fluoride daily in tablets or drops is beneficial if it is done regularly during the more than ten years teeth are being formed in the jaws. A dentist or a physician must supervise the taking of fluoride because the supplement must be adapted to the child's age and intake of fluoride from other sources. Improper use of concentrated fluorides can be dangerous. As a precaution no large quantities of fluoride should be kept in the home and all quantities should be stored out of reach of children.

A less effective method of application is regular use of special fluoride toothpaste. Even if fluoride is available from other sources, fluoridated toothpaste may be of value. Moreover, studies of toothpaste containing fluoride indicate that its regular use can prolong the effectiveness of the dentist's fluoride treatments.

See also MINERALS; TEETH AND MOUTH DISORDERS; TOOTHPASTE.

FOAM, VAGINAL See BIRTH CONTROL.

FOLIC ACID See ANEMIA; VITAMINS.

FOOD ADDITIVES are a mixed blessing.

Of more than 2,000 additives that turn up in food, some are used to maintain or improve color, flavor, texture. Some are used for sweetening and thickening. Some can boost nutrition. Some retard spoilage, inhibit bacterial growth, cure meats. Some serve no useful purpose but become components of food through contact with processing equipment or packaging materials.

Under the law the Food and Drug Administration (FDA) must approve all new food additives. In addition the FDA maintains a list of substances identified as GRAS (generally accepted as safe), and these are currently undergoing review for safety. On the basis of new evidence the FDA can allow continued use, limit their use, or ban them altogether.

When a substance is cleared, the FDA assures that "risk of adverse effects . . . is at an acceptably small level," but adds that "there is no way in which absolute safety can be guaranteed."

Even if a food additive is generally safe for the public, it may not be safe for you. There is always the possibility of an adverse allergic reaction. Anyone on a low-sodium diet must read labels carefully to avoid products with added sodium compounds like salt or MSG (monosodium glutamate, a flavor enhancer).

Some people with an allergy to MSG experience what is called "Chinese restaurant syndrome." They suffer headache, facial pressure, and chest pain after eating Chinese meals that contain large amounts of MSG.

Many food additives considered safe at present levels of usage may present health hazards when given in extremely high doses. On the other hand, the FDA points out, *any* food eaten in large quantities may be harmful: "It is likely that all substances, either natural or synthetic food ingredients or additives, when fed at a high enough level for a period of time, will produce some chronic biological injury."

Go light on additives. Since the cumulative effect of eating many food additives over many years is unknown, it may be prudent to select foods with the fewest and least controversial additives.

You need not fear most compounds used to improve nutrition. Vitamins and iron enrich many juices, breads, and margarines. Amino acids, components of protein, are added to some foods.

But many so-called convenience foods consist of virtually nothing but synthetic chemical additives with a sprinkling of vitamins and a heavy dose of sugar. This is true, for example, of some imitation fruit drinks. Many other foods, such as most commercial cereals and frozen dinners, contain natural ingredients plus many synthetic food additives.

To reduce your consumption of additives, use fresh or minimally processed foods as much as possible. Drink real fruit juices, not "drinks." Read labels carefully, and select packaged goods with fewer additives.

Two classes of food additives of particular concern are:

Artificial sweeteners. The quest goes on for an artificial sweetener with the fewest possible calories—and no harmful medical effects.

After cyclamate was banned in the United States for being carcinogenic, saccharin became the only permitted noncaloric sweetener. Its greatest use has been in low-calorie sodas and in tabletop sugar substitutes. It's also been used as a sweetener in dietetic foods and in a wide range of products including toothpaste, mouthwashes, drugs, and cigarette paper.

Then a 1977 Canadian study found a relationship between saccharin and cancer of the bladder in rats. Canada banned saccharin, and there was a threat the FDA would do the same. Although saccharin is still available, questions about its ability to cause cancer have not been fully resolved.

The most recent review of the saccharin evidence by the National Academy of Sciences concluded that saccharin is a weak carcinogen in animals and is probably also capable of causing cancer in human beings. Saccharin might act as a cocarcinogen, promoting other cancer-causing agents.

In the United States all saccharin-containing products bear this label: "Use of this product may be hazardous to your health. This product contains saccharin which has been determined to cause cancer in laboratory animals."

Not only is saccharin possibly harmful, but it also may work against efforts to lose weight. There is evidence that saccharin enhances appetite, causing an overall weight gain. Animals that got saccharin-sweetened drinks increased their intake of solid food, more than offsetting any calories saved by using a substitute for sugar.

If you've used saccharin as a diet aid, you're safer—and possibly more likely to lose weight—if you consume sugar instead. Simply eat less elsewhere in your diet to compensate for the sugar (at 18 calories per teaspoon).

The latest artificial sweetener to hit the market is Aspartame. It is used as a sweetener in breakfast cereals, powdered beverages, gelatin, puddings, fillings, whipped toppings, and chewing gum. Under the trade name Equal, it is also available as a tablet or in powder form for table use.

Aspartame is certainly sweet—about 180 times the sweetness of sugar. The equivalent sweetness of 1 teaspoon of sugar is only .10 of a calorie. But as with saccharin, the long-term safety of Aspartame remains to be determined.

Nitrites. Used in bacon, frankfurters, bologna, corned beef, other cured meats, and some smoked fish, nitrite gives the meat its red tint and helps preserve it against spoilage. It particularly protects against the botulism microorganism, which can be fatal.

There is considerable laboratory evidence that when nitrite is taken into the body, it can join with compounds called amines to form nitrosamines, a group of substances known to be carcinogenic.

Does this pose a significant health hazard? No one really knows. A recent report by an expert committee convened by the National Academy of Sciences at the request of the FDA and the Department of Agriculture found some evidence to suggest that high exposure to nitrites might be associated with an increased risk of cancer of the stomach and esophagus. The committee recommended that the use of nitrites in meat products be reduced "to the extent that protection against botulism is not compromised," and that alternative curing agents be sought.

At the same time, the committee came to the conclusion that cured meats accounted for only a small proportion of the average person's exposure to nitrosamines, and that eliminating nitrites from meats would "not have a major effect on the risk" of cancer.

Other sources of nitrosamines include cigarette smoke, cosmetics, soaps, shampoos, some drugs, and new car interiors.

Nitrates—which can be converted to nitrites by bacterial action—are naturally high in many vegetables, including beets, celery, endive, lettuce, parsley, radishes, rhubarb, and turnip greens. But the committee noted that the vitamin C in these vegetables could block the formation of nitrosamines. Vitamin E may have a similar effect. But it is not yet known if supplemental vitamin C or E could completely protect against nitrosamine formation.

Nitrates are also found in baked goods, cereals, fruit juices, and some other foods. Some drinking water is high in nitrates because of fertilizer runoff.

Nitrosamine exposure is highest among people who work in such industries as rubber manufacture, leather-tanning, and rocket fuel.

Until the question of nitrite hazard is resolved, it seems prudent to limit your exposure. Eat cured meats sparingly. In some specialty stores you can find frozen bacon and hot dogs, free of nitrites.

When you do have a product cured with nitrites, have some food high in vitamin C at the same time. Add a sliced tomato to your bacon sandwich, for example, or glaze a cured ham with orange and pineapple juice. It might also help to add foods rich in vitamin E to the meal —cereal grains or vegetable fats, for example.

If you grow your own vegetables, use a low-nitrate fertilizer.

When you eat fresh vegetables naturally high in nitrates, cook only the amount you expect to eat at one meal. After vegetables are cooked, bacteria act to change nitrates to nitrites. Store cooked vegetables for only a day or two in the refrigerator. Commercially frozen cooked vegetables are not a problem—freezing stops the action of the bacteria.

See also NUTRITION.

FOOD ALLERGY One man's meat may be another man's poison. Eating a food you are sensitive to may be followed by asthma, hay fever, hives, eczema, migraine, eye symptoms, nausea, intestinal cramps, and diarrhea. A food allergy can also cause itching of the palms, scalp, and hairy areas of the body.

Allergic inflammation of the lips and mouth may result from contact with foods or with cosmetics, toothpaste, mouthwashes, or dental plates and adhesives. Canker sores are sometimes due to food sensitivity.

Anaphylactic shock, fortunately rare, is the most startling response to allergenic foods. The symptoms consist of generalized itching, restlessness, labored breathing, perspiration, weakness, and pallor. There also may be chest and abdominal pains, and nausea, vomiting, and diarrhea that is sometimes bloody. Hives and swelling often break out. Occasionally the condition leads to suffocation and circulatory collapse. Anaphylactic symptoms usually occur immediately after the food is eaten.

An allergy to milk, wheat, or other substances can be the cause of seeming retardation or behavioral problems in children. Some food-sensitive children become irritable, sluggish, unpredictable in behavior. The child may be tired after a full night's sleep, pale, and be puffy and have dark circles around the eyes.

Some victims react even before the food is swallowed, while it is still in the mouth. At other times there may be a delayed response: hours or even a day may elapse. It is thought that in immediate reactions the offending allergen is the whole food protein. With delayed reactions the cause may be some product formed during the process of digestion. This may explain why skin tests with whole food extracts often fail to demonstrate causes of food allergies.

Which foods cause the allergy? Diagnosis depends mainly on a careful dietary history and sometimes an elimination diet, in which you eat only a few foods. Other foods are then restored to the diet one by one. If symptoms reappear after a food is restored, omit it from your diet.

Such common foods as fish, chocolate, nuts, beans, eggs, and milk widely cause allergic reactions. Some doctors urge that you keep chocolate in particular from any child with any allergy. Evidence shows the sweet adds to the allergic youngster's already abundant troubles.

In infants the foods that most often cause gastrointestinal problems—from swelling of the lip to cramps and diarrhea—are eggs, milk, wheat, and some vegetables such as peas, squash, and beets. After the age of 20 months the commonest offenders are peanuts, peanut butter, watermelon, cantaloupe, apples, all nuts, chocolate,

coconut, cheese, cottonseed oil, shellfish, and occasionally corn and popcorn.

When a food allergy causes bladder problems—urinary burning, painful urination, feelings of urgency—the foods most frequently responsible are in the pea-bean family, barley, cabbage, nuts, peanuts, soybeans, licorice, and fish.

Eggs are contained in many prepared foods. They may provoke reactions in allergic people who were unaware of their presence. If you are allergic to eggs, you may get a reaction to custards and various other puddings; ice creams and sherbets; some candies; almost all cakes, including macaroons, griddle cakes, and muffins; some cake and pancake flours; waffles; egg noodles; and mayonnaise and some salad dressings. While hardly visible, the white of egg brushed on breads, rolls, and pretzels to provide a glaze may cause an allergic problem.

Milk is often an unsuspected ingredient in many types of white bread, cakes, custards, candies, ice creams, cream soups, cream sauces, noodles, macaroni, spaghetti, and instant foods. But if you are sensitive to fresh milk, you may be able to tolerate it heated, boiled, or evaporated.

Food contaminants can cause allergic symptoms. Infants may react to sulfa drugs or penicillin taken by a nursing mother. Cow's milk may contain traces of penicillin used in treatment of the animal. In one instance infants with eczema were wrongly diagnosed as allergic to milk. Actually they were allergic to fish: the cows producing the milk had been fed meal containing ground fish.

The vegetable gums—karaya, tragacanth, and acacia—used in the food industry to thicken foods, may cause allergic symptoms. These substances are used in fillings of candies, processed Cheddar cheese, cream cheese, whipped-cream cake icing, toothpastes, commercial potato salad, mustard, Jell-O, and wheat cakes. If you are sensitive, be cautious of labels that merely say "vegetable gums" without specifying the exact product.

Reactions may vary. Some people have symptoms only if the food is eaten in large quantities or in a certain season. Some people don't have symptoms if one allergenic food is eaten, but eating 3 or 4 at the same meal may cause a reaction. Similarly, a food may cause symptoms only when taken along with alcohol.

In most cases you'll find cooked or canned, rather than raw, foods less allergenic. Omissions of foods or other changes in diet may result in unbalancing the diet so that you may lack sufficient proteins, minerals, or vitamins. Diet regulation needs to be under the guidance of a physician.

It is sometimes better to take frequent small meals, perhaps as often as five a day, than to stick to the routine of three main meals. Avoid heavy, greasy foods, difficult to digest. Since there may be a loss of water in allergic attacks, take plenty of liquids.

Sometimes desensitization can be achieved through very gradual reintroduction. The allergen is removed from your diet. Then minute amounts are restored and your tolerance is carefully watched. The amounts are gradually increased. An average of three or four months of gradual feeding is needed to achieve results, and even then you must watch carefully for any return of sensitivity.

Another approach is to avoid the food for 2 years, then reintroduce it gradually. Often the allergy is eliminated.

See ALLERGY.

FOOD, HEALTH See HEALTH FOOD.

FOOD POISONING (food-borne illness). Seventeen-year-old Jeff Cooley was an incoming freshman at East Tennessee State University. With his parents he was attending an open house. They toured the campus, chatted with staff members, and ate a box lunch. About two hours after eating they began to feel ill.

Along with the Cooleys some 300 people were developing nausea and vomiting, diarrhea, abdominal cramps, fever with chills. Some collapsed and dozens were rushed to a hospital emergency room. All were victims of a toxin produced by staphylococci bacteria, the most common cause of poisoning from food.

Self-help in such cases: Do nothing to retard your vomiting and diarrhea. Your gastrointestinal tract is ridding itself of the irritant.

Warm compresses on the abdomen, plenty of fluids, and bed rest usually bring about complete recovery in a few days. Children, the elderly, and the infirm especially need extra fluids to ward off dehydration.

Most cases of staph food poisoning result from food being prepared by an infected person who shows no symptoms. The food is left unrefrigerated long enough for the staph to multiply. They release a toxin that resists heat—so even if the food is then cooked and the bacteria killed, the food may remain poisonous, though it looks and tastes fine.

Nearly everyone harbors staph bacteria from time to time, commonly on the hands and arms, in the nose, on the hairy regions of the body. At the East Tennessee campus the outbreak was traced to a staph-infected kitchen worker who had mixed macaroni salad for the box lunch. This alone would not cause the poisoning outbreak. But the salad was kept out of the refrigerator for about six hours. By the time it was eaten, it was alive with staph.

Preventing food poisoning. Keep cold foods cold (below 40° F) and hot foods hot (above 140° F). Bacteria thrive in between, when temperatures range from merely chilly to warm. Dump without tasting any food that by odor or appearance makes you suspect its safety—a mere taste of some toxins can cause illness. Be particularly careful in hot weather.

Put cooked food into the refrigerator or freezer while still hot. The old practice of cooling food to room temperature first (so as not to "strain the refrigerator"—a fallacy) gives bacteria a running head start. Also refrigerate leftovers right away. Leaving them on the table invites contamination.

Thaw frozen foods in the refrigerator, not at room temperature.

When you shop, buy frozen foods last, and buy only packages stored deep in the freezer—the top layer often thaws. Go right home and put perishables in the refrigerator; the temperature in most cars is ideal for bacterial growth. Don't refrigerate in deep containers—food acts as an insulator, and the center of large masses of food can stay warm for long periods even though the outer layers may be almost frozen.

Refrigeration doesn't kill bacteria, merely slows their growth, so even refrigerated food can spoil. For storage longer than three or four days, maintain a temperature of 40° F or below. Leave space around stored foods for air to circulate. Don't block air flow by lining refrigerator shelves with foil or paper. Don't let more than 1/4 inch of ice collect on the cooling coils, or cooling efficiency will nosedive. To make sure cold air is not leaking out, close the refrigerator door on a dollar bill. If you can slip the bill out easily, it's time to replace the rubber gasket.

Your freezer temperature needs to be −10° F for storage up to six months, colder if you'll keep foods longer. If your freezer goes off in a mechanical breakdown or power failure, don't open the freezer door. Insulation will keep food frozen up to 48 hours in a full freezer, 24 hours in a partially filled one. If the freezer will be out of commission for more than 48 hours, transfer the food to a commercial locker, or pile dry ice on top of the food (you'll need about 50 pounds for a full-size freezer).

Don't refreeze any food that has completely thawed and warmed to above 45° F. Contamination may have already begun. If you can't use the thawed food within a day or so, cook and refreeze it, or discard it. You may safely refreeze foods that have thawed to refrigerator temperatures, though with refreezing you may lose some vitamin C and impair the food's taste and texture.

Be especially careful with foods high in moisture and protein. Disease-causing bacteria flourish in milk, milk products, eggs, meat, poultry, fish, shellfish—and such products as cream pies, custards, sandwich fillings, salads (especially tuna, chicken, potato). Some tips on specific foods and locales:

Milk. Drink only pasteurized milk. Pasteurization eliminates the risk of tuberculosis, brucellosis, and other milk-borne infectious disease.

It is a myth that pasteurization makes milk significantly less nutritious. While pasteurizing removes some vitamin C, this has no appreciable effect on your diet. It is also untrue that poisoning can result from consuming milk with seafood or with acid fruits.

Eggs. Don't eat cracked eggs, which are breeding grounds for bacteria. Avoid raw eggs, which may carry illness from infected birds. Contrary to myth, raw eggs are no more nutritious than cooked eggs.

Wash eggs before breaking to prevent the raw egg from coming in contact with bacteria on the shell. Keep egg products like cream fillings, custard, and meringue continuously refrigerated, or cook them just before serving.

Meat and poultry. Beware trichinosis from pork products. Don't eat raw beef. It may carry toxoplasmosis and tapeworms, plus bacteria called *Salmonella,* which are responsible for many outbreaks of food poisoning.

Don't wash meat—the added moisture promotes bacterial growth. Have meat ground in your presence. Since hamburger is extremely susceptible to contamination even in a refrigerator, eat it or freeze it within a day.

Mold on cooked meat in the refrigerator is generally a sign the meat is so spoiled you should throw it away. On raw meat, however, mold is a harmless aid to an "aging" process that improves flavor.

Don't stuff poultry until immediately before you cook it. The moist interior of a bird is a good environment for bacteria. Keep raw fowl away from other food—infection may spread from a diseased bird. Cook poultry to an internal temperature of at least 165° F.

"Freezer burn," appearing as grayish specks, may make meat and poultry less palatable but does not render it unsafe to eat. The discoloration results from drying out, and can be avoided with moisture-proof wrapping. Airtight packaging also protects meat from oxygen that can make fat rancid, imparting an off-flavor.

Seafood. Don't eat raw fish, which can carry parasites. Be especially careful to properly refrigerate members of the scombroid family of fish—tuna, swordfish, mackerel, albacore, bonito, skipjack—which release a poison as they decompose.

Buy (or pick) shellfish only from sources you absolutely trust. Shellfish from contaminated waters can carry infectious hepatitis. Some unscrupulous merchants have sold clams and mussels gathered from coasts struck by red tide. The one-celled red organisms can cause anyone who eats the shellfish to develop a possibly fatal paralytic poisoning.

Oysters are verboten from May through August on the East Coast, from May through October on the West Coast. During these months the shellfish can develop a high level of saxitoxin, a substance that can cause severe illness.

Fruits and vegetables. Wash them before eating. Pesticides used against insects and rats may leave a residue that can cause illness. Also a large number of parasites—pinworms, roundworms, amebiasis, shigellosis—can be transmitted through dirt on food, particularly on food that is fertilized with human excrement.

Cut away green patches on potatoes before cooking. They could be concentrations of solanine, a toxic agent. Similarly, while rhubarb stalks are perfectly safe, cut away the leaves—oxalic acid in them can cause illness. On the other hand it used to be believed that raw cucumbers are poisonous unless eaten with salt. That's not so.

Never pick mushrooms unless you've been shown in the field by an expert precisely which kinds of mushrooms are safe, which are poisonous. There is no rule of thumb to distinguish mushrooms from toadstools—poisonous mushrooms don't turn silver black or peel any differently from safe ones. Being guided by a book is extremely risky. Even experienced mushroom pickers get fooled, with tragic consequences, so you're safest buying mushrooms commercially.

Don't store fruit juices or fruits in ceramic containers because of a risk of lead poisoning from the glazes. Zinc (in galvanized iron), antimony, and cadmium make for toxic cookware and food containers. On the other hand, despite scare stories to the contrary, aluminum and Teflon—the no-stick coating for cookware—are harmless.

Keep an eye out for sanitation. One mother poisoned her family with staph from an infected hangnail. If you have an infection on your hand, wear gloves before touching food.

As basic a precaution as washing your hands before handling food can go a long way toward eliminating food-borne illness. So too be sure work surfaces and utensils are clean. Don't mix food with your hands when you can use a clean spoon or fork.

Restaurants. Before eating in a restaurant, it's a good idea to inspect the kitchen. Food critic Duncan Hines used to walk out of any establishment that balked. He found that the best restaurants are proud to give a kitchen tour.

Even high-priced restaurants can be pigpens. At one mid-Manhattan restaurant the New York City Health Department uncovered: "Heavy fly infestation in kitchen, butcher shop and dining room area. . . . No sterilization facilities for glasses. . . . Accumulation of grease, soot, and dust. . . . Rat burrows in the cellar. . . . Roach infestation."

Other indicators of a low level of sanitation: Employees have colds or other illnesses that can spread germs to food. The waiter's fingernails are dirty. A person who handles food also handles money—a study reported in the *Journal* of the AMA found that 42 percent of a sampling of dollar bills carried staph or other food-poisoning bacteria.

Outdoors. When picnicking, hiking, or camping, plan your meals around preserved, dehydrated, or canned food and fresh fruits and vegetables, which are least subject to infection.

Unless you have a heavily insulated container, don't try to transport hot food. Instead chill cooked food well and reheat just before the meal.

Make a practice of freezing foods you're planning to take on a picnic. As your portable ice chest warms up, food taken from the refrigerator is likely to get to bacteria-spawning temperatures. Frozen food will last longer and help keep the ice chest cold, be ready to eat when you arrive. You can make sandwiches by using frozen slices of bread and well-chilled or frozen fillings.

Keep your ice chest in the shade. For long trips pack it with dry ice. Limit food quantities so there will be no leftovers. You may be better off throwing leftovers out rather than trying to eat them later.

Bring along paper plates and cups and throw them away. Washing dishes when picnicking can be both a nuisance and a sanitary problem.

"Ptomaine poisoning," an old name for food poisoning, is a misnomer. Ptomaines are protein substances found in decayed food, and were once considered responsible for the effects of food poisoning. It has since been discovered that ptomaines are destroyed by your digestive system and cause no harm.

For severe types of food poisoning, see AMEBIC DYSENTERY; BOTULISM; LEAD POISONING; POISONOUS PLANTS; SALMONELLOSIS; SHIGELLOSIS. Also see INFECTIOUS DISEASE; TRAVEL HEALTH.

FOOTBALL is the "roughest and most dangerous" of sports, warns the National Safety Council. About 1 in 12 players are injured in football accidents every year. Some 15 boys a year die, mainly from head injuries. Many others suffer permanent damage.

Before you let your child play football, the council urges you to be sure of these safeguards:

His helmet should protect his head. Look for certification that the helmet meets the American National Standards Institutes Z-90 level of performance. Demand that your child's school team buy only headgear that meets this standard. A knee striking a head can transmit 400 foot-pounds of energy, far more than most helmets in general use can protect against.

A helmet should have an around-the-head inside padding of plastic foam that protects ears and neck. There should be 1 inch of airspace between the shell and canvas or nylon suspension webbing, which should adjust to head size so the helmet neither falls over your child's eyes nor turns on his head. There should be a plastic-coated aluminum face guard. If possible, find a helmet with *outside* as well as inside padding. The hard-shell helmet can cause injury on impact.

Helmets that start at $2.29 are actually toys: thin plastic shells, with minimal webbing, that offer virtually no protection against impact. Such helmets should never be used in an actual game.

Testimony before the National Commission on Product Safety showed that even expensive helmets could be hazardous to your child's head. Witnesses revealed that some manufacturers did almost no scientific testing and had little knowledge of what blows might be expected in a game or what good their helmets might do. One maker of expensive helmets was said to have advertised them as the finest in the field without having tested any competitive product.

Old helmets should be discarded, never passed down. Perspiration and wear play havoc with the all-important inner lining, especially around ears, forehead, temple.

His equipment must protect him from face to feet. A mouthpiece not only prevents a lot of damage to his lips and teeth but also provides a cushion against blows to his head and chin that might otherwise cause concussion.

His shoulders, hips, thighs, and knees must be properly fitted with full-weight pads. Effective shoulder pads are provided with a cantilever arrangement.

He should wear stockings to protect his legs from cuts and infections. His shoes should be waterproofed for playing on wet fields and need to be kept in good repair.

He must have a thorough physical exam. Before he joins the team, take your youngster to a doctor for a physical examination that includes X rays of any past injuries, a urinalysis, and an electrocardiogram. No child who has a heart abnormality should play football.

Make sure the coach is qualified to administer first aid in case of the inevitable minor injuries. Only a doctor (and not a trainer or coach) is qualified to decide whether a player can return to the game after being hurt. If an injury causes fainting or unconsciousness, he needs to see a doctor immediately. Any concussion calls for X-ray and encephalogram studies.

He should play only against youngsters of comparable size and skill. See to it that opposing teams are evenly matched.

The ideal arrangement is for freshmen to play freshmen, and so forth. Opposing schools should also be about the same size, since a small school has a smaller pool to draw on for first-rank players and replacements.

His coach should be safety-minded. "Unfortunately," comments the AMA, "coaches are sometimes hired primarily to win games; and it is made known to them in no uncertain terms that their jobs depend on a winning record. Is it any wonder that the interests of the boy become secondary under these conditions?"

When it comes to football safety, any boy will obey the rules of his coach on the field rather than the rules of his parents back home. It is essential to have a coach who will insist that his players wear complete equipment for practice scrimmages because these can be as risky as real games. He will always arrange for a doctor to be on call during games and scrimmages.

Most injuries occur when a player is blocking, tackling, or being tackled. A safety-minded coach prohibits dangerous tactics such as "spear tackling," in which the tackler aims his head at the breastbone of the ball carrier. This has caused tacklers spinal injuries resulting in paralysis. It can also damage the liver, spleen, and heart of the player being speared.

Expect your child's coach to teach the art of taking falls without getting hurt. There needs to be at least one week of practicing before the squad plays a game. Players need to be kept active and warmed up during all phases of practice. Watch that substitutes are thoroughly warmed up before being sent into a game, and that the whole team warms up before the kickoff of each half.

In general, be sure your child's coach is giving higher priority to health and safety than to winning games. Since youngsters are often reckless with their health, a coach must be prepared to enforce safety practices despite a boy's opposition.

A 16-year-old Trenton, New Jersey, high school student died of heat stroke after a football practice session of more than two hours in hot weather of 90°. The coach explained that though the boy had complained of fatigue, he was allowed to play, since he said he didn't want to rest while others practiced.

See also HEAD INJURIES; SPORTS.

FOOT PROBLEMS Abraham Lincoln is reported to have complained: "When my feet hurt, I can't think." The estimated 80 percent of adults who suffer from foot problems may share this sentiment.

Some foot problems are the result of congenital deformities of the feet, legs, or hips. In other instances foot pain is related to conditions such as arthritis, gout, diabetes, or poor circulation.

By far the most common cause of foot pain is related to structural deformities of the foot. Shoes that are too tight, too loose, or too high-heeled may cause stiff toes and tight heel cords. Pressure and friction from ill-fitting shoes often result in corns, calluses, and blisters. Bunions commonly cause problems when the shoe is cramped across the ball of the foot.

A shoe that doesn't give good support under the arch may aggravate fallen arches (flat feet) and cause foot pain. Tight shoes, stockings, or socks pressing against the toe may contribute to ingrown toenails.

Overweight can compound the discomfort resulting from a poor shoe or even from walking or standing too long in a good shoe. Similarly, pregnant women often develop foot problems when their feet are taxed with the added weight of pregnancy.

Athlete's foot is a common foot infection characterized by itching, redness, and swelling between the toes. It is caused by a fungus. Plantar warts may develop on the soles or balls of the feet, often making walking painful.

Foot problems are the special area of podiatric physicians (podiatrists, chiropodists), graduates of four-year colleges of podiatric medicine who are licensed in every state to treat the foot medically and surgically. Some foot-related problems require the care of a medical doctor or orthopedic surgeon (orthopedist). See illustration for care of injured toe.

WHEN A TOE IS INJURED
For broken, stubbed, crushed toes
Splinting can relieve pain, help healing

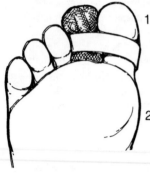

1. Wrap gauze around injured toe
(Reduces sweating, friction, blisters)

2. Tape to adjacent toe
(Healthy toe acts as splint)

Check a baby's feet. Proper foot care for babies and children may help avert many foot problems. Have a baby's feet checked regularly. Your child may have a congenital foot deformity that requires correction.

Children who walk with severe toe-in or toe-out may suffer from a twisting in the leg that has very little to do with the feet. The condition may warrant placing the child in a cast or brace to straighten the legs. Never buy orthopedic shoes or arch supports on a shoe salesman's advice.

Most doctors believe that the best foot covering for infants is nothing. Loose booties or socks can be worn on chilly days. But be wary of tight stretch suits that may press too tightly on a child's toes and cause them to overlap.

When a child begins to walk, he should be fitted for shoes. The young child's shoes should have a soft, flexible sole and a rounded toe. They should be at least a thumb's width longer than the big toe and sufficiently wide so that a small amount can be pinched up.

Many people buy children's shoes with high tops with the mistaken notion that such shoes will strengthen a child's ankles.

Sneakers may be the best shoes you can buy for your child's feet. They are softer and more elastic than leather and will give his feet more freedom to develop. You needn't buy sneakers with arch supports. Normal feet provide their own support.

Relieving foot discomfort. For relief of swollen, aching, tired feet: Try resting your feet by elevating them several times a day. At night soak your feet for about ten minutes, alternating between tubs of lukewarm and cold water.

Women often experience calf cramps after switching from high heels to flats. This is because the calf muscles, shortened by the wearing of high heels, cause pain when they try to lengthen again. You can help your calf muscles adjust more easily by walking around barefoot on your heels with your toes off the ground. Do this three or four times a day regularly.

Tight heel cords are another problem of women who regularly wear high heels. You can relax the heel cords by doing the following exercise daily: Place your palms against a wall and move toward it by using your ankles only. As your cords relax, you'll be able to stand farther and farther from the wall.

Buying shoes. Changing to properly fitting shoes may improve foot comfort. Here are some hints for buying the best shoe for you:

Buy shoes in the afternoon. Feet expand in the course of a day, and the shoes you buy in the morning may be too small in the afternoon. Feet also expand in hot weather, so it's unwise to buy summer shoes in the winter.

A good shoe should be wide over the ball and fit the heel snugly. Make sure the shoe gives firm support along the inner border of the arch. Make sure you can wiggle your toes freely. The shoe should extend 1/2 inch beyond your longest toe. Don't buy too-tight shoes with the thought of breaking them in. It's more likely that instead of the shoe conforming to your foot, your foot will conform to the shoe.

If you have foot problems, buy leather- instead of rubber-soled shoes. The rubber sole is generally too soft to give adequate cushioning and it produces more friction on contact with the ground.

Have the shoe salesman measure your shoe size whenever you buy shoes. Always stand when your feet are being measured.

If you are a woman with foot problems, buy low-heeled rather than high-heeled shoes. While high-heeled shoes (over 2 inches) don't cause most foot problems, they may accentuate them. This is particularly true of pointed-toe shoes. The higher heel exerts more force of gravity on already cramped toes.

Foot care. Good foot care may help prevent foot problems. Keep your feet clean and dry. A good foot powder will help if your feet perspire a great deal. When washing your feet, take care not to rub between your toes. The vulnerable skin may crack, inviting infection.

Buy properly fitting socks. Too-tight socks

can crowd the toes and force them into an awkward position. Too-loose socks can cause blisters. Always wear socks or stockings when you wear shoes. They guard against chafing and absorb perspiration.

If the skin of your feet is dry or chapped, wash with warm water, then rub gently with petroleum jelly, cream, or oil. Take care of minor irritations before they become major problems.

If your work requires you to stand for long periods, protect your feet by standing on a stiff rubber pad. Alternate between different pairs of shoes, trying not to wear the same shoe two days running. This is particularly necessary for women, so that their feet and legs can become accustomed to several heel heights.

Walking is the best exercise for the feet. It helps the muscles maintain strength and elasticity. You can also keep your feet in shape by regularly exercising the muscles of the foot.

See also ARTHRITIS; ATHLETE'S FOOT; BLISTERS; BUNIONS; CALLUSES; CORNS; DIABETES; FALLEN ARCHES; GOUT; INGROWN TOENAILS; WARTS.

FRACTURES (broken bones). First aid for fracture victims includes the following:

· Give first aid for SHOCK (which see).
· If the bone is showing, gently apply a sterile dressing or clean handkerchief to the wound. Control bleeding by direct pressure of your hand (see BLEEDING). Apply a tourniquet only if the person's life is in danger. Do not push a protruding bone back.
· Never test for fracture by having the victim try to move the injured part or walk on a possibly broken leg.
· Give him nothing to eat or drink. He may need surgery, and food complicates the administration of anesthesia.
· Have X rays made of all suspected fractures. Some—like finger fractures—may seem like mere sprains.

A fracture victim may also be suffering internal injuries. Unless it is absolutely essential, refrain from moving the injured person.

If a fracture victim must be moved, immobilize the injured part with a splint to prevent further pain and injury (see illustration). Use a sling for broken arms, ribs, collarbones (see illustration).

To transport a fracture victim in an emergency, you can fashion a makeshift stretcher by buttoning a coat or shirts around two sturdy branches. Or use a door. Alternatively, have several people support every part of the victim's body, keeping it in a straight line.

Standard medical treatment for a fracture is to reduce it (replace the bones in normal position, sometimes through surgery). A limb is often immobilized in a plaster cast until it heals. A bandage is used for some types of fractures, especially of the elbow, heel, and foot, where a cast might cause stiffness.

Open or closed. Fractures are either *open* (compound), in which there is an open wound from the skin to the fracture area, or *closed* (simple), in which the skin is unbroken.

Young children often suffer from a type of closed fracture called a *greenstick fracture,* in which the bone is not completely broken through. The relatively soft and pliable bones of children make greenstick fractures fairly easy to treat. (See illustration for types of fractures.)

In an open fracture the wound usually is inflicted by a broken bone end that tears through the skin and usually slips back again. Or it can be caused by an object that penetrates the skin and breaks a bone. Open fractures are generally more serious than closed ones because the fracture area is likely to become infected.

In many cases there are no clear indications of

TYPES OF FRACTURE

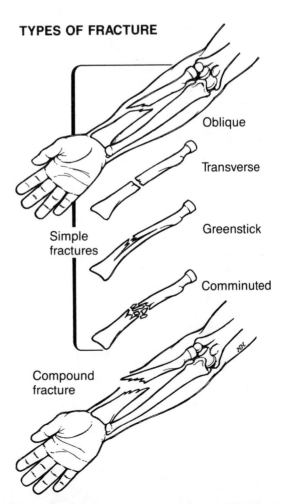

Oblique

Transverse

Greenstick

Simple fractures

Comminuted

Compound fracture

HOW TO APPLY A SPLINT

Keep bone from moving!
Use any immobilizing object
(newspaper, pillow, stick, etc.)

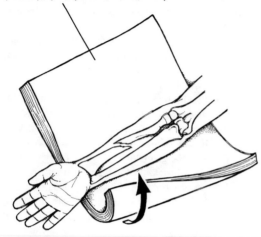

Tie so bone can't move

Use scarf, belt, necktie, etc.

Above break

At break

Below break

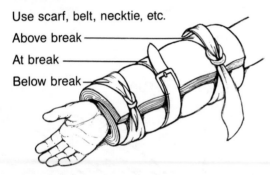

HOW TO MAKE A SLING
Use bandage, towel, blanket, etc.

fracture, even though it may be severe. But suspect a fracture if you hear or feel a "pop." You may also experience tenderness, pain—often sharp—and swelling.

In arm or leg fractures, you may see a deformity, such as the limb dangling at a grotesque angle. There may be a grating sensation when you move, and you are likely to have difficulty moving the fractured part. If you see a wound with a bone visible or projecting, you can be fairly certain it's a fracture.

Fractures of deep-lying bones, such as back, neck, collarbone, or pelvic fractures, are particularly hard to detect. Swelling, tenderness, and deformity may be absent. Rib fractures may give virtually no sign, but can cause pain with movement and deep breathing.

See also ACCIDENTS; ARM FRACTURES; BACK FRACTURES; BANDAGES; BLEEDING; COLLARBONE FRACTURES; FINGER FRACTURES; LEG FRACTURES; MOVING THE INJURED; NECK FRACTURES; PELVIC FRACTURES; PLASTER CASTS; RIB FRACTURES; SHOCK; SPORTS; SPRAINS; X RAYS.

FRECKLES are spots of the pigment melanin. In sunlight melanin granules darken and freckles may blossom across your exposed skin.

If you have freckles, leave them alone. Avoid sunlight and they will become less evident in time. Much of the success attributed to freckle creams may be due to this natural loss of color.

Older people often have brown spots on the backs of the hands, face, and neck. Although they resemble the freckles of youth, they are larger and more irregular. Their color is darker

Support arm   Tie behind neck   Pin or tie at elbow

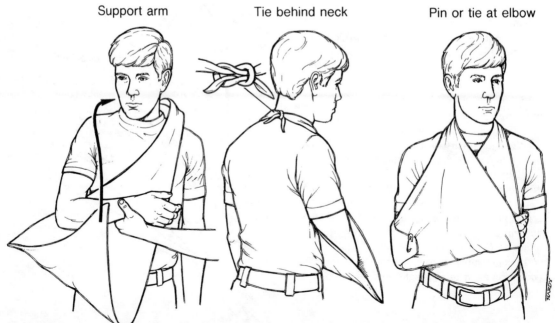

and uneven, and they do not fade in the winter. The spots are termed old-age or senile freckles, liver spots, or senile lentigines.

There is no connection between these spots and liver disease. Nor is mere age the principal cause. The spots are signs of irreversible skin damage from long exposure to sun and wind.

Treatment consists of preventing further irritation. Avoid sunbathing and extreme exposure to sunlight. Use a sunscreen when exposure is unavoidable. See a doctor if the spots enlarge, become thicker, or develop a crust. These symptoms may indicate cancer of the skin.

Don't bleach. Bleaching creams are of little value and potentially injurious. While most mercury preparations have been ordered off the market, some bleaching creams remaining on the shelves may contain ammoniated mercury, which is a peeling agent that temporarily reduces the amount of pigment by removing outer skin layers. If used for more than a few months at a time, they may cause a bluish-black discoloration that looks worse than the freckles. Mercury from the cream is deposited permanently in the skin—there is no way to remove it.

Mercury causes severe contact dermatitis in some people. Never apply an ammoniated mercury bleaching compound to irritated, cut, or broken skin or to large areas of the body. Don't use it on children under 12. If any type of skin disorder such as redness or soreness develops, stop using the product immediately.

Beware of "skin tone creams" containing hydroquinone. Hydroquinone bleaching creams are moderately effective when used to treat limited areas where excess pigmentation is caused by disease or skin injury. Hydroquinone is considerably less effective as a depigmenting agent on normal skin.

Some hydroquinone drugs are powerful depigmenting agents and can produce blotchiness and other undesirable effects when not properly used. These drugs require close medical supervision.

Some hydroquinone products are promoted to blacks as "skin lighteners." They rarely work. After treatment is stopped, repigmentation almost always occurs.

See also CANCER OF THE SKIN; SKIN DISORDERS; SUNBURN.

FRIGIDITY commonly refers to a condition in which the female is unable to respond to any form of sexual stimulus and cannot achieve orgasm. Applied to an individual woman, the preferred term is *nonorgasmic,* since the word *frigid* has many negative connotations.

This condition is almost always due to psychological stress rather than physical causes. But inability to achieve orgasm may result from illness or medication, so a thorough physical examination is in order.

Often a woman's inability to respond sexually or have an orgasm is due to societal conditioning and ignorance about sex. Lack of communication between sex partners is another major factor.

General anxiety or hostility toward the sex partner can keep a woman from achieving an orgasm. Sex researchers Dr. William H. Masters and Virginia E. Johnson include distractions, fatigue, and preoccupation as basic barriers to satisfying sexual experience. Failure to have an orgasm is sometimes due to a woman's fear of letting go or losing control.

The myths about orgasm. There is only one kind of orgasm. Many women feel they are frigid, or at least sexually inadequate, because they can't achieve what Sigmund Freud called a "mature" vaginal orgasm as opposed to an "immature" clitoral orgasm.

Later researchers have disputed Freud's theory. The clitoral orgasm was supposedly achieved by masturbation, petting, and sexual intercourse only when the clitoris was directly stimulated. This, Freud said, was an immature kind of orgasm, related to childhood sexual experiences. Freud considered the mature, ultimate sexual experience for a woman to be vaginal orgasms, thought to occur through the movement of the penis in and out of the vagina.

In fact, from a biological point of view, clitoral and vaginal orgasms are the same. This is true even though all orgasms do not feel the same to a woman and may be reached in different ways—through intercourse, oral stimulation, masturbation, breast stimulation, direct clitoral stimulation, and so on.

Orgasm in the female is usually brought about by direct or indirect stimulation of the clitoris, whose sole functions are sexual arousal and orgasm. The lower third of the vagina also has extremely sensitive tissue capable of producing orgasm.

The clitoris is richly supplied with nerves. If you are not sure where your clitoris is, feel your outer genitals until you touch the most sensitive spot. Look with a mirror. Get to know your body.

During vaginal intercourse the thrusting of the penis moves the inner lips (labia minor) at the entrance of the vagina. These lips come together above the vaginal opening and the urethra to form the hood of the clitoris. This rhythmic motion can stimulate the exquisitely sensitive glans of the clitoris.

The human sexual response cycle for women can be divided into four parts. The first is the excitement phase, characterized by the moistening of the vagina and the erection of the nipples of the breasts. The plateau phase follows: the rate of breathing increases, muscle tension is heightened. The tissues around the vagina swell. The clitoris becomes erect and the inner lips change from pink to deep red.

Orgasm is the third phase, consisting of rhythmic muscular contractions of the vagina. In the fourth phase the body returns to its preorgasmic condition.

Some women are capable of having multiple orgasms. Masters and Johnson demonstrated that some women experience from 5 to 20 recurrent orgasms, and sometimes more, "until physical exhaustion terminates the session."

Multiple orgasms are more apt to occur during masturbation than during intercourse. This is because few men can maintain an erection long enough to produce multiple orgasms in their partners.

Like men, women are capable of having orgasms and enjoying sex well into old age. The Masters and Johnson research shows that *regularity* of sexual expression is the most important factor in maintaining sexual responsiveness. Some women past menopause experience drying and thinning of the tissues of the vagina, which can make intercourse uncomfortable. Hormone replacement and/or lubrication with a water-soluble cream like K-Y can correct this condition.

Education for sexual satisfaction. Sexual dysfunction can often be cured through sex reeducation. Some women are able to reach an orgasm for the first time after receiving a simple explanation of female sexual physiology and sex instruction.

Many women never achieve an orgasm during penetration, but can be brought to climax by manual stimulation of the clitoris. The clitoris doesn't lubricate like the vagina, so it may be helpful for the sex partner to spread the vaginal secretion, his own saliva, or a lubricant to the clitoris to prevent irritation.

Experimenting with different sex techniques or positions helps many women. Oral sex may bring a woman to orgasm where vaginal intercourse does not. Intercourse with the woman on top, or the man and woman side by side, allows for more direct contact with the clitoris and may bring an orgasm.

Women who have found it difficult or impossible to have an orgasm may discover how their bodies work through masturbating. Dr. Mary S. Calderone, executive director of the Sex Information and Education Council of the U.S., advises nonorgasmic women: "You, yourself, must reawaken your body, rediscover it, re-educate it . . . find out for yourself how it feels to touch yourself in certain places. Find out which places arouse the most pleasure in you when touched. Communicate these discoveries to your husband."

Many women find, for example, that direct stimulation of the clitoris is irritating and counterproductive. Dr. Milton Abramson, a Minneapolis specialist in obstetrics and gynecology, advises a nonorgasmic woman to "show how she prefers manual stimulation by placing her hand on his to guide and exert pressure where it pleases her." This will often be along the side of the clitoral shaft, not on the head of the clitoris.

An electric vibrator can often induce orgasm. It should be used only as a last resort. The continuous, rhythmic stimulation may be particularly helpful for women who have never experienced orgasm. Once the woman has learned that she is capable of experiencing orgasm, it is then usually possible for her to reach orgasm by other means.

Erotic literature or fantasy may also be helpful for nonorgasmic women. Psychologist Albert Ellis advises women who have difficulty in becoming sexually aroused or reaching a climax to "focus, and keep focusing, on something sexually exciting whatever that may be . . . anything, as long as it gets you more interested in your current relations."

Exercises may be of help in achieving orgasm. One such exercise is starting and stopping the urine stream with legs apart, contracting and holding for about three seconds. This will tighten up the vagina, heightening feeling during intercourse.

Psychotherapy has been successful in curing many cases of sexual dysfunction, especially when the woman's inability to have an orgasm results from deep-seated personal problems or hostility toward her sex partner or all males.

See also MASTURBATION; MENOPAUSE; SEX DISORDER.

FROSTBITE requires getting the victim indoors as fast as possible. Meanwhile cover the frostbitten part with a warm hand or heavy clothing or blankets (see illustration). If his hand or fingers are frostbitten, have him hold his hand in his armpit, next to his body. Give him hot drinks, no alcohol.

IF YOU'RE FROSTBITTEN
Outdoors, keep frozen part warm

Cover it with hand

Wrap it up
(Blanket, clothing,
sleeping bag)

Put frozen hand in
armpit

*Hurry indoors—
thaw in warm water*

Immerse whole body
Keep water about
104° F

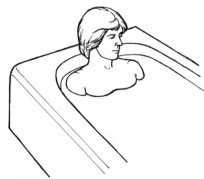

Quickly thaw the frozen part in warm water (104° F to 108° F), immersing the victim's entire body if possible. This may take 45 minutes or longer, until the tips of the part flush. Aspirin can help relieve any pain.

A second-best treatment consists of hot, wet towels constantly changed. Less preferably, use an electric blanket to raise body heat. Or place the patient in a sleeping bag with another person. Don't use hot-water bottles, heat lamps, or a hot stove—burns can result without your realizing it.

Treat the frozen part with extreme gentleness. Contrary to folk remedy, don't rub or massage it —especially not with cold water or snow—or exercise it, for these measures increase the risk of gangrene.

Thawed parts are extremely sensitive to injury and infection. Avoid putting weight on a thawed part or reexposing it to cold.

Don't open blisters. Don't put bandages, salves, ointments—anything—on the frostbitten part. If fingers and toes are involved, keep them separated by wedges of cotton.

Avoid thawing and refreezing. If you are far from help, you are better off not trying to thaw the part immediately. If it becomes refrozen, it will cause more severe injury than if you don't thaw it at all. Walking on a frostbitten foot is not recommended. But you can walk a great distance on a frostbitten foot and do much less damage than if you allow it to thaw and then refreeze.

Frostbite sneaks up on you. In white people the skin turns pink, then white or grayish-yellow. Dark-skinned blacks need to be especially wary—a warning color change is not obvious.

The skin becomes hard and glossy. Generally any pain quickly subsides, and the part merely feels cold and numb. The victim may not be aware of frostbite until someone observes changes in his skin. Most often attacked are the hands, feet, ears, and nose, in that order. If the part thaws but is injured, you may feel throbbing, burning pain, and a pins-and-needles sensation. Blisters may appear in a day or two.

First-degree frostbite injures surface skin, causing swelling and tenderness up to several weeks. Second-degree frostbite intensifies into blisters, which may develop thick black crusts. Joint stiffness may be long lasting. Third- and fourth-degree damage deep tissues and much of the frozen part generally needs to be amputated. Damage is often similar to burns.

A delayed form of frostbite of the fingers, called epiphyseal necrosis, usually doesn't strike until six or eight months after the exposure, which means that symptoms may not show up until midsummer. Pain and rigidity are the initial symptoms. Treatment may include special night splints to reinforce weakened muscles, sometimes surgery to repair damaged finger joints.

How to avoid frostbite. To prevent frostbite, stay dry. Moisture, including perspiration, ruins the insulating qualities of clothing. Get warm and dry immediately after falling through ice. Wear a water-repellent, windproof covering— but not waterproof clothing, which holds in the moisture produced by your body.

Wear several layers of light clothing rather than one bulky or heavy garment. Avoid overexertion. If you begin sweating, ease up or take off one or more garments. You're better off being slightly chilly than too warm.

Waffle-weave underclothing is helpful because air is trapped between the skin and the fabric and serves as insulation. If the underclothing is made of cotton or is cotton-lined, it will absorb perspiration and reduce heat loss. For the next layer nonpermeable, close-woven shirt and slacks are ideal. Over these a lightweight sweater and down-filled parka provide excellent protection. Wool and polyester down substitutes retain some protective value when wet; cotton and goose or duck do not.

Your feet are best protected by light cotton socks next to the skin, and over them woolen or synthetic socks. Prefer mittens to gloves—they allow the fingers to help keep each other warm. Wear lightweight gloves under mittens for protection if you need to remove the mittens. Carry extra mittens and socks in case you need to switch to a dry pair.

Don't touch freezing metal with your bare hands—your skin may freeze to the metal and tear badly if you pull it away. In most circumstances body heat will eventually warm the surface and release your hand. Otherwise moisten the area with warm water. Saliva or urine can be helpful in an emergency. Or use heat—warm the area with a match or heated object.

Wear loose clothing and boots, which don't slow circulation. Scarves are great neck-warmers, though possibly hazardous (see SCARVES). Wear a face mask. Protect your head with a hat or hood.

Don't drink alcohol or smoke. Smoking constricts the blood vessels, thereby reducing circulation. Alcohol opens up the small blood vessels, exposing greater quantities of blood to cooling in the extremities and at the surface of the body. Even though the alcohol feels warm in the stomach, it reduces body heat.

Use a buddy system if outdoors with a companion. Watch his face for white spots, and have him watch yours.

Windy days. Dress extra warm on windy days. Merely reading the thermometer can be dangerously deceptive. With no wind 20° F is reasonably comfortable and poses little danger of frostbite for an adequately clothed person. But a wind of only 20 miles per hour drops the equivalent temperature by 30°. It makes 20° F feel as bitterly cold as −10° F on a still day, and 10° F threatens the freezing of exposed flesh.

A rough measure of how hard the wind is blowing: If you just feel it on your face—wind velocity is about 10 miles an hour. If small branches move, or dust or snow is raised—20 miles per hour. If large branches are moving— 30 miles per hour; and if a whole tree bends, wind velocity is about 40 miles per hour.

Altitude increases susceptibility to frostbite. So do exhaustion, injury, shock, poor circulation, and old age.

Stranded motorists. Dress for the weather when you drive. Many people become frostbitten when their cars have mechanical failures. If you don't want to wear your high boots and parka to a party or while you are driving, be sure proper clothing is available in your car.

If the weather is subfreezing and your car fails or you get a flat, don't take your mittens or gloves off to make repairs. Paying a towing fee is cheaper than the frostbite you court if you try to make repairs yourself in subzero cold. Avoid getting gasoline on your hands. It doesn't freeze, but it does take on the temperature of the surrounding area and cools skin by evaporation.

If stranded with a car in very cold weather, swab your skin with grease or crankcase oil, recommends the Royal Canadian Mounted Police. Burn a tire to keep warm. Use a hubcap as a shovel, seat covers as blankets, floor mats packed against doors and windows to help shut out cold air. To signal rescuers burn a quart of oil in a hubcap.

Don't walk through snow in low shoes. If you don't have boots and other proper clothing, stay in the car. As a rule a rescue team is more likely to find an individual if he remains close to his vehicle, be it a car or plane.

Keep moving if heat cannot be provided by a fire or auto heater, but especially if you are outdoors and unable to find shelter (even when you are properly dressed). Walking or moving your arms and legs will help keep your circulation up and help reduce the chance of frostbite.

If caught in a car during a blizzard, don't leave the car. Run the motor to warm up the car, but open the car window a crack for circulation. Since the blizzard may strand you for a long time, save on gasoline by running the motor only when the cold becomes too uncomfortable. If snow piles up high enough to block the exhaust, you risk gas poisoning from carbon monoxide. Get out of the car long enough to clear away the snow from the exhaust.

If the car runs out of gas, close all windows immediately and keep them closed. Stuff all cracks or open places around doors and windows with rags, handkerchiefs, or whatever is available.

Don't go to sleep under any circumstances. Exercise occasionally—stamp your feet, swing your arms, and slap your hands.

If more than one person is in the car, huddle together for warmth and use all clothing, blankets, or other covering. Rubbing and slapping each other's feet or hands will help. If the extremities get too cold, place them next to another person's stomach or other warm part of the body until they are warmed.

If alone, remove your shoes, rub your feet, and sit on them to keep them warm.

If you live in heavy snow areas, keep in your car heavy socks, mittens, blanket, emergency rations, rags to stuff in car openings, and a covered tin or box for body eliminations.

If you're on foot or horseback and get caught in a blizzard, head immediately for any type of shelter. If visibility is nonexistent, determine some sure course, such as following a fence to a known destination or staying in the ruts of a road.

To prevent suffocation from the wind and snow tie a handkerchief, scarf, or any available cloth over your face to cover your nostrils and mouth. This also affords some protection to keep your face and ears from freezing.

See also COLD WEATHER; FALLS THROUGH ICE.

FUNERALS   See DEATH.

FUNGI   See INFECTIOUS DISEASE.

GAGGING is a choking reflex you may experience when a doctor is trying to examine your throat. It's involuntary but is a discomfort to you and a nuisance to the examiner.

To keep from gagging pretend to sing a high note. Without the use of a tongue depressor this often will allow the doctor to see the back of your throat. Or place your index finger on your tongue, advancing the finger backward with increasing pressure.

If the doctor requires a tongue depressor, you can keep from gagging by panting rapidly like a dog while he performs the examination. It may help to also grasp a spare depressor tightly in both hands while you're panting.

See also RESPIRATORY DISEASE.

GALLBLADDER DISEASE (gallstones) may cause sudden attacks of "gallbladder colic."

A typical attack includes nausea and vomiting. Fever and chills may accompany severe, unrelenting pain in your upper abdomen, mainly on the right side. You may have difficulty breathing. The pain generally lasts up to several hours, then subsides spontaneously.

Many people confuse a first gallbladder attack with indigestion or heart attack.

Call a doctor immediately. Lie down in as comfortable a position as possible. Loosen your clothing.

The gallbladder, part of the digestive system, is a small sac located underneath the liver. It stores bile, a product secreted by the liver for digestion of fats. Compounds in bile form hard gallstones.

Inflammation of the gallbladder is almost always due to gallstones. Attacks usually occur when gallstones try to pass through the narrow duct leading from the gallbladder to the common bile duct, which connects with the intestine. Emergency surgery may be necessary.

Gallstones can also cause chronic gallbladder inflammation. Besides occasional attacks you may have a feeling of fullness and discomfort in your abdomen, especially after overeating. You may experience nonspecific symptoms, such as nausea and vomiting, belching, and intestinal gas. The chronically inflamed gallbladder is usually scarred and largely nonfunctioning.

Gallstones. About 15 million Americans have gallstones. They range from nearly invisible grains to the size of a walnut. Some people have only one, others have many.

Most stones are largely composed of a cholesterol (see FATS). Many people are untroubled by their gallstones and may be unaware of having any.

Gallstones usually develop with increasing age, afflicting mainly people over 40. Normally bile contains agents that keep cholesterol soluble. If your body produces too much cholesterol, or too little of these solubilizing agents, cholesterol crystals may precipitate out and form gallstones.

Avoid overeating with gallbladder disease. Reduce to normal weight if you're overweight. Routine exercise is recommended.

The traditional gallstone diet called for the avoidance of fats and rich foods. Now doctors are finding that, by and large, what a gallbladder patient eats makes little difference. Most physicians advise their patients to avoid foods that consistently upset them.

In most people gallbladder disease can be cured only by surgically removing the gallbladder and any stones in its ducts. The body can function well without a gallbladder. In selected cases, medications such as chenodiol (Chenix) have the potential for dissolving gallstones.

Complications of gallbladder disease can be severe. If the common bile duct is blocked by a stone, bile will accumulate in the bloodstream. The result is a yellowed skin (jaundice) and possible liver damage.

Other complications include rupture of the gallbladder and obstruction of the intestine with a stone, both potentially fatal. A chronically inflamed gallbladder increases the risk of cancer.

Don't fall for the olive oil "cure." This bit of folklore involves drinking a large amount of fruit juice and olive oil.

See also GAS; SURGERY.

GAS (belching, burping, farting, flatulence) is a common symptom of indigestion.

To reduce intestinal gas, try cutting down on gas-producing foods, such as cabbage, beans, brussels sprouts. Too much starch and sugar in the diet may also cause gas. Swallowing air is gas-producing and results from emotional stress.

After surgery flatulence is a common occurrence. It may also be a symptom of a gastrointestinal disorder, especially when accompanied by diarrhea or constipation, fever, or nausea and vomiting.

Gallbladder disease, ulcerative colitis, and peptic ulcer are among the conditions that may produce gas and gas pains. See a physician if you are often troubled by gas.

If you burp a lot, you may be swallowing a lot of air, either consciously or unconsciously. A small amount of air swallowing is unavoidable during eating and drinking. The amount is increased by smoking, gum chewing, gulping food, or eating foods with air whipped into them such as milkshakes and sponge cakes.

In some people swallowing air may be a habit with emotional roots requiring psychotherapy.

See also INDIGESTION.

GAS POISONING To rescue a victim of gas poisoning—including smoke inhalation—hold your breath and quickly ventilate the room even if you have to smash windows. If the gas is flammable, this also will help eliminate the danger of fire and explosion.

Pull the victim to fresh air. Loosen his clothing and keep him warm. Give artificial respiration if his breathing is impaired. Call a doctor. Don't give alcohol in any form.

Dangers of carbon monoxide. In the home by far the greatest danger is from carbon monoxide. This gas is a product of incomplete burning of carbon-containing fuels, charcoal, or trash.

Carbon monoxide displaces oxygen from red blood cells. And while it is strangling the tissues, it cannot be detected by the senses. It is invisible, odorless, colorless, and tasteless, and can overcome you without a hint of danger.

First symptoms may be a tightening across the forehead and a throbbing headache. These are followed by drowsiness, lethargy, nausea, unconsciousness. If the victim is not rescued until he has been unconscious for a long period of time, he may have suffered permanent brain damage.

Breathing low concentrations of carbon monoxide for prolonged periods can result in dizzy spells, nervous irritability, circulatory impairment. Prolonged exposure to high concentrations of the gas is generally fatal.

To prevent carbon monoxide accidents:

Never run the engine of a car or gasoline-fueled lawn mower in a closed garage.

Don't tamper with the burner orifice or pressure regulator of gas-burning appliances. You may alter the gas/air mixture, generating carbon monoxide.

Don't drive with the rear window of a station wagon open. Exhaust fumes may seep in.

If you are snowbound in your car and must keep the engine running to get heat, make sure you have at least one window open. Check that your exhaust pipe is not blocked by snow.

Never burn charcoal indoors. Barbecuers have been overcome by carbon monoxide after a burning grill was brought into the garage, basement, back porch, kitchen, or living room during rainy or cool weather. Campers have been asphyxiated by trying to heat cabins, tents, and automobiles with charcoal briquets. Unless you are sure your chimney has a good draft, don't put a grill in your fireplace. Despite the claims of some manufacturers, Japanese-style hibachis are unsafe in an unventilated room.

Give up smoking. Carbon monoxide in cigarette smoke can injure smokers, even nonsmokers who must breathe the smoke of others.

Chlorine fumes. Chlorine is another poisonous gas that often causes household injuries. Never mix chlorine-containing bleaches (Clorox, Rose-X) or scouring powders (Comet with Chlorinol 3) with any other cleaning agent. The chemical reaction with an acid or acid-producing substance—like vinegar and most toilet bowl cleaners—may liberate pure chlorine, which is extremely irritating to the mucous membranes of the eyes and respiratory tract. Irritating gases will also be released if the chlorine compound is mixed with alkaline substances like ammonia, lye, oven cleaner.

Don't make the mistake of one housewife who thought that if one cleaning agent is good, two must be better. She was dissatisfied with how a toilet bowl cleaner was removing stain, so she added some bleach and stirred with a brush. Inhaling the resulting cloud of chlorine produced pulmonary edema. She died from this flooding of her lungs.

After an exposure to such irritating gases, flush the eyes and other affected tissues with large amounts of water. Treat as for poisoning with corrosives.

Gas fuels. Natural gas and liquefied petroleum gas (bottled gas) are not toxic, but are a fire hazard. It is possible for a large leak to give off gas, displacing enough oxygen in a room to cause asphyxiation, but the National Safety Council considers this unlikely.

Unburned utility gas escaping into confined spaces can be explosive, set off by a flame, static electricity, or operation of an electric switch or doorbell.

If you smell gas, don't light a match or use a light switch. Turn off the gas supply at the main valve near the meter. Open doors and windows.

Call the gas company for emergency investigation.

Tear gas causes redness of the eyes and a burning flow of tears. You may run afoul of police tear gas if you're at the scene of a demonstration or riot. Irritation of the upper-respiratory tract causes nasal congestion, coughing, and hoarseness. If exposure is in the open, symptoms usually disappear within a few hours, though eyes may remain red for half a day. Prolonged or intense exposure can cause lung injury.

If you've been exposed to tear gas, flush out your eyes with plenty of water. Rinse out your mouth as well. Wash exposed surfaces of your body, ideally with a diluted alcohol solution.

See a doctor if exposure was severe or if you were sprayed in the eyes.

See also ACCIDENTS.

GERMAN MEASLES See RUBELLA.

GIARDIASIS (lambliasis) is an infectious disease that results from swallowing cysts of *Giardia lamblia,* microscopic, one-celled animals, in contaminated food or water. The parasites become active in the small intestine, attaching themselves to the intestinal wall.

The most common symptom is watery, foul-smelling diarrhea. The infected person may also feel weak, lose weight, and suffer nausea and abdominal cramps. He often has greasy stools, a swollen abdomen, and intestinal gas.

Giardiasis is this country's major protozoal intestinal infection. The Centers for Disease Control have identified over 12,000 cases in a single year.

Food handlers carrying the disease may spread it by not adequately washing their hands. Food can be contaminated by flies, cockroaches, and other insects harboring the parasite. Leafy vegetables may spread infection if fertilized with human excrement or washed in polluted water.

Among adults there is also a significant amount of sexual transmission as a result of oral-anal contact. Statistically, sexual transmission of giardiasis is most prevalent in male homosexual communities.

Outbreaks of the disease are especially likely to strike communities where surface water (streams, rivers, lakes) rather than well water is used; where chlorination is the main method for disinfecting water; or where water treatment does not include filtration, or existing filters are defective. Recent waterborne outbreaks have been as widespread as California, Washington, Colorado, Pennsylvania, New York, and New Hampshire.

G. lamblia is also a common cause of traveler's diarrhea. The Soviet Union is ranked as the area of greatest risk to travelers. Other high-risk areas are western South America, the Middle East, Mexico, and Southeast Asia and other parts of the Far East.

Drugs can usually eliminate the symptoms and parasites. To help prevent giardiasis follow safeguards against water contamination, food poisoning, and insects.

See also DIARRHEA; FOOD POISONING; INFECTIOUS DISEASE; INSECTS; TRAVEL HEALTH; VENEREAL DISEASE; WATER CONTAMINATION.

GINGIVITIS is an inflammation of the gums (or gingivae), marked by soreness and bleeding. The "pink toothbrush" of toothpaste ads is a sign of gingivitis. Gingivitis may develop into periodontal disease (pyorrhea), so consult a dentist if the condition persists.

Some causes are accumulation of plaque and tartar deposits, and the impacting of food debris between the teeth. Prevention includes plaque control, regular visits to a dentist, and adequate diet. A severe form of gingivitis is trench mouth.

Gums that are only mildly irritated may be nursed back to health at home. Brush and floss them thoroughly at first, even if this is painful and causes some bleeding. As an adjunct to toothbrushing use a dental irrigator (Water Pik) to spray out foreign particles. Irrigate gently to avoid forcing particles under the gums.

If your gums are puffy and inflamed, it may help to try a saltwater rinse. Use a teaspoon of salt in a glass of water as warm as you can stand. Take a sip, swish it back and forth over your gums and between your teeth, then spit it out. Keep doing this until you've used up the entire glassful. Repeat hourly.

If, after several days of these rinses, your gums are still irritated, they probably have gone past the first stages of gingivitis and require treatment by a dentist.

Massaging your gums is likely to be a waste of time. For years dental patients were advised to "stimulate circulation" by using interdental stimulators like the little rubber tip on some toothbrush handles, toothpicks, strips of balsa wood, or plastic. However, says the ADA, recent dental research shows that the real benefit of such devices is that they remove plaque, much as dental floss does in a program of plaque control. Massaging per se does little or no good.

Avoid picking your teeth with pins or other sharp or metal instruments. They can injure your gums, scratch tooth enamel, and lead to infection. There is no special value in "medicated" toothpicks.

See also PERIODONTAL DISEASE; TEETH AND MOUTH DISORDERS; TRENCH MOUTH.

GLANDULAR FEVER See MONONUCLEOSIS.

GLASS soda bottles can explode unexpectedly, causing severe cuts and eye injuries.

The National Commission on Product Safety says pop bottles present an "unreasonable risk to consumers." Faulty manufacture plus internal pressures generated by the gas make the bottles booby traps.

Glass bottles account for about one in six consumer-product insurance claims. Some 34 different brands of carbonated beverages were involved in spontaneous explosions in one study.

Protect yourself by storing unopened pop bottles in a protected place—in a refrigerator or in a cabinet away from heat. In a refrigerator don't store bottles on the door shelves, where temperature changes are rapid and you're exposed to the bottle each time you open the door. Have your grocer wrap each large bottle in a separate bag, to keep them from clinking together. Transport the bottles in the trunk rather than the passenger compartment of your car.

Open a bottle without shaking it or clinking it against any hard surface. Aim the bottle away from everyone when handling or opening it.

Avoid having glass in the bathroom or at swimming pools or other places where broken glass may cut feet. Transfer soaps and shampoos from glass bottles to plastic containers.

Cuts from sliding glass doors, storm doors, and shower enclosures hurt about 225,000 people a year, estimates the Public Health Service.

Insist on safety glass in any door you buy, and replace ordinary annealed glass in doors with safety glass. Tempered glass, the most economical, is about four times as strong as ordinary glass and crumbles when broken into dull bits resembling rock salt. Laminated glass contains a layer of plastic to which broken glass clings. In wired glass embedded mesh strengthens the glass and prevents it from shattering.

Most collisions with glass doors occur because the glass isn't noticed. Put up warning signals of colored tape or decals, at both child and adult eye level. Consider installing push-pull bars that prevent contact with glass surfaces. Block a glass door with a chair or table so as to slow down traffic.

Keep doorways clear of scatter rugs, which can cause falls into the door. Glass shower enclosures increase the necessity for skid-proof bathmats and nonskid tub surfaces. Don't let children play near glass doors.

See also ACCIDENTS; BLEEDING; CUTS.

GLAUCOMA is an eye disorder in which increased fluid pressure within the eye gradually destroys sight.

The eye is partially filled with a fluid, the aqueous humor, which is constantly being formed in the eye and normally is drained off into the bloodstream. In glaucoma the fluid does not drain out as quickly as it forms. Pressure builds up inside the eyeball and the optic nerve fibers are slowly destroyed.

As the pressure persists, side vision is lost first. Gradually the field of vision straight ahead diminishes into a narrower and narrower circle. If neglected, glaucoma can lead to complete blindness.

One out of every 8 blind persons in the United States lost his sight because of glaucoma. It is the leading cause of blindness, and affects the eyesight of more than 1 million persons in this country. An estimated 1 out of every 50 people age 35 or over have glaucoma, but about half do not know it and therefore are not under proper treatment. Blacks are at special risk.

Sneak thief. Chronic glaucoma—the most common type—has been termed "the sneak thief of sight" because it gradually destroys vision without symptoms. It is usually completely painless—there is no redness or other alarming external sign. It is rarely discovered by the patient until some degree of irreversible visual loss has occurred.

The most frequent signs and symptoms suggesting chronic glaucoma are as follows:

Glasses, even new ones, not seeming to help.
Trouble in adjusting to darkened rooms such as at the movies, sometimes followed by vague headache.
Reduction of side vision of one or both eyes. (If you look straight ahead and stretch your arms out sideways, you normally should be able to see your thumbs wiggling.)
Blurred or foggy vision, often clearing up after a while.
Rainbow-colored rings around lights.
Difficulty in focusing on close work.
Excessive tearing.

The best preventive is an eye exam by an ophthalmologist or optometrist every 2 years for persons at risk and those over age 35. The doctor measures the pressure inside the eye with a tonometer. The normal eyeball is semisoft. In glaucoma it can become hard to the touch.

Also, the doctor looks directly into the eye with an ophthalmoscope and views the optic disk around the optic nerve for signs of abnormalities. He may take a picture of the disk for further study. In addition, a visual field test checks the patient's side vision.

STAGES OF GLAUCOMA

Normal
(You see front and sides)

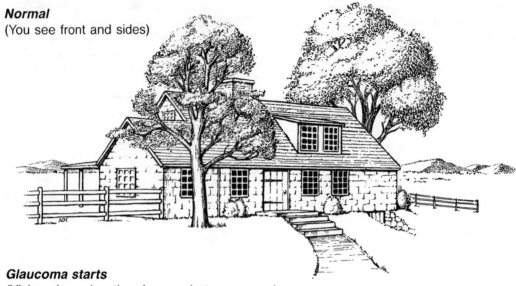

Glaucoma starts
(Vision closes in—there's no pain to warn you)

Glaucoma progresses
(Vision narrows further)

Glaucoma seems to run in families. If you have a close relative with glaucoma, have a medical examination at least once every two years. If you have glaucoma yourself, be sure to alert your relatives about your eye condition, so they may get checkups.

Treatment to reduce the tension in the eye most often consists of eyedrops that help expand the draining channels and increase the outflow of fluid. Other drugs may be administered to reduce the inflow.

If glaucoma is discovered late, or if medication doesn't work, surgery—either traditional or laser—may be needed to open up an extra drainage channel.

If you have glaucoma, avoid situations that make you emotionally tense. They can raise the pressure in your eyeball. Fluids, if taken in large quantities within a short period, may raise the pressure in your eyeball. Smoking may cause constriction of the blood vessels supplying the optic nerve and adversely affect your glaucoma.

An acute form of glaucoma attacks suddenly and painfully. Because patients agonized by acute glaucoma require immediate medical care, the condition is usually detected in time for early treatment. Drugs may help, but surgery is often needed.

Stay away from remedies that may lead you to neglect glaucoma symptoms. Eye exercises and eyewashes are valueless. "Swaying," a rhythmic turning of the body with the eyes closed, has been advertised as a "cure" for the disease. Since glaucoma can be arrested only if treated early, any delay in treatment because of misplaced hope in quick cures may be disastrous.

Glaucoma is not contagious, as is believed by some people who confuse it with the highly contagious trachoma. Also contrary to popular belief, the fluid in glaucoma has nothing to do with tears. Nor has the disease anything to do with crying "too much" or "too little."

Similarly, glaucoma is absolutely unrelated to cancer or high blood pressure. It is not caused or made worse by using your eyes for reading, writing, sewing, watching TV, or any other visual activity.

See also EYE DISORDER.

GLUE SNIFFING is dangerous. If you accidentally inhale solvents, step outside and breathe fresh air.

Warn youngsters away from breathing in the fumes of airplane glue, gasoline, lighter fluid, paint thinner, varnish, shellac, nail-polish remover, or other volatile hydrocarbons. Since the products are widely available, some youngsters deliberately inhale them for kicks.

The solvents can cause a state of intoxication much like that of alcohol. But enough vapor to produce a high is also likely to damage the liver, kidneys, lungs, or bone marrow. Injury also can result from accidents while the child is intoxicated from the sniffing.

Deaths from suffocation have been caused by plastic bags containing glue being held against the face. A related hazard is inhaling the gas in spray cans.

See also ARTS AND CRAFTS; CHOKING; SPRAY CANS.

GOITER   See THYROID DISEASE.

GOLF, as every golfer knows, can cause head injuries if a golf ball makes a hole-in-one with your head. So experienced golfers are careful to observe greens safety rules.

But many golf-related accidents take place at home—from the liquid in golf balls. Don't cut into a golf ball or leave one where a child may be seized by a powerful temptation to find out what's inside. Golf balls with liquid cores contain a chemical compound under pressure of up to 2,500 pounds per square inch. If the core is cut or punctured, it may explode.

Common ingredients—all corrosive chemicals —are sulfuric acid, barium sulfate, and zinc sulfide. A number of cases have been recorded in medical literature of curious youngsters who cut into golf balls and were rewarded by a painful shot in the eye with what the case reports tend to describe as "white, tenacious material."

A number of cases have required surgery to remove the core contents from in and around the eyes. Less serious cases have usually involved severe eye injuries. The National Society to Prevent Blindness warns that if a child doesn't receive immediate first aid, he can be permanently blinded.

See also SPORTS.

GONORRHEA is a very widespread venereal disease in the United States, about 20 times more common than syphilis.

An estimated 2 million Americans are infected for the first time each year. This infectious disease is particularly common among teenagers and young adults. In a typical high school of 2,000 students chances are some 16 have the disease.

Gonorrhea is caused by gonococcus bacteria, which thrive in the moist, warm mucous membrane tissue that lines body openings such as the penis, vagina, throat, and rectum. It is passed from one person to another during intimate sexual contact.

The gonococci cannot survive long after exposure to air. Thus there is almost no chance of contracting the disease from public toilets, towels, doorknobs, or other objects that might be contaminated.

Also known as "clap," "dose," "gleet," and "strain," gonorrhea is hardly confined to heterosexual intercourse. A significant percentage of reported infections involve contacts between members of the same sex. In male homosexuals rectal infections are common.

If there is any chance that your sex partner has gonorrhea, take the following precautions: Wash your genitals with soap and water both before and after sexual intercourse. Use a condom (a rubber sheath) on the penis during intercourse. For a man, urinating directly after intercourse may help ward off infection.

There is some evidence that women who use copper-containing intrauterine devices for birth control may be protected from gonorrhea. Investigators at the Mount Sinai School of Medicine have found that small amounts of copper or copper compounds can destroy gonococci.

If you have any suspicion that you have gonorrhea, go to a doctor or a clinic immediately. In general, minors can be treated for venereal disease without their parents' consent.

Symptoms of gonorrhea appear about three to eight days after sexual contact with an infected person. In the male there is usually a burning sensation when urinating and a white, puslike discharge from the penis. This discharge may contain millions of infectious gonococci. The man may remain infectious for as long as two years unless he seeks treatment.

Although the early symptoms of gonorrhea will disappear without treatment, men with the disease are usually uncomfortable enough to go to a doctor. But perhaps one in five show no symptoms.

Most women, on the other hand, have no early symptoms. If a woman has a discharge, she may mistake it for symptoms of a less serious condition. According to the Public Health Service between seven and nine out of ten women with gonorrhea do not realize they are infected.

A woman is usually suspected of having the disease only when she is named as a sexual partner of someone with a diagnosed case of it. It is often weeks or months after first contracting the disease that women experience their first discomfort: Pain in the reproductive organs.

Damage from gonorrhea. Untreated, gonorrhea can cause severe permanent damage. Gonococci usually remain in the genital and urinary tracts, later attacking the internal reproductive organs.

In a woman gonorrhea may lead to infertility from pelvic inflammatory disease when germs mutilate the linings of the fallopian tubes, blocking the passages through which an egg must pass to be fertilized. About 25 percent of women with gonorrhea eventually need hysterectomy to arrest the disease.

In a man gonorrhea can cause sterility by blocking the tubes through which sperm must pass to fertilize an egg. Gonorrhea bacteria may migrate to the prostate, seminal vesicles, or testes. Surgical removal of the infected organs may become necessary.

When gonococci attack a man's urethra, a permanent condition known as urethral stricture may result. The urethra is sealed off by scar tissue, making urination at first difficult and then impossible. Pressure resulting from the buildup of urine in the bladder causes extreme pain. Relief can be obtained only by frequent visits to a physician to have the urethra stretched, allowing the passage of urine.

Gonorrhea germs may also cause a condition known as gonococcal arthritis, a particularly painful and destructive form of the disease. Symptoms are usually rash, fever, and aches and pains in the joints. It must be treated immediately, since joints can be rapidly damaged by the gonococci.

Eventually gonorrhea can affect the linings of the heart or brain. Pain usually makes the victim see a doctor long before this happens.

At one time many infants were blinded when the gonococci from an infected mother entered her baby's eyes in the birth canal. Now, with laws requiring drops of silver nitrate or penicillin placed in babies' eyes at birth, the problem has been virtually eliminated.

Diagnosis. Gonorrhea is diagnosed by taking a smear of the discharge. The gonococci are identified through microscopic examination. It is often very difficult to detect gonorrhea in women, since there may be no discharge or a discharge may not show the presence of gonococci. Making a culture of smears from several different sites (cervix, vagina, urethra, rectum) can result in a more accurate diagnosis for women. A newly marketed mass-screening blood test promises to make gonorrhea easier to catch in its early stages.

Gonorrhea cannot be detected by the blood test for syphilis. Nor can syphilis be detected by the laboratory test for gonorrhea. It is possible to suffer from both diseases at the same time.

What's more, having the disease once does not confer immunity. A person can be infected any number of times.

Treatment for gonorrhea is large doses of penicillin or other antibiotics. The disease can almost always be cured, but organs and tissue already damaged cannot be repaired.

More virulent strains of gonorrhea are becoming resistant to the usual dose of penicillin. Doctors have had to resort to massive doses of penicillin or combinations of other antibiotics. Treatment may be continued for several months.

See also VENEREAL DISEASE.

GOOFBALLS See BARBITURATES.

GOUGES (avulsions) are injuries that tear a whole piece of skin loose or leave it hanging as a flap. After gouging accidents follow procedures for cleansing minor wounds with soap and water.

IF SKIN IS GOUGED

Cleanse with soap and water

Put gouged-out tissue back

Bandage tissue in place

Stop bleeding with direct pressure on the wound with a sterile pad.

Restore a flap of tissue to its proper spot in the injured area before putting a bandage on the wound (see illustration). It may graft itself back in place. Even if it dies, it will help cushion the healing wound.

Large gouges require restoration by a physician. Collect all gouged-out tissue and take it in ice water to a doctor. Add 1/4 teaspoon of salt for each 8 ounces of water.

See also ACCIDENTS; BLEEDING; CLEANSING MINOR WOUNDS; SEVERED PARTS.

GOUT (or gouty arthritis) is a disease of the joints and kidneys, developing from excess uric acid in the tissues. Uric acid, manufactured in the body and supplied by foods, normally is excreted in urine and feces. Most gout patients both overproduce and underexcrete uric acid.

Gout is a form of arthritis and can attack any joint or combination of joints. In nine out of ten gout victims the big toe is affected. Gout attacks are characterized by inflammation, swelling, redness—and always severe pain. "Now it is a violent stretching and tearing of the ligaments—now it is a gnawing pain, and now a pressure and tightening," described Dr. Thomas Sydenham in the 1600s. "So exquisite . . . is the feeling of the part affected, that it cannot bear the weight of the bedclothes nor the jar of a person walking in the room."

A current-day sufferer says the pain is "as though a large, angry dog has sunk his teeth to the bone and is trying to bite your toe off."

A typical attack begins suddenly. It progresses rapidly, lasts several days, and disappears completely, leaving no residual symptoms. Attacks may recur at intervals of weeks, months, or years.

Attacks may be brought on by events unusual in a patient's life, such as severe emotional stress or injury to a joint. Sometimes attacks follow taking medications, especially diuretics. People with gout frequently suffer attacks after surgery. Always inform a surgeon beforehand if you have the disease.

Gout is unusual in women. In men symptoms are most likely to start in middle age.

Tophaceous gout is characterized by the presence of tophi, deposits of monosodium urate monohydrate—a white, chalky substance derived from uric acid—which gradually accumulate in the tissues. In people with gout, tophi can occur in or near the joints. They are also commonly observed around the elbow or in the rims of the ears. They are generally painless, but as the disease advances, they can grow to the size of golf balls and interfere with joint motion. Tophi usually form only after a patient has had gout for a number of years without adequate treatment.

What to do about gout. Gout can be treated and controlled in almost every case. To ease an attack doctors often prescribe colchicine, a centuries-old remedy made from autumn crocus plants. It should be taken at the first sign of an attack. A powerful drug, colchicine may cause abdominal cramps and diarrhea until the precise dosage need is determined. Colchicine usually brings considerable relief within 12 hours. Allopurinol (Zyloprim) is another potent drug for resolving tophi and uric acid crystals.

Other drugs used to relieve gout attack include phenylbutazone and indomethacin, both of which can have severe side effects and are usually prescribed for short periods only. Steroids such as cortisone, corticotrophin, and ACTH are also often used.

Prevention of further attacks is accomplished either by ridding the body of excess uric acid or reducing the production of uric acid in the body. Probenecid (sold under the brand name Benemid) is the drug prescribed most often to increase the excretion of uric acid by the kidneys, thus depleting the body of abnormal stores. Colchicine is often used as preventive therapy; the dosage is increased at the first sign of an attack.

Preventive therapy may include dietary restrictions. The gout sufferer is well advised to keep weight as close to normal as possible, since overweight people tend to have more trouble with gout than others.

In addition patients are often warned to avoid foods high in purines, the substance from which the body manufactures uric acid. Such foods include lobster, beer, and the organs of animals—sweetbreads, brains, kidney, and liver. But no diet can eliminate all the substances from which the body manufactures uric acid.

Patients are often advised to drink a lot of fluid—perhaps up to 3 quarts a day—to help increase the discharge of uric acid and prevent the development of kidney stones, a frequent tendency in gout.

Who gets gout? Myths about gout have a long history. Does gout tend to single out the talented and eminent as its victims? Alexander the Great had gout. So did Henry VIII, Martin Luther, Chief Sitting Bull, J. P. Morgan, Theodore Roosevelt, John Foster Dulles, and a host of other notables. One theory has been that high uric-acid levels in the body stimulate the cortex of the brain. A recent study has found that male college professors with high uric acid tend to outstrip their colleagues in "drive, achievement and leadership."

Clinicians in the field tend to be skeptical. "It's entertaining to talk about," says one. The British humor magazine *Punch* decided several years ago that gout had become democratic. The magazine commented: "It is ridiculous that a man should be barred from enjoying gout because he went to the wrong school."

Similarly, gout has been falsely associated with high living, possibly because high-purine foods are often delicacies. But physicians are quick to point out that gout is a metabolic disorder at least as likely to afflict people of modest means as the rich. Indeed many doctors feel that diet as a cause of gout has been overemphasized, that anxious gout sufferers often eat more sparsely than they need to.

See also ARTHRITIS.

GRAND MAL See EPILEPSY.

GRASS (Marijuana) See DRUGS.

GRIPPE See INFLUENZA.

GROWING PAINS don't exist as a diagnosis. Many children complain of leg pains in the evening, and the notion persists that these are the pains of growing.

Actually these pains are almost always caused by just plain tiredness. In a very small number of cases the pain may be due to foot, knee, hip, or low-back problems.

Bathing in hot water before bedtime will bring the child relief. Massage and aspirin may be necessary after a particularly strenuous day. Consult a physician if relief does not follow these measures.

GUNSHOT WOUNDS require immediate attention. Cover the wound, ideally with a sterile bandage. Control bleeding. Take steps to prevent shock.

Watch out for fractures. Take special care of chest injuries. Get medical help immediately.

Don't try to remove the bullet. Though the wound may be dirty, don't wash it with water or antiseptics.

Guns are dangerous. More people are accidentally shot at home than while hunting. Never keep a loaded gun in the house. Keep guns hidden from children, locked up if possible. Store guns and ammunition in separate places so if a child finds one, he won't have the other.

Hunters are most frequently injured by loaded guns when they stumble and fall, when they catch the trigger on a bush or other object, when they put the gun in or take it from the car, or when they cross a fence. The National Safety Council offers this advice to hunters:

Wear fluorescent orange. It stays visible longer after sunset than other colors, and is more easily seen by people with color blindness or other eye disorders. Yellow is next best but doesn't show up at sunset. The traditional red is worse than either—it appears black at dawn or dusk and can't be distinguished by color-blind hunters.

Handle every gun as if it were loaded. Carry it with the muzzle pointed up or toward the ground. Leave the safety on until just before the shot.

While you climb a fence or jump a ditch, slip the shells out, break the action, or hand your gun to a companion. Never prop a loaded gun against anything. Check after a fall that the barrel isn't plugged with dirt or snow.

Stay in line with companions. Don't get ahead or behind. Call to each other in thick cover.

Have your youngster take the National Rifle Association gun-safety course. Teen-agers have more hunting accidents than any other age group—but those who've taken the NRA course have far fewer accidents. In addition your child is ready for a gun only if he's over 12 and exhibits responsibility in other areas, says the NRA. A .22 rimfire single-shot rifle is safest for beginners.

See also ACCIDENTS; BLEEDING; CHEST INJURIES; FRACTURES; SHOCK.

HAIR BLEACHING can cause hair to break off and become thin. Hydrogen peroxide used for bleaching attacks hair protein as well as the pigments, causing the hair to lose its elasticity and strength.

Any hair loss is usually temporary because damage affects hair above the scalp, not the roots. But since hair grows only about 1/2 inch a month, it may take many weeks to get back to its normal length. During this time suspend bleaching and exercise extreme care in dyeing, curling, straightening, or even brushing—any of which may cause further damage.

Although sunlight has a bleaching effect on hair, it is not a good alternative for chemical bleaching. It often causes dryness and uneven streaking. Sunlamps similarly are undesirable for bleaching and raise a risk of sunburn.

Frosting or tipping the hair, which gives a dramatic flare of color around the face, may be less risky since the bleach does not touch the scalp.

When bleaching, scalp irritation may occur if the solution comes in contact with cuts and bruises or a tender scalp. Solutions applied too frequently or use of a solution that is too strong may irritate the skin. An allergic reaction, such as contact dermatitis or hives, may come from boosters or accelerators added to the bleaching solution.

Overbleaching causes hair to become harsh and strawlike. For color changes that need more than one operation, spread the process over several days. This allows enough time for the hair to be coated with scalp oil, an added protection against bleach damage.

If your hair is naturally red or auburn, it will be more resistant than other colors to peroxide bleaching. If peroxide turns your hair a harsh yellow, use a toner to soften the color.

For bleaching a whole head of hair you're likely to get a better job if you buy a commercial preparation and follow the manufacturer's directions. Homemade solutions are best suited to bleaching limited areas.

See also ALLERGY; SKIN DISORDERS.

HAIR BRUSHING in excess can irritate your scalp and contribute to breakage, split ends, and hair loss.

Forget about brushing 100 strokes a day. Chances are that 20 to 30 strokes are more than enough to distribute oil along the hair shafts, remove tangles, whisk away dust and dandruff. Don't brush immediately after washing, when your hair is wet and at its weakest.

The best brushes have natural bristles (usually boar hairs) with smooth, tapered ends, or are made of textured nylon that resembles natural bristle. Ordinary nylon filaments are cheaper but may be jagged and can injure the scalp and hair. If your hair is brittle and dry, it is more vulnerable to damage, so avoid nylon or extra-stiff natural bristles. Also, fine-toothed combs can cause hair breakage.

Choose a curved or all-around brush if you brush with top-to-bottom strokes (for long hair). Flat-backed brushes are better for front-to-back strokes. If you have an abnormal scalp condition such as seborrheic dermatitis or psoriasis, your doctor may suggest a specially constructed brush (for example, one with the bristles cushioned in a rubber pad) that will be gentler on your scalp.

See also SKIN DISORDERS.

HAIR CURLING preparations for permanents can cause brittleness, frizziness, split ends, and breakage close to the scalp. This damage ordinarily results from the hair-waving solution being left on the hair too long. Or the hair may be inadequately neutralized—the oxidizing after-rinse was too weak or improperly applied. Other possible reactions include contact dermatitis and burns on the scalp or skin.

If you use a home preparation, follow the directions for that specific brand. Damaged or overbleached hair demands special attention.

Electric hair setters that use electricity to heat the rollers may cause excessive dryness if used too frequently. Curling irons, whether heated by electricity or flame, are much hotter than electric curlers, and hair and scalp damage can result from careless or excessive use. Generally, if the curling iron is hot enough to burn your fingers, it will also burn your hair. On the other hand if heat is too low, your hair won't curl adequately.

The heat generated by most electric curling irons is low enough to be relatively safe. However results are rarely as satisfactory or long-lasting as ads claim. A curling iron may serve as a supplement when there is no time for the regular wet, set, and dry method, but can seldom replace it.

Quick-set rollers. Plastic "quick-setting" hair rollers, which you boil in water before using, can be about as effective as curling irons. The rollers are filled with a paraffin-type wax, which melts and holds heat. The technique is best suited for a softly turned-up hair style. When a tight set is desired, the regular wet, set, and dry method will give better results.

The quick-set rollers are unlikely to harm the hair or scalp but are a potential fire hazard. In numerous cases the rollers have caught fire when water was allowed to boil out. The pan overheated and the wax inside the roller spilled out and ignited. Attempts to extinguish with water caused splattering of the molten wax and a spread of the fire.

If you use these rollers, check on them during the boiling. If the rollers ignite, cut off the oxygen supply by covering the pan with a flat cookie sheet or close-fitting lid. Never put a pan with burning grease or wax under the kitchen faucet or pour water on the flames.

It is a myth that permanent waving cannot be successful during pregnancy. Sometimes the degree of oiliness changes during pregnancy, but this won't affect the action of permanent waving preparations.

See also SKIN DISORDERS.

HAIR DRYNESS results from loss of the hair's protective oily film. It is sometimes an inherited trait. But it often results from overexposure to sun and water, and from improper use of curling, straightening, dyeing, and bleaching preparations. Dull, brittle hair can accompany an illness or dietary deficiency.

The best remedy is washing with a mild shampoo formulated for dry hair, soaping only once. Follow the shampoo with a rinse or dry-hair conditioner. These products leave a light film on the hair that reduces tangling and counteracts static electricity that causes hair to fly up. Pat your hair dry, since vigorous rubbing can remove oil. A hot-oil treatment by a competent beautician may be of temporary help.

In summer protect your hair with a scarf or hat. Rinse your hair thoroughly after swimming in salt or chlorinated water. Better yet wear a bathing cap.

Avoid excessive use of hair spray and wave sets. Brushing daily can be helpful for appearance, but don't brush or handle brittle hair more than necessary.

See also SKIN DISORDERS.

HAIR DYEING may be hazardous. Hair dyes contain chemicals that can be absorbed into the body through the skin and scalp. In large doses many of these chemicals have been known to cause cancer and genetic defects in laboratory animals—and are thought to pose a similar threat to human beings.

The strongest evidence of carcinogenicity was found in a chemical called 4-MMPD (or 2, 4-DAA), which was found in most permanent dyes, more than 400 products in all.

Many of the suspect chemicals in hair dyes were banned for use in foods and other cosmetics because of their cancer-causing properties. But a 1938 congressional statute exempts hair dyes from the safety regulations of the Food and Drug Administration. Thus even if a hair dye is found to cause cancer or other injury in people, the FDA is powerless to ban it. The most it can do is to require that products with the hazardous chemical bear a warning label. This is what the FDA proposed for 4-MMPD.

To avoid this requirement, most hair-dye manufacturers have removed this and other known cancer-causing chemicals from their dyes. But in many cases manufacturers have replaced them with ingredients that are thought to be as potentially dangerous. In one case, for example, 4-MMPD was replaced with 4-EMPD, a formulation that is identical except for the addition of three atoms. Many experts—according to research by Consumers Union—believe that the cancer-causing potential of this chemical is the same as the original. But if the FDA chooses to investigate the new formulation, it will take at least four years and cost several hundred thousand dollars.

About $400 million is spent on hair dyes each year. Roughly three fourths goes for permanent dyes, which include Nice'n Easy, Miss Clairol, Clairesse, Preference, Excellence, and Radiance.

Since most of the research has concentrated on permanent dyes, less is known about the hazards associated with temporary rinses (such as Fanci-Full, Nice Change, and Come Alive Gray, which usually last until the next shampoo), and semipermanent hair dyes (which last through four to six washes). Some of the coal-tar chemicals in semipermanent dyes are known to penetrate the skin; but none of the ingredients in the country's leading semipermanent product—Clairol's Loving Care—are among the untested chemicals believed to be potential human carcinogens.

While the risk associated with hair dyes is by no means conclusive, it is wise not to use these products at all. Besides their potential cancer-causing risk, hair dyes may cause allergic reactions or blindness if used carelessly.

Take these precautions. If you do choose to dye your hair, take these precautions:

- Don't use hair dyes if you are pregnant. Chemicals in dyes may cause mutations. It's also prudent to avoid hair dyes if you expect to have children in the future: mutations in the immature eggs in the ovaries may possibly result in birth defects. It's best to put off using hair dye as late in life as possible: The shorter your period of exposure, the less your risk.
- Take a patch test. This is essential before each and every use of a permanent dye, one that will last until the hair grows out. You also absolutely need a patch test before each use of a semipermanent dye, which lasts through several shampoos.

  Follow the instructions on the package. Reread them with each package in case they've changed. This test also applies to hair spray, which some dermatologists believe is even more likely than hair coloring to cause a reaction.

  Generally a patch test requires that you apply a small amount of dye, mixed as for actual use, to the skin behind your ear or on the inside of your arm at your elbow. Keep the test area uncovered and untouched by eyeglasses, combs, or other objects for 24 to 48 hours. If redness, burning, itching, blisters, or eruptions appear at this site during that time, you have an allergy and under no circumstances should you use the dye.

  Insist that your beauty shop schedule a patch test before each hair-coloring appointment. Many shops do a patch test the first time a woman comes to have her hair colored but omit it on repeated applications. This is an error because you may have become sensitized as a result of the last application. The allergy may not be evident until the next dyeing.
- Never apply hair dyes to your eyebrows or eyelashes. To do so may cause serious eye injuries, even blindness. Use only special colorings safe for use around the eyes.
- If there is the slightest indication of a skin eruption during the dyeing operation, discontinue it at once. The reaction will show more prominently on the forehead, neck, and face than on the scalp itself.

  Treat the skin eruption with nothing more than cold, wet compresses of Burow's solution diluted 1 part to 15 parts of cold tap water. If the reaction is severe, consult a physician immediately. Once you have an allergic reaction to a dye, never use it again.

- Thoroughly shampoo the hair with soap and water to remove as much dye as possible.
- Leave at least four weeks between each dyeing. More frequent applications increase your potential risk, and may cause overlapping of colors, streaking, or hair dryness or brittleness. Don't try to change the color of your hair too often or too radically—as from dark brown to red. You may get green hair instead.
- Don't leave dye on your head any longer than the package instructions advise.
- If possible, use a method that requires less direct contact of the dye with the scalp, such as frosting, tipping, or streaking. Shampoo-in methods involve much more scalp contact.
- Don't use hair color unless your scalp is free of scratches, sore spots, and other types of skin disorder.
- Don't mix hair color in or with anything metal—a chemical action may result.
- Don't save leftover hair color. Chemical formulas can change when exposed to the air.
- Call up the hair-coloring manufacturer if you have a question. A "hot-line" number is usually printed on the package insert.

Progressive dyes. Metallic or "progressive" dyes are not toxic and pose little allergy hazard. These dyes (Grecian Formula, Sun Ray Hair Color) are applied daily until the desired shade is reached.

Because of the slow buildup of color on the hair, an illusion of natural color restoration is created and the products are falsely called "hair color restorers."

The metallic salts coat the hair shaft, often imparting a lifeless appearance. Excessive use, especially of silver salts, may develop a metallic-appearing coating on the hair shaft. The dye is adversely affected by permanent waving. There is no proven danger of lead poisoning from external use of metallic hair dyes.

Henna, made out of a plant substance, is considered safe. But it gives only an orange-red color, and it cannot be washed out; the color stays until the hair grows in.

See also ALLERGY; SKIN DISORDERS.

HAIRINESS (hirsutism, hypertrichosis) in women may be biologically normal though not always fashionable. Some ethnic groups have more noticeable hair growth than others—Mediterranean and Semitic peoples, for example, are generally hairier than Anglo-Saxons.

Many women normally develop some hair on the upper lip or chin following menopause. A glandular disorder may be present, however, if a young woman has a sudden increase of hair on the face, chest, abdomen, or extremities. And consult an endocrinologist if a child, regardless of sex, develops hirsutism.

Excess hair can be a side effect of taking steroids and some other drugs. An overgrowth of hair is occasionally induced by X-ray therapy, or by plaster casts or heavy straps that rub against the skin. Discuss such growth of hair with a doctor.

It is a myth that facial creams can cause excess hair. Often women start using such creams around their menopause, when skin dryness is likely to become a problem. Hair resulting from menopause may be attributed to the creams.

Removing excess hair. When, as in the great majority of cases, excess hair is a cosmetic rather than a medical problem, you have the following choices:

Bleaching is the simplest cosmetic aid and is harmless to the average skin. At best it conceals hair, particularly on the upper lip and arm. At worst it may cause the hair to break off or it may color the skin slightly. Excessive bleaching may make hair harsh and strawlike.

Before bleaching, degrease your hair with acetone (nail-polish remover). Then rub it off. Use a commercially prepared bleach or home preparation: 1 ounce of 6 percent hydrogen peroxide (20 volume peroxide), 20 drops of household ammonia, and a few soap chips to form a paste. Test on a patch of skin for possible irritation and reduce proportions accordingly.

Shaving is the best and fastest method for removing leg and arm hair. Despite a near taboo against a woman's shaving her face, there is nothing medically harmful in it.

Shaving's only disadvantage is that it must be done frequently and carefully. Minimize cuts by wetting the skin, applying shaving cream, and shaving in broad strokes in the direction of hair growth.

It is a fallacy that shaving coarsens or darkens hair. Every hair, whether it be dark or light, long or short, is darker and thicker in the portion closest to the skin. The root, which determines hair structure, is unaffected by anything you do to the hair above the skin's surface.

Tweezing may be best for facial hair since it retards regrowth. It is recommended for long solitary hairs such as on the breasts.

Apply a hot cloth to the area to be tweezed. Use a magnifying mirror if on the brows or face. Tweeze in the direction the hair grows or the follicle will become enlarged. Be cautious in the use of a magnifying mirror as what may appear to be a dark hair in the mirror may not in reality be that dark. Don't tweeze unnecessarily.

Tweezing is the best method for shaping eyebrows. Tweeze hairs underneath your natural brow. Pluck above the brow only for stray hairs or if brows are very bushy.

Tweezed hairs do not grow back thicker than before, although it may appear that way. Shorter hair is always rougher. Tweezing removes the hair just above the papilla or root of the hair follicle. It is not true that tweezing promotes cancer of the skin. Since an irritation may develop from tweezing hairs in moles, clipping mole hairs is preferred.

Waxing (zipping) is a method of plucking hair en masse, if a bit painfully. Apply a thin layer of melted wax to the skin and allow it to cool with a cloth laid over it. As you grip the cloth and strip it off, the hair imbedded in the wax is plucked out. Strip it off quickly against the direction of hair growth or the hair will stretch, become distorted, or break off above the skin. Beware of wax that is too hot.

Female hormones (estrogens) don't make waxing creams any more effective, despite advertisers' claims. The AMA can find no scientific evidence to support claims that the use of estrogen creams in conjunction with zipping would result in permanent hair removal.

Chemical depilatories can be dangerous on the face, besides being messy and time-consuming. Thioglycolates, the basic ingredient, reduces protein bonds and dissolves the hair.

Follow instructions on the package carefully, for you may develop an allergy such as eczema or contact dermatitis. Milk and cold compresses relieve irritation, as do steroid ointments.

Abrasion with pumice is rarely a good idea. It's impractical for large areas and, if used too vigorously, may cause irritation. After hair removal with a pumice use cream or lotion.

Electrolysis is the only permanent method to remove hair. One method, electrocoagulation, is done by inserting a thin needle down the hair shaft to the follicle base and sending a shortwave heat-producing current to burst the cell of the root. It is a long, expensive, and sometimes uncomfortable process.

Properly performed by a licensed operator, it is safe. But you can expect a destruction rate of only 30 to 50 percent. If it is 100 percent, too high a current was used.

Ask a dermatologist to give you the names of electrologists he's found honest and competent. Make sure your operator is licensed, uses sterilized needles, and has adequate lighting. A shallowly implanted needle doesn't destroy the root. One planted too deeply destroys healthy tissue. Improper electrolysis can cause infection, distorted hair growth, or pitting and scarring.

Don't buy a home electrolysis device. The likelihood of regrowth and scarring is great, since it is difficult for an untrained person to gauge the direction of the hair follicle, locate the base of the hair, and judge the amount of current needed. At best such devices are suited for removal of hair on readily accessible parts of the arms and legs.

Drugs may be used in cases of severe hirsutism in women. Recently improvement has been reported after treatment with spironolactone (Aldactone) and cimetidine (Tagamet).

Don't use X rays to destroy hair follicles. No matter how carefully they are administered, there is serious risk of permanent skin damage and possibly skin cancer.

See also SKIN DISORDERS.

HAIR LOSS (baldness, alopecia) in men is hereditary. It is triggered by the male hormone testosterone reaching a level that causes shrinkage or disappearance of hair follicles, the skin depressions containing hair roots.

Men who are becoming bald tend to have finer, less pigmented hair than normal, the result of their follicles getting smaller. Their hair is generally short when it falls out, since their cycle of hair growth lasts only three to six months instead of the normal two to three years.

This type of baldness is not a skin disorder, but has been described as a disability of individual follicles, which die before their owner does.

Male-pattern baldness most often begins at the temples. The hair gradually recedes from the temples until the frontal hairline looks like the letter M. By the time this happens, the crown has usually thinned out to join the bare front area. Eventually there may be only a fringe of hair around the base of the scalp.

It is estimated that two out of five of all Caucasian men will have male-pattern baldness, which usually begins in their late twenties or early thirties. Men with a strong family history of baldness may start to lose their hair shortly after adolescence and be bald before 30. They are much more likely to end up with a horseshoe fringe than are the men who become bald in their fifties.

Since baldness begins with testosterone, there is a myth that bald men are more virile than men with a full head of hair. But their baldness only indicates a level of male hormones high enough to start their hair thinning.

Baldness in women. Women may inherit a tendency to hair loss. Female-pattern hair loss develops much like male-pattern baldness. The loss is not as severe as in men because women produce less testosterone and also produce neutralizing amounts of female hormones.

Women with this type of hair loss usually develop thinning hair on top of the head and a mild receding on the upper sides of the forehead. Both sexes have a normal daily loss of up to 100 hairs. But thinness and baldness become evident only when loss so exceeds regrowth that 40 percent of the hair is lost, a condition rare for women.

About 15 percent of all women are troubled with thinning hair before menopause; 50 percent after. Women virtually never become completely bald.

Pulling causes most bald spots in women. Barettes, bobby pins, and curlers can pull hair out by the roots.

Any type of roller can cause hair loss if the hair is pulled too tightly. When curling hair, wind the hair firmly around the roller but keep the hair loose between the scalp and the roller. Foam rubber rollers do not pull the hair from the scalp as tightly as other types, therefore are less likely to cause hair loss. Rollers with brushes inside are particularly likely to cause hair loss. Metal or plastic clips don't cause undue hair breakage or loss, but if you use bobby pins to hold rollers in place, select those with rubber tips.

Avoid hair styles that require excessive pulling of hair. When hair has been pulled back severely into a ponytail or tight braids, thinning and bald spots often occur. This can cause permanent hair loss. When the hair is held loosely in the same fashion, there are rarely problems.

Brushing with sharp nylon rather than natural or tapered bristles can split and fray hairs. Hair straightening, bleaching, dyeing, and excessive washing leading to dryness may cause hair to become brittle and break off. Unless chemicals affect hair roots, any hair lost this way will usually regrow.

Contrary to what some people believe, oiliness does not cause baldness, nor does dandruff. Split ends, or singeing or cutting split ends, also do not cause hairs to stop growing.

Hair loss from illness. Some illnesses cause temporary hair loss. Ringworm of the scalp, diabetes, influenza, scarlet fever, syphilis, leukemia, and other forms of cancer can all lead to patches of hair falling out. Other illnesses may cause hair to become dry and brittle and to break off close to the scalp, especially if accompanied by high fever.

Human hair grows in cycles. A long period of growth is followed by a short rest when the hairs stop growing entirely and are shed. A new growing cycle starts in a few months and the lost hairs are replaced. In a normal scalp various hairs are at different stages of their own individual cycles. When an illness influences your metabolism or endocrine glands, this increases the number of hairs in the resting phase of their growth cycles and shows up as temporary hair loss. X-ray therapy and some drugs may cause loss of hair.

Diet and severe weight loss can affect your hair. A shortage of vitamins or proteins may contribute to lack of sheen, dryness, and—in the case of chronic starvation—to some hair loss. Excessive vitamin A may cause hair to fall out.

Hair is often lost during and after pregnancy. Such loss is related to the many bodily changes that occur in expectant mothers. Hair loss may persist for several months after delivery, but hair growth eventually returns to normal. Women who take birth control pills may experience similar hair loss. A woman going off the pill also may lose hair.

To preserve hair during such times brush your hair with a natural-bristle brush, and manipulate it as little as possible. Wash your hair gently, using a mild shampoo. Pat hair dry instead of rubbing it. Wear it in simple styles that avoid the necessity of setting or combing out.

Baldness from stress. Hair may fall out from psychological causes. Emotional stress is linked to a type of baldness (alopecia areata) in which round bald spots suddenly appear on the scalp. A person may wake up to find small heaps of hair on his pillow. This type of baldness is usually spotty. But it may denude the entire scalp, the eyebrows, the eyelids, or other parts of the body. The disorder is thought to be hereditary, and precipitated by emotional stress.

About three quarters of those who experience a complete loss of hair remain bald all their lives. A cure is less likely the more extensive the condition, the longer it lasts, and the earlier in life it begins—children as young as three suffer this affliction.

When the hair regrows spontaneously, at first it is fine like baby hair. Then comes a new growth of thicker hair that lacks color, which gives the head the splotchy look of a piebald pony. Usually within two years the normal color and quality of the hair returns. The condition may reappear, triggered by emotional upset.

In some cases regrowth can be induced by steroids. Many physicians think that for most victims the disease is self-limiting and any treatment other than simple reassurance may only prolong it by calling attention to it. Meanwhile a sufferer can rearrange his hair to cover the bare spots, color the new growth of unpigmented hair to match the rest of his head, or wear a hairpiece.

Babies may cause bald spots by pulling out their hair, a habit like thumb-sucking. If the infant swallows the hair, a hair ball may form, possibly obstructing his stomach or intestine. You can break the habit by cutting his hair very short or shaving his head. A temporary bald spot may appear if an infant's head rubs against his bedding, breaking hair off close to the scalp.

Transplants. Hair transplants are the only cure for baldness. A transplant is a surgical procedure that can be done in the doctor's office under local anesthesia. It may require dozens of visits, depending upon the expanse of bald spot to be covered. As many as 20 to 100 transplants can be made in one session by the following method:

Small plugs of skin containing 8 to 12 hairs are taken from the sides and back of the head where the hair is thickest; and each plug is placed in a hole that has been made on the bald scalp. The new hair is spaced over the bare area so that as it grows it can be combed to cover the surrounding bald head. After about a month all the grafted hairs fall out.

Some two months later new hair starts growing from the roots. The areas from which the grafts were taken heal within two weeks. Because of shrinkage during the healing and the coverage of overlying hair, as many as 100 to 150 transplants can be taken from the back and sides of the head without leaving obvious bare spots.

Any discomfort after hair transplanting is usually mild and relieved with aspirin. Complications are rare. Scars are usually hidden by surrounding hair.

Before undergoing transplanting, check the doctor's qualifications. You're best off with a board-certified dermatologist or plastic surgeon. Because hair transplanting is an office procedure and seems easy, many unqualified physicians have tried their hands at it—and have been known to place grafts on the scalp backwards so that new hair grew in the wrong direction. Others have placed hair too low on the forehead.

If the grafting is extensive, the procedure may be time-consuming and expensive. The cost is usually about $10 to $25 per graft. A very bald man may require as many as 600 grafts. Insurance rarely covers hair transplantation unless hair loss resulted from disease, accident, or surgery.

In extensive baldness hair transplantation alone may not suffice, and the physician may recommend a procedure called scalp reduction. An incision is made down the center of the scalp, some skin is removed, and the scalp is sewn together. This procedure reduces the bald area that needs to be covered. The scar is eventually covered by grafted hair. In another procedure a hair-bearing flap from in front of the ear or behind it may be transplanted all at once.

Stitched-on hairpieces can pose medical problems. In this technique small loops of plastic-coated stainless steel wire are stitched into the scalp. Thread is woven between the loops to form a meshlike base. Then hanks of hair are woven through the loops and mesh and cut to blend into wearer's own hair.

There may be degrees of discomfort and pain, and the body may reject the wire loops stitched into the scalp. If scalp disorders develop, they could be exaggerated or difficult to treat without removing the close-fitting mesh base.

The Federal Trade Commission wants you to understand that implantation is a surgical procedure. There is a high probability of pain and a risk of infection, skin disease, and scarring. The system has been in use for too brief a time to determine all the side effects.

Follow-up care is necessary after implantation to reduce the risks. This may involve additional costs for assistance and medication. Consult your personal physician about a hair-stitching system before you decide to buy it. Many dermatologists advise against it.

Hair weaving doesn't always work out well. This method of disguising baldness claims to provide a semipermanent hairpiece. You need enough natural hair to be braided to form a base. Nylon thread is used to reinforce these base sections and to attach matching hair that is styled to blend into your own hair.

Because the hairpieces are attached to living hair, they will move away from the scalp as your hair grows. The pieces must be relocated on the scalp about every eight weeks. But they can be shampooed, trimmed, and combed as easily as natural hair, and unlike hairpieces that are attached with tapes or glue, physical activity need not be limited.

The tight braiding can pull hair out by its roots. Another problem is to find operators sufficiently skilled in the art. New York City's Department of Consumer Affairs has received many complaints from dissatisfied customers.

One man complained of intense headaches lasting 72 hours after his first weaving. Others who had paid from $250 to $450 for a weaving found that the process was not as durable as they had been led to believe. One customer complained that after he took a swim, the new hairs separated to reveal the nylon base, making his head look so shaggy that he had to go into hiding.

Wigs. Watch out for wig sellers' deceptions. Don't buy wigs by mail. You may get stuck like thousands of women who "won" a supposedly free wig, but had to pay a $21 "styling fee." The scruffy, synthetic wigs they got were worth about $1.

Some promoters' aids show people said to be wearing hairpieces. In fact they have full heads of their own hair. Photographs may be retouched to make the hairline appear more natural than is actually the case.

The frequent wearing of a well-made, attractive wig won't cause your hair to fall out or stop growing. It can, however, cause increased perspiration, dandruff, and itching, all of which may be remedied by more frequent shampooing (of your own hair, not the wig).

False promises for baldness. No product can cure baldness. Warns the AMA: "Hair treatments and remedies claiming to prevent, postpone, or correct baldness have been promoted for centuries, and they all have one thing in common—they fail to grow hair."

It is among victims of patchy, self-curing alopecia areata that hair-restorer quacks strike gold. Victims often are lured by ads featuring "before and after" pictures of a customer who claims that his hair loss was cured by the advertised treatment. Actually, if the claim is true at all, the hair grew back in the natural course of events and not because of any "tonic" or "professional" scalp treatments.

Massage is useless. Quacks promote electric brushes and vibrators to increase blood circulation in the scalp, claiming that this stimulates cell activity and the growth of hair. Their ads warn that your hair is dying from lack of a sufficient blood supply.

In fact there is no proof that a temporary increase in the supply of blood influences baldness in any way. At best, and very rarely, continued massage might produce a colorless fuzz, invisible except under a strong light. Promoters often claim credit for this, maintaining that it's the beginning of a real growth of hair. But the fuzz drops off after reaching about 1/2 inch in length and is not replaced.

All commercial antibaldness shampoos, lotions, hormone creams, miracle formulas, ultraviolet lights, hair nourishers, and vitamins are frauds. There's a baldness cure in the first known medical record, the 4,000-year-old Ebers papyrus. It calls for equal parts of the fat of a lion, a hippopotamus, a crocodile, a goose, a serpent, and an ibex, rubbed liberally on a bald spot. The AMA observes that this ancient remedy is "quite as effective as most of the modern over-the-counter preparations."

Ointments for baldness seemed to get medical support some years ago. Quacks jumped on the bandwagon when publicity was given to an experimental treatment involving applications of the male hormone testosterone. By anointing bald scalps with a cream containing this hormone, two doctors did manage to achieve a scraggly bit of hair growth on a few of their experimental subjects.

But, as the physicians reported in the *Journal* of the AMA, this did not mean they had discovered a cure for baldness. The growth was too scanty, and side effects possibly produced by the absorption of testosterone through the skin had not been evaluated. The investigators strongly warned against the indiscriminate use of the hormone by unsupervised patients. They completely ruled out its use by women of reproductive age. Attempts by other investigators to duplicate even the meager results of these researchers have been unsuccessful.

Another line of research is seeking to develop a shampoo and cream treatment that reduces the testosterone levels in a man's scalp. While promising, the treatment thus far is wholly experimental.

Also under investigation are scalp applications of minoxidil, which is ordinarily used for lowering blood pressure. In terms of achieving cosmetically acceptable hair growth, successes range from 0 to 30 percent.

See also SKIN DISORDERS.

HAIR OILINESS can't be cured. It's an inherited trait, and is a special problem in adolescence. But frequent washing, perhaps daily, can remove oil that has collected on the scalp and hair.

Shampoo and rinse. Then shampoo again, leaving the lather on for five minutes, before rinsing thoroughly. Look for a commercial shampoo with high detergent or drying characteristics. If none works, ask a physician to prescribe a medicated shampoo.

A short haircut can make frequent shampooing easier and reduces the hair's ability to collect oil. Some types of skin problems, most often DANDRUFF and SEBORRHEIC DERMATITIS (which see) can result from excessive oiliness of the scalp.

Also see SKIN DISORDERS.

HAIRS, INGROWN See INGROWN HAIRS.

HAIR STRAIGHTENING products need to be used with care and moderation. There is no permanent way to change curly or kinky hair to completely straight hair, whether it be with a pomade, hot comb, or chemical hair straightener.

The Afro hair style can cause scalp infection, hair breakage, and even premature baldness. The harsh chemical straighteners, hot combs, and petroleum-based cosmetics, all used to make the hair stand out, if used daily over several years can cause infection of hair follicles.

While temporary hair straightening can often be achieved, all straighteners have their drawbacks, especially with long use. Pomades or heavy oils and petrolatum-type products contribute to excessive oiliness. Hot combs and pressing can burn the scalp, cause dryness, break the hair. Chemical curl relaxers can cause burns and eye injuries, break the hair, and damage roots, leading to hair loss.

Use products that cause the least damage: pomades, and ammonium or sodium bisulfite curl relaxers. These are milder than alkaline or sodium hydroxide creams and thioglycolate lotions or creams.

If you find your hair becoming dry, brittle, or damaged, immediately discontinue straightening. If your hair has been bleached, color-treated, or previously straightened by other methods, a curl relaxer should be used with caution.

Test a product on a small section of your hair before proceeding. Follow the manufacturer's instructions. Don't use a curl relaxer if your scalp is sensitive, scaly, scratched, sore, or tender. Use a curl relaxer with special caution if you've previously straightened with other methods or if you've recently undergone bleaching or dyeing.

See also SKIN DISORDERS.

HAIR WASHING as a rule is best done with a shampoo. Unless you're in an area with very soft water, ordinary soaps will form a curd that's hard to rinse off your hair. Most commercial shampoos have detergents that operate without forming curds in hard water.

Most people need to shampoo their hair about once a week, when it becomes dull or seems unclean. Oily hair will need to be washed more often. Shampoo less frequently if your hair is dry. Frequent washing won't cause hair to fall out, though it can make dry hair brittle.

Brushing before shampooing helps get rid of tangles and surface dirt. Wet your hair thoroughly before lathering up the shampoo. Massage your scalp with your fingertips rather than nails to avoid scratches.

After flushing your hair with water, you may

want to use a rinse. Creme rinses contain an antistatic compound that makes hair more manageable. Most contain protein ingredients that coat the hair with a film, making it shinier and giving it more body. Home preparations like egg, stale beer, and gelatin are also effective texturizers.

Mildly acidic rinses—vinegar, lemon juice, coffee, tea—are useful for removing soap scum. They're unnecessary if you use a detergent shampoo or if your water is soft.

If you suffer from a skin condition that causes severe dandruff—such as seborrheic dermatitis, psoriasis, eczema, or ringworm—ask your doctor for special instructions regarding shampooing and rinsing.

Transfer any shampoo products from glass to plastic containers. Glass bottles are likely to slip out of wet hands and cut bare feet.

If a shampoo or rinse gets in your eyes, flush your eyes thoroughly with water. The products can irritate and possibly damage eyes.

See also SKIN DISORDERS.

HAIRY TONGUE refers to an overgrowth of the filiform papillae, tiny hairlike projections on the surface of the tongue. Eliminate all agents often found as causes: irritating dentifrices, lozenges, mouthwashes containing peroxides, antibiotics, excessive smoking.

Your dentist can advise treatment, which ordinarily includes improved hygiene regimen for the tongue. Brushing the tongue with a toothbrush (see TOOTHBRUSHING) and rubbing it vigorously with a moistened washcloth wrapped around the index finger may be beneficial.

See also TEETH AND MOUTH DISORDERS.

HALITOSIS See MOUTH ODOR.

HALLOWEEN raises the threat of accidents for pint-size spooks who go trick-or-treating. Here's how to make Halloween safe for them:

Accompany young children.

Avoid masks. They may block a child's vision as he's dashing from one doorbell to the next. Instead paint false faces on with eyebrow pencil, greasepaint, burnt cork, cosmetics.

Buy flame-proof costumes and decorations.

To keep children from being struck by cars, use reflective tape liberally on costumes, jack-o'-lanterns, broomsticks, loot bags.

No lighted candles or torches. It's a good idea for the child to carry a lantern or light, but make sure it's powered by flashlight batteries.

No knives or other sharp instruments. Make a dummy knife or sword out of cardboard.

Alter costumes so they don't catch on fences or hedges. Long skirts invite falls.

Tell children not to eat any of their collected goodies until these have been examined by an adult. There have been episodes of deliberate poisoning, and real-life ghouls have given children pins, razor blades, slivers of glass.

Around your own home cover holes and keep an outside light on so excited kids don't trip over stairs, lawn furniture, or other obstacles. Keep dogs inside. They may snap at ghosts, witches, and goblins.

See also ACCIDENTS.

HALLUCINOGENS See DRUGS.

HAND, FOOT, AND MOUTH DISEASE (HFM), caused by a virus, and unrelated to the well-known foot and mouth disease of cattle, has recently been added to the list of childhood illnesses. The disease occurs with greatest frequency during the warm months, sometimes in epidemics.

The first signs of infection, appearing three to five days after exposure, are usually slight fever, sore mouth, and loss of appetite. Small blisters or ulcers may then appear in the mouth and throat, and painless blisters may also appear on the skin. The skin areas most frequently affected include the backs and sides of hands and feet, and skin between fingers and toes. Less often blisters develop on palms and soles. Other symptoms that may occasionally occur include rash (often on the buttocks), sniffles, and digestive upset.

Especially in cases where there is no obvious skin involvement, HFM may be mistaken for cold sores. The disease mainly affects children between the ages of one and five, although some adults are also susceptible. It is highly contagious and children continue to carry the virus for some weeks after their apparent recovery. Exposed persons showing no sign of illness may also carry the agent.

HFM usually is very mild, and little treatment is needed. A child whose mouth is sore may be offered ice cubes to suck for relief. Aspirin may also be used if discomfort is severe. The disease usually runs its full course in less than a week and offers little reason for serious concern.

See also INFECTIOUS DISEASE.

HANGOVER refers to the collection of uncomfortable symptoms that follow a night of overindulgence in alcohol. They may include headache, nausea, vomiting, diarrhea, shakiness, and an ache-all-over feeling.

The best way to avoid a hangover is simply not to drink too much. But if you are likely to overindulge, there are some preventive measures you can take. Much of the headachy, weak, muddleheaded feeling comes from an imbalance of the water content of your body, since it takes 8 molecules of water to burn 1 molecule of alcohol.

To restore the water balance, have a chaser after each drink. Drink a glass of water or a nonalcoholic beverage after each strong drink. Or have one or two glasses of water every time you go to the bathroom.

Avoid drinking on an empty stomach, since this is likely to keep you intoxicated longer.

Your body oxidizes or burns up alcohol at the rate of about 1/2 ounce an hour. This is the amount of alcohol in an average drink. Thus you can avoid a drunken feeling by drinking no more than one drink an hour.

Take 2 tablespoons of Kaopectate or Pectocel before you go out, to counteract drinkers' diarrhea. Both are nonprescription items. An upset stomach can usually be avoided by taking antacids. Swallow 2 teaspoonsful or thoroughly chew 2 tablets with a glass of water before going out; take a few more in the course of the evening.

After you've been drinking. Antacids will help combat morning-after upset. Raw or coddled eggs—a traditional hangover remedy—may also help neutralize stomach acids and soothe the stomach lining. Until your stomach feels better, cooked cereals, fruit juices, soups, and boiled eggs are recommended.

Black or strong coffee is another traditional sober-upper. Coffee has no effect on the rate of alcohol oxidation, but the stimulation of the caffeine may help keep you awake.

Hangover headaches often respond well to a restored salt-and-water balance. Aspirin will also bring relief, as will an ice bag or a cold wet towel on the head.

Increasing the flow of fluid from your body will help flush out the alcohol and terminate your hangover. You can drink a lot of fluid, so that your kidneys will excrete more.

See also ALCOHOL; ANTACIDS.

HANSEN'S DISEASE   See LEPROSY.

HARELIP   See CLEFT LIP.

HAY FEVER, an inflammation of the eyes and nasal passages, is the most common allergic disease in the United States, afflicting about 1 in 15 Americans. The name is a misnomer: it is not caused by hay, nor is there a fever.

Seasonal hay fever occurs in the spring, summer, and fall. It is caused almost entirely by an allergy to plant pollens and mold spores present in the air.

Year-round or perennial hay fever—also called allergic rhinitis—occurs at all times of the year. It is caused by nonseasonal allergens such as dust, feathers, animal hairs, foods, or by bacterial infections.

The victim of either type is troubled with attacks of sneezing; redness and itching of the eyes; itching of the ears, nose, throat and mouth; stuffy nose with annoying watery discharge; and fullness of the ears, often with diminishment of hearing. There may be a cough and wheezing in the chest.

Difficulty in breathing at night may make sleeping difficult or impossible. The sufferer may constantly sniff and snort. But blowing the nose helps very little because the stuffiness comes not from mucus but from swelling of the nasal membranes.

Hay fever can produce serious complications. Infections of the ears, nose, throat, or sinuses are common. Some hay fever sufferers develop asthma, which may lead to permanent bronchial trouble and damage to the lungs and heart, crippling the victim permanently.

Seasonal hay fever can result from a variety of pollens. In the Midwest and East the most severe and most common type is produced mostly by ragweed in late summer and early fall. Close contact with zinnias, cosmos, golden glow, and goldenrod may cause symptoms in ragweed-sensitive patients.

Summer hay fever—which some people wrongly call "rose fever"—is caused by grasses such as timothy and bluegrass. Spring hay fever (April and May) is caused by trees, such as oak, birch, or poplar. The plants and seasons vary in different parts of the country.

The severity of seasonal hay fever depends on the amount of pollen in the air and the degree of sensitivity. On a cool, cloudy, windless, or rainy day the average sufferer may have few symptoms. Then the weather may become hot, dry, sunny, and windy, raising invisible clouds of pollen or molds, and hay fever will return in full force. Some people are susceptible to cold or dampness, usually when the barometric pressure falls. Their hay fever or asthma may become worse during periods of high humidity. Pollens are usually thickest in the air between dark and noon. Sensitivity to dust, animal dander, insects, and foods may aggravate the symptoms of seasonal hay fever.

Year-round hay fever is often heralded, especially in children, by the "allergic salute." This upward-outward rubbing of the nose with the hand or sleeve is an attempt to scratch the itch and elevate the tip of the nose to widen clogged nasal passages.

The rubbing can make the nose red and raw; in time the upward pressure may cause a crease to develop. Other common signs are "allergic shiners," slightly blackened eyes that often persist through adult life.

Parents often believe that their child is subject to colds or has a lingering cold, so they fail to get professional help. Actually colds normally last only a few days. If symptoms are persistent or lingering, they usually are due to allergy.

Nasal allergy can cause severe earache and hearing loss, especially in babies and small children. A sufferer's head may feel heavy or blocked or full, and he may feel or hear fluid in his ear when he turns his head.

Be suspicious if a child persists in using a louder voice than usual, since it may be a result of partial hearing loss. Sometimes neither parent nor child realizes the hearing problem and the child may be thought inattentive, slow in understanding, or even disobedient.

Sinus trouble is a common complication (see SINUSITIS). The sinuses are hollow areas in the bones of the forehead and cheeks. Small openings join some of them to the upper air passages of the nose. When the nasal membranes are swollen, they obstruct these openings so that mucus and infection are trapped.

Polyps inside the nose are another complication, more common in adults than in children. Grapelike clusters grow out of the nasal mucous membranes that block the airways. In the past polyps were usually removed by surgery. More recently they have been successfully removed by applying steroids to them.

Loss of sense of smell in year-round hay fever is not unusual. In some cases the sense of taste is also destroyed. Usually these senses can be regained after proper treatment. But in cases where the condition is allowed to persist, they are sometimes lost permanently.

Because of the obstructed airways a child becomes accustomed to breathing through his mouth. For most small children retraining is possible once the allergic condition has been brought under control. If the condition continues into adulthood, it is much harder to correct. The persistent nasal blockage that makes mouth breathing necessary can also produce so-called buck teeth and also adenoid facies, a pushed-in appearance or flattening out of the cheekbones.

Finding relief. Antihistamines can provide rapid temporary relief for most hay-fever sufferers (see ANTIHISTAMINES). A Food and Drug Administration (FDA) advisory panel found these products to contain safe and effective ingredients, in recommended dosages: Chlor-Trimeton Allergy Tablets, Chlor-Trimeton Allergy Syrup, Decapryn Syrup, Dimetane Elixir, and Dimetane Tablets.

If one brand doesn't work, or if it makes you drowsy, or if it loses its effectiveness for you, try another. Unless prescribed by a physician, avoid products containing a combination of antihistamines, or extraneous ingredients like caffeine, aspirin, or acetaminophen. Similarly, unless prescribed, stay away from "timed-release" or "sustained-action" products—they're unreliable in how they release their ingredients in any individual.

Avoid nonprescription nose drops and nasal sprays, which can be addicting and injurious (see NOSE DROPS). You're far safer with an oral decongestant, one in the form of a tablet or syrup.

In general, you're better off taking antihistamines and oral decongestants as separate medications, since you can treat each symptom with the appropriate drug. A fixed-combination product may relieve your stuffy nose, but give you so much unnecessary antihistamine that you get sleepy. If you feel that the convenience of a combination product offsets the possible drawbacks, select a product whose ingredients the FDA panel found safe and effective in recommended dosages. These include Allerest Allergy Tablets, A.R.M. Allergy Relief Medicine Tablets, Chlor-Trimeton Decongestant Tablets, Fedahist Tablets, Fedahist Syrup, Novafed A Liquid, and Novahistine Elixir.

Eyedrops are sometimes prescribed, containing a local anesthetic, adrenaline, and antihistamines, hydrocortisone, or related products. Hormones (steroids, hydrocortisone, prednisone, prednisolone) have been used for hay-fever symptoms but usually are needed in only the very severe case.

The standard long-term treatment for hay fever consists of desensitizing injections given just prior to the hay-fever season, during the season, or all year round. There is some difference of opinion among allergists as to which is most effective and practical. A recent development is the repository emulsion injection. In this "one-shot" treatment the offending particles are fed slowly into the system in an oil medium that is absorbed very slowly by the body. But not all patients can take advantage of it, and the exact dosage for best immunization with least hazard is still to be determined.

Getting free from pollen. There usually is less pollen near a large body of water. But driving, particularly in the country, exposes you more. Open windows will increase the pollen in the home.

On days with high pollen counts wear a mask available from your pharmacy, or tie a handkerchief over your mouth and nose. Wear glasses when outdoors to keep pollen from blowing directly into your eyes. Avoid gardening, and don't keep cut flowers in your home.

Air conditioning often gives relief provided you spend much of your time indoors. It is important that the cooling be moderate and the temperature within the room not be more than 12° below the outside air. Extreme cooling will often irritate the membranes of the nose and bronchial tubes.

Relief is provided by the filtering of the air conditioner, not the cooling. Even on cool days, if the pollen count is high, you may find relief by turning on the air conditioner. Electronic air filters or electrostatic precipitators, which can usually be attached to an air conditioner, are more effective than the mechanical filter found on most air conditioners. These devices remove particles by giving them an electric charge.

In humid areas, particularly if you are sensitive to mold, a dehumidifier may help. In dry climates the low humidity may aggravate—though not cause—hay-fever symptoms, so you may benefit from a humidifier (see HUMIDITY).

Once the cause of your seasonal hay fever has been identified, you may wish to live or vacation in parts of the country where that particular pollen or mold is absent or markedly decreased. If ragweed is the offender, you can go to the central Adirondacks, the extreme southern tip of Florida, the wooded areas of Maine, New Hampshire, northern Minnesota, extreme northern Michigan, the regions west of the Cascade Mountains in Oregon and Washington. The desert regions and forests of the Rocky Mountains and intermountain states are also largely free from ragweed.

If your hay fever is from grasses or trees, your chances of complete escape are more limited. These allergy sources are much more widespread and no territory is entirely free of them. The seasonal allergy to Christmas trees may be avoided by using an artificial tree in your home or spraying the natural tree with a dust sealer.

Check maps that give the pollen pollution in different sections. You can find information about the kinds and amount of pollen in various areas of the United States by referring to a brochure entitled *Hay Fever Holiday* by O. C. Durham. Copies may be obtained by writing to the American Academy of Allergy, 611 East Wells Street, Milwaukee, Wisconsin 53202.

Keeping a dust-free home is a basic precaution for year-round hay-fever sufferers. A sensitivity to molds is closely related to hay fever.

See also ALLERGY; MOLD ALLERGY.

HEADACHE is often due to emotional stress.

If you have an occasional headache, try aspirin or acetaminophen. Rest, fresh air, quiet, and sleep may help. You may get relief from massaging your head and the back of your neck, or applying hot compresses, or bathing in warm water. Relaxation exercises may help. Try head rolls: Let your head hang forward, slowly roll it to the right side, drop it back, then to the left side; continue slowly rotating your head, first in one direction, then in the other. Also try tightly tensing muscles of your shoulders, scalp, face, neck, and jaw; hold to the count of 30; then relax completely.

Eating can ease a headache compounded by hunger. Drinking a cup of coffee may provide quick relief if the headache is due to caffeine dependency.

But a headache can be a symptom of many medical conditions. Among them are infectious disease, teeth and mouth disorders, and eye problems. Colds and acute sinusitis are often accompanied by headache. Some people get headaches from food additives such as monosodium glutamate (MSG), commonly added to Chinese food as a flavor enhancer.

Headache may also be a symptom of anemia, gastrointestinal disorders, and very high blood pressure. Head injury often results in headache. Only rarely is headache a symptom of allergy or brain disorders.

Gas poisoning is another cause of headaches. If you and other members of your family wake up with a dull headache each day, have a repairman check your heating system.

Headaches that need attention. Consult a physician if you suffer any of the following:

A headache associated with fever or convulsions.

A sudden, severe headache.

A headache accompanied by confusion, unconsciousness, or loss of balance or hearing.

A headache following head injury.

A headache that repeatedly wakes you in the early morning.

A headache associated with pain elsewhere in your body.

A headache associated with brief dimming of vision.

A headache that gets progressively worse over days or weeks.

A headache unlike any other you have previously had.

A frequent or incapacitating headache.

Also get medical help for a child with recurrent headaches, and for an older person who hasn't had many headaches before.

Headache clinics in medical centers may be your best bet for diagnosis and treatment of chronic headache. For the names of clinics, study projects, and physicians specializing in headache contact the National Migraine Foundation (5252 North Western Avenue, Chicago, Illinois 60625).

Most headaches are tension (or muscle-contraction) headaches. In tension headache a dull, tight, steady pain spreads through the entire head, usually lasting several hours.

Almost everyone has a tension headache at one time or another. Men and women suffer equally. The tension-headache sufferer is typically worried and fretful. He may have had an argument, missed a train, or just had a trying day. Or he may have a sense of dull annoyance or chronic unhappiness about his life. He often holds his head stiffly and tenses his scalp and neck muscles without realizing it. Tight muscles themselves can cause aches. Contracted head and neck muscles also irritate sensitive nerve endings and constrict local blood vessels. Frequently people with chronic tension headache are suffering from depression.

Tension headache can occur with migraine or with headache from other sources. Pain relievers, muscle relaxants, and antidepressants may be prescribed for recurrent tension headaches. If they become chronic and disabling, psychotherapy may help.

See MIGRAINE (including cluster headache) for another type of headache.

HEADACHE, CLUSTER OR HISTAMINE
See MIGRAINE.

HEAD INJURIES require prompt medical attention. Call a physician or ambulance immediately, whether or not the person is unconscious.

Keep the victim lying down. If his face is flushed, raise his head and shoulders. If it is ashen or normal, keep him flat. If he vomits, lay him abdomen down, face turned to one side.

Otherwise avoid moving him. Don't disturb him in any way that may raise his blood pressure, as by handling him or engaging him in conversation.

Prepare to give ARTIFICIAL RESPIRATION (which see) if he has trouble breathing, and

closed chest massage if there's HEART STOPPAGE (which see). Keep him warm. Watch for SHOCK (which see). Give no stimulants such as coffee or ammonia, no alcohol or other fluids.

Control bleeding by applying pressure. In an area of a possible skull fracture avoid pressing more than needed to stop blood flow.

The commonest clue to a head injury is headache, especially a severe headache after an interval of mild or no headache. Sometimes a drop or two of blood appears in the ear canal. There may be bruises or wounds of the head. The eye pupils may be unequal in size, and vision may be slurred or double. There may be nausea and vomiting. Speech may be blurred or incoherent. The person may experience convulsions.

Unconsciousness following brain injury may be brief or prolonged, deep or light. It may appear at once or be delayed by more than half an hour.

Even people with minor head injuries need to be followed carefully by a physician for changes in vision, memory and thinking. For months after an accident, the person may have a postconcussion syndrome, marked by headaches, dizziness, blurred vision, and loss of appetite and ability to concentrate.

Brain concussion—a blow leading to brain damage—is a major cause of death following car accidents and falls. When the brain is violently jarred, it may swell. The pressure of the swelling against the rigid skull may cut off circulation of blood to parts of the brain.

See also ACCIDENTS; ARTIFICIAL RESPIRATION; BLEEDING; HEADACHE; HEART STOPPAGE; MOVING THE INJURED; SHOCK; SKULL FRACTURES; UNCONSCIOUSNESS.

HEAD LICE See LICE.

HEALTH CLUBS (reducing salons, health spas, health studios) can be unscrupulous in their pitches to overweight people who wish to slim down with (or without) exercise.

The best bargain in gym programs is almost certainly the local YMCA or YWCA. While lacking the wall-to-wall carpeting and Roman bath decor of some commercial clubs, the Ys offer professionally supervised programs at rock-bottom rates. Or perhaps a local school or church offers courses in physical fitness, which are apt to be reliable and inexpensive.

If you've made many unsuccessful stabs at exercise programs, you're not likely to benefit from a high-priced contract with a commercial club. An estimated 40 percent of those who sign up soon drop out. After the first flush of good intentions they attend less and less. Though they stop going altogether, they generally remain obligated to pay off their legal contract.

Watch out. In dealing with commercial health clubs, be wary of these common deceptions, cautions the FTC:

"Special reduced price" is often advertised to attract customers. Frequently the "special" rate is really the regular price.

Bait and switch. A special offer—such as 10 treatments for $10—may be made just to get you in the door. Once in you may be told that 10 sessions are of no value. If you demand the offered special, you may be told that you must take 2 treatments on each visit to the spa, or that only limited facilities for limited hours are available under the offer. The salesperson will nearly always try to sign you up in a more expensive, long-term program.

"Free visits" are sometimes awarded to everyone who signs up at registration tables set up in high-traffic areas. Winners often find that their visit amounts to a high-pressure sales pitch to accept a "discount" on an inflated membership fee.

"Before" and *"after"* photos may show two different people. Or in the before photograph, the person is unkempt, frowning, slumping, and poorly lighted, while in the after photo he is standing straight, smiling, with stomach in, chest out, in a tight swimsuit, and flattered by lighting and camera angle. In other cases the pictured person may have never even visited the advertised spa.

"Weight loss without exercise" is a frequent false claim. Many spas advertise that exercise devices will contribute to weight loss and better muscle tone without effort on your part. There is no evidence that devices that simply vibrate or shake the body will aid in weight reduction or improving muscle tone.

"Personal programs" and "specifically developed" or "personally designed" programs may prove to be standard calisthenics and exercises that vary little from person to person.

"Application" forms may be given you supposedly to reserve a place in the spa, when in reality you are signing a legally binding contract for long-term membership.

Guarantees of weight loss, inch loss, changes in dress size, or medical cures are often meaningless. The health spa may be the sole judge of whether you followed the program to the letter and can claim that since you did not "exactly" follow the program, the guarantee does not apply.

A reputable health spa will let you consider joining without pressuring you. Don't fall for claims that it is the "last day" before membership fees go up, when in fact no price increase is being considered.

Make sure you understand what happens if you decide to cancel your membership. A high percentage of people who sign contracts discontinue using spas in a very short time. Requests for membership cancellation are frequently denied.

In an ideal cancellation arrangement you get a refund based on the proportion of time used during the contract. Under present collection practices used by some spas, you could be harassed and even sued for the full contract price—even if you never used the spa's facilities.

See also EXERCISE; OVERWEIGHT.

HEALTH FOOD (organic food, natural food), for all its benefits, sometimes lends itself to exaggerated claims.

Think of a health food store as a specialty grocery store, not as a temple of purity. Like an Italian, Armenian, or any ethnically oriented food shop, a health food store carries some good foods not readily available elsewhere. In many areas only a health food store sells unroasted nuts and many kinds of seeds, grains, and rice.

Health food stores make available many valuable foods. Wheat germ, the embryo of the wheat seed, is high in protein and many vitamins. It can boost the nutritional value of cereals, casseroles, and foods breaded with it. Soybeans, yogurt, sprouts, unusual vegetable juices, whole grain products, and brown rice are other nutritious health food store staples.

The popularity of the thousands of U.S. health food stores has prompted big food companies to market brands with a minimum of food additives, and supermarkets have been spurred to stock many items formerly found only in health food stores. All to the good. But:

Don't use health food to cure illness. Unless you have a nutritional deficiency disease, such as anemia from iron deficiency, specific foods won't cure sickness. Nor will particular foods prevent any ailments. Pumpkin seeds will not help men with prostate trouble; carrot juice doesn't cure cancer or heal a peptic ulcer.

Vitamin E will not reverse impotence or infertility. Kelp won't cure indigestion. Honey is not a remedy for whooping cough. Fraudulent medical claims are made for countless other food, including bone meal, brewer's yeast, "tiger's milk," halibut liver oil.

Some health foods are downright unhealthful. Apricot kernels—available in many health food stores—contain amygdalin, which the body can convert to cyanide, a lethal poison.

Crushed apricot kernels have been sold in capsule form as Aprikern and Bee-Seventeen. The Food and Drug Administration (FDA) warned that 20 capsules of Aprikern could be fatal to an adult and only 2 packets of Bee-Seventeen could poison a child.

Some herbal teas sold in health food stores may be harmful. Teas containing buckthorn bark, senna leaves, dock roots, and aloe leaves may cause severe diarrhea. Burdock root tea can result in blurred vision, dry mouth, inability to urinate, bizarre behavior and speech, and hallucinations. Other plants that may cause hallucinations include catnip, juniper, hydrangea, jimsonweed, and wormwood. Ginseng has been reported to cause swollen and painful breasts. Chamomile tea has been associated with allergic reactions in people who are allergic to ragweed pollen. Nutmeg can cause severe headache, cramps and nausea, hallucinations. In very high doses it may cause liver damage and death.

Also avoid bitter almonds, the pits of apples, cherries, peaches, pears, plums, chokecherries, and cassava beans, all of which contain amygdalin. If you're an enthusiast of fruit pits the best way to detoxify them is to steam-distill them at 140° F for more than 12 hours.

Avoid raw, unpasteurized milk. Drinking such milk—from goats as well as cows—is another health-food practice fraught with danger. You may risk tuberculosis, brucellosis, and other milk-borne infectious disease.

Some health food faddists mistakenly believe that raw milk is healthier than pasteurized milk. While a tiny amount of vitamin C is lost in pasteurization, it's not enough to make much difference. Milk is not considered a good source of the vitamin in any case.

Honey is nutritionally little better than sugar. Other health foods favored by many health foodists items are of questionable value.

So-called raw sugar is actually a partially refined cane sugar. Like brown sugar it retains a bit more nutrients than white sugar, but not enough to justify its higher price.

Sea salt has not been proven to be better than regular salt, but it is much more expensive. The vitamin and mineral preparations you buy in a health food store are likely to cost considerably more but are no better for you than those sold in drugstores.

Your body can't tell the difference between natural and synthetic vitamins. In any case if you eat a wide variety of good foods, you have no need for supplemental vitamins and minerals unless your doctor prescribes them.

Organic food. Organic fertilization has no advantage over chemical fertilization. Plants can't tell the difference. A plant cannot absorb organic fertilizer until it is broken down by the soil into chemical elements, such as potassium, phosphorous, and nitrogen. The same elements are supplied more quickly and directly by chemical fertilizers.

Laboratory tests are unable to determine whether a plant has been fertilized organically or chemically. There is no evidence that organic plants are nutritionally superior. Moreover, organic fertilizer containing human excrement may contribute to the spread of hookworms, infectious hepatitis, shigellosis, and amebiasis.

Organic food may be a fraud. Because of the great demand, and in the absence of government standards, some chemically fertilized or pesticide-sprayed food is sold as organic. Allen Grant, West Coast editor of *Organic Gardening and Farming,* estimates that as much as 50 to 70 percent of the food labeled organic is identical with supermarket food—and it's much more expensive.

Nor are organically fertilized foods likely to be any more free of contamination by filth, mold, bacteria, or natural toxins than chemically fertilized foods.

Read natural-food labels carefully. You may be surprised that the foods contain additives and are little different from ordinary brands.

Natural cereals. Many so-called natural cereals, while made with nutritious whole grains, are loaded with sugar. Those put out by major cereal manufacturers—Heartland and Quaker 100% Natural Cereal—contain about 20 percent sugar.

Natural cereals are likely to be higher priced than regular cereals, and substantially more caloric. In a ½ cup serving the natural cereal Alpen has 220 calories while Cheerios has 44.

Nutritionally, natural cereals may have no advantage over ready-to-eat fortified cereals. A serving of Alpen contains 10 percent of the FDA's recommended daily allowance (RDA) for protein—the same amount as in a serving of Kellogg's Special K, at a lower price.

Alpen's vitamin and mineral content is significantly lower than that of most fortified cereals. Ordinary brands like Total, Corn Total, and Product 19 are enriched to 100 percent of the RDA of vitamins and iron.

Crunchy granola, a health food favorite, stacks up little better. Store-bought granolas frequently list sugar and oil as the second and third major ingredients, after rolled oats. A granola sold by a California food co-op was found only slightly more nutritious—and much more caloric—than the popular cereals Cheerios, Wheaties, and Special K.

If you want a delicious, whole grain, sugar-free, chemical-free, nutritious, inexpensive, ready-to-eat (but relatively high-calorie) cereal, make your own granola:

In a $13 \times 9 \times 2$-inch baking pan, mix 4 cups of rolled oats; 1½ cups unsweetened wheat germ; ½ cup unsweetened coconut; 1 teaspoon cinnamon; 1 teaspoon vanilla; 2 tablespoons vegetable oil; ¼ cup water; and chopped nuts, sesame seeds, and shelled sunflower seeds.

Bake 45 minutes in a 300° oven, stirring a few times. Then—to boost nutrition (but also calories)—you might add chopped dried fruit and raisins. If you want it sweetened, sprinkle a small amount of brown sugar to taste. Stir a few times during cooling. Store in a covered jar.

See also NUTRITION; QUACKERY.

HEALTH INSURANCE is protection you need against skyrocketing medical costs. A catastrophic illness—heart disease, cancer, stroke, or a severe accident—can reduce a middle-income family to poverty.

The illness can hurt every member of the family. Houses sold and lifetime savings depleted are common hardships. Because adults in the family have to help care for the stricken person, many lose opportunities for promotion or are forced to retire early or change careers. Most families cut back on food, clothing, and health care for themselves, and eliminate plans for vacations and major purchases.

Most families have inadequate coverage. Fewer than two in five patients in a National Cancer Foundation study got payments exceeding $10,000, though costs rapidly mounted far above that.

Before buying new insurance, check what benefits you're already entitled to. First look into public programs you may qualify for—under the Veterans Administration, Medicare, Medicaid, Public Health Service, state and local health departments, plus any national health insurance that develops. Such programs, if not free, are almost always cheaper than privately funded plans.

Then explore group coverage. As a fringe benefit your employer may provide comprehensive insurance at no cost to you or with a minimal contribution. If you leave your job, see about converting your group policy to an individual one. It sometimes is cheaper than a policy you initially buy as an individual.

By buying in quantity, unions, professional associations, and other organizations can negotiate coverage at lower rates than would be available to you as an individual purchaser. Though you're a nonjoiner, it may pay you to sign up with an organization if only to get into their insurance plan.

Supplement—don't duplicate—such programs with insurance you buy individually. Do not try to overinsure. Cover the really big items, the ones that would cause financial distress if you weren't insured against them. Insurance is so expensive that you're generally better off paying for minor services yourself.

HMOs: Your best bargain? Health maintenance organizations (HMOs) have been around for decades—one of the first, the Kaiser Foundation Health Plan, began in 1933. But only in the past few years have HMOs become a widespread alternative to conventional hospital and medical insurance. For a monthly fee, with little or no extra cost, HMOs generally provide nearly all the medical and hospital care you're likely to need—including all visits, tests, X rays, drugs, surgery, and hospitalizations.

Despite its coverage, such a prepaid group plan may actually cost less than a fairly comprehensive insurance plan. For example, if you were a worker whose employer made the usual basic contribution, you could join a typical Blue Cross/Blue Shield plan for $61 a month. Thereafter, you'd pay the first $150 of office visits per year and 20 percent of office-visit costs after that. But for only $59 a month, in the same city, you could join an HMO and your office visits would be free.

Health economist Harold Luft of the University of California at San Francisco compared total costs—premiums plus out-of-pocket charges—paid by people in HMOs and by people in conventional health insurance plans. Luft found HMO costs between 10 and 40 percent lower.

What about quality of care? Even the AMA, which long opposed the HMO concept, has been favorably impressed. After studying HMOs, the AMA's Council on Medical Service reported that the "medical care delivered by the HMOs appears to be of a generally high quality." Among HMO advantages, the council cited the availability of medical care at all hours, centralized medical records, ready access to specialists, a good screening process in hiring new physicians, and the peer review system (in which doctors evaluate each other's work).

You're likely to find HMOs in your area falling into one of four types: In the *staff model,* the HMO employs physicians and other specialists directly in a health center or clinic. In the *group model,* the HMO contracts for medical services with a group of physicians. In the *network model,* the HMO contracts for services with several medical groups or multispecialty medical centers. In the *individual practice association (IPA),* the HMO contracts with physicians who, most often, provide services in their own offices.

Before joining any such plan, check out the physicians available to you just as you would if you were choosing an individual doctor. If a plan owns its own hospital, satisfy yourself that the institution is of suitable quality. Ask HMO members how well they've found the plan to be administered. Think twice about joining if you hear frequent complaints of impersonal care, rudeness, long delays for appointments, or bureaucratic foul-ups.

For a list of group prepayment plans, write the Group Health Association of America, 624 Ninth Street, N.W., Washington, D.C. While HMOs are being pushed by government and employer health programs eager to lower costs, you may not find an acceptable one near you. Or you may wish to continue with a physician who is not affiliated with one. If so, you'll need to consider more traditional forms of health insurance.

Hospital insurance. Your most important coverage is for hospitalization, the most expensive part of nearly any major illness.

Nonprofit Blue Cross often offers the best deal. Typically, of every $1 in premiums, it returns perhaps 90¢ in benefits.

Blue Cross pays "service" benefits—within limits it pays your entire bill directly to the hospital. Some commercial carriers pay service benefits too. More typical of commercial carriers is an "indemnity" policy, which pays a fixed amount and you owe the rest. Thus you might collect $50 a day from an indemnity policy—but if the hospital charges $150 a day, you need to come up with the remaining $100 yourself.

With hospital costs rising steadily, you're likely to be way ahead with a service policy, though it's somewhat more expensive than one with indemnity benefits. If daily hospital costs increase $20, you're still fully covered under a service policy. With an indemnity policy you're out the additional $20 a day.

Some local Blue Cross plans cover a hospital stay of 365 days; others, no more than 21 days. The larger number of days is preferable, but shorter-stay coverage may prove adequate: The average hospital stay is only 8 days; only 14 days for people over 65.

Doctor bills. For meeting doctors' bills consider Blue Shield or prepaid health plans. Local

Blue Shield plans vary considerably. In general their emphasis is on physicians' and surgeons' services *in the hospital*—where the costliest services usually mount up.

Like Blue Cross, nonprofit Blue Shield pays about 90 percent of its premium dollar back in benefits, indicating you're likely to get your money's worth. In many Blue Shield plans member doctors accept Blue Shield's check as payment in full if you earn below a specified income. Above that income Blue Shield's payment is only an indemnity—so many dollars toward, say, an appendectomy—and you pay the rest. Out-of-hospital services typically receive scant coverage.

Major medical. Get major medical to fill in the gaps. Major medical policies pick up on doctor and hospital bills where your other coverage leaves off. They also cover other services that can add up during a major illness—private-duty nursing, prescription drugs, out-of-hospital physician care and lab work, blood transfusions, treatment for mental illness.

"Since the odds of a major illness are slim, the coverage costs less than you'd think," notes the consumer-minded Pennsylvania Insurance Department. Here are tips derived from the department's pamphlet *A Shopper's Guide to Health Insurance* and other authoritative sources:

Your best insurer may be one of these companies listed below. Each returns in benefits at least 50¢ of each premium dollar and does not specialize in mail-order insurance. In addition each has a stability rating of excellent or very good from *Best's Insurance Reports.*

Here's how companies that met these criteria ranked in a department study of the 25 largest commercial insurers:

1. American National General Agencies
2. Equitable Life Assurance Society of the United States
3. Metropolitan Life Insurance Company
4. American Republic Life Insurance Company
5. New York Life Insurance Company
6. Mutual of Omaha Insurance Company
7. Travelers Insurance Companies
8. Continental Insurance Companies
9. Prudential Insurance Company of America
10. Bankers Life Company

Have at least $100,000 in maximum benefits. Treat major medical as disaster insurance—and running up $100,000 in medical bills is not only disastrous but all too possible. The $10,000–$20,000 maximum that some families' policies will pay is far too little.

Many insurers offer maximums of up to

$250,000 at little extra cost. Some provide unlimited benefits for a bit more. If you already have an adequate major medical policy and want to add to it, you get at reasonably low cost an "umbrella" policy that begins coverage where your regular benefits end.

Make your deductible $750 or more. The deductible is the amount you pay before the insurer's payments start. The higher the deductible, the less you pay for the insurance—the difference between a zero deductible ("first-dollar coverage") and a $1,000 deductible can often mean a doubling of the premium. You're better off having a high deductible—which you can meet from income, savings, or loans—and applying your premium dollars toward a higher maximum benefit.

Seek a policy in which the deductible can be satisfied by combining all family members' medical expenses, rather than just one individual's sickness.

Coinsure up to $5,000. Most major medical policies require you to "coinsure"—pay a percentage of any expense over your deductible. For a bill of $100 you typically pay $20 or $25, the company paying the balance.

Pay no more than the standard 20 or 25 percent. And have a cutoff point of $5,000, after which the company pays 100 percent. Otherwise if you were required to coinsure to the policy maximum, you could wind up paying 25 percent of a $100,000 bill.

Be sure coverage is adequate. Try to avoid "internal limits," the maximum your policy will pay toward a particular item. If you can't avoid a hospital-expense limit, it should be at least as high as your hospital's daily semiprivate room charges. Read your policy over every year or so to be sure its benefits are still in line with medical costs.

Be fully covered for intensive and cardiac care, blood and plasma, and prosthetics and other rehabilitation devices. Also seek coverage for private nursing care both in and out of the hospital, and for convalescent home care of 60 to 120 days.

Look into your family's needs to determine what else to cover. A couple planning to have children may do well to provide for pregnancy and childbirth; singles, and couples who've had their kids, may save money if they can omit such coverage. If you have a youngster who will require orthodontic treatment, see about dental coverage. Decide whether psychiatric benefits would be a good buy for you and your family.

Avoid "dread disease" policies, which are so narrow in coverage they pay only if you get a particular illness, usually cancer. Some policies cover leukemia, meningitis, rabies, polio, and other scare diseases. Warns the Pennsylvania Insurance Department: "When you buy these policies, you're not insuring, you're gambling."

Seek guaranteed renewability. Be sure the insurer can't cancel your policy no matter how many claims you make. After age 65 your policy should be convertible to supplement Medicare.

For your part, you don't build up equity with a policy, so switch companies if you can do better. Do this cautiously, however. If you're under treatment for an illness or injury, you're likely to be better off sticking with your present insurer. A new insurer would ordinarily refuse to cover such pre-existing conditions.

Watch the fine print. Seek the shortest possible waiting period. Some policies won't cover new illnesses until your policy is 30 days old; some require a six-month wait for specified illnesses like heart disease, cancer, tuberculosis if hitherto undiagnosed. For maternity coverage a waiting period of nine or ten months is acceptable. Newborn infants should be covered from *birth* (not two to four weeks old as is common) because birth defects and other problems can require immediate costly care.

Most policies restrict coverage on pre-existing illnesses, those you had at the time you took out the insurance. That's so you don't buy a policy one day, then check into the hospital the next day for a long-needed operation. Avoid policies that exclude pre-existing conditions for more than a year.

Resist riders that limit your coverage in important respects. For example, if a medical questionnaire or physical examination shows you have heart disease, the company will ordinarily exclude it from coverage or include it for reduced benefits or an increased premium. If there are too many such loopholes, you come out with what labor leader Walter Reuther once called a "buffalo policy": You can collect only if you are run over by a herd of buffaloes at noon.

Mail-order frauds. Beware mail-order health insurance. People who have other coverage don't need it and people who buy it as their only health insurance are not being adequately protected.

The field is full of gyps. The companies typically advertise widely on TV and in the press that you'll get "$1,000 a month tax-free extra cash" if hospitalized. In fact even $1,000 a month is only about $33 a day, far less than daily hospital costs—and much less coverage than you need.

And you may not collect anything. The Senate Antitrust and Monopoly Subcommittee found that for a typical policy, the nation's leading mail-order insurer one year rejected fully 38.5 percent of all claims.

Mail-order companies often get out of paying by tucking away in fine print a requirement that you spend three to eight days in the hospital before you start collecting. By the time you're eligible for payments, you're likely to be on your way home. Most mail-order policies pay nothing toward home care; nursing, convalescent, rehabilitation, or extended-care facilities; government hospitals; tuberculosis sanatoriums.

A "pre-existing condition" may be pulled on you. Mail-order companies widely advertise "No physical examination required," suggesting your previous health is irrelevant. In fact they flood physicians with questionnaires about your health, asking dates when illnesses began. Then the company may reject your claim for tenuous reasons. In New Jersey an elderly man was denied benefits for an intestinal infection because years before he'd had varicose veins.

Mail-order insurers widely claim that their rates are lower because they pay no salesmen's commissions, thus presumably give you more benefits for less money. Not necessarily. The Pennsylvania Insurance Department found that of each premium dollar received one year by mail-order insurers, as little as 32¢ was paid back in benefits. Union Fidelity paid back less than 36¢; Bankers Multiple Life, less than 32¢.

Moreover, the lack of a salesman means you have no one to explain a policy to you.

Hypocrisy and high-pressure tactics are rife in mail-order insurance sales. A folksy show-business personality appeared on TV declaring: "You know me. I wouldn't recommend anything I honestly didn't believe in." Drawing on the public's affection for him, he said: "I've looked over the policy very carefully . . . That's why I cannot imagine *anybody* passing up a chance to enroll in this health plan."

He in fact was paid $50,000 a year for promoting the policy. What's more, he was a stockholder and director of the insurance company. The Florida insurance commissioner levied a $20,000 penalty against the company, charging that his commercials were deceptive. Though the ads portrayed him as a public-spirited citizen, the commissioner concluded, he in fact was acting as an unlicensed insurance agent.

Avoid Medicare frauds. If you're on Medicare, supplement it with a low-cost Blue Cross–Blue Shield "65-special" policy. This will cover Medicare's deductibles and coinsurance requirements, hospitalization beyond Medicare maximums, etc.

Steer clear of mail-order policies that have sprung up around Medicare. As with other types of mail-order coverage their payments are inadequate and ads often misleading.

A favorite tactic is to suggest a policy is endorsed by the U.S. Government or has some other official status. One company, charged with mail fraud, pretended to be linked with the government and had return cards addressed to "Medicare 65, Washington, D.C."

Another company sends retirees an IBM card in an official-looking envelope. It appears to come from the government and offers information on Social Security benefits you may be entitled to. Returning the card opens your door to a high-pressure spiel for commercial insurance.

Disability insurance. A policy that provides an income if you can't work can be at least as important as life insurance. In terms of hard cash, long-term disability can pose a greater threat than death.

A good policy pays so much a month for five to ten years, perhaps to age 65, for any one bout of disability from sickness. It's liberal in its definition of disability—for example, it will pay benefits if you are unable to do your regular job (rather than require that you be too incapacitated to do any work at all). It pays lifetime benefits for disability from an accident. Some policies provide additional cash benefits for accidental death or dismemberment, but this optional feature may overlap your life insurance.

Shop for a policy among the reputable companies mentioned earlier. Insist on a policy that's noncancellable—some companies are quick to cancel after the first hint of trouble. Seek guaranteed renewability until you reach at least 65.

It should cover any and all illnesses—there are policies that don't cover heart disease but pay off handsomely on such unlikely ailments as cholera. It should make no distinction between "confining" and "nonconfining" ailments; there's no reason you should be hospitalized or housebound to collect. It should cover "accidental bodily injury," a phrase that indicates *any* injury—including one from an accident related to a medical condition or your own negligence, for example.

Other desirable features: Guaranteed level premiums (no sudden rise in cost) for as long as you hold the policy. Waiver of premiums during disability—you don't pay premiums while you're unable to work. Coverage of recurrent disability from the same cause: you collect during relapses even though you went back to work between bouts of the illness.

Don't miss out on a broad range of public disability programs. If you're under 65 and unable to work for a year or more, ask a Social Security office about disability benefits and Supplemental Security Income. Workmen's compensation and the Veterans Administration also provide benefits for which you may qualify.

See also HOSPITAL; MEDICAL DEDUCTIONS; PHYSICIAN.

HEALTH SPAS See HEALTH CLUBS.

HEARING AIDS can improve hearing in certain types of deafness. Consult an otologist, a medical specialist, to determine if you need treatment. If your hearing loss is correctable through drugs, surgery, or the simple removal of earwax, you won't need a hearing aid at all.

A hearing aid is a miniature amplifier that picks up and transmits sounds to the ear. Using electrical energy supplied by tiny batteries, it changes sound waves into electrical impulses. These impulses are then converted into amplified sound and transmitted to the ear. A complete hearing aid has an amplifier, a microphone, a battery, a receiver, and controls for adjusting sound.

The basic kinds of hearing aids include:

Air conduction hearing aids, which direct the sound into the opening of the ear canal.

Bone conduction hearing aids, which apply the sound to the bone behind the ear. These are less efficient than air conduction hearing aids at getting sound vibrations to the inner ear, but they may be made necessary by a medical condition such as chronic ear infection. Their use is rare.

Monaural hearing aids, which are used for one ear only.

Binaural hearing aids, which consist of two complete aids, one for each ear.

CROS (contralateral routing of signal) or "cross-over" hearing aids, which place the microphone beside the poor ear and feed the amplified signal to the better ear. This system may help those who have moderate or severe loss in one ear and useful hearing in the other ear.

Hearing aids can be worn on the body or at ear level. On-the-body models can be carried in a pocket, pinned to clothing, or worn in a special carrier. A cord leads to a receiver button in the ear. About 10 percent of all users find this style more suitable for their use. It is meant for severe hearing loss.

Ear-level models include behind-the-ear models, eyeglass models, and in-the-ear models. Behind-the-ear aids can be worn fairly inconspicu-

ously, held in place by a thin, short piece of tubing that connects to a small ear mold in the ear. In eyeglass models the hearing aid is built into the frame.

In-the-ear models are so small that all of the parts can be inserted into the ear. Many people feel that their hearing impairment is less apparent with very small hearing aids, and thus prefer in-the-ear aids. But doctors caution that some people need the greater amplification of larger models. Follow a professional's recommendation as to which hearing aid will be best for you.

If a hearing aid is indicated, your doctor may decide that your hearing loss may also need to be evaluated by a certified audiologist, a nonmedical professional trained in the testing, rehabilitation, and counseling of people with hearing disorders. His examination will determine how well speech is understood, what the specific dimensions of the hearing loss are, and what characteristics the hearing aid should have.

All certified audiologists are listed in the *American Speech-Language-Hearing Association* (ASHA) *Directory,* published annually and available at libraries, hospitals or clinics, or from societies for the hard of hearing. A certified audiologist can make an impartial recommendation, since he does not profit from the product he prescribes.

Hearing-aid audiologists, on the other hand, usually are either hearing-aid dealers or work for dealers, and are not required to meet the same stringent educational requirements set for certified audiologists. They often have a conflict of interest, since they are likely to make a direct profit on the hearing aids they sell.

After his examination the audiologist may prescribe an aid, specify several models from which to choose, or specify what the aid should accomplish, allowing the dealer to match a model to the patient's requirement. Often an audiologist will have several hearing-aid models you can try on to see which provides the greatest improvement for you. You can then buy the aid through an audiologist or a hearing-aid dealer.

Selecting a hearing aid. Compare for comfort and convenience. Controls should be easy to operate. Batteries, parts, and minor repairs should be available locally.

Compare for clarity and quality of sound. Listen to familiar voices with each of the aids. Compare how well you understand speech with each.

Listen in noisy places as well as in quiet. Try the aids outdoors as well as indoors. But bear in mind that a hearing aid requires time to get accustomed to. Don't expect sounds to be perfect when you first try using it.

In fact a hearing aid will never give you perfectly natural sound. But a good hearing aid should be able to filter out as much noise as possible so as to make speech more intelligible. All hearing aids have some degree of sound distortion; try to pick one with the least possible degree of distortion.

The high cost of hearing aids discourages many hard-of-hearing people from buying them. Most good hearing aids cost several hundred dollars.

Don't be afraid to compare costs—a low-priced aid may be just as satisfactory as a high-priced one, depending upon your needs.

Find out exactly what the price includes. Ask about the cost of batteries for each aid, and the expected life of the battery.

Also compare extra services included in the price. Does the dealer give you a convenient repair and replacement service? How long is the aid guaranteed for free repairs? Will the dealer help you to learn to use your aid? Insist that the dealer agree to a money-back guarantee if the aid does not work properly for you, and have him put it in writing.

If you cannot afford the high cost of most hearing aids, you may get assistance through the federal Social and Rehabilitation Service program. Contact your state division of vocational rehabilitation.

For a child ask the doctor, audiology center, or local or state health department for information on a program financed in part by the Children's Bureau of the Department of Health and Human Services. Or it may be possible to save some money when buying the aid through a group willing to set up a buying program and to negotiate with dealers or manufacturers. Some dealers will give discounts to the elderly.

Some hearing-aid dealers may urge you to buy two aids, one for each ear (binaural hearing aids), to aid you in identifying the direction of sound. But a binaural system does not work for everyone, and it is usually double the price of a monaural system. Consider the binaural system only if it gives you a great improvement in hearing over one aid, or if your audiologist recommends it.

Adjusting to a hearing aid. Don't be discouraged if you have some trouble adjusting to a hearing aid. Most people do. At first a hearing aid will bring unaccustomed sounds to your ears —background sounds you have not heard for years—typewriters, street noises, doors closing,

power lawn mowers, airplanes, footsteps, distant radio, and many other neighborhood noises.

You may find some of these noises jarring and distressing. You may have trouble following what's being said at a party. Like everyone else, you'll be uncomfortable with a person who does not enunciate clearly or who talks with a cigarette in his mouth.

In time you will develop a screening ability and learn to disregard background noises much as does the person with normal hearing. You will learn to listen only to what you want to hear and to adjust the hearing aid to suit your specific needs.

To get used to a hearing aid, wear it only at home at first. Try sitting quietly and tune in on noises around you. Turn a radio or TV to a low volume and get used to it. After a few days of such practice, try talking quietly to just one person.

Gradually increase the amount of time you wear the hearing aid at home, then use it in selected social situations, starting with groups of two or three people.

Experiment for a while to find the adjustment that generally lets you hear best. After that don't keep fiddling with the controls. Hearing and speech centers frequently offer courses in how to use a hearing aid properly and can assist you in adjusting to it. Many audiologists believe such courses are essential for getting the best use of the hearing aid.

To care for your hearing aid remember it is a delicate instrument. Avoid leaving it in direct sun, near radiators, or locked in a hot car. Read the booklet the dealer furnishes with your particular hearing aid.

In your daily inspection of your aid, be sure the ear insert is free from ear wax and the battery is not leaking and threatening to corrode the aid. If you have a cord, be sure it is not frayed. At night be sure to disconnect the battery by removing it or swinging out the battery case.

Keep the aid dry. Store it at night or during any long period of nonuse in a closed container with silica gel or some other material that absorbs moisture. Following this rule is especially important in humid weather. Don't forget to remove it when you swim, bathe or shower.

Avoid sharp blows to your hearing aid—treat it gently and don't drop it. Don't sit under a hair dryer or use a hair spray while wearing your hearing aid.

Hearing-aid frauds. Beware of high-pressure or fraudulent sales tactics. Remember that not everyone can be helped with hearing aids, so don't be misled by ads that promise miracles.

In the past few years the FTC has frequently asked hearing-aid manufacturers and promoters to discontinue misrepresenting their products by making false claims. The industry typically sells hearing aids like vacuum cleaners or storm windows.

Be particularly suspicious of mail-order advertisements. It's likely to be nearly impossible to get satisfaction if something goes wrong. The same is true if you buy the aid from a salesman merely passing through your town. Also be wary of any over-the-counter drugs that are advertised as a cure for poor hearing.

Many hearing-aid dealers are skilled only in high-pressure salesmanship. Often they have no expertise about the problems of the hard of hearing, or about the delicate appliances they sell.

To help guard against incompetence use a hearing-aid dealer who is certified by the National Hearing Aid Society. Members of this organization undergo instruction to become proficient in the use of all hearing-aid equipment.

In addition about half the states have licensing laws for dealers. In these states complaints can be directed to the State Hearing Aid Licensing Board, in care of the state capitol.

To protect yourself further, insist that the aid be bought on a trial basis only. Most reputable dealers will rent you the aid for a month. If you aren't satisfied, they'll take it back. If you buy the aid, they'll deduct the rental fee from the price. During the trial period, return to your otologist or audiologist so that he can check whether the aid is working properly.

If a disagreement should arise that cannot be solved by direct negotiations with your dealer, you can write to the president of the hearing-aid dealers association in the state in which the hearing aid was purchased.

See also HEARING LOSS.

HEARING LOSS (deafness) afflicts an estimated 8.5 million Americans. About 71,000 may be totally deaf, about 235,000 have a severe hearing loss, and more than 8 million are inconvenienced or handicapped by a lesser degree of hearing loss. About 1 million American children have a significant handicap in hearing.

Suspect a loss of hearing:

If you hear better some days than others.

If you often fail to catch words or phrases.

If you find yourself unable to follow conversations in a group.

If you find you can better understand what a person is saying when you are facing him.

If you frequently feel that your family and friends mumble instead of speaking clearly.

If you have a running ear, or pain or irritation in the ear.

If you suffer from dizziness, loss of balance, or head noises.

Audiologists determine the type and extent of a hearing loss with an audiometer, a machine that gauges a patient's responses to variable pitches and intensities of sound tones. By recording these measurements on an audiogram, it's possible to tell not only where the damage is, but how great the loss is at each sound frequency. In addition he may use special tuning forks and word-discrimination tests to confirm the diagnosis.

Otologists will evaluate you and determine if the hearing loss is medically treatable. Most otologists for convenience divide hearing impairments into three main types: conductive deafness, sensorineural (perceptive) deafness, and mixed deafness.

Conductive deafness results from interference with the passage of sound to the inner ear. It may be caused by chronic infection of the sinuses, tonsils, and adenoids. Other causes include infection or fluid in the middle ear, inflammation of the eustachian tube connecting the throat and the middle ear, perforation of the eardrum, or chronic mastoiditis, and restriction of motion of the stapes bone.

These conditions impede sound and interfere with the conduction of sound waves through the middle ear to the inner ear, where the hearing apparatus is located. Even though the nerve endings in the hearing apparatus may function normally, sound cannot get to them.

Sensorineural deafness exists when the sound is transmitted intact to the hearing nerve, but there is degeneration of the organ of hearing, the nerve that transmits impulses to the brain, or of the brain itself. These changes can be caused by retarded circulation, nerve damage, injury, or the aging process.

Mixed deafness is a combination of the two.

Hearing loss has many causes. An infant who is deaf at birth may have had his hearing injured by infection or trauma in the uterus. Rh disease from a blood incompatibility between the mother and the unborn infant may also cause hearing loss. If the mother has had rubella (German measles) in the first three months of pregnancy, deafness in the child is a common result. Physicians have found that the incidence of ear damage in premature births is nearly seven times greater than in full-term deliveries. Hearing loss can also be a hereditary trait.

In children hearing loss frequently results from ear infections, particularly of the middle ear, often accompanied by earache. Some childhood diseases, such as measles, mumps, and scarlet fever, can lead to hearing deficiencies. Meningitis and encephalitis may result in ear damage, as may head injuries and blows to the ear. Other causes of hearing loss include allergies, inner-ear tumors (such as acoustic neuroma), cancer of the brain, and Ménière's disease. A common cause of slightly impaired hearing is the accumulation of earwax.

Hearing may also be affected by overuse of drugs, such as certain antibiotics or salicylates. Some industrial chemicals can cause hearing impairment.

Hearing losses on account of aging result primarily from arteriosclerotic and degenerative changes in the inner ear (known as presbycusis). Almost no one over 65 can hear as well as he did at 25.

Otosclerosis is one of the most common causes of hearing loss. In this condition for unknown reasons new bone starts to grow in the middle ear. If the process continues, it soon renders the stapes—one of the three tiny bones in the middle ear that transmit sound—rigid and motionless. The condition is usually hereditary, and often begins in early adulthood. This hearing loss may frequently be aided by surgery and a hearing aid.

Noise can cause hearing loss. A panel appointed by the U.S. Department of Commerce has reported that "millions of workers are now exposed to noise levels that have been shown conclusively to produce hearing damage."

The Federal Council for Science and Technology estimates that at least 6 million and possibly as many as 16 million workers in this country experience noise conditions unsafe to hearing.

Most of the endangered workers are unaware of the hazard and do not act to protect themselves. Crewmen on aircraft carriers, for example, are regularly subjected to about 160 decibels of sound whenever jet planes are launched. Scientists generally agree that a short burst of sound of about 150 decibels can do permanent damage to the hearing, and a danger point may be reached at 85 to 90 decibels. Repeated exposure to noise at high levels increases the risk of permanently impaired hearing.

Loud music—such as roaring rock music—can have the same effect. Typically loud rock music registers about 100 to 120 decibels, well in the potential danger range. A guinea pig subjected to music played at that volume was found to have destroyed cells in his cochlea, the organ that translates sound waves into nerve impulses.

Rock musicians are particularly endangered, but researchers are finding that many teen-agers have measurable hearing losses, and they suggest that listening to loud music may be to blame. A case in point: A significant number of entering freshmen at the University of Tennessee were found to have hearing losses in the high-frequency range. Some investigators have suggested legislation limiting the sound in discotheques to 100 decibels.

Turn the volume down if you have buzzing or tickling sensations in your ear or if your ears hurt. If you hear noises in your ear after listening, or if you have trouble hearing for five or ten minutes, you'll know the music was too loud. Musicians and others exposed to loud noise should equip themselves with customized ear defenders, which would reduce the intensity level of the noise by 20 to 30 decibels.

Hunters may be endangering their hearing by firearm noise. An Air Force study has found significant hearing loss in men who have practiced for the routine Army small-arms qualification course. Mufflers on guns will cut the noise and help protect hearing. Similarly, if you routinely operate loud machines such as power saws, wear ear protection.

Hearing-loss detection. Early detection of hearing loss—especially in young children—can help prevent later difficulties. The child with undetected and uncorrected hearing loss is almost certain to develop speech problems as well. Furthermore his unresponsiveness may cause peers and teachers to label him dull or retarded.

Ask your family doctor or pediatrician to refer your infant to an audiologist to determine if his hearing is normal. Any child with a speech, learning, or behavior problem should be checked for hearing loss by an audiologist. A child may be showing hearing problems if he habitually ignores a passing fire engine, hangs up the phone without speaking, turns up the volume on the radio or television, or frequently says "What?" or misunderstands.

Restoring hearing. In some cases mere removal of earwax will improve hearing. People with conductive deafness can often have their hearing restored with the use of medication or surgery. For example, hearing loss arising from temporary ear infections can usually be cured with antibiotics. The removal of infected tonsils and adenoids may often improve hearing.

A surgical procedure, called stapedectomy, is available for the treatment of otosclerosis, improving hearing in a large percentage of cases. In this operation, the immobilized stapes is removed and replaced with an artificial stapes of plastic or stainless steel.

An operation called tympanoplasty reconstructs the middle-ear structure, improving hearing in those with a diseased mastoid or infected middle-ear bones. Under development is the cochlear implant (bionic ear), which may restore some sound reception in people who have severe hearing loss in both ears and cannot be helped with hearing aids.

Hearing loss resulting from excess fluid in the middle ear can be relieved by surgical drainage. A myringoplasty can repair a perforation of the eardrum.

In most cases of sensorineural hearing loss surgery is of little avail. Disorders that arise in the inner ear seldom respond to surgery or treatment. An exception is Ménière's disease, in which the symptoms can often be controlled. And drugs that dilate the blood vessels can improve hearing loss due to a reduction of blood supply to the inner ear.

However many people with sensorineural hearing loss will benefit from the use of hearing aids. But never buy a hearing aid except on the advice of an otologist or audiologist—and then make sure you are getting unbiased, professional help in its selection.

If possible consult a hearing-rehabilitation center. Most of these centers have physicians and audiologists who make evaluations of hearing loss and advise about the type of hearing aid needed.

Learning to read lips can often help people with hearing aids communicate better. Lip-reading is often called speech reading, since it involves observation of gestures, expressions, and other supplements to words formed by the lips. Most hearing centers have professionals qualified to give instruction in lip-reading.

If a deaf child or adult cannot learn lip-reading, he may be able to learn to communicate by finger spelling and by the language of signs. This sometimes speeds up a deaf child's acquisition of language and may provide an impetus to learn to talk.

Help for the hard of hearing. Other aids for the hard of hearing include:

A telephone with an amplifier. It costs a little more than a regular telephone, but it looks the same and people with normal hearing can use it. A few public telephones equipped with amplifiers can generally be found in large cities; the telephone company would know about them.

An electronic device that flashes a light when the telephone or the doorbell rings or the baby cries.

Headphones, with built-in volume controls, for listening to television, radio, and the phonograph.

An inexpensive device called an inductor, used with a hearing aid, which substantially improves the clarity of television, radio, and the phonograph.

Intercom systems that pick up sounds in one room, such as the baby's, and deliver them amplified to another, such as the kitchen or the bedroom.

Ear banks. To further research in hearing loss, a network of ear banks has been set up in leading medical centers and universities throughout the country. Called Temporal Bone Banks (the temporal bones contain the middle- and inner-ear structures), these centers function as laboratories for studying inner-ear structures bequeathed to the program.

The Temporal Bone Banks Program is particularly interested in encouraging people who are hard of hearing to bequeath their ears after death. Since inner ears cannot be examined during life, after-death studies are essential in determining how various conditions affect the hearing. In hearing loss because of mumps, for example, studies have shown that the virus had destroyed parts of the cochlea having to do with the blood supply.

For information about ear banks write to The Deafness Research Foundation, 55 East Thirty-fourth Street, New York, New York 10016.

Eardrum transplants have been performed in recent years, largely under the auspices of Project HEAR in Palo Alto, California, the first regional eardrum bank program in the nation. Eardrums can be more easily transplanted because they don't cause the rejection problems that have plagued heart, kidney, and liver transplants.

Eardrum transplants are being done in increasing numbers to replace damaged eardrums and to restore hearing loss from infections of the middle ear and mastoid. The transplants cannot, however, correct inner-ear or perceptive deafness.

Help for children. If your child has severe hearing problems, enroll him in a special preschool center for hard-of-hearing children where specially trained teachers will help him with his particular problems. A child with a severe hearing deficiency will need a lot of practice in learning to speak and read lips. He may also need help in learning to use a hearing aid.

In many states the public schools have programs to help children with hearing and speech problems. Your local school system or your state department of education can supply information on these programs. The Department of Health, Education, and Welfare's Office of Education offers consultation services on school programs for the hearing-handicapped.

At home parents can help with word and speech drills prescribed by the center. Parents are advised to speak to a nonhearing child a great deal, standing on a level with his face a few feet in front of him and in good light. In this way he gets a lot of practice in lip-reading.

Remember that almost all deaf children have some residual hearing. You can help develop it by constantly exposing your child to sound, experimenting with the sounds he seems to respond to.

Try to treat the deaf child as much like a hearing child as possible. Encourage other people to talk to him, to play with him, to show him things and tell him about them.

In order to have a full command of language and to learn to use it vocally and intelligently, your deaf child will have to use all his senses to the fullest possible extent. You can help by providing as rich and varied an environment as possible.

For more information about coping with the problems of hearing loss write to the following:

American Speech-Language-Hearing
  Association
10801 Rockville Pike
Rockville, Maryland 20852

The association offers information to consumers, literature, and referrals.

The Alexander Graham Bell Association for
  the Deaf, Inc.
3417 Volta Place, NW
Washington, D.C. 20007

The association has more than 200 parent groups affiliated with it throughout the country and publishes *The Volta Review,* a lay and professional journal. *Speaking Out* is a newsletter specially written for parents that goes to all affiliated parent groups each month.

National Association of the Deaf
814 Thayer Avenue
Silver Spring, Maryland 20005

The association offers a catalog of materials relating to education and problems of the deaf of all ages. It also publishes *Deaf American,* a monthly magazine for laymen and professionals who are concerned with deafness.

These and other organizations can put you in touch with a selection of special services for the hard of hearing, such as summer camps, schools, athletic associations, homes for aged deaf, insurance programs, housing, and many others. A complete *Directory of Services for the Deaf in the United States* is published by the *American Annals of the Deaf.* Write to the Editor, American Annals of the Deaf, Gallaudet College, Washington, D.C. 20002.

See also ACOUSTIC NEUROMA; ALLERGY; ANTIBIOTICS; CANCER OF THE BRAIN; EARACHE; EAR INFECTIONS; EARWAX; ENCEPHALITIS; HEAD INJURIES; HEARING AIDS; MEASLES; MÉNIÈRE'S DISEASE; MENINGITIS; MUMPS; NOISE; RH DISEASE; RUBELLA; SCARLET FEVER.

HEART ATTACK (coronary occlusion, coronary thrombosis, myocardial infarction) is a blocking of one or more arteries that supply the heart muscle with blood.

Minutes count. Of the nearly 600,000 Americans killed by heart attacks each year, most die before they reach a hospital.

If you suffer a heart attack: Call a doctor immediately. If you can't reach one, get to a hospital emergency room by the fastest means possible. Unless an ambulance can reach you within ten minutes, go in a private car. A bumpy ride won't hurt you, but delay can be fatal.

While riding to the hospital, sit upright unless you feel like fainting. Heart pain tends to worsen if you lie down. Too, shortness of breath is eased in a sitting or half-sitting position.

If you're helping a heart-attack victim, arrange the foregoing for him so he stays quiet. Be sure he isn't in fact choking on a piece of food— a "café coronary" is often mistaken for a heart attack (see CHOKING). Give nothing to eat or drink.

Be on guard against HEART STOPPAGE (which see). If his heart stops while you're driving to the hospital, stop the car immediately. Place him on a hard surface outside the car and apply closed-chest massage.

Symptoms of heart attack. Usually there is a heavy, prolonged sensation of pressure, fullness, squeezing, or aching in the center of the chest, behind the breastbone. The pain may spread across the chest, possibly to the shoulder, arm, neck, jaw. It is likely to be accompanied by sweating, nausea, vomiting, breathing difficulties.

The pain may be in the arms alone, where it is commonly mistaken for arthritis, bursitis, or a muscle strain. Or it may be only in the neck, where it may be thought to be a toothache or stiff neck, or in the upper abdomen, where it may feel like indigestion. It may be in the back, and be confused with backache or charley horse. It may be in combinations of these.

There are many causes of chest pain besides heart attack. In particular a sharp, jabbing pain on the left side of the chest is often experienced by tense people, but the pain of heart attack is rarely sharp or jabbing.

"Silent" heart attacks can be an even graver hazard. A heart attack may be signaled by less severe pain, sometimes by merely mild fluttering. Don't be reassured if the discomfort subsides or disappears. Many people ignore repeated warnings of this type, only to have a damaging or fatal attack. If they have alarming symptoms, they are more likely to get to a hospital fast—and may have a better chance of surviving.

At least a third, and possibly half, of all heart attacks happen so subtly as to go undiscovered. In a silent no less than a frank attack, you need prompt treatment. Victims of both types of attacks share a danger that the underlying blockage of the arteries to the heart will cause a second attack. The National Heart Foundation study in Framingham, Massachusetts, found that one in three victims of silent attacks have another, probably more severe, attack within five years.

The cause of heart attack. Most heart attacks result from atherosclerosis, a form of arteriosclerosis in which the arteries become roughened and narrowed by fatty deposits. Around these patches scarlike tissue forms.

Blood fighting its way through such an artery may form a clot (a thrombus) that seals off the channel, halting blood flow through that vessel and all of its downstream branches. The segment of heart muscle normally fed by the blocked artery dies. This kind of attack, called a coronary thrombosis, can happen during sleep as well as during excitement.

In a second type of heart attack, the fatty deposits themselves plug the vessel, without a clot. The deposits become so enlarged that they merge and shut off the flow of blood.

An attack occurring in either way may be preceded by angina pectoris. How mild or severe the pain is depends on the size of the blocked vessel and the extent of the area damaged by blood starvation. This damaged or killed region of heart muscle is called a myocardial infarct.

Take these measures to sidestep major "risk factors" in heart disease:

Reduce your intake of cholesterol and saturated fats.
Control high blood pressure.
Give up cigarette smoking.

HOW MOST HEART ATTACKS HAPPEN
A clot blocks circulation to heart muscle

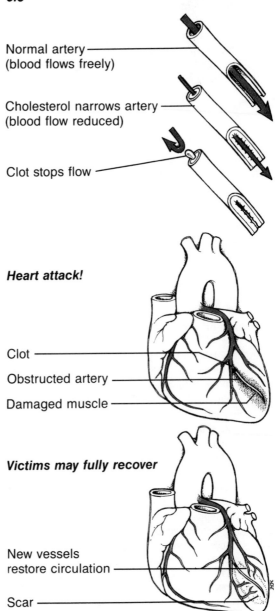

Normal artery
(blood flows freely)

Cholesterol narrows artery
(blood flow reduced)

Clot stops flow

Heart attack!

Clot

Obstructed artery

Damaged muscle

Victims may fully recover

New vessels
restore circulation

Scar

Free yourself of emotional stress.
Keep your weight down.
Get regular exercise.
Have periodic physical examination.

Take special care if you have close relatives who died between ages 40 and 60 from heart attack. This could mean a tendency to arteriosclerosis runs in your family. But even if you are coronary prone by heredity, you are likely to be spared a heart attack if you avoid the risk factors.

Men are more susceptible to heart attacks than women. The difference is largely due to estrogen, the female hormone, which delays the development of arteriosclerosis. But once menopause has begun, women become progressively more susceptible. Until age 45 men have 13 times as many heart attacks as women. Between 45 and 62 men have twice as many. After 62 the incidence is about the same.

Teach your children health habits that will help them avoid heart attack. Early in life, train them to control their body weight, keep down their intake of saturated fats, abstain from cigarettes, and take part in sports and other physical activities they can enjoy all their lives.

If you have diabetes, you need to bring it under control. Untreated diabetes is associated with a rise in cholesterol and other fats in the blood, and promotes the development of atherosclerosis.

Personality and heart attacks. A hard-driving personality may put you in a high-risk category. Cardiologists Meyer Friedman and Ray H. Rosenman of the Mount Zion Hospital and Medical Center in San Francisco found that more than nine out of ten heart-attack victims had a compulsive, always-on-the-go behavior pattern they labeled the Type A personality.

In contrast to the easygoing, tranquil Type B, a Type A has "hurry sickness." He is aggressively involved in a chronic struggle to get more and more done in less and less time. He walks fast, talks fast, constantly consults his wristwatch.

He's competitive and quick-tempered. While donating blood one Type A glanced at the donor at the next table and complained, "Hey, how come his blood is coming out faster than mine?" The typical Type A has a great need to accumulate material goods, and tends to measure his life in terms of numbers—he made so many dollars, completed so many jobs, etc.

Drs. Friedman and Rosenman estimate that 50 to 60 percent of urban Americans exhibit a Type A personality. One reason Type A behavior may lead to heart attacks: There's evidence that blood cholesterol rises in response to stressful situations. Conclude Friedman and Rosenman: "In the absence of Type A Behavior Pattern, coronary heart disease almost never occurs before 70 years of age, regardless of the fatty foods eaten, the cigarettes smoked, or the lack of exercise. But when this behavior pattern is present, coronary heart disease can easily erupt in one's 30s or 40s."

Their recommendation: If you're behaving in a Type A manner, stop it. They offer a program for "re-engineering" your personality in their book *Type A Behavior and Your Heart* (Knopf, 1974).

To free yourself from hurry sickness, they advise, review your successes—and realize that the most important ones came not from doing a job faster than anybody else but from doing it better. Generally a self-imposed grind is an effort to appease a gnawing sense of insecurity with ever-increasing conquests. Take stock of what you really want out of life—and make these your goals.

Revise your schedule to eliminate as many activities as possible. Retain only those that serve your goals. Allot more time to each thing you schedule. Take time to relax and daydream if you finish earlier than expected. Arise earlier in the morning to stave off the rush common to commuters. Have a second cup of coffee and take a stroll.

At work get rid of clutter—it's a prod to hurry. Rather than rush to finish a project by 5:00 P.M., stay at work a little longer. During lunch hours see friends or wander about rather than waste this needed break on business affairs.

Make a point of being alone to muse and reflect. Talk less and listen more. Check a tendency to see every situation as a challenge. Call on your sense of humor to cope with irritations. Drop Type A friends, and cultivate friendships with interesting Type Bs. As you re-engineer your personality, note that you feel better and in more control of your life. (For related tips, see STRESS.)

A related strategy: Concentrate on avoiding risk factors during times of great change—illness, retirement or dismissal from a job, marriage, separation from a spouse, death of a loved one. Researchers in Finland studying heart-attack victims found a marked increase in such life changes in the six months immediately preceding the attacks. The investigators felt that moderate or marked increase in recent life changes was almost as reliable as high blood pressure or an elevated cholesterol level in predicting potential coronary victims.

Seek a family and community life that brings you peace and harmony. The serenity of daily life in Roseto, Pennsylvania—an Italian-American community of 1,700—may be responsible for the nation's lowest heart-disease rate, less than half that of the United States as a whole.

The usual risk factors such as overweight and smoking are present in Roseto, and relatives living in New York and Philadelphia have a death rate from heart attack close to the national average. World Health Organization investigators concluded that the only feature that could be found to account for Roseto's low occurrence of heart disease was the "cohesive structure of the community." There is little poverty or crime. The elderly retain their influence over family affairs. There is great civic pride and prompt and generous financial assistance to neighbors in need. "The total effect is one of mutual support and understanding."

Avoiding the risk factors is essential for those who have had a heart attack. One attack invites another—and may lead to congestive heart failure.

Caring for a heart-attack patient. Treatment of heart attack is aimed at giving the heart time to mend itself. Though you may feel fine after the first week, you ordinarily need to rest in a bed or chair to give your heart time to heal. With such precautions, the chances of your surviving a heart attack are from three to one to four to one in your favor.

Sometimes the body can prepare an auxiliary system, called collateral circulation, in which nearby blood vessels widen or small new ones form so that blood can be sent around the affected artery to the injured heart muscle. The collateral system can provide an uninterrupted supply of life-sustaining blood, as well as mend the damage inflicted on the heart.

On being admitted to a hospital, a heart-attack victim is likely to go directly to a coronary care unit or an intensive care unit. There he is wired to a machine that monitors the heart rate and rhythm. These units impose routines many patients find senseless and irritating—sedation, small semisolid or liquid feedings, no visitors, no phone calls, bed rest. Dr. Arnold L. Abrams of White Plains, New York, finds patients are better able to accept routine aimed at reducing their activity when it is explained this way:

"When you break an arm or leg, we immobilize the bone by putting on a cast. When the heart is damaged, we cannot stop it for maximum healing, but we can permit the heart to relax between beats. Within a normal range, the slower your heart beats with longer periods of time between beats, the more quickly the heart can repair itself."

The chances are better than four to one that people who survive heart attacks will be back at work in less than a year. Heart-attack patients usually can return to their old jobs at their former level of activity. In some communities chapters of the American Heart Association sponsor work-evaluation units to determine how much and what kind of work heart patients can do.

The majority of those who recover from a heart attack are able to take walks, play golf, fish, swim, and engage in similar activities without trouble. Such exercise in moderation is beneficial, provided it does not cause pain, shortness of breath, or other symptoms.

Sexual relations are usually not harmful after convalescence. With a doctor's permission, most coronary sufferers can resume sexual activity about six weeks after their attack, or about the time they undertake other activities like climbing steps. It is not the orgasm that may cause problems, but the physical exertion needed to achieve it. To relieve sexual tension, masturbation is virtually always harmless.

One caution: While the usual sexual activity of married couples puts little strain on the heart, an extramarital affair may subject the coronary sufferer to undue stress. Embarrassment, fear, guilt, a high degree of expectancy and excitement—all make an affair far more taxing to the heart than the usual low-keyed sex of the marriage bed. Indeed a heart attack may be one of the most convincing arguments yet discovered in favor of marital fidelity.

If you've suffered a heart attack, your physician may prescribe various drugs to help avert the possibility of another attack: Coronary vasodilators improve the blood flow, supplying more oxygen to the heart muscle. Anticoagulants help prevent clotting. Other drugs can increase the pumping ability of the heart. Propanolol (Inderal) seems promising as a preventive for repeated heart attacks. In some cases coronary bypass surgery may be recommended (see ARTERIOSCLEROSIS).

See also ARTERIOSCLEROSIS; BLOOD CLOT; CHEST PAIN; CORONARY ARTERY DISEASE; HEART DISEASE; SMOKING.

HEART BLOCK (Adams-Stokes syndrome) calls for the installation of an artificial pacemaker to maintain the heartbeat. The condition involves damage to the heart's natural pacemaker, a group of fibers that produce and transmit electrical impulses that cause the heart muscles to contract and pump blood.

If the impulses are blocked or become irregular, the heart may slow down, or pause in its beat for a few seconds at a time, or stop beating altogether.

Heart block most often affects people over 60 who have had arteriosclerosis. The condition can also result from other types of heart disease; in young people it may be a congenital heart defect or the consequence of rheumatic fever.

First signs of heart block are generally fainting spells, dizziness, fatigue on exerting effort, convulsions. The more beats skipped, the worse the symptoms. Victims are often invalids.

The pacemaker. Implanting a pacemaker can clear up the condition. At least 100,000 Americans have pacemakers. Their ranks increase by more than 10,000 a year.

A typical pacemaker is about the size of a pack of cigarettes—its batteries, circuitry, and wires embedded in plastic, with a metal shield. The type most often used is implanted above the breast. Its leads are threaded through a vein to lodge in the heart.

Implanting such a "transvenous" pacemaker is considered relatively minor surgery requiring only local anesthesia. The recipient is generally up in a day and out of the hospital in a week. Other types of pacemakers involve placing electrodes directly on the heart wall and involve major surgery through the chest wall.

The type of pacemaker used is dictated by precisely which fibers in the heart are blocked. Another consideration is whether the condition calls for a pacemaker that has its own constant rate, or a rate based on its sensing of the heart's activity.

Pacemaker precautions. If you wear a pacemaker, your major concern is battery depletion. The typical pacemaker must be surgically replaced after two years or so. (Externally chargeable batteries and nuclear-powered pacemakers are under development.) You need to see your family doctor or cardiologist for regular checkups, increasing in frequency as the replacement date approaches.

Worn-down batteries and (much rarer) mechanical failures are signaled by a return of heart-block symptoms. Call your doctor immediately if you suffer blackouts, dizziness, chest pain, shortness of breath, prolonged hiccups, muscle twitching.

Get to a hospital emergency room if you suffer several closely spaced fainting episodes. Carry emergency medical identification, setting forth the type of pacemaker you wear, its manufacturer, paced rate, etc. Tell your dentist and any new doctor that you have a pacemaker.

Your doctor may want you to take your pulse daily. On the other hand physicians often feel this puts added stress on the patient, who is already anxious, who regards the pacemaker as a kind of time bomb ticking away in his chest. If you have such fears, or are depressed over having to wear a pacemaker, discuss your feelings with your physician.

The pacemaker puts very few limitations on you. Rules governing exercise and overweight are the same as they would be if you weren't wearing the device. There are no special limitations on sexual activity.

The only restrictions are those that might damage the instrument. For example, replace football with noncontact sports. Hunting is unwise if your shotgun would recoil against the device.

Avoid microwave ovens and diathermy. They may interfere with the pacemaker's functioning. Since the shielding has been improved, other types of machines are unlikely to cause interference. Gasoline engine ignition systems, electric shavers and toothbrushes, and various types of motors used to affect pacemakers, but no longer do so.

See also HEART DISEASE.

HEARTBURN See INDIGESTION.

HEART DEFECTS, CONGENITAL See CONGENITAL HEART DEFECTS.

HEART DISEASE refers to a number of illnesses that affect the circulatory system. A more exact name is cardiovascular diseases (cardio = heart; vascular = blood vessel).

At least 41 million Americans have some form of cardiovascular ailment, and these diseases are responsible for more than 52 percent of all U.S. deaths, about 1 million a year.

Most cardiovascular conditions begin with clogging of the arteries. (This and many of the following conditions are described separately. See list at end of this entry.)

In atherosclerosis, the most common form of arteriosclerosis, there is a thickening of the artery walls from accumulations of fats, particularly cholesterol and triglycerides. Coronary artery disease develops as atherosclerosis impairs circulation to the heart.

A heart attack occurs when a section of heart muscle is deprived of its blood supply, often because of closing of a coronary (heart) artery or a blood clot related to atherosclerosis. Stroke occurs when the blood supply to a part of the brain is reduced or cut off. A blood clot resulting from surgery or inactivity may cause a blockage of an artery in the lung.

High blood pressure (hypertension) causes the circulatory system to overwork, and, because there are no symptoms, is a widely ignored hazard, causing heart attack, stroke, kidney disease, and eye disorders. Smoking aggravates hypertension and is a contributor to heart disease.

Rheumatic fever and the rheumatic heart disease that may follow it account for much of the cardiovascular disease among young people, because of damage to a heart valve. Congenital heart defects occur when the heart or a major blood vessel near the heart has failed to develop normally during fetal growth. Congestive heart failure results when the heart's ability to pump blood has been weakened by a disease—chiefly high blood pressure—and generally calls for a diet low in sodium.

Heart damage may result from diabetes and thyroid disease. Heart disease may also be caused by the germs of syphilis and diphtheria.

Heart block results from abnormalities in the heart's natural pacemaker, causing it to beat abnormally. Heart palpitation is an irregularity in heartbeat, often harmless. Heart murmurs, especially in children, are rarely cause for concern.

Among circulatory conditions, varicose veins are bulging, distorted veins that appear mainly in the legs. In thrombophlebitis inflammation of a vein is combined with a blood clot. Leg pain is often a result of arteriosclerosis obstructing circulation. Spider veins are merely cosmetic defects.

Symptoms. Watch for symptoms of heart conditions. Chest pain is a common sign, though more often than not it is unrelated to heart disease. Another symptom is increasing shortness of breath, on exertion or at night. Be sure to see a doctor if you awaken from sleep at night with a choking sensation or a feeling of suffocation. Some people with heart trouble find they require a number of pillows to prop them up in order to make breathing easier.

Edema (swelling) of the ankles may indicate a circulatory impairment, like congestive heart failure. If your ankles swell at the end of the day, consult your doctor, especially if it interferes with putting on your shoes, or if you can make a deep mark by pressing with a finger.

An erratic or bounding pulse, dizziness, fainting spells, blue lips, attacks resembling asthma, and extreme fatigue are other possible symptoms of heart conditions. Spitting up or coughing up blood, or a cough that persists in spite of treatment, warrant investigation for heart disease.

Almost all cases of heart disease can be helped, especially if diagnosed early. Drugs, diet, and changes in living habits can ordinarily put the heart patient back on his feet again. Surgery can help many hearts and blood vessels that were improperly formed at birth or were damaged later. Progressive exercise, under a doctor's supervision, is part of most heart patients' rehabilitation.

Your heredity may predispose you to a heart condition. But you may set the disease process in motion if you add the risks of smoking, overweight, a diet rich in animal fats (cholesterol), emotional stress, and lack of exercise.

Reducing risks. At the least reducing the risks can result in good general health. Children stand to benefit by learning early in life to avoid eating and living patterns that may lead to heart disease in adulthood. Thus to reduce your risk of heart disease:

Have periodic medical checkups. If you have a condition that needs treatment, a regular physical examination may enable your doctor to discover it early. Most heart exams include an electrocardiograph (ECG or EKG) reading. The ECG records on a moving strip of paper tiny electrical impulses the heart generates with each beat. The zigzag pattern reveals whether the heart's rhythm is regular. It also tells much about the origin of the impulse that makes the heart contract and shows whether this impulse spreads through normal pathways at its normal speed. A stress cardiogram—taken after exercise —may detect irregularities that don't show up in ECGs taken at rest.

A person may have a serious heart condition and yet have a normal cardiogram. It is estimated that ECG recordings contribute about 15 percent to an overall heart diagnosis. Physical examinations contribute another 25 percent, X ray or fluoroscopic examinations 5 percent, and laboratory tests another 5 percent. The remaining 50 percent of the information needed to complete any diagnosis of a heart disorder must come from the patient's summary of his complaints and the physician's evaluation of them.

Guard against high blood pressure (hypertension). If you're diagnosed as having high blood pressure, don't fall into the trap of ignoring it because it has no symptoms. Hypertension is a silent killer.

Watch your diet. Cholesterol and some other types of fats (chiefly triglycerides) are implicated in atherosclerosis, heart attack, and stroke. If you're overweight, reduce. Extra body fat puts a strain on your heart. Cut down on use of salt, which some studies find associated with fluid retention and congestive heart disease.

Don't smoke. Smoking can increase the risk of heart attack, make the heart beat faster, raise the blood pressure, and narrow the blood vessels of the skin. It is especially dangerous for people with peripheral vascular diseases (varicose veins, thrombophlebitis, Buerger's disease) because it constricts blood vessels that are already narrowed and damaged. Peripheral vascular victims who continue to smoke increase their risk of gangrene, amputations, even death.

Keep physically active. An impressive amount of research suggests that a well-planned program of exercise can help ward off heart trouble.

Reduce psychological stress. Tension, frustration, and anxiety have a close link to heart attack and other physiological conditions.

Driving and heart disease. If you have heart disease, check if you should drive. About one in five people with cardiovascular conditions risk having accidents.

The driving risk is based on the likelihood of sudden death, temporary unconsciousness, or unexpected bouts of extreme pain. A past heart attack does not necessarily mean you should not drive.

Among specific conditions that can temporarily or permanently make you a driving hazard are those that cause constriction of blood vessels, with sudden pain or inability to react to traffic demands. This group includes arteriosclerotic heart disease, angina pectoris, coronary insufficiency, congenital heart disease, peripheral vascular disease, Raynaud's disease, Buerger's disease, and scleroderma.

Uncontrolled high blood pressure can make you unsafe behind the wheel. So can congestive heart failure and stroke.

Living with heart disease. Stay active—within the limits prescribed by your doctor. Exceedingly few heart-disease sufferers are so badly incapacitated that they must vegetate.

If you pursue a life as nearly normal as possible, you can expect to fare better both physically and mentally than those who resign themselves to invalidism. Chances are you are no more obliged to lead a completely sedentary life than anyone else is.

A woman with heart disease needs to consult her physician before becoming pregnant. Pregnancy and childbirth are not likely to be banned to her, but may call for special care.

Dental irrigators should not be used by persons with chronic rheumatic heart disease without consulting a physician. The strong jet of water from this appliance could force bacteria from the gums into the bloodstream, where they might lodge and multiply on a defective heart valve and have dangerous—potentially fatal—effects. Other heart diseases in the same category include calcific aortic stenosis, congenital heart disease, and many cases involving open-heart surgery.

Watch out for quackery. Vitamins and health foods are of no special value in preventing or treating heart disease. Postal authorities brought a mail-fraud action against the so-called Cardiac Society of Detroit, actually a group of promoters selling vitamin E under the pretense that it would be of benefit in circulatory disorders.

Massagers, saunas, and special baths are also valueless in treating circulatory conditions. The Food and Drug Administration (FDA) stopped the sale of wedge-shaped foam accessories for beds, falsely touted as good for varicose veins and heart conditions.

See also ARTERIOSCLEROSIS; BED REST; BLOOD CLOT; BLOOD PRESSURE; CHEST PAIN; CHOKING; CONGENITAL HEART DEFECTS; CORONARY ARTERY DISEASE; COUGHING.

DIABETES; DIPHTHERIA; DIZZINESS; EDEMA; EXERCISE; EYE DISORDER; FAINTING; FATIGUE.

FATS; HEART ATTACK; HEART BLOCK; HEART FAILURE; HEART MURMURS; HEART PALPITATION; KIDNEY DISEASE; LEG PAIN.

OVERWEIGHT; PHYSICAL EXAMINATION; PULSE; QUACKERY; RHEUMATIC FEVER; SHORTNESS OF BREATH; SMOKING; SODIUM; SPIDER VEINS.

STRESS; STROKE; SURGERY; SYPHILIS; THROMBOPHLEBITIS; THYROID DISEASE; UNCONSCIOUSNESS; VARICOSE VEINS; VITAMINS.

HEART FAILURE (congestive heart failure, cardiac insufficiency, dropsy) occurs when the heart's ability to pump blood has been weakened. The heart muscle lacks strength to keep the blood circulating normally throughout the body. As a result, the flow of blood is inadequate to meet the body's needs.

To say that the heart is "failing" does not mean that it will stop beating. The heart goes on working, but with less strength than is needed for good health.

Failure may be caused by a severe heart attack; by the effects of disease, especially rheumatic fever; or by congenital heart defects. Or the heart may be weakened by high blood pressure. Coronary artery disease—involving gradual narrowing of the arteries that nourish the heart (atherosclerosis, a form of arteriosclerosis) —also can cause failure, especially in elderly people.

When the heart fails to pump efficiently, the flow of blood slows down. Blood returning to the heart through the veins tends to back up, causing congestion in the tissues. (In the language of medicine *congestion* means excessive or abnormal accumulation of blood in a part of the body.) Some of the fluid is forced out through thin blood-vessel walls into surrounding tissues.

The result is edema, most often in the legs and ankles. Fluid may accumulate in the abdominal and chest cavities and in the lung. This used to be called "dropsy." Fluid in the lungs may interfere with breathing and cause shortness of breath.

Heart failure also affects the ability of the kidneys to dispose of sodium and water. Sodium normally eliminated in the urine stays in the body and holds water. Fluid retained in this way adds to edema.

Spotting heart failure. The most common indications of heart failure are difficulty in breathing and edema. Consult a doctor if activities you usually perform without trouble begin to cause shortness of breath—climbing a flight of stairs, hurrying for a bus, working around your house. Waking at night with shortness of breath is another possible symptom. Sometimes heart-failure sufferers must prop themselves up in bed with two or more pillows before they can breathe comfortably and sleep.

Swelling in the legs, ankles, or abdomen is another sign. So is increasing weight caused by an accumulation of water in the tissues.

If you suffer from heart failure, treating the underlying causes is an important part of care. For instance, high blood pressure can generally be lowered. If defective heart valves are causing failure, they may be corrected by surgery.

Digitalis is usually prescribed to strengthen the action of the heart muscle. If you take digitalis, don't use kaolin-pectate antidiarrhea preparations like Kaopectate, which interfere with the drug. Similarly, separate digitalis and an antacid by at least six hours.

When edema is present, your physician may also prescribe a diuretic to help the kidneys get rid of excess sodium and water. You are likely to need a sodium-restricted diet to prevent or reduce edema.

You may need bedrest, with a gradual return to activity. To avoid strain on your heart, adjust to a slower pace of living and avoid emotional stress.

See also HEART DISEASE.

HEART MURMURS are unusual sounds produced by the heart as it sends blood through its valves and chambers. The normal heart sound that the doctor hears is *lub-dupp, lub-dupp, lub-dupp*. A murmur is a little extra sound sometimes heard before, after, or during these normal sounds (e.g., *lubb-shdupp*). Each kind of murmur—be it a hiss, rumble, grunt, click, twang, coo, whoop, honk—may mean something different.

Some murmurs may be caused by serious conditions such as a scar on a heart valve or a narrowing of a channel that blood must pass through. But far more often the murmur may be "innocent" or "functional," and indicate no heart disease or defect. Adults with perfectly healthy hearts may have murmurs after sports or vigorous exercise. Stress can cause murmurs.

Innocent murmurs are so common that more than half of any group of children between three and seven are likely to have them. The off sounds usually disappear in adolescence. Meanwhile the children are not heart patients and need no special care. In one study more than 15,000 Denver children were examined and no fewer than 83 percent of them were found to have innocent heart murmurs. About half the murmurs could not be heard at a second examination.

Don't overprotect a child with a murmur. Parents often turn children with murmurs into cardiac cripples who sit on the sidelines when they could be as active as other youngsters. The psychological damage can be permanent.

In Seattle 93 children with murmurs had been told they had bad hearts. In fact, pediatricians found, 75 of them were normal. At least 30 of the children were being needlessly restricted in activities. Some normal youngsters were even being kept home from school.

If your child has a heart murmur, talk it over with your family doctor or a pediatrician or cardiologist. Learn if the murmur is serious or harmless. Find out if there really needs to be any restrictions on the child's activity.

Don't be alarmed if the doctor does not declare the murmur innocent right away. Heart murmurs are sometimes hard to diagnose, and the physical examination may be especially inconclusive if the child is restless or frightened.

Thus it is not unusual for a doctor to want to see a child more than once. While murmurs may conceivably indicate congenital heart defects or heart damage from rheumatic fever, such a follow-up visit does not necessarily mean that the child has a heart condition.

See also HEART DISEASE.

HEART PALPITATION (cardiac arrhythmia) is irregularity in the heartbeat. People who experience palpitations often describe them as pounding, racing, turnovers, kicks, flutters, thumps, knocks, jumps, or flip-flops. In general, they're the result of an irregularity in the electrical impulses that govern the heart's pumping.

See a physician if palpitations persist, or if you're distressed by symptoms such as dizziness, shortness of breath, or frequent urination. An erratic or speeded heartbeat may be a sign of coronary artery disease or heart block. Some drugs, notably diuretics given for heart failure and high blood pressure, can have palpitation as a side effect.

Heart irregularity may be an aftermath of a heart attack, including one the victim doesn't realize he had. Damage to the heart may cause ventricular fibrillation—the heart races wildly, writhing like a worm—which is soon fatal unless the victim is treated with an electric counter-shocking machine that restores the heart's normal electrical impulses.

Normal irregularities. In most cases a departure from your usual heart rate is perfectly normal. After monitoring the heartbeat of normal middle-aged men for six hours each, Dr. Lawrence E. Hinkle, Jr., of Cornell University Medical Center concluded that more than three in four had some irregularities ranging from isolated premature beats to bursts of extremely rapid beats. Not one of the men had been aware, much less disturbed, by the irregularities.

Emotional stress is the most frequent cause. When your heart skips a beat out of fear, or goes pit-a-pat when you're in love, or races in excitement, you're experiencing an arrhythmia of psychological origin. Palpitations also may be brought on by excess coffee, alcohol, or smoking —and can be relieved by a few days' abstinence. Fatigue and overactivity of the thyroid gland may also affect the heartbeat.

Under normal circumstances, auxiliary pacemaker tissue within the heart may initiate an electrical impulse out of sync with the heart's principal pacemaker. This may give an extra beat. A longer-than-usual compensatory pause may follow, feeling like a skipped beat. The heart may fill up with more blood than usual, so there may follow an extra-forceful beat, sensed as a thump.

Abnormal pacemaker centers may suddenly trigger tachycardia—a pulse racing up to 240 beats a minute. Most types of palpitation that have been declared by a doctor to be no cause for worry will pass in a few minutes.

You may be more comfortable if you sit or lie down until the palpitation passes. Contrary to myth, however strong the racing or pounding is, it can't "loosen" your heart or knock it from the strong bands of fibrous tissue that suspend it in your chest cavity.

See also HEART DISEASE.

HEART RATE See PULSE.

HEART STOPPAGE (cardiac arrest) causes the death of thousands of Americans each year who might have been saved by external (closed-chest) heart massage. The heart stops beating most commonly as a result of heart attack. Heart stoppage may also result from poisoning, drowning, choking, smoke inhalation, and electric shock.

Cardiac arrest is not necessarily fatal. But victims are often assumed to be dead—and first-aid measures are discontinued prematurely.

External cardiac massage works by rhythmically squeezing the heart between the breastbone (sternum) and the backbone, compressing the heart and forcing blood into the arteries. When the pressure is removed, the chest expands, causing the heart to fill with oxygenated blood.

Signs of heart stoppage are unconsciousness, absence of breathing and pulse, and a weak or fluttering heartbeat or no heartbeat at all. If the victim's pupils are very large and don't contract in bright light, it's a sign that the brain is receiving insufficient oxygen and the heart needs massage.

Begin rescue work immediately. Irreparable damage generally occurs 4 to 6 minutes after the heart stops beating. After 6 minutes, permanent brain damage is likely, and death almost surely follows.

To restore the heartbeat, first give artificial respiration (which see for details and illustrations), going on to do external cardiac massage if necessary.

See also ARTIFICIAL RESPIRATION; HEART ATTACK.

HEAT CRAMPS usually occur in people who do strenuous work at high temperatures and drink large quantities of water—without replacing salt lost in sweating. This can usually be avoided by the liberal use of salt at mealtimes during periods of very hot weather.

In less severe cases, arms and legs will tingle and the abdomen may hurt slightly. More serious cases may be preceded by headache, vertigo, faintness, and abdominal distress.

Or the attack of cramps may occur without warning. The person will feel excruciating pain in arms and legs, and sometimes abdominal muscles. He may writhe with pain. His skin will be gray, cold, and clammy, his pulse rapid. But body temperature will remain normal.

The condition can usually be quickly corrected if the person is taken to a cool place, put to bed, and given salted water or salted lemonade (1 teaspoon salt to 1 quart). If the pains don't respond to this treatment within a few minutes, see a doctor.

See also HOT WEATHER.

HEAT EXHAUSTION comes about when the heart is unable to maintain proper blood pressure because of excessive heat and physical exertion. Often the body has lost too much water and salt in sweating. Its victims are often people who are not used to heat.

Symptoms usually build up over several days and include headache, fatigue, confusion, and drowsiness. In severe cases these are followed by loss of appetite, vomiting, and unconsciousness. The person's skin feels cold and clammy, blood

IN CASE OF HEAT EXHAUSTION
Rest in a cool place

Raise feet

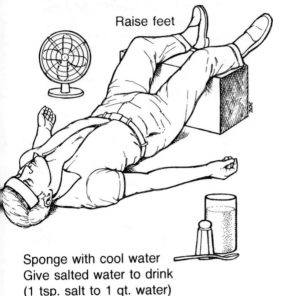

Sponge with cool water
Give salted water to drink
(1 tsp. salt to 1 qt. water)

pressure is low, temperature is normal or below, sweating is profuse.

Since the early symptoms of heat exhaustion are so debilitating, the victim usually seeks medical help before the condition becomes serious. To give first aid to someone suffering from heat exhaustion, move him to a cool place and have him lie down with his feet elevated. Take off his clothes and sponge him with wet, cool cloths.

Give him salted water (1 teaspoon of salt to 1 quart of water). In cases of severe vomiting or unconsciousness a salt solution may have to be given intravenously by a physician. After an attack of heat exhaustion the victim should rest for two or three days.

See also HOT WEATHER.

HEAT STROKE (sunstroke) is the most serious ailment caused by hot weather. If untreated it is fatal. The condition is more likely to occur on a hot, humid day than on a hot, dry one. It is more likely to strike someone who is doing active physical work. The elderly and people who consume great quantities of alcohol are especially vulnerable.

In heat stroke the body's temperature-regulating mechanism collapses. The person stops sweating and develops a high fever (105° F to 110° F) and may go into shock.

The first symptoms may be those of heat exhaustion: headache, numbness and tingling, dizziness, restlessness, and confusion. On the other hand, the victim may suddenly have convulsions and fall into unconsciousness. Breathing and pulse will be fast, blood pressure high.

Since unconsciousness can be a symptom of both heat exhaustion and heat stroke, you can distinguish the conditions by the feel of the skin: In stroke the skin is dry, red, and very hot; in exhaustion it is wet and normal in temperature.

Summon an ambulance for any case of heat stroke. Give emergency treatment as follows to lower the body temperature (see illustration):

ACT FAST AGAINST HEAT STROKE
Bring down body temperature—safely!

Rush to cool place

Remove clothes

Wrap in cold wet cloths
(Pour on alcohol or cold water)

Fan victim
(By hand if necessary)

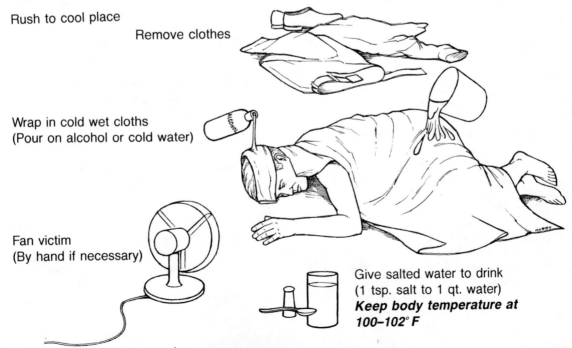

Give salted water to drink
(1 tsp. salt to 1 qt. water)
Keep body temperature at 100–102° F

1. Get the victim out of the sun to the coolest place possible, preferably to an air-conditioned room with a fan on.
2. Remove his clothes and wrap his body in a cool, wet sheet or towels. Cool his head with cold cloths. Keep the materials cold with water.
3. Fan the victim to help moisture on the skin evaporate.
4. Don't put him in an ice-water bath or massage him with ice.

   Continue treatment for several minutes, then observe the patient. If he seems cooler (100° F to 102° F), stop for a while. If his temperature starts climbing again, resume treatment.
5. Continue cooling treatment until the victim reaches the hospital.
6. If he is fully conscious, have him drink salted water (1 teaspoon of salt to 1 quart of water). Do not let him drink alcohol in any form.

See also HOT WEATHER.

HEIGHT   See SHORTNESS.

HEMANGIOMAS   See BIRTHMARKS.

HEMOPHILIA (bleeders' disease) is an inherited disease in which the clotting of blood is abnormally delayed, most often by a deficiency of a chemical agent (clotting factor) in the blood. It is more widespread than is commonly thought. In serious form it occurs in 1 of 10,000 males, about as often as polio before the Salk vaccine. There are many mild cases, often undetected until accident or surgery causes a bleed.

When a bleeding episode occurs, a person with hemophilia can be treated with an intravenous infusion of concentrated clotting factor. In hemophilia treatment centers, people with hemophilia and family members and friends are taught to give such infusions.

If a hemophiliac starts bleeding, he should be treated as soon as possible. Bleeding may be slow but persistent in his joints.

Don't allow him to make his own way home if he becomes ill, or walk home if he develops a swollen or painful leg. For some sufferers nosebleed is fairly common. It is not a cause for immediate alarm and can be treated by simple measures, such as rest and pressure on the nose. If bleeding doesn't stop quickly, he needs medical attention.

Scrapes and cuts call for first aid in the normal fashion, with a bandage firmly applied. Cold compresses may be placed on the injured part or wrapped around it to relieve pain and swelling as first aid. If bleeding persists, a physician's care is required. Mouth bleeds require special care.

How hemophilia is inherited. The disease is sex-linked, carried by the chromosome that determines sex. The most common form shows up only in males and is passed on only through females. None of the sons of a hemophiliac inherits or transmits the infirmity. But all of his daughters, while not themselves hemophiliacs, are carriers.

A carrier has a 50 percent chance with each pregnancy of having a child affected with hemophilia. A woman whose mother is a carrier of hemophilia may have a test done to estimate the chance that she too is a carrier.

Searching the family history is important in establishing a diagnosis of hemophilia. Sometimes several generations pass before the condition appears again. Some cases of hemophilia are due to new mutations, with no history of a bleeding problem in the family.

Hemorrhage may occur in infancy. Often hemophilia is first evident following circumcision. In early childhood the bleeding tendency is often manifested by the appearance of unexplained bruising.

Repeated hemorrhage into the joints frequently leads to crippled arms and legs. Free blood in the joints can erode bone and injure the nerves. Brain damage can result from hemorrhage into the brain because of injury or spontaneous bleeding.

With proper education and care, people with hemophilia can enjoy reasonably normal lives. It is important for people with hemophilia to be under the management of a family physician. Surgical and dental procedures need to be performed in medical centers by physicians who are familiar with hemophilia.

People with hemophilia do well to register with a local chapter of the National Hemophilia Foundation (110 Greene Street, New York, New York 10012). The foundation sends literature on the disorder to patients and physicians, and keeps them abreast of new developments.

See also BIRTH DEFECTS; BLEEDING.

HEMORRHAGE   See BLEEDING.

HEMORRHOIDS (piles) are swollen veins in the anus. They affect perhaps one in three Americans.

A common symptom of hemorrhoids is rectal bleeding. But bleeding can also be due to more serious conditions, such as cancer of the colon and rectum and ulcerative colitis. See a physician if you experience any bleeding from your rectum.

Other frequent symptoms of hemorrhoids are

pain and itching. Sometimes the enlarged veins protrude out of the rectum.

Untreated hemorrhoids occasionally cause complications. A painful blood clot can form in the hemorrhoids. They can rupture and bleed, sometimes resulting in anemia.

Don't self-treat hemorrhoids. No over-the-counter preparations can heal or cure hemorrhoids. One widely advertised product was enjoined by the FTC from claiming that its use will "avoid the need for surgery."

While some commercial products may give temporary relief of pain or itching, their use can delay your seeking necessary medical treatment. Moreover, some anesthetic ointments (such as benzocaine) may cause contact dermatitis and allergic sensitivity.

Commercial creams may seem to work because the hemorrhoids often disappear, then recur. Don't assume you're cured when your symptoms abate. Once hemorrhoids have developed, they tend to reappear unless they're treated.

Recommended treatment. For a mild case of hemorrhoids your physician may recommend soothing creams, suppositories, or ointments—although there is some medical controversy about their effectiveness. Sitz baths in warm water 3 or 4 times a day—including after each bowel movement—may provide relief. The water should be between 100° and 110° F. Remain in the bath for 15 minutes each time.

Stay off your feet as much as possible to relieve pressure on blood vessels. Don't do any heavy lifting.

If you have painful bowel movements because of hemorrhoids, eat a diet high in FIBER (which see)—with lots of fruits, vegetables, whole grains. Fiber adds bulk to stool and makes it easier to pass. Drink plenty of water—1 to 2 quarts a day.

To ease defecating, you might also try a stool softener, such as docusate sodium (e.g., Colace, Regutol), or an agent that makes stools bulkier (Effersyllium, Hydrocil, Metamucil).

A tablespoon of mineral oil also has a softening effect. But mineral oil may leak from the rectum and, if overused, can deplete the body of vitamins A, D, E, and K. Reduce the drawbacks by taking the smallest effective amount of mineral oil on an empty stomach and by not lying down for at least a half hour thereafter.

Acetaminophen or aspirin is often recommended for relief of pain associated with hemorrhoids. Take two tablets every four hours.

Witch hazel compresses often bring relief. Apply a compress every 4 hours for 30 minutes.

You can use a clean handkerchief soaked in full-strength witch hazel, or buy witch hazel pads (such as Tucks) at a pharmacy.

When surgery is required. Surgery is usually recommended for a severe case with pain and bleeding. In most cases it is a permanent cure. But even after surgery some people develop more hemorrhoids, since not all rectal veins can be removed.

If your physician recommends surgery, ask about a procedure called rubber band ligation. In this method a rubber band is applied around the base of the hemorrhoid, cutting off circulation and destroying it. Patients who undergo a series of such ligations generally suffer little or no pain, do not require hospitalization, and lose no time from work.

Rubber band ligation is generally suitable only for internal hemorrhoids (those occurring in the rectum), not for external hemorrhoids (those that protrude out of the anus).

After hemorrhoid surgery, there may be some bowel soiling for a while. Both men and women can use sanitary napkin pads. Wash after bowel movements with a warm cloth.

Causes of hemorrhoids. People with chronic constipation who frequently strain to pass hard, dry stools are prone to develop piles. To reduce your chances of getting hemorrhoids, avoid straining while moving your bowels.

Women may develop hemorrhoids during pregnancy, when the enlarged uterus may press on veins, interfering with the blood supply and causing irritation. Chronic coughing and jobs involving heavy lifting or long standing can predispose you to the condition.

Hemorrhoids can also occur when a tumor presses on veins in the rectum. Other disorders, including liver conditions, may also be responsible. People who are overweight are more likely to develop hemorrhoids than people of normal weight.

See also CONSTIPATION; FIBER; PREGNANCY; SURGERY.

HEPATITIS (viral hepatitis) is a virus inflammation of the liver. Hepatitis A (formerly called infectious hepatitis) and hepatitis B (formerly called serum hepatitis) both have the same symptoms but are caused by different viruses. Hepatitis that cannot be identified as either A or B is called non-A, non-B hepatitis.

In hepatitis A the virus is swallowed in contaminated food or water, or spread by direct contact with an infected person. In most cases of hepatitis B the virus gets to the liver directly through the blood, although it can also be passed through direct contact. The two types occur with about equal frequency, with hepatitis B causing slightly more deaths.

The most characteristic sign is yellowing of the whites of the eyes. This results from bile pigments entering the blood from the diseased liver. In some—but not all—victims the skin may develop a yellowish, "jaundiced" color.

The most common first symptoms are tiredness, loss of appetite, and upset stomach with or without vomiting. There may also be headache, pain in the abdomen on the right side, and itching. A fever may occur at first but generally stops in a few days. Victims of hepatitis B are more likely to have skin rash and joint pains.

The liver may enlarge and become tender. Urine becomes darker until it resembles diluted coffee. One curious symptom is that smokers may find the taste of tobacco so nauseating that they give up smoking (every cloud has a silver lining).

Hepatitis A may begin two to six weeks after exposure to the disease and usually lasts one to two weeks in children, four to six weeks in adults. Hepatitis B may not show symptoms for two to four months after exposure, and the disease lasts longer.

Treatment in most cases is bed rest. A diet of at least 2,000 calories a day is usually recommended. To counteract poor appetite eat foods that appeal to you. Foods low in fat may cause less nausea. If you have no appetite for large meals, try eating many snacks in the course of a day.

Take care not to drink any alcoholic beverages until your doctor tells you that your liver function is back to normal. Also check before taking any medication, prescription or nonprescription.

Hepatitis requires a physician's care. Inflammation of the liver is also caused by alcoholism, yellow fever, and many drugs and chemicals. Jaundice is a sign as well of gallstones, cancer that obstructs the bile ducts, leptospirosis, malaria, mononucleosis.

Immune serum globulin, a blood fraction containing antibodies, can prevent or ameliorate hepatitis A if given within two weeks of exposure. Ask your physician for a vaccination if you have been in household or sexual contact with a hepatitis victim, or if you are traveling to an area with a high incidence of the disease.

Avoiding hepatitis. Hepatitis A is one of the diseases spread by water polluted by human fecal matter. Take precautions against water contamination when traveling, hiking, or camping. Fourteen members of a South Carolina Boy Scout troop came down with the disease after a campout in which they swam and washed dishes in a polluted lake.

Teach children to keep dirty objects out of their mouths and to wash their hands thoroughly with soap and water after using the toilet.

If a member of your family gets either type of hepatitis, avoid all intimate contact with him until the doctor says his condition is no longer contagious. Wash your hands thoroughly after touching him or anything he uses.

Don't eat raw clams, oysters, and other seafood from lakes and ocean shores that may be polluted. Hundreds of people a year develop hepatitis because they fail to cook contaminated shellfish thoroughly.

Cleanse all food that may have been in contact with polluted water. Hepatitis A struck over a third of a Tennessee farming community. The victims had eaten raw watercress gathered from contaminated streams.

Both hepatitis A and B can be spread by carriers of the virus, people who have the disease but don't show symptoms. In a county in Michigan, 63 cases were traced to a baker's assistant who was a carrier.

Blood used in transfusions may carry hepatitis B, although more careful screening of blood donors in recent years has reduced its incidence. The disease can be spread by any instrument that punctures the skin, such as needles used for ear piercing and tattoos. Among narcotics users, hepatitis B may be passed from one person to another on the tips of contaminated hypodermic needles.

Hepatitis B can also be spread by close contact—including sexual contact—with an infected person. The disease is common among people with many sexual contacts, particularly homosexual males. Non-A, non-B hepatitis is not known to be transmitted sexually but is otherwise spread much like hepatitis B.

A vaccine against hepatitis B is now available. Given in three injections over six months, it is thought to give protection for at least five years. Ask your physician about hepatitis B vaccine if you are among those considered at high risk of infection: medical workers; hemophiliacs; kidney dialysis patients; and others who need frequent blood transfusions; those in close contact with infected people; narcotics addicts; and people with numerous sexual contacts.

People who have had any type of hepatitis won't contract that type again—although they can still get any other type of hepatitis.

See also ALCOHOLISM; ANIMAL DISEASE; BLOOD TRANSFUSION; CANCER; GALLBLADDER

DISEASE; INFECTIOUS DISEASE; LEPTOSPIROSIS; MALARIA; MONONUCLEOSIS; RUBELLA; WATER CONTAMINATION; YELLOW FEVER.

HERNIA (rupture) is due to a weakness or opening in the muscle of the abdominal wall, allowing intestines or other organs to bulge out.

When a great deal of the intestine pushes through, there is the danger that the hernia may become strangulated: its blood supply is cut off and gangrene may result. Emergency surgery is necessary.

Abdominal-wall weakness is thought to be a birth defect, although a hernia may not develop for many years, if at all.

Umbilical hernias occur at the navel in infants, especially in premature and poorly nourished infants. Girls have umbilical hernia twice as frequently as boys. Often bandaging can control it until the abdominal wall strengthens. Only about 1 in 50 infants with umbilical hernia will require surgery.

Inguinal hernia occurs low in the abdomen, at the groin. In males it can extend into the scrotum.

A child with an inguinal hernia may experience vomiting and fever. Adults will often complain of pain in the groin, but a hernia can be present with no pain. Frequently there is a swelling or lump in the groin.

Inguinal hernia—much more common in males—may develop from the pressure of chronic constipation or from prostate trouble, in which the man must strain to urinate. Any condition that causes frequent coughing may lead to a hernia; it may also result from straining to lift heavy objects.

Surgery is the recommended treatment. Local anesthesia is widely used because it allows the doctor to check the hernia repair under stress: Still on the operating table, the patient is asked to cough. Hernia patients who have had local anesthesia often walk from the operating room and resume normal activity within three days.

In cases where the patient is a poor surgical risk—a sick older person, for example—doctors may recommend the use of a truss until the surgery can be performed.

Buy a truss only on your doctor's advice. Beware mail-order trusses or other treatment advertised as a cure for hernia. Ill-fitted trusses are more likely to strangulate hernias than cure them.

For some people, the hernia recurs after surgery, particularly in older people or when it is aggravated by an unresolved condition, such as a bad cough. Have the underlying condition treated, if possible before your operation. Ask your doctor about the safety of air travel.

Hiatal hernia usually causes little or no discomfort. Also called hernia of the diaphragm, it occurs where the esophagus passes through the diaphragm to the stomach. A weak spot in the muscle of the diaphragm allows the upper part of the stomach to push up through the diaphragm. Acid stomach contents may regurgitate into the esophagus.

People troubled by hiatal hernia usually experience heartburn and feelings of indigestion, with chest pain, belching, and hiccups after meals. Symptoms may be worse after a large meal or when lying down. Exercise that involves bending forward may increase discomfort. So may bending, stooping, strenuous lifting, or collapsing into a soft chair (especially after eating).

Hiatal hernia may be alleviated by avoiding irritating foods and taking small, frequent meals. Antacids may be prescribed. Raising the head of the bed about 8 inches with blocks may help you sleep at night. Nothing should be eaten for at least 3 hours before bedtime.

Weight reduction often helps. Corsets, belts, or other tight clothing should be avoided. Surgery is necessary only for the most severe cases.

Incisional hernia can occur after an operation. Intestines can push through a wound left by abdominal surgery. Additional surgery may be necessary.

See also SURGERY.

HEROIN   See DRUGS.

HERPES (herpes genitalis). Herpes simplex virus (HSV) can attack the coverings and linings of the sex organs, and can be transmitted through sexual intercourse. Genital herpes is a common —and dangerous—venereal disease. It is also painful and returns over and over again.

An estimated 5 to 20 million Americans suffer from genital herpes infections, and the disease is spreading at the rate of 500,000 new cases a year. Infections are usually spread through intimate sexual contact. But recent research suggests that the virus can survive for a brief time on surfaces outside the body—on towels, toilet seats, clothing, for example. This raises the possibility that genital herpes can be spread in ways other than direct contact. To minimize the possibility of such infection, cover public toilet seats with toilet paper or a paper seat cover. Don't share towels, sheets, or clothing with anyone with an active herpes infection.

HSV type 1 is generally responsible for "cold sores" and "fever blisters," type 2 for genital infections. Both types of herpes simplex can be spread through oral sex. Type 1 can cause painful genital sores. Conversely, type 2 can affect lips, mouth, and tongue. So it is unwise to engage in oral sex when either partner has a cold sore. In general, however, type 1 is considerably less serious than type 2.

Herpes and cancer of the cervix. A genital herpes infection can be serious for a woman, since it seems to be associated with a greater incidence of cancer of the cervix. The virus has been isolated from cervical cancer cells. In large part because of the link with HSV, cancer of the cervix is considered to be a venereal disease. It is most prevalent in women who engage in intercourse at an early age and with numerous sexual partners. It is practically unheard of in nuns and celibate women.

A woman who has genital herpes should have a Pap smear twice a year. This quick, simple, inexpensive test can help detect cervical cancer in its early stages, when it can almost always be cured.

The herpes virus may also attack the eyes, nose, mouth, throat, lungs, intestines, and the central nervous system, including the brain.

Recurrent attacks. Herpes sores first appear in the genital area three to six days after sexual contact. They sometimes itch, but they are more likely to go unnoticed until they ulcerate and become painful, especially while one is walking or urinating.

A woman may be a silent carrier of the disease. She may have no symptoms if the infection is on her cervix. Yet she can spread the virus to others. The infection can be detected through a Pap smear.

The first attack of herpes may last three weeks or so. The sores heal without treatment. Then at unpredictable intervals attacks are likely to recur—each lasting from a few days to two weeks. The average sufferer has four or five outbreaks a year—although some people go for many years without a flare-up, and a few are never again troubled after one attack.

An attack may start with tightness, stinging, tingling, or burning of the infected areas. Clusters of small blisters usually follow. These break down in a couple of days, becoming crusty-looking sores. During an attack of herpes there may be a fever, swollen glands, and a feeling as though one were coming down with flu. Attacks may be triggered by fever, sunburn, premenstrual changes, emotional stress, sexual intercourse, and other factors.

Sexual intercourse or other skin contact should be avoided until sores have healed entirely. The disease can spread easily between sex partners. Moreover, the virus can shed between attacks, so there is a risk of transmitting the disease even when there are no symptoms.

To minimize your chances of contracting herpes, be selective in your sex partners. Avoid sex with partners with genital lesions or cold sores. The use of a condom may provide some protection.

Pregnancy. If a woman with genital herpes is pregnant, her baby's life is especially threatened by the disease, principally by spontaneous abortion or by herpes encephalitis—a crippling, often fatal brain infection. She can usually have a baby by vaginal delivery if she has no active sores in her vagina or on her labia. But if such sores are present, she may require a cesarean birth—delivery through an abdominal incision—so that the baby will not be exposed to the herpes virus as it passes through the birth canal.

If you are pregnant and have had herpes, have regular tissue cultures taken during the final weeks of pregnancy. This can detect the presence of the virus in the absence of symptoms.

Treatment. There's no definitive treatment for herpes. No current treatment can cure the disease or prevent future attacks. Large doses of the amino acid lysine (about 1,000 mg per day) appear to promote healing, according to anecdotal reports. Recovery also seems to be speeded by contraceptive creams and foams containing nonoxynol 9 and by exposing the sores to fluorescent light and keeping them clean and dry. Acyclovir (Zovirax) seems to speed recovery from the initial attack, reduce recurrences, and reduce the severity of outbreaks. Sitz baths and soothing ointments may bring relief. Painkillers may be helpful.

For more information contact the Herpes Resource Center, Box 100, Palo Alto, California 94302. The organization has local chapters with support groups, a quarterly newsletter, and a telephone hotline.

See also VENEREAL DISEASE.

HERPES SIMPLEX   See COLD SORES.

HERPES ZOSTER   See SHINGLES.

HIATAL HERNIA   See HERNIA.

HICCUPS (hiccoughs) can usually be cured by this incredibly simple remedy: swallow a dry spoonful of ordinary table sugar. After a moment you can chase it down with water if you wish. Forget about holding your breath, having a friend yell unexpectedly in your ear, or putting your head in a paper bag.

The remedy, apparently a folk cure, was brought to light in a letter to the prestigious *New England Journal of Medicine.* The experimenters—Dr. Edgar G. Engleman of the University of California School of Medicine and Drs. James and Barbara Lankton of the University of Miami School of Medicine—reported that it worked for 19 of 20 chronic hiccupers.

The sugar is thought to activate an enzyme that ends the spasmodic contractures of the diaphragm, an involuntary reflex action. If you suffer a recurrence of the hiccups, simply take more sugar.

The most common cause of hiccups is rapid eating or drinking, particularly of irritants such as spices or alcohol. Tobacco may set off the rhythmic cycle of spasms, or hearty laughter after a big meal. An overloaded stomach or indigestion may be involved.

Long-term hiccups. Hiccups that persist become a medical problem. There can be many causes: Gastric irritation, ballooning of the stomach, irritation of the lining of the lungs or heart, electrolyte imbalances in the blood, calcium deficiency, central nervous system disease following encephalitis, and probably many emotional disorders. Hiccups also can appear as a postoperative complication of chest or pelvic surgery.

The sugar treatment should be tried before more drastic remedies. Sometimes these have meant emptying the stomach by induced vomiting or irrigation to reduce distension and irritation. Sedatives or anesthetics, or hypnosis, have been used to put the person to sleep and interrupt the spasm rhythm.

Antispasmodic, blood-vessel dilating, stimulant, or antinausea medicines have also been used. In certain severe and long-lasting cases of hiccups it was deemed necessary to inject, freeze, crush, or sever the right and left phrenic nerves, the two motor nerves that carry impulses to the diaphragm.

If an episode of hiccups persists for more than an hour despite all your efforts, check with your doctor.

See also INDIGESTION.

HIGH BLOOD PRESSURE See BLOOD PRESSURE.

HIKING To reduce hiking and climbing accidents:

Wear sturdy, broken-in shoes that cover your ankles. A less-than-perfect fit leads to blisters. Wear cotton socks inside woolen ones. Wool absorbs perspiration and dries quickly. If your feet get wet, you can wring out woolen socks and wear them without much discomfort.

If you wear sneakers or other light shoes on rough ground, you'll invite sprains and strains and soon tire. Depending on the climate you can expect on the hike, dress appropriately for hot or cold weather. If hiking on snow, remember the need for sunglasses and protection against sunburn as well as frostbite.

Equip yourself for emergencies with a selection of first aid supplies. Also take along a compass, sharp knife, matches in a waterproof case, canteen of fresh water, flashlight, whistle. For snacks pack some easily carried high-energy food like dried fruit or chocolate bars. Insect repellent is usually welcome, and a snakebite kit is a good idea.

When heading into unfamiliar territory, take a map of the region. U.S. Geological Survey maps are excellent. Study the map until you know the elevations, waterways, landmarks, trails. If you lose your map or compass, you'll have your memory to rely on.

Allow time to return by daylight. Darkness, especially over unfamiliar ground, can be perilous for hikers. Especially in mountain areas, distance is often much greater than it looks.

The average walking time is about 20 minutes per mile, estimates the Boy Scouts of America. Thus to walk 3 miles figure you'll need 1 hour plus 10 to 20 minutes of rest—longer in rough terrain.

With companions walk far enough apart so that each hiker handles branches for himself. If you try to hold a branch for the hiker behind, it may snap back and cause injury. Don't explore caves unless you have special equipment and an experienced guide.

To avoid gunshot wounds don't carry loaded firearms unless the safety catch is on. Disassemble fishing rods—hooks on the line may snag someone.

You'll cover more ground if you rest often. On a moderate hike pauses of five or ten minutes every half hour will help ward off exhaustion.

If you suffer from a respiratory or heart disease, take only easy hikes to avoid overexertion, and remember that high altitudes make breathing more difficult.

Eat lightly and rest before as well as after eating. Don't drink from strange wells or springs unless a reliable local person tells you it's safe. If in doubt take precautions against contamination.

Leave strange dogs and wild animals alone, even if they seem friendly. Besides inflicting bites, unusually docile wild animals may carry a form of rabies.

Before you set out, tell someone where you're headed and when to start searching. If you're away from home, the Sierra Club recommends that you phone a friend or family member with this information—and the number of the local sheriff to call if you don't phone back by such-and-such a day and time.

If you get lost, try to recall where you made a wrong turn. Then, using your map and compass, attempt to retrace your steps. Mark your trail in some way so rescuers can follow you. If you can't pick up your trail, stop and wait for rescue. Avoid climbing on rocks or in thick underbrush —an injury while you're lost is doubly danger-ous.

You'll be safest if you travel in a group of three or more. If you get separated from them, stay put. You'll be missed.

Don't run or take shortcuts. Both are signs of panic, and will take you in circles or in the wrong direction.

The universal distress signal is a group of three. Make three fires (made smoky by green or damp leaves) about 50 feet apart. Every so often blow your whistle three times. If you have a gun, every hour or so fire it three times. If you can manage none of these signals, periodically yell three times at five-second intervals.

If you know your general direction and are positive no one will be looking for you, search for a running body of water and follow it down-stream, leaving a smaller stream for a larger one. It will eventually lead you to civilization. Since undergrowth is generally thickest near a stream, you may find walking easier on a ridge parallel to the stream.

Similarly, any trail in the mountains that goes downhill will lead you to civilization.

To find your direction without a compass use the sun's shadow. Push a foot-long stick verti-cally into the ground and make a mark at the tip of its shadow. Wait a half hour and make an-other mark at the shadow's tip. A line drawn from the second mark to the first will point ap-proximately west.

Alternatively, moss generally grows on the north side of a tree. But be sure you can tell moss from lichen.

Worry about water, not food. You can survive for weeks without food, but only about eight days without water. You need some 2 quarts a day to avoid dehydration.

If you're hungry, catch and eat insects. Grass-hoppers, crickets, worms, grubs, slugs, snails, beetles, bees, flies, caterpillars—all are safe and nourishing. No one need ever starve in the wil-derness. Avoid, however, the legs and wings of grasshoppers, which are indigestible. You may roast, fry, or boil the bugs—or in a pinch eat them raw.

Snakes are also good food. So too is tree bark —the white-and-green inner bark of evergreens, birches, willows. Porcupines are called the "woodsman's friend" because they are the only wild animal a starving woodsman can run down and immobilize with a stick.

See also ACCIDENTS; ANIMAL BITES; CAMP-ING; COLD WEATHER; FIRST AID SUPPLIES; HOT WEATHER; INSECTS; SNAKEBITE; WATER CON-TAMINATION.

HISTOPLASMOSIS, often called histo, is fre-quently mistaken for other diseases. What was termed "summer influenza" in the Midwest is now believed to be largely histo. Although it is not catching from someone who has it, the respi-ratory disease is often confused with tuberculo-sis.

Few Americans have even heard of it. Yet ac-cording to conservative estimates 30 million peo-ple are infected with histoplasmosis, with 600,000 new cases occurring every year. In some regions—chiefly in parts of the Mississippi, Ohio, and Missouri river valleys—histo is as fa-miliar as the common cold. For 2 percent of cases (about 600,000 persons in this country) the disease is severe, debilitating, even fatal.

Histo is caused by a fungus. Once breathed in, the fungus seeds, called spores, get down into the lungs and, in effect, take root. The tiny plants increase in number within the lungs by dividing themselves in two, over and over again. The area becomes inflamed. There is often severe localized damage to the lymph nodes and lung cells. Scars and calcium deposits form. Cavities may appear within the lung tissue.

Such severe injury does not take place with most people who are infected by histo spores. When the fungus invades the lungs, the body's defenses often wall off the spores. When this happens, the little plants become starved for ox-ygen and nutrition. Although they remain in the body, they are made harmless and no longer multiply. This provides some protection from further development of the disease.

Symptoms of histo. Depending upon the de-gree of exposure, histoplasmosis symptoms vary in intensity—from unnoticed to extremely se-vere. The most frequent symptoms are almost identical with those of flu: fever, tiredness, some-times slight coughing or chest pains. After a few weeks patients usually recover, thinking they have had the flu or some other virus.

A large dose of the fungus may bring more serious symptoms: loss of weight, extreme tired-ness, and weeks or months of convalescence. In an even more serious type of histo the spores spread from the lungs throughout the body. This condition may cause various organs to enlarge, fever to rise, and bring about anemia.

In chronic, long-lasting cases injured areas may be found in the lungs and at times in the throat and nasal passages. If cavities are formed in the lungs, there may be a great deal of spitting up—sometimes of blood. These severe cases, although rare, can be fatal.

Most cases of histo require little or no treatment. After their flulike symptoms, patients recover of their own accord.

A drug, amphotericin B, is effective in the more severe cases. Its use requires hospitalization because the drug must be introduced into the bloodstream almost daily for a period of weeks or months, and because severe side effects may develop. Surgery—removal of sections of the lung that are embedded with histo spores—is sometimes effective when there has been extensive damage.

Histo used to be considered a rural midwestern disease. But it has been discovered recently in cities in the East and other parts of the country.

Where histo thrives. Histo spores need warmth, moisture, and preferably some darkness in order to flourish. These conditions are found most often in accumulated droppings from bats and from chickens, pigeons, starlings, and other birds. The points of infection for many people are chicken houses, barns, belfries, pigeon lofts, caves.

One outbreak of histo affected a troop of Boy Scouts who had cleaned up an old city park in which many starlings roosted. The dank, damp undergrowth of the park was disturbed for the first time in years—and the boys breathed in a sufficient quantity of fungus-bearing dust to get the disease.

The American Lung Association offers rules that might prevent histoplasmosis or cut down its severity:

Keep farm buildings as clean and dry as possible. Before sweeping them out, wet down the floor to prevent dust from rising. A high-quality filter mask may offer some protection. But the histo fungus is very small and may slip through loosely woven masks.

Always wet down chicken droppings before cleaning out chicken houses.

Keep storm cellars clean and dry.

See also RESPIRATORY DISEASE.

HIVES are burning, itching swellings, usually caused by an allergy. The two main types are urticaria (eruptions on skin) and angioneurotic edema (giant swellings that may erupt internally).

If large, hives may cause swellings of the eyelids, tongue, mouth, hands, or feet. Hives can be accompanied by difficulty in breathing or swallowing, stomach disturbances, and fever. Pain, nausea, and vomiting may occur if the swelling is in the stomach.

If the swelling is in brain tissue, headache and other symptoms may be the result. Hives may come and go. They may last a few hours to a few days, or they may be chronic and last for months or years.

In an attack of hives avoid foods and drugs known to be frequent causes of allergy. Foods most likely to cause hives are chocolate; eggs and cheese; nuts, including peanuts; all seafood; tomatoes, berries, watermelon, cantaloupe, coconut, and other raw fruit; and highly spiced or seasoned foods. But any food, drug, or skin contact may cause hives in any person sensitive to it.

Drugs that may produce hives are aspirin and related products, certain laxatives, some arthritis medicines, and barbiturates and tranquilizers. About 4 percent of patients who receive penicillin break out in urticaria or giant swellings. Other frequent offenders are quinine, codeine, morphine, atropine, heparin, and vitamins B_1 (thiamine) and B_{12}.

In a large number of instances, particularly in chronic cases, no allergic cause can be found. Emotional stress is often a culprit. In some cases the swellings are produced by sensitivity to heat, cold, or sunlight. In a few the outbreaks may be due to chemical changes taking place as a result of mechanical irritation, as from wool rubbing against skin.

Nickel in jewelry, especially in earrings for pierced ears, is a common but seldom suspected cause. Infections may produce hives, as can rheumatic diseases and forms of cancer like Hodgkin's disease. So too may endocrine changes such as menstruation, menopause, hypothyroidism, and hyperthyroidism.

A physician can often relieve symptoms by prescribing an antihistamine. Some drugs are good preventives—for example, if you develop hives from cold weather, you may benefit from taking a drug like Periactin for a few days before a skiing trip. Desensitization is considered rarely worthwhile, since recurrent attacks of urticaria usually don't get worse.

Warning: Some people who get hives from cold have died after diving into cold water and going into shock. In addition, life-threatening angioedema requires aggressive treatment, possibly even an opening in the windpipe (tracheostomy) to permit breathing.

See also ALLERGY; ANTIHISTAMINES; DRUG ALLERGY; FOOD ALLERGY; ITCHING; STRESS.

HOARSENESS (laryngitis) means something has gone wrong with your vocal cords so they do not align perfectly when they vibrate.

See a doctor if hoarseness lasts more than three weeks. This may be the only early warning sign of cancer of the larynx.

Emotional reactions to stress commonly lead to hoarseness.

Most hoarseness however, comes from overuse that injures the vocal cords—parents and teachers yelling at children, singers and salesmen projecting their voices improperly. A voice that is too low and monotonous causes the vocal cords always to vibrate together in the same way, which may cause an ulcer at the point of contact. Hoarseness from voice overuse is likely to become worse in the afternoon, since rest at night restores some of the normal tone.

Hoarseness that lasts weeks or months often results from irritation and drying of the larynx membranes from smoking, alcohol, air pollution. Infections such as colds and sore throat and other types of respiratory disease may have hoarseness as a symptom.

To relieve hoarseness due to overuse or irritation do all of the following:

Avoid irritants. No smoking. No hot, spicy foods. No alcoholic beverages. Get away from polluted environments.

Rest your voice for a few days. No talking or whispering (which strains the vocal cords as much as talking). Use a pencil and pad. Make a practice of being completely silent for several specified periods each day.

Inhale menthol steam. Bring a pan containing 1¼ quarts of water to a boil. Take the pan off the stove and add a pinch—no more than ⅛ teaspoon—of menthol crystals (toxic, available only on prescription). Put a towel around your head and over the edge of the pan and inhale the vapors until the water cools down. Repeat every 2 hours until your voice becomes normal.

See also CANCER OF THE LARYNX; RESPIRATORY DISEASE.

HODGKIN'S DISEASE, the commonest lymphoma (cancer of the lymph glands), most often occurs in people between the ages of 20 and 40.

Most patients treated in the early stages of Hodgkin's disease may be cured. Since the condition can often be arrested, even patients with advanced disease may lead normal, productive lives for many years. Cure is possible in a large percentage of advanced cases.

The lymphatic system is part of the circulatory system that plays a major role in a person's ability to fight infection. The lymph glands manufacture lymphocytes, a type of white blood cell that fights the spread of infection. In Hodgkin's disease (first described in 1832 by Thomas Hodgkin, an English physician) these cells proliferate in a variety of abnormal forms, leaving the body fewer normal lymphocytes to fight infection.

Hodgkin's disease may begin in one area of the lymph system. If unchecked, it spreads throughout the system and to other tissues and organs. Anemia may develop. The body becomes less able to combat infections. Damage to vital organs occurs.

The most common first symptom of Hodgkin's disease is a painless swelling of lymph glands, usually in the neck, sometimes in the armpits or groin. Other symptoms may include pain in the abdomen or back. There may be persistent night sweats, fatigue, fever, and loss of weight, with itching, nausea, and vomiting.

Since each of these symptoms may occur in other, often minor diseases, only a qualified physician can make a definite diagnosis. Lymph glands may be enlarged as a result of infections or other illnesses, such as rheumatoid arthritis or mononucleosis. Consult a physician if any lymph gland remains enlarged for three weeks.

Biopsy, lab tests, and diagnostic X rays aid in the "staging": determining if the disease is confined to a single lymph node or organ (Stage 1) or if it has spread to other regions (Stages 2, 3, or 4).

A diagnostic X-ray examination called lymphangiography is often used to help determine the stage of the disease. It consists of injecting into the lymph system a dye that shows on X rays. The X-ray outline of the lymph system can be examined for abnormalities.

Radiation therapy is usually the most effective treatment for early stages of Hodgkin's disease. Evidence is strong that X ray is curative in at least half of such cases.

Several drug treatments can be useful in more advanced stages of Hodgkin's disease. A number of combination treatments produce encouraging results.

Related cancers. Including Hodgkin's disease, cancers of the blood and lymph tissues affect about 40,000 Americans a year and take 21,000 lives.

Non-Hodgkin's lymphomas share many of the symptoms of Hodgkin's disease, although the cancer may affect different types of lymphatic tissue. The most prevalent form is lymphosarcoma, which is fast-growing and often widespread on diagnosis. It usually affects people age 50 to 80.

Multiple myeloma is a cancer of the blood-forming system. It begins in the bone marrow with the uncontrolled production of plasma cells. When malignant plasma cells proliferate, bone marrow is destroyed, impairing production of red blood cells (which carry oxygen), white blood cells (which fight infection), and platelets (which control clotting).

Multiple myeloma usually affects people 40 or older, especially those over 55. It's typically signaled by bone pain, concentrated in the back. Other symptoms include weight loss, weakness, bone fractures, anemia, and repeated infections. Chemotherapy is the most effective treatment.

See also CANCER.

HOME NURSING   See BED REST.

HOOKWORMS are parasites, 3/8 inch long, with a ring of sharp, hooklike teeth. In the United States these worms occur mainly in the South and in Puerto Rico. Hookworm disease (ground itch, ancylostomiasis) is the malady resulting from severe infestation with the parasite.

Hookworms thrive in areas where winters are mild and the soil is moist and sandy. They are most common in poor rural areas, in soil surrounding outhouses. Feces from infected humans carry eggs into the soil, where they hatch into microscopic larvae.

When the soil is cool and moist, the worms crawl to the nearest high moist area and extend their bodies into the air. They remain there—waving their bodies to and fro—until they come into contact with the skin of a suitable host or until they are driven back down by the heat.

Most people with hookworm disease get it from walking barefoot on infected soil or handling it. You can't feel the larvae entering through your skin. When they've worked their way in, you may itch where they have pierced the skin and bored through, or you may notice an itching sore. These sores are most likely to appear between or under the toes, or on the hands around the fingers. Commonly called toe itch, it is generally a sign of hookworm disease.

Once the larvae are in the body, the blood carries them to the heart and lungs. There they bore through the membranes and get into the bronchial tubes, then into the throat. They are swallowed and travel through the stomach to the intestines, where they stay.

With its hooks the worm clamps onto the intestines and sucks blood and tissue juices to nourish itself. Thus housed and fed, the larvae grow to adults that lay thousands of eggs daily. These pass out of the body in the feces, get onto the ground, hatch into larvae, and the cycle starts all over again.

Symptoms of infection. By draining the host's blood the worms can cause severe anemia, especially in people suffering from malnutrition. Severe infestation is now rare in the United States, but even in mild cases hookworm disease can make a person listless and weak. As a result many a child and adult has been called stupid or lazy—when actually he is a victim of hookworm disease.

People suffering from the disease grow noticeably pale. Frequently they suffer from indigestion and diarrhea. Their skin may be pasty-yellow, their gums and lips almost colorless. Their legs, abdomen, and face may become swollen.

Puberty is often delayed and sexual development frequently recedes. Impotence may occur in men; menstruation may cease in women. When one person in a family has hookworm disease, the chances are that other members have it too, since they are all exposed to the same unsanitary environment. It spreads rapidly in schools where toilet facilities are inadequate and in towns that do not have sanitary sewage systems.

Most health departments supply free anti-hookworm medicine to any doctor who requests it for people unable to buy it. The drugs are extremely effective, but reinfection often occurs because the victim is reexposed to the parasite.

Wearing shoes outdoors in hookworm areas is a prime preventive. If your child insists on going barefoot in a hookworm area, see if he'll compromise by wearing sneakers or sandals.

Prevention of soil pollution is the only sure way of wiping out hookworm disease. A first step is to replace unhygienic outhouses with sanitary ones. Your local or state health department will furnish advice on building sanitary outhouses if you live in an area needing them.

Since hookworm larvae can migrate only a few inches in soil, deepening the pit of a privy may be all that's needed to keep the parasite from surfacing before it dies.

Hookworm is also an animal disease and may be spread by dog and cat feces. Penetration of the skin may take place, but the larvae from nonhuman hosts cannot complete their migratory cycle. Instead they move through layers of human tissue just below the skin. This tissue becomes inflamed and the skin bears red serpentine markings. These heal from one end as the larvae move forward. The condition is referred to as creeping eruption or cutaneous larva migrans.

For other parasitic worms common in the

United States see PINWORMS; ROUNDWORMS; TAPEWORMS; TRICHINOSIS. For diseases caused by parasites in other parts of the world, see MALARIA; SCHISTOSOMIASIS. See also INFECTIOUS DISEASE; TRAVEL HEALTH.

HOSPITAL In an emergency if you or one of your family must enter an unfamiliar hospital, phone your regular physician immediately. Ask him to call the doctor in charge of your case and to investigate the qualifications of the hospital.

If he has any doubt about the hospital or doctor, ask him to recommend another hospital for you to transfer to. No hospital can legally hold you against your will, or against the family's will if the patient is a child or mentally incapacitated.

Be extremely selective about hospitals. Since you'll want access to a first-rate institution if you need one, locating a good hospital is your first step in choosing your regular physician.

What to look for in a hospital. Phone the administrator and ask if his institution meets these criteria:

1. It's accredited. The Joint Commission on Accreditation of Hospitals sets minimum standards for patient care and building facilities. The standards are enforced by periodic visits from inspectors for the commission, which represents the AMA, the American Hospital Association, American College of Physicians, and American College of Surgeons, among other professional groups.

Accreditation is voluntary. It is a long jump up from mere state or local licensing, which may assure you of nothing more than that someone's paid a license fee. About one in three hospitals is *not* accredited, so beware.

2. It's a teaching hospital. A hospital affiliated with a medical school is likely to have the services of qualified family doctors and specialists in all fields available as needed. Such institutions attract high-caliber physicians and generally enforce a high level of performance. Unfortunately there are only about 600 such hospitals, concentrated near medical schools.

Next best and far more numerous are hospitals approved for residency training in at least the four major specialty fields—obstetrics and gynecology, internal medicine, surgery, and pediatrics. Lacking this, look for a hospital that has a nursing school or internship-training program.

Howard Berman of Blue Cross Association recommended that you give first choice to a hospital whose interns and residents are chiefly graduates of U.S. rather than foreign medical schools. Hospitals that can't attract graduates of American schools may be deficient in important areas. Also you may have difficulty being understood by staff physicians who are weak in your language.

3. It's well administered. Given two hospitals that meet the foregoing criteria, prefer the institution that has the earmarks of being well run.

A hospital should have at least one registered nurse (R.N.) to every five or six on-the-job personnel. At night there should at least one R.N. for every 10 to 15 patients.

Look for a preadmitting procedure that can save you a long wait. Except in emergencies, a good hospital should get basic information over the telephone about Blue Cross numbers, previous admissions, and so on.

When confronted with hospitalization, deal with these questions:

Is hospitalization really necessary? Ask your doctor if there is definite need for special services that cannot be provided on an office or outpatient basis or at home. Hospitalizing children and elderly persons especially imposes psychological stress.

Nearly all hospitals have shortages of staff, which means that the quality of their nursing and supportive services may be inferior to what the family could supply at home. Furthermore strains of staphylococcus and other bacteria that are resistant to many antibiotics are more likely to be encountered around a hospital than in your home.

Inquire about home care, aimed at people whose needs are so minimal they can be met at home. A visiting nurse may be able to take blood and urine samples, dress wounds, supervise feeding through veins. Some cities have Meals-on-Wheels programs, to deliver prepared meals to families in which the housewife is ill. Your community may have a personalized service bureau to perform minor repairs, arrange visits from clergymen, transport patients for short trips.

How short can you cut your hospital stay? Even if you have health insurance, loss of income from not working may be a bigger blow to you than the medical costs.

Ordinarily you're admitted to a hospital the afternoon before surgery, to leave time for the compilation of your history, a physical examination, and lab work. In many cases you can save that extra night in the hospital if your doctor handles your history and physical in his office and the hospital does your tests on an outpatient basis. You spend the night at home—and all preoperative work will be ready when you're admitted early the next morning.

Friday's the ideal day for short-term surgery, since you have the weekend to recover with no workdays lost. Otherwise enter a hospital between Sunday night and Friday noon, if you have any choice. Only small crews perform lab work and X rays on weekends. You may be paying for a weekend in bed when no serious medical work will start until Monday.

If your doctor will be away over the weekend, be sure the physician covering for him is authorized to discharge you if you can possibly go home.

What kind of rooms are available? Sharing a room with one or more other patients can save you money, but can also give you an overdose of togetherness. The best way to get privacy in a hospital is to get a private room. You'll pay 10 to 25 percent more than what a semiprivate room would cost. Most insurance plans stipulate either a semiprivate room or a maximum daily rate—any difference is your expense.

Even if you're willing to pay the price, it's often not easy to get a private room. Be certain your doctor knows in advance that you want one —and that he makes this clear to the hospital. Call and remind the hospital admitting office of your request. If you can't wait for a private room, when you arrive let the admitting office know you want one as quickly as possible.

Conversely, you may not want a high-priced room though it's the only one available. Unless it's an emergency, go to the hospital toward the end of the year or during the summer months, when hospitals in many areas are less crowded.

Will you get the attention you need? Don't suffer in silence. Let your nurse know when you first begin to suffer from pain. If it lingers, the nurse may have to contact your physician, who may want to order a particular type of medication. An hour or two could elapse while you suffer needlessly.

Pain is worse when you're bored. To beat the boredom of hospital routine, rent a television set. Make sure you have a telephone; use it to schedule friends for visits (and to discourage visits of acquaintances who would tax you). Invite a guest in for dinner—having a relative or friend join you at a meal can be refreshing.

Beware lapsing into "hospitalitis," the state of lethargy and apathy fostered by being weak and dependent in an impersonal institution. Assert yourself, though it may be discouraged by some hospital staff members who want you to be a "good" patient—passive and no trouble.

Learn when your treatments and medications are scheduled. If they're forgotten by busy personnel, don't hesitate to call forth a reminder.

Dress up your room with pictures and personal possessions. Wear your own pajamas. Get out of the sick role as soon as possible: Put on your street clothes. Get up and about. Even go off the hospital grounds—with permission from your doctor. Complain about poor food or service—a justified beef is stimulating and may correct a fault.

See also HEALTH INSURANCE; HOSPITALIZING CHILDREN; MEDICAL DEDUCTIONS; PHYSICIAN; SURGERY.

INSIST ON YOUR RIGHTS

The American Hospital Association has confronted the most common troublesome situations and issued a "Patient's Bill of Rights" for the guidance of hospitals. In effect it codifies minimum standards you should expect from your hospital, although it has no force in law. According to this policy statement you have the right to:

1. Considerate and respectful care.
2. Complete current information from your doctor about diagnosis, treatment, and prognosis in terms you can understand.
3. Information from your doctor that enables you to give informed consent prior to any procedure.
4. Prohibition of treatment to the extent the law allows, and explanation of the medical consequences of your refusing recommended care.
5. Privacy concerning your medical care.
6. Confidentiality of communications and records concerning your case.
7. Reasonable response to your request for services, and complete information as to the reasons for transfer to another institution (including the alternatives to such a transfer).
8. Information about any relationship between your hospital and other health-care or educational institutions connected with your case, and about any relationship between individuals who are treating you.
9. Refusal to participate in experimentation.
10. Reasonable continuity of care—including knowledge of availability of doctors and your requirements for care after your discharge.
11. Explanation of your bill, regardless of who pays it.
12. Information as to what hospital rules and regulations apply to your conduct.

HOSPITALIZING CHILDREN can be traumatic. To a child the hospital means separation from his parents. It is often a terrifying interruption in his life.

Failure to give him the psychological support he needs produces stress that often becomes evident only after he leaves the hospital. In some children this can lead to bedwetting, trouble in school, nightmares, deteriorating relationship with parents—the seeds of psychiatric problems that can last into adulthood.

Moreover, a young patient whose psychological adjustment to hospitalization is poor may refuse to participate in physical therapy, learn a self-treatment procedure, eat properly—any of which can deter progress.

If possible avoid surgery in a child under six. In this stage of development children are emotionally vulnerable to symbolic threats. Unfortunately these are the years when most tonsil and adenoid operations seem necessary.

Your child's fears are inevitable. Many young children fear that they'll be abandoned at the hospital, that they'll be left behind if they can't be properly fixed. Reassure your child that he'll be coming home.

The child may associate being sent to the hospital with punishment, abandonment, death. Even simple things like a surgical mask may appear ominous. The size, smell, and sounds of a hospital are likely to be frightening. Your youngster may be in the hospital only a week, but how long does it seem to him?

He may think a hospital is a place where you die, as perhaps his grandfather did. He may tell you, "The hospital is a place where you go to get well"—but in fact believe, "It's a place where people hurt you." If he is due for surgery, he may not know that after someone cuts him, the cut will be sewn up. He may be convinced that a hernia operation will leave him permanently disabled.

Telling the child. How should you tell your child? Be matter-of-fact about his need to go to a hospital to get better. Reassure him that you'll spend a lot of time with him, that there'll be other children there his age.

Give a clear and honest explanation at his level of comprehension. To the older child you might volunteer an explanation of where the tonsils and adenoids are located, what purpose they serve, and why they occasionally cause trouble. A younger child might be given the simple statement like: "You're going to the hospital where the doctor can fix your tonsils so you won't be sick anymore."

Tell the child about some of the things he can expect to see in the hospital—beds that crank up and down, the kind of gown he'll wear. But avoid belaboring the point. Too much advance buildup of the coming hospitalization through books, records, and so on may intensify impending events unnecessarily.

Good books to help you prepare your child include *Curious George Goes to the Hospital* by H. A. Rey, and *What Happens When You Go to the Hospital* by Arthur Shay.

Give your child ample opportunity to express his fears about hospitalization. To get at hidden concerns and misapprehensions, ask your child to tell you why he has to go to the hospital, and what he expects to happen there. Or have him draw a picture of a hospital scene or enact it with dolls.

To help a child better understand what will happen, ask your doctor for photographs or drawings, in simplified form, of the anatomical part or procedure. Make sure the child realizes where the part is, and how it is to be removed or treated. One three-year-old girl thought her tonsils were in her abdomen. If the appendix is to be removed, reassure the child that a relatively small cut will be made, not the huge gash many children fear.

If a young boy is having surgery for an inguinal hernia or an undescended testicle, anticipate a common concern and reassure him that his penis will not be cut off.

It is important to let your child know where you'll be during each procedure, and when he'll see you again.

Anticipate the possibility that your child may feel to blame. Repeat several times that nothing the child said or did or thought caused the illness or the need for surgery.

Lying will backfire. Don't try to dispel a child's fears by telling him he is merely going on a little trip that will be fun and no pain. Your manner is apt to give you away and he's bound to discover the falsehood sooner or later. His trust in you will be shaken, and thereafter he may take your reassurance to mean real danger.

At the same time, the child's capacity to absorb much information at one time is limited. Incomplete answers may be satisfactory from his standpoint. Don't map out the expected course of an illness. There may be unforeseen complications that may make you seem a liar. Instead explain things one step at a time as they develop.

Let his physician and nurses know about what may be bothering him or any behavior that indicates problems you feel require their special attention. Besides checking his physical progress, the doctor's responsibility includes providing him with information about his illness and giving him the opportunity to vent his anxieties.

Pain is always a concern of the child. Discuss all procedures with him in advance and tell him if they will hurt. Stress the positive—"It won't hurt much." "It won't take long." "The injection will be like a little beesting."

Explain why the treatment is necessary. Emphasize that it will help him recover. Make sure that everyone gives him a similar explanation. As important to the child as the information itself is hearing the *same* reassuring story from every quarter.

It helps if the child sees how the instruments the doctor is using work, and touches them. If a doctor or nurse uses anesthetic or even an alcohol swab, stress its "magical" protecting and pain-blunting properties. Children believe in magic and are strengthened by talismans.

In the hospital. Visit the hospital with your child in advance to get acquainted. Your doctor may want to admit him a day before surgery so he can adapt to the new surroundings and personnel. Some doctors, on the other hand, oppose advanced hospital admittance on the ground that it prolongs separation from home.

Bring the child's favorite toy or personal possession as a comforting security object. If the child is young, also leave one of your own personal belongings (a comb, a scarf), which may be of comfort after you depart. (But check with the hospital first to make sure that such articles may be brought in.)

Be with the child just before surgery and again when the child returns to the room. Remind him frequently that you'll be there—and also that there'll be periods when he'll be taken care of by others.

For the child under five it's best if the mother or father is on hand during his waking hours. For older children, including adolescents, parent visits a few hours each day may suffice. For an infant under four months, constant parent attention is not essential if he gets attention from the hospital staff.

If you can't be with the child yourself, arrange for visits by someone he knows. Recruit on a scheduled basis relatives, neighbors, schoolmates.

Unless he is desperately ill, a child should be in a room or small ward (four to six beds) with other children, preferably of his own age. Usually a pediatrics ward has older children who are up and about. To get special attention for your youngster, hire one of them to be an "assistant nurse" or baby-sitter.

In addition to contact with people the hospi-

talized infant, even one month or younger, needs stimulation to avoid lapsing into a trancelike lassitude that may persist after he is discharged. He requires only what he'd have at home—a brightly colored mobile above his crib, a toy that hangs across it, small noisy objects, or scraps of colored cloth.

You have a right to sensitivity from the doctors and hospital. Parents need an opportunity to discuss their anxieties about their child's illness. Select a doctor who'll provide this for you. Establish a schedule for making contact with the doctor at the hospital or by phone.

Beware holding yourself responsible for the illness. Such guilt can harm your relationship with the child and may make you reluctant to spend as much time with him as you otherwise would.

Select a hospital where you'll be welcome. Often a fear of "being in the way" or "being a nuisance" prevents parents of a sick child from becoming involved or asking questions.

Most authorities agree that even if a mother is a poor nurse and underfoot, she should still be around to give the child the loving support he needs. In many hospitals pediatric-service visiting hours are extensive and flexible. Rooming-in is often possible. In less enlightened hospitals, you may have to arrange special visiting privileges through your doctor.

Hospitalization may affect your child's behavior. Since it is a period of great stress, aberrant behavior is a natural consequence.

Often what appears to be good behavior is in fact an indication of depression and withdrawal. In contrast the unruly behavior so easy to label as bad (especially in the traditional hospital setting) is usually a healthy child's response to a confusing, frightening experience.

Upon returning home, your youngster may be cranky, tearful, demanding, hostile, clinging. There may be some night terrors, hypochondria, and a return to bedwetting. This regressive behavior is normal, especially if you immediately try to treat him in the same way as before he was hospitalized. If behavior problems and difficulties persist beyond the usual couple of weeks, discuss them with the doctor.

See also HOSPITAL.

HOT WEATHER   With the growth of air conditioning, many people are becoming less acclimatized to seasonally high temperatures. As a result there are more cases of heat cramps, heat exhaustion, and heat stroke.

The businessman who goes from air-conditioned home to air-conditioned office Monday through Friday is a candidate for a collapse on the golf course on a hot Saturday afternoon. Even inactive people exposed to unusual heat may fall victim to it. As humidity rises, discomfort worsens (see illustration)—and you need to take extra precautions because the air won't absorb as much sweat as your body needs to get rid of.

Also take extra care when the official temperature is over 85° F. Official readings are often taken from cooler places, like towers. When the weather man says it's 90° F, your street may be more than 100° F, even in the shade.

Beating the heat. To help avoid heat discomfort and disorders:

Refrain from unaccustomed amounts of exercise on weekends or vacations during hot weather. The best times for strenuous activity are the cool early morning and late afternoon. When possible avoid outdoor activity between 10:00 A.M. and 2:00 P.M.

Acclimatize to the heat slowly. Start with 15 minutes of strenuous activity the first hot day, and add 15 to 30 minutes each day for a week or so. Spend a few minutes outdoors (like a walk to lunch) on hot days. When doing hard work, rest 5 or 10 minutes every half hour.

Drink plenty of water, even if you don't feel thirsty. In hot, dry weather you may not feel that you're sweating because the water you're losing evaporates quickly. It's a myth that drinking water when you're hot and active will bring on stomach cramps.

Hot coffee or tea will leave you feeling cooler than an iced drink. Sugar-loaded soft drinks can make you feel hotter. Abstain from alcohol, which draws water from your tissues and will make you thirstier.

Salt food heavily at mealtimes, but don't take salt tablets unless advised by your doctor. Eat light meals. Several small meals a day are better than the customary three large ones.

Wear loose-fitting, light-colored clothing to reflect the sun's rays and help sweat evaporate. Wear a wide-brimmed hat if you have to be under the sun during the heat of the day.

Keep cool by bathing your hands and wrists under cold tap water and soaking your feet in tepid or cool water. A lukewarm bath or shower can have longer-lasting effects than a cold shower. Before going to bed on a torrid night, take a warmish shower, dry yourself lightly, let evaporation cool you further.

Since heat disorders can occur indoors as well as out, make interiors cooler with air conditioning or fans. You can keep a house cool by closing windows and drawing blinds in the morning,

opening them again at dusk to capture the cool night air.

Avoid overcooling with an air conditioner—going from a 70° F room to 100° F outside can be stressful. Before getting into a car that's been parked in the sun, open it up for a few minutes.

If you're on a low-salt or salt-free diet—or if you have heart disease, hypertension, diabetes, or lung disease—high heat and humidity put an especially heavy burden on you. Consult your doctor before engaging in any unusual activity.

Get medical attention as soon as possible if you feel the effects of heat and humidity—unexplained stomach or arm and leg cramps, extreme fatigue, nausea, headache, or dizziness.

WILL THE HEAT GET YOU DOWN?

In general, the higher the relative humidity at a given temperature, the more discomfort you suffer and the more heat precautions you need to take.

At This Temperature	This Relative Humidity Makes You	
	Uncomfortable	Extremely Uncomfortable
75° F	100%	—
76	91	—
77	82	—
78	75	—
79	68	—
80	61	—
81	55	100%
82	49	93
83	43	86
84	38	78
85	33	71
86	29	65
87	25	59
88	20	54
89	17	49
90	14	43
91	10	38
92	7	34
93	5	30
94	3	26
95	1	23
96	Any humidity	20
97	"	16
98	"	13
99	"	11
100	"	8
101	"	6
102	"	3
103	"	1
104	"	Any humidity

See also BATHING; DEHYDRATION; EXERCISE; FOOD POISONING; HEAT CRAMPS; HEAT EXHAUSTION; HEAT STROKE; HUMIDITY; INSECT STINGS; SUNBURN.

HUMIDITY, moisture in the air, is important in proper amounts for helping to prevent and relieve respiratory disease. At the minimum, air that is too dry in your house causes coughing, sore throat, skin dryness, parched mouth, chapped lips.

Keep relative humidity at 30 to 50 percent. Relative humidity is the amount of water vapor air has, compared with how much it could hold at the same temperature. When relative humidity is 50 percent, air contains half the moisture it can potentially hold. At 100 percent, it holds all the water vapor it can. Beyond that are fog, clouds, rain, and snow.

Excessive humidity, as in damp climates in summer, can pose problems for allergy sufferers. A dehumidifier, or an air conditioner with a humidity control, may help.

Maintaining proper humidity is an even greater problem in winter. The warmer the air, the more moisture it can hold—thus the more moisture it needs to maintain a comfortable relative humidity.

At 20° F outside air needs very little moisture to have a relative humidity of 80 percent. Brought indoors and heated to 75°—as happens in cold climates in winter—the relative humidity becomes an arid 10 percent, drier than air in the Sahara. The air becomes so thirsty it sucks up moisture wherever it can find it.

Dangers of dry air. Dry air invites respiratory disorders. It sucks up moisture from the mucous membranes of your nose, throat, and lungs. The normally watery mucus secreted by the membranes helps keep your airways clean. The fluid traps germs and dirt so that tiny hairlike cilia carry them up to the throat to be ejected.

When mucus is dried, it thickens, slowing the cilia and providing a growth medium for bacteria. The thick mucus makes breathing difficult. This worsens colds, influenza, hay fever, and sinusitis—and can be extremely serious in such conditions as asthma, croup, and pneumonia.

On top of this, excessive dryness keeps dust suspended in air, providing a vehicle for bacteria to be inhaled. Static electricity is worse in dry air, so you get a shock if you touch metal or another person after walking across a rug.

You are likely to feel somewhat chillier than you would in moister air of the same temperature. When humidity is 10 percent you need to heat a house to 77° F to get the same feeling of

warmth you'd get at only 70° F if humidity were 75 percent.

Humidifiers. Should you get a humidifier? In a northern climate you may feel better even if there is no disease present and be less likely to wake up in the morning with a dry, semisore throat.

You can tell your house is too dry if you suffer buildups of static electricity, if your piano constantly goes out of tune, if tables and chairs become rickety from glued joints shrinking and coming apart. The most accurate way to measure relative humidity is with a hygrometer, but the Vaporizer-Humidifier Council offers this quick test: Stir three ice cubes in a glass of water. If, after three minutes, there's no moisture on the outside of the glass, your house needs humidification.

Beware getting a humidifier if your house lacks a vapor barrier—a layer of polyethylene film, metal foil, or a suitable asphalt-saturated paper—inside every outer wall, which seals off the warm side of the wall from the insulation. The purpose of the vapor barrier is to prevent too much moisture from migrating through outer walls of the rooms into the insulation space. The weather side of this space on cold days may be so much colder than the interior side that condensation may take place inside the wall.

Too much dampness there can result in rotting of structural wood, development of mildew, or blistering of paint. Meanwhile the insulation may become less effective through being watersoaked or frozen. In a loosely constructed house, even if such condensation is not a problem, a humidifier may not be of much use because the water vapor it produced would escape outside at so great a rate that the indoor air would continue to be too dry.

Putting a pan of water on a radiator is not an adequate substitute for a humidifier. It takes a gallon or two of water a day to humidify a room in a dry northern house. Usually a pan puts out only a quart of water in a day.

A humidifier alone will not prevent illness such as colds or necessarily reduce their incidence. Despite this a number of humidifier manufacturers in listing the benefits of humidification make unqualified promises of protection against colds and nosebleeds, alleviation of allergy and asthma symptoms, and cures for sore throat, sleeplessness, and skin irritation. The Food and Drug Administration (FDA) has seized makes of humidifiers because of such health claims.

Vaporizers. An electric vaporizer can be a

boon to a sickroom. It won't cure any ailment. But it can reduce the symptoms of respiratory ailments by helping to liquefy mucus and soothe irritated membranes.

Some vaporizers have cups for medications such as menthol—you can damage your unit by putting medication in the water. But some consultants feel there is little therapeutic value in airborne medications. The concentrations in the air are too small to be more effective than plain water alone.

Cool mist vaporizers, which atomize water and spray it into the air, are safer than steam models—which heat water and may cause burns if spilled. The two types of models are equally effective.

Where a bathroom adjoins a bedroom, an occasional running of hot shower water to produce steam may generate the desired humid effect. Otherwise, try using a steam kettle or an evaporating pan placed over an electric hot plate. Keep this equipment at a safe distance from a child lest he knock it over and burn himself.

See also HOT WEATHER; RESPIRATORY DISEASE.

HYDROCEPHALUS ("water on the brain") is a birth defect in which excessive amounts of cerebrospinal fluid accumulate within the spaces of the brain and spinal cord, usually because of some obstruction in drainage. It occurs about once in every 500 live births.

There is no known cause, nor does it seem to be associated with any conditions of pregnancy. In some cases, hydrocephalus is a complication of spina bifida.

The baby with hydrocephalus may be irritable because of headaches caused by the pressure of the fluid. He may eat poorly and vomit frequently. As the fluid builds up, the soft bones of the baby's skull begin to spread apart, and his skull becomes enlarged. Mental retardation and difficulties in movement can result from impairment of the nervous system. Untreated, two out of three children with hydrocephalus will die.

However surgery that bypasses the obstruction will allow the fluid to drain, and two out of three children who have this operation will survive.

See also BIRTH DEFECTS; SPINA BIFIDA.

HYDROPHOBIA See RABIES.

HYPERTENSION See BLOOD PRESSURE.

HYPERVENTILATION (overbreathing) is the act of forced deep breathing. It depletes the lungs—and eventually the blood—of carbon dioxide. This results in dizziness, tingling and numbness of fingers and toes, and occasionally mental confusion.

As an emergency measure breathe into a paper or plastic bag to return exhaled carbon dioxide to the lungs. For repeated episodes doctors prescribe mild tranquilizers or phenobarbital.

Anxiety is the cause of most unconscious hyperventilation. The hyperventilation-anxiety syndrome lurks behind much unexplained dizziness. The sufferer may also feel light-headed, giddy, sweaty.

Beware deliberate hyperventilating. Some youngsters take very deep breaths in rapid succession for a drugless trip. The practice itself rarely does physiological harm. But after becoming dizzy or unconscious, you can injure yourself falling to the ground or hitting a sharp edge.

Never hyperventilate before swimming. Swimmers who want to stay underwater a long time sometimes take a number of deep breaths before diving in, because they mistakenly think they can pump more oxygen into the bloodstream. Even with normal breathing, blood is almost completely saturated with oxygen all the time.

What actually happens is that hyperventilation empties the lungs of carbon dioxide and thus removes the normal danger signal that cries "Breathe!" when you can't hold out any longer. Swimmers who hyperventilate run out of oxygen without feeling the need to breathe and can easily become unconscious and drown.

HYPNOTICS See BARBITURATES.

HYPOGLYCEMIA (low blood sugar) is a condition in which the sugar content of the blood is abnormally low. Two to five hours after each meal, a person with hypoglycemia may experience weakness, tremulousness, dizziness, sweating, anxiety, hunger sensations, palpitation, headache, and fainting. These symptoms usually disappear with some sugar intake or with the next meal.

Symptoms of a more severe form of the disorder may include convulsions and coma. In rare cases hypoglycemia is fatal.

One frequent cause of a hypoglycemic reaction occurs in a person with diabetes who has taken too much insulin or eaten too little food.

Functional (or reactive) hypoglycemia accounts for about 70 percent of cases. Blood sugar is burned up too rapidly, but there is no organic abnormality. In functional hypoglycemia, the symptoms will usually spontaneously disappear after a short time, even without sugar intake, when the liver releases glucose (stored sugars) to compensate for the low sugar level in the blood.

Many cases of functional hypoglycemia result from the overproduction of insulin by the pancreas, which abruptly lowers blood-sugar levels. Excess carbohydrates (sugars and starches) in the diet may cause the pancreas to overreact. Sometimes emotional stress triggers the pancreas into oversecretion. Alcoholic excess may also bring on functional hypoglycemia.

The condition is likely to occur in people with a family history of diabetes—the condition in which blood sugar is abnormally high. In some cases hypoglycemia is an early forerunner of diabetes.

Functional hypoglycemia usually responds to a change in eating habits. If you have this condition: Maintain a diet high in proteins and fats, low in carbohydrates. Proteins and fats are absorbed into your bloodstream much more slowly than carbohydrates, hence they are less likely to bring on a surplus of insulin.

Also eat five or six small meals a day; large meals, widely spaced, may flood the body with carbohydrates and overstimulate the pancreas. Avoid rapidly absorbable carbohydrates (candy, ice cream, pies, pastry). But always carry some sweets with you for emergencies. A sweet can quickly restore some sugar to your blood, possibly averting dizziness or unconsciousness while, say, you're driving.

If emotional stress accounts for your overproduction of insulin, tranquilizing drugs or psychotherapy may be recommended in addition to diet changes.

Organic (or fasting) hypoglycemia results from organic disorders in the body, such as a tumor of the pancreas, liver disease, drug intoxications, hormonal malfunctions of the pituitary, or, in rare cases, the adrenal glands. In liver disease, for example, hypoglycemia may come about when the malfunctioning liver releases insufficient glucose into the bloodstream. Treatment of the underlying condition will usually correct the low blood-sugar condition. Symptoms of organic hypoglycemia often occur during the night or early in the morning.

Infants with hypoglycemia are rare, but if undiagnosed they can suffer severe brain damage. Symptoms may be absent altogether, or they may include lowered body temperature, irregular breathing, poor color. An infant is most likely to have hypoglycemia at birth if he is the child of a diabetic mother, or is premature or abnormally small, or has liver disease.

Organic hypoglycemia has often been undetected or misdiagnosed, possibly because its symptoms so closely resemble those of migraine, ulcers, heart disease, brain tumor, and various kinds of mental illness. What's more, patients with hypoglycemia may also suffer from emotional problems, further complicating diagnosis.

Nonhypoglycemia. As more people become aware of the possible hazards of low blood sugar, many are erroneously diagnosing themselves as hypoglycemic, a potentially dangerous practice. Don't assume you have hypoglycemia simply because you suffer from one or more symptoms associated with the condition. Above all don't treat yourself for undiagnosed hypoglycemia.

Hypoglycemia can be diagnosed by means of a blood test called the glucose tolerance test. Administered during a hypoglycemic attack, it will show how much sugar is in the blood. Other tests can determine whether the condition is functional or organic.

A person with hypoglycemia should be under a doctor's care for as long as symptoms or physical abnormalities exist. Be wary of over-the-counter drugs or diets that purport to cure all types of hypoglycemia.

See also DIABETES.

HYPOTHERMIA   See COLD WEATHER.

HYPOTHYROIDISM   See THYROID DISEASE.

HYSTERECTOMY is the surgical removal of the uterus. If you're told you need this operation, get another doctor's opinion.

Many hysterectomies are unnecessary—a situation ethical gynecologists call the "rape of the pelvis." A study of 246 hysterectomies at 10 hospitals found that fully 31 percent of the uteri removed were normal. In more than 9 percent of the cases the hysterectomies were performed for such nonspecific complaints as irritability, fatigue, and headache. An additional 17 percent of the patients had no complaints at all.

Some women are rushed into such operations though their complaints are entirely unrelated to gynecology. One surgeon removed both ovaries, both fallopian tubes, and the uterus of a 25-year-old woman when she was, in fact, suffering from eye trouble.

These abuses are the exception rather than the rule. Your best bet is to consult a specialist, a board-certified fellow of the American College of Obstetricians and Gynecologists.

Fibroid tumors may not be large enough to justify the hazards of surgery. Fibroids, the commonest reason for hysterectomies, are hard, noncancerous growths ranging from grape- to grapefruit-size. Their cause is unknown. They usually appear between ages 35 and 40.

It is estimated that one out of every four or five women has fibroid tumors. If they cause no pain or discomfort, most physicians prefer to do nothing about them, since after menopause the fibroids sometimes disappear. Rapidly enlarging fibroids require surgery.

In some cases the fibroid may push against the lining of the uterus, causing heavy bleeding during menstruation or between periods. If the tumor presses against the bladder, it may cause frequent urination; if against the rectum, it may cause constipation.

Sometimes fibroids can be removed without removing the uterus. This procedure—called a myomectomy—is a good alternative for a woman who may wish to bear children in the future.

But the fibroids often grow back after the operation. If you become pregnant after a myomectomy, your uterine walls may be weakened. Your baby will most likely need to be delivered by cesarean section.

Other common reasons for hysterectomy include severe hemorrhaging; life-threatening infection; and cancer of the endometrium (uterine lining), cervix, ovary, or fallopian tube.

Removal of the uterus terminates menstruation and brings an end to childbearing. For many women these changes require psychological adjustments that merit frank discussion with the doctor. Unlike tubal ligation hysterectomy is not a preferred surgical method of birth control.

Hysterectomy and sex. Hysterectomy needn't affect your ability to enjoy sex. Along with other sensations of orgasm, some women can perceive the uterus contract, a feeling lost with hysterectomy. But the vagina and the clitoris, which respond to sexual stimuli, are not affected by removal of the uterus. In fact many couples find increased pleasure in sex once the possibility of pregnancy is eliminated.

A woman's ovaries are not removed in a simple hysterectomy. If the ovaries are diseased and must be removed at the same time as the uterus, the operation is known as an oophorectomy and hysterectomy. Removal of the ovaries will bring about premature menopause.

Removal of the uterus alone does not bring on premature menopausal problems. Contrary to widespread misapprehension, a hysterectomy will not cause wrinkles or hairiness. It is also untrue that either type of hysterectomy makes a woman grow fat, shrinks her breasts, or causes emotional problems.

Ask your surgeon about having a vaginal rather than an abdominal incision. The vaginal hysterectomy requires more skill than the abdominal and is generally considered quicker and safer. It often requires a briefer hospital stay and a briefer convalescence than the abdominal hysterectomy. A hysterectomy usually requires about a week in the hospital and three to four weeks for recovery.

See also MENOPAUSE; SURGERY.

ICE See FALLS THROUGH ICE.

ICE SKATING outdoors will be more comfortable if you wear two pairs of socks, a light cotton pair next to the skin and a woolen or synthetic one on top. Your feet will be warmer and you'll get fewer blisters. For figure skating indoors wear one pair of lightweight socks.

Make sure your skates fit properly. A too-tight skate can cut circulation and cause frostbite of toes. More falls occur because of improper fit than any other factor.

Wear protective headgear if you play hockey. Don't skate alone at night unless the area is well lighted and supervised.

If possible restrict youngsters' ice skating to flooded fields or shallow ponds where water is only 1 or 2 feet deep. These areas usually are the safest and form the smoothest surface.

Check the thickness of ice with a pick, or contact local authorities about skating conditions. Ice on rivers and lakes should be at least 12 inches thick for safe skating. You're safest if you skate near the shore, where water is no more than waist-deep. If you skate over deeper water, carry two ice awls and a rope with you.

The novice skater is less likely to be involved in collisions if he skates with other beginners. Learners do best with double-edged or thick-bladed hockey skates.

To prevent cuts when carrying skates, have your child cover the blades with safety guards.

See also ACCIDENTS; COLD WEATHER; FALLS THROUGH ICE; SPORTS.

ICHTHYOSIS (fish scale disease) is a fairly common hereditary skin disorder. There is a dry scaling and thickening that causes the skin to resemble fish scales. In severe forms it may affect the whole body, but in other cases it may be limited to the palms of the hands and soles of the feet.

Ichthyosis (IK-thee-O-sis) usually becomes evident shortly after birth. It may become less marked at puberty, when the activity of the oil glands greatly increases. It is often accentuated with aging when the skin becomes drier and more scaly.

The dryness, scaling, and itching are always worse in cold weather. For the person with a severe condition warmth and high humidity are most desirable. A dermatologist can recommend bath oils and skin ointments.

See also SKIN DISORDERS; SKIN DRYNESS.

IMMUNIZATION An epidemic of measles erupted in Texarkana, a Texas-Arkansas border town. Some 621 of the Texas residents became ill. But hardly any of the Arkansas side contracted the disease. Not long before, Arkansas had held an immunization drive that cut susceptibility to the disease.

Such immunity is now possible against more than a dozen types of infectious disease. But Public Health Service surveys suggest that some one of three preschool children are not adequately protected. Three out of four adults have also failed to get necessary immunizations.

Americans continue to get diphtheria, tetanus (lockjaw), whooping cough (pertussis), polio, measles, mumps, rubella (German measles)—all illnesses for which immunization should be routine (see table).

In addition for special purposes (unusual risk, exposure to infection, travel to affected areas) immunization is available against chickenpox, cholera, infectious hepatitis, influenza, Type C meningitis, plague, pneumococcal pneumonia, rabies, Rh disease, smallpox, tuberculosis, typhoid, typhus, and yellow fever.

You may be able to get many of these vaccinations free or at reduced cost through government health agencies. Ask your local health department about immunization clinics.

Keep a record of all immunizations for each member of your family, in case you change doctors or your doctor's records aren't available when you need them. Carry on your person emergency medical identification noting your most recent tetanus immunization or booster for quick reference in case of accidents.

Be realistic with children about the pain of shots. Many parents are themselves scared of the needle, and a child may sense their apprehension.

Don't tell a child a needle won't hurt when obviously it will. Instead tell him, "It'll hurt less than a beesting." Offer soothing words like "Everything will be all right before we're ready to go." Give a choice: "In which arm will it hurt less?" Ask that your child be given an ice cube in a plastic bag to rub on the site before the injection. The shot will hurt less.

Most doctors think it's a good idea to let your child watch himself being injected if he wants to. Telling him to turn his head suggests that an injection is too terrifying to be seen.

Don't tell him not to cry. That's going against nature. A better tack to take is, "Cry for two more minutes and then we'll go."

And don't make the doctor's office the subject of threats—don't say, as one mother did, "If you don't behave, I'll march you right back in for another shot!" Such threats often make children afraid of doctors.

Dangers from epidemics. Where immunization levels against a particular disease in the population fall off, it is not long before there is an upswing in the disease. Failure to immunize significant numbers of children against diphtheria was followed by epidemics of the disease in Texas and Alabama.

The neglect affects every racial, economic, and geographic group.

Because public health in recent years has been generally good, many people have been lulled into believing these myths:

"These diseases have been wiped out in this country." Not so. Scores of deaths occur every year from immunizable diseases, and incidence of some is on the rise.

"Immunizations aren't really necessary until children reach school age." On the contrary, in-

---

SPECIAL VACCINES

The following are recommended only for cases of unusual risk, exposure to infection, travel to infected areas, or the like. Consult your local health department for recommendations as to immunizations for foreign travel.

Chickenpox (zoster immune globulin)
Cholera
Hepatitis, infectious/Type A (immune serum globulin)
Hepatitis, serum/Type B
Influenza
Meningitis (Types A and C meningococci)
Plague
Pneumonia, pneumococcal
Polio (for adults)
Rabies
Rh disease (Rh immune globulin)
Smallpox
Tuberculosis (BCG vaccine)
Typhoid
Typhus
Yellow fever

---

fants are the most frequent fatalities from diphtheria and whooping cough.

"Immunizations are only for children." In fact rubella is most hazardous to women of childbearing age because the fetus may be damaged if a woman is infected with rubella in pregnancy. Perhaps the most serious effect of mumps is on the fertility of young men and women past puberty. Adults are the prime victims of tetanus and may fall victim to diphtheria.

"If you were immunized once, you're protected for life." Not true. Diphtheria and tetanus vaccines need boosters every ten years. Some other diseases—among them hepatitis and influenza—require revaccination.

How immunization works. The surest way to become immune to many infectious diseases is to contract them—and recover. When measles viruses, for example, first invade the body's tissues and begin to multiply, an intricate biochemical assembly line (in blood cells, lymph nodes, some other sites) begins to manufacture tailor-made protein molecules called antibodies. Measles antibodies react specifically with measles virus particles, thereby preventing them from invading additional cells and multiplying.

Such antibodies may help to terminate the initial illness. Thereafter if measles viruses invade the body, the antibodies are ready to keep them from multiplying and causing illness. You may develop these antibodies even though an attack of invading microorganisms did not cause symptoms. Thus by the time you're an adult, you almost certainly are protected against whooping cough or measles, though you never had the disease.

Almost all forms of preventive immunization trigger this natural line of defense without causing the initial illness. The immunizing agent must be so much like the disease-causing agent that—even though it causes no significant disease itself—it induces the production of antibodies that neutralize the real thing.

Polio or measles viruses can be killed by chemical or heat treatment. Toxins like the poisons produced by the bacteria that cause tetanus or diphtheria can be altered so they cause no illness. Yet the antibodies produced in response to these will react with polio or measles viruses and tetanus or diphtheria toxin and prevent illness.

Or, for the same purpose, living—but still harmless—agents can be used. The cowpox virus, though seldom harmful to humans, is so similar to the smallpox virus that the antibodies it stimulates also protect against smallpox. When no such close cousin occurs in nature, sci-

WHAT IMMUNIZATIONS DO YOU NEED?

Here are the recommendations of public health authorities. Consult a physician about your individual immunization. Some people are prone to side effects, and immunization practices may vary depending on local needs.

Adults (16 and over)		
All adults, any age	DT (diphtheria–tetanus) booster	Repeat every 10 years
"	Mumps	If not immune (from disease or vaccine)
All females, any age	Rubella	If not immune. Must not be pregnant or become pregnant for 2 months

Infants (in first year)		
2 months old "	1st DTP (diphtheria tetanus–pertussis) 1st oral polio	Usually given together
4 months old	2nd DTP	Can be given together
	2nd oral polio	
6 months old	3rd DTP	

Older Children (to 16)		
15 months old	Tuberculin test	At least 2 days before measles vaccination (Recommended mainly for high-risk areas.)
" " "	Measles Mumps Rubella	Can be given together
18 months old	3rd oral polio	
	4th DTP	
2–6 years old	Meningitis	Protects against *Haemophilus influenzae* bacteria (most common cause)
5–6 years old	DTP booster	On beginning school—and every 10 years thereafter
"	Polio booster	On beginning school
Up to 15 years old	Measles	If not immune. (There is little danger of getting measles after 15.)
15–16 years old	DT booster	And every 10 years thereafter

entists can sometimes create one. To make live-virus polio vaccine, disease-causing polio viruses are "tamed" by repeated passage through tissues to produce a new strain that produces no significant illness but still triggers the production of polio antibodies.

These are techniques of active immunization, which causes the body to make its own antibodies. In time the antibodies to a particular disease may gradually decline in number and your ability to ward off the disease may diminish. But some sort of biochemical memory device remains. When a comparatively small booster dose of the vaccine is given, additional antibodies are made until a high level of protection is reestablished. Thus the need to get boosters against tetanus and diphtheria at least every ten years.

In passive immunization antibodies already made by other human beings or animals are injected to provide partial or temporary protection, generally in the form of serum globulin, as against hepatitis, chickenpox, or Rh disease. These borrowed antibodies gradually disappear. They leave no biological memory behind and require fresh vaccinations. The relatively short-lived immunity of newborn infants to many infectious diseases is based on antibodies borrowed from the mother before birth.

See also INFECTIOUS DISEASE.

IMPETIGO is an infection of the skin that is caused by either staphylococcus or streptococcus bacteria, both of which commonly inhabit the nose and throat. The infection may be introduced by minor scratches, insect bites, or rashes. It is most common in young children.

An impetigo sore starts with a blister that can be as tiny as a pinpoint or as large as a pea. It itches somewhat, and soon breaks, leaving a shallow, open patch that is then covered by a honey-colored crust. When this crust is moistened and removed, a red, weeping surface of skin is exposed which quickly crusts over again. The favorite sites for impetigo are usually those areas of the skin that are uncovered, such as the face, arms, and legs.

See a physician. Prompt treatment with an antibiotic, usually penicillin, can prevent serious complications.

Try to keep a child from scratching, which can spread infection. If you like, you can remove crusts with soap and water, using a soft washcloth and gentle rubbing.

If this seems painful to a child, fill the bathtub with warm water, add soap, give him some toys to play with, and let him stay in the tub for half an hour to an hour. The crusts will float off without causing pain.

Children are often infected by bodily contact with playmates or brothers or sisters who have the condition. To help stop the spread of infection, wash an infected child's hands and face three or four times a day with rubbing alcohol. As a general preventive, have all members of your family use separate washcloths and towels.

See also SKIN DISORDERS.

IMPOTENCE, the inability to achieve or sustain an erection, is most commonly caused by fatigue from working too long or hard.

Every man experiences times he's unable to have an erection. If he attempts sexual intercourse on such occasions, he's certain to be impotent. Contrary to the myth of the ever-ready male, such episodes of transient or acute impotence are normal, indeed virtually inevitable. But if a husband or wife becomes anxious about the supposed failure, emotional stress is likely to build up and the problem may become chronic.

Much of the anxiety couples suffer in respect to impotence stems from what Dr. William H. Masters and his wife/associate Virginia E. Johnson call "phallic fallacies." Masters and Johnson, whose work at the Masters & Johnson Institute in St. Louis has revolutionized the understanding and treatment of sexual dysfunction, note that more misinformation has been perpetrated about the penis than about any other organ.

An erection develops when muscles close off a vein leading from the penis. Blood flowing into the penis through arteries fills spongy tissue called the corpora cavernosa. This engorgement causes the organ to enlarge and stiffen.

Myriad factors can interfere with the process. Here are the major reasons a man may not be able to have an erection:

He's trying too hard. Our culture makes sexual prowess essential to the self-esteem of most men. The villain in many cases of impotence is a mythic great lover some sex therapists call Super Stud. This fantasy bedroom athlete—with his push-button erection and monumental staying power—has as little relation to real-life lovemaking as Batman has to crime-fighting. But Super Stud sets the standard for much of America's sex life.

Such unrealistic expectations can place tremendous pressure on men. "Impotence is very commonly caused by fear of failure and anxiety over performing," notes psychologist Wardell Pomeroy, formerly of the Institute for Sex Research. "Pressures over *having* to achieve an erection (sometimes applied by the wife but more often by the husband) need to be eliminated first. The act of 'willing' oneself to get or maintain an erection is the very pressure that must be avoided."

Just the attempt to will an erection may breed failure. Then a vicious circle begins. Each failure weakens confidence, and the next attempt becomes more difficult. Anxiety increases—and leads to repeated failure. Finally the man becomes convinced he has lost his sexual powers.

He's ill. Any debilitating acute illness—influenza, for example—can render a man incapable of intercourse until recovery is complete. Chronic diseases—especially diabetes, Addison's disease, hypothyroidism—may have impotence as a symptom.

It was long believed that 90 percent of impotence was due to emotional causes. Now, however, it appears that illness and injury contribute to or cause about half of all cases. Thus if you suffer from impotence, seek a thorough physical examination.

A man who's had a heart attack is often impotent out of baseless fear of incurring another attack during orgasm. Talk to your doctor about when you can safely resume sexual activity.

He's blocked by medication. Some drugs for lowering high blood pressure commonly have impotence as a side effect. The antihypertensives most often implicated include reserpine (Serpasil), guanethidine (Ismelin), hexamethonium (Methium), and methyldopa (Aldomet).

Many tranquilizers—Librium, Valium, Equanil, Miltown—and antidepressants (Tofranil, Parnate, Marplan) can cause impotence. Amphetamines, used in diet and pep pills, can produce impotence and general loss of interest in sex. So can a wide variety of other medications. Ask your physician if medication you are taking could be interfering with sexual response.

Merely switching to another medication for the same condition may restore some men's potency.

He's drunk too much. Many men try to overcome inhibition or sexual difficulty by drinking to loosen up. But the alcohol itself leads to impotence.

Dr. Sallie S. Schumacher, program director of the sex clinic at the Long Island Jewish Medical Center, finds that as little as two drinks can block an erection. That one drink too many explains why many couples, after returning from a party, are disappointed when they try to make love.

He resents his wife. There may be disagreements over managing the children or budget. Or perhaps a wife assumes a more dominant role in the household because the husband is passive or absent. If he resents this, psychiatrists believe

that he may not be able to express it—except by becoming impotent.

Fear of causing pregnancy can cause impotence. Some men become impotent only during the times of the month their wives are most likely to conceive.

He feels inadequate. Job tensions can leave a man feeling worthless and unable to perform. Often impotence follows a symbolic loss of potency in work: not getting a raise, losing a job, being passed over for promotion.

Unconsciously some men still regard themselves as little boys. Their fear of sex may be masked by Victorian attitudes or by excessive complaints of tiredness. Psychiatrist Robert N. Rutherford of the University of Washington believes the typical such male comes from a household dominated by a mother who controlled him by threatening to withdraw her love if he wasn't a good boy. Among the evils of life she conveyed to him was sex.

When impotence arises as a problem early in marriage, notes Dr. John Reckless, it may be due to the man's fear of his wife in orgasm. "He may have been brought up to believe, 'Nice girls don't enjoy sex that much!' "

He's overeaten. After a heavy meal the blood rushes to the stomach, liver, and intestines, which may make it difficult to sustain an erection.

Overweight and poor physical condition impair sexual performance. Active sexual intercourse requires a vigorous body.

He's worried about aging. Once impotent under any circumstances, report Masters and Johnson, many older men conclude, "It's all over for me." They withdraw from sexual intercourse altogether rather than face the ego-shattering experience of repeated impotence.

In fact men—and women—can remain sexually active through their eighties, at least.

Starting at 50 or so a man may notice it takes him longer to achieve an erection and it may be somewhat softer. In addition, with age, he may feel less need to ejaculate or ejaculation may take longer. Counsels Dr. Wardell Pomeroy: "He should think of it as a delightful prolongation of an always pleasurable act." The changes need not interfere with the effectiveness or pleasure of intercourse.

Psychiatrist Beverley T. Mead of Creighton University School of Medicine draws this comparison for older men: "At 70 you're not the sprinter or tennis player that you were at 20 or 30, but it doesn't mean you have to give up the game. In fact if you keep playing the game regularly, you'll remain pretty good, but if you remove yourself the road back is harder."

He's depressed. A man may not be aware of an underlying mental depression. But along with a case of the blues he may lose his desire or ability for sex. The condition often occurs in the forties or fifties as part of a midlife crisis, when a man feels he's peaked out at work and everything—job, home life, health—is downhill from now on.

Other signs pointing to mental depression are impaired energy, difficulty getting to sleep or getting up, forgetfulness, bouts of agitated behavior. Clearing up the depression usually clears up the impotence.

Quack impotency cures. In this field quackery runs amok. Steer clear of unlicensed "practitioners" and "sex counselors." Dozens of impotent men who have come to Masters and Johnson had suffered further psychological damage at the hands of unscrupulous promoters.

The only medications and devices of help in impotence require a doctor's prescription. A physician may find value for you in a type of splint for use in keeping a penis erect or in a battery-operated mechanism that raises an erection through electrical stimulation of the groin. For organic impotence—caused by disease, surgery, injury—a new development is an inflatable silicone device that can be implanted in the penis.

All advertised drugs are junk, despite their suggestive brand names. Nor has any food any value as a sexual stimulator. Olives, ginseng, plover's eggs, oysters, radishes, mangoes, and countless other edibles and not-so-edibles have been used as aphrodisiacs. There is no evidence that any has more than a placebo effect—if you believe something increases your potency, it well may, since your most important sex organ is your brain.

Recently multivitamin and vitamin E preparations have been promoted as aids to sexual vigor. Vitamins are of no value in impotence. One supposed impotence pill widely sold at health food stores contained such useless ingredients as papaya leaves, prickly ash bark, ground cockleburrs, and radish powder.

Royal jelly, from bees, has been found worthless for restoring potency. Be wary of products that contain male hormones. Their value in the treatment of impotence is limited to specific medical conditions, and they can be dangerous if used without medical supervision.

For remedies that work see SEX DISORDER. For a sex problem sometimes regarded as a form of impotence see PREMATURE EJACULATION.

INCONTINENCE   See BEDWETTING.

INDIGESTION (hyperacidity, heartburn, upset stomach, intestinal gas) bothers everyone at one time or another. Typically, after a meal you repeatedly burp and may feel a pressure or burning sensation below your ribs. You may feel bloated and pass gas. Nausea is common.

When your stomach is upset, eat light, nonirritating foods such as tea and toast. Drinking milk may help.

Antacids neutralize stomach acid and will usually bring relief. A bout of indigestion is a good time to cut down on smoking, which aggravates heartburn.

Prevent indigestion by not overeating. Don't eat too fast. Avoid spicy dishes and other foods that upset you.

Emotional problems can cause stomach upset. Stress may result in indigestion in children as well as adults.

Children's stomach upset is occasionally caused by swallowing foreign objects. If you know your child has eaten something inedible, call your doctor.

Usually small objects pass harmlessly through the stomach and intestines and are excreted. Examine the child's bowel movements for the object. The child should have a normal diet.

Don't give a child laxatives. Only rarely do swallowed objects have to be removed by surgery.

Don't ignore chronic indigestion. If your stomach feels upset after nearly every meal or if your indigestion is severe, see a doctor. There are many serious conditions that might account for chronic abdominal discomfort.

See also ANTACIDS; APPENDICITIS; CANCER OF THE STOMACH; DIVERTICULITIS; FOOD POISONING; GALLBLADDER DISEASE; GAS; HEART ATTACK; HERNIA; INFECTIOUS DISEASE; NAUSEA; PEPTIC ULCER.

INFANT DEATH SYNDROME, SUDDEN   See CRIB DEATH.

INFANTILE PARALYSIS   See POLIO.

INFARCTION, MYOCARDIAL   See HEART ATTACK.

INFECTIOUS DISEASE can often be avoided merely by washing your hands. Many doctors believe that the current careless attitude toward hand-washing substantially increases the spread of illness.

A simple, thorough washing can remove from the skin many disease-causing microorganisms, virtually all of which can be transmitted via the hands. Few adults and fewer children take the time to wash thoroughly.

Follow a procedure adapted from surgical

scrub-downs: Remove rings, watches, bracelets, and roll up your sleeves to the elbows. Scrub your skin and nails with soap and water. Keep on hand fresh, dry towels or disposable paper ones—damp towels are a favorite breeding ground for microorganisms.

If you wash like this before and after caring for a sick person, you'll do much to keep his illness from spreading. Also cleanse your hands before each meal, before preparing food, before handling a baby, after doing housework, after going to the toilet.

To reduce the risk of infection at home, keep your family physically clean, follow standard hygienic measures, and prevent excessive accumulation of dirt and dust. However it is impossible to keep a germ-free house and compulsive cleaners generally cause their families more emotional damage than the physiological benefits justify.

Don't fall for the claims or warnings of so-called germicides. They cannot kill all the germs anywhere. Nor is it usually necessary to. Even in a closed hospital operating room, strong germ-killing solutions do not eliminate but merely reduce the number of the organisms present. In a home with people constantly coming and going, germicidal preparations have little effect.

Also think twice before buying any electrical gadget to fight household germs. The Food and Drug Administration (FDA) has seized any number of "ozone air purifiers" on the grounds their claims of destroying airborne microorganisms are false and misleading. Other mechanisms that supposedly combat infection, like the Thermatic Pulsed Shortwave Device and the Diapulse Electromagnetic Energy Generator, have also been seized.

Microorganisms. Infectious disease results from organisms, termed pathogens, whose invasion interferes with normal body functioning.

Man's microscopic enemies have annihilated armies, destroyed empires, laid regions waste. A single epidemic of the Black Death (plague), starting in Venice in 1348 and spreading across Europe, killed a quarter of the population.

It is a military axiom that victory can rest with the best medical services. Until World War II the United States always lost more men to disease than in battle. The lengthening of human life in this century, adding about 25 years of life expectancy, stems almost wholly from the reduction in deaths before age 45 from infectious diseases.

Viruses are the smallest pathogens. For the most part they are visible only under an electron microscope. The attack by viruses on cells pro-duces chickenpox; colds; most cases of encephalitis; hand, foot, and mouth disease; infectious hepatitis; influenza; measles; infectious mononucleosis; mumps; polio; rabies; rubella; shingles; smallpox; and yellow fever. Cat scratch disease, whose agent is unknown, is thought to be virus caused.

A virus is a protein substance that occupies a special kingdom between the living organism and the nonliving chemical. Viruses can reproduce with explosive rapidity—yet they do not eat or breathe. The virus acts on cells like an independently existing gene.

When a virus invades a susceptible cell, it chemically combines with the genes that command the cell's activity. The cell stops its normal function and begins serving the needs of the virus, manufacturing new viruses and dying in the process. The viruses spewing forth go on to infect other cells.

Viruses generally resist drug therapy. Since the virus exists as an integral part of the cell it has infected, the only way to kill it is to also kill the cell. The injury would not end there, for a drug that will kill infected cells will also kill noninfected ones.

Viruses are little damaged by cold or by chemical disinfectants. Medicine's best weapon against viruses is prevention, primarily through immunization. Once infection begins, the body's natural defenses may destroy the invader. To build up your resistance you'll almost always benefit from supportive care: rest, warmth, plenty of fluids and high-protein food, aspirin to relieve headache and fever. In addition doctors often prescribe antibiotics to prevent secondary infections.

The body is thought to produce a natural antivirus substance called interferon, which may be a major factor in natural recovery from virus infection. Attempts to treat virus infection by injecting interferon have been uniformly disappointing. Therefore much current research is being directed toward finding artificial ways of stimulating the body to produce larger amounts of interferon. An especially promising method involves injections of ribonucleic acid (RNA), in natural form a vital ingredient of all living cells and many viruses. Experimenters report that RNA injections have met with success in treating rabbits infected with herpes simplex, a common viral pathogen in man.

Rickettsiae are microorganisms larger and more complex than viruses. They are complete cells carrying out basic life functions. But, like viruses, they multiply only within susceptible cells.

The organisms are named for Dr. Howard Taylor Ricketts, a Chicago physician who observed them in his studies of Rocky Mountain spotted fever. Ricketts was himself killed by rickettsiae while studying another disease they cause: epidemic typhus.

Antibiotics are effective in early stages of rickettsial disease and vaccines are available. The most effective preventives are pesticides commonly used for control of insects, since most rickettsial disease is carried by infected fleas, ticks, lice, and mites. Rickettsiae have nothing to do with rickets, a disease caused by vitamin D deficiency.

Bacteria are some 10,000 times larger than viruses. They are usually classified as plants, although many are capable of locomotion by means of long filaments called flagella that enable them to swim about. Bacteria are described by their characteristic shapes: bacillus (rodlike), coccus (round), spirillum (spiral), spirochete (coiled). To help categorize a type of organism or a kind of disease, you may speak of tuberculosis bacilli and meningococcal meningitis.

Unlike viruses and rickettsiae, bacteria generally exist outside the cells they attack, usually in the spaces between cells. Most bacterial diseases result from poisons, called exotoxins, secreted by the organisms as they feed off the body cells. These exotoxins are far more damaging to body tissues than the most potent snake venom: a needle dipped in tetanus exotoxin could kill several people; a thimble of botulism exotoxin could wipe out New York City. Other bacterial diseases include brucellosis, cholera, diphtheria, gonorrhea, leprosy, leptospirosis, plague, syphilis, tularemia, typhoid, and whooping cough.

Bacteria are responsible for many cases of food poisoning and food-borne illnesses, including salmonellosis and shigellosis. Staph infections, the most common cause of food poisoning, also appear as boils and styes. Streptococci, bacteria that form necklacelike chains, cause erysipelas, rheumatic fever, scarlet fever, sinusitis, and sore throat. Both viruses and bacteria can be responsible for pneumonia.

Most bacterial infections can be relieved by penicillin and other antibiotics. For some conditions vaccination is possible.

Fungus growths—yeasts and molds—are related to mushrooms but are much smaller. Yeast cells are usually smooth and round and dwell independently. Molds generally have filaments and grow in tangled masses. Aside from structure the two organisms behave much the same. Some fungi can grow in either the yeast or mold form.

The commonest fungus disease is tinea or ringworm, a group of closely related forms of skin disorder that includes athlete's foot.

While fungus growths on the body surface can be prevented, the air and soil are so rife with easily inhaled yeast and mold that internal fungus diseases are considered virtually impossible to avoid. Histoplasmosis and coccidioidomycosis are types of respiratory disease caused by fungi.

Other causes of infectious disease:

Protozoa are one-celled animals possibly 50 times larger than bacteria. They can react readily to such stimuli as heat, chemicals, and light. Most can move about easily.

Amebas may attack the intestinal wall, causing amebiasis. Protozoa cause one of the world's most widespread diseases: malaria. A one-celled animal causes toxoplasmosis, which may cause birth defects if contracted in pregnancy.

Parasitic worms are made up of many cells. While some are microscopic, many may be seen with the naked eye. Tapeworms may grow in the intestines to a length of 30 feet.

Other intestinal worms common in this country include roundworms, pinworms, and hookworms. A roundworm causes trichinosis. In tropical countries schistosomiasis is a major parasitic disease.

You may catch many of the aforementioned illnesses from pets (see ANIMAL DISEASE). Compared with most of the rest of the world, the United States is antiseptic. As a result Americans lack resistance to diseases that are rampant elsewhere on the globe. Infectious disease is a major problem for travelers, especially in areas where water is contaminated from sewage.

See also AIDS; AMEBIASIS; ANTIBIOTICS; ATHLETE'S FOOT; BIRTH DEFECTS; BOILS; BOTULISM; BRUCELLOSIS.

CAT SCRATCH DISEASE; CHICKENPOX; CHOLERA; COCCIDIOIDOMYCOSIS; COLDS; DIPHTHERIA; ENCEPHALITIS; ERYSIPELAS; FEVER; FLEAS; FOOD POISONING.

GIARDIASIS; GONORRHEA; HAND, FOOT, AND MOUTH DISEASE; HEADACHE; HEPATITIS; HISTOPLASMOSIS; HOOKWORMS; IMMUNIZATION; INFLUENZA; INSECTS.

LEPROSY; LEPTOSPIROSIS; LICE; MALARIA; MEASLES; MENINGITIS; MONONUCLEOSIS; MUMPS.

PINWORMS; PLAGUE; PNEUMONIA; POLIO; QUACKERY; RABIES; RESPIRATORY DISEASE; RHEUMATIC FEVER; RINGWORM; ROCKY MOUNTAIN SPOTTED FEVER; ROUNDWORMS; RUBELLA.

SALMONELLOSIS; SCARLET FEVER; SCHISTOSOMIASIS; SHIGELLOSIS; SHINGLES; SINUSITIS;

SKIN DISORDERS; SMALLPOX; SORE THROAT; STYES; SYPHILIS.

TAPEWORMS; TETANUS; TICKS; TOXOPLASMOSIS; TRAVEL HEALTH; TRICHINOSIS; TUBERCULOSIS; TULAREMIA; TYPHOID; TYPHUS; WATER CONTAMINATION; WHOOPING COUGH; YELLOW FEVER.

INFECTIOUS HEPATITIS   See HEPATITIS.

INFERTILITY (sterility) affects about one in eight U.S. couples of childbearing age. A couple is considered infertile when pregnancy has not occurred after a year of normal sexual relations without the use of birth control.

If you've been trying to conceive for a year, see a doctor. If you're a woman over 35, see a doctor after six months. With treatment perhaps half of infertile couples may be able to conceive.

For a pregnancy to occur, a man must produce and discharge an adequate number of normal, moving sperm cells. The woman must ovulate, expelling a normal egg from the ovary. This egg must pass through one of the fallopian tubes, be fertilized by the sperm, carried to the uterus, and embedded there. Any disruption in this series of events can result in infertility.

The causes of infertility may lie in the man or the woman or both. Both husband and wife need to undergo an examination, including examination of their reproductive organs. For a doctor who specializes in fertility problems, seek a board-certified urologist for the man, a board-certified gynecologist for the woman. Many hospitals have outpatient fertility clinics.

Chronic medical problems may contribute to infertility. Endocrine disturbances, such as hypothyroidism, and deficiencies in the hormones from the pituitary, adrenal, and reproductive glands, all may prevent conception. Often the trouble may be traced to chronic infections, malnutrition, overweight, anemia, and various metabolic problems. Genital anomalies may be a factor.

Excessive smoking and use of alcohol may also affect fertility. When these problems can be fairly easily corrected, pregnancy may result within a few months.

Severe emotional stress—job tensions, family discord, fear of pregnancy—can slow or stop the flow of hormones, inhibiting ovulation or sperm production.

While emotional problems alone rarely cause infertility, they are an important element that needs to be considered in diagnosis and treatment.

You may be helped by altering habits surrounding intercourse. A woman who wishes to

become pregnant does well to lie in bed for a while. If she immediately gets up or if she douches after intercourse, she loses a lot of semen, thereby reducing her chances of conceiving.

A man might try having intercourse no more than every second or third day. More frequent intercourse can cause his sperm to be ejaculated before they have matured. Conversely, of course, excessively infrequent intercourse reduces chances of conception.

Sperm are damaged by excessive heat. Avoid taking long, hot baths, which can interfere with sperm production. Men who work in extremely high temperatures sometimes need to change jobs to resolve an infertility problem.

Have intercourse at times of the month when the woman is most likely to conceive. This is when she is ovulating (when her ovary has discharged an egg), about 2 weeks before her next menstrual period. In a woman with a 28-day menstruation cycle ovulation would most likely occur at about 14 days. A man who travels a lot may need to schedule his trips so he'll be home when his wife is ovulating.

If you'd like to establish the probable time of your ovulation, keep a basal body temperature graph. Just before ovulation your body temperature dips, then shows a rise that remains fairly stable until your next menstruation. Charted over several months, the graph can help you become familiar with your ovulatory pattern.

The male-superior position of sexual intercourse, with the man on top and the woman below, is thought to be best for conception. This position allows the sperm to be delivered high in the cervical canal and makes it less likely that semen will leak out. Another position may be advisable if a woman has a severely tilted uterus.

Some organic causes. Blockage of the fallopian tubes is a common cause of infertility. An obstruction may result from infection or the effects of gonorrhea. Emotional stress can cause the tubes to go into spasm.

About one in five infertile women cannot become pregnant because they fail to ovulate. Or a woman may ovulate but produce an abnormal egg. In some cases the uterus may not be properly prepared for accepting the fertilized egg because of an inadequate secretion of the female hormone progesterone. Tumors, polyps, or infections in the uterus may also prevent pregnancy. A small or tilted uterus alone will rarely keep a woman from conceiving.

Sometimes a woman has thick mucus obstructing the cervix, instead of the thin, clear mucus needed for conception. Or sperm may be repelled or destroyed by the chemical nature of the mucus, or by bacteria or other organisms. Some women develop antibodies to their husband's sperm; in effect they become immune to conception.

Men are responsible for or contribute to more than 40 percent of the cases of infertility. Too few sperm cells is a common cause of male infertility. Or the sperm may be poor swimmers, or underdeveloped. A small number of men produce no sperm at all.

Mumps may have injured the testicles, destroying their ability to produce adequate sperm. Scars from venereal disease may be obstructing the tubes through which sperm pass.

Many infertile men have congenital defects in their reproductive system. Chronic infection of the prostate may be a cause of infertility. So may undescended testicles.

Men commonly confuse infertility and virility, considering a diagnosis of sterility a blow to their manhood. But one has nothing to do with the other. A sexually active male may have poor semen, while a man with little interest in sex can be perfectly fertile.

Here is how medical science is treating some common causes of infertility:

For the woman who fails to ovulate, drugs that stimulate the ovaries to produce mature eggs are available. These drugs sometimes induce multiple ovulation, and may lead to twins, triplets, and other multiple births.

Mildly blocked fallopian tubes frequently open during the examination procedure. Several types of surgery are used—with varying degrees of success—to treat severely blocked tubes.

Cervical mucus hostile to sperm is usually treated with the female hormone estrogen. Or the husband's semen may be injected directly into the wife's uterus. Antibiotics are used to treat any bacterial infections that may be interfering with conception.

When a man has a low sperm count, it may be possible to achieve a pregnancy by obtaining a split ejaculate: The first part of the ejaculated semen—which has the highest number of active healthy sperm—is caught in a container and transferred directly into the wife's cervical canal through artificial insemination.

When a woman has severely blocked fallopian tubes that cannot be surgically opened, the egg can sometimes be fertilized with the husband's sperm in the laboratory, then injected into the woman's uterus. Several so-called "test-tube babies" have thus far been conceived through this method.

The use of tranquilizers and psychotherapy is frequently part of the medical treatment for infertility.

See also BIRTH CONTROL; PREGNANCY.

INFLUENZA (flu, grippe, catarrhal fever) is a highly contagious respiratory disease that usually occurs in epidemics beginning in the late fall and winter. Each epidemic lasts locally from four to six weeks. The word *influenza* comes from the Italian word for *influence,* which expressed the medieval concept that this mysteriously recurring ailment was due to the influence of the stars.

Most flu is caused by two strains of viruses, A and B. Type A epidemics tend to occur every two to three years, Type B—generally milder—every four to five. There is little cross-immunity between strains, even between families within a strain. A person who has recovered from a Type A_1 flu may still catch Type A_2 as well as any of the Type Bs.

A pandemic consists of a worldwide spread of a virus. In an ordinary year only a small percentage of the population comes down with influenza. In a pandemic from 20 to 40 percent of the population may become ill with influenza.

Great pandemics seem to return at intervals of 10 to 12 years. The pandemic of 1918 is said to have killed 21 million people, second only to the plague in the fourteenth century as a medical catastrophe. Swift modern transportation makes for even faster transmission of the influenza epidemic virus.

In an epidemic flu is most likely to strike children 5 to 9 years old and adults 25 to 35. The death rate is highest in infants and in those over 50. Flu is also especially perilous to people with heart disease and such chronic lung diseases as tuberculosis, chronic bronchitis, and emphysema. Pregnant women too have an increased fatality rate from influenza.

The onset of flu is sudden. There are chills, headache, muscular aches in the back and limbs. Temperature goes up quickly to 101° F or as high as 104° F. There may be frequent coughing. The face is often flushed, the throat red. There may be some inflammation of the eyelids and a watery nasal discharge.

How can you tell if you have influenza or just a bad cold? If you have a fever—particularly a high fever—you most likely have influenza. Colds are rarely accompanied by fever.

Symptoms develop one to three days after exposure. Two or 3 days of fever may leave you exhausted and in low spirits for some time.

Complicating bacterial infections are a great

danger, particularly pneumonia, sinusitis, ear infections, and bronchitis. Hence consult a doctor for fever lasting longer than a few days and for such unusual symptoms as shortness of breath, continuing hoarseness, hard coughing, blood-stained sputum, pain in the chest.

What to do. Go to bed when symptoms start. Keep warm and out of drafts. Wear a warm robe and slippers if you have to get out of bed. Eat simple foods that agree with you. Drink plenty of water or other fluids. Take aspirin or acetaminophen for headache.

No known medicine will cure influenza. Sulfa, penicillin, and other antibiotics have no effect upon it, although they are used to combat some of the complications that may follow. Getting well without developing complications depends on giving your body every advantage while it fights the infection.

Ignore antiflu promises made by manufacturers of remedies for colds. None is more effective than plain aspirin.

During an epidemic the community air becomes laden with viruses. It is almost impossible to avoid getting in the path of a few coughs and sneezes. However practicing good health habits such as getting plenty of rest and eating regular, well-balanced meals will help keep up your resistance to infection.

For the short duration of an epidemic avoid crowded places, such as movies and dances. At school or work keep a distance from people who do not cover their coughs and sneezes with a handkerchief or tissue.

If you have flu, cover your nose and mouth with paper tissue whenever you cough or sneeze, and drop these tissues at once into a paper bag. Replace these bags frequently and wash your hands after disposing of the used bags. Take special care during the early stages of the illness, when influenza is most easily transmitted.

Flu shots. Vaccines are now available that protect against the current strains of Types A and B virus. Protection lasts only through one flu season; so people who need flu shots should get one every year.

Should you have a flu shot? In general, the answer is yes if you are over 65 or if you have:

Pulmonary disease (bronchitis, bronchial asthma, emphysema, pulmonary fibrosis, tuberculosis).

Cardiovascular disease (heart trouble of any kind, hypertension, arteriosclerosis).

Kidney disease (nephritis, pyelonephritis, uremia).

Metabolic disease (diabetes, gout, hypoglycemia, thyroid disease).

A neurologic disease (epilepsy, multiple sclerosis, Parkinson's disease).

Weak or paralyzed respiratory muscles.

The U.S. Public Health Service Advisory Committee on Immunization Practices recommends that people who are elderly or have chronic diseases receive influenza immunization before the start of the flu season. If a new strain raises the threat of severe epidemic, the committee may advise widespread vaccination.

Routine vaccination for healthy infants, children, and adults is not recommended. In these persons flu is comparatively mild and a quick recovery is usual. Moreover, at best immunization is effective for only about 65 percent of people inoculated.

The vaccine is dangerous for patients with an allergy to eggs (the growth medium) or chickens and for those with a history of allergic reactions. Pregnancy is not a bar to being vaccinated, but should be avoided in the first trimester if possible.

If you need a flu shot, don't wait until influenza is already in your neighborhood. The human body requires two weeks to build up full resistance.

Your immunization will require two injections if you have never had a flu shot. The first one should be given in midautumn and the second shot two months later. A single booster shot sometime in late fall is sufficient if you have been previously inoculated.

Reactions to flu shots are usually mild and can be relieved by aspirin. But flu shots may interfere with your body's ability to metabolize other medication—such as asthma medication or anticoagulant drugs. If you are taking medications such as these at the time of your flu shot, you should be carefully monitored by your physician for several weeks.

Flu vaccines are under constant revision. So if you need the shot, check with your doctor every fall to arrange for a booster shot of the latest vaccine.

From time to time new strains of influenza develop. Epidemics may then occur because people have not had any previous exposure to the new strains and have not acquired any immunity. Existing flu vaccines may not be effective against the new strain, and a new vaccine must be developed.

The daily use of amantadine (Symmetrel) may also help prevent influenza A (but not B) infections. Starting before or immediately after exposure to influenza A, and continuing throughout the period of exposure for up to 90 days, amantadine prevents the flu in about 70 percent of healthy adults. In people who have been previously vaccinated, the effectiveness of the drug is enhanced. Its main usefulness is in nursing-home patients or other high-risk patients during a widespread outbreak in the community. Amantadine has also been shown effective in early treatment (within 48 hours of the onset of symptoms) of influenza A infections.

When it is not flu. One type of flu has nothing to do with influenza. The bug responsible for much of midwinter misery is the more modest Coxsackie virus.

It is one of the most common forms of viral infection. Named after the small Upstate New York town where it was first identified in 1948, the bug usually causes diarrhea and sometimes nausea, as well as muscular pains, fever, and a general ache-all-over feeling.

Coxsackie viral infections begin increasing during the late summer and reach a peak in the late winter. Rarely serious, the infection also rarely if ever succumbs to medical treatment. It runs its course by itself. Aspirin may relieve the discomfort.

See also INFECTIOUS DISEASE; RESPIRATORY DISEASE.

INFLUENZA, SUMMER See HISTOPLASMOSIS.

INGROWN HAIRS may develop after shaving when the ends of coarse, curly beard hairs curve back and reenter the skin. Skin disorders such as irritation, swelling, and infection may result. To avoid ingrown hairs:

Don't shave too close or against the grain. Clipping off whiskers beneath the surface of the skin encourages ingrowing.

Use a sharp blade. The more pressure you must exert because of a dull blade, the greater the angle of the cut edge of the whisker. A sharply angulated hair is more likely to curl inward.

Experiment to find out whether electric or wet shaving gives you the least trouble.

Grow a beard, if not permanently, then during a vacation, to allow irritation and infection to clear up.

If the problem persists, consult a physician to discuss removing the ingrowing hairs by electrolysis.

See also HAIRINESS.

INGROWN TOENAILS result when the edges of the nail curve downward, penetrating the soft flesh of the toe. The big toe is most often affected.

The tendency for the corners of the nail to curve downward is sometimes hereditary. Much more commonly, the problem develops because tight shoes or socks put pressure on the toenails, or because toenails are clipped like fingernails—to an oval or pointed shape.

Ingrown toenails are usually swollen, red, painful, and may become infected.

Have a physician or a podiatrist treat your ingrown toenail. He may pack wet dressings under the nail at its edges and thin the nail at its center to encourage flattening. One doctor recommends placing adhesive tape under the edge of the nail, so that the nail will grow over the tape instead of through the skin.

Severe and recurrent cases may require surgery that includes removing the nail at its origin in the nail bed, in an attempt to permanently correct the sharp arc.

To prevent ingrown toenails trim your toenails off straight, leaving the corners exposed. They're easier to cut after a bath. Wear properly fitted socks, stockings, and shoes.

See also FOOT PROBLEMS.

INGUINAL HERNIA See HERNIA.

INSECTS and similar vermin transport armies of viruses, bacteria, and other causes of infectious disease. Chief disease carriers include flies, mosquitoes, and ticks. Insects cause other problems as well.

Insect stings—from bees, hornets, wasps, red ants—are a frequent cause of severe allergy. Toxic reactions can result from caterpillars, centipedes, scorpion stings, spider bites. Maddening itching is a major symptom of scabies (infestation by mites) and a result of attacks by bedbugs, chiggers, fleas, lice. Cockroaches are nuisances and may be harmful.

Insecticides. Any chemical for use against pests may cause poisoning. All have some degree of toxicity—despite label claims like "safe" or "nonpoisonous to children and pets." Inhaling and skin contact can be as poisonous as swallowing. You can die from getting in your eye a single drop of parathion, one of the highly toxic organophosphates.

In case of insecticide poisoning call a physician or get to a hospital emergency room. The most valuable information you can have at hand is often on the container: the chemical formulations of the insecticide and the recommended first aid.

Most household insecticides are slow enough acting in humans to allow time for calm, deliberate first aid. Severe poisoning from a single, short exposure to an insecticide spray is rare, since concentrations in sprays are low. If symptoms worsen, or persist after an hour, consider yourself poisoned and get medical help.

For children the insecticide hazard is more critical. Consult a physician in any case of possible poisoning of a youngster, especially a baby or small child. About half of all deaths attributable to insecticides occur in children accidentally exposed at home.

Never use insecticides on nursery walls, playpens, cribs, toys, or places where infants creep. Use as little of any product as will do the job. Don't mix or store pesticides in bowls, pans, or bottles normally used for food.

Try not to stock insecticides. Buy them only as they are needed. When they must be stored in the house, keep them in a locked cabinet, preferably not in a room that is constantly lived in. Spray cans of insecticide can explode or leak under some storage conditions, as in a hot closet.

Use no pesticides in the home unless absolutely necessary. Insect pests are not likely to be attracted to your kitchen if you keep foods, garbage, ripe fruit, and dry staples well covered and if you rinse out glasses promptly. Insects have little interest in dry, well-aired, uncluttered basements.

Screens are the most important barrier against flying insects. Where small, biting sand flies or eye gnats are troublesome, use the finer 18 × 18-mesh rather than the common 16 × 16-mesh screening. Frames should fit snugly to block ants and other crawlers.

Seal cracks. Caulk thoroughly around window, pipe, and door openings, at the top of the foundation, and under eaves. Cement cracks in basement floors or walls and putty holes in siding. Cover attic ventilators and other apertures with fine-mesh screening.

If nonchemical measures prove inadequate, use the least hazardous chemical that will do the job. Read the label to determine contents, and start off with a product that poses the least hazard. Only if that doesn't work, use the next most dangerous preparation.

First choice: For both flying and crawling insects the least hazardous products are based on pyrethrins or allethrin plus agents such as piperonyl butoxide or MGK 264. These substances are low to moderate in toxicity and last from merely an hour to a few days. Asthmatics and people sensitive to pollen should avoid pyrethrins.

Second choice: Moderately hazardous for indoor use are methoxychlor, propoxur, diazinon, and chlordane. They can form a residual coating that may contaminate surfaces for many months. Don't use them in a household with small children or pets. For gardens, use carbaryl (Sevin), chlordane, diazinon, and malathion.

Third choice: Highly hazardous are traps for crawling insects that contain Kepone, a chemical high in toxicity and lasting-power. Don't use such ant and roach traps where there are small children or pets.

Don't use: Too hazardous for household use are dichlorvos—common in sprays and vaporizing strips—and lindane, widely used in fumigating smoke, shelf paper, and floor waxes. Both highly toxic chemicals continue to vaporize for months and are suspected of being health hazards to those who inhale them.

Also avoid ant and roach traps that contain arsenicals. These compounds are highly toxic and long-lasting. If spilled from the trap, they may be swallowed or come in contact with the skin.

In fruit and vegetable gardens never use systemic pesticides sold for flowers and other ornamentals. These chemicals poison the entire plant, including supposedly edible parts. Most systemic pesticides contain organophosphates and carbamates, which are highly toxic and best avoided.

When spraying or dusting pesticide, cover or remove all foodstuffs and cooking and eating utensils. Clear everybody else out of the room. Remove pets, birds, and fish. Outdoors, spray with the wind so solution or dust doesn't blow in your face.

Wear plastic or rubber gloves when you mix or apply insecticides, and follow label directions to the letter. Wash your face and hands and other exposed parts of the skin with soap and water afterward. If insecticides are accidentally spilled, remove all contaminated clothing immediately and wash your skin thoroughly. Launder or clean the clothes before wearing them again.

Before using a space spray, close the windows. Start spraying at the far side of the room. Spray your way out of the door, and close it. Do not reenter for at least 15 minutes. Ventilate the room thoroughly when you do.

When the more hazardous longer-lasting poisons are called for, use a liquid brand to be brushed on. Apply only in spot applications when possible, and only on baseboards, edges of floors, lower parts of walls, and shelves below table height. If you find it necessary to apply the more hazardous chemicals by spraying, be sure the room is well ventilated.

Avoid breathing sprays and dusts. When using dusts in quantity, wear a gauze mask available at drugstores. Never use spray near an open flame or while you are smoking—it may explode.

Repellents. In personal insect repellents look for a product registered with the EPA (Environmental Protection Agency), a sign of its safety and effectiveness. If a particular type of bug bothers you, buy only products that list it on an EPA-approved label. All EPA-registered repellents work against mosquitoes; none discourages such stinging insects as bees or wasps.

The best all-around repellent is "deet," which may be identified on the label as diethyl toluamide or N,N-diethyl-metal-toluamide. Another repellent, oilier on the skin and not as versatile as deet, is ethyl hexanediol (or 2-ethyl-1,3-hexanediol).

Sprays are the most convenient to apply to skin and clothing, but are bulky to carry and contain relatively low percentages of active ingredients. Sprays with the highest percentages of deet include Sportsmate II Spray, Deep Woods Pressurized Formula Off!, Cutter Foam, and Cutter Spray. Other types of repellents highest in deet include Sportsmate II Cream, Off! Towelettes, Deep Woods Formula Off! Lotion, Cutter Cream Formula, and Cutter Stick.

When applying repellent, avoid the lips and areas around the eyes. Don't use a spray directly on your face. Spread the product as you would a liquid, with your palms.

Warn children not to rub their eyes after their skin has been coated. Keep containers out of the reach of children. Repellents can be toxic if swallowed. You'll keep children out of harm's way if you buy a repellent with a safety cap.

You may need to reapply repellent several times if you perspire heavily, or each time you swim. The same application may protect you against some types of mosquito for as long as eight hours, against other types for only three hours, against deer flies and gnats for even less time.

On clothing apply repellent in a half-inch band on the inside edges of all openings. Treat socks from the top down below to the shoe level. On fabrics repellent isn't rubbed off as from skin, so it will often last for days.

If you're allergic to one repellent, before using another make a patch test as for hair dyeing. You may get a slightly warm feeling on the skin immediately after applying any one of them, but usually this soon goes away.

Consider a "black light insect trap" for indoor

The active ingredients of pesticides are here referred to by their *common* names. You may find that the labels on some pesticide containers in stores call the active ingredients by their *chemical* names. The accompanying table will aid you in buying the right pesticide; it shows the common and chemical name for each active ingredient.

COMMON AND CHEMICAL NAMES OF PESTICIDES

Common name	Chemical name
Diazinon	0,0-diethyl 0-(2-isopropyl-6-methyl-4-pyrimidinyl) phosphorothioate or 0,0-diethyl 0-(2-isopropyl-4-methyl-6-pyrimidinyl) phosphorothioate
Dichlorvos (DDVP)	2,2-dichlorovinyl dimethyl phosphate
Kepone	Dechachlorooctahydro-1,3,4-metheno-2H-cyclobuta(cd)pentalen-2-one
Lindane	99+%gamma-1,2,3,4,5,6-hexachlorocyclohexane
Malathion	S-[1,2,-bis(ethoxycarbonyl)ethyl] 0,0-dimethyl phosphorodithioate
Methoxychlor	1,1,1-trichloro-2,2-bis(p-methoxyphenyl) ethane
MGK 264	N-octyl bicycloheptene dicarboximide
Piperonyl butoxide	Butyl-carbityl (6-propylpiperonyl) ether
Propoxur	2-(1-Methylethoxy)phenol methylcarbamate or o-Isopropoxyphenyl methylcarbamate

use. These devices attract flying bugs with ultraviolet ("black") light and electrocute them.

Outdoors, however, such traps are a waste of money, despite promoters' promises of insect-free living in patios and other open areas. The only way such devices can work is the way commercial pest-control operators employ them around drive-in restaurants and the like: with hundreds of units positioned to draw insects away from the premises. Few families can afford that many units or have enough land around their houses to properly position the traps.

See also ALLERGY; ANTS; BEDBUGS; CATERPILLARS; CENTIPEDES; CHIGGERS; COCKROACHES; FLEAS; FLIES.

INFECTIOUS DISEASE; INSECT STINGS; ITCHING; LICE; MOSQUITOES; POISONING; SCABIES; SCORPIONS; SPIDER BITES; SPRAY CANS; TICKS.

INSECT STINGS If you are stung by a bee, wasp, yellow jacket, hornet, or red ant, your life may be in danger. Every year more Americans die from allergic reactions to insect stings than from snakebite. You can have a severe reaction if you've had merely mild reactions before, or even if you've never previously been stung.

Remove beestingers quickly as if they were splinters, tweezing or scraping them out with your fingernail. Be careful not to press the venom sac atop the stinger, for this will squeeze in more of the fluid. The female honeybee worker is the only one of the hymenoptera—this group of insects—that loses its stinger, then dies. The others can sting repeatedly without committing suicide.

Lessen the spread of venom by sucking the site of the sting and by placing a loose tourniquet above the site (see TOURNIQUET). Meat tenderizer—1/4 teaspoon in 1 or 2 teaspoons of water—rubbed on the site promptly relieves the sting (the tenderizing ingredient papain breaks down venom). A drop of household ammonia, an alkali, also reduces the stinging by neutralizing the acid venom. Ice compresses relieve the pain and swelling. Because the stung person may be in SHOCK (which see), keep him warm, lying down, with legs elevated and head lowered.

Time is the crucial factor. If within a half hour you have *any* symptoms in addition to the local swelling—or if you have a severe local reaction to a sting on the face or neck—get to a doctor as rapidly as possible. The shorter the interval between sting and development of symptoms, the greater the risk. Standard treatment calls for an emergency injection of Adrenalin. Some doctors give a shot of a local anesthetic like Xylocaine to reduce the pain.

In a highly allergic person one sting can produce shock and prove fatal within minutes. In moderately sensitive people reactions may cause widespread swellings or hives, wheezing, faintness, dizziness, vomiting, abdominal cramps, or diarrhea. There may be some shortness of breath, nasal discharge or stuffiness in the nose, and some tightness in the throat.

Occasionally there is aching and swelling of the joints, and a bruised appearance of the skin at a site distant from the sting. In mild reactions all that may develop is a large local swelling at the sting area, which may last several days and itch intensely.

Another kind of reaction can result from insect stings—a toxic reaction, which resembles the reaction to venom in snakebite, spider bites and scorpion stings. A toxic reaction may result after multiple insect stings, perhaps 30 or more at one time in healthy adults—fewer for children, the elderly, the disabled. Venom attacks the red blood cells and the nervous system to produce hemorrhages, anemia, and forms of nervous paralysis.

Precautions. If you are allergic to insect stings, ask your doctor for an emergency kit. Carry it at all times, but especially when working in the yard, on outings or picnics, while golfing, and on vacation trips. Also carry emergency medical identification warning of your allergy and giving instructions for the use of your kit.

Kits are available through pharmacies for a few dollars. Good ones are made by Center, Dome, Hollister-Stier, International Medication Systems, and Meridian Laboratories. Most commercially available kits contain a syringe of Adrenalin (epinephrine), antihistamines, barbiturates, and a tourniquet. Add coins so you can phone for help. Also add a tweezer or razor for removing a stinger and an antiseptic towelette (like Wash 'n Dri). Check the Adrenalin regularly since it may lose its effectiveness and turn brown. The medication will last longer if kept away from light, refrigerated if possible.

Desensitizing treatment is a prolonged process, but can be lifesaving. It is recommended only for people who have had severe systemic reactions to insect stings. A small amount of the insect's venom is injected once a week in increasing doses for 8 to 15 weeks or longer—until it reaches the amount injected by the insect in one or two of its stings. Once the maintenance dosage has been reached, treatment gradually works down to once a month. In many cases therapy must continue for the rest of the sufferer's life.

Even after desensitizing treatment, it is wise to be equipped with an emergency kit. You may receive multiple stings by the insect you're sensitive to, and your protection may not be adequate for such a large amount of venom. You may be stung by an insect you have not been immunized against. You may be among the small number of treated patients (about 5 percent) who do not become adequately immunized, and thus may experience severe reactions if they are stung.

To help avoid stings stay away from known nest sites. Sit quietly—without swatting—if a stinging insect lands on any part of your body. If you have an allergy to stings, avoid eating outdoors and air-condition your car so car windows can be closed during warm weather. Be especially careful around flowers, since most of these insects feed on pollen and nectar.

Keeping food covered until the moment of disposal, meticulous cleanliness about the garbage area, repeated spraying of patio and garbage cans with insecticide—all will help keep insects away. Yellow jackets like protein and are attracted by hot dogs and hamburgers set out by unwary picnickers.

Garden carefully. Electric hedge clippers, tractors, and power mowers should not be used by persons sensitive to insect stings. Accidentally penetrating a bumblebee's nest or mowing over a yellow jacket's nest will infuriate the insects.

If you're sensitive, don't use hair spray, perfume, pomade, suntan lotion, or other aromatic cosmetics that attract insects. Smooth clothing is less attractive to insects than rough; clean is safer than sweaty. Wear white, green, tan, and khaki. Avoid bright colors, flowery prints, and black.

Don't kick dead logs—the vibrations may disturb nearby yellow jackets. Stay away from public trash baskets at parks. Keep an insecticide bomb in the glove compartment of your car, and wear shoes when outdoors except on a hard, sandy beach. (One type of wasp spends most of its life on dune grass.) Sandals are not adequate protection, but sneakers are.

Removing nests is essential, but get help if you're allergic. Although some types of hymenoptera are more combative than others, every type will sting readily if its hive is molested (see illustration).

Get rid of a wasp's nest at night, when the insects are less active. Scrape the nest into a jar or pail and cover quickly. Spray the area with an insecticide for two to three days to discourage rebuilding.

Yellow jackets build in the ground and emerge through a small hole. Mark the hole with a thin stick. At dusk, when all the insects have re-

STINGING INSECTS—AND WHERE THEY LIVE

Yellow Jacket

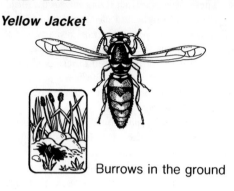

Burrows in the ground

Wasp

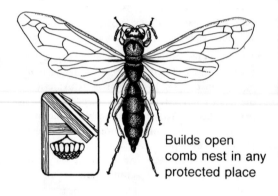

Builds open comb nest in any protected place

Honeybee

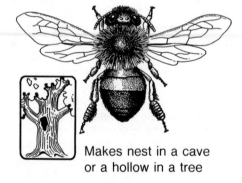

Makes nest in a cave or a hollow in a tree

Hornet

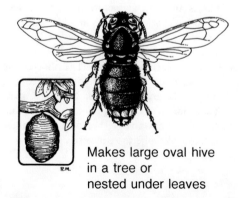

Makes large oval hive in a tree or nested under leaves

turned for the night, pour gasoline or kerosene freely down the hole. It need not be lighted. Lye may be used in the same way. Repeat the following evening in case the fumes have not penetrated to every crevice. Never point a water hose at the hole, for this can cause the enraged insects to sting you unmercifully.

Hornets build gray football-shaped hives, usually in shrubs or trees, often high or far out on a branch. If the nest cannot be reached by a flaming torch or cannot be clipped into a jar or pail, an exterminator with poison gas, or the fire department with the aid of extension ladders, may succeed in removing it.

Honeybees, whether swarming on a twig or nesting in a hollow tree, may be removed by a beekeeper, who frequently is delighted to have an extra colony for his trouble.

See also ALLERGY; INSECTS.

INSOMNIA See SLEEPLESSNESS.

INSURANCE, DISABILITY See HEALTH INSURANCE.

INTESTINAL CANCER See CANCER OF THE COLON AND RECTUM.

INVALIDS See BEDREST.

IODINE See MINERALS; THYROID DISEASE.

IRON is necessary for forming red blood cells. Insufficient iron can sometimes result in iron deficiency anemia, the chief symptom of which is excessive tiredness.

Lack of iron is the most widespread nutritional failing in the United States. Women of childbearing age are most frequently deficient, largely because of blood lost in menstruation. Children under two are also frequently deficient.

Iron—one of several minerals your body needs—is particularly important during pregnancy and breastfeeding. A physician often prescribes supplemental iron to ensure a woman is getting enough.

Sources of iron. Eat dark-green vegetables, seafood, and meat. Iron-rich green vegetables include kale, watercress, turnip greens, beet greens. (See the table of food values under NUTRITION for amounts of iron in various foods.)

Seafood, such as clams, shrimp, and oysters, is high in iron. So are lean meat, fish, and poultry. Organ meats—liver, heart, kidney—provide a particularly rich supply.

Other good sources include eggs, dried beans and lentils, dried fruit, nuts, brewer's yeast, and whole grain or enriched breads and cereals.

Many iron-rich foods—particularly meat, fish, poultry, and eggs—are also high in protein and vitamins.

Don't force a child to eat spinach. It was once thought a particularly good source of iron. Actually it is not as iron rich as many other foods.

Iron supplements. Don't buy supplemental iron products to self-treat tiredness. Fatigue is a symptom of many conditions besides anemia. And anemia can result from many conditions besides inadequate iron intake.

Your physician can determine whether you need more iron and can prescribe supplemental iron preparations. If you have trouble getting sufficient iron in your diet, he may recommend some form of continuous iron supplementation, perhaps an over-the-counter iron product. The iron may make your bowel movement black; it is no cause for worry.

If you already have normal iron levels, a supplement will do you no good. Unnecessary iron supplements may cause constipation, cramps, or diarrhea. An overdose of iron can be fatal to children.

Let your doctor know you're taking iron supplements before he prescribes any other medication. Iron can cause adverse reactions in combination with penicillin, phenothiazine tranquilizers (Compazine, Phenergan, Thorazine), and some drugs for high blood pressure and gout.

If you're taking iron supplements, drink alcohol sparingly. Alcohol increases iron absorption and can overload the blood with iron. People who try to counter the effects of heavy drinking with doses of vitamins and iron are following a useless and dangerous practice.

See also ANEMIA; NUTRITION.

IRRITABLE COLON See COLITIS.

ISOMETRICS See EXERCISE.

ITCHING (pruritus) "It is easy to stand a pain, but difficult to stand an itch," observed the seventeenth-century Chinese philosopher Chang Ch'ao. Although this teasing irritation is the worst symptom of many conditions, scratching can further damage the affected tissue.

Rubbing *around* the area can often bring quick relief with no injury. So can rubbing an itchy rash with an ice cube. Other ways to relieve itching:

Hot water. In some conditions—including eczema, poison ivy, and insect stings—the brief application of very hot water to the affected area can bring immediate and complete relief lasting as long as 12 hours. The water should be hot enough to cause considerable discomfort when it is applied, but not hot enough to burn.

The range of 120° F to 130° F is suggested, subject to cautious trial. If a chronic or recurrent condition is to be treated, buy a thermometer. Momentary application, with a washcloth or under running water repeated several times, may be sufficient. If large areas are to be treated, apply the water to a small area at a time.

Caution: The required temperature is much too high to be used safely in a bath or shower. Water that is hot, but not hot enough, may worsen the itch. Prolonged heat may be harmful in some types of skin disorders.

Wet compresses. Make compresses of Burow's solution diluted 1 part to 25 parts of water. Prepare the dressing from a clean piece of soft sheet, pillowcase, or napkin, folded six to eight ply and cut to fit slightly larger than the affected area. Immerse it in the solution, which should be kept at room temperature, and wring it out until it is sopping wet (neither running wet nor merely damp). Place it on the affected area and, if necessary, keep it in place with a gauze bandage. At intervals frequent enough to keep the dressing sopping reimmerse it in the solution.

Starch solution baths. Stir from 1/2 to 1 pound refined soluble cornstarch (preferably unperfumed Linit starch) into a tubful of water—any temperature will do. Stay in the bath from 15 minutes to several hours.

Calamine lotion may be applied to the affected areas.

If none of the above works, a physician may prescribe antihistamines and in severe cases steroids. Ointments containing hydrocortisone or related hormones are so effective in relieving itching that some allergic patients take them indiscriminately—a dangerous practice because of possible side effects.

The Medical Letter warns against the use of anesthetic sprays and medicated wipes offered for the relief of itching or pain. The anesthetic agents in these products do not relieve itching or pain on skin that is not injured. Some local anesthetics, such as benzocaine, are likely to cause an allergic reaction.

Furthermore the antimicrobial agents have only slight antibacterial and antifungal action in the concentrations used, and almost all of them can induce skin reactions.

See also JOCK ITCH; SCABIES; SKIN DISORDERS.

IUD   See BIRTH CONTROL.

IVY, POISON   See POISON IVY.

J

JELLYFISH tentacles are thickly studded with stinging capsules containing a paralyzing acid venom. While jellyfish are thickest in warm waters, they also appear in large numbers in northern seas. Bathers need to beware even those washed up on shore.

Jellyfish float with the current and are incapable of attacking. But a bather who bumps one—or a detached tentacle of one—may experience burning pain, followed by a linear rash and possible blistering. A severe sting, such as often occurs in U.S. waters from the giant Portuguese man-of-war, may produce muscular cramps, nausea, and breathing difficulties. Some people suffer an allergic reaction, much like that to insect stings, especially after repeated contact (see illustration).

If you're stung by a jellyfish, don't rush into a shower—fresh water activates the stingers. Instead wash the area with ocean water, heated if possible. If jellyfish tentacles cling to the skin, remove them with a gloved hand or a towel—don't touch them with your bare hand.

Then deactivate the venom by applying alcohol—rubbing alcohol, perfume, liquor—household ammonia, or a meat tenderizer containing papain. Cover the area with flour, baking powder, shaving soap, or—as a last resort—dry sand. Scrape these off and wash again with saltwater.

A topical corticosteroid analgesic can then be applied, preferably by aerosol. If lymph glands, such as those in the groin, swell, apply ice compresses for 20 minutes out of each hour.

For severe stings a physician may prescribe an analgesic cream containing antihistamines. In some cases Adrenalin may be needed, plus strong analgesics like morphine or meperidine (Demerol) to relieve the pain.

This advice applies not only to jellyfish but also to fire-coral, sea anemones, and the Portuguese man-of-war (which is technically not a jellyfish but a hydroid).

See also ACCIDENTS; STINGRAYS.

JET LAG (time-zone displacement, desynchronosis) is the physical and emotional fatigue you

IF YOU'RE STUNG BY THESE

Apply ammonia, meat tenderizer, alcohol

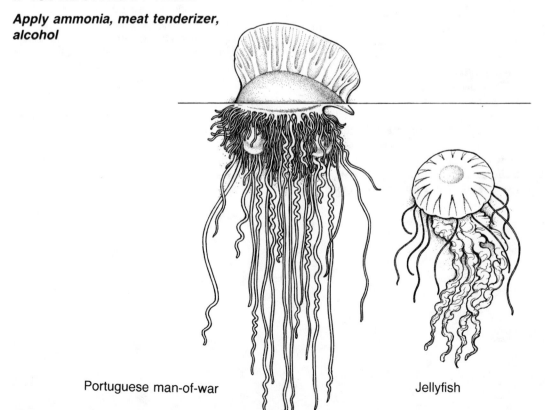

Portuguese man-of-war   Jellyfish

suffer after high-speed air travel across several time zones.

Your metabolism, temperature, digestion, elimination, and sleep work on a cycle of almost exactly 24 hours. All this can be grossly disrupted if, for example, you leave home from New York at noon on a flight to Paris—where during daylight saving time it's 5:00 P.M.

When you land, seven hours later, it will be 7:00 P.M. your body's time, but midnight for Parisians. Four or five hours later, about the time you're ready for bed, Paris will start waking up.

Even if you cut your sleep short to get in step with Paris, your metabolism and other functions will remain on their New York schedule for several days. Until you completely adjust, your highs and lows will be out of sync with your Paris activities, causing abnormal irritability and tiredness.

In reverse, suppose you leave Paris at noon (7:00 A.M. in New York). By the time you land in New York, your body will be closing down for the day—while New Yorkers will be having lunch. If you have an 8:00 P.M. engagement, you're likely to find yourself bleary-eyed and yawning, since your body will still be on Paris time; 1:00 A.M. the following morning.

The National Aeronautics and Space Administration estimates that it takes one day for your body to recover completely from each hour of time-zone change you undergo. On a flight to Western Europe crossing five time zones, you might be noticeably out of sorts for only the first couple of days. But you won't be completely back to par for five days—and that's half of a ten-day vacation abroad.

The older and more out of shape you are, the longer it takes you to recover.

How to reduce the effects of jet lag? When flying eastward schedule a night flight so you can sleep on board and reach your destination more or less in sync with activities there. If your flight leaves New York at 11:00 P.M., you'll arrive at 11:00 A.M. Paris time, with minimal disruption from the hours you've lost en route. Take sleeping pills if necessary to help you slumber on the plane.

Conversely, leave Paris at 9:00 or 10:00 A.M. after a good night's sleep. When you arrive in New York, it'll be about noon. Other suggestions for reducing the effects of time-zone fatigue:

1. Avoid working immediately on arrival.
2. Catch up on some sleep as soon as you can.
3. Try to stay on your regular eating and sleeping schedule as closely as possible.
4. Pace yourself so as not to do too much the first few days.
5. Get some light exercise before bedtime.
6. Try to make some of the time adjustment a few days before you leave. Go to bed an hour earlier each night if you plan to travel east; an hour later for westerly trips.

Altered eating patterns before and during a flight can help reduce jet lag, the fatiguing disturbance of body rhythm that's commonly suffered by long-distance travelers.

Here's a recommended regimen for jet flights going *east:*

Three days before the flight, "feast" (eat three full meals). Two days before the flight, "fast" (eat three low-calorie, low-carbohydrate meals). One day before the flight, feast again. On the day of the flight, fast again. En route, drink coffee or tea without milk or sugar; refrain from drinking alcohol or eating the meal; try to sleep; eat a high-protein breakfast.

For jet flights going *west,* do the same, except that it's advisable to drink lots of coffee or tea early on the flight day but none after noon.

See also AIR TRAVEL; TRAVEL HEALTH.

JOCK ITCH is a popular name for any rash on the groin and inner thighs. It is often caused by ringworm fungi. Other causes are yeast infection, contact dermatitis, seborrheic dermatitis, and psoriasis. See a doctor to determine the cause and appropriate treatment.

See also SKIN DISORDERS.

KELOIDS are excessive growths of scar tissue. They are a major complication of EAR PIERCING (which see). In some instances a keloid fails to stop growing and produces large masses. This abnormality of the healing process is most common in blacks and others with highly pigmented skin. The condition is believed hereditary. It is sometimes possible to control keloids early in their development with injections of cortisone derivatives. Contrary to popular belief, keloids are unrelated to cancer and are not caused by vitamin deficiency.

Surgical removal of a keloid is often necessary, but there is a risk the keloid may redevelop in the surgical wound. Some surgeons recommend that keloid scars be treated with small doses of X rays to prevent the overgrowth.

Because keloids may shrink as a child grows older, most pediatricians and surgeons tend to be more conservative with young children. Moreover, many people who develop keloids when young are free of them later in life.

See also SKIN DISORDERS.

KIDNEY CANCER See CANCER OF THE BLADDER.

KIDNEY DISEASE affects about 13 million Americans, of whom 78,000 die each year.

See a physician if you experience any of these symptoms:

· Swelling of hands and feet.
· Unexplained fever.
· Chronic fatigue.
· Puffiness around the eyes, especially in children.
· Pain in the back, below the ribs.
· Burning on urination, or increased frequency of urination.
· Tea-colored, cloudy, or bloody urine.

But you can have kidney damage without any symptoms. An annual physical examination will help to detect kidney disorders.

The kidneys, located on either side of your spine just below your rib cage, produce urine as they remove waste products from your blood and regulate the amount of water and chemical substances such as sodium in your body.

Many disorders can interfere with the proper functioning of the kidneys. A common type of kidney disease is called glomerulonephritis, nephritis, or Bright's disease. It's an inflammation that often develops after sore throat from streptococcal bacteria, most commonly in children under seven.

Bed rest, a diet low in protein and salt, and drugs cure the disease in almost all children and in roughly three out of four adults. Full recovery may take several months.

Some children and adults develop chronic glomerulonephritis, and may experience progressive kidney damage.

Another condition, nephrosis, most commonly affects children between ages 1 and 6. In this condition proteins leak from the kidneys and are present in the urine. The most obvious symptom is severe swelling.

Medication—usually steroids, sometimes antibiotics—cures eight out of ten. Others may suffer progressive kidney failure.

The relapse rate is high. Children who have had nephrosis need to be rechecked periodically.

Another cause of kidney disorder is urinary tract infection, an inflammation caused by bacteria invading the kidneys, bladder, or urinary passageways. Very rarely do infections lead to kidney damage or failure. However, if a person has a blockage or similar abnormality of the urinary tract, then infection may contribute to progressive damage to the kidneys.

Some drugs can result in kidney malfunction. Diseases such as diabetes, gout, and tuberculosis may affect the kidneys. The kidneys can fail because of accidents, poisoning, or reactions to incompatible blood transfusion.

High blood pressure (hypertension) and the kidneys are closely related. Hypertension can cause kidney disorders, and kidney disorders can cause hypertension.

High pressure in the blood vessels of the kidneys causes them to become thickened and rigid. As this reduces the blood supply to the kidneys they can no longer function efficiently. Therefore, the kidneys become unable to remove waste products from the body. Salt is retained, which causes the body to hold fluid, putting a burden on the heart.

The decrease in blood supply also results in dysfunction of kidney tissue, which leads to further decline of kidney function. Eventually, if blood pressure is uncontrolled, total kidney failure can ensue, with uremic poisoning.

Avoid self-medication. Don't treat kidney problems yourself. No over-the-counter preparation can relieve or cure kidney ailments. Treatment for kidney disease requires a doctor's close supervision.

Drugs can often control infections and inflammations affecting the kidney. Obstructions such as kidney stones causing impaired function may be treated with medicine, surgery or pulverization through shock waves.

Hemodialysis. For people with chronic kidney disease hemodialysis or kidney transplant may be necessary. Without treatment, failure of both kidneys can be fatal in two to three weeks. Kidney failure causes the body's waste products to accumulate in the blood, a condition called uremia. Its later stages are characterized by headache, nausea and vomiting, blurred vision, convulsions, coma, and death.

Hemodialysis is the use of an artificial-kidney machine. The machine performs the functions the patient's own kidneys are unable to: It cleanses the blood of waste products and restores proper chemical balance.

The machine is connected to the person's arm or leg through a tube inserted into an artery. His blood passes over the machine's thin cellophane membrane where its impurities are filtered through a solution almost identical to normal blood plasma. Necessary chemicals pass from the solution into the blood. Another tube carries the blood back to a vein in the person's body.

Many people require hemodialysis two or three times a week for sessions lasting up to ten hours. Such treatments allow many kidney patients to lead productive lives. Many are able to maintain full-time jobs. Joining a dialysis support group may help patients adjust to their dependence on a machine.

Home hemodialysis is less expensive and can be more convenient than hospital or clinic treatments. Many people feel that they adjust better to the use of the machine at home. Machines can often be borrowed or rented. After a waiting period is completed, Medicare pays 80 percent of the cost of hemodialysis for people of any age.

A recent development in home hemodialysis is CAPD—continuous ambulatory peritoneal dialysis. In this procedure a flexible hollow tube is implanted through the abdominal wall. A sterile dialyzing solution flows through the tube from a plastic container into the patient's body. Once empty the container can be rolled up and placed under the patient's clothing. The patient can then engage in normal activities for many hours, while toxic wastes and excess water pass from the bloodstream into the solution. Four times in each 24 hours the patient empties the waste solution into the plastic bag, and then infuses fresh dialyzing solution. This process takes about 30 to 45 minutes. While CAPD means much greater freedom for selected patients, it requires training and meticulous care to avoid serious complications.

Transplantation offers new hope for kidney patients. Techniques for transplanting healthy kidneys to replace diseased ones have greatly improved in recent years. Several thousand successful kidney transplants have been performed, liberating many from hemodialysis treatments. People with kidney transplants can lead near-normal lives.

Kidneys for transplantation are either donated by a relative with two healthy kidneys— one kidney can perform the functions of both— or removed from a person at death.

The main problem in kidney transplantation is rejection. The body's defense system attacks all foreign substances. More effective drugs and better tissue typing (techniques for matching tissue of the donor and recipient) have greatly improved the chances for a successful transplant.

Long-term success is most likely when the kidney comes from a twin. Next best is a brother or sister. After that, parents.

If you wish to donate a kidney, contact the National Kidney Foundation (2 Park Avenue, New York, New York 10016). For other information about donating your body or organs, see DEATH.

Also see KIDNEY STONES; URINARY TRACT INFECTION.

KIDNEY STONES were said by Hippocrates to cause the "most exquisite pain known to man."

The main symptom of a kidney stone passing through the urinary system is an excruciating pain originating in the back or side and radiating across the abdomen and into the groin, genitals, and inner thigh. Any movement may be agonizing, and there may be sweating, chills, nausea, vomiting. Pain and bleeding on urinating are other common symptoms.

Your urine may be strained to catch small particles of stone to determine their exact composition. About 90 percent of all kidney stones contain calcium.

The kidney stone is allowed to be excreted spontaneously if X rays show that it is moving freely and kidney function is good. In cases of obstruction or infection, however, the stone may have to be removed surgically. Sometimes stones can be removed through "closed" surgery: an instrument attached to a catheter inserted into the urinary tract may be able to snare the stone; other devices can crush stones into smaller pieces or pulverize them with shocks. Some stones can be dissolved by medication.

What causes stones. Dehydration may contribute to kidney-stone formation in susceptible people. People who live in hot, dry climates are nearly twice as susceptible to kidney-stone formation as others.

An infection in the gastrointestinal tract may contribute to dehydration, as may chronic diarrhea. Disorders of calcium or uric acid metabolism may account for the formation of stones. Physical inactivity may promote their development.

A person being treated for stomach ulcers may develop a kidney stone as the result of the combination of milk and calcium carbonates or other calcium-containing antacids. A diet containing excessive amounts of foods containing oxalate (cranberries, chard, rhubarb, gooseberries, spinach, beet leaves) and calcium (see MINERALS) can also promote the tendency to stone formation in susceptible people. Age is another factor—stone formation is more common in middle age. Men are much more susceptible to kidney-stone formation than women.

Drinking plenty of fluid may help to lower your risk of stone formation. There is strong evidence that drinking too little fluid decreases the amount of urine and increases the concentration of substances that accumulate to form stones.

See also KIDNEY DISEASE.

KITES When flying a kite, do it so you avoid accidents, especially electric shock and burns when kites tangle with power lines.

Fly your kite in a level, open space.

Fly your kite only in dry weather. A wet cord is a conductor of electricity. Wet shoes on wet earth increase the hazard since they enable a charge to be grounded more readily, and this is dangerous.

Don't risk your life climbing up a tree or pole to try to get a kite from an overhead wire or roof.

Use a safe cord, never of wire or tinsel. If you build your own kite, don't use metal, such as umbrella stays, in place of wood or plastic sticks.

Use reels and wear gloves when flying large kites. These help to avoid friction burns in case the string runs through your hands too fast.

See also ACCIDENTS; BURNS; ELECTRIC SHOCK.

KNEE, TRICK See TRICK KNEE.

KNEE, WATER ON THE See WATER ON THE KNEE.

KNIVES For treating a stabbing, see PUNCTURES.

Keep knives sharp to avoid cuts and other accidents. A sharp knife requires less pressure to do its work, so doesn't slip as easily when being used. Don't dull a knife, or risk its breaking, by using it to open jars or cans.

It's safest to use the correct size and type of knife for each job—a small knife for paring vegetables, carving wood; a large knife for slicing bread, carving meat. Keep your eye on the cutting edge, your fingers out of its path. As a guide use a block of wood rather than your fingers.

Store knives in slotted racks or drawers. If they're loose in a drawer with other tools or utensils, you may get cut while rummaging around. Similarly, wash and dry knives separate from other utensils, keeping their handles together and their blades pointed in the same direction.

Keep knives out of reach of small children. For cutting tasks give them scissors. When a youngster is approaching school age, train him to carry a knife with the blade pointed to the ground; never to run when carrying a knife; never to toss a knife to another person; always to hand someone a knife with the handle toward the recipient.

When hiking or camping bring along a Boy Scout knife rather than a sheath knife. A strong pocketknife will handle all your camp needs—a sheath knife is just too tempting to kids.

See also ACCIDENTS; CUTS; PUNCTURES.

KWASHIORKOR See PROTEIN.

L

LACERATIONS See CUTS.

LARYNGITIS See HOARSENESS.

LAXATIVES See CONSTIPATION.

LAZY EYE See AMBLYOPIA.

LEAD POISONING among children is a cause of mental retardation, injuries to the nervous system, permanent brain damage, and death. The Public Health Service estimates that each year 400,000 U.S. children—rich and poor—suffer from lead-poisoning accidents. About 200 die, 800 are permanently impaired, and 32,000 suffer moderate to severe brain damage.

The symptoms of low-level lead poisoning are common to many diseases. A child may have a headache, be mopy and cranky. He may eat very little and often throw up or have stomachaches. Suspect lead poisoning if a child suddenly develops behavior or learning problems.

General ways to avoid lead poisoning: Whenever you paint cribs or anything else a small child might chew on, use lead-free paint. Look for the word *nontoxic* on the label of the paint can.

Discourage chewing on pencils. True, the "lead" in a pencil is not lead but a form of carbon called graphite that's not poisonous. However the *paint* coating some pencils contains lead.

Also discourage your child from eating or licking magazine pages. The yellow coloring in some color inserts contains lead in quantities that could be dangerous to a child.

Don't use pottery or glazed earthenware for storing foods that are high in acid, such as fruit, fruit juices, soft drinks, tomatoes, cheese, wine, anything that contains vinegar. Lead is a normal and usually a safe part of ceramic glazes. But if the glaze is improperly mixed or fired, the lead in it can leach out on prolonged contact with acid. There is no danger, however, from using ceramic glazed dinnerware merely for eating and drinking.

Be especially watchful if your child suffers from pica, a compulsion to eat unfoodlike substances. Children who eat dirt may ingest lead accumulated in soil from exhaust fumes.

Most victims are ghetto children who eat old, lead-containing paint that peels off the walls. Until about 1940 lead-containing paint was frequently used in interiors as well as exteriors of houses. In large cities there is such a marked concentration of poisoning in tenements that these areas are called "lead belts." Lead in exhaust fumes from automobiles also contributes to children's exposure to lead in large cities.

If you live in an older house, take your child to a doctor if you see him putting pieces of paint or plaster in his mouth, or find that he's chewed on a painted railing or windowsill. In the beginning stages of lead poisoning a child may not seem really sick. Don't wait for signs of poisoning.

Get a broom or stiff brush and remove all loose pieces of paint and plaster from walls, woodwork, and ceilings. Cover lower parts of walls within children's reach by pasting paper or nailing board over them. Old sheets and burlap can also be used as coverings.

See also ACCIDENTS; CRIBS.

LEECHES are bloodsucking worms ranging from dot-size to as long as 2½ inches. They are found mainly in warm fresh waters and may attack anyone venturing into infested lakes, ponds, and rivers, especially in spring and early summer.

Remove a leech from your skin carefully, lest its jaws be left in the wound, promoting infection.

Any of these methods will usually get a leech to release its hold: Flush the attached leech with a strong salt solution; drop vinegar on the site of the wound; apply a flame or the end of a lighted cigarette to the worm.

A leech's saliva prevents coagulation of blood, so the wound may continue bleeding. Wash it with soap and water. Then press to stop the blood flow and apply a sterile bandage.

In addition to attaching themselves to the skin, leeches may enter the urinary passages and vagina. If swallowed, while swimming or by drinking infested water, they may dangerously obstruct the digestive and respiratory passages. Internal leeches cause bleeding, blockage, and pain. They require the attention of a physician.

Insect repellents are generally effective against leeches. But no repellent will last long in water, so the best preventive against aquatic leeches is to avoid going into infested waters.

Be aware of leeches while traveling. In Asia and South America some land leeches climb shrubs and rain down on passersby.

See also INSECTS; TRAVEL HEALTH; WATER CONTAMINATION.

LEG FRACTURES, including ankle fractures, should never be tested by trying to walk on the injured leg. It won't prove anything. For while it is possible to hobble even with a broken leg, the damage done by trying may be irreparable.

Symptoms of a broken leg include pain, swelling, and tenderness—all signs of sprains as well. Fractures of the ankle are particularly difficult to distinguish from sprains, since swelling may be mild and come slowly. As a precaution have X rays made of all ankle injuries.

Avoid moving an injured person without the help of an ambulance crew. If you must move him, support the fractured leg firmly, preventing the foot from sagging or twisting. Tie a splint—a broom handle or tree branch will do—to the leg. Or strap the victim's legs together by tying at several points (see illustration).

Standard treatment for fractures of the legs is to immobilize them in a plaster cast until the fracture is healed. Surgery may be required.

See also ACCIDENTS; FRACTURES; PLASTER CASTS.

IF AN ANKLE OR FOOT MAY BE BROKEN

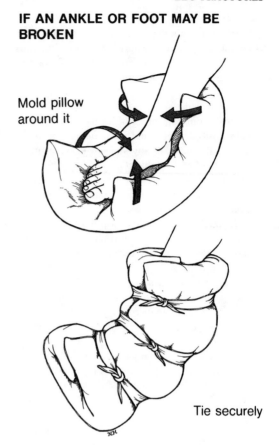

Mold pillow around it

Tie securely

IF A LEG MAY BE BROKEN
Splint it

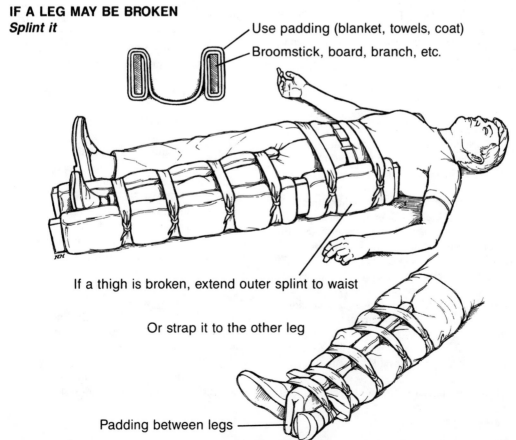

Use padding (blanket, towels, coat)

Broomstick, board, branch, etc.

If a thigh is broken, extend outer splint to waist

Or strap it to the other leg

Padding between legs

LEG PAIN often results from arteriosclerosis blocking circulation to one or both legs. This condition, termed arteriosclerosis obliterans (ASO), is the most frequent cause of cramps, limping, and fatigue after walking short distances, and unaccountable aches like those of charley horse.

Other common causes of leg pain are varicose veins, osteoarthritis, and nerve damage from diabetes. If you suffer any such pain, see a physician. Don't assume that it will go away by itself, or that it is merely a normal part of aging. Prompt attention can keep the underlying condition from worsening.

If you suffer from ASO, stop smoking or using tobacco in any form. It further constricts your blood vessels, and its continued use can create severe problems.

Sleep with the head of your bed raised 4 to 6 inches on blocks of wood or bricks. This enables gravity to promote circulation to your legs and feet. Just putting pillows under your head is not enough.

The principal therapy is walking, which helps stimulate the growth of new blood vessels around the blockage in your arteries. Walk for at least 30 minutes at least twice, but preferably three, times a day.

Each time out walk until your muscles demand that you halt, well past the point of mere discomfort. When the pain goes away, continue until you absolutely must stop again. Gradually you'll go longer and longer before feeling pain.

In severe cases, where reduced circulation threatens to require amputation of the leg, a bypass around the blocked area or a blood-vessel graft may restore circulation.

Reduced circulation raises the threat of infection. Therefore protect your foot and leg from injuries and blisters. An estimated 40 percent of the amputations due to complications of arteriosclerosis could be avoided by simple precautions like these:

Outdoors wear comfortable leather shoes with a firm toe and heel. Break in new shoes by wearing them indoors until they're comfortable. Otherwise when indoors always wear slippers. Change socks or stockings daily.

Wash your feet daily with a mild soap, removing any scales between the toes. Dry well, and apply lanolin to prevent dryness and cracking. Use an orangewood stick to clean under the nails.

Once a month, after washing your feet, trim your nails straight across. Don't cut them too close.

Don't cut, file, or self-treat corns or calluses.

Use only medication prescribed by a physician or podiatrist, never over-the-counter chemicals. Consult a physician before permitting surgery for ingrown toenails. Tell a podiatrist before he begins treatment that you have impaired circulation in the legs.

Take strict precautions against athlete's foot. See a physician if athlete's foot or any other infection doesn't clear up within four days.

Avoid exposing your legs and feet to extremes of temperature in hot weather or cold weather. Protect your legs and feet from sunburn.

Don't wear clothes that constrict your legs and feet. Avoid elastic stockings, circular garters, tight girdles.

See also ARTERIOSCLEROSIS; DIABETES; HEART DISEASE; OSTEOARTHRITIS; VARICOSE VEINS.

LEGIONNAIRE'S DISEASE   See PNEUMONIA.

LEPROSY (Hansen's disease)   The panic that greets leprosy differentiates it from virtually every other disease and keeps it from being understood by a large segment of the public.

Deep-seated fears most people have toward leprosy originate with the Bible, which presents the leper as loathsome and deserving of such scriptural phrases as "Unclean, unclean." Research has amply proved that the "leprosy" spoken of in the Bible was a miscellaneous grouping of skin diseases such as psoriasis, eczema, and ringworm. The Hebrew general term for all these types of skin disorders was translated into the Greek *lepra,* meaning a scaly skin condition. An error in translating *lepra* to English made the English Bible call all the skin disorders "leprosy."

International Congresses of Leprosy have urged the public to drop the word *leper* from the language since, unfairly for the afflicted, it signifies everything repulsive and reprehensible. There has been a campaign to change the name to "Hansen's disease," after the Norwegian scientist who first isolated the bacillus.

Despite its bad reputation leprosy can be successfully treated. It is an infectious disease caused by bacteria closely resembling the bacillus that causes tuberculosis.

Who gets it. There are roughly 15 million cases in the world, with the highest rates in central and western Africa, French Guiana, and Burma. The United States has some 2,600 known cases, most from other countries.

How the disease spreads remains a mystery. Some authorities believe it is transmitted to a susceptible person by direct skin-to-skin contact with a person who has an untreated case. But half the cases develop without apparent exposure to an existing case. Conversely, long and close contacts by medical personnel, even by spouses of sufferers, rarely result in infection. Dr. Robert G. Cochrane, a British leprologist, believes that 90 percent of the human race is naturally immune, 1 percent is highly susceptible, and the rest would become infected only after long exposure.

Transmission may be largely via cuts and needle pricks. Two U.S. Marines in Melbourne, Australia, during World War II caught the disease from a needle in a tattoo parlor. In India barefoot residents of rocky regions are stricken more often than those elsewhere.

How it progresses. There are two major types of the disease. They are termed tuberculoid (loosely termed "nerve type") and lepromatous ("skin type")—although all cases of leprosy present both nerve and skin lesions.

The nerve type usually is first evident with a red spot or several spots resembling ringworm. The spots may grow larger, and the center of a spot may lose its coloring and become insensitive to touch, pain, heat, or cold. Nerve damage may produce severe pain.

In the skin type, the victim may come down with bouts of nosebleed, headache, and fever. Small lumps often appear on the skin, growing larger and more numerous. They may break down and ulcerate. Meanwhile other areas of the skin may thicken and show exaggeration of the natural folds of the skin. When this happens on the face, the sufferer may develop lionlike features. In advanced cases the mucous membranes of the nose may be involved, and the septum of the nose may be destroyed.

Without treatment nerve-type leprosy sometimes runs its course within two years, leaving only residual nerve damage. By contrast skin-type leprosy may lead to blindness and kidney damage, and may require many years of treatment.

One problem in both types stems from the loss of nerve sensitivity. Leprosy victims need to be on guard against burning themselves while smoking, cutting themselves when shaving, wearing ill-fitting shoes. They may cause injury and invite infection without realizing they've been hurt.

Shedding parts of the body is one of the horrifying myths of leprosy. Leprosy patients do not drop off fingers, toes, noses, lips, chins, and feet. The myth probably is rooted in the fact that the bones may shrink through absorption. Rather than falling off, fingers and toes can shorten and

conceivably can recede altogether over 10 to 20 years.

Cases rarely progress this far in the United States, thanks to standard use of sulfones, drugs developed in the 1940s, and the more recent rifampin. The drugs may arrest a case immediately, but can take a long time to wipe out the bacteria—five years or more in skin-type cases.

Some leprosy sufferers go to the Public Health Service hospital maintained at Carville, Louisiana. Most cases are treated privately or by local agencies. Hospitalization permits medical supervision for drug reactions and rehabilitative therapy. Patients are thought not to be infectious while they are receiving treatment.

Most leprosy patients' worst problems are social and economic. The disease may be cured or arrested, but even after leaving the hospital the sufferer bears the brand "leper." He is often shunned by family and friends and barred from earning a living.

Your chances of getting leprosy are virtually nil, especially if you take normal precautions in foreign areas with high leprosy rates. The National Institute of Allergy and Infectious Diseases puts leprosy in perspective with this advice: "Anyone who has a persistent skin lesion or sore should consult his physician. The diagnosis is not likely to be leprosy, but there are other, far more serious skin diseases."

Leprosy organizations warn Americans against responding to direct appeals for clothing and money from leprosy patients in foreign countries. Such letters, many originating in the Philippines, usually complain of severe deprivation and are in the same handwriting. Notes American Leprosy Missions: "Obviously they are often written by the same person as a part of a planned solicitation program exploiting the American recipient's generosity."

See also INFECTIOUS DISEASE.

LEPTOSPIROSIS (swineherd's disease, mud fever, Weil's disease) is an animal disease group caused by leptospires, a family of spiral bacteria. Carriers include cattle, swine, sheep, goats, horses, mules, dogs, cats, foxes, opossums, skunks, raccoons, wildcats, mongooses, rats, mice, voles, and bats.

Leptospires infect the kidneys of animals and are shed through their urine. Humans can get this infectious disease by drinking or swimming in contaminated water or walking on moist soil that contains the infected urine.

Some people get the disease either by handling a sick animal or by handling the kidney and other infected tissues of an animal that has had leptospirosis. The disease is most prevalent among farmers and other workers who handle animals and animal products. The leptospirosis organism enters the human body through the nose, mouth, or eyes or through a break in the skin.

After a four- to ten-day incubation the victim suffers fever, headache, chills, muscle pains, and sometimes nausea and vomiting. Jaundice, skin rashes, blood in the urine, and a stiff neck are other common symptoms.

Because of the numerous and varied symptoms it is sometimes hard to distinguish this disease from other infectious diseases.

Most cases are mild and the sufferer recovers in one to two weeks. When the infection is severe, however, the kidney, liver, or heart may be damaged and death can result.

The symptoms in animals are usually similar to those in humans, but may be so slight that the illness is not detected. Infected dogs will sometimes shed the leptospirosis organisms in their urine for a year or more after they have recovered from the disease. Therefore you can be infected by an apparently healthy pet.

If you suspect infection, call a physician promptly. Give him a report of possible exposure to leptospirosis organisms. Although the best treatment for leptospirosis has not been clearly established, it is generally believed that antibiotics, if given early, will shorten the course of the disease and lessen the severity of the symptoms.

A host of animals, both domestic and wild, harbor the disease. Sanitation measures can reduce the danger of spread. Drain muddy farm areas. Destroy rats. Protect drinking water—for animals as well as for humans—from contamination. Avoid swimming in waters where cattle and other animals frequently wade and drink. Take precautions against water contamination.

Cattle and dogs can be vaccinated against leptospirosis. The animal vaccines are effective for about six to nine months. However they do not give immunity against all types of leptospirosis organisms.

When an animal continues to shed leptospirosis organisms after it has recovered from the disease, this condition, known as the "carrier state," can sometimes be corrected by injections of appropriate antibiotic drugs. Have a veterinarian examine animals believed to have been infected.

See also ANIMAL DISEASE; INFECTIOUS DISEASE; WATER CONTAMINATION.

LEUKEMIA means "white blood," the name given the disease when it was first identified. One of the common symptoms is an oversupply of abnormal white cells (leukocytes) in the blood. The disease strikes about 25,000 Americans a year and takes some 17,000 lives.

Leukemia is not, as commonly called, "blood cancer." It is a cancer of the tissues in which blood is formed: mainly the bone marrow, the lymph nodes, and the spleen.

These tissues release hundreds of millions of new, normal blood cells of all types each day. When leukemia strikes, too many of these cells are white cells, often only partly developed. In advanced disease leukemic cells crowd out the production of normal white cells (needed to fight infection), platelets (which clot blood, preventing hemorrhage), and red blood cells (lack of these causes anemia).

A patient with early leukemia may feel and look completely well. Early cases are usually picked up in routine blood examinations—an excellent argument for regular health checkups.

Because leukemic cells circulate throughout the blood and lymph systems, the patient may develop a variety of symptoms. The most frequent are fatigue, pallor, nosebleed and other hemorrhages, night sweats, bone pain, and sore throat. In children the symptoms may resemble those of infection or rheumatic fever.

Advanced leukemia is marked by great fatigue, massive hemorrhages, and pain. There is often high fever and enlargement of spleen, liver, kidneys, and lymph nodes. There may be swelling of the gums, and various skin disorders.

About 90 percent of leukemia involves two types of white cells—granulocytes formed in the bone marrow, and lymphocytes formed in lymphatic tissue.

For practical discussion the forms of leukemia are *granulocytic* (or myeloid) and *lymphocytic.* In addition a leukemia can be *chronic*—which develops slowly—or *acute,* which grows rapidly and can cause death in a few weeks or months without treatment. The two types of cells and two rates of growth give four main types of leukemia.

Acute lymphocytic leukemia strikes children in 80 percent of cases. Drugs and radiation can achieve complete remission for about 90 percent of affected youngsters. About half can discontinue therapy because they're cured. The brightest prospects are for those between ages one and nine, and those whose treatment was started early.

Acute granulocytic leukemia about 90 percent of the time affects adults. For most patients intensive therapy can bring about remissions averaging 12 to 18 months. Younger patients (those under 55) and those with minimal bleeding problems tend to fare best.

Chronic granulocytic leukemia usually occurs in adults. Treatment has not greatly improved survival, which averages about 36 months. Most patients die soon after the beginning of a terminal stage, which resembles the acute form.

Chronic lymphocytic leukemia is seen only in older people, usually in the 50 to 80 age range. Survival typically lasts from six to eight years, although the disease often runs a very long course and does not necessarily shorten life.

For best results, prompt referral to a special treatment center is essential. Many of the effective drugs are still experimental, restricted to certain research institutions. For the name of the nearest hospital specializing in leukemia, contact the local chapter of the Leukemia Society of America or the American Cancer Society, or the National Cancer Institute, Research Information Section, Bethesda, Maryland 20024.

Once in a remission a patient can be treated at home by the family physician or pediatrician. The Leukemia Society provides some financial aid to help outpatients pay for drugs, radiation, transportation, and lab studies.

Leukemia patients do not usually die of the disease but of its effects, mainly hemorrhage and infection. These can be controlled with supportive therapy: antibiotics, special germ-free environments, and platelet transfusions to prevent hemorrhage. Newly developed machines allow relatives to give platelets as often as twice a week without damage to themselves, unlike whole-blood transfusions, which can only be given about once in two months.

See also CANCER.

LICE (pediculosis), small bloodsucking insects, have skyrocketed as a health problem for middle-class Americans because of longer hair, relaxed sexual standards, and a lessening of personal hygiene in some antiestablishment circles.

Lice cause maddening itching and often raise a skin irritation of small reddish blisters. Scratching frequently causes sores and scabs, with subsequent infections. Lice come in three types—pubic, head, and body:

Pubic lice (crab lice) usually fasten themselves to the hairs of the genital region. Sometimes crab lice adhere to the eyebrows and eyelashes and the hair of armpits and chest. They often leave a tiny bluish or slate-colored stain under the skin where they've fed. Other calling cards are their nits (eggs), small grayish bodies glued to the hairs.

Infestation is common where people work or live under crowded conditions, and is often

HEAD LOUSE

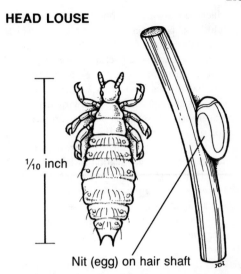

1/10 inch

Nit (egg) on hair shaft

spread by sexual contact. A case of pubic lice also merits a check for its frequent companion: venereal disease, particularly gonorrhea.

Head lice mainly infest the hair at the back of the head. You may contract them merely by leaning back in a chair, as at the movies. Nits are usually abundant, showing up first near the scalp and later all over the hair; they resemble dandruff but don't brush off.

Children, especially girls, are most likely to become infested. An epidemic that closed the schools of Anderson, Indiana, was laid in part to students exchanging hats.

Body lice may carry typhus. They ordinarily dwell in the seams of clothing, especially undergarments. They leave minute blood specks on the skin, most often around the collar, belt line, underarm, and wherever seams touch the body. Nits are usually found in the seams.

Lack of personal cleanliness is a common cause of infestation. But any child or adult may get the parasites through contact with infested people, bedding, or clothing. Treatment is a shampoo, lotion, or cream containing gamma benzene hexachloride (Kwell, Gamene). Use precisely as directed—if taken into the mouth or overused, the drug can cause convulsions and death. A nonprescription item, Rid, is also effective against lice.

For head lice the shampoo is usually used as follows: Wet your hair. Apply 1 tablespoon or less of the shampoo and work it into a lather. Shampoo hair for four minutes, carefully working the lather all over your head and scalp. Rinse hair thoroughly and towel dry it. Comb the nits out with a fine-toothed comb, from the scalp out. In 90 percent of cases one treatment is effective.

Machine-wash on the hot cycle or dry-clean all clothing, bed linens and towels with which you've had contact for the past week. Articles not easily washed or dry-cleaned—such as caps or leather garments—can be sealed tightly in a plastic bag for ten days. This kills the lice.

Caution children not to borrow or lend hats, combs or brushes, scarves, hairpins or barrettes.

For pubic lice removal the lotion or cream is applied after a bath to all hairy areas in the affected region. The medication is left on for 12 hours, then washed off in a second bath. If a shampoo is used, apply 1 tablespoon to the affected area, lather for 5 minutes, then rinse thoroughly and towel dry. Nits left on hair shafts can be fine-tooth-combed or picked out with a tweezers.

If eyelashes are infested, the physician will prescribe a special product that is nonirritating to the eyes.

To destroy body lice disinfect clothes by boiling them, ironing them with a hot iron, or having them dry-cleaned (or by dipping them in gasoline or naphtha). Regular washing and dry cleaning of clothes thereafter will generally prevent infestation. Avoid wearing clothing worn by others. *The Medical Letter* warns that lindane-containing sprays are unnecessary and potentially dangerous.

Frequent bathing is a general preventive. If one member of a family becomes infested, all other members and their sexual contacts need to be examined. An entire household may need to undergo disinfection to avoid a recurrence.

See also INSECTS.

LIFE EXPECTANCY See DEATH.

LIGHTING can help you avoid accidents and eyestrain. The eye sees small details better with more light on the task. In addition the eye sees faster with more light. Depth perception, the ability to recognize differences in distances away from the eye, also improves with more illumination. Here are lighting recommendations of the Better Light Better Sight Bureau:

Provide two types of lighting—general and local. General, or fill-in, lighting gives a moderate level of background lighting throughout a room. It is provided by upward light from floor, table, and wall lamps, by wall and ceiling fixtures, and by lighted valances and cornices. Lighting will be more effective if walls, ceilings, and floor coverings are of a light to medium color, since light colors reflect light while dark colors absorb it.

Local, or functional, lighting is needed where any visual task such as reading, sewing, studying, desk work, food preparation, and grooming takes place. Lamps are usually preferred for lo-

cal lighting in living areas (such as living, family, dining rooms, and bedrooms) because they can be easily positioned and adjusted for the user's comfort. Fixtures are desirable in fixed locations: at the bathroom mirror, in the kitchen (over the range, sink, or work counter), over a workbench.

Check your home for these common enemies of good seeing:

Glare is raw, irritating light direct from unshaded bulbs or from improperly placed lighting equipment. Avoid glare by being sure to have lamps and fixtures properly shaded.

Contrast—differences between lighted and unlighted areas in the room—can cause eye fatigue. Avoid too much contrast by using lamps and fixtures that send light upward as well as downward, over a wide area. Don't confine your lighting to one spot, leaving the rest of the room in semidarkness.

Shadows cast from poorly placed lamps and fixtures can make it difficult to see and can be eye-tiring. Avoid shadows cast by the hand on writing, sewing, or drawing, by lighting from the left for right-handed people—and from the right for left-handed people.

Not enough light may result from too few lamps or fixtures, bulbs that are too small, room colors that are too dark. Have properly placed lamps and fixtures where you need them. Be sure that the light bulbs or fluorescent tubes are the proper size to light the seeing task.

Select and place lamps so that they provide comfortable and efficient seeing. If a lamp is too short, light will be confined to a narrow area. If it is too high, your eyes will receive glare from the bulb or from the shade interior.

The eye-level height of a person seated in upholstered furniture is normally about 40 inches above the floor. Lamps placed on tables that are about 25 inches high should thus measure about 15 inches from the tabletop to the bottom of the shade (40 − 25 = 15).

Floor lamps usually measure from 42 to 49 inches from the floor to the bottom of the shade. Position floor lamps used for reading behind your right or left shoulder.

Be sure lampshades are equipped to provide upward light on walls and ceilings; wide enough at the bottom to permit the light to spread over the entire working area; designed to conceal the light bulb from view when either seated or standing; equipped with white or near-white lining to reflect as much light as possible; sufficiently dense to prevent glaring bulb brightness from shining through the material of the shade, but not opaque.

Follow these recipes for good lighting:

For desk and table work. Place a table lamp 12 inches from the front edge of the desk and 15 inches from the task. Use at least a 150-watt bulb or 40 watts of fluorescent. For serious study you need 200 watts. Even better is studying between two lamps 30 inches apart, each with a 100-watt bulb.

To cut contrast have a light desk top, perhaps by adding a large, light blotter. Have a light-colored wall behind the desk. If the wall is dark, hang a light bulletin board of cork or insulation board.

Prop or tilt books and other reading matter 30 degrees toward the eyes. If the book is flat on the work surface, the type is foreshortened and reading is more difficult.

At an easel or music rack, use 300 watts of incandescent light in a floor lamp or wall- or ceiling-mounted pull-down fixture. Or use a 150-watt reflector flood lamp in an adjustable fixture, mounted on or recessed in the ceiling, and positioned so that you don't cast a shadow on the work.

When painting light both your subject and easel. The type of lighting (incandescent, fluorescent, or natural daylight) can affect the appearance of colors.

Hand sewing. You need 300 watts of incandescent lighting (a 100/200/300-watt bulb on high position). If there is much fine detail, or if you're to be sewing for long periods, use a 75-watt reflector bulb in addition to a floor lamp, and positioned much closer to the work. This can be in an adjustable socket clamped to the stem of a floor lamp. Position it below eye level, and about 15 inches from the sewing.

See also EYE DISORDER; EYESTRAIN.

LIGHTNING, a discharge of atmospheric electricity, can cause severe electric shock with heart stoppage and burns, and require artificial respiration.

Lightning seeks the quickest path to the ground. Despite the old saw, it is likely to strike the same place more than once—many tall buildings have been struck hundreds of times. A direct hit is not needed to fry a victim. Voltage in a bolt can be so great that the electricity can travel for some distance through conductors like soil or water. About 150 people in the United States are killed in lightning accidents each year. If you are with someone who has been struck by lightning, give mouth-to-mouth resuscitation and treat for heart stoppage, if necessary.

During a lightning storm if you're indoors, don't stand in doorways or near open windows. Keep away from large metal objects, the fire-place, plumbing fixtures, telephone, and television. All these can conduct lightning into your house.

If you're outdoors, seek shelter in a building. If no other shelter is available, stay low in a ditch, under a cliff, in a cave, or flat on the ground.

Never allow yourself to become the tallest object in an area. Lightning usually chooses high targets. If you are on a field when lightning starts, don't stand under an isolated tree. The lone tree is lightning's favorite target, and the charge is likely to reach you through the soil. You're safer in a grove, under the lower trees. As a last resort crouch down in the open with only your feet touching the ground.

Among the worst places to be in a lightning storm is on a boat, which not only sticks out above its surroundings but is afloat on a prime conductor. At the first sign of lightning make for shore. Also avoid being in water, atop a hill, on a horse or bicycle, or near a wire fence, overhead wires, or towers.

A car can provide good protection, but avoid touching metal parts. During one storm a friend was leaning against a car talking to the driver. Lightning struck the car. The driver, insulated from the charge, was unharmed. The other man provided a ground for the bolt and was killed.

Protect your house with a lightning rod. This equipment conducts lightning to the ground with no damage to the building or surroundings. If you are installing a lightning rod system, select one with a Master Label, indicating it meets Underwriters Laboratory specifications.

Ground your television mast. Have an electrician install a lightning arrestor, which protects your household wiring from surges of electricity.

See also ACCIDENTS; ARTIFICIAL RESPIRATION; BURNS; ELECTRIC SHOCK; HEART STOPPAGE.

LIP CANCER   See CANCER OF THE MOUTH.

LIP, HARE   See CLEFT LIP.

LIPIDS   See FATS.

LOCKJAW   See TETANUS.

LOW-BACK PAIN   See BACKACHE.

LOW BLOOD PRESSURE   See BLOOD PRESSURE.

LOW BLOOD SUGAR   See HYPOGLYCEMIA.

LSD   See DRUGS.

LUMBAGO   See RHEUMATISM.

LUNG CANCER   See CANCER OF THE LUNG.

LYMPHATIC CANCER   See HODGKIN'S DISEASE.

LYMPHOMA   See HODGKIN'S DISEASE.

MACHINES account for one in ten work accidents. Advice to the machine operator:

Use only tools and equipment you are authorized to use. Get checked out first by a qualified person.

Wear protection against eye injuries. Don't wear long sleeves, neckties, jewelry, loose trousers—or anything else that may get caught in a machine. For the same reason, avoid gloves when operating machinery in motion. Tie back long hair. Wear safety shoes with steel caps to protect your toes.

Before turning on a machine, be sure everyone is in the clear, and guards and safety devices are properly adjusted.

When adjusting or lubricating is needed, turn off the power and wait until the machine has come to a standstill. Don't try to slow down machinery with your hand or a makeshift device.

Keep your machine clean. Remove chips from a moving machine with a brush or stick, not your hands.

See also ACCIDENTS.

MAGNESIUM See MINERALS.

MALABSORPTION is the body's inability to take in sufficient nutrients through the small intestine. Common symptoms are unexplained weight loss, malnutrition, foul-smelling diarrhea, fatigue, poor appetite, weakness, and anemia.

Malabsorption often results from diseases of the small intestine. Chief among these is nontropical sprue. In children the condition is called celiac disease. The most frequent symptoms are a failure to thrive, poor appetite, and an abnormally large abdomen.

In sprue an intolerance to gluten (the protein portion of some grains) causes changes in the small intestine which lead to impaired absorption of fats, some vitamins, and sometimes carbohydrates and proteins.

Children with celiac disease may show symptoms at a few months of age. The disease often disappears by age five, and may reappear in adulthood.

Most children with the condition respond well to a diet free of gluten. Excluded are wheat, rye, oats, and barley. Rice, corn, and soybean flour can be substituted for these grains. Iron and vitamin supplements may be prescribed.

If you or your child must be on a gluten-free diet, be sure to read food labels. Soups, sauces, stews, and other foods may be thickened with wheat flour. When dining out, avoid breaded foods. At home you can bread foods with cornmeal, cornflake crumbs, or crushed potato chips. Cornstarch can be used to thicken soups and gravies.

Explore gluten-free breads, cakes, and cookies. Ask your doctor or local health department where you can get recipes for gluten-free foods.

Malabsorption may also result from massive doses of X rays to the small intestine, or surgical removal of part of the small intestine. Gallbladder disease and diseases of the pancreas and liver may result in malabsorption. So may some drugs and strong laxatives (see CONSTIPATION).

In children malabsorption may also be due to cystic fibrosis.

MALARIA was eradicated from the United States through mosquito control, and most doctors have never seen a case.

But it is now occurring more frequently, as more Americans venture into tropical countries —and as more people from such countries visit the United States. By not being recognized, a large number of cases go untreated and lead to the victim's death. Among the casualties of the Vietnam War were the servicemen—some 3,000 a year—who returned to this country with malaria.

In the rest of the world, there are more than 200 million cases and 2 million deaths every year. The problem is becoming more critical as strains resistant to medication become more widespread.

Anopheles mosquitoes, which can transmit the plasmodium parasites that cause malaria, still exist in many parts of the United States, and reintroduction of this infectious disease is a possible but unlikely event. For example, a summer camp counselor in New York State came down with the disease seemingly inexplicably. But, investigators found, the *Anopheles* mosquito is native to New York—and in the area was a young man from Africa who had just been treated for the same type of malaria. Presumably a mosquito had bitten him, then transmitted the disease to the counselor.

Like serum hepatitis, malaria can be spread in

blood transfusions. It may be passed from one user to another through infected needles.

Before going to a malarial region, take preventive medication. The Public Health Service recommends that all travelers to such areas take chloroquine phosphate once a week. Begin medication a week before arriving in the malaria region, and continue taking it for six weeks after you leave. Other drugs are available for travel to areas where malaria is resistant to chloroquine phosphate.

This and similar drugs are also used in treating the disease. On returning from a malarial region, be watchful for symptoms.

Check the malaria status of anyplace you plan to stop, even briefly. A group of airline passengers traveling between two areas free of malaria got the disease while they were off their jet at a refueling stop in a malarial area.

The malaria belt girdles the globe. It includes much of Mexico and Central and South America; nearly all of Africa, except South Africa and portions of the Sahara; large parts of the Middle East; most of Southeast Asia. The World Health Organization publishes a guide to malarial regions that may be available through your local health department.

Symptoms usually develop 10 to 35 days after exposure. Ancient Chinese thought the symptoms were caused by three demons—one equipped with a hammer causing the headache; another, a pail of cold water for the chills; the third, a stove for the fever. Other symptoms include loss of appetite, nausea, and vomiting. Complications may include anemia, encephalitis, and internal bleeding. Symptoms usually come in periodic attacks.

The Romans associated the disease with bad air (mala aria in Italian). They drained swamps as early as the fifth century B.C., a precaution some countries are just now getting around to.

See also INFECTIOUS DISEASE; MOSQUITOES; TRAVEL HEALTH.

MALIGNANT MELANOMA See CANCER OF THE SKIN; MOLES.

MALOCCLUSION (crooked teeth, buck teeth, faulty bite) is any abnormal tooth arrangement, including irregularities of tooth position (malalignment). It also refers to occlusion, the fitting together of the teeth on closing the jaws (see illustration).

Malocclusion may lead to other teeth and mouth disorders and to deformities of the jaws and face. The condition is a cause of tooth decay and pyorrhea, since food particles lodge more readily between teeth not in proper position and

teeth that overlap or are crowded are more difficult to clean. Crooked or protruding teeth detract from appearance and can result in emotional problems. Malocclusion also may result in poor speech, faulty chewing and swallowing habits, and misshaping of the roof of the mouth.

It is estimated that about half the children of any age need care by an orthodontist, the dental specialist who diagnoses and treats malocclusion. While malocclusion may occur at any age,

START ORTHODONTIC TREATMENT EARLY

The younger the child, the more likely his

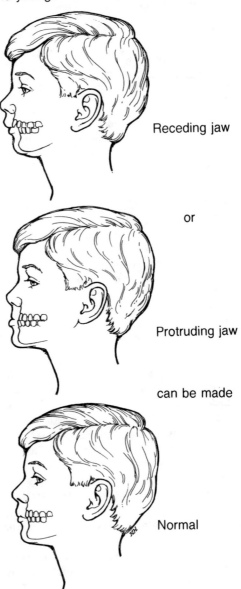

Receding jaw

or

Protruding jaw

can be made

Normal

it is most common during the time the baby teeth are being shed and the permanent teeth are erupting.

Adults often can profit from orthodontic treatment. Orthodontics can be performed at any time during a person's life if the bones, teeth, and gums are healthy. The earlier the start, though, the shorter the length of treatment.

The sooner you take a child to an orthodontist, the better. At one time parents were advised to wait until a youngster's permanent teeth were fully erupted. Now orthodontists feel treatment can often begin upon the eruption of the six-year molars. One reason for taking children to the dentist every six months starting at age two or three is so he can watch for malocclusion as teeth emerge.

If a child with an orthodontic problem is seen early enough, a great deal can often be done without braces to eliminate or at least alleviate developing malocclusion. The most obvious problem is extreme crowding of the front teeth or a severe protrusion commonly called the "Bugs Bunny" appearance. If not treated at an early age, the child is likely to fracture the protruding teeth in a fall, or develop psychological scars from playmates' teasing.

Seek a dentist's advice if a child has:

· Crowded, spaced, or twisted teeth.
· Protruding upper front teeth.
· A lower jaw that appears to be prominent, deficient, or swung to one side.
· Overly prominent lips as a result of front teeth (upper or lower) that stick out.
· Front teeth that do not meet when the back teeth are closed.
· Upper teeth that completely cover the lowers when the back teeth are closed.

Your dentist may feel you need to do nothing for the present. It's often normal for the permanent upper and lower front teeth to come in tipped, flared, or winged upward. Lip and tongue pressure, and biting pressure as the child's dental arches develop, usually will straighten these teeth. If they don't show any signs of adjustment within a year of eruption, early orthodontic treatment can often solve a problem that could call for extensive treatment later.

Head off problems. Beware of abnormal thumb-sucking. Some sucking of thumbs or fingers (or tongue-thrusting or lip-sucking) is part of the normal behavior pattern of infants. But a bored, unhappy, or overfatigued child or one who's not fed enough may engage in an abnormal amount of vigorous sucking.

In general, thumb-sucking during the first two years of a child's life need not cause any concern. Any irregularity in the position of teeth that is directly due to sucking habits will probably correct itself. But, especially if continued beyond age five, thumb- or finger-sucking may affect the position of the incoming permanent teeth and the shape of the jaws.

Even the slight pressure exerted in thumb-sucking may force teeth out of position and narrow the dental arches, making eventual orthodontic treatment necessary.

There are special hazards in tongue-thrusting, the poking of the tongue against the front teeth. It can misshape teeth and, if not corrected early, can ruin orthodontic work. This extremely common problem may require the attention of a myofunctional therapist—often a dental hygienist or certified speech therapist experienced in helping children retrain the muscles of the tongue.

Malocclusion sometimes is caused by a sleeping posture that produces prolonged pressure on the jaws.

If baby teeth are lost too early, the adjoining teeth may then shift, reducing the space intended for permanent teeth. On the other hand, if baby teeth are retained too long, incoming permanent teeth may be prevented from erupting at the normal time or may erupt in an undesirable position.

Children may inherit teeth that are unduly large, or a jaw that is too small to accommodate the teeth regardless of their size. Or a child may have extra or missing teeth, or there may be an abnormally wide strip of gumlike tissue between the front teeth, forcing them far apart.

A very prominent or an underdeveloped lower jaw is found more readily in children of parents who have these characteristics.

Any inherited tendency toward a dental or facial deformity can be aggravated by excessive thumb-sucking or other habits that exert pressures that interfere with growth.

Orthodontia. What does an orthodontist do? In a typical case with fixed steel appliances (braces) he puts a stainless steel band around each tooth that is involved—about 24 in the average teen-ager's mouth. Then he attaches wires to each band, and adjusts the tension and direction of force to move the teeth through the bone.

As a tooth moves, bone is built up on one side of it and taken off on the other side. In most cases rubber bands are used in addition to wires.

When a youngster comes out of braces, he's

generally given a wire and plastic retainer that can be snapped on and off, to be worn all day for a few months and then only during sleep. Orthodontists often like to check on patients intermittently until the major growth of the face is completed—for girls until 15 or 16, for boys until about 18. Consider orthodontic care completed only after the third molars (wisdom teeth) have erupted normally or otherwise been taken into account.

Although severe pain is rare in orthodontic treatment, during the first few days of wearing the appliances there may be discomfort or soreness. After the child gets used to the appliance, the discomfort generally will disappear. Additional periods of discomfort may occur as the appliances are adjusted.

To save money ask your orthodontist about the Andresen's appliance, a removal mouthpiece developed in Europe and coming into wider use in the United States. It's best suited to children under age nine, and is worn only at night. Results are generally not esthetically perfect, as fixed appliances might achieve. But the Andresen's appliance generally gets results well within the normal range, is more comfortable for the wearer, and costs perhaps one half to two thirds as much. The ADA adds this caution about the Andresen appliance: "While this *may* be a desirable option for the patient, it should be the qualified dentist and not the layman who makes the choice. After all, good oral care and not just economics should be the final determinant."

If you're a patient, you need to cooperate by keeping your teeth and appliances scrupulously clean. Appliances may lodge food particles between the teeth, so you can wind up with straight teeth full of cavities. Brush your teeth after every meal. Practice plaque control scrupulously. Avoid bubble gum, which when hard can bend the wire of an appliance and pull teeth in the wrong direction. Also go easy on apples, carrots, and other hard foods.

Since orthodontic care usually requires considerable time, most orthodontists require an initial payment to cover the cost of diagnostic materials and construction of the appliance. The remaining cost usually can be spread over a period of years. If you are unable to afford private treatment, check your local dental schools or clinics. They often accept orthodontic patients free or at nominal cost.

See also PLAQUE; TEETH AND MOUTH DISORDERS; TOOTHBRUSHING.

MALPRACTICE   See PHYSICIAN.

MALTA FEVER   See BRUCELLOSIS.

MARIE-STRÜMPELL DISEASE   See ANKYLOSING SPONDYLITIS.

MARIJUANA   See DRUGS.

MASTURBATION is not harmful. Contrary to the warnings of old wives and puritans, it does not cause warts on the hands, blindness, insanity, or any other physical damage.

Masturbation is the normal practice of sexual self-stimulation. It is estimated that more than 90 percent of males and more than 60 percent of females masturbate at least occasionally. This includes adults as well as children, married people as well as singles.

Babies usually discover the pleasure of fondling their genitals at a few months of age. This will not harm the child either physically or mentally. The only injury that could result is the child's feeling guilty and anxious if its parents react by scolding or punishing.

Young children normally masturbate when they are tired, bored, or irritable.

Parents may be embarrassed when a young child handles its genitals in public. If your child does this, explain that you know that what he or she is doing is enjoyable and that it's okay with you. But, like other bodily functions, it is the sort of thing people do in private.

No physical harm results even from extremely frequent masturbation—from a medical point of view there is no such thing as "excessive masturbation." A child's compulsive masturbation, however, may be a symptom of emotional stress.

An adolescent may try to relieve nonsexual tensions—loneliness, conflicts with peers or parents, feelings of inadequacy—through frequent masturbation. These youngsters may require professional counseling—not for the masturbation but for the underlying problems.

See also SEX DISORDER.

MEASLES (rubeola) is one of the most serious childhood diseases. This infectious disease could be wiped out by immunization. But many U.S. preschool children have not been vaccinated—so that epidemics are still a threat.

Don't be lulled by the commonness and "cute" name of measles (it comes from a Middle English word for *spots).* Many parents fail to realize that one case in six is followed by complications including ear infections, sinusitis, pneumonia, and encephalitis. Permanent deafness, blindness, and brain damage can result. Even a mild case of measles can result in irregular eating habits, emotional disturbances, and poor general health up to a year after the initial illness.

The lethal potential of measles is seen in West Africa, where an estimated 25 to 50 percent of measles cases are fatal, and in Chile, where measles is thought to account for half of all deaths from acute communicable diseases.

When to vaccinate. Children should be vaccinated at about 15 months old, recommends the Public Health Service. The measles vaccine can be combined with those for mumps and rubella.

The vaccine can usually prevent measles if given within two days after a child has been exposed to the disease. When an epidemic threatens, a child can be vaccinated at six months. Children vaccinated before they are ten months old need to be revaccinated to assure full protection.

Children should not be vaccinated if they are running a high fever or show other evidence of illness. A physician may advise against vaccinating children with certain serious diseases, such as leukemia, generalized cancer, tuberculosis, or epilepsy. If your child has an allergy to eggs, tell your doctor; vaccines prepared in canine cultures are available. Conversely, vaccines prepared in chick cultures can be used for those allergic to dog hair or dog dander. Allow a month to elapse between a measles vaccination and one for polio. Vaccination should be avoided during pregnancy.

Some children may develop a high fever (103° F or more) or a mild rash 7 to 12 days after vaccination. The reaction should last only 1 or 2 days. If your child develops high or persistent fever or shows other signs of illness, consult a physician.

Symptoms of measles. If measles occurs, the first symptoms usually suggest a severe cold. They include a runny nose, red watery eyes, and a hacking cough and appear 10 to 14 days after exposure to infection. The child may run a temperature ranging from slightly above normal to as high as 103° F or 104° F.

Almost always he will develop an inflammation of the mucous membrane lining the eyes, which causes sensitivity to light. About four days after the cold symptoms start, a blotchy red rash appears first on the head and neck and later on other parts of the body. A week later this rash begins to fade, accompanied by the forming of fine powdery scales on the skin. The disease is contagious from the start of the cold symptoms to five days after the appearance of the rash.

Treatment consists primarily of keeping the youngster comfortable and in comparative isolation. Isolation is important to keep him from giving the disease to anyone else, and to protect him from other infections he might get from visitors.

During the period the rash and fever are most severe, keep the child in bed for as much rest as possible. He should drink plenty of water and other fluids like broth, fruit juices, and soft drinks.

Although it is not necessary to keep his room dark, avoid strong light because the disease makes the eyes very sensitive to brightness. Light will not damage the eyes—nor will reading or watching television—but it may cause discomfort.

By the time the rash fades, the child is convalescing and cannot give his disease to anyone. For his own health, however, give him another week to regain his strength before he goes back to school and full activity.

This disease is also known as "common," "seven-day" or "ten-day" measles. German measles (rubella) is a wholly different disease.

See also INFECTIOUS DISEASE; RUBELLA.

MEDICAL DEDUCTIONS can lower your income tax. Federal tax law states simply that you can deduct what you pay for the "diagnosis, cure, mitigation, treatment, or prevention of disease." You may be able to claim many medical expenses provided you can show that they were necessary or related to medical care. A letter from your doctor will ordinarily suffice as proof.

If you have a question, call your local IRS office or see an accountant or other tax adviser. Be up to date in your information, since tax rulings and tax laws change frequently. Medical expenses are deductible only to the extent they pile up to more than 5 percent of your adjusted gross income. Since rules may change, be sure you're getting the maximum deduction the law currently allows.

Also explore health-related *exemptions*—income that's free of taxes. Did you get paid while away from your job ill? Sick pay can be tax-exempt within certain limits. Social Security or Veterans Administration benefits may be exempt from taxes. So may be payments from health, disability, and life-insurance policies. So too are workmen's compensation benefits.

Here are major expenses you can deduct to soften your tax bite:

Fees. Save your bills from medical and osteopathic physicians and surgeons, and from dentists, podiatrists, optometrists, and opticians. You also may tax-deduct fees for such specialists as midwives and lip-reading teachers. Although scientific medicine expresses doubts about the value of acupuncturists, chiropractors and

Christian Science practitioners, the IRS allows their fees to be deducted.

Hospitalization and medical insurance. The law lets you tax-deduct medical insurance premiums with your other medical expenses, subject to the 5 percent limitation.

Health-related travel. If you used a car to go to and from dental and medical offices for treatment, simply figure your travel costs at the allowable amount (now 9 cents) per mile and add any tolls and parking fees. The IRS says you can deduct parking only for the actual time involved with the health care.

If out-of-town travel is required for medical reasons such as physical examination or treatment, you may be able to deduct the travel expenses. Lodging (not meals) may be deducted at $50 per night for the taxpayer and one other person needed to care for him. Side trips aren't deductible.

You can deduct travel expenses to a climate essential to your treatment (such as a winter trip to Florida on doctor's advice for a heart patient). Your spouse's travel may also be deductible if you're too sick to travel alone. Ambulance hire is of course deductible.

Special equipment and furnishings. Deduct what you pay for items directly related to the treatment of an illness, such as crutches or a wheelchair.

Also deduct items that help a handicapped person get around—like a Seeing Eye dog, or hand controls on a car driven by someone who doesn't have full use of his legs.

Under certain circumstances and subject to certain limits, if you have an allergy, you may be able to deduct the cost of installing an air-conditioning system.

Other cases that may serve as models for you: A father could deduct the cost of a clarinet and lessons for his son because an orthodontist had advised him it would relieve the boy's malocclusion. A heart-disease sufferer was allowed to deduct the cost of a reclining chair because a cardiologist stated that the chair gave him the rest he needed.

Facilities for health care. Don't overlook what you paid to a hospital or to another facility. Nursing-home care can be claimed if the main reason for being there is medical treatment. If the stay is for personal or family reasons, you may deduct only the medical care. For a person at a therapeutic center for drug addiction you can deduct expenses including meals and lodging.

Nursing care. You can deduct for nursing care even though the person providing it has not had special training. If you can show you paid for *nursing*—rather than ordinary household, cleaning, or child-care services—you can claim payments to domestics.

Keep a log of the time a nonnurse spends on nursing as opposed to household duties, since the IRS allows deductions only for the portion of wages spent on nursing. If the outlays are not deductible as medical expenses, check the rules for deducting costs of caring for children and disabled dependents.

Drugs and special food. Save all your pharmacy receipts, since drugs prescribed by a physician can be included as medical expenses to the extent they exceed 5 percent of your income when combined with other medical costs.

Vitamins and similar diet supplements are deductible only if prescribed or recommended by a doctor. The IRS won't allow deductions for such items if they're taken merely for general health purposes.

Also deductible are costs of foods and beverages prescribed by a physician. But the item must be in addition to the normal diet and not part of nutritional needs. One taxpayer on a low-sodium diet was allowed by the tax court to deduct the difference between what he paid for the special food he needed and what it would have cost him for regular food.

Mental health. Claim fees paid to a psychiatrist, psychologist, or sex therapist. Costs of a special school may be deductible if you can show they're primarily for the purpose of preventing or easing a physical or mental defect.

See also HEALTH INSURANCE; HOSPITAL; PHYSICIAN.

MEDICAL IDENTIFICATION, EMERGENCY See EMERGENCY MEDICAL IDENTIFICATION.

MEDICAL SUPPLIES widely sold at drug counters should be available in every household. In your medicine chest keep on hand at least these basic items:

Aspirin or acetaminophen (see ASPIRIN).
Liquid antacid (see ANTACIDS).
Calamine lotion (see ITCHING).
Oral decongestant (see NOSE DROPS).
Enema syringe (see CONSTIPATION).
Rubbing alcohol (see ANTISEPTICS).
Adhesive bandages (Band-Aids), the nonmedicated type, for minor wounds.
Roll bandage, 2 inches wide.
Sterile gauze pads, 4 inches square, separately wrapped.
Elastic bandages, about 3 inches wide (see SPRAINS).

Adhesive tape, one roll 1 or 2 inches wide.

Scissors, large and sharp enough to cut gauze or cloth.

Ice bag (see COMPRESSES).

Electric heating pad (see COMPRESSES).

Clinical thermometer (see FEVER).

Sunscreen (see SUNBURN).

Electric vaporizer (see HUMIDITY).

Tweezer with fine points for removing SPLINTERS (which see).

Hydrocortisone skin medication, such as Cortaid, for itching and rashes, insect bites, poison ivy.

Safety pins (to use with bandages or slings).

Antidiarrheal preparation containing paregoric or polycarbophil, such as Kaopectate (see DIARRHEA).

Syrup of ipecac and activated charcoal (see POISONING).

Tape to your medicine chest door a list that includes the telephone numbers of:

Your physician

Your dentist

Ambulance service (or 24-hour taxi service)

Nearest emergency room

Poison control center

Pharmacy (an all-night one if possible)

Police department

Fire department

At least as important as a well-stocked home medicine cabinet is a kit of first aid supplies stored in your car for emergencies. Assemble a special kit for camping hazards.

See also ACCIDENTS; CAMPING; FIRST AID SUPPLIES.

MEDICATIONS See DRUGS.

MEDITERRANEAN FEVER See BRUCELLOSIS.

MELANOMA, MALIGNANT See CANCER OF THE SKIN; MOLES.

MÉNIÈRE'S DISEASE results from an imbalance of the fluid pressures in the inner ear. Its symptoms are some degree of hearing loss, usually in just one ear; tinnitus (noise in the involved ear); and episodes of extreme vertigo (dizziness), often lasting several hours. The vertigo may be so severe as to produce sweating, nausea, and vomiting.

The disease tends to recur and comes in attacks of varying degree and frequency of dizziness. An acute attack may end without any treatment, but the sudden and severe onset may make driving unsafe.

Though the exact cause is unknown, it seems to be related to emotional stress. One of the goals of medical treatment is to try to reduce that stress.

Drugs to suppress dizziness or control excess fluid in the ear may help relieve the vertigo. Physicians usually advise restricting use of salt, coffee, tobacco, and alcohol.

Surgery may be required when the attacks are frequent and severe and cannot be controlled by other measures. One approach to the treatment of the condition is the use of special sound waves (ultrasound), which destroys the area of the inner ear responsible for the vertigo, yet leaves the hearing unimpaired.

Other approaches include draining the inner-ear fluid into other parts of the skull and cutting the vestibular (balance) nerve. Dizziness may also be permanently relieved by a total labyrinthectomy (complete destruction of the portion of the inner ear regulating balance) if hearing has already been severely impaired and has not returned with treatment.

See also HEARING LOSS.

MENINGITIS is an inflammation of the meninges, the membranes covering the brain and spinal cord. It is a medical emergency. Survivors may be left with disabilities such as deafness, paralysis, and mental retardation, though with early treatment most recover fully.

The most severe and contagious form is caused by bacteria, principally *Haemophilus influenzae* and three strains of a type called meningococci. It chiefly affects children and young adults. With about 18,000 cases and 1,000 deaths a year bacterial meningitis kills or damages as many youngsters as polio ever did.

Meningitis is also caused by viruses and can be a complication of a wide range of conditions: cancer, cat scratch disease, chickenpox, coccidioidomycosis, encephalitis, infectious hepatitis, lead poisoning, leptospirosis, measles, mononucleosis, mumps, rubella, sinusitis, stroke, syphilis, toxoplasmosis, and trichinosis.

Bacterial meningitis usually begins with a high, fluctuating temperature. The fever is accompanied by a severe headache, shivering fits, and perspiration. There is likely to be an inflammation of the nose and throat and violent vomiting. Frequently a skin rash of tiny bright red spots occurs.

A typical feature of all types of meningitis is a rigid neck, with stiffness in the back and shoulders. The neck muscles may be cramped and the head bent backward. In severe cases, the body may form an arc as spasms draw the head and feet backward.

If you suspect meningitis, get medical help immediately. Persons exposed to meningitis caused by bacteria may require preventive antibiotics. Victims need to be isolated until 24 hours after the start of antibiotic treatment.

The bacteria causing meningitis generally enter the body through the nose and mouth. They are spread by direct contact or by droplets sprayed into the air through sneezing and coughing.

During an epidemic several thousand times more people carry and spread the bacteria than become ill. It is thought that most people carry antibodies naturally—and those who lack them are susceptible to the disease.

Cleanliness and personal hygiene—taking care to cover the mouth when coughing or sneezing—help prevent spread of bacteria. This is particularly important when people live in close groups. Beds in barracks or dormitories should be placed as far apart as possible.

A vaccine against *Haemophilus influenzae* is recommended for children beginning at age 2.

Immunization against meningococci strains Type A and Type C is available for people at special risk. Epidemics used to recur on military reservations, but now that all recruits routinely get meningitis vaccine, the problem has virtually disappeared.

See also INFECTIOUS DISEASE.

MENOPAUSE (climacteric) refers to the two- to five-year span during which a woman's body undergoes the physiological changes leading to the end of menstruation. Thereafter she can no longer bear children.

Most women experience menopause between 44 and 53, although it may begin as early as 36 or as late as the sixties. The age when a woman began menstruating—be it early or late—has no bearing on when she will reach menopause. Cigarette smoking accelerates menopause—at age 48 a woman who smokes a pack or more a day is twice as likely to be past menopause as a woman who never smoked.

The onset of menopause causes changes in the menstrual pattern—you may have a heavier or lighter flow than normal or you may completely miss periods.

As menopause nears, the ovaries produce less and less estrogen, the principal female sex hormone. Ovulation stops, and the production of the hormone progesterone abruptly declines. The pituitary reacts by attempting to stimulate production of these hormones. The intricate glandular balance of the body goes into turmoil, attempting to achieve a new balance.

Hot flashes. The most common symptom of the menopause is the hot flash or flush, a feeling of heat that spreads over the body. There may be visible blushing, which starts at the chest and rises up to the neck, face, and head. From there it may spread all over the body. You may alternately sweat and shiver.

If you take your temperature during an episode, you'll find that you don't have any real fever.

These hot flashes may start from two to five years before the actual menopause, and may continue for several years thereafter. They may occur by day or night. Some women experience as many as 20 or more a day, and may be awakened by this sensation several times at night. Other women are barely troubled.

Hot flashes are thought to be caused by the sudden excessive dilation of small blood vessels close to the skin's surface. This results in more blood being brought to the area, which produces increased local heat and activates the sweat glands.

The instability of the blood vessels that causes the flashes is probably due to changes in hormone production.

Other common symptoms associated with menopause are dizziness, weakness, insomnia, nervousness, headache, and backache. There may be sharp changes in blood pressure, heart palpitations, or stomach upsets. There may be weight gain or redistribution of weight, and breast pains. Brown patches may develop, especially in areas exposed to light, such as in the face, hands, arms, or legs. A woman may also experience a recurrence of skin allergy.

Late in the menopausal period, vaginal tissues may become thin and shrunken. They lose their elasticity and become dry and easily irritated. Known as atrophic vaginitis, this condition can make sexual intercourse painful. A water-soluble jelly such as K-Y can be used as a lubricant. Treatment with estrogen creams can relieve the problem, but are absorbed into the body and may be no safer than estrogen taken orally.

Don't assume all physical symptoms are related to your menopause. This is the time of life when diabetes, cancer, high blood pressure, and other diseases are most likely to occur. Although of menopausal age, if you're starting to miss periods, be sure the cause isn't pregnancy.

Report all symptoms to your doctor, especially heavy bleeding between periods, and any vaginal bleeding after your periods have stopped. After menopause continue to have periodic pelvic examinations at least once a year.

Depression in menopause. Anxiety and depression sometimes afflict menopausal women. Emotional stress may result from a multitude of changes, in addition to menopause, facing a woman at this time of her life.

A woman who devoted her life to raising a family suddenly finds herself with grown children who do not need her. A career woman may find herself pressured by younger women. A woman may find herself depressed by wrinkles and overweight in a culture that puts a premium on youth. She may be depressed by the realization that she will never again be able to bear children.

Psychotherapy may be needed for a woman suffering severe emotional disturbances. Some women, on the other hand, go through the climacteric without any negative psychological symptoms. These are usually women who have managed other stressful situations effectively. To clarify what menopause entails (and scotch prevalent misconceptions), it's a good idea for husband and wife to have a joint visit with her doctor.

Sex and menopause. Normal sex urges remain after menopause. Indeed many couples welcome release from the possibility of pregnancy and find sex more enjoyable than before.

Since the ovarian cycle is unpredictable during menopause, use contraception for a year after the last menstrual period. A woman taking birth control pills will continue to menstruate.

A younger woman who has had both ovaries surgically removed will go through a so-called artificial menopause. It is often more troublesome than a natural menopause since the cessation of hormone production is abrupt. Hormone therapy is usually called for.

After several months to a year or more, a woman's body adjusts to the hormonal changes, and the menopause-related symptoms disappear. Many women report a new vigor and excellent health after menopause.

Estrogen replacement therapy can help relieve menopause symptoms. It may be helpful in the treatment of hot flashes, atrophic vaginitis, and osteoporosis, a bone problem often accelerating at menopause.

But many doctors are cautious about prescribing it, since long-term users of estrogens are at a considerably higher risk of cancer of the endometrium (the lining of the uterus) than women who do not use estrogens.

Because of this and other potential hazards, estrogen therapy should be given in the lowest dose that will be effective.

Before a woman starts on estrogen replacement therapy, she should have a thorough physical examination—including a Pap smear for detection of cancer of the cervix, and an examination of the uterus for precancerous changes. Estrogen therapy should not be given to women who have liver disease, breast or endometrial cancer, hypertension, or heart disease.

Most doctors prescribe estrogen in the lowest possible dose for three weeks each month, adding progestin for the last 10 days. This combination of estrogen and progestin seems to reduce, and may even eliminate, the risk of endometrial cancer associated with estrogen therapy alone. On balance, most authorities now believe that the potential benefits of estrogen replacement therapy outweigh the risks.

See a doctor every 6 to 12 months while on estrogen therapy. Report any unscheduled vaginal bleeding. Estrogen therapy does not prevent wrinkles or other visible signs of aging.

See also BIRTH CONTROL; MENSTRUATION; OSTEOPOROSIS.

MENSTRUATION need not limit a woman's physical activity.

Except for a possibly increased susceptibility to colds, a woman is no more susceptible to illness during menstruation than at any other time. She can engage in sports, and neither bathing nor swimming need be restricted during her period.

The menstrual cycle. Most girls begin to menstruate between 11 and 13½, although it is not uncommon to start menstruating as early as 9 or as late as 18.

The lining of the uterus sloughs off at intervals of roughly four weeks. It is discharged in a flow of blood, carrying with it the unfertilized eggs. A menstrual period generally lasts from three to seven days. An average of about 3 ounces of blood is lost.

Menstrual periods continue until a woman reaches the end of menopause. Menstruation also ceases during pregnancy and often during breastfeeding.

During the first years menstruation may be irregular, but most women eventually establish a regular pattern. It is common for intervals to be as brief as 21 days or as long as 45.

Some women never become entirely regular, but this does not affect their health. Irregularity is also common in the older woman just before menopause.

A woman of any age needs a physical examination when her irregularity is more than slight, as when there are many months between periods. Amenorrhea—failure to menstruate—is not a disease itself but a symptom of other conditions.

In *primary amenorrhea* a woman 18 or older has never menstruated. This may be due to a large number of physiological conditions, many of them genetic. She may have an obstruction of the cervix or the vagina. She may have been born with a deformed or missing uterus. Her ovaries may be malfunctioning. She may be suffering from hormonal deficiencies. Psychological stress may also play a part.

If menstruation begins and then ceases for six or more cycles, the condition is called *secondary amenorrhea*. It may be due to an ovarian cyst, or a pituitary or ovarian tumor. Tuberculosis, heart disease, diabetes, and hyperthyroidism may also interrupt the menstrual cycle.

Rapid weight loss (such as 30 pounds in as many days) may cause periods to stop. So may overweight. Emotional stress is responsible in a large number of cases. A woman having premarital or extramarital affairs sometimes stops menstruating because of anxiety and guilt—frightening her further into believing she is pregnant.

It's normal to gain weight and retain fluids during menstruation. You may also experience a dull ache in the lower abdomen and mild cramping. Some women break out in acne, probably related to hormones secreted by the ovaries. Breasts may be swollen and tender.

Toxic shock syndrome (TSS). This is a rare, sometimes fatal, disease that strikes primarily at young women who use tampons. A recently recognized disorder, TSS symptoms include sudden high fever, almost always over 102° F; vomiting and diarrhea; rapid drop in blood pressure; a sunburnlike rash, particularly on the palms and soles. There may also be dizziness; headache; muscle and joint pain; sore throat; shock. The vast majority of cases of TSS have been in menstruating women who were using tampons.

The disease is caused by an infectious toxin-producing bacterium called *Staphylococcus aureus*. Tampons appear to be related to the development of TSS. In experiments, some highly absorbent synthetic fibers were found to absorb magnesium, which can enhance the production of the toxin. Tampon manufacturers have removed these fibers, making for generally safer tampons.

TSS usually lasts four or five days, with one or two weeks of convalescence. Most deaths have occurred within a week; the mortality rate is 5 to 6 percent.

Treatment for TSS is hospitalization in an intensive care unit. Large volumes of intravenous fluids and medication are given to help raise blood pressure. Antibiotics may be given.

You can almost entirely eliminate your risk of TSS by not using tampons. If you choose to use tampons, do so intermittently. Use sanitary napkins at night and on days of light menstrual flow. Avoid high-absorbency tampons, which seem to be associated with a greater risk of TSS. Most such tampons are labeled "super-plus." Avoid tampons if you have had TSS, and for six to eight weeks after giving birth. If you experience symptoms of TSS, stop using tampons immediately and consult a doctor.

Sex during menstruation. There is no physiological reason to abstain from sex. Indeed many women report an increased sex drive during menstruation.

It's prudent to use birth control even during menstruation. It is almost impossible for a woman to conceive during her menstrual period, since the uterus is sloughing off its lining and cannot harbor a pregnancy. Still pregnancy occasionally does occur during menstruation.

Take particular care to use contraception if a menstrual period is very long. Ovulation—the production of an egg—may begin even while blood is showing. There is a slight chance that sperm could survive long enough for fertilization to take place.

If you use an IUD, check to see that it's in place after each menstrual period.

Menstrual problems. See a doctor if menstrual pain is so severe it interferes with your daily activities. Called dysmenorrhea, this condition is sometimes due to organic causes, such as infections, tumors, or pelvic inflammatory diseases.

In most cases painful menstrual cramps are thought to be caused by the body's production of hormonelike chemicals known as prostaglandins. Painful menstruation is estimated to afflict half of all women at one time or another. It is especially common in young women and in those who have not given birth.

Severe menstrual pain can usually be relieved with nonsteroidal anti-inflammatory drugs, such as nonprescription ibuprofen (Advil, Nuprin). Aspirin often works for mild to moderate menstrual pain.

Many women experience premenstrual symptoms. For a day or two before menstruation begins, they may feel tense, irritable, or tired. There is usually quick relief once menstruation begins.

About 5 percent of women in their reproductive years are thought to experience severe, incapacitating psychological symptoms before menstruation. This is called premenstrual syndrome and is usually marked by cyclical anxiety, depression, or irrational behavior. The cause is unknown. It is thought to be related to hormonal changes preceding menstruation. Some women have reportedly obtained relief with a regimen of progesterone suppositories, exercise, changes in diet (alcohol, sugar, and salt are eliminated), and vitamin supplements.

Be watchful for excessive menstruation (menorrhagia). It is often hard to judge the amount of flow that should be considered abnormal. In general, be concerned if ordinary pads changed several times a day do not afford protection, or if the menstrual blood forms into large clots.

Cancer, tumors, polyps, inflammations, and diseases such as rheumatic fever can cause excessive bleeding. It can also be due to hormone disorders or abnormalities of the reproductive organs. Emotional factors may precipitate excessive menstruation.

Also see your doctor if you bleed between periods or after intercourse.

See also BIRTH CONTROL.

MENTAL RETARDATION afflicts more than 6 million people in this country. Between 100,000 and 200,000 babies born each year are mentally retarded.

A child who is mentally retarded has unusual difficulty in learning and in coping with the problems of everyday life. Depending on the degree of retardation, he may seem just mildly slower than other children, or he may be incapable of doing virtually any tasks for himself. He may have problems of speech, vision, and hearing and impairments of motor coordination.

Get diagnosis and help as soon as you suspect mental retardation. While there is no cure, most retarded children can be helped through special classes and vocational training centers. Most states have clinics for diagnosis and evaluation of mentally retarded children. Contact your local health department.

Counselors can advise you whether the child should be placed in an institution or raised at home, now the recommendation in most cases. They can help you seek a way of life for a child suited to his abilities, and aid you in dealing with your own problems in coping with a retarded child.

For more information and assistance contact the following: National Association for Retarded Citizens, 2501 Avenue J, Arlington, Texas 76011; President's Committee on Mental Retardation, Washington, D.C. 20201; National Easter Seal Society for Crippled Children and Adults, 2023 West Ogden Avenue, Chicago, Illinois 60612; Closer Look Information Center, Box 1492, Washington, D.C. 20013.

How you can help. If your child seems to be progressing slowly and you and your pediatrician suspect mental retardation, it may be many months before you can get confirmation. In the meantime you can help your child reach his fullest potential by doing the following to stimulate his development:

Place bright toys and pictures around his crib, playpen, and other areas where he spends a lot of time. Mobiles or mechanical toys are particularly interesting for a baby to watch. Once or twice a day, move a bright object slowly in front of his eyes.

Change his position often and encourage him to look around.

If he doesn't move much on his own, set aside a few minutes twice a day and move his arms and legs up and down and around.

When he is four months old, begin pulling him from a lying position on his back up to a sitting position. Be sure to support his head if he doesn't have sufficient control of it.

Provide him with objects of various textures. If he doesn't hold on to objects by four months, help him learn by placing an object in his hand and closing his fingers around it.

Introduce him to a wide variety of sounds—music, the telephone, singing. When your child makes a sound on his own, repeat it.

Set aside time to play with your child—all games are learning experiences. The organizations listed above can provide you with suggestions for activities that can help improve a wide variety of skills.

Causes of retardation. No specific causes can be found for most mental retardation. Sometimes it is due to birth defects such as Down's syndrome or hydrocephalus. About half the children born with cerebral palsy are mentally retarded. Metabolic problems such as PKU may also be responsible.

Sometimes it has been traced to diseases in the mother during early pregnancy, such as rubella, meningitis, or toxoplasmosis. Syphilis in the mother and Rh disease can also result in mental retardation.

A mother in poor health and poor nutritional condition runs a higher than average risk of having a retarded infant; retardation is often accompanied by premature delivery and low birth weight.

Problems during delivery can injure the child's brain; accidents later in life can do the same. Some childhood diseases—especially whooping cough and measles—can lead to retardation. Lead poisoning or malnutrition may have the same effect.

Since some kinds of mental retardation are due to hereditary factors, if you have a retarded child, consult a genetic counselor before deciding to have more children.

See also BIRTH DEFECTS.

MESCALINE See DRUGS.

MESOTHELIOMA See ASBESTOS.

METHADONE See DRUGS.

MICROWAVE OVENS emit a form of radiation that can cause injury by raising the temperature of body organs.

Microwaves are very short electromagnetic waves that can cook food rapidly. The waves increase the motion of molecules, which generates heat. Microwaves leaking from an oven can cause burns deep within the body without a heat sensation to serve as a warning, since the body's temperature sensors are principally in the skin.

The eye is especially vulnerable to microwaves because it can't dissipate heat readily. Animal experimentation has established that microwaves can cause cataracts. Reliable human data are not yet available on this, but preliminary studies suggest that microwaves can cause cataracts in humans as well.

Heart-disease victims who have cardiac pacemakers need to avoid microwave ovens, which may cause the pacemaker to malfunction. Animal experiments suggest that microwaves may injure unborn infants and impair the ability of white blood cells to fight disease.

If you can live without a microwave oven, you may be safer. The FDA's Bureau of Radiological Health has set leakage-control standards that it feels make all new ovens safe. However over a long period of use and possible abuse the safety features may fail. And even the allowable leakage may be hazardous. The bureau itself has declared that "a great deal of research" is needed to assess the health effects of long-term low-level microwave radiation.

In any case any radiation leakage from an oven does not affect the food cooked in it. No radiation remains in the food.

If you do buy a microwave oven, be sure that it is received in good condition. Operate it according to the manufacturer's instructions. Check that it bears a statement that it meets Bureau of Radiological Health standards.

To help minimize the danger of radiation hazards keep the oven very clean and unplug it when you're not using it. Keep several feet away from an operating oven, taking care not to peer into it while it's on. Keep children away.

If the door seal or interlock fail, don't operate the oven until it has been repaired. Don't poke objects into the viewing screen, door seals, or other openings. Inspect the oven periodically to make sure all screws and hinges are tight. Never operate the oven when it's empty.

Out of prudence you can have your oven checked for leakage at a service center authorized by the manufacturer. Or you may be able to have the Bureau of Radiological Health check it for you.

See also RADIATION.

MIGRAINE (sick headache) pain results from a temporary dilation of the blood vessels in the head.

Migraine is a throbbing, usually one-sided headache that begins slowly and typically lasts from 12 to 18 hours. One out of three migraine sufferers experiences an aura 10 to 30 minutes before an attack. There may be flashes of light, numbness, and partial, temporary blindness. This type of migraine is called a classic migraine. Where there is no aura, it is a common migraine.

Migraines usually appear at regular intervals —two to four attacks per month is typical. Attacks usually occur more frequently during periods of emotional stress. Sometimes eating particular foods seems to set off an attack. Common culprits are ripened cheeses, chocolate, chicken livers, sausage, citrus fruits, and caffeine. Alcohol may also precipitate attacks. So may fatigue, hunger, weather and temperature changes, menstruation, ovulation, and pregnancy.

The migraine headache is often accompanied by nausea, vomiting, and a sensitivity to light. The headache is often severe and may sometimes be incapacitating. A migraine sufferer usually feels better lying down.

The typical migraine sufferer is a woman who is hardworking, productive, perfectionistic, rigid, and meticulous. She usually has a family history of migraine.

Migraine attacks can often be ended if the sufferer breathes slowly and deeply into a bag, inhaling his expired air to raise the carbon dioxide level of his blood. One physician reported in the *British Medical Journal* that patients using a plastic bag and mouth valve terminated attacks in 10 to 30 minutes.

Migraines may also be relieved by the drug ergotamine tartrate (Cafergot, Ergostat, Wigraine). Methysergide (Sansert) and propranolol (Inderal) may help prevent recurrences. Aspirin is unlikely to help. Psychotherapy is sometimes recommended.

In a new type of treatment some migraine sufferers are being trained to relieve their migraines by concentrating on moving blood to their hands at the first sign of an attack. This biofeedback technique works, some doctors speculate, by diverting blood that might otherwise go to the head during a migraine attack.

If you're subject to migraines, avoid birth control pills. They may precipitate attacks or cause severe complications.

In children food allergy may be a cause of migraine. Cheese, nuts, and chocolate most often trigger an attack.

Cluster headaches (histamine headaches) are similar to migraine, but usually worse. Men are the usual victims of such headaches. Cluster headaches start fast and usually last fifteen minutes to three hours. The pain is intense, sometimes so severe that the sufferer becomes suicidal.

Cluster headache often wakes the sufferer out of sleep. His eyes may tear and his nose may be stuffy. Unlike the migraine sufferer he is usually too agitated to lie down. He may have several headaches a day for six to eight weeks. Then they may disappear for a year or more.

Cluster headache may be precipitated by alcohol, vasodilators, nitrates, or histamine. Heredity plays no part in cluster headache. It may be treated with drugs, chief among them a nasal solution of 4 percent lidocaine (xylocaine), methysergide (Sansert), and steroids. A recent study suggests that cluster headache may be relieved by taking two Sinutabs, a nonprescription decongestant, at the first sign of an attack. But Sinutabs should not be taken by anyone with high blood pressure.

Migraine and cluster headaches are called vascular headaches because they involve changes in blood vessels. For more information, contact The National Migraine Foundation (5252 North Western Avenue, Chicago, Illinois 60625).

See also HEADACHE.

MINERALS are necessary in small amounts for many body processes. Without enough iron, for example, anemia will develop. Sodium is essential for maintaining a proper water balance in your body.

If your diet is nutritionally balanced, you're likely to be getting sufficient minerals, for they occur in many foods rich in protein and vitamins (see tables of food values and mineral requirements under NUTRITION). Supplemental minerals may be needed during pregnancy, in the elderly, and when the diet is inadequate.

Other minerals you need are:

Calcium—the most abundant in your body—is necessary for healthy teeth and bones and proper functioning of the heart and nervous system. Next to iron calcium is the mineral most likely to be deficient in your diet. Women past menopause need a diet high in calcium in order to help avoid osteoporosis. Calcium supplements may be necessary for many.

Best sources of calcium are milk and milk products, including skimmed milk, yogurt, cheeses—but not butter or margarine. One cup of skimmed milk provides nearly a third of your daily requirement.

Dark-green leafy vegetables—kale, collard greens, mustard greens, turnip greens—also contribute significant amounts of calcium. Soybeans are another good source, as are canned sardines and salmon if you eat the bones.

Sufficient calcium is especially important for children and for women during pregnancy and breastfeeding.

Don't count on coffee whiteners or nondairy creamers. They're made with chemicals and oils —and are likely to be deficient in milk's protein, vitamins, and other minerals.

"Filled" or "imitation" milk is a product in which milk fat is replaced by a vegetable oil. It usually costs less than whole or skimmed milk and has many of the nutrients of nonfat milk. But since ingredients vary, check a particular brand's nutritive value.

Fluoride occurs naturally in the water supply in many areas. It is plentiful in some fish, cheeses, plants, meats, and especially tea. Adding it to water helps in the prevention of tooth decay (see FLUORIDATION).

Iodine deficiency can cause thyroid disease. If you live in inland areas where soil is deficient in iodine, use iodized salt. Fish is another good source of iodine.

Magnesium is necessary for bones, teeth, and many body functions. It is available in many foods. Among the best sources are whole grain breads and cereals, dry beans and peas, nuts, and dark-green vegetables.

Phosphorus is necessary for strong bones and teeth and for good muscle and nerve responses. It is found in milk and milk products, meat, and cereals.

Potassium helps maintain a normal water balance and normal cell growth. Foods high in protein are generally also high in potassium. It's especially high in bananas, raisins, baked potatoes, winter squash, and oranges. Potassium is also plentiful in green vegetables, and in apples, cantaloupes, cherries, dates, figs, and prunes.

If you're taking a diuretic to lower your blood pressure, you're likely to lose potassium as well as sodium in your water outflow. In making up potassium lost from a diuretic, in general eat fresh or frozen food rather than canned food. Potassium leaches out in the water canners use to cook or store vegetables; moreover, canners generally add salt, which contains sodium. To conserve potassium use as little water as possible in cooking—and save leftover liquid for soups or stews.

If you need to take potassium chloride supplements, you may find commercial preparations unpalatable. Better-tasting and often lower-priced is a plain 10 percent aqueous solution of potassium chloride mixed by your pharmacist. Drink it in fresh squeezed or low-sodium tomato juice.

Trace elements are minerals needed by the body in minute quantities. They include zinc, copper, manganese, molybdenum, nickel, tin, silicon, vanadium, chromium, cobalt, and selenium. A diet with adequate protein will usually provide sufficient trace elements.

Except for iron, iodine, zinc, and calcium, mineral deficiencies are uncommon. But you can suffer from mineral depletion after a severe bout of vomiting or diarrhea. People who suffer from malabsorption and ulcerative colitis are also prone to mineral deficiencies. Some drugs, such as diuretics for high blood pressure and edema, can cause deficiencies.

There is no truth in the notion that the American soil is depleted and unable to provide you with properly nourishing foods.

Zinc supplements may be needed by people with vision problems because of alcohol-caused cirrhosis of the liver, and by those with an inherited disorder of zinc malabsorption called acrodermatitis enteropathica.

A frequently recurring health swindle is the sale of bottled ocean water or sea salt with the claim that it supplies minerals that are essential to life. Actually foods in a normal diet contain all necessary minerals in much greater abundance than ocean water.

Don't self-prescribe mineral supplements. Many minerals are toxic in large doses. The trace minerals, needed in minute quantities, are particularly dangerous—sometimes fatal—in overdose.

See also IRON; NUTRITION; SODIUM.

MINIBIKES These small motorized bicycles are very vulnerable to accidents. They rarely have windshields, so there is no protection if the rider crashes into a wire fence or cable. Because of their size they have a low profile on the highway, making it hard for car drivers to see them.

They generally have inadequate lights, weak acceleration, low visibility, poor handling. Their design is inherently faulty because they are built like toys, with small wheels, a short wheelbase, and minimal braking capacity.

You'll do your child a favor by *not* buying him a minibike. There is considerable evidence that youngsters under 14—the principal market for the vehicles—lack the discipline or skill to handle them safely.

If you must buy a minibike, at least reduce the hazards by having your youngster use it only away from roads and pedestrians. Require that he wear a safety helmet and sturdy shoes and clothing.

Secure experienced off-road instruction. Join or form a safety-conscious minibike club. Don't permit the bike to be lent to inexperienced friends. For your legal protection, check your insurance carrier for what additional coverage you need.

See also ACCIDENTS; BICYCLES.

MISCARRIAGE See ABORTION; PREGNANCY.

MOLD ALLERGY is an abnormal sensitivity to the microscopic spores (similar to seeds) of mold, a type of fungus. Mold spores are major causes of asthma, hay fever, and eczema. They often complicate pollen sensitivity and are particularly common offenders in allergic children. For ideas on reducing mold around your house, see illustration.

The outdoor mold allergy season is long—molds may be present at all times of the year. Household molds may grow in profusion in a cool, damp atmosphere, as in a basement. In hot, humid climates they will thrive on stale bread and other foods. They also flourish in log piles, compost heaps, and dark, damp garages.

Air-conditioning systems may harbor one type of fungus, leading to shortness of breath, chills, and fever. A wintertime allergy is caused by a similar fungus that grows in heating systems. Yet another type of mold grows on old books, causing victims to suffer nasal congestion and eye inflammation soon after entering bookstores and libraries.

Because of their lightness and tininess, spores are readily wind-borne and widely disseminated. When in the air in significant quantities, they may be responsible for allergic symptoms similar to those caused by plant pollen.

In the northern United States the most common mold spores begin to appear in May and rise to a peak in October. Molds can be found year round in the southern states, and they are of prime importance as causes of respiratory allergy for at least nine months of the year. In agricultural areas a great atmospheric concentration of molds results from the turning of the soil. The greatest overall exposure to molds occurs in the Midwest grain belt.

Identifying a mold allergy. Symptoms in most cases begin before age 20. Asthma is most fre-

12 WAYS TO CUT MOLD

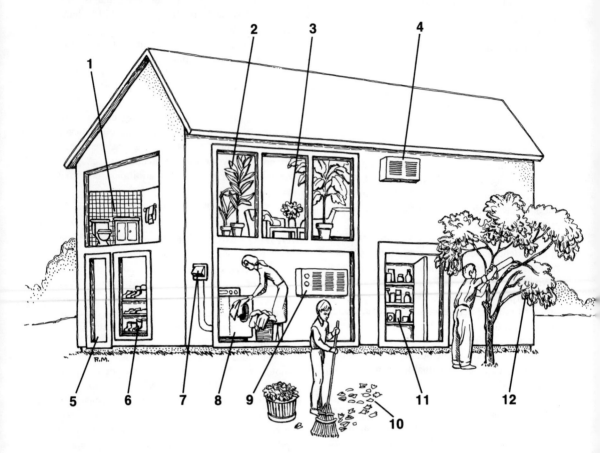

1. Wash tiles and grout frequently
2. Indoor plants may breed mold in potting soil
3. Dried flowers often contain mold
4. Air conditioners, humidifiers, and dehumidifiers should be checked frequently for a musty smell. Spray them with a mold inhibitor
5. Paint basements with a mold-inhibiting paint
6. Allow damp footwear to air out and dry
7. Vent clothes dryer to the outside, instead of to the basement
8. Dry clothes immediately after laundering
9. Dehumidify your cellar
10. In the fall, keep yard free of fallen leaves
11. Periodically check stored food for possible mold growth
12. Avoid heavy vegetation around the house, as it encourages dampness and mold growth

quently the predominating condition, sometimes occurring only in the summer. Rhinitis (stuffy or running nose) may be present, with or without asthma.

Frequently mold symptoms begin when there is no pollen in the atmosphere and continue long after ragweed pollination has ceased. Symptoms may last until frost. Attacks that occur in musty rooms, in damp basements, or in barns also suggest mold sensitivity.

Year-round symptoms as a rule occur in people exposed to large numbers of molds in their home or occupation. Job exposure is likely to be suffered by someone who works with bedding and overstuffed furniture, vegetation or grains, or in damp or musty places.

In the house furniture and mattress dust and stuffed animal toys particularly harbor molds. Molds also attack paper products and wallpaper paste, paint, wood, natural and synthetic fibers, and leather. They often flourish in air conditioners and humidifiers, and in the rubber gaskets around refrigerator doors.

Damp cellars are fertile grounds, as are summer residences, since they are closed for long periods. The molds may lie dormant throughout the winter, but will flourish with the first rise in temperature.

Desensitization injections are often successful, although treatment of mold allergy begins with avoidance. Remove all suspicious material such as old books, old furniture, and bedding. Dry damp cellars with dehumidifiers. Use synthetic materials for furniture and bedding. Spray mold-inhibiting products on walls and in cellars. Use mold-proof paint in place of wallpaper.

See also ALLERGY; HAY FEVER.

MOLES (nevi) are ordinarily harmless. But they can become the sites of a fast-spreading form of skin cancer called malignant melanoma.

See a doctor immediately if you note *any* change in a mole—such as if it suddenly becomes elevated, ulcerated, scaly, or painful, or if it bleeds, darkens, or itches. Any such change may mark the beginning of cancer.

Be on special guard if you are a light-skinned, blue-eyed blond who burns on short exposure to sunlight, or if you are a redhead with a sandy complexion who freckles in the sun. Almost 80 percent of victims of malignant melanomas fit this description.

Also be alert if a close blood relation has had malignant melanoma. Some forms of melanoma tend to occur in families.

Tell your doctor if you have moles on the soles of your feet, palms of your hands, or in your genital area—there's a greater incidence of melanomas in these areas.

A mole that lies in the growing area of a toenail or fingernail, which leaves a streak of brown pigment incorporated into the nail, may signal melanoma in a white person. Many blacks show such brown streaks in the nail normally.

Moles range in appearance from skin color to pink, from light tan to brown to blue-black. They may be round, oval, or an irregular shape; flat, raised, large, or small; with or without hairs; mottled or evenly colored. Because of the risk of cancer, see a doctor if the appearance of a mole worries you—or if it changes in any way.

Harmless moles. *Un*changing moles are rarely cause for concern. The average white person has about 30 of these pigmented spots on his skin; Negroes average only 2.

Infants generally have no moles at birth. Moles develop through early life and reach the maximum number at age 25 or so. After 40 they start to disappear. By 90 there are few if any moles left.

It is a myth that irritations such as shaving or rubbing by clothing will cause a mole to become cancerous. You may, however, want to have moles in the beard area removed because they are annoying or are frequently nicked in shaving.

If you wish to remove a hair from a mole, clip rather than tweeze. Constant tweezing will not prevent future hair growth and irritation may develop around hair follicles within the mole because of tweezing. Surgical removal of the mole will remove the pigmented spot and the hair at the same time. Electrolysis by a qualified practitioner can remove the hair permanently, leaving the mole untouched.

If you find a mole annoying or unsightly, see a dermatologist about getting rid of it. A mole may be destroyed with an electric needle or by surgical excision. Most procedures used to remove moles can be performed in a doctor's office, though large moles may require hospitalization. Brown scaling spots (superficial keratoses) that develop with age can be removed by freezing with dry ice or liquid nitrogen.

The doctor frequently will have an excised mole examined by a pathologist to determine whether it's malignant. Never have a mole removed by anyone who is not a licensed physician. Improper surgery can cause infection and possibly delay treatment of a malignancy. Similarly, burning off a mole without biopsy can miss the diagnosis of melanoma.

See also CANCER; SKIN DISORDERS.

MONGOLISM   See DOWN'S SYNDROME.

MONONUCLEOSIS (infectious mononucleosis, glandular fever) is sometimes called the "kissing disease"—the virus is transmitted through secretions from the nose and throat. It is primarily a disease of the teen-ager and young adult—some 75 percent of cases occur between the ages of 15 and 30—yet physicians are seeing it with increasing frequency in younger children.

Though an infectious disease, it is only slightly contagious. There is no need to isolate a patient. Mono is rarely passed through casual contact in a household. It is thought to be spread through direct oral contact. But it has not proved generally possible to spread the disease experimentally, even by spraying mono patients' saliva into the throats of volunteers. Authorities disagree on the incubation period. Estimates range from 30 to 50 days, possibly 10 to 14 days in children.

Symptoms are like other diseases. The "medical mimic" is another nickname for mono. Its symptoms may imitate those of a dozen other diseases: the sore throat of strep throat or diphtheria; the painful stiff neck of meningitis; the abdominal pains of acute appendicitis or hepatitis; the cough of whooping cough or tuberculosis; the rash of scarlet fever; the swelling around the eyes of trichinosis; the abnormality of the lymph nodes which can be mistaken for toxoplasmosis, leukemia, or Hodgkin's disease. Considering the grave possibilities, it usually comes as a relief when a three-minute blood test in a doctor's office shows the patient merely has mono.

Mono nearly always starts out with a fever of 100° F or 101° F, a sore throat with a pinpoint rash on the palate, and a general feeling of fatigue. Some sufferers may also have chills, nausea, headache, and abdominal or muscular pain. In the early stage of the disease there may be a blotchy rash on the trunk. Some lymph node ("gland") enlargement is always present, and those in the neck and armpits will be firm and tender.

The disease is usually mild, with the longest lasting symptoms being irritability, lack of appetite, and tiredness. While fatalities are extremely rare, complications occur in about 15 percent of cases.

A possibly fatal complication is rupture of the spleen, which occurs most often during the third week of illness. A warning of difficulty may come with sudden abdominal pain and tenderness. The pain may also be felt in the left shoulder. If you have an enlarged spleen because of mono, avoid all possibilities of trauma to the abdomen—contact sports, lifting heavy objects, straining while having a bowel movement. If rupture occurs, prompt surgery is essential.

Liver involvement (detectable by enlargement of this organ or by specific blood tests) is common in mononucleosis and may occur in about 75 percent of the patients. Only about 10 percent of these will have jaundice (yellowing of the skin and eyes).

Treating mono. The usual treatment is bed rest and convalescent care. For painful sore throat warm saltwater gargles may be helpful. Drink plenty of fluids; take aspirin for general discomfort and headache. Cortisone is occasionally used in unusually severe cases and may help relieve symptoms.

Acute symptoms may last a week or two, and the period of reduced activity and convalescence ranges between two and six weeks. Absolute bed rest is not necessary; indeed prolonged bed rest may itself cause fatigue. But remain inactive until signs of liver inflammation and fever disappear.

Avoid strenuous physical activity as long as there is any enlargement of the spleen, liver, or lymph nodes. Rest when you feel fatigued. It's rarely necessary for students to leave school, but curtailing extracurricular activities is often advisable.

People who have had mono are thought to remain carriers for a year or more. Don't give blood until at least a year after you have had the disease.

See also INFECTIOUS DISEASE.

MORPHINE   See DRUGS.

MOSQUITOES inject saliva into the skin that makes bites itch and swell. To reduce discomfort, as soon as possible after you're bitten, press an ice cube to the bite for 20 to 30 seconds. Or quickly pass a lighted match close to the wound.

Scrub the bite with soap and water. If itching persists, apply compresses of very hot water.

Mosquitoes are least likely to bother you if you:

Wear light clothing—white, yellow, light green, rather than black, dark red, dark blue.

Stand still rather than either lie down or move about.

Keep freshly bathed or cool rather than sweaty.

Avoid perfumes, colognes, after-shave lotions.

Stay in a cool, dry room rather than a warm, moist one.

If you have dark skin, you may need to take more antimosquito precautions than someone with light skin. Women are likely to find mosquitoes more troublesome when they are secreting higher amounts of estrogen hormone in the menstrual cycle.

Mosquitoes are the principal carrier of encephalitis, malaria, and yellow fever. Follow precautions against insects to repel or get rid of mosquitoes. As with flies your first weapon is a swatter. In heavy invasions spray rooms with relatively safe insecticides like pyrethrins, allethrin, or rotenone.

Mosquitoes hatch in stagnant water, so keep a tight cover on septic tanks, cisterns, and rain barrels. Twice weekly drain standing water from birdbaths, plastic wading pools, and swimming pools. Empty and store indoors all containers like watering cans, buckets, flowerpots, children's sand pails. Establish drainage for any low spots in the yard where water may stand.

Screen all windows and doors. Fill cracks in

walls and floors. Clean up junk from your environs, since the debris may harbor stagnant water. In some mosquito-eradication programs block-by-block searches are made for old tires, broken crockery, and rusting cans. Despite their harmless appearance, all are ideal breeding places for some type of mosquito.

See also INSECTS.

MOTION SICKNESS (airsickness, car sickness, seasickness) will cause sweating, pallor, and nausea, frequently progressing to vomiting. It is thought to be related to the effect of motion on the inner ear, although psychological stress also appears important. Some sufferers feel nauseated on stepping aboard a motionless plane or boat, even on watching a movie depicting motion. One physician calls it *"emotion* sickness."

People differ greatly in their susceptibility to motion sickness. Children under two and the elderly rarely get sick, evidently because of the structures of their inner ears. Young women seem more susceptible than men, fat people more so than thin.

Prevention. If you're prone to motion sickness, eat lightly before embarking. Overeating or traveling on an empty stomach increases the risk of sickness. On a boat or plane sit amidships. In a car sit in the front seat.

Be well rested before a trip and wear loose-fitting clothing and comfortable shoes. Avoid alcohol before and during your trip. Also avoid tobacco smoke and unpleasant odors. Move your head slowly.

If you sense an imminent attack, you may control it by lying down or reclining as far as possible. Hold your head firmly against a pillow or headrest. Breathe cool air deeply.

Refrain from reading. It may help to close your eyes. Or fix your gaze on a still point to keep movement from causing a blur that can make you sick. Following a bout of vomiting, you'll hasten recovery if you drink plenty of liquid to replace lost fluids.

Most drugs that prevent or relieve motion sickness are antihistamines—except for scopolamine, which is also used—and all are more or less effective. The results of many clinical tests indicate that no one drug is of outstanding effectiveness—and often a placebo affords as good protection as the active medication.

The most popular antihistamine drugs for motion sickness are Benadryl, Bonine, Dramamine, and Marezine. Each causes drowsiness at times (and hence should be avoided by anyone driving a car), but Benadryl is particularly likely to do so. Dramamine is less likely to cause drowsiness, and Bonine generally gives protection for a longer period than the others. A number of these drugs can be obtained without a prescription in this country at present, and you may want to carry along enough for your whole trip.

Many over-the-counter remedies depend upon scopolamine (also known as hyoscine) for their motion-sickness benefits. If they have helped you in the past, go ahead and use them again. But such side effects as dry mouth and blurred vision have made the use of scopolamine difficult for many persons, particularly during long exposure to motion. Avoid it if you have any indications of glaucoma.

A recent development is scopolamine in a small plastic disc that continuously releases the drug through the skin. The disc (e.g., Transderm Scop) is placed against the skin just behind the ear. It generally takes two to four hours after application to achieve an effective concentration of scopolamine in the blood; so apply the disc at least that long before exposure to conditions that usually cause motion sickness. Don't drive or use potentially dangerous machinery while you are taking scopolamine in any form.

As you travel more, the tendency to become sick is likely to decrease sharply. If it persists, consult an otologist about a possible abnormality in your ear.

See also TRAVEL HEALTH.

MOTORCYCLES may be 15 times as likely as cars to cause injury or death in accidents.

Small wonder. In automobile accidents even the flimsiest car surrounds you with some sort of protection, whereas on a motorcycle it's your body that usually bears the brunt of the impact. Furthermore any two-wheel vehicle is easily upset. And drivers of cars tend not to see motorcyclists, even when they are not deliberately trying to make their lives miserable.

Ride defensively. Always expect the worst from drivers around you. Other tips to improve your odds:

Get an engine of about 250 cc. This allows a motorcycle to keep up with most traffic, yet not be too heavy to push or hard to maneuver at low speeds. Too small an engine can be dangerous because any vehicle that travels substantially faster or slower than the surrounding traffic is much likelier to get into an accident than a vehicle that keeps up with traffic flow.

Avoid motorcycles with protruding parts. Drivers can be castrated by flip-open fuel caps, luggage racks mounted on the fuel tank, steering controls in front of the driver's groin. Insist on a metal fuel tank—those of fiber glass tend to rupture in an accident and may set the driver on fire.

The larger the wheels and tires, the more stable the machine. Conventional-tread road tires corner better on paved roads, especially in wet weather, than do "knobby" or "off-road" tires with a blocky tread. Proper tire pressure is more critical on a motorcycle than on a car.

Have an electrical starter. It can get you going faster than a kick starter can if you stall in traffic.

Road-test a motorcycle for noisiness and vibration, which can tire you and dull your senses. Some machines vibrate so badly that after a half hour your feet may be too numb to properly shift or operate the rear brake.

Wear a helmet. Wear a fiber glass helmet that meets Snell Memorial Foundation standards. Other standards (read the label) are too low, and polycarbonate helmets may be fragile because of sloppy manufacturing. Head injuries account for more than 60 percent of all motorcycle fatalities.

Helmets deteriorate in the sun. Replace yours every four years, immediately if it's involved in a crash or develops cracks or stress lines. Clean your helmet with a damp rag. Solvents, cleaning materials—and paints—may be destructive unless certified by the manufacturer.

You need goggles or a face shield to protect your eyes against dust or flying objects. The "uniform" of many cyclists—leather jacket and pants, heavy riding boots, and gloves—is practical as well as stylish. It can take a lot more abrasion than cloth or skin.

Always ride with headlight on. The increased ability of car drivers to see motorcyclists has caused a drop in motorcycle accidents in states that have passed daytime-headlight laws.

Wear bright-colored, reflective clothes, especially at night. Stick reflective tape on your helmet. If you're not sure a motorist sees you, use your horn or rapidly switch your headlight beam on and down.

Be extra cautious at intersections. The most common type of accident involves a car making a left turn across the path of an oncoming motorcycle. Don't pass on the right, or squeeze between two lanes of traffic, or share a lane with a car. If the car edges over, you may have no escape path.

Motorcycles often spill on obstructions that wouldn't affect a car. Avoid snow, slippery surfaces like wet manhole covers and metal bridges, ruts, potholes, rocks, patches of sand, ice, water, oil. If you can't avoid a rock or other small obstacle, hit it straight on, not on an angle. Reduce speed at night, when obstacles on the road are hard to see.

See also ACCIDENTS.

MOUTH CLEFT is a birth defect in which the lip or the roof of the mouth has an abnormal split. One out of every 750 babies is born with a mouth cleft—in the United States more than 6,000 infants a year. More than 250,000 Americans have some form of mouth cleft. It is one of the commonest birth defects and by far the commonest congenital malformation of the face. It can usually be repaired surgically or remedied by a mouth appliance.

See also BIRTH DEFECTS; CLEFT LIP; CLEFT PALATE; TEETH AND MOUTH DISORDERS.

MOUTH ODOR (halitosis, bad breath, breath odor) is often prevented by plaque control. Special preparations are rarely necessary.

Mints, mouthwashes, and flavored toothpaste do not cure halitosis but may temporarily mask the condition. Chlorophyll in dentifrices, chewing gum, and the like reduce mouth odor for only a limited period. Some chlorophyll compounds are even selective—they neutralize only certain odors, leaving others unaffected.

Laxatives do not improve the quality of the breath. Nor does constipation necessarily contribute to halitosis.

Many breath odors originate from mouth conditions: decaying food debris, stagnating saliva, gingivitis, pyorrhea, unclean dentures. Correcting these with proper dental care usually improves the breath.

To combat other causes, cut down on smoking and odor-producing foods like garlic, cabbage, onions. Reducing the intake of fatty substances, particularly milk and butter fats, may be of value.

The pronounced odor that some foods like garlic give to the breath for as much as a day does not primarily originate in the mouth. It is caused chiefly by aromatic material absorbed from the intestines, carried in the bloodstream to the lungs, and excreted by the lungs into the breath. Rinsing the mouth may rid it of a few particles of garlic, but has no effect on intestinal absorption. The only way to avoid the odor is to avoid the food.

Malodorous breath on arising results from the increase in bacterial activity in the mouth during sleep, and usually disappears with the first toothbrushing. Proper brushing before retiring will do much to lessen the "brown" morning taste. Mouth breathing when awake or asleep can add to breath odor and should be avoided.

Some women develop unpleasant breath for several days before menstruation. Emotional stress, which upsets the metabolism, may also be a factor.

There are other causes: sinusitis, postnasal

drip, emphysema, asthma. Chronic tonsillitis produces the odor of Limburger cheese; digestive malfunctioning often gives the breath a sour tinge. Sufferers of diabetes may breathe of acetone; kidney patients, of urine. Blood on the breath may signal intestinal bleeding.

It is generally impossible to smell one's own breath. A bad taste in the mouth need not mean bad breath—and a sweet mouth taste can be accompanied by breath odor. A coated tongue may or may not be associated with a bad taste, bad breath, or both.

Thus people with halitosis rarely know it. With the prodding of dentifrice manufacturers this has given rise to a national near-neurosis. "Not even your best friend will tell you," said one recurrent toothpaste theme.

If concerned, ask about your breath on your next dental or medical visit. And if a friend suffers from halitosis, you'll be compassionate—and almost certainly appreciated—if you give lie to the ads and tell him his breath is sour. See PLAQUE; TEETH AND MOUTH DISORDERS; TOOTHBRUSHING.

MOUTH SORES may signal mouth cancer. There are also at least four types of noncancerous oral sores.

See COLD SORES or fever blisters—common names for herpes simplex—which can cause birth defects if the disease is contracted during early pregnancy. CANKER SORES (which see) are blisterlike sores inside the mouth and on the lips. Less common, though usually far more severe, is ERYTHEMA MULTIFORME (which see)—blisters that are thought to result from an allergic reaction and may spread over the body and possibly cause blindness. Most severe, and rarest, is PEMPHIGUS (which see)—in which half the patients die from generalized blistering.

Attempts at self-treatment are dangerous. The wrong mouthwashes or ointment may only irritate tender and painful tissues. If you have a sore in the mouth, especially one that recurs, consult a dentist or physician.

See also TEETH AND MOUTH DISORDERS.

MOUTH-TO-MOUTH RESUSCITATION See ARTIFICIAL RESPIRATION.

MOUTHWASHES may be cosmetically pleasant for rinsing the mouth. But they do not prevent or treat diseases of the mouth and upper-respiratory tract, and claims that they do may delay patients from seeking professional care for underlying teeth and mouth disorders.

No medicated mouthwash has any merit for unsupervised use by the general public, warns the American Dental Association Council on Dental Therapeutics. Specifically, the council does *not* recognize "any substantial contribution to oral health" from these widely sold mouthwashes: Cepacol, Chloraseptic, Kasdenol, Micrin, Oral Pentacresol, Sterisol, or Vince.

The normal mouth has not been shown to need mouthwashes containing astringents or germicides. Dentists may use mouthwashes as pleasant-tasting solutions for rinsing and spraying after drilling, filling, and the like—water without coloring or flavoring is often used just as well. Sometimes a salt or baking-soda solution is used to relieve mouth inflammation.

Germ-killing properties of mouthwashes have received only limited verification—and in fact the so-called "antiseptic" or "germicidal" ingredients may be harmful. Those that contain alcohol can dry out the mucous membranes of the mouth and aggravate existing conditions.

The ADA feels that the general use of mouthwashes can serve no greater purpose than as an aid in the removal of loose food and debris.

Don't leave mouthwashes within reach of children. Youngsters have died of poisoning after drinking these products.

See also MOUTH ODOR; TEETH AND MOUTH DISORDERS.

MOVING THE INJURED by nonexperts is likely to cause further damage. Wait for a physician or ambulance crew unless you are certain the victim will be hurt more by staying where he is, as in a fire.

The fact that traffic is tied up by the accident is rarely reason for moving a severely injured person. Direct traffic around an accident scene. Similarly, rather than move a victim out of rain or snow, shield him with coats and blankets until expert help arrives.

When moving an injured person is necessary, if at all possible first be sure he is breathing. Give ARTIFICIAL RESPIRATION (which see) and massage for HEART STOPPAGE (which see) if needed. Also, if possible before moving him, control BLEEDING (which see) and splint any FRACTURES (which see).

If you must move a car-accident victim who is complaining of head, neck, or back pain, first tie a padded board to support his spine.

If you're alone and must pull a victim to safety, don't pull him sideways. Ideally place a blanket, rug, or coat beneath him to act as a skid and pull him headfirst.

If no such skid is available, pull him headfirst, lifting him under the shoulders, or drag him by his collar or the back of his shirt.

If he's too heavy for any other method, pull him feet first, taking care to protect his head.

IF YOU MUST MOVE AN INJURED PERSON

If spine may be injured

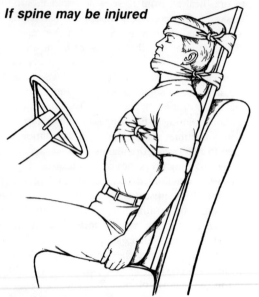

If you have a helper, improvise a stretcher from a door, removed by pulling its hinge pins. If no door or similar board is available, button a coat or two shirts over broomsticks, branches, pipes. Or wrap a blanket in thirds around such poles. As you lift the victim onto the stretcher, support his entire body in a straight line.

If you can't make a stretcher, you and your helper can slide a chair under the victim and carry him on the chair. But don't use this technique for people with neck, back, or leg injuries.

If the victim is unconscious, use the fore-and-aft carry: One of you stands between the victim's legs and grips him under the knees; the other supports the victim around his chest from behind.

If driving a person to medical aid, keep him lying down. A station wagon or flatbed truck is better suited to this than a passenger car.

Keep head and neck from moving
Tie padded board to back with several strips of cloth

Pull him on a blanket, coat, rug, etc.
Padding protects him from bumps

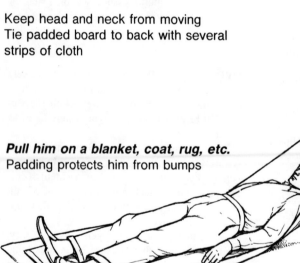

Or make stretcher from door (remove hinge pins)

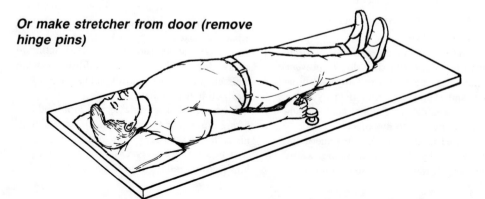

Drive within the speed limit. Contrary to popular belief, minutes saved are rarely of importance if you've protected the victim against breathing difficulties, bleeding, and shock.

See also ACCIDENTS.

MOWERS can be manglers. Because of the many severe accidents involving the power mower, consumer advocate Ralph Nader condemns it as the "most dangerous household product in existence."

Amputations and severe fractures and cuts are common when a limb comes in contact with a whirling power blade. Always turn off the machine before reaching toward the blade, and use the machine only in adequate daylight.

Buy only a mower that permits no more than 1¼ inches of blade to be exposed. As you shop, look for the triangular label bearing the letters OPEI (for Outdoor Power Equipment Institute), an assurance that the machine meets this and other minimal safety standards.

Never leave a machine running unattended, even in neutral. The vibrations can make the clutch engage, causing the mower to take off on its own. On a riding mower have a dead-man switch that stops the machine if pressure is released from a foot pedal.

Feet are most often caught in mowers when the operator slips or pulls the mower back over his foot. Get a mower that has a rear safety shield to protect your feet, and an upstop latch so you can't raise the handle high enough to walk under the blade.

Don't mow on wet grass, which invites slipping. Be especially wary on inclines, where mowers are likely to tip over or run away. Wear tough leather shoes, preferably with safety toes, rather than sneakers or sandals.

Attach a grass-catcher device to catch objects propelled by the blade. You can be shot by an object expelled from a mower. At 300 revolutions per second a mower blade can fire a steel bolt through the side of a car 90 feet away.

Before mowing, pick up loose stones, sticks, and debris from the lawn. Keep bystanders at least 200 feet away.

To avoid fires fill a mower with gasoline outdoors and only when the engine is cool. With electric mowers beware electric shock. Lay out the cord so as to avoid cutting it with the blades.

Best safety suggestion of all: Use a hand-power mower. You'll cut down on noise and air pollution, save money on fuel purchase cost, and get exercise. Some manual mowers can do the job almost as fast as power models—and

are lighter and less nerve-wracking to handle, and easier to store.

See also ACCIDENTS.

MULTIPLE MYELOMA See HODGKIN'S DISEASE.

MULTIPLE SCLEROSIS (MS) usually affects young adults between 20 and 40. It is one of the most common chronic disorders of the central nervous system.

Symptoms are due to patchy lesions on the nerve sheaths of the brain and spinal cord. These multiple sites are replaced by hard scar (sclerotic) tissue, hence the name of the disease. Once the nerve fibers themselves are affected by scar tissue, their function is permanently lost.

The cause of MS is unknown. A virus or disturbance of the immune system—or both—are suspected. Hereditary susceptibility may play some part. MS is not contagious. Slightly more women than men develop MS.

Symptoms vary greatly from one person to another. Common symptoms may include fatigue, weakness, tremors of the arms and legs, sensitivity to heat, unsteadiness and stiffness in walking, disturbances of vision and speech, numbness, and—in advanced cases—various degrees of paralysis. Impaired bladder and bowel function may occur in more severe disease. Onset of MS may be sudden or gradual.

Some victims of the disease are able to carry on near-normal activity, while others are severely incapacitated. Life expectancy is close to normal.

It is impossible to predict the course of the disease. Many times early symptoms disappear, often for years. Then they may reappear in new or more severe forms. In other cases symptoms remain the same over many years. For still others the disease progresses slowly but steadily.

The condition is thought to be aggravated by injuries, infections, allergy, and emotional stress. A mild form of MS occurs in one out of four patients. They have few serious symptoms many years after onset. Three out of four MS patients are still active many years after a firm diagnosis is made.

Treatment. Many drugs and therapies have been used, but none is of proven value to all patients. Physical therapy may be beneficial, particularly for helping those whose symptoms are in remission to regain lost skills. Exercise and massage reduce spasms and help maintain optimal condition of unaffected muscles.

MS patients need to avoid fatigue and stress. Exposure to extremes of heat and cold should also be avoided. Infections need to be treated promptly lest they aggravate the disease. MS patients should take care to avoid overweight, which can put stress on already weakened muscles.

Good nutrition is important, although no special diet is of proven value. Some studies suggest that a high-protein, low-fat regimen—much like the Weight Watchers' diet—may bring improvement.

Medications can control muscle spasticity. An eye patch can reduce double vision. Special instruction can minimize speech difficulties. For some people ACTH or adrenal steroids (such as prednisone) may help lessen the intensity of an acute attack, or shorten its duration.

MS occurs most frequently in cold, damp climates. But there is no evidence that moving to a warmer climate will cure or control the disease. Indeed heat commonly worsens MS problems. Steer clear of any practitioner who claims to be able to cure multiple sclerosis with an unorthodox therapy.

The National Multiple Sclerosis Society (205 East 42nd Street, New York, New York 10017) helps maintain clinics and centers for MS patients. Local chapters of the society provide counseling services, recreational programs, help in securing good medical care, and other valuable services for MS patients and their families.

MUMPS developing after puberty is serious enough to warrant vaccination if you have never had the disease—and women need protection as well as men.

In children the disease is ordinarily mild enough so that the youngster's swollen cheeks are the most troublesome discomfort. The swelling is caused by a viral infection of the parotid gland, a salivary gland below the earlobe. (Mumps is from an old word meaning "grimace.") In adults and adolescents, however, symptoms are likely to last longer than the usual week and be severe.

In about one in five cases after puberty the disease produces inflammation of the testicles or ovaries. Furthermore, in about 1 in 500 males, sterility results. In females, while no cases of sterility are on record, there is some evidence that mumps can lead to spontaneous abortion during the first three months of pregnancy.

In older patients generally the virus is more likely to involve other areas such as the pancreas, and to result in nausea, abdominal pains, and inability to take food or fluid. Another possible complication is encephalitis.

The Public Health Service recommends that all children be routinely vaccinated for mumps after their first birthday. The vaccine confers

IN MUMPS . . .

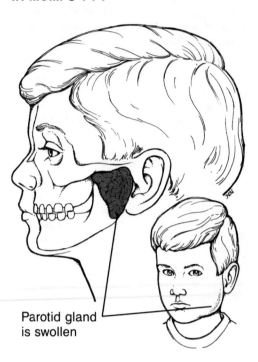

Parotid gland is swollen

lifetime immunity. It may be combined with those for measles and rubella.

The incubation period for mumps is about 18 days. But immunization after exposure is too late—the vaccine may not work in time.

No one running a high fever or showing other signs of illness should be vaccinated. Before getting mumps vaccine, tell your doctor if you have an allergy to eggs, chicken, chicken feathers, or neomycin, or if you are taking cortisone or other steroids or receiving X-ray therapy.

The first symptoms consist of 24 to 48 hours of fever (rarely going over 102° F), malaise, and headache. These are followed by the characteristic facial swelling on one or both sides (see illustration). Mumps generally produces a tender, smooth, firm (not hard) swelling that covers the corner of the jawbone where it turns upward toward the ear. Fever may then rise to 103° or 104° F.

Inside the cheek the opening of the parotid gland, next to the upper second molar tooth, will swell and look like a mosquito bite with a bright red center.

Use aspirin when needed for reducing temperature and the discomfort of mild headache and muscle aches. Warm compresses over the side of the face may relieve some tenderness. No dietary restrictions are necessary, except that a mumps patient is likely to prefer soft foods for easier swallowing. He'll usually find sour and acid foods—fruit juices, pickles, and the like—painful to take into the mouth.

A child with mumps will not appear to be very sick but is contagious from the onset of the first symptoms until fever and/or swelling disappear. Mumps is spread by direct contact and droplet infection. Isolate the patient and keep his cutlery, dishes, and towels for his use only.

In contrast with children, adults need to go to bed with the first sign of mumps and stay there until both fever and swelling subside. With adults the greater the physical activity, the greater likelihood that there will be complications.

If the infection spreads to the ovaries or testicles, the doctor may prescribe a sedative and a stronger pain-reliever than aspirin. The testicles may become painful and swollen one to three days after the symptoms of mumps have disappeared. Temperature may rise to 106° F. To reduce the strain, the swollen scrotum can be supported by a pillow or by a cradle of gauze or tape stretched hammocklike from the thighs.

There is about a 1 in 400 chance of getting mumps twice. But most cases of "mumps the second time" are actually the first case of the disease. The earlier illness usually was not mumps but swollen neck glands from an infected throat.

See also INFECTIOUS DISEASE.

MUSCULAR DYSTROPHY refers to a group of diseases characterized by progressive wasting and weakness. It affects the voluntary muscles, such as those of the face, arms, and legs. Its victims are frequently young children, and males are affected five to six times more frequently than females. Most forms of muscular dystrophy are hereditary.

There is no cure, but physical therapy can delay weakening and crippling. Braces will support muscles, and deep-breathing exercises can keep the lungs in good shape.

When the condition develops in adulthood, it usually progresses slowly. For years the only symptom may be weak facial muscles. An adult may have the disease for 30 years or more. When the disease strikes in childhood, it is likely to progress much more quickly. Afflicted children often do not live to adulthood.

Types of muscular dystrophy include:

Duchenne's disease (or pseudohypertrophic) is the most common type and affects boys between two and six. It begins in the large muscles of the lower trunk and upper legs. The boy may first show difficulty walking and may frequently fall. The calf muscles typically appear enlarged, because of deposits of fat and connective tissue. Progression is usually rapid; a wheelchair is usually needed by adolescence, and life expectancy is short.

Duchenne dystrophy is a sex-linked recessive trait. Sisters and maternal aunts of affected boys should be tested to determine if they are carriers. Testing and genetic counseling are available through the Muscular Dystrophy Association.

Facioscapulohumeral dystrophy begins in muscles of the face (facio), shoulder (scapulo), and upper arms (humeral). The disease usually occurs in early adolescence. Severity varies greatly. Facial muscles are weak, with difficulty in closing eyes. Shoulders characteristically slope forward, and there is difficulty in raising arms over the head. Progression is usually very slow, and life span may be normal. The disease is inherited through a dominant gene from one parent.

Limb-girdle dystrophy usually appears in late childhood or early adolescence. The disease begins in either the shoulder muscles or the muscles of the lower trunk and upper legs. If shoulders are affected, the victim has difficulty raising arms and lifting objects. Shoulders droop. If legs are affected, there is generally a waddling walk, with frequent falls and difficulty in rising and climbing stairs. Progression varies greatly but is likely to be slower if the disease begins in the shoulder muscles. Eventually severe disability usually occurs, with a shortened life span. Limb-girdle dystrophy is inherited through a defective gene from both parents.

Myotonic dystrophy (Steinert's disease) most frequently occurs between 20 and 35. Most common first signs are facial weakness and delayed relaxation of muscles after contraction. Weakness of hands and feet is another early sign.

As the disease progresses, weakness spreads, but disability rarely becomes severe until 15 to 20 years after onset. The disease affects other body systems: Many myotonic dystrophy patients develop eye cataracts. In men receding hair and atrophy of testicles may occur. Myotonic dystrophy is inherited through a dominant gene from one parent.

If your child is afflicted with muscular dystrophy, your state's crippled children's program may provide diagnostic and treatment services. Ask your local public-health service about nurses or physical therapists for home treatment. Your physician may teach you some exercises for helping your child.

For information and help, contact the Muscular Dystrophy Associations of America, 810 Seventh Avenue, New York, New York 10019, or the National Foundation for Neuromuscular Diseases, 555 West 57th Street, New York, New York 10019.

MYASTHENIA GRAVIS (MG) literally means "serious muscle weakness."

Weakness is the most common characteristic of the disease. Muscles tire very quickly and take much longer to recover. The first sign is often weakness of the eye muscles, resulting in drooping eyelids and double vision.

Other muscles commonly affected include those of the lips, tongue, throat, and neck. Speech, swallowing, and breathing may be impaired. In some cases the onset of MG occurs suddenly with extensive paralysis.

Drugs can often control the disease, particularly when it affects the arms and legs. Some MG sufferers benefit from the surgical removal of the thymus gland, which is frequently enlarged or tumorous. A promising experimental treatment is plasmapheresis, or plasma exchange, in which blood cells are separated from plasma, reconstituted in artificial plasma, and restored to the patient.

The condition often goes into remission, leaving the person symptom-free for months or years. Sometimes a person with mild symptoms will spontaneously and completely recover. For others, without treatment the weakness becomes progressively worse.

The disease seems to involve a defect at the junction between the nerves and muscles that may be due to an immunological disorder. Hereditary factors may be involved.

MYOCARDIAL INFARCTION See HEART ATTACK.

MYOPIA See NEARSIGHTEDNESS.

MYXEDEMA See THYROID DISEASE.

N

NAIL-BITING is often the result of emotional stress.

If you want to stop biting your nails, try using one of the foul-tasting commercial preparations, such as Thum. Some people conquer the compulsion to nail-bite by promising themselves something special at the end of, say, a month's abstinence. It often helps to write yourself a promise not to bite your nails for ten days, sign it, and post it prominently.

Don't nag, scold, or shame a child who nail-bites. This may simply worsen his tension or anger. Try using encouragement: Praise him on days he doesn't bite. Reward him with gold stars or his favorite dessert. Promise a special toy or trip when his nails are grown. Tell him how grown-up he is to give up the habit, how nice his nails look.

It may be best to ignore the problem entirely. Many children stop spontaneously. For others nail-biting may be a symptom of severe anxiety and emotional conflicts that require professional help.

See also STRESS.

NARCOTICS   See DRUGS.

NATURAL FOOD   See HEALTH FOOD.

NAUSEA and vomiting can sometimes be relieved by folk remedies: Eat small meals without drink, and drink moderate amounts of fluid between meals. If you're prone to nausea in the morning, as some women are in early pregnancy, eating a cracker before getting out of bed may help.

Nausea and vomiting may result from many different conditions. In some people, especially children, nausea is a reaction to anxiety and emotional stress. It's a common symptom of hangover, food poisoning, and indigestion, and the predominant effect of motion sickness. It may also be a side effect of some drugs—such as digitalis or aspirin in large doses.

Get medical help if nausea and vomiting are persistent or severe. There are drugs the doctor can prescribe or he may need to treat the underlying cause, which may vary from minor viral intestinal infections and other infectious diseases to appendicitis and other serious disorders.

See also APPENDICITIS; ASPIRIN; FOOD POISONING; HANGOVER; INDIGESTION; INFECTIOUS DISEASE; MOTION SICKNESS; PREGNANCY; STRESS.

NEARSIGHTEDNESS (myopia), the inability to see distant objects clearly, usually comes from a defect in the shape of the eyeball. As a result the retina receives only a blurred image of light rays from distant objects.

Eyeglasses and contact lenses are the only proven correctives. Surgery of the cornea (radial Keratotomy) is a new procedure whose long-term effects have not yet been documented. Except for a few isolated cases eye exercises have not been shown to make any measurable improvement. Restricting eye use by cutting down on reading, TV, and other close work doesn't correct the condition. Nor does drinking carrot juice for its vitamin A. It doesn't do any harm, but it doesn't help myopia.

Have a child's eyes tested if he stumbles and falls easily. Nearsighted children may also squint in an effort to see more—it's the commonest sign of myopia. Failing to see in the distance, the child's world may become a closed-in,

IF YOU'RE NEARSIGHTED

Your eye focuses in front of retina

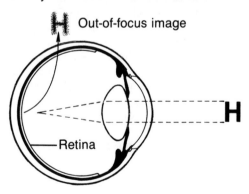

Out-of-focus image

Retina

Normal

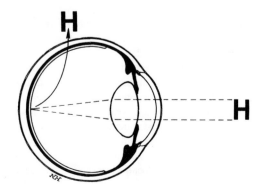

smaller sphere, often leaving him timid and withdrawn.

In contrast to those who are farsighted, the nearsighted child usually likes reading and other close work for which his vision is suited. He frequently avoids outdoor games where distant vision plays such an important part. Facial expressions, direction of movement required to gauge plays—these are the details lost to him.

When a child's vision grows worse, parents often feel he should do less eye work. There was a time when increasing nearsightedness, since it developed during school years, frequently caused children to be taken out of school, or their reading was curtailed. Now most doctors believe such restriction is unwarranted, particularly since it does not seem to decrease the myopic tendency and may cause emotional problems.

See also EYE DISORDER.

NECK FRACTURES can cause permanent paralysis or instantaneous death if head movement causes pressure against the spinal cord. Make sure the victim's head does not bend forward or tilt sideways.

Neck fractures, like back fractures, are fractures of the spine. The victim is likely to have an ache, with swelling and tenderness over the injury. If the spinal cord is injured, his legs or arms may be paralyzed.

Avoid moving someone with a suspected neck fracture unless you have expert help. If in an emergency you must move him, keep his head immobile. Slide thick padding—rolled-up clothing, towels, blankets—under his neck and around his head. Never bend his head forward to insert the padding.

See also BACK FRACTURES; FRACTURES; MOVING THE INJURED.

NEPHRITIS; NEPHROSIS See KIDNEY DISEASE.

NEURITIS is the inflammation of one or more nerves. It is usually associated with nerve pain (neuralgia). Other symptoms may include a burning sensation, numbness or paralysis, and sensitivity to pressure. There may be reddened skin along the course of the nerve, and sensations of heat and cold.

Neuritis may be caused by injury, lead poisoning or poisoning from arsenic and mercury, infectious disease, or alcoholism. It often seems to attack people who are weakened by illness and exposed to cold and damp. Malnutrition—particularly the lack of sufficient vitamin B as in bread or cereal—may be a cause.

Most neuritis is localized in one nerve. Sciat-

ica, for example, involves the sciatic nerve, which runs along the back of the leg. Generalized neuritis, involving many nerves, is far less common and much more serious. A person with untreated generalized neuritis can lose all feeling in his hands and feet, and become paralyzed and bedridden.

See a doctor if you have any of the symptoms of neuritis. Many people can be successfully treated. Steer clear of mail-order products that offer miracle cures.

See also PARALYSIS; SCIATICA.

NEUROBLASTOMA See CANCER IN CHILDREN.

NIACIN See VITAMINS.

NOISE control (sound conditioning) has become more important with the realization that the proliferation of noises is actually injurious to health. Hearing loss is a particularly common result of frequent exposure to loud noises. Noise may also contribute to mental illness and may be related to such stress ailments as peptic ulcer, heart disease, colitis, high blood pressure, migraine, and allergy.

Sound is measured in terms of decibels, 1 decibel being the smallest sound difference the human ear can detect. In rural areas the average sound level is 20 decibels; in residential suburbs it's 25 to 35 decibels; and in cities it's about 40. One jet 50 feet away may measure as much as 135 decibels. You can help protect your health and sanity by controlling the decibel level of your home.

Here are some tips on keeping the noise level down:

Soften the sound-reflecting surfaces in your home. Rugs will dull sharp sounds. Padding under rugs and felt lining under linoleum will cut noise. Upholstered furniture and pillows also soak up sound. Put up curtains or drapes, as large expanses of glass reflect noise. A well-filled bookcase will absorb more sound than a bare wall.

Carpeting or rubber treads on stairs will help, as will rubber pads under table and chair legs.

Kitchens can be sound-conditioned with an acoustical ceiling of tiles or panels, reducing noise by up to 75 percent. Applying acoustical tile to the ceiling and walls around heavy appliances, such as a dishwasher or washing machine, will also help. Keep appliances well serviced and lubricated.

In central air-conditioning and heating systems ducts should be acoustically insulated. Replace faulty plumbing fixtures that may be causing gurgling, banging, or sucking sounds.

FOR MOST NOSEBLEEDS

First try this

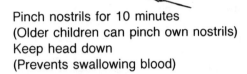

Apply ice
Forehead, upper lip, or back of neck

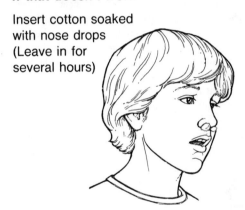

You can reduce vibrations from radio, television, and hi-fi sets by putting a 2-inch waffle padding with a foam-rubber back under the set.

Silent light switches are available, eliminating that click every time a light goes on.

Soundproofing. If you're building a new house, use solid-core doors for outside entrances. Make sure all doors and windows are tight-fitting to keep out street noises. You can use weatherstripping around the edges of windows and doors. If the street noises are particularly loud, consider year-round air conditioning, so the windows can remain closed. Trees, shrubs, and fences will do little to soften sound.

In a new home reduce sound by using sound-deadening insulation board in interior walls. For best results nail the board on both sides of *staggered* studs, so that the two walls have no mechanical connection. For nonbearing walls slitting the studs to within 6 inches on either side will reduce sound transmission, but not as effectively as insulation board.

Zone your home so that quiet areas and activity areas are kept apart. Locate windows sparingly on the street side of the house. Never install new outlets and wall switches back to back, as they create tunnels for noise.

Place insulation between the floor joists to cut down sound. This is particularly necessary where the floor is also a ceiling. For ground-level floors a resilient or spongy underlayment can be placed under the subfloor.

Sound travels in straight lines, so plan your home so that sound must change direction. Interior doors should be staggered, not facing each other across hallways. Have stairwells open into halls that turn a corner.

Install plumbing with cushioning material between pipe hangers and major plumbing connections. Install quieter toilets and garbage disposers.

If you're planning a courtyard, make sure it's open on one side to let sound escape.

See also HEARING LOSS.

Pinch nostrils for 10 minutes
(Older children can pinch own nostrils)
Keep head down
(Prevents swallowing blood)

If that doesn't work

Insert cotton soaked
with nose drops
(Leave in for
several hours)

Pinch nostrils for 10 minutes more with steady pressure

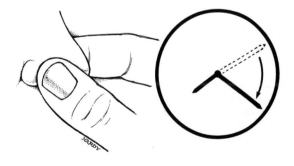

NOSEBLEED (epistaxis) usually is more annoying than serious. If—as is most often the case—the bleeding area is near the inner tip of the nose, first gently blow the nose to remove any clots. Then pinch the nostrils together for about ten minutes (see illustration) with a steady pressure. Applying ice to the forehead, upper lip, or back of the neck sometimes helps to constrict blood vessels and reduce bleeding.

If this doesn't work, insert into each nostril a small piece of sterile absorbent cotton wet with nose drops, hydrogen peroxide, or water. Press the nostrils firmly together for about ten minutes. Then slowly and gently remove the cotton.

Keep a child's head tilted forward to prevent his swallowing blood, which may cause nausea. If the bleeding is coming from the back of the nose, pinching the nostrils will not help. In such cases—or at other times when bleeding is prolonged, profuse, or recurrent—see a doctor. Occasionally the physician will need to cauterize (burn) the ulcerated area. Nosebleeds that occur following tonsillectomy or adenoidectomy (see TONSILLITIS) need to be treated by a physician. Also call your doctor if you are taking anticoagulants (blood thinners) or large doses of aspirin.

For two to three days after a nosebleed, treat your nose very gently. If you feel a sneeze coming on, try pinching your nostrils together and sneezing through your mouth. If you have to blow your nose, do so as gently as possible. Keep your nostrils moist by applying petroleum jelly or bacitracin ointment several times a day.

Nosebleed without apparent cause is common in childhood, especially in girls during early menstruation. Nosebleeds often occur at night when a child rubs or picks the nose during sleep. The most common cause is dryness of the mucous membranes. You may correct this condition by improving humidity in the home. Also helpful is the application of petroleum jelly to the inside of the nostrils.

Older people often get nosebleeds with such conditions as arteriosclerosis and high blood pressure. Nosebleeds are also commonly brought on by colds and accidents involving the nose. Some people are affected following strenuous exercise or unaccustomed exposure to high altitude. Nosebleed is sometimes an early sign of rheumatic fever or leukemia.

See also ACCIDENTS; BLEEDING.

NOSE DEFORMITIES may cause breathing difficulties. Deformities inside the nasal passages may lead to headache and postnasal drip, and worsen sinusitis. A deviated septum—a crooked nasal partition—increases chances of nosebleed.

Rhinoplasty is the name given to the plastic surgery for the nose designed to correct external deformities. The operation consists of removing excess bone or cartilage and rearranging and reshaping the new nose. Most rhinoplasties are performed because the patient wishes to improve his or her appearance.

If you feel you need rhinoplasty, select a sur-

geon trained to perform nasal plastic surgery: most often an otolaryngologist specializing in facial plastic surgery or a general plastic surgeon. Consult your family physician or a medical center for the names of qualified surgeons. Surgeons who do this kind of work are usually members of the American Association of Plastic Surgeons, the American Society of Plastic and Reconstructive Surgeons, or the American Academy of Facial Plastic and Reconstructive Surgery. The academy offers these words of caution:

Don't expect to see a perfectly shaped nose as soon as the dressings are removed. More likely the nose will appear stiff and turned up too much because of the effects of the bandage and swelling of the tissues.

A great deal of swelling disappears within three or four days after removal of the bandage. You are likely to sense more swelling than is apparent to other people. It generally takes upward of a year for the last 1 or 2 percent of the swelling to disappear. This won't usually bother you or detract from your appearance. Since the work is usually done inside the nose, there are rarely scars on the outside.

The tissues within the nose are somewhat swollen after surgery. Expect decreasing amounts of nasal blockage.

The thicker your skin, the longer it takes for the nose to return to its final shape. Nasal plastic surgery can't change skin that is inherently thick and oily. Such skin limits the amount of correction that can be obtained.

There are other limits to the corrective procedures possible. The surgical goal is improvement, not matching an ideal that might be in your mind. Some of the limiting factors in rhinoplasty, in addition to the texture and thickness of your skin, are the contour and shape of your face; the slope of your chin, lip, and forehead; the depth of the angle between forehead and your nose; your height; and the healing power of your tissues.

See also SURGERY.

NOSE DROPS and nasal sprays can turn victims of colds, hay fever, postnasal drip, and sinusitis into nasal medication addicts.

The compounds, termed *decongestants* or *vasoconstrictors,* shrink swollen mucous membranes, providing short-lived relief for stuffed noses and clogged sinuses. When the drops wear off, the membranes tend to swell even more than before because the compounds damage the tissues. The result of this "rebound congestion" is that you use more and more of the medication, constantly trying to relieve a perpetually swollen nose.

Moreover, the indiscriminate use of inhalants, nose sprays, and nose drops may lower the tissues' resistance to infection and paralyze the cleansing mechanisms of the respiratory tract. When this happens, many bacteria that normally inhabit the nose and throat without causing trouble may multiply and cause infections leading to respiratory disease.

Safer than drops and as effective is simple irrigation. Mix 1/4 teaspoon salt and 1/4 teaspoon baking soda (sodium bicarbonate) in 8 ounces water. Or use 1 part of the commercial mucus solvent Alkalol to 3 parts water. With a nasal douche run the solution from your nose to your throat and spit it out. Spray each nostril two or three times, several times a day, until the mucus has been dissolved.

The best vasoconstrictors are *oral*, taken by mouth. D-Feda Syrup, Novafed Liquid, and Sudafed Tablets are safe and effective in recommended dosages. Oral decongestants have a longer-lasting effect than drops or sprays, are less damaging to nasal tissues, and cause less rebound congestion.

If you feel you must use nose drops, follow to the letter the directions that accompany the medication. Never use drops or sprays for more than two or three days at a time, and never more than two or three times a day.

To wean yourself from an addiction, put drops in only one nostril to let the other side heal. In less than a week, the other side is usually back to normal and you can stop the drops completely.

Decongestants, whether tablets or drops, may cause increased general nervousness, sleeplessness, and tremor. You may suffer heart palpitations, sweating, urinary retention or frequency, and skin eruptions. You also may have urinary problems, either being unable to urinate or needing to urinate frequently. Don't use these preparations without your doctor's advice if you have high blood pressure, heart disease, diabetes, or thyroid disease.

Nose drops for children. Your doctor may advise nose drops for children. In small children, particularly infants, it is important to keep the nose clear, because many don't breathe well through the mouth. Those still on a bottle won't eat if the nose is clogged. Nose drops may have a use in cases of nosebleed and nose obstructions.

Be sure you don't use the long-acting adult drops. Many children get excited by vasoconstrictors, especially by oral vasoconstrictors. If the child is under two, convulsions may result. Therefore oral vasoconstrictors should be used

cautiously under this age and never with an infant under one year.

In giving nose drops to small children tilt the child's head back so the drops will enter properly. Hold a baby over a bed with his head downward and administer the drops one at a time. You may need to wrap a frisky toddler tightly in a sheet or bedspread so his movements are restricted.

Sharing bottles of nose drops may spread germs. When an upper-respiratory ailment strikes a family and it is felt that nose drops would be helpful, buy individual bottles for each person. This helps stop the spread of germs. Moreover, the ingredients and/or strength of children's nose drops may vary significantly from those sold for adults only.

Discard any remaining medication after each illness. When the drops are administered, almost inevitably germs are picked up on the dropper or inhaler. These bacteria may cause a reinfection or be passed on to the next person who receives the medication, producing a secondary infection, such as earache in children.

Prevent secretions from being drawn into the container by not letting suction take place in the nose. Withdraw the inhaler from your nostril before releasing your fingers from the bulb or spray.

Throw away any drops that are cloudy or otherwise suspect. Store drops in the refrigerator. If exposed to heat and light, the solutions may undergo chemical changes that can irritate the nasal membranes.

Misleading advertising. Are advertised sprays any better? Not much, a Senate subcommittee investigating patent drugs was told. As an example of misleading advertising claims a commercial for one nasal spray boasts of "soothing, cooling vapors."

Actually the product merely contains menthol, which has a physiological cooling effect that may be mistaken for air flowing through blocked nasal passages.

Commercials for another nasal spray claim that a special antihistamine and a decongestant control sneezing, thus implying that it prevents the spreading of colds. But there is no clinical evidence that either decongestants or antihistamines reduce or eliminate sneezing when applied in the nose. Further, the references cited by the manufacturer are primarily in texts of pharmacology and internal medicine, and in only a very general way refer to the question of sneezing.

See also COLDS; HAY FEVER; POSTNASAL DRIP; SINUSITIS.

NOSE FRACTURES are common and frequently

unrecognized. If you have a nosebleed after a hard blow, suspect a fracture and see a doctor. An unrepaired broken nose—particularly in children—may result in permanent deformities and obstructed nasal passages.

See also FRACTURES.

NOSE OBSTRUCTIONS   If a child gets a foreign body—an insect, peanut, etc.—up his nose, don't try to remove the object with a tweezer or cotton-tipped stick. You may push it up farther.

Instead ask the child to blow his nose gently. If this doesn't dislodge the object, press the unobstructed nostril closed. Encompass the child's mouth with your mouth. Blow sharply once or twice.

Because you have created a closed system, the only exit available to the air is the nostril containing the foreign body. If it doesn't work the first time, use two to three drops of nose drops and repeat the procedure. Then, if you still haven't moved the object, get medical help.

NURSING   See BREASTFEEDING.

NURSING, HOME   See BED REST.

NURSING, HOSPITAL   See HOSPITAL.

NUTRITION   Attaining good nutrition is a national problem. Many Americans fail to eat the proper foods for maintaining good health. In most cases the malnutrition is borderline, resulting from inadequate intake of calories or specific nutrients. The overuse of alcohol, fats, and sugar are common causes of malnutrition.

Malnutrition causes deficiency diseases such as anemia, rickets (from vitamin D deficiency), and kwashiorkor (from severe protein deficiency). When women are badly undernourished during pregnancy, there is a much greater risk that their infants will not thrive.

In young children, particularly those under 18 months, severe malnutrition can cause permanently stunted growth and possibly irreversible brain damage. Severe long-term malnutrition can be fatal.

Ignorance about nutrition accounts for much of the problem. People don't eat properly because they don't know enough about food. The problem is compounded by advertising that glorifies processed foods that are often of low nutritional value.

Teen-agers are especially likely to suffer from poor nutrition. An overscheduled life leaves little time for family meals. Young people come to rely on vending machines and snacks for much of their food. They thus eat a greal deal of junk food with little nutritional value. People following fad diets for overweight may also become undernourished.

What you should eat. To be well nourished, your daily diet needs to include adequate amounts of protein, fats, carbohydrates, vitamins, and iron, calcium, and other minerals. To avoid dehydration you also need sufficient water from food and drinks.

Consume food from these six categories daily:

1. Meat and other sources of protein. You need 2 servings every day of 1 of the following: meat, fish, poultry, eggs, dried peas, beans, lentils, nuts. A serving is 2 to 3 ounces of meat, fish, or poultry; 2 eggs; 1 cup of peas, beans, or lentils; 1/2 cup of nuts. This group provides the bulk of protein in your diet, and a considerable amount of iron.

2. Dairy products. Two servings (8-ounce cups) of skim or whole milk and milk products give you calcium, protein, some vitamins, and minerals. Included in this group are cottage cheese and other cheeses (but not cream cheese), yogurt, and buttermilk. Children and pregnant and nursing mothers should have at least 3 servings.

Ice cream is in this group. But to get the food value of 1 cup of milk (160 calories) or skim milk (90), you have to eat about 2 to 3 large scoops—and you'll be taking in lots of fat and sugar and at least 500 calories.

3. Bread and cereals. Three to 4 servings of bread, cereal, pasta, for protein, B vitamins, iron, and energy. A serving is 1 slice of bread, 1 roll or muffin, or 1/2 to 3/4 cup of cooked cereal or pasta.

Buy whole grain or enriched breads and cereals. Whole grains such as whole wheat, buckwheat, and rye retain the bran (the outer covering) and the germ—the most nutritious portion of the grain.

If you buy white breads, cookies and cakes, crackers and cereals, as well as cornmeal, pasta, and rice, make sure the product is enriched with vitamins and iron.

4. Fruits and vegetables rich in vitamin C. One serving or more of citrus fruits (oranges, grapefruits, tangerines, lemons) or tomatoes, or fruit juices, provides you with a day's supply of vitamin C. Or you can substitute other foods rich in vitamin C: cantaloupe, strawberries, cabbage. A serving is 1 medium orange or 1 tomato, 6 ounces of juice, 1/2 cup of berries, half a cantaloupe, 1 cup of cabbage.

5. Green and yellow vegetables. Two servings (1/2 cup) of a leafy green or a yellow vegetable give you important vitamins and some minerals. Particularly nutritious are kale, turnip and mustard greens, watercress, carrots, winter squash, and sweet potatoes.

6. Miscellaneous nutritious vegetables and fruits. One serving (1/2 cup) or more of the following round out your diet: potatoes, broccoli, cauliflower, green peppers, bananas, melons, peaches. They provide vitamin C, minerals, and protein.

Eat a wide variety of foods within each of the categories. To help ensure good nutrition, don't get stuck in food ruts. Many foods overlap categories—pizza, for example, or soups, fish stews, meat and vegetable casseroles, macaroni and cheese.

Eat high-fiber foods daily. These include whole grain breads and cereals, cabbage, lettuce, carrots, and fruits. They provide the bulk that helps move waste products through the intestines at a proper rate.

There's evidence that if food lingers too long in the intestines, it might contribute to diverticulosis, ulcerative colitis, appendicitis, colon polyps, and cancer of the colon and rectum.

It's particularly important to eat a wide range of vegetables and grains if you practice vegetarianism. You would also benefit from milk products and eggs if you don't eat meat.

The Prudent Diet. Under Dr. Norman Jolliffe the New York City Department of Health launched a study of the effect of diet change on a group of men dubbed the Anti-Coronary Club. Members of the club followed a so-called Prudent Diet, low in calories, cholesterol, and saturated fats.

Compared with a control group that received no dietary instruction, club members had less than half the incidence of heart attacks. The American Heart Association recommends the essentials of the diet. It conforms to basic nutritional requirements.

To be a Prudent Dieter: Limit your intake of meat, eggs, shellfish, and whole-milk cheeses to but a few servings a week. Substitute skim milk and buttermilk for whole milk, polyunsaturated vegetable oils and margarine for butter.

Avoid butter, cream, sour cream, ice cream, fatty gravies. High-fat meats (such as spareribs, corned beef, bacon, frankfurters, cold cuts) are also banned. So are high-calorie, high-fat snacks such as potato chips, chocolate, coconut. Reduce your consumption of salt and sugar.

Have frequent servings of fish, chicken, turkey, and lean veal; citrus fruits; other fruits and vegetables; cottage cheese; whole grain or enriched bread or cereal. (For more detailed recommendations, see FATS; FIBER; PROTEIN.)

Snacks that are good for you. Make snacks nutritious. There's nothing wrong with snacking between meals or even eating many snacks a day instead of two or three big meals—*if* the snacks are nutritious mini-meals instead of fat-and-sugar-laden calorie bombs. Substitute real food for pretzels, candy, soda, cookies, potato chips.

Yogurt is one example of a healthful snack. It contains good amounts of calcium and protein. Plain yogurt made from skim milk is low in fat and gives you only about 125 calories a cup. You can make yogurt into a meal in miniature and boost its nutrition by adding fresh fruit or berries and topping with wheat germ.

Other suggestions for nutritious snacking: Roasted soybeans or peanuts; fresh or dried fruit; raw vegetables and pickles; hard-boiled eggs; cottage cheese mixed with cut-up fruit or melon.

Still other ideas: Pizza; green pepper or celery stuffed with peanut butter or soft cheese; cheese cubes or peanut butter on whole grain or enriched crackers.

Don't overlook unsugared dry cereals as snacks. They're particularly good mixed with nuts, seeds, and raisins. Cut up leftover meat, fish, or poultry for nibbling, or add such leftovers to canned soup. For drinks substitute milk and fruit and vegetable juices for soda.

Medical problems like heart disease may require a special diet, such as one low in sodium. Elderly people may suffer from vitamin D deficiency if they consume little milk and don't get enough sun.

Feeding children. Infants can be fed many of the same foods you eat, following your physician's instructions for your baby's requirements. Blenders make it easy to prepare vegetables, meats, and fruit.

Suppose your child doesn't eat. Many children between two and six seem to eat very little. This is a period of relatively slow growth, and healthy children of this age often require less food than infants. If you have doubts that the child is thriving, get him a physical examination to rule out medical problems.

Don't coax or bribe a child to eat or punish him for not eating. Instead take your child food shopping, and encourage him to select foods he'd like to try. Serve foods you know he likes.

Set out small, attractive portions of a variety of foods. Children who reject cooked vegetables may happily eat raw ones. Serve a second helping only if he asks for it—otherwise a child may balk because he feels pressured to eat.

Make sure low-nutrition snacks are not available between meals. When a family meal is over, remove your child's plate, without discussion about what he has or has not eaten. You thus avoid making food a weapon in a possible battle between parent and child.

Reading labels. Under Food and Drug Administration (FDA) regulations any food to which a nutrient is added, or any food for which a nutrition claim is made, must carry nutrition information on its label. For other foods nutrition information is voluntary.

You can find out from a label the number of calories in a serving, and the amount of protein, carbohydrates, fats, and seven vitamins and minerals. Amounts are in grams (gm). Equivalents are: 1 pound = 454 grams; 1 ounce = 28 grams; 1 gram = 1,000 mg; 1 mg = 1,000 mcg.

A label with optimal nutrition information may look like the one printed below.

Armed with such information, you can compare brands of similar food to get the best nutritional value for your money.

The information can be of immeasurable help to people who must restrict their intake of cholesterol, saturated fats, and sodium for medical conditions.

Bear in mind that a product must list ingredients in order of decreasing amounts. All products must list food additives, including artificial colors and flavors and chemical additives. This can be helpful if you have a food allergy.

For some foods the FDA has set a standard of identity. This is the minimum standard for a particular kind of food.

For example, when you see strawberry jam on the shelf, by government regulation it must contain at least 45 parts of strawberries to 55 parts of sugar. A product can't be called raisin bread unless it has raisins equal to at least half the weight of the flour. Diluted orange juice drink should be labeled as such, and should tell you the percentage of orange juice it contains.

A standardized food is not required to list all its ingredients on the label, except when the standard requires the manufacturer to list some or all of them. Frequently added ingredients, but not basic ones, must be listed. The FDA has requested manufacturers to voluntarily list all ingredients.

See also ALCOHOL; ANEMIA; CARBOHYDRATES; DEHYDRATION; FATS; FIBER; FOOD ADDITIVES; FOOD ALLERGY; HEALTH FOOD; HEART DISEASE; IRON; MINERALS; OVERWEIGHT; PHYSICAL EXAMINATION; PREGNANCY; PROTEIN; SODIUM; VEGETARIANISM; VITAMINS.

NUTRITION INFORMATION
(Per Serving)
Serving Size = 8 Oz.
Servings Per Container = 1

Calories	560	Fat (Percent of	
Protein	23 gm	Calories 53%)	33 gm
Carbohydrate	43 gm	Polyunsaturated*	2 gm
		Saturated	9 gm
		Cholesterol*	
		(20 mg/100 gm)	40 mg
		Sodium (365 mg/	
		100 gm)	830 mg

Percentage of U.S. Recommended Daily Allowances (U.S. RDA)

Protein	35	Riboflavin	15
Vitamin A	35	Niacin	25
Vitamin C		Calcium	2
(Ascorbic Acid)	10	Iron	25
Thiamin (Vitamin B₁)	15		

* Information on fat and cholesterol content is provided for individuals who, on the advice of a physician, are modifying their total dietary intake of fat and cholesterol.

What Nutrients You Need

Here are recommended daily dietary allowances, designed for the maintenance of good nutrition of practically all healthy persons in the U.S.

Sex-age category	Persons							Food energy	Protein	Minerals			Vita-min A	Thia-min	Ribo-flavin	Nia-cin	Ascor-bic acid
	Age		Weight		Height					Cal-cium	Phos-phorus	Iron					
	Years																
	From	To	Kilo-grams	Pounds	Centi-meters	Inches		Calor-ies	Grams	Milli-grams	Milli-grams	Milli-grams	Inter-nation-al units	Milli-grams	Milli-grams	Milli-grams	Milli-grams
Infants	0	0.5	6	13	60	24		kg x 11.5 lb 52.3	kg x 2.2 lb x 1.0	360	240	10	1,400	0.3	0.4	6	35
	0.5	1	9	20	71	28		kg x 10.5 lb 47.7	kg x 2.0 lb x 0.9	540	360	15	2,000	.5	.6	8	35
Children	1	3	13	29	90	35		1,300	23	800	800	15	2,000	.7	.8	9	45
	4	6	20	44	112	44		1,700	30	800	800	10	2,500	.9	1.0	11	45
	7	10	28	62	132	52		2,400	34	800	800	10	3,300	1.2	1.4	16	45
Males	11	14	45	99	157	62		2,700	45	1,200	1,200	18	5,000	1.4	1.6	18	50
	15	18	66	145	176	69		2,800	56	1,200	1,200	18	5,000	1.4	1.7	18	60
	19	22	70	154	177	70		2,900	56	800	800	10	5,000	1.5	1.7	19	60
	23	50	70	154	178	70		2,700	56	800	800	10	5,000	1.4	1.6	18	60
	51+		70	154	178	70		2,400	56	800	800	10	5,000	1.2	1.4	16	60
Females	11	14	46	101	157	62		2,200	46	1,200	1,200	18	4,000	1.1	1.3	15	50
	15	18	55	120	163	64		2,100	46	1,200	1,200	18	4,000	1.1	1.3	14	60
	19	22	55	120	163	64		2,100	44	800	800	18	4,000	1.1	1.3	14	60
	23	50	55	120	163	64		2,000	44	800	800	18	4,000	1.0	1.2	13	60
	51+		55	120	163	64		1,800	44	800	800	10	4,000	1.0	1.2	13	60
Pregnant								+300	+30	+400	+400	18+	+1,000	+.4	+.3	+2	+20
Lactating								+500	+20	+400	+400	18	+2,000	+.5	+.5	+5	+40

Source: *Nutritive Value of Foods*, Home and Garden Bulletin No. 72, U.S. Department of Agriculture.

YOUR FOOD'S NUTRITIONAL VALUE

This table tells you how many nutrients and calories you get in most foods you eat. Values for prepared dishes are calculated from typical recipes. Cooked vegetables are without added fat. Gm. = grams. Mg. = milligrams. I.U. = International Units. Cal. = calories. Tr. = trace. Ounce refers to weight; fluid ounce to measure.

Source: *Composition of Foods—Raw, Processed, Prepared,* Handbook No. 8, U.S. Department of Agriculture.

Food, and Approximate Measure	Food Energy Cal.	Protein gm.	Fat gm.	MINERALS Calcium Mg.	Iron Mg.	Vitamin A Value I.U.	VITAMINS Thiamine B₁ Mg.	Riboflavin B₂ Mg.	Niacin Value Mg.	Ascorbic Acid Mg.
A										
Apple, raw, 1 medium 2½″ in diam.	76	.4	.5	8	.4	120	.05	.04	.2	6
Apple betty, 1 cup	344	3.9	6.7	34	.2	370	.13	.09	1.1	3
Apple butter, 1 tbs.	33	.1	.1	3	.1	—	Tr.	Tr.	Tr.	Tr.
Apple juice, fresh or canned, 1 cup	124	.2	—	15	1.2	90	.05	.07	Tr.	2
Applesauce, canned unsweetened, 1 cup	100	.5	.5	10	1.0	70	.05	.02	.1	3
sweetened 1 cup	184	.5	.3	10	1.0	80	.05	.03	.1	3
Apricots, raw, three	54	1.1	.1	17	.5	2,990	.03	.05	.9	7
canned, sirup pack, 4 medium halves, 2 tbs. sirup	97	.7	.1	12	.4	1,650	.02	.03	.4	5
dried, uncooked, 1 cup (40 small halves)	393	7.8	.6	129	7.4	11,140	.02	.24	4.9	19
cooked, unsweetened, 1 cup (25 halves approx.)	242	4.8	.3	80	4.6	6,990	.01	.14	2.8	9
cooked, sweetened, 1 cup (25 halves approx.)	400	4.9	.3	78	4.6	6,860	.01	.13	2.9	10
frozen, 3 ounces	70	.6	.1	9	.3	1,410	.02	.03	.4	3
Asparagus, cooked, 1 cup cut spears	36	4.2	.4	33	1.8	1,820	.23	.30	2.1	40
canned, green, 1 cup cut spears	38	4.2	.7	33	3.3	1,400	.11	.14	1.7	31
Avocado, raw, ½ peeled, 3½ × 3¼″ diam.	279	1.9	30.1	11	.7	330	.07	.15	1.3	18
B										
Bacon, crisp, 2 slices	97	4.0	8.8	4	.5	—	.08	.05	.8	—
Bananas, raw, 1 large, 8 × 1½″	119	1.6	.3	11	.8	570	.06	.06	1.0	13
Barley, pearled, light, dry, 1 cup	708	16.6	2.0	32	4.1	—	.25	.17	6.3	—
Bean sprouts, Chinese, 1 cup	21	2.6	.2	26	.7	10	.06	.08	.5	14
Beans:										
Red kidney, canned or cooked, 1 cup	230	14.6	1.0	102	4.9	—	.12	.12	2.0	—
Other (including navy, pea bean—raw), 1 cup	642	40.7	3.0	310	13.1	—	1.28	.44	4.1	3
Baked—pork and molasses, 1 cup	325	15.1	7.8	146	5.5	90	.13	.09	1.2	7
pork and tomato sauce, 1 cup	295	15.1	5.5	107	4.7	220	.13	.09	1.2	7
Beans, lima immature, cooked, 1 cup	152	8.0	.6	46	2.7	460	.22	.14	1.8	24
canned, solids and liquid, 1 cup	176	9.5	.7	67	4.2	330	.09	.11	1.3	20
Beans, snap:										
green, cooked, 1 cup	27	1.8	.2	45	.9	830	.09	.12	.6	18
canned, drained solids, 1 cup	27	1.8	.2	45	2.1	620	.04	.07	.5	7
wax, canned, drained solids, 1 cup	27	1.8	.2	45	2.1	150	.04	.07	.5	7
Beans, soya (See Soybeans)										
Beef cuts, cooked:										
Chuck, 3 ounces without bone	265	22.0	19.0	9	2.6	—	.04	.17	3.5	—
Flank, 3 ounces without bone	270	21.0	20.0	9	2.6	—	.04	.17	3.5	—
Hamburger, 3 ounces	316	19.0	26.0	8	2.4	—	.07	.16	4.1	—
Porterhouse, 3 ounces without bone	293	20.0	23.0	9	2.6	—	.05	.15	4.0	—
Rib roast, 3 ounces without bone	266	20.0	20.0	9	2.6	—	.05	5.1	3.6	—
Round, 3 ounces without bone	197	23.0	11.0	9	2.9	—	.06	.19	4.7	—
Rump, 3 ounces without bone	320	18.0	27.0	7	2.1	—	.04	.13	2.6	—
Sirloin, 3 ounces without bone	257	20.0	19.0	9	2.5	—	.06	.16	4.1	—
Beef, canned:										
Corned beef hash, 3 ounces	120	11.7	5.2	22	1.1	Tr.	.02	.11	2.4	—
Roast beef, 3 ounces	189	21.0	11.0	14	2.0	—	.02	.19	3.6	—
Strained (infant food), 1 ounce	30	4.9	1.0	3	1.2	—	Tr.	.06	.9	—

Food, and Approximate Measure	Food Energy Cal.	Protein gm.	Fat gm.	MINERALS Calcium Mg.	Iron Mg.	Vitamin A Value I.U.	VITAMINS Thiamine B₁ Mg.	Riboflavin B₂ Mg.	Niacin Value Mg.	Ascorbic Acid Mg.
Beef, corned, canned:										
Lean, 3 ounces	159	22.5	7.0	18	3.8	—	.01	.21	3.0	—
Medium fat, 3 ounces	182	21.5	10.0	17	3.7	—	.01	.20	2.9	—
Fat, 3 ounces	221	20.0	15.0	16	3.4	—	.01	.19	2.7	—
Beef, dried or chipped, 1 cup	336	56.6	10.4	33	8.4	—	.12	.53	6.3	—
Beef, dried or chipped, 2 ounces	115	19.4	3.6	11	2.9	—	.04	.18	2.2	—
Beef and vegetable stew, 1 cup	252	12.9	19.3	31	2.6	2,520	.12	.15	3.4	15
Beer (average 4 pct. alcohol), 8 ounces	114	1.4	—	10	—	—	Tr.	.06	.4	—
Beets, red, raw, 1 cup diced	56	2.1	.1	36	1.3	30	.03	.06	.6	13
cooked, 1 cup diced	68	1.6	.2	35	1.2	30	.03	.07	.5	11
Beet greens, cooked, 1 cup	39	2.9	.4	171¹	4.6	10,790	.07	.23	.6	22
Beverages, carbonated:										
Ginger ale, 1 cup	80	—	—	—	—	—	—	—	—	—
Other, including kola type, 1 cup	107	—	—	—	—	—	—	—	—	—
Biscuits, baking powder, 1–2¹/2″ diam.	129	3.1	4.0	83	.2	—	.02	.03	.2	—
Blackberries, raw, 1 cup	82	1.7	1.4	46	1.3	280	.05	.06	.5	30
canned, sirup pack, 1 cup	216	1.8	.5	45	1.8	460	.03	.05	.5	16
Blanc mange (vanilla cornstarch pudding), 1 cup	275	8.7	9.7	290	.2	390	.08	.40	.2	2
Blueberries, raw, 1 cup	85	.8	.8	22	1.1	400	.04	.03	.4	23
canned, sirup pack, 1 cup	245	1.0	1.0	27	1.2	100	.03	.03	.5	33
frozen without sugar, 3 ounces	52	.5	.5	14	.7	200	.01	.01	.2	12
Bluefish, cooked, baked, 1 piece 3¹/2 × 3 × ¹/2″	193	34.2	5.2	29	.9	—	.15	.14	2.8	—
fried, 1 piece 3¹/2 × 3 × ¹/2″	307	34.0	14.7	28	.9	—	.16	.16	3.1	—
Bouillon cubes, 1 cube	2	—	.1	—	—	—	—	.07	1.0	—
Brains, all kinds, raw, 3 ounces	106	8.8	7.3	14	3.1	—	.20	.22	3.8	15
Bran (breakfast cereal almost wholly bran), 1 cup	145	7.2	2.0	56	6.2	—	.22	.23	11.5	—
Bran flakes, 1 cup	117	4.3	.8	24	2.0	—	.19	.09	3.5	—
Breads:										
Boston brown, unenriched, 1 slice 3 × ³/4″	105	2.3	1.0	89	1.2	70	.04	.06	.7	—
Cracked-wheat, unenriched, 1 sl. ¹/2″ thick	60	2.0	.5	19	2.2	—	.03	.02	.3	—
French or Vienna, unenriched, 1 pound	1,225	36.8	12.3	109	3.2	—	.21	.28	4.2	—
Italian, unenriched, 1 pound	1,195	39.5	3.6	59	3.2	—	.23	.30	4.5	—
Raisin, unenriched, 1 slice ¹/2″ thick	65	1.6	.7	18	.3	Tr.	.02	.02	.2	—
Rye, American, 1 slice ¹/2″ thick	57	2.1	.3	17	.4	—	.04	.02	.4	—
White, unenriched, 4 per cent nonfat milk solids, 1 slice ¹/2″ thick	63	2.0	.7	18	.1	—	.01	.02	.2	—
Toasted, 1 slice ¹/2″ thick	63	2.0	.7	18	.1	—	.01	.02	.2	—
Whole wheat, 1 slice ¹/2″ thick	55	2.1	.6	22	.5	—	.07	.03	.7	—
Bread crumbs, dry, grated, 1 cup	339	10.5	4.0	98	2.3	—	.24	.19	2.7	—
Broccoli, cooked, 1 cup	44	5.0	.3	195	2.0	5,100	.10	.22	1.2	111
Brussels sprouts, cooked, 1 cup	60	5.7	.6	44	1.7	520	.05	.16	.6	61
Buckwheat flour:										
Dark, 1 cup sifted	340	11.5	2.4	32	2.7	—	.56	.15	2.8	—
Light, 1 cup sifted	342	6.3	1.2	11	1.0	—	.08	.04	.4	—
Buckwheat pancake, 1 cake 4″ diam.	47	1.6	2.3	67	.3	30	.04	.04	.2	Tr.
Butter, 1 tbs.	100	.1	11.3	3	—	460²	Tr.	Tr.	Tr.	—
Buttermilk, 1 cup	86	8.5	.2	288	.2	10	.09	.43	.3	.3
Buttermilk, 1 quart	348	34.2	1.0	1,152	.7	40	.35	1.74	1.1	13
C										
Cabbage, raw, 1 cup shredded finely	24	1.4	.2	46	.5	80	.06	.05	.3	50
cooked, short time, 1 cup	40	2.4	.3	78	.8	150	.08	.08	.5	53
Cabbage, celery or Chinese:										
Raw, leaves and stem, 1 cup 1″ pieces	14	1.2	.3	43	.9	260	.03	.04	.4	31
Cooked, 1 cup	27	2.3	.6	82	1.7	490	.04	.06	.6	42
Cakes:										
Angel food, 2″ sector	108	3.4	.1	2	.1	—	Tr.	.05	.1	—
Foundation, plain, 1 sq. 3 × 2 × 1³/4″	228	3.8	7.6	82	.3	100³	.02	.05	.2	—
With fudge icing, 3″ sector	314	4.0	10.4	88	.4	100³	.02	.07	.2	—
Fruit, dark, 1 piece 2 × 2 × ¹/2″	106	1.6	4.1	29	.8	50⁴	.04	.04	.3	—

Food, and Approximate Measure	Food Energy Cal.	Protein gm.	Fat gm.	MINERALS Calcium Mg.	Iron Mg.	Vitamin A Value I.U.	VITAMINS Thiamine B_1 Mg.	Riboflavin B_2 Mg.	Niacin Value Mg.	Ascorbic Acid Mg.
Cupcake, 1 2³/4″ in diam.	131	2.6	3.3	62	.2	50	.01	.03	.1	—
Iced layer cake, 3″ sector	241	3.9	4.6	88	.3	70	.02	.05	.2	—
Iced cupcake, 1 2³/4″ in diam.	161	2.6	3.1	58	.2	50	.01	.04	.1	—
Pound, 1 sl. 2³/4 × 3 × 5/8″	130	2.1	7.0	16	.5	100[5]	.04	.05	.3	—
Rich, 1 square 3 × 2 × 2″	294	3.8	13.3	79	.4	160[6]	.02	.06	.2	—
Plain icing, 3″ sector	378	4.4	14.7	88	.5	170	.02	.07	.2	—
Sponge, 2″ sector	117	3.2	2.0	11	.6	210	.02	.06	.1	—
Candy:										
Butterscotch, 1 ounce	116	—	2.5	6	.5	—	—	Tr.	Tr.	—
Caramels, 1 ounce	118	.8	3.3	36	.7	50	.01	.04	Tr.	Tr.
Chocolate, sweetened milk, 1 ounce	143	2.0	9.5	61	.6	40	.03	.11	.2	—
Chocolate creams, 1 ounce	110	1.1	4.0	—	—	—	—	—	—	—
Fondant, 1 ounce	101	—	—	—	—	—	—	—	—	—
Fudge, plain, 1 ounce	116	.5	3.2	14[7]	.1	60	Tr.	.02	Tr.	Tr.
Hard, 1 ounce	108	—	—	—	—	—	—	—	—	—
Marshmallows, 1 ounce	92	.9	—	—	—	—	—	—	—	—
Peanut brittle, 1 ounce	125	2.4	4.4	11	.6	10	.03	.01	1.4	—
Cantaloupe, 1/2 melon 5″ diam.	37	1.1	.4	31	.7	6,190[8]	.09	.07	.9	59
Carrots, raw, 1, 51/2 × 1″	21	.6	.2	20	.4	6,000	.03	.03	.3	3
Grated, 1 cup	45	1.3	.3	43	.9	13,200	.06	.06	.7	7
Cooked, 1 cup diced	44	.9	.7	38	.9	18,130	.07	.07	.7	6
Catsup, tomato, 1 tbs.	17	.3	.1	2	.1	320	.02	.01	.4	2
Cauliflower, raw, 1 cup flower buds	25	2.4	.2	22	1.1	90	.11	.10	.6	69
Cooked, 1 cup	30	2.9	.2	26	1.3	108	.07	.10	.6	34
Celery, raw, 1 stalk, 8″ long, 1″ wide	7	.5	.1	20	.2	—	.02	.02	.2	3
Celery, raw, 1 cup diced	18	1.3	.2	50	.5	—	.05	.04	.4	7
Cooked, 1 cup diced	24	1.7	.3	65	.6	—	.05	.04	.4	6
Chard, cooked, 1 cup	47	4.6	.7	184[1]	4.4	16,960	.07	.28	.5	30
Cheese:										
Camembert, 1 ounce	85	5.0	7.0	30	.1	290	.01	.21	.3	—
Cheddar, 1 ounce (1″ cube)	113	7.1	9.1	206	.3	400	.01	.12	Tr.	—
Cottage from skim milk, 1 cup	215	43.9	1.1	216	.7	50	.04	.69	.2	—
Cottage from skim milk, 2 tbs.	25	6.0	.1	27	.1	10	.01	.09	Tr.	—
Cream cheese, 1 ounce	106	2.6	10.5	19	.1	410	Tr.	.06	Tr.	—
Limburger, 1 ounce	97	6.0	7.9	167	.2	360	.02	.14	Tr.	—
Parmesan, 1 ounce	112	10.2	7.4	329	.1	300	.01	.21	.1	—
Swiss, 1 ounce	105	7.8	7.9	262	.3	410	Tr.	.11	Tr.	—
Cherries, raw, sour, sweet, 1 cup pitted	94	1.7	.8	28	.6	960	.08	.09	.6	13
Canned, 1 cup	122	2.0	.8	28	.8	1,840	.07	.04	.4	14
Chicken raw, broiler, 1/2 bird (8 oz. bone out)	332	44.4	15.8	31	3.3	—	.18	.36	22.4	—
Roasters, 4 oz. bone out	227	22.9	14.3	16	1.7	—	.09	.18	9.1	—
Hens, stewing, 4 oz. bone out	342	20.4	28.3	16	1.7	—	.09	.18	9.1	—
Fryers, 1 breast, 8 oz. bone out	210	47.0	1.0	28	2.2	—	.13	.18	21.1	—
1 leg, 5 oz. bone out	159	29.1	3.8	21	2.6	—	.14	.34	8.0	—
Canned, boned, 3 oz.	169	25.3	6.8	12	1.5	—	.03	.14	5.4	—
Chile con carne, canned, 1/3 cup (without beans)	170	8.8	12.6	32	1.2	130	.01	.10	1.9	—
Chili sauce, 1 tbs.	17	.5	.1	2	.1	320	.02	.01	.4	2
Chocolate, bitter, 1 ounce	142	1.6	15.0	28[1]	1.2	20	.01	.06	.3	—
Sweetened, plain, 1 ounce	133	.6	8.4	18[1]	.8	10	.01	.04	.2	—
Chocolate beverage, 1 cup (made with milk)	239	8.2	12.5	260	.5	350	.08	.40	.3	2
Chocolate sirup, 1 tbs.	42	.2	.2	3[1]	.3	—	—	—	—	—
Cider—See apple juice										
Clams, raw, meat only, 4 ounces	92	14.5	1.6	109	7.9	120	.11	.20	1.8	—
Canned, solids and liquid, 3 ounces	44	6.7	.9	74	5.4	70	.04	.08	.9	—
Cocoa, breakfast, plain dry powder, 1 tbs.	21	.6	1.7	9[1]	.8	Tr.	.01	.03	.2	—
Cocoa beverage made with all milk, 1 cup	236	9.5	11.5	298	1.0	400	.10	.46	.5	3
Cola beverage, carbonated, 1 cup	107	—	—	—	—	—	—	—	—	—
Coconut, fresh, 1 piece, 2 × 2 × 1/2″	161	1.5	15.6	9	.9	—	.04	Tr.	.1	1
Dried, shredded, 1 cup	344	2.2	24.2	27	2.2	—	Tr.	Tr.	Tr.	—
Milk only, 1 cup	60	.7	1.0	58	.2	—	Tr.	Tr.	.2	4
Cod, raw, 4 ounces edible portion	84	18.7	.5	11	.5	—	.07	.10	2.5	2
Dried, 1 ounce	106	23.2	.8	14	1.0	—	.02	.13	3.1	—
Coffee, clear, 1 cup	—	—	—	—	—	—	—	—	—	—

Food, and Approximate Measure	Food Energy Cal.	Protein gm.	Fat gm.	MINERALS Calcium Mg.	Iron Mg.	VITAMINS Vitamin A Value I.U.	Thiamine B₁ Mg.	Riboflavin B₂ Mg.	Niacin Value Mg.	Ascorbic Acid Mg.
Coleslaw, 1 cup	102	1.6	7.3	47	.5	80	.06	.05	.3	50
Collards, cooked, 1 cup	76	7.4	1.1	473	3.0	14,500	.15	.46	3.3	84
Cookies, plain, 1 3″ diam., 1/2″ thick	109	1.5	3.2	6	.2	—	.01	.01	.1	—
Corn, 1 ear 5″ long	84	2.7	.7	5	.6	390[9]	.11	.10	1.4	8
Canned, solids and liquid, 1 cup	170	5.1	1.3	10	1.3	520[9]	.07	.13	2.4	14
Corn bread or muffins, 1, 23/4″ diam.	106	3.2	2.3	67	.9	60[10]	.08	.11	.6	—
Corn flakes, 1 cup	96	2.0	.1	3	.3	—	.01	.02	.4	—
Corn flour, 1 cup sifted	406	8.6	2.9	7	2.0	370[11]	.22	.06	1.6	—
Cornmeal (whole) cooked, white or yellow, 1 cup	119	2.6	.5	2	.5	100[12]	.04	.02	.3	—
Corn sirup, 1 tbs.	57	—	—	9	.8	—	—	Tr.	Tr.	—
Crabs, canned or cooked, 3 oz. (meat only)	89	14.4	2.5	38	.8	—	.04	.05	2.1	—
Crackers, graham, 4 small	55	1.1	1.4	3	.3	—	.04	.02	.2	—
Saltines, 2, 2″ square	34	.7	.9	2	.1	—	Tr.	Tr.	.1	—
Soda, plain, 2, 21/2″ square	47	1.1	1.1	2	.1	—	.01	.01	.1	—
Cranberries, raw, 1 cup	54	.5	.8	16	.7	50	.03	.02	.1	13
Canned or cooked sauce, 1 cup	549	.3	.8	22	.8	80	.06	.06	.3	5
Cream, light, table, 1 tbs.	30	.4	3.0	15	—	120	Tr.	.02	Tr.	Tr.
Heavy or whipping, 1 tbs.	49	.3	5.2	12	—	220	Tr.	.02	Tr.	Tr.
Cress, garden, cooked, 1 cup	73	7.6	2.5	380	5.2	5,940	.11	.23	1.3	52
Cress, water, raw, 1 pound (leaves & stems)	84	7.7	1.4	885	9.1	21,450	.37	.71	3.6	350
Cucumbers, raw,1, 71/2 × 2″	25	1.4	.2	20	.6	—	.07	.09	.4	17
Currants, red, raw, 1 cup	60	1.3	.2	40	1.0	130	.04	—	—	40
Custard, baked, 1 cup	283	13.1	13.4	283	1.2	840	.11	.49	.2	1
D										
Dandelion greens, 1 cup cooked	79	4.9	1.3	337	5.6	27,310	.23	.22	1.3	29
Dates, fresh and dried, 1 cup pitted	505	3.9	1.1	128	3.7	100	.16	.17	3.9	—
Doughnuts, cake type, 1	136	2.1	6.7	23	.2	40	.05	.04	.4	—
E										
Eggs, boiled, poached, 1	77	6.1	5.5	26	1.3	550	.05	.14	Tr.	—
Omelet, 1 egg	106	6.8	7.9	50	1.3	640	.05	.17	Tr.	—
Scrambled, 1 egg	106	6.8	7.9	50	1.3	640	.05	.17	Tr.	—
Yolk, raw,1	61	2.8	5.4	25	1.2	550	.05	.06	Tr.	—
White, raw,1	15	3.3	—	2	.1	—	—	.08	Tr.	—
Endive, Escarole, 1 pound raw	90	7.3	.9	359	7.7	13,600	.30	.53	1.8	49
F										
Farina, cooked, 1 cup	104	3.1	.2	7	.2	—	.01	.02	.2	—
Fats, cooking (vegetable), 1 tbs. See also Lard, Oils	110	—	12.5	—	—	—	—	—	—	—
Figs, raw, 3 small, 11/2″ diam.	90	1.6	.5	62	.7	90	.06	.06	.6	2
Canned, sirup pack, 3, and 2 tbs. sirup	129	.9	.3	40	.5	60	.03	.04	.4	1
Dried, 1 large	57	.8	.3	39	.6	20	.03	.02	.4	—
Fig bars, 1 small	56	.7	.8	11	.2	—	Tr.	.01	.1	—
Flounder, summer and winter, 4 oz. (raw) edible portion	78	16.9	.6	69	.9	—	.07	.06	1.9	—
Frankfurters, 1	124	7.0	10.0	3	.6	—	.08	.09	1.3	—
Frog legs, raw, 4 oz. edible portion	82	18.6	.3	20	1.2	—	.16	.29	1.3	—
Fruit cocktail, canned, 1 cup (solids & liquid)	179	1.0	.5	23	1.0	410	.03	.03	.9	5
G										
Gelatin, dry, plain, 1 tbs.	34	8.6	—	—	—	—	—	—	—	—
Dessert powder, 1/2 cup (3 ounce pkg.)	324	8.0	—	—	—	—	—	—	—	—
Dessert, ready-to-serve, 1 cup	155	3.8	—	—	—	—	—	—	—	—
Ginger ale, dry, 1 cup	80	—	—	—	—	—	—	—	—	—
Gingerbread, 1 piece 2 × 2 × 2″	180	2.1	6.6	63	1.4	50	.02	.05	.6	—
Gooseberries, raw, 1 cup	59	1.2	.3	33	.8	440	—	—	—	49
Grapefruit, raw, 1/2 medium (41/2″ diam.)	75	.9	.4	41	.4	20	.07	.04	.4	76
Grapefruit, raw, 1 cup sections	77	1.0	.4	43	.4	20	.07	.04	.4	78
Canned in sirup, 1 cup solids & liquid	181	1.5	.5	32	.7	20	.07	.05	.5	74
Juice, fresh, 1 cup	87	1.2	.2	20	.7	20	.09	.05	.5	99
Juice, canned sweetened, 1 cup	131	1.3	.3	20	.8	20	.08	.04	.5	87
Juice, canned unsweetened, 1 cup	92	1.2	.2	20	.7	20	.07	.04	.4	85
Juice, concentrate, frozen, 1 can, 6 fluid ounces	297	3.8	.8	63	2.4	60	.24	.13	1.4	272

Food, and Approximate Measure	Food Energy Cal.	Protein gm.	Fat gm.	Calcium Mg.	Iron Mg.	Vitamin A Value I.U.	Thiamine B$_1$ Mg.	Riboflavin B$_2$ Mg.	Niacin Value Mg.	Ascorbic Acid Mg.
				MINERALS			VITAMINS			
Grapes, raw—Concord, 1 cup skins & seeds	84	1.7	1.7	20	.7	90	.07	.05	.3	5
Malaga, Muscat, 1 cup (40 grapes)	102	1.2	.6	26	.9	120	.09	.06	.4	6
Grape juice, bottled, 1 cup	170	1.0	—	25	.8	—	.09	.12	.6	Tr.
Griddle cakes (wheat), 1 cake, 4" in diam.	59	1.8	2.5	43	.2	50	.02	.03	.1	Tr.
Guavas, common, raw, 1	49	.7	.4	21	.5	180	.05	.03	.8	212
H										
Haddock, cooked, 1 fillet 4 × 3 × 1/2"	158	19.0	5.5	18	.6	—	.04	.09	2.6	—
Halibut, broiled, 1 steak 4 × 3 × 1/2"	228	33.0	9.8	18	1.0	—	.08	.09	13.9	—
Ham, See Pork										
Hamburger, See Beef										
Heart, beef, lean, raw, 3 ounces	92	14.4	3.1	8	3.9	30	.50	.75	6.6	5
Chicken, raw, 3 ounces	134	17.4	6.0	20	1.4	30	.10	.77	4.4	5
Herring, smoked, kippered, 3 ounces edible portion	180	18.9	11.0	56	1.2	—	Tr.	.24	2.5	—
Hominy grits, cooked, 1 cup	122	2.9	.2	2	.2	100	.04	.01	.4	—
Honey, 1 tbs.	62	.1	—	1	.2	—	Tr.	.01	Tr.	1
Honeydew melon, 1 wedge 2 × 7"	49	.8	—	26	.6	60	.07	.04	.3	34
I										
Ice cream, plain, 1/7 of quart brick	167	3.2	10.1	100	.1	420	.03	.15	.1	1
J										
Jams, marmalades, 1 tbs.	55	.1	.1	2	.1	Tr.	Tr.	Tr.	Tr.	1
Jellies, 1 tbs.	50	—	—	2	.1	Tr.	Tr.	Tr.	Tr.	1
K										
Kale, cooked, 1 cup	45	4.3	.7	248	2.4	9,220	.08	.25	1.9	56
Kidney, beef, 3 ounces (raw)	120	12.8	6.9	8	6.7	980	.32	2.16	5.5	11
Pork, 3 ounces (raw)	97	13.9	3.9	9	6.8	110	.50	1.47	8.4	11
Lamb, 3 ounces (raw)	89	14.1	2.8	11	7.8	980	.44	2.06	6.3	11
Kohlrabi, raw, 1 cup diced	41	2.9	.1	63	.8	Tr.	.08	.07	.3	84
cooked, 1 cup	47	3.3	.2	71	.9	Tr.	.06	.06	.3	57
L										
Lamb:										
Rib chop cooked, 3 ounces without bone	356	20.0	30.0	9	2.6	—	.12	.22	4.8	—
Shoulder roast, 3 ounces without bone	293	18.0	24.0	8	2.2	—	.10	.19	3.9	—
Leg roast, 3 ounces without bone	230	20.0	16.0	9	2.6	—	.12	.21	4.4	—
Lard, 1 tbs.	126	—	14.0	—	—	—	—	—	—	—
Lemons, 1 medium	20	.6	.4	25	.4	—	.03	Tr.	.1	31
Juice, fresh, 1 tbs.	4	.1	—	2	—	—	.01	Tr.	Tr.	7
Lettuce, loose leaf, 1 head	32	2.6	.4	48	1.1	1,200	.10	.18	.4	17
Lettuce, loose leaf, 2 large leaves	7	.6	.1	11	.2	270	.02	.04	.1	4
Limes, 1 medium	19	.4	.1	21	.3	—	.02	Tr.	.1	14
Juice, fresh, 1 cup	58	1.0	—	34	.2	—	.11	.01	.3	65
Liver, beef, 2 ounces cooked	118	13.4	4.4	5	4.4	30,330	.15	2.25	8.4	18
Calf, 3 ounces raw	120	16.2	4.2	5	9.0	19,130	.18	2.65	13.7	30
Chicken, 3 ounces raw	120	18.8	3.4	14	6.3	27,370	.17	2.10	10.0	17
Lamb, 3 ounces raw	116	17.8	3.3	7	10.7	42,930	.34	2.79	14.3	28
Liver, canned, strained, 1 ounce (infant food)	30	4.5	1.1	7	2.0	5,440	.01	.61	1.8	—
Lobster, canned, 3 ounces	78	15.6	1.1	55	.7	—	.03	.06	1.9	—
Loganberries, raw, 1 cup	90	1.4	.9	50	1.7	280	.04	.10	.4	34
M										
Macaroni, enriched, cooked, 1 cup (1" pieces)	209	7.1	.8	13	1.5	—	.24	.15	2.0	—
Macaroni & cheese baked, 1 cup	464	17.8	24.2	420	1.1	990	.07	.35	.9	Tr.
Mackerel, canned, 1, 3 ounces solids & liquids	153	17.9	8.5	221	1.9	20	.02	.28	7.4	—
Mangos, raw, 1 medium	87	.9	.3	12	.3	8,380	.08	.07	1.2	55
Margarine, 1 tbs.	101	.1	11.3	3	—	460[13]	—	—	—	—
Marmalade, 1 tbs.	55	.1	.1	2	.1	Tr.	Tr.	Tr.	Tr.	1
Mayonnaise, 1 tbs.	92	.2	10.1	2	.1	30	Tr.	Tr.	—	—
Milk, cow: fluid, whole, 1 cup	166	8.5	9.5	288	.2	390	.09	.42	.3	3
Fluid, nonfat (skim), 1 cup	87	8.6	.2	303	.2	10	.09	.44	.3	3
Buttermilk, 1 cup	86	8.5	.2	288	.2	10	.09	.43	.3	3
Canned, Evaporated (unsweetened), 1 cup	346	17.6	19.9	612	.4	1,010	.12	.91	.5	3

	Food Energy Cal.	Protein gm.	Fat gm.	MINERALS Calcium Mg.	Iron Mg.	Vitamin A Value I.U.	Thiamine B₁ Mg.	VITAMINS Riboflavin B₂ Mg.	Niacin Value Mg.	Ascorbic Acid Mg.
Condensed (sweetened), 1 cup	981	24.8	25.7	835	.6	1,300	.16	1.19	.6	3
Dried, whole, 1 tbs.	39	2.1	2.1	76	—	110	.02	.12	.1	1
Dried, nonfat solids (skim), 1 tbs.	28	2.7	.1	98	—	Tr.	.03	.15	.1	1
Malted beverage, 1 cup	281	12.4	11.9	364	.8	680	.18	.56	—	3
Half & Half (milk and cream), 1 cup	330	7.7	29.0	261	.1	1,190	.08	.38	.2	3
Chocolate flavored, 1 cup	185	8.0	5.5	272	.2	230	.08	.40	.2	2
Milk, goat, 1 cup	164	8.1	9.8	315	.2	390	.10	.26	.7	2
Molasses, cane, light, 1 tbs.	50	—	—	33	.9	—	.01	.01	Tr.	—
Medium, 1 tbs.	46	—	—	58	1.2	—	—	—	—	—
Blackstrap, 1 tbs.	43	—	—	116	2.3	—	.06	.05	.4	—
Barbados, 1 tbs.	54	—	—	—	—	—	.01	.04	—	—
Muffins, plain, 1, 2¾″ in diam.	134	3.8	4.0	99	.3	50	.02	.06	.2	—
Mung bean sprouts, raw, 1 cup	21	2.6	.2	26	.7	10	.06	.08	.5	14
Mushrooms, canned, 1 cup solids & liquid	28	3.4	.5	17	2.0	—	.04	.60	4.8	—
Muskmelon, ½ melon 5″ diam.	37	1.1	.4	31	.7	6,190	.09	.07	.9	59
Mustard greens, cooked, 1 cup	31	3.2	.4	308	4.1	10,050	.08	.25	1.0	63
N										
Noodles, unenriched, containing egg, 1 cup (dry)	278	9.2	2.5	16	1.5	140	.15	.08	1.7	—
Cooked, 1 cup	107	3.5	1.0	6	.6	60	.05	.03	.6	—
Nuts:										
Almonds, shelled, 1 cup	848	26.4	76.8	361	6.2	—	.35	.95	6.5	Tr.
Brazil, shelled, 1 cup (32 kernels)	905	20.2	92.3	260	4.8	Tr.	1.21	—	—	—
Cashew, roasted, 1 ounce	164	5.2	13.7	13	1.4	—	.18	.05	.6	—
Peanuts, roasted, 1 cup medium halves	805	38.7	63.6	107	2.7	—	.42	.19	23.3	—
Peanuts, roasted, 1 tbs. chopped	50	2.4	4.0	7	.2	—	.03	.01	1.5	—
Pecans, 1 cup halves	752	10.2	78.8	80	2.6	50	.77	.12	1.0	2
Pecans, 1 tbs. chopped	52	.7	5.5	6	.2	Tr.	.05	.01	.1	Tr.
Walnuts, 1 cup halves	654	15.0	64.4	83	2.1	30	.48	.13	1.2	3
Walnuts, 1 tbs. chopped	49	1.1	4.8	6	.2	Tr.	.04	.01	.1	Tr.
O										
Oatmeal or rolled oats, 1 cup dry	312	11.4	5.9	42	3.6	—	.48	.11	.8	—
Cooked, 1 cup	148	5.4	2.8	21	1.7	—	.22	.05	.4	—
Oils, salad or cooking, 1 tbs.	124	—	14.0	—	—	—	—	—	—	—
Okra, cooked, 8 pods, 3 × ⅝″	28	1.5	.2	70	.6	630	.05	.05	.7	17
Oleomargarine, 1 tbs.	101	.1	11.3	3	—	460	—	—	—	—
Olives, green, 10 large	72	.8	7.4	48	.9	160	Tr.	—	—	—
Ripe, Mission, 10 large	106	1.0	11.6	48	.9	40	Tr.	Tr.	—	—
Onions, mature, raw, 1, 2½″ diam.	49	1.5	.2	35	.6	60	.04	.04	.2	10
Onions, mature, raw, 1 tbs. chopped	4	.1	—	3	—	Tr.	Tr.	Tr.	Tr.	1
Cooked, whole, 1 cup	79	2.1	.4	67	1.0	110	.04	.06	.4	13
Onions, young green, 6 small	23	.5	.1	68	.4	30	.02	.02	.1	12
Oranges, 1 medium, 3″ diam.	70	1.4	.3	51	.6	290	.12	.04	.4	77
Orange juice, fresh, 1 cup	108	2.0	.5	47	.5	460	.19	.06	.6	122
Canned, unsweetened, 1 cup	109	2.0	.5	25	.7	240	.17	.04	.6	103
Canned, sweetened, 1 cup	135	1.5	.5	25	.8	250	.18	.05	.6	105
Orange juice concentrate, canned, 1 ounce	65	1.2	.2	17	.5	140	.10	.02	.3	63
Frozen, 1 can (6 fl. oz.)	300	5.5	1.4	69	2.0	670	.48	.11	1.5	285
Oysters, meat only, raw, 1 cup (13–19 med.)	200	23.5	5.0	226	13.4	770	.35	.48	2.8	—
Stew, 1 cup (6–8 oysters)	244	16.6	13.2	262	7.0	820	.21	.46	1.6	—
P										
Pancakes (griddlecakes)										
Wheat, 1 cake, 4″ diameter	59	1.8	2.5	43	.2	50	.02	.03	.1	Tr.
Buckwheat, 1 cake, 4″ diameter	47	1.6	2.3	67	.3	30	.04	.04	.2	Tr.
Papayas, raw, 1 cup, ½″ cubes	71	1.1	.2	36	.5	3,190	.06	.07	.5	102
Parsley, common, raw, 1 tbs. chopped	1	.1	—	7¹	.2	290	Tr.	.01	.1	7
Parsnips, cooked, 1 cup	94	1.6	.8	88	1.1	—	.09	.16	.3	19
Peaches, raw, 1 medium	46	.5	.1	8	.6	880	.02	.05	.9	8
Peaches, canned, sirup pack, 2 medium halves, 2 tbs. sirup	79	.5	.1	6	.5	530	.01	.02	.8	5
Strained (infant food), 1 ounce	17	.2	.1	2	.3	180	.01	.01	.2	1
Frozen, 4 ounces	89	.5	.1	7	.5	590	.01	.03	.6	5
Dried, cooked, no sugar, 1 cup, 10–12 halves, 6 tbs. liquid	224	2.4	.5	38	5.9	2,750	.01	.16	4.3	11
With sugar added, 1 cup, 10–12 halves, 6 tbs. liquid	366	2.4	.6	37	5.8	2,750	.01	.15	4.3	12

Food, and Approximate Measure	Food Energy Cal.	Protein gm.	Fat gm.	Calcium Mg.	Iron Mg.	Vitamin A Value I.U.	Thiamine B₁ Mg.	Riboflavin B₂ Mg.	Niacin Value Mg.	Ascorbic Acid Mg.
Peanut butter, 1 tbs.	92	4.2	7.6	12	.3	—	.02	.02	2.6	—
Pears, raw, 1, 3 × 2¹/₂" diam.	95	1.1	.6	20	.5	30	.03	.06	.2	6
Canned, sirup pack, 2 medium halves, 2 tbs. sirup	79	.2	.1	9	.2	Tr.	.01	.02	.2	2
Strained (infant food), 1 ounce	15	.2	.1	3	.1	10	Tr.	.01	.1	Tr.
Peas, green, 1 cup	111	7.8	.6	35	3.0	1,150	.40	.22	3.7	24
Canned, 1 cup drained solids	145	7.2	1.0	51	3.4	1,070	.19	.10	1.6	15
Canned, 1 cup solids & liquid	168	8.5	1.0	62	4.5	1,350	.28	.15	2.6	21
Peppers, green, raw, 1 medium	16	.8	.1	7	.3	400	.02	.04	.2	77
Persimmons, raw,										
Seedless kind, 1, 2¹/₄" diameter	95	1.0	.5	7	.4	3,270	.06	.05	Tr.	13
Kind with seeds, 1, 2¹/₄" diameter	74	.8	.4	6	.3	2,570	.05	.04	Tr.	10
Pickles: Dill, 1 large	15	.9	.3	34	1.6	420	Tr.	.09	.1	8
Bread & butter pickles, 6 slices	29	.4	.1	13	.8	80	.01	.02	Tr.	4
Sour, 1 large	15	.7	.3	34	1.6	420	Tr.	.09	Tr.	8
Sweet, 1 average	22	.2	.1	3	.3	20	—	Tr.	Tr.	1
Pies: Apple, 4" sector	331	2.8	12.8	9	.5	220	.04	.02	.3	1
Blueberry, 4" sector	291	2.8	9.3	14	.7	160	.02	.04	.3	5
Cherry, 4" sector	340	3.2	13.2	14	.5	530	.04	.02	.3	2
Custard, 4" sector	266	6.8	11.3	162	1.6	290	.07	.21	.4	—
Lemon meringue, 4" sector	302	4.3	12.1	24	.6	210	.04	.10	.2	1
Mince, 4" sector	341	3.4	9.3	22	3.0	10	.09	.05	.5	1
Pumpkin, 4" sector	263	5.5	12.5	70	1.0	2,480	.04	.15	.4	1
Pimientos, canned, 1 medium	10	.3	.2	3	.6	870	.01	.02	.1	36
Pineapple, raw, 1 cup diced	74	.6	.3	22	.4	180	.12	.04	.3	33
Canned, sirup pack, 1 cup crushed	204	1.0	.3	75	1.6	210	.20	.04	.4	23
Canned, sirup pack, 1 large slice & 2 oz. juice	95	.5	.1	35	.7	100	.09	.02	.2	11
Frozen, 4 ounces	97	.5	.2	16	.3	110	.07	.02	.2	22
Pineapple juice, canned, 1 cup	121	.7	.2	37	1.2	200	.13	.04	.4	22
Plums, raw, 1, 2" in diam.	29	.4	.1	10	.3	200	.04	.02	.3	3
Canned, sirup pack, 1 cup (fruit & juice)	186	1.0	.2	20	2.7	560	.07	.06	.9	3
Popcorn, popped, 1 cup	54	1.8	.7	2	.4	—	.05	.02	.3	—
Pork, fresh:										
Ham cooked, 3 ounces without bone	338	20.0	28.0	9	2.6	—	.45	.20	4.0	—
Loin or chops cooked, 1 chop	293	20.0	23.0	10	2.6	—	.72	.21	4.4	—
Pork, cured:										
Ham, smoked, cooked, 3 ounces without bone	339	20.0	28.0	9	2.5	—	.46	.18	3.5	—
Luncheon meat: Boiled ham, 2 ounces	172	12.9	12.9	5	1.5	—	.57	.15	2.9	—
Canned, spiced, 2 ounces	164	8.4	13.8	5	1.2	—	.18	.12	1.6	—
Pork sausage, links, raw, 4 ounces	510	12.2	50.8	7	1.8	—	.49	.19	2.6	—
Pork, canned, strained,1 ounce (infant food)	36	4.8	1.7	4	.5	—	.10	.08	1.3	—
Potatoes, baked, 1 medium, 2¹/₂" diam.	97	2.4	.1	13	.8	20	.11	.05	1.4	17
Boiled in jacket, 1 medium, 2¹/₂" diam.	118	2.8	.1	16	1.0	30	.14	.06	1.6	22
Peeled and boiled, 1 medium, 2¹/₂" diam.	105	2.5	.1	14	.9	20	.12	.04	1.3	17
French fried, 8 pieces 2 × ¹/₂ × ¹/₂"	157	2.2	7.6	12	.8	20	.07	.04	1.3	11
Hash-browned, 1 cup	470	6.4	22.8	35	2.3	60	.15	.11	3.3	14
Mashed, milk added, 1 cup	159	4.3	1.4	53	1.2	80	.16	.10	1.7	14
Mashed, milk and butter added, 1 cup	240	4.1	11.7	53	1.2	500	.15	.10	1.6	13
Steamed or pressure cooked, 1 medium	105	2.5	.1	14	.9	20	.12	.05	1.5	18
Canned, drained solids, 3–4 very small	118	2.8	.1	16	1.0	30	.11	.05	1.3	18
Potato chips, 10 medium, 2" diam.	108	1.3	7.4	6	.4	10	.04	.02	.6	2
Pretzels, 5 small sticks	18	.04	.2	1	—	—	Tr.	Tr.	Tr.	—
Prunes, dried, uncooked, 4 large	94	.8	.2	19	1.4	660	.03	.06	.6	1
Cooked, no sugar added, 1 cup	310	2.7	.7	62	4.5	2,210	.07	.20	2.0	2
Cooked, sugar added, 1 cup	483	2.9	.6	64	4.4	2,200	.09	.18	1.8	3
Prunes, canned, strained, 1 ounce (infant food)	28	.3	.1	7	.4	210	.01	.01	.2	1
Prune juice, canned, 1 cup	170	1.0	—	60	4.3	—	.07	.19	1.0	2

Food, and Approximate Measure	Food Energy Cal.	Protein gm.	Fat gm.	MINERALS Calcium Mg.	Iron Mg.	Vitamin A Value I.U.	VITAMINS Thiamine B₁ Mg.	Riboflavin B₂ Mg.	Niacin Value Mg.	Ascorbic Acid Mg.
Prune whip, 1 cup	200	3.8	.4	35	2.4	1,160	.05	.15	1.0	3
Pudding, vanilla, 1 cup	275	8.7	9.7	290	.2	390	.08	.40	.2	2
Puffed rice, 1 cup	55	.8	.1	3	.3	—	.06	.01	.8	—
Puffed wheat, 1 cup	43	1.3	.2	6	.4	—	.01	.02	.6	—
Pumpkin, canned, 1 cup	76	2.3	.7	46	1.6	7,750	.04	.14	1.2	—
R										
Radishes, raw, 4 small	4	.2	—	7	.2	10	.01	Tr.	.1	5
Raisins, dried, 1 cup	429	3.7	.8	125	5.3	80	.24	.13	.8	Tr.
Raisins, dried, 1 tbs.	26	.2	—	8	.3	Tr.	.02	.01	Tr.	Tr.
Cooked, sugar added, 1 cup	572	3.2	.6	112	4.7	60	.18	.12	.6	Tr.
Raspberries, black, raw, 1 cup	100	2.0	2.1	54	1.2	—	.03	.09	.4	32
Red, raw, 1 cup	70	1.5	.5	49	1.1	160	.03	.08	.4	29
Frozen, 3 ounces	84	.7	.3	24	.5	70	.01	.03	.2	14
Rhubarb, raw, 1 cup diced	19	.6	.1	62¹	.6	40	.01	—	.1	11
Cooked, sugar added, 1 cup	383	1.1	.3	112¹	1.1	70	.02	—	.2	17
Rice, brown, raw, 1 cup	784	15.6	3.5	81	4.2	—	.66	.10	9.6	—
Cooked, 1 cup	204	4.2	.2	14	.5	—	.10	.02	1.9	—
White, raw, 1 cup	692	14.5	.6	46	1.5	—	.13	.05	3.1	—
White, cooked, 1 cup	201	4.2	.2	13	.5	—	.02	.01	.7	—
White, precooked, dry, 1 cup	420	9.7	.2	4	.9	—	.02	.02	.1	—
Wild rice, parched, raw, 1 cup	593	23.0	1.1	31	—	—	.73	1.03	10.0	—
Rice, flakes, 1 cup	118	1.8	.2	6	.5	—	.02	.03	.3	—
Rolls, plain, pan rolls, unenriched (12 per pound), 1	118	3.4	2.1	21	.3	—	.02	.04	.4	—
Sweet, unenriched, 1	178	4.8	4.3	35	.3	—	.03	.07	.6	—
Rutabagas, cooked, 1 cup cubed or sliced	50	1.2	.2	85	.6	540	.08	.11	1.1	33
Rye flour, light, 1 cup sifted	285	7.5	.8	18	.9	—	.12	.06	.5	—
Rye wafers, 2	43	1.6	.2	6	.6	—	.04	.03	.2	—
S										
Salad dressings:										
Commercial, plain (mayonnaise type), 1 tbs.	58	.2	5.5	1	.1	20	Tr.	Tr.	—	—
French, 1 tbs.	59	.1	5.3	—	—	—	—	—	—	—
Mayonnaise, 1 tbs.	92	.2	10.1	2	.1	30	Tr.	Tr.	—	—
Salad oil, 1 tbs.	124	—	14.0	—	—	—	—	—	—	—
Salmon, broiled, baked, 1 steak 4 × 3 × ½″	204	33.6	6.7	—	1.4	—	.12	.33	9.8	—
Canned, solids and liquid:										
Chinook or King, 3 ounces	173	16.8	11.2	131	.8	200	.02	.12	6.2	—
Chum, 3 ounces	118	18.3	4.4	212	.6	50	.02	.13	6.0	—
Coho or silver, 3 ounces	140	17.9	7.1	197	.8	70	.02	.15	6.3	—
Pink or humpback, 3 ounces	122	17.4	5.3	159	.7	60	.03	.16	6.8	—
Sockeye or red, 3 ounces	147	17.2	8.2	220	1.0	200	.03	.14	6.2	—
Sardines: Atlantic type, canned in oil:										
Solids and liquid, 3 ounces	288	17.9	23.0	301	3.0	—	.01	.12	3.3	—
Drained solids, 3 ounces	182	21.9	9.4	328	2.3	190	.01	.15	4.1	—
Pilchards, Pacific type, canned, solids and liquid natural pack, 3 ounces	171	15.1	11.5	324	3.5	20	.01	.26	6.3	—
Tomato sauce, 3 ounces	184	15.1	12.6	324	3.5	20	.01	.23	4.5	—
Sauerkraut, canned, 1 cup drained solids	32	2.1	.4	54	.8	60	.05	.10	.2	24
Sausage: Bologna, 1 piece 1 × 1½″ diam.	467	31.2	33.5	19	4.6	—	.37	.40	5.7	—
Frankfurter, cooked, 1	124	7.0	10.0	3	.6	—	.08	.09	1.3	—
Liver, liverwurst, 2 ounces	150	9.5	11.7	5	3.1	3,260	.10	.63	2.6	—
Pork, links or bulk, 4 ounces (raw)	510	12.2	50.8	7	1.8	—	.49	.19	2.6	—
Vienna sausage, canned, 4 ounces	244	17.9	18.6	10	2.7	—	.11	.14	3.5	—
Scallops, raw, 4 ounces edible muscle	89	16.8	.1	29	2.0	—	.05	.11	1.6	—
Shad, raw, 4 ounces edible portion	191	21.2	11.1	—	.6	—	.17	.27	9.6	—
Sherbet, ½ cup	118	1.4	2.0	48	—	—	.02	.07	—	—
Shortbread, 2 squares, 1¾ × 1¾″	81	1.1	3.9	2	.1	—	.01	Tr.	.1	—
Shredded wheat, 1 large biscuit, plain	102	2.9	.7	13	1.0	—	.06	.03	1.3	—
Shrimp, canned, 3 ounces drained solids	110	23.0	1.2	98	2.6	50	.01	.03	1.9	—
Sirup, table blends (chiefly corn sirup), 1 tbs.	57	—	—	9	.8	—	—	Tr.	Tr.	—

Food, and Approximate Measure	Food Energy Cal.	Protein gm.	Fat gm.	Calcium Mg.	Iron Mg.	Vitamin A Value I.U.	Thiamine B₁ Mg.	Riboflavin B₂ Mg.	Niacin Value Mg.	Ascorbic Acid Mg.
Soups, canned:										
Bean, ready-to-serve, 1 cup	191	8.5	5.0	95	2.8	—	.10	.10	.8	—
Beef, ready-to-serve, 1 cup	100	6.0	3.5	15	.5	—	—	—	—	—
Bouillon, broth, and Consomme, ready-to-serve, 1 cup	9	2.0	—	2	1.0	—	—	.05	.6	—
Chicken, ready-to-serve, 1 cup	75	3.5	2.5	20	.5	—	.02	.12	1.5	—
Clam chowder, ready-to-serve, 1 cup	86	4.6	2.3	36	3.6	—	—	—	—	—
Cream soup—asparagus, celery, mushroom, 1 cup	201	7.0	11.7	217	.5	200	.05	.20	.1	—
Noodle, rice or barley, 1 cup	117	6.0	4.5	82	.2	30	.02	.05	.7	—
Pea, ready-to-serve, 1 cup	141	6.4	2.0	32	1.5	440	.17	.07	1.2	5
Tomato, ready-to-serve, 1 cup	90	2.2	2.2	24	1.0	1,230	.02	.10	.7	10
Vegetable, ready-to-serve, 1 cup	82	4.2	1.8	32	.8	—	.05	.08	1.0	8
Vegetable, strained, 1 ounce (infant food)	12	.7	.1	7	.3	700	.02	.02	.1	Tr.
Soybeans, whole, mature, dried, 1 cup	695	73.3	38.0	477	16.8	230	2.25	.65	4.9	Tr.
Soybean flour, medium fat, 1 cup stirred	232	37.4	5.7	215	11.4	100	.72	.30	2.3	—
Soybean sprouts, raw, 1 cup	49	6.6	1.5	51	1.1	190	.24	.21	.9	14
Spaghetti, dry, unenriched, 1 cup 2" pieces	354	12.0	1.3	21	1.4	—	.09	.06	1.9	—
Cooked, 1 cup	218	7.4	.9	13	.9	—	.03	.02	.7	—
Spinach, raw, 4 ounces edible portion	22	2.6	.3	92[1]	3.4	10,680	.13	.23	.7	67
Cooked, 1 cup	46	5.6	1.1	223[1]	3.6	21,200	.14	.36	1.1	54
Strained (infant food), 1 ounce	4	.5	.1	22[1]	.4	1,190	.01	.03	.1	2
Squash, summer, cooked, 1 cup diced	34	1.3	.2	32	.8	550	.08	.15	1.3	23
Winter, baked, mashed, 1 cup	97	3.9	.8	49	1.6	12,690	.10	.31	1.2	14
Winter, canned, strained, 1 ounce (infant food)	8	.3	.1	9	.1	560	.01	.02	.1	1
Starch, pure (corn), 1 tbs.	29	—	—	—	—	—	—	—	—	—
Strawberries, raw, 1 cup capped	54	1.2	.7	42	1.2	90	.04	.10	.4	89
Frozen, 3 ounces	90	.5	.3	19	.5	30	.02	.04	.2	35
Sugars:										
Granulated, cane or beet, 1 cup	770	—	—	—	—	—	—	—	—	—
1 teaspoon	16	—	—	—	—	—	—	—	—	—
1 lump 1⅛ × ⅝ × ⅛"	27	—	—	—	—	—	—	—	—	—
Powdered, 1 cup (stirred before measuring)	493	—	—	—	—	—	—	—	—	—
1 tbs.	31	—	—	—	—	—	—	—	—	—
Brown, 1 cup (firm-packed)	813	—	—	167[14]	5.7	-	—	—	—	—
1 tbs.	51	—	—	10[14]	.4	—	—	—	—	—
Maple, 1 piece 1¾ × 1¼ × ½"	104	—	—	—	—	—	—	—	—	—
Sweet potatoes, baked, 1, 5 × 2"	183	2.6	1.1	44	1.1	11,410[15]	.12	.08	.9	28
Boiled, 1, 5 × 2½"	252	3.7	1.4	62	1.4	15,780[15]	.18	.11	1.3	41
Candied, 1 small	314	2.6	6.3	63	1.6	10,940[15]	.07	.07	.9	16
Canned, 1 cup	233	4.4	.2	54	1.7	19,300	.12	.09	1.1	31
Swordfish, broiled, 1 steak 3 × 3 × ½"	223	34.2	8.5	25	1.4	2,880	.06	.07	12.9	—
T										
Tangerine, 1 medium	35	.6	.2	27	.3	340	.06	.02	.2	25
Juice, unsweetened, 1 cup	95	2.2	.7	47	.5	1,040	.17	.06	.6	75
Tapioca, dry granulated quick cooking, stirred, 1 cup	547	.9	.3	18	1.5	—	—	—	—	—
Tomatoes, raw, 1 medium, 2 × 2½"	30	1.5	.4	16	.9	1,640	.08	.06	.8	35
Canned or cooked, 1 cup	46	2.4	.5	27	1.5	2,540	.14	.08	1.7	40
Juice, canned, 1 cup	50	2.4	.5	17	1.0	2,540	.12	.07	1.8	38
Tomato catsup, 1 tbs.	17	.3	.1	2	.1	320	.02	.01	.4	2
Tomato puree, canned, 1 cup	90	4.5	1.2	27	2.7	4,680	.22	.17	4.5	69
Tongue, beef, medium fat, raw, 4 ounces	235	18.6	17.0	10	3.2	—	.14	.33	5.7	—
Tortillas, 1, 5" diameter	50	1.2	.6	22	.4	40[16]	.04	.01	.2	—
Tuna fish, canned, 3 oz. solids & liquid	247	20.2	17.8	6	1.0	180	.04	.08	9.1	—
Tuna fish, canned, 3 oz. drained solids	169	24.7	7.0	7	1.2	70	.04	.10	10.9	—
Turkey, medium fat, raw, 4 oz. edible portion	304	22.8	22.9	26	4.3	Tr.	.10	.16	9.1	—

Food, and Approximate Measure	Food Energy Cal.	Protein gm.	Fat gm.	MINERALS Calcium Mg.	Iron Mg.	VITAMINS Vitamin A Value I.U.	Thiamine B₁ Mg.	Riboflavin B₂ Mg.	Niacin Value Mg.	Ascorbic Acid Mg.
Turnips, raw, 1 cup diced	43	1.5	.3	54	.7	Tr.	.07	.09	.6	38
Cooked, 1 cup diced	42	1.2	.3	62	.8	Tr.	.06	.09	.6	28
Turnip greens, cooked, 1 cup	43	4.2	.6	376	3.5	15,370	.09	.59	1.0	87
V										
Veal, cooked, cutlet, 3 ounces without bone	184	24.0	9.0	10	3.0	—	.07	.24	5.2	—
Shoulder roast, 3 ounces without bone	193	24.0	10.0	10	3.1	—	.11	.27	6.7	—
Stew meat, 3 ounces without bone	252	21.0	18.0	9	2.6	—	.04	.20	3.9	—
Veal, canned, strained, 1 ounce (infant food)	24	4.5	.5	4	.5	—	.01	.09	1.6	—
Vinegar, 1 tbs.	2	—	—	1	.1	—	—	—	—	—
W										
Waffles, 1	216	7.0	8.0	144	.8	270	.05	.14	.3	—
Watercress, raw, 1 pound (leaves & stems)	84	7.7	1.4	885	9.1	21,450	.37	.71	3.6	350
Watermelon, 1/2 slice 3/4 × 10″	45	.8	.3	11	.3	950	.08	.08	.3	10
Wheat flour, whole, 1 cup stirred	400	16.0	2.4	49	4.0	—	.66	.14	5.2	—
Wheat products:										
Breakfast flakes, 1 cup	125	3.8	.6	16	1.0	—	.03	.06	1.7	—
Puffed, 1 cup	43	1.0	.2	6	.4	—	.01	.02	.6	—
Rolled, cooked, 1 cup	177	5.0	.9	19	1.7	—	.17	.06	2.1	—
Shredded, plain, 1 small biscuit 2½ × 2″	79	2.0	.6	10	.8	—	.05	.03	1.0	—
Whole meal, cooked, 1 cup	175	6.6	.7	22	1.7	—	.25	.08	2.3	—
Wheat germ, 1 cup stirred	246	17.1	6.8	57	5.5	—	1.39	.54	3.1	—
White sauce, medium, 1 cup	429	10.0	33.1	305	.3	1,350	.09	.41	.3	1
Wild rice, parched, raw, 1 cup	593	23.0	1.1	31	—	—	.73	1.03	10.0	—
Y										
Yeast, dried, brewer's, 1 tbs.	22	3.0	.1	8	1.5	—	.78	.44	2.9	—
Yogurt, commercial made with whole milk, 1 cup	170	11.0	8.0	560	.2	380	.10	.45	—	3

1 Calcium may not be available because of presence of oxalic acid.

2 Year-round average.

3 If fat used is butter or fortified margarine, the Vitamin A value would be 350 I.U. per square and 520 I.U. per 2-inch sector iced.

4 If fat used is butter or fortified margarine, the Vitamin A value would be 120 I.U.

5 If fat used is butter or fortified margarine, the Vitamin A value would be 300 I.U.

6 If fat used is butter or fortified margarine, the Vitamin A value would be 620 I.U. per square.

7 The calcium contributed by chocolate may not be usable because of presence of oxalic acid; in that case the value would be 11 mg. per ounce.

8 Vitamin A based on deeply colored varieties.

9 Vitamin A based on yellow corn; white corn contains only a trace.

10 Based on recipe using white corn meal, if yellow used, Vitamin A value is 120 I.U.

11 Vitamin A based on yellow corn flour, white contains only a trace.

12 Vitamin A based on yellow corn meal, white contains only a trace.

13 Based on the average Vitamin A content of fortified margarines. Most margarines manufactured for use in the U.S. have 15,000 I.U. of Vitamin A per pound; minimum Federal specifications for fortified margarine require 9,000 I.U. per pound.

14 Calcium based on dark brown sugar; value would be lower for light brown sugar.

15 If very pale varieties only were used, the Vitamin A value would be very much lower.

16 Vitamin A value of tortillas made from yellow corn; tortillas made from white corn have no Vitamin A value.

OAK, POISON See POISON IVY.

OBESITY See OVERWEIGHT.

ODOR, MOUTH See MOUTH ODOR.

OILS, VEGETABLE See FATS.

ORAL CANCER See CANCER OF THE MOUTH.

ORGAN DONATIONS See DEATH.

ORGANIC FOOD See HEALTH FOOD.

OSTEOARTHRITIS (degenerative joint disease) is a form of arthritis that seems to result from a combination of aging, injury to the joints, and normal wear and tear. It is far more common than rheumatoid arthritis and as a rule less damaging. Older people are its most frequent victims.

Common symptoms of osteoarthritis are pain, aches, and stiffness and loss of mobility. With soreness and loss of joint mobility the muscles serving the joint become weakened and overall body coordination and posture may become affected. Severe loss of motion, however, is unusual. Although osteoarthritis associated with enlargement of the finger joints can be painful and unsightly, good function of the hands can be maintained and significant impairment is not likely.

While osteoarthritis can occur in any joint, certain joints are more prone to become involved than others. The most commonly involved joints are those that bear weight, such as the hips, knees, and spine. Also involved frequently are the terminal joints of the fingers and joints at the base of the thumb and big toe.

Heredity, hormonal changes, obesity, and repeated slight injuries are thought to be underlying factors. Some people develop osteoarthritis early in life, without having experienced unusual strain on the joints involved. This is sometimes called primary osteoarthritis and occurs most frequently in women, particularly at the time of the menopause.

Others develop the disease only after unusual strain on the joints over many years. This "wear and tear" variety is sometimes labeled secondary osteoarthritis. Contributory factors are overweight, poor posture, injury, or strain from one's occupation or recreation.

Though there is no cure for osteoarthritis, the disease can be controlled and symptoms can be alleviated.

Aspirin is the single drug used most widely. It is generally prescribed in large doses, which may produce more side effects (like ringing in the ears) than when it is taken for headaches or colds. Indomethacin (Indocin), another anti-inflammatory drug, is particularly successful in relieving pain from osteoarthritis of the hip. Many patients, however, cannot tolerate it.

Physical therapy in the treatment of osteoarthritis aims at restoring the maximum degree of physical function. Physicians and physical therapists usually specify a series of exercises in which the affected joints are moved through their full range of motion several times a day. Canes, crutches, or walkers may be used to take the weight off affected joints.

Heat—in the form of hot baths, warm packs, heated wax, heat-lamp treatments, or electric pads—often bring some relief. Since overweight places an abnormal strain on joints, weight reduction is advisable for all patients with osteoarthritis of weight-bearing joints.

Orthopedic operations on joints can be effective in preventing some deformities, in relieving pain, and in improving overall function. Surgery is playing an increasing role in the rehabilitation of the handicapped patient and is useful in preventing deformities. Artificial hip joints have made operations on the hip and knee particularly effective in alleviating severe osteoarthritis of those joints.

See also ARTHRITIS.

OSTEOPATHS See CHIROPRACTORS; PHYSICIAN.

OSTEOPOROSIS is a gradual decrease in the density and strength of bone tissue. The bones can actually become soft. It is an extremely common condition of the elderly.

The vast majority of osteoporosis sufferers are over 60 years of age. Women—particularly those who have passed menopause—are especially vulnerable.

Osteoporosis most commonly begins with the bones of the spine. These thinned bones are compressed or mashed down by the weight of the body, resulting in low-back pain, a round-back deformity, and loss of height. The person's capacity for physical activity progressively decreases.

Eventually the bones of the spine fracture by mashing down and collapsing. As the disease advances, other bones become thinned, particularly those of the pelvis, arms, and legs. Osteoporosis is responsible for many of the fractures that disable elderly people.

Many people suffer from osteoporosis without being aware of it. The bones are neither painful nor tender until they have become so weak that they break.

Osteoporosis is thought to be due to a combination of factors. In the normal adult old bone is continually reabsorbed by the body and new bone is produced to replace it. In a person with osteoporosis, however, the normal breaking up of bone continues while the regeneration of bone slows.

This is thought to result in part from the aging person's decreasing production of the hormones that help stimulate bone regeneration.

Another important factor in osteoporosis seems to be a long-term shortage of calcium. Every adult loses calcium daily, and it must be replaced with new calcium from food and drink. If the amount of calcium in the diet is insufficient, bone strength will lessen.

A third possible factor is lack of exercise. A normal degree of activity helps keep bones strong and solid. A person who is inactive suffers from bone loss because of a substantial increase in bone resorption. When younger people are immobilized because of illness or injury, their bone loss is reversible when they resume activity. In older people, bone once lost usually cannot be regained.

Osteoporosis is usually treated with a diet rich in calcium and protein. Adequate doses of vitamin D are needed for normal absorption of calcium. Some physical activity is recommended. After menopause, estrogen replacement therapy may be prescribed to retard bone thinning. Such measures may halt or slow the progress of the disorder, but are unlikely to reverse it.

A possible preventive measure is a high calcium, vitamin D, and protein intake, especially after age 40—combined with regular physical activity. This is best done with a physician's advice. Excessive calcium can cause kidney stones and other problems.

See also EXERCISE; MENOPAUSE; NUTRITION.

OVERBREATHING See HYPERVENTILATION.

OVERWEIGHT (obesity, fatness) if excessive may shorten your life. In general the fatter you are, the greater your vulnerability to premature death from heart disease, high blood pressure, diabetes, and respiratory disease.

Fat people are more prone to a host of other medical conditions, including liver and gallbladder disease, kidney disease, appendicitis, and hernia. A Milwaukee study of 75,532 overweight women found that even those who were slightly overweight tended to be ill more often than those of normal weight. Overweight people are also more prone to accidents.

Excess weight can worsen many conditions and complicate their treatment. This is particularly true of cardiovascular conditions, among them varicose veins, and also osteoarthritis and other bone and joint diseases. Overweight can severely complicate pregnancy and childbirth.

Overweight also increases cancer risk. Compared to women of normal weight, overweight women have a greater incidence of cancer of the gallbladder, uterus, and ovaries. After menopause, overweight women also have a heightened risk of breast cancer. Overweight men are at increased risk of cancer of the colon, rectum, and prostate.

Are you too fat? At least 34 million Americans are too fat. To see if you're among this number, check the accompanying table of desirable weights. If you remain in doubt, take a pinch test and a ruler test.

For the pinch test, grab the skin on the inside of your upper arm between your thumb and forefinger. If you can pull out much more than an inch of flab, you're probably too fat.

For the ruler test, lie flat on the floor on your back and place one end of a yardstick on your breastbone. Like a bridge, the stick should also touch your pubic bone, above your genitals. If the stick gets hung up on your middle, you have too much fat there.

A very muscular person built along the lines of a football player may weigh more than normal, since muscle weighs more than fat: he is technically overweight without being overfat. For most people, though, overweight means overfat. You are considered obese if, due to fat, you are 20 percent or more over your desirable weight.

Everyone meeting that standard definition of obesity should reduce, urged a panel of experts convened by the National Institutes of Health. For some people, the panel warned, even five pounds can threaten health. Observed the panel chairman: "Fat is not just a cosmetic affair. At surprisingly low levels, it's a biologic hazard."

Some obesity experts are less restrictive about higher weights, especially as one ages. Dr. Reubin Andres of the National Institute on Aging's Gerontology Research Center contends that the lowest death rates are associated with leanness in the 20s followed by a moderate weight gain into middle age. Dr. William R. Hazzard of Johns Hopkins University adds that a little extra fat appears to help the elderly endure illness. These, however, remain minority views. Comments the American Heart Association, which recommends a relatively restrictive table of desirable weights: "Few health problems are improved by gaining weight."

Eating too much. If you're overweight, you almost certainly eat too much. When you take in more energy in food than you expend in growth, vital functions, and physical activity, the excess is stored as fat. The process is devilishly efficient —eating merely 1 extra Fig Newton a day can add up to a gain of more than 5 pounds in a year.

One pound of body fat equals 3,500 calories. A calorie is a unit of energy, the amount needed to heat 1 kg of water 1° C. A Fig Newton contains 55 calories. Times 365 days, that's 20,075 calories—or (since 3,500 calories = 1 pound) nearly 5¾ pounds of body fat for the year.

Most moderately active people require about 15 calories a day for each pound they weigh. Thus if you weigh 150 pounds, about 2,250 calories a day (15 × 150) will maintain you at that weight. If you consistently eat more, you're likely to gain weight. If you consistently eat less, you'll lose.

Very active people can eat much more without gaining weight. A lumberjack may need as much as 6,000 calories a day to maintain his 150 pounds. A man with a desk job who does virtually no physical labor may need less than 2,000 calories to maintain that same 150 pounds.

Regular exercise can help you use up many excess calories, and is an invaluable adjunct to dieting. (See the table under EXERCISE for the energy expended by various activities.) If you become less active, you may need to compensate by eating less or you're likely to put on weight. To illustrate the impact of light, regular activity: A typist who saves effort by switching from a manual to an electric machine could gain three pounds a year from the unexpended calories.

You may have a special tendency to put on weight and need to work extra hard to take it off. Many authorities believe that, compared with people of normal weight, an overweight person has more and larger fat cells—and converts more food intake into body fat. It's also theorized that everyone is "programmed" to maintain a certain "set-point" weight, and the body will lower its metabolism rather than go below that weight. Thus diets often fail, although some investigators find that extensive exercise can alter the body's set point.

Where are you fat? Recent evidence suggests that where you're fat may be more important than how fat you are. "Male type" obesity—the bulging abdomen sometimes known as beer belly or executive spread—seems to pose more of a threat than fat lower down around the hips and buttocks ("female type" obesity). Bulging bellies appear to increase the risk of developing cardiovascular disease and diabetes. For men, risk seems to increase sharply when the waist-to-hip ratio exceeds 1 in men (if a man has more than, say, a 36-inch waist to go with his 36-inch hips). For women, the waist-to-hip ratio should not exceed 0.8 (24-inch waist, 30-inch hips).

A woman whose fat is concentrated in her hips, buttocks, and thighs may be physiologically unable to become as slim as she'd like. Lower-body obesity seems to arise from oversize fat cells that are difficult if not impossible to reduce. After strict dieting, such a woman may find herself slender on top and still fat from the waist down, as if she were two different women joined at the waist. If she persists in dieting, the resistant fat cells may steal energy from muscle tissue, including the heart.

In rare cases endocrine or brain disorders may alter appetite or metabolic rate (see THYROID DISEASE), and account for the weight increase. Suspect such factors if you have a sudden gain in weight or a greatly increased appetite.

Older people have a tendency to gain weight because they reduce their activity but continue to eat as usual. Metabolic rate—the rate at which the body burns up food—may also slow down with age.

People who quit smoking often notice a weight gain: They increase their food intake to compensate for the loss of cigarettes. Most smokers who quit gain no more than 5 to 7 pounds, then slowly begin to take it off.

Don't resume smoking in an effort to reduce. You're likely to be healthier as an overweight nonsmoker than as a lean smoker.

The permanent diet. To lose weight and keep it off, reform your eating habits. Untold millions go on reducing diets and lose weight. Within a year 90 percent gain it back—and frequent weight gains and losses may be even more harmful than remaining fat.

Think of a diet not as a temporary state, but as a new way of life. If you tend toward overweight, you'll always need to watch what you eat. Food addiction is like alcoholism: a lifelong battle.

If you need to lose more than 10 pounds, see a doctor. He can help determine what factors— physical or emotional—may be contributing to your overweight. He'll fashion a diet to suit your needs and habits, taking into consideration any medical problems you may have.

Eat a wide variety of foods, but in smaller quantities. Make sure your diet is balanced in terms of nutrition. Don't eliminate any one category of foods (see NUTRITION). Familiarize yourself with the calorie and nutrient chart, and select foods high in nutrition but low in calories.

For a main course your best bets are chicken, fish, and veal. Shellfish and liver are low in calories but high in cholesterol, so are best suited to occasional use. Low-calorie vegetables include mushrooms, celery, spinach, radishes, broccoli, asparagus, and green beans. Substitute lemon juice for butter or margarine on cooked vegetables.

Among dairy products, choose skim milk, plain yogurt made from skim milk, and cottage cheese. Neufchâtel cheese and dietetic salad dressings are also caloric bargains. Cut down on oil by using nonstick spray coating and water-packed rather than oil-packed tuna. Have fresh fruits for dessert.

Reduce your intake of fried and breaded foods. Butter, sauces, candies, and rich desserts are loaded with calories. So are cream, pork, nuts, and dried fruits. Beware sugary foods and snack foods like potato chips.

Before you begin a diet, calculate the number of calories you normally consume. Keep a food diary for about a week. You may find that some foods you routinely eat contain large amounts of calories.

Half a pound of fatty steak can run 800 calories. Half an avocado is about 275. A glass of whole milk, 160. Replace them with low-calorie items, like chicken for steak, tomatoes for avocado, skim milk for whole.

A sensible diet. When dieting, cut down your usual food intake by no more than 500 to 1,000 calories a day. Since each pound represents 3,500 calories, you'll lose weight at the rate of about 1 to 2 pounds a week: 500 fewer calories a day adds up to 3,500 over a week, or 1 pound; 1,000 fewer is 7,000, or 2 pounds.

When your weight levels off, again reduce

HOW MUCH SHOULD YOU WEIGH?

This is the table of desirable weights recommended by the American Heart Association. Weight is in pounds and includes indoor clothing. Other authorities have devised tables permitting higher weights, especially for the middle-aged and elderly.

MEN
(Age 25 and Over

HEIGHT (with shoes on) 1-inch heels Feet Inches	SMALL FRAME	MEDIUM FRAME	LARGE FRAME
5 2	112–120	118–129	126–141
5 3	115–123	121–133	129–144
5 4	118–126	124–136	132–148
5 5	121–129	127–139	135–152
5 6	124–133	130–143	138–156
5 7	128–137	134–147	142–161
5 8	132–141	138–152	147–166
5 9	136–145	142–156	151–170
5 10	140–150	146–160	155–174
5 11	144–154	150–165	159–179
6 0	148–158	154–170	164–184
6 1	152–162	158–175	168–189
6 2	156–167	162–180	173–194
6 3	160–171	167–185	178–199
6 4	164–175	172–190	182–204

WOMEN
(Age 25 and Over)

HEIGHT (with shoes on) 2-inch heels Feet Inches	SMALL FRAME	MEDIUM FRAME	LARGE FRAME
4 10	92–98	96–107	104–119
4 11	94–101	98–110	106–122
5 0	96–104	101–113	109–125
5 1	99–107	104–116	112–128
5 2	102–110	107–119	115–131
5 3	105–113	110–122	118–134
5 4	108–116	113–126	121–138
5 5	111–119	116–180	125–142
5 6	114–123	120–135	129–146
5 7	118–127	124–139	133–150
5 8	122–131	128–143	137–154
5 9	126–135	132–147	141–158
5 10	130–140	136–151	145–163
5 11	134–144	140–155	149–168
6 0	138–148	144–159	153–173

For girls between 18 and 25, subtract 1 pound for each year under 25.

your usual intake by 500 to 1,000 calories. And so on, until you reach your desirable weight (see weight chart).

Don't plan to lose weight at a faster rate. Crash diets for quick weight loss are likely to leave you tired, irritable, and more vulnerable to disease. What's more, pounds shed quickly are often just as quickly regained.

Nor should you reduce your caloric intake to less than 1,200 calories a day. You're likely to miss out on essential nutrients when your intake is cut so low (see accompanying sample diet).

Don't confuse pounds of food with pounds of body weight. If you eat a pound of tomatoes, you're taking in only about 100 calories. By contrast a pound of butter (about 3,200 calories) in excess of your body's caloric needs is likely to be stored in your body as nearly a pound of fat.

Here's a smorgasbord of tips for succeeding in your diet. Choose those that suit your personality and eating preferences:

Eat meditatively. This is a sure-fire method for losing weight while enjoying food more. Take a tiny amount on your spoon or fork—one bean tastes the same as a mouthful. Chew it very, very slowly. Let it liquefy before you swallow it.

People who eat fast take in more food than they need to feel full. Put down your utensils between bites. Really experience the taste and texture of what you eat.

Make a production out of each meal, with a proper table setting. Luxuriate through the meal in a series of small steps—preparing, arranging it on a plate, and so forth.

Eat at your leisure in quiet, comfortable surroundings. The reduced tension may aid you in eating less. If people raise your level of tension or distract you, you may be better off eating alone. Don't read or watch TV while you eat. Shut your eyes and concentrate on your food.

Eat only in one room, preferably the dining room. And eat only when you're seated. Stand-up eating promotes gulping.

Eat only when you're hungry, not because food is in front of you. You may need to train yourself to recognize hunger. Rather than responding to feelings of hunger or fullness, most fat people are guided by visual cues. They see food and eat it.

Never go grocery shopping when you're hungry. Make a list beforehand and stick to it. Store food in covered containers, out of sight.

Before sitting down to eat, decide the number of calories you'll eat. If you then have an avocado, subtract something else so you don't go over your limit.

Make enough food for only one meal. Serve portions in the kitchen. Have no extra amounts of food on the table—its availability encourages you to take second helpings you don't need. If you think you'll want two of something—pieces of toast, for example—first eat one, and then prepare a second only if you really want it.

Put a small portion on a small plate instead of a large plate. You'll feel less deprived. Slice food thin and spread it out on the plate. Eat with a small spoon and fork.

Eat several small meals a day instead of three larger ones. This means you won't have to go hungry for many hours, and you'll never get so hungry that you stuff yourself before you realize what you're doing.

Space your meals throughout the day. Don't skip breakfast or lunch.

Face up to your fatness. Most fat people are out of touch with what they look like. Look at yourself nude in the mirror frequently. Familiarize yourself with your contours, and follow your progress toward slimness.

To give yourself a boost, have pictures of yourself taken as you lose weight. Meanwhile, post an overweight picture of yourself on the door of your refrigerator.

Weigh yourself once a week. You'll get added reinforcement from the drop in weight, or a prod if you've slipped.

Don't be discouraged when you know you've been dieting but the scale refuses to acknowledge this. You may be temporarily retaining water or a bowel movement. Eat less salt to retain less water. A few days before menstruation women may show a weight gain that soon disappears. If you've been exercising, you may be gaining muscle, which weighs more than fat.

Visualize your fat as a tumor, advises Dr. Theodore Isaac Rubin, a formerly fat psychiatrist. This unpalatable image may help reduce your appetite. Dr. Rubin also suggests thinking of high-calorie foods as poisons. He lost 60 pounds by visualizing a skull-and-crossbones painted over high-calorie dishes.

Make foods work for you. Drink a glass of water or bouillon before each meal. It will help fill you up.

Experiment with low-calorie food combinations, adapting higher-calorie recipes. Make deviled eggs with cottage cheese and herbs instead of mayonnaise. Bake skinned chicken in soy sauce or low-calorie salad dressing. Substitute plain yogurt or buttermilk in recipes calling for sour cream, or use a low-fat sour cream substitute.

Use herbs and spices to perk up foods. For

example, sweet marjoram sprinkled over cooked green beans can make butter unnecessary.

For a nutritional bargain, increase your intake of such fiber-rich foods as fruits, vegetables, and whole grains. They're relatively low in calories. They also take longer to chew and are bulky, thus fill the stomach and small intestine before many calories are consumed.

You can also stay full longer by increasing your intake of protein. It's digested more slowly than sugars, which are high in calories and soon leave you hungry.

Get a meat scale and weigh the meat, fish, or poultry you plan to eat. Otherwise it's nearly impossible to know how much you're eating. You may be surprised to find that the 3-ounce steak you planned for dinner is actually twice as large. Remove bones and visible fat from meat before weighing.

At parties drink water, tea, or lemon-flavored club soda instead of alcohol. A 2-ounce martini or Manhattan runs 160 calories. Whiskey is 110 calories for a 1½-ounce shot. Liqueurs run about 100 calories an ounce. The lowest-calorie alcoholic beverage is beer, at about 13 calories an ounce, but beer drinkers tend to down 8 to 12 ounces at a time.

If there's a buffet, stay on the other side of the room—you may find the spread irresistible. Have someone bring you a sampling.

Indulge your food eccentricities. Eat only what you really want to eat, where and when you want to eat it. This may mean potato salad for breakfast in bed, or sipping tea while your family eats steak and potatoes. You'll derive satisfaction from eating foods that really turn you on—instead of depriving yourself of them or eating them guiltily. Over the long run, researchers find, your nutritional intake generally will be balanced, and you'll wind up losing weight.

Adopt a strategy for snacking. Keep a supply of fresh, raw vegetables in the front part of your refrigerator. Carrots, cauliflower, and cabbage are tasty low-calorie snacks. A nibble of chicken can feel like a treat, yet add minimal calories.

Don't leave snack food out on tables or near the TV. Better still, don't buy any. Nor should you buy any food you find impossible to eat in moderation. Peanuts can be the instrument of the devil.

If you tend to overindulge in the evening, plan an activity that occupies your hands, or leave the house until bedtime. Or if you're in the habit of snacking at night, save part of your supper.

If there's a high-calorie treat you cannot do without, include a small portion in your diet once or twice a week. Half a cup of chocolate ice cream may make you feel indulged, and will set you back only 200 calories.

Enlist the help of friends. Tell friends you're dieting. Good friends will encourage you, tell you how well you're starting to look, prepare low-calorie meals when you visit.

Beware that friends and family members may try to keep you fat rather than adjust to a new you or be shown up by your self-assertiveness and success. Such saboteurs say things like "You don't need to diet," "Just a small portion won't hurt you," and "I'm insulted—you don't like my food." If you can't stand up to them, stay away until you've reached a desirable weight.

Plan time with friends around activities other than eating. Go bowling. Walk. See a movie. Make a point of *not* eating in company—many people act as if calories don't count when they're consumed with friends.

Diet with a friend. Call the friend when tensions mount and you feel an eating binge coming on. It may help to have a small bet with a friend, say $1 a pound. If you lose 10 pounds to your friend's 8, you'll make $2.

Join a group of dieters. Several national organizations—such as TOPS (Take Off Pounds Sensibly), Overeaters Anonymous, and Weight Watchers—have local chapters that provide dieters with support, recipes, diet tips.

Stay out of restaurants. The quantity and variety of food and the urge to eat your money's worth pose a special challenge to dieters. If you need to dine out, order a la carte so you won't be tempted to eat the whole dinner merely because you're paying for it.

Before being tempted by the menu, decide generally what you'll eat. Start with melon, grapefruit, clear consommé, or shrimp cocktail. For an entrée choose broiled fish, lamb, or chicken.

Steer clear of sauces. Many are made with some combination of cream, flour, cheese, or wine. Also avoid cheese or oil dressing on your salad. Substitute lemon juice or vinegar with salt and pepper. Skip dessert, or request fresh fruit, melon, or berries.

Have the restaurant pack to go any food you don't finish. You might pass up an entire baked potato (90 calories) and make it the next day's lunch.

Seafood restaurants are good places for dieters. So are Chinese restaurants. Select a Chinese meal with a lot of vegetables and fish or chicken. Avoid pork, rice, and breaded or deep-fried dishes.

Be suspicious of franchised restaurants. Food

packaged centrally for serving at local restaurants are usually high in salt and fat.

Reprogram your responses to food. Keep a diary, noting what, when, and with whom you eat. Also note your degree of hunger (not hungry = 0, ravenous = 5). And jot down your mood while eating (anxious, bored, tired, depressed, angry, happy, other). Keeping such a diary can help overcome a fat person's biggest problem: Lack of control.

A diary helps make eating less of a reflex action and more a conscious effort. It also can give you clues to why you eat. Perhaps you reach for food almost automatically while watching television, or unconsciously when depressed or angry.

To resist a high-calorie food think of an unpleasant image having to do with your fat. At a meat counter examine what 5 pounds of suet (animal fat) really looks like. Then realize that's on you. Using behavior-therapy techniques, here are some types of "thought punishment" you might try out: You die from overeating. You see yourself as a hugely overweight corpse. Rolls of fat come off your abdomen like hot, sticky taffy, then grow back. Invent your own horrifying images.

Similarly, reward yourself with a beautiful image for selecting a low-calorie food. For example, a vision of yourself thin and attractive, walking the beach at sunset with someone you love.

Give yourself a reward when you're down to a particular weight or size—an article of clothing, a trip, a special present. If food is a special incentive, have a wonderful dinner or dessert—but don't undo a week's dieting with one meal.

Get in the habit of leaving some food on your plate. Just a bit of your portion set aside will remind you that you're in charge of your eating —and no law says you have to finish every last morsel on your plate. Once this becomes habitual, you'll probably find it easier to push your plate away when you're full—not when it's empty.

Diet one day at a time. Envisioning weeks or months of deprivation may overwhelm you and make you give up prematurely. It may help you to stick to your resolve if you promise yourself each day—in writing, with your signature—that you'll stay on your diet.

Plan your meals the day before. Determine just how much you'll eat of which foods at what times. The rigidity of this plan may help you resist temptations.

One behavior-modification program awards points for weight-reducing behavior, such as stopping between bites, leaving food on the plate, and counting calories before the meal.

You can adapt this experiment by setting up a point system for yourself. An example of the point system:

Behavior Control Act	Points
Left food on plate	5
Paused after each mouthful	3
Invoked thought punishment to refuse high-calorie food	15
Called friend when anxiety occurred	10
Counted calories before meal	5

Deduct the same number of points if you fail. At the end of the week have a friend or a spouse give you a penny for each point. If it's a minus week, *you* pay up. The amount of money is less important than the symbolic reward or punishment.

When you've finished supper, give your teeth a good brushing. If you're like most people, brushing your teeth signals the end to the day's eating, and having to clean your teeth all over again will help discourage you from snacking after dinner.

Identify the emotions that send you to the refrigerator. Do you often stuff yourself when you're tense? Angry? Frustrated? Try to find another outlet for these feelings. If you're angry, tell the person off. If you can't do that, try battering a pillow or hitting a bed with a tennis racket. If you're tense, try knitting or jumping rope.

Since overweight is often complicated or caused by emotional problems and stress, psychotherapy may be a useful aid in weight reduction. Even brief therapy may help you break the vicious circle of being unhappy so you overeat, which makes you unhappy so you overeat, and on and on.

The last resort. As a last resort only, consider drastic measures. They are suitable only if you are grossly obese (perhaps 100 pounds overweight or more) and are unable to diet successfully.

You can fast under a doctor's supervision. In a hospital obese people have been put on diets of water and vitamins for months. After a day or so they stop being hungry. Impressive weight losses have been recorded.

But often the people regain the weight once they return home. Fasting puts a strain on the liver and kidneys. Even in a hospital setting it is barred to people suffering from infections, diabetes, or heart, liver, or kidney disease—and to women who are pregnant or breastfeeding.

You can have the fat cut off. The surgery is called lipectomy (cutting away of fat). It usually involves removing the fat pad over the abdomen. Flabby upper arm and inner thigh skin can also be surgically removed by a plastic surgeon experienced in this procedure.

You can have your jaw wired shut, in the same procedure used for treating broken jaws. With your mouth wired shut, you subsist on a liquid diet. The effects of a liquid diet on healthy people have not been studied. And of course it's still possible to cheat: you could sip malteds all day.

Lastly you can have an intestinal bypass operation. This experimental surgery should be used only as a lifesaving measure for people at least 100 pounds overweight for whom all other measures of weight loss have failed.

The operation creates a shortcut through the small intestine, so that less food is absorbed. Some people report a decrease in appetite after the operation. Many people have lost a lot of weight after this operation—but at a great price. Expected complications include diarrhea, pain and hemorrhoids, tiredness, thirst, and nausea.

More severe complications are dehydration, drastic metabolic changes, and severe anal disease. There may also be chronic diarrhea, nausea and vomiting, abnormal liver function, and fatal liver failure.

As with all major surgery some people fail to survive the operation. General anesthesia and abdominal surgery are much more hazardous for obese people than for those of normal weight. The long-range effects of the operation are not known.

Some people's systems cannot accommodate to the bypass and their intestinal function must be restored by additional surgery. The operation is unsuitable for heart patients and alcoholics.

Avoid obesity in childhood. Take care not to stuff children. A fat child is not necessarily a healthy one—and is likely to grow into a fat adult.

Overfeeding in childhood is thought to lead to an excessive number of fat cells. The normal-weight person has roughly 27 trillion fat cells, according to Dr. Jules Hirsch of Rockefeller University, while the "naturally obese" have about three times as many. This abnormality persists even when they lose weight: the fat cells shrink, but they don't disappear.

People who have been overweight since childhood may thus be fighting the natural inclination of their bodies to fill up its fat cells. This may help explain why so many reducing diets ultimately fail.

To help your child grow up thin, wait until a baby is four months old before introducing solid foods. Refrain from giving food or milk to pacify a baby in distress. Try rocking, walking, using a pacifier instead.

Give a baby high-calorie desserts sparingly or not at all. Concentrate on vegetables, lean meats, poultry, and fish. Give a child unsweetened juices and water if he's thirsty after drinking sufficient milk. Check with your doctor about giving your child skim milk.

Make sure your child gets exercise. Overweight children don't necessarily eat more than their leaner contemporaries: They often exercise less. Encourage a fat child to engage in more sports and physical activity. Play running games with him. Do less chauffeuring so that the child has to walk more.

Examine family eating patterns to see if they're contributing to the problem. Don't have high-calorie snacks or desserts available. Cut down on fatty meats, fried foods, heavy sauces.

Serve the whole family low-calorie nutritious foods, so that the overweight youngster won't feel deprived or punished. Try not to make an issue of what he eats. An overweight child is unlikely to voluntarily eat fewer calories unless he is very highly motivated, a state of mind even rarer in children than in adults. You can tactfully deny a child a cookie or second helping by telling him, "That's not good for you." But nagging to get an overweight youngster to reduce is likely to exacerbate an already tense situation. Give your child the feeling that you love and accept him, fat and all.

Summer camps for overweight children are unlikely to be of lasting benefit without a change in family eating habits. Most fat children who lose weight at camp only gain it back after returning home.

Have a physician examine a grossly obese child for organic conditions. A multitude of emotional problems may contribute to childhood obesity.

The danger of drugs. Take drugs only under a doctor's supervision. Most appetite-curbing drugs contain amphetamine and are not meant for long-term use. They lose their effect after about a month, and the dieter resumes his normal eating pattern. Many people suffer side effects such as sleeplessness, sweating, irritability.

Amphetamines can be addictive. Taken over long periods, such drugs can damage the cardiovascular and central nervous systems.

For most people thyroid hormones do little good and may be dangerous.

The same is true of diuretics, drugs to decrease water being retained by your body. Such drugs may be prescribed for some people at the beginning of a diet if they are retaining a lot of fluid. Diuretics are not meant for prolonged use: they can cause severe kidney damage, among other medical problems.

Laxatives have no place in a weight-reduction diet. With overuse, they can cause constipation, nutritional deficiencies, and metabolic disturbances.

Digitalis to cause loss of appetite is not justified, according to *The Medical Letter*, because it poses "an unacceptable risk to the patient." Pills that contain combinations of thyroid hormone, digitalis, and other agents can be particularly dangerous, possibly fatal, as in the prevalent "rainbow pill" diet treatment. The Food and Drug Administration (FDA) charged that these pills are neither safe nor effective in treating obesity.

Beware of pills. Over-the-counter diet pills are likely to be overpriced, ineffective, and possibly dangerous. Most falsely promise astounding weight loss in a very short time—with barely any effort on your part.

Currently one of the most widely used ingredients in over-the-counter diet pills is phenylpropanolamine (PPA), found in Dexatrim, Dietac, Ayds, Control, Prolamine, and many others. Ads for these products are likely to claim that PPA, ordinarily a nasal decongestant, was proved effective as an appetite suppressant by "a panel of experts for the U.S. Government" or in "U.S. Government tests," implying government endorsement. In fact PPA was evaluated in an extremely preliminary way by a group of nongovernment experts serving as an advisory panel to the FDA, drawing on industry studies that scientific authorities have attacked as defective.

Even if PPA diet aids suppress appetite in some individuals, their effect at best is modest and temporary. Worse yet, the drug can cause sharp rises in blood pressure. PPA has also been linked to psychotic behavior.

Typical of fraudulent tablets attacked by federal agencies:

Placidon capsules, advertised as "miraculous reducing capsules," contained an ordinary vitamin B complex, useless in reducing. Packages that sold for $5.98 had ingredients worth 32¢.

One brand promised to help you "lose up to 10 pounds every week . . . the most effective, fastest reducing tablet of all time." It contained minerals, vitamins, and other ingredients of no effect in taking off weight. The U.S. Postal Service found its manufacturers guilty of "false representations."

Other diet plan tablets contained the vegetable product methylcellulose, a so-called bulk producer widely sold as a diet aid. These products swell up when they absorb water. Taken before meals, they are supposed to enlarge in your stomach and diminish hunger pangs. But bulk producers pass rapidly into the small intestine on an empty stomach. Even when they remain in the stomach, there is no evidence that they reduce overeating.

Before-meal candies contain sugar, which is supposed to raise your blood-sugar level and thus diminish your appetite. One such product had a dose of about 3 teaspoons sugar. This amount has little effect on blood-sugar levels though it gives you 50 empty calories. Nor is there evidence that a rise in blood sugar depresses appetite.

The fad diets. Virtually all diets work, but not because of any magical properties of any food or combinations of food. If you lose weight, it's because the diet is likely to be lower in calories than your regular diet. Boredom with the diet may cause you to eat less. Merely going on a diet will make you more aware of what you're eating; hence you'll probably eat less.

You'll thus initially tend to lose weight on any new diet you go on. But diets that concentrate on one food or group of foods are boring and can't be sustained for long. They're likely to be injurious to your health if they eliminate whole categories of necessary foods. Because they don't teach you lifelong eating habits for weight control, you're likely to start gaining back the pounds as soon as you go off the diet.

Avoid fad diets like these:

Low-carbohydrate diets. Carbohydrates (starches and sugars) are essential to health. On a diet very low in carbohydrates the body has to provide carbohydrates for the brain by breaking down its own protein. Carbohydrate deficiency can thus cause extreme fatigue, lowered blood pressure, and many undesirable metabolic changes.

People at greatest risk from this diet are those

with a propensity for kidney stones, gout, osteo-porosis, nausea, mineral depletion. It can harm the fetus during pregnancy.

The high concentration of fats in the diet may lead to high blood cholesterol, possibly predis-posing you to heart attack and arteriosclerosis. The clincher for dieters may be this fact: The rapid weight loss many people experience on a low-carbohydrate diet is largely due to loss of water, not fat. Thus your scale may go down but not your bulk. If you do get thinner on this diet, it's because you're eating fewer calories.

The Simeons HCG diet plan proposes daily in-jections of human chorionic gonadotropin, a hormone-stimulating substance found in the urine of pregnant women, in combination with a 500-calorie-per-day diet. Authorities believe that the 500-calorie diet, not the injec-tions, promotes the weight loss.

The lecithin-plus diet calls for supplementing a low-calorie diet according to the following the-ory: lecithin to help emulsify fat; vitamin B_6 to help metabolize fat; apple-cider vinegar to pro-vide potassium; and kelp to make the thyroid speed up metabolism. Research at the University of California shows that the plan does not speed up weight loss.

Liquid diets. Metrecal, Slender, and other liq-uid formulas are usually designed to supply nec-essary nutrients and 900 calories a day. They are often used successfully at the beginning of a weight-reduction regimen, or to replace one meal.

In the long run most people find the liquid diet monotonous and unpalatable. They often eat along with drinking the liquid, winding up with more calories than they consumed before. Within a year most people on liquid diets inch back up to their original weight.

Grapefruit diets feature that citrus fruit plus various foods that are supposed to create a weight-losing combination. Some variations are misleadingly called the "Mayo diet." In fact it has no connection whatever with the Mayo Clinic.

Contrary to claims, grapefruit has no special properties as a metabolizer of fat. If the diet were followed for a long time without supervi-

1,200-CALORIE SAMPLE DIET

Breakfast

Fresh fruit or juice	1 serving—1/2 cup
Egg—cooked without fat	1
or	
Cereal	1 small serving
Bread	1 slice
Butter or margarine	1 level tsp.
Skim milk	1 glass—6 oz.
Clear coffee or tea	

Lunch

Cottage cheese or lean meat	1/2 cup cheese or 2 oz. meat
Vegetables (raw or cooked)	1/2 cup cooked; raw, freely
Skim milk	1 glass—6 oz.
Fruit (raw, cooked, or canned without sugar)	1 serving—1/2 cup

Dinner

Lean meat, fish, or poultry	4 oz. (cooked)
Vegetables (raw or cooked)	1/2 cup cooked; raw, freely
Potato or bread	1 small potato or 1 slice bread
Butter or margarine	1 level tsp.
Skim milk	1 glass—6 oz.
Fruit (raw, cooked, or canned without sugar)	1 serving—1/2 cup

sion, it could be harmful to people with heart or kidney disease.

The rice diet consists of rice, fruit, sugar, nonfat milk, or butter. Like other diets that play up particular foods, this one contains gross nutritional deficiencies, particularly in protein, iron, niacin, and salt.

The worthless gimmicks. Beware of gimmicks for weight reduction. Phony slimming products —often associated with health clubs—promise you effortless shedding of fat. Items like these will make your wallet slimmer, not your paunch:

Reducing creams are of no value in weight reduction. A New York State court ruled against one sales company for promoting a "smooth away" cream that would "literally melt the fat and inches away." The $6 cream contained about 32¢ worth of lanolin.

Massage, vibrating devices, and electronic muscle stimulators purportedly will "roll away ugly fat" and are "ideal as a spot reducer." Such devices have no fat-reducing value. Nor will they reduce in spots or remove bumps and bulges.

The FDA charged the promoters of several such devices with false and misleading claims. The devices bore names such as Figurecare, Figuremagic, Isotron, Muscle Stimulator, Electronic Exerciser, Exertronic.

Sleep-slimming devices are worthless. The Everslim Sleep-and-Slim Garment, among many others with similar names, was charged with false and misleading claims to induce weight loss while sleeping.

Belts, girdles, body-wraps, rubber or plastic garments advertised as slimmers, may make you look thinner, but they don't reduce fat or weight.

Postal authorities clamped down on a "sauna girdle," whose manufacturers claimed it would allow users to spot-reduce hips, abdomen, waist, and thighs. The best it can do, a medical expert testified, is cause temporary weight loss through water given off in excessive sweating.

In a government-sponsored experiment, men who wore a brand of "girth-reducing" sauna shorts lost no more than other men who did the exercises alone, without wearing the shorts. Exercise, not the shorts, takes the credit for any weight and girth reduction.

Steam baths and saunas: Any device that promotes sweating can result in a temporary loss of water. But as soon as you drink, the weight will come back. Sweating is of no value for permanent weight reduction.

See also EXERCISE; HEALTH CLUBS; HEART DISEASE; NUTRITION; VITAMINS.

PACEMAKER   See HEART BLOCK.

PAGET'S DISEASE   See CANCER OF THE BONE.

PAIN   See ANALGESICS.

PAINT REMOVERS are among the most dangerous products used in the home. If splashed, they can cause contact dermatitis and eye injuries. If accidentally swallowed, they can blind or kill. If used in an inadequately ventilated area, they can sicken with their noxious fumes.

To remove paint from skin—especially if the paint is on your face, near your eyes or mouth, or in other sensitive areas—apply mineral oil or baby oil to gauze or cotton and wipe the paint away. The paint will ordinarily come off without doing any damage to the skin or adjacent mucous membranes.

When handling chemical paint removers, wear goggles and neoprene rubber gloves. If possible work outdoors. Besides being poisonous, most paint removers are fire hazards. Indoors make sure there's plenty of ventilation, produced either by a window fan to exhaust air from the room or at least by a cross-draft between open doors and windows, and stand upwind of the surface on which the work is being done. If you splash yourself, immediately wash the affected area with soap and water.

Avoid opening a warm container. When uncapping a container, cover the cap with a cloth and point it away from you. Avoid storing paint remover by buying only enough for the job at hand.

Keep children away from the stuff, both in the container and at any work site. In the event that a child swallows paint remover, follow label instructions for treating poisoning and call a doctor at once.

Don't buy remover with a paper label, for if a label is torn or falls off, you may be unaware of the hazards in the can.

See also ACCIDENTS; POISONING.

PALSY   See CEREBRAL PALSY; PARKINSON'S DISEASE.

PARALYSIS (plegia) is loss of control of part of the body. Feelings of temperature, touch, and pain may also be gone.

Paralysis typically results from damage to nerves or to the spinal cord. If the injury is to a peripheral nerve, say in the arm or leg, the cut or damaged ends can often heal or be sewn together. New nerve tissue grows around the wound, and the paralysis may diminish or disappear.

Paralysis from spinal-cord injury is generally permanent. When the spinal cord is damaged, usually from accidents or disease, scar tissue forms between the severed or bruised ends, and nerve impulses cannot be transmitted. Nerve regrowth does not occur in the spinal cord.

Diseases that can cause paralysis include stroke, cancer and other tumors of the spinal cord, and infections and abscesses of the cord. Multiple sclerosis, polio, meningitis, encephalitis, and some birth defects may lead to paralysis. Severe stress may cause psychosomatic loss of sensation or paralysis, which may reverse spontaneously or through psychotherapy.

When the damage to the spinal cord occurs at the level of the chest or lower back as in back fractures, both legs and the lower part of the body may be paralyzed (paraplegia). An injury to the spinal cord at the neck level, as in neck fractures, may result in paralysis of both arms and both legs (quadriplegia).

Most large medical centers and university hospitals provide special services for severely paralyzed people. Much can be done to help paraplegics and quadriplegics make the best use of their remaining abilities and lead fulfilling lives.

See also ACCIDENTS; BACK FRACTURES; NECK FRACTURES; POLIO.

PARATYPHOID FEVER   See SALMONELLOSIS.

PARKINSON'S DISEASE (parkinsonism, shaking palsy) affects brain centers that regulate movement. It afflicts about 1 million Americans, most over age 50.

The first symptom of Parkinson's disease is often a fine tremor of the hands. Tremors of the feet and head may develop.

Muscles may become stiff or rigid, often resulting in a shuffling gait, slow movements, and difficulty in any movement that requires complicated muscle coordination. It can become hard, for example, to get out of a chair or out of bed. There may be a tendency to fall. Facial muscles may be affected, making speech slurred and the face expressionless, with an unblinking stare. Emotional stress often worsens the course of the condition.

Untreated, Parkinson's disease usually becomes slowly but progressively crippling. Vision and hearing are rarely affected, but intellectual function may become somewhat slowed. Depression often develops. The disorder does not usually shorten the life span.

There is no cure, but parkinsonism can often be relieved. The drug levodopa (Sinemet, Larodopa) reduces tremor and rigidity in most sufferers, sometimes completely.

Dosage of levodopa must be carefully regulated by a physician, since it can have such side effects as nausea and vomiting and lowered blood pressure. A small number of people experience mental changes, including restlessness, agitation, and sleeplessness. Involuntary movements, usually of the face or head, are a common sign of too large a dose. These jerky movements usually disappear when the dose is decreased. The chance of side effects is reduced by combining levodopa with other drugs. The drug Sinemet combines levodopa with carbidopa, and is effective in many cases.

Large amounts of vitamin B_6 may reverse levodopa's effects. Levodopa users need a physician's advice before taking multivitamin preparations.

Levodopa is usually most effective in the first years of treatment. Prolonged use may cause increasing side effects, and benefits may diminish. Many physicians reserve levodopa for more severe cases and begin treatment with other drugs —usually anticholinergic drugs (such as Artane, Cogentin, Parsidol, Disipal) or amantadine (Symmetrel).

Exercise and physical therapy are helpful in keeping muscles flexible and recovering some lost functions. Speech therapy can help Parkinson's disease patients learn to speak more clearly. Brain surgery, once thought promising, is now very rarely recommended. Its benefits are generally minimal and temporary. The operation may lead to severe speech impairment.

Parkinson's disease results from a deficiency of the chemical dopamine, which mediates the transmisson of nerve impulses. Other chemical imbalances may be involved as well. In most cases the cause is unknown. In some people the parkinsonism develops after encephalitis. Some drugs can cause parkinsonism-like symptoms. The disease is not contagious. There is no firm evidence that it is hereditary.

To protect the parkinsonism patient at home, remove all loose or scatter rugs. Make sure carpets are properly fastened to the floor. If possible remove all doorsills between rooms. Remove any sharp pointed tables or precarious bric-a-brac. If the patient must climb stairs, they should have rails on both sides. It's a good idea to install handles on walls adjacent to doorknobs of all doors in the house. This gives the patient more stability in standing. He can hold the handle in one hand while pulling or pushing the doorknob with the other.

A tipped-forward chair is easier for the Parkinson's disease patient to use. You can place a 2-inch block under the back legs of a sturdy armchair. To get out, place feet back underneath you about a foot apart and push against the arms of the chair.

Clothing should be simple to get into and out of. Zippers are easier to use than buttons. Shoes without ties (such as loafers) are best, but be sure they fit well—floppy shoes are easy to trip in. Bowling shoes have slightly upturned toes and may reduce scuffling and stumbling. Shoes with snaps or zipper closings are another good alternative. Wide-sleeved jackets are easier to get into. Clip-on ties should be substituted for long neckties.

Surgical-supply stores have special elevated toilet seats that may be easier for the Parkinson's disease patient. Or a plumber may be able to raise the seat of an ordinary toilet 2 inches above the bowl.

When walking, quick turns should be avoided. Legs should be set wider apart than normal. Conscious effort should be made to swing arms back and forth, for balance, and to lift toes with every step and place heels down first.

Constipation is often a problem with Parkinson's disease. A diet high in fiber content (whole grain breads and cereals, fresh fruits, and raw vegetables) is recommended. Increase the amount of fluid with this diet.

Because eating is slow and swallowing may be difficult, maintaining adequate nutrition and weight may be a problem. Select nutritious foods; plan several small easy-to-prepare meals a day. A food warmer at the table can be helpful.

It is important for Parkinson's disease patients to maintain as much independence as possible. Ample time should be allowed for accomplishing tasks.

For more information about Parkinson's disease and help in dealing with it get in touch with National Parkinson Foundation (1501 NW 9th Avenue, Miami, Florida 33136); Parkinson's Disease Foundation (650 West 168th Street, New York, New York 10032).

PELLAGRA   See VITAMINS.

PELVIC FRACTURES usually heal after about a month of bedrest. However they are often complicated by injuries to the urinary, genital, and digestive tracts. In these cases, surgery is often necessary.

IF PELVIS MAY BE BROKEN

1. Improvise a "corset"

2. Tie victim onto stretcher
(Door, board, etc.)

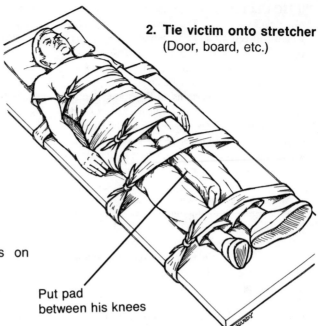

Strips of blanket, sheet, etc.
(2 inches above hips, 2 inches on thighs)

Put pad
between his knees

Be alert to the possibility of pelvic fracture if you have pain when walking, particularly in the lower abdomen or crotch. Another sign is pain when the hips are pressed inward. The pain will not necessarily be severe.

Refrain from moving an injured person with a possible pelvic fracture. If you must move him, have him lie down on a flat board (see illustration). If you place padding between his knees, he is likely to be more comfortable.

See also FRACTURES; MOVING THE INJURED; SURGERY.

PEMPHIGUS is one of the most severe types of mouth sores. The most common type, pemphigus vulgaris, appears most frequently among people 40 to 70 years of age, Jews, and persons of Mediterranean origin. The cause of the disease and why it attacks these particular groups are mysteries.

The onset of pemphigus is insidious, for at first the blisters are not painful. The victim feels a dryness in his mouth and a slight discomfort when eating hot or spicy food. He may have difficulty swallowing. Next, large blisters form on the lips, tongue, cheek, palate, or gums. Often these blisters are not seen because they break easily, leaving a reddish erosion with ragged edges. It is after they break that the blisters become very itchy and painful. Salivation increases, often tinged with blood.

In about three fourths of the cases of pemphigus, blisters form first in the mouth. Lesions on the skin may not appear for several months, sometimes never. When they do appear, they form over the entire body—face, trunk, arms, and legs. These blisters are thin-walled and translucent, filled with a yellow fluid. When they break, they form a foul-smelling yellow membrane. The top layer of skin can be rubbed off with slight pressure.

In the early stages of the acute form of the disease, there may be periods of remission with complete healing of the sores. Later, with each attack the blisters and following erosions gradually become larger until the whole mouth is involved. Eating and drinking become extremely painful. The skin, covered with large blisters, has the appearance of severe burn.

Acute pemphigus runs a rapid course. Mortality is high. About half of the patients succumb to the continual loss of body fluid through the breaking blisters and to the malnutrition and final involvement of the vital organs.

The prognosis of chronic pemphigus vulgaris is much more hopeful. This form of the disease may last for years, causing only minor discomfort to the patient. The blisters do not break easily and tend to heal well.

Treatment of pemphigus can only be palliative, for there is no known cure. Cortisone has been used to alleviate symptoms and penicillin to prevent secondary infection. Mild mouthwashes can help relieve pain in the mouth. These should be used only on the advice of a doctor.

See also MOUTH SORES; TEETH AND MOUTH DISORDERS.

PENICILLIN   See ANTIBIOTICS.

PEP PILLS   See AMPHETAMINES.

PEPTIC ULCER develops in more than 3 million Americans each year. The typical ulcer victim is a man between 45 and 55, though it can afflict young children and the elderly, and women as well as men. Roughly one in ten people will at some time in their lives have an ulcer.

The term *peptic* pertains to digestion. Peptic ulcer includes both stomach (gastric) ulcers and duodenal ulcers (those occurring in the duodenum, the first few inches of the small intestine where it connects to the stomach). Duodenal ulcers are about ten times more prevalent than stomach ulcers.

An ulcer develops when stomach acids eat away at stomach or duodenal tissue. This leads to an open sore. Hereditary factors may predispose a person toward the development of ulcers: Ulcers are three times more common among blood relatives of ulcer patients.

Emotional stress often plays a large part in the development of an ulcer. Hormonal changes caused by emotional upsets can trigger the vagus nerve to call forth the production of the stomach hormone, gastrin. Released into the bloodstream, gastrin causes the stomach glands to release increased amounts of hydrochloric acid. In the absence of food the acid begins digesting the body's own mucous membrane.

Stomach ulcers seem to be related more to a weakness in the stomach lining than to the oversecretion of acid. Regurgitated bile from the duodenum may be implicated.

So-called "stress ulcers" often develop during a period of intense emotional trauma or after a serious illness or injury. They progress quickly, often healing just as quickly when the stress is relieved.

Ulcer pain. Most ulcer sufferers experience a burning or gnawing pain in the abdomen. The pain is usually between the navel and the breastbone, and comes between 30 minutes and 2 hours after a meal.

Relief usually comes with the next meal. As a result, ulcer sufferers may become overweight as they nibble all day to relieve the ulcer symptoms, which they may interpret as hunger.

Other common ulcer symptoms may include feelings of indigestion, nausea, and a full, gaseous feeling. Black, tarry stools may indicate slow bleeding from ulcers, and this may lead to anemia. Some people have ulcers with no symptoms at all.

Most ulcers heal in about six weeks, some spontaneously. Treatment usually consists of ANTACIDS (which see). Take enough to neutralize stomach acids. Antacids should usually be taken 1 and 3 hours after meals, and before bedtime. Use a product containing aluminum or magnesium hydroxide. With large doses, expect diarrhea. Reduce the dosage as ulcers heal.

Other drugs can relieve pain and lower acid secretion. Cimetidine (Tagamet) and Ranitidine (Zantac) are the drugs most commonly used. Sucralfate (Carafate), which acts locally on the stomach lining, can also be effective. Occasionally bed rest is prescribed. Some people need to be in a hospital during an acute flare-up.

Sedatives and tranquilizers may be prescribed. A technique for freezing the stomach, popular some years ago, has not proved effective.

The ulcer diet. A bland diet is not necessary for ulcer treatment. The traditional ulcer regimen called for dairy products, white meat, rice, and other bland foods. Now it is clear that a more varied diet promotes healing just as fast. During an acute ulcer flare-up, on the other hand, physicians may prescribe a very bland diet.

Your doctor may recommend that you cut down on or avoid caffeine and alcohol, which stimulate acid secretion. This may mean eliminating coffee (including decaffeinated coffee, which has also been shown to increase secretion), tea, and some sodas—colas in particular, which contain caffeine.

Also avoid any food that seems to upset your condition. There is no evidence that spices necessarily aggravate ulcers.

Give up cigarettes if you have an ulcer. (Or if you don't.) Smoking, especially on an empty stomach, worsens ulcer symptoms.

Some drugs like aspirin and steroids can aggravate ulcers. People with arthritis, who must take a great deal of aspirin, seem prone to ulcers.

Major complications can include heavy bleeding if the ulcer erodes a blood vessel. If the ulcer perforates through the duodenum or stomach wall, stomach contents may leak through the hole into the abdominal cavity. Immediate surgery is usually necessary. Surgery may also be required for an obstruction in the digestive tract caused by ulcer scar tissue or inflamed, swollen ulcers.

Surgery may be necessary when other measures are ineffective, and this is more likely with stomach ulcers than duodenal ulcers. Acid-producing areas of the stomach are removed in an operation called a gastrectomy. Another operation involves severing parts of the vagus nerve, which stimulates stomach secretions. Some people have both types of surgery.

By itself, a stomach ulcer is not a precancerous condition. Nonetheless, the symptoms of stomach cancer and stomach ulcer are much the same, and stomach cancers often ulcerate.

A nonhealing stomach ulcer thus raises a suspicion of underlying cancer. Gastroscopy is extremely important to rule out this possibility. Duodenal ulcers rarely cause concern about malignancy.

Ulcers often recur. Once an ulcer has healed, antacids and other medication may prevent a recurrence. Consult a physician as to how long to continue treatment.

Although the stereotype of the ulcer-prone personality is the high-powered executive, ulcer is even more likely to strike a blue-collar worker frustrated over his status. On the other hand some ulcer sufferers are relaxed, calm people who outwardly at least don't fit the ulcer personality type at all.

See also ANTACIDS; STRESS; SURGERY.

PERIODONTAL DISEASE (perio, periodontitis, pyorrhea) is the major cause of tooth loss in people over 35, affecting the gums, fibers, and bone that support the teeth. Although the teeth themselves may be sound, the underlying structure may become so deteriorated that some or all of the teeth cannot be retained.

A major cause is the accumulation along the gum line of plaque, a sticky film that mineralizes if not promptly removed, and also contributes to tooth decay.

Layer builds upon layer, irritating and inflaming the gums to cause gingivitis. Impacted food debris often decays in the crevice where the tooth and gum tissue meet. The bacteria add to the destruction of the tissue, and get further nourishment from the gums' bleeding.

Healthy gum tissue is firm and pink. It hugs the tooth tightly and terminates in a fine margin. As disease develops, the gums take on a swollen, bluish-red, blunted appearance and the tissue becomes separated from the teeth.

A pocket soon forms between the gum and the root. Tartar enters, and local infection and inflammation may set in, aggravating the pyorrhea. The old term "pyorrhea" means "flow of pus," which may occur from the infection.

The end result is the gradual loosening of the tooth from its moorings. If the process is not halted, the loosening continues until the tooth falls out. Periodontal disease often is nearly asymptomatic and can be diagnosed only by a professional using probes and X rays.

Other causes. Bad alignment of the teeth makes them difficult to clean. Irregular spacing encourages food retention, with resultant gum inflammation. Moreover, tilted, rotated, or malpositioned teeth subject the periodontal structures to undesirable stresses when food is chewed. The stresses may contribute to the breakdown of the supporting tissue. Constant clenching, clamping, or grinding of the teeth during waking or sleeping hours may have similar results.

Diabetes and other circulatory disorders often contribute to periodontal disease. A rarer cause is poisoning by heavy metals such as lead, arsenic, and mercury. In some industries with exposure to these metals workers often complain of soreness and bleeding of the gums.

Prevention entails keeping your gums clean. Practice plaque control. Visit your dentist regularly to have the rough, hard tartar removed.

With the aid of instruments to reach between the gum and root, the dentist cleans out deposits of tartar and debris from the periodontal pocket and smooths the tooth root. Such curettage eliminates important sources of irritation. In severe cases of pyorrhea the dentist may refer you to a periodontist, a specialist in gum disease.

Only a dentist or dental hygienist can remove hardened tartar from the teeth. Don't believe toothpaste ads to the contrary. If a toothpaste could remove these cementlike deposits, it would be so abrasive or corrosive as to be harmful to tooth enamel. There is no drug or other patent remedy effective for curing pyorrhea.

See also PLAQUE; TEETH AND MOUTH DISORDERS.

PERSPIRATION ODOR is in only small part due to sweat, which is virtually odorless when secreted.

Most of the odor is caused by the action of the skin's natural bacteria on organic material secreted by the apocrine sweat glands, which are concentrated in the armpits, around the nipples, and in the genital region. The armpits and groin perspire heavily in cool weather as well as warm, and air circulation is poor in hairy areas covered by clothes where moisture cannot readily evaporate. Thus bacteria have a field day, with odorous results.

The glands are stimulated by emotional stress (as when you break out in a cold sweat), fear, pain, sexual excitement. The glands become active only after puberty and remain so as long as the sex glands are active. Body odor is rarely a problem among young children or the elderly.

Another type of sweat gland, the eccrine, contributes little to perspiration odor. Eccrine glands cover your entire body, but leave little organic residue for bacteria to act on. They help control your body temperature and are active almost entirely in response to heat, exercise, nervous tension. Eccrine glands can be a problem in cases of sweaty palms and when feet perspire excessively, causing odor and possibly athlete's foot.

Combating odor. To control normal body odor, personal cleanliness is a must. Frequent bathing with ordinary soap will get rid of bacterial growth on your skin. Clothing and underwear collect odors and bacteria and need to be changed often. Avoid tight clothing, which impedes air circulation. Shaving under the arms gets rid of moist hair that breeds bacteria.

Try various commercial antiperspirants to determine which works best for you. Most contain salts of aluminum that temporarily reduce the amount of sweat reaching the surface of your skin. Aluminum chlorohydrate is the active ingredient most commonly used. Other ingredients may combat bacteria and give a scent to mask perspiration odor.

Most antiperspirants on the market cut perspiration by 20 to 46 percent. Lotions are likely to be most effective, followed by creams, sticks, liquids, and roll-ons. Least effective are aerosols —and they are usually considerably more expensive. Since there is also some doubt about the safety of inhaling spray every day over many years, aerosols are best avoided. The safety and effectiveness of deodorant soaps has not been established, and they are likewise best avoided.

Like antiperspirants deodorants are effective in reducing perspiration odor. But unlike antiperspirants, which diminish sweating, deodorants simply reduce odor. They contain perfume, to mask body odor, and antimicrobial chemicals, to inhibit odor-causing bacteria.

If you suffer from abnormally heavy sweating —a condition called hyperhidrosis—regular antiperspirants will do little to help. A prescription product, Drysol, can reduce excessive sweating from armpits, palms, and soles. But use it with caution: It contains a form of aluminum chloride, which can irritate skin and discolor and corrode fabrics.

If your underarms become irritated or develop other types of skin disorder, change antiperspirants. But also check that you're not irritating yourself by shaving too close or toweling too hard. You may eliminate irritation by shaving at night and applying your antiperspirant next morning. It's wise to apply an antiperspirant well before you need it, since antiperspirants are not effective immediately after being applied to the skin.

Men don't need stronger antiperspirants or deodorants than women do. The amount of sweat and odor is about the same for both sexes, though fewer men than women shave underarms and so have to work harder to avoid body odor. Be wary of claims for "extra strength" products. Putting more of the active ingredient in an antiperspirant does not make it more effective.

See also SKIN DISORDERS.

PERTUSSIS See WHOOPING COUGH.

PETIT MAL See EPILEPSY.

PHENYLKETONURIA See PKU.

PHLEBITIS See THROMBOPHLEBITIS.

PHOSPHORUS See MINERALS.

PHYSICAL EXAMINATION A complete physical examination is a prime safeguard against such severe but silent conditions as cancer and heart disease.

How often do you need a physical? If you have a chronic medical problem, your physician will develop an examination schedule that is best for you. What if you have no symptoms? For many years an annual examination was deemed necessary by most medical authorities. Now there is a general feeling that a less frequent schedule is adequate—and certainly much easier on your pocketbook.

Most authorities are largely in agreement with the Mayo Clinic's recommendations for the typical adult: Have exams at 18 and again at 25. Between 31 and 40, get 3. Between 41 and 50, get 4. Between 51 and 60, get 5. Over 60, get 1 every year.

In any case every time you see a physician in a medical field, whatever the reason for your visit, get your blood pressure checked. Hypertension can erupt between regular checkups.

Children need a complete examination just before entering school, at age five or six. A schedule of four other physicals suffices to safeguard most children: at about the fourth grade, seventh grade, tenth grade, and upon graduation from high school.

The checkup. Just what constitutes a complete physical examination depends on your age and your medical history.

A complete examination should include the taking of a thorough medical history on the first visit, preferably by the physician—rather than by questionnaire or computer. Your medical history includes current medical complaints, past illnesses or surgery, illnesses in your family, vaccinations, and allergies. Your physician should also ask questions about your diet, exercise program, alcohol consumption, smoking habits, and stresses in your life.

After the history taking, the physician will examine you. A good physical examination generally includes measurement of height and weight;

measurement of blood pressure; examination of ears, nose, and mouth; palpation of the thyroid gland; breast examination; palpation of the abdomen; examination of the heart and lungs with a stethoscope; examination of the lymph nodes; examination for hernias; examination of the skin; brief neurological examination; and examination of the rectum.

A woman will generally have a gynecologic checkup as part of the exam. In addition many doctors evaluate hearing and eyesight as part of a general physical. Some physicians examine the inside of the eye and test for glaucoma. Necessary immunizations are also given at the time of the physical.

In addition to taking a medical history and examining the patient a complete physical examination generally includes several diagnostic tests. Following are common tests and how often you should have them:

- *Urinalysis* should be done every time you have a physical. This simple, inexpensive test can detect diabetes, infection, and the possible presence of tumors.
- *Complete blood count* is another simple, inexpensive test that should be done at each checkup. It can detect anemia and other blood disorders.
- *Blood-chemistry analysis* is a more thorough blood study that can detect a wide variety of disorders. Have one at each checkup.
- *Pap test,* for the detection of cervical cancer, is an inexpensive, easy-to-do procedure. Although the American Cancer Society recommends it once every three years after negative tests two years in a row, it's most prudent to have an annual Pap test. Women should have their first Pap test at age 20, or when they begin having sexual intercourse, whichever comes first. Women with multiple sex partners are best off having annual examinations.
- *Tests for breast cancer.* At every checkup the physician should palpate a woman's breasts. Breast self-examination should be done once a month after age 20. Routine mammograms (X rays of breasts) are recommended starting at 40, earlier if there is a family history of breast cancer.
- *Tuberculosis skin test.* It's wise to have this quick, inexpensive test every time you have a physical.
- *Tests for colorectal cancer.* Have a digital rectal examination as part of every checkup after age 40. After age 50 (some physicians recommend starting at age 40) have an annual Hemoccult test (to detect hidden internal bleeding), and a sigmoidoscopy (examination

of the rectum and colon with an instrument) every three years following two initial negative tests a year apart. Have tests for colorectal cancer more frequently if you have ulcerative colitis, or a personal or family history of polyps or colorectal cancer.

- *Electrocardiogram (ECG)* measures the heart's electrical activity. Have a baseline ECG at about age 35 for men, age 40 for women. Thereafter have an ECG every five to ten years. Have ECGs more frequently if you smoke, have high blood pressure, have a high serum-cholesterol level, have a family history of heart disease, are obese, or lead a very sedentary life.

A stress test—an ECG that is taken while the patient is exercising—should be limited to people who have chest pain despite a normal resting ECG. Also get a stress test if you're over 35 and plan to begin a program of vigorous exercise—especially if you smoke, are overweight, lead a sedentary life, or have a personal or family history of heart disease.
- *Chest X ray.* Have a baseline X ray at about 35, then at five- to ten-year intervals. Have chest X rays more frequently if you've smoked more than a pack a day for 20 years, or if you work with asbestos or toxic chemical fumes.

Get another opinion if your doctor diagnoses a major problem requiring surgery. Also consider getting a second opinion if you are confused about your options, if the treatment seems controversial, or if the condition doesn't respond to treatment.

Tell your doctor, "I'll welcome a consultation." If he objects or acts offended, flee. Medical ethics, as well as the law and common sense, give you the clear right to confirm his opinion.

Seek a consultant who's a board-certified specialist in the area of your problem—a dermatologist for a skin condition, a urologist for a kidney disorder, and so forth. If your family physician can't suggest one who satisfies you, phone a nearby medical center and ask for the names and office addresses of faculty members in your locale.

You're likely to cooperate fully with a course of treatment only if you have confidence in it. If you harbor any doubts about the correctness of a diagnosis, your disbelief can impede your recovery.

What's more, the original diagnosis may well be wrong. In one classic case of improper diagnosis doctors removed a man's right kidney. He died almost immediately—the doctors had neglected to notice a birth defect: he had only the one kidney.

Tests cost money. Make a point of asking, "Is this test necessary?" A George Washington University study found that some doctors just tend to order more unnecessary and expensive lab tests than other doctors.

When you see a consultant, you may be able to avoid the trouble and expense of unnecessary duplication of tests. Ask your family doctor to send the consultant the reports or originals of lab studies, X rays, electrocardiographs, and other tests you've already undergone.

Another possible money saver: Ask that the lab bill you directly, or that your doctor itemize the lab charges on his bill. Don't accept a bill lumping lab costs and the physician's professional fee, like one that says merely: "Complete physical examination $100." Itemizing helps you catch common bookkeeping errors, and discourages the rare doctor who buries with the lab costs a fee that's too high.

Physicians often overtest out of fear of a malpractice suit. With an eye toward demonstrating, if need be, that they weren't negligent, many physicians order more extensive lab work than is actually needed.

Don't push your doctor into ordering unnecessary studies. Some physicians order unnecessary tests because otherwise the patient would think them negligent. Many such people, physicians find, tend to discount the intuition of an experienced clinician and have confidence only in objective laboratory tests.

Such faith in tests is not always justified. People tend to forget that fancy machinery is only an accessory to clinical judgment. For example, the electroencephalogram (EEG) is widely used to help diagnose brain injury. But if a neurologist relied on an EEG alone, he'd misdiagnose a large number of his cases. At least 15 percent of people with convulsive disorders never have an abnormal EEG. On the other hand at least 15 percent of the general population have abnormal EEGs though they have no disorder.

Interpretation is similarly imprecise. As many as 24 percent of radiologists differed with each other in their readings of identical films, even in cases of extensive disease, reported Dr. L. Henry Garland in his presidential address to the Radiological Society of North America. When the same radiologists read the same films later, fully 31 percent disagreed with their own earlier diagnoses.

A similar study was conducted on electrocardiographic (ECG) tracings. The reports of the ECG readers varied by 20 percent between doctors, and 20 percent on rereading of the same tracing by the same doctor at a later date. An editorial in the *Journal* of the AMA warned that ECG variations were so great—depending on time of day, activity, digestion, and so on—that many normal people showed changes usually regarded as evidence of heart disease.

Fraudulent diagnostic techniques. Beware of diagnosis by quacks. Mail-order testing is a ripe field for quackery. A promoter in Texas claimed he had perfected an effective urine test for cancer. More than 15,000 tests were mail-ordered at $10 each before postal investigators found the tests were fakes.

Some promoters send you a fake urinalysis report showing you have various illnesses. The "lab" recommends that you treat these supposed conditions by buying food supplements or drugs from it or from a company in cahoots.

Reliable labs report only to physicians, never to laymen. Urinalysis or blood testing by mail is fraught with danger. Results are of value only if part of a general examination by a competent physician. You may in fact be seriously ill, but normal as far as your blood or urine shows.

Quack practitioners may try to sucker you in with so-called diagnostic machines. After all, if X rays work, why not an equally complex-looking machine called the Electron-O-Ray? And if you can use an X ray for both diagnosis and therapy, then what's odd about the Pathoclast, which claims to do the same? After the Pathoclast operator reaches a diagnosis, he applies to the "affected" area of your body a rod attached to the machine that will "cure" you.

The Better Business Bureau of Cleveland offered a $1,000 reward for proof that any of these types of devices had the slightest diagnostic or curative value. No manufacturer or user has ever even tried to claim the reward. The AMA exhibits these machines in a medical chamber of horrors, publicly labeling them fakes and frauds. None of the manufacturers has dared sue for libel.

See also PHYSICIAN.

PHYSICIAN selection is your most important health-care decision.

Every member of your family needs a regular doctor, a "medical manager" familiar with your history. Ideally, he (or she) can be freely consulted; he can treat most problems; he will direct you to well-qualified specialists when needed; he will serve as your advocate and guide in your dealings with the complex world of medicine.

Choosing your doctor(s) is a *plural* task for many families. One member may see a general practitioner, another an internist (specialist in internal medicine). A child may go to a pediatrician. Women and older girls may have as their regular doctor an obstetrician-gynecologist. There may be frequent contact with other specialists to meet particular needs. Your family may be best off with one family physician who can coordinate health care for the whole family.

If you have a doctor you're satisfied with, of course stick with him. However if you are looking for a doctor, here are some things you should know:

While the great majority of physicians perform with competence and honor, many are guilty of substandard practices. The laws governing medicine are extremely weak, and state licensing boards generally fail to police the profession. In many states the law makes no provision for suspending a license even when it is proved that the doctor is grossly negligent, or that he exploits his patients, or even that he is mentally incapacitated.

A medical license is virtually a blank check. The licensee can legally perform any medical or surgical services he wishes, even if they are far beyond his skills. Moreover, once a medical license is granted, it is virtually permanent, subject only to the paying of a periodic fee. One retired GP in his eighties is nearly blind. But by paying his annual fee he has kept up his medical license. He is amused that legally he can do brain surgery.

At least 1 physician in 20—possibly 1 in 9—is a severe disciplinary problem, estimated Dr. Harold E. Jervey, Jr., a past president of the Federation of State Medical Boards, the principal association of medical-licensing officials. Most of these physicians commit offenses that are unethical rather than prosecutable: substandard care, abandonment of patients, overcharging. But, Dr. Jervey concluded, between 2,500 and 7,500 are actually breaking the law through narcotics violations, frauds, and other felonies.

Other estimates of medical wrongdoing are even higher. While on the staff of New York's Bellevue Hospital, Dr. Vincent J. Fisher evaluated the prehospital care given by patients' private physicians. He reports that he found "poor and even harmful care" in one case out of ten. A surgeon writing in *Medical Economics* under the name of Michael V. Corio said, "If patients brought malpractice suits against *all* guilty doctors—and against guilty doctors only—the courts would probably be flooded with three times the number of suits now in litigation."

But it's not always easy to find out whether a doctor is competent. "Most people can find out more about a car they plan to buy than they can

about a doctor who may hold their life in his hands," observed Ralph Nader's Public Citizen Health Research Group, which compiled a pioneering *Consumer's Directory* of information about physicians in Prince Georges County, Maryland.

"Neighbors and friends can be helpful, if you're lucky enough to get a good recommendation. Sometimes the medical society has a referral bureau that will give you the name of a few doctors—but they never say whether the doctor is any good. . . . And of course the Yellow Pages in the phone book usually lists *all* the doctors practicing in your area."

To point up the value of doctor-shopping, the Health Research Group notes that doctors aren't required to be reexamined each year—and that the AMA estimates some 5 percent of U.S. physicians are either drug addicts, alcoholics, or mentally ill. "Would you ride on an airplane if you knew that pilots never had to be relicensed and that at least 5 percent of all pilots were drug addicts, alcoholics, or mentally ill?"

Watch out for doctors who engage in shady advertising practices. While physicians may legally and ethically advertise, they should follow the guidelines suggested by the Council of Medical Specialty Societies. Appropriate advertising can contain the qualifications of the physician, his specialty board, the hospital to which he admits patients, his office hours, fees, and location. He may also describe diagnostic services, terms of payment, and languages spoken by himself and his staff.

By contrast inappropriate advertising includes false or misleading statements, pictures or testimonials claiming cures that are not the experience of the average patient, and undocumented claims that the physician is superior to other physicians of similar training and experience. Also be on your guard when a physician's advertisement comes in the guise of a news story.

Shop for a doctor. To find the best doctor for you, first get about six recommendations from authoritative sources. Other physicians are most knowledgeable, and pharmacists and R.N.'s often have a good idea of how various doctors perform. They're likely to give you a straight answer if you ask, "If you were I, which doctor would you go to?" Or turn to the best nearby hospital and ask for names of attending physicians who meet your specifications.

Be skeptical of patients' recommendations. No one wants to believe he is using the "wrong" doctor—it would be a reflection on his own judgment. Conversely, a patient who's had a bad experience with a physician may go overboard in condemning him.

With a list of qualified candidates in hand, make a survey to find one who suits you. While individual variations are enormous, you're most likely to be satisfied if a doctor has these characteristics:

He should inspire your confidence. Visit a prospective physician before illness strikes, perhaps for a minor service like a shot. It pays to invest in an office visit just to decide if you want him to be your doctor.

A good relationship with a physician can be curative in itself. The good feelings the right doctor engenders in you can ease the pain of an illness and free your mind while you're recovering. This personal chemistry can be more important and is certainly safer than the drugs you take.

By contrast if you don't like or trust a doctor, you may subject yourself to a great deal of stress that can impair your health. You're likely to see him only with reluctance. You may follow his instructions grudgingly, with anxiety and doubt. If anything goes wrong, even if it's not his fault, out of resentment you may hold him responsible —and kick yourself forever afterward for not switching to another doctor while you had the chance.

He should be associated with the best hospital in your area. That's where you'll want to go if you ever need hospital services. Your doctor can admit you only to a hospital whose staff he's on. Too, first-rate hospitals tend to be choosy about who's on the staff, so hospital privileges may be an indicator of quality.

Another sign of quality: The doctor teaches. As a rule private practitioners who participate in the education of medical and nursing students, interns, and residents tend to stay sharp. University appointments in particular show a doctor is believed by his peers to be a good practitioner.

He should be certified in his field. This means he has a diploma from a certifying body in his specialty (the American Board of Internal Medicine, for example).

To receive board certification a doctor must normally complete a specified period of residency (postinternship) training in his field, then pass an examination. Physicians who have met the residency requirement without the exam sometimes refer to themselves as board-eligible. Such residency training is a sign of the breadth and depth of a doctor's background.

The *Directory of Medical Specialists,* available in many public and hospital libraries, can help you identify board-certified specialists in your

area and research their backgrounds. Also look for membership in a "college" or "academy," an honorary society whose main concern is continuing education in a specialty. After a doctor's M.D., he may have such initials as FACP (Fellow of the American College of Physicians, for internal medicine), FACOG (. . . American College of Obstetrics and Gynecology), or FAAP (. . . American Academy of Pediatrics).

If you're considering a general practitioner, look for membership in the American Academy of Family Physicians. To stay in the AAFP a physician needs to complete a specified amount of postgraduate study. A similar credential: Being certified by the new American Board of Family Practice, which requires periodic reexaminations for continued certification.

One credential you need *not* look for is membership in a county or state medical society or the AMA. These organizations are open to virtually any M.D. Nor is it necessarily pertinent what medical school the doctor went to. All U.S. medical schools are of relatively high quality, and there's no demonstrated link between a physician's school and his abilities as a practitioner.

Following the M.D., some physicians use the initials *PC.* This is not a medical credential but merely stands for "professional corporation," a mechanism for saving taxes.

Doctors of osteopathy (D.O.'s) receive an education similar to that offered in medical schools, and are gaining increasing recognition from organized medicine. As with an M.D. look for a D.O. who is certified by a specialty board or is a member of the AAFP. Don't confuse osteopaths with chiropractors, who are no substitute for medical professionals.

His office or hospital should be close to your home. If you're nearby, you're more likely to get prompt care in an emergency. When you interview a physician, ask about his willingness to make house calls. This is especially important if you're housebound.

His practice should always be covered. It's a relatively rare plus if a physician is in a partnership or group that has a doctor on call nights and weekends.

At the minimum, expect a doctor to be reachable through his answering service after hours and to have a specific colleague covering his practice when he's on vacation. If you're referred to a hospital emergency room or medical society coverage system, you're not as assured of high-quality, personalized care. See the accompanying list of when (and when not) to call your doctor after hours.

He should have an appointment system that

works. If you're seen promptly—within perhaps 15 to 30 minutes of when you're scheduled—it's a sign his office is well managed. A competently run office generally does a good job on record keeping, billing, form filling, and other administrative matters that could prove troublesome to you if mishandled.

He practices preventive medicine. Look for a doctor who is interested in helping you maintain good health. He should ask about your diet, smoking and alcohol habits, exercise program, occupational risks—and make appropriate recommendations to help you avoid illness. Also look for a doctor who will exhaust simple remedies before prescribing potent drugs.

Fees. Talk turkey about charges to any doctor you visit. Get used to asking, "How much will that cost?" The Health Research Group urges that in comparing doctors you phone their offices and ask the costs of an initial office visit (which may include a complete physical examination), routine office visits, and, if appropriate, whether the doctor accepts Medicare or Medicaid.

While specialists generally charge more than GPs, there is no clear correlation between how much a doctor charges and his competence. (Many patients believe otherwise. Often a doctor raises his fees to cut his practice and finds he's getting more patients than ever.) Thus if two physicians appear to be equally satisfactory in other respects, there's no reason you shouldn't go to the one whose fees are lower.

Expect to pay the "going rate." This is the approximate fee charged within a community by most doctors of comparable training. Health insurance plans, medical societies, and courts use the going rate as their guide to reasonable charges. Within a community, however, medical fees can vary greatly. *Money* magazine found that in one city some pediatricians charged four times as much as others for a routine office visit, some GPs two and a half times as much as others for a house call.

Worrying over how much a condition will cost you can be almost as stressful as the disease itself, so clear up any questions beforehand. Find out what the fee includes, and what other costs you should expect. In addition to your physician's charges you're also responsible for any lab fees, diagnostic tests like X rays or electrocardiograms, fees charged by other doctors, and all hospital charges and drugs.

Health insurance can absorb much of the shock. If your insurance fails to cover the full fee, you're responsible for the balance.

Tell your doctor if you can't afford a service.

If nothing else you'll be able to work out an easy-payment plan. The Principles of Medical Ethics holds that a doctor's fee "should be commensurate with . . . the patient's ability to pay," and in genuine hardship the typical doctor will consider giving a reduction. He may be able to arrange for you to get the service free or at greatly reduced cost as a clinic patient.

Challenging the bill. What if you don't agree with a doctor's bill? Take it up with him right away and ask for an itemizing. Often the problem is not that the doctor's fee is too high but that it's not adequately explained—it may include lab fees, injections, other services you're not aware of.

Suppose after discussion the bill still seems high. Find out the going rate. Ask a doctor, nurse, lawyer, or someone connected with hospitals or insurance. From their contacts they can determine fairly quickly if your bill's out of line.

If the problem's with a bill from a specialist you were referred to by your regular doctor, ask your physician to run interference. Many family physicians will do that as part of their feeling of responsibility for a patient. A doctor, especially a referring physician, has a lot more clout with a colleague than a layman is likely to have.

Offer a settlement you've been told is fair. One way to do this is to send a check with a note on the back, "Full payment for services rendered through [date of your last visit]." If the doctor cashes your check, he's not likely to pursue the matter further, though you probably won't be able to go back to him.

If the doctor turns down your settlement, don't send a check for the full amount with the hope of getting restitution later. Most courts deem paying a bill an admission on your part that the charge was proper.

Instead take the matter to the county medical society's grievance (ethics) committee. Keep the summary of your complaint brief and free of rancor. Enclose copies of all related correspondence. In about half of all cases, if only for good public relations, grievance committees recommend a fee reduction.

The committee's recommendation has no force in law, but it's a rare physician who refuses to go along with it. If an offending physician persists and takes you to court, you have a powerful case if you point to a committee's finding in your favor. If the committee rules against you, your position in court is much weaker, and if the doctor employs a collection agency, you may get a black mark on your credit rating.

On the other hand you may win a suit over a fee if you can get other doctors to testify that the

PHONE YOUR DOCTOR AFTER HOURS IF . . .

No responsible physician objects to being phoned outside regular office hours if a delay may cause you harm. But in fairness, why disturb him at home for a minor condition that can wait? An AMA-convened panel of family physicians offers these dos and don'ts about phoning after hours:

For adults: DO call for any possible danger signal like:

Serious injuries such as animal bites, falls with possible head or spinal injuries, puncture wounds, wounds with heavy bleeding, possible fractures, severe burns, possible poisoning.

Sudden, severe abdominal pain or cramps.

Impairment of any vital function—marked by a noticeable rise or fall in pulse rate; or a drop in blood pressure, leading to faintness; or difficulty in breathing.

Unconsciousness, however brief.

Sudden worsening or inexplicable persistence of a symptom: fever accompanied by pain or joint swelling, or shooting up over 102° F; an itch that becomes unbearable; a headache that fails to respond to aspirin.

Any unexplained discharge of blood or another substance from a body opening.

Any sudden neurological symptom: Impairment of vision or hearing, mental confusion, convulsion, amnesia, numbness, paralysis.

Continual or severe diarrhea or vomiting.

Sudden, severe chest pain.

For children: DO call for all symptoms as for adults, plus:

Any unexplained drowsiness, if accompanied by difficult breathing and difficulty in arousing the child from a nap.

Any stomachache.

Any earache.

Any slight fever (over 100.5° F) in an infant under three months.

Any projectile vomiting (throwing up with great force).

Any diarrhea *or* vomiting in an infant; any diarrhea *and* vomiting in an older child.

Any two of these symptoms: Fever, rash, bad cough, stiff neck; swollen lymph nodes in the neck, armpits, groin; markedly decreased appetite; generally acting sick.

Before picking up the phone: DO make these preparations:

Be ready to report exactly where the pain is and how it feels; the temperature if there's a fever; anything that can account for the condition—an injury, exposure to infection, etc. If the doctor's out, leave a precise message with this information.

Search your medicine cabinet for any drugs prescribed for similar conditions in your family. Keep them near the phone so you can describe them to the doctor, possibly saving a trip to the drugstore.

Have a pad and pencil handy. Jot down any questions you have. Take down his instructions.

If a child can talk, let him take the phone and describe his own symptoms and answer the doctor's questions.

In a nonemergency such as the following DON'T call but wait for regular office hours:

Clearly minor ills, such as colds, however uncomfortable.

Rashes or low fever (under 102° F for adults and children above three months) if unaccompanied by other symptoms.

One or two episodes of diarrhea (for adults and older children) if not accompanied by severe abdominal pain.

Questions about shots, physical examination results, insurance forms, and the like.

charge was outrageous. A Louisiana physician billed a business executive $1,939 for care after a heart attack. Testimony by doctors got the fee trimmed to a third of that amount.

You'll need another doctor's opinion if you suspect you've been overtreated. The deliberate performing of unnecessary services to justify a higher bill is harder to prove than plain fee gouging. Fees generally fall within a fairly narrow range. But in matters of medical judgment doctors enjoy extremely wide latitude.

It is relatively easy to show that a fee gouger charged about twice the going rate for an injection. It is far tougher to prove that an overtreater gave twice the number of injections actually called for.

When it's malpractice. If you suspect malpractice, hold off before signing any release offered you by a doctor, hospital, or insurance company. First speak to a lawyer experienced as a plaintiff's attorney in this specialized branch of law. Ask for a referral to such a specialist from your family lawyer, the local bar association, or the Association of Trial Lawyers of America (1050 31st Street, NW, Washington, D.C. 20007). If you've suffered substantial damages, consider attorneys outside your community—for a big case major malpractice lawyers travel all over the country.

Don't be surprised if lawyers advise you *not* to sue. Medical malpractice is extremely difficult to prove. The law is generally weighted in favor of the physician. You may need to get a local doctor to testify against the defendant, a virtual impossibility in many communities.

In only about one out of three cases does the patient collect—and the patient's lawyer gets perhaps a third to a half. If you lose, you may be well into the red after paying witness fees, court costs, out-of-pocket expenses.

Listen to your lawyer if he questions your motives for suing. Patients often become angered enough to claim malpractice if they feel a doctor is overzealous in trying to collect his fee. In many cases the patient resents a lack of tact, warmth, or interest on the part of the doctor—and retaliates by filing a suit.

You may, however, have a case if your rights as a patient are violated. Here are the principal grounds for suit and what you need to prove:

Negligence. The doctor failed to meet the lowest acceptable standard of skill and learning common to physicians in his community.

In question is only the physician's level of performance, as compared with that of other local doctors. Bad results alone in no way prove a doctor negligent, since things can happen in the course of treatment for which he is not to blame.

Assault. You were treated without your informed consent. Not only must you give your permission, you must be informed of the possible risks. Justice Benjamin Cardozo stated the guiding principle: "Every human being of adult years and sound mind has a right to determine what shall be done with his body."

An exception to this general rule is an emergency in which you're in no mental or physical condition to give consent. Similarly, courts have waived the consent requirement if it would endanger the life of a minor or other person incapable of speaking for himself, or would jeopardize the health of the community.

Abandonment. A physician treating you for a specific condition left you in the lurch. You didn't dismiss him. Nor did he formally withdraw, giving you time to find another doctor. "After a physician has accepted employment in a case," ruled the Virginia Supreme Court of Appeals, "it is his duty to continue his services as long as they are necessary."

Legally a physician has no obligation to accept a patient. As long as no doctor-patient relationship exists, he can refuse to treat a critically ill person even if he is the only doctor available and doing nothing else at the time. Ethically, however, he violates a principle that says in an emergency a physician "should render service to the best of his ability."

Some doctors are reluctant to be good Samaritans, fearing they'll expose themselves to a charge of abandonment or negligence. But emergency treatment does not establish a doctor-patient relationship and is not expected to meet the caliber of care rendered in a physician's office or hospital. The AMA Law Department scoured court records and couldn't find a single good Samaritan suit, concluding: "In a roadside emergency or any similar case there'd be absolutely no special risk for the doctor."

See also HEALTH INSURANCE; HOSPITAL; PHYSICAL EXAMINATION; QUACKERY; SURGERY; X RAYS.

PILES   See HEMORRHOIDS.

PILL, THE   See BIRTH CONTROL.

PINK EYE (conjunctivitis) is an inflammation of the conjunctiva, the delicate covering of the eyeball and lining of the lids. The bright pink inflammation usually covers the entire white of the eye and often the lining of the lids. One or both eyes may be inflamed. It can occur at any age, and appears most often in the fall and spring.

Causes include infections by bacteria and viruses, allergy, and irritants.

There is no actual pain associated with conjunctivitis, although sunlight, bright lights, or TV may hurt the eyes. The discomfort is a scratchy, itchy, stinging sensation of the lids. A discharge of pus may cause the lids to stick together upon awakening. There is no true impairment of vision, simply a temporary blurring from the discharge.

If you have red, sore eyes, see a physician. Treatment is usually antibiotic ointment or drops applied to the eyes or lids. If you experience pain in your eyes or head, and have difficulty in seeing, you may have a more serious eye disorder than conjunctivitis.

Cold or warm compresses on the eyes will relieve some of the irritation. Warm water can help remove the dried pus and crusty discharge.

Pink eye can be highly contagious, sometimes epidemic. A basic preventive is separate towels for every resident in a household.

See also EYE DISORDER.

PINWORMS (seatworms, oxyuriasis, enterobiasis), unlike most intestinal parasites, do not chiefly infect the rural and the poor—they are found even in the seats of the mighty.

An estimated 18 million Americans have this infectious disease. Pinworms are tiny, delicate, white worms, the largest of them less than half an inch long. Infestation occurs when the microscopic eggs are swallowed and hatch in the small intestine. The young worms then migrate to the large intestine where they attach their heads to the mucous lining, usually in the appendix or nearby.

In about two months the mature worms emerge, usually at night, at the anus. The females lay eggs by the thousands in the moist folds of skin around the rectal opening.

The most common symptom of pinworm infestation is an itch around the anus. A pinworm sufferer, especially a child, frequently reinfects himself. He scratches and gets the sticky eggs on his hands; later he puts his hand to his mouth, or transfers the eggs from his hand to food.

If the anal itching is prolonged, it can lead to sleeplessness and nervousness—a source of the old notion that fidgety children have worms. Infected children sometimes have dark circles under their eyes and are pale, in part from lack of sleep. Restlessness, loss of appetite, loss of weight, and sometimes nausea and vomiting occur. Infected children are apt to be irritable, hard to manage, and inattentive at school.

In women and girls migrating worms may enter the vulva and vagina, frequently causing vaginal irritation and discharge. After a bowel movement it is wise to wipe away from the vaginal opening, to lessen the chance of infection. Occasionally pinworms cause intestinal inflammation with symptoms much like appendicitis.

When one member of a household gets pinworms, the others are likely to get infested as well. The eggs may contaminate toilets, nightclothes, bedding, underwear. They may be carried on air currents and inhaled or swallowed. They can infest pets, especially dogs, which may then infect their owners. Students in classrooms, residents of a dormitory or institution, coworkers may infect each other.

Sometimes you can see worms on a freshly passed stool or in bed. Giving a shallow enema may bring out worms. Worms may be sighted at night if you separate the sufferer's buttocks and shine a light on the anus.

If you can't find worms by these methods, visit a physician or public-health laboratory. In preparation wrap about 2 inches of cellulose tape, sticky side out, around a flat surface like an ice-cream stick, tongue depressor, or the blade of a blunt knife (see illustration). First thing in the morning, press this swab firmly on the anal region. Any pinworm eggs will adhere to it and show up under a microscope. Since the worms deposit eggs erratically, it may be necessary to make a swab on four or five consecutive days before pinworms can be ruled out.

Treating pinworms. Every member of a household should be treated. Even those showing no symptoms may be infested and thus a possible source of reinfection. Treatment needs to be in the hands of a physician, who may prescribe pyrantel pamoate (Antiminth), pyrvinium pamoate (Povan), or piperazine citrate (Antepar), the standard medications prescribed for pinworms.

Don't be surprised if pyrvinium pamoate turns your bowel movements bright red. Avoid patent medicines; they are less effective and possibly more dangerous.

Use 5 percent ammoniated mercury ointment around the anal area each night at bedtime for two weeks. This furthers destruction of the eggs. Cut short the fingernails of small children who may do much rectal scratching and have them sleep in tight-fitting pajamas.

Pay close attention to personal hygiene. When under treatment for pinworms make a point of showering or bathing daily and scrubbing your anal region.

Dryness and heat tend to kill the eggs. Every morning the underwear, nightclothes, and towels of a family in treatment should be run

IF YOU SUSPECT PINWORMS

Sample rectal area for eggs
Collect specimens 4–5 mornings
Wrap tape sticky side out
(Use ice-cream stick,
cardboard strip, etc.)

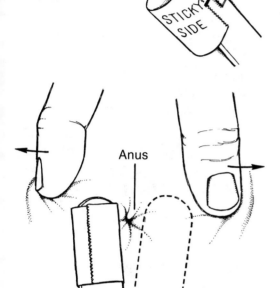

Anus

Press around anus
immediately on awakening

Keep specimens in jar
Take to your doctor

through an electric dryer, boiled, or at least heated to 150° F for several minutes. Dust the house thoroughly. Vacuum rugs and furniture. If a house is kept vacant for about five days, any pinworm eggs in it will ordinarily die.

As general preventives keep fingers and any potentially infected objects out of your mouth. Wash your hands frequently with running warm water, especially after the toilet and before handling food. Keep your fingernails trimmed and clean.

For other parasitic worms common in the United States, see HOOKWORMS; ROUNDWORMS; TAPEWORMS; TRICHINOSIS. For parasites that may be acquired elsewhere, see MALARIA; SCHISTOSOMIASIS.

See also INFECTIOUS DISEASE; TRAVEL HEALTH.

PKU (phenylketonuria) is a hereditary metabolic disorder. It usually causes mental retardation if it is not detected and treated soon after birth.

Most states have laws which require screening newborn infants for PKU before they leave the hospital. A few drops of blood are taken from the baby's heel and analyzed.

The PKU screening test is usually done about the third day after birth. If you leave the hospital before your baby is three days old, don't neglect to bring him back in a few days for PKU testing.

Babies who are found to have PKU must be put on a diet that contains little phenylalanine, an amino acid found in all natural protein foods, since PKU babies lack an enzyme needed to convert it into a form the body can use. Without the special diet phenylalanine and its byproducts accumulate in the body, causing damage to the brain.

Babies with PKU tend to have blue eyes, blond hair, and fair skin. They appear normal at birth and have normal intelligence, but phenylalanine buildup can cause brain damage by three months. Once brain damage has occurred, it cannot be reversed.

Hospital screening tests for PKU are often positive for infants who don't actually have the disorder and are occasionally negative for infants who do have it. Therefore positive test results always require definitive testing. Many authorities also recommend that negative results be confirmed by retesting a few weeks after birth. Definitive testing and any needed treatment call for the services of a pediatric center that specializes in PKU.

Physicians and nutritionists can fashion a diet that restricts foods with phenylalanine while providing enough protein and other nutrition for normal growth. The diet therapy may have to be continued for many years, with periodic tests to keep a check on the child's condition.

PKU runs in families. So if one of your children has PKU, have other children checked for the disorder.

Women who were successfully treated for PKU as children are now beginning to bear children of their own. These babies are at very high risk for congenital brain damage and malformations unless their mothers resume a medically supervised low-phenylalanine diet very early in pregnancy, preferably even before becoming pregnant.

See also BIRTH DEFECTS.

PLAGUE (Black Death) A 32-year-old hunting guide was admitted to a hospital in rural Idaho with a fever of 106° F and swellings and gangrenous ulcerations of the lymphatic glands in the groin and under the skin. These "buboes" alerted doctors to an infectious disease usually associated with medieval Europe but also found in present-day America: bubonic plague. The man died three days later.

Bubonic plague is usually transmitted by fleas from infected animals. Rats can be carriers, but chipmunks, squirrels, prairie dogs, and other wild animals can be infected as well. Public-health officials believe the Idaho hunting guide might have contracted the disease from fleas on a rabbit he skinned during the two- to six-day incubation period.

Pneumonic plague (or primary plague pneumonia) results from inhaling plague bacteria, usually coughed up by plague victims. Its onset is explosive—marked by high fever, rapid breathing and heartbeat, and extreme restlessness. Antibiotics are often successful in treating bubonic plague. Pneumonic plague needs to be treated within the first 10 to 15 hours of fever or is almost invariably fatal—it played a large part in the Black Death of some 5 million people in fourteenth-century Europe.

While human plague in the United States is extremely rare—only about a dozen cases a year are reported—a danger persists because the disease is harbored in the wild rodent population of the western third of the country: Arizona, California, Colorado, Idaho, New Mexico, Oregon, Utah, Washington. Public-health officials fear that as cities expand into the countryside, plague-carrying fleas may be passed from wild to urban rodents, causing an epidemic. In Denver one or more wild squirrels evidently infected the local squirrel population, prompting an all-out effort to dust city squirrels with insecticide that would destroy their fleas. It is also possible for domestic rats to become infected by rats off a ship from a plague-ridden area like Vietnam.

Get vaccinated if you face special risks. The Public Health Service recommends immunization for everyone going to Vietnam, Cambodia, and Laos, and for people whose work would bring them into contact with wild rodents in plague-infested areas of the western United States, South America, Africa, or Asia.

The PHS does *not* recommend routine vaccination for people simply living in plague areas like the American West, or for travelers merely going to most countries where plague exists. Except in Indochina you'd need unusual exposure to wild rodents to warrant vaccination. While the vaccine reduces your chances of getting the disease, and its severity if you get it, its total effectiveness is open to question.

The vaccination series consists of three injections. The first two are given a month apart; the third, 4 to 12 weeks after the second. If you are short of time, you can get satisfactory but less than optimal protection with but two injections 3 weeks apart. If you remain in a plague area, get boosters every 6 to 12 months.

See also INFECTIOUS DISEASE.

PLAQUE control is the surest way to avoid tooth decay, periodontal disease, gingivitis, and mouth

THE BEST WAY TO CLEAN YOUR TEETH

Your goal: remove red stain
1. Color teeth red
Tablet or liquid shows plaque

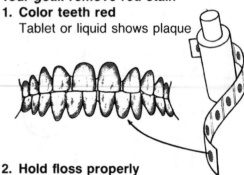

2. Hold floss properly
Wrap 30 inches around middle fingers

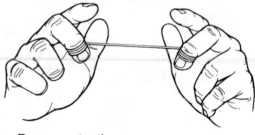

For upper teeth

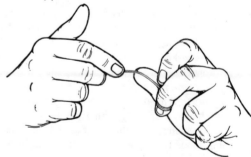

For lower teeth

odor. This technique, a landmark in preventive dentistry, is the most effective way of defeating the major cause of most teeth and mouth disorders.

Plaque (pronounced plack) is a sticky, colorless film of bacteria constantly being formed in the mouth. It adheres to tooth surfaces and gum

---

3. Scrape floss between teeth

Work floss up and down, back and forth

Work below gum line

4. Use toothbrush
See TOOTHBRUSHING entry
Don't use toothpaste now

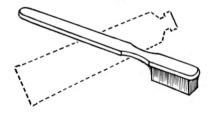

5. Irrigate mouth
Or rinse vigorously

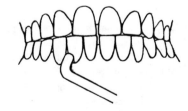

6. Again color teeth red

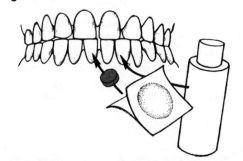

crevices. If you don't remove plaque, the bacteria it harbors thrive in its sugary environment—and give off acids that cause cavities.

Furthermore calcium salts in your saliva turn plaque into tartar (calculus), a hard, razor-sharp crust that clings to the tooth above and below the gum line. This irritating buildup, combined with mouth bacteria, leads to most gum diseases.

Toothbrushing alone won't remove all plaque. The film collects between teeth, in deep tooth fissures, on other surfaces your toothbrush can't reach.

Thus the program called plaque control. The entire combination of methods will take you perhaps five minutes once a day. Some people can get by doing it only every other day, providing they brush their teeth daily. Here's what you need to do (see illustrations):

1. Swish a disclosing chemical around in your mouth. The tablet or liquid contains food coloring that stains invisible plaque a vivid red. Your goal is complete removal of all the red markings.

2. Work dental floss around each tooth. Pull a taut inch or so of floss between two teeth and slightly under the gum line. Then move it up and down from the gum so it scrapes the side surface of each tooth. You can clean these areas only by using floss or similar products like dental tape.

3. Brush your teeth. With a soft nylon brush remove red stain on the inside, outside, and chewing surfaces, which floss doesn't cleanse

---

7. Remove remaining red areas
Use tissue or brush

8. Toothbrush again
This time with fluoride toothpaste

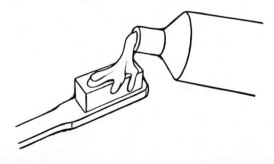

well. Don't use toothpaste, which would make the stained plaque difficult to see.

4. Rinse your mouth. To remove all dislodged bacterial masses and food particles, swirl water vigorously around in your mouth. Better yet use a dental irrigator (Water Pik), shooting a stream or pulse of water between your teeth and under your gum line. Keep the spray gentle, since it can damage gums and impact them with debris.

In some forms of heart disease don't use a dental irrigator without consulting your physician. The jet of water could force bacteria from your gums into your bloodstream, where they might lodge and multiply on a defective heart valve, with dangerous—potentially fatal—effects. Heart conditions in this category include chronic rheumatic heart disease, congenital heart defects, calcific aortic stenosis, and many cases involving open-heart surgery.

5. Double-check. Use the disclosing compound a second time. When red still appears, use floss, your toothbrush, or tissue to wipe it away. Then brush again—this time with a toothpaste containing fluoride.

Despite the effectiveness of plaque control— and its enthusiastic endorsement by the American Dental Association and the American Society for Preventive Dentistry—it is not widely practiced. Many dentists are not spreading the word. Even when patients are told of it, they are often reluctant to change their toothbrushing habits.

Ask your dentist for instruction in plaque control. It's a good motivator, especially since on your own it's difficult to learn how to use the tools properly. There are devices and methods for people with special problems—for example, a nylon yarn is an aid for a person with wide spaces between his teeth.

See also TEETH AND MOUTH DISORDERS; PERIODONTAL DISEASE; TOOTHBRUSHING.

PLASTER CASTS are applied to many types of fractures to render the broken bones immobile and keep them set in place. Most casts are worn for several weeks and require special care.

If you are wearing a cast, to reduce swelling most physicians recommend that you keep your broken arm or leg elevated as much as possible for the first 24 hours. Take care not to lean or press on an arm cast for at least two days. Don't walk on a leg cast for at least two days.

Your doctor may recommend placing cracked ice over a particular spot to reduce swelling. Make cold compresses of an ice bag or a plastic bag wrapped with a towel.

General recommendations when you wear a cast:

Keep your cast dry at all times. A wet cast will weaken and break. When you bathe, cover your cast with a plastic bag (like a garbage bag) secured and made waterproof with tape or rubber bands. Or purchase a reusable waterproof covering from a medical-supply store.

If you itch in the cast, try cooling the cast with an ice bag. Also you may get relief by rubbing a battery-powered vibrator on the cast.

If the itching becomes unbearable, call the doctor. Don't insert sharp objects into the cast to scratch yourself. And warn children not to shove articles under a cast. A pencil, bottle top, or marble can lodge under the cast and cause a pressure sore and infection.

You can use a vacuum cleaner to suction out food crumbs or other debris that collects under the cast, causing itching and irritation. Use your cleaner's long, narrow "crevice" attachment. To soothe irritated skin under the cast, switch to the blow cycle.

If the cast's rough edges catch on clothing, cut the foot off a nylon stocking, slide the stocking over the cast, and tuck it in around the edges.

If you'll be exposed to very hot or very cold temperatures, get special instructions from your doctor. Extreme temperatures can injure the skin inside the cast.

Call your doctor if you experience severe pain; rubbing or pinching; seepage of fluid from the cast; breaks, cracks, or softness in the cast; looseness or slipping of the cast. Other signs of trouble with your cast include unusual swelling, coldness, numbness, tingling, or bluish or purplish discoloration of your fingers or toes.

See also FRACTURES.

PLASTIC SURGERY   See EAR DEFORMITIES; NOSE DEFORMITIES; WRINKLES.

PLEURISY is an inflammation of the pleura, a two-layer membrane that lines the chest cavity. This wrapping fits closely around the lung, with only a thin lubricating layer of fluid between the two layers. Ordinarily, with the help of the fluid, the smooth linings serve to allow the lung free movement within the chest for normal breathing. In pleurisy this movement is restricted.

A primary pleurisy arises in the pleural tissues from a germ that attacks them directly, or from an injury or growth. A secondary pleurisy is an effect of some other respiratory disease—for instance, pneumonia, in which the germs reach the pleura as well as the lungs themselves. Or tuberculosis. Or lung cancer. The symptoms and course of primary and secondary pleurisy may be exactly the same, with only the cause different.

Dry pleurisy is an inflammation that has not formed fluid. It can be extremely painful, especially when the swollen outer layer is stretched on breathing. A grating sensation may be felt when the two layers, both perhaps stiffened and swollen, rub against each other.

The inflammation of dry pleurisy may subside and the pain go away, even though the grating of the roughened tissues may still be felt. Or it may turn into wet pleurisy, with the accumulation of fluid. The fluid may be absorbed and become a dry pleurisy again.

When dry pleurisy heals, it may leave adhesions—strands of tissue strung between the lung and the wall of the chest. Sometimes these adhesions are so extensive that they limit the movement of the lungs. But usually the soreness disappears and the adhesions stretch so much that they no longer cause any difficulty.

Wet pleurisy (pleural effusion) is marked by excess fluid that intrudes into the space between the pleural linings. The fluid may arise from an outpouring of blood and lymph or from a chest injury with bleeding.

In wet pleurisy the fluid in the pleural cavity may restrict the movement of the lungs and therefore the ability to breathe. If the fluid becomes infected, it turns into pus and may lead to a serious condition called empyema. The pus sometimes breaks through the lung wall and into the air passages, where it may be coughed up. Removal of the pus by drainage is usually needed for the empyema patient to recover.

When pleurisy is painful, you feel each movement of your chest wall. Each breath induces a stabbing, knifelike pain. With a deep breath or a cough or sneeze the pain is severe. This may go on night and day.

Other symptoms of the infection causing pleurisy may be dry coughing, weakness, headache, and loss of appetite. There may be chills, fever, and rapid pulse beat.

To relieve the pain of pleurisy, limiting the movement of the lungs may be desirable so as to reduce the stretching of the sore tissues. The doctor may suggest that you lie on the sore side on a firm surface to limit breathing movement on that side. In wet pleurisy the doctor may remove the fluid by drawing it out with a needle. See also RESPIRATORY DISEASE.

PNEUMONIA has recently begun to appear with increasing frequency. As late as 1936 it was the number one cause of death in the United States.

Then sulfa drugs and penicillin brought it under control. But today there is a resurgence of this often deadly respiratory disease.

Bacteria that resist antibiotics are one important factor. Also there are greater numbers of elderly people, who are the prime victims of pneumonia. And an increase in air pollution causes lung damage that can predispose people to pneumonia.

Pneumonia isn't a single infectious disease, but some 30 different acute lung infections. In all forms the spongy, air-filled tissues of the lungs become infected. Inhaled oxygen can no longer diffuse properly into the bloodstream.

Many types of pneumonia are caused by bacteria.

Pneumococcal pneumonia is the most common type of bacterial pneumonia. It is caused by pneumococcus bacteria that are often found living in your nose or throat. They may move into your lungs when your body's resistance to infection is low, or when you have a cold impairing your lungs' defenses. Each year there are some 500,000 cases of pneumococcal pneumonia alone, with a 5 to 10 percent fatality rate.

A pneumococcal pneumonia infection usually settles in one lung. Once the infection is established, a whole section of the lung can quickly become filled with so much mucus and pus that air can no longer move in and out of the infected area. These bacteria also produce debilitating toxins that contribute greatly to the severity of the illness. Pleurisy is a common complication.

First symptoms usually include sudden chills and a temperature spiking to 103° F to 106° F. There may be an increasing sense of tightness in the chest, shortness of breath, dry coughing that soon becomes extremely painful. The victim often becomes delirious from the fever and toxicity of the illness.

The face and lips often seem bluish. Breathing is rapid. The victim tends to lie on the affected side to reduce the pain. There are often fever sores on the lips.

The infection can progress so swiftly that an apparently normal person may become mortally ill within a matter of hours. He soon begins coughing up sticky mucus mixed with pus and a rusty-colored spit from the infected lung. If the condition goes untreated, the fever and chills may continue for as much as two weeks while the victim becomes increasingly weak and short of breath.

Those who survive typically go through a crisis. The temperature drops sharply in the midst of drenching perspiration, and great quantities of infectious debris are coughed up from the diseased lung. A long period of convalescence is required before healing is complete. In some cases lung tissue is so scarred that the victim remains highly vulnerable to infections for many years.

Get medical help as soon as possible. Chances of survival are greatest if treatment is begun within five days. The sulfa drugs and penicillin are usually effective in fighting the bacteria causing the disease. But in recent years more and more antibiotic-resistant strains of these organisms have begun to appear. Those who die of pneumococcal pneumonia are usually babies and elderly people.

Pneumonia in general poses its greatest threat as a secondary infection, moving in on the heels of virus infections such as measles or influenza, or complicating less dangerous bacterial infections such as sore throat or bronchitis.

A vaccine against pneumococcal pneumonia is now available. Vaccination is recommended for people at high risk for pneumococcal pneumonia: those who have impaired spleen function, cirrhosis, or kidney disease; "brittle" diabetics; those with cardiopulmonary disease or emphysema; people with sickle cell anemia; people over age 65. The vaccine is also recommended for people whose immune systems are impaired by drugs or disease.

After vaccination a moderately painful reaction at the injection site occurs in one of three patients. Slight fever is also common. The vaccine is thought to confer immunity for at least five years. Vaccination is not recommended for children under two.

Other forms of pneumonia have similar symptoms, but usually are slower and less deadly.

Bronchial pneumonia (or bronchopneumonia) infects small patches of lung tissue throughout both lungs, rather than settling in one lobe. It often develops after an attack of bronchitis but has a wide range of possible causes—fungi, animal parasites, bacteria, rickettsiae, viruses, inhaled irritants, chemical or physical injury, even a blow on the chest.

Legionnaire's disease is a type of pneumonia, so called because it occurred at an American Legion convention in Philadelphia in the summer of 1976, attacking 182 people. This type of pneumonia does not seem to be transmissible from person to person. Instead the bacteria collect in the water of air-conditioning systems, cooling towers, even shower heads. The infection spreads when people inhale bacteria in the form of fine mists and water droplets in the air. Legionnaire's disease is treatable with the antibiotic erythromycin.

Viral pneumonia is impervious to antibiotic treatment. It is usually slow in onset, with early symptoms resembling those of colds, and rarely is fatal. Usual treatment is plenty of bed rest, aspirin, and medication for coughs.

The Food and Drug Administration (FDA) has approved the use of amantadine HCl in the treatment of viral pneumonia caused by Type A influenza. If given within 48 hours of the onset of symptoms, it reduces the severity of the disease. The drug may also be used as a preventive in highly susceptible people.

Chemical pneumonia is pneumonia that can arise from inhaling irritating gas fumes. The danger is greater than generally realized, and many products are potentially harmful if inhaled. The FDA seized containers of graphite-penetrating oil because its labels did not carry warnings that it could cause chemical pneumonia (particularly in children) if its fumes were inhaled.

Oil (or lipid) pneumonia can be similarly caused by inhaling oily products. Medicated rubs (such as Vicks Vaporub) can cause lipid pneumonia if accidentally taken into the lungs. Drinking furniture polish, a frequent cause of accidental poisoning of children, can lead to lipid pneumonia.

Aspiration pneumonia can arise from inhaling material from the stomach into the lungs while vomiting. This is a frequent problem for people unconscious from alcohol or narcotics. Aspiration pneumonia is also a hazard to surgical patients under general anesthesia.

Stasis pneumonia can result from remaining in bed for too long during an illness.

Don't rush recovery from pneumonia. It is not unusual for pneumonia that has been aborted by antibiotics to be only partially healed. When the patient begins to feel better, he may stop his medications and start moving about. The term *walking pneumonia* is applied to people who don't feel sufficiently sick to be in bed. But they risk possible damage to lung tissue if the pneumonia is not treated and if they do not get sufficient rest.

See also RESPIRATORY DISEASE.

POISONING   Speed is essential. If someone has been poisoned, it's important to act before the body has time to absorb the poison:

1. Immediately call a physician, hospital emergency room, or poison control center (your telephone operator can connect you with the nearest one). If possible one person

should begin treatment while another phones.

2. Begin ARTIFICIAL RESPIRATION (which see) if the victim has difficulty breathing. Keep him warm.

3. Give milk or water (unless he is unconscious or in convulsions). Give one glass (8 ounces) for children under five, and two glasses for anyone older. This dilutes the poison and helps the victim vomit without overloading his stomach.

4. If you can't get immediate medical advice, make him vomit—except in the following circumstances:

If he has burns around the mouth or is known to have swallowed a corrosive such as toilet-bowl cleaner, lye, acids, iodine, washing soda, ammonia water, household bleach—vomiting would aggravate burns in the throat and mouth.

If the poison is a convulsant (such as strychnine in mouse pellets)—vomiting may cause convulsions.

If he has swallowed petroleum products such as kerosene, gasoline, furniture polish, cleaning fluids, lighter fluid, and many automotive compounds—petroleum seeping into the lungs can cause pneumonia. Any vomiting needs to be under medical supervision.

If he is unconscious or in convulsions—vomiting could make him choke to death.

To induce vomiting: Give 2 tablespoons (1 ounce) of syrup of ipecac—1 tablespoon (1/2 ounce) for a child. If there's no vomiting within 20 to 30 minutes, repeat the dose. If you have no ipecac on hand, after giving the victim water or milk, tickle the back of his throat. Use the end of a napkin or a handkerchief-padded spoon instead of your finger—a child may bite down.

Never use fluid extract of ipecac, a hazardous concentrate that's 14 times stronger than the syrup. Never use saltwater, mustard, or bicarbonate of soda—home remedies that are dangerous or ineffective.

When retching and vomiting begin, place the victim facedown with his head lower than his hips to prevent vomitus from entering his lungs.

5. Administer activated charcoal in water in a dose at least 10 times the estimated amount of poison ingested. Give the charcoal about 30 minutes *after* the ipecac syrup; otherwise the charcoal will be vomited up.

Don't use charcoal with corrosives. It's also ineffective with cyanide, ethyl or methyl alcohol, mineral acids, and iron salts.

For a child mix about 1/2 cup of charcoal with 1 2/3 cups of water. An adult usually requires 1 cup of charcoal in the same amount of water.

The mixture looks like black mud and tastes gritty. If possible give it to a child in a dark container with a wide-bore straw to bypass the tastebuds. If the child won't drink the mixture, add a small amount of ice cream, sherbet, jam, jelly, or fruit syrup. Alternatively mix a *full cup* of activated charcoal with 1 2/3 cups of vanilla ice cream.

6. Don't try to neutralize a poison. By giving, say, vinegar to neutralize an alkali, you can cause further burns from the chemical reaction.

Forget the supposed universal antidote of burned toast, milk of magnesia, and weak tea. It's ineffective. There is no such thing as a universal antidote.

7. Save and give to the physician or hospital the poison container with its intact label and any remaining contents. If the poison is unknown, bring along the vomitus for examination. The nature of the poison may determine the treatment.

8. Do not follow instructions on the product label for specific antidote treatment. These instructions may be outdated or incorrect. Specific antidotes should be administered only on the advice of your physician or the poison control center.

Suspect poisoning if you detect any of the following:

Odor of poison on the victim's breath.

Unusual stains on his skin or clothing.

Discoloration of his lips and mouth.

Actions that make you think he has pain in his mouth or throat.

Unconsciousness, confusion, severe nausea and vomiting, or stomach pains when access to poison is possible.

Open bottles or packages of drugs or poisonous chemicals in the presence of children.

Evidence in mouth of eating wild berries or leaves (see POISONOUS PLANTS).

Hide toxic substances. Chances are you have at least 40 toxic substances in your home. There are more than 250,000 available. Many are not generally recognized as poisons. Others are stored where children have easy access to them.

As a result 500,000 children a year swallow poisons. As many as 400 deaths occur in a year to children under 5, while more than 40,000 children of this age are hospitalized. Youngsters in this age group are particularly susceptible to poisoning accidents because they learn by exploring their environment. What they see, they try to reach—and what they reach, they often put into their mouths.

Aspirin is the most commonly ingested agent in poisoning accidents. Next come detergents, iron tablets, and pesticides. Disinfectants are major hazards. Then come tranquilizers, furniture polishes and stains, and lighter fluids, especially charcoal lighter. Amphetamines used for weight reduction and caustics such as drain-cleaning products are also common causes of child poisoning.

Be especially watchful between 4:00 and 6:00 P.M. That's when children get hungry and are likely to poison themselves while hunting for food. Another "arsenic hour" occurs around 11:00 A.M. Sundays, when children forage for breakfast while their parents sleep late. To discourage such foraging keep crackers, fruit, and milk in easy reach so a child can get a snack.

Some children are poison prone. If at least one poisoning has occurred in your family, be on guard. Accidental poisoning is more likely to strike your household again than a family where it's never happened.

To prevent poisoning. Search out hazards in the home, garden, and outbuildings. Destroy those dangers, through child-proof storage, careful use of all medicines and household supplies, and by destroying all hazardous items when no longer needed.

The FDA reports that 95 percent of poisonings to children under five occur while they are under the supervision of parents, baby-sitters, or other responsible people. While the older person's attention is elsewhere, the child gets into a poison.

Since you can't keep your eye on your children every minute, careful storage is critical to safety and should be varied to meet the changes in children. If a child is in the crawling stage, keep household products somewhere other than below the kitchen sink or on floors and lower shelves of unlocked cabinets.

If a child is able to climb, be certain that all hazardous substances are on shelves completely beyond the child's reach or, better yet, locked in a cabinet or closet.

Avoid packaging that makes poisons attractive. Manufacturers of liquid furniture polishes have a practice of masking the normal odor— and the lethal nature—of petroleum-based polishes with fruit-flavored scents and beveragelike appearances.

Children will sample anything, no matter the taste. Hundreds of preschoolers swallow household ammonia products every year. One company marketed ammonia with an appealing storybook figure on the label. The ammonia was scented lemon and pine mint and sold in 1-quart translucent plastic bottles—all of which made the ammonia look like soda pop marketed for kids.

Don't buy hazardous compounds when relatively safe ones will do. Some dishwashing detergents contain extremely caustic soda ash.

Don't buy liquid drain cleaner at all. All but the most stubborn drain blockages will yield to hot water, or a plunger or plumbing snake. The University of Kansas Medical Center treated seven children who had swallowed a small amount of liquid drain cleaner, which is a highly corrosive alkali. Each child sustained such damage to the esophagus that it had to be replaced surgically with a piece of the colon and involved a hospital stay of from six months to a year.

Medicine that can poison. Medicines account for fully half of accidental poisonings. Reduce the hazard as follows:

Lock the medicine cabinet.

Go through your medicine chest and throw out unused portions of prescriptions unless told by your doctor it's safe to keep them. Get rid of any unlabeled preparations. Flush them down the drain and wash out the containers before putting them in the garbage can. Many drugs become toxic if kept too long.

Replace all torn or lost drug labels. Cover labels with transparent tape to keep them legible. Pour liquid medication away from the label side to prevent streaking.

Never give medication of any kind without reading the label carefully. Never give or take medicine in the dark.

Avoid medications that look or taste like candy. Never refer to medicine as candy to get a child to take it, nor make the giving a game. Don't take medicine or give it to another adult in front of a child, who may then mimic the adult.

Keep purses out of reach of children. Dangerous medications and cosmetics are found in purses.

Don't economize by buying large bottles of aspirin or other drugs. Be sure your pharmacist puts all prescription drugs in containers with safety closures that make it difficult for a child to open.

If medicine is to be taken during the night, place only one night's supply on the bedside table. Much drug poisoning takes place when children find medicine that is not in its usual safe place, such as in a bedroom.

Store a child's medications in the refrigerator. He's less likely to play in and around a refrigerator than around a medicine cabinet or a bedside table. Also medicine is more palatable when cold, and when the mother opens the refrigerator at meal-fixing time, she'll be reminded not to miss doses.

Other safety precautions. To avoid poisoning from household products:

Move detergents, ammonia, bleach, and other poisonous substances from under the kitchen sink, where they are easily reached by children, to high shelves, locked if possible.

Don't put poisonous household substances in beverage bottles or other food containers. Keep these substances in their original containers and away from food supplies.

Frequently check areas such as the shed, garage, cellar, attic, laundry room, and back porch, which may become catchalls for dangerous chemical mixtures such as insecticides, fungicides, paints, paint thinners, gasoline, bleaches, rust removers, and spot-removing fluids.

Check the bathroom in your home to be sure that toilet-bowl cleaners, cosmetics, beauty preparations, as well as medications, are out of reach of children.

Use only a safe, nontoxic shoe polish on a toddler's shoes. Many are toxic. To be safe lock away all brands of shoe polish as potential poisons.

Keep cosmetics out of the reach of children. Many contain lethal ingredients. Your dressing table can be as deadly to a toddler as your medicine cabinet.

See also ACCIDENTS; ARTS AND CRAFTS; DRUGS; GAS POISONING; LEAD POISONING; MEDICAL SUPPLIES; PAINT REMOVERS; POISONOUS PLANTS.

POISON IVY and related plants. The sticky sap of poison ivy, poison oak, and poison sumac contains urushiol, an oily, irritating substance. All three plants cause similar allergic skin reactions and require the same treatment.

Reactions don't occur if you merely get near the plants. Urushiol, which is present in all parts of the plant, must make contact with your skin.

The plant is poisonous even after long drying, even if roots and stem are dead. It's particularly irritating in the spring and early summer when full of sap.

Never try to get rid of these plants by burning them. The smoke carries droplets containing urushiol, which can get on the skin or enter the nose, throat, and lungs. Children sometimes eat the berries, which can cause an allergic reaction in the mouth, or in the rectal area as the plant is excreted. Clothing or garden tools that touch the plants, or pets that rub against them, can pick up the sap and pass it to a person.

Don't assume you have natural immunity, since apparent resistance one year may be followed by explosive sensitivity the next. Sensitivity to these plants varies markedly among people, even in different periods of the same person's life. In general, sensitivity is highest in childhood and diminishes with age. Farmers, foresters, and others who spend much time outdoors in areas where these plants are common may acquire a degree of resistance.

Poison ivy, oak, and sumac are limited to North America. A type of primrose is their counterpart in Europe. Similar poisoning is possible from a Japanese plant used in making lacquer. This type of dermatitis sometimes afflicts fishermen who use lacquered gear manufactured in Japan.

The rash may develop within a few hours or up to seven days after contact. The reaction may occur wherever the sap has touched the body. The first symptom is a burning and itching sensation, followed by a rash and swelling and probably by blisters.

If there are large blisters or severe inflammation, or if the inflammation is on your face or genitals, seek the help of a physician. He may prescribe steroids and antihistamines to relieve discomfort and guard against the swelling shut of eyes and urinary tract.

Stubborn cases may be due to repeated contact with contaminated clothing. The rash doesn't spread by itself. Dry-clean or wash any suspected garments. Scrub under your fingernails, a frequent harboring place.

If at any time you realize you have accidentally handled one of these plants or brushed against it, cleanse your skin as soon as possible. A highly sensitive person needs to wash within five minutes, a moderately sensitive person within an hour.

Yellow laundry soap is best. There is no improved value in the more expensive tincture of green soap or other soaps that claim special solvents. Lather several times, and rinse in running water after each sudsing. This should remove or make less irritating any oil that hasn't already penetrated the skin. Change exposed clothes and wash them thoroughly to remove that source of contact.

When there are only a few small blisters on the hands, arms, or legs, they can be treated at home. For relief use methods listed under ITCH-

STEER CLEAR OF THESE PLANTS!

POISON IVY
Shrub, vine, small plant

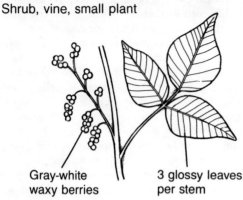

Gray-white waxy berries

3 glossy leaves per stem

EASTERN POISON OAK
A form of poison ivy

WESTERN POISON OAK
Shrub
3 oak-shaped leaves per stem

White berries

POISON SUMAC
Tree 5–6 feet tall
Mainly in swampy areas

Drooping green berries

ING (which see). Don't use oily ointments or alcoholic solutions; they serve to spread the irritation. A host of other agents thought by some to be beneficial—bromine, kerosene, gunpowder, iodine, buttermilk, cream, marshmallows—are actually ineffective.

Efforts for hyposensitization are of possible value only for people with extreme reactions who cannot avoid contact with the plants. Benefits are limited. Frequently severe side effects include rectal itching, rashes, and digestive problems.

Don't eat the fruit or leaves to gain immunity. You can suffer severe internal complications.

Avoid the plants. Staying away from the plants is the best way to avoid a rash. Long sleeves, long pants, and gloves will help guard against exposure in heavily weeded areas. Bar-

rier creams, including recent silicone preparations, have been tested and found not effective.

Poison ivy (see illustrations) grows in the form of climbing vines, shrubs which trail on the ground, and erect shrubbery growing without support. It clings to stone and brick houses, and climbs trees and poles. It grows abundantly along fences, paths, and roadways, and is often partially hidden by other foliage.

The leaves vary in length from 1 to 4 inches. They are green and glossy in summer. In the spring and fall they are red or red-brown. The berries are gray-white and waxy, and resemble mistletoe.

Poison oak closely resembles poison ivy, though it is usually more shrublike, and its leaves are shaped somewhat like oak leaves.

Although poison ivy and poison oak assume

many forms and display seasonal changes in leaf coloring, they have one constant characteristic that makes them easy to recognize: the leaves always grow in clusters of three per stem. The old jingle "Leaflets three, let it be" has helped children and adults to recognize poison ivy or oak at a glance and avoid it.

Poison sumac, a small tree about 5 or 6 feet high, grows primarily in swampy areas. It is distinguished by its drooping green berries. Harmless sumacs have red, erect berry clusters.

To destroy poison ivy and oak the U.S. Department of Agriculture recommends such herbicides as amitrole (considered most effective), silvex, and ammonium sulfamate, which are sold under a variety of brand names. Since these chemicals can damage valuable vegetation, they should be carefully sprayed or even painted on the plant leaves. Grubbing out poison ivy and oak is a good method of eradication. Grubbed-out plants should be buried, not burned or left for an unsuspecting trash collector.

Methods of plant eradication are described in *Farmer's Bulletin No. 1972,* prepared by the U.S. Department of Agriculture and sold by the Superintendent of Documents, United States Government Printing Office, Washington, D.C. 20402.

See also ALLERGY; CONTACT DERMATITIS; POISONOUS PLANTS.

POISONOUS PLANTS   In case of poisoning or suspected poisoning from eating plants, follow the procedure for POISONING (which see).

Induce vomiting immediately. When you phone for help, give the name of the plant involved. If you don't know it, secure a specimen of the plant for identification.

Teach children never to eat any part of a plant without your approval, no matter how pretty a flower or bright a berry.

Weed out the riskiest plants around your house. Store bulbs, which are often poisonous, out of the reach of children. There's no safe test for poisonous plants. Because an animal can eat a plant without harm, it doesn't mean that it is safe for humans.

Recently many adults have been poisoned while searching for foods that grow wild. It is extremely difficult to identify plants from drawings in such guides as *Stalking the Wild Asparagus.* The classic advice, "Don't pick mushrooms unless you're with someone who's picked them before," applies to other wild plants as well. The leaves of the deadly foxglove resemble those of the comfrey plant—and have killed people who picked "comfrey" to make herbal tea.

The dangerous ones. One part of a plant may be edible while another is poisonous. The leaves and all green parts of tomatoes and potatoes are poisonous. Remove the eyes of sprouting potatoes before cooking.

Rhubarb stalks are safe—but the *leaves* contain oxalic acid, and have caused many accidental deaths by destroying the kidneys. The seeds of apples, apricots, cherries, peaches, and plums contain cyanide. In quantity they can cause breathing difficulty, kidney failure, even death.

The time of year also can be critical. In the South the young tender leaves and stems of pokeweed are widely served. They're safe if gathered in the spring and boiled in two waters. By late summer pokeweed berries and mature leaves can be lethal. Since poke juice is always hazardous, the plants should be gathered with gloved hands.

The deadliest plants found commonly in gardens are lantana, foxglove, delphinium, narcissus, castor bean, and oleander. There is no antidote for ricin, the poison found in the mature seed of the castor bean. As little as one can kill a child, four or more an adult.

More than 700 U.S. plants can cause poisoning. Some, like wisteria, may cause mild to severe digestive upset. Others, like the yew, can produce sudden death without symptoms. Biting dieffenbachia embeds crystals of calcium oxalate in the tongue and mouth, causing intense burning, swelling, and irritation.

Here are the commonest plants with poisonous parts:

House plants: Hyacinth, narcissus, daffodil (bulbs); dieffenbachia or dumb cane, elephant ear (all parts); rosary pea, castor bean (seeds), philodendron (stems, leaves).

Garden plants: Larkspur, delphinium (young plant, seeds); monkshood (fleshy roots); autumn crocus, garden amaryllis or naked lady, star of Bethlehem (bulbs); hydrangea, lily of the valley (leaves, flowers); iris (underground stems); foxglove (leaves); bleeding heart, or Dutchman's breeches (foliage, roots).

Ornamental plants: Daphne, holly (berries); wisteria (seeds, pods); golden chain (beanlike capsules in which the seeds are suspended); laurels, rhododendron, azaleas, jessamine (all parts); lantana or red sage (young plants, green berries); yew (berries, foliage).

Trees and shrubs: Wild and cultivated cherries (twigs, foliage); oaks (foliage, acorns); elderberry (shoots, leaves, bark); black locust (bark, sprouts, foliage); English ivy (leaves, berries); peach (leaves); buckeye or horse chestnut (leaves, fruits); oleander (the whole plant, including vase water in which the flowers have been placed). ·

Plants in wooded areas: Jack-in-the-pulpit (all parts, especially roots); moonseed (berries); mayapple (apple, foliage, roots).

Plants in swamp or moist areas: Water hemlock (all parts).

Plants in fields: Nightshade (all parts, especially the unripe berry); buttercups, poison hemlock, jimsonweed, or thorn apple, (all parts); milkweed (leaves, stems).

See also ACCIDENTS; FOOD POISONING; POISONING.

POLIO (poliomyelitis, infantile paralysis) The first week of January 1964 stands out in red letters in the annals of public health. It was the first week on record without report of a new case of polio. By contrast, in the peak week of the worst epidemic year (1952), the number of reported new cases of this infectious disease totaled 4,180.

Polio immunization has spelled the difference. The dramatic change brought by polio vaccine is so great that it is hard to grasp by adults who are too young to recall polio "seasons" and polio-caused panics. In 1952 there were 58,000 cases of polio and more than 3,000 deaths in the United States. In some recent years there have been less than 10 cases.

But new epidemics threaten. More than a third of the nation's children are inadequately vaccinated. In city slums, among migratory and marginal farm workers, in impoverished ethnic groups, many children have no protection or less than adequate protection. It's fortunate that a large percentage of these youngsters are in fact protected, mainly because taking merely one dose of the recommended three-dose regimen offers substantial immunization.

The polio virus. Three types of viruses cause polio. All can damage spinal nerve cells, which control movement of the body below the neck. They also may injure the cranial nerves and other nerve centers in the base of the brain, the most vital of which control breathing, circulation, and swallowing. Type I causes most polio epidemics. Type III (bulbo-spinal polio), while least frequent, is usually the most serious form of the disease.

Polio viruses are believed to enter through the mouth, lodge in the mouth region and intestines, then spread to nerve centers. The incubation period is usually 7 to 14 days but may be as long as 35 days. Human carriers, who show no symptoms but nonetheless bear the virus, may spread the disease.

In its early stages polio may resemble influenza and sore throat. There is usually a fever, and other early symptoms may be headache, vomiting, fretfulness, and drowsiness. There may be stiffness and pain in the neck. Paralysis of the muscles, most commonly in the legs, occurs in severe cases.

In mild cases there is no paralysis, and sometimes there are no actual apparent symptoms and no crippling aftereffects. Many people thus acquire a degree of immunity without knowing they had the disease. Some of them, however, remain carriers and can infect susceptible persons.

There is no cure for polio. Once it strikes a person, it runs its course.

The vaccine. Protection against all three types of polio virus is needed. Immunity to one type—either by vaccination or infection—does not immunize you against the other two. A dose of vaccine may be monovalent (acting against just one type of virus) or trivalent (acting against all three).

The first polio vaccine was developed by Dr. Jonas E. Salk and introduced in 1955. It contains killed polio viruses, is trivalent, and is injected into the muscle. In 1961 an oral (taken by mouth) live-virus vaccine developed by Dr. Albert B. Sabin was licensed for use in this country. The original Sabin vaccine was monovalent, but in common use now are live-virus oral vaccines that are trivalent.

A battle over the Salk versus Sabin vaccines still rages in medicine. The Sabin vaccine produces a higher degree of resistance and works more rapidly. Swallowed on a sugar cube or in syrup, it is easier to administer than the Salk injectable.

On the other hand oral live-virus vaccine has in rare instances produced polio in recipients or people in close contact with them, mostly adults. The Salk vaccine is not now manufactured in the United States, but is the vaccine of choice in many other countries. A Canadian product licensed for use in the United States is now available.

Despite the common name *infantile paralysis,* the disease can be a threat to older persons. Franklin Delano Roosevelt was 39 when he caught it. In epidemics 25 to 30 percent of the victims were over age 15.

Begin infant immunization at two to three months, advises the Public Health Service. The oral vaccine is usually given at the same time as the first injection against diphtheria, tetanus, and whooping cough.

After six to eight weeks, schedule the second polio vaccination. Then, 8 to 12 months later, schedule the third. A booster is needed at five or six years of age, when the child begins school.

If your child has received one or two doses of vaccine but not the whole course, ask your physician how the child's protection can be improved.

Routine vaccination for adults in the United States is not recommended. Adults need to be vaccinated only if in contact with a polio case—or if going to areas where polio is epidemic or occurs regularly. They should receive injectable—not oral—vaccine. Pregnant woman should avoid vaccination.

See also IMMUNIZATION; INFECTIOUS DISEASE.

POLYUNSATURATED VEGETABLE OILS
See FATS.

POSTNASAL DRIP arises from abnormal accumulations of secretions in the upper throat, the nasopharynx, which lies above and behind the soft tissue at the rear of the mouth.

The nasopharynx warms and moistens air drawn into the lungs through the nose and catches dust and bacteria on its moist surfaces. The nasal passageways produce two types of fluids—a watery secretion and a thick mucus. When an oversupply accumulates in the nasopharynx, particularly an oversupply of mucus, the result is postnasal drip.

Its worst effects are encountered during the night or early in the morning. When a sleeper moves and changes position, he coughs, perhaps even retches, and spits up mucus.

The condition often is closely related to sinusitis. Other causes include allergy, air pollution, smoking, changes in barometric pressure. The condition may also arise from chemical or physical damage to the membranes, nose deformities affecting the airways, and individual responses to such conditions as climate, altitude, and humidity.

Consult your physician if you suffer from postnasal drip. If the drip is untreated for a long period, tissues can thicken and this may result in permanent deformities that require surgical correction. To make breathing easier, he may prescribe nose drops and suggest that you increase household humidity.

Mouthwashes and gargling are not effective against the drip or the mouth odor that frequently accompanies it. Gargling reaches only the front two thirds of the oral cavity, and the secretions causing the trouble are in the rear third.

See also RESPIRATORY DISEASE.

POT (marijuana)   See DRUGS.

POTASSIUM   See MINERALS.

PREGNANCY occurs when a male's sperm cell unites with a female's egg, usually in the fallopian tube between the ovary and uterus. The fertilized egg travels to the uterus and implants in its lining. Conception is most likely to occur at about the midpoint of a woman's menstrual cycle, around the fourteenth day for a woman who has a regular 28-day cycle.

Most women suspect they are pregnant when they skip menstruation. Other common first signs include enlarged, tender breasts, sometimes with a sensation of tingling and fullness; sleepiness; and increased urination.

See a physician as soon as you suspect you're pregnant. Your family doctor can confirm your pregnancy. For care and delivery you're likely to be best off with a board-certified obstetrician-gynecologist, a surgeon who specializes in childbirth and women's medical problems.

Early diagnosis of pregnancy and good prenatal (before-birth) care can help prevent many of the complications of pregnancy and reduce your risk of having a child with birth defects. An early prenatal examination can spot potential problems. A small number of women, for example, have ectopic pregnancies, those occurring outside the uterus, usually in the fallopian tube. These need to be detected early and surgically removed.

Don't rely on do-it-yourself pregnancy tests. They may give false results.

During the first six months of your pregnancy your doctor will probably want to see you about once a month. At each visit he'll check your weight, blood pressure, urine, and the growth of the fetus. After a few months he'll be able to listen to its heartbeat. From about the sixteenth week he'll be able to feel the unborn baby in the uterus. Between the eighteenth and twenty-fourth weeks, the baby's movements can be felt by the mother.

In your seventh and eighth months you'll probably see your doctor every second week; and in your last month every week. Full-term delivery occurs at about 40 weeks, or 280 days, but a baby born after the twenty-eighth week can generally survive with proper medical care.

Proper weight gain. Try not to gain more than 2 or 3 pounds a month. If you're of normal weight when you start your pregnancy, aim for a total weight gain of about 25 pounds.

Where do the pounds come from? In addition to the weight of the infant, the placenta and amniotic fluid weigh more than 3 pounds. The larger uterus weighs 2 pounds. The enlarged breasts weigh nearly another pound, the increased blood volume several ounces.

An additional few pounds of unaccounted-for weight appears to be in the form of fat around the hips and thighs. It is evidently a built-in safety factor for energy storage. A woman not usually overweight generally can easily lose it after the delivery.

Pay close attention to a proper diet. When a pregnant woman suffers from malnutrition, her baby is likely to be smaller and to have a higher risk of dying during the first few weeks. A woman who eats poorly also has a greater chance of bearing a baby with birth defects such as mental retardation or physical deformity.

A balanced and varied diet during pregnancy should include the following foods every day:

At least four glasses of whole or skim milk.
Six ounces of a protein food such as lean meat, poultry, fish, cheese, or eggs.
Two or three servings of vegetables and fruits, including one dark-green or deep-yellow vegetable and one citrus fruit.
Two or three servings of whole grain or enriched bread or cereal.

Your diet needs to be particularly rich in calcium for the proper development of the baby's skeleton and teeth. Milk and cheeses are good sources. If you don't like drinking milk, try using it in soups and casseroles. Or eat plain yogurt, perhaps with fresh fruit.

Phosphorus is essential. It's found in milk and dairy products, some fruits and vegetables. Foods high in vitamin A (carrots, spinach, liver) are important, as are iron-rich foods (leafy green vegetables, liver, clams). Many doctors recommend iron and folic acid supplements during pregnancy. But don't take them without a prescription.

Eliminate or severely cut down on foods with empty calories, such as candy, pastry, cake, fatty foods. Unless you have a medical problem, there is no need to restrict your salt intake. But don't binge on salty foods like potato chips and salted nuts, which promote your body's retention of water. If your water supply doesn't include fluoridation, your physician or dentist may prescribe a fluoride supplement. Never try to lose weight during pregnancy.

Stay physically active. Exercise helps you control your weight and keep your muscles strong. Most doctors urge healthy pregnant women to continue with the kind of exercise they are used to until it becomes uncomfortable to do so. Walking is particularly good.

Do what is comfortable for you but avoid overtiring yourself. Pregnancy is no time to learn a new sport, but if you are accustomed to tennis or waterskiing, you need not give it up before your growing abdomen compels you to.

Wear comfortable, loose-fitting clothing. As your breasts become larger and heavier, wear a bra for support. Your doctor may recommend an abdominal support such as a panty girdle or a special maternity girdle late in pregnancy. Don't wear tight-fitting garters on your legs—they impair circulation.

Pregnancy problems. If you suffer from nausea and vomiting in early pregnancy, eat five or six small meals a day instead of three large ones.

Try sucking a lollipop. Very hot or very cold liquids may help. If you feel especially nauseated in the morning, keep a few dry crackers next to your bed for munching before you get up. Try starting the day with a carbonated beverage instead of coffee, tea, or orange juice. Avoid overtiring yourself.

Indigestion can usually be prevented by avoiding fried foods. Small sips of water or milk may also help. Talk to your doctor before taking any antacids.

Constipation can often be relieved by eating plenty of fruits and vegetables and drinking lots of water. Prunes, raisins, or prune juice help.

Leg cramps can often be relieved by massage, or the application of hot compresses like a hot-water bottle. If you get leg cramps frequently, tell your doctor about it. These cramps may be due to an excessive accumulation of phosphorus caused by drinking too much milk.

Dizziness and fainting affect some pregnant women. If you feel a spell coming on, sit down or lie down quickly and wait for the feeling to pass. Lie on your side, preferably your right side. Lying flat on your back may interfere with circulation in your abdomen.

To avoid fatigue rest frequently. Take a nap every afternoon if you feel like it.

Shortness of breath may bother you and may interfere with your sleep. If so prop up your head and shoulders with several pillows. If the problem is persistent and troublesome, consult your physician. Overweight women are especially likely to suffer from this.

Low backache may bother you late in pregnancy. Try to stand with your buttocks tucked under. It may help to straighten your back out along a wall, pushing the small of your back against the wall or floor. Low-heeled shoes may improve your balance, relieving back strain.

Varicose veins often appear or are aggravated during pregnancy, especially in overweight women. Elevating your feet several times a day will usually help. Support stockings may also be necessary. The condition usually improves greatly after delivery.

Some women develop phlebitis. It is an inflammation of the veins, particularly affecting those of the upper leg. It may be caused by poor circulation, overweight, infection, or blood clots. Phlebitis may take months to heal. It usually has no effect on the fetus, but can be painful to the mother and requires a doctor's care.

Increased urination is not unusual. If it is especially troublesome, have your doctor check to see if you're suffering from a urinary tract infection. Excessive sweating may be bothersome, causing perspiration odor and calling for more frequent bathing.

Mood swings may result from hormonal changes. You are likely to find yourself inexplicably depressed or unaccountably joyful. It's normal. But if you feel deeply troubled by anxiety or depression, talk to your doctor about it.

If it's your first baby, attend a child-care class while you're pregnant. Women who take such courses tend to have significantly fewer emotional upsets after the birth of the baby.

Some swelling (edema) because of increased water retention is normal. Your fingers may be somewhat puffy and stiff in the morning. Since swelling is one of the symptoms of a serious condition—toxemia—report it to your doctor.

Your skin may discolor. A darkening of pigment may show up as brownish spots and patches on your forehead, cheeks, abdomen. This "mask of pregnancy" is most common in brunettes and women with dark skin. Dark moles, freckles, birthmarks, and circles under the eyes tend to become darker during pregnancy.

These are temporary and almost always disappear after the delivery. In the meantime use cosmetics to camouflage any skin discolorations you find unattractive. Since these pigmentations are intensified by exposure to the sun, block out the sun with a sunscreen preparation (see SUNBURN). A regular suntan lotion won't do.

Stretch marks (striae)—thin white scars on the abdomen—often occur as the skin stretches with the growth of the baby. They may disappear eventually but more often are permanent. Use an emollient cream to keep the skin of your abdomen soft and to help relieve the taut feeling and minimize itching. It is questionable that such creams or lotions can keep stretch marks from forming.

Enlarged blood vessels may show up as red spots or spiderlike tracings anywhere on the body. These are normal.

Toxemia is a severe complication. It is a metabolic disorder marked by the excretion of protein in the urine, edema, hypertension (high blood pressure), and sometimes excessive vomiting and sudden weight gain. Blurred vision and severe headaches may also occur.

Unchecked, toxemia (also called preeclampsia) can progress to eclampsia, a potentially fatal stage characterized by convulsions and coma. Half the women suffering from eclampsia die of it. It can also result in the death of the fetus.

Nutritional deficiencies, particularly lack of protein, may be a cause. Toxemia occurs most often in first pregnancies, after the twenty-fourth week. It is most likely to affect women who have diabetes and women who are carrying more than one fetus. If you had a mild case in your first pregnancy, you are likely to have mild toxemia in subsequent pregnancies.

Good prenatal care can detect toxemia in its early stages and generally get it under control. A woman suffering from any of the symptoms associated with toxemia is usually put on a high-protein diet with supplements of folic acid, iron, and vitamin D.

In cases of severe hypertension drugs may be prescribed. Bed rest alone, at home or in the hospital, can often control mild or moderate hypertension. A low-salt diet and diuretics (drugs that induce increased urination) are no longer recommended during pregnancy. If symptoms of toxemia persist after treatment, your physician may recommend inducing labor. Toxemia disappears within a few days after delivery.

Placenta previa is a rare complication. The placenta (the organ through which the fetus gets its nourishment from the mother) is attached near the cervix instead of high up on the uterine wall. It can thus be torn by the expanding cervix, causing painless bleeding and premature childbirth.

Premature separation of the placenta is another rare complication. A blood clot separates the placenta from the uterine wall.

Both conditions occur during the last three months of pregnancy. The warning sign for both is vaginal bleeding. Brain damage in the baby resulting in mental retardation is a risk in these conditions.

Immediate medical treatment is necessary to save the baby, which must often be delivered by cesarean section. The mother is given blood transfusions to replace the blood she has lost.

Intercourse during pregnancy. Sexual intercourse can ordinarily continue during a normal pregnancy. A side-by-side position for sex may be the most comfortable. Another good position is with the woman on top. Pregnant women often have increased sexual desire, particularly in the last several months.

Some doctors prohibit intercourse during the last month of pregnancy. A study of 27,000 pregnancies suggests a link between potentially harmful infections of the amniotic fluid and intercourse in the month before delivery. Besides abstinence possible preventive measures may include the use of a condom and careful washing of the genitals of both partners before intercourse.

Some other cautions:

A woman who habitually miscarries may be advised by her doctor not to have intercourse or orgasms for the first three months.

A woman who is prone to premature labor should avoid having an orgasm during the last weeks of pregnancy, as it may bring on labor.

A woman who experiences vaginal or abdominal pain or bleeding during intercourse or at any other time should abstain from sex until she has talked with her doctor.

A woman should not have intercourse after her amniotic sac has ruptured because of the possibility of infection.

Throughout pregnancy couples who engage in oral-genital sex should take care that no air is blown into the vagina. Death to a few mothers-to-be has resulted when the forced air passed into the blood vessels of the placenta, causing bubbles that blocked circulation to the heart.

Also avoid vaginal douching during pregnancy unless your doctor recommends it for a medical condition.

Seat belts. Don't stop wearing a car seat belt when you're pregnant. There is no evidence that seat belts pose any threat to the fetus, and in accidents they could save the lives of both of you.

But wear the belt low, snugly fastened across the pelvic bones and upper thighs, not across the uterus. For added protection wear a shoulder harness too. You can continue to drive as long as you can fit behind the wheel.

Air travel in a pressurized cabin poses no special hazards. But avoid long airplane trips during the last weeks of pregnancy because of the possibility of labor or delivery during the flight. Arm yourself with a note from your physician before going to the airport. Some airlines require a doctor's note to the effect that childbirth en route is unlikely before they'll permit an obviously pregnant woman to board.

Most doctors recommend that a pregnant woman remain at her job as long as she feels comfortable working, even well into the ninth month. Check with your own physician to see what he suggests for you.

Drugs. Take no drug during pregnancy unless there is a strong medical need for it. Virtually all drugs pass through the placenta, entering the unborn child's circulation and possibly harming it.

The Medical Letter recommends that physicians give pregnant women as few drugs as possible. It cautions that "except for urgent indications, all drugs should be withheld during the first trimester [three months]."

Since 1962, when the drug thalidomide was found to cause severe physical abnormalities in the fetus, many other drugs—including some antidepressants, antibiotics, and antihistamines—have been implicated in potential birth defects. Iodides, contained in many preparations to suppress coughing, can cause large goiters and respiratory distress in newborn infants. Progestogen, estrogen, and androgenic hormones can cause masculinized external genitals in the female fetus. Antibiotics containing tetracyclines may inhibit fetal bone growth or produce teeth discoloration.

Other drugs that are suspected of causing fetal damage include antinauseants, anticoagulants, and anticonvulsants.

If your doctor prescribed a drug, take it only in the doses and at the times indicated. Never take a drug that has been prescribed for someone else.

If you are leading an active sex life without using birth control and you have missed a period, before getting a prescription tell your doctor you are *potentially* pregnant—even if no pregnancy has been confirmed. Because many women are pregnant and don't know it when prescribed drugs that may harm the fetus, some physicians advocate making pregnancy testing routine for all women of childbearing age who are admitted to hospitals for any reason.

Cut out all nonprescription drugs when you are pregnant or potentially so. Except on your doctor's advice, don't take aspirin, vitamins, remedies for colds, laxatives, or medicated nose drops. Avoid lotions or ointments containing hormones or other drugs.

It's advisable for a pregnant woman to put up with a certain amount of discomfort and sleeplessness rather than resort to drugs. If she can get away without taking any antacids, aspirins, and sleeping pills, she and her fetus will be better off.

Avoid illicit drugs such as marijuana or LSD

during pregnancy, since their effect on the fetus is unknown. Heroin, morphine, or methadone addiction in the mother can cause severe physiological problems or death in the newborn.

Immunization with live-virus vaccines (for mumps, measles, polio, rubella) may be harmful to the fetus. If you are exposed to these or other communicable diseases, consult your physician about possible preventives.

On the other hand tetanus toxoid is recommended if your immunization has lapsed. The shot will also protect your baby through the first month.

X rays can be dangerous to the fetus, particularly during the first three months. Postpone all nonessential abdominal X rays until after delivery, or at least until the fourth month or later. If you must have an X ray elsewhere on your body —such as a dental X ray—make sure your reproductive organs are protected with a lead apron.

Chronic medical conditions require particularly careful supervision. Women with heart disease, diabetes, cancer, and severe hypertension are much more likely to have problems during pregnancy.

Viral diseases such as measles, mumps, hepatitis, and influenza may also complicate pregnancy, as well as pose a threat to the unborn child. If a woman less than three months pregnant contracts rubella (German measles), her baby is likely to suffer from mental retardation or other severe birth defects.

If you are pregnant and have been exposed to rubella, see your doctor. Laboratory tests can determine whether you've really become infected. You may have had such mild symptoms that you missed them entirely. Abortion is usually recommended for a pregnant woman who's contracted the disease.

Toxoplasmosis—an infectious parasitic disease usually transmitted through raw meat or the feces of infected cats—is also associated with birth defects. Its symptoms often resemble the common cold, and it may go unnoticed.

Cut out cigarettes. Women who smoke during pregnancy have a greater than average risk of stillbirths or early infant deaths. The Public Health Service's report to Congress on cigarette smoking estimates that 4,600 stillbirths a year can almost certainly be attributed to the smoking habits of the mothers.

Smoking during pregnancy also tends to reduce the size of the infant. The woman who gives up smoking by her fourth month of pregnancy apparently eliminates the risk to her baby.

The danger to the fetus seems to come from the toxic effects of the nicotine.

Keep your intake of alcohol way down—or better still, drink no alcoholic beverages when you are pregnant. Alcohol appears to adversely affect the fetus. Infants born to heavy drinkers have a high rate of birth defects, including mental retardation, physical deformities, and general failure to thrive. Even moderate alcohol use (two to four cocktails, beers, or glasses of wine twice a week) may increase a woman's chances of miscarriage.

Use vitamin supplements only on the advice of your physician. An excess of certain vitamins may harm the fetus.

It's wise to reduce or eliminate your intake of caffeine—in coffee, tea, chocolate, and cola drinks. Research with animals shows that high doses of caffeine may increase the frequency of birth defects.

Miscarriage. One in ten pregnant women has a miscarriage (spontaneous abortion). Most women miscarry during the first 12 weeks of pregnancy. Typically the first sign of an impending miscarriage is vaginal bleeding—which should be reported to your doctor immediately. Other symptoms may include cramps, backache, and nausea.

Very little can be done to avert a threatened miscarriage, especially if you have heavy bleeding and severe cramps. If the bleeding is slight, with little or no abdominal cramps, your doctor will most likely advise you to go to bed and stay there until 24 hours after the bleeding has stopped. He will also probably recommend that you avoid vaginal douching and have no sexual intercourse or strenuous physical activity until the bleeding has completely stopped for 24 to 48 hours. There is a possibility that these measures may save the infant.

In the past synthetic estrogens such as diethylstilbestrol (DES) have been used to prevent miscarriage. Now they are in disfavor, since they have been associated with a type of vaginal cancer in girls who were in the womb when their mothers took the drugs. Sons of women who took DES while carrying them are often infertile and have genital abnormalities. All children born from a DES-aided pregnancy need to be examined regularly for possible problems arising from the drug.

A woman who experiences an incomplete spontaneous abortion—in which part of the fetal tissue remains in the uterus—must have the remaining material removed. This is done either by a D & C (dilation and curettage: stretching the cervix and scraping the uterus), or by the use of a drug that stimulates the uterus to contract and expel the remaining material.

A woman in her second pregnancy is more likely to miscarry than a woman in a first pregnancy. Women past 40 are more likely than younger women to miscarry.

Don't feel guilty about miscarrying. The pregnancy that ends in miscarriage usually was an abnormal pregnancy.

In other cases the miscarriage may be due to a medical condition in the mother, such as a genital infection, anemia, diabetes, hepatitis, or heart disease. A woman suffering from malnutrition is also more likely to miscarry. Severe emotional stress may play a role.

Most normal pregnancies can withstand a good deal of strenuous physical activity, even accidents, falls, and blows.

The chances are that if you have one spontaneous abortion you won't have another. A few women habitually abort. Various preventive treatments are used to try to help such women carry a baby to term, including surgery to correct a prematurely opening cervix, and psychotherapy.

See also ABORTION; BACKACHE; BATHING; BIRTH CONTROL; BIRTH DEFECTS; BIRTHMARKS; BREAST SAGGING; CHILDBIRTH; FAINTING; FATIGUE; INDIGESTION; INFERTILITY; MENSTRUATION; NAUSEA; NUTRITION; OVERWEIGHT; POLIO; RUBELLA; SHORTNESS OF BREATH; SMOKING; STRESS; TOXOPLASMOSIS; URINARY TRACT INFECTION; VAGINAL DOUCHING; VITAMINS; X RAYS.

PREMATURE BIRTH All babies who weigh less than 5 pounds are treated as premature. This accounts for about one U.S. childbirth in ten.

A very small premature baby may weigh little more than 2 pounds. A premature baby's chances of survival increase with his birth weight and how close he is to full term. If your child is only a little below 5 pounds, his chances for survival and normal development are excellent.

Much smaller babies are more likely to suffer from infections and birth defects such as cerebral palsy, crossed eyes, brain damage, and visual and hearing defects. Some very small premature infants succumb to hyaline membrane disease, a condition that makes it difficult for them to expand their lungs.

Incubator. If you have a premature infant, he'll be put into an incubator. This see-through box simulates conditions inside the uterus. It is controlled for heat, moisture, and oxygen, and provides portholes so that nurses and doctors

can care for the child without removing him from his special environment. Monitoring equipment keeps track of the baby's breathing and body temperature.

If he has breathing problems, a respirator may be used. He may need to be fed intravenously, through a tube passed through his nostril into his stomach, or through an eyedropper. Some premature babies need blood transfusions.

A premature infant usually remains in the incubator or in the hospital until he is 5 to 5½ pounds. This may be six or more weeks from the time he is born.

When you take your preemie home, he'll need extra care. Since he's more susceptible to body-temperature changes, make sure that he's neither too hot nor too cold. For the first few weeks keep him out of public places and away from strangers because of the increased danger of infections. A premature baby may need to be fed more often during the first few weeks at home, and he may be slow in starting to gain weight.

Calculate a preemie's development not from his birth date but from his probable date of conception. Thus if your baby was born two months early, his development eight months after delivery will be roughly on a par with a full-term baby of six months. The smaller a premature baby is, the longer it takes him to catch up. Within two or three years he's likely to be of average size.

A few preemies, though, will always be small. Their reading ability, emotional maturation, and muscular development may lag somewhat behind those of their age peers. It is often advisable to start a preemie in kindergarten at six, instead of five, so he'll be more on a par with his classmates.

Don't feel it's your fault if your baby is premature. The cause of most premature births is unknown. Contributing factors include abnormalities of the cervix or uterus, infection in the mother, toxemia, and premature separation of the placenta. High blood pressure, heart disease, tuberculosis, and other chronic illnesses may also lead to prematurity.

Women who are carrying more than one baby are more likely to give birth prematurely, as are women under 16 or over 40. Underweight or malnourished women have more preemies than normal-weight women. Pregnancies closely spaced also seem to promote premature delivery.

Prolonged pregnancy can also have an adverse effect on the baby. Babies delivered several weeks after full term frequently require incubator care, oxygen, and intravenous feedings. Their mortality rate is significantly greater than babies born on time; those who survive are likely to have poorer health for the first three years.

Make sure your dates are correct if you think you're overdue. Calculate the length of your pregnancy from the first day of your last normal menstrual period. If your baby is definitely more than two weeks overdue, your doctor may suggest inducing labor to avoid the hazards of late delivery.

See also CHILDBIRTH; PREGNANCY.

PREMATURE EJACULATION is a common sexual problem, sometimes regarded as a form of impotence. This sex disorder involves the man's ejaculating before penetration or shortly thereafter.

Premature ejaculation is generally a conditioned response, a habit outside the man's conscious control. Most cases arise from the man's being introduced to sex in a way that emphasizes ejaculating rather than satisfying his partner. A young man may develop a hair-trigger reaction if he starts by having intercourse in situations that call for a hurried response: in the back seats of cars, in rooms with parents nearby, with prostitutes who want to turn as many tricks as possible in record time.

Squeeze technique. The condition is almost completely reversible through the "squeeze technique" developed by urologist James H. Semans of the Duke University School of Medicine. Assuming you're a married man:

Just before you have an urge to ejaculate, your wife presses your frenulum—the sensitive spot at the bottom edge of the crown of the penis—firmly with her thumb for three or four seconds. She holds the opposite side of the crown with two fingers.

The goal of the squeeze technique is to keep you sexually excited at a level short of ejaculation. If you're uncircumcised, your frenulum can be located with a little practice. If your wife worries about how hard she can press without hurting you, show her by placing your fingers over hers.

From 10 to 50 percent of the erection is usually lost after the squeeze is applied, but it's generally soon regained. Over several weeks men become more and more able to bring the urge to ejaculate under their own control.

Sex therapists William H. Masters and Virginia E. Johnson report a 98 percent success rate applying the squeeze technique to a regimen that begins with four days of "pleasuring," love play without intercourse (see SEX DISORDER).

This is followed by three or four days of slow genital play. The man is masturbated by his partner at the rate of one stroke every three seconds or so. As soon as he feels the urge to ejaculate, he tells her—and she applies the squeeze technique. After 15 to 30 seconds, she resumes masturbating him.

This training teaches the man the level of sexual excitement he can sustain without ejaculating. It also encourages open communication about sex. About 20 minutes of sex play can thus be experienced without ejaculation. There's no attempt to have intercourse or bring the woman to orgasm.

Finally the couple engages in intercourse, at first with the woman on top. She holds the penis in her vagina and refrains from moving. When he feels the urge to ejaculate, she withdraws from his penis—and applies the squeeze. After three or four days of practice, the man generally can provide just enough pelvic thrusting to maintain his erection without ejaculating.

After control increases, couples generally prefer a lateral coital position, lying on their side with the woman's hip on the man's inner thigh, his other leg between her legs. This allows greatest freedom of movement, and permits the woman to apply the squeeze if necessary.

It usually takes between 6 and 12 months to achieve complete ejaculatory control. The squeeze technique should be practiced at least once a week for six months. Once a month, during the woman's menstrual period, practice slow genital play.

Only as a last resort, ask your physician about prescribing tricyclic antidepressants such as Tofranil or Presamine. Minute doses can slow down ejaculation without impairing erection.

In any case avoid nonprescription drugs like anesthetic creams and jellies, which are supposed to prolong intercourse by reducing penis sensitivity. They are a waste of money and can trigger a drug allergy.

Masturbating before intercourse rarely delays ejaculation. Nor does wearing two condoms. Nor do attempts by the man to distract himself by pulling his hair, thinking about his job, or counting backward from 100.

See also IMPOTENCE; MASTURBATION; SEX DISORDER.

PREMENSTRUAL SYNDROME See MENSTRUATION.

PRESBYOPIA is a problem with close-up vision that usually occurs around the age of 45. The eye disorder affects almost everyone who lives long enough.

Presbyopia is caused by the natural aging of the eye. The ability of the eye to change its focus to different distances gradually wanes. Focusing for near vision becomes increasingly difficult.

Reading matter must be held farther from the eyes, causing some to complain that their arms aren't long enough. Eventually small print becomes blurred. The effort to see close objects causes eyestrain.

Presbyopia is corrected by reading glasses. You can have reading lenses added to the glasses you already wear. In such glasses, called bifocals and invented by Benjamin Franklin, distant vision is obtained through the upper part of the lens and near vision through the lower portion. It may take a few weeks to get used to bifocals— you need to learn to move reading matter or detail work to where you can see it most comfortably.

In new models there's no line marking the lens segments, a boon to those who think bifocals look "old." Unless the lens is "progressive" (clear at all distances), you'll need to get used to blurring at the transition zone.

The half-eye lens—the framed lower reading segment of a bifocal—is another idea. But you'll have to adjust to the top-frame line that cuts your line of vision. A better idea, if you need glasses for reading but not for distance, may be a lens with clear glass in the top half.

For some people bifocal contact lenses are a possibility.

Trifocal lenses are also effective. They have a top section for distant vision, a middle section for viewing objects 20 to 40 inches away, and a reading section for use at 14 inches. They are no more difficult to use than bifocals, and often are easier to become accustomed to.

Waiting to get reading lenses may prolong eyestrain unnecessarily. Don't use a magnifying glass to help you read. It is much less efficient than a reading lens and may prolong eyestrain.

See also EYE DISORDER.

PRICKLY HEAT (miliaria) is a skin disorder in which there is a temporary blockage of the sweat duct openings on the skin surface. Perspiration cannot reach the surface, so may break through the wall of the sweat duct and cause an inflammation in the skin.

Numerous pinhead-size pimples and blisters cause itching and burning. Infection may be caused by invading microorganisms. Prickly heat is especially common in areas where two skin surfaces are close together, as in the skin folds of plump babies and overweight adults.

To treat or avoid the condition keep the skin cool and dry. Wear light, loose-fitting clothes, use air conditioning or fans. Take cool showers followed by liberal sprinklings of cornstarch or dusting powder.

See also SKIN DISORDERS.

PROSTATE TROUBLE refers to a variety of conditions involving the prostate gland, a small organ located at the base of the bladder in the male. It is wrapped around the urethra, the tube through which urine passes.

The prostate is part of a man's reproductive system. The ducts that carry sperm pass through tunnels in the prostate. At ejaculation the muscles in the prostate squeeze the embedded glands to discharge a fluid that helps to transport and nourish the sperm.

Prostatitis, the commonest prostate trouble, is an inflammation of the prostate, often caused by bacteria. Another common cause is congestion. Its most frequent symptoms are pain on urinating or sexual intercourse, frequent urination, and aching in the groin, testicles, and lower back.

To relieve the discomfort of prostatitis take sitz baths at least twice a day for 10 to 20 minutes at a time. Sit in 6 to 10 inches of very hot water.

Avoid any foods and drinks that seem to aggravate your symptoms. These often include coffee (also decaffeinated), tea, cocoa, cola, alcohol, spicy foods, chocolate, and nuts (especially cashews).

Avoid sitting for prolonged periods of time, and avoid bouncy rides on trucks, motorcycles, etc.

If your prostatitis is not caused by bacteria, ask your physician about engaging in sexual activity—ejaculation may help relieve the inflammation.

If your condition is caused by bacteria (acute prostatitis), try to avoid sexual arousal until the infection is under control. Take your medication exactly as directed for the recommended number of days. Don't discontinue taking the pills when you start to feel better.

Prostate enlargement. After age 50 one of every three men will have difficult passage of urine. There may be related discomforts, such as frequent urination. In most cases the cause is a hypertrophied prostate, a benign enlargement of glands surrounding the urethra. Have the condition checked by a physician early—many of the same symptoms mark cancer of the prostate.

The cause of enlarged prostate is uncertain. It does *not* result from sexual excesses, masturbation, or gonorrhea.

An enlarged prostate puts pressure on the urethra and the bladder, interfering both with the starting of the urine stream and the complete emptying of the bladder. This results in a sensation of irritation and a need to empty the bladder frequently. The stream of urine lacks force and becomes weak and dribbly. Straining to urinate may cause pain and the appearance of blood in the urine.

During the months or years of increasing discomfort obstruction of urine flow contributes to complications. The muscles of the bladder wall must force urine through the narrowing urethra. These muscles become enlarged from the extra exercise, thickening the bladder wall and reducing the bladder's capacity. Occasionally the increased muscular effort forces weak spots on the wall of the bladder to become pockets called diverticuli. This can lead to urinary tract infection.

Eventually the kidneys may be damaged, preventing the filtering of waste products from the blood, which can be fatal.

No medicine currently available can shrink or dissolve the enlarged glands. In the early stages prostate massage may be helpful.

Prostate surgery. Surgery is the recommended treatment when enlargement greatly obstructs the urine flow, or when there is a chronic infection.

There should be no loss in sexual function following what is called a transurethral resection. Although the operation is called a prostatectomy (which means removal of the prostate gland), the gland itself is not removed, merely the mass of overgrown tissue inside the prostate. The man will be able to have an erection, engage in intercourse, and experience orgasm. At worst he will no longer produce an ejaculate—a problem only in the event that he wants more children.

When impotence follows prostate surgery, it is usually emotional in origin, possibly because the operation leads to infertility. Physiologically, men who functioned sexually before the surgery can almost always continue to do so after it.

Be wary of devices advertised as do-it-yourself treatments for prostate trouble, such as prostate massage implements. Even in skilled hands such devices have limited value, and prostate-gland disorders include many conditions too serious for self-treatment.

See also CANCER OF THE PROSTATE; SEX DISORDER.

PROTEIN is an element of nutrition necessary for growth, maintenance of body functions, and tissue repair.

Next to water, protein is the most plentiful substance in your body: it's the main component of muscles, tendons, skin, red blood cells, antibodies.

Crippling protein deficiency is rare in this country. But many people in poor countries suffer from kwashiorkor, a potentially fatal protein deficiency disease characterized by stunted growth, skin sores, edema, hair discoloration.

Men need about 55 grams of protein a day. Women need about 45, more during pregnancy and breastfeeding. Children's needs vary from about 25 grams for young children to about 50 for children over 12. (See the table of nutrient needs under NUTRITION.)

Sources of protein. Every day eat two or three portions of animal protein, plus a variety of fruits and vegetables, breads and cereals.

A day's protein can be amply provided by 1/4 cup of cottage cheese (11 grams); 3 ounces of tuna fish (24 grams); 2 ounces of hamburger (11 grams); 2 slices of bread (4 grams); 1 cup of broccoli (5 grams); 1/2 cup of baked beans (7 grams).

Many foods high in protein also provide you with other nutrients, including vitamins and minerals. Particularly good sources of protein are milk and milk products (but not butter or margarine), eggs, meat, fish, poultry, eggs.

Half a chicken and a cup of cottage cheese each gives you almost 44 grams of protein; a cup of clams, about 28 grams; a medium-sized egg, about 6 grams. Other foods rich in protein: Soybean products, peas, beans and lentils, peanut butter, nuts, some grains (wheat, oats), and seeds (sunflower, sesame).

There is no point in eating extra protein. Any excess over your caloric needs is stored as fat. Eating too much protein is an expensive way to gain weight. A diet exceptionally high in protein—say, 100 to 150 grams—can be dangerous for people with kidney disease and may interfere with calcium metabolism.

On the other hand if you're on a diet for overweight, you may find that a somewhat higher proportion of protein in your diet keeps you fuller longer.

Proteins from animal sources—meat, fish, poultry, eggs, milk and milk products—are generally of high quality. They provide all eight amino acids, the components of protein, which are essential to your body.

Plant proteins are also valuable sources of these essential amino acids. Soybeans and soybean products are the most nearly complete nonanimal sources of protein. A mixture of animal and plant proteins is most likely to provide all the essential amino acids in adequate amounts.

People who practice strict vegetarianism—excluding all meat, eggs, milk, and milk products from their diets—may have difficulty obtaining all the essential amino acids. Nutritionists therefore suggest that vegetarians eat a wide variety of grains, vegetables, and fruits. Some animal protein, if only a glass of milk or a cup of yogurt a day, will also help ensure adequate nutrition.

If you're counting calories, fish is your best bet. It provides you with the greatest amount of animal protein for the calories. About 3½ ounces of cod yields more than 18 grams of protein for less than 100 calories.

Next best are chicken and eggs. Veal and lean beef also give you a good deal of protein for the number of calories.

With pork, sour cream, or peanut butter, on the other hand, you have to consume a lot of calories for the protein you get. One tablespoon of peanut butter (100 calories) gives you only 4 grams of protein.

Of the plant foods, soybean cakes (tofu) and other soybean products provide the most protein in relation to calories. Other plant sources with a good protein-calorie ratio include lentils, mung beans, lima beans, peas, chick-peas, and sunflower seeds.

By contrast, rice, wheat, barley, sesame seed, and some nuts are high in calories for the amount of protein you get.

To help ward off heart disease, select a majority of protein foods that are low in saturated fats (including cholesterol). These include fish, cottage cheese, pot cheese, chicken, turkey, whole grain or enriched breads or cereals, dried peas, beans, lentils.

Cutting costs. To cut protein costs, eat more dried beans, peas, lentils. They can be mixed with eggs or cheese—other good buys—for soups or casseroles with a good balance of animal-plant proteins.

Soybean extenders for hamburger meat can cut the cost without significantly affecting the taste. Soy products made to taste like liver, ham, and other meats are available in some supermarkets and health food stores. To cook soybeans soak them overnight, then simmer them for a few hours until soft. Add them to soups, vegetable dishes, cheese casseroles. For a nutritious snack sprinkle them with oil after soaking and roast in a 150° F oven until browned.

Absurdity: Most soybeans are now fed to pigs and cows. Nutritionally, it's a poor exchange. The protein derived from these animals is much less than that fed to them, and it's vastly more expensive.

Try Chinese-style cooking. Small bits of shredded chicken, beef, or seafood are stir-fried (quickly cooked in a pan) with lots of vegetables. This is a good way to cut down on the high cost of protein.

Add nonfat dry milk to soups or casseroles, an economical way of boosting protein content. Extend hamburger or meat loaf with low-priced grains like oatmeal.

See also NUTRITION.

PROTOZOA   See INFECTIOUS DISEASE.

PSORIASIS may have been the skin disease that afflicted many so-called lepers of biblical times—especially those who had miraculous cures. Psoriasis (so-RI-ah-sis) often goes into remission and all the characteristic lesions may even disappear for a year or more, which does not happen with leprosy.

In psoriasis, which is thought to be inherited, abnormal changes in the cells cause the outer layer of skin (the epidermis) to reproduce itself every three or four days instead of the usual month. Such fast growth produces imperfectly formed cells, which become itching, reddened scales.

There is no known cause for psoriasis, nor is there a cure. The disorder is not contagious, but people with severe psoriasis may be shunned because it is so unsightly. Anxiety and distress about psoriasis can seriously disrupt the sufferer's life.

The condition needs to be diagnosed by a dermatologist, since there are many other scaling skin disorders. Sufferers often fall for patent-remedy ads and treat themselves for psoriasis—when they are really suffering from contact dermatitis, eczema, ichthyosis, or seborrheic dermatitis.

Psoriasis usually appears as red patches with thick, silvery scales. Major sites are the elbows, knees, and trunk, less often the scalp, underarms, and genital area. Some cases of jock itch are psoriasis. At the hairline the patches shed quantities of silvery-white scales that look like dandruff. Affected fingernails and toenails develop small pits on their surfaces, lose their luster, and become loose. The face is rarely affected.

Psoriasis usually begins gradually. The first small bright red spots develop thin layers of sticky, dry scales. These spots increase in size and may combine to form larger patches that spread. Often the first spots appear at the site of minor injuries, such as cuts, burns, or bruises.

An eruption called exfoliative psoriasis can be serious enough to require hospitalization. There can be a painful reddening of the whole skin, severe chills, cracking of the skin around the joints, and shedding of large scaly areas.

Arthritis is a complication for about one in ten persons. Sometimes both diseases appear together, but usually psoriatic arthritis follows a longstanding case of psoriasis and affects the joints of the fingers in particular.

Treating psoriasis. Sunlight is the most effective treatment for many sufferers, and the doctor will urge them to sunbathe as much as possible, but to avoid bad sunburn. (In some cases sun worsens the problem.)

To increase the therapeutic value of sunlight apply an over-the-counter tar preparation such as Tarpaste 20 minutes before going outdoors. Remove excess ointment before going out. The tar remains active for about 24 hours—so, to avoid burning, be cautious in exposing tar-treated skin to sunlight. Tar derivatives may be applied in ointment form (e.g., Estar) or added to the bath (Balnetar).

Remove scales daily with soap and water. Then apply petroleum jelly (such as Vaseline) or any other mild lubricant.

A pumice stone can help remove psoriasis scales. The soft abrasive, usually employed for removal of foot calluses, can scrub off scales without tearing the skin. For maximum effectiveness a keratolytic agent (Keralyt) is first applied, then covered with a dressing for a few days. Then before using the pumice stone the sufferer should soak in a tub for 10 to 15 minutes to soften the scales further for easy removal.

Many over-the-counter moisturizers used daily can help to control scaling and improve appearance. For psoriasis of the scalp use such medicated shampoos as Sebutone, Zetar, or Polytar. If scales are very thick, apply a preparation like Unguentum Bossi or Bakers P & S Liquid to your head at night and shampoo it out the next morning.

Avoid irritation and injury to the skin. Steer clear of irritating cosmetics, ointments, or chemicals. Wear loose clothing.

Eliminate alcohol from your diet—flare-ups of psoriasis often follow heavy drinking. Overweight also aggravates psoriasis. So may emotional stress.

Corticosteroids may help. They are often applied in a cream or ointment, then covered with a plastic film overnight. Steroids should not be used over large areas of the body. Systemic steroids are not recommended because massive doses are generally required to suppress the disease, and the risk of serious side effects is great. Resistant cases may call for hospitalization and supervised use of coal tar ointments and ultraviolet radiation for two weeks or more.

Some drugs are of value for disabling psoriasis, but may have severe side effects. Among them is methotrexate (Mexate), used for resistant psoriasis with severe psoriatic arthritis. Patients using this drug should be examined at intervals for signs of toxic effects to the liver, blood, and kidneys.

Ultraviolet light, type B (UVB), is commonly used to clear psoriasis. It is normally administered in a dermatologist's office.

A treatment for severe psoriasis is PUVA therapy (psoralen ultraviolet-light A-spectrum). An oral drug—methoxsalen (Oxsoralen)—is given, then the patient is exposed to long-wave ultraviolet light. Treatment is given several times a week for two to three months, with maintenance treatments for some months thereafter. The university medical centers testing this method report that it often induces remission even in patients with severe, resistant psoriasis over large parts of their bodies. But the long-term side effects of this treatment are unknown.

Psoriatic arthritis is treated the same as rheumatoid arthritis, except that steroids and antimalarial agents may not be used.

For further information contact the National Psoriasis Foundation, Suite 210, 6443 SW Beaverton Highway, Portland, Oregon 97221.

See also RHEUMATOID ARTHRITIS; SKIN DISORDERS.

PSYCHOSIS See TRANQUILIZERS.

PSYCHOSOMATIC ILLNESS See STRESS.

PULSE (heart rate) is a count of the contraction of your heart—it is the rate at which your heart beats. To take your pulse, place the first two fingers of one hand against the bone on the thumb side of your other wrist (see illustration). You'll feel an artery in your wrist give a little jump every time your heart beats. The number of times per minute this artery pulsates is your heart rate.

Experiment a bit and select the best spot on your body to take your pulse. A better location than your wrist may be at your neck, just over your collar line and to the right or left of your windpipe. Or try the inside of your elbow just above the bend.

Don't take a pulse with your thumb. The thumb has its own slight pulse, which may be confusing.

When taking your pulse at rest, simply count the number of pulsations for a full minute, using a watch with a second hand for accuracy. At

HOW TO TAKE A PULSE

Feel with fingers (not your thumb)

At wrist
(thumb side)

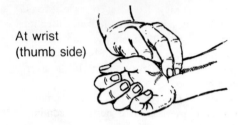

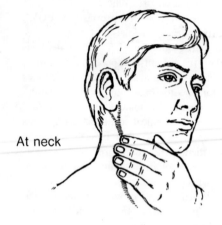

At neck

At elbow

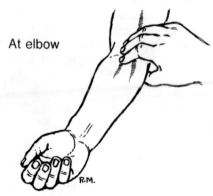

rate slows quickly after you stop your activity; if you took a full minute's count, your rate for the last ten seconds would be different from your rate for the first ten.

A rapid, bounding pulse may signal stress or high blood pressure. After accidents check the victim's pulse frequently. The absence of a pulse may be a sign of heart stoppage. A rapid, weak pulse may indicate shock.

See also HEART DISEASE.

PUNCTURES result from penetration of the tissues by pointed objects such as knives, scissors,

DON'T REMOVE AN IMPALING OBJECT
DO

1. Leave object in wound (knife, arrow, stick, etc.)

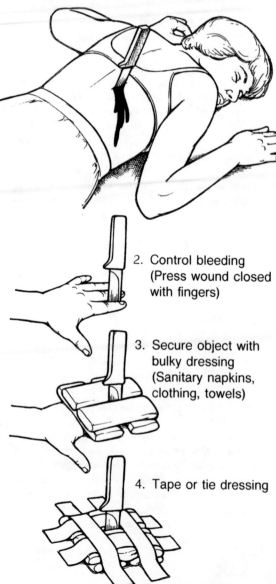

2. Control bleeding (Press wound closed with fingers)

3. Secure object with bulky dressing (Sanitary napkins, clothing, towels)

4. Tape or tie dressing

rest the following pulse beats per minute are about normal: men, 54–70; women, 75–80; children, 82–180. Fever may cause a sharp rise in the pulse, about 10 beats per minute for each degree above the normal range.

If you're ill, keep a record of pulse and fever every two hours or so to tell your doctor. In some diseases, rises and falls in heart rate and temperature help in diagnosis. Also note the pulse's general character—full, bounding, weak, irregular—for this may be significant.

In heart disease you may be asked to keep track of how exercise affects your heart. *Immediately* after exercising, count the beats for the first ten seconds only. Then multiply this number by six to get a per-minute reading. The heart

PUNCTURES

or needles; splinters of wood, metal, or glass; or a nail or bullet.

Squeezing the puncture gently to promote bleeding may help to clean it. All punctures that are deep or resist bleeding need to be seen by a physician. In severe injuries combat shock and any heavy bleeding.

Don't probe into the wound to remove the object. Don't remove a knife, for example, even if it's sticking out of the victim (see illustration). You may cause severe bleeding and further damage nerves and muscles.

Move an injured person as carefully as possible. In an extreme emergency, if the victim is impaled on a stick or other object that impedes his transportation, *shorten* the object rather than remove it. Touch it as little as possible, since its slightest movement may cause severe pain and damage.

Don't try to cleanse a large puncture. Cover it with a clean bandage and seek medical help.

Check your immunization against tetanus, a particular hazard of puncture wounds. Although there may be less visible bleeding than from a cut, a puncture can be much more serious. The risk of infection is greater, since germs can be deeply implanted and cannot be easily washed away.

In addition the object may puncture a vital organ in the chest or abdomen.

See also ABDOMINAL INJURIES; ACCIDENTS; BLEEDING; CHEST INJURIES; GUNSHOT WOUNDS; HEART STOPPAGE; MOVING THE INJURED; SHOCK; TETANUS.

PYORRHEA See PERIODONTAL DISEASE.

QUACKERY is fraud or incompetence in health care—the term derives from an old Dutch word, *quacksalver,* meaning *charlatan.*

Purveyors of quackery owe their apparent successes in healing to the fact that most diseases are self-limiting. Given time, they cure themselves regardless of treatment. Similarly, many diseases ordinarily go through stages of worsening and improving. A normal remission may be attributed to a quack cure. Pain and many other symptoms are highly subjective. If a sufferer feels better after being treated by a quack, he may regard the practitioner as a miracle worker.

However such relief comes at considerable risk and cost. The quack is unqualified to treat, often even to recognize, a major condition that requires prompt care. For this bad medicine you pay good money. About $1 of every $9 spent for health goes to purveyors and manufacturers of quack products and services. The amount, some $2 billion a year, is about three times that spent for all medical research.

How quacks prosper. You need to protect *yourself* against quackery. Enforcement by the authorities is extremely weak. It took ten years for the Food and Drug Administration (FDA) to halt the sale of the worthless Hoxsey cancer treatment. The FTC fought for 16 years before getting the word *liver* removed from Carter's Little Liver Pills. Though the FDA, FTC, and Post Office Department were massed against a man named Paul Case, who sold a useless rheumatism remedy, he stayed in business for at least 28 years. Ultimately he was fined but $250, an example of the flimsy penalties against quackery.

The diseases supposedly treated are limited only by the charlatan's imagination. To an unscrupulous seller of a health product a disease is a "market"—and the more markets he can reach, the likelier he is to make a profit. The manufacturer of one device claimed it could diagnose 33 conditions by measuring electrical currents in the body. Actually, the machine could not detect the difference between a live person and a corpse.

There's only one sure way to avoid quackery. That is to put your health care under the guidance of a reliable physician and narrowly limit your self-diagnosis and self-medication. For the care of teeth and mouth problems rely on a reputable dentist.

How quacks operate. Quackery strives to appear legitimate, which can make it hard for you to detect health frauds. It's common for a quack to wear a white coat, call himself "Doctor," and display walls full of diplomas and certificates. He may set up a "clinic," "foundation," or "institute."

Typical was the Drosnes-Lazenby Cancer Clinic in Pittsburgh, which pushed a worthless mold called Mucorhicin. As for the medical backgrounds of the founders, Drosnes had been a tire salesman and Lazenby, a manager of a hospital cafeteria.

A favorite gimmick of clinics is to offer you free a supposed physical examination. Ads may be mailed out by the thousands; in Manhattan two chiropractors operating such a clinic had 31 telephone solicitors on their premises. If you bite, you're given a once-over with a stethoscope and blood pressure device, then informed you need X rays at such and such a charge.

The X rays in most cases "reveal" a dire ailment—cancer or whatever—and you're told you desperately need a course of "treatment." A Florida clinic operating in precisely this fashion took in an estimated $100,000 from so-called examinations that invariably showed the need for a $350 series of weekly enemas.

Many purveyors of quack goods and services are out-and-out con men. They know that what they're peddling is worthless, but they hustle fraudulent health care the same way they would junk cars, shoddy storm windows, or watered stock. A few such charlatans are M.D.'s who knowingly betray their patients and profession by engaging in quackery.

Still other quacks are very nice people who are well intentioned and sincerely believe they are offering a product or treatment that will help you. They don't think of themselves as "quacks" and would be offended if you told them that's what they are.

Quacks in general are disarming. Far from being sleazy, they are often well dressed and seem kind and sympathetic.

Nonetheless all of them—whether dishonest or deluded—are hazards to your health and pocketbook. Deliberately or not, they shortchange you on the first requirement of sound health care: Their product or method has no scientific basis.

What distinguishes modern medicine from

witchcraft is its application of sciences like biology, chemistry, and physics to healing and the preservation of health. In this requirement, the foundation of medical effectiveness, quackery fails you.

How to spot a quack. Watch for clues. Quackery has certain earmarks that distinguish it from legitimate medicine. Avoid a practitioner or product if you detect *any* of the following:

Quacks promote secrecy. There are no secret machines or formulas in medicine. If a doctor tells you that you can be cured only by him, he's either lying or no doctor. A guarantee of a cure is not worth the paper it's written on.

No reputable physician ever promises, much less guarantees, a quick or easy cure. Not only would such a promise open him up to a breach-of-contract suit, it would fly in the face of what every doctor knows: You cannot predict exactly how any individual patient will respond to any given course of treatment.

Quacks sell worthless gadgets. Laymen are often impressed by medical devices. Thus many quacks rig up gadgets with so many dials and gauges they look like the instrument panel of an airliner.

Despite the array of knobs, flashing lights, buzzes, and clicks, the machines are medically worthless. Emphasizes the FDA: "There are no cure-all machines that are capable of diagnosing or treating different kinds of disease simply by turning dials and applying electrical contacts to the body. Such devices are fakes!"

These machines often have space age names—Radioclasts, Depolarays, Neurolinometers. One electronic device, the Oscilloclast, earned a doctor more than $2 million. He claimed that his machine could diagnose and cure all diseases, which were supposedly caused by "disharmonious vibrations" in the body's electrons.

In a test, a sample of blood was tested with the machine. It diagnosed diabetes, malaria, cancer, and syphilis. Actually, the blood came from a rooster.

Quacks promote their cures. Ethical practitioners don't try to get you to buy a particular product or service from them. They clarify your choices and make recommendations. Some physicians dispense—most often drugs or eyeglasses. But rather than push you into buying from them, they give you a prescription that you are free to take to a druggist or optician of your choice.

Only a quack uses testimonials from "satisfied" patients. Laymen, however big in show business or government, are rarely competent to judge medical matters. A U.S. senator was a leading proponent of the fake cancer cure Krebiozen. Blind people sincerely lent their names to a drug they believed was growing them new eyes. People who swore that they were cured by a diabetes remedy actually never had the disease.

Some quack products are sold door-to-door by salesmen who represent themselves as "health and nutrition specialists." One diet supplement containing vitamins and minerals had 75,000 salesmen ringing doorbells and promising homemakers the product would help with cancer, alcoholism, ulcers, arthritis.

Be extremely skeptical of medical reports in the popular press. Quacks constantly try to steal space through news releases, and editors often print an article without being certain of its accuracy.

Television and radio promotion is no less specious. Talk shows may give quacks enormous exposure, with no equal time for a spokesman for medical accuracy. Don't trust any product whose commercials bandy about words like *safe* and *cure,* or promise sensational "fast relief," or use actors pretending to be doctors. All such stratagems raise doubts about the manufacturer's reliability. An actual physician or dentist endorsing a product violates his profession's ethics.

Books advancing quack theories may be most hazardous of all, since a book smacks of authoritativeness and stays available a long time. Glenn D. Kittler's book, *Laetrile: Control for Cancer,* is blamed for sending thousands of cancer victims to Mexico for the worthless drug, sometimes tragically delaying the care they need. Some quack books are written by M.D.'s, like Dr. Herman Taller's *Calories Don't Count* and Dr. D. C. Jarvis's *Arthritis and Folk Medicine.*

Quacks use the mails. Diagnostic tests and treatments are offered by mail for every major condition, and too many people have faith in mail-order advertising. An Iowan was indicted for mail fraud for a scheme aimed at diabetics. His treatment called for withdrawing from insulin and replacing it with sugar. Any diabetic who did this was courting death.

The list of mail-order quackery is endless. Promoters have been convicted of selling defective hearing aids through the mail, their prime victims being the impoverished elderly. Phony sex products galore are hustled via the postal service, like Persuasion X-19, an aphrodisiac; Erectopen, an impotence cure; booklets for "virility exercises"; oils and incenses for sexual attraction.

Your mailbox can be flooded with do-it-yourself hypnosis schemes, tablets, special garments and foods for losing weight—none of which works.

A quack may be hostile to the medical profession. Here's a quick test for quackery: Ask a practitioner to consult with your family physician. If he refuses or tries to dissuade you, you can assume he's up to no good.

Merely dissenting from policies of the AMA and organized medicine (the informal network of societies within the profession) is not a sign of quackery. Many reputable doctors do it. But their basic disagreements are nearly always on grounds that are political and economic, not scientific. A competent physician may disagree with the AMA's stand on questions like government regulation, but he or she surely supports the profession's methods of research and proof.

By contrast, quacks often seek to discredit medical science, refusing to accept established procedures for investigation. As in the case of Krebiozen (see CANCER) they may clamor for recognition—but avoid tests or stop short of giving data needed for proper evaluation. Some quacks claim that medicine is afraid of their competition. A quack may tell you that his method of treatment is better than surgery, X rays, or drugs prescribed by physicians.

Quacks may claim miracles. Some faith healers have been taken seriously in scientific circles because they evidently cured patients whom doctors regarded as absolutely hopeless.

Because such apparent miracles do in fact occur, spiritual therapy cannot be wholly dismissed. And many quacks cash in on this. Don't delay getting standard medical care while pinning your hopes on a miracle. Self-deluding quacks who deem themselves miracle workers can be at least as dangerous as outright frauds.

Don't fall for quacks who use churches as a gimmick, calling themselves "ministers," "prelates," "bishops." The National Council of Churches knows of more than 400 such "churches" with at least 150,000 members. Typically, in Turlock, California, the so-called Universal Life Church offered cures with a Multiple Wave Oscillator, actually an automobile spark coil. State investigators caught the minister of the church using the device to treat a parishioner who had throat cancer.

Christianity is similarly exploited. The Christian Medical Research League was the principal outfit distributing the worthless cancer remedy Glyoxilide.

Resist the claims of religious groups that hold out the promise of cures through the occult. You'll be wasting money if you buy a product like the Oriental Mystic Magnetic Health Bracelet, which claims to cure fatigue, menopause, sleeplessness, neuralgia, and headache.

You risk a lot more if you put yourself in the hands of a "yogi healer and clairvoyant reader" like "Dr. Abn Donahji," actually a factory worker who got no closer to India than his native Kansas. From a house rechristened a temple, he took in about $400,000 from people he treated personally and by mail for cancer, heart disease, and multiple sclerosis.

A growing army of witches and warlocks (male witches) seek to lure you into buying cures from the beyond. "You literally go into the other world to do battle with the disease," a Berkeley, California, witch told a cancer victim, then cast a spell over a bubbling cauldron.

Bookshops specializing in the occult also sell books like *Back to Eden: Healing Herbs, Home Remedies, Diet & Health*—which contains a disastrous self-medication for cancer—and magazines like *Occult Gazette,* which advertises remedies to induce abortion. Many occult bookstores have bulletin boards overflowing with ads for spiritual healers.

Nor is there value in voodoo or root medicine, widely practiced in black communities. One root doctor got at least $25,000 from people who followed such advice as, "Touch the place where it hurts with 13¢. Then send the 13¢ along with an additional $6."

One Professor Senoj (try it backwards) claimed to be descended from African kings and to know their secrets of brewing roots and herbs to cure all ills. He came complete with a snake and a talking parakeet, and wore flowing black robes and a white headgear with a ruby. After drawing blood with a razor blade, he'd prescribe a liquid found to be turpentine and vinegar mixed with roots, house dirt, and roaches. Cost: $10.

Don't be lured by supposed American Indian tribal medicine. A woman calling herself Princess Yellow Robe sold a laxative-liniment combination for treating bedwetting, sinusitis, earache —and also cows with sore udders.

Indian folklore can be dangerous. In Arizona a badly burned Indian asked to have a medicine man perform the appropriate ritual at bedside. His physician agreed, unaware that the ritual entailed spitting on the burns. The patient developed septicemia (a blood infection) that killed him.

Why quackery flourishes. Texas Tech University researchers interviewed patients who had been detoured from conventional to quack care and concluded that they fall into four categories:

1. The miracle seekers, who turn to religion in

time of trouble. One woman with breast cancer used a prayer cloth each night for six months, expecting each morning to find that the condition disappeared. Finally she was convinced that her sinfulness and lack of faith were responsible for the failure of her treatment. She turned to conventional care, too late.

2. *The restless,* who are looking for a quick cure. They tend to be impatient, uncooperative, often angry. They assume the attitude toward conventional physicians, "If you can't do it now, I'll go somewhere else."

3. *The uninformed,* who know little or nothing about doctors and medical practice. If someone says so-and-so is a cancer specialist, they accept the statement as a fact without further investigation.

To the uninformed every newsworthy advance in medical therapy can make quack treatment seem more reasonable. If hormones are effective in a number of conditions, so too might be Liefcort for arthritis or Laetrile for cancer. If penicillin can be a wonder drug though derived from lowly mold, who can discredit this or that drug whose origins are no more improbable?

4. *The straw-graspers,* desperate people who've been told by their physicians that nothing more of a curative nature can be done for them. In a panic they seek someone who offers hope—and fall into the hands of the first quack who promises a cure.

In *Death Be Not Proud* the distinguished journalist John Gunther relates the story of his 16-year-old son's fight against brain cancer. Told by foremost specialists that there was no hope,

the otherwise sophisticated Gunther tried everything. One practitioner prescribed doses of vegetable juice combined with freshly squeezed blood from calf's liver. To get the precise regimen, Gunther placed the boy in the quack's hospital.

Quacks may fill emotional needs not met by the patient's physician. Being sick can make adults childish in thought and feeling. Often the patient seeks an all-powerful "parent" to relieve the illness, a need that is met by the quack's emotionally gratifying reassurances and guarantees.

The quack generally holds out hope, where the regular physician may not. Although the quack can't cure the disease, he has for a brief time soothed the patient and helped the family to believe they have left no stone unturned in seeking a cure. Doctors who have studied why people turn to quacks urge their colleagues to try to meet a patient's emotional needs, to give them a little sympathy and reassurance.

For specific information on worthless remedies see also ACNE; ALLERGY; ANEMIA; ARTHRITIS; BEDWETTING; BREAST SMALLNESS; CANCER; CHIROPRACTORS; COLDS; COLITIS; DENTURES; DIABETES; DRUGS; EPILEPSY; EXERCISE; EYEGLASSES; FATIGUE; FRIGIDITY; HAIR LOSS; HEADACHE; HEALTH FOOD; HEARING AIDS; HEART DISEASE; HOSPITAL; IMPOTENCE. MENOPAUSE; MINERALS; MULTIPLE SCLEROSIS.

NUTRITION; OVERWEIGHT; PHYSICAL EXAMINATION; PHYSICIAN; POLIO; RESPIRATORY DISEASE; RHEUMATISM; SEX DISORDER; SKIN DISORDERS; SLEEPLESSNESS; SMOKING; STRESS; SURGERY; TUBERCULOSIS; VITAMINS; WRINKLES; X RAYS.

RABBIT FEVER See TULAREMIA.

RABIES (hydrophobia) has had an upsurge among wildlife—particularly bats, skunks, foxes, and raccoons, somewhat less so among coyotes, bobcats, woodchucks, minks. The Center for Disease Control warns families that wild animals as pets are a danger.

All warm-blooded animals can carry this infectious disease. Dogs and cats continue to be responsible for most of the 20,000 people who need antirabies vaccinations in the United States each year, and many cases occur in such farm livestock as cows, horses, goats, sheep, and hogs.

The rabies virus is transmitted almost exclusively in saliva injected by a rabid animal's bite. A rare case results from a rabid animal's licking a scratch or sore.

Once rabies develops, it is almost invariably fatal, with the symptoms becoming progressively more severe. Vigorous supportive therapy has occasionally saved a rabies victim.

The rabies virus attacks the nervous system. After an incubation period ranging from ten days to a year or more, depending on the severity of the bite and its closeness to the brain, the victim often develops a tingling sensation at the site of the wound. His muscles may stiffen, his nerves tense, and he becomes overcome with anxiety, often maniacal terror.

The disease can cause an increased flow of saliva, the "foaming at the mouth" of folklore. Convulsions may be brought on by a light touch or even by currents of air. When the patient attempts to drink, he may suffer strangling contractions in the muscles of the throat.

After several such seizures he may develop hydrophobia—fear of water. Even the sight of water or mention of the word can induce a convulsion. Death generally results from respiratory failure.

Rabies in animals. Rabies can make an animal unusually hostile ("furious rabies")—or just the opposite ("dumb rabies"). One of the first symptoms is a noticeable change in the animal's disposition. In dumb rabies, a previously playful dog becomes sullen, prefers to be alone, refuses food. It may appear ill and may die without any evidence of furious behavior.

In furious rabies, the animal may attack without warning. As the disease progresses, the animal snarls viciously, barks and growls at imaginary objects, and may chase and bite other animals—thereby spreading the disease. If free it may wander long distances from home, biting as it goes, until it drops from paralysis or exhaustion and dies.

Dumb rabies is more difficult to recognize. The symptoms of excitement and irritability are absent or slight. Indeed a usually wild animal like a skunk or raccoon may seem tame, posing a danger to children who may wish to adopt it as a pet.

Paralysis is frequently first noted in the lower jaw, and the appearance and choking of the animal may lead one to believe that it has a bone in its throat. Any attempt to relieve the animal is dangerous, since it may result in getting infectious saliva into some skin wound.

If you are bitten, cleanse the wound immediately with soap and water. If one is available, use a syringe—like that of a douche—to flush the full depth of the wound. Then get to a doctor as quickly as possible. He most likely will irrigate the wound with a medical detergent and give you an injection against tetanus, in addition to taking rabies precautions.

If the animal is a pet dog or cat, it should be kept under observation for ten days. If it appears normal at the end of this period, there need be no fear of rabies. If you need to kill a wild animal or unwanted pet, or if an animal dies, pack the head in ice and have it examined for rabies at the nearest health department laboratory.

If the animal is not available, your physician will have to determine whether to subject you to treatment. Your risk of exposure to rabies will be greatest if the biting animal was a carnivorous animal or bat, if its bite was unprovoked, or if rabies is in the area.

The best treatment is human rabies immune globulin plus human diploid cell vaccine. The course of treatment lasts up to 28 days. Most people experience mild swelling and redness at the injection site. There may also be fever, nausea, abdominal pain, muscle aches, and headache.

Immunization before exposure to rabies is possible. But it is recommended only if you are traveling to a region where rabies is a constant threat, or if you are in frequent contact with potentially rabid animals. If you're bitten, it's essential to get a booster dose of the vaccine.

See also ANIMAL DISEASE; INFECTIOUS DISEASE.

RADIATION is a process—natural or man-made —by which energy is emitted and carried through space in the form of electromagnetic waves or infinitesimal particles. Anything that stops the radiation absorbs the energy. This absorption can damage living tissue. Radiation at any level can be potentially dangerous.

The most common form of radiation is from the sun, and solar radiation has been linked to skin cancer, as well as to sunburn and premature aging of the skin leading to wrinkles and senile freckles. X rays used in diagnosis and treatment may cause burns and birth defects. Faulty color television sets may emit X rays. Emissions from microwave ovens may lead to cataracts.

Radioactivity is a property of some elements —radium, uranium, plutonium—that involves the emission of special types of radiation. Men who worked for many years mining uranium and pitchblende, a source of radium, were prone to lung cancer. Painters of luminous watch dials often developed cancer of the bone. Over a long period they unknowingly swallowed small quantities of radium while moistening their paintbrushes with their lips. Today such occupational exposure to radiation is rare, except for workers in nuclear energy plants.

In nuclear war or a severe nuclear accident the effects of heavy acute radiation exposure may appear immediately or not until many years later. Called radiation sickness, the short-term effects may include nausea, fatigue, and blood and intestinal disorders. There may be temporary hair loss and, at very high doses, severe or fatal damage to the central nervous system. Survivors of the atomic bombings of Hiroshima and Nagasaki suffered an increased incidence of leukemia.

However exposure to any dose of radiation does not necessarily mean cancer and death. You are exposed to minute background radiation constantly from cosmic rays, radioactivity in the earth, building materials, even from food and body substances such as potassium. While exposure to potentially harmful radiation should be kept to a minimum, the body is generally able to repair almost all exposures to small doses.

The body also can tolerate a substantial dose of radiation. A dose of 450 rads to the entire body is likely to be lethal, but the National Council on Radiation Protection and Measurements estimates that a single dose of even 200 rads to the entire body would probably not require medical care.

See also BIRTH DEFECTS; CANCER; CANCER OF THE BONE; CANCER OF THE LUNG; CANCER OF THE SKIN; CATARACT; FRECKLES; HAIR LOSS; LEUKEMIA; MICROWAVE OVENS; SUNBURN; TELEVISION; WRINKLES; X RAYS.

RATS are too dangerous to be allowed around your home. They often attack sleeping humans —particularly babies.

Rats also carry leptospirosis, plague, trichinosis, and typhus. Rat-bite fever is marked by stiff joints and long-lasting, painful ulceration in the bite area. Rickettsialpox, spread by rats in cities, causes pimples around the body, accompanied by fever, headache, and muscular pain.

To keep down the rat population, eliminate the conditions in which they thrive. First look for rat signs like droppings, tracks, and rub marks. The droppings of rats are fairly large— up to 3/4 inch long and not less than 1/2 inch. Mouse droppings are only about 1/4 inch.

Track marks may be left on the ground or on dusty surfaces and are a good clue. Along walls an inch or so from the floor, look for rub marks. Rats like to stay close to walls, which they feel with sensitive hairs in their whiskers and on their bodies.

Trap or poison them. If you decide to use traps, don't just set one or two but many—so you catch a lot of rats before they become "trap wise." Place traps along baseboards in corners and near possible ratholes.

You can buy poisoned rat bait at drugstores, grocery stores, and garden shops. Closely follow directions on packages. But make sure to lock up extra poison where children cannot possibly reach it.

Tin pans make good containers for poisoned bait if nailed to the floor so rats can't turn them over. Put the pans of bait in out-of-the-way places where you think rats might go. If there are a lot of rats around, you may have to set out a large number of baits. Inspect and rebait often.

Starve them out. Don't let rats get to your garbage. Teach children not to play with lids, leaving cans open so rats can get in.

Garbage cans should be strong, with lids that fit. It is best to put cans on platforms with guard rails so they cannot be turned over.

Destroy their living places. Pick up old lumber, bottles, boxes, and other junk from yards and alleys. Rats don't like to come out in the open and so they often hide behind trash.

Ratproof your house. Put metal hardware cloth over even very small holes. A mouse can get through hardware cloth larger than 1/4-inch mesh and a small rat through hardware cloth larger than 1/2-inch mesh.

Fill openings around pipes with sheet metal patches or concrete. Rats can cross wide city streets by walking telephone wires, and they can climb the vertical walls of most brick buildings. Vine-covered walls are perfect runways.

With a running start and a bounce against a vertical wall, rats can jump more than 3 feet. They are also good swimmers and have been known to swim up through toilets and floor drains—probably coming from a manhole or other break in the sewer.

They can gnaw through almost anything— even lead pipes, oak planks, and poorly mixed concrete. Since their front teeth grow at least 4 inches a year, rats must gnaw to wear them down.

Get your neighbors to cooperate. When rats infest a neighborhood, they are more than an individual problem. Your local health department can help you clean out rats. But rats will come back unless you and your neighbors keep things cleaned up to deny them food and shelter.

See also ANIMAL BITES; ANIMAL DISEASE.

REFRIGERATORS and freezers can be lethal traps, and suffocation in them has become more common as people buy new models and either store their old ones or throw them away with the door intact. Children coming upon a discarded refrigerator are tempted to use it as a playhouse, jail, or hiding place. If trapped in an airtight box, a child will consume all the oxygen in 15 minutes, less if he screams and pounds.

Before abandoning or storing a refrigerator, remove the door. It isn't enough to remove the latch, since the door may be too heavy for children to push it open. Three fourths of the victims in refrigerator deaths are under the age of six.

If a box is temporarily out of use, use rubber bumpers or wooden blocks to keep the door from closing. Or chain and padlock or tie the door closed. Or face it against a wall so the door

can't be opened. Warn baby-sitters of this hazard.

See also ACCIDENTS.

RESPIRATION, ARTIFICIAL See ARTIFICIAL RESPIRATION.

RESPIRATORY DISEASE is any condition that interferes with breathing or other functions of the respiratory system. Respiratory-disease sufferers are the target of a wide variety of patent medicines, virtually none of which is more effective than inexpensive home remedies.

The most common symptoms of respiratory disease—coughing, sore throat, hoarseness, and shortness of breath—may indicate grave conditions. Don't ignore them or rely on patent medicines to treat them yourself. If they persist more than a very few days, see a doctor.

Colds are by far the commonest respiratory disease, indeed the leading U.S. cause of acute illness. A cold may lower your resistance and make you more vulnerable to other respiratory forms of infectious disease such as pneumonia, sinusitis, and tonsillitis.

In small children croup may be a life-threatening result of colds. Bronchiectasis and pleurisy are among other secondary respiratory problems that may develop.

Influenza is an acute illness that may have severe complications.

Repeated infections may turn acute bronchitis into a chronic condition. Emphysema, though not well known to the general public, is a major crippler among chronic diseases. Tuberculosis, while now curable with drug therapy, is still widespread, and many people don't know they have it.

Some respiratory diseases—notably asthma and hay fever—may result from an allergy. Others, like histoplasmosis and coccidioidomycosis, are caused by fungi. Cystic fibrosis is an inherited condition. Workers in a number of occupations suffer from dust disease, although asbestos dust is a hazard to everyone.

Smoking and air pollution are major contributors to respiratory disease. Both are linked to lung cancer.

Maintaining proper humidity can be helpful in relieving respiratory disease. Nose drops are of benefit in some conditions but must be used with extreme caution or they may be habit-forming.

Postnasal drip aggravates respiratory conditions. If it results from nose deformities, it may be correctable by plastic surgery.

Hyperventilation can be hazardous to swimmers. Breath-holding, on the other hand, while scary to parents, is rarely serious to the child.

NOT USING A REFRIGERATOR?
It can be a death trap for kids!
Remove doors

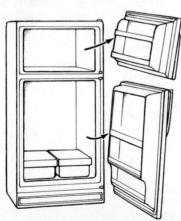

Distinguishing Common Respiratory Diseases

Symptom	Common Cold	Allergic Rhinitis (Year-round hay fever)	Sinusitis	Bronchitis	Influenza	Strep Throat
Duration of illness	At least 5–7 days	Weeks or months	Days; months if not treated		About 10 days	Symptoms clear after 3 days with or without treatment
Cough	Dry, hacking, clear mucus if any	None, unless caused by post-nasal drip	None	Severe; pus in sputum	Severe	Treat for 10 days
Fever	Low if any	None	Over 100°F, variable	Over 100°F, variable	Over 100°F, perhaps as high as 104°F	Over 100°F at times
Discharge	Clear, copious; runny nose	Clear; runny nose	Pus-laden, thick, yellow-green discharge from nose	No nasal discharge	Pus-laden discharge from nose	None
Pain	None, except a few aches before or at onset	None	Pain over involved sinuses	In chest, on coughing or drawing deep breath	Generalized aches	In throat
Sore throat	Should be gone in 3 days	None	None	None	Yes	Red, inflamed
Other			Possible sore throat due to sinus drainage		Possibly diarrhea, vomiting	Often headache; sometimes abdominal pain; Breath odor; Speech nasal.

Hiccups, another nuisance, is easily remedied. So too is gagging.

See also AIR POLLUTION; ALLERGY; ASBESTOS; ASTHMA; BREATH-HOLDING; BRONCHIECTASIS; BRONCHITIS; CANCER OF THE LUNG; COCCIDIOIDOMYCOSIS; COLDS; COUGHING; CROUP; CYSTIC FIBROSIS.

DUST DISEASE; EMPHYSEMA; GAGGING; HAY FEVER; HICCUPS; HISTOPLASMOSIS; HOARSENESS; HUMIDITY; HYPERVENTILATION.

INFECTIOUS DISEASE; INFLUENZA; NOSE DEFORMITIES; NOSE DROPS; PLEURISY; PNEUMONIA; POSTNASAL DRIP; SHORTNESS OF BREATH; SINUSITIS; SMOKING; SORE THROAT; TONSILLITIS; TUBERCULOSIS.

RESUSCITATION, MOUTH-TO-MOUTH See ARTIFICIAL RESPIRATION.

RETARDATION, MENTAL See MENTAL RETARDATION.

Rh DISEASE results from a blood incompatibility between a mother and her unborn child. The Center for Disease Control estimates that it kills about 6,000 babies a year in the United States alone, and burdens another 20,000 with congenital anemia, heart disease, hearing loss, jaundice, or mental retardation. About one out of every eight expectant mothers is a potential bearer of a child with Rh disease.

Now a dramatically effective medication can make Rh disease a problem of the past. The drug is called Rh immune globulin, and is marketed under the trade names RhoGam, HypRH-D, and Gamulin Rh. The American College of Obstetrics and Gynecologists recommends that it be administered to all Rh-negative women within 72 hours of childbirth, miscarriage, or abortion.

An injection costs about $50. Clinics operated by Planned Parenthood may provide the medication free to their abortion patients who need it. Some states make it available at no cost through hospital obstetric services.

The disease itself is unique. To begin with there is nothing wrong with either the baby or the mother. It is the interaction between the two that causes the trouble. Even more curious, it is the interaction between the mother and her first baby that can make trouble for a later baby.

Rh disease can occur only if the mother is Rh negative. This means that a blood component present in most people (85 to 90 percent of American females) happens to be missing. The component is called the Rh factor because it was first isolated in a Rhesus monkey.

When the Rh factor enters the bloodstream of an Rh-negative woman, it is a foreign substance. Her body's immune system springs into action and starts manufacturing antibodies to fight it off, just as if it were a horde of infectious microbes.

This is precisely the set of circumstances that comes about if an Rh-negative woman becomes pregnant and if her baby is Rh positive—that is, if the baby's blood contains the Rh factor. The incompatibility does not seriously endanger the first baby because the placenta separates the two blood circulations. About halfway through the pregnancy, however, some of the baby's blood begins to seep through. Then, just before birth, with the ripping away of the placenta, a great spurt of the baby's blood enters the mother's bloodstream.

In some women this blood interchange will cause the mother's system to start manufacturing antibodies, and in a small percentage of cases these antibodies will pose a danger in future pregnancies, damaging or even destroying the fetus if it is Rh positive.

Before the development of Rh immune globulin, there was no way to prevent Rh disease and its aftereffects. An Rh-negative mother could limit herself to having only one child if her first was Rh positive, and she had begun to develop antibodies. Or Rh-negative people could exercise genetic control by marrying only other Rh negatives, thus ensuring Rh-negative offspring but severely limiting their choice of mates.

However it was possible to monitor the mother's blood during pregnancy, and if the level of antibodies rose to a dangerous level, the newborn child's blood supply was completely replaced by transfusion. In some cases doctors were able to accomplish such transfusions while the child was still in the mother's womb. This did save many babies, but it could not reverse or alleviate whatever defects had already been suffered.

The Rh immune globulin, which contains anti-Rh antibodies, has changed all that. Injected into an Rh-negative mother, it tricks her body into foregoing its normal antibody-making activity. This prevents her from inflicting Rh disease on her future babies.

The vaccine does not work on Rh-negative mothers who have already acquired their own permanent active antibodies by having given birth to an Rh-positive child. It has, however, proved 99 percent effective on Rh-negative women when it is administered within 72 hours after the birth of the first baby, or after a miscarriage or abortion. Because the vaccine's immunizing effects are only temporary, the mother must be revaccinated with each birth.

See also BIRTH DEFECTS; PREGNANCY.

RHEUMATIC FEVER is said to "lick the joints and bite the heart."

This inflammation of the joints is accompanied by heart disease in about one out of three cases. The American Heart Association believes rheumatic fever causes more prolonged disabling illness in children than any other disease.

Initially rheumatic fever can weaken the heart muscle, harm the heart's pumping function, deform its valves, and enlarge the whole organ. It may leave permanent damage, most often in the valves of the left side.

Many cases of rheumatic heart disease hidden for years are discovered during a routine examination when heart murmurs are detected.

An estimated 98 percent of the acquired heart disease suffered by people under 20 years old is caused by rheumatic heart disease. Adults may develop the disease as well.

An aftermath of strep. Take special care in strep infections. Rheumatic fever is always triggered by an infection of streptococcal bacteria, such as a strep sore throat, scarlet fever, or strep ear. Some 10 to 30 days after the original infection signs of rheumatic fever may appear in about 1 to 3 percent of untreated strep infections. The greatest percentage of these are in children 5 to 15; the next largest groups are very young children and adolescents.

Rheumatic fever itself is not contagious, but strep infection is, and can spread among close contacts at home and at school.

To prevent rheumatic fever the strep infection needs to be treated with a ten-day course of penicillin—and it is vital that all of the penicillin be taken, even after symptoms disappear.

Rheumatic fever symptoms include tenderness and swelling of the joints. Some, but usually not all, of the following major symptoms may also be present: Heart inflammation, often with murmurs, involuntary jerky movements of the body, nodules under the skin, a pink rash. There may be fever, nosebleed, abdominal pains.

A victim who has had rheumatic fever is particularly susceptible to another attack, with additional heart damage.

Rheumatic fever mimics several other diseases: Rheumatoid arthritis, leukemia, sickle cell anemia, tuberculosis, brucellosis, appendicitis. This makes it so difficult to diagnose that some specialists suspect there are three or four cases of rheumatic fever for every case that is brought to a doctor and diagnosed.

Although drugs can cure strep infections, no medication will cure rheumatic fever. If there is no heart involvement, aspirin can relieve the symptoms. If the heart is involved, then the physician may prescribe steroids to reduce inflammation and subsequent heart disease.

The most important treatment for rheumatic fever is bed rest. This gives the child's natural strength a chance to combat the illness. Hospitalizing children is often best so they can have constant expert care.

The first attack may be over in a few weeks, or it may take months. Then the victim needs to continue to rest in bed until the doctor is sure the active stage is over, even though he may look well and feel fine.

About half the children who have rheumatic fever suffer no aftereffects. Many whose hearts are affected escape serious damage. Surgery can repair some heart valves that have been injured.

Once a child has had rheumatic fever, it is doubly important to prevent a strep infection that could bring on another seige of the disease. One method calls for a monthly injection of long-lasting penicillin. Another preventive requires a small dose of penicillin, or of a sulfa drug, taken by mouth every day.

But don't make a child a hypochondriac. Only strep bacteria bring on a recurrence of rheumatic fever. Cold weather and exercise do not. Thus it is unnecessary—and possibly psychologically harmful—to overdress children who have had rheumatic fever or to needlessly restrict their participation in sports or other activities.

A life-threatening complication can arise if the rheumatic fever patient develops aortic insufficiency (aortic regurgitation), in which some of the blood pumped to the aorta flows back into the heart through a damaged valve. It's important for the doctor to check early for a high-pitched heart murmur. Otherwise ten years may pass before the appearance of such advanced symptoms as heart palpitations caused by exercise, followed by problems with breathing and fatigue.

A patient with a value defect has a lifelong predisposition to a heart infection called subacute bacterial endocarditis, which can lead to heart and kidney failure and blood clots in the brain and lungs. To prevent infection the person should get antibiotics before any tooth extraction or other type of surgery. He also should consult a physician at the first sign of fever, chills, sweats, fatigue, joint pains, or loss of appetite.

See also HEART DISEASE; INFECTIOUS DISEASE; SORE THROAT.

RHEUMATISM is a term for pain in joints or

muscles, usually recurrent. The causes are legion. Although there are products valuable for relieving temporary minor aches and pains associated with rheumatism, there is no single product that is a cure for it.

The commonest rheumatic condition that does not affect the joints directly is fibrositis, or muscular rheumatism. Lumbago is pain in the lower back. Fibrositis is not a proven disease entity, but a combination of symptoms including pain, stiffness, or soreness of fibrous tissue, especially in the muscle coverings. Attacks may follow an injury, repeated muscular strain, prolonged mental stress, or depression.

The condition may disappear spontaneously or respond well to treatment. Other cases persist for years. However chronic sufferers are rarely crippled. Fibrositis is not a destructive, progressive disease.

See also ARTHRITIS; RHEUMATIC FEVER.

RHEUMATOID ARTHRITIS is a chronic illness associated with inflammation of the connective and supporting tissues of the body. It is most destructive in the joints. This form of arthritis occurs more often in women than in men. Unlike osteoarthritis it is most likely to strike people from 20 to 50, but can occur at any age.

The disease usually begins with general fatigue and—especially on waking—soreness, stiffness, and aching, followed by the gradual appearance of localized symptoms of pain, swelling, warmth, and tenderness. Sometimes there is a sudden onset of these symptoms. In most cases several joints become involved, particularly those of the hands and feet. Usually there is weakness and fatigue, loss of appetite, and loss of weight. Frequently sufferers have cold, sweaty hands and feet.

Gradually joint motion can be lost, and in time deformities of the joints may occur. In addition to joint symptoms patients may have other changes such as lumps under the skin, inflammation of the eyes, pleurisy, and anemia.

Permanent damage during the early years of the disease may be kept to a minimum with prompt treatment. There is always some tissue inflammation even when it cannot be detected by X ray. In more serious forms there may be erosion of the cartilage and bones and scarring of the soft tissues around the joint. Sometimes in severe cases joint surfaces are affected to the point where the joint cannot bear weight or is unstable. In other cases the joint surfaces grow together so they cannot be moved.

But for every person who may have serious crippling or deformities, there may be hundreds who don't even realize their aches and pains are caused by rheumatoid arthritis. The disease varies widely in severity. Many people have a mild form of the disease.

Rheumatoid arthritis is typically a disease of ups and downs. Even someone with a severe case may have periods lasting weeks, months, or years in which pain and stiffness are much reduced or even absent. Sometimes—in one out of every five people with the condition—it seems to disappear completely. Doctors may still find evidence that the disease is present, but as far as the patient is concerned, it is gone.

The cause of rheumatoid arthritis is unknown. Some scientists speculate that an infection triggers a chain of events leading to the development of the disease, even though the infectious agent (perhaps a virus) itself may be gone by the time the disease appears.

Another theory holds that the body's chemistry may be thrown out of kilter so that the body produces antibodies that attack its own joints and tissues. The suspected process is known as autoallergy.

It seems clear that emotional stress may be an important factor in aggravating the disease. You may notice the beginning of symptoms following a disturbing event such as a death in the family, divorce, separation, or an emotional strain or shock. If you already have rheumatoid arthritis, such events may seem to make the disease worse. Even worrying about having arthritis sometimes seems to delay improvement. When emotional stresses are relieved, improvement follows. You can help yourself a great deal by discussing personal problems frankly with the doctor.

There is no cure for rheumatoid arthritis. However the disease can often be controlled and the pain considerably relieved. Treatments include a combination of drugs, exercises, rest, posture rules, hydrotherapy, heat, splints and braces, gold therapy, and surgery.

Aspirin is the drug of choice initially. In sufficient quantities it relieves joint pain and reduces inflammation. Several small meals a day, with antacids between meals and at bedtime, can relieve the gastric distress aspirin may cause.

Indomethacin is an anti-inflammatory and analgesic drug that has proved effective in many patients with moderate symptoms, although it seems of little value in severe disease. While it has some side effects, it is generally considered the safest antirheumatic drug next to aspirin.

Other drugs—phenylbutazone, antimalarials, and corticosteroids—have been effective, but all can have marked side effects and should be used only under a doctor's supervision.

To provide temporary relief of a painful joint, medication—such as corticosteroids—may be injected directly into the joint. Relief may last from a few days to several weeks. After an injection take special care not to put too much strain on the joint, since overuse may accelerate joint destruction.

Chemical compounds containing gold have long been used. Gold injections may be especially helpful during the early stages of the disease. Because of dangers of toxicity, doctors often prefer to use this therapy only if other measures have failed for six or more months. A newer drug, penicillinamine, often has the same effect as gold therapy, and is also used for patients who have not responded to other medications. As a last resort immunosuppressive drugs, usually used in cancer therapy, may be prescribed.

Orthopedic operations on joints can be effective in preventing some deformities. Surgery also may help in relieving pain and improving overall function. An operation called a synovectomy—removal of the membrane that encloses joints—has been used with considerable success in improving function and correcting deformities, particularly in knee, hand, and wrist joints. However, the disease tends to return within two or three years after synovectomy. Other types of surgery can help joints of the hip, spine, neck, and foot.

In the past doctors used surgery only after extensive damage had already been done. Now surgery is sometimes considered as much a preventive as a corrective measure.

Juvenile rheumatoid arthritis. In children rheumatoid arthritis exists in several forms, some different from the type that affects adults. It is usually much milder in children than in adults. Most often children become afflicted before the age of seven, but occasionally the disease occurs in the first year of life. It may last into adult life.

A child's arthritis begins gradually and usually affects the knees. Frequently it is painless and without the morning stiffness prominent in adult rheumatoid arthritis. Some children have the disease in one joint only. All of this makes early recognition a problem.

Parents should also be aware that juvenile rheumatoid arthritis may begin with little or no evidence of joint involvement. A high fever, one that may reach 105° F, appears first, accompanied by a measleslike rash that is distinctive by lasting for weeks or months.

Although few children succumb to this disease, the great hazard of untreated juvenile rheumatoid arthritis is the potential danger to internal organs or eyes, which may become affected. The disease may also retard normal growth and development during adolescence.

Though there is now no cure for juvenile rheumatoid arthritis, children can be greatly helped by proper care and treatment, which must be under a physician's continued supervision. This includes the use of aspirin, steroids, and other drugs as well as physical therapy. Chances of avoiding permanent crippling are excellent if the child receives prompt and continuing medical care.

See also ARTHRITIS; SURGERY.

RHINITIS, ALLERGIC See HAY FEVER.

RIB FRACTURES can come and go unnoticed. Often the ribs adjacent to the broken rib act like splints to immobilize the fracture and allow it to heal.

Frequently, though, the person with a rib fracture will feel pain when he breathes or rolls over in bed. If so he will get relief if bandages are tied around his chest while he is awaiting medical help (see illustration).

Do not use a bandage if the fractured ends of the ribs seem to be pushing inward. A bandage might drive them deeper into soft tissue and penetrate the lung.

Multiple fractures of ribs may cause a "stove-in," "crushed," or "flail" chest. The flail, or loose segment, will not move with the rest of

IF A RIB MAY BE BROKEN

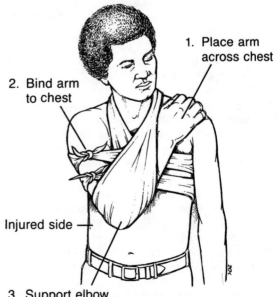

1. Place arm across chest

2. Bind arm to chest

Injured side

3. Support elbow with sling

WHEN MANY RIBS ARE BROKEN
Treat for flail chest

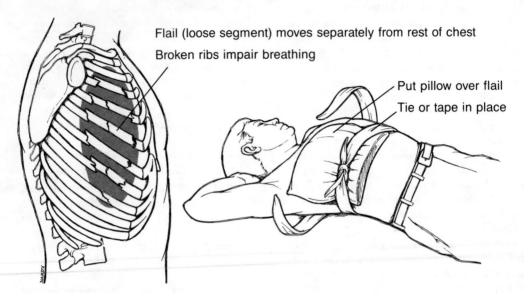

Flail (loose segment) moves separately from rest of chest

Broken ribs impair breathing

Put pillow over flail

Tie or tape in place

the chest cage in breathing. It will move out on an inhale, in on an exhale—and severely impair breathing.

Cover the flail with a pillow, binding it in place with tape or strips of cloth (see illustration). The splint will make it easier for the victim to breathe. Stand by to administer artificial respiration.

See also CHEST INJURIES; FRACTURES.

RIBOFLAVIN See VITAMINS.

RICKETS See VITAMINS.

RINGWORM is a fungus disease that gets its name from the circular, raised lesions that develop on the body. Athlete's foot, or ringworm of the feet, is the most common type. The groin infection jock itch may be caused by ringworm fungi. Other types:

Ringworm of the nails occurs when the fungus grows in or under the nails. The fungus growth can penetrate the nail, causing it to become thickened and misshapen, discolored, chalky, pitted, grooved, and brittle. This is the most stubborn form of ringworm infection.

Ringworm of the body is spread by contact with infected people or by touching their clothing and other contaminated articles. Ringworm of the body can be spread by cats, dogs, and other animals.

Infection is usually in the form of one to four flat, ring-shaped sores that may be dry and scaly, or crusted and moist. As the sores enlarge, the center of the ring frequently clears and leaves apparently normal skin. Ringworm of the body

can be transmitted from one person to another, or from animals to people, as long as the sores remain on the skin.

Ringworm of the scalp also can be spread from person to person or from animals to people. Clothing contaminated by an infected pet or person, unsterilized barber's tools, backs of theater seats, combs and brushes—all are possible sources of the fungus.

Scalp ringworm generally begins in the form of a small pimple or sore, then spreads into a ringlike shape to leave an area of scaly baldness that may be permanent. Infected hairs become brittle and break easily.

Treatment of all types of ringworm requires a physician. The medication most often prescribed is griseofulvin (Grifulvin, Fulvicin, Grisactin), which can have as side effects headaches, gastrointestinal disturbances, and allergic reactions.

Griseofulvin can also cause a reduced tolerance to alcohol. If you're taking the drug, you may get drunk easily and should steer clear of alcohol if you need to drive or to operate machinery. If pets or livestock have ringworm, consult a veterinarian. Check your animals often for the characteristic "moth-eaten" look of the fur.

Ringworm of the body can be prevented by wearing clean cotton garments, which absorb moisture. If you sweat a lot, either because of climate or emotional stress, change your hose and underwear as frequently as is practical and use talcum powder at each change.

Avoid scalp and body ringworm by never wearing another person's clothing or using another's towel or toilet articles. Be sure your barber sterilizes his instruments. Change and wash bedding frequently, especially between uses by different people.

To keep the infection from spreading to others, a person with ringworm of the scalp should not go to the barber or to any public place where his head will rub against the back of a seat.

See also ATHLETE'S FOOT; INFECTIOUS DISEASE; SKIN DISORDERS.

ROCKY MOUNTAIN SPOTTED FEVER (tick-borne typhus) is a severe infectious disease transmitted to man through the bite of ticks. The disease, originally believed to be limited to the Rocky Mountain region, is nationwide, being most prevalent in the Southeast. It is most likely to strike in spring and summer, when ticks are most active in brush and woods. The disease is a special hazard of camping, hiking, fishing, and other recreation in wooded areas.

The first symptoms appear 4 to 12 days after the bite. The attack is characterized by a chill, rapid rise in temperature, severe headache, restlessness, and sleeplessness. About three to four days after the fever begins, a pinkish skin rash appears. The individual spots are small and distinct.

The rash usually breaks out first on the arms and legs, especially around the wrists and ankles. Later it may spread over the entire body, including the face, palms, and soles of the feet. The victim suffers chiefly from headache. He is often restless and may become delirious. The disease is easily confused with measles and may lead to encephalitis or be fatal if untreated.

Call a doctor at the first appearance of symptoms. The danger of death from spotted fever has been radically reduced by broad-spectrum antibiotics.

Prevention is largely a matter of avoiding ticks and removing them if attached. It's generally believed that a tick must remain attached for several hours to transmit the infection.

See also INFECTIOUS DISEASE; TICKS.

ROSE FEVER   See HAY FEVER.

ROUGHAGE   See FIBER.

ROUNDWORMS (ascariasis) are large, tubular worms that look like ordinary earthworms and may be as much as 16 inches long and as thick as a pencil. The parasites infect some 3 million Americans, chiefly in the South. Children are most likely to be infested. Most victims harbor about a dozen worms, but in severe cases there may be hundreds.

Roundworm eggs are most often found in soil around unsanitary toilet facilities: poorly constructed outhouses, homes with inadequate sewage disposal, shallow field latrines, etc. The eggs generally are carried to the mouth by dirty hands and objects, and by vegetables and fruits fertilized with human excrement and not properly washed. The adult worm settles in the channel of the small intestine. Each day it expels some 200,000 eggs, which are carried out in the host's feces and may spread infection.

In mild infestations, symptoms are usually vague and erratic. The first clear sign of worm infection may come only with the victim's vomiting a worm or finding one in his bowel movement or in his bed. Heavy infection may cause such digestive disturbances as cramps, abdominal pain, and vomiting. The victim may tire easily but sleep poorly because of general restlessness.

Allergic reactions, most often hives, occur in people who are sensitized to the worms or their products. If the worms migrate from the intestine, they may cause severe damage to the liver and gallbladder. Fatal cases of peritonitis have resulted from worms penetrating the intestinal wall. Before settling in the small intestine, larvae of the worm migrate to the lungs, where they may cause a respiratory disease called pneumonitis.

Effective treatment is possible through drugs administered by a physician, most often piperazine citrate (Antepar) and pyrvinium pamoate (Povan). Povan can stun the unsuspecting by turning bowel movements brilliant red. Self-medication against worms can be dangerous. Children have died from taking over-the-counter preparations.

Prevention primarily consists of sanitary disposal of human excreta. Fruits and vegetables grown in areas where human feces is used for fertilizer need to be thoroughly washed and preferably cooked. Children need to be taught to wash their hands after using the toilet and before touching food, and to keep dirty hands and objects out of the mouth. Since contaminated soil may be carried into the house on shoes, train youngsters early to wash off or throw away food that has dropped on the floor.

For other parasitic diseases see HOOKWORMS; MALARIA; PINWORMS; SCHISTOSOMIASIS; TAPEWORMS; TRICHINOSIS. See also INFECTIOUS DISEASE; TRAVEL HEALTH.

RUBELLA (German measles) was for generations considered a common unimportant infectious disease of childhood. The first hint that it was a threat to unborn babies came when an Australian eye specialist, Dr. Norman M. Gregg, noticed a sharp increase in the number of babies brought to him with cataracts and other birth defects. From questioning Dr. Gregg learned that almost all the mothers had had rubella early in pregnancy.

Rubella that occurs in the first three months of pregnancy can penetrate the womb, infect the growing embryo, and cause drastic damage. When the disease strikes during the first month of pregnancy, it is estimated that half of the babies are born with malformations. These include brain damage (often accompanied by mental retardation, hearing loss, eye disorders, and congenital heart defects.

Twenty-two percent of babies whose mothers have rubella in the second month of pregnancy and 7 percent in the third month are born with such defects. There is evidence that rubella just before conception, or in the fourth month of pregnancy, can also trigger birth defects.

In addition an estimated 10 to 20 percent of the pregnancies in which rubella occurs end in miscarriage. Although a rubella-infected baby may appear normal at birth, abnormalities can show up some six months later. As a result of a U.S. rubella epidemic in 1964–65 more than 50,000 babies were born dead or with birth defects.

Rubella umbrella. All children need to be vaccinated against rubella. This immunization—widely hailed as the "rubella umbrella"—cuts down the major source of infection for susceptible pregnant women.

Have a child vaccinated between age one and puberty—the earlier the better, though before age one the vaccination may not take. The vaccine may be combined with those for measles and mumps.

Adolescent girls and adult women also need rubella immunization. They must not be pregnant at the time of vaccination—or become pregnant for at least three months thereafter.

The vaccine should not be administered if a person has cancer or a severe illness with fever, is taking steroids or some other drugs, or is undergoing X-ray treatment.

Rubella can be such a mild disease that many people have it without showing symptoms. But even these undetected cases in a pregnant woman can cause severe damage to an unborn infant. Conversely, other viruses can cause a mild, rashy disease which imitates rubella, and some women who think they've been made immune to rubella may not actually have had the disease. A blood test can determine whether you have antibody protection against rubella.

Typically, rubella causes a slight rash, a mild sore throat, and swollen glands in the neck. There may be fever, seldom higher than 100° F or 101° F, and it rarely lasts more than two or three days. In childhood there are almost never serious complications. One of the severest is rubella arthritis, which strongly resembles rheumatoid arthritis—and even that rare complication disappears completely, usually within a week.

Treatment is aimed mainly at keeping the sufferer comfortable. Aspirin and bed rest ordinarily suffice.

See also BIRTH DEFECTS; INFECTIOUS DISEASE.

RUPTURE See HERNIA.

SALMONELLOSIS (paratyphoid fever) most frequently results from food poisoning by salmonella bacteria. It's extremely common, probably amounting to 20 million cases a year. Victims of salmonellosis often think they have "intestinal flu." The symptoms can appear 8 to 48 hours after eating infected food, and are usually marked by fever, cramps, diarrhea, nausea, vomiting, and headache.

Do nothing to stop the diarrhea and vomiting, which are efforts by the body to purge itself of the poison. Drink plenty of milk or water to correct loss of fluids and to encourage the vomiting.

While this infectious disease is rarely fatal, it can be dangerous for the very young, very old, and people already weakened by illness. Otherwise healthy adults generally recover within a week if they stay in bed, drink lots of fluids, and apply warm compresses to the abdomen.

Salmonella most often infect meats, poultry, eggs, dry milk, and dairy products. Especially in regard to these foods, follow precautions against food poisoning. Salmon, the fish, has nothing to do with these bacteria, which derive their name from their discoverer, pathologist Daniel Elmer Salmon.

Turtle carriers. Keep pet turtles out of your home—they frequently harbor the disease. At the minimum wash your hands after handling one, and keep a pet turtle away from human food and dishes.

The sale of turtles as pets is illegal, but the animals are nonetheless widely available. Of the people who get salmonella from turtles, most are children who suck their fingers after handling pet turtles, kiss the animals, put them in their mouths, or drink the water or suck the pebbles from turtle bowls.

Even turtles certified as free of salmonella may carry the disease. Breeders can use chemicals to fool the salmonella test, and turtles may contract and transmit the bacteria after they're purchased.

Other pets that can carry this disease are dogs, ducklings, chicks, rabbits, guinea pigs, hamsters, and snakes.

See also FOOD POISONING; INFECTIOUS DISEASE.

SALT   See SODIUM.

SCABIES (sarcoptic itch) results from burrowing under the skin by mites, arachnids (close kin of spiders) barely 1/50 inch long (see illustration).

Major signs of the condition are reddish zigzag furrows, accompanied by intense itching that is heightened at night. Scratching doesn't help, and may lead to impetigo.

Scabies occurs most often in skin folds, especially in the webbing between the fingers and around the wrists. The elbows, genital area, breast, and feet are also often infected. Mites travel from person to person through handshaking, close physical—including sexual—contact, and bedclothes and public towels.

Scabies often spreads through a family; bedmates frequently infect each other. The mite thrives where people live in crowded conditions and do not bathe. During times of upheaval caused by natural disasters and war the incidence of this disease increases enormously.

Differing only slightly from the mites that cause scabies in humans is a second type that causes mange in dogs, cats, horses, and other domestic animals. People sometimes become infected with this disease from riding a horse or

IN SCABIES . . .

Mites burrow under skin

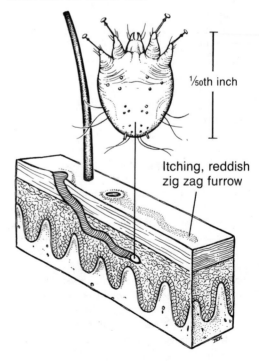

1/50th inch

Itching, reddish
zig zag furrow

Relieve with bathing, medication
Dry-clean or boil family's clothes, bedding

holding a puppy. Another type, nodular scabies, forms red-brown lumps in covered parts of the body. Norwegian or crusted scabies results from millions of mites infesting the skin, usually of a bedridden or institutionalized person.

Consult a physician or a hospital clinic when the disease first appears. Scabies is often confused with eczema, syphilis, contact dermatitis, hives, and infection by lice or other insects.

Effective treatment begins with bathing in warm water, using a soft brush and drying thoroughly with soft towels. For application after the bath your doctor may prescribe gamma benzene hexachloride USP (Kwell, Gamene) or crotamiton (Eurax).

Work the cream or lotion into your skin from your chin to your toes, especially in hairy parts and folds. Leave the medication on for 24 hours. Use shampoo for scalp mites. Two applications may be needed; more may trigger a drug allergy.

Intense itching may persist after treatment. Your doctor may prescribe steroids to relieve it. If small, hard nodules have developed in response to the mites, they may need to be removed.

Every member of a family, even close household contacts—plus any sexual contacts—need to be treated. Everyone's clothing and bedding need to be dry-cleaned or washed in boiling water. Use a hot iron on clothing—especially in the seams—to cut down reinfection.

See also INSECTS.

SCARLET FEVER (scarlatina) is caused by streptococcal bacteria. These are the same organisms that cause strep throat (see SORE THROAT), but of a strain that produces a toxin causing bright red skin rashes.

As with strep throat there is a danger that untreated scarlet fever will lead to rheumatic fever and heart disease. Thus it is essential that you see a physician and follow a complete course of penicillin therapy even after symptoms disappear.

Scarlet fever is usually accompanied by sore throat, chills, headache, and vomiting. Its characteristic rash generally spreads from the trunk to the arms and legs, though the rash may appear only in the armpits and groin. When the face bears the rash, there is usually a pale area around the mouth. There is often a "strawberry" or "raspberry" tongue—bright red with bumps.

The disease usually erupts three to five days after exposure. It may be communicable for up to three weeks after symptoms appear. Aspirin helps the sore throat, headache, and fever.

See also INFECTIOUS DISEASE; RHEUMATIC FEVER; SORE THROAT.

SCARS may become less prominent if you gently rub plain cold cream into the scar areas for a minute or two each night before bed. During the day, until they fade, apply a masking cosmetic with the proper tint for your complexion.

Wash scar areas with tepid water and a mild, unscented soap.

Dermabrasion (skin planing), performed by a dermatologist or plastic surgeon, is a technique for removing scars from acne and other sources. Scars may also be removed by means of surgery, X rays, and freezing. Keloids often require such special measures. Some scars, especially pitted ones, can be treated with injections of collagen, a protein material in skin and other tissue.

See also SKIN DISORDERS.

SCARVES can strangle you if they become entangled in such machines as ski lifts, snowmobiles, or motorcycles. A team of Boston doctors that documented the danger of such accidents concluded that dangling scarves should be banned on ski slopes and snowmobile trails. Indeed it is safest not to wear long scarves at all. No one can predict when they might get caught in the door of a car, bus, or elevator.

See also ACCIDENTS; CHOKING.

SCHISTOSOMIASIS (bilharziasis) is man's most widespread parasitic infection next to malaria. Some 200 million people suffer from it.

Though the continental United States is free of the parasite, it occurs in Puerto Rico. It is infecting more and more Americans because of the increasing number of travelers who are spending time in out-of-the-way areas of tropical and subtropical countries where it is most prevalent.

The schistosome—or blood fluke—is a flat worm in the same family as tapeworms. In fresh water its eggs hatch into larvae, which invade snails—and there develop in a fork-tailed free-swimming form called cercariae.

On contact with humans the cercariae can penetrate the skin, enter the bloodstream, and lodge in the liver, where they become adult worms. Eventually they may cause severe damage to the liver, intestines, and urinary tract— and lead to cancer of the bladder. Early symptoms include bloody and frequent urination, hepatitis, abdominal tenderness, fever. There also is generally headache, dysentery, muscle pains, and loss of appetite.

Ironically schistosomiasis is on the rise as a result of progress. Underdeveloped countries expand irrigation projects for food production, introducing the parasites and their host snails into new areas. As this infectious disease spreads, the malaise that afflicts local populations renders them ever less able to work. In consequence promising agricultural projects are being let go to waste and the areas are often worse off than before.

Drugs that kill the adult worms are generally effective but can have side effects—vomiting, dizziness, abdominal pain—so severe that the patient has to stay in bed during treatment. To avoid the disease drink only water that has been treated against contamination.

If you fall into a fresh-water pond, stream, or lake where schistosomiasis exists, you can obtain considerable protection by drying yourself quickly. The cercariae don't usually penetrate the skin until it starts to dry. Bathing in chlorinated pools or saltwater is usually safe.

At the time the cercariae penetrate the skin, they often cause an itching eruption called "swimmer's itch." In North America a form of swimmer's itch can occur after exposure to fresh water or saltwater containing snails that harbor the cercariae of the schistosome parasites of birds and rodents. In this condition only the skin is affected; there is no damage to internal organs. The skin eruption usually clears up within a few days and requires no specific treatment.

For parasitic worms common in the United States see HOOKWORMS; PINWORMS; ROUND-WORMS; TAPEWORMS; TRICHINOSIS. See also IN-FECTIOUS DISEASE; TRAVEL HEALTH; WATER CONTAMINATION.

SCHIZOPHRENIA   See TRANQUILIZERS.

SCIATICA is a severe pain that follows the sciatic nerve—the longest in the body—through the hip and down the leg to the foot. Sciatica is a symptom, not a diagnosis.

The condition usually results from the sciatic nerve being pinched or irritated between the spinal cord and the hip. Ninety percent of sciatica is caused either by arthritis of the lower spine or by a ruptured or "slipped" disc—in which part of a cushiony disc separating two spinal vertebrae is pushed out of place. When a slipped disc causes the sciatica, it may be accompanied by backache.

The discomfort of sciatica may be relieved by strict bed rest on a firm mattress and the use of pain-relieving drugs. Adhesive strappings or a brace may be required. If a vertebral disc is damaged or if severe pain persists, surgery may be needed.

See also ARTHRITIS; BACKACHE; SLIPPED DISC.

SCISSORS are generally safer than knives for children to use. Give beginners scissors with rounded tips.

Teach youngsters early to keep out of the path of the scissors when cutting and to be careful of the hand supporting the material. Also train children to walk—not run—carrying scissors with the blades downward, and to hand (never throw) scissors to another person by the handle.

As with other tools, when not using scissors, store them closed in a case or box. Keeping a cork on the sharp tip of grown-up's scissors is a good safety practice.

See also ACCIDENTS; CUTS; PUNCTURES.

SCORPIONS are generally deadly only to children under the age of six, and then only if the stinging scorpion is of a species in the Southwest that is small (not more than 2 inches long) and colored cream to light amber (see illustration).

Death occurs from the child's exhausting himself from constant, running-type convulsive movements. The activity is so vigorous that a victim is often passed from one person to another because no one can hold on to him. The child is comatose and salivates freely.

If a child has been stung by a deadly scorpion and has not yet developed symptoms, immerse the stung part in ice water and keep it there for an hour. No treatment is needed thereafter. Don't use a tourniquet. Sucking the wound, as for snakebite, is of little value because of the minute amount of venom injected.

If convulsions have begun, take the child to a hospital emergency room. In most cases he will be given barbiturates in doses sufficient to stop the movements and be discharged after a day or so.

The small, deadly scorpion generally causes only local reactions in adults and larger children. The sting of the large, hairy scorpion also produces only minor itching and swelling. It can be relieved by applying ammonia, which neutralizes the acid injected in a sting. Ice compresses reduce the swelling.

Scorpions are mainly a problem in warm climates. During the day they hide in attics and closets, in shoes and folded blankets. Scorpions sting only when provoked, and you'll avoid accidents if you inspect these items before using them. At night scorpions frequent kitchens and bathrooms, preferring rooms with a water supply.

As a general preventive, locate indoor hiding places and apply by spot treatment a liquid product containing 2 percent chlordane. If you live in the country, chickens and ducks can quickly eliminate most scorpions from your vicinity. Remove all loose rocks, old boards, bricks, and other debris under which scorpions may hide. Scorpions like to burrow in sand, so don't have a children's sandbox if there are scorpions in your area.

See also INSECTS.

THIS SCORPION CAN KILL CHILDREN

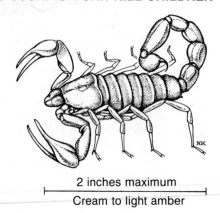

2 inches maximum

Cream to light amber

Immerse stung part in ice water

Soak for 1 hour

Treat convulsions at hospital

SCRAPES (abrasions) are superficial wounds with little bleeding, as in a skinned knee. Scrapes frequently contain bits of foreign matter like pebbles or soil.

Flush the area with soap and water. If the foreign matter cannot be easily washed out, see a doctor—for if the skin heals over it, infection may develop and there may be a permanent, tattoolike scar. Cover a scrape with a sterile bandage.

See also ACCIDENTS; CLEANSING MINOR WOUNDS.

SCUBA DIVING is a much more dangerous sport than is generally realized. Using any self-contained underwater breathing apparatus can be hazardous.

To avoid accidents get scuba certification through training offered by the National Association of Underwater Instructors, YMCA, or Boy Scouts of America. Then rigorously follow rules for diving safety. Besides drowning, these are the major risks of scuba diving:

Air embolism, bubbles of air in the blood, can

result if you hold your breath in a rapid dive. The depth may be merely 6 feet—but unless you exhale before diving, air from your lungs may be forced under pressure into your blood. The bubbles can plug arteries to the heart and brain, possibly causing death.

A victim of air embolism may suffer blotching and itching of his skin and pain in his muscles, joints, and abdomen. There may be froth in his nose and mouth, with difficult breathing and chest pain. He may be dizzy and nauseated and have difficulty seeing. Paralysis and coma sometimes occur.

The required treatment is recompression: placing the victim in a pressure chamber. Call the Coast Guard, which not only knows where the nearest pressure chamber is but generally will transport the victim to it. The victim will need to be rushed to a chamber, even if it's thousands of miles away.

At the scene of an air embolism accident, provide ARTIFICIAL RESPIRATION (which see) if needed, and be on guard against HEART STOPPAGE (which see) and SHOCK (which see). Don't let a victim dive again. An attempt to force the air bubbles out of his blood with water pressure will only make the condition worse.

The bends (caisson disease) are more common in areas of deep diving—off California and the Hawaiian Islands and in the Caribbean. They occur when a diver ascends too rapidly (more than 60 feet a minute). Normally nitrogen gas from the compressed air the diver breathes is absorbed into fat, then is released slowly into the blood. In a rapid ascent, the nitrogen can escape in bubbles large enough to block arteries to the muscles, heart, and brain.

The bends may show first as pain in the region of a joint—usually an elbow, shoulder, or knee —within two hours after the dive was completed. More serious cases cause dizziness, difficulties in breathing and hearing, possibly paralysis and unconsciousness. As with air embolism the condition calls for prompt recompression.

Nitrogen euphoria (rapture of the depths, nitrogen narcosis) is the result of nitrogen poisoning during deep diving (below 200 feet). "It's like having martinis on an empty stomach; it makes you feel tipsy," says Navy physician William H. Spaur.

Under its influence, the diver fails to realize the danger of his situation. He may take out his mouthpiece or swim down instead of up. When he surfaces, he usually needs to be treated for drowning.

Squeeze injuries are caused during diving by pressure buildups in the ears, sinuses, lungs, eyes. The pressure ruptures blood vessels in these areas and may collapse the lungs and impair the heart.

General signs are blood in the ears, throat, and nostrils. There is usually extreme dizziness, deafness, lack of coordination.

Emergency oxygen therapy is required. Until this is available, stand by to give mouth-to-mouth resuscitation and closed-chest massage.

Avoid scuba diving during pregnancy and if you have seizures, heartbeat irregularities, insulin-dependent diabetes, active chronic obstructive pulmonary disease, or sickle cell anemia.

If you have a history of allergic or infectious rhinitis, you are prone to difficulty in equalizing pressure between the middle ear and nasopharynx during scuba diving, and you risk a squeeze injury.

Patients with bronchitis or asthma are at risk of air embolism when diving. If you smoke, you're at greater risk of nitrogen poisoning.

Avoiding hazards. To scuba-dive more safely, take the following precautions:

· Never dive with earplugs. Pressure can push them deep into your ear canal.
· Don't fly for 24 hours after scuba diving.
· Resurface if you feel pain in your ears—or any other part of your body.
· Don't use antihistamines if you are going to dive. They may make you drowsy and interfere with coordination. Check labels on cold-remedy packages.
· Avoid touching sponges, which can give you a rash. If you are stung by a JELLYFISH (which see) or fire coral, wash with saltwater (preferably heated). Then apply rubbing alcohol, ammonia, or meat tenderizer.
· Don't breathe rapidly in and out (hyperventilate) before a free dive. If you get rid of too much carbon dioxide, there won't be enough to trigger your craving for another breath of air. You can quickly lose consciousness.
· Rub down with a rough towel when you get out of the water. This can usually prevent "swimmer's itch" caused by organisms called schistosomes.
· Dry ears by gently pulling on the cartilage over the lobe. If trapped water fails to run out, use a soft tissue. Don't use cotton-tipped swabs.

See also ACCIDENTS; DROWNING.

SCURVY See VITAMINS.

SEASICKNESS See MOTION SICKNESS.

SEBORRHEIC DERMATITIS (cradle cap) is a result of seborrhea, a skin disorder in which the sebaceous (oil-producing) glands of the skin produce an excessive amount of sebum (oil).

Seborrhea most often occurs on the scalp and face, as the oil glands in these areas are especially plentiful and active. It may merely give rise to excessive oiliness of the hair and skin. More severe forms may cause scaling, irritation, and inflammation of the skin and scalp.

The condition may also affect the abdomen, armpits, chest, back, and groin region. Cracking of the skin may introduce infection.

Cradle cap in babies is a mixture of grease and scales that pile up on the crown of the head. Temporary baldness may occur when hairs are dislodged by the crust.

Some parents promote a scaly condition of the scalp by not bathing the area because they mistakenly fear they'll hurt the soft spot of the scalp. In such cases gentle shampooing will usually clear up the condition.

In affected children cradle cap often appears during the first two or three months of life and recurs most frequently during the first two or three years. No treatment will prevent its recurrence, although with time the child generally has less trouble with it.

Treatment. Seborrhea generally improves in sunshine and gets worse in winter. In milder cases shampoo at least twice a week—some dermatologists say daily—with a sulfur-base antiseborrheic shampoo (Sebulex, Meted, Head & Shoulders, Enden). When the scaly element is severe but oily scalp is not a big problem, try a shampoo containing tar (Sebutone, Pentrax, Tersa-Tar, Zetar).

Don't get these strong shampoos in your eyes. If you do, flush your eyes with plenty of water.

For infants with cradle cap, your doctor may prescribe nightly application of a water-washable ointment consisting of sulfur and salicylic acid. The ointment can be shampooed out the next morning.

Some specialists advise mothers of children who have seborrheic dermatitis on other parts of the body to use a preparation such as Sebulex instead of soap in the daily bathwater. Lesions in the armpits and groin may call for applications of steroids and antibiotics.

See also ALLERGY; JOCK ITCH; SKIN DISORDERS.

SEDATIVES See BARBITURATES; TRANQUILIZERS.

SEIZURES See CONVULSIONS.

SEVERED PARTS of the body can often be salvaged. When a hand, foot, arm, finger, or toe is cut off, it may be surgically replanted.

To give first aid to the victim of a severed part, first stanch the BLEEDING (which see) by applying direct pressure. Treat the victim for SHOCK (which see).

Cool the dismembered part by wrapping it in a piece of plastic or a towel or clean cloth, then pack it in ice (see illustration). In the absence of ice, immerse the wrapped part in cold water. Lowering the temperature of the tissues slows the damage to the skeletal muscles that begins when blood supply stops. Get to a hospital as quickly as possible.

See also TOOTH SALVAGING.

IF PART OF THE BODY IS CUT OFF
Chill it quickly!
It may be rejoined

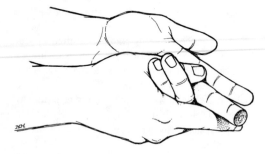

Wrap it in cloth or plastic

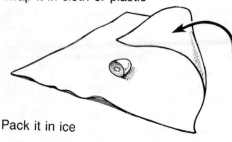

Pack it in ice

Take it to hospital with victim

SEX DISORDER affects about half of all marriages, according to a "guesstimate" by Dr. William H. Masters and Virginia E. Johnson of the Masters and Johnson Institute in St. Louis and authors of the authoritative *Human Sexual Response* and *Human Sexual Inadequacy.*

The most common sex disorders are impotence, premature ejaculation, and orgasmic problems ("frigidity"). Diminished sexual desire is another common problem.

In some people sexual problems are the result of illness, medications, surgery or other treatments, or congenital malformations of the urogenital system.

Far more people suffer sexual problems because of emotional stress. Frequently fears about sexual performance lead to sexual problems. Job tensions often play a large part in causing sexual difficulties. Myths about sex contribute to stress.

Sexual dysfunction in a marriage may result from other tensions and difficulties—and vice versa. Marital problems that might easily be solved become aggravated by poor sexual functioning.

But if a husband and wife really want the marriage to work, are willing to try to communicate with each other, and seek competent therapeutic help, they can often resolve their sexual difficulties.

The first step is to break free of sexual myths. These common fallacies are barriers to sexual fulfillment:

It's not true that the larger the penis, the more satisfied the woman. Actually the vagina is a sleeve of soft tissue, not an empty cavity that must be filled. The flexible vaginal wall will enclose a penis of almost any size with essentially the same sensation for the woman.

It's not true that the larger the clitoris, the greater the woman's orgasm. There is no relationship whatever between these. Nor is the size of the woman's vagina important in the production of orgasm.

It's not true that men enjoy sex more than women do. On the contrary. Physiological studies show that women in general have a greater potential for sexual responsiveness than men. Women react more intensely and longer to sexual stimulation.

It's not true that the man should always be active, the woman passive. The reverse can be equally satisfying, depending on the couple and how they feel at the moment.

As Virginia Johnson puts it, in the past sex was something the male did *to* the female. Then as more women began to demand sexual fulfillment, the male had the responsibility of doing something *for* the female. Increasingly sex is coming to be accepted as a mutual undertaking —something the male does *with* the female.

It's not true that simultaneous orgasm should always be the goal. This idea, says psychiatrist Leon Salzman of the Georgetown University

School of Medicine, ignores the "enormous complications in the production of the orgasm both in the male and in the female."

Simultaneous orgasm is difficult to achieve and not necessarily desirable—you each may gain more pleasure watching the other's pleasure. Don't strive for simultaneous orgasm at the expense of your overall enjoyment. Indeed you can have extremely satisfactory intercourse without orgasm at all, depending on how you feel at the moment.

It's not true that there is a so-called normal frequency. Dr. Sherwin A. Kaufman of the New York University School of Medicine and medical director of Planned Parenthood of New York City advised couples that "frequency of intercourse should be as spontaneous as any other aspect of sex, with no special rules to be followed."

Don't rate yourself a failure if you have sex less than a given number of times a week, be it 1, 10, or 20. There is no minimum score you must achieve. Or, for that matter, a maximum you must not exceed.

Sexual frequency is extremely variable from one couple to another and from one week to the next. Activity may decline to zero in periods of busyness or stress and increase accordingly at other times. You have a problem only if one or both partners are dissatisfied.

It's not true that you have to master some specified technique. The best technique is affection for your sex partner and a wish to give pleasure while receiving it. Concentrate on having fun.

"We don't think sexual technique has any importance at all," compared with "getting across to the general public that sex is a *natural function*" like eating, says Virginia Johnson. "Some people are hungry at different times, some people eat for different reasons, at differing speeds, in different amounts." The same is true of sexual appetites.

Once people learn to accept and express their own sexuality, their own sexual pace and preferences, she believes, 75 to 80 percent of sexual problems will disappear and "technique will come on the scene automatically."

Increasing sexual response. Most therapists suggest that you each take responsibility for your own good time. Communicate to your partner what pleases you.

Psychologist Wardell Pomeroy, a coworker of the late Dr. Alfred Kinsey at the Institute of Sex Research, urges couples to vocalize their pleasure during intercourse. "It will probably help you enjoy sex more," and it is one way of communicating to your partner what you enjoy. This is much preferable, he believes, to sex "performed in a sort of deadly silence."

Therapist Audrey Resnik of Chevy Chase, Maryland, encourages women to explore the range of their sexual responses through masturbation. "Self-stimulation is extremely beneficial in helping you learn what you like, so you can express this to your husband."

Experiment freely. Exploration can help relieve bedroom boredom, which can exacerbate sexual dysfunction. Counsels Dr. Milton Abramson, a consultant to the Minneapolis Clinic of Psychiatry and Neurology, "Experimentation is not sexual depravity and is a very definite part of any good sexual relationship so long as it's acceptable to both partners." Whatever pleases both of you is normal.

For one thing the male-superior (man on top) position is not necessarily best. With the female superior the man can delay ejaculation longer, since he's not so physically active and the woman gets deeper penile thrusting. A position in which you each lie on your side—with the woman's hip resting atop the man's thigh, his other leg between her legs—allows both partners full use of their hands and arms.

Says Dr. Wardell Pomeroy: "There is no limit to the number of positions that can be used in intercourse." Invent your own.

Sexual fantasies. Encourage your sexual fantasies. Psychologist Pomeroy urges people to enjoy their erotic musings. "Almost all normal people indulge in sex thoughts and fantasies, and . . . these visions are often helpful in arousal during intercourse."

Nor should you feel guilty about sexual stimulation you may derive from looking at erotic pictures, books, or films. "Pornography can be a great aid to fantasy," says Dr. Pomeroy. "It can teach new techniques that might not otherwise be imagined, and it can be useful as erotic stimulation."

What's more, you can no more censor your unconscious than you can determine what you will or will not dream. To try to shut out unwelcome thoughts is to invite anxiety and guilt. You're better off giving your fantasies free rein.

Don't be alarmed if your daydreams include members of your own sex. There's a great deal of evidence that "bisexuality is normal and healthy," said Dr. Lonny Myers, director of medical education at Chicago's Midwest Association for the Study of Human Sexuality—and that society dictates that this erotic feeling should be channeled only to appropriate members of the opposite sex.

Dr. Duane E. Spiers, psychologist and director of Creighton University Medical School's Behavioral Sciences Division, agrees. "I think we're all born potentially bisexual and are conditioned by social and family experiences to develop either hetero-, homo-, or ambisexual patterns."

Since your unconscious is not controlled by culture, you may well be turned on by male or female, young or old, married or single. There's little or no danger of your *acting* on such fantasies, so enjoy them for the harmless flights of the imagination that they are.

Learning to pleasure each other. Engage in pleasuring. "Pleasuring" or "sensate focus" is a technique developed by Masters and Johnson to overcome sexual dysfunction. It promotes a loving, sexually arousing relationship while freeing a couple from the pressure of intercourse.

If impotence or orgasmic dysfunction is a problem, deliberately refrain from having intercourse. Instead set aside an hour a day for love play for at least four days. Indulge yourselves in the sensations of touching and being touched. "Relax and have a lot of fun," suggests psychiatrist Rebecca Liswood, a New York specialist in family counseling. "This is sex too."

Please each other by kissing, stroking, patting, massaging, playing with each other's hair. Take a bath together, washing one another. Try using a feather along your bodies. Vocalize your pleasure. Share your erotic fantasies.

For these first few days avoid the pelvic area. Even if the male partner gets an erection, don't try to take advantage of it—lest there be failure and a setback. If it happens once, it can surely happen again.

Pleasuring can help you see that your whole body is an erogenous zone. Couples have come to orgasm from massage of the low back or shoulders. One man told sex therapists Dorothy and Armando DeMoya of Washington, D.C.: "You know what? I have 21 penises!" In addition to the usual appendage he and his wife had discovered the erogenous potential of massaging his fingers and toes.

From nongenital pleasuring, move on to exploring stimulation techniques for several days. In most cases intercourse comes casually, after the man's ability to sustain an erection becomes virtually taken for granted.

Finding medical help. If your sexual problem persists despite these measures, seek competent help promptly.

Beware of charlatans. Quackery is rampant in the field of sex therapy. There are no legal restraints on who can claim to be a sex therapist.

Thus a classified ad for "sex therapist" or "sex clinic" can as easily be placed by a high school student or a prostitute as by a qualified therapist. Thousands of sex clinics have proliferated in recent years, the vast majority of them staffed by unqualified people. Only a few hundred can be considered legitimate.

Even worse, some self-styled therapists exploit people with sexual difficulties. The Hippocratic Oath specifically prohibits "lasciviousness" on the part of the doctors, and a ban on sexual contact with patients is fundamental to every ethical code. The American Psychiatric Association and the American Psychological Association have revised their codes to specifically prohibit sexual contact between therapists and patients. Yet sex therapists encounter scores of patients who have been seduced as part of their "therapy."

Many people naturally turn to the family physician for help with sexual difficulties. This may be a good choice, for many physicians have become aware of the great need for sex counseling. Most medical schools are responding to a new recognition of this need by providing human-sexuality courses. In 1960 only three medical schools in this country had formal courses in sexuality.

Your family physician may be in a unique position to help with sexual counseling. A family doctor often knows the total family situation and presumably has rapport with the patient. The doctor also knows of medical problems or medications that may be interfering with sexual functioning.

On the other hand many physicians may fail to help—out of ignorance or prudishness. Even among M.D.'s sex is often a charged topic. As individuals doctors are likely to have the same hang-ups as anyone else. Often a physician's prejudices may interfere with treatment. Further, unless a doctor supplements the basic courses provided by most medical schools, he may not know much more about sex than many of his patients.

It may be a good idea for a patient to ascertain a physician's comfort and experience with sexual counseling by asking such questions as: "Do you feel qualified to give sexual advice?" Or, "Have you studied sexual dysfunction?" The patient can also ask where the physician received training and what affiliations he or she has with academic institutions. If a doctor is obviously uncomfortable talking about sex, it is wise for a patient to ask for a referral to a qualified sex therapist or clinic.

Many patients with sexual problems require only reassurance that their functioning is normal. Others need to have myths dispelled. Some benefit from physiological explanations of sexual functioning. Many physicians can resolve such difficulties in two or three office visits. If sexual problems persist, a referral for sex therapy may be in order.

Among the most reliable sources of treatment are outpatient clinics in increasing numbers of hospitals across the country. These may be staffed by physicians, nurses, social workers, psychologists, psychotherapists, or others who have been trained in techniques for treating sexual dysfunction.

If there is no such hospital clinic locally, contact the American Association of Sex Educators, Counselors, and Therapists, 11 Dupont Circle, NW, Washington, D.C. 20036.

Referrals can also be sought through local medical societies and social service agencies.

Some of the best sex-therapy programs are modeled after the pioneering program of William H. Masters and Virginia E. Johnson at the Masters and Johnson Institute in St. Louis. This is an intensive two-week program using a male-female therapy team. There is a one- to two-year follow-up program.

Both partners undergo therapy, and the focus of the therapy is on improving the couple's relationship—for a couple's sex problems are usually more a symptom than a cause of problems in their relationship.

Further, while one partner may seem to have the sexual problem, the situation is usually much more complex. A woman who enters therapy because she fails to have orgasms may have a husband who ejaculates prematurely, compounding her problem.

The focus of the Masters and Johnson approach is on educating the couple and helping them improve their skills at communication. Underlying the therapy is a view of sex as a natural function. Sexual dysfunction is seen not necessarily as a symptom of an underlying personality conflict or a deep-rooted psychological problem. Rather, Masters and Johnson believe, most people suffer from sexual problems as a result of ignorance about physiology, anxiety about sex, and assuming a spectator role in sexual activity—watching themselves, monitoring their responses, judging how well they are succeeding in realizing their goal.

A medical examination identifies people whose problem is largely or entirely organic. Others may have medical problems that contribute to the sexual dysfunction, and they are given concurrent medical treatment.

The Masters and Johnson program utilizes a wide range of psychotherapeutic techniques. The focus of the therapy is on the present, rather than the history of behaviors and attitudes.

Central to the therapy in most cases is teaching the couple sensate focus techniques, or pleasuring. In the privacy of their hotel room the couple experience the pleasures of touching and being touched—without the pressure to perform sexually.

Sex therapy usually works best when the sexual problems do not result from a major conflict or mental disorder. In cases where they do, referral to a psychiatrist may be in order.

Some sex therapists use a format of one or two sessions per week for 10 or 12 weeks. This approach allows the couple to live at home during the therapy. It also has the advantage, some therapists feel, of allowing the couple to absorb the therapy slowly.

The therapy is done by either a male-female team or an individual therapist. While most sex therapists prefer to treat sexual difficulties in the context of a relationship, many accept individuals for treatment—for a person with a longstanding or severe sexual problem may not at the time be involved in a relationship. For some people group therapy has been effective in alleviating sexual difficulties. It has been used successfully for some women with orgasmic problems.

How well does sex therapy work? Nobody really knows. Recently even the methods used by Masters and Johnson for evaluating patients' therapy outcomes have come under attack.

Such controversy stems from the fact that it is unusually hard to ascertain what constitutes success—or failure—in sex therapy. A patient may consider failure what the therapist counts success, and vice versa. There may be relapses; so a couple considered cured may still have unresolved sexual problems. The reverse also happens: Initial failures may well yield to success as a couple slowly incorporates knowledge and communication skills. Sometimes the therapy may help one partner but not the other.

Whatever the success statistics—and they have a wide range, depending on the nature of the complaint and the particular therapist—it is undoubtedly true that hundreds of couples and individuals have benefited from sex therapy over the last 15 years.

See also FRIGIDITY; IMPOTENCE; MASTURBATION; PREMATURE EJACULATION; QUACKERY; STRESS.

SHAVING advice for those who prefer a wet shave:

1. Wash your face with soap and hot water for at least one minute before starting. This softens your whiskers and removes perspiration, oil, and grit.
2. Rinse with water as hot as you can comfortably stand.
3. Apply shaving cream, which works better than ordinary soap in holding water to soften hairs and in keeping them upright. Keep lather on for two minutes before shaving. If your water is hard, use more soap and more shaving cream.

If your skin is dry or sensitive to soap, select a brushless spray or tube shaving cream, which provides more lubrication because it is an emulsion of oil in water.

In case of oily skin choose a lather type of shaving cream and apply it with a brush. These creams are really soaps and therefore remove oil better than do the brushless creams. Mentholated lather will have an even greater degreasing action on your skin.

4. Wet the razor with hot water before you begin. Keep both your face and the razor wet all through the shave. Use a sharp blade. Some shavers expect too much from stainless steel and other special alloy blades, and overuse them.
5. Shave your upper lip and chin last. These are where most of the coarsest whiskers grow and need the longest contact with water. Contrary to popular belief, shaving does not coarsen hairs or make them grow faster.
6. Don't wipe a blade dry—you'll dull its edge. Simply rinse with hot water, shake, and let dry.

The foregoing applies to shaving underarms and legs as well as faces.

Electric shaving. Electric versus wet shaving is a matter of personal preference. There is no proof that either method is best for all skins, though one study suggested that you can get a closer, smoother shave with a razor and lather. The study showed that an electric shaver left hair ends ragged and split while a razor left them smooth. It also showed that the razor cut the hair closer to the skin surface and left a stubble of more uniform length than the electric shaver.

Use of preshave lotion can help remove perspiration that interferes with electric shavers. But for the average person, *after*shave lotions are of no real value. Unless you like a particular fragrance you might just as well apply rubbing alcohol, witch hazel, or plain water.

If you have a skin disorder like acne, an alcohol-containing lotion or rubbing alcohol may be of some help by reducing bacteria on the skin surface, though this benefit has not been evaluated. If you use a body refresher after bathing or showering, you may use the same preparation as an aftershave lotion. It has a higher alcohol content than most lotions.

Be skeptical of TV ads for shaving creams. Most creams are equally effective and hucksters may exaggerate or falsify supposed advantages. The FTC won an action against the makers of Rise after one commercial showed that the "ordinary lather" of competing brands dried out. The next sequence revealed Rise staying thick and foamy.

The truth was that the ordinary lather was no lather at all. It was an imitation made up of 90 percent water with a foaming agent, and contained none of the soaps or fatty acid salts that are used to keep shaving cream foamy. Small wonder that when this "lather" puffed out of the can, it rapidly dried up and disappeared.

The FTC also cried "Fake!" over a commercial that purported to demonstrate the moisturizing powers of Rapid Shave. The picture showed an actor putting Rapid Shave on what looked like sandpaper. Right after applying the cream, the actor shaved the "sandpaper" clean with one stroke of a razor. "Apply—soak—and off in a stroke" was the slogan.

It so happens that real sandpaper looks like plain, colored paper on TV, and it cannot be "shaved" until it has soaked for about one hour. As imitation sandpaper, therefore, the advertisers had used a piece of Plexiglas covered with a jellylike substance over which sand had been sprinkled. The FTC held that the commercial was deceptive, and found that Rapid Shave could not shave real sandpaper even after it had been soaked for an hour.

See also ACNE; INGROWN HAIRS; SKIN DISORDERS.

SHIGELLOSIS (bacillary dysentery) is marked by diarrhea containing blood, pus, and mucus. The victim has abdominal cramps, fever, and nausea.

This infectious disease is usually spread by food and water contaminated by shigella bacteria borne by human excrement and unwashed hands. The bacteria attack the large intestine. Symptoms begin one to four days after exposure.

Children under two, the elderly, and debilitated adults may die from loss of fluids. Otherwise healthy adults generally recover spontaneously within a week, though severe cases may take up to six weeks. The wisest course is to see a doctor, since antibiotics, particularly ampicillin, are effective. Without laboratory tests shigellosis is often confused with ulcerative colitis.

The disease is a problem for travelers, especially in the tropics—it is epidemic in Mexico and Central America.

See also AMEBIASIS; DIARRHEA; INFECTIOUS DISEASE; TRAVEL HEALTH.

SHINGLES (herpes zoster) is an inflammation of nerve cells that produces pain and then a rash. Its worst and most common complication is a fierce and long-lasting pain.

First symptoms may be chills and fever, malaise, and gastrointestinal disturbances. After three or four days pain may begin—a pulling, nagging, or burning sensation in or under the skin, usually on the face, chest, or abdomen. Some people do not experience pain with shingles infection.

After several days, small watery blisters on reddened skin generally appear, at first along the infected nerve, often later on other body surfaces. Until the telltale blisters appear, the pain in the abdomen may be confused with appendicitis; that on the chest, with heart disease or pleurisy.

Shingles usually occurs only once and lasts about two to five weeks. Pain may be excruciating and may sometimes persist for months or years after the infection is gone. There may be some scarring of skin from the rash.

Shingles develops only in people who have previously had chickenpox; it is caused by the same virus. In most people the virus is thought to be harbored in an inactive form in nerve cells for many years after a bout with chickenpox. Then—triggered by an injury, emotional stress, certain drugs, exposure to cold, and other factors—the virus becomes activated and results in an attack of shingles. Shingles attacks are also common in cancer patients and others debilitated by a severe illness, and in people who have weakened immunological defenses. Elderly people are particularly prone to shingles. The disease afflicts about 10 to 20 percent of adults, most of whom are over 50. Deaths are rare.

You cannot catch shingles from a person undergoing an attack. But if you come in direct contact with a shingles rash, you may contract chickenpox if you have never had it before.

Shingles most commonly affects the nerves around the chest and waist area. Pain often comes in spasms, sometimes triggered by even the slightest touch. Sometimes nerves in the eye are involved, causing temporary blindness. In some cases the cornea may be permanently scarred. Excruciating pain and paralysis may result if facial nerves are affected.

Shingles in the early weeks of pregnancy may injure the developing baby, leading to birth defects resembling those caused by rubella: brain damage, often accompanied by mental retardation; hearing loss; eye malformations; and congenital heart defects.

Treatment. Shingles calls for a physician's care. Analgesics such as aspirin and/or codeine can help relieve the pain. Lukewarm wet compresses often bring some relief.

Corticosteroids given early in the disease may relieve pain and reduce the chances of long-lasting pain, but can have severe side effects. Corticosteroids should never be used in people who may have a related virus, herpes simplex, of the eye.

If blisters appear on the forehead, nose, or eyelid, shingles may affect the eye. See an ophthalmologist in such cases, to prevent scarring of the cornea. And seek an otologist's care if shingles affects the ear.

For pain that persists, treatments include antidepressants, acupuncture, electrical nerve stimulation, and anticonvulsant drugs.

For further information write to Shingles, National Institute of Neurological and Communicative Disorders and Stroke, Building 31, Room 8406, Bethesda, Maryland 20205.

See also BIRTH DEFECTS; CHICKENPOX; INFECTIOUS DISEASE.

SHOCK is a severe drop in blood pressure that brings on a depression of breathing and circulation. Shock can be a hazard in accidents involving bleeding, burns, or poisoning. It may result from stroke, heart attack, or heat stroke. If not treated, shock can be more life-threatening than the condition that caused it.

Symptoms of shock include weakness, faintness, and mental sluggishness. The victim's face is generally pale, with the skin cold and clammy, possibly in a cold sweat. Eyelids are often drooping, eyes vacant and dull, pupils dilated. Breathing is often rapid and shallow. There may be chills, nausea with or without vomiting, thirst and restlessness. The pulse may be weak, fast, irregular, or too weak to feel.

The victim of shock needs immediate medical attention. Until help comes:

Control any bleeding. Provide ARTIFICIAL RESPIRATION (which see) if necessary. Be on guard for HEART STOPPAGE (which see).

Keep the victim lying down with his legs and trunk elevated 8 to 12 inches above his head—

HOW TO TREAT SHOCK VICTIMS
Cover all shock victims for warmth

If you're in doubt whether head is injured

Keep victim flat

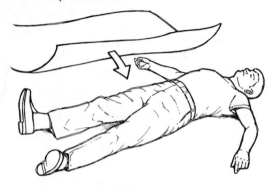

If chest is injured
If breathing is difficult
Raise head and shoulders

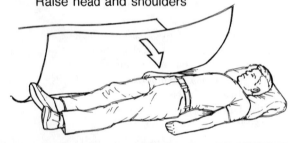

For all other conditions
Raise legs

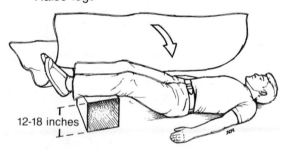

12-18 inches

unless he is suffering from a head injury, chest injury, or breathing difficulty (see illustration).

For a head injury, lay him flat with his head resting off the injured side. For a chest injury or breathing difficulty, raise his head and shoulders. If in doubt about the proper position, keep him lying flat.

If the victim is unconscious or has severe wounds of the lower part of the face and jaw, place him on his side to allow drainage of fluids and to avoid airway blockage of vomitus or blood.

Keep him warm with blankets under and over him. But take care not to overheat him—cover him only enough to prevent loss of body heat.

If he vomits, turn his head to the side to prevent his choking on the vomitus.

If he is conscious, get him to drink fluid—about 4 ounces every 15 minutes. Ideally use a formula of 1 quart of water mixed with 1 teaspoon salt and ½ teaspoon baking soda (sodium bicarbonate). Orange juice, soda pop, cool water with sugar, are also helpful.

Don't give fluids if the victim is unconscious or semiconscious, or if there is an abdominal injury. Also avoid fluids in cases of brain injury, convulsions, vomiting, bleeding from the rectum, or if surgery is likely to be required. Never give alcoholic beverages.

See ACCIDENTS.

SHORTNESS is determined by a person's heredity—plus environmental factors. In general, children of short parents will most likely be shorter than average, although probably taller than their parents. Children of tall parents are likely to be taller than average.

Children also may follow a family pattern of developing late. They're less mature than their peers through much of childhood and adolescence. Ultimately they catch up, and as adults are of average height and sexual development. The reverse phenomenon is seen in children who mature unusually early.

Both types of children often think they're freaks. Parents who've gone through the same experience can reassure the youngsters that they'll come out normal.

Disease, poor nutrition, emotional stress—all can retard growth and keep a person from reaching his genetic potential for height. Children from troubled homes are often undersized, and not from lack of food or medical care. Their growth is evidently stunted by emotional factors that suppress the pituitary gland, which regulates bone growth.

A child who is short because of a pituitary deficiency may benefit from injections of human growth hormone. The hormone can cause diabetes and other side effects and is recommended only for children whose shortness as adults will present severe problems.

The hormone is in extremely short supply. It may be secured free through an endocrinologist doing research for the National Pituitary Agency. If bought commercially, it runs about $2,500 a year for typical dosages.

Little can be done to increase the height of a child with a family tendency toward shortness. Drugs containing sex hormones may bring on early puberty or premature bone development. The AMA cautions that drugs that include the male sex hormone "should not be used to stimulate growth in children who are small but otherwise normal and healthy."

Children, principally girls, whose above-average height is deemed a problem may be stopped from growing with injections of estrogens. The female hormone brings about puberty and bone maturation. Estrogens, however, have been linked to cancer (see BIRTH CONTROL). Moreover, girls of eight or nine are often not ready for budding breasts, pubic hair, and menstruation.

Predicting height. To estimate the adult height a child will attain, physicians need X rays showing the child's "bone age," the degree to which his bones have matured from cartilage in comparison with average children.

A 13-year-old whose bone age is 10 still has a lot of growth ahead of him. If he's shorter than his friends, he'll probably at least catch up with them; if he's taller, he'll probably wind up a very tall adult. A short child whose bone age matches his chronological age is likely to remain short.

Height alone at one age is no reliable indicator of what height will be at another age. It's a poor rule of thumb to double the height of a child at two and a half in the hopes of estimating his adult height.

In general, children go through growth spurts. The most rapid is before two years, when children may grow from 15 to 18 inches. Growth usually slows down between three and six years, then is fairly steady until adolescence, perhaps 1½ or 2 inches a year. Adolescence brings another great spurt in growth—often 3 or 4 inches a year for two or three years. Girls usually have the spurt around 11, boys around 13.

When do youngsters stop growing? Children studied at the Fels Research Institute in Yellow Springs, Ohio, reached their adult stature at median ages of 21.2 for boys, 17.3 for girls. For 10 percent of the boys growth continued until 23.5; for 10 percent of the girls until 21.1

Steer clear of any appliances or systems of exercise that purport to increase the height of adults. None works, and some may cause injury.

SHORTNESS OF BREATH (dyspnea) may afflict anyone at any time—for any of a number of medical reasons.

Often it is nothing more than a sign that the body is making a temporary, normal adjustment to unusual physical exertion. But in some cases shortness of breath can signal a serious underlying illness.

Some people suffer shortness of breath as a result of emotional stress. In most cases excessive shortness of breath results from one of four general types of problems:

Respiratory obstructions that interfere with movement of air in and out of the lungs, and hinder the exchange of oxygen and carbon dioxide between the lungs and the blood, result in labored, difficult breathing. In bronchitis the bronchial tubes leading to the lungs fill with sticky mucus. An infection such as pneumonia can prevent oxygen from passing into the capillaries. During asthma attacks the muscles that line the walls of the breathing tubes go into spasm, squeezing the airways shut.

Severe and continuing shortness of breath may develop as a result of emphysema or dust disease.

Most shortness of breath due to respiratory obstruction is aggravated by exertion and is often accompanied by coughing. When mucus plugs are coughed up and expelled, the condition may be temporarily relieved.

Heart disease may be associated with severe or recurrent shortness of breath. In congenital heart defects oxygen-exhausted blood may be sent back into circulation through abnormal openings between the heart chambers without first being returned to the lungs for oxygen replenishment.

In congestive heart failure a damaged or overworked heart muscle loses its capacity to circulate the blood efficiently. Oxygen is carried to the tissues too sluggishly. Fluid from the capillaries seeps out into the lung tissue, impairing the intake and distribution of oxygen.

A coronary heart attack can precipitate heart failure suddenly, with shortness of breath among the symptoms. In other cases heart failure may develop over days or weeks. Shortness of breath is sometimes the earliest symptom, appearing during episodes of mild exertion or when the victim is reclining so that he must prop himself up on two or three pillows to sleep.

Anemia may make you short of breath because the blood cannot handle the job of transporting oxygen. The dyspnea at first occurs only on exertion, but in advanced cases may be present even at rest.

Poor physical conditioning is perhaps the commonest cause of shortness of breath. Ordinarily during periods of exertion the lungs can expand somewhat more than usual and the heart can beat faster than usual, circulating the blood more swiftly as the respiratory rate increases. Once the exertion is over, these changes revert quickly to normal.

As long as these natural cardiorespiratory reserves are exercised more or less regularly through daily activity or exertion, they remain in good order indefinitely, ready for use whenever the body needs them. But if you lead a sedentary life, you may allow your natural physical reserves to deteriorate. Then even moderate exertion leads to noticeable shortness of breath.

As a first aid measure, if you are short of breath, rest. There is no other specific treatment for shortness of breath in itself. If rest does not bring immediate relief, send for a doctor right away.

Shortness of breath on little or no exertion is never normal, regardless of your age or how out of condition you are. In such cases, even when rest does bring relief, get a thorough checkup to find out what is wrong.

The best prescriptions for the likeliest cause—poor physical conditioning—is dieting to get rid of excess weight, exercising regularly, and quitting smoking. Other possible causes need a doctor's attention.

See ANEMIA; EXERCISE; HEART DISEASE; OVERWEIGHT; RESPIRATORY DISEASE; SMOKING.

SICK HEADACHE See MIGRAINE.

SICKLE CELL ANEMIA is a hereditary blood disease in which the red blood cells sometimes assume a shape like a crescent or sickle. Normally red blood cells are shaped like doughnuts and float easily through the bloodstream.

Sickle-shaped cells are shorter-lived than normal red cells. Their rapid destruction causes the symptoms of anemia—mainly pallor, fatigue, and shortness of breath. Sickle cells tend to join together and become gelatinous masses that block tiny blood vessels and prevent oxygen from reaching tissues. When this occurs, the victim undergoes attacks of pain in his arms, legs, back, and abdomen.

His eyes take on a yellow cast. His joints sometimes swell up. He has a low resistance to infections. Chronic "punched-out-looking" ulcers often appear about his ankles.

Symptoms generally appear between the ages of six months and four years. Infants may be irritable without apparent reason. The child may have colic, distention of the abdomen, repeated bouts of fever.

His appetite may be poor. He may vomit frequently and be pale and jaundiced. Some infants have symmetrical painful swelling of both hands and/or feet.

Attacks of pain, known as crises, are more readily recognized in older children than in infants. Frequently an infection such as a sore throat or cold precedes or accompanies a crisis.

The interval between crises varies but usually lasts several months.

During these periods patients may feel quite well and be without any complaints, despite a moderate degree of anemia. Others complain that they tire easily.

An African mutation. Sickle cell anemia affects the black population more than any other. The sickle cell gene evolved from a mutation of the normal blood pigment (hemoglobin) gene thousands of years ago. At that time malaria was common on the African continent. People with the sickle cell trait tended to enjoy some immunity to the malaria microorganism and lived to pass the gene on to future generations.

The disease occurs when a child inherits two sickle cell genes, one from each parent. About one in every ten blacks in the United States is estimated to have one such gene, which is called the sickle cell trait. One in every 500 is thought to have the disease.

Some whites, particularly people whose ancestors came from the Mediterranean area, the Middle East, and parts of India, may also have the disease.

Symptoms may be relieved with painkilling drugs. Hot compresses placed on painful joints may ease the pain. So may propping up the painful arm or leg. Blood transfusion and bed rest may also relieve painful attacks. It's important to drink plenty of fluid during pain episodes—at least 2 quarts a day for a 100-pound patient—since liquid may help move sludged cells.

People with the disease and carriers of the trait are advised against high altitudes and unpressurized air travel, or any situation that might cause a moderate lack of oxygen, such as running a long distance. A lowered amount of oxygen may lead to an attack of abdominal pain, nausea, and vomiting, even in carriers who may be otherwise symptom-free. Travel in commercial pressurized airplanes is as safe as for other passengers.

There is no cure. Death can result from infections, heart or kidney failure, or from damage to a vital organ because of lack of oxygen. Until recently most victims did not live beyond age 40. Today their life expectancy has been increased considerably through treatment of infections with antibiotic drugs.

Because sickle cell trait—one abnormal gene—normally causes no problems, people with it usually don't know they have it. But when both a man and woman have sickle cell trait, each of their children has a one in four chance of having sickle cell anemia and a one in two chance of having sickle cell trait.

New blood tests make it simple to detect those who have the trait. In view of this physicians sometimes warn carriers who are considering marriage of the risk that their children may be born with the disease. Such genetic counseling is the only known way of preventing the disease.

See ANEMIA; BIRTH DEFECTS.

SINUSITIS (sinus trouble) is an infection of the lining of the sinuses, which are air spaces in the bones of the head and face. Small openings connect the nose with the sinuses, permitting sinus fluids to drain into the nose. Inflammation of the nasal passages may close the sinuses, interfering with the emptying of sinus secretions and trapping air in the cavity.

If a sinus is closed, the air in it may be absorbed and a vacuum may form, causing severe pain. Pus and mucus may press on the sinus wall, also causing intense pain. The air spaces most commonly infected are those above the eyes, between and behind the eyes, and in the cheekbones below the eyes.

Usually there is headache or pain over the infected sinus in the morning, easing in late afternoon. There may be pain in the cheek or upper teeth. The forehead is likely to be tender to pressure.

The nasal passages often are dry and clogged because of the swollen membranes and lack of drainage. There may be a yellow-green discharge of pus from the nose, or a postnasal drip. Sometimes the sense of smell is partially lost. Other symptoms may be fever, sore throat, and coughing. There often is swelling of the cheeks, eyelids, or forehead.

An acute infection of the sinuses may clear up in several days—or it may develop into chronic sinus trouble. Sometimes a chronic case shows few symptoms except susceptibility to frequent and prolonged colds. But persistent, uncured sinusitis may lead to other, more serious diseases like bronchitis and ear infections. The infection sometimes spreads to the nervous system, and causes meningitis and brain abscesses.

It's not always sinusitis. Most people who complain of "sinus trouble" don't really have it. They've picked up the term from TV commercials for purported cold and sinus remedies.

They usually have a stuffed nose and a tension headache. You can tell the difference. Sinus headaches get worse when you lie down, because lying down impedes drainage. Tension and eye-fatigue headaches get better when you lie down and relax.

Tooth decay, periodontitis, eye disorder, and other causes of headache have to be ruled out. Some people react to stress by developing nasal symptoms. Depressed patients are especially prone to excessive nose and eye discharge.

Colds are the commonest cause of acute sinusitis. Other frequent causes are infections of the nose and throat such as influenza, scarlet fever, and whooping cough.

When you have a cold, blow your nose gently and don't dive or swim with your nose under water—or you may force infectious material into the sinuses.

Frequent use of nose drops, oils, and antiseptics in the nose may injure the mucous membrane and bring on sinus trouble.

An allergy, such as mold allergy or hay fever, was present in 65 percent of chronic sinusitis cases in one survey. Respiratory allergies cause continual irritation of the mucous membranes in the nose and sinuses, which then makes these more susceptible to infection. The infections serve to aggravate the allergic reaction, and so on in a vicious circle.

Another complicating factor can be a deviated septum, which impedes the natural drainage of the nose. This condition is often caused by injuries to the nose that twist the septum, or center wall of cartilage of the nose, partly or completely blocking one side.

Treatment. If you have the yellow-green mucus symptom of sinusitis more than three days after the onset of a cold, cautiously try taking one of the over-the-counter decongestants or antihistamine-decongestant combinations, preferably in pill form. Keep in mind the fact that some decongestants also raise the blood pressure, while some antihistamines cause drowsiness that can make you a dangerous automobile driver.

If the symptoms don't clear up in two days, see your doctor. He'll seek to keep acute sinusitis, if that is what it is, from becoming chronic. He may pass a needle directly into the infected sinus to flush out the pus and infection and apply a decongestant. An antibiotic may be prescribed. A last resort in chronic sinusitis consists of a surgeon's creating openings in the bone leading to a congested sinus to allow more drainage.

Sinus headache and pain may be relieved with plain aspirin. In addition, when you wash in the morning, soak your washcloth in water as hot as you can stand and hold it to your forehead and face. Repeat this for 15 to 30 minutes at least five times a day.

An electric pad, infrared lamp, or hot-water bottle may similarly bring relief. Because of the risk of burns, don't use shortwave diathermy devices.

Avoid chilling exposures. Have a muffler over part of your face when you are outside.

To ease congestion try washing out the nasal cavity with warm saltwater (1/4 teaspoon of salt per 8-ounce glass—add 1/4 teaspoon baking soda, sodium bicarbonate, if possible). Flush a child's nose gently with a small bulb syringe. An adult can immerse his nose in a pan of the solution and sniff. The mucus and pus are then more easily discharged, just as a swimmer discharges a noseful of ocean saltwater.

Maintain adequate room humidity—a vaporizer or humidifier may help. Avoid the irritating effect of tobacco smoke. Don't drink alcohol—it closes air passages still further by dilating the blood vessels. If the sinuses above the eyes or behind the bridge of the nose are involved, sit up in bed to facilitate drainage.

See also COLDS; HUMIDITY; NOSE DROPS; RESPIRATORY DISEASE.

SKIING can be a downhill trip all the way. Of the 5 million Americans who go skiing each year, some 105,000 go home with fractures, dislocations, sprains, and cuts, estimates the Insurance Federation of Pennsylvania.

It has been calculated that for every 1,000 skiers who take to the slopes for even a day, 6 are injured, 2 of them seriously, making skiing one of the most hazardous sports.

The vast majority of these injuries are caused by the force of a forward fall and/or an outward twist of the leg during a fall. Films show that when a skier falls forward, one leg with its ski becomes fixed while the body's momentum continues forward. Something has to give, and usually the bone of the fixed leg breaks or the Achilles' tendon in its heel is sprained. If the leg is twisted outward at the instant of the fall, the ankle may be fractured and/or the knee or ankle tendons sprained.

To avoid ski injuries:

Get yourself into shape before the season. Conditioned skiers have fewer injuries. Differences in conditioning and strength may account for women being injured twice as often as men.

Warm up before you begin to ski hard. Start with a short cross-country run or a few easy warm-up runs. Contrary to what you've probably heard, you're most likely to be injured on one of your *early* runs. Late-afternoon injuries are common only because many more skiers, especially beginners, are on the slopes at that time.

Dress for the slopes. Being cold and uncomfortable increases your chances of getting hurt.

Wear long johns, thermal socks, and waterproof mittens, pants, and outer jacket. Don't wear an outfit of blue jeans, heavy sweaters, and knit gloves, as many beginners do. You may start out feeling snug, but between sweating and falling your clothes may soon be soggy. Ski slopes typically face north and turn frigid early in the afternoon when the sun disappears behind the mountain.

Wear shatterproof sunglasses. Glare can cause temporary snow blindness that seriously reduces night vision. Every year there are automobile accidents because skiers driving home at night have great difficulty seeing the road.

High altitude and snow reflection increase the likelihood of sunburn, so put on a good sunscreen. Without adequate sun protection warm-weather skiing in a bathing suit can land you in a hospital for burns. See TRAVEL HEALTH for high-altitude precautions.

Take lessons from a professional instructor. The better the skier, the fewer the injuries. Many ski instructors now start beginners on short skis. You learn faster than on long skis, and in a fall there is less chance of your breaking a leg.

The main purpose of the long skis is to keep you from sinking into deep snow. But today most trails are so well cared for that you won't have that problem even after a heavy snowstorm. Many experienced skiers prefer the safety and maneuverability of short skis, though as you become more skillful you can graduate to longer skis for their generally greater speed.

Rent top-quality gear while you're learning. Later decide how much you want to invest in your own equipment. Poor equipment contributes to injury, especially among children and beginners.

Make sure your bindings are in working order and are set loosely enough to release if you get into difficulties. With another skier standing on the back of your ski, you should be able to just disengage your foot by leaning forward with your full weight.

Don't expect more protection from any safety bindings than they can give you. The rate of severe ski injuries is as high now as when safety bindings were rare. Improvements in lifts and ski equipment that allow you to cover a great deal more ground, and to cover it faster, have increased your risk of injury.

Avoid the cable-type release bindings. They are much less reliable than other release bindings.

If you carry your skis on a rack outside your car, they can pick up salt spray from the road. Clean the bindings after every trip and spray them with silicone.

To prevent runaway skis strap your skis to your boots with leashes.

Stay on the trail that's right for you. Follow the maps that show which trails are for beginners, intermediates, experts. If you find at the top that you've overestimated your skill, get back on the lift and reach the bottom safely.

Ski with a companion and keep an eye on each other. If you must be alone, never leave marked trails. In cross-country skiing don't venture onto any frozen body of water without first checking its safety.

On lifts watch out for loose clothing. There are cases on record of people being dragged to their death by dangling scarves, long hair, or loose jackets.

Don't stunt. "Hotdogging" or acrobatic skiing, an innovation in the sport, is causing neck and back fractures and spinal-cord injuries. In one season in Colorado alone three hotdoggers became totally paralyzed from stunting accidents. Another permanently lost the use of his legs.

The rise in such accidents prompted the Colorado Medical Society to urge ski areas not to promote acrobatic stunting because the activity can cause an "extremely limited future life-style in mostly young people." Commented the society's president, "Unfortunately, skiers . . . do not realize the potential high risk . . . almost like Russian roulette."

See also ACCIDENTS; COLD WEATHER; FRACTURES; SPORTS.

IN A SKIING INJURY

Signal for help!
Cross skis

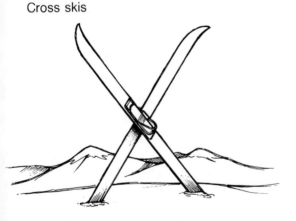

SKIN DISORDERS, the province of the dermatologist, involves health problems of the body's largest organ. It has a weight in the average adult of about 6 pounds, twice that of the brain or liver. It protects the body against invasion of bacteria, against injury to more sensitive tissues, against the rays of the sun, against loss of moisture. It is an organ of perception for the nervous system. It helps regulate the body's temperature.

Its complexity is rarely appreciated. One square cm (about 2/5 inch) of skin contains, on the average, 1 yard of blood vessels, 100 sweat glands, 3,000 sensory cells at the end of nerve fibers, 4 yards of nerves, 25 pressure apparatuses for the perception of touch, 200 nerve endings to record pain, 2 apparatuses for sensing cold, 12 apparatuses for sensing heat, 10 hairs, and 15 sebaceous (oil) glands.

The skin's ailments. Skin is subject to attack by germs. Fungi, as agents of infectious disease, can cause ringworm and athlete's foot. A virus is linked to warts. Bacteria can cause the pimples of acne, which may worsen into boils. Bacteria also are responsible for impetigo. Commonly confused with boils are cysts, which are noninfectious growths.

Allergic reactions of the skin account for the lesions of contact dermatitis, eczema, and hives. Beware poison ivy, one common cause of dermatitis. Also avoid tattoos, which can cause allergy and infection.

Itching is a frequent symptom of skin disorders. So is scaling, as in dandruff, seborrheic dermatitis, psoriasis, and ichthyosis.

The skin is vulnerable to the sun, a major cause of skin cancer. Sunburn can be as serious as other types of burns. The sun promotes wrinkles and premature aging of the skin, and brings out freckles.

Warm weather also can give rise to prickly heat, especially in babies. The most common skin disorder among infants is diaper rash.

Skin and heredity. Many skin conditions are inherited. Most birthmarks go away by themselves or can be covered with cosmetics. Moles bear special watching since they may develop into a virulent form of skin cancer. Vitiligo can be masked with cosmetics. Dermographism and sweaty palms are mainly nuisances, though if serious enough they can be treated.

Since the skin is the body's first line of defense, it often requires first aid for splinters, scrapes, cuts, blisters, and bruises. In some people scars may become overgrown into keloids.

Perspiration odor and vaginal odor can usually be corrected by proper cleansing. Bathing is a good remedy for skin oiliness and can be relaxing besides. Excessive exposure to water and cleansers, however, can cause dry skin and brittle nails.

Circles under the eyes are a cosmetic problem

and may be resolved with eye makeup. On the other hand bags under the eyes and xanthoma generally develop with aging and require surgery for permanent correction.

The hair. Hair, unlike skin, serves no essential biological function. Bald people live as long as hairy ones.

Washing it often is the best corrective for oily hair. But if it is dry, brittle, and seems to be falling out, be careful when brushing, curling, straightening, dyeing, or bleaching.

Shaving may require special care, especially if ingrown hairs are present.

Cosmetics. Use cosmetics cautiously. These preparations, though usually harmless, can cause skin eruptions, loss of hair, severe allergic reactions, burns and itching—all serious enough to restrict activity or require medical attention. A National Commission on Product Safety survey of U.S. insurance companies found that beauty aids account for the second largest group of personal injury claims (after glass containers).

The most dangerous products are hair cosmetics, including bleaches, dyes, shampoos, straighteners, and wave sets. They account for fully 30 percent of the complaints received each year by the Food and Drug Administration (FDA). Bath preparations, particularly bubble baths, account for 11 percent of the complaints. Some 9 percent stem from mouthwashes, toothpaste, and tooth powders (one offending ingredient—chloroform—has since been excluded from most of these products).

Deodorants and antiperspirants added 7 percent. Other frequent offenders were eye preparations, nail products, and face creams.

Keep cosmetics out of the reach of children, who may be poisoned if they swallow any.

Unlike food and drugs, cosmetics are almost completely unregulated. Most cosmetics are reasonably safe. Dr. Joseph B. Jerome, secretary to the AMA Committee on Cutaneous Health and Cosmetics, observes: "There are virtually no cosmetic products available on the market today that, when used according to the manufacturers' directions, represent a health risk to any significant group of consumers."

Nonetheless there are no mandatory standards for cosmetics. Nor are there requirements for premarketing testing. The burden of proof is on the Food and Drug Administration to show that a product is harmful, rather than on the manufacturer to prove it is safe.

One woman wrote to her legislator about a cuticle massage cream that caused her fingertips to swell, blister, and drain: "I have had five children, and I can say that childbirth is a snap compared to the agony I went through after using this product." A foundation cream caused another to suffer "big blisters" on her face and left scars around her mouth and eyes.

Selling hope. Watch out for wild promises. "The consumers don't *have* to buy a $10 or $15 face cream, but they do, out of hope," noted an editor of the trade magazine *Drug & Cosmetic Industry.* "That's what the industry sells—hope."

Cosmetic ads abound in made-up words, offering products like "aqualizing" creams, "dermatizing" scrubs, "lubrifying" toners. They also promise results like a "rich-girl mouth" and a "liquefied eye."

Products often couch their promises in legally unchallengeable phrases. A cream "helps fight" skin eruptions. Nobody says it won the fight. "May help" makes the promise even weaker. Most "miracle" ingredients are cosmetically worthless. They generally sound romantic and are included to add to the mystique that sells cosmetics.

There has been a cream with an ingredient "created from the precious pollen of the orchid" and a powder that "actually contains pulverized pearls." Mink coats are presumed to be beautiful, so mink oil is touted to make the wearer "beautiful." Turtles live long, thus turtle oil is promoted as a skin rejuvenator.

Polyunsaturates are receiving a lot of attention for their role in the prevention of heart disease. Cosmetics manufacturers have jumped on the bandwagon and come up with creams with polyunsaturates for "feeding" the skin. Natural proteins are of interest to fanciers of health foods. Sure enough, cosmetic products have been developed with natural proteins as ingredients. Collagen, a protein substance getting a lot of attention in medical research, is another "wonder" ingredient.

None of the aforementioned ingredients is of the slightest benefit in cosmetics. Nor is royal jelly, the food of the queen bee that for years has been touted for its healthful effects. Nor is aloe vera, the juice of a plant purportedly cited in the Bible. Nor is such hocus pocus as "placenta extract" or "milk serum" or "formula X9" (or any other "secret formula").

The price is high. There is little or no relationship between effectiveness and price. A simple, low-priced product is likely to be at least as satisfactory as one whose price is jacked up by advertising costs or special ingredients.

Indeed, the high- and low-cost products may be exactly the same but for the label. Dimestore brands are often identical to "better store" brands getting their components from the same supplier. One manufacturer of eyebrow-pencil cores supplied the same product to seven of the leading cosmetic companies. When it was discovered that he was illegally using toxic dyes, millions of pencils of many brands had to be recalled.

One reason cosmetics manufacturers fight labeling legislation is that the difference between brands is merely which standard ingredients they use in what proportions.

The ingredients in a $2 lipstick cost perhaps 6¢. So do the ingredients in a $3 lipstick, or a $5.50 lipstick. Except for the perfume used and the particular blend of colors, they are the same. The packaging often costs more than the product.

Far from trying to lower prices, companies give considerable thought to how they can stake a claim to the top of the market. One of Estée Lauder's first products was Re-Nutriv, a cream that sold for $115 in the 16-ounce economy size and was billed as the most expensive in the world. Charles of the Ritz met the challenge with a cream called Novesscence, priced at $150 for a mere 12 ounces. Neither really tries to defend its pricing in any but mystic terms. "How much is the canvas and oil in a Renoir worth?" Leonard Lauder demands. "What counts is the artistry."

Use medicated cosmetics only under a doctor's direction. In most cases a drug added to a commercial cosmetic is there only for show. Though raising the price, it does no more than orchid pollen or pulverized pearls to make the cosmetic more effective.

Worse yet, a medication may have severe side effects. Many people feel that cosmetics are harmless because they are simply applied to the skin and washed off, or wear off, without entering the body. Actually the skin is not altogether impermeable. Cosmetic ingredients can penetrate intact skin, or enter the body through the eyes, mouth, or lungs.

Since medicated cosmetics are sold over the counter, there is a great danger of overdosing. No drug has been shown so far to have no absorption at all. In the case of cosmetics that are applied once or several times daily and often on relatively large surfaces, the amount absorbed and permitted to have systemic effects is entirely uncontrolled.

Even lemon extract can produce allergic reactions. Innocent-seeming and common as lemon juice or oils from lemon peel are, you're likely to be better off without them in cosmetics. About all a lemon ingredient accomplishes is a short-lived lemony fragrance. Yet, like many other unnecessary additives, they can be sensitizing.

Antibiotics in cosmetics can trigger a drug allergy. They also can lead to disease resulting from overgrowth of fungi and other antibiotic-resistant organisms that are normally kept in check by the bacteria the antibiotic eliminates. In addition indiscriminate use of antibiotics promotes the development of antibiotic-resistant strains of bacteria, which can cause illness.

Hormone creams. Avoid hormone creams unless prescribed. The female hormone estrogen is widely used in face creams. It is absolutely useless for avoiding wrinkles or for any other rejuvenating effect.

However hormones can be absorbed through the skin and produce profound systemic effects. In one instance a woman ten years past menopause applied an estrogen cream. She thought she had begun to menstruate again. In fact the estrogen was causing her uterus to bleed. Estrogens also can upset the skin's chemistry and lead to increased pigmentation of the face.

Vitamins in cosmetics are similarly valueless and hazardous. Vitamins A and D particularly may be absorbed in excessive quantities and cause side effects. There is no reliable evidence to support the grandiose claims made for the supposedly restorative or healing powers of vitamin E.

Shop for cosmetics as if they were groceries. Take the romance out of them, and treat them as consumer products that merely do a job. Read the labels—the Food and Drug Administration (FDA) requires that they list all ingredients—and avoid products containing chemicals that may harm you.

Look for bargains, trial offers, store-label brands, other money-savers. Take advantage of package deals that have attached samples you can try—then return the larger package if the sample doesn't suit you. Try one product at a time in its smallest size. Resist being sold sets of cosmetics because they "go together." The fewer products you buy, the less likely you'll be disappointed.

Return any product that makes a promise it doesn't live up to. Look for guarantees of satisfaction, and hold the product to them. Return products that produce wrong reactions. If you have trouble with the store, complain to the president of the manufacturing company. He's likely to be nervous enough about the FDA and FTC to yield to your complaint.

See also ACNE; ALLERGY; ANTIBIOTICS; ATHLETE'S FOOT; BAGS UNDER THE EYES; BATH-

ING; BIRTHMARKS; BLISTERS; BOILS; BRUISES; BURNS.

CANCER OF THE SKIN; CIRCLES UNDER THE EYES; CONTACT DERMATITIS; CUTS; CYSTS; DANDRUFF; DERMOGRAPHISM; DIAPER RASH; DRUG ALLERGY; ECZEMA; EYE MAKEUP.

FINGERNAIL BRITTLENESS; FIRST AID SUPPLIES; FRECKLES; HAIR BLEACHING; HAIR BRUSHING; HAIR CURLING; HAIR DRYNESS; HAIR DYEING; HAIRINESS; HAIR LOSS; HAIR OILINESS; HAIR STRAIGHTENING; HAIR WASHING; HIVES.

ICHTHYOSIS; IMPETIGO; INGROWN HAIRS; ITCHING; KELOIDS; MOLES; MOUTHWASHES; PERSPIRATION ODOR; POISON IVY; PRICKLY HEAT; PSORIASIS.

RINGWORM; SCARS; SCRAPES; SEBORRHEIC DERMATITIS; SHAVING; SKIN DRYNESS; SKIN OILINESS; SPLINTERS; SUNBURN; SWEATY PALMS; TATTOOS; TOOTHPASTE.

VAGINAL ODOR; VITAMINS; VITILIGO; WARTS; WRINKLES; XANTHOMA.

SKIN DRYNESS (chapped skin, winter skin, winter itch) results from loss of moisture from the outer layer of the skin.

It is generally most pronounced in cold weather, when the humidity of outside air decreases and inside air tends to be dry because it is heated. Cold wind also can dry the skin, causing windburn, a dry redness resembling sunburn.

Excessive washing or frequent contact with water tends to cause dryness by removing the skin oil (sebum) and water in the skin. Bathing is likely to dry your skin if you use very hot water or soaps containing a detergent. Some chemicals, especially solvents, dry skin by stripping away the oils.

In summer your skin may become dry if you're constantly exposed to air conditioning, especially to the draft of air outlets. The problem is likely to be worse in houses than in offices or public buildings. Industrial conditioners often humidify the air, whereas home models rarely do.

Too much exposure to sun—or sunlamps—can result in skin dryness. So can frequent swimming in chlorinated pools.

Some people are born with an oil-deficient skin condition. Age causes a general reduction in skin oil, making dry skin a common complaint of the elderly. What's more, thanks to hormones, you can have areas of oily skin—perhaps an oily forehead or nose—but dry skin elsewhere on your body.

Dry skin may flake and itch. Conditions called "winter skin" and "winter itch" usually are little more than cases of skin dryness.

Chapped skin occurs when the outer layer of the skin loses its flexibility as water is lost from the keratin, the protein substance making up this layer. Dehydration causes brittleness, which leads to cracks. Inflammation of the skin may follow.

Children are frequent victims of dry skin. Their pink, chapped cheeks and lips may look healthy, but chapping can be painful. The usual cause is improper drying before running out to play. Youngsters can get chapped, cracked lips from bubble gum. Another cause, for both children and adults, is nervous licking of the lips.

Excessively dry skin may lead to fine, superficial lines. But it is not an important factor in the formation of premature wrinkles.

Overcoming dryness. What to do about dry skin? Follow these rules:

Keep the heat in your home below 72° F. Feed moisture into the air with a humidifier.

Limit bathing to once or twice a week. Substitute a quick shower, or a short warm bath, for a long hot soak in the tub. Go easy with the soap. Adding a bath oil to the water may help reduce postbath itchiness (but be careful—it can make the tub slippery).

If a baby's skin is dry, don't use soap. Think of the bath as play and let the water do the cleaning.

Use rubber gloves when you wash dishes. Use the gloves, too, when you handle strong soaps and detergents and solvents such as gasoline, kerosene, benzene, or turpentine.

In winter stay away from tight clothing, which can rub against dry winter skin. Protect your lips with lipstick, greasy lip cream, or lip balm.

Apply a moisturizing cream or lotion every day. These emollient preparations make the skin soft and smooth by retarding evaporation and by leaving a film of oil to cement down the skin's rough surface. It's likely to work best if you put it on when your skin is moist.

Choose whichever product is cheapest and appeals to you because of its texture, washability, scent. Most are variations of the basic formula for cold cream—oil, water, perfume and emulsifiers—and are about equally effective. No cream penetrates beneath the top layer, no matter what the manufacturer claims.

Products containing vitamins or hormones are no improvement over ordinary cold cream—though they cost much more and may trigger an allergic reaction. *The Medical Letter* reports that for simple dry skin, urea creams have not been proven more effective or safer than older products, despite their being extremely expensive.

Men who object to the scent of lubricating creams or oils may use plain petroleum jelly, mineral oil, or vegetable shortening (such as Crisco), with equal effectiveness. Women can apply a foundation cream under makeup. If your skin is very dry, skip the powder and use only a creamy makeup. Alternate the use of soap and water with cleansing cream. Avoid egg facials and astringents (alcohol, witch hazel), which tend to irritate dry skin.

For other conditions that resemble dry skin, but require different treatment, see CONTACT DERMATITIS; DANDRUFF; PSORIASIS; SEBOR-RHEIC DERMATITIS.

See also SKIN DISORDERS.

SKIN OILINESS varies with how much you perspire. The skin's surface oil will spread out on a film of water. Thus when you sweat a great deal, as in summer or when under emotional stress, your skin will appear oilier.

The amount of oil that is constantly being delivered to the surface can't be reduced. But most oiliness can be controlled by washing with soap and water three or four times a day. When washing is inconvenient, use premoistened cleansing pads.

Avoid complexion brushes or abrasive soaps. They offer no advantage for removing surface oils. If used frequently, they may irritate the skin. Despite old wives' tales oiliness will not prevent wrinkles.

Cosmetics for oily skin that work best are loose powder and nonoily foundation lotions. Oily substances may only add to the problem.

Many women complain they have "combination" complexions, with both oiliness and dryness. The midforehead, nose, and chin tend to be oilier than the cheeks and temples.

No single cosmetic will care for all skin areas. Use a nongreasy cleanser to decrease oiliness in the center areas of the face. Relieve dryness on the cheeks, temples, and eyelids with a moisturizing cream, applied sparingly once or twice daily. If excessive oiliness persists, use an astringent (a strong alcohol solution) two or three times daily on the forehead, nose, and chin.

DANDRUFF and SEBORRHEIC DERMATITIS (which see) may result from excessive oiliness.

See also SKIN DISORDERS.

SKULL FRACTURES can be serious because they may be associated with potential damage to the delicate structures of the brain or to the blood vessels that supply it. A fracture may oc-cur to any portion of the skull, but those near the back of the head are particularly dangerous.

It is possible to have a severe skull fracture without a visible wound. Any unconscious or semiconscious person who has had a head injury should be treated as though he had a skull fracture.

There may be one or more of these symptoms: Confusion; severe, persistent headache; unconsciousness; bleeding or oozing of watery fluid from one or both ears, from the nose and mouth, or from all; eye pupils of unequal size; repeated vomiting.

Get medical help as soon as possible. For first aid:

1. Treat for SHOCK (which see). Keep the victim on his back, with his head flat.
2. Turn his head slightly away from the injured side so as to relieve pressure. Don't interfere with drainage of watery cerebrospinal fluid from his ears and nose.
3. Keep him absolutely quiet and unmoving.
4. Never give stimulants or any painkilling agent. These may increase the degree of unconsciousness and slow up respiration.
5. Avoid moving him. If you must transport him, keep him flat on his back on a stretcher or board, firmly immobilized. Don't raise his head.
6. Don't remove impaled objects (knives, rods, etc.).

See also FRACTURES; HEAD INJURIES; MOVING THE INJURED.

SKUNKS are major carriers of rabies. Indeed in many parts of the United States skunks must be considered rabid unless proven otherwise.

Skunks are normally shy animals and avoid humans. Beware any that come toward you even if it seems friendly. Tameness is one sign a skunk may have rabies. Another clue: A rabid skunk is ordinarily unable to discharge its scent. Don't try to make a wild skunk into a pet.

If a skunk bites you, scrub the wound and get to a doctor immediately. If possible kill the skunk without unnecessary damage to its head and bring it with you for a disease check. Skunks also may carry leptospirosis and tularemia.

Skunk spray. If you are sprayed by a skunk: Flush the discharge from your face and eyes with plenty of water. The oily discharge released from paired glands just inside the skunk's rectum contains a general irritant that affects all mucous membranes. Intense pain will result if the spray makes contact with the lips, eyes, or nasal passages.

You can temporarily deodorize skin by washing with diluted vinegar. Or, less effective, use diluted laundry bleach, tomato juice, shaving lotion, gasoline, or ammonia.

The odor may return as soon as the sprayed portion of the body becomes wet. After several days it will dissipate substantially. You may find the characteristic skunk odor, from the chemical butyl mercaptan, to be quite tolerable in small quantities.

Hang clothing in the sun and wind for several weeks. Multiple washings are only moderately helpful.

Noxious skunk odors in buildings may be partially masked by using a deodorant called Neutroleum Alpha, available in concentrated or water-soluble form from the manufacturer, Fritzsche Brothers, Inc., of New York, or from hospital suppliers or pest controllers.

Give skunks you encounter a chance to amble away. They rarely let fly unless disturbed. Take off in the opposite direction if you see one in firing position—tail lifted toward you, head curved around.

Don't kill skunks needlessly. They eat insects and may help to rid your lawn of cutworms and grubs as they dig and uproot turf.

If a skunk sets up housekeeping under a building, close all but one opening and sprinkle a little flour in front of it. Examine this patch after dark. If tracks show that the skunk has left, close the opening. To speed its exit scatter mothballs, naphthalene flakes, or paradichlorobenzene around the entrance and under the floor.

Skunks avoid light. Illuminate an area to help keep them away. You can keep them from uprooting lawns by using a soil insecticide to kill off their food supply.

See also ANIMAL BITES; ANIMAL DISEASE; RABIES.

SLEEPERS, SLEEPING PILLS See BARBITU-RATES.

SLEEPING SICKNESS See ENCEPHALITIS.

SLEEPLESSNESS (insomnia)—too little sleep—falls into three patterns: (1) You have difficulty in falling asleep; (2) you awaken intermittently; or (3) you wake up too early.

The minimum sleep requirement varies considerably from person to person, even in the same person from time to time. On the average adults need to sleep from six to nine hours a night. The best way to determine if you are sleeping the proper number of hours is to ask: Do you fall asleep easily? Do you awake refreshed? If not, adjust your bedtime earlier or later.

Like adults, youngsters vary greatly in the amount of sleep they require. The average 5-year-old needs 11 to 13 hours; 10-year-old, 10 to 12 hours; 15-year-old, 9 to 11 hours; 20-year-old, 8 to 9 hours.

As important as the amount of sleep you get is the quality. Normal sleep consists of drifting up and down through different levels of consciousness—from light slumber to deep sleep approximating unconsciousness, to periods of rapid eye movement (REM sleep) when dreams occur. The deep-sleep period is the most restful and restorative.

Infants spend about half their sleeping time in the dreaming stage. By the end of their first year their dreaming-sleep periods drop to 20 percent.

This percentage remains about the same up to age 50, then decreases. Older persons spend less time in dreaming and deep-sleep stages, more in the light stage. This may account for an elderly person's complaints about sleeping poorly.

What keeps you up? Difficulty in sleeping results mainly from anxiety, worry, or depression. If emotional stress is not at fault, look for bodily illness. Sleeplessness can be an early symptom of acute infectious disease. A person with unrecognized heart disease may be able to breathe only in a sitting position and may thus have difficulty sleeping. Asthma, chronic pain, and itching can likewise produce insomnia. Insomnia may be due to a variety of prescription drugs. Another's snoring may also keep you awake.

While even one night of tossing and turning can make you miserable, there is little evidence that even chronic insomnia takes any lasting toll. Poor sleepers almost always sleep more than they think they do. Merely lying in bed, even without sleep, helps refresh the body.

If you have trouble getting to sleep, here are some tips that may help you:

Make your sleeping conditions as ideal as possible. Usually the quieter the room the better, although soft music or the low hum of an air conditioner may be soothing. Wear loose-fitting nightclothes.

Sleep in a cool room, about 60° F. Use one warm blanket instead of several lighter ones which can become twisted and uncomfortable. Soft light and dark colors in a bedroom may be conducive to sleep.

Do relaxing things before bedtime. Bathing in warm (98° F–104° F) water can help relax your muscles. For an hour before bedtime try reading, playing solitaire, listening to restful music. TV may not work—bad late news or a disturbing movie can keep you up.

It may also help to go to bed at around the

same time each night. The regularity of the routine may make you more relaxed.

Do some light exercise. A walk, a slow, rhythmic exercise, or just a few minutes of deep breathing may help you sleep. If it's too strenuous, it may have the opposite effect. Sexual intercourse before bedtime often promotes sleep.

Eat and drink sparingly before retiring. Avoid stimulants like coffee, alcohol, and cola drinks. No smoking either—tobacco is a stimulant.

A light, bland snack such as an apple or crackers and a beverage probably will satisfy any hunger you may feel, yet won't stimulate your bladder and digestive tract and make you restless and uncomfortable. Milk, hot or cold, is an excellent sleep-inducer.

If you feel tense in bed, do a squeeze and stretch: Sit up with your arms around your knees, pressing your heels into your buttocks. Bury your face in your thighs. Then squeeze into as small a space as you can. Clench your fists, arms, legs, buttocks. Hold this position until it becomes unbearable, at least a minute.

Then release and instantly do the reverse: stretch; re-al-ly stretch, so that you occupy as much space as you can. Pull apart your arms, legs, toes, fingers. Stretch your face, with your eyes and mouth open wide, your tongue sticking out.

Hold for a minute or two. Release, and breathe deeply and slowly. Let your body sink into the bed. A great wave of peace is almost certain to engulf you.

Further: Try relaxing each muscle individually, starting with your toes and slowly working your way up to your head. Chances are you'll be asleep before you try relaxing your ears.

Worthless products. Be skeptical of gadgets advertised to cure insomnia. While these may help in individual cases, they are likely to be expensive and unlikely to relieve a severe, long-term sleep problem.

Thus be wary of claims made to insomniacs for ear plugs, eye shades, phonograph records to provide hypnotic sound, special bed lamps and mattresses.

One unproved sleep-suggester is a plaster representation of a widely yawning head to be hung in view of the insomniac. Other products, rarely of help, are bedroom paints, wallpapers, and curtains, all promoted as being relaxing, restful, or sleep-inducing. There are "special" foods and drinks, which accomplish little more than the snack suggestions cited earlier.

Nonprescription sleep preparations are best avoided. Americans spend more than $25 million a year to dose themselves with drug products promising sleep. But such products may be ineffective—and can have pronounced side effects.

These preparations generally contain antihistamines, usually used to treat allergies. Antihistamines used in sleep aids can cause such side effects as nausea, vomiting, dizziness, fatigue, double vision, and dryness of the mouth, nose, and throat.

If you use over-the-counter sleep preparations, be particularly careful not to exceed the recommended dosage. Do not give to children under 12. Avoid taking in combination with alcohol, which can worsen side effects and cause respiratory difficulties. Don't use nonprescription sleep aids if you suffer from asthma, glaucoma, or enlargement of the prostate.

Someone with a serious sleep disorder may benefit from the services of a sleep clinic. For a list of sleep clinics write to Peter Bent Brigham Hospital Sleep Clinic (721 Huntington Avenue, Boston, Massachusetts 02115).

If your insomnia is persistent and severe, your physician may prescribe BARBITURATES or TRANQUILIZERS (which see).

See also ANTIHISTAMINES; SNORING; SLEEP-WALKING; STRESS.

SLEEPWALKING (somnambulism) usually affects children between the ages of 5 and 12.

Typically a sleepwalker will get out of bed and wander around for a few minutes before returning to bed. Unlike sleepwalkers in the movies his hands are in a normal position at his sides, not outstretched, and his eyes may be open. Also contrary to myth, sleepwalking occurs not during dreams but during deep dreamless sleep. On awaking, the sleepwalker has no memory of his travels.

Sleepwalking in children is thought to be mainly a symptom of an immature nervous system. It often runs in families. In most cases it occurs only occasionally and is outgrown in two or three years. Where sleepwalking occurs frequently, it may be a sign of anxiety or other psychological stress. Parents should consult a physician.

Adults who live alone may discover they are sleepwalkers when they find their rooms messed. Or they may find breadcrumbs in their beds in the morning, evidence of a sleepwalking snack. Extremely overweight people are sometimes compulsive sleep-eaters. Psychotherapy is often needed to cure sleepwalking in adults.

Sleepwalkers can harm themselves on their jaunts: some have left their homes and crossed busy streets. Others have climbed out of windows. Protect the sleepwalker by having him sleep on the first floor. Fasten windows and lock outside doors. Put away dangerous objects and car keys.

Don't awaken a sleepwalker if you can avoid it. If it is necessary to awaken him, try not to frighten him. Tap him gently on the shoulder and repeat his name until he hears you. Never punish a child for sleepwalking.

See also STRESS.

SLIPPED DISC refers to a condition in which a disc of the spinal column is partly forced out of place or ruptured. The discs—made of a firm but cushiony substance—serve as shock absorbers between the bones of the spine, called vertebrae.

With aging, a disc's elastic tissue weakens, and its supporting mechanism is damaged. When a condition of sufficient strain occurs—sometimes merely a sneeze—the disc may tear or move out of place.

The cover surrounding the disc tears, and the central portion protrudes through the tear.

The chief symptom of slipped disc is a pain in the leg. Back pain may occur early, probably due to the tear, and tends to subside over a few days. If the injured disc puts pressure on the sciatic nerve, it causes the severe hip and leg pain called sciatica.

Slipped disc requires a doctor's attention. Some people respond well to bed rest, exercises, traction, or corrective corsets. Surgery may be required.

See also BACKACHE; SCIATICA; SURGERY.

SMALLPOX has been wiped out. The eradication of smallpox from the globe represents a triumph of preventive medicine. In the late eighteenth century it infected half the population of Europe and was responsible for one in ten deaths. If not fatal, smallpox often led to complications, such as blindness, arthritis, and deep pitting or scarring of the skin. There is no known cure.

The turnabout began on May 14, 1796. A Gloucestershire physician named Edward Jenner set about testing a folk belief that dairymaids who had had cowpox, a mild animal disease, would not contract smallpox. Jenner removed matter from a cowpox sore on the hand of Sarah Nelmes, a milkmaid, and injected it into the arm of a boy named James Phipps.

Seven weeks later Jenner sought to infect Jimmy with smallpox. No disease developed; the boy's immunity was complete.

From this monumental experiment has sprung the entire field of immunization. The episode is memorialized in the words *vaccine* and *vaccination,* which are derived from *vaccinia,* the medical term for *cowpox.*

With worldwide vaccination and careful surveillance, smallpox has been conquered. At the World Health Assembly in May 1980, the World Health Organization (WHO) declared the world free of smallpox. There is no evidence of smallpox transmission anywhere in the world.

Routine smallpox vaccination is not recommended, except for laboratory workers directly involved with smallpox or closely related viruses, such as monkeypox.

Nor do you need a smallpox vaccination for international travel. WHO has recommended that all countries no longer require a certificate of vaccination for incoming travelers.

See also INFECTIOUS DISEASE.

SMOKING, observed the British Royal College of Physicians, is now as important a cause of death as the great epidemics of typhoid, cholera, and tuberculosis in the past.

Reports of the surgeon general of the U.S. Public Health Service have left no doubt that smoking is a serious health hazard, endangering the lives of millions of Americans. Some findings:

At every age over 30 there are more deaths among cigarette smokers than among nonsmokers. These are called excess or unnecessary deaths. There are 300,000 unnecessary deaths of smokers each year in the United States.

If you're a smoker, you're likely to die earlier in proportion to the number of cigarettes you've smoked. The more years you've smoked, statistically the younger you die. The earlier the age you started, odds are the earlier you die.

Men over 30 who smoke less than one half pack a day have a death rate about 35 percent higher than that of nonsmokers. A man who smokes one to two packs a day increases his chances of dying by about 95 percent. If he smokes two or more packs a day, this risk of dying is 125 percent above normal.

Heavy cigarette smokers, on the average, lose about one minute of life for every minute they smoke. A man of 25 who smokes a pack of cigarettes a day may be giving up five and a half years of life, compared with a 25-year-old man who doesn't smoke cigarettes. If he smokes two or more packs a day, on average, he cuts eight years, four months out of his life.

There are fewer statistics on women, because women haven't been smoking as long as men. But according to present evidence the death rate of female smokers has been climbing. It is now going up as fast as the male rate, but is still at a lower level.

Moreover, women are starting to smoke at an

earlier age. An increasing percentage of women are becoming heavy smokers. Once a woman takes up smoking, she is less likely than a man to give it up.

In the last 30 years deaths from lung cancer among women have increased fourfold. About 25,000 women a year die of lung cancer; most were smokers.

Women smokers are also more likely than nonsmokers to suffer heart attacks, cerebral hemorrhages, cancers of the larynx and bladder, chronic lung diseases, and a host of respiratory ailments. All evidence shows that women are just as likely as men to die from the effects of cigarettes.

Cigarettes and heart disease. Cigarette smoking contributes to the development of coronary artery disease, which leads to heart attack and stroke.

Nicotine and related substances in cigarette smoke put stress on the coronary arteries by raising blood pressure and heartbeat. Nicotine may cause an increase in the heart muscle's demand for oxygen—while the carbon monoxide absorbed from smoking decreases the available blood oxygen.

Nicotine also causes free fatty acids to pour into your blood, thus promoting arteriosclerosis. Smoking apparently can accelerate blood clotting. This may increase death from thrombosis —blood clots blocking arteries in the heart and brain.

Twice as many heart attacks are suffered by heavy cigarette smokers (two or more packs a day) as by nonsmokers. Death rates from heart attacks in men range from 50 to 200 percent higher among cigarette smokers than among nonsmokers, depending on age and the amount smoked. The average increase is 70 percent.

Smoking presents a special hazard to women taking birth control pills. The total death rate resulting from smoking plus the Pill is greater than from either factor alone. Of 100,000 women age 40 to 44, heart attack kills 11 who use the Pill but don't smoke, 16 who smoke but don't use the Pill—and 62 who both use the Pill and smoke.

Smoking is especially dangerous for patients with diseases of blood vessels in the arms and legs (peripheral vascular diseases). It constricts blood vessels that are already narrowed and damaged, makes them more susceptible to infection, and slows the healing of cuts, burns, and bruises. Patients who continue to smoke increase their risk of gangrene, amputations, death.

Buerger's disease occurs almost exclusively in men who smoke. It affects the small arteries of toes and fingers in early stages, but may later involve larger blood vessels. When the patient stops smoking, the condition almost always is arrested. A return to smoking causes it to recur.

Smoking and cancer. An estimated 30 percent of all cancer deaths—about 130,000 a year—are attributable to smoking. People who smoke more than a pack a day are three times as likely to die of cancer as nonsmokers. Smoking is considered the "major cause" of cancers of the lung, larynx, oral cavity, and esophagus, and a "contributory factor" in cancers of the bladder, kidney, and pancreas.

Smoking as a cause of lung cancer far outweighs all other factors. The average male smoker is ten times more likely to develop lung cancer than nonsmokers. The risk is as much as thirtyfold for heavy smokers. It is estimated that 85 percent of all lung cancer deaths could have been avoided if the victims had not smoked.

Tobacco smoke contains some 30 chemicals capable of causing cancer, plus others (known as cocarcinogens) that promote the action of cancer-causing agents. Skin cancer has been produced in animals with chemicals found in cigarette smoke and with tars condensed from smoke. Some pesticides used in tobacco cultivation and found in tobacco smoke increase the incidence of cancer in laboratory animals.

Male cigarette smokers aged 45 to 64 have ten times the normal risk of dying of mouth cancer. Smoking pipes and cigars, which generate more heat than cigarettes, may be even more important than cigarettes in the development of oral cancer. A cause-and-effect relationship has been established between pipe smoking and cancer of the lip.

Cancer of the larynx causes six times as many deaths among cigarette smokers aged 45 to 64 as among nonsmokers. Cigarette smokers are four to five times likelier to die of cancer of the esophagus than a nonsmoker. Deaths from cancer of the bladder are more than three times as numerous among cigarette smokers as among nonsmokers aged 65 to 79.

Smoking and respiratory disease. A smoker's risk of death from emphysema or chronic bronchitis is 6½ to 15 times that of a nonsmoker, depending on the number of cigarettes smoked.

Respiratory disease is promoted by the damage tobacco smoke does to the cilia—tiny, hairlike projections of tissue that move constantly, sweeping impurities out of the respiratory tract. When tobacco smoke is inhaled, the cilia slow down and may stop. This allows smoke particles, dust, tars, smog chemicals, and bacteria to irritate the lungs and throat, establishing a foothold for disease.

Smokers tend to have a lower breathing capacity—less ability to provide the body with oxygen in emergencies. Smoking thickens the lining membranes of the air passages and obstructs them with secretions. It contracts the muscles in the air-passage walls, which narrows them and further reduces air flow. A single cigarette will markedly reduce the air flow of a smoker.

A smoker's larynx may have thicker, swollen vocal cords, audible as hoarseness or a raspy voice. Irritations from smoke cause swelling and increased secretion in the air passages and lungs. This results in "smoker's cough," which is believed to predispose a person to emphysema or chronic bronchitis.

Carbon monoxide, a component of tobacco smoke, prevents red cells from picking up enough oxygen. It also inhibits the cells from giving up oxygen as fast as the tissues demand. Because of this effect a cigarette smoker who lives at sea level is getting as little oxygen as someone who's more than 8,000 feet above. A smoker may thus feel winded under mild stress, even if he smokes only five or six cigarettes per day.

Some smokers get "tobacco angina," a dull, boring sensation under the breastbone. The chest pain appears as soon as they begin smoking a cigar or cigarette. It disappears when they stop smoking.

Smoking and sex. Sexual functions seem to be interfered with by smoking. Some evidence suggests that cigarette smoking may lower the libido and impair the fertility of both sexes. Nicotine may speed the passage of an egg through the fallopian tube, an effect that could reduce the possibility of its being fertilized. For some infertility patients stopping cigarette smoking was all the treatment needed to bring about a long-awaited pregnancy.

A study among 5,000 women revealed that those who smoked had a greater incidence of sterility, menstrual disturbances, miscarriages, and difficulty reaching orgasm. A pregnant woman who smokes is smoking for two. Nicotine constricts the blood vessels in her unborn child, cutting down on fetal blood flow, while carbon monoxide cuts down the amount of oxygen in the reduced blood supply. The fetus doesn't get as much blood or oxygen to grow as fast as it normally would.

Babies born to smoking mothers average 5 to 8 ounces less than those borne by women who abstain from smoking during pregnancy. Their babies more often weigh less than 5½ pounds—which is considered premature—and are exposed to more risk of disease and death. Pregnant women who smoke have a greater number of stillbirths than nonsmoking women. Their infants are more likely to die within the first month.

Mouth damage. Smoking can damage teeth and gums. Not only does it yellow teeth and leave an odor on breath, it ages the mouth. Relatively young smokers have oral health as poor as that of nonsmokers who are 15 years older.

Trench mouth occurs more often among heavy smokers than among light smokers or nonsmokers. Smokers of both sexes have significantly more of the severe, advanced form of pyorrhea than people who don't smoke.

Smoking hastens the destruction of the alveolar bone in which teeth are anchored, thus leading to eventual tooth loss. A study of nearly 10,000 people in Michigan found significantly more loss of teeth among men and women who smoked than among nonsmokers of the same ages. Women between the ages of 20 and 39 and men between 30 and 59 were twice as likely to have lost their teeth if they were smokers.

Other effects of smoking. Tobacco may cause reactions in the stomach and intestines that affect normal digestion or make gastrointestinal disorders become worse. Smoking appears to slow down the healing of peptic ulcers and tends to make an ulcer chronic.

Smoking may prematurely age the skin. In a study of more than 1,000 adults internist Harry W. Daniell reported that among both sexes the amount of cigarette smoking was clearly related to the degree of facial wrinkling. The association between smoking and wrinkles becomes striking soon after age 30. Smokers in the 40 to 49 age group have as many wrinkles as nonsmokers 20 years older.

Tobacco and tobacco smoke are associated with allergy. Reactions include asthma, hay fever, hives, and skin eruptions. Exposure to tobacco leaf or smoke also may trigger migraine.

Even nonsmokers can suffer from smoking. Exposure to a smoke-filled environment causes nonsmokers to suffer increases in heart rate, blood pressure, and the amount of carbon dioxide in the blood.

Other effects are eye and nose symptoms, headache, sore throat, cough, hoarseness, nausea, and dizziness. Cigarette smokers in a crowded, ill-ventilated room or automobile can raise the level of carbon monoxide past the danger point. Allergy-prone people are especially likely to be in distress on exposure to smoke.

Recent evidence suggests that "passive" (or

"involuntary" or "second-hand") smoking can be a "possible serious public health problem," according to the surgeon general. Children of parents who smoke are more likely to suffer bronchitis and pneumonia in the first year of life. Nonsmoking spouses of heavy smokers seem more prone to respiratory disease and death from lung cancer.

More than 25 percent of all U.S. fires are caused by smokers. In one year 163,900 fires were traced to smoking or matches used in smoking, and resulted in 1,800 deaths and property loss of more than $95 million.

Why people smoke. In young people smoking may represent freedom to do as one pleases, or may be a reaction against adult authority. A young person is more likely to become a smoker if his parents, older brothers and sisters, or—especially—his friends smoke. At first the taste and the effect of tobacco are not pleasant—the smoker must learn to like cigarettes. He does this primarily for social reasons: to appear more adult, to be like his friends, to give himself poise.

Feelings of inadequacy may spur smoking. Dr. Ian M. Newman of the University of Tennessee found that teen-age boys and girls who smoke cigarettes generally see themselves as failing to measure up to expectations of parents and school. They are more likely than nonsmoking counterparts to fail courses and to be tardy or truant. Nonsmokers are more likely to be listed on academic honor rolls and to be active in extracurricular activities.

The smoker who begins in his teens with a few cigarettes is likely to become a habitual smoker. Thus, concluded the American Public Health Association, if present trends continue more than 1 million children now in school will die of lung cancer before they reach age 70.

Reaching the young. Cigarette advertising is a major seducer of the young. "Between the time a kid is 18 and 20, he's going to make the basic decision to smoke or not to smoke," said Liggett & Myers's vice president and advertising director. "If he does decide to smoke, we want to get him." Some admen call this game "Hooking the Kids."

Cigarette ads often portray and seem to be directly pitched at young people. A Federal Trade Commission study found a recurrent theme of cigarette ads in "outdoor activity of an athletic nature, engaged in by youthful, fit and personable appearing models."

You can reduce the health risks of smoking. Choose a cigarette with less tar and nicotine. The FTC publishes ratings of all leading brands of cigarettes, showing some with ten times the

tar of others. Reduce your tar and nicotine intake by switching to another brand or to another version of the brand you are presently smoking.

But beware that you don't start smoking more low-nicotine cigarettes to satisfy your nicotine addiction. You may also smoke a low-nicotine cigarette to a shorter butt, increase the size of each puff, draw smoke deeper into your lungs, or take more puffs per minute. Any of these efforts to compensate for the lesser nicotine can increase your intake of harmful tars.

Don't smoke any cigarette all the way down. The most tar and nicotine is in your last few puffs. The tobacco retains a portion of the tars and nicotine that pass through it, so the last half yields about 60 percent of the total of these harmful ingredients. This fact points up the added risk of the longer cigarettes. Their extra puffs are really extra perils.

Take fewer draws on each cigarette. With practice some people find they can substantially cut their actual smoking without really missing it.

Reduce the depth of your inhaling and its frequency. It's the smoke that enters your lungs that does most of the damage. About 90 percent of the nicotine is absorbed into the body when smoke is inhaled. Only 10 percent is absorbed when smoke is puffed without inhaling.

Switch to a pipe or cigars. Despite a higher incidence of oral cancer pipe and cigar smokers have less risk of heart disease, lung and kidney cancer, and many of the other diseases associated with cigarette smoking—probably because the pipe and cigar smoker usually does not inhale.

Quitting is the only really safe answer. There is risk even in moderate cigarette smoking. People who smoke more than five cigarettes a day show a higher death rate than nonsmokers.

Conversely, even if you've smoked a long time, your risks go down when you quit. The death rate from heart attack decreases among those who give up cigarette smoking until it is close to the death rate of people who have never smoked. When you stop smoking, some body tissues that have been damaged—such as in the lungs or bronchial tubes—gradually return to normal. Young smokers have the best chance of quitting, a good reason for youngsters to stop before they're as hooked as older people who have smoked for 15 or 20 years.

Filter tips reduce only moderately the harmful substances in cigarette smoke. There is no evidence that filters are the answer to "safe" smoking. Indeed some filter cigarettes have a higher content of nicotine and tars than some unfiltered cigarettes. The death rate of filter-tip smokers who smoke heavily is still five times that of non-smokers.

Menthol is merely an additive that changes the taste of the smoke. It does not actually make smoke cooler or less dangerous.

What about switching to so-called little cigars, products that are the size and shape of cigarettes but are wrapped in tobacco rather than paper? The switch may actually increase the hazard if you still inhale. One FTC study found that the smoke of little cigars contained more nicotine and tars than an equivalent amount of cigarette smoke. What's more, the mildest little cigars—those whose smoke is less alkaline and so likelier to be inhaled—were the very brands posing the greatest threats from tars and nicotine.

How to quit. Different types of smokers need different ways of quitting. The American Cancer Society estimates that 50 percent of successful quitters did it cold turkey. The other 50 percent quit gradually.

Don't feel guilty if you can't stop quickly. Many smokers fail in their first, second, even fifth attempts, and then finally succeed. It's not a failure of "willpower," but a need to learn a new behavior pattern.

If you break down and have a cigarette, don't be discouraged. Just start over. Every cigarette you don't smoke is that much less smoke in your lungs. It helps put you one-up statistically.

To think of stopping as self-denial is also an error. You are not giving up an object of value, however dependent you may be on it. If you begin to feel sorry for yourself and brood on your sufferings, they may well become unendurable.

How hard it is for you to give it up may depend on what kind of smoker you are. Dr. Silvan Tomkins of the City University of New York distinguishes these general types:

The habitual smoker, who may hardly be aware he has a cigarette in his mouth. He may once have regarded smoking as an important sign of status. But now smoking is automatic. He must first become aware of when he is smoking.

The positive affect smoker, for whom it serves as a stimulant that produces pleasure. Or he uses it as a relaxant to heighten enjoyment, as at the end of a meal. This smoker may enjoy most the handling of a cigarette or the sense and sight of smoke curling out of his mouth. He may find giving up cigarettes relatively painless.

The negative affect smoker, to whom it is a sedative, used to reduce feelings of distress, fear, shame, disgust. This smoker may not smoke at all when things go well, but under tension he reaches for a cigarette. He gives up often, but when pressure hits, he finds it very hard to resist a cigarette. A strong substitute, like nibbling ginger root, may be useful.

The addictive smoker is always aware when he isn't smoking. Lack of a cigarette builds need, desire, discomfort. But his enjoyment of the cigarette is brief and may be disappointing.

For the addictive smoker, tapering off doesn't seem to work. The only solution is to quit cold. For the week before going cold turkey some such smokers find it useful to increase the number of cigarettes they smoke—to go from two packs to four, to force themselves to smoke so that their bodies will be in revolt against the double dose of tar and nicotine.

How to taper off. If you decide to taper off, do it within three days, advises the U.S. Department of Health, Education, and Welfare. You may take less time but not more. Each day smoke less than half the cigarettes you smoked the day before. If you smoked a full pack yesterday, cut back to nine cigarettes today, four tomorrow, and one on the third and final day.

For a more gradual plan give yourself up to four weeks to quitting day. Set a date and, as it approaches, cut down. Smoke only once an hour, then extend the nonsmoking time by half an hour, one hour, two hours. Or reduce by half the cigarettes you smoke week by week.

Dr. Donald T. Fredrickson of the New York City Smoking Withdrawal Program suggests that you begin by making a list of when and why you smoke. Eliminate the least important cigarette, then the next least important, and so on. You may find that you are largely a social smoker or that cigarettes play a large part in your picture of yourself as a mature and successful person. Go without a cigarette and convince yourself that people like and respect you for more important reasons than your cigarette.

To bring your habit to conscious awareness, hold the cigarette in the hand opposite the one you usually use or between two different fingers. Place it in a part of your mouth where you don't normally smoke it. Ask yourself each time you light up: "Do I really want this cigarette? Or am I just doing this out of habit?"

Don't carry matches or a lighter. Keep cigarettes in an out-of-the-way place, such as a drawer or cabinet. If you always carry your pack in one pocket, put it in another so you'll have to fumble for it. Shift from cigarettes you like to an unpalatable brand.

Get others to help you quit. Tell your friends and family you're quitting. A smoking withdrawal clinic may give you the boost you need. Public commitments bolster willpower.

Find one other person to stop when you do so you can work on it together. A husband and wife may form a successful team. They can support each other with sympathy or, occasionally, through antipathy, since neither may want to exhibit a lack of willpower to the other.

Form a betting pool of ex-smokers. A group of people can each put up $50. The ones who stop smoking get their money back. The others lose.

On the day you stop, resolve that the time to quit is *right now*—not New Year's Day, not during Lent, not when you finish the pack or carton. Burn your bridges behind you. Crumple whatever cigarettes and matches you have and toss them in the wastebasket. Throw away your cigarette case and lighter.

The first 48 hours are critical for most people. Once you pass them, it will be easier for you each day. After a week you're likely to be over the hump.

Center on something that holds your interest for a long period of time so you aren't tempted to smoke. Look for enjoyment. Line up a relaxing schedule for the next few weeks. Include good movies, a ball game, plan a party.

For a few days spend as much time as possible in libraries or other places where smoking is forbidden. Ride in "no smoking" cars.

Keeping all cigarettes, ashtrays, matches, etc., out of sight so you aren't reminded of your renunciation. For two weeks keep away from friends who are heavy smokers.

Have your favorite food on quitting day. But avoid drinks, such as coffee and liquor, that customarily stimulate a desire to smoke. Give yourself other things that you like best. For some the cigarette after a meal is very important. Instead of a cigarette try a mouthwash.

Resist sudden cravings for a smoke. The urge generally subsides within ten minutes. Tide yourself over with a supply of chewing gum, cough drops, carrot sticks, other low-calorie nibbles. Drink water. Chew bits of fresh ginger or clove.

When you've saved a bit of money by not smoking, buy yourself a present.

Find something to do with your hands. Try playing the harmonica or sketching cartoons or knitting socks or painting the kitchen or whittling—anything to avoid feeling empty-handed just because you're not fingering a cigarette.

Refrain from the first cigarette in the morning. This one is easiest to omit, and it usually sets the day's pace.

Stay off a day at a time. Tell yourself you're stopping only for a day, promising that the situation will be reevaluated the next day. This does away with the fear of long years without a smoke. Each day free of the habit makes it easier to stay off the next.

Exercise whenever possible. Long walks, calisthenics, strenuous physical activity, can be helpful in working off irritation and tension at not having a cigarette. Vacation is a good time for some people to stop. Try camping, mountain climbing, tennis.

Practice breathing deeply. Inhaling is part of the relaxing effect of smoking. Deep breathing may replace this attraction. When you feel like smoking, slowly fill your lungs as full as you can. Then, very slowly, empty them, keeping your lips partly closed as you exhale. The effect is a sigh.

When not smoking you may tend to hypoventilate—breathe too shallowly—and then feel tense and uncomfortable from not getting enough air. Retrain your breathing through an exercise of first exhaling and then inhaling rhythmically 16 times a minute. Practice this for three minutes, eight or ten times a day, for three or four weeks. It's a good idea to do this exercise in the weeks before you stop smoking, then continue for ten days after you've quit smoking.

You may have a spurt of weight gain when you quit smoking, the result of nervous eating. The best tactic is to forgive yourself this for a few weeks, and take care of the extra pounds after your smoking habit is licked.

Products of dubious value. Commercial antismoking products rarely work. Possibly the most useful are pacifiers like plastic cigarettes (e.g., Resty). Flavored to taste somewhat like the real thing, they provide something to hold between the fingers and lips.

Tobaccoless cigarettes which you light up don't have to bear the notice, WARNING: THE SURGEON GENERAL HAS DETERMINED THAT CIGARETTE SMOKING IS DANGEROUS TO YOUR HEALTH. But, cautioned the National Better Business Bureau: "There still is no evidence that smoking lettuce or cabbage cigarettes is less hazardous in regard to lung cancer or respiratory and circulatory ailments."

The most common pills and tablets to "break the tobacco habit" consist of nothing more than spices and flavorings such as licorice, cloves, coriander, ginger, and menthol. The AMA advises that it is difficult to see how confections of this kind can be of any physiological value in the treatment of the tobacco habit. Ordinary chewing gum or candy normally do just as well and are less expensive.

Another type of product contains silver nitrate, alum, or other metallic substances. One or more of these ingredients, incorporated into a mouthwash or lozenge, acts as an astringent on the mouth membranes, tending to make the taste of smoke so unpleasant that the use of tobacco is distasteful immediately after taking the product. Such products, however, have no effect on the desire for the pharmacologic satisfaction provided by nicotine. They won't help permanently if the nicotine effect is the reason for smoking.

Benzocaine, a local anesthetic, is sometimes used in antitobacco tablets, lozenges, and chewing gum. Its effect is to numb the mouth and throat membranes, thereby negating the desire to eat or smoke. Again this treatment is a temporary one, since the desire for oral gratification generally returns once the anesthetic effect has worn off. Indeed repeated use of benzocaine may cause a drug allergy.

Lobelia, or lobeline sulfate, has essentially the same actions in the body as nicotine. Authorities such as *The Medical Letter,* however, doubt that lobeline preparations provide enough of the drug to be a pharmacological substitute for the amount of nicotine in cigarettes. Though lobeline appears to work for some people, once you stop taking it, you may expect any craving for tobacco to return.

Further, lobeline may cause some people stomach pain and nausea. If you have peptic ulcers or other digestive disturbances, you're generally advised not to use lobeline preparations.

Nicotine chewing gum (e.g. Nicorette), on the other hand, has helped some people kick the cigarette habit. It's best used as part of a formal program. Nicotine gum needs to be prescribed by a physician. It may sometimes stick to dentures.

Formal programs. An increasing number of formal programs—using group therapy or individual counseling—are being offered to people who want to quit smoking. Various success rates are claimed. In general, 20 to 40 percent of participants find such programs effective.

Group clinics sponsored by the American Cancer Society, American Heart Association, and American Lung Association are offered free of charge or for a nominal fee.

The Seventh Day Adventist Church offers a five-day plan for a very low fee. Another five-day plan is offered by Schick Laboratories at about two dozen centers nationwide. Cost is $495 with a money-back guarantee. SmokEnders offers programs in about 30 cities. Nine weekly meetings cost about $175.

Medical authorities advise that you do well to adopt some specific plan of attack. But it has not yet been scientifically proven that any of the commercial plans or programs now on the market is any more effective than a simple do-it-yourself program. Indeed the surgeon general reports that 95 percent of people who have stopped smoking have done so without an organized program.

For more information on quitting smoking, contact the following:

American Cancer Society
90 Park Avenue
New York, New York 10016

American Heart Association
7320 Greenville Avenue
Dallas, Texas 75231

American Lung Association
1740 Broadway
New York, New York 10019

National Interagency Council on Smoking and Health
419 Park Avenue South, Suite 1301
New York, New York 10016

Schick Laboratories
1901 Avenue of the Stars, Suite 1530
Los Angeles, California 90067

SmokEnders
Memorial Parkway
Phillipsburg, New Jersey 08864

General Headquarters
5 Day Plan To Stop Smoking
Seventh Day Adventist Church
Narcotics Education Division
6840 Eastern Avenue, NW
Washington, D.C. 20012

Office on Smoking and Health
U.S. Department of Health, Education, and Welfare
200 Independence Avenue, SW, Room 622E
Washington, D.C. 20201

Office of Cancer Communications
National Cancer Institute
National Institutes of Health
Bethesda, Maryland 20205

See also CANCER; HEART DISEASE; RESPIRATORY DISEASE.

SNAKEBITE can cause severe illness and death. But about two thirds of people bitten by poisonous snakes in this country survive with no treatment. Treatment with antivenom within 30 to 60 minutes (depending on your size and health) can usually counteract the effects of the venom. In recent years there have been fewer than 20 deaths a year.

If you are bitten by a poisonous snake, seek help immediately. If you are with friends, have them carry you. When you must walk, do so slowly. Never run. Ideally stay motionless to retard the spread of the venom through the body.

First aid. Keep the area below the rest of your body. If possible immobilize the bitten part with a sling. Do not apply cold water or ice. If bitten on the arm or leg, tie a tourniquet (preferably a piece of cloth, but a shoestring, tie, or belt can be used in an emergency) 2 to 5 inches above the bite.

In snakebite the tourniquet is meant not to stop circulation but to retard the spread of venom. It should be loose enough to wedge a finger under. Make sure the flow of blood is not stopped. The pulse should be felt in blood vessels below the tourniquet. The binding should not produce a throbbing sensation. As swelling appears, remove tourniquet and place it 2 to 4 inches above the first site.

Symptoms of the bite may include severe local pain, skin discoloration around the bite, nausea, vomiting, thirst, sweating, fever. Reactions usually begin within ten minutes after the bite. When a great deal of venom has been injected, there may be numbness and tingling of the face, violent muscle spasms or convulsions, drop in blood pressure, difficulty in breathing.

Removing the venom. In a widely accepted first aid measure, wash the area around the bite, and sterilize a knife or razor with a match. Whiskey is a fair antiseptic for the wound—but, despite its reputation as a remedy for snakebite, don't drink any: alcohol speeds circulation and thus the spread of venom. For cleansing, soap and water is better if available.

Make a shallow (1/8 inch deep) lengthwise incision through each fang mark—not an *x* as is popularly believed. Simply pinch the skin and make a cut through the ridge 1/8 to 1/4 inch long. You'll have two parallel cuts in the direction of the fangs' path of entry.

Suck out the venom for half an hour. Spit the venom out. Since the venom is not poisonous in the stomach, there is no danger in sucking it unless you have a cold sore or other open wound in your mouth or digestive tract. If you are alone and can't reach the site with your mouth, try pushing the venom out with your fingers.

A snakebite kit (available for about $5 at many pharmacies and camping-supply stores) will simplify the procedure. A kit usually contains a tourniquet, an antiseptic, a small knife, and suction devices for sucking out the venom. Such kits should be standard equipment for anyone who goes hiking in snake-infested woods.

After the venom is sucked out, the wound should be covered with a sterile or clean bandage. The victim can sip water unless he is unconscious, nauseated, vomiting, or having convulsions. No alcoholic beverages should be given.

Get to the nearest hospital emergency room as soon as possible. If possible telephone ahead so that antivenom serum can be made ready. If you can, capture and kill the snake and take it with you. Otherwise describe it as well as you can.

If you know you've been bitten by a coral snake, do not tie off the bite area with a tourniquet. Nor should you try to remove the venom. Symptoms of coral-snake bite may not appear for several hours. They include slight pain and swelling at the site of the bite; blurred vision and drooping eyelids; drowsiness; heavy drooling; speech difficulties; heavy sweating; nausea and vomiting; breathing difficulty and paralysis. Seek medical help as soon as possible at a hospital emergency room.

If you're with a snakebite victim, give artificial respiration if necessary. Watch for signs of shock, and treat accordingly.

Poisonous snakes. The great majority of snakes are harmless to man, indeed beneficial as devourers of insects and rodents. While most, if they bite at all, can inflict only scratches, a few of the large species are capable of giving a nasty bite. Treat as for other animal bites.

In general, a poisonous snake leaves one or two distinct puncture wounds while a harmless snake leaves multiple small punctures (see illustration). Sometimes people think they've been bitten by a snake in the dark when actually they've encountered a thorn, insect, or furry animal. Blood oozing from the wound generally distinguishes a snakebite.

In the continental United States the poisonous types are coral snakes and pit vipers—which include copperheads, water moccasins, and more than a dozen species of rattlesnake (see illustration).

Coral snakes, which are found only in the South and Southwest, have pure black heads and body bands of red, yellow, and black. The yellow bands always separate the other two colors—"red next to yellow will kill a fellow." Harmless look-alikes can be distinguished from the coral snake since nonpoisonous varieties have black rings rather than yellow separating the bands.

Pit vipers have a depression (or pit) between the eye and nostril on each side of the head. They have "cat eyes"—vertical, oval-shaped pupils. All species of rattlesnakes have rattles at the end of the tail. Water moccasins—also

IF A POISONOUS SNAKE BITES YOU

Stay calm—move slowly
Excitement speeds spread of venom

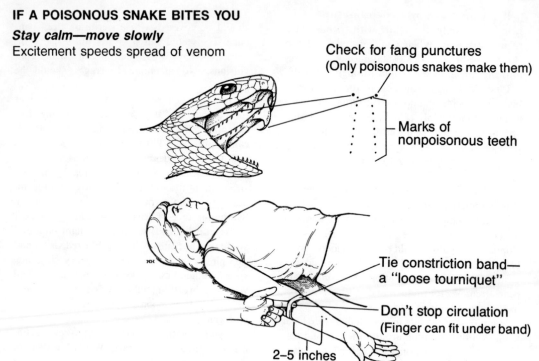

Check for fang punctures
(Only poisonous snakes make them)

Marks of
nonpoisonous teeth

Tie constriction band—
a "loose tourniquet"

Don't stop circulation
(Finger can fit under band)

2–5 inches

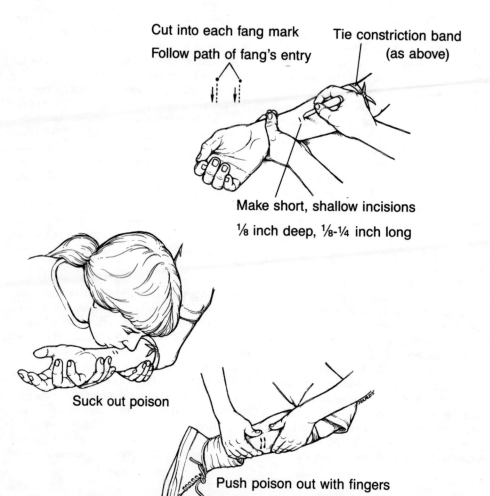

Cut into each fang mark

Follow path of fang's entry

Tie constriction band
(as above)

Make short, shallow incisions
⅛ inch deep, ⅛-¼ inch long

Suck out poison

Push poison out with fingers
If you can't suck wound

BEWARE OF THESE POISONOUS SNAKES

Eastern and western diamondbacks
Aggressive, deadliest bite

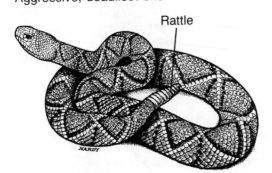

Rattle

Eastern: dark brown, black diamond markings
Yellow border
Tan, light brown background
8 feet
Ala., Fla., Ga., Miss., N.C., S.C.

Western: light brown to black diamond markings
White border
Light gray, tan, pink background
8 feet
Ariz., Cal., N.M., Okla., Tex.

Copperhead
Invades suburbs, unaggressive, rarely lethal

Large chestnut brown bands
Pinkish, reddish brown background
Coppery head
4 feet
Ala., Ark., Conn., Del., Fla., Ga., Ill., Iowa, Kan., Ky., La., Md., Mass., Miss., Mo., Neb., N.H., N.J., N.Y., N.C., Ohio, Okla., Pa., R.I., S.C., Tenn., Tex., Vt., Va., W.Va.

Cottonmouth (water moccasin)
In swamps, marshes; moderately dangerous

White mouth

Dark blotches
Thick brown or olive body
5 feet
Ala., Ark., Fla., Ga., Ill., Ky., Miss., Mo., N.C., S.C., Tenn., Tex., Va.

Coral snake
Extremely poisonous, rarely bites

Narrow yellow ring

Wide black ring

Wide red ring

Black snout

3 feet
Ala., Ark., Ariz., Fla., Ga., La., Miss., N.M., N.C., S.C., Tex.

known as "cottonmouths"—are obvious because of their white mouths. Copperheads have distinctive hourglass markings of chestnut brown on a pale pinkish- or reddish-brown surface, and a coppery tinge of the head.

Snakes can be sorted out as follows:

Extremely dangerous: The eastern and western diamondback rattlers are aggressive and inject a large quantity of potent venom. Although they account for only 10 percent of poisonous snakebites, they cause 95 percent of deaths. Numbness around a bite during the first 5 to 15 minutes indicates a medical emergency. The Mojave rattler is also deadly but attacks rarely.

The coral snake has extremely potent venom but accounts for only about 2 percent of reported snakebites. A well-aimed bite, usually on fingers or toes, can lead to respiratory failure (which may not show symptoms for 18 hours). More typically, coral snakes are shy and unable to penetrate clothing because of short fangs and a small mouth.

Snake fanciers sometimes get bitten by cobras, mambas, kraits, and other exotics. A nationwide list of antivenom sources for foreign snakes is maintained by the Oklahoma Poison Information Center in cooperation with the Oklahoma City Zoo. The phone number is (405) 271-5454.

Moderately dangerous: The water moccasin and most U.S. rattlesnakes other than those named fall into this category.

Not potentially fatal: The copperhead delivers the vast majority of snakebites in several states but produces few severe effects. Though unaggressive it's often a culprit because it invades human habitats where the rattler and moccasin seldom venture. The pigmy rattler and the massasauga are similar.

Being realistic about snakes. Heavy clothing and high boots will afford some protection. It's a good idea to carry a stick. Snakes are rarely aggressive, but one accidentally cornered or stepped on may become aroused.

When you are in an unfamiliar area, find out what kind of snakes inhabit the region. Don't stick your hands into holes in rocks or trees or under them. When crossing a fallen log, don't plant your foot on the other side before you can see what is there. Don't sit on a pile of rocks or a tree trunk before examining it closely.

Snakes are the subject of much folklore. To explode some common myths:

A snake doesn't have to be coiled up to bite. Snakes can bite from any position, though rattlers, water moccasins, and copperheads usually strike (or lunge) from a coiled position. The distance a snake can strike may be from a third to half its length. So don't think you're safe if you are 2 feet away from a 6-foot snake.

Sitting in the center of a circle made by a horsehair rope is no insurance against snakebite —it's a myth that a snake won't cross a horsehair rope. Nor can a snake milk a cow, roll itself into a hoop, or break apart.

Snakes are good swimmers and can bite underwater as easily as above. Also a dead snake can bite since its reflexes still work for quite a while. Handle a dead snake with a stick, staying at least 1 foot away from its mouth.

Young snakes are just as poisonous as the adult kind. In fact the baby western diamondback rattler can give a bite that is fatal.

Snakes will bite at night—actually many snakes are most active at night. When camping, gather all your firewood before nightfall.

Rattlesnakes don't always rattle a warning before striking. It would be nice if they did, but they only do it occasionally.

See also ACCIDENTS; ANIMAL BITES; CAMPING; HIKING.

SNORING may result from lying on your back when you sleep. Your tongue tends to fall back and obstruct your breathing.

If your snoring keeps others awake, try sleeping on your side. If you keep rolling onto your back, tie a strip of cloth around your chest and knot it at your back. The discomfort you feel from the knot pressing into your back will probably make you roll onto your side or front.

If you continue snoring while sleeping on your side, you may have an obstruction in your respiratory tract. See a physician.

Persistent snoring may result from bronchitis, colds, hay fever, or sinusitis. In combination with excessive sleepiness, snoring may be a symptom of sleep apnea—a frequent cessation of breathing during the night that has also been tagged as a possible factor in crib deaths.

If your snoring began or increased after age 60, the outer sides of your nostrils may have collapsed with age. To keep them from being drawn in with every breath, causing snoring, you can insert little dilators into your nose at night.

Overweight can cause snoring by swelling the nasal passages with excess body fluid. Surplus poundage also encourages you to sleep on your back and breathe through your mouth.

Even if you're slim, avoid heavily salted foods just before bedtime. They can cause fluid to gather in your nasal tissues.

See also SLEEPLESSNESS.

SNOWMOBILES have been causing deaths rising at an average rate of about 60 percent a year. The fatalities are largely the result of collisions with cars, drowning from falls through ice, brushes with barbed wire. There are unexpected flights over cliffs, and late-night encounters with unseen obstacles.

If you're a snowmobiler, save that first drink for when you are safely at home. Alcohol is involved in about half of all accidents.

Wear a fiber glass helmet. In nearly half of the fatalities in one year death was attributed to head injuries. Plastic helmets, which are cheaper, shatter easily on impact. Watch out for dangling scarves that may cause choking.

Whenever possible stay on or near trails frequented by snowmobilers. You lessen your chances of getting lost, and if you break down, help won't be far away.

Drive especially carefully at night. More than half of deaths result from accidents in the dark, most between 10:00 P.M. and 2:00 A.M. Snowmobile headlights won't allow you to see barbed-wire fences, ravines, parked automobiles, or branches in time to avoid them unless you are traveling slowly.

Guard against frostbite. When you travel at 35 mph on a still day, you create your own 35-mph wind. If the temperature that day were 0° F, the effective temperature for you would be −51° F.

Wear ear plugs or mufflers. Prolonged exposure to noises as loud as snowmobiles generate will cause temporary hearing loss. Sustained exposure may cause permanent impairment.

Use sunglasses to guard against snow blindness. Protect yourself against sunburn.

Machine versus man. Be wary of snowmobile jumping. Spinal fractures commonly result. The force on the spine after a drop of only 4 feet is estimated to be 20 to 30 times the force of gravity. If you do jump, take up the shock with your legs by lifting your buttocks off the seat. Take it slow on unfamiliar terrain.

Ride with your legs inside the vehicle. Dragging them to brake or turn causes many fractures.

Don't start out with an impaired machine. A leisurely half-hour drive at 30 mph can leave you with a walk of 15 miles through the snow if your machine breaks down.

Take special precautions for cross-country or overnight trips: Travel in pairs. Inform others where you plan to go and when you expect to arrive. Carry an emergency kit that includes first aid supplies, spare spark plugs, a drive belt, fuel, rations, flares, a knife or small ax, waterproof matches, a rope, a flashlight, a tool kit, and an extra ignition key.

Remember these rules if you should become stranded:

Planning will help you; panic won't. Stay together and conserve your energy and warmth.

Melted clean snow will give you all the moisture you'll need to survive.

Make a shelter using snow and evergreen boughs.

Build a fire. If you have no matches, use an engine spark, flashlight batteries, and steel wool or other thin wire, or use ice to focus the rays of the sun as you would with a magnifying glass.

Make a signal with fire, branches, or messages tramped in the snow.

See also ACCIDENTS; COLD WEATHER; FALLS THROUGH ICE.

SODIUM, a mineral found in nearly all foods, tends to hold water in the body tissues, a hazard to sufferers from high blood pressure, congestive heart failure, or edema.

To prevent this your doctor may reduce the sodium in your diet to the amount your body can handle. He may also prescribe a diuretic, a drug to help the body get rid of excess fluid.

Restricting water in itself serves no purpose. In fact drinking large quantities of liquid may promote excretion of water.

Even if you have no medical problem that requires a low-sodium diet, you would do well to decrease your intake of sodium—most familiar in the form of salt. Most Americans consume salt far in excess of the body's needs. This may pose a health hazard, since salt appears to be a major precipitating cause of high blood pressure (hypertension), which may lead to kidney failure, stroke, and heart disease. A high-salt diet may also cause extreme symptoms of premenstrual tension, with bloating, headache, irritability, and crying.

Checking for sodium. If you're on a sodium-restricted diet, read labels and avoid products bearing the words *sodium* or *soda,* or the symbol *Na* (for *natrium,* a word for sodium that may appear on foreign labels). Ask your local heart association for low-sodium diets and meal-planning guides. Explore salt-free and low-sodium products where dietetic foods are sold.

To be sure that the water you drink is not high in sodium, check your local supply with the heart association or health department. Don't use home water softeners that add sodium to the water. Use soft drinks sparingly—they may be made with water high in sodium. Distilled water, on the other hand, is usually safe.

Cut out table salt (sodium chloride)—only ¼ teaspoon contains the entire 1,000 mg per day allowed in many diets. Don't use a salt substitute unless your doctor recommends a specific kind. Some salt substitutes and low-sodium meat tenderizers can be harmful in certain diseases. Also watch out for monosodium glutamate (MSG), a flavor enhancer widely used in prepared foods as well as sold in retail form.

If you use a dietetic sweetener, avoid sodium compounds like sodium saccharin, which is often sold as "soluble saccharin" or just plain "saccharin." Avoid artificially sweetened products—diet beverages and the like—unless you know they contain a sweetener you are permitted.

Some foods, such as brains and kidneys, are particularly high in sodium. So are canned, salted, or smoked meats (bacon, bologna, chipped or corned beef, frankfurters, ham, luncheon meats, salt pork, sausage, smoked tongue). Kosher meat is sometimes packed in salt before it reaches the consumer.

Dairy products. Regular (whole) milk, evaporated milk, skim milk, and powdered milk are generally low in sodium. So is plain buttermilk —but some dairies add salt to buttermilk, so check with your dairy before you buy. The sodium content of these foods is likely to be high: chocolate, ice cream, sherbet, malted milk, milk shakes, instant cocoa mixes, chocolate milk, condensed milk, all other kinds of milk and fountain drinks.

Shellfish (clams, crabs, lobsters, oysters, scallops, shrimp) have a high sodium content. So do frozen fish fillets; canned, salted, or smoked fish (anchovies, caviar, salted cod, herring, sardines, etc.); and ordinary canned tuna or salmon.

Canned soups and sauces contain salt. Canned vegetables are packed in salt water even though the label doesn't say so. Look for frozen vegetables specifically not processed with salt.

Some vegetables in any form are too high in sodium for a low-sodium diet: artichokes, beet greens, beets, carrots, celery, chard, dandelion greens, whole hominy, kale, mustard greens, sauerkraut, spinach, white turnips.

Regular breads, crackers, cereals are generally heavy on sodium, as is any product made with self-rising flour. Potato chips and pretzels are loaded with salt.

When you bake, use yeast or a special sodium-free baking powder. Instead of baking soda (sodium bicarbonate), use potassium bicarbonate.

Use butter or margarine sparingly unless it's specifically unsalted. Avoid ordinary commercial salad dressings or mayonnaise.

Away from home, in restaurants, order broiled chops or steaks. You can also have boiled or poached eggs (poached in unsalted water), fruit or vegetable salads without dressing, baked potatoes. Other fairly safe choices: an inside slice of roast beef, lamb, or fresh pork (no gravy), or roast chicken or turkey (without skin or gravy). Outer layers are likely to have been salted and spiced before cooking.

Don't order cooked vegetables, because restaurants use salt and monosodium glutamate in seasoning them. For the same reason avoid foods that are breaded or fried in a batter, unless you can remove the crust.

On short trips pack a lunch. Before undertaking plane travel or a long trip by train, be sure special meals can be provided. On long trips or in visiting out-of-the-way places, take along a supply of low-sodium foods.

Medication should be checked with your doctor if he has not prescribed it. These are some drugs that are likely to contain sodium: antacids and "alkalizers" for indigestion, headache remedies, cough medicines, laxatives, antibiotics, sedatives.

Seasonings and relishes that contain one or more sodium compounds include celery salt, garlic salt, onion salt, catsup, chili sauce, prepared mustard, horseradish if prepared with salt.

Cooking wine, meat and vegetable extracts (unless from foods allowed), meat sauces, meat tenderizers, soy sauce, and Worcestershire sauce contain sodium.

So do barbecue sauces, bouillon in any form (unless homemade), celery leaves or flakes, celery seeds, olives, pickles, relishes.

Flavorings instead of salt. Try some of these ideas:

For beef: Bay leaf, dry mustard, green pepper, grape jelly, sage, marjoram, mushrooms, nutmeg, onion, pepper, thyme, tomato.

For chicken: Cranberries, mushrooms, paprika, parsley, poultry seasoning, thyme, sage.

Lamb: Curry, garlic, mint, pineapple, rosemary.

Pork: Apples, applesauce, garlic, onion, sage.

Veal: Apricots, bay leaf, curry, currant jelly, garlic, ginger, marjoram, mushrooms, oregano, paprika.

Fish: Bay leaf, curry, dill, dry mustard, green pepper, lemon juice, marjoram, mushrooms, paprika, tomato.

Eggs: Curry, dry mustard, green pepper, jelly, mushrooms, onion, paprika, parsley, tomato.

See also BLOOD PRESSURE; HEART DISEASE.

SOLAR PLEXUS BLOWS are hits below the belt. Rest the victim on his back and moisten his face with cool water. Loosen his clothing around his waist or chest. Call a doctor if pain or dizziness persists for more than 12 hours. If necessary, treat for TESTICLE BLOWS (which see).

See also ACCIDENTS.

SORE THROAT can be a symptom of a serious ailment. Call a doctor if:

Your sore throat is severe.

You have a fever over 100° F.

The sore throat is accompanied by coughing, hoarseness, and difficulty in breathing.

You have in the past had rheumatic fever.

The soreness has recurred several times in recent weeks.

The sore throat—however mild—has lasted more than a week.

You can have these conditions without being seriously ill. However precautions are wise because inflammation of the throat, or pharynx— the corridor from the back of the nose past the mouth to the larynx (voice box)—may be an early symptom of leukemia and diphtheria. It may also be a sign of tonsillitis, mononucleosis, or trench mouth.

To get a good view of a sore throat use a flashlight. Depress the tongue with a wooden blade or spoon handle.

Strep throat. The most common serious sore throat is caused by bacteria called beta hemolytic streptococcus. The same germ also causes tonsillitis and scarlet fever. If strep throat is not promptly treated, it can lead to kidney disease or rheumatic fever and permanent heart damage.

A strep throat usually comes on suddenly, often starting with a high fever followed by pain in the throat 12 to 24 hours later. Other symptoms may include headache, skin rash, stomachache, vomiting, and a general sick feeling. In most cases there are swollen, tender glands in the neck. Fiery redness and swelling mark the throat.

The extent of soreness in the throat does not indicate how serious the illness may be. In the most dangerous strep cases leading to rheumatic heart disease, the pain can be so mild that a child never even mentions it. It can also be so severe that it interferes with speech and swallowing.

You need to get rid of strep as soon as possible. By delaying, you may come down with rheumatic fever several days or weeks after you have apparently recovered. Other complications of strep throat include ear infections and abscesses in the throat that may require minor surgical treatment.

To pin down a diagnosis a doctor will usually take a throat swab and let the germs grow in a laboratory dish overnight. The usual treatment is a course of penicillin for ten days (or a similar antibiotic in the case of penicillin allergy).

If you don't receive adequate treatment, the bacteria may persist in your throat for months, during which you can spread it to others. The bacteria may be transmitted by direct contact, by droplets such as from a cough or sneeze, or by indirect contact with contaminated objects such as bedclothes or eating utensils.

No cough drop, lozenge, or any other patent medicine can aid in the treatment of strep throat. Manufacturers make such claims despite the possible consequences of untreated strep. In one decision the FTC ordered the makers of Sucrets and Children's Sucrets to discontinue TV ads that repeatedly emphasized that Sucrets would "kill even . . . strep germs."

Minor sore throats. Most sore throats clear up in a few days. Cold viruses are the most frequent cause.

Such a sore throat tends to start out slowly, often as a feverish feeling accompanied by headache and loss of appetite. The raspy, slightly reddened throat that follows is often joined by dry coughing and runny nose. If you have a fever, it isn't likely to go higher than 100° F.

A viral sore throat, known as herpangina or "summer sore throat," is one of the commonest summertime illnesses of young children. It is a mild disease that often occurs in epidemics in summer camps. Its characteristic symptoms are fever (in this case the temperature may go up to 105° F), loss of energy, and very painful, small, raised sores in the back of the mouth. Usually all symptoms are gone by the fourth day.

Caring for a sore throat. No remedy hastens recovery by as much as five minutes. A variety of simple measures can make you more comfortable:

Increase room humidity. It lessens drying out of membranes. Take aspirin or acetaminophen for pain relief.

Suck hard candies to keep your throat moist. Medicated lozenges are no more effective than candy—and may be harmful. The medication may mask symptoms of a more serious illness and may sensitize you into a drug allergy.

Avoid such irritants as smoking and eating spicy foods.

Gargle every few hours with a glass of warm saltwater (1/2 teaspoon of table salt is recommended). Saltwater, more so than plain water, helps wash away irritants and mucus that may add to the discomfort of a sore throat. The warmth of the water increases blood flow in the throat, bringing more of the body's natural disease-fighting machinery to the site of the infection.

Drink plenty of fluids. Commercial gargles are no more helpful than warm saltwater. Mouthwashes do not materially reduce the number of germs in the mouth and throat. Any temporary reduction, as from an antiseptic gargle, is offset by new bacteria entering your mouth the next time you breathe and by the remaining bacteria's multiplying.

Moreover, sore throat results from an invasion by bacteria of the tissues beneath the surface membranes. The infected area includes not only the visible part of the throat, but also the hidden nasopharynx behind the nose. Even the most thorough gargling reaches only a small portion of the visible pharynx and none of the nasopharynx. Germs deeper in the tissues are not touched at all.

See also COLDS; RESPIRATORY DISEASE; RHEUMATIC FEVER.

SPEED See AMPHETAMINES.

SPERMICIDE See BIRTH CONTROL.

SPIDER BITES of most species—including the fierce-looking tarantula—are temporarily painful but not dangerous. Only two spiders in the United States are considered poisonous to humans—the black widow, found throughout the country, and the brown recluse, found mostly in the South and Midwest (see illustration).

If you think you have been bitten by one of these spiders, kill or capture it. Positive identification may be helpful in getting you proper care or determining if treatment is required. Be sure to see a doctor.

Black widows are long black spiders with a red hourglass marking on the belly. They mainly inhabit dark, still corners—under houses, in basements and barns. The widow's venom causes extremely severe abdominal cramps and muscular tenseness, sometimes accompanied by pain in the extremities. Death is rare except in small children and aged people with heart disease, but the pain is nightmarish.

Immediately after the bite keep the victim quiet. If the bite is on the arm or leg, apply a tourniquet loose enough for a finger to pass under. Put an ice pack over the bite. Keep the bitten area lower than the victim's heart. Give artificial respiration if necessary. Seek prompt medical attention.

The brown recluse is also called the fiddleback.

BEWARE THESE POISONOUS SPIDERS

Black widow

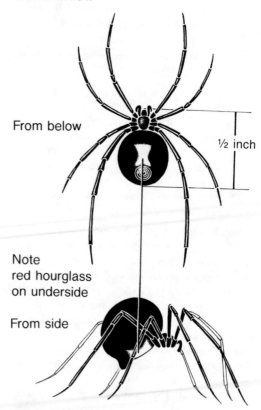

From below

½ inch

Note red hourglass on underside

From side

Brown recluse
From above

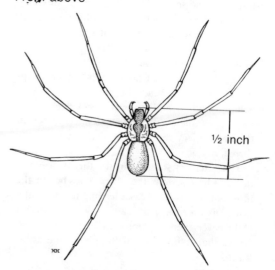

½ inch

Note fiddle-shaped marking

Its color varies from gray brown to deep red-brown, but it always has a dark fiddle-shaped area on the front half of its back. These spiders are found in nearly any corner, indoors or out.

Immediately after being bitten, scrub the fang punctures to help prevent infection. Apply cold compresses to the area surrounding the bite.

Don't treat the wound as you would snakebite. Don't cut the fang punctures. Don't apply suction. Don't employ a tourniquet.

Although there is no specific antidote for the bite of the brown recluse spider, patients have responded well to treatment with steroids, antihistamines, and antibiotics.

The bite is usually followed by intense pain. Sometimes the victim is not immediately aware that he has been bitten, and an hour or more may pass before he experiences discomfort.

The first visible symptom of brown recluse poisoning is a small white blister at the site of the fang punctures. The affected area enlarges and becomes inflamed. It is hard to the touch.

Eventually affected tissues begin to die and peel away. The center of the bitten area becomes sunken and the skin around the bite becomes raised slightly. An ulcerating sore then develops. It may be so extensive that skin grafts are necessary.

See ARTIFICIAL RESPIRATION; INSECT STINGS; SCORPIONS.

SPIDER VEINS (telangiectases) are reddish or bluish roadmaplike markings that may appear spontaneously just under the skin, most often on the legs, nose, and cheeks. They are slightly enlarged blood vessels of no medical consequence. They almost never cause pain or any other problems. Their cause is unknown.

If you feel your spider veins are unsightly, try covering them with a cosmetic paste like Covermark or Lydio-Liri. If this doesn't sufficiently hide the spider veins, you may wish to try sclerotherapy. In this procedure a physician injects into the vein a substance that causes the walls of the vessel to join together. A bandage is applied to help keep the vessel walls joined.

Sclerotherapy is most often done on legs. Several treatments may be necessary if many vessels are involved. The procedure itself is rarely painful—but the tight bandages may cause itching or pain. Call your physician if you are very uncomfortable.

Daily exercise is necessary to the success of sclerotherapy on the legs. Do your usual daily activity, including participation in sports, and walk at least 2 miles every day. But don't kneel or do deep knee bends while your bandages must still be on.

In the first few weeks after sclerotherapy the leg may look bruised. But the discoloration usually disappears completely in a few weeks.

Avoid electrical or surgical attempts to destroy the spider veins. There is a high risk of scars, discoloration, and other complications.

See also SKIN DISORDERS.

SPINA BIFIDA (literally "cleft spine") is one of several spinal birth defects. It occurs in 1 out of every 1,000 U.S. live births.

In spina bifida one or more of the spinal vertebrae fail to close completely. These partially open bones form an abnormal passageway through which the contents of the spinal canal can slip. In its mildest form—called *occulta*—the defect may go unnoticed.

A more serious form is called a *meningocele,* in which the protruding material contains nerve roots. In still more severe cases the sac will contain the coverings, part of the spinal cord, and may leak spinal fluid. This condition is called a *meningomyelocele.*

The baby will have an obvious lump or cyst-like lesion, usually on the lower spine. At birth the sac may be covered with skin, or the nerves may be exposed. The baby's legs may be weak or paralyzed. Children with severe conditions often have no bladder or bowel control.

Infection of the spinal cord and brain coverings is a danger in spina bifida. Another common complication is hydrocephalus. If not treated promptly, this buildup of fluid in the skull could cause mental retardation.

The specific causes are not known. Recent research suggests that women with poor diets and poor health have a greater chance of having babies with this birth defect. More cases occur within some families than chance would account for, possibly because of the mother's health or hereditary factors.

Prompt treatment is recommended as soon after birth as possible to prevent infection, hydrocephalus and additional loss of nerve function. Most children will require physical therapy to prevent paralyzed muscles from stiffening and shortening. Corrective shoes, braces, or crutches may be needed.

Because of the possibility of a hereditary factor, if you have a child with spina bifida, consult a genetic counselor before deciding to have more children. For additional information, write Spina Bifida Association of America, 343 Dearborn Street, Chicago, Illinois 60604.

See also BIRTH DEFECTS; SURGERY.

SPLINTERS just under the skin can often be flicked out with a fingernail.

Or remove a splinter by using a sterilized needle—pass it through a flame until it glows (see illustration). Clean the skin and a pair of tweezers with soap and water. Then split the skin the length of the splinter with the needle. Gently pull the splinter out with the tweezers. Wash the area again with soap and water and cover with a small bandage.

For splinters embedded under fingernails, file the surface of the nail with an emery board until it is paper thin. Make a small cut in the filed area with a sterilized scissors or razor blade to expose the splinter for easy removal. This is considerably less painful than the traditional practice of cutting through an intact nail.

For nearly invisible metal splinters—such as wire particles from buffing wheels or steel wool —cover the affected area with a strip of cellophane tape. Lift the tape gently, and the tiny splinters are likely to come out with it.

If the splinter is large or lies deep in the skin, have it removed by a doctor. Treat deep splinters as PUNCTURES (which see).

See also ACCIDENTS; CLEANSING MINOR WOUNDS.

SPORTS raise the risk of injuries, usually bruises and minor muscle pulls. About 10 percent of sports injuries are more serious, most commonly affecting the knee, ankle, head, neck, and shoulders.

Fractures are common sports injuries—especially in skiing and football—as are sprains, strains, and dislocations.

The knee is a particularly vulnerable joint. Injuries to the knee include conditions referred to as trick knee, which involves damaged knee cartilage, and water on the knee, in which excessive lubricating fluid accumulates in the knee.

Unaccustomed participation in sports often results in charley horse, or sore muscles because of spasm. Weekend tennis or golf players may develop an ache in the swinging arm known as tennis elbow.

Football injuries often include head injuries, which may result in skull fractures. Divers and surfers are prone to neck fractures as well as skull fractures when their heads collide with underwater obstructions or hit bottom.

Dangerous sports practices add to the likelihood of injury. Spearing is a football tactic in which a blocker or tackler uses his head as a battering ram. Continued over a long period, the practice is likely to cause degenerative changes in the neck. The greater risk is that spearing may cause possibly fatal damage to the head and neck, and gravely injure the opponent.

Another risky practice is injecting an injured player with local anesthetics or steroids to enable him to continue the game. Unable to feel pain in the damaged part, the player may injure himself far more seriously.

Sending a player with any degree of injury back into a game prematurely can have serious consequences. The decision should rest with a physician, not the coach or the parents.

Some traditional conditioning exercises can lead to injury. The deep knee bend—in which the athlete moves alternately from a standing position to a full squat—is now generally disapproved of by medical authorities.

This exercise can seriously damage the knee joint. A similarly dangerous exercise is the duck waddle, in which the athlete walks in a squatting position.

In addition to being potentially injurious these

TO GET A SPLINTER OUT

1. Cleanse area

2. Sterilize needle

3. Split skin over splinter

4. Lift splinter

5. Tweeze it out

exercises are now thought to have little value in football conditioning, where they have mainly been used. Few of the player's activities involve fully bending the knee joint.

Don't use drugs or hypnosis to improve performance. The AMA has labeled the practice as potentially dangerous.

Hypnosis has sometimes been used to enable an athlete to play to the peak of his ability. But the dangers far outweigh the possible benefits. The athlete may exceed the limits of fatigue and overexert himself. Under the influence of hypnosis he may aggravate injuries of which he is unaware. He may also become oblivious to safety measures he usually follows.

The use of oxygen and stimulants like amphetamines may have much the same effect. Further, the AMA has condemned the use of drugs to improve athletic performance, calling the practice "inconsistent with the . . . ideals of sportsmanship."

Preventive measures. To help protect yourself against sports injuries, you can do the following:

Have a thorough physical examination before you try out for any sport, particularly rough contact sports like football and hockey. A sports checkup should include measuring your ability to adapt to heat changes.

Certain conditions may keep you from engaging in contact sports. These include having only one eye or one kidney, an enlarged spleen, or a history of unconscious episodes. Hepatitis should disqualify an athlete for one year. Your physician can tell you if you have any conditions that might pose a threat to you on the playing field.

Be in proper condition for your sport. Participation in sports requires year-round conditioning, since the strength you develop dwindles if you don't maintain it by continued exercise.

Protect yourself against heat illnesses. Heat exhaustion is dangerous and heat stroke can be fatal. Get accustomed to working hard in heat. To replace lost fluid drink small amounts of water (2 to 4 ounces) at frequent intervals (perhaps every 15 minutes) instead of great gulps after a prolonged period. You can add salt to iced water (1 teaspoon to 6 quarts) to replace salt lost in heavy perspiration. Salt taken in tablet form may cause some gastric irritation and is not generally recommended.

Protect yourself with proper equipment. Goggles or sunglasses reduce injuries in skiers. Plastic helmets with outside padding—not the usual hard shell—are recommended for protection of the head in football.

To help prevent ankle and knee injuries, ankle wraps are suggested, particularly in basketball and football. A nonelastic cotton bandage—about 2½ inches wide by 8 feet long—is wrapped over the athletic socks, with several turns over the heel. Friction tape can hold the wrap in place. Physicians usually recommend that previously injured ankles be taped with adhesive tape.

Eat, drink, and rest properly. Be careful not to fatigue yourself. A study of injuries to skiers found that the peak of accidents occurred at about 3:00 P.M., when the skier was very likely overtired.

Athletes require a well-balanced diet, with possibly a higher consumption of carbohydrates than nonathletes.

The healthy athlete on a proper diet does not need supplementary vitamins. They have not been proven to prevent colds or in any way improve performance. Taken in excess, vitamins can be harmful.

Some players prefer a liquid diet drink before games. Liquid meals are particularly valuable between events in track, wrestling, and swimming meets. Avoid eating fats and hard-to-digest foods before engaging in sports.

See also ACCIDENTS; BICYCLES; BOATING; BRUISES; CAMPING; CHARLEY HORSE; COLD WEATHER; DISLOCATIONS; DROWNING; EXERCISE.

FISHING; FOOTBALL; FRACTURES; FROSTBITE; GUNSHOT WOUNDS; HEAD INJURIES; HEAT EXHAUSTION; HEAT STROKE; HIKING; HOT WEATHER.

ICE SKATING; MOTORCYCLES; NECK FRACTURES; SKIING; SKULL FRACTURES; SNOWMOBILES; SPRAINS; STEROIDS; STRAINS; TENNIS ELBOW; TRICK KNEE; VITAMINS; WATER ON THE KNEE.

SPRAINS usually occur at the ankle, wrist, or knee. They are the result of sudden bending or twisting at a joint. The supporting tissues (ligaments) are greatly stretched. Connective tissue strands, muscle fibers, and tiny blood vessels may be torn. Like strains, which involve muscles and tendons, sprains are common sports injuries.

The usual signs of a sprain are swelling, tenderness, and pain, particularly when moving. The sprained part will become black and blue if the blood vessels are injured.

Since these signs often also indicate fractures, have X rays taken.

To give first aid for sprains:

1. Slightly elevate the part.
2. Cover the area with ice or apply cold com-

presses to relieve swelling, preferably within a half minute after the injury.

3. If you can't get medical help for some time, continue the cold applications. If the victim is elderly or has poor circulation, every five minutes remove the injured part from the cold for 30 seconds or so.

4. Massage the area three times a day. For ten minutes, using your index and middle fingers, stroke the area above the swelling, and then the section below it. Stroke toward the heart to help move the fluids away from the injury and back into circulation. Then, working from the injury outward, gently massage the most tender spots.

See also ACCIDENTS; FRACTURES; SPORTS; STRAINS.

SPRAY CANS hold an active ingredient—insecticide, shaving cream, paint, etc.—plus a propellant gas under high pressure. If exposed to enough heat, the pressure may build up so that the can explodes.

Familiarity may cause you to get careless. A baker may thoughtlessly set a half-used can of spray frosting on a hot stove. A motorist may leave a container of windshield cleaner in the trunk of a car. Resulting explosions have killed bystanders and severed parts of bodies.

Your safest course is to avoid spray cans altogether. Most spray products are sold in nonpressurized form as liquids or creams. Tubes, bottles, and jars are much cheaper, too, since you don't have to pay for the costly spray mechanism or the propellant (which is about 70 percent of the product's net weight).

Keep spray cans in cool places, under 120° F. They can explode in the sun, in overheated sheds, near heating units. Cans of suntan lotion have exploded on the beach and at poolside, injuring bathers with fragments.

Many spray products are fire hazards. Avoid smoking while using a flammable spray.

Don't puncture a can. A small tear can cause it to explode like a balloon. Instead of incinerating a discarded can, expel all the gas through the nozzle. Put the can with trash for dumping rather than garbage to be burned.

Beware spray can vapors. About 50 young thrill-seekers a year die from sniffing fluorocarbon, a common propellant gas. The gas, also called Freon, can cause freezing of the air passages, choking, and heart stoppage. Store spray cans out of the reach of children.

Keep sprays away from your face and from food. Spray with plenty of ventilation. The droplets are often poisonous and can cause eye injuries.

See also ACCIDENTS.

SPRUE See MALABSORPTION.

SQUINT See CROSSED EYES.

STERILITY See INFERTILITY.

STEROIDS (adrenocorticosteroids, corticosteroids) are extremely useful drugs, but often cause severe side effects.

If you're taking steroids (ACTH, cortisone, prednisone, triamcinolone, dexamethasone), phone your physician immediately if you feel faint on arising from a chair or bed. This can be an extremely important early sign of circulatory impairment that may be due to the drug.

Also alert the doctor if you experience dizziness, nausea or vomiting, thirst, or any sort of pain. Call right away after any episode of unconsciousness or convulsions.

Let him know promptly if you develop any infection or infectious disease. Steroids can suppress the ordinary symptoms of an infection until it is far advanced. Have your family be watchful for signs of emotional stress such as depression or nervousness and notify your doctor as soon as you start acting strangely—steroids can bring on a psychosis.

You may suffer from a sudden failure of the adrenal glands if you take steroids in large amounts or for more than two weeks. This is especially likely to follow severe emotional upset or falls or other accidents.

Other serious side effects of steroid use may include peptic or duodenal ulcer, bone disease, potassium loss, inflammation of the pancreas, cataracts, elevated blood pressure, increased eye pressure. With long-term steroid therapy, cushingoid syndrome may develop. This is an unusual type of obesity in which fat is distributed between the shoulders, creating a buffalo hump, and around the waist.

Some conditions make steroids especially risky. If you're to undergo surgery, be sure your surgeon knows of any steroids you've taken in the past two months.

If your doctor is contemplating steroids for you, tell him if you suffer from diabetes, high blood pressure, any infection (bacterial, viral, or fungal, including yeast infections), glaucoma, thrombophlebitis, tuberculosis, peptic ulcer, or pancreatitis.

Other conditions that may preclude steroid therapy are pregnancy, shortness of stature for a child's age, central nervous system disease, Cushing's syndrome, or psychosis.

Precautions with steroids. Don't do heavy

work if you're on steroids. Long-term use may cause osteoporosis, raising your risk of back fractures.

Also, if you're on steroids, stick to the prescribed dosage. Since the drug is so effective in relieving symptoms, some people are tempted to take "a little extra"—with ill effects.

Also avoid taking the drug more often or for a longer period of time than your doctor has ordered.

If you are taking steroids as long-term therapy, it's a good precaution to carry an Emergency Medical Identification or to wear a Medic Alert bracelet.

Do not take aspirin or any aspirin products (such as Anacin or Excedrin) without first checking with your doctor.

Before you start taking steroids, let your doctor know what prescription or nonprescription drugs you are taking.

Tell every doctor or dentist who treats you that you are taking steroids.

Do not abruptly stop taking steroids. Steroid medication must usually be tapered off to avoid unpleasant withdrawal effects.

If your doctor prescribes a low-salt or potassium-rich diet, follow it carefully.

Keep away from anyone with a contagious disease—chickenpox is particularly hazardous. Don't get any immunization without first consulting your doctor.

Expect some weight gain and edema, and possible rounding of your face. Acne and bruises often develop. There's also a likelihood of headache, sleeplessness, fatigue, indigestion, and emotional reactions ranging from euphoria to irritability.

There may be an increased need to urinate, especially at night. While a woman is on steroids, menstruation may stop and hair may develop on the face and body.

Physicians consider the foregoing "acceptable" side effects—they're not so serious as to preclude taking steroids. However if they worsen, or otherwise interfere with your normal life, tell your doctor. He may be able to relieve a side effect by changing the steroid or adding another medication (for example, a diuretic to counter water retention). Most physicians want to see a patient on steroids at least once every one to two months.

What steroids can do. Steroids reduce inflammation. Ordinarily your tissues react to injury— from infection, allergy, trauma, most other causes—by becoming "inflamed." Blood vessels dilate, increasing blood flow in the area. Fluid seeps into the affected tissues. White blood cells accumulate. There is pain, heat, redness, swelling.

A group of steroids called glucocorticoids can counteract these effects and protect the tissues from the effects of injury. In conditions like severe asthma, pemphigus, and some blood-vessel inflammations, steroids can be lifesaving, since the inflammation can interfere with vital functions or cause widespread damage.

In a chronic painful disease like rheumatoid arthritis or ankylosing spondylitis steroids can bring the sufferer to a more comfortable day-to-day existence. In ulcerative colitis steroids can give the tissues a chance to heal. In skin disorders—including contact dermatitis, poison ivy, psoriasis, seborrheic dermatitis—steroids can reduce itching and overcome discomfort. Steroids are used in a wide variety of other medical conditions.

Another category of steroids—the mineralocorticoids—promote proper sodium and potassium balances in the blood and cells, and help regulate the functions of the kidneys.

The steroids are derived from the adrenal glands. These glands, which sit atop each of your kidneys, have an inner part—the medulla, which secretes adrenaline—and the outer, bark-like cortex, which gives forth some 50 steroids that regulate many biochemical reactions. They're called steroids because they contain carbon rings typical of the sterol family of chemicals; the terms *corticosteroid* and *adrenocorticosteroid* indicate that they come from the adrenal cortex.

Normally the output of the adrenal cortex is governed by the pituitary gland, which issues a hormone called ACTH (for adrenocorticotropic hormone; the suffix *tropic* means "acting upon"). Administering ACTH therefore stimulates the adrenal cortex and acts much the same as taking steroids.

See also DRUGS.

STIFF NECK most commonly results from strains on the neck muscles. Typically a person with a stiff neck experiences pain on moving the head, and sometimes pain in the shoulders and arms as well.

A stiff neck usually disappears spontaneously within four days. To ease the discomfort while it lasts, take aspirin. Hot compresses often help— you can use a heating pad or warmed towels. Or use a hot-water bottle partly filled with very hot water.

Cold applications may also give relief, but most people don't find cold as comfortable as heat. You can fill a hot-water bottle or an ice bag with crushed ice and cradle your neck on it.

Gentle massage of the neck area—with an analgesic cream or warmed baby oil—may also bring relief.

You may be able to avoid stiff neck if you're careful about your posture when you're performing various tasks. Stiff neck may be due to such activities as sitting bent over a desk for many hours or reaching above your head to paint a wall.

If you have to do repeated bending, for example, be sure to squat—don't stoop. Use a ladder for doing work above eye level. Make sure your pillow allows your head to rest in a comfortable position. Too many pillows—or no pillow at all —may contribute to stiff neck.

Frequent, prolonged, or severe neck pain can be a symptom of several conditions requiring a doctor's attention, among them osteoarthritis or cervical disc disease, so don't neglect it if it persists.

Emotional stress is believed to contribute to many cases of stiff neck. One sufferer has discovered that he gets a stiff neck every time he has an important decision to make. He can't make up his mind—and physiologically as well as mentally is looking in two directions at once.

See also STRESS.

STINGRAYS (whip rays) have whiplike tails bearing a venomous stinger near the base and many smaller venomous spines. These flat, fan-shaped fish are common along warm ocean shores, where they bury themselves in sand or mud. Although they never attack humans, they are often stepped on by barefoot bathers, inflicting an extremely painful lash and generally leaving the stinger in the wound.

The area around the wound is usually white for a half hour or so, then becomes black and blue, with painful swelling. Nausea, weakness, and fainting are common. In rare severe cases there may be convulsions, muscular twitching, and irregular heartbeat and breathing.

Immediately flush the wound with cold saltwater, trying to wash out venomous cells. Apply a tourniquet as for snakebite, and remove any remains of the stinger. Then soak the wound in the hottest water you can stand for 30 to 90 minutes, to help relieve pain and destroy the toxin.

Consult a physician for severe cases. While most stings occur below the knee, divers and swimmers occasionally get stung through the abdomen or chest. Emergency surgery is sometimes required.

When wading where stingrays may be hiding, shuffle your feet in the sand as you walk. The vibrations will send the fish scurrying. Don't

TO AVOID BEING STUNG LIKE THIS

Shuffle your feet when wading
Ground vibrations chase stingrays away

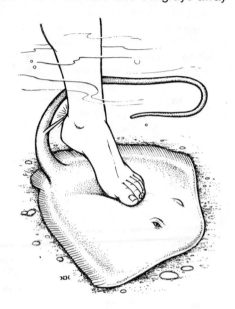

confuse stingrays with skates, similar long-tailed fish which are harmless.

See JELLYFISH, another venomous hazard of ocean bathing. Treatment for their stings also applies to stings by the Portuguese man-of-war, sea anemone, and fire coral.

See also ACCIDENTS.

STOMACH ULCER   See PEPTIC ULCER.

STOMACH, UPSET   See INDIGESTION.

STONECUTTER'S DISEASE (silicosis) See DUST DISEASE.

STRAINS are caused by the wrenching of a muscle or its tendon, the fibers connecting muscle to bone. Dancers, for example, frequently strain a muscle in the inner thigh when doing the split, in which the legs are spread out in opposite directions and the pelvis rests on the floor. Like sprains, which affect joints, strains are common sports injuries.

Damage can range from the minor stretching of a few muscle fibers to the complete tearing of the muscle or tendon. Untreated strains can be incapacitating, since ruptured muscles may become fixed in a shortened position within a few days.

Symptoms generally include pain, swelling, and loss of movement. Sometimes there may be internal bleeding, visible as bruises.

To reduce the swelling apply cold compresses immediately. Firmly tape the area with adhesive strips to limit movement and help support the injured tissue. Heat, usually applied after five to seven days, and aspirin may help relieve the pain.

Build up strained muscles gradually. Too much activity after a strain often results in another injury. If pain lasts more than a day or if loss of movement is severe, see a physician.

A common type of strain is "tennis leg" or "golfer's leg," occurring in the Achilles' tendon at the back of the heel or in the big muscle in the calf. When the strain occurs in the calf muscle alone, it is commonly called charley horse. To treat gently massage above and below the points of greatest tenderness. Apply a strip of adhesive along the back of the leg and down the heel.

See also ACCIDENTS; BACKACHE; CHARLEY HORSE.

STREP THROAT See SORE THROAT.

STRESS is one of the important factors in the psychosomatic approach to health. The word *psychosomatic* comes from the Greek *psyche,* which means *soul,* and *soma,* which means *body.* In this approach, which is gaining increasing recognition among physicians, each individual is seen as a mind-body unity and physical health is considered in the context of a whole way of life.

It begins with the recognition that mind and body are inseparable parts of a single biochemical process. Merely recall how you felt the last time you drove your car through heavy traffic, worked at a frustrating job, quarreled with your spouse, or were told by someone, "I have bad news for you." Chances are your reaction did not stop in your head. You may have felt a knotting in your gut, a tightening in your throat, a cold sweat, or your heart skipped a beat. All are common physiological reactions to emotional stress.

Experiments show that emotions can alter the output of endocrine glands, impair blood supply and blood pressure, impede digestion, cause abnormalities in breathing rate and body temperature.

Stress and disease. A sustained state of emotional stress can produce changes that lead to disease. The heart and circulatory system are especially vulnerable to emotional stress, sometimes reacting in hypertension and heart attack. Many types of respiratory disease, from common colds to tuberculosis and asthma, can have a strong emotional component. A skin disorder, backache, headache, fatigue may all reflect emotional difficulties. So may hyperthyroidism, rheumatoid arthritis, peptic ulcer, and ulcerative colitis.

For women guilt and frustration can interfere with menstruation and childbirth. For men resentment toward women can lead to impotence.

For both men and women, sex problems are often largely a matter of emotional factors. Indeed virtually every medical condition is affected by emotional states. And troubled emotions are also likely to make a person more prone to accidents.

How can you reduce stresses in your life? A simple formula, medically approved, is this: Be good to yourself.

Specifically, doctors experienced with psychosomatic illness offer these pointers:

Sidestep stressful situations. The typical ulcerative colitis victim tends to suppress rage. Would he be better off learning how to control it? Not by a long shot, says psychiatrist Ari Kiev of the Cornell University School of Medicine. You do better by bypassing situations that make you feel enraged. Advises Dr. Kiev: "Find out what makes you happy. Do that as much as possible, and—whenever you can—avoid what makes you unhappy."

Much emotional stress, in Dr. Kiev's view, comes from doing not what you want to do but what others expect of you. "You feel guilty if you 'fail' to live up to your 'obligations.' Meanwhile it's natural to feel frustrated and resentful over all the tasks heaped on you that you don't enjoy."

Keep changes to a minimum when you can. A study in Sydney, Australia, shows that in the year following bereavement 32 percent of a group of widows suffered a marked deterioration in health. Illness occurred among them 16 times more frequently than among married women of the same age and background. Similarly, a widower in the first six months following his wife's death is half again more likely to die of coronary disease than are married men his age.

Psychiatrist Thomas H. Holmes of the University of Washington School of Medicine has found that such major changes—or a cluster of lesser ones—are likely to be followed by a physiological illness within a year. (See the accompanying chart for red-flag events.) Surprisingly, good events—winning the lottery, marrying a dreamboat—may be as stressful as bad ones.

Dr. Holmes theorizes that the connection between stressful life events and disease is based on the functioning of the immunity system. Fear, excitement, any emotional jolt, may weaken it. Stressful events may also upset hormone production. Either way big events in your life may mean that you'll be ill, so keep other stresses to a minimum.

Watch for early-warning signals that your emotional reactions follow certain patterns. Many factors contribute to illness, and particular patterns of behavior are thought to be among them. People suffering from certain diseases are often found to have similar emotional conflicts. Those prone to peptic ulcers, for example, tend to seek love via achievements—doing super-well on their jobs, trying to be perfect in everything they attempt. Neurodermatitis victims crave to be touched and held, perhaps as a result of not being fondled enough as infants. Rheumatoid arthritics often seek to control others through sacrifice. The typical hypertension victim is overcompliant but resentful of the burdens he stacks upon himself.

One early-warning sign is a sense of hopelessness and helplessness. Don't give up, physicians advise. Marshal your psychological resources and fight off the depressing effects of a series of misfortunes, for your bodily health may depend upon it.

In a study of cancer patients psychologist Lawrence LeShan of the Institute of Applied Biology in New York City discovered that three out of four shared a feeling of "bleak hopelessness about ever achieving any real feeling of meaning or enjoyment of life." One cancer victim said: "It's as if all my life I'd been climbing a very steep mountain. And the mountain has no top."

Conversely, patients with plenty of fight left in them have a better chance of recovering. Dr. Kathleen M. Stavraky and her associates at the Ontario Cancer Treatment and Research Foundation Clinic found that people with the most favorable cancer outcome tend to be more hostile than average. They had not given up. They were not hopeless and helpless. They were still fighting back.

Learn how to relax. Some techniques can help you better cope with stress and reduce anxiety.

Deep muscle relaxation. Lie down comfortably. Beginning with your toes, first tense for a few seconds, then relax, each muscle in your body. Concentrate on relaxing; when other thoughts enter your mind, disregard them and return your attention to your muscles. Don't forget muscles of the stomach, buttocks, scalp, forehead, pelvic area, eyebrows, back of neck, mouth, and tongue. Breathe slowly as you tense and relax.

When your whole body is completely relaxed, keep your eyes closed and allow random thoughts to float through your mind. Breathe slowly and calmly, following the steady rhythm of your breathing. On exhaling, think of a single word or sound, such as *here* or *ah*. Concentrate on the color blue—a calm blue sea or a cloudless

blue sky. Do this for five to ten minutes before resuming other activities.

Meditation promotes relaxation and reduces tension. To adapt techniques of transcendental meditation, try the following:

· Select a word (a mantra) you find pleasant and soothing. It can be a real word you have nice associations with (such as *peace* or *love)* or a meaningless syllable you find beautiful.

· Set aside 15 to 20 minutes twice a day, and find a place where you will not be disturbed. You might also take the phone off the hook.

· Sit in a comfortable position, close your eyes, and think your word over and over, slowly and silently.

· If you become aware that your mind is wandering, think your word again. If worries intrude, go back to meditating again, with the attitude: "I can worry and make plans later. Right now it's pleasant to think this nice word."

· If you fall asleep, it was a sign that your body required sleep. Finish meditating when you awaken.

· With time there may be periods when your mind becomes a complete blank, a very relaxing experience. If your thoughts are tumultuous and disruptive during meditation, take the attitude of an outsider observing how tense you are. Then slowly and gently go back to thinking your word over and over. Thoughts during meditation are mostly a sign of the release of tensions by your mind. The aim of meditation is not to experience a "high" but to release yourself from thoughts that cause tension.

· After meditating for 15 to 20 minutes, rest for a minute or two before doing something else.

Accept your limitations. Why not regard yourself with the same tolerance you'd accord someone else. Nobody had perfect parents. Nobody has perfect genes. Learn to accept yourself with your assets as well as your liabilities.

By the same token, it helps to be mindful of your basic strengths and keep adversity in perspective. When troubles get you down, tell yourself: "There is more to my life than these instances of hard luck. I can live with them."

Get regular exercise. Working up a good sweat is great for washing out tension and relieving anxiety, apart from the well-known psychological benefits. Even just 20 minutes of walking, bicycling, or floor exercises each day can significantly reduce stress.

Schedule regular vacations. You need time off from home and work pressures, or your health may suffer. Vacations are necessities, not luxuries. Take care, however, not to build stress into your vacation. Leave more than enough time for everything you want to do. Travel with snacks to avoid between-meal letdown and irritability. Take along a good book for the inevitable delays. Expect some disappointments and frustrations, and accept them as part of the experience. If you are traveling with other people, plan some private time each day. Get some exercise each day—walking is a fine vacation exercise. But a vacation is not a good time to start a diet.

Seek psychotherapy if you need it. Problems causing stress—and possibly illness—may reach into your unconscious. Professional counseling may help you gain insights needed for working out hidden emotional conflicts involved in a bodily illness.

Psychoquackery. Charlatans prey upon people in need of psychological counseling. Ask your family physician to refer you to a qualified psychotherapist. You are likely to be in the most competent hands with a board-certified psychiatrist—an M.D., who can prescribe drugs (such as tranquilizers or antidepressants) if needed—or with a clinical psychologist or social worker who works under a psychiatrist's supervision. Or, for less expensive therapy, ask your physician to recommend a clinic or agency.

Any supposed therapist, however well intentioned, should be treated with skepticism if he minimizes the possible seriousness of an emotional disturbance and denigrates "establishment" practitioners, promising a quick, inexpensive cure. Be wary if he displays testimonial letters from patients.

Also be leery of a practitioner who refuses to consult with your physician. Any respectable therapist knows of the indivisibility of an emotional disorder and the patient's physiological well-being.

Be skeptical if his degrees come from institutions of questionable stature. Many such training programs have arisen with the growth of encounter groups. These groups are no substitute for professional psychotherapy. They cannot solve complex personality problems and are only useful for the average person who is functioning adequately; whose emotional problems, to the extent they exist, don't severely interfere with his family life or work; who nonetheless wants to gain insight into his feelings and behavior; and who can profit from developmental experiences.

Avoid chiropractors. Though they may call themselves "doctor," they have no competence in psychotherapy.

Be wary of mail-order psychotherapy. The postal service cited one firm for offering computerized psychoanalysis by mail.

Also steer clear of psychotherapy gimmicks and gadgets. One victim of a nervous ailment paid $28,600 in one year for treatment with a machine represented as being capable of performing psychoanalysis.

See also PHYSICIAN.

HOW MUCH STRESS ARE YOU UNDER?

Psychiatrist Thomas H. Holmes and his colleagues devised this scale, which indicates the relative amount of stress caused by typical life events.

THE SOCIAL READJUSTMENT RATING SCALE	
LIFE EVENT	IMPACT VALUE
1. Death of spouse	100
2. Divorce	73
3. Marital separation	65
4. Jail term	63
5. Death of close family member	63
6. Personal injury or illness	53
7. Marriage	50
8. Fired at work	47
9. Marital reconciliation	45
10. Retirement	45
11. Change in health of family member	44
12. Pregnancy	40
13. Sex difficulties	39
14. Gain of new family member	39
15. Business readjustment	39
16. Change in financial state	38
17. Death of close friend	37
18. Change to different line of work	36
19. Change in number of arguments with spouse	35
20. Mortgage over $10,000	31
21. Foreclosure of mortgage or loan	30
22. Change in responsibilities at work	29
23. Son or daughter leaving home	29
24. Trouble with in-laws	29
25. Outstanding personal achievement	28
26. Wife begin or stop work	26
27. Begin or end school	26
28. Change in living conditions	25
29. Revision of personal habits	24
30. Trouble with boss	23
31. Change in work hours or conditions	20
32. Change in residence	20
33. Change in schools	20
34. Change in recreation	19
35. Change in church activities	19
36. Change in social activities	18
37. Mortgage or loan less than $10,000	17
38. Change in sleeping habits	16
39. Change in number of family get-togethers	15
40. Change in eating habits	15
41. Vacation	13
42. Christmas	12
43. Minor violations of the law	11

STROKE (cerebral vascular accident, apoplexy, shock) If you're with someone who has a stroke, keep him lying comfortably and call a physician or ambulance. Immediate hospital care can reduce stroke damage—indeed, it can be lifesaving.

Watch for breathing difficulties that may call for ARTIFICIAL RESPIRATION (which see). If unconsciousness or paralysis has set in, the victim risks choking on his own saliva. Give him nothing to eat or drink, since his throat may be paralyzed. Be prepared to treat HEART STOPPAGE (which see).

Don't handle him needlessly—you can aggravate the stroke. However be sure that a possibly paralyzed arm or leg is safe: not crushed beneath him, twisted uncomfortably, too close to a heating unit.

Though unable to speak, he may be conscious and in a panic. Speak to him calmly and reassuringly. Let him know you've called for help.

A stroke is an interruption in the blood supply to a part of the brain. When the brain cells die, the part of the body controlled by these cells cannot function.

More than 2 million Americans are currently disabled by strokes. Strokes take more than 200,000 lives a year, making it the country's third leading killer (after heart disease and cancer). Risk of stroke increases with age.

How strokes develop. The commonest cause of strokes is cerebral thrombosis, the blocking by a blood clot (thrombus) of an artery supplying the brain. The clot frequently results from atherosclerosis (see ARTERIOSCLEROSIS).

In about three out of four cases a tiny blood clot in one of the smaller arteries causes a momentary blocking—a little stroke (transient ischemic attacks, or TIAs)—in which a very small area of brain tissue is affected. Little strokes also occur when a large artery is narrowed by atherosclerosis so that adequate blood fails to reach the brain.

These little strokes sometimes serve as warning attacks. Their immediate impact may be slight: a brief dizziness or feeling of confusion. People who have little strokes over the years may scarcely be aware of them. A slight clumsiness of the hand may show up in a change of handwriting, or there may be sudden difficulty in speech. After one or more little strokes the victim may undergo personality changes, often becoming extremely irritable and quick-tempered.

A wandering blood clot is another cause of stroke. Carried in the bloodstream, usually as a result of a heart attack, this embolus can become wedged in one of the brain arteries. Such a cerebral embolism thereby interferes with the flow of blood to the brain.

Yet another cause of stroke is cerebral hemorrhage, internal bleeding within the brain. A diseased artery in the brain can burst and flood the surrounding brain tissue with blood. The cells nourished by the artery fail to get their supply of food and oxygen.

A cerebral hemorrhage is more likely to occur when the victim suffers from a combination of atherosclerosis and high blood pressure. Sometimes a clot and a hemorrhage are present at the same time.

Brain hemorrhage may also be caused by head injuries. Or there may be a bursting of an aneurysm, an abnormal blood-filled pouch that balloons out from the wall of an artery somewhat like a weak spot in a tire's inner tube. An aneurysm may be present at birth but usually does not cause trouble until some years later. It often accounts for strokes that occur in adolescents.

Warning signs. Since little strokes are likely to precede major ones, bring any symptoms suggesting advancing thrombosis to a physician. Little strokes often occur as early as one's thirties. Here are the warning signs you're likely to recognize:

A sudden, temporary weakness or numbness of the face, arm, or leg.

Temporary difficulty or loss of speech, or trouble understanding speech.

Sudden, temporary dimness or loss of vision, particularly in one eye.

An episode of double vision.

Unexplained headaches, or a change in the pattern of your headaches.

Temporary dizziness or unsteadiness.

A recent change in personality or mental ability.

Depending on the diagnosis you may be prescribed anticoagulants and other drugs. Surgery can open a blocked section of artery, or bypass a diseased artery with a graft.

Other preventives are generally the same as for heart disease: Have a periodic physical examination. Quit smoking. Take regular exercise. Cut down on cholesterol and saturated fats in your diet. Reduce if you're overweight. Control high blood pressure. Avoid emotional stress.

These measures are all the more important if you have reason to believe you've had a little stroke—or if you suffer from one of the conditions often leading to stroke: diabetes, hypertension, atherosclerosis, and other heart and blood-vessel diseases.

Therapy for stroke damage. Begin rehabilitation right away. Often within 24 hours victims of major strokes can be started on assisted movements to restore use of an affected arm or leg. Only one in ten victims of hemiplegia—paralysis of one side of the body—need accept permanent helplessness, estimates the National Institute of Neurological and Communicative Disorders and Stroke. Of the nine in ten who can learn to walk, at least three can return to work. The younger the victim is, the greater his chances for complete rehabilitation.

If you have a stroke victim in your family, ask your doctor about a rehabilitation center, generally the best source of specialized help. If no such center is available, ask him to recommend a physical therapist, occupational therapist, speech therapist.

Your local heart association is a good source for information (including useful booklets like *Strokes: A Guide for the Family* and *Aphasia and the Family*). Your local health department or Visiting Nurse Association may provide nursing help. Many hospitals and Red Cross chapters give short home-nursing courses.

Tips for the family of a stroke victim:

Encourage his independence by easy steps, advises the American Heart Association. Don't frustrate him with overly difficult tasks. "It calls for fine judgment . . . to stimulate progress and still not to encourage unrealistic expectations." If he can brush his teeth, shave, comb his hair, dress himself, let him do so even though it may take a long time.

Praise any effort he may make. Don't be discouraged by his failures.

Have him participate in as many family activities and as much family planning as he can. Encourage visitors if his condition permits it. Don't relegate him to the sidelines with only radio and TV to occupy him.

He's likely to suffer from loss of language (aphasia), marked by inability to remember the names of people and things. Reassure him that this is part of his illness, that he is not "losing his mind."

To encourage his regaining speech, speak simply but naturally. Encourage him to respond in any way he can: with gestures, in writing, or with inaccurate—even bizarre—use of language if that's the best he can do for now.

Meals, dressing time, other routine activities are good times for speaking. Encourage greetings and social exchanges like "Hello," "Thank you," "How are you?" Ask lots of direct questions requiring simple yes or no answers. Don't

confuse him with idle chatter or too many people speaking at once.

To help him do for himself, secure or make self-help devices. If he has difficulty walking, fasten handrails along the walls. Protect him from falls by installing no-skid strips or rubber mats in the bathtub. Keep in easy reach of his bed toilet articles, a bell for summoning help, a light switch.

Warn unknowing visitors, especially children, against committing common but demeaning errors in dealing with stroke victims. Tell them: Don't finish sentences for him or make fun of the way he speaks (some people think that will help motivate him to relearn to talk). Don't address him as if he were a child or deaf or retarded—his hearing and intellectual faculties are likely to be intact. Don't talk about him in his presence.

Personality changes are common for weeks or months after a stroke. Some common problems are involuntary laughing or crying, irritability and temper tantrums, cursing, mood swings, unreasonable anger. Brain centers that regulate such behaviors have been damaged, and the patient may have little control over these outbursts. He may know, however, that his behavior is inappropriate, and it will help if you let him know you understand that he is embarrassed and wishes he could control these emotions. Also reassure him that this sort of behavior almost always disappears with time.

If the stroke victim is excessively self-pitying or depressed, professional assistance is called for. Inappropriate crying or laughing can sometimes be controlled if the patient squeezes something in one or both hands. Do not give in to unreasonable demands the patient makes: you slow his recovery if you do too much for him.

Vision problems are common after stroke, and include double vision, rapid eye movements, blindness in one eye, or a loss of peripheral vision. Arrange for an eye examination by an ophthalmologist. Remember to stand where the patient can see you. Keep objects out of his path on the impaired side.

Spacial perceptions and sense of balance may also be impaired. A patient may believe he is standing straight, for example, when he is actually leaning to one side. The stroke patient's attention span, reasoning ability, and memory may be seriously impaired as well. Don't expect that something he has learned in one setting will necessarily be generalized to another. Written reminders and instructions around the house may be useful. It may help, for example, to post a checklist in the bathroom to make sure the patient doesn't forget routine bathroom chores.

Loss of control of the bladder or bowels after a stroke is usually temporary. While it lasts, the patient is likely to feel embarrassed, hopeless, and guilty. You can help by reminding him that this is a common problem after stroke, and control will probably return as he gets stronger.

You and your family may benefit from joining a "stroke club." Contact the Easter Seal Society or the American Heart Association for information about such clubs in your area.

For more information, contact the following:

American Heart Association
7320 Greenville Avenue
Dallas, Texas 75231

National Institute of Neurological and
    Communicative Disorders and Stroke
Department SBH, Room 8A06, Building 31
National Institutes of Health
Bethesda, Maryland 20205

American Physical Therapy Association
1156 15th Street, NW, Suite 500
Washington, D.C. 20005

American Occupational Therapy Association
1383 Piccard Drive
Rockville, Maryland 20850

Vocational Guidance and Rehabilitation
    Services
2239 East 55th Street
Cleveland, Ohio 44103

American Speech-Language-Hearing
    Association
10801 Rockville Pike
Rockville, Maryland 20852

National Association for Hearing and
    Speech Action
6110 Executive Blvd.
Rockville, Maryland 20852

See also BED; HEART DISEASE.

STYES are usually minor infections that appear in the form of a red, tender pimple at the base of an eyelash. A stye feels as if there's something in the eye, and the eye itself may be teary and sensitive to light.

Apply warm compresses every two or three hours for ten minutes at a time—a wet warm tea bag is especially soothing. The stye should open, drain, and heal in a few days. If it does not, or if you have styes often, consult a doctor.

See also EYE DISORDER.

SULFA DRUGS See ANTIBIOTICS.

SUMMER INFLUENZA See HISTOPLASMOSIS.

SUNBURN is as serious as any type of burn, and

can cause chills, fever, even delirium. Peeling of the skin after a severe burn is inevitable.

For relief take aspirin. Apply cold compresses using any of the following: Burow's solution, cornstarch in water, or emulsions such as Cetaphil Lotion. If large areas of the body are burned, a solution of colloidal oatmeal (e.g., Aveeno) can be especially effective. These measures increase cooling by evaporation—usually the body's ability to cool itself by perspiration is impaired by the burn.

Take a soothing, lukewarm bath with at least a teacup of both cornstarch and baking soda. Don't take a cold shower—it may irritate your skin.

Of the commercial sunburn remedies, only those that contain benzocaine (Solarcaine, Exocaine) are at all effective. However, many dermatologists recommend against using these products because of a high risk of developing contact dermatitis. A bland cold cream may be soothing, but baby oil or petroleum jelly is often irritating in a burn's early stages.

If you dust yourself with talcum, turning in bed will be easier. Avoid calamine lotion—it's very drying.

Even if your burn is slight, don't get any more sun until your skin returns to normal. Spend the daytime indoors if possible, and avoid midday sun. The slightest glare or reflection can cause further damage.

If you must go outside, use a good sun-blocking agent. Wear clothes that cover your burn. Stay in the shade, even if it's just the shade of a beach umbrella or a large hat.

If you suffer severe pain or extensive blisters, see a doctor. He can prescribe steroids and painkillers that can bring substantial relief.

The dangers of too much sun. Sunburn isn't the worst effect of too much sun: skin cancer is. Excessive exposure to sunlight can cause skin problems that become cancerous, such as actinic keratoses (see CANCER OF THE SKIN).

Too much sun prematurely ages the skin. The young woman in her twenties who relentlessly bakes herself in the sun may find in her forties, when she most wants to look youthful, that her skin has become leathery. Wrinkles, dryness, loss of elasticity, thickening, a yellowish or blotchy brown color, are among the effects of too much exposure to the sun for too long a time.

Getting overheated in the sun is dangerous for anyone, especially those with heart disease. Tuberculosis may worsen after exposure to the sun, and the disease called systemic lupus erythematosus is believed to be precipitated or aggravated by sunburn. Sunlight may promote skin lesions in people with severe malnutrition resulting from alcoholism.

Sunlight is of little benefit to health. Though it can be helpful in relieving acne and psoriasis, the chief benefit is psychological.

A suntan is a status symbol—especially out of season. But the reverse was true in earlier times, when only common folk spent enough time outdoors to get tanned. Then the lady of leisure clutched her sunbonnet and parasol to retain her dazzling whiteness.

There is also a popular theory that since sunlight is beneficial and necessary to plants, it must be beneficial and necessary to humans. It just isn't true. Sunbathing will not make you healthy. It will not bake out germs. It won't cure colds or any other ailment.

The sun does help your body produce vitamin D (important for strong bones), so it's a help to growing children. But adults' bones aren't growing—they need only enough vitamin D to maintain skin and bone health.

Excessive buildup of vitamin D in the body—produced by a combination of sunlight and food supplements—may ultimately cause joint and vein damage. In any event vitamin D is available from so many foods (it's added to milk) that even children don't need exposure to the sun.

Sun allergy. An allergic reaction to the sun, termed *photosensitivity,* may cause redness, itching, inflammation, rash, and discoloration. Even sunlight passing through glass windows can trigger the reaction. So can artificial light sources, including fluorescent tubes.

Taking certain drugs can induce this sensitivity to sunlight. Among such drugs are the sulfonamides; tetracyclines (especially Declomycin); griseofulvins, used for ringworm and athlete's foot (Fulvicin, Grifulvin, Grisactin); thiazide diuretics (Diuril and others); and nalidixic acid (NegGram), a urinary antibiotic. Others less frequently implicated are barbiturates, salicylates, estrogens, gold salts, quinine, and local anesthetics of the procaine group. It has also been reported that chlorpromazine (Thorazine) and other tranquilizers of the phenothiazine family may do the same.

Occasionally you may find a greater sensitivity to the sun after use of eau de cologne or perfumes containing bergamot or citron oils, or after skin contact with tars. Some people get a reaction after touching (not necessarily eating) such plants as figs, carrots, celery, citrus fruits, and parsnips—all of which contain sensitizing chemicals. Antibacterial agents in some deodor-

ant soaps, body powders, and other toilet articles have also been implicated.

When going on vacation in sun country, ask your doctor if you're likely to be photosensitized by any drug you take regularly or are carrying with you. Report to him any exaggerated sunburn response. The first remedy usually is to cut down on or cut out the possibly offending product.

One type of sun allergy is commonly called sun poisoning. It affects mostly the hands, mouth, and feet. It can be extremely painful but there is no visible rash or redness. Relief comes from antihistamines, cold compresses of Burow's solution, and avoidance of the sun.

Getting a tan. To tan without burning take the sun slowly. Tanning results from the sun's ultraviolet rays causing the top layer of the skin to thicken and a brownish pigment called melanin to be produced in greater quantities.

Tanning begins to show about two days after your first exposure. It can't be speeded up. Contrary to popular belief, a burn does *not* change to tan. If you blister and peel, you'll lose the top layer of skin and be back where you started.

Start with 10 to 20 minutes of sunbathing on each side of your body. Each day increase your exposure by about 10 minutes a side. Shorten your first exposures if you burn easily. Fair-skinned people have little melanin except in freckles and so tend to burn rather than tan. But even dark-skinned people are not necessarily resistant to sunburn.

Children have less resistance to the sun than adults. Their exposure to the sun should start out at about five minutes, with five-minute increments. The rest of the time protect them with shirts or robes.

During the midday hours—10:00 A.M. to 2:00 P.M. standard time, 11:00 A.M. to 3:00 P.M. daylight savings—rays are always too strong for small children and others with sensitive skin. Anyone is more likely to burn on a hot day—heat accentuates the effects of ultraviolet radiation. The sun also tends to be stronger at higher altitudes, where there's less protective atmosphere. It also beats down more strongly at the equator. Never use a reflector to speed a tan. You'd merely invite a burn from the concentrated rays.

To prevent burning. Light-colored or loose-woven clothing, particularly if wet, can allow the sun's rays to get through. Don't depend on an umbrella. Rays reflected from sand and concrete can burn even though you are not directly exposed. Do not be fooled by overcast days. Haze and fog scatter the sun's burning rays and may produce a severe sunburn.

Also keep in mind that ultraviolet rays penetrate water, so you need to apply a sunscreen if you spend a lot of time swimming or scuba diving.

Take extra care at the beach. The sand bounces sunlight right back at you, increasing the dose. Water and wind on a cool, breezy day can make you feel so comfortable that you fail to notice when you've been out too long.

During cold weather a bright sun, especially if reflected off snow, can cause severe burns. Windburn can be a problem even in hot weather. Wind hastens evaporation of protective perspiration from the skin, thus increasing susceptibility to the sun's rays.

Protect your hair. Too much sun can make hair temporarily discolored and promote brittleness and temporary hair loss.

Your eyes cannot build up immunity to the sun and are always vulnerable to injury. When lying down, cover them with cotton pads. At other times wear sunglasses.

Sunscreens. Most commercial preparations contain chemicals called sunscreens, which absorb some of the burning rays of sunlight, thus allow you to stay in the sun longer with less risk of burning.

Products containing 5 percent PABA (para-aminobenzoic) or one of its derivatives provide the best protection. These compounds not only block out more rays than other types of sunscreens—they also stay on the skin longer. PABA products help prevent sunburn but do allow some tanning. To increase its effectiveness apply a PABA product for a few days before you expect to be out in the sun for greater than normal periods, such as on a vacation. Some of the sunscreen penetrates and remains in the skin, providing extra protection.

Since you may be sensitive to a particular sunscreen, apply some on a small area of your skin. If the area reddens or itches within 24 hours, don't use that sunscreen.

Among the most effective PABA products are PreSun and Pabanol. Less effective than PABA sunscreens but acceptable are benzophenones (Solbar, Piz Buin, Uval), which are easily washed away by bathing and sweating. Also recommended, although somewhat less effective than PABA preparations, are dimethylaminobenzoates (Block Out, Pabafilm).

To help you choose an appropriate sunscreen, the FDA has rated products in terms of their "Sun Protection Factor," or SPF. SPF ranges from 2 (minimal protection) to 15 (super protec-

tion). You'll usually find this information on the sunscreen's label.

If you always burn easily and never tan, choose a sunscreen with an SPF of 15 (PreSun 15, Super Shade 15, and others). If you usually burn easily and tan minimally, choose a sunscreen with an SPF of 6 to 12 (such as Eclipse, Pabanol, Piz Buin 6). If you burn moderately and tan gradually, a sunscreen with an SPF of 4 to 6 may be best (Sundown, ProTan, Sea & Ski 6). If you tan readily and rarely burn, a sunscreen with an SPF of 2 to 4 may do the job (Coppertone 2, Piz Buin 2).

Reapply all suntan products at least every two hours, after each swim, and whenever the protecting film may have rubbed off or washed away. Sunscreens may stain fabrics, so take care.

For total screening use a sunblocking agent. Opaque chemicals like zinc oxide or titanium dioxide provide complete protection by preventing the sun's ultraviolet rays from reaching the skin. Zinc oxide ointment—the white stuff on lifeguards' noses—is cheap, resists washing off, and is effective for small sensitive areas like the nose. Pancake makeup and ordinary lipstick can be good blocking agents if applied thickly enough.

Mineral oil or baby oil, though commonly used, won't prevent burning or promote tanning. The addition of iodine to the oil does nothing more than stain the skin. Too much grease on the skin, combined with perspiration and skin irritation from sun exposure, can produce an itchy rash and inflamed hair follicles.

Vinegar mixtures and other homemade concoctions do nothing to screen the sun. Nor do so-called tanning aids. These are lotions, oils, and butters that moisturize your skin while you sunbathe, but contain no sunscreening chemicals.

But do moisturize your skin after sunning by rubbing in an emollient like cold cream. It will replace some of the oils dried out by the sun and reduce skin dryness.

Artificial tanning preparations can give you a tanned appearance without the dangers of sunlight exposure. But they provide no protection against the sun. They merely stain the skin. A chemical called dihydroxyacetone (DHA) combines with proteins in the outer layer of your skin to produce a tan coloration.

The products are safe provided you haven't an allergy to their ingredients. The process takes three to five hours and won't wash off. But it does wear off in four or five days if not renewed, sometimes leaving unsightly streaks.

With prolonged use the skin can become dry and scaly. Rough skin, warts, and moles often pick up extra color from the chemical tanners—it may not be harmful, but it won't help their appearance. Don't use any tanning preparation on sores or areas of infection.

Sunlamps, another substitute for the real thing, are treacherous. To avoid burning yourself, follow the manufacturer's directions about exposure time and wait a day between exposures. One minute under a sunlamp may be the equivalent of one hour under the sun. If you burn easily, make your first exposure shorter than the recommended time. So you don't fall asleep, buy a lamp with a built-in timer or set an alarm clock—and put it out of reach, so you don't turn it off in your sleep.

Measure your distance from the lamp carefully. At 30 inches, an exposure of six minutes under a bulb lamp is safe for most people. But if you move the lamp to 15 inches, you get the same effect in less than two minutes.

Protect your eyes which are easily burned. Wear safety goggles under a lamp. Ultraviolet rays can penetrate the eyelids, causing conjunctivitis and, in extreme cases, cataracts. Even when wearing goggles, don't stare into the lamp or read under it.

Make sure the same precautions are taken if you get your tan in a "tanning booth" at a tanning center. Such establishments, which have proliferated in recent years, offer you a quick total body tan in a small room with as many as two dozen sunlamps. People who never tan from the sun will not tan from a sunlamp.

Beware of claims that a lamp is "safe," and that it poses no increased risk of skin cancer. Visits to suntan parlors, as to the beach, add to the cumulative damage to the skin that leads to the development of wrinkles and cancer. Stay away from so-called suntan pills except under a doctor's direction. Publicized as providing protection for "easy burners" such as blondes and redheads, they also can be dangerous.

The pills contain a chemical known as psoralen, which hastens tanning—but it does not thicken the skin so there is little protection from future sunburn, as there would be with a natural tan. This potent drug is sometimes prescribed for vitiligo. However misuse can cause severe, blistering dermatitis, and other side effects such as nausea, vomiting, and vertigo.

See also BURNS; HOT WEATHER; SKIN DISORDERS.

SUNGLASSES, if worn unnecessarily, can make your eyes oversensitive to light. This tempts you to wear them even more, thus increasing your sensitivity.

To help protect your eyes, wear tinted lenses only in bright sunlight. They can be especially valuable in places where reflection of infrared and ultraviolet rays can actually injure your eyes, such as at the beach, on water, or in snow-covered areas.

But in average daylight the contraction of the pupil and the pigment of the iris are protection enough. As a rule of thumb the National Society to Prevent Blindness recommends: "If you squint, furrow your brow, constrict the muscles of the eyelids, and end a day in the sun with tired, teary, or inflamed eyes—sunglasses may help."

Use sunglasses sparingly while driving, when available light is most needed for safety. Remove sunglasses before driving into a tunnel. The sudden dimness may make it impossible for you to see.

Don't wear sunglasses at night or in fog, certainly not while driving. Although they may cut down some of the glare of oncoming headlights, even lightly tinted glasses can dangerously reduce your ability to see dimly lighted objects. Take off your sunglasses indoors. If you wear them in normally lighted rooms or while watching TV, you risk eyestrain.

Sunglass safety. To prevent injuries wear only glasses with impact-resistant lenses. Look for glasses that are tagged as meeting minimum standards of the National Bureau of Standards, an indication of at least minimum acceptability. Any other claims that glasses are "certified" or "guaranteed safe" are meaningless. Also discount promises that sunglasses will sharpen your vision in mist or fog, increase the amount of visible light, or give complete eye protection.

Select uniform-density lenses to get the same color throughout regardless of the thickness of the glass. This is a special consideration in prescription lenses, where the thickness of the lens can vary substantially from edge to edge and from one eye to the other.

Odd shapes—triangles, squares, oversized circles—won't cause any problems, though a lens that is too small may not protect against side glare. Heavy, wide temple bars on sunglasses can be hazardous while driving because they restrict side vision.

To avoid color distortion, choose neutral gray. Tan and pale green are second for color fidelity. The world looks discolored through rose-colored glasses—as well as through red, red-orange, yellow, amber, and blue. Besides giving poor color perception, these tints do a poor job of filtering out sun rays.

No sunglasses, no matter how dark, are safe

for staring at the sun or for viewing an eclipse. Nor do they protect properly against sunlamp glare. Direct rays—including invisible infrared rays during a solar eclipse—can burn the retina of an eye in seconds, causing permanent blind areas.

Tips on buying. Buy sunglasses that transmit 10 to 20 percent of visible light. They are best for all-around use. A density value of 21 to 30 percent is almost as good. Color tones in this range are usually labeled "medium" or "general use." Glasses labeled "dark" transmit less than 10 percent and are too dark, even under extreme conditions such as in snow or at sea. Those labeled "light" transmit more than 30 percent and do little more than keep dust out of your eyes.

Photochromatic lenses are made of glass and contain fine silver crystals that allow the lenses to change color depending on the degree of ultraviolet light: they darken in the sunlight, lighten in shade or indoors. About 20 percent of all prescription lenses sold today are photochromatic.

These may be a good choice for people—such as door-to-door salespeople—who constantly go from bright sunlight to darker interiors. But photochromatic glasses are not a perfect solution: they take several minutes to complete the change. Also the effect depends on ultraviolet rays, which are absorbed by window glass. So you won't get much of a sunglass effect in a car.

Polarizing lenses are rarely worth the extra cost. Supposedly light is filtered through a thin sheet of polarizing material to improve clarity and reduce glare. In practice the effect is generally negligible. Indeed the lenses may prove too dark for general use.

Plastic sunglasses and plastic clip-ons for people who wear regular glasses can work well. Handle plastic lenses with particular care because they scratch easily.

Be sure clip-ons are properly fitted. They often fail to cover the entire clear lens, and the space between the clip-ons and your regular glasses may let in glare and play havoc with your vision. In general, prescription sunglasses are a better bet since they guarantee good-quality lenses with adequate sun protection. Keep a pair of clip-ons as spares.

Before buying any type of sunglasses, examine them for scratches, bubbles, and distortion. These defects, especially common in bargain-counter glasses, can warp vision and cause discomfort, often with headache, nausea, and eyestrain.

See also ECLIPSES; EYE DISORDER; EYEGLASSES.

SURGERY should be performed when it's the best or only way to relieve a problem—and it can be lifesaving. But too many people tend to glamorize it, by overemphasizing the miraculous cures and minimizing the dangers. Submit to surgery only if there's no possibility that a nonsurgical approach will be effective.

All surgery carries a risk of complication, disability, or death, depending on the type of operation. Despite advances a significant number of patients do not come out of the hospital alive. The major life-threatening hazards of surgery are heart stoppage, shock, pneumonia, infections, thrombophlebitis, and blood clots in the lung.

The administration of anesthesia alone is hazardous. Even if an anesthesiologist takes every normal precaution, general anesthesia carries a small risk that the patient will unforeseeably die.

The pain and scars of surgery can be mental as well as physical. Merely being in a hospital can be a source of emotional stress. And even with health insurance, surgery is your most expensive service in medicine.

Too many surgeons. An oversupply of general surgeons can lead to abuses. There are about one third more general surgeons in practice than are needed to serve U.S. civilian needs. In many parts of the country, there aren't enough patients to go around. "I could easily do five times as many operations as I'm doing," *Medical Economics* quotes one surgeon as saying. "Of the 200 surgeons in my town, I estimate that only 6 are working at more than 80 percent of capacity."

Moreover, the oversupply is worsening. Residency programs are turning out new general surgeons at a faster rate than the growth in population. Even existing surgeons have less and less to do as more conditions yield to medical treatment.

But despite the increasing competition surgeons are earning more than ever. *Medical Economics* reports the net incomes of surgeons average among the highest in medicine.

The reasons for this seeming paradox spell trouble for the patient. Some surgeons perform unnecessary operations; many operate beyond their competence; surgical fees are high, and sometimes tainted by fee splitting.

Pennsylvania Insurance Commissioner Herbert S. Denenberg estimated that 2 million needless operations (out of a total of 12 to 15 million) are performed in the United States each year. According to Dr. Sidney M. Wolfe, director of Ralph Nader's Public Citizen-sponsored Health Research Group, that estimate is conservative.

In Britain, with free medical care but less aggressive surgeons, the rate of surgery per capita is about half that of the United States.

"We have surgical manpower creating its own demand," observed Dr. John H. Knowles, president of the Rockefeller Foundation and former director of Massachusetts General Hospital. "The more surgeons you have, the more surgery is going to be done, simply because the surgeons are there and have to make a living."

Strategy to follow. If your regular physician tells you that you need an operation, follow this strategy:

Be sure an operation is really needed. When he refers you to a surgeon, ask your doctor and the surgeon, "What would happen if I didn't have the operation?"

With knowledge of the alternatives you may well choose surgery rather than suffer continuing distress or inconvenience. A hernia repair, for example, is more desirable than a lifetime of wearing a truss and limiting your activity. You may prefer to have a gall bladder operation if it is indicated rather than put up with chronic indigestion. In cases such as these elective operations are usually justifiable.

But many others are not. A surgeon writing under the name of Lawrence P. Williams estimates in his book *How to Avoid Unnecessary Surgery* that half of all tonsillectomies and adenoidectomies are unnecessary. In about one in three cases, he estimates, hysterectomy is unjustified.

See at least two surgeons—and make sure they are qualified. You're likely to be in competent hands if your regular physician refers you to a board-certified surgeon who is a fellow of the American College of Surgeons. Many health-insurance plans cover the cost of a second opinion.

The ACS has stiff membership qualifications and continuing-education requirements. A member may identify himself with FACS after his name. The *Directory of Medical Specialists* lists M.D.'s certified in general surgery and in surgical specialties like gynecology, orthopedics, urology.

Even if your regular doctor and the surgeon agree that surgery is necessary, get an independent evaluation from one or more other surgeons of equal qualifications. The Pennsylvania Insurance Department notes that such consultations reduce operations by 20 to 60 percent. The department's publication *A Shopper's Guide to Surgery* quotes a surgeon who suggests that the best way to avoid unnecessary surgery is to get three independent opinions without advising any of the surgeons about the conclusions of the other two.

Being sure of a surgeon's qualifications helps you steer clear of general practitioners who do surgery part time.

Find out exactly what to expect. You have a right to give informed consent, based on a full understanding of the procedure and its possible hazards. You also ought to know the details of pre- and postoperative measures so that you will not be frightened, for example, when you wake up in the recovery room attached to various tubes, bottles, and equipment.

Ask your surgeon beforehand to describe the experience step by step, from preparations you need to make at home to your discharge from the hospital. Have a relative or friend with you. As the surgeon proceeds with his narrative, both of you ask questions and take notes. Your understandable anxiety may make you neglect to ask for information and forget what the surgeon tells you.

If the surgeon lapses into medical terminology, have him reexplain it in plain English. If, for example, a man is told by his surgeon that he needs a "transurethral prostatic resection," he should understand that this surgery will possibly render him sterile.

If a child faces surgery, ask the surgeon to give him a detailed rundown on what's going to happen: where the incision will be made; what's going to be removed or corrected; why the operation is necessary; what might happen if it is not done. Tell the youngster about others who have benefited from it. If possible cite someone the child knows. Assure him that it won't hurt because he'll be anesthetized.

Have the surgeon explain how he'll feel afterward. Emphasize that the operation won't permanently disrupt normal functions. For example, a six-year-old boy who faces a hernia repair needs reassurance that the procedure won't affect his ability to urinate or the growth of his genitals. If he secretly fears that his penis is going to be cut off, set the record straight.

Surgical fees. Surgery can be expensive. Discuss charges frankly with the surgeon. Find out all the costs you should expect—fees for him, any assistants he needs, the anesthesiologist, special nursing, charges for the hospital, laboratory, X rays. Compare the charges with your health-insurance coverage.

If you can't afford the operation, let the surgeon know beforehand so that he can recommend a service—his own or someone else's—that is available at lesser cost.

Be sure you know the surgeon's charge for the

complete service, including care both before and after the operation. It is likely to be bill padding if a surgeon charges separately for preoperative or postoperative care, if he levies an extra charge for a so-called tough case, or if he breaks down a routine operation into several stages with an individual charge for each stage.

If you suspect a surgeon's charges are out of line, check authoritative sources (see PHYSICIAN). The AMA Medical Disciplinary Committee tells of a surgeon who charged $2,000 for working on a woman's bunions and calluses. At most such work should cost $200.

Some ways to save money on surgery:

Office surgery. If the surgeon offers to do a minor procedure in his office, don't refuse. You'll not only save the costs of a hospital bill, but the physician's own charges are likely to be much less—he makes more efficient use of his time and avoids the necessity of conforming to a hospital's minimum charges.

Outpatient surgery. If an operation can't be performed in your surgeon's office, ask if it can be done at a hospital without an overnight stay. Even some operations requiring general anesthesia can be performed on an outpatient basis, with the full resources of the hospital on call.

With proper preparation outpatient surgery is suited to operations that ordinarily have few complications and little blood or postoperative pain. It's ideal for children, who need not be separated from their parents for the night. On the other hand surgeons generally prefer an overnight stay for a patient who's over 60 or suffering from anemia, heart disease, or other possible complicating conditions.

Local anesthetic. Whenever a local rather than a general anesthetic can be used safely, it may do away with the need for an anesthesiologist. In addition a local is safer than a general anesthetic. It can be administered without delay even if the patient has recently eaten, a hazard in general anesthesia (if a patient throws up under the mask he may inhale his vomit).

Fee splitting. It is unethical, indeed illegal in many states, for a surgeon to pay another doctor for referring patients. The practice is less of a problem than formerly, but it's well for patients to be on guard.

Fee splitting can lead to unnecessary surgery. If a sizable kickback is in the offing, a physician is tempted to refer you for surgery you don't need. The surgeon is usually obliged to operate, since if he doesn't, the "feeder" may not send him any more business.

The care you receive is likely to suffer. An ethical physician refers you to a specialist whose skill he has confidence in. By contrast, when fees are split, money, rather than the best medical care, is the deciding factor.

Instead of handing over part of his fee, a surgeon may engage the feeder as a "surgical assistant" and have him stand around the operating room or pass him instruments. This stratagem is widely preferred by fee splitters. No money changes hands between doctors, and proving that an assistantship was a payoff is nearly impossible. Moreover, *you* pay the kickback, in the form of an additional charge for the assistant's services.

And this can be disastrous for the patient. A main purpose of engaging an assistant is to have present a second surgeon competent to continue the operation if the surgeon in charge is suddenly incapacitated.

Because the feeder lacks surgical skill, he often merely adds to the operating time and increases the likelihood of complications.

Another kickback arrangement is to have the feeder needlessly supplement the surgeon's postoperative care and bill you accordingly. Even among physicians who wouldn't dream of splitting a fee, the referring doctor is often no more competent to handle postoperative care than he is to perform the operation. A medical man may miss complications that a well-trained surgeon would catch.

Fee splitting can be stopped in a community if every surgeon submits to an audit of his financial records, patient lists, and income-tax returns. Such a plan was begun in Columbus, Ohio, and has been duplicated with great success elsewhere. Short of that the most effective policeman against fee splitting is yourself.

Before agreeing to surgery, discuss with your physician and the surgeon who gets how much for what. The American College of Surgeons calls this "a matter of self-protection." To discourage fee splitting: *Don't* let the referring physician assist in the surgery or administer anesthesia. *Do* have postoperative care included in the surgical fee and administered by the surgeon. *Do* have each doctor on the case submit a separate, itemized bill.

Psychic surgery: a fraud. Don't be taken in by practitioners of "bloodless surgery." These quacks claim to operate with their bare hands, without pain or an anesthetic. They purport to remove affected tissue without making an incision or leaving a scar.

Those who perform this so-called psychic surgery are sleight-of-hand artists. After prayers and massage they appear to plunge their hands into the patient's abdomen and take out what seems to be an organ or mass of tissue. Actually they merely dent the soft flesh—and bring forth animal tissue that's been concealed. A pathologist who analyzed the supposed cancer removed in one such operation guessed the tissue was part of the intestine of a small animal, perhaps a rabbit.

See also HEALTH INSURANCE; HOSPITAL; PHYSICIAN.

SWAY BACK   See BACKACHE.

SWEATY PALMS (hyperhidrosis) are socially embarrassing. People with hyperhidrosis—more women than men—cannot shake hands properly. Nor can they enter a profession such as stenography or drafting, because their hands may begin sweating at any moment to such a degree that it would spoil their work.

Excessive perspiration also affects other parts of the body with concentrations of sweat glands —the soles, forehead, armpits. The condition is thought to be hereditary, and is aggravated by emotional stress, though tranquilizers and psychiatric treatment are generally not effective.

Avoiding stimulants such as coffee and tea is often helpful. Drysol, a prescription antiperspirant, may be effective. A surgical operation involves excision of the nerves associated with sweating of palms. Iontophoresis, which uses a direct current to seal off sweat glands, also can be effective.

See PERSPIRATION ODOR; SKIN DISORDERS.

SWELLING   See EDEMA.

SWIMMING POOLS have become a major source of accidents. To enjoy the use of your pool without courting danger, follow these safeguards:

"Kidproof" your pool. Youngsters under ten account for more than half the cases of drowning in pools. Nearly three out of four of these children are under age five.

Build a fence at least six feet high, with a self-locking gate. To warn off trespassers, install an automatic alarm system activated by electric eyes, foot pressure, or water movement. Dump and store a portable wading pool at the end of each use. (*Legal note:* Without such efforts to keep children out of the pool, you may be held liable for having an "attractive nuisance" if a young trespasser has an accident.)

Adult supervision is a must. "Temporarily unattended children" contributes to more drownings than any other single cause. Even an adult needs another adult around when swimming or working about the pool. Injury or exhaustion may lead to drowning.

Locate a float line in the shallow end about 1 foot before the slope begins. It will serve as a lifeline and help keep weak swimmers in shallow water. Keep on hand a floatable pole with a metal hook at one end. It will enable even a non-swimmer to pull a distressed bather to safety.

Post complete emergency instructions, with rescue techniques and telephone numbers to call. Warn of the dangers of hyperventilation. Strictly forbid horseplay, running on the deck, riding bicycles near the pool, having toys and glass objects that may cause cuts to bare feet.

Protect divers. Head injuries and neck and back fractures commonly result from dives into unsuspected shallow spots. Some cheaper pools, made of metal with plastic liners, are deep enough for a toddler to drown in, yet too shallow for an older child to dive into safely.

Depth markings on the deck need to be clear and show variations. The depth in any given section needs to be uniform. The pool should not be shallower at the sides than in the middle because an inexpert diver may not land where he aims.

Keep divers and swimmers apart. One solution if your pool gets overcrowded is to have separate swim times for children, teen-agers, adults.

Beware electricity. Have underwater and poolside lights put in only by electricians experienced in pool work.

As a further preventive against electric shock, be sure no electrical conduits are exposed anywhere near the pool area. Ban from the pool area electric appliances, including radios and television sets.

See also ACCIDENTS; DROWNING.

SYPHILIS is the most severe of all the venereal diseases and ranks as a major killer among infectious diseases.

With the introduction of penicillin it was thought that syphilis could be quickly eradicated. For many years there was a sharp decline in the incidence of the disease. In recent years, however, the number of syphilis cases has risen markedly, and health authorities now feel that it has reached epidemic proportions in the United States.

The syphilis germ is nearly always passed by an infected person through direct sexual contact, either heterosexual or homosexual. If a syphilis sore is on the mouth, the disease may be transmitted through kissing. Oral-genital contact can also transmit the disease.

The spiral-shaped bacterium, called the *spirochete,* which causes the disease, thrives in the mucous membrane tissues that line body openings such as the mouth, anus, and sex organs.

The spirochete cannot endure great temperature changes. Nor can it survive in open air for more than a few seconds. Thus, contrary to myth, it is highly unlikely that the disease can be contracted from towels, doorknobs, or toilet seats.

The stages of syphilis. Syphilis typically goes through five stages.

1. The primary stage is usually characterized by a sore called a chancre, which appears from 10 to 90 days (average 21) after exposure. This primary chancre appears where the syphilis germ first entered the body. It may look like a pimple, a blister, or an open sore. It usually does not hurt or itch.

The primary chancre is the most contagious sore of syphilis, containing millions of spirochetes. These germs can be passed to any person whose mucous membrane tissues come in contact with the sore. An untreated person can remain infectious for as long as two years.

On the other hand the primary chancre may not appear at all or it may be so small it is overlooked. In women it may be hidden inside the sex organs. It may develop in the back of the mouth or throat, or in the anal area.

The chancre can easily be ignored or mistaken for something else. Some people, not realizing they have a syphilis sore, attempt self-treatment with salves or ointments. With or without treatment the chancre will heal spontaneously within a few weeks. This means only that the spirochetes have moved away from that particular site. It does not mean that the disease is cured.

2. A symptom-free period usually lasts from two to ten weeks. It may last up to six months.

3. The secondary stage follows. By now the syphilis germ will have multiplied enough to produce symptoms throughout the body.

The victim may suffer fever, sore throat, severe headache. Skin reactions are common, ranging from a fine rash to large pox, a measles-type rash or oozing sores. Scalp hair may fall out in patches. Or the victim may suffer from sores around the mouth and lips or on the palms of the hands or soles of the feet.

Like the primary chancre secondary symptoms of syphilis may escape notice or be ignored. The rashes don't itch or sting and will always heal spontaneously. The symptoms of the secondary stages are often mistaken for something else, such as prickly heat or an allergy.

Throughout the secondary stage the person remains infectious. Anyone who has intimate contact with that person may contract the dis-

ease. At the end of this period, which may last from six months to two years, the victim is no longer able to transmit the disease to others—though it is still there, ready to do more harm.

4. A latent stage may last a few years or a lifetime. The victim may feel perfectly healthy and the disease is no longer contagious. Only a blood test can now detect its presence.

5. The late stage is characterized by severe damage to body organs.

Roughly 23 percent of people with untreated late syphilis develop crippling or fatal forms of the disease. Most common among these are heart disease, central nervous system damage, syphilitic insanity (paresis), and blindness.

A woman with untreated syphilis can infect her unborn children. Many such infants are stillborn. If alive, they often suffer from birth defects. An infant with congenital syphilis may become deaf, blind, or insane if not treated immediately after birth.

Every pregnant woman needs to be tested for syphilis as early as possible.

Tests for syphilis. Syphilis can be detected by a blood test that reveals antibodies the body produces to fight the spirochetes. These are not always found in the first blood test. If you've been exposed to syphilis, you should be retested several times over a three-month period.

The blood test for syphilis will not detect gonorrhea. It is possible to have both gonorrhea and syphilis at the same time.

Medical treatment. Syphilis can be cured in almost any stage with penicillin or other antibiotics, administered in large doses by a physician.

Don't attempt to treat syphilis by yourself. Treating chancres or rashes with salves and ointments—especially those containing penicillin—will only disguise the symptoms of the disease. Some salves, especially those containing steroids, may even speed up the production of spirochetes. Nor should you attempt to treat yourself with leftover penicillin pills. The large doses of penicillin that are necessary must be taken under a doctor's supervision.

The person treated in the early stages of syphilis can usually be completely cured. In its later stages the disease itself can be cured but any damage it has done to vital organs cannot be repaired.

There appears to be no immunization, either natural or acquired, for syphilis. The disease can be cured and contracted again—any number of times. Nor are there any preventives, although use of condoms and care in choosing sexual partners will decrease your chances of infection.

See also VENEREAL DISEASE.

SYSTEMIC LUPUS ERYTHEMATOSUS

(SLE), an inflammatory disorder of the body's connective tissues, is associated with arthritis in nine out of ten cases. It runs a chronic and irregular course, with periods of flare-up alternating with periods of improvement. The disease attacks five times more women than men and occurs most often in persons 20 to 40 years of age.

The cause is unknown, but some scientists believe it may involve a disorder in the body's production of antibodies, perhaps triggered by an infectious agent such as a virus.

SLE may appear with any number and combination of symptoms. Frequently the skin is affected. In some victims a facial rash takes the form of an open butterfly, spread over the bridge of the nose and cheeks. This was once thought to resemble the bite of a wolf (*lupus* in Latin). Other notable features include weakness, lack of energy, loss of appetite, and loss of weight. Some people develop anemia and may have a low white blood cell count. Infections are frequent. The kidney is affected early in severe cases.

The heart and blood vessels are often involved. Some SLE patients suffer from spasms of the small blood vessels at the fingertips or toes, often following a slight exposure to cold or emotional stimulation. Such exposure also causes pain and blanching of the skin. When SLE affects the heart, it may mimic the effects of either a blood clot in a coronary artery or rheumatic heart disease.

Joint symptoms are a source of considerable discomfort to almost every patient. The membranes surrounding the heart, lungs, and abdominal organs are prone to inflammation. SLE may attack the nerves, affecting the patient's thinking and movements, and may affect the brain to the point of causing neurological and mental changes.

The disease may begin in any organ. Then it may progress to any combination of organ systems or may affect only a single organ or system. In many cases it is a mild nonprogressive disease. In others episodes of active disease may be short-lived or arrested by therapy and the patient remains completely well for long periods. Frequently such patients suffer no recurrence of symptoms.

When the skin is affected, avoid exposure to the sun. Also avoid emotional stress, which can trigger flare-ups. The general measures of supportive care, including relief of pain and maintenance of good nutrition, are essential. Sufficient rest is important, especially during periods when the disease is most active.

Antimalaria and anti-inflammatory drugs have been effective in many cases. Aspirin, the most conservative of the anti-inflammatory agents, often works very well. Steroid hormones can suppress most of the disease activity. To secure the brightest future for an SLE sufferer, strict medical supervision is required.

For further information, write the SLE Foundation of America, Inc., 95 Madison Avenue, Room 1402, New York, New York 10016; or The Arthritis Foundation, 1314 Spring Street, N.W., Atlanta, Georgia 30309.

See also ARTHRITIS; STEROIDS.

TALLNESS See SHORTNESS.

TAPEWORMS are flat, ribbonlike parasites sometimes found in the intestines of human beings.

Although the common tapeworm seldom produces much physical disturbance, there may be anemia, abdominal pain, nausea, or diarrhea. Simply knowing that the worms are in the intestines often causes worry and queasiness.

Dwarf tapeworm, less than an inch long, is believed to be the most common U.S. tapeworm and is especially prevalent in the South among children. Eggs are expelled in human feces, then may infect a person's hands, food he touches, and objects he puts in his mouth. If swallowed by a human being, the eggs hatch in the person's intestines and develop into mature worms.

Beef tapeworms are from 12 to 25 feet long and sometimes have enough segments to fill a 2-quart container. Eggs are eaten by cattle grazing on moist pasture contaminated with infected feces or sewage. The eggs hatch into larvae, which lodge in the muscle tissues.

They develop a protective capsule, cysts about ¼ inch in diameter; when swallowed by man, the cysts dissolve and free the larvae. The infection is especially common among people who eat beef that is raw or merely seared.

Fish tapeworms grow up to 30 feet long. Eggs are discharged with human feces into fresh water. The embryos are eaten by small shellfish, which are then consumed by larger fish. Tapeworms are most often found in fresh-water fish (carp, perch, pike, trout, whitefish) originating in Canada, northern Michigan, and Minnesota, all endemic areas. They're also found in Alaskan salmon that may be prepared as sushi.

People may get the infection by eating raw or insufficiently cooked fish.

Beef tapeworm segments may appear in stools. Their identity should be verified by your doctor, especially because pork tapeworms give off similar segments. Dwarf and fish tapeworms don't give off segments, and their eggs can be seen only under a microscope.

Several drugs are used with success against tapeworm, but need to be administered by a physician. No patent medicine is as effective as these prescription drugs, and some OTC drugs may be toxic.

As a basic preventive don't eat raw beef, pork, or fish. Buy only meats produced under federal or equivalent inspection. Use sanitary methods for disposing of feces. Train children to wash their hands before eating or preparing food, and to keep dirty objects out of the mouth.

For other parasitic worms common in the United States see HOOKWORMS; PINWORMS; ROUNDWORMS; TRICHINOSIS. For parasites in other parts of the world, see MALARIA; SCHISTOSOMIASIS. See also ANIMAL DISEASE; INFECTIOUS DISEASE.

TATTOOS are bad news. The pigment itself can trigger an allergy. A contaminated needle can expose you to the possibility of skin infections and to hepatitis B. The hazards have prompted some dermatologists not only to warn against tattooing, but also to call for the shutting down of tattoo parlors.

Removal of tattoos is often difficult. Surgery and lasers may excise small tattoos with minimal scarring, but large tattoos usually require dermabrasion (skin planing), a technique used to remove other types of scars. Dermabrasion may leave the tattoo site hairless and lighter in color than surrounding skin. For superficial tattoos some dermatologists scrape the skin with ordinary table salt, causing an inflammation that carries away tattoo pigments.

See also HEPATITIS; SKIN DISORDERS.

TEETH AND MOUTH DISORDERS can be prevented to a great extent by taking simple measures. But most people fail to attend to their dental health. The American Dental Association estimates that more than half of all Americans go for a year or more without seeing a dentist and that fewer than a third of the population brush their teeth more than once a day.

Some results of poor dental habits: The average two-year-old has at least one decayed tooth. More than 100,000 teen-agers are completely without teeth. More than three out of four people over 60 require full or partial sets of replacement teeth.

"The majority of these dental problems would be vastly reduced with proper care, both at home and in the dental office," concludes the ADA. The association urges you to follow four basic dental health rules:

Rule 1. Keep up a program of PLAQUE CONTROL (which see), using dental floss as well as brushing regularly. This will remove the major cause of tooth decay. It will also protect you against gingivitis, a gum inflammation that can worsen into periodontal disease, the major cause of tooth loss for adults.

Rule 2. Cut down on sweet foods. Sugar contributes to decay and development of plaque.

Rule 3. See your family dentist at least twice a year, or as often as he advises. He will be able to catch many conditions early, which may, if left untreated, lead to loss of teeth or other serious conditions.

Rule 4. Drink fluoridated water—and support community-wide fluoridation in your area. Use a toothpaste containing fluoride. In areas without fluoridation protect children's teeth with prescribed fluoride drops or tablets. Even with fluoridation a dentist's fluoride treatments can be valuable.

The importance of calcium. Tooth enamel begins to form before birth and continues until the teeth are calcified at about age 13. If there is insufficient calcium during this time, the enamel may be poorly formed or pitted.

Don't give a child calcium tablets without the advice of your dentist or physician. If a child eats a balanced diet and drinks an adequate amount of milk, he will obtain all the calcium he needs. Once his teeth are completely formed and calcified and have erupted in the mouth, no more calcium is necessary for their growth. Nor will they benefit from further intake of the mineral.

It is a common fallacy that drinking lots of milk prevents tooth decay. Milk is the best dietary source of calcium, which is needed throughout life to maintain bone strength. But once decay starts, no amount of milk will repair the cavity or stop its progress.

Nor will eating foods with plenty of vitamins and minerals prevent tooth decay. A balanced diet will maintain the health of all the tissues of the body, including the gums and other mouth tissues. But be skeptical of any vitamin product promising dental benefits—no product can reverse decay once it has begun.

Care of baby teeth. It is wrong to believe, as many parents do, that it's not important to take care of baby teeth because they'll be replaced anyway.

Baby teeth maintain the shape of the jaws and the necessary space so that permanent teeth will erupt in the proper position. If a baby tooth is lost six months or more before the permanent tooth replacing it is due to erupt, a space maintainer may be needed. Like permanent teeth baby teeth are needed for chewing and speech. Decayed baby teeth may become infected and abscessed.

Many parents also believe that six-year molars

are eventually replaced by permanent teeth, so it's not necessary to take care of them. Six-year molars *are* permanent teeth, the first that appear in the mouth. They'll never be replaced, except by dentures.

Begin dental care for a child between the ages of two and three, after all baby teeth have erupted. The sooner the dentist can check for any dental problems, such as decay or faulty bite, the less need there will be for major treatment as the child grows older.

Children learn fear of the dentist from parents, brothers, sisters, friends, sometimes from TV shows. Before a child's first dental appointment speak about the dentist as a friend. Tell the child honestly what's going to happen.

Don't threaten a visit to the dentist as punishment for misbehavior. Don't offer a bribe for going. During the visit be prepared to let the child go into the treatment room alone. Let the dentist do the talking.

Choosing a dentist. Too many people have less than competent dental care. "It can be conservatively estimated that at least 15 percent [of dentists] are incompetent, dishonest or both," says the consumer-oriented Pennsylvania Insurance Department.

Neither state-licensing agencies nor dental associations police dentists adequately. It is rare for a state to revoke a dentist's license or a dental society to expel a member. Most dentists work alone in their own offices, and are not subject to monitoring by colleagues (as are practitioners who work in hospitals or groups).

How do you find a family dentist? The Pennsylvania Insurance Department recommends that you go beyond the usual advice of friends and relatives and seek out professionals who can evaluate a dentist's work.

Ask a dental specialist: an *orthodontist* (who specializes in correcting malocclusion); a *periodontist* (gum diseases); or an *endodontist* (root-canal work, dealing with the tooth's pulp interior and nerve). Such specialists are in a position to see which dentists do careful work, which take shortcuts. They are often called on to correct family dentists' mistakes.

Alternatively, phone a university dental school for names and addresses of faculty members. Faculty affiliation, even part time, is generally a sign of above-average skill and conscientiousness. If a school is far from you, ask one or more faculty members to recommend a practitioner in your area.

Before you let a dentist treat you, look for practices that indicate quality. Select only a dentist who does at least the following:

He takes your medical history. If a dentist unwittingly extracts a tooth of someone with hemophilia, the patient may bleed to death. Other medical conditions that require special dental precautions are diabetes, heart disease, and drug allergy.

He's available for emergency care. If he can't be reached through his office, he should give a phone number to be called, even if it's that of a hospital or local dental society. If he's away, he should have another dentist taking his calls.

He's prevention oriented. He educates his patients on plaque control, an indication he's out to save your teeth and money. He recalls you for a checkup once or twice a year, with dental X rays generally once a year (using proper safeguards against radiation hazards). One sign of prevention orientation: He belongs to the American Society for Preventive Dentistry.

He spells out procedures and what they'll cost. He explains alternative treatments and possible complications. He itemizes bills and is willing to give you a written estimate to avoid misunderstandings.

He inspires your confidence. "You should feel free and comfortable . . . to ask him about any aspect of your examination, treatment, or fees," advises the Pennsylvania Insurance Department. "If your dentist doesn't serve you well, drop him and find another. Worry about your teeth and not some dentist's feelings!"

He takes trouble. He polishes fillings, which not only enhances their durability and appearance but shows good dental technique. He protects you with a lead apron while taking X rays. He and his office are clean and neat. He's compassionate.

He's well organized. He works without interruption for relatively long periods. He uses such auxiliary personnel as dental hygienists and dental assistants. His equipment is up to date.

Making fees painless. Get a firm estimate before your dentist starts work. You'll avoid being shocked later on. An estimate isn't legally binding, but most dentists are reluctant to exceed it. Don't be shy about comparison shopping among equally qualified dentists.

Be wary of the dentist whose charges are unusually low. He may be skimping on essential steps or material. You're better off going to a top-notch practitioner and, if you can't afford his full charge now, arranging for payments spread over several months. Or ask about doing the same job with less expensive material. Or about having the most urgent work done now and postponing the rest—though you don't want to let a condition deteriorate, and cost more

later. If the dentist says no, cautions the ADA, "There may be good oral health reasons. . . . The dentist, not the patient, is trained in the complexities of oral health materials, and should be the final judge."

Sign up for dental insurance if it's available, usually through employers, unions, employee groups. Such plans are similar to hospital and medical insurance, and can help you meet dental costs.

Consider going to the clinic of a dental school, where dental students will work on you under the supervision of a faculty member. Fees are very low.

If you feel a dentist has overcharged you, discuss with him if an adjustment is called for. If you're not satisfied with his response, take it up with the grievance committee of the local dental society.

A case of malpractice may justify getting an attorney experienced in negligence work. Ordinarily he'll try to secure a settlement with the dentist's insurance carrier or follow through with a lawsuit.

Avoiding unqualified dentists. Beware bootleg dentistry. There are perhaps 100 prosecutions each year for the unlicensed practice of dentistry. Bootleg dentists huckster their "buy-direct-and-save" bargains via shop windows, direct mail, newspapers, magazines, telephone directories, handbills. Some even make personal solicitations in public places such as parks, beaches, bus depots, taverns.

The bootlegger may impress victims with one or two dental chairs placed in a room adjoining his laboratory facilities. He may go through the motions of a dental examination and may not hesitate to do extractions. He and his assistants are always dressed in professional white.

The public generally is not able to distinguish a bootlegger from a licensed dentist. Some bootleggers are employed by day as technicians in a law-abiding dental laboratory. At night or on weekends they make dental appliances for whatever customers they can pick up. They may operate from a kitchen, a garage, a backroom in a barbershop. But they have had no training that would enable them to actually work on a patient's mouth.

The racketeering technician most likely has had two or three years of high school and probably learned the trade from some other technician. Many of the illegal operators received their training in schools that offer "master's certificates" for a program of study lasting six weeks.

But even a few dentists take part in this illegal practice. The Chicago Dental Society estimates that some 35 to 40 renegade dentists are tied in with illegal labs. In every city where bootleg dentistry is common, you will probably find licensed dentists who front for illegal labs.

Usually the dentist occupies a separate room equipped as a dental office, but uses the same front door and the same reception room as the lab. Often he subleases his space from the lab owner and splits fees with him.

See also CANCER OF THE MOUTH; CANKER SORES; CLEFT LIP; CLEFT PALATE; COLD SORES; DENTURES; ERYTHEMA MULTIFORME; FLUORIDATION; GINGIVITIS; HAIRY TONGUE; HEMOPHILIA; MALOCCLUSION; MINERALS; MOUTH CLEFT; MOUTH ODOR; MOUTH SORES; MOUTHWASHES; PEMPHIGUS; PLAQUE; PERIODONTAL DISEASE; TOOTHBRUSHING; TOOTH DECAY; TOOTH EXTRACTION; TOOTHPASTE; TOOTH SALVAGING; TRENCH MOUTH; VITAMINS; X RAYS.

TELEVISION sets can pose fire and electric shock hazards. Major brand names are not necessarily a guarantee of safety. The Consumer Product Safety Commission found fire and shock hazards in 93,000 portable color TV sets bearing the brands Admiral, Zenith, Wards, Philco-Ford.

Television won't "ruin your eyes." But take precautions to avoid eyestrain.

Color TV. Some years ago color TV sets were found to be emitting X rays, but engineering changes have now eliminated most of the features that posed radiation problems in earlier models. According to Dr. Robert Elder, deputy director of the Food and Drug Administration's (FDA) Bureau of Radiological Health: "Color television sets manufactured after January 1970 and all older sets which have been serviced since that time will not present any radiation hazards."

Don't attempt to check your own TV set for radiation. The Public Health Service has warned that do-it-yourself kits for TV X-ray detection are usually useless.

If you are in doubt about the safety of your early-model color set, call a reliable TV repairman and ask him to make certain that your high voltage is adjusted to the manufacturer's recommended limit and that all shielding is in place.

When buying a new color TV set, check the back of the set for the tag certifying that it meets FDA standards. When your set needs servicing, call a qualified technician to ensure safe viewing.

When color TVs were first found to be emitting radiation, the surgeon general cautioned viewers to sit no closer than 6 feet from an operating set. The FDA no longer feels this precaution is necessary, stating that "there should be no significant health hazard in watching TV at a distance at which the image quality is satisfactory to the viewer."

See also RADIATION.

TEMPERATURE   See FEVER.

TENNIS ELBOW refers to several maladies involving chronic strain and inflammation of the muscle attachments at the elbow. The aching elbow results from excessive use of weak muscles in the arm. Sometimes small tears in tendons or ligaments contribute to the pain.

If you feel elbow pain after playing tennis or similarly overusing your elbow muscles, apply ice packs for 30 minutes. Hot compresses before a tennis game may ease the pain. Aspirin may also help, as may vigorously rubbing the elbow and forearm before playing.

If the pain persists, see a doctor. You may need injections of anti-inflammatory agents and anesthetic. In rare cases surgery is necessary.

While most commonly afflicting the intermediate to advanced tennis player, tennis elbow is also suffered by golfers, bowlers, even by total nonathletes. Industrial workers who perform the same motion with the wrist or elbow hundreds of times a day are also possible sufferers.

To avoid tennis elbow, wind a 4-inch strap tightly around your forearm just below the elbow before you engage in the aggravating activity. Make sure the strap does not impede blood flow.

Strengthen your wrist and forearm muscles with exercises: Put rubber bands around all your fingers and strain against them. Squeeze a tennis ball repeatedly. Grip your steering wheel tightly when you're stopped in traffic; relax and repeat. Do some stretching and bending exercises for a few minutes before the game. Warm up with some practice volleys before you start playing competitively.

Learn to swing the racket properly, stepping into the ball and using your body for power (rather than leaning back and slapping). Use your shoulder muscles as well as the force of your whole body. Backhand strokes put particular strain on elbow muscles and account for over 90 percent of sore elbows from tennis playing. A two-handed backhand stroke will help avoid tennis elbow.

Select a lighter racket. Stainless-steel rackets tend to exert the least force against the elbow in swinging.

See also SPORTS.

TESTICLE BLOWS can be painful, but are usually not dangerous. Have the victim rest on his back. Apply an ice bag or cold compress to his groin.

See a doctor if pain persists, or there's suspicion of an inguinal hernia. See also ACCIDENTS; HERNIA.

TESTICLES, UNDESCENDED See UNDESCENDED TESTICLES.

TESTICULAR CANCER See CANCER OF THE TESTICLES.

TETANUS (lockjaw)   The cut the father received from his daughter's plastic toy was tiny, so he cleansed it with antiseptic and forgot about it. Five days later his arms and legs felt sore and his jaw and neck hurt. His face assumed an unearthly leer, with the corners of his mouth drawn out, eyebrows lifted, forehead wrinkled. After four days of convulsions he was dead of tetanus.

His death was unnecessary, because routine immunization makes tetanus virtually completely avoidable.

Of every five people who develop tetanus, three die of it. It is one of the deadliest preventable diseases. More than half of deaths occur in the least protected group, people over 50.

You need to be revaccinated against tetanus every ten years. Immunization is ordinarily combined with that against diphtheria. Failure to get such boosters accounts for most adult deaths.

For a child the Public Health Service recommends initial immunization at two to three months of age with DTP, standing for diphtheria-tetanus-pertussis (whooping cough) vaccine. The second DTP comes four to eight weeks later; the third, four to eight weeks after that; a fourth, a year after the third. A booster shot is needed at five to six years, on beginning school, then at ten-year intervals thereafter.

After an injury a physician may give further tetanus protection with a booster (which is a toxoid, made up of detoxified toxin of tetanus bacteria). Whether or not you get it is largely determined by how many vaccinations you've received and when, and the cleanliness of the wound. For a large or dirty wound, you are likely to get not only the toxoid but also tetanus immune globulin (TIG), a blood fraction containing tetanus antibodies. TIG has largely replaced antitoxin made from serum drawn from a horse or cow, which has caused many allergic reactions.

The American College of Surgeons and the Public Health Service have been alerting physicians not only to give boosters every ten years—but also *not* to give them too frequently. If given over too short a period, tetanus boosters can cause arm swelling and other overdose reactions.

Though some schools and camps require it, boosters should not be administered routinely at annual intervals.

Where tetanus originates. Tetanus germs are everywhere. This infectious disease is caused by spores—reproductive cells or "seedlings"—of a bacteria common in household dust, soil, and manure. Tetanus can result when the spores enter the injured tissues through scratches, cuts, punctures, insect stings, or animal bites. It is a myth that tetanus will develop only if a puncturing nail is rusty.

Over an incubation period of five to ten days, the spores "hatch" into bacteria that release a poison that attacks the nerves, particularly in the head and neck. Among other symptoms chewing muscles grow rigid, producing "lockjaw." Muscle spasms and convulsions can be so severe that some victims have been known to fracture a vertebra.

Tetanus bacteria are anaerobic—they thrive in the absence of air. In a clean, free-bleeding cut the spores are usually washed out or may be destroyed by oxygen in the blood. But when blood flow is slight—as in a deep puncture, or when spores are insulated by imbedded debris—the tetanus bacteria may gain a hold within the body.

Half of all tetanus cases occur in people with no apparent injury, or with an injury that seemed too trivial for a doctor's care. Puncture or tear wounds, especially those that are soiled by dirt or have bits of clothing or other contaminated matter in them, require special attention by a physician.

Tetanus often follows in the wake of disaster in unimmunized populations, adding to the hazards of fire, floods, and tornadoes as well as common accidents. The risk of tetanus increases with the coming of spring and the upsurge in outdoor activities.

See also ACCIDENTS; IMMUNIZATION; INFECTIOUS DISEASE.

TETRACYCLINE See ANTIBIOTICS.

TETRALOGY OF FALLOT See CONGENITAL HEART DEFECTS.

THALASSEMIA See ANEMIA.

THROMBOPHLEBITIS is a condition in which the veins of the leg are clotted (in a state of thrombosis) and inflamed (phlebitis). Often the skin is reddened and the ankles swollen. There may be fever and leg cramps. The greatest danger is that a piece of the blood clot will break off, travel through the bloodstream, and block circulation in some vital organ, such as the heart, lung, or brain.

Thrombophlebitis most often occurs as a result of varicose veins, excessive weight, stagnation of blood, injury, and infection. It sometimes comes about as a complication of surgery, pregnancy, or heart failure. Some women have developed thrombophlebitis from wearing high, tight boots.

Anticoagulants are generally prescribed to prevent further clotting. To relieve pain and swelling, treatment may also include use of hot compresses and elastic stockings or bandages.

When you have pain, tenderness, redness, or swelling at any point on the leg, report it to your doctor. After surgery and childbirth getting up and about early cuts down the likelihood of thrombophlebitis.

If you're in bed more than five days, use a footboard, pushing on it at least 1,000 times a day. Practice breathing deeply. Frequent turning and elevating your legs may also be of benefit.

See also BLOOD CLOT; HEART DISEASE; PREGNANCY; SURGERY; VARICOSE VEINS.

THYROID DISEASE comes from a malfunctioning of the thyroid gland, one of the more common hormone disorders.

The thyroid is a small butterfly-shaped gland just in front of the windpipe at the front of the neck. Its two hormones, thyroxin and triiodothyronine, regulate the speed of most body processes and are vital for normal growth.

When the thyroid gland becomes noticeably enlarged, it is called a goiter. This condition is sometimes due to insufficient iodine in the diet. In this country the soil is deficient in iodine in the so-called goiter belt: from the Pacific Northwest through the Great Lakes basin to the Appalachians.

An absence of iodine in the soil means that food grown in those areas also lacks iodine. If you live in the goiter belt, protect yourself by using iodized salt. Eating fish, which is rich in iodine, can also help.

In parts of the country where the soil is rich in iodine, the mineral can be found in grains, some vegetables, fruits, and milk.

The thyroid gland may also become enlarged because of benign tumor, inflammation, or—very rarely—cancer. In recent years, the incidence of goiters caused by dietary deficiency of iodine has decreased dramatically, probably due to the common use of iodized salt and the availability in stores in the goiter belt of foods shipped in from iodine-rich areas of the country.

Certain kinds of goiters will often shrink or disappear with thyroid hormone medication. Iodine is rarely effective for treating (as opposed to avoiding) goiters. Sometimes surgery is necessary.

Excess thyroid hormone. Goiters may also be associated with too much thyroid hormone, a condition called hyperthyroidism, which sometimes seems to be brought on by emotional stress.

The symptoms can be alarming: heart palpitation, extreme nervous irritability, sleeplessness, high blood pressure, sharp weight loss, protruding eyes, hand tremors. Sufferers often fear they are going crazy or have heart disease or both.

With all the body's processes speeded up, an extra burden is put on the heart. In people whose hearts are already weak, hyperthyroidism can be extremely serious, even fatal.

People with long-term, severe hyperthyroidism may experience a thyroid crisis or storm. All their symptoms suddenly worsen, sometimes because of injury or illness. They frequently also suffer delirium, high fever, rapid and irregular heartbeat, sweating, vomiting, dehydration, shock. This condition, now rare with better control of hyperthyroidism, is fatal in two out of three cases.

Medication may be prescribed that interferes with production of thyroid hormones. This leads to long-term or permanent remission in some people, but others may have to take the drugs all their lives or switch to an alternative treatment.

For some people—mainly those for whom medication is ineffective—surgery may be advised. Part of the thyroid gland is removed, reducing thyroid hormone production.

Many patients are treated with radioactive iodine, which reduces thyroid hormone production to normal levels or below. This kind of therapy is usually reserved for adults and should not be used during pregnancy.

Insufficient thyroid hormone. Too little thyroid hormone is called hypothyroidism. People with this condition—termed myxedema—may be overweight, have coarse skin, hoarseness, and memory loss. They may suffer chronic fatigue, muscle cramps, intolerance to cold, and a general slowing down of physical and mental activity.

In a newborn infant hypothyroidism is called cretinism. The child is sluggish, pale, with subnormal temperature, constipation, and coarse skin. His appetite is poor and he fails to grow properly. He may have a goiter. Untreated, he will become both physically and mentally retarded. Women who take iodine-containing drugs during pregnancy are somewhat more likely to have babies with hypothyroidism.

The condition is occasionally caused by the

malfunction of the pituitary gland or by disorders of hormone-regulating mechanisms. The most common causes of hypothyroidism are the destruction of thyroid gland function by an autoimmune process and as a result of treatment for the opposite condition, hyperthyroidism (too much thyroid hormone).

The symptoms of hypothyroidism often improve dramatically with taking thyroid hormone in the form of pills.

Not a weight-reduction drug. Thyroid hormone is generally not recommended for weight reducing. Only a small fraction of the population is overweight because of thyroid deficiency.

For most overweight people thyroid hormone is useless and, in fact, dangerous. Particularly dangerous are pills containing a combination of thyroid hormone and digitalis, a heart stimulant.

Thyroid disorders may be a cause of INFERTILITY (which see).

See also OVERWEIGHT.

TIC DOULOUREUX (trigeminal neuralgia) is a disease characterized by severe facial pain, usually occurring in attacks that last one or two minutes. The pain affects the trigeminal facial nerve, which has branches reaching to the skin of the eye, nose, and cheek.

During an attack the victim's face may contract as the pain hits in searing, agonizing stabs. This "tic" and the pain are the only symptoms. The condition may have an emotional component—sufferers are often tense and under stress.

Victims are usually over 50. The pain is almost always on just one side of the face.

An attack is usually precipitated when a hypersensitive spot, the trigger point, is touched, sometimes by as little as a smile or a breeze. Trigger points are most frequently on the lower lip, the side of the nose, the mouth, or the cheek. Shaving, talking, washing one's face, even eating, may sometimes trigger an attack.

Attacks tend to come closer together as the disease progresses, until a victim may have several attacks an hour throughout the day. Then the condition may go into remission for several weeks or months.

The drug carbamazepine has been used successfully to relieve and prevent attacks. But it can have severe side effects, such as blood disorders and liver damage, and cannot be tolerated by some people. It should not be taken by pregnant women.

Other drugs or combinations of drugs may afford relief. But analgesics such as aspirin are rarely effective.

Alcohol injections directly into the nerve may work, sometimes permanently. If necessary, the root of the nerve can be cut surgically, which usually brings permanent relief, but often leaves a feeling of numbness.

TICKLISHNESS, an oversensitivity of the surface nerves, is no joke to a busy parent or doctor who needs to touch to perform a procedure.

People can't tickle themselves. So let the ticklish person take charge of the touching.

Suppose you're ticklish and a doctor needs to palpate your abdomen. You would put your hand on top of his, and push down at his command. When he is checking for a hernia, have him hold his finger motionless and allow you to move onto it.

TICKS feed entirely on blood. Their bites can spread Rocky Mountain spotted fever and tularemia. A toxin in the saliva of some ticks causes a paralysis that can be fatal if the tick is not removed before the muscles that control breathing are affected. Ticks also are responsible for Colorado tick fever, a condition marked by high fever and internal bleeding.

These arachnids—wingless eight-legged creatures related to spiders—are flat, usually brown, and about 1/3 inch long. As a tick feeds, it begins to swell. After several hours it is about the size and shape of a jellybean.

Most bites occur in woods and brush, and through contact with tick-infested sheep, cattle, dogs, and rabbits. Although ticks cling tenaciously, their bite is painless and may go unnoticed. Ticks feed for several days, and the longer one is attached, the greater the chance it will transmit an infectious disease. Fatalities in tick paralysis usually result from the tick's being hidden in long hair.

Removing a tick. To remove a tick touch a lighted match to its rear. Or use a lighted cigarette or heated paper clip (see illustration). The heat will cause it to remove its embedded head. Shake or tweeze onto a piece of paper. Then crush it and throw it away.

Don't try to yank it out. You may break off its mouth parts, leaving them embedded in the skin. And don't use chemicals like gasoline or alcohol. These will kill the tick, leaving its head embedded.

Take care not to crush the tick, which is fragile when engorged. If its head is embedded, you may inject yourself with dangerous material. If smeared on the skin, it may cause infection.

After removing the tick, cleanse the bite with soap and water. Scrub your hands and any tweezer or other implement you used. Use the foregoing procedure also to remove ticks from animals.

In tick-infested areas avoid sitting or sleeping

HOW TO REMOVE A BITING TICK

Don't yank or squeeze! Imbedded head may infect you

1. Touch heat to rear
   Use hot metal, match, cigarette

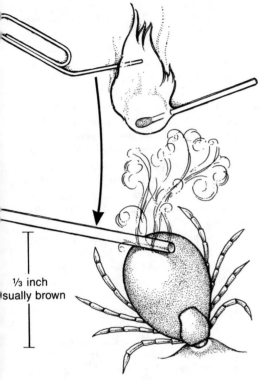

⅓ inch
usually brown

2. Shake it off and crush it
3. Check scalp, body, clothes for others
   Be alert for tick-borne fever, paralysis

on the ground. Protect your head with a hat or hood. Wear long sleeves, preferably with the cuffs tied over the top of gloves. Tie trouser legs over the top of boots.

After spending time in woods or brush, check your clothing and body, especially the scalp. When children play outdoors in wooded places, inspect them from top to toe at least once, preferably twice a day.

As a general preventive follow precautions for controlling insects. Keep your lawn closely cut and the yard well policed. Clearing vegetation from an area eliminates most ticks. Filling chinks and cracks in walls helps keep them out of the house.

Dogs and cats that run at large in tick-infested areas may bring ticks into the house. If it is too difficult to inspect your pet often, learn your lo-cal tick season from your health department. For the duration keep the animal either in or out of the house.

The hazard of tick infestation from pets is reduced if you dust them frequently with a powder containing 0.75 percent to 1 percent rotenone. Destroy the bedding of an infested animal, and treat a dog house with rotenone powder.

See also ANIMAL DISEASE; INSECTS; ROCKY MOUNTAIN SPOTTED FEVER; TULAREMIA.

TINNITUS refers to noises in the ears. In different people—and in the same person at different times—it can range from barely audible to quite loud. Most people with tinnitus report a high-pitched ringing; others a buzzing, hissing, roaring, or other sound. The sound may be constant or may come and go.

Tinnitus is often caused by exposure to loud sounds. It also can be a symptom of many conditions, accompanying virus infections, allergies, and blood and circulatory disorders. Some medications—such as aspirin or quinine—may cause it. Brain cancer, meningitis, and head injuries can be implicated, as can diseases of the nervous system that involve the auditory nerve.

Mild tinnitus is common. The American Tinnitus Association estimates that 9 million people have it severely, making it one of the major unattended medical problems.

Tinnitus is usually accompanied by hearing loss. In some cases a hearing aid may help to mask the ringing by amplifying outside sounds.

Tinnitus often disappears when the offending drug, infection, hypertension, or other condition is removed or brought under control. Tranquilizers can relieve symptoms and help the sufferer sleep better.

Another way to get to sleep: Use a transistor radio with an ear attachment. FM static can mask the bothersome sounds. Tinnitus sufferers should avoid loud sounds.

A promising new development is a tinnitus masker, a hearing aid–like device that produces a noise that may obscure the tinnitus.

For more information about tinnitus, write to:

American Tinnitus Association
P.O. Box 5
Portland, Oregon 97207

See also HEARING LOSS.

TIREDNESS See FATIGUE.

TONGUE CANCER See CANCER OF THE MOUTH.

TONSILLITIS is an inflammation of tonsil tissue, which consists of several sets of spongy, glandular masses arranged in a ring in the throat and behind the nose. In most cases surgery—formerly the cure-all for tonsil problems—is unwise and unnecessary.

The tonsils are a pair of small almond-shaped structures on each side of the throat just behind and above the level of the tongue. When infected, they become greatly enlarged and may almost meet in the middle of the throat.

The adenoids are a mass of tonsil tissue located above and behind the soft palate, where the nose and mouth come together. When infected, they may grow large enough to block the flow of air into the throat from the nostrils and thus force one to breathe through the mouth. They may also cause ear infections leading to loss of hearing from accumulation of fluid in the middle ear.

Tonsils act as a defense against infections that invade the body through the nose and mouth. They are part of the lymphatic system of the body, a protective system whose cells attack and literally devour bacteria. They frequently get involved in respiratory disease such as colds and sore throat and may themselves become overwhelmed by infection. Not every swelling of the tonsils is tonsillitis, however. They often swell, then subside without being seriously infected.

Tonsillitis strikes as a sore throat with a fever as high as 106° F. There is a washed-out feeling, headache and other pains, rapid pulse, and chill. Inside the mouth the tonsils are fiery red and swollen. After a couple of days of soreness the tonsils have white spots on them. Adults and older children tend to suffer more than younger ones.

An even worse kind of tonsil infection is quinsy, an abscess that forms behind the tonsil. It usually has to be lanced and drained, lest it burst and the pus find its way into the lungs, where pneumonia and other severe complications can develop.

Unnecessary surgery. Tonsils and adenoids are now only rarely removed. Medical opinion has undergone a turnabout since not long ago when every child's tonsils were removed after he had a couple of sore throats.

Now acute tonsillitis responds well to antibiotics, largely rendering unnecessary the operation called T & A, which stands for tonsillectomy (surgical removal of the tonsils) and adenoidectomy (removal of the adenoids). T & A is a difficult surgical procedure and with anesthesia and postoperative complications results in 100 to 300 deaths in the United States each year.

Moreover, hospitalization is a traumatic experience for most children. Many otolaryngologists refuse to do T & As on children under eight except when it's unavoidable.

Don't try to talk a doctor into removing your child's tonsils because you believe in any of these misconceptions:

"Tonsils are useless. Why not yank them out?" Medical scientists continue to report new evidence that the tonsils are a valuable part of the body's defense mechanism against invading germs and viruses.

"They're swollen." That may be their normal size. The tonsils attain maximum size in normal children at about age 12, making them disproportionately larger than other body parts. Mere enlargement is no basis for surgery.

"My child is always sick." Chances are he's in a normal stage of growth, irrespective of his tonsils. Before a child can build up his own defense system of antibodies against infectious-disease agents, he must be exposed to them. So a certain number of mild respiratory diseases must be expected during a child's early years. These illnesses are likely to increase when a child starts school and is exposed to a number of new infectious agents.

"He'll be healthier with them out." It's a myth that a T & A makes a child less susceptible to colds, sore throat, and other respiratory diseases. Nor does it relieve an allergy such as asthma.

When is a T & A called for? Tonsils and adenoids are removed when they are so enlarged that they obstruct breathing, distort speech, or cause swallowing difficulties with weight loss and poor nutrition. Tonsils are also removed in the rare case of a malignant tumor. Doctors may also recommend surgery for chronic, severe, stubborn tonsillitis that doesn't clear, or a history of repeated quinsy.

Tips for care following T & A: After the operation the patient's throat will be sore for perhaps a week. An earache may last about a day.

Pain in swallowing can be relieved by pressing the thumbs against both ears while swallowing. Serve soft foods—custards, soups, ice cream—and bland drinks (tart beverages like orange and tomato juice burn the throat).

Call a doctor at once if any bleeding occurs, if temperature is more than 101° F by mouth, or if pain keeps getting more intense. Also phone the doctor if the child cannot sleep, is restless, or refuses all fluids or nourishment.

If you notice bleeding, tell the child to spit out the blood gently and lie quietly. Administer a cold cloth or ice pack around his throat. If you are alarmed and can't reach the doctor, take your child to the hospital emergency room.

In a T & A you can tell a child his hospital stay will usually be only a day or two. Within a week after his operation he can look forward to playing as usual and going back to school. The older child may take longer, because his operation covers a larger healing area.

See also HOSPITALIZING CHILDREN; INFECTIOUS DISEASE; RESPIRATORY DISEASE; SURGERY.

TOOLS that use electric power need safeguards against electric shock. Look for the safety seal of the Power Tool Institute, a sign that the manufacturer claims to have inspected a tool for shock hazards.

Even with such a seal check all tools and attachments for dangers. One researcher shook a new wire wheel brush—and found it shedding many loose wires and metal fragments that would have flown off at first use under power.

For protection against eye injuries use a hood-type wheel guard when operating a grinding machine. Where fragments may fly, wear goggles or a face shield, or eyeglasses made of safety glass.

Do without a tool until you can afford a safe one. Cheaper models often break or dull quickly, which makes them slip and cause cuts. Tools and chemicals for arts and crafts pose a variety of hazards.

Hand tools. Don't use excessive force on a hand tool. Other tips on avoiding accidents with hand tools:

Chisels. Grind the head of a cold chisel frequently to prevent excessive mushrooming. When using a wood chisel, always work cut away from your body. Use a large enough chisel for the job. Never try to catch a chisel if it falls. Store chisels immediately after using them—they're too sharp to be left around.

Files. Don't use a file without a handle. Don't use a file for a pry, as it is brittle and breaks easily.

Hammers. Use a machinists' hammer for machine work and a claw hammer for carpentry. When using a sledge or maul, look behind you before you begin your backswing.

Pry bars. Be sure your bite is secure by applying a slight pressure at first. Then check your own balance before you exert full force. This will prevent you from falling in case the pry slips.

Saws that are sharp and free of rust are less likely to bind or jump. When using wood saws and hacksaws, start cuts by guiding the blade with your thumb. Thereafter keep fingers out of the saw's path.

Screwdrivers. Use the right size and type for the job. Hold the work on a surface rather than the palm of your hand—the screwdriver may slip and injure you. File a screwdriver when nec-

essary to prevent slipping. Don't hammer on one as you would a chisel or use one for a pry.

Wrenches. In using any wrench it is better to pull than push. If necessary to push, use your open palm. When using an adjustable wrench, exert pressure toward the movable jaw.

Lest you slug yourself, stand to one side when pulling down on a wrench above your head. Don't hammer on wrenches or use a pipe extension. Instead use a proper-size wrench.

See also ACCIDENTS; ARTS AND CRAFTS; AXES; KNIVES; MACHINES; MOWERS; SCISSORS.

TOOTHACHE may be excruciatingly painful because the inflammatory process is confined by the hard tissues of the tooth or within the jawbone. Meanwhile, decay is working its way toward the pulp, which contains the nerve.

Consult a dentist even if the pain goes away. A toothache is commonly a warning that something is seriously wrong deep within the tooth. If the pain stops after a few days, it may mean that the pulp and nerve are destroyed by the disease.

Until you see a dentist, you may find some relief in rubbing oil of cloves ointment on the painful area. Taking aspirin may help. But *swallow* the aspirin. Don't use the home remedy of putting aspirin on the gum next to an aching tooth—it can burn the tissue.

A toothache only rarely means it is too late to save the tooth. Generally prompt treatment can bring relief without extraction.

See a dentist if heat or cold ever causes pain in a tooth, for this may be an early sign of an impending ache or may signal a gum or tooth disorder.

Toothbrushing or cold may trigger painful spasms, because of hypersensitive teeth. Youngsters and adults over 35 are most affected by dental hypersensitivity. The condition is possibly caused by recession of the gums—often involving periodontal disease—or by tooth erosion or improper brushing. In youngsters hypersensitive teeth may be due to inadequate development of the protective enamel.

A dentist can diagnose the cause of tender teeth in minutes. With the aid of special toothpaste, you can usually relieve the sensitivity until the underlying condition clears up.

See also TEETH AND MOUTH DISORDERS.

TOOTHBRUSHING is an essential part of plaque control for prevention of teeth and mouth disorders. The best manual toothbrush, advises the ADA, ordinarily has:

A comparatively small head (1–1¼ inches long, 5/16–3/8 inches wide) to let you clean every surface of every tooth. Young children need smaller brushes than adults.

A flat brushing surface with soft, end-rounded bristles.

Firm, resilient bristles. Too stiff a brush may not get into crevices, and can scratch teeth and cause gums to bleed. Buy a new brush as soon as it becomes bent or frayed, which makes the brush ineffective.

Brush at least once a day with fluoride toothpaste (see illustration). It's better to brush more often. But brushing alone, without practicing plaque control, won't prevent decay.

Because bacteria act so rapidly, to get results you need to brush thoroughly within minutes after eating—not very practical for most people.

Moreover, you'd have to be an expert brusher to remove every bit of plaque and debris. Brushing first thing in the morning makes the mouth feel clean, but does little to prevent decay.

Electric toothbrushes. The conventional toothbrush, powered by hand, can be the most effective cleaning device if used properly.

But, for the person who's not inclined to devote adequate time and effort to oral hygiene, an electric toothbrush may do a better job. A motor in the handle drives the brush section in short strokes as fast as 2,000 times a minute.

Several studies with children have shown that the electric brush produces superior dental cleanliness, at least partly because the gadget makes children more interested in caring for

ONE GOOD WAY TO BRUSH YOUR TEETH

1. Hold brush flat on teeth
   Press bristles against gum

2. Rotate brush toward teeth
   Sweep from gum to edge
   Repeat 4–5 times

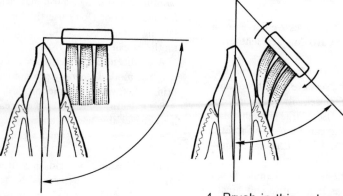

4. Brush in this order

3. Clean chewing surfaces

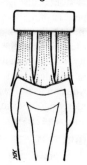

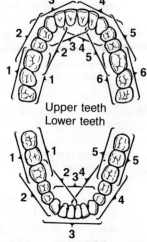

Upper teeth
Lower teeth

Do outside, inside,
and chewing surfaces

their teeth. Adults report getting a pleasant tingle in their gums and a feeling of cleaner, more attractive teeth.

See also PLAQUE; TEETH AND MOUTH DISORDERS.

TOOTH DECAY (dental caries) can best be avoided through control of plaque.

Bacterial decay of teeth is believed to be the most common single ailment of man. Studies have found decayed teeth in 50 percent of youngsters two years of age, 96 percent of those of high school age. The ADA estimates Americans have 700 million unfilled cavities, enough to keep practicing dentists working full time for two and a half years on fillings alone.

Contrary to popular belief, teeth do not decay because they are soft. There is little difference in the hardness of people's teeth, and this difference has no bearing on tooth decay.

Nor is it true that pregnancy increases tooth decay, or that a mother loses a tooth for every child. If tooth decay increases during pregnancy, it generally is because of poor mouth hygiene or increased eating of sweets.

What causes decay. Decay results from a complex chain of events. The chief factors are mouth bacteria, food, dental plaque, and a susceptible tooth surface.

The bacteria thrive on food debris in the mouth, breaking it down and producing acid. The dental plaque—a combination of saliva components and other substances (including some bacteria and food debris) that adheres tenaciously to the teeth—collects the acid and holds it against tooth surfaces. The acid then attacks the tooth surface with varying degrees of success, dependent on the tooth's susceptibility to decay.

At first glance bacteria seem the most obvious target in this chain. The public is attuned to disease prevention through germ control, and indeed dental researchers are seeking to develop a vaccine against tooth decay. Attacking the bacteria directly is the theory on which much of dentifrice advertising is based.

But the mouth harbors such extremely large numbers of different acid-producing bacteria that it is impossible to immobilize or kill sufficient numbers of them to significantly reduce acid formation. No antiseptic can kill all the germs in the mouth, or prevent the residue from multiplying rapidly.

Many dental researchers feel that even if it were possible to reduce oral bacteria significantly, it would be harmful because some bacteria in the mouth limit the growth of fungi and other harmful microorganisms.

Food debris is a more practical target. The problem here is timing. Acid production begins as soon as food gets in your mouth. The more food debris there is and the longer it remains in your mouth, the more acid the bacteria can produce.

Proper toothbrushing can help prevent decay, especially if used with dental floss, fluoridated water, and fluoridated toothpaste. Mouthwashes do little or nothing to prevent decay—plain water is generally as effective for rinsing food away.

Eliminating carbohydrates. Carbohydrate foods (candy, soda, sweetened cereals, cookies, etc.) cause a great deal of the problem—they are an ideal medium for bacterial action, and acid builds up in the mouth with great rapidity after they are eaten.

The Eskimos in Alaska had very little tooth decay until they began eating the type of sugar-heavy diet most Americans eat. Now the Eskimos have about the same rate of decay as other Americans. Public Health Service dentists say they can almost tell how close an Eskimo lives to the white man's trading post by looking at his teeth.

For people whose teeth decay readily, some dental scientists suggest this diet adjustment: Stop eating between meals. Repeated eating during the day adds to the total time of rapid acid formation.

Also avoid foods that will stay in your mouth for a long time. Hard candies and chewing gum are prime examples. The longer the bacteria have to act on a food—especially a sweet—the more acid will be formed. Also, the stickier the sweet (e.g., raisins, taffy, caramels), the longer it takes to leave the mouth, increasing its potential for causing decay.

At one time it was believed that chewy "detergent" foods like firm fresh fruits and raw vegetables would help keep your mouth clean from being forced over the teeth and gums. Dental research has disproved this effect. These foods do not remove plaque. On the other hand they are good for the diet, since they are likely to be low in sugar and don't stick to the teeth as much as soft foods.

To help prevent tooth decay in babies and young children, wipe your child's teeth and gums with a damp washcloth or gauze pad after each feeding. When all the child's primary teeth have grown in (at about two or two and a half), teach the child to brush and floss. Make an appointment for a dental checkup.

Never allow your child to go to bed with a bottle of milk or a sweetened liquid. During the day saliva helps wash some of the liquid out of the mouth. But at night or nap time the saliva flow decreases, and the liquid pools around the teeth, attacking them with acids and causing serious decay. Dentists call this the "bottle mouth syndrome."

The introduction of the chemical fluorine into drinking water is the most promising means of building decay-resistant tooth surfaces, but it has met with bitter opposition in many communities.

See also FLUORIDATION; PLAQUE; TEETH AND MOUTH DISORDERS.

TOOTH EXTRACTION ought to be avoided if at all possible. "Losing your teeth should be viewed as a disaster," warns the consumer-minded Pennsylvania Insurance Department.

You are often well rid of wisdom teeth that erupt diseased or wedged against other teeth. Also, extraction is often warranted to correct faulty bite, or in cases of periodontal disease, if the tooth has lost its supporting tissue.

But otherwise the more teeth you lose, the more you are susceptible to other teeth and mouth problems. Any tooth that is extracted must be replaced to keep teeth from shifting and loosening.

Beware the family dentist who's quick on the draw. In most cases when you have a toothache, cavity, or infection, teeth can be salvaged, perhaps through root-canal therapy. A competent family dentist can handle most such problems. A difficult case may require treatment by a board-certified endodontist, a specialist in diseases of the pulp and nerve of the inner tooth.

Before consenting to an extraction, get a consultation with either an endodontist or a board-certified oral surgeon, who specializes in the extraction of teeth and surgery of the mouth and jaws. If your family dentist argues against such a consultation, you need a new family dentist.

After an extraction. Extraction wounds usually heal quickly if you take simple precautions. Reduce your activity as much as possible for several hours. This helps reduce bleeding and permits the formation of a clot in the tooth socket, which is necessary for healing.

Much pain and swelling can be prevented if you apply cold compresses to the affected side of your face immediately after the extraction. Use an ice bag or cold moist cloth for 15 minutes of every hour, continued for several hours. Swelling itself is rarely cause for concern, and don't be surprised by a sudden rise in pain as the anesthetic wears off.

Don't rinse your mouth during the rest of the day. The blood clot needs time to form and should not be disturbed. After the first day use warm saltwater (1/2 teaspoon salt in 1 glass warm water) to rinse your mouth gently after meals. Continue toothbrushing as usual. Good oral hygiene will help prevent infection.

Some oozing of blood is normal for a day after an extraction. If flow is heavier, bite on a fresh tea bag—the tannic acid may help stanch the wound. Or gently wipe the blood from the wound with a clean gauze pad. Place another clean, folded gauze pad directly on the bleeding spot. Close the teeth tightly, pressing the pad against the wound. Maintain pressure for about 30 minutes. Repeat if necessary. If bleeding persists, notify your dentist.

To help the healing process try not to miss a meal after the extraction. You may eat soft, nutritious foods—soft-boiled eggs, chopped meat, custards, milk, soup, foods mixed in a blender—without disturbing the clot.

Eat often for the first few days. Add solid foods as soon as they can be chewed comfortably.

See also DENTURES; TEETH AND MOUTH DISORDERS.

TOOTHPASTE containing fluoride is your best bet—it helps strengthen tooth enamel against tooth decay in young people under 25, whose teeth are still developing. There is some evidence that fluoride toothpaste can benefit older people as well by slowing down the rate of decay.

Best choices are toothpastes accepted by the ADA Council on Dental Therapeutics as being useful in preventing decay. Included are Aim, Colgate MFP, Crest (mint and regular), Aqua-Fresh, and Macleans Fluoride. Look for the ADA seal on the toothpaste.

But even these dentifrices are only aids to combating decay—they are not cure-alls, warns the ADA council. They must be used in conjunction with plaque control, proper diet, and regular visits to a dentist. They will not substitute for fluoridation of community water and are less effective than a dentist's application of fluoride on a child's teeth.

No other special ingredient of dentifrices has therapeutic merit. Ammonium compounds, urea, chlorophyll derivatives, "antienzyme" compounds, antibiotics—the council has found not one of these highly touted additives has any value in preventing or controlling decay. Nor has the council seen evidence justifying claims for Sensodyne, Thermodent, or any other dentifrice promoted for relief of pain from hypersensitive teeth.

The ADA has campaigned for many years

against deceptive advertising; they emphasize that:

- No toothpaste can take the place of regular toothbrushing.
- No toothpaste can permit unrestricted consumption of carbohydrates.
- No toothpaste will prevent oral disease.
- No toothpaste gives all-day protection with one brushing.
- No toothpaste provides an "invisible shield" giving unlimited protection.
- No toothpaste can prevent "bad breath," which may be due to diseases of the nose, sinuses, lungs, or gastrointestinal tract.

Abrasives may be too harsh. Individuals vary markedly in their need for an abrasive in a dentifrice. Many people can maintain their teeth free from stains by using a suitable brush and plain water. If only a slight degree of abrasion is necessary to keep teeth from staining, ordinary baking soda (sodium bicarbonate) or powdered table salt will usually suffice.

The ADA warns that dentifrices containing harsh abrasives may be dangerous. Generally speaking, tooth powders are more abrasive than toothpastes.

Virtually no popularly sold brand of toothpaste is abrasive enough to injure enamel, the hard surface of normal teeth. But some dentifrices may injure dentin, a softer layer of the tooth just under the gum. As you age, gums may recede, exposing dentin at the neck of the tooth to possible damage by abrasion. After many brushings with abrasives, the teeth tend to show tiny notches, which harbor food debris and thus promote decay. And teeth that are worn away leave the nerves more exposed to pain from heat and cold.

Crest is a low-abrasive fluoride toothpaste accepted by the ADA. Other less-abrasive toothpastes include Craig-Martin, Listerine, and Pepsodent. Toothpastes that are advertised as "whitening" or "brightening" teeth are apt to be more abrasive. Use only special cleaners for dentures.

Use dental stain removers with special caution. Unlike ordinary dentifrices these liquids, powders, and pastes claim they remove tobacco and other types of stains, as well as bad taste and odor.

One type of remover uses hydrogen peroxide to bleach out stains. At best, notes the ADA, this procedure is "ordinarily time-consuming and laborious." While a dilute solution (up to 3 percent) may be safe if used occasionally, peroxide in any strength should not be used exten-

sively or on a sustained basis. It can cause black, hairy tongue, alter tooth enamel, and change the bacterial balance of the mouth.

The National Better Business Bureau warns that dental stain removers sold directly to the public should be advertised as clearly limited to simple superficial or surface stains. In no case are they appropriate for regular or sustained use. Difficult or deep stains cannot be removed by such treatment and often do not respond even to professional care. In general, such products should be used only under a dentist's recommendation or supervision.

See also PLAQUE; TEETH AND MOUTH DISORDERS.

TOOTH SALVAGING Contrary to popular belief, a tooth need not necessarily be lost if it's broken, if its nerve dies, even if it's knocked out. Dental procedures can often salvage such teeth or save them from extraction.

If a tooth is accidentally knocked out of your jaw, immediately place it in a glass of milk. Or transport it in your mouth, where it can receive its natural bath of saliva. Bring it to a dentist at once. Don't clean it, for this may remove vital tissue. The sooner the tooth is replanted in the jaw, the better the chance that it will reattach to its bony socket for long-term if not permanent retention.

If you suspect a tooth is cracked or broken, get to a dentist immediately. Cracked or broken teeth can become discolored and infected.

You may need to see an endodontist. He is a specialist in the branch of dentistry concerned with diseases of the tooth pulp, the soft interior tissue containing nerves and blood vessels. Deep decay or injury may cause the pulp to become infected, generally causing toothache if infection hits the nerve. When the infected pulp is removed, healing can take place much as in any other living part of the body.

If infection spreads to the pulp within the tooth root—the root canal—it may reach the jawbone. In severe cases—when bone has been destroyed or the root tip damaged—it may be necessary to trim the tip of the root and remove the diseased tissue, after which the bone will grow back normally.

When a tooth is fractured and the nerve or pulp of the tooth is exposed or dies, the nerve is ordinarily removed and the remainder of the tooth restored to normal function. The tooth will not be "dead," because it has another source of blood and nerves by way of tissues which attach the tooth to its socket. These will continue to function even though the pulp is removed.

A tooth sometimes darkens after root canal

treatment. It sometimes can be brought back to its original color through a bleaching process. The ADA estimates that upward of 90 percent of teeth treated endodontically last as long as other teeth not requiring this treatment. If the bone has been infected, success is somewhat less sure, depending on your health and your body's ability to repair the damaged bone.

Root-canal treatment of a single tooth can cost enough to make some patients question its value. However the alternative is extraction and replacement, which is generally even costlier. Where there's a choice, dental authorities prefer endodontic treatment, feeling that artificial substitutes rarely function quite so well as natural teeth.

See also TEETH AND MOUTH DISORDERS.

TORNADOES Take shelter in a basement in the corner closest to the oncoming tornado. This is usually the southwest corner, since tornadoes most often move in a northeasterly direction. You thus gain protection against the tornado's action on the walls, which first burst outward and then are blown away.

If you are caught in the open, run at a right angle to the oncoming twister's path. Find a hollow or sheltered place in the earth, such as a ditch, creek, or riverbank. Cover your face with any kind of cloth to prevent choking from dust.

Warning signs preceding tornadoes are dark, thick storm clouds; heavy rain or hail; a tremendous roaring or rushing sound like that of several trains speeding through a tunnel. When local weather forecasts include tornado warnings, keep your first aid supplies nearby.

See also ACCIDENTS; ELECTRIC SHOCK; FIRE; FLOODS; FOOD POISONING; WATER CONTAMINATION.

TOURNIQUET Never use a tourniquet to control bleeding—unless, to save a life, you must sacrifice a limb.

Once a first aid standby, the tourniquet has fallen out of favor, for it cuts off the blood supply with the risk of gangrene. Use only in a rare

ONLY IF A TOURNIQUET'S A MUST

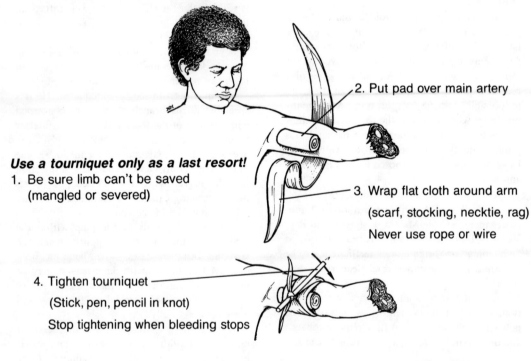

2. Put pad over main artery

Use a tourniquet only as a last resort!
1. Be sure limb can't be saved
   (mangled or severed)

3. Wrap flat cloth around arm
   (scarf, stocking, necktie, rag)
   Never use rope or wire

4. Tighten tourniquet
   (Stick, pen, pencil in knot)
   Stop tightening when bleeding stops

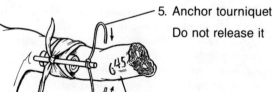

5. Anchor tourniquet
   Do not release it

6. Mark time tourniquet was applied

case when bleeding in an arm or leg cannot be controlled in any other way, or when a limb is severed or so mangled it will probably have to be amputated in any case.

If you have no alternative but to use a tourniquet, follow these precautions (see illustration):

Use padding under the tourniquet.

Use a flat material for the tourniquet, about 2 inches wide (a tie, stocking, scarf). Don't use anything that will injure the skin, like rope or wire.

On the victim's forehead mark with pen, blood, soot—anything—the code letters *TK* and the time the tourniquet was applied. Don't cover the tourniquet—and point it out to the doctor or ambulance attendant.

Making a tourniquet. To apply a tourniquet place it between the injury and the heart. Leave a small amount of normal skin between the wound and the material. Wrap the tourniquet cloth tightly twice around the limb and tie a half knot.

Place a short, stout stick, pencil, or similar article on the half knot and tie two full knots to secure it. Twist the stick to tighten the tourniquet until the flow of blood ceases. Anchor the stick in place.

Don't loosen or remove the tourniquet once it's been applied. Doctors formerly recommended loosening it several times an hour to let blood flow through the limb. But this practice lost more lives than it saved: When the tourniquet is loosened, toxins from the injured limb get into the victim's circulation and can cause a condition called "tourniquet shock," which can be fatal. The tourniquet should be loosened or removed only by a physician who is prepared to treat the tourniquet shock.

See also ACCIDENTS; BLEEDING.

TOXIC SHOCK SYNDROME   See MENSTRUATION.

TOXOPLASMOSIS is an animal disease that is particularly dangerous for pregnant women. The infection—caused by the one-celled toxoplasma parasite—may injure the unborn baby's nervous system and cause other birth defects, especially eye damage. It has been held responsible for miscarriages and stillbirths.

In most cases there are no symptoms and an infected woman might be unaware of her exposure. However some people with the disease react with symptoms like those of colds or mononucleosis: a low fever, malaise, muscle pain, moderate anemia, and swollen lymph nodes. Liver function may be slightly abnormal. The disease usually runs its course in a few weeks. In rare cases chronic toxoplasmosis can cause severe damage to the heart, eyes, and central nervous system.

An estimated 30 percent of adults in this country have had the disease, usually without knowing it. A blood test for toxoplasma antibodies can determine whether you've had it. In that case you are presumed to be immune. There is no vaccine to prevent it.

Toxoplasmosis is common in cats, dogs, cattle, swine, sheep, rabbits, and some domestic birds. One way the organisms are thought to be transmitted to man is through uncooked or undercooked meat.

The disease is prevalent in cats, and transmitted easily through their feces.

Warning for pregnant women: If you've been eating raw meat or have been in close contact with cats during pregnancy, have a blood test to see if you've had the disease. If not take the following precautions:

Cook all meat to an internal temperature of at least 140° F. In restaurants specify that you want your meat well done. Never eat raw meat.

Don't feed your cat raw or rare meat. Commercial cat food is best. Keep the cat from hunting mice, birds, or coming into contact with other cats.

Wash hands thoroughly after handling raw meat and after working in open soil.

Don't empty the cat's litter box yourself. The person who does empty it should do the chore daily, since the feces, which carries the parasite, is not infectious until two to four days after excretion.

Cat feces should not be buried in the garden, where the expectant mother may inadvertently dig it up.

If you do contract toxoplasmosis during pregnancy, a combination of drugs can control the disease. However these drugs can cause undesirable side effects and your doctor may recommend against your taking them. He may discuss abortion.

See also ANIMAL DISEASE; PREGNANCY; BIRTH DEFECTS.

TOYS   A large dart about 1 foot long and weighing about ½ pound is sold under several trade names.

You flip the dart in the air so it will come down and stick in the ground. A pediatrician tells of one child who lost an eye to a dart, another who suffered a penetrating wound of the brain and has required two skull operations.

Some toy.

An estimated 700,000 youngsters are injured in accidents involving toys each year. Under the Child Protection and Toy Safety Act, the Food and Drug Administration (FDA) bans hazardous toys by the hundreds. But real protection of your children is up to you and your baby-sitters.

The industry tends to point to children and their parents as misusers and abusers of the products. New York attorney Norman Landau disagrees. "Toys are regarded by children as parts of the world around them, which they are constantly exploring and experimenting with. It's normal for children to bite, taste, stamp on, and even throw the objects they encounter, including toys. [Toy manufacturers should] know better than anyone else the need for maximum safety precautions in design and manufacture."

The right toy. Choose toys appropriate for the child's age and development. Heed warnings such as NOT INTENDED FOR CHILDREN UNDER 3 YEARS OF AGE, and remember that younger brothers and sisters may have access to toys intended for older children.

Teach children to put toys away. Proper storage may help prevent misuse of toys by another child. Getting toys off the floor reduces the likelihood of falls.

Inspect your children's toys frequently for loose parts, sharp edges, defective wiring. Safely constructed toys and play equipment become defective as a result of constant use or misuse. Teach children to look for defects and to report them to you.

Here are toy hazards to beware:

Loudness. Avoid toys that produce excessive noise. Toy cap pistols fired too close to a child's ear can cause deafness.

A single shot from one such gun is louder than a jackhammer. A child who fires such a gun indoors many times in succession exposes himself and others to a noise level 16 times louder than that considered dangerous by hearing specialists.

Breakableness. Many fragile or brittle toys that break easily leave sharp-pointed edges that can cause cuts and small pieces that can be swallowed.

Speed. Most toy-associated injuries are caused by bicycles, minibikes, roller skates, sleds, and other vehicles. You can reduce the risk of accidents by being sure that off-street vehicles—tricycles, sleds, and the like—are used in protected areas away from traffic.

Flammability. Check fabric labels for "non-flammable," "flame-retardant," or "flame-resistant" notices. Dolls with flammable hair and faces recurrently appear on the market. A toy

tunnel was made of an iron framework covered by cloth that caught fire and burned in seconds.

Explosives. Stay away from fireworks and from projectiles powered by caps or other explosive chemicals. They may be fairly safe when used just as instructed. But children often try putting in two or three caps at once. This can produce speeds of more than 80 mph—and cost a child his sight.

Chemistry sets on the market are rarely dangerous if only the chemicals sold with the sets are used. But combinations of chemicals bought at drugstores or chemical-supply houses, or found at home, can be explosive or cause gas poisoning. Under no circumstances should a child mix substances to see "what might happen."

Sharpness. Check dolls, rattles, tops, and other toys to make sure that no spikes or sharp pins are used to hold them together. The National Commission on Product Safety uncovered a stuffed rabbit whose ears easily came off the sharp spikes on which they fitted, a doll whose hair ribbon was fastened with a straight pin, a rattle that came apart and disclosed spikes used to hold it together.

Rubber protective parts, such as rubber-tipped arrows, should be very hard to remove.

Edges of toys should be rolled or turned in and corners rounded. Tea sets should be made of material which, if broken, will not produce sharp edges. Sleds should not have sharp-edged hooks on the runner ends.

Projectiles used with slingshots, such as space rockets or flying birds, should not be pointed or sharp-edged. Blowguns that eject darts are not only a hazard to anyone who may be in front of them, but children frequently put the wrong end in their mouths and ingest the dart. Your best bet is not to buy any such item.

Key-winding toys should have their springs and gears enclosed. Otherwise a child's finger might be mashed or cut if he picks the toy up before it has run down. The key should not revolve when the toy is in action.

In studying walker-jumpers for infants, the FDA found some baby bouncers that had holes and crossbars that could amputate a child's finger. The National Electronic Injury Surveillance System reports cases of children's fingers being crushed and amputated by the hinges of swing sets.

Electricity. To ensure safe construction of electric toys that operate on house current, look for the UL (Underwriters Laboratories) marker on the cord and toy. Whenever possible electric toys should operate through a transformer that reduces 110-volt house current to 6 to 12 volts. Battery-operated toys eliminate electric shock hazards completely.

Electric toys should never be handled with wet hands or when in wet clothing (for example, after playing in the snow). Teach youngsters to bring to your attention defects that can cause electric shock. At the first sign of a defect repair or discard the toy.

Don't buy electric toys for the very young. Show a child how to insert a plug safely into an electrical outlet and how to unplug the cord by holding the plug and never the wire.

Be sure electrical elements are well covered. Science kits or other toys with electric transformers should not have live terminals that can be easily touched.

Play ovens, irons, and similar toy appliances should never heat to extraordinary temperatures. One oven got up to 660°—higher than a real one. Such playthings should be nonelectrical —it's doubtful that a child's enjoyment depends on so much realism.

Model airplanes and kites need to be controlled by nonconducting string or well-insulated wire. The National Safety Council tells of a 14-year-old boy flying a model airplane controlled by fine wire. He was killed when his plane struck an electric wire.

Stranglers. When choosing a toy for small children, make sure it is too large to be swallowed and does not have detachable parts that can lodge in the windpipe, ears, or nostrils.

Watch out for squeakers on dolls and other toys that detach easily; rattles and maracas that come apart, revealing loose pellets that can be swallowed and inhaled. Rattles that have lead buckshot may cause lead poisoning if the pellets are swallowed.

When you buy a stuffed toy, yank on the ears, nose, and button eyes. They're likely to come off —and it's better to have a faceless animal than a choking child.

Avoid toys with long cords, such as telephones, for infants or very young children. Some of these advertised as "crib toys" have caused strangulation.

Plastic film for packaging dolls, games, and other toys could smother or be swallowed by small children. Destroy it promptly.

Toy chests can trap and smother small children, much like refrigerators. When selecting a toy box, be certain that it has a lightweight lid and provides adequate ventilation. Make sure it has no automatic locking device.

Don't allow young children to play with deflated balloons. A child who breathes in instead of out while blowing up a balloon can easily inhale the rubber and choke to death.

See also ACCIDENTS.

TRACE ELEMENTS See MINERALS.

TRACHEOSTOMY See CHOKING.

TRACHOMA is a highly contagious infection attacking the conjunctiva, the membrane that lines the eyelids and covers the front of the eye. Further infection leads to permanent scarring of the cornea.

Someone with the infection will have a tearing, burning sensation and the constant feeling of something caught in the eye. His eyes will hurt in the light.

Trachoma is the world's leading cause of blindness. In the United States it is a common problem in southwestern Indian and Mexican populations, though sporadic cases do occur in the white population, especially in the West and Northwest.

As a rule the disease spreads by close contact among family members. Poor hygiene, particularly in desert areas where lack of running water makes cleaning difficult, encourages the spread of the infection. Flies and eye gnats are thought to be carriers.

Medical treatment with eye ointments and oral antibiotics usually arrests the disease.

Preventive measures: Use separate towels and washcloths. Don't share mascara brushes, eye-liner pencils, or any eye cosmetics.

See also EYE DISORDER.

TRAINS in many parts of the country run so rarely that motorists no longer take necessary precautions when they approach a railroad crossing. As a result deaths from accidents involving cars at grade crossings are on the rise. In addition each year more than 100 children under age 15 are killed or injured while trespassing on railroad property.

When driving, stay alert for the railroad warning sign. Trains move faster than ever, often 60 to 100 mph. Don't race an oncoming train to a crossing.

Be particularly alert during the most hazardous months of December and January, when early hours of darkness and inclement weather cut visibility. Inadequate traction on snowy and icy highways, tightly closed cars, and the distracting noises of heaters and radios also lead to accidents.

Keep children away. Under no circumstances let children use railroad property as a playground. An electric or diesel locomotive is much less noisy than a steam locomotive and may strike a person on the tracks before he hears it.

Hopping rides on trains is a quick way to lose arms or legs or be killed. While swinging on or off even a slowly moving train, you can be thrown under the wheels.

Trespassers have been accidentally locked inside boxcars and have frozen or starved to death. Entering a freight car also puts you under suspicion of attempted theft. Trestles and bridges are often wide enough only for a train, forcing you to jump from perilous heights, perhaps into water.

Even if not injured himself, a child may cause fatal wrecks. Youngsters have brought about the deaths of many passengers by tampering with signals, switches, communications lines, or uncoupling cars.

See also ACCIDENTS.

TRANQUILIZERS—including antianxiety, antidepressant, and antipsychotic drugs—can make it unsafe for you to drive or handle dangerous tools or machines.

They can produce such a feeling of relaxed indifference that you can disregard the existence of a traffic light as well as its importance. They can make you drowsy, impair your judgment, cause fainting by lowering your blood pressure when you stand up suddenly.

After you're first placed on tranquilizers, don't drive or handle hazardous machinery until your next medical checkup. Tranquilizers are most dangerous when you begin taking them, since they often call for a large initial dose followed by a tapering off to maintenance level.

Avoid other drugs. Don't drink alcohol or take antihistamines or pills (such as barbiturates) for sleeplessness unless your physician says it's okay. The drugs enhance each other, working like $2 + 2 = 5$. The multiplied effect on judgment and driving skills can be disastrous. Also inform your physician about any other medications you are taking.

You need to watch your diet if you're taking antidepressants that inhibit monoamine oxidase (MAO)—Parnate, Eutonyl, Marplan, Nardil. These medications can raise your blood pressure dangerously if you eat foods that contain high concentrations of substances called tryptamine and tyramine.

Among the highest levels of tyramine are in ripened cheeses: cheddar, Emmenthaler, Gruyère, Stilton, Brie, and Camembert. (Cottage cheese, cream cheese, and yogurt are safe unless allowed to ferment.) Also avoid bean pods, dried salt herring, and fermented sausages—bologna, salami, pepperoni, and summer sausage. Chicken liver and pickled herring that have been left unrefrigerated can develop levels of tyramine hazardous to a person on MAO inhibitors.

Beer, sherry, and red wine have caused reactions in some patients. Bananas, avocados, and canned figs can cause mishaps, especially if overripe. Yeast extract, chocolate, and fava beans can be dangerous.

If you're taking an MAO inhibitor, also stay away from these drugs: Adrenaline (epinephrine), noradrenaline (norepinephrine), methyldopa, L-dopa, dopamine.

People on antipsychotic drugs (Thorazine, Sparine, Trilafon, Stelazine, Vesprin, Compazine) need to continue taking them until taken off them by a psychiatrist. Most of the people who benefit from these drugs have been hospitalized for schizophrenia—their symptoms include hallucinations, delusions, emotional withdrawal, hostility, feelings of persecution. Some two in three need the drugs for years, even for life, to remain relatively free of symptoms. Yet about half the admissions in some state mental hospitals are *re*admissions—former patients who have gone off the drug and suffered relapses.

The most common side effects of antipsychotic drugs mimic the symptoms of Parkinson's disease: slurred speech, tremors, uncontrollable restlessness, and jerkiness of motion. These can be relieved by switching to another drug, or adding the use of antiparkinsonian medication.

When a drug is needed. Do you really need an antianxiety or antidepressant drug? Such drugs are often overprescribed or wrongly prescribed.

The side effects make them more of a hazard in many cases than justified by the benefits they bring. Often, on the other hand, drugs alone are not enough—the patient needs psychotherapy to find longer-lasting relief.

For anxiety: "In threatening situations, anxiety is a normal reaction and does not call for the use of drugs," notes *The Medical Letter.* However an antianxiety or other sedative drug may be prescribed when anxiety—the constant apprehensiveness over a nameless dread—interferes with your sleep, work, pleasures, or relationships with others.

But—and this is not generally realized by the public—common antianxiety drugs (Miltown, Equanil, Librium, Valium, Solacen, Tybatran) are likely to be habit forming. (So, of course, are barbiturates widely taken as sedatives.) You may find yourself taking ever larger amounts to get the same effect. With abrupt withdrawal there can be a severe reaction, including insomnia, depression, tremor, sweating, nausea, twitching, and rapid heartbeat. Some people experience convulsions and psychosis. After high doses or prolonged use the drug should be tapered off over ten days under medical supervision.

The use of antianxiety drugs is very extensive, and such drugs are widely considered to be overprescribed. It is estimated that 10 to 15 percent of adults in the U.S. take antianxiety drugs on a reasonably regular basis.

Don't overuse antianxiety drugs. Anxiety is usually episodic, and most people really need antianxiety medication only during times of acute stress.

Before you take antianxiety drugs, let your physician know if you may be pregnant, or if you are breastfeeding. Tell your physician if you suffer from asthma, emphysema or other lung disease, glaucoma, kidney disease, liver disease, myasthenia gravis, or depression. Antianxiety drugs may worsen these conditions.

Inform your physician if you notice excessive drowsiness, difficulty in walking, dizziness, difficulty in concentrating, nightmares, or increased tension or irritability.

For depression: Similarly, antidepressants may be unnecessary or accompanied by side effects. Almost everyone has mild depression occasionally, and drug therapy is usually not required. Medication is needed only in cases of moderate to severe depression, often associated with anxiety, severe neuroses, or psychoses.

Antidepressants are mainly suited to a depression that has no external cause. These drugs are not notably successful in dealing with depression that results from real-life losses, such as of a loved one, or of a job.

Amphetamines are dangerous. Don't use them to counter a depression.

Nonprescription tranquilizers. These are best avoided. Many are antihistamines also sold for insomnia. They are nearly worthless either for inducing sleep or for easing tension, and for some people they can provoke dangerous allergic reactions. Common side effects include drowsiness, dizziness, confusion, dry mouth, nausea.

See also ALCOHOL; BARBITURATES; DRUGS.

TRAVEL HEALTH Discuss your travel plans with your physician if you need immunizations, if you have a chronic medical condition, or if you'll be traveling to an underdeveloped country.

In your Emergency Medical Identification, have your physician record any information that may prove important. Ask him to note his phone number as well, so he may be called in case additional information is needed. The most a three-minute person-to-person call costs is about $5 in this country, $15 from Europe. A call is much cheaper and faster than diagnostic tests a strange physician may need to get findings your own doctor has on file.

In case of accidents away from home get directions to the emergency room of the closest general hospital.

Carry first aid supplies in any car you drive. Take with you spare pairs of eyeglasses and prescription sunglasses, or at least a copy of your Rx. Prudent wearers of dentures take a spare set with them. Wear broken-in, comfortable shoes—foot problems can ruin your vacation.

Before traveling with a child, ask your pediatrician about special health precautions and about altering a baby's formula. A pregnant woman needs to check with her obstetrician.

Beware of unaccustomed exercise. Tourists with heart disease often go slow at the outset, then try to get their money's worth and wind up overexerting themselves. Going from sea level to a high altitude can cause oxygen deprivation and tax the heart. Other symptoms of "mountain sickness" are headache, rapid heart rate and breathing, dizziness, sleeplessness, weakness. Ignoring these symptoms can lead to dangerous buildups of fluid in the lungs and skull, possibly leading to death.

Mention an upcoming high-altitude trip to your doctor. Problems can often be avoided by small doses of Diamox (acetazolamide) taken a few days before and after your ascent. Rest for a day or two on arrival to give your body time to acclimatize. Don't drink alcohol or smoke, and stick to a high-carbohydrate, low-calorie diet. If symptoms persist or worsen, you may need oxygen therapy and evacuation to an altitude at least 5,000 feet lower.

On vacation resist the temptation to overeat and overdrink. Changes in your diet and daily routine can bring on indigestion, diarrhea, or constipation.

An aching tooth can spoil your vacation. Well before your trip have a complete dental examination and any necessary treatment. If you are in the process of root-canal therapy, your periodontist can consult the directory of the American Academy of Periodontology, which lists foreign members in many countries. Travel with a few names for each country you plan to visit. If a problem develops, you'll have someone to call on.

Do not fly for at least 12 hours after such procedures as extractions, root-canal work, and fillings. If any gas is trapped in the tooth, it can expand with the change in atmospheric pressure in an airplane, causing great pain. If your dental problem persists after treatment, call your own dentist for advice.

Precautions overseas. At least two months before you're due to leave this country, call your local health department and ask for immunizations that may be required or recommended for countries you're to go to. These change constantly.

For a trip to tropical and developing countries the Public Health Service advises immunization against polio. If you've previously been immunized, it's wise to receive at least one supplementary immunization. Some areas pose a malaria risk, and travelers should take preventive medication. Long-term travelers to rural regions of tropical countries should be vaccinated against typhoid. Still other countries, or regions within countries, may warrant protection against infectious hepatitis, influenza, plague, rabies, Japanese encephalitis, meningococcal disease, dengue, cholera, and yellow fever.

Have your diphtheria and tetanus shots up to date—these diseases are far more common abroad than in the United States. If you have never had measles or measles vaccine, it's wise to be vaccinated before traveling. Smallpox vaccine is no longer necessary.

In addition ask your health department what requirements the countries you plan to visit set for incoming travelers. There are virtually no restrictions against people coming directly from the United States. But if you pass through country A, you may be barred from country B without proper immunization.

Watch your diet. Don't drop your guard against food-borne illness. Americans abroad are all too familiar with traveler's diarrhea, variously called "the GIs," "Rome runs," "Greek gallop," "Turkey trots," "Montezuma's revenge," "Aztec two-step," or *"la turista."*

It can be provoked by the stress of traveling and change in diet—as by switching from the ordinary American diet to an Italian diet rich in olive oil, salads, and pasta. To avoid this eat lightly of local foods for the first few days.

Some bouts of diarrhea are mild and pass in a few days. As long as you're not sick and have no fever, blood in the stool or severe weakness, you can generally ignore the diarrhea.

For diarrhea without cramps, nausea or malaise, you might use a prescription antidiarrheal such as Lomotil or Imodium. Ordinary, over-the-counter Pepto-Bismol is effective for relief of diarrhea, cramps, and nausea. Take 2 tablespoons every 1/2 hour for 4 hours. Relief generally comes in a day for uncomplicated *turista.*

You may benefit from antibiotic treatment if you develop diarrhea with 3 or more loose stools in an 8-hour period, especially if you also have nausea, vomiting, abdominal cramps, fever, or blood in the stools. A typical 3- to 5-day illness can be shortened to 1 to 1 1/2 days by trimethoprim-sulfamethoxazole (Bactrim, Septra), trimethoprim (Proloprim, Trimpex), or doxycycline (Vibramycin). The drugs should be taken for 2 or 3 days. See a physician if the diarrhea persists and is accompanied by fever, serious fluid loss, and blood or mucus in the stools.

What about taking drugs to prevent diarrhea? A National Institutes of Health panel recommends *against* that, mainly because of the risk of side effects. The panel, however, adds: "Some travelers may wish to consult with their physician and may elect to use prophylactic antimicrobial agents for travel under special circumstances, once the risks and benefits are clearly understood."

Pepto-Bismol has also been successfully used as a preventive. But the dosage recommended for this purpose contains as much salicylate as eight 5-grain aspirin tablets. Travelers should therefore be warned against Pepto-Bismol if they are sensitive to aspirin, or if they are already taking large daily doses of salicylates for arthritis. It's also not recommended for patients taking oral anticoagulants such as warfarin (Coumadin, Panwarfin) and dicumarol, uricosuric drugs such as probenecid (Benemid) and sulfinpyrazone (Anturane), or methotrexate.

Antibiotics may have side effects that can include allergies, rashes, heightened sensitivity to sunlight, and the staining of the teeth in children. The antibiotics may also kill off some of the body's normal bacteria and thereby cause diarrhea and vaginitis from an overgrowth of other organisms.

Replace fluids. When you suffer from traveler's diarrhea, it's important to drink plenty of fluid—best is fruit juice laced with honey or corn syrup (1/2 teaspoon in 8 ounces of juice) and a pinch of salt. Alternate with bottled carbonated or boiled water mixed with 1/4 teaspoon baking soda.

Severe or prolonged diarrhea requires medical attention. See a doctor if you have more than ten loose stools per day, blood or mucus in your stool, or persistence of symptoms for more than five days. Severe diarrhea can cause dangerous dehydration and electrolyte imbalance. If medical care is not immediately available, ask a pharmacist for packages of glucose and premixed electrolytes, which can be mixed in water. In a pinch mix your own: To 1 quart of water, add 1

549

TRAVEL HEALTH

teaspoon salt, 1 teaspoon baking soda, and 4 teaspoons sugar.

In most of Europe you're no likelier to get
sick than you are in the United States, but salmonellosis and other forms of food poisoning
are as common there as here. So even in antiseptic Sweden or sterilized Switzerland, be as careful in the choice of restaurants as you are at
home.

In most areas of the globe you're generally
safe in good hotels and restaurants in major cities and tourist centers. If you rent a house, you
may bring a native maid or cook into your
home. If so it's a wise precaution to have the
person checked by a physician. Since local sanitary practices are likely to be different from

those you're used to, give very clear instructions
about hygienic precautions you want observed.

Where you suspect food handling is faulty or
refrigeration is lacking, avoid cold meats, meat
and potato salads, cold egg mixtures, cream,
milk, and foods—including ice cream—containing milk. Unpasteurized dairy products (milk,
cheese, ice cream) are prime sources of brucellosis.

Wherever you go, choose thoroughly cooked
meat, fish, and poultry—preferably served hot.

Take special precautions in tropical areas,
where many of the local people are carriers of
infection and where human feces may be used
for fertilizer, a source of dysentery, round-

Traveling Medical Kit—Two Weeks

Condition		Medication	Amount & Strength	Dosage
Respiratory infection: Cold symptoms, sinuses, allergy or other signs of upper congestion	Select 1 or more	Chlor-Trimeton (OTC)	14–16 tablets	1 tablet every 3–6 hours (taken during the day)
		Ornade (Rx)	14–16 spansules	1 twice a day
		Coricidin-D decongestant (OTC)	14–16 tablets	1 tablet every 4 hours (not to exceed 4 tablets per day)
		Benadryl (OTC)	10 capsules	1 or 2 capsules every 4–6 hours for severe allergy or for sleep
Diarrhea: explosive or watery stool more than twice in 24 hours		Lomotil (Rx)	30 tablets	1 or 2 tablets 4 times a day (half-dose for children)
Constipation		Milk of Magnesia (tablets) (OTC)		Taken as directed (half-dose for children)
Gastrointestinal upset		Donnatal (Rx)	30 tablets	1 tablet 4 times a day (half-dose for children)
Motion sickness		Dramamine (OTC)	15 tablets	1 or 2 tablets 4 times a day (half-dose for children)
Aches and pains		Empirin Compound with Codeine (Rx)	24 tablets	1 every 4 hours, not to exceed 6 tablets
Misc. Supplies	Adhesive tape Antacid Aspirin	Bandages First aid book Gauze	Clinical thermometer Insect repellent Suntan lotion	2% tincture of iodine Electric heating coil

worms, and other parasites. Eat no raw fruit unless it has an unbroken skin and you yourself peel it just before eating it. Otherwise eat only thoroughly cooked foods, freshly prepared.

If you want leafy vegetables (lettuce, cabbage, celery) in a salad, drop them one leaf at a time into boiling water and keep them there for at least five minutes. Since this is more of a chore than most tourists care to endure, it may be best to do without salads in the tropics. Soaking vegetables in potassium permanganate or chlorine solutions is not protective, and it tastes terrible.

Avoid contaminated water. Mexico City's pipes are cracked from earth tremors. Even in Paris some water mains are a shaky 600 years old. Less developed areas make no attempt to send out water that is pure. In Bangkok the canals, which are open sewers, leak into the city's drinking supply.

In areas of dubious sanitation don't even brush your teeth with tap water, much less drink it. Whatever you drink, don't put ice in it. The cold won't kill harmful organisms, nor will alcohol. Don't use ice on airplanes unless you know it was prepared and loaded in a safe area.

Drink bottled water, but only if you open the bottle seal yourself—it's too easy to get an open bottle that was refilled from the tap. The universally safest drink is beer. Bottled carbonated water and soft drinks are likely to be pasteurized and safe to drink—though in developing countries bottling hygiene is often slipshod. Coca-Cola maintains generally high standards worldwide—if you can be sure the drink you're getting is really Coke.

Coffee and tea are safe if properly boiled. Learn to drink them without milk or cream during tropical travel. Fresh milk is safe in the tropics only if it's been pasteurized. You need to boil water used in reconstituting evaporated, condensed, and powdered milk. Bring along an electric heating coil for boiling water in your room.

Before swimming in the tropics, check against schistosomiasis.

Medical supplies. Take with you any special drugs you need, enough for the entire trip. Also take along prescriptions, since drugs can be lost. Have your doctor write any Rx by generic rather than brand name—abroad, the drug is likely to have a different brand name than here.

Ask your doctor for medications to meet common emergencies. Tablets are easier to carry than liquid medicines, which might spill. The accompanying sample kit for a two-week trip is based on suggestions by Drs. John Tobin and C. Craig Wright, consultants to the journal *Patient Care.* Some items you can buy over the counter

(OTC); others require a doctor's prescription (Rx). In addition, ask your doctor about antibiotics you might carry for diarrhea.

Note: The iodine suggested in the kit is for use in decontaminating drinking water, not as an antiseptic (use soap and water for minor injuries). Because you may have an allergy to an untried foreign suntan lotion or insect repellent, take brands you've been happy with at home. If you're going to a tropical area, ask your doctor about the advisability of taking drugs against malaria.

Getting help. Suppose you need a doctor in a non–English-speaking country. To locate a top-caliber one who speaks English, phone the nearest U.S. embassy or consulate. If there's a U.S. military installation in the vicinity, you may get help from a doctor there. In an emergency call an ambulance or taxi and get to the nearest university hospital, or one in the nearest large community.

Through the directory of the International Association for Medical Assistance to Travelers (350 Fifth Avenue, New York, New York 10118), you can find competent English-speaking doctors in more than 250 cities in about 70 countries around the world. All 3,000 affiliated physicians have had specialty training in the United States, Canada, or Great Britain, and are pledged to provide 24-hour service at a reasonable set fee.

IAMAT will send you the directory and a membership card free. But—search your conscience—it is a nonprofit organization surviving mainly on contributions from directory users. The IAMAT directory can make mighty comforting bedside reading at 3:00 A.M. if you have a 104° F fever in Budapest.

See also ACCIDENTS; AIR TRAVEL; AMEBIASIS; BOATING; BRUCELLOSIS; CAMPING; CARS; CHOLERA; COLD WEATHER; CONSTIPATION; DIARRHEA; DIPHTHERIA; EMERGENCY MEDICAL IDENTIFICATION; FIRST AID SUPPLIES; FISHING; FOOD POISONING; HIKING; HOT WEATHER; IMMUNIZATION; JET LAG; MALARIA; MOTION SICKNESS; PLAGUE; POLIO; ROUNDWORMS; SALMONELLOSIS; SCHISTOSOMIASIS; SHIGELLOSIS; SMALLPOX; SUNGLASSES; TETANUS; TRACHOMA; TYPHOID; TYPHUS; WATER CONTAMINATION; YELLOW FEVER.

TRENCH FOOT is a breakdown in circulation of the feet caused by prolonged exposure to cold and moisture. It is usually associated with wearing wet shoes for days, and may be intensified by lack of movement and constriction caused by tight shoes or clothing. It's more likely to occur in slushy, wet cold than in dry cold with lower, below-freezing temperatures.

It sometimes takes 36 hours for trench foot to develop. Like frostbite little or no pain is noticed at first, but the feet feel numb or become hard to control. In later stages the feet swell, become red, form blisters, begin to hurt. In the final stage, the flesh dies and the foot may have to be amputated.

To prevent trench foot, keep your feet dry. If they get wet, warm them with your hands, apply foot powder, and put on dry socks. When your shoes or socks are wet or when the weather is very cold, never keep your feet still for long. Jump up and down or run in place a few steps back and forth. Flex and wiggle your toes in your boots.

If you see signs of trench foot, don't try to walk. Allow no pressure on the foot. Get someone to wrap you in warm blankets or clothing. Handle the affected parts carefully to avoid injury, and keep the injured feet dry, cool, and elevated. Take warm, sweet drinks.

Immersion foot, a similar condition, results from prolonged immersion of the feet in very cold water, and can happen to fishermen and sailors wrecked at sea. It calls for the same treatment as trench foot.

See also COLD WEATHER; FROSTBITE.

TRENCH MOUTH (Vincent's disease, acute necrotizing ulcerative gingivitis)—a disease of the gums, throat, and mouth—was named in World War I because of its prevalence among combat soldiers.

Symptoms include inflammation and ulceration of the gums, with foul odor, pain, bleeding, and sometimes sore throat. Consult a dentist for proper care. It is far more serious than ordinary gingivitis.

Treatment may entail removing dead tissue. Antibiotics may be administered if the condition is severe and widespread and accompanied by fever. Therapy ordinarily includes a program of plaque control; rest; a bland, soft diet; and a multivitamin preparation in therapeutic doses. Many dentists also recommend mouthwashes of warm saltwater, mild hydrogen peroxide, or a mild alkaline solution. Surgery may be needed to reshape tissue if much has been destroyed.

The disease is believed not to be contagious. Its cause is unknown, but is thought related to poor hygienic conditions and a lowering of tissue resistance in the mouth because of physical and emotional stress.

See also GINGIVITIS; PLAQUE; TEETH AND MOUTH DISORDERS.

TRICHINOSIS The kitchen crew of a Manhattan banqueting hall raided the icebox for an end-of-work snack. Finding ground meat, they made hamburgers. Four of the men cooked their patties rare. The meat was not ground beef, as the men thought, but pork. All fell ill of trichinosis. A fifth man, who ate two patties raw, died of the disease.

Trichinosis is a parasitic infection caused by small, threadlike worms called *trichinae,* and results almost always from eating raw or insufficiently cooked pork. An infrequent hunter gets it from eating underdone bear meat.

Some butchers dilute ground beef with pork, an illicit practice that sometimes infects people who never knowingly eat pork. Beef can also be contaminated if it goes through a grinder that has ground infested pork. Even a minute amount of contaminated meat can produce symptoms. Medical journalist Berton Roueché tells of a Detroiter who suffered a violent seizure of trichinosis as a result of merely eating a piece of bread buttered with a knife that had been used to slice an infested sausage.

The disease is so prevalent in U.S. hogs that some other countries prohibit imports of American pork products. The incidence of trichinosis has sharply decreased. Nonetheless, there are still about 100 cases reported a year, and several times that number probably go unreported because of wrong diagnosis.

Irritation produced by the activity of the worms in the intestines causes nausea, vomiting, and diarrhea. The hundreds of parasites traveling through the body make the patient sick with fever, headache, and prostration, sometimes lasting for months. The larvae can enter so many organs and cause such a variety of symptoms that mimic other diseases that misdiagnoses are common.

Symptoms include swelling of the face and other parts of the body, soreness in the eyes, hemorrhages under the skin, pain in the muscles, and difficult breathing. The patient may show symptoms of heart disease or brain involvement such as delirium or coma.

Treatment. If trichinosis is suspected, within the first weeks attempt to kill with drugs the adult worms in the intestine. This would remove the females before they have produced all their larvae, but there is no proven drug that will kill the larvae that have already burrowed into muscles.

Medical treatment is necessary, to treat symptoms and to prevent complications. A regimen to build up the patient's resistance usually consists of bed rest, plenty of fluids, and a high-calorie, high-vitamin diet. Steroids have been effective in relieving swelling, fever, and muscular pain.

The death rate from trichinosis is low. Even in severe cases the chance of recovery is good.

Cook pork properly. Cook all pork until it is grayish-white. Thorough cooking is necessary even for cured or smoked pork and for partially cooked pork products such as sausages and frankfurters. Merely smoking or pickling meat does not kill the parasite.

You can help assure that pork is safe and also at its best flavor by cooking it slowly. Braise a chop 3/8 to 1/2 inch thick for 40 minutes over very low heat, about 175° F. Cut into the meat near the bone to see if a chop is done. The least sign of pinkness means that it has not been cooked enough for safety.

In preparing large cuts such as hams and shoulders, a meat thermometer stuck into the center of the thickest part—not touching the bone—will show when the meat is roasted through. An internal temperature of 160° F results in a safe, juicy cut. Without a thermometer cook roasts at least 50 minutes to the pound at 325° F to 350° F. If the roast is put into the oven frozen or partially frozen, allow 70 to 75 minutes per pound. The center rib needs 30 minutes to the pound, 50 if frozen.

Tenderized hams stamped FEDERALLY INSPECTED AND PASSED have been processed to kill parasites. They can safely be eaten with less cooking if desired.

In packing plants operating under federal inspection, pork products usually eaten without further cooking are treated to destroy parasites. When these foods—salami, cervelat, mettwurst, and Italian-style ham—have been made safe for eating as is, they are stamped in pure vegetable dye, FEDERALLY INSPECTED AND PASSED. Look on the cellophane wrappers for this stamp.

Since not all of these pork products have been treated and government inspected, feel free to ask about this protection when eating them in restaurants and always when buying for your own table. Have your butcher grind beef in your view. Always scour a grinder after putting pork through it. Never eat raw sausage meat to test it for seasoning. For safety cook a morsel before tasting it.

Freezing of pork cuts is also a good way to kill trichinosis organisms. For a block of pork up to 6 inches thick you need a freezer temperature of 5° F for 20 days, −10° F for 10 days, −20° F for 6 days. Freeze blocks of pork between 6 and 27 inches thick at 5° F for 30 days, −10° F for 20 days, −20° F for 12 days.

As a public-health precaution farmers are required to cook garbage properly before feeding it to hogs. Swine can get parasites through eating scraps of infested pork. This usually occurs through feeding them raw garbage from municipal dumps. Canada and all but one of our states require that municipal garbage be cooked before it is fed to swine. But until all garbage is cooked or otherwise safely disposed of—and until safeguards are universally enforced—trichinosis will persist as a threat to health.

For other parasitic worms common in the United States see HOOKWORMS; PINWORMS; ROUNDWORMS; TAPEWORMS.

See also INFECTIOUS DISEASE; MALARIA; SCHISTOSOMIASIS; TRAVEL HEALTH.

TRICHOMONIASIS, a vaginal infection, causes a foamy, yellow-green discharge and a burning sensation on urinating. Most women also experience an intense vaginal itch. There may be soreness, swelling, and bleeding of the vaginal walls. The urethra and the bladder may also be affected.

Like a yeast infection trichomoniasis is diagnosed by a pelvic examination and a smear of the discharge.

Trichomoniasis is usually spread through sexual intercourse. Some physicians regard it as a venereal disease. The organism—a one-celled animal called *Trichomonas vaginalis*—can be carried from the rectum to the vagina by anal intercourse followed by vaginal intercourse, or by wiping bowel movements from the rectum toward the vagina.

Because the protozoa can survive outside the body in a warm, moist place, it may also be possible to contract it through clothing, toilet seats, towels, washcloths, and other personal articles.

Men often harbor the organisms in the urethra, prostate gland, or bladder without any symptoms. Thus a woman who has been successfully treated can be repeatedly reinfected by her sex partner.

For this reason the male partner usually needs to be treated at the same time as the female. It is advisable that the man use condoms during intercourse for several weeks to lessen the possibility of reinfection.

Trichomoniasis is usually treated with the drug metronidazole. Don't take it if you are pregnant or nursing, or if you have a history of blood diseases or diseases of the central nervous system. There has also been some research that links the drug with cancer.

Since metronidazole changes the environment of the vagina, it may result in a yeast infection. Other possible side effects include nausea, diarrhea, cramps, dizziness, dry mouth and vagina, and a glossy tongue. It's best to avoid alcoholic drinks, since the drug blocks the metabolism of alcohol and one drink affects you like several.

Alternative therapy may include vinegar douches, vaginal suppositories, creams, and jellies. Since *Trichomonas* lives in an environment less acidic than normal, you may be able to control the infection at its first signs by douching with a solution of 2 tablespoons vinegar in 1 quart of water.

Even with these many methods of treatment eradicating the organism may prove difficult. There is a high recurrence rate. Research suggests an association between infertility and a history of trichomoniasis.

See also VAGINAL INFECTION; VENEREAL DISEASE.

TRICK KNEE usually refers to a split or broken cartilage of the knee. A little piece of the cartilage locks the joint and makes bending the knee difficult.

An orthopedic surgeon may prescribe a bandage or brace to support the knee. For football players and others who don't recover, surgery may be performed to correct the condition.

See also SPORTS.

TRIGEMINAL NEURALGIA See TIC DOULOUREUX.

TUBERCULOSIS is still with us though many laymen believe it has been eradicated and many physicians fail to suspect its presence.

Despite enormous progress in drug therapy, an estimated 16 million Americans have live TB germs in their bodies and 30,000 develop active TB each year. By the time symptoms appear—fever, weight loss, tiredness, coughing, perhaps blood spitting—this respiratory disease has reached a point at which control is difficult. Over 4,000 victims still die from TB each year.

The rod-shaped bacilli that cause TB are spread by coughing, sneezing, and spitting. Infection is *not* spread by handling a TB patient's bedsheets, books, furniture, or eating utensils. Brief exposure to a few TB germs rarely infects a person. Close continuous contact is ordinarily needed.

Resisting the bacteria. Infection doesn't always mean disease. White blood cells attack the invading bacteria. If general resistance is good and there aren't too many germs, some are killed by the body's defenses and others are walled up where they can do no harm in a small mass, called a tubercle.

Millions of people go through life with tubercles in their lungs without ever getting sick. But sometimes bodily resistance goes down, perhaps because of excessive physical activity, poor diet, an illness. Then the bacteria walled up in the tubercles break out, multiply, and invade other parts of the lungs.

At this stage the victim may still feel healthy, but active tuberculosis has begun. If left unchecked, it will continue spreading. The broken tubercles cause cavities in the lungs, impairing lung function.

New medication. Anti-TB medicines now available make it possible for all patients to recover. The cure takes nine months to two years because the drugs work only on germs that are reproducing. Even when active tuberculosis is present, many bacteria are in a resting phase. Treatment needs to be continued for many months to handle the resting germs when they start to multiply.

Isoniazid, streptomycin, ethambutol, and rifampin are the primary medicines used in the treatment of tuberculosis. They are generally used in combinations, because some germs may be resistant to one or another.

Most patients stop spreading tuberculosis soon after they start treatment and no longer need to be isolated for extended periods. Some don't need any hospitalization.

Preventive treatment for one year is recommended for those with an inactive infection. In addition a drug regimen is advisable for family members and other close associates of active TB cases, even those (especially children) who show up negative on TB tests.

Skin test. Get a tuberculin skin test several times in your lifetime. Children should get it starting around age one. A small amount of tuberculin, a harmless protein derived from TB germs, is put into the skin of your forearm. In two or three days a doctor can tell by measuring the spot on the arm if your reaction is positive.

If so, living TB germs are in your body, though not necessarily causing disease. An X ray and laboratory tests tell if active disease is present in your lungs. Your doctor may recommend preventive treatment. He may suggest periodic X rays to make sure germ activity has not started.

You also may be urged to return for checkups if you are in a group running the greatest risk of TB. This includes you if you have been with someone with active TB; you are under 20; you are elderly; you are taking steroids.

Some medical conditions can activate or reactivate tuberculosis. For this reason tuberculin tests are needed by people with diabetes, Hodgkin's disease, leukemia, dust disease, unexplained respiratory disease, and those who have had a recent gastrectomy.

Ask your doctor about BCG vaccine if you face special risks. It contains living but greatly weakened tuberculosis germs that can stimulate the body's defense mechanism enough to cause development of active resistance. In this country there is no need for wholesale immunization, but it is used as a protective agent for nurses and physicians in tuberculosis institutions, and for social workers who meet many people with active tuberculosis as part of their daily work.

If you're planning to live abroad, especially in a high-TB area, BCG vaccine is likely to be a wise precaution.

See also RESPIRATORY DISEASE.

TUBERCULOUS ARTHRITIS is a joint infection caused by tubercle bacilli. It occurs in about 4 percent of those with tuberculosis, usually as a result of spread from the primary infection in the lung. The chances of a cure have greatly improved in the past two decades with the development of effective antibiotics and medications for tuberculosis itself.

See also ARTHRITIS; TUBERCULOSIS.

TULAREMIA (rabbit fever) was named for Tulare County, California, where this animal disease was first studied in 1911.

It's rarely transmitted from person to person. Most cases occur in autumn during the rabbit-hunting season, and you are most likely to get it by handling the carcass or eating the undercooked flesh of infected animals. The bites of sick animals, or of insects that have bitten sick animals, also spread the disease. People have also been infected by drinking water from streams inhabited by diseased animals such as beavers and muskrats.

Though rabbits are the most common victims, a variety of other animals—including dogs and cats—sometimes become infected. Insects and birds are also known to be susceptible; a biting fly, called the deerfly, and certain kinds of ticks are common carriers.

Symptoms. The bacteria causing tularemia need no visible wound for entry into the body. They are able to go through apparently healthy skin. Infection often results from rubbing the eyes with contaminated fingers.

An ulcer usually develops at the place where the germs enter the body—on the hands, around the eyes, or at the site of the insect or animal bite. Lymph glands in the neck, armpit, or groin —near the part of the body that has been infected—are likely to become enlarged and are sometimes abscessed. The victim has chills and fever, sometimes accompanied by extreme exhaustion.

The incubation period is usually about three days. If ten days have passed without symptoms since suspected exposure, there is little chance that the disease will develop.

Antibiotics, used as soon as diagnosis is made, are highly effective, although sufferers usually remain ill for several weeks. Recovery results in permanent immunity.

Butchers and meat handlers run a higher than average risk of infection, particularly if they handle wild game. Wear rubber gloves while skinning or dressing wild game, especially rabbits. If you find any whitish spots on the dark organs such as liver or spleen, bury or burn the carcass. If your hands have been soiled, immediately wash and scrub them with soap and water.

Other precautions: Keep free of ticks. Thoroughly cook wild game before eating it. Avoid drinking water from streams in areas where the disease is known to exist. When purity of water is in question, treat it for contamination.

See also ANIMAL DISEASE; INFECTIOUS DISEASE; WATER CONTAMINTION.

TYPHOID Ordinarily the water supply of Keene, New Hampshire, met generally accepted sanitation standards. Then heavy rains soaked the countryside, flushing waste from a distant lumber camp into a brook that fed the city reservoir. One of the loggers unknowingly was a typhoid carrier. Typhoid bacilli he excreted were swept down the brook into the reservoir. The bacteria got through a defective filter—and 14 residents of Keene came down with typhoid. One died of complications.

Exposure to the urine or feces of a carrier accounts for most cases of this infectious disease. It is a special menace during floods, when sewage and drinking water are likely to be mixed. In the United States, most cases are transmitted through food prepared by a carrier.

Typhoid abroad. Before leaving the country, check your local health department about the need for typhoid vaccination. While typhoid is relatively rare in the United States, it is a major problem in other countries, such as Mexico.

The Public Health Service recommends immunization for travelers to typhoid-infected areas and for anyone in the midst of a typhoid outbreak or in contact with a typhoid carrier. Routine vaccination is not recommended in the United States.

The vaccine is administered in two doses at least four weeks apart. Boosters are needed at least every three years.

At one time immunization procedure called

for vaccination against both typhoid and paratyphoid, a similar but milder infection. Authorities now recommend that plain typhoid vaccine be used instead of the combination, since this reduces the frequency and severity of the reactions in some people. There is no clear evidence that inoculation against the paratyphoid germs is effective.

First signs. Typhoid symptoms usually begin with a feeling of being tired and out of sorts. There is mild fever, coughing, headache, dullness. Over about a ten-day period the fever increases. The victim may have some abdominal pain and tenderness, and either constipation or diarrhea. He may have chills and severe headache and suffer from weakness and confusion.

Rose-colored spots appear on the body around the second week of illness. Victims usually have a high fever for about ten days.

During the first week after symptoms appear, physicians can usually confirm the diagnosis of typhoid by laboratory tests. They nearly always recommend that the victim be cared for in a hospital, since all his body discharges must be disinfected in order to prevent spread of the disease. The effectiveness of treatment has been increased in recent years by the use of antibiotics.

Prevention. To prevent typhoid: In rural areas privies or cesspools need to be located at least 100 feet away from the water supply and, if possible, downhill. Treat water for contamination if sanitation is in doubt. Most U.S. cities add chlorine to the public water supply to kill harmful microorganisms, including typhoid bacilli.

Milk and milk products, if not pasteurized, can carry typhoid germs. If you are not sure of the purity of milk, boil it. Typhoid germs can be carried in shellfish that have been grown in contaminated water. Buy only shellfish that come from government-approved sources.

To avert outbreaks, health departments keep some 3,000 known carriers under supervision. Typhoid carriers are usually people who have recovered from typhoid fever; a few have picked up typhoid bacilli but never been ill from them. The bacilli often lodge in the carrier's gallbladder, removal of which may eliminate the germs.

Carriers can take special precautions to prevent infecting other people. They especially need to wash their hands after using the toilet, and avoid handling food, drink, or dishes that are to be used by others.

See also INFECTIOUS DISEASE; WATER CONTAMINATION.

TYPHUS has ravaged armies and changed the course of history. During World War II the Russian army was in retreat from the Germans when typhus broke out on the German side, contributing in large part to the shift in battle and the German defeat.

Epidemic typhus is caused by rickettsiae spread by the human body louse. The lice defecate the microorganisms while feeding. Scratching by the host rubs the rickettsiae into the skin. Once high fever makes the host too warm for the louse's comfort—or death too cold—it seeks out another host. Typhus may be contracted even by people not louse infested, if they breathe air containing rickettsiae-bearing louse feces.

The rickettsiae invade small blood vessels throughout the body, causing irritation and obstructions. After an incubation period of about 12 days, the first symptoms are usually a severe headache and aches and pains over the entire body. A fever of 104° F, with chills, is common. Reddish spots appear on the back and chest, spreading and becoming darker. Areas of skin tissue die, and gangrene develops in portions of the body—the extremities, penis and scrotum, tips of the nose and ears—where circulation is poor. Pneumonia is a frequent complication.

Antibiotics are generally effective if administered early. A basic preventive measure is dusting louse-infested people with an insecticide.

Today the disease most often occurs in colder climates among impoverished people who live in close quarters and rarely bathe. The last U.S. outbreak of epidemic typhus occurred in 1922, and for Americans today the disease is rarely encountered, even while traveling, if visits are limited to urban areas with modern hotel accommodations.

However immunization—two injections of vaccine four or more weeks apart—may be advisable for travelers to remote highland and rural areas of Mexico, the Andean region of South America, Eastern Europe, and mountainous regions of Asia and Africa. Booster shots every 6 to 12 months are recommended if you stay in infested areas.

Another form of typhus, murine (or rat) typhus, is chiefly spread by rat fleas, and may be transmitted by pets. It is found in mice and rats worldwide, with some cases reported in the United States each year. Symptoms are usually high fever, headache and backache, and a reddish, spotted rash. Deaths are extremely rare.

See also FLEAS; INFECTIOUS DISEASE; LICE; RATS; TICKS.

ULCERATIVE COLITIS   See COLITIS.

ULCER, DUODENAL   See PEPTIC ULCER.

UMBILICAL HERNIA   See HERNIA.

UNCONSCIOUSNESS differs from sleep in that the person can't be aroused. Unlike fainting, unconsciousness is long-lasting and generally is a result of severe accident or illness. Coma is prolonged, deep unconsciousness.

If you're with someone who's unconscious, assume there is a possible head injury. Call for medical help immediately. Note such important details as how long the person is out, and whether he comes to intermittently or responds to your voice or other stimuli. Never give anything to eat or drink.

For emergency first aid measures see ARTIFICIAL RESPIRATION; BLEEDING; and HEART STOPPAGE.

Unless absolutely necessary avoid moving the victim until professional help arrives. Don't move the head if there is bleeding from the nose, mouth, or ears, or you may aggravate head injuries. Even though recovery may seem to occur spontaneously, secure medical attention.

Finding the cause. Try to determine the cause of unconsciousness. Check for EMERGENCY MEDICAL IDENTIFICATION (which see). Observe the skin color of the victim: red, white, or blue.

Red unconsciousness—marked by a flushed face—often indicates stroke, hypertension, heat stroke, epilepsy, skull fracture, or coma resulting from diabetes. Raise the victim's head and shoulders on pillows. Apply cold compresses to the head.

White unconsciousness, characterized by pallor, may indicate shock, bleeding, heat exhaustion, poisoning, frostbite, convulsions, or insulin shock. Lay the victim flat, with his head down. Loosen his clothing.

Blue unconsciousness usually indicates choking, drowning, gas poisoning (especially by carbon monoxide), electric shock, or heart attack. If you know the cause, take appropriate first aid measures.

Intoxication from alcohol may be a cause of red, white, or blue unconsciousness.

See also ACCIDENTS; MOVING THE INJURED.

UNDERWEIGHT is generally a boon to health. "The thinnest people live longest and are least affected by the so-called degenerative diseases—heart, liver, and kidney disorders," reports Harvard nutritionist Jean Mayer. "They even seem to have fewer accidents." Extremely thin people do tend to tire easily and often complain of feeling chilled and weak. But the main problems associated with thinness are more related to appearance than health.

Some people are constitutionally thin; they're born with a body structure and physiology that keep them from gaining weight. Many of them try desperately to gain weight in order to "look better." Although the vast overweight population may be incredulous, some thin people feel as unhappy about their shape as fat people.

If underweight is your problem, here are some tips for adding pounds:

Keep track of what you eat for a week. You may be taking in too few calories (see the table of food values under NUTRITION).

Add 500 calories a day to your normal diet in order to gain a pound a week. It takes about 3,500 excess calories to gain a pound. Make sure your diet remains balanced.

If you're unable to eat large meals, have several smaller meals a day.

Gradually increase the portions of food you eat. Check portion sizes with a measuring cup to be sure.

Drink high-calorie liquids with meals—milk, hot chocolate, eggnog. Avoid water, tea, coffee, to leave more room for food.

Have a snack before bed—a high-calorie drink, cheese and crackers.

Identify the high-calorie nutritious foods, and eat more of them. Among these are cheese, nuts, dried fruit, creamed soups, peanut butter, ice cream, sour cream, beans (except green beans), potatoes, winter squash. You can afford to indulge in sodas and desserts, but don't substitute empty calories for real food.

Avoid smoking or drinking alcohol before meals. Cigarettes and liquor can dull your appetite.

Plan for leisurely, relaxed meals.

Fashion tricks can help you look heavier. Clothes striped across give a larger appearance. So do bright colors and prints, and such fabrics as fluffy wool and airy gauze.

For women blouson waists, full sleeves, soft cowl necklines, and dresses and skirts that flare at the hips will probably be more flattering than form-fitting fashions. Layering adds interest and disguises thinness. A short, curly hairdo rounds the face, whereas long, straight cuts make faces seem longer.

If you're 10 percent or more under the desirable weight for your age, sex, body build, and level of activity, see a physician to rule out illness. Also consult a doctor if you suddenly lose weight for no apparent reason. Marked weight loss can be an early sign of infection, diabetes, anemia, hormonal imbalance, and many other diseases.

Emotional stress sometimes leads to weight loss—under trying circumstances, many people lose their appetite. An extreme form of food revulsion that causes severe weight loss affects mainly young women. Called anorexia nervosa, the condition causes some to become so emaciated that they starve themselves to death. Anorexics need immediate psychiatric intervention.

See also NUTRITION; STRESS.

UNDESCENDED TESTICLES (cryptorchidism) in adults are linked to infertility and to a higher risk of cancer of the testicles.

In the male fetus the testicles are normally inside the abdomen. They pass into the scrotum shortly before birth. Sometimes one or both testes fail to descend. This may be due to physiological immaturity or to an obstruction in the inguinal canal (through which the testicles normally descend).

Some testicles will spontaneously descend in the first few years of life. If the testes fail to descend, most physicians recommend that surgery be performed before the boy reaches puberty.

The operation involves opening the canal, removing any obstructions, and placing the testicle in the scrotum. Hormone therapy is sometimes recommended as an alternative.

See also INFERTILITY.

UNDULANT FEVER   See BRUCELLOSIS.

UPSET STOMACH   See INDIGESTION.

UREMIA   See KIDNEY DISEASE.

URINARY TRACT INFECTION (UTI) results from one or more types of bacteria infecting the bladder, urethra, or other parts of the urinary tract. When the bladder is infected, it is called cystitis.

The most common symptoms are a burning sensation on urinating and frequent urination. Backache, fever, and pain above the pubic area may accompany the infection. There may be blood in the urine.

Children may show only high fever. Very young children may have vomiting and diarrhea. Some adults and children have no symptoms at all. Many more women than men develop urinary tract infections.

The infection is diagnosed by obtaining a urine specimen and urine culture. These will show an abnormal number of bacteria and white blood cells. Many doctors advise a urine test for children as part of the routine physical examination. Other diagnostic tests—such as X rays—may be necessary if the infection fails to respond to treatment.

Untreated, the infection may pass from the bladder to one or both kidneys, resulting in nephritis—and this in turn may ultimately cause uremic poisoning.

Obstructions. UTI often results from obstructions to the normal flow of urine. The obstruction may be congenital, such as an abnormally narrow urethra, the tube through which urine passes. Infants and children with UTI often have some relatively minor abnormality in the urinary tract.

The obstruction may also be acquired. In some women tissue damage caused by childbirth may result in some disruption of the normal flow of urine. Other causes are tumors in nearby organs, scar tissue, and kidney stones.

When urine stagnates in the bladder because of an obstruction, germs that are usually present in small numbers multiply rapidly, and infection results.

Treatment. Usually, treatment consists of sulfa drugs or antibiotics or a combination of drugs. In some cases, if the infection recurs or persists, a physician may prescribe a long course of treatment—up to several months. When an obstruction is responsible, surgery is usually recommended.

If you're being treated for UTI, drink a lot of water or juices—cranberry juice, an American Indian remedy, may be effective. Avoid coffee, tea, and alcohol, which may irritate the urinary tract.

Pregnancy poses special problems for a woman with urinary tract infection, since antibiotics may possibly cause congenital malformations in the fetus during the first three months. Some physicians postpone treatment if the infection is not too serious. Several consultants of *The Medical Letter* recommend large doses of ascorbic acid (vitamin C) as a possibly effective treatment.

A woman with recurrent cystitis may feel less discomfort during sexual activity if she urinates before intercourse. An empty bladder can reduce the likelihood of irritation in the pelvis by allowing more space. Adequate lubrication also helps.

To help prevent UTI teach girls to wipe away from the vagina, not toward it, after bowel movements. To protect against urine stagnation, drink at least five glasses of water a day, and urinate frequently.

See also KIDNEY DISEASE.

URTICARIA   See HIVES.

VAGINAL DOUCHING Irrigating and cleansing the vagina is both unnecessary and unwise under normal circumstances.

In a healthy woman the vagina is self-cleansing. Some clear vaginal discharge is perfectly normal. It should be colorless and odorless. If you are troubled with excessive foul-smelling or greenish-yellowish discharge, consult your doctor. You may have an infection.

Some women believe there will be a vaginal odor unless they douche regularly. But in the absence of an abnormal condition, odor usually results from poor hygiene of the *external* genitals. Regular bathing or washing with soap and water will prevent most odors.

Strong chemicals in a douche solution can injure cells in the lining of the vagina. Further, the normal secretions of the vagina contain protective bacteria that tend to prevent infections of the vaginal tract. By habitually flushing out the vagina, a woman is inviting the very condition she hopes to avoid by douching.

Don't use douching as a means of birth control. It is an extremely unreliable method.

When a doctor recommends douching for the treatment of certain vaginal infections or some other conditions, he will usually prescribe the powder or liquid to be used. Many doctors recommend a douche solution consisting of 1 tablespoon white vinegar to 1 quart water, which helps maintain the normal acid medium of the vagina.

Douche precautions. Be wary of over-the-counter douching solutions and products. They can be extremely dangerous. An electric douche which costs $40 was found to be capable of causing a fatal electric shock.

Many women have permanently damaged their vaginal membranes by using strong douching formulas passed on from mothers and grandmothers—such as phenol household disinfectants, bichloride of mercury, and potassium permanganate. Other douche solutions may contain harmless, but useless, ingredients—such as borax and soda or perfumed salt.

When douching is prescribed, some women injure themselves by improperly using the douche. Here are some tips for successful douching:

Read the directions on the douching preparation. It is particularly important not to use too much of the chemical.

Put the water in the douche bag before the chemical. Otherwise the concentrated chemical at the bottom of the bag reaches the vagina first, possibly injuring the delicate tissues.

Don't use too much pressure, since the solution can thus be forced into the uterus or the peritoneal cavity. Never connect the douche bag directly to a faucet.

Use lukewarm—not hot—water. Use your elbow to test the water temperature—water that feels warm to your hand could be too hot for douching.

After you fill the douche bag, suspend it from a hook so that the lower end of the bag is not more than 2 feet above your hips when you administer the douche. The most convenient place to douche is a dry bathtub. Lean back on your elbow at a 45-degree angle to the tub's bottom. Elevate your knees slightly and spread them apart. In a shower enclosure, lean against the wall at the same angle.

Gently insert the nozzle slightly downward about 2 inches into the vagina. Release the clamp to allow the douche solution to flow into the vagina.

Press the lips of the vulva around the nozzle with the thumb and forefinger of one hand so that no solution escapes. When you feel a sense of fullness and pressure, pinch off the flow, count to 15, and let the fluid gush out. Repeat the process until you've used up all the douche solution.

Keep the douche bag hygienic. Thoroughly wash and dry the bag after every use, then store it in a clean place.

See also BIRTH CONTROL; VAGINAL INFECTION; VAGINAL ODOR.

VAGINAL INFECTION constitutes the most common women's disease. It may be caused by bacteria, fungi, or other microorganisms. A woman can have more than one type of vaginal infection simultaneously.

The most common symptoms are vaginal itching, a cloudy discharge, an unpleasant vaginal odor, and possibly a burning sensation when urinating.

Form-fitting pantyhose and girdles—particularly those made of nylon or other synthetics—have increased the incidence of all types of vaginal infections. Nylon undergarments raise body temperature and keep moisture from evaporating, and the organisms that cause vaginal infections flourish in such a moist, warm environment. Women who have recurrent infections are urged to substitute regular stockings for pantyhose, cotton underpants for nylon.

Besides yeast infection, gonorrhea, and trichomoniasis, the most common vaginal infection is nonspecific vaginitis. Bacteria that normally inhabit the vagina, such as streptococci, staphylococci, colon bacteria, or *Hemophilis vaginalis,* may cause an infection under certain conditions.

Changes in the vaginal environment can allow these usually harmless bacteria to become troublesome. The acid/alkaline balance of the vagina changes during ovulation, menstruation, and pregnancy. Douching also may change the vagina's chemical environment.

Another infection in the body can set the stage for a vaginal infection, as can exhaustion or poor diet. So too can aggressive intercourse that causes inflammation of the cervix or the vaginal walls. Women taking the birth control pill seem more prone to vaginal infections. And if you're taking antibiotics for an infectious disease, resistant bacteria in your vagina may flourish unchecked.

Symptoms of nonspecific vaginitis include a pus-containing yellow or white discharge, possibly streaked with blood. One of the early symptoms may be frequent and burning urination, since the infection can quickly spread to the urethra.

The infection can also spread into the uterus and fallopian tubes. Chronic infections can cause the cells of the cervix to grow abnormally, and make you more susceptible to cancer of the cervix.

Other symptoms of nonspecific vaginitis may be lower-back pain, cramps, and swollen glands in the abdomen and thighs.

To diagnose nonspecific vaginitis the physician examines the cervix and vagina. (Don't douche for at least 24 hours before your appointment.) The discharge examined under a microscope will show a large number of bacteria and white blood cells.

Treatment. Nonspecific vaginitis is usually treated with sulfa drugs and creams or suppositories, to be used morning and evening for 10 to 14 days. Alternative treatment is available to women allergic to sulfa.

During the first five days of treatment refrain from intercourse. Take the medication for as long as your doctor prescribes, even if all your symptoms disappear. Chronic nonspecific vaginitis may take several months to respond to therapy. To help speed recovery keep the area

dry and wear cotton underwear instead of nylon.

See also ANTIBIOTICS; BIRTH CONTROL; CANCER OF THE UTERUS; GONORRHEA; TRICHOMONIASIS; VAGINAL DOUCHING; YEAST INFECTION.

VAGINAL ODOR—like perspiration odor—is caused by bacteria acting on the perspiration, mucus, and oil on skin, hair, and clothing. It's a problem in all body areas that are normally warm and moist.

To combat normal vaginal odor wash daily with soap and water. Wear fairly loose-fitting cotton underwear. Close-fitting nylon underwear, panty girdles, and pantyhose delay the evaporation of perspiration and may thus accentuate the odor.

If you have an abnormally strong and persistent odor, consult a physician. You may be suffering from a vaginal infection or other pathological condition.

What not to do. Don't try to eliminate odors by douching.

Steer clear of vaginal deodorants. They are unnecessary and potentially harmful. This is particularly true of genital deodorants in spray cans.

Most feminine deodorant sprays consist of oils of the type used in cosmetics with antibacterial agents, perfume, and a propellant. But they have been found not as effective as soap and water in promoting a hygienic and odor-free external genital surface.

In addition some women have severe allergic reactions to the sprays; many more develop a skin disorder.

The Food and Drug Administration (FDA) has received scores of complaints from women injured by genital deodorant sprays. The most common complaint involves burns. There are many cases of rashes, blisters, itching, irritations. Other reactions include infections with vaginal discharge and a feeling of urinary urgency with pain, swelling, open sores.

Part of the problem may stem from confusing advertising. The spray is not intended for use inside the vagina—it is meant to be applied to the *external* genital area only. It can easily injure the delicate mucous membranes of the vagina.

Another potential hazard of vaginal deodorants: Widespread advertising may persuade many women with vaginal infections or an unsuspected cancer to put off seeking medical advice.

There are also strong objections to the implications of the advertising for deodorant sprays: that women will be offensive to men unless they are completely deodorized. Testifying before a

Senate subcommittee on the promotion and advertising of over-the-counter drugs, psychiatrist Natalie Shainess remarked that ". . . the implication of need for such a spray conveys a message of women as being dirty and smelly—extremely damaging to a woman's sense of self-esteem and self-worth, as well as to man's view of her."

If you feel you must use a vaginal deodorant spray, here are some tips on using it safely:

Spray it only on the external genital area, not into the vagina.

During menstruation spray only your skin or a sanitary napkin. Don't spray onto a tampon, which would bring the deodorant in contact with vaginal tissue.

Don't use a spray just before sexual intercourse. It can cause genital irritation for men as well as women.

Don't use an underarm antiperspirant spray on your genital area. It may contain aluminum salts, which are very irritating to the mucous membranes of the genitals.

Spray at least 8 inches from your skin.

Use the spray sparingly, and not more than once a day.

Don't use the spray on broken, irritated, or itching skin. If you develop any such disorder in your vaginal area, see a doctor.

See also VAGINAL INFECTION.

VARICOSE VEINS are enlarged veins (*varicose* means "swollen"). The condition affects one out of every two women over 40, one out of every four men. They often can be seen as bluish ropy vessels just under the skin on the inner side and back of the calf and on the inner side of the thigh.

One early symptom is a feeling of heaviness in the legs, especially after you've been standing for a long time. The leg muscles seem to be fatigued; ankles swell and itch at the end of the day. The veins themselves are tender and sore. You may suffer a dull or stabbing pain, and cramps in the legs at night.

If untreated, varicose veins tend to grow worse. Over months or years the veins toughen and thicken, sometimes becoming as big around as a thumb. Leg ulcers and bleeding are frequent complications.

What causes swollen veins. Ordinarily valves every few inches in leg veins keep blood moving toward the heart. When the valves are weak, or leaky, the column of blood in the legs flows backward into the vessel. Blood pressure in the vein below the faulty valve increases, and the veins become stretched and swollen.

Standing still for a long time places the greatest strain on the veins. People in occupations that require standing all day—dentists, salespeople, barbers, policemen, elevator operators—seem more prone to varicose veins than people who can sit while they work. Anything that interferes with circulation of the blood, such as tight clothing, can cause varicose veins to become worse.

Heredity is a contributing factor. If you've inherited weak veins or valves, any extra strain on blood circulation can affect the valves. When varicose veins have affected others in your family, you'd be better off in an occupation that doesn't require long hours of standing.

If it is likely that you'll develop varicose veins, act as if you already have them. Steps for preventing the condition are essentially the same as measures for treating it.

Women frequently develop varicose veins during pregnancy. Increased abdominal pressure from the enlarging uterus and increased blood flow to and from the lower abdominal and pelvic areas hinder return flow from the leg veins. Unless severe the condition generally improves after delivery without treatment.

Treating varicose veins. If you have varicose veins, wear elastic bandages or stockings to support the vein walls and keep the veins from becoming distended. A woman with a mild condition can wear elastic pantyhose. Don't wear tight girdles, garters, or other constricting garments.

Avoid prolonged sitting, and when possible elevate your legs. On a plane or on long bus or train trips, get up and walk around every half hour or so. Make frequent rest stops while driving.

Don't stand for long periods. If prolonged standing is unavoidable, exercise the muscles in your legs by raising up on your toes every 15 minutes or so.

If you are overweight, reduce. The more weight you carry, the more strain on the veins.

Walk 1 to 2 miles a day, wearing elastic bandages or support hose. Climb stairs rather than use an elevator or escalator. Swimming, even merely walking in water, is good for your legs. A regular exercise program can greatly reduce fatigue and swelling.

For one hour each day, elevate your legs above the level of your heart. Use a tilt-back chair. Or lie in bed with pillows raising your knees, calves, feet.

In moist heat like a steam bath, small veins in your legs may swell and rupture. Lie down, elevate the leg, and apply pressure to stop the bleeding.

Beware of false claims by manufacturers of water massagers and whirlpool baths—the devices are of no value in treating varicose veins.

Surgery only when necessary. Surgery is a last resort, needed only by those with a severe condition that causes constant tiredness, aching, and fullness. Removing ("stripping") the vein unnecessarily can impair leg circulation.

Varicose veins are sometimes treated with sclerotherapy—a series of injections of a hardening material that blocks off the part of the vein that is swollen. When successful, the procedure causes the vein to wither and disappear. But effects have most often proved merely temporary, and sclerotherapy is generally used only for small veins.

See also BLOOD PRESSURE; FIBER; HEART DISEASE; LEG PAIN; SURGERY; THROMBOPHLEBITIS.

VASECTOMY is a surgical operation for male sterilization. It prevents sperm from entering the man's semen.

Vasectomy is an increasingly common form of birth control. An estimated 600,000 men a year are vasectomized.

The surgery involves removing a small part and tying off, cauterizing, or clipping the ends of the vas deferens, the tubes that carry sperm cells from the testicles. To do this the surgeon—preferably a urologist—generally makes one or two incisions about 1/2 inch long in the scrotum. The operation is usually performed in his office under local anesthesia and takes about 20 minutes. Some doctors prefer to do vasectomies in the hospital under a short-acting general anesthesia.

If you undergo a vasectomy, you may be able to return to work and resume normal activities the day after the operation. You're likely to experience discomfort for several days.

Infections and other complications are extremely rare. There is no evidence that vasectomy causes any harm to a man's heart or blood vessels. No deaths have been reported from vasectomies.

If you've undergone a vasectomy, get examinations of your semen for several months. Use another form of contraception in the meantime. Sperm may remain in the seminal tract (the path the sperm follow) for weeks or months, depending on how frequently you ejaculate. You can help flush out your sperm by ejaculating three or more times the day before your operation. Ten to 15 ejaculations are usually required to clear the ducts of residual sperm.

Rarely, the severed ends of the vas deferens grow together and fertility is restored. Until the surgeon has verified that your semen is free of sperm, use other methods of birth control.

Vasectomy and sex. Vasectomy need have no effect on your sexual performance. The glands that manufacture semen are not affected by the operation. So you can continue to have intercourse, ejaculate normally, and enjoy orgasm as before. The vasectomy has no effect on the production of the male sex hormones, or on the appearance of the genitals.

The sole physical effect of vasectomy is that there will be no sperm in the semen, hence no possibility of pregnancy. The sperm cells—still produced by the testicles but now having no outlet—dissolve and are harmlessly absorbed into the bloodstream.

You may have intercourse as soon as you desire after the vasectomy. Couples often report that they enjoy sex more since they feel confident that there will not be a pregnancy.

In rare cases a man may mistakenly associate virility with the ability to produce a child. Vasectomy may make him feel like less of a man, and may result in emotional stress and impotence. But these psychological disturbances usually occur in men who already had doubts about their sexual adequacy, or who have serious conflicts with their sex partners.

Psychological aftereffects may also result when a man unwillingly submits to the operation under pressure from his wife, or when he has a vasectomy against his wife's wishes. It's a good idea to have a frank, open talk with your doctor before a vasectomy. Ask questions and discuss any fears you have.

Regard vasectomy as irreversible. Consider it only if you are certain you never want to have more—or any—children. Attempts to reverse the vasectomy are often unsuccessful. And, unlike the vasectomy, reversal is a risky, lengthy, and expensive operation. Even when the operation is successful and sperm are once more ejaculated, there is a possibility that the sperm will not be alive and able to cause pregnancy. Further, sperm cannot be taken directly from the testes of vasectomized men for artificial insemination of the partner—for sperm undergo further maturation after they leave the testes to be ejaculated. Without this natural maturation the sperm are unable to cause pregnancy.

Some men place quantities of their sperm in sperm banks to be frozen, and subsequently used in artificial insemination. While thawed sperm has produced some pregnancies and healthy babies, don't count on it. Frozen sperm declines in fertility. The longer the sperm is frozen, the less likely it is to cause pregnancy.

Scientists are currently trying to develop a reversible vasectomy device—a silicone valve placed in the sperm duct that could be turned on or off by a doctor.

For more information, contact the Association for Voluntary Sterilization, Inc. (122 East 42nd Street, New York, New York 10168).

See also BIRTH CONTROL.

VEGETABLE FIBER See FIBER.

VEGETARIANISM—the practice of eliminating all meat from your diet—can provide adequate nutrition. What's more, a well-balanced vegetarian diet tends to promote proper weight and low blood-cholesterol levels—good preventives against heart disease. On the other hand, a vegetarian diet can be harmful if the food you select does not contain enough protein, calcium, iron, or other important nutrients.

Not all vegetarians follow the same diet. A "vegan" is most restricted, eating neither meat nor animal products of any kind. "Lacto-vegetarians" eat no meat, poultry, or fish, but will consume milk and milk products (including cheese, of course). A "lacto-ovo-vegetarian" also eats eggs.

Eating meat, fish, or poultry is not essential in order to obtain all the nutrients necessary for good health. Lacto-vegetarians and lacto-ovo-vegetarians can easily be well nourished on a diet of grains, fruits, vegetables, nuts, beans, milk, and dairy products.

However vegans must plan their meals carefully and must eat a wide variety of grains, vegetables, beans, seeds, and nuts to get all the protein that everyone needs for good nutrition.

Balancing the diet. All grains and vegetables lack one or more of the essential amino acids, components of protein. A diet concentrating on just a few plants is likely to be lacking in some necessary amino acids.

One way vegetarians can improve protein nutrition is by eating such high-protein legumes as peanuts, dry beans, soybeans, and peas.

Vegan diets are likely to be low in calcium and iron. Calcium deficiency can pose a serious threat to nursing mothers. Insufficient iron is particularly likely to be a problem for infants, young males from 11 to 18, and women who menstruate. Take care to include foods high in calcium and iron. Dark-green leafy vegetables—kale, broccoli, turnip greens, collards, etc.—are good sources of both. Infants and young children may need iron-fortified formula and iron-enriched cereals.

Vitamin B_{12}—found almost exclusively in animal products—is difficult to get enough of on a vegan diet. Seaweeds and fermented soybean foods (such as tempeh) may contain sufficient B_{12}. Or you may need a synthetic supplement or B_{12}-fortified soy or nut "milks." Unless you live in a sunny climate, vitamin D may also be hard to get. But take supplements only on your doctor's advice.

If you are breastfeeding, make particularly sure your intake of vitamin B_{12} is adequate. Without enough vitamin B_{12} breast-fed infants may suffer a severe and potentially fatal deficiency. Your baby may also need supplemental iron, and vitamins D and K.

Avoid the zen macrobiotic diet, a dangerous form of quack vegetarianism that progresses through ten stages, eliminating more and more foods until it consists only of cereal.

Claimed to prevent or treat more than 80 diseases, the diet will be more likely to cause severe nutritional deficiencies, anemia, kidney malfunction, bone and tissue damage. The Food and Drug Administration (FDA) has charged that at least five people have died of starvation after following this regimen.

See also IRON; MINERALS; NUTRITION; QUACKERY; VITAMINS.

VENEREAL DISEASE (VD) is the general term for those infectious diseases that are transmitted mainly through intimate sexual contact.

It is estimated that at least 2 million cases of gonorrhea occur each year. Some 600,000 persons need treatment for syphilis and do not know it. At any given time an estimated 14 million Americans have syphilis or gonorrhea or both. VD is particularly on the rise among the young. One in four reported cases involves a person 20 or younger.

How VD is increasing. Ignorance about VD is widespread. Many people fail to realize that they've been exposed, and don't recognize the early symptoms. They don't seek treatment, and continue to infect others. Embarrassment also keeps infected people from seeking help.

Relaxed attitudes about sex and widespread use of birth control pills, which have allowed more sexual activity without fear of pregnancy, have contributed to the VD epidemic.

Formerly, condoms (rubber sheaths for the penis) were the most popular form of birth control for the young. Since they prevent direct penis-vagina contact, condoms provide a measure of protection against VD, especially gonorrhea. Contraceptive foams, too, seem to protect users against VD. However the widespread use of birth control pills—or the use of no contraception at all—virtually eliminates these preventive measures.

At present there is no immunization against VD. A person can be reinfected many times. Infection may be transmitted to a partner of one's own sex as well as to a partner of the opposite sex.

Venereal diseases (also called sexually transmitted diseases or STDs) can be spread through oral-genital contact.

Many venereal diseases are more serious than most people realize. They can lead to sterility, arthritis, paralysis, and death. Babies of women with VD may be stillborn or suffer from birth defects.

Many venereal diseases are easily cured—but damage already done to tissues cannot be repaired.

Newly worrisome forms of VD. AIDS (acquired immune deficiency syndrome), which is often fatal, is spreading into the drug-free heterosexual population.

Another growing venereal disease is genital herpes. It can be particularly serious in women, since it seems to be associated with a greater incidence of cancer of the cervix (see HERPES).

Nongonococcal urethritis (NGU) is a highly contagious disease spread through sexual contacts. It is caused by a variety of organisms, chief among them *Chlamydia trachomatis.* Many male NGU victims suffer from painful urination, irritation of the urethra (the canal through which urine passes), and occasionally a mucous discharge. But some men, and virtually all women, can have NGU without symptoms.

Untreated women carrying NGU may give birth to infants who have eye infections that can lead to scars and blindness. The only way to find symptom-free victims is by tracking down sexual contacts of known carriers—lab tests that reveal NGU in men can fail to show definitive results for women.

NGU was long thought to be a minor condition, self-limiting and without complications. Now it is regarded as essential to treat with a two- to three-week course of tetracycline therapy. Untreated NGU may lead to infertility.

Other venereal diseases. Beware exotic venereal diseases outside the United States. Especially in tropical areas these can constitute major problems for travelers.

Chancroid attacks the genital area, producing a shallow, ragged ulcer with grayish pus. Lymph glands in the groin swell and may develop abscesses. Chancroid responds well to treatment, but tissues already damaged cannot be restored.

Lymphogranuloma venereum affects the genitals, causing ulceration of the lymph nodes in the groin. The infection may spread to the lower opening of the bowel, with bleeding, discharge, and scarring. Early treatment can prevent permanent damage.

Granuloma inguinale is less infectious than either chancroid or lymphogranuloma venereum. It produces sores on the sex organs and the lymph glands. It can be easily controlled with antibiotics.

Pubic lice may also be caught through sexual contact. Vaginal infections such as trichomoniasis and yeast infection may likewise be passed on through sexual intercourse. So may intestinal infections such as amebiasis and giardiasis.

Stopping the ravages of VD. If you suspect you have VD, consult a physician or clinic immediately. Your doctor is required to report some venereal diseases to the Public Health Service, though many fail to do so out of a misguided wish to spare their patients embarrassment. But such reporting is necessary to identify others who may be infected and can spread the disease even further.

All VD records are confidential. Neither you nor your contacts will be identified to one another or to anyone else. In most states minors can receive treatment without informing or receiving permission from their parents. Many communities have established free clinics for the diagnosis and treatment of VD.

Several measures can help reduce your likelihood of contracting sexually transmitted diseases: Be selective in your partners—the fewer the number of sexual contacts, the lower the risk. Use a condom with anyone but an exclusive partner. Urinate and wash your genitals after intercourse.

Public and school education programs can do much to check the spread of VD. In Los Angeles, for example, two years after the introduction of VD education in the schools, public-health authorities noted a drop of 72 percent in teenage syphilis. Health officials also mounted an intensive public-information campaign to explain the school program to the community. As a result the general population became more knowledgeable, and the incidence of syphilis outside the school system dropped more than a third.

See also AIDS; AMEBIASIS; BIRTH CONTROL; CANCER OF THE UTERUS; GIARDIASIS; GONORRHEA; HERPES; IMMUNIZATION; INFECTIOUS DISEASE; LICE; MENTAL RETARDATION; SYPHILIS; TRAVEL HEALTH; VAGINAL INFECTION.

VIRUSES See INFECTIOUS DISEASE.

VISUAL TRAINING See EYE EXERCISES.

VITAMINS are organic compounds needed in

small amounts for proper nutrition (see accompanying chart). Many medical authorities believe that there is a great deal of nutritional quackery about vitamins, which can lead you to waste your money and overdose yourself.

The Recommended Dietary Allowance (RDA) for vitamins is provided by the Food and Nutrition Board of the National Academy of Sciences–National Research Council. Set deliberately high to preclude mild deficiencies, the RDA is a rough guide to how much of each vitamin is needed each day to assure an adequate intake. In general, infants and young children need less of each vitamin. More is needed by women who are pregnant or breastfeeding.

If you eat a well-balanced diet, you normally don't need vitamin pills. With a daily intake that includes milk and milk products, breads and cereals, vegetables, fruits, and meat, fish, or poultry, you are probably getting all the vitamins you need.

Supplemental vitamins may be necessary if your diet is poor or if you're ill. Vitamins may be prescribed if your diet is imbalanced because you suffer from food allergy, if you have a strong distaste for a particular class of food such as green vegetables, or if you're on a severely restricted diet to lose weight.

Supplemental vitamins are often prescribed for pregnant and breastfeeding women and for alcoholics. Women on oral contraceptives may also need supplemental vitamins. Sometimes vitamin deficiencies result from illness, such as ulcerative colitis, malabsorption, and any condition resulting in chronic diarrhea.

Preserving vitamins. The way in which you prepare food can help retain vitamin content. Cut a salad just before serving, since exposure to air destroys some of the vitamin content.

Don't overcook vegetables. They're tasty and richest in vitamins if slightly crisp. Cook vegetables in a very small amount of water. Then use the water as a base for soups and sauces—it contains vitamins. Better still, steam vegetables instead of boiling them. Bake potatoes instead of boiling. Cook vegetables and fruits whole, in their skins.

There is little difference between the vitamin content of fresh and processed foods. Modern methods of canning and freezing fruits and vegetables retain most vitamins.

Meat loses more B vitamins when it is cooked at high heat, for long periods, or in water. You'll retain more vitamins if you broil or fry meat than if you stew it. If you eat the stewing liquid you'll recoup some of the vitamins. With tougher cuts of meat roast slowly in a dry open pan rather than braising or cooking in liquid.

The myth of organic vitamins. Contrary to the claims of some food faddists, there's no difference between "organic" and "synthetic" vitamins. Each vitamin has a specific molecular structure, whether it grows naturally or is manufactured. Vitamin C, for example, has the same effect on your body whether it's synthesized in a laboratory or whether you eat it in an orange.

Nor is there any material difference between the brands of vitamins you buy in a drugstore and the so-called organic or natural vitamins—usually higher-priced—available in health food stores or from chiropractors.

Buy vitamins only on a doctor's advice for a particular vitamin deficiency. Vitamins lose much of their potency after about eight months. It's thus wise to buy no more than a few months' supply at a time. Capsules have more staying power than tablets or liquids.

Don't take vitamin pills for fatigue or lack of pep. These conditions may be a sign of illness, emotional stress, sleeplessness, or illness that requires a doctor's care.

What vitamins won't do. Vitamin pills won't grow hair, nor will they make you more youthful. They won't curb your appetite or help you lose weight. Nor will they cure sex disorder or nonnutritional diseases.

The Food and Drug Administration (FDA) prevents vitamin manufacturers from making such claims for their products. And you should not believe vitamin promoters' assertions that it is impossible to get enough vitamins from foods because of soil depletion or overprocessing.

The dangers of overdose. Vitamin overdoses can cause major medical problems. The fat-soluble vitamins—A, D, E, and K—are stored in the body, and can build up to dangerous levels. Vitamin A excess over a prolonged period can produce loss of appetite and weight, irritability, and drying and cracking of the skin, especially at the corners of the mouth. Other symptoms of vitamin A poisoning are headache, bone pain, hair loss, and enlargement of the liver and spleen.

Intracranial pressure mimicking cancer of the brain may be the most serious effect of vitamin A overdose, since it has caused several people to undergo unnecessary, hazardous brain surgery.

If you are taking vitamin A for acne treatment, discuss your diet with your doctor to make sure you are not getting too much by eating foods enriched with vitamin A.

Chronic vitamin D excess can cause nausea, constipation or diarrhea, high blood pressure.

There also may be loss of appetite and weight, bone deformities, increased urination, kidney damage. Calcium deposits may develop in the soft tissues of the heart, kidneys, blood vessels, and stomach. Excess vitamin D during pregnancy may be harmful to the fetus.

Vitamin K in excess can be harmful to newborn babies, particularly premature ones.

In a few people a chronic, large excess of vitamin E has caused disturbances of reproductive functions, gastrointestinal upsets, and muscle weakness.

If you take no supplemental vitamins, you're unlikely to suffer from vitamin A or D excess unless your diet is severely unbalanced. However check food labels for vitamin fortification.

The water-soluble vitamins—the B vitamins and vitamin C—are not stored as extensively in the body, and excesses are largely excreted. However, massive doses of vitamin B_6 may be toxic. Massive doses of vitamin C may cause severe diarrhea and, in some susceptible people, gout. Niacin overdose can cause liver damage. Moreover, your body's adaptation to large doses of vitamin C—and possibly the B vitamins too—can create an unnatural need for continued high doses.

Overdose in children. Children are often the victims of vitamin overdoses administered by overzealous parents. The National Clearinghouse for Poison Control Centers reports about 3,000 cases of vitamin poisoning each year.

In children vitamin A excess can retard growth. Vitamin D overdoses can impair physical and mental development. Overdoses of vitamins fortified with iron can be particularly hazardous.

Don't succumb to your child's pressure to buy him candy vitamins advertised on television.

Vitamin E. Many unsubstantiated claims have been made for vitamin E. Sales have skyrocketed of large doses (often more than 20 times the daily requirement in a single capsule).

The vitamin is promoted as a cure, preventive, or treatment for scores of ailments, including cancer, muscular dystrophy, peptic ulcers, burns, and skin disorders. Claims also include protection against the effects of air pollution, slowing of the aging process, and prevention of heart attack.

The greatest lure is the suggestion that vitamin E can enhance your sex life and cure infertility and impotence. There is no scientific proof for any of these claims. Nor is there evidence that vitamin E has any beneficial effect in cosmetics.

The clamor over vitamin E is based mainly on a misinterpretation of animal experiments and

WHAT YOU NEED TO KNOW ABOUT MAJOR VITAMINS

Vitamin	Adult Recommended Dietary Allowance (RDA)	Good Sources	Use in Body	Symptoms of Deficiency	Comments
A	4,000–5,000 IU	Carrots, liver, whole milk, butter, egg yolk, fish-liver oil, dark-green leafy vegetables, yellow fruits and vegetables	Vision in dim light; new cell growth; bone development; healthy skin and mucous membrane tissues	Night blindness and other eye disorders, including blindness; dry, rough skin, susceptible to infection	Stored in body; deficiency rare
B_1 (Thiamine)	1.0–1.5 mg	Pork, beans, soybeans, liver, peas, brewer's yeast, nuts, whole grain breads or cereals	Aids carbohydrate metabolism, normal function of heart and nervous system	Loss of appetite; leg-muscle pain and intestinal disorders; edema and nerve irritation; deficiency disease is beriberi	
B_2 (Riboflavin)	1.1–1.7 mg	Green leafy vegetables, dried yeast, liver, kidneys, meat, milk, eggs, whole grain or enriched breads or cereals	Aids carbohydrate and protein metabolism	Skin disorder with lip sores and cracking; dimmed vision	

Vitamin	Adult Recommended Dietary Allowance (RDA)	Good Sources	Use in Body	Symptoms of Deficiency	Comments
Niacin	12–19 mg	Meat, fish, poultry, peanuts, milk, eggs, liver, kidneys, brewer's yeast, green vegetables, whole grain and enriched breads and cereals	Food metabolism; healthy skin	Pellagra, disease characterized by rough skin, mouth sores, diarrhea, mental disorders	Formerly a major deficiency disease, now rare
B₆	2.0 mg	Potatoes, green vegetables, corn, whole grains, red meat, egg yolk, bananas, milk	Necessary for utilization of protein and for proper growth	Dizziness; nausea; weight loss; mouth soreness	Deficiency rare
B₁₂	3 mcg	Liver, kidneys, shellfish, fish, meat, milk	Normal development of red blood cells; functioning of all cells, particularly those in bone marrow, intestines, nervous system	Pernicious anemia	Strict vegetarians may suffer from deficiency, since very little B₁₂ is present in plants
Folic acid	400 mcg	Dark-green leafy vegetables, navy beans, liver, nuts, whole wheat products, fresh oranges	Normal metabolism and manufacture of red blood cells	Anemia	
C (ascorbic acid)	60 mg	Citrus fruits, tomatoes, cantaloupe, strawberries, currants, cabbage, spinach, kale, broccoli	Normal bone and teeth formation; promotes healing of wounds	Scurvy, disease marked by bleeding of gums and loose teeth, weakness, weight loss, irritability	Deficiency rare; large doses are promoted for prevention and treatment of colds, but evidence is inconclusive
D	400 IU	Fortified milk, egg yolk, fish-liver oils, canned fish such as herring, salmon, and tuna; also formed in skin by sun's rays	Bone formation	In children rickets with bone deformities, bowed legs, deformed spine, sometimes stunting of growth; in adults weakened bones	With milk fortification, rickets very rare
E	8 mg	Whole grain breads and cereals, meat, eggs, vegetable oils, nuts, beans, liver, fruits, vegetables	Prevents oxygen from destroying other substances, particularly stored fats	Deficiency severe enough to produce symptoms extremely rare, since vitamin present in so many foods	Subject of many unsubstantiated claims
K	70–140 mcg	Green leafy vegetables, cauliflower, liver, egg yolk	Blood clotting; liver function	Heavy bleeding	Premature infants sometimes born with too little

IU = International Units.   Mg = milligrams (1,000 mg = 1 gram)   Mcg = micrograms (1,000 mcg = 1 mg) their misapplication to human beings. Rats deprived of vitamin E became sterile. But large doses of vitamin E are *not* useful in treating human sterility or sex disorders.

As far as is known, vitamin E supplements are necessary and beneficial only for premature infants suffering from a specific kind of anemia, for people with intestinal disorders involving poor absorption of fats, and for intermittent claudication, a weakness due to poor circulation in the legs.

See also COLDS; NUTRITION.

VITILIGO is a skin disorder of unknown cause in which areas of the skin fail to produce melanin, the dark pigment for normal skin color.

This results in smooth, light-colored patches of skin, which may cause an undesirable appearance, especially in dark-skinned people. In the summer, as normal areas of the skin tan, the unpigmented areas become more noticeable.

Drugs called psoralens may be taken, followed by daily exposure of the areas to sunlight or ultraviolet light. However, this treatment does not always work.

The lightened areas can be camouflaged with preparations such as special masking cosmetics designed to cover birthmarks, and various stains including a special walnut stain (not furniture stain) and dihydroxyacetone, the ingredient in artificial suntanning preparations. If vitiligo is very widespread, bleaching the few remaining islands of normal skin color may be the most practical way of achieving uniform appearance.

See also SKIN DISORDERS.

VOMITING   See NAUSEA.

WARTS are benign tumors of the skin, apparently caused by viruses. Contrary to myth, common warts do not develop into a cancer.

There can be an epidemic of warts among members of a family. It is sometimes possible to trace the source of such an outbreak to a single neglected wart on the mother or father. But rarely do people contract warts through casual contact, such as handshaking. Warts often spread: when a wart is scratched, other warts may appear along the line of broken skin.

Warts can appear on any part of the skin, but occur most often on the hands, fingers, and soles of the feet. They are most troublesome where they are subject to trauma (fingers, knees, soles); in the beard area, where they interfere with shaving; and on the genitals.

Warts are usually not painful, except for plantar warts, which appear on the soles and range in diameter from a pinhead to a tennis ball. Since they can't bulge outward as do warts on other parts of the body, they develop a callus and are pushed inward with every step, feeling like a stone in the shoe. This can cause so much pain that the sufferer can't walk until the wart is treated.

Warts usually go away by themselves. Almost all warts eventually disappear without treatment, although they may persist for many years.

Suggestion therapy is often effective in hastening their departure. One dermatologist asks children to give him a tracing of the hand or the foot that has the warts. He then burns this diagram and tells the children that their warts will be gone in a few weeks. And they usually are.

This kind of suggestion therapy is undoubtedly the reason why so many folk cures work. One common folk remedy involves rubbing the wart with a slice of raw potato, then burying the potato by the light of the full moon.

Warts also respond to hypnosis therapy. In one experiment, conducted among people who had warts on both sides of their bodies, the hypnotic suggestion was that the warts on the left side of the body would disappear. Within a few weeks most of the people reported that most or all of the warts on their left sides were indeed gone. There was one notable exception, a person whose *right*-side warts had disappeared: he was found to habitually confuse left and right.

Treating warts. See a doctor if you want your warts treated. While warts will most likely eventually disappear, treatment is warranted if a wart is irritated, itchy, or unsightly. Also seek treatment if your warts are spreading. Plantar warts are usually so painful that you'll certainly want them removed.

Proper medical therapy is surer and quicker than attempts at self-treatment. Among the many methods of treatment is cryotherapy, which involves freezing of the wart by dry ice or liquid nitrogen, then lifting it out after about a week. A wart can be destroyed by electric current, or the doctor may use an acid or a medication containing cantharidin, a blistering substance obtained from dried, powdered blister beetles.

Some physicians apply ordinary corn plasters containing salicylic acid, which acts on the wart so that it can be scraped away. In scraping a plantar wart a doctor may use formaldehyde, and may recommend the wearing of pads or special shoes to remove the pressure from painful spots.

Surgical removal of the wart is not recommended—it may cause lasting or painful scars or tissue damage. X-ray therapy should not be used.

Even after warts are treated or spontaneously disappear, the virus may remain. About one in three people will get warts again. Eventually, however, they will develop immunity.

See also SKIN DISORDERS.

WATER CONTAMINATION can lead to dysentery, infectious hepatitis, or typhoid. In disasters like floods and tornadoes, ordinarily safe water supplies may become contaminated. When hiking and camping, it's often impossible to know whether water is safe. Any natural water source may be contaminated from animal excrement, no matter how pure the water looks.

The simplest and cheapest purification method for a camper or hiker is to add a drop or two of ordinary 2 percent tincture of iodine to a glass of water and let it stand for ten minutes. It is easy enough to carry along a small bottle of iodine for this purpose.

Or you can boil water for a half hour to make it safe to drink. However for large quantities you may prefer a chemical purifier.

Mix 2 drops of common household laundry bleach (4 to 6 percent chlorine) to 1 quart clear water, 4 drops to 1 quart cloudy water. After letting it stand for 30 minutes, you should be able to detect a slight chlorine odor, an assurance the water is safe. It not, repeat the dosage and let stand 15 minutes more.

If the bleach has 7 to 10 percent chlorine, use only 1 drop to 1 quart clear water, 2 drops for cloudy water. If the concentration of chlorine is 1 percent or not labeled, use 10 drops for clear water, 20 for cloudy.

Alternatively, buy water purification tablets (Halazone) at a drugstore or camp supplier. Or 5 drops of common 2 percent tincture of iodine after a half hour will purify 1 quart clear water, 10 drops 1 quart of cloudy.

Emergency water supplies. At home in an emergency you can get water by draining your hot-water tank, melting ice cubes, dipping into the toilet-flush tank (not the bowl). Water-packed fruits and vegetables provide a good source of water.

Outdoors, look for water from an underground source such as a well or spring. If you must get water from a creek, stream, lake, or pond, avoid water that has an odor, is dark, or contains floating particles. Try to get water upstream from an inhabited area. Dip deep below the surface.

Water abroad. Unsafe drinking water can be a hazard to travelers, especially in tropical and subtropical countries. Drinking water contaminated by bacteria or parasites is a source of cholera and other intestinal disorders.

In larger cities the water supply where tourists ordinarily go is generally safe. But where it is customary for tourists to drink bottled water or mineral water, follow the custom. Make certain that the seal has not been broken—the bottle may have been filled from a local tap. Don't trust water bottled in a hotel or restaurant.

You may care to stick to beer, wine, or such commonly available soft drinks as Coca-Cola and Pepsi-Cola, which are unlikely to be contaminated. Beware too of food poisoning from foods washed or prepared with unsanitary water.

Water for swimming may concern you too. European saltwater beaches are likely to be safe for bathing, although many are contaminated by fresh-water streams or sewage outlets—inquire locally. If you contemplate swimming at a tropical or subtropical beach, consult the local public-health officer or the U.S. consulate.

A different kind of contamination is the danger, in saltwater, of being stung by jellyfish or stingrays. Fresh-water health hazards include leeches and—in tropical and semitropical countries—SCHISTOSOMIASIS (which see).

See also INFECTIOUS DISEASE; TRAVEL HEALTH.

WATER LOSS See DEHYDRATION.

WATER ON THE KNEE is a colloquial term referring to the excessive accumulation of lubricating fluid in the knee joint. It is a response to irritation of the joint from injury or disease.

An injury to the knee may cause excessive fluid to be produced or may prevent its normal absorption.

Water on the knee requires a doctor's attention, since there is a possibility of permanent damage if the knee is used prematurely.

See also SPORTS.

WEBBED FINGERS (syndactylism) is a congenital defect in which two or more fingers (most frequently the third and fourth) are fused together. Physicians usually recommend surgical separation of the fingers when the child is four or five years old.

See also BIRTH DEFECTS; WEBBED TOES.

WEBBED TOES (syndactylism) is a condition in which two or more toes are fused together, most often the second and third. It presents no physical problem, since it does not affect walking.

Nothing need be done about it. Surgery can separate the toes if desired.

See also BIRTH DEFECTS; WEBBED FINGERS.

WHIPLASH is the common name applied to a neck injury that most frequently occurs in automobile accidents when a car is hit from behind. It also occurs in some falls and sports injuries.

As the lower back is snapped forward, the neck jerks backward like the end of a cracking whip. The injury can range from strains to sprains to fractures of the vertebrae, neck, and back. The spinal cord may also be damaged. Infants, whose neck muscles are weak, may be crippled or killed by even playful shaking or tossing.

Following a rear-end collision you may feel pain in your neck. Some people also experience dizziness, headache, vomiting, gait disturbances, and rigidity or numbness in the arms. The neck pain often disappears after a few weeks but may last a year or more. Sometimes it returns months later. You may also feel pain from scar tissue within the neck pressing on nerves. The pain may involve your shoulders, upper back, and arms.

If you experience a whiplash injury, see a doctor. X rays will determine the extent of the injury. The doctor may prescribe a supportive collar and neck exercises. A mild analgesic—such as aspirin with codeine—will help relieve pain.

Muscle relaxants may also be prescribed. Hot showers and warm compresses often ease pain.

The combination car seat belt/shoulder strap may afford some protection against the whiplash motion. A properly positioned headrest (2 or 3 inches behind your head, not too low) may also help.

See also ACCIDENTS; CARS.

WHOOPING COUGH (pertussis) is a disease that need not occur. Babies can be immunized beginning at two to three months of age. Three doses are needed at four- to six-week intervals, with a fourth a year after the third injection. Children need a booster at five to six years, when they begin school.

Before whooping cough vaccine was used extensively in the United States, nearly all children contracted this infectious disease and thousands died of it every year. Even today laxity in getting children immunized results in thousands of cases a year.

For most childhood illnesses the infant is protected for several months by immunity passed on by its mother. Not so whooping cough, and three out of four deaths occur before the age of one year.

Whooping cough at first often resembles an ordinary cold. There is a running nose and a slight, hacking cough. These signs usually develop about seven days after exposure. Within two weeks the cough develops into a series of violent coughs to expel sticky mucus from the air passages and throat. This is followed by the whooping sound as the victim attempts to catch his breath. These coughing fits often end with vomiting.

During the coughing attack the face gets red and the eyes watery and bloodshot. Hernia may result from severe paroxysms. Hemorrhages into the brain, eyes, and skin may occur. Emphysema occurs in nearly every severe case, and resistance to pneumonia is lowered.

A child with whooping cough will generally awaken from a deep sleep to cough and get his breath. Very young infants, and adults who have typically mild cases, are sometimes spared the whoop.

The whooping stage lasts from four to six weeks, passing gradually into a stage when attacks of coughing are less frequent. The final stage usually takes another two or three weeks, but some children cough for many months. The disease is generally easy to recognize by the coughing spasms, but mild cases sometimes can be detected only through laboratory tests.

Treating the disease. Call a physician in suspected cases of whooping cough. Hospitalization is recommended for seriously ill infants. The doctor may prescribe sedatives and other drugs to make the victim more comfortable.

Afternoon naps help to rest the child who suffers from coughing seizures at night. Elevating his head and use of an oxygen tent may help him breathe. If he chokes from mucus getting in his lungs, place him on his stomach with his head lowered, or apply gentle suction with your mouth or a suction-bulb device available from drugstores.

Foods such as nuts, crackers, toast, highly seasoned dishes, and very hot or very cold foods should be avoided since they may start a coughing spell and get breathed into the lungs. If severe vomiting occurs, feed the child smaller quantities with greater frequency.

If one child contracts the disease, other unprotected children in the family most likely will become infected. The disease is spread by bacteria found in the discharge of the nose and throat. Talking, sneezing, and coughing spray these germs into the air. The disease can also be caught by drinking from an infected glass or by handling things that have touched a sufferer's nose or mouth.

Whooping cough is highly contagious in its early stages, but can be considered not communicable three weeks after onset of the coughing fits. While the disease is running its course, keep the victim away from susceptible children, out of school and other public places. This isolation protects him from catching other diseases to which he may be particularly susceptible at this time. Keep other children in the family household away from outside susceptible children for 14 days.

The eating utensils of the patient should be kept separate or boiled after every use. Other infected articles can be sterilized by boiling for three minutes. Burn tissues used for sputum and nasal discharges.

See also IMMUNIZATION; INFECTIOUS DISEASE.

WOLVES attack human beings and are especially dangerous in packs—right?

Wrong. There has never been an authenticated case of wolves attacking a person. When you are in wild areas, wolves are nonproblems.

See also CAMPING; HIKING.

WRINKLES (aging skin) may most often be caused by changes in the skin's supporting tissues. The deeper layer of the skin (the dermis) becomes thinner, retains less water, and loses elasticity. The fatty layer that supports the skin diminishes, and sagging from gravity changes the facial contours.

Preventing wrinkles. There is no way to prevent wrinkles. But some practical approaches will help to retard their development. Premature development has been linked to heavy smoking.

Avoid excessive exposure to sunlight, and use sunscreens. Sun damage can make your skin age faster. This is seen vividly in studies where physicians have compared the skin from different parts of the body for effects of aging. The buttocks show the least amount of degenerative changes in the skin since they are least exposed to the sun. Faces and arms are the most severely damaged.

Thus from childhood on, it's wise to follow precautions against sunburn. You may also be able to retard wrinkles by exercising, eating well, getting plenty of sleep, and avoiding smoking and the overuse of alcohol.

Use a plain face cream. Your skin may become dry and scaly as you get older. Any emollient cream—a soothing, softening cream like cold cream—will help it retain more water. Avoid excessive bathing or use of soap and detergent in cold, dry weather.

No so-called antiwrinkle cream or lotion, no matter how expensive, will do more than ordinary cold cream. Emollients may aid in smoothing out very fine facial lines caused solely by skin dryness or temporarily soften or postpone the appearance of lines or wrinkles. However there are no known creams, lotions, peels, astringents, plasters, or other products which will prevent, correct, or remove wrinkles.

Nor will applying creams with upward and outward strokes be of special benefit in preventing the sagging of tissues from the aging process. The chief value of "upstroking" is psychological —the woman feels she's doing something. Any gentle method of application will be equally effective.

Products that don't work. The antiwrinkle market abounds in quack products. Hormones in creams raise the price astronomically. But they make cream no more effective in relieving skin dryness or remedying wrinkles. Overuse of hormone creams can affect the system and thin the skin.

Royal jelly, supposedly the stuff queen bees are made of, is useless outside the beehive, and powerfully expensive besides. Whether taken in capsules or lotions, it will do nothing for aging skin.

Products containing ingredients such as algae, buttermilk, placental extract, turtle oil, mineral oil, baby oil, cod liver oil, shark oil, mink oil, natural proteins, polyunsaturates, or "secret formulas" are usually safe to use. But they have not been scientifically proven to rejuvenate aged skin. They are merely good cold creams or vanishing creams at a high price, and will do only what any good low-cost emollient creams or lotions will do.

No exercise, gadget, or beauty treatment will improve wrinkles or sagging skin. Facial isometrics or any other kind of exercise are valueless in erasing signs of aging skin. Although face muscles may be exercised, the structural changes associated with aging primarily involve the skin. There is no evidence that improving the tone of such muscles will prevent sagging and flabbiness or improve contour.

Facial massage is equally useless. Vigorous massage may temporarily increase blood flow to the skin, and perhaps produce some swelling by increasing the amount of fluid in the tissues. However such changes are of no lasting benefit.

Facial saunas are a waste. All they do is temporarily increase the circulation in your skin and make your face warm and wet. Though they are relaxing, the same effect can be achieved with a hot towel.

Face packs and face masks provide only temporary psychological relief through warmth and a sense of tightening. Your skin may feel refreshed and surface dirt may be washed off along with the mask. But the treatment in no way alters the aging process. If you have extremely dry skin, you may find masks irritating.

Plastic surgery. To smooth out facial creases, plastic surgeons and dermatologists often inject collagen, a protein material in skin. Periodic touch-up injections are generally needed.

A face-lift operation can take years off your face. This is done by smoothing out wrinkles and pouches, removing excess skin and fat, and tightening the remainder.

In a typical face lift, called a rhytidectomy, the surgeon makes an incision inside the hairline from your temple past the front of your ear to the back of your skull. Then the cheek, jaw, and neck skin is separated from the fatty tissue and muscle below. Some fat tissue may be removed. The underlying fascia (fibrous tissue) and muscle layers are usually tightened. The skin is pulled taut to smooth out wrinkles.

The excess skin is then trimmed away and the remainder is stitched under the hairline, making the scar almost invisible. The operation may be done in a hospital, or in an office or outpatient surgical facility. The swelling and black-and-blue or yellowish bruising on the face may remain for 2 to 3 weeks. The operation is often performed in conjunction with one to remove bags under the eyes and skin above the eyes. A forehead lift, done in combination with a conventional face lift, can relieve overhanging eyebrows, horizontal forehead wrinkles and vertical frown lines.

Recovery is rarely painful. Feelings of tightness or unnaturalness around the face usually disappear in a few weeks. For a successful operation you need a qualified plastic surgeon. Membership in the American Association of Plastic Surgeons, the American Society of Plastic and Reconstructive Surgeons, or the American Academy of Facial Plastic and Reconstructive Surgery is an indicator of the physician's special interest in this type of work.

If you are considering a face-lift, remember that it is major surgery, and has some risk of complications, including a very rare risk of death. In addition the results of face lifts are extremely variable, and often depend on how lined and wrinkled the skin is.

A face lift, moreover, will do nothing for crow's feet around the eyes, mouth lines, or deep frown lines.

Face lifts are expensive procedures, usually costing several thousand dollars, and most insurance policies do not cover such elective cosmetic surgery—except for victims of disease or accident.

So-called mini-face-lifts are office procedures in which a triangle of skin is cut out in the area of the temple above the hairline. The edges of the skin are sewn together, lifting the lower part of the face. Mini-face-lifts are not widely done since they give only minor improvement, and are not lasting.

"Temporary face lifts" are provided by elastic headbands that are tied around your head and concealed by your hair or a wig. The headbands, sold at department stores, are supposed to pull up and tighten the skin around the lower part of your face. If as tight as they need to be, the bands may cause headache. Headbands rarely give significant improvement.

Skin peeling. Chemical skin peeling may remove fine facial wrinkles. In this superficial chemosurgery your neck and face are swabbed with a mild phenol solution and covered with an adhesive tape mask. The mask is kept on for one or two days, during which time the phenol burns away your epidermis and hardens your connective tissues.

When the mask is removed, the skin appears to have a second-degree burn, but after two months your face will be smoother. However the treated area of your face may appear lighter, for phenol removes skin pigment.

Dermabrasion (skin planing), widely used to remove acne scars, is another method to remove the epidermis and smooth the skin.

Stay away from face peels by nonphysicians. Beauticians and spa owners who attempt "chemical face-lifts" are responsible for many severe and disfiguring burns. One 38-year-old former actress and model required ten skin grafts to reduce the horrible burns and scars on her face and neck.

Also avoid electric-needle wrinkle treatment. Its results are only temporary and the side effects of using a needle to transmit an electric current under the skin include skin irritation, scarring, and the formation of dark spots.

See also BAGS UNDER THE EYES; SKIN DISORDERS; SURGERY.

XANTHOMA is a skin disorder marked by soft yellowish lumps of fat, often around the eyelids. The tendency to develop these deposits is believed to be an inherited metabolic defect. The lumps are unrelated to cancer.

Treatment sometimes consists of a diet low in cholesterol, a constituent of the fatty material. Since the lumps may present a cosmetic problem, see a dermatologist about removing them by surgical excision or electric needle.

See also SKIN DISORDERS.

X RAYS can save lives. But if used carelessly or excessively, they may cause cancer, burns, or birth defects.

Don't refuse a necessary X ray out of fear of radiation. At the same time try to keep your exposure to X rays to a minimum. And beware cumulative effects of repeated doses.

The risk associated with good diagnostic X-ray technique is small. In most X-ray examinations the dose to the skin where the beam enters is less than 1 rad, well within the bounds of safety. It is even less to tissues deeper in the body, and much less to tissues outside the main X-ray beam.

With the use of X rays physicians can obtain images of bones to detect fractures and to view arteries, soft tissues, and many organs, and thus detect disease at a much earlier stage. Dentists use X rays to detect tooth decay and other oral problems.

In addition to diagnosis, X rays are used in therapy. The beams are particularly effective in destroying some kinds of cancer.

But overexposure to X rays has been also linked to cancer and to birth defects. Leukemia has developed several years after prolonged X-ray therapy, especially in people who were treated for arthritis of the spine. Extensive exposure to X-ray therapy, not diagnostic X ray, has also been correlated with an increase in bone cancer.

X rays are known to produce changes in the genes and chromosomes in the reproductive organs and from this, genetic mutations—deformities, blindness, mental retardation—may be passed on to future generations. *Any* X-ray exposure of the reproductive system of children or adults of reproductive age carries some risk of damaging the reproductive cells and causing a genetic mutation in their offspring. And, as the Food and Drug Administration (FDA) points

out: "The full impact of any damage to the genetic heritage may not become evident for many generations."

In pregnancy there are indications that even low doses of radiation can be injurious to an embryo. This is particularly true in the first six weeks, when the woman may not even know she is pregnant.

In some cases injuries may surface after many years. A Harvard study of more than 700,000 infants in 39 U.S. hospitals showed a 40 percent increase in leukemia and cancer of the brain and central nervous system in children whose mothers were X-rayed during pregnancy.

Particularly likely to be harmful to the fetus are fluoroscopic examinations of the pregnant woman's abdominal area—such as the abdominal section of the aorta and other arteries in the abdomen, and the bladder.

Preventing X-ray damage. Many X rays are thought to be unnecessary. The FDA's Bureau of Radiological Health estimates that at least 30 percent of the X rays taken in this country are unproductive, contributing no diagnostic information to the doctor.

Some X rays are taken merely to protect the doctor in the event of a future malpractice suit. A litigation-shy doctor may order X rays chiefly to avoid being sued for failing to do so.

Because diagnostic X rays are responsible for the major share of the total exposure of the population, every physician should keep patient exposures to the minimum compatible with good medical practice. The physician should weigh the risks against the possible benefits in each case. Physicians and dentists should also see to it that their X-ray machines are kept in good repair and are equipped with the most up-to-date exposure-reducing devices.

To help reduce the amount of radiation people are exposed to, some X-ray procedures have been discouraged. The FDA, American College of Chest Physicians, and American College of Radiology have recommended the discontinuation of mass screening programs to detect tuberculosis by means of mobile X-ray equipment. The small number of cases detected, it was felt, did not justify exposing large numbers of people to radiation. What's more, the amount of radiation on these vans was far in excess of that in the average hospital.

Fluoroscopic examinations are no longer part

of the routine physical examination because of the large X-ray dosage they require. Fluoroscopes give a continuous X-ray image, and have the advantage of enabling a physician to see your internal organs in operation. But they may subject you to roughly 200 times the dosage required for a good X-ray film.

Similarly, shoe-fitting fluoroscopes—in which the foot is X-rayed in a new shoe to see how the shoe fits—represents an unnecessary hazard to health. In most states these machines are banned or carefully regulated.

The American Dental Association reports that many dentists no longer take routine full mouth X rays once a year. Instead they now take a full set of X rays of new patients and additional X rays for particular problems, such as periodontal disease. Full mouth X rays are taken at regular, but less frequent, intervals.

To protect yourself from excess radiation from X rays: Ask your dentist or doctor if it wouldn't be better to use a gonadal shield—a strip of lead—if you are of reproductive age. Children should also have this shield to protect their genitals against radiation. If you're a woman of childbearing age and must have an X ray of the pelvis or lower abdomen, tell your physician when you had your last menstrual period. He can then schedule the X ray for a time of the month when there is little possibility of damaging a newly formed embryo. During the first ten days after the onset of menstruation, pregnancy is least likely.

If you are pregnant, postpone all X rays that are not urgent until after the baby is born. When you change from one physician or dentist to another, arrange to have your X rays transferred.

When a doctor recommends an X ray, ask if it is essential to your health. Make sure that the exposure is limited to the part of your body which needs to be X-rayed. Don't agree to a fluoroscopic examination where an X ray will do. And don't press your doctor to take an X ray when he feels it's unnecessary.

X-ray therapy requires doses far in excess of those used for taking X rays. It is usually used only when the benefit may outweigh the hazard, as in the treatment of cancer. For nonmalignant conditions, such as bursitis or eczema, most medical authorities discourage the use of X-ray therapy where other treatment will work as well.

Thus if a physician recommends X-ray treatments without first trying other kinds of therapy, get another opinion. And if you do opt for X-ray therapy, be sure the practitioner is specially qualified. Seek a radiologist (a medical doctor who specializes in X rays) or a specialist in the field of your illness, such as a dermatologist for a skin disorder.

See also RADIATION.

YEAST INFECTION (moniliasis, candidiasis, fungus infection) is a vaginal infection caused by the fungus *Candida albicans*. It is characterized by itching in and around the vagina and by a thick, cheesy discharge with white patches. The vagina and outer genital area may be reddened, raw, and irritated. Intercourse may be painful. Some sufferers feel a need for frequent urination, sometimes with a burning sensation.

Yeast spores, which are in the air, usually inhabit the rectum and vagina, causing no harm. But when the normal balance of bacteria, fungi, and other organisms in the vagina is disturbed, the yeast may cause infection. Women often develop yeast infections while taking antibiotics that kill the normal bacteria in the vagina, allowing yeast to grow unchecked.

Pregnant women and women with diabetes are more susceptible to yeast infections because their balance of organisms is changed. Taking birth control pills may promote yeast infections, since the pills lessen the acidity of the vagina. Vaginal douching can also change the normal acid/alkaline balance of the vagina.

You are also more susceptible to yeast infections when your resistance is low from another infection (even another vaginal infection, which changes the content of the vagina), poor diet, insufficient sleep, or drug taking.

Transmitting yeast infections. The infection is sometimes transmitted through sexual intercourse. Many men who have yeast infections show no symptoms. But they can pass the infection to women during intercourse. A woman who seems to have a chronic yeast infection may actually be recurrently reinfected by her mate.

If a woman is suffering from a yeast infection when her baby is born, the baby may acquire the fungus as it passes through the birth canal. The infection affects the baby's mouth, and is called thrush.

Physicians diagnose yeast infection by noting the characteristic discharge and redness in the vagina. A vaginal smear examined under a microscope confirms the diagnosis.

A number of remedies have been used successfully, but yeast infections tend to recur. Sometimes, the infection seems to be gone, only to flare up after the next menstrual period alters the environment of the vagina.

Many doctors advise their patients to stop using oral contraceptives and also advise against having sexual intercourse while infected. Some physicians recommend using condoms.

An effective traditional treatment is the use of aqueous solution gentian violet. The physician paints it on the vagina, cervix, and outer genitals. Then the patient can use gentian violet gels, creams, or tampons daily. The major drawback of gentian violet is its messiness. Everything it touches is stained purple. If your doctor prescribes gentian violet, wear a sanitary napkin for the duration of the treatment.

Many doctors prefer to prescribe miconazole (Monistat 7) vaginal cream. It is used once daily at bedtime for seven days. Among other effective treatments are nystatin vaginal suppositories, used daily for at least 14 days. If suppositories alone are not effective, oral nystatin tablets three times daily may be prescribed concurrently. This may control a possible intestinal source of the yeast infection. Since the symptoms may disappear even though the infection remains, a woman should be checked four to six weeks after treatment is discontinued.

To help prevent yeast infections, wear cotton instead of nylon underwear. Keep your vaginal area clean and dry, making sure to spread the labia apart when bathing. Wipe yourself from the vagina toward the rectum, so that organisms from the rectum won't get into the vagina.

Thoroughly wash panties, bathing suits, and tub surfaces. If you use a diaphragm, wash it particularly thoroughly with soap and water. If you've had recurring and persistent yeast infections, it may be best to throw it away and get a new one.

At the first sign of an infection try to restore the normal acid/alkaline balance of your vagina by douching with 2 tablespoons vinegar in 1 quart water. Or try 2 tablespoons plain, active-culture yogurt in 1 quart water. But don't douche if you're pregnant.

See also VAGINAL INFECTION.

YELLOW FEVER used to sail into the United States on wooden ships that sheltered mosquitoes in crevices and holes. In one year alone 13,000 people died from "yellow jack" in towns along the Mississippi River.

Today the yellow-fever virus does not exist in the United States. But in Africa and South America the virus is harbored by enormous numbers of monkeys. A jungle mosquito, after biting an infected monkey, may pass the virus on to man. If an infected person finds his way to a town, the yellow fever virus may be spread to other humans by the *Aedes aegypti* mosquito, which is common in our southern states and in Africa and South America.

Fortunately, outbreaks of urban yellow fever have become rare. But yellow fever remains a threat to Americans who travel in the countryside near jungle or savanna in much of Africa or South America. With jet planes a person could be infected with the virus abroad, then before showing symptoms, could find his way to what the Public Health Service terms our "yellow-fever-receptive areas," the ten-state region including Alabama, Arkansas, Florida, Georgia, Louisiana, Mississippi, North and South Carolina, Tennessee, and Texas, plus Puerto Rico and the Virgin Islands. Here an *Aedes aegypti* biting him could pick up the virus and spread it, igniting an epidemic.

Immunization—a single shot with a booster in ten years—is recommended by the Public Health Service for anyone traveling to areas where there is a risk of infection. Check with your local health department for the latest report of such regions.

A few African and South American countries require incoming travelers to have an International Certificate of Vaccination showing yellow-fever immunization. Moreover, if you travel to an infected region—even pass through one—you won't be able to enter some countries unless you have a valid yellow-fever vaccination certificate. They will ordinarily accept a physician's letter stating medical reasons why you couldn't be vaccinated.

In the United States immunization against yellow fever is not available through private physicians. It must be obtained at clinics and other installations authorized by the Public Health Service. Your local health department can direct you to the nearest center.

The wild yellow fever virus attacks the liver, often causing the jaundice that gives the disease its name. After an incubation period of 3 to 6 days, the victim may suffer a sudden fever of 104° F or more, with severe hemorrhaging in the stomach and intestines, which produces black vomit (in Latin America the disease is termed *el vomito negro)*. About 1 in 10 cases proceeds to coma, followed by a period of wild delirium, then death.

There is no specific treatment, short of relieving symptoms and restoring fluids. Some jungle adventure stories describe heroic efforts to get a yellow fever victim to a district hospital. In most cases, the patient would be better off if he were kept quiet in bed.

See also INFECTIOUS DISEASE; TRAVEL HEALTH.

Z

ZIPPERS can be treacherous for small boys who don't wear underpants. Big boys, too. Zippers may also trap other areas, such as the skin of the neck.

In such accidents don't jiggle the zipper. Merely cut across the fabric of the zipper below the trapped skin (see illustration). The zipper will come apart easily and painlessly.

A word of caution from Dr. Lucian A. Arata of Shelbyville, Indiana: "Reassure the child about what is to be cut or he will strenuously, and properly, object to the prospect of being separated from this important bit of his anatomy!"

See also ACCIDENTS.

ZOONOSIS See ANIMAL DISEASE.

IF SKIN IS TRAPPED IN A ZIPPER

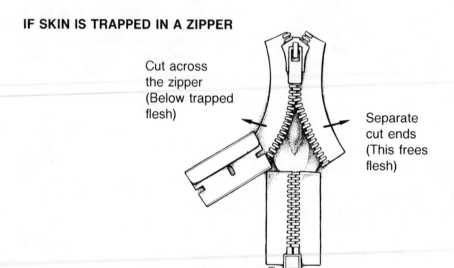

Cut across
the zipper
(Below trapped
flesh)

Separate
cut ends
(This frees
flesh)